W9-AKV-755

THE BAR & BEVERAGE BOOK

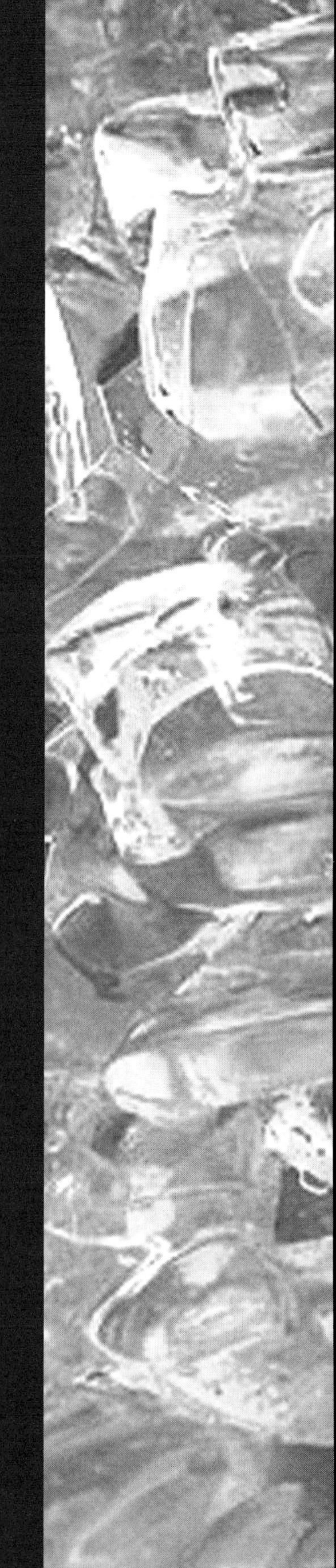

THE BAR & BEVERAGE BOOK

FOURTH EDITION

Costas Katsigris
Chris Thomas

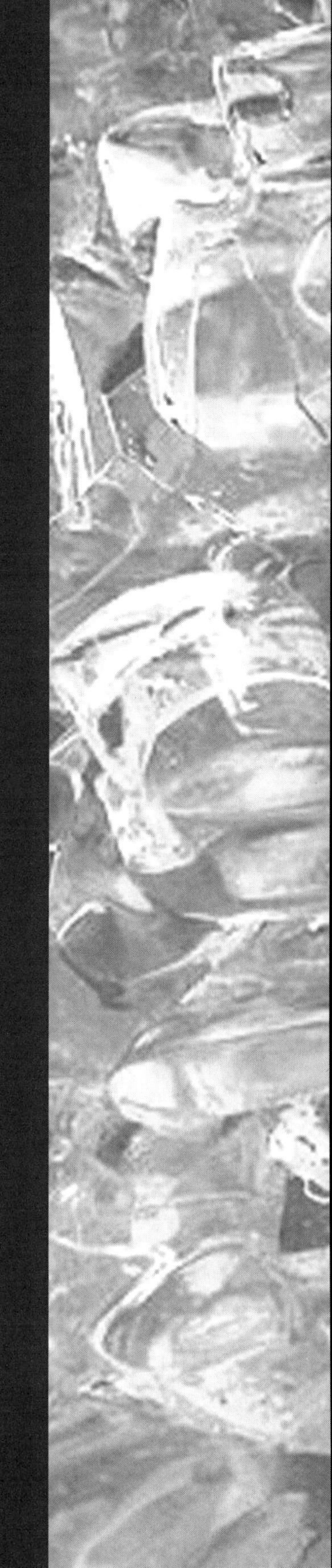

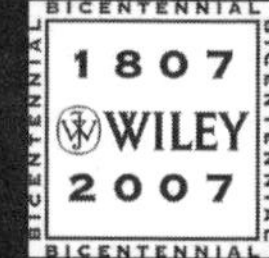

John Wiley & Sons, Inc.

This book is printed on acid-free paper. ♾

Published by John Wiley & Sons, Inc., Hoboken, New Jersey
Published simultaneously in Canada

For general information on our other products and services or for technical support, please contact our Customer Care Department within the United States at (800) 762-2974, outside the United States at (317) 572-3993 or fax (317) 572-4002.

Wiley also publishes its books in a variety of electronic formats. Some content that appears in print may not be available in electronic books. For more information about Wiley products, visit our web site at www.wiley.com.

Library of Congress Cataloging-in-Publication Data:

Katsigris, Costas.
The bar and beverage book / Costas Katsigris, Chris Thomas. — 4th ed.
p. cm.
Includes index.
ISBN-13: 978-0-471-64799-7 (cloth)
ISBN-10: 0-471-64799-3 (cloth)
1. Bartending. I. Thomas, Chris, 1956– II. Title.
TX950.7.K37 2006
641.8′74—dc22

2006025101

Printed in the United States of America

10 9 8 7

Contents

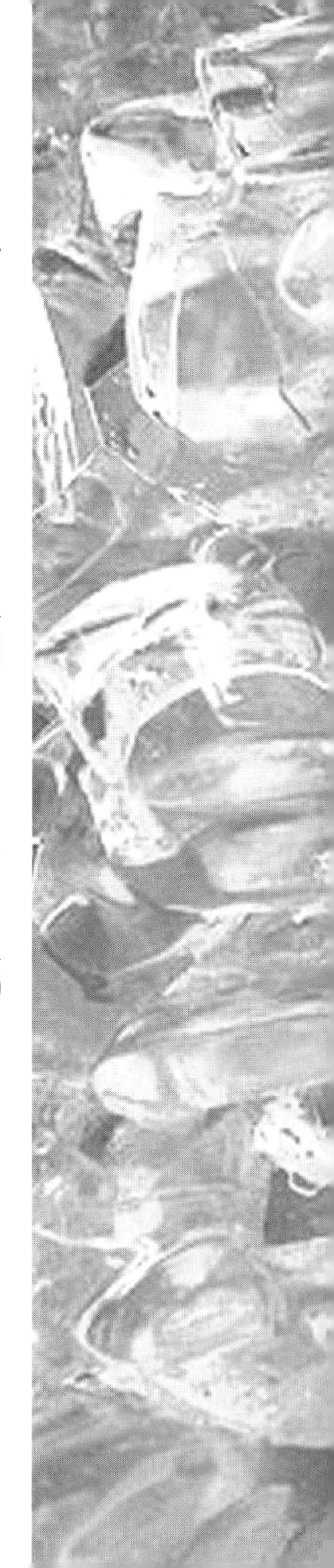

CHAPTER 7

WINE SALES AND SERVICE 275

CHAPTER 8

BEER 307

CHAPTER 9

SANITATION AND BAR SETUP 361

CHAPTER 10

MIXOLOGY, PART ONE 401

CHAPTER 11

CHAPTER 12

CHAPTER 13

CHAPTER 14

Preface

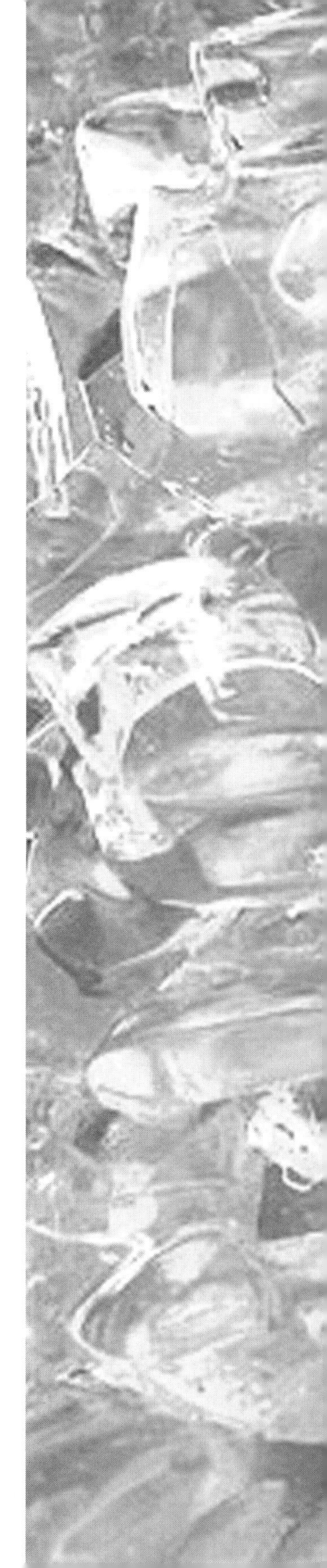

Owning a bar seems like the ultimate way to make friends and have fun while building a successful business. In this fourth edition of *The Bar and Beverage Book,* we've tried to prepare prospective bar owners, managers, servers, and bartenders for the hard work and planning that are required in order to realize the payoffs—e.g., friends, fun, and profit!

Since the first edition of this book was published in 1983, the years have thrown challenges at the bar and beverage industry that few observers could have predicted. The changing demographics of America have changed drinking habits, as well as beverage preferences. The trends are discussed in Chapter 1, after a brief history of the industry.

A climate of caution has overtaken the legal and law enforcement communities, with higher legal drinking ages, more stringent drunken-driving laws, and stiffer penalties for breaking them. For anyone who serves alcohol, the increased responsibilities—legal, ethical, and moral—are huge considerations. We cover them thoroughly in Chapter 2, along with information about alcohol's impact on human health and nutrition. Then, Chapters 3 and 4 encompass the many details of how to plan and organize a new bar business, from doing market research on potential customer groups, to designing and equipping the bar itself.

A visit to any local liquor store will confirm the plethora of flavored liquors and eye-catching packaging and advertising to make each and every product "the next big thing." And yet, almost all of them begin with the same basic distillation steps covered in Chapter 5. Our in-depth discussion includes current trends in *mixology,* food-pairing, and demographics of "who's drinking what." It is the longest chapter in the book, covering all the major brown goods and white goods, plus liqueurs and specialty products. The art (and science!) of bartending is covered in Chapters 10 and 11, including plenty of cocktail recipes and discussion of techniques.

Winemaking is the topic of Chapter 6, with new information about all ten of the world's top wine-producing countries, and why some wineries are choosing alternatives to traditional corks as bottle closures. The discussion continues in Chapter 7 with new sections on creating and pricing wine lists and by-the-glass programs. We have retained basic information about decanting, storage, and how to open wine and Champagne bottles.

The hotly competitive beer industry is the focus of Chapter 8, in which we have greatly expanded the definitions of ale and lager types and styles and included a discussion of *malternative* beverages. We have added hints for promoting beer sales, training serving staffs, and maintaining draft beer systems.

Chapter 9 covers the basic bar sanitation and set-up procedures and the importance of creating these routines, with expanded HACCP-based food-safety guidelines.

Like any service industry, bars have numerous budget challenges. In the latter chapters of the book, we delve into the fiscal realities of the following:

- Employee management (Chapter 12)—Interviewing and hiring, staff training, calculating wages, paying benefits, and requiring dress codes or uniforms.
- Purchasing and inventory considerations (Chapter 13)—The consolidation of suppliers and its impact on purchasing, using the Internet for research and purchasing, product freshness, and how to determine the value and turnover rates of inventory.
- Budgeting and planning (Chapter 14)—Pricing drinks profitably, preventing theft, and shopping for point-of-sale systems to track transactions.
- Managing the business (Chapter 15)—Creating a business plan and using it as a touchstone for ongoing operations; how to determine the worth of the business, and what to do to protect your successful concept from being stolen or copied.
- Obeying the laws (Chapter 16)—The federal-agency changes (from BATF to TTB), product labeling and disposal requirements, insurance coverage, learning about state and federal alcohol regulations, and how and why bars are audited.

To the Student: We've worked hard to ensure that this textbook is useful and easy to read, and we have tried to offer many options for you to consider if you're serious about making a career in the beverage industry. Pay special attention to the question-and-answer segments found at the end of the chapters. Also, read carefully the profiles of people from all facets of the industry. You will find their comments enlightening and fun, and their enthusiasm contagious.

To the Instructor: This text presents a comprehensive treatment of a topic that is ever changing. We've tried to organize the material in logical, sequential teaching units; there is also an *Instructor's Manual* (ISBN 0-471-78201-7) to help you create both in-class activities and enrichment assignments beyond the classroom walls. The *Instructor's Manual* is available to qualified instructors on the Wiley web site at www.wiley.com/college

To the Prospective (or Current) Bar Owner: This book is comprehensive enough to use for planning your business profitably. From layout and equipment, to hiring and staffing, to purchasing and budgeting, to responsible alcohol service, you can use this text both as your road map and as a springboard for testing your own ideas and creating a solid, money-making, crowd-pleasing business.

As you can tell there's a whole lot more to this business than mixing a good drink. The year 2005 marked the 20-year anniversary of *Nightclub & Bar* magazine, the joint effort of publisher Ed Meek and a small group of bar owners. The group holds its well-attended annual convention, known as "The Show," in Las Vegas. Judging from the photos on the magazine's web site, a *very* good time was had by all at the 2005 gathering! But beneath the revelry was an undercurrent of true concern for the future of the industry. Comments from participants, excerpted with permission from the July 2005 issue of *Nightclub & Bar,* sum it up quite well:

"The next 20 years will prove to be even more challenging than the last. The days of just serving alcohol and being successful are over. Licensed establishments need to provide more value-added products and services to create a unique experience for our guests. We will face more and more competition for that consumer entertainment dollar while also battling the 'new Prohibitionists' who distort the facts and continue to push us toward their ultimate goal of criminalizing beverage alcohol."

George Borello, Vice President of Marketing, Top-Shelf Marketing, a division of Progressive Specialty Glass, Buffalo, New York

"We cannot segment by music anymore. Today, gang members listen to the same music as 21-year-old girls do. That is part of the reason we have such a huge burden on security and safety. When we do concepts today, we really look hard at how to position it from an entertainment standpoint so that it drives revenues but doesn't pull an undesirable element. Once you put in a dance floor, that becomes a real challenge."

John Taffer, Chairman, Taffer Dynamics, Inc., West Palm Beach, Florida

"Everything from tip reporting to sexual harassment has become the responsibility of owners and managers. As a result of Mothers Against Drunk Driving (MADD), state regulatory agencies and the pot of money available through an operator's liquor liability insurance, guests' responsibility for over-consumption and driving under the influence has been shifted in part—or in some cases, entirely—over to restaurant and bar operators and their staff members. In many states, operators are now responsible for policing their guests' smoking. And there's more to come."

Bill Asbury, President and CEO, Pencom International, Denver, Colorado

These salient quotes should give prospective bar owners pause for reflection, but certainly not cause them to give up their dreams. These trends (and others) point to the need for well-trained bar managers with common sense, people skills, financial flexibility, and marketing savvy. You'll get a taste of all these topics in the next 16 chapters. The only things we *haven't* provided . . . are tastes of the beverages themselves!

Costas ("Gus") Katsigris
Chris Thomas

Acknowledgements

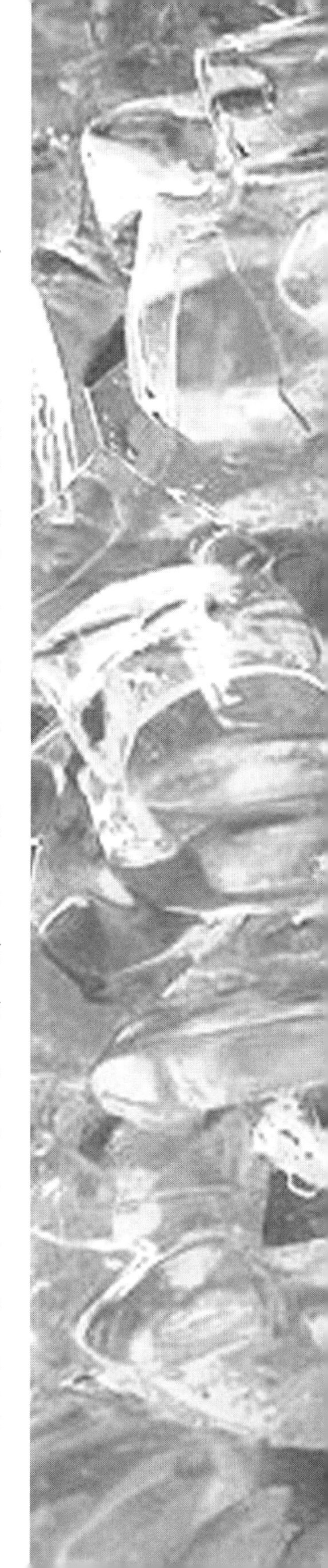

Successful books, like successful bars, are extremely collaborative efforts. First, the authors are grateful to all of the sources of our photos, charts, and sidebars. These items add a great deal to a book because they make the chapter topics come alive and increase students' understanding of trends and issues.

In addition to the people mentioned in the first three editions of *The Bar and Beverage Book,* the authors would like to add sincere thanks to the following people, listed here in alphabetical order:

Bianca Benevides Anderson, for introducing us to the intricacies of North American whiskeys and bourbons.

Darryl Beeson, a food, wine, and travel writer and educator, for his honest insights about sommeliers and the importance of their restaurant sales functions.

Alfonso Cevola, an Italian wine expert and longtime friend of Gus Katsigris from the days of Cracker's Restaurant in Dallas, Texas.

Chris Dains of Remy-Amerique, for his knowledge of French wine.

Cynthia Bozzelli Duke, the FHSV computer lab coordinator at El Centro College in Dallas, Texas. She and her colleagues served as Gus's own personal "help desk" in his ongoing quest for computer literacy!

Jim Fleming of Eclipse Distribution Services, for sharing his information about Spanish wines.

Andrew Frankel of Vineyard Brands, for his tireless marketing efforts on behalf of South African wines.

Ron Gay of Glazer's, for sharing his training materials and making us aware of the myriad types of craft and imported beers.

Regina Gowans, an administrative assistant in the El Centro College Business Division, for design assistance with the book's charts and tables.

Russ Kempton, who continues to update our information on scotch in general, and on single malt scotches in particular.

Emily Kennedy of Glazer's, for her enthusiastic input about Cognacs and brandies.

Gary A. Konke of Lone Star Wine Cellars, for his down-home advice on Texas-made wines.

Beat A. Kotoun of Kobrand Corporation, for inspiring additional research into Ports and Champagnes.

Anthony J. ("Tony") LaBarba, a legend in the Texas wine industry. Tony died in 2003, but he was an early inspiration to Gus, both to learn and teach about wine. In Texas, the land of six-packs, LaBarba managed to create a wine culture that continues to thrive.

John A. Laudenslager of Glazer's, who began as a student in Gus's classes at El Centro College and who continues his love affair with tequila research.

Camille McBee of La Buena Vida Vineyards, for information on Texas wines.

Randy C. McLaughlin of Sigel's Beverages LLP, for his wealth of California wine and wine-history information.

Eric Moore, of Sigel's Liquor and Fine Wines, for his perspective on the off-premise side of the beverage industry.

Al Moulin, a retired wine educator and industry leader. Al and Tony LaBarba urged Gus to write the first *Bar and Beverage Book* in the 1970s! At a youthful age 86, Al continues to be a vigorous cheerleader for each new edition.

Jace Patton and Pat Reynolds, both of Ben E. Keith Beers, for sharing their beer-sales and -promotion knowledge.

Robert Schafer of Classical Wines of Spain, for his limitless knowledge of wines in general, and Spanish wines in particular.

David P. Shanahan of Delaney Vineyards, for his knowledge of Texas viticulture.

David Ward, a training manager for Glazer's, for his expertise on brandies and Cognacs.

Barry White of Horizon Wines, for helpful information on the Rhone wines of France, as well as New Zealand wines.

We would like to thank the following people for reviewing this book in its various stages: John Bandman of the Art Institute of New York, Michael Barnes of State University of New York–Delhi, Robert P. Maidl of Harrisburg Area Community College, Terry McDonough of Erie Community College, Gary Ward of Scottsdale Community College, and Stephen Zagor of the Institute of Culinary Education.

And finally, special thanks to Evelyn Katsigris, who missed movie dates, ate dinner late (or alone), went without the garage being cleaned out, and postponed planned trips to visit friends and relatives, all so that Gus could finish his portions of this project.

Best wishes to all.

Gus Katsigris
Chris Thomas
July 2006

CHAPTER 1
THE BEVERAGE INDUSTRY, PAST AND PRESENT

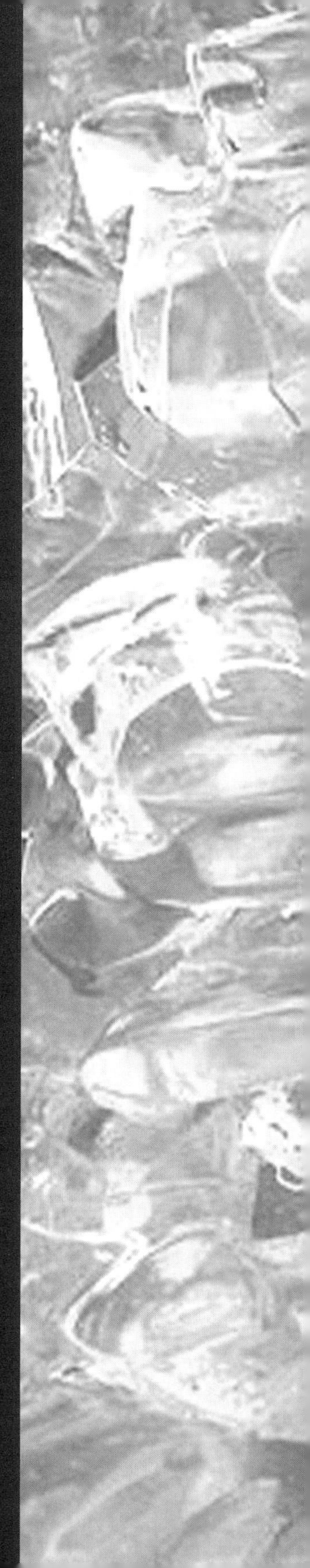

The drinking of alcoholic beverages is as old as human history, and the serving of drinks for profit is as old as the concept of profit itself. In most cultures over the centuries, these beverages have been accepted as an essential part of everyday life. And yet they also possess a magic that can sometimes take the edge off human troubles or add a special dimension to a ceremony or celebration.

There has always been a dark side to alcoholic beverages, too, which we will examine in coming chapters. The purpose of this chapter, however, is to offer a glimpse into the past and the present, both good and bad. It will provide you with important background to help you understand the challenges that the bar and beverage industry faces today.

THIS CHAPTER WILL HELP YOU . . .

- Learn the historical importance of alcohol in religious rites, ceremonies, and medical treatment; in meals; in fellowship; and in humankind's search for wisdom and truth.
- Learn about how wine, beer, and distilled spirits were created.
- Trace the history of the tavern in Europe and America and recount the role that taverns played in the American Revolution.
- Examine the impact of Prohibition on the bar industry.
- Compare and contrast the types of businesses that make up today's beverage-service industry.

In the last century in the United States alone, the bar and beverage business has gone from an illegal enterprise, carried on behind the locked doors of a **speakeasy,** to one of the nation's most glamorous and profitable businesses. Together with the foodservice or restaurant business, the two form the country's fourth-largest industry. In fact, it is impossible to separate them.

In the 1930s the United States was nearing the end of **Prohibition,** which was an unsuccessful attempt to regulate alcohol consumption by outlawing it entirely. History tells us that such attempts have never worked because people find other ways to get what they want. From earliest times, human beings seem to have wanted alcoholic beverages. Indeed, some historians theorize that one of the reasons our nomadic forebears settled into civilized life was to raise grain and grapes to ensure supplies of what they looked upon as sacred beverages.

THE EARLIEST WINES

Perhaps 8,000 to 10,000 years ago someone discovered that when fruit (or grain, milk, or rice) was fermented, the results tasted good, made one happy—or both. The Bible mentions wine consumption in both the Old and the New Testaments. When Noah settled down after the flood, he planted a vineyard ". . . and he drank of the wine and was drunken." With all of alcohol's benefits and hazards, it was a universal feature of early civilizations.

At least one legend claims that wine was discovered accidentally, by a neglected member of a Persian king's harem. She attempted to end her loneliness by ending her life, drinking from a jar marked "Poison." It contained grapes that had fermented. She felt so much better after drinking the liquid that she gave a cup of it to the king, who named it "the delightful poison" and welcomed her back into active harem life.

Early peoples all over the world fermented anything that would ferment: honey, grapes, grains, dates, rice, sugarcane, milk, palms, peppers, berries, sesame seeds, pomegranates. Almost all of the world's wines (the ones made from grapes, that is) can be traced to a single Eurasian grape species, **Vitus vinifera.** We know that grapes were being cultivated as early as 6,000 B.C. in the Middle East and Asia. The Egyptians, Phoenicians, and Chinese were all tending their vines at about the same time. It is believed that the ancient Greeks got their **viticulture** knowledge from the Egyptians, and began to make wine about 2,000 B.C.

Historians continue to debate the exact origin of the term *wine,* but there is wide agreement that the Hittite characters that spell *wee-on* are probably the first recorded word for wine, around 1,500 B.C. The Oxford English Dictionary credits the old English word *win,* which derived from the Latin *vinum* and is further traced to the ancient Greek word *oinos.* Indeed, the Greek term *oinos logos* ("wine logic") is the origin of the modern word for the study of wine: enology (the U.S. spelling) or oenology (the British spelling).

The practice of aging wines was first discovered by the Greeks, in cylinders known as **amphorae.** Made of clay, they were remarkably airtight. Fifteen hundred years later, the Romans tried a similar method, but their clay was more porous and didn't work as well. So they began coating their clay vessels with tar on the insides, a process known as **pitching.** Yes, it prevented air from mixing with wine, but can you imagine what the addition of tar must have done to the quality of the wine?

By 1,000 B.C. grapevines were found in Sicily and Northern Africa. Within the next 500 years, grapevines reached the Iberian Peninsula, Southern France, and even Southern Russia. Conquering Saracen (Arab) tribes in the Middle Ages brought both winemaking and **distillation** skills with them. The words *alcohol* and *still* are Arabic in origin.

As the Roman Empire spread it brought grapes to Northern Europe, too. After the fall of the Roman Empire, the Catholic Church was the most prominent promoter of viticulture. Monasteries became the vanguards of wine production and knowledge because wine was needed both in everyday life and in sacramental activities. The Portuguese are credited with shipping the first corked bottles of wine to England, but not until the year 1780.

In one of the more fascinating discoveries of this century—at least, for wine lovers—a bottle of wine from the 1700s was discovered in 2002, bobbing around in the North Sea off the coast of The Netherlands. Although the cork was soft, no appreciable amount of seawater had seeped into the flask-like glass bottle. A tasting panel of seven experts gathered to sip and study the contents. They decided it was an early variant of dry port that had been colored with a small amount of elderberry juice. Its alcohol content was estimated at 10.6 percent, it showed no traces of oxidation, and its acidity compared favorably to present-day wines.

In many cultures people associated intoxicating beverages with wisdom. Early Persians discussed all matters of importance twice: once when they were sober and once when they were drunk. Saxons in ancient England opened their council meetings by passing around a large, stone mug of beer. Greeks held their famous symposiums (philosophical discussions) during hours of after-dinner drinking. In fact, the word *symposium* means "drinking together." As the Roman historian Pliny summed it up, *"In vino veritas"* ("In wine there is truth").

Alcoholic beverages, often in combination with herbs, have been used for centuries as medicines and tonics. Indeed, herbs and alcohol were among the few ways of treating or preventing disease until about a century ago. But probably the most important historic use of alcoholic beverages was also the simplest: as food and drink. Bread and **ale,** or bread and wine, were the staples of any meal for an ordinary person, with the drink considered food. For centuries these hearty beverages provided up to half the calories needed for a day's heavy labor. In addition, they were considered the only liquids fit to drink, with good reason. Household water was commonly polluted. Milk could cause *milk sickness* (tuberculosis). But beer, ale, and wine were disease-free, tasty, and thirst-quenching, crucial qualities in societies that preserved food with salt and washed it down with a diet of starches.

Both wines and grapevines were imported from France to the New World in the 1700s. As U.S. Minister to France Thomas Jefferson was one of the primary supporters of the fledgling winemaking industry, and tried (passionately but unsuc-

FIGURE 1.1 Bacchus, the Roman god of wine. Photo courtesy the Picture Collection, The Branch Libraries, The New York Public Library.

cessfully) to grow his own grapes at Monticello. By the early 1900s about 1,700 wineries dotted the United States, and they were mostly small, family-owned businesses.

Wine was still considered an effete beverage until the 1800s, when Italian immigrants came to the United States with their home winemaking skills and a hospitable culture that accepted wine as a simple, everyday part of mealtimes and celebrations. Many of today's best-known California winemakers, with names like Gallo and Mondavi, are descendants of these immigrant families.

Today the world's largest wine museum is located in Briones, a town in the Rioja region of Spain, about 180 miles northeast of Madrid. From a thirteenth-century wine vessel, to more than 3,000 corkscrews, you can learn about the history of winemaking in English or Spanish. The facility is a five-story building owned by the Vivanco family, on their Dinastia Vivanco winery property.

 WINE AND RELIGION

Early beers, ales, and wines were considered gifts from the gods—that is, miracle products with magical powers. People used them universally in religious rites, and they still do. The Israelites of the Old Testament offered libations to Jehovah. The Romans honored **Bacchus,** god of wine (see Figure 1.1). Christians used wine in the sacrament of Communion. Primitive peoples used fermented beverages in their sacred rites. Victories, weddings, and other sacred and joyous occasions were celebrated with wine or ale. Camaraderie and fellowship were acknowledged with a "loving cup," passed around the table and shared by all until it was emptied.

Of all alcoholic beverages wine has the greatest religious connection. In the book *Religion and Wine: A Cultural History of Wine-Drinking in the United States* (University of Tennessee Press, 1996), author Robert Fuller traces the development of winemaking from the French Huguenots, Protestants who settled along the East Coast of North America in the 1500s, to the Pilgrims in Plymouth Bay in the 1600s, to the Franciscan friars and Jesuit priests who built the early missions in California during the 1700s and 1800s. Whether these early Americans were Baptists, Methodists, or Mormons, they permitted and enjoyed limited wine consumption as part of their worship. According to Fuller the United States did not have "grape-juice Protestants" (a nickname for those who decried the alcohol content of wine and replaced it in ceremonies with grape juice) until the late eighteenth century. Interestingly this alternative was first developed by Thomas Welch, a dentist and Methodist minister. His name later became a famous trademark for juice products.

At that time attitudes about alcohol changed as some religious groups (Fuller calls them "ascetic Christians") began to espouse the theory that the road to heaven required total self-discipline, including the denial of all earthly pleasures. Some groups feared that consuming alcohol would weaken sensibility, ethics, and moral values and diminish self-control in an age where many churches sought greater control over their members.

Conversely other religious groups felt just as strongly that rituals using wine could mediate God's presence and foster greater enjoyment of what life had to offer. These included Roman Catholics, Eastern Orthodox, Episcopalians, and Lutherans. And so the rift widened.

Since the 1800s, the relationship between alcohol and religion has been the subject of debate and ambivalence. Almost two centuries later, in 1990, California winemaker Robert Mondavi designed a new label for his wines that included a paragraph extolling the beverage's longtime role in culture and religion. In part it read, "Wine has been with us since the beginning of civilization. It is a temperate, civilized, sacred, romantic mealtime beverage recommended in the Bible . . ." Mondavi was prohibited from using this wording by the U.S. Bureau of Alcohol, Tobacco and Firearms.

A BRIEF HISTORY OF BEER

The Sumerians (a generic name for the ancient inhabitants of Mesopotamia) are said to have discovered the beer fermentation process quite by chance. They must have liked it: They had a goddess of brewing, **Ninkasi,** and a hymn to her, which was the beer-making recipe put to music.

Their successors, the Babylonians, knew how to brew 20 different types of beer. The recipes were recorded by scribes as early as 6,000 B.C. The ancient Egyptians made note of Ramses III, the pharaoh whose annual sacrifice of about 30,000 gallons of beer appeased "thirsty gods." The Egyptians passed on their brewing knowledge to the Greeks and Romans. In each of these civilizations wine was considered the trendy beverage, and beer was brewed on the outer fringes of the empires, where wine ingredients were apparently more difficult to get. Thus, we find beer brewed on German soil for the first time around the year 800 B.C.

The word *beer* comes from the ancient Latin word *biber,* a slang term for the beverage made by fermenting grain, adding hops for flavoring. In ancient times biber was considered lower class compared to ale, which was made in similar fashion but without the addition of hops. Hops became popular in Europe in the Middle Ages when it was discovered they served as a natural preservative; other herbs had been tried, sometimes with disastrous (i.e., poisonous) results. Not until the year 1516, however, did the Duke of Bavaria proclaim the German Beer Purity

Law, establishing for the first time that only barley, hops, and pure water could be used to make beer in that region. (The use of yeast was not yet known.) It is the oldest valid food and/or beverage law in the world. Today the European Union will permit importation of beers that are not brewed in accordance with the Beer Purity Law—but only if this fact is clearly stated on the label.

Until the Middle Ages both beer-brewing and bread-baking were viewed largely as women's work. In ancient Babylon only priestesses made beer, connecting it with religion for the first time. This connection became even stronger in Europe around A.D. 1,000 when monasteries turned their attention to brewing, for profit and their own mealtime use. Even during periods of fasting, monks were permitted to have beer.

During this time period the brewing process was also fine-tuned for different purposes. There were everyday, lower-alcohol beers, and others with higher alcohol content for special occasions. The modern term *bridal* joins the words *bride* and *ale;* a *bride's ale* was brewed by a young woman's family in preparation for wedding festivities.

Just about every civilization has made some type of beer, from whatever grain or root or plant was available in abundance. African tribes made their beer from millet; in Japan, the chief ingredient was rice; in Europe and North and South America, it was barley. The brew was hearty and filling, and provided calories and nutrients to fuel manual labor. The significance of beer in the average person's diet was demonstrated at the landing of the Mayflower at Plymouth, in what is now Massachusetts. The Pilgrims were headed for Virginia, but the ship was running out of beer. So they were "hasted ashore and made to drink water that the seamen might have more beer," wrote Governor Bradford later.

Before 1850 the beverage preference in the United States was ale, which had been popular in England. It was made like beer, but fermented more quickly, at higher temperatures than beer.

Beer production and sales played colorful parts in U.S. history. The first American brewery was opened in Lower Manhattan by the Dutch West Indies Company in 1632. There is speculation that the crude streets of New Amsterdam (later New York City) were first paved to help the horse-drawn beer wagons make better progress, which were so often stuck in the mud! Brewing became an aristocratic and popular business. William Penn, the Quaker leader who founded the state of Pennsylvania, Revolutionary War leaders Samuel Adams and Ethan Allen, and even George Washington, all were brewery owners. (Adams is credited with suggesting to Washington that he supply the Revolutionary Army with two quarts of beer per soldier, per day.)

By the mid-nineteenth century, brewing dynasties that are still household names among today's beer drinkers had begun in the United States. In Detroit, Michigan, Bernard Stroh, from a beer-making family in Rhineland, Germany, opened his brewing company in 1850. Five years later Frederick Miller purchased an existing facility, Best's Brewery in Milwaukee, Wisconsin. In St. Louis, Missouri, Eberhard Anheuser purchased a struggling brewery in 1860. His daughter married Adolphus Busch, a German immigrant whose family supplied grains and hops, and the mighty

Anheuser-Busch Company was born. A dozen years later, Adolph Coors, another German immigrant from the Rhineland, started to brew beer in Colorado.

The Germans brought with them a different brewing style that produced a lighter beer known as **lager,** which is paler and clearer in appearance than ale and has a drier flavor. Its name comes from a German word for *storage* or *storehouse;* it was routinely stored for several months in cold temperatures before serving. Making lager-style beer required ice, so it was typically brewed in winter and stored until summer, when the demand was highest. Milwaukee emerged as the nation's brewing center for the most practical reason: Ice was easily available from Lake Michigan, and there were plenty of local caves to store the beer. When refrigerators and icemakers were invented, lager could be brewed anytime, anyplace.

Heat was just as important as cold to the fast-growing beer-making industry. The French chemist Louis Pasteur discovered in the 1800s that, like milk or cider, beer could be heated to sufficient temperature to kill harmful bacteria without diminishing the quality of the brew. This process of **pasteurization** enabled beer to be bottled for shipment.

Pasteur also experimented with live brewer's yeast to prompt fermentation. Yeast had been around for many centuries and used for cooking and medicinal purposes. With the advent of reliable and sanitary methods of propagating yeast, the brewer's ability to make consistent beers, batch after batch, was greatly improved. By the 1960s stainless-steel barrels were replacing the old wooden ones in modern breweries. These metal barrels are considered to be more hygienic, and easier to fill and tap.

DISTILLED SPIRITS IN BRIEF

The art of distillation—first heating, then cooling and condensing liquids to extract and concentrate their alcohol content—was known in crude form even in ancient times. The Chinese and the peoples of the East Indies distilled liquids and used the resulting potions for medicinal purposes as early as 800 B.C. About the time the Pilgrims ran out of beer at Plymouth Rock, these forms of concentrated alcohol were coming into favor in Europe.

Distilled spirits made from fermented liquids were much more potent than the original liquids. The first ones were called **aqua vitae** (water of life) and used as medicines, but they were quickly assimilated into society as beverages. Highland Scots and Irish distillers made whiskey. The French distilled wine to make brandy. A Dutch doctor's experiments produced gin, which is alcohol flavored with the juniper berry. In Russia and Poland the distilled spirit was vodka. In the West Indies rum was made from sugarcane, while in Mexico, Spaniards distilled the Indians' native drink to make mescal, the great-grandfather of today's tequila. With increasing supplies of spirits and their high alcohol content, excessive drinking became a national problem in several European countries. In England cheap gin became the drink of the poor. They could and did get "drunk for a penny, dead drunk for two pence," as one gin mill advertised. This particular mill, in the same advertisement, mentioned that it also provided "free straw" (a bed of hay) for sleeping it off.

Across the Atlantic Americans welcomed the new spirits, and soon rum became the most popular drink and New England became a leading manufacturer. George Washington put rum to political use when he ran for the Virginia legislature, giving each voter a barrel of rum, beer, wine, or hard cider. By the end of the century whiskey was challenging rum in popularity.

Seeing a potential new income source, the new U.S. Congress enacted the first tax on whiskey production in 1791. Many of the distillers, still trying to recover financially from the Revolutionary War, did not have much money and refused to pay the taxes. By 1794 President Washington had a real problem on his hands. He mustered 12,000 troops and marched into Pennsylvania to avert the so-called Whiskey Rebellion. It ended without a shot being fired, but many angry distillers packed up and moved farther west to enjoy greater freedom and avoid future confrontations.

When Washington's presidency ended in 1797, he was once again a forerunner in the distilling business, making his own rye from his own grain in his own stills at Mount Vernon, Virginia. In one year his distillery produced 11,000 gallons of whiskey and showed a profit of $7,500, which is equal to about $105,000 today.

Here's his recipe, called a **mash bill:**

1. Start with 65 percent rye, 30 percent corn, and 5 percent malted barley, each ground (separately) into a coarse meal.
2. Mix the rye and corn. (This was done in a wooden vessel called a *hogshead.*) Add hot and cold water, and stick your hand into the mash to make sure it is not too hot. If it does not burn, the temperature is just right. Add the barley and stir.
3. Cool the mixture a bit more and add yeast. Let the mixture ferment for a few days.
4. Pour the mixture into a copper still and let it boil. The alcohol will vaporize and condense, flowing out of a tube (also known as a *worm*).
5. Collect the liquid and run it through the copper still one more time.

Washington probably barreled his whiskey and sold it immediately. Today distillers would age it for a few years. A few of today's top U.S. whiskey makers followed the recipe in 2003 to create a special batch for an auction to benefit the Mount Vernon estate, now an historic landmark. The Distilled Spirits Council, a trade group, is spending more than $1 million to excavate the site where the original distillery stood and re-create it as an educational exhibit.

The distillers who relocated to Tennessee and Kentucky after the Whiskey Rebellion inadvertently discovered a gold mine of sorts there: cold, clear water supplies that are still famous for their role in whiskey production. The spirit soon became known as **bourbon** since some of the first distillers set up shop in Bourbon County, Kentucky. As the American West was settled, whiskey was easier to store and transport than beer or wine; in great demand, it became a very popular commodity in the trade-and-barter commerce of frontier life.

Distillation gained momentum as the process was refined. **Rectification** (described more fully in Chapter 5), or distilling a liquid more than once, yielded a much cleaner and almost 100 percent pure spirits than previous efforts. Before rectification was perfected, spirits contained flavor impurities. Herbs, honey, and/or flowers were added to mask them. After rectification these items were also routinely added, but now, to enhance the flavor. Some of today's grand liqueurs are the results of these early flavor concoctions. Cognac, for instance, was a pale, acidic French wine for which there was little public demand—until it was concentrated in the 1600s as an *eau de vie,* French for *aqua vitae.* It became enormously popular and still is today.

ALCOHOL AND HEALTH IN HISTORY

Alcoholic beverages, particularly wines, were the prime medicinal agents of our ancestors from the ancient world into the early nineteenth century. Wine was the most common ingredient in the medicines of ancient Egypt, Syria, and Mesopotamia, either taken by mouth or topically applied. The Roman scholar Pliny the Elder recommended a mixture of wine and rue (a strongly scented, bitter-tasting shrub) for just about any type of insect sting or animal bite. Jewish Talmudic tradition maintained that impotence could be cured by heating and drinking a mixture of wine and ground saffron. The oddest prescription we found while researching this topic came from ancient Egypt: a combination of wine and ground-up donkey testicles was fermented and used to treat epilepsy.

In addition to alcohol's anesthetic properties, early physicians and folk healers recognized its ability to act as a disinfectant. Remember old Western movies in which whiskey is guzzled by the cowboy before the country doctor removes the bullet from his leg—and then also poured on the open wound to sterilize it? The doctors of olden times couldn't see and didn't know about things like germs, single-cell yeasts, and antioxidants, but they did see cause-and-effect relationships. Centuries ago people who drank alcohol (not to excess, of course) were healthier and hardier than those who did not due to its nutritional value. They lived longer and reproduced more. Armies were "inoculated" against disease on their foreign campaigns by mixing wine with the local water supply to kill bacteria. Early beermakers realized that unless their brew fermented for a certain time and reached an alcohol level of at least 5 percent, it would contain detrimental microorganisms that produced "off" flavors and odors and might even be dangerous to drink.

The curative compounds found in alcoholic beverages were not isolated and purified to be used on their own until the 1800s. Today remnants of folk medicine still abound, from rubbing whiskey on a teething baby's gums to ease pain, to sipping a glass of wine to aid digestion. You will learn more about alcohol, health, and nutrition in Chapter 2.

THE TAVERN: PLEASURES AND POLITICS

Pouring for profit developed hand in hand with civilization. The clay tablets of Old Babylon's King Hammurabi refer to alehouses and high-priced, watered-down beer. A papyrus document from ancient Egypt warns, "Do not get drunk in the taverns . . . for fear that people repeat words which may have gone out of your mouth without you being aware of having uttered them." Greek and Roman cities had taverns that served food as well as drink; excavations in Pompeii (a Roman city of 20,000) have uncovered the remains of 118 bars. In both Greece and Rome some taverns offered lodging for the night, or gambling and other amusements.

After the fall of the Roman Empire, life in most of Europe became much more primitive. When next the taverns reappeared, they were alehouses along the trade routes, which provided a stable for the horses, a place to sleep, and sometimes a meal. In England the public house, or **pub**, developed during Saxon times as a place where people gathered for fellowship and pleasure. An evergreen bush on a pole outside meant ale was served. Each pub was identified by a sign with a picture of, for example, a Black Horse, White Swan, or Red Lion. These early "logos" were used because most people could not read.

As time went on the tavern became a permanent institution all over Europe. There were many versions: inns, pubs, cabarets, dance halls, and "meetinghouses." Neighbors gathered at these establishments to exchange the latest news and gossip over a mug or a tankard. In cities men of similar interests met for a round of drinks and good talk. In London's Mermaid Tavern Shakespeare, dramatist and poet Ben Jonson, and other famous literary figures met regularly. Lawyers had their favorite taverns; students, theirs. Members of Parliament formed political clubs, each meeting in its favorite tavern for lively discussion of strategy.

Whatever its form, the tavern was a place to enjoy life, to socialize, to exchange ideas, and to be stimulated. The beverages intensified the pleasure, loosened the tongue, sparked the wit, or, as Socrates said, "moistened the soul." When Europeans immigrated to America, they brought the tavern with them. It was considered essential to a town's welfare to have a place providing drink, lodging, and food. In Massachusetts in the 1650s, any town without a tavern was fined! Often the tavern was built near the church so that parishioners could warm up quickly after Sunday services held in unheated meetinghouses. A new town sometimes built its tavern before its church. As towns grew into cities and roads were built connecting them, taverns followed the roads. In parts of Pennsylvania today it is possible to find towns named for such early taverns as Blue Bell, Red Lion, and King of Prussia. In some towns the old tavern is still standing.

It was also in the taverns that the spirit of revolution was born, fed, and translated into action. These were the rendezvous spots for rebels, where groups like the Sons of Liberty were formed and held their meetings. The Boston Tea Party was planned in Hancock Tavern, while in the Green Dragon, Paul Revere and 30 companions formed a committee to watch the troop movement of British soldiers. In Williamsburg the Raleigh Tavern was the meeting place of the Virginia patriots, including Patrick Henry and Thomas Jefferson. In New York's Queen's Head Tavern, a New York Tea Party was planned, and many patriot meetings were held there during the Revolutionary War. After the war Samuel Fraunces, its owner, renamed the tavern Fraunces Tavern (to eliminate any reference to the Queen). It was here that General George Washington said good-bye to his fellow officers in 1783. When Washington became President, Fraunces became his chief steward. Today, Fraunces Tavern is a New York City landmark.

When Americans pushed westward taverns sprang up along the routes west. As towns appeared the tavern was often the first building. Homes and merchants grew up around it. By the middle 1800s the "modern" American tavern was becoming a large-scale inn for the travelers and businesspeople of a nation on the move. At the same time drinking places without lodging were appearing. These kept the name *tavern,* while more elaborate inns adopted the term *hotel.* But the hotel kept its barroom; it was often a showplace, with a handsome mahogany bar and a well-dressed bartender who might wear gold and diamonds. Some hotel bars became famous, including the Menger in San Antonio where Teddy Roosevelt recruited Rough Riders, and Planter's Hotel in St. Louis, home of the Planter's Punch.

By the turn of the century the successors to the early taverns had taken many forms. There were glittering hotels that served the wealthy in cities and resorts. There were fashionable cabarets, such as Maxim's in Paris, where rich and famous men consorted with rich and famous courtesans, and music halls, such as the Folies Bergères. There were private clubs, cafes ranging from elegant to seedy, big-city saloons that provided free lunches with their drinks, and corner saloons of working-class districts, where many a man toasted his victories and/or drowned his sorrows in drink (see Figure 1.2). The restaurant industry also made its appearance in the nineteenth century, serving wines and other beverages to enhance the diner's pleasure.

PROHIBITION AND ITS EFFECTS

Meanwhile, in the United States a growing number of people sought to curb the use of alcoholic beverages. At first this movement went by the name **Temperance** and its target was "ardent spirits" (distilled spirits), but proponents soon included beer and wine and expanded their goal from temperance, or moderation, to total prohibition. In a century-long barrage of propaganda and moral fervor, the movement succeeded in convincing many Americans that drink of any kind led inevitably to sin and damnation. If you outlaw "demon rum," they believed, sin would disappear and Utopia would naturally emerge. Along with this belief went the notion that those engaged in making or selling alcoholic beverages were on the devil's side of this battle between good and evil or, as it was also dubbed, **"Dry" and "Wet."**

FIGURE 1.2 The typical bar setup today doesn't look much different than it did in the 1880s, when this photo was taken in Pocatello, Idaho. Courtesy of the Idaho Historical State Society, Boise, Idaho, photograph number 70-47.1.

The fervor was fed by the proliferation of saloons opened by competing breweries to push their products, many of them financed by money from abroad. By the late 1800s there was a swinging-door saloon (also called a *joint*) on every corner in small towns and big cities. These establishments often became unsavory places because there were far too many of them to survive on sales of beer and whiskey alone, so many became places of prostitution, gambling, and other illegal goings-on.

In 1851 Maine became the first state to pass its own prohibition law. By 1880 Kansas was the first state to pass a constitutional amendment that outlawed both the manufacture and sale of alcohol, although the new law was selectively enforced or often simply ignored.

In Kansas, Carry A. Nation was a woman who decided "enough was enough." A combination of a frustrating marriage to an alcoholic and disgust at the lack of enforcement of the law led Nation to take her own kind of action. Calling herself a "Home Defender," she waged a two-year, vigilante-style campaign, rallying women to show up at bars swinging bats and hatchets—and singing hymns—as they literally destroyed the places! Her crusade made her the darling of national Prohibition advocates. By 1901 Nation addressed the Kansas legislature on behalf of families. She also went on the lecture circuit, billing herself as "The Famous and Original Bar Room Smasher," although she was neither the first nor the last activist to employ violence for the cause (see Figure 1.3).

FIGURE 1.3 Anti-alcohol activist Carry Nation took her "show on the road" in the early 1900s, destroying Kansas barrooms with hatchets and baseball bats as "The Barroom Smasher." Photo courtesy of the Kansas State Historical Society, Topeka, Kansas.

While the Prohibition movement gave some women (who could not yet vote) their first taste of political activism, it was also an expression of religious and ethnic antagonisms. It pitted fundamentalist middle-Americans against the new German and Irish Catholic immigrants. The brewers were German and the bartenders were Irish, and both brought with them cultures that included alcohol intake as a fact of everyday life. The movement also pitted small-town and rural America against what was perceived as big-city licentiousness. During World War I the Dry side won its battle. The **Eighteenth Amendment,** passed during the wartime fever of patriotism and self-denial, prohibited the "manufacture, sale, transportation, and importation of intoxicating liquors" in the United States and its territories. Ratified by all but two states, Connecticut and Rhode Island, it went into effect in 1920.

Despite the zeal of its proponents, Prohibition had a short and unhappy life of not quite 14 years. As Kansans had discovered decades earlier, there was simply no way to enforce it. While legal establishments were closing their doors, illegal "speakeasies" began opening theirs to those who could whisper the right password. Legal breweries and distilleries closed down, but illegal stills made liquor by the light of the moon in secret hideouts, hence the nickname **moonshine.** Illegal spirits also were smuggled into the country from Canada and Mexico and from "Rum Rows" offshore; these were bootleg supply ships that sold to small, fast boats whose entrepreneurial captains made the run to shore. Some folks just decided to make their own beer, wine, and gin at home.

Prohibition affected the wine industry as dramatically as it did other alcoholic beverage producers. Many winery owners simply plowed their fields under and planted different crops. A few received special licenses to make sacramental wines, or permits to make wines strictly for home use, only up to 200 gallons per year.

Ironically, rather than decreasing drinking, Prohibition seemed almost to invite it: Flouting the law became, to some, the fashionable (or, at least, enterprising) thing to do. After nine years of Prohibition New York City had 32,000 speakeasies, about twice as many as the number of pre-Prohibition saloons! To add to the problems of enforcement, organized crime took over the bootleg business in many cities. Gangsters quickly became rich, powerful, and seemingly immune to the law. The combination of racketeering, gang warfare, and bootlegging became a major national problem. Everyone, even those who first vehemently supported it, agreed that things had gotten out of hand under Prohibition. In 1933 Congress passed the **Twenty-first Amendment,** repealing the Eighteenth.

Before Prohibition shut it down, beverage manufacturing had been the fifth largest industry in the United States. After passage of the Twenty-first Amendment, it made a quick comeback, despite stiff taxes and heavy regulation by federal and state governments. Today alcoholic beverages are an accepted part of the American scene, and have been for some time; the sale of liquor is legal in every state and the District of Columbia. The serving of liquor in bars and restaurants is a normal part of the culture, and restaurant patrons expect to be able to buy mixed drinks, beer, and wine with their food. In fact restaurants that don't serve liquor often have a hard time competing. But the "Wet versus Dry" controversy never really ended. Control of the issue was given to states, counties, towns, and precincts, resulting

A FORMER SPEAKEASY CELEBRATES ITS COLORFUL PAST

December 2003 marked the seventieth "anniversary" of the end of Prohibition, and New York City's famous '21' Club was among the celebration sites. The '21' Club had been a speakeasy, complete with passwords, secret knocks, and trick doors for its clientele.

The front entrance was guarded by tall, spiked gates, and there was a peephole in the door. In a cramped cellar below the main kitchen, a number of 18-inch meat skewers hang on a hook. Insert one of the skewers into the "correct" hole in the wall, even today, and it unlocks a heavy door that protects a million-dollar inventory of fine wine—the former site of the illegal bar. Its backbar shelves were rigged to dump their liquor contents into the city sewer system at a moment's notice!

Similar "secret taverns" existed in just about every block of the downtown area. '21' Club legend has it that once, when federal agents showed up for a raid, New York City's good-timing Mayor James J. Walker was among the guests! He called the police and had the agents' cars towed away.

(Information adapted from a *New York Times* article, December 6, 2003.)

FIGURE 1.4 The trick door of New York's '21' Club, opened by pushing a metal bar into a tiny hole. Today the door still works and the area behind it is used as a wine cellar. Courtesy of the '21' Club.

in a mishmash of local liquor laws that has made America into a "Wet-Dry" checkerboard. Even today this pattern mirrors our society's longstanding mixed feelings about alcohol use.

Historically alcohol has always had its dark side as well as its benefits, from the drunkenness in the taverns of ancient Egypt, to the cheap gin consumed by the poor in eighteenth-century England, to the corner saloons of small-town America 100 years ago. Today the problems are just as critical, with drunk-driving accidents taking thousands of lives each year and some 10 percent of drinkers becoming alcohol-addicted. What is it about alcohol that can "moisten the soul," yet cause so much harm? We will discuss this issue at length in Chapter 2.

TODAY'S BEVERAGE-SERVICE INDUSTRY

Since 1990 alcohol consumption in the United States has gradually declined. Expert observers relate the drop to lifestyle changes for many busy Americans, many of whom now focus on fitness and preventive health care. They've stopped smoking, they exercise, they watch their weight and their cholesterol count, and they keep their heads clear during working hours. The "three-Martini lunch" is now a relic, replaced by bottled waters, flavored iced teas, and, on rare occasions, perhaps a single glass of wine. These moderate drinkers limit their consumption to one or two drinks a day. At the same time they are very much interested in the quality of whatever drink they choose. When they do imbibe they tend to choose premium or super-premium liquors and wines. "Drinking less but drinking better" has become the norm.

What People Are Drinking

Beverage Digest magazine tracks U.S. beverage-consumption figures and graciously shared them with us for this chapter. Perhaps the statistic that says the most about American lifestyle changes at the turn of the most recent century is the per capita consumption figure for bottled water: It has risen from 8.7 gallons per person per year in 1993, to 16.6 gallons per person per year in 2003.

In contrast Americans drank the highest amount of distilled spirits—two gallons per person per year—back in the 1970s. Since 1993 consumption figures have hovered between 1.2 and 1.3 gallons per person per year.

When the fitness enthusiast does drink, he or she wants a "light" drink, one that is perceived to contain less alcohol and fewer calories. (Some of these drinks do and some don't, as we will see). But overall, sales of spirits continue to decline. **"White goods"** (vodka, gin, tequila, and rum) generally do better than **"brown goods"** (bourbon, scotch, and other whiskies) even though they all have similar alcohol contents.

Wine enjoyed its largest upsurge in popularity in the 1980s, reaching a high of 2.4 gallons per person per year. Wine is still popular and boasts a loyal following, but overall consumption has remained steady, at about 2 gallons per person per year since 1990. Despite jam-packed supermarket wine-section shelves and all kinds of exotic choices, the three best sellers continue to be Chardonnay, Cabernet Sauvignon, and White Zinfandel.

Beer sales look very impressive when compared to wine and spirits. Americans consume a little more than 21 gallons of beer per person per year. However, this is a slump compared to the 24-gallon-per-person figures of the 1980s, and it is less than half the amount of soft drinks we consume annually.

To slow sales erosion and attract health-conscious consumers, beer companies busily introduced some major product extensions in the 1990s: light beers (lower in alcohol and calories than their "regular" counterparts), dry beers (crisply flavored, and touting "no aftertaste"), and nonalcoholic beers. Light beers now account for 47 percent of all beer sales in the United States.

Imported beers and beers from small, regional breweries, or *microbreweries,* have gained substantial followings, and there's a small but lively home-brewing hobbyist market. In most major cities you'll find at least one beer-making store where home brewers can buy equipment and supplies and get advice. For a fee some allow you to brew on-site, let the beer age in their storage tanks, and then come back and bottle your own creation yourself!

In recognition of customers who drink less, almost all restaurants offer wines by the glass, not just by the bottle. (In Chapter 7, you'll learn more about creating a workable wine list.) They also do more to publicize their nonalcoholic offerings: mineral waters, soft drinks, flavored teas, juice drinks, and even no-alcohol beers and *mocktails.* The latter, alcohol-free versions of the Bloody Mary, Piña Colada, and other drinks, are mixed and served with the same care and flair as the bar specialties.

This does not mean that Martinis or Gin and Tonics are obsolete, or that fewer people are patronizing bars or ordering drinks with their meals. There has been renewed interest in the traditional cocktails (Martini, Bloody Mary, Screwdriver) and *tall drinks* (Scotch and Soda or Bourbon and Soda, Gin and Tonic or Vodka and Tonic). There is also strong interest in **call brands,** the slang term for premium brands that are asked for, or "called for," by name. Super-premium imports, such as single-malt scotches, Irish whiskeys, Cognac and Armagnac brandies, also have loyal followings. They are popular with customers who have developed a taste for and interest in "buying the best" and are willing to pay more for it. They are also interested in experimenting with new brands and learning more about beverages. In contrast most brown-goods customers are in the upper age groups and are comfortable with their reliable favorites, such as Scotch and Soda or Bourbon and Water.

But be wary. By the time you read this it all might have changed! New drinks will be invented, and new twists will be added to old favorites. Managing a bar means keeping your finger on the pulse of the market and making the changes necessary to stay ahead.

Next, consider a few different types of beverage service, as well as the challenges associated with them. Though it is impossible to divide bars into just a few categories—there are almost as many variations as there are bars—certain kinds have distinct characteristics and styles of service, and it may be revealing to see how they differ and what they have in common.

The Beverage-Only Bar

The simplest kind of beverage enterprise is the bar that serves beverages alone, with no foodservice except snacks: peanuts, pretzels, cheese and crackers. This type of bar serves beer, wine, or mixed drinks, or any combination of the three, plus nonalcoholic beverages. It might be a neighborhood gathering place, a way station for commuters on their homeward treks, or a bar at an airport or bus terminal or bowling alley.

Business at such bars typically has a predictable flow: a daily pattern of peaks and valleys, a weekly pattern of slow days and heavy days, with the heavy days related to paydays and days off. There might also be seasonal patterns. In airports and bus terminals, business is geared to daily, weekly, and seasonal travel patterns, and according to the time of day; light beverages are served during morning and afternoon, and heartier drinks are served as the working day ends. Because only one type of product is sold and business is generally predictable, the operation of a beverage-only bar is relatively simple, from production, to staffing and purchasing, to keeping track of the beverages, money, and profits.

This type of bar also usually has a specific reason for success, perhaps its location, its reputation as a friendly place (or for pouring well-made drinks), or simply its lack of competition; or perhaps it has just "always been the place where everybody goes." Often such bars thrive by being the same as they always were. Customers become sentimental about them and would not tolerate change.

That said, as the mood of the country changes, many neighborhood bars are adding food to their offerings. Hotel chains, such as Marriott, Radisson, and Hyatt, have phased out their cocktail-only lounges in favor of food and beverage combinations. The decision is practical: Some states do not allow beverage sales without food sales; other bar owners have decided that it is simply more responsible to offer people food if they will be drinking. Master concessionaires, such as Host Marriott, now run more than 1,800 restaurants in 73 airports, and the trend has been to upgrade these facilities to pour more premium beverages, serve better food, partner with brewpubs (see p. 21), and offer entertainment for travelers awaiting their flights.

In short, beverage-only bars are definitely a minority today. Although some are highly profitable, most bars find that serving liquor alone is not enough to attract and keep customers. So the majority of bars offer something else: entertainment or food or both.

Bar/Entertainment Combinations

Bars offering entertainment range from the neighborhood bar with pool, pinball, dartboards, or giant televisions, to nightclubs with big-name entertainers, to comedy clubs, to ballrooms with big bands. In between are cocktail lounges and nightclubs with live-entertainment piano bars, country-and-western dancing, jazz or folk duos, or rousing rock-and-roll groups. This concept must include the decision to make room for a stage area, sound system, and dance floor. Having entertainment also means hiring someone knowledgeable to book the bands or entertainers whom people will want to see (negotiating contracts at a fair but affordable price) and always thinking ahead to the next fad or hottest music trend to attract the fickle public. A concept that includes regular entertainment of any kind also includes the fixed costs and additional financial risk of hiring and paying the entertainers.

In most cases the entertainment may draw the crowd, but it is the drinks that provide the profits. If there is a **cover charge**, which is an admission fee per person paid at the door, at least part of it is likely to go to the entertainers. The fortunes of this type of bar will rise and fall with the popularity of its entertainers, unless the place has something else going for it.

Probably the most stable type of bar/entertainment combo is the smaller place with an attractive ambience, good drinks, and local entertainment to draw a loyal, local crowd. The success potential of this kind of establishment is much the same as the bar-only enterprise. Larger operations featuring out-of-town entertainers have a higher but riskier profit potential. It is likely to be either feast or famine. The bar gears up for each crowd with temporary extra help, a large investment in liquor inventory, and possibly extra security personnel. Weather, holidays, location, and weeknight versus weekend crowds all heavily impact this type of business.

Casinos are another enduring combination of entertainment and beverage service. Today's casinos might be run by a huge corporation or a Native American tribal council, and might include everything from big-name stage productions and professional boxing matches, to restaurants and nongambling arcades that attract families instead of adults only.

Sports bars offer a different type of entertainment. In the mid-twentieth century, the term *sports bar* was a nickname for popular watering holes frequented by sports figures and sports writers, who bought each other drinks and traded stories and colorful quotes. Today, however, you are more likely to have your conversation yelling at a big-screen television than at a sports columnist. Modern-day sports bars are designed for group viewing of popular sporting events. Equipped with large television screens (or plenty of strategically placed smaller ones), the sports bar often sets a fixed price or cover charge to guarantee a good profit because customer turnover is so small (see Figure 1.5). Large sports bars serve a menu of full-course meals, and many take reservations in advance of popular events—boxing matches, baseball's World Series, a Triple Crown horse race—that will draw a crowd.

Food and Beverage Combinations

The most common form of beverage operation is one that is linked with some kind of foodservice. One type is the restaurant/bar, where drinks and wine are part of the meal service, served by the same waitstaff that serves the meal. The bar is often used as the waiting area for the restaurant during busy times. Drinks may be poured at a service bar out of public view or at a pickup station in a bar that serves customers while they are waiting for a table. The major portion of the sales comes from the foodservice. However, the beverage sales often turn the profit for the enterprise. The only added costs are for the wine and liquor, the bartender, and a minimum investment in equipment; the other necessities, service personnel and the facility itself, are built into the restaurant operation.

Another type of food-beverage combination is the bar that offers light food in addition to drinks. In this case the beverages and the bar atmosphere dominate, and the major sales volume comes from the bar. But the food is a nice sidelight that attracts customers and prolongs their stay. Typical menu items are appetizers: nachos, chips or crudités and dips, spiced chicken wings, and stuffed potato skins.

FIGURE 1.5 Some sports bars offer full-service dining but the focus is on cheering on your favorite teams, not necessarily on food and drink. Disney Regional Entertainment.

A special variation of the food-beverage combination is the **wine bar,** which first appeared during the 1970s as Americans discovered and learned to appreciate wines. Here the customer can choose from a selection of wines by the glass or by the bottle, beginning with inexpensive house wines and going up in quality and price as far as the entrepreneur cares to go. Some wine bars offer inexpensive one-ounce *tastes* (or groups of these one-ounce samples, known as **wine flights**) to enable guests to sample a number of wines. A full menu, or fruit and cheese platters and upscale hors d'oeuvres, can be served.

There are inherent problems in running wine bars. The first is, of course, that serving only wine tends to limit the clientele to wine lovers. Some urban areas have enough wine enthusiasts to support a profitable enterprise; they respond to quality and expertise, and they attend and appreciate special wine tastings, classes, and wine-centered celebrations. This enthusiasm, however, raises a second difficulty:

Purchasing appropriate wines requires an expertise few people have and may require a financial investment few are willing to make. As a result many wine bars serve liquor and beer as well. This broadens their appeal and allows them to realize the necessary profit margin. In effect they are simply bars that specialize in wine sales and wine knowledge.

Other wine bars may broaden their offerings by serving meals, thereby becoming restaurants with an emphasis on wines. Some also sell wines at retail, offering customers discounts for volume (one case or more) purchases. This combination of on-premise service and take-home sales is not an option everywhere. Beverage laws in many areas do not allow it.

Beer aficionados also have their own version of the wine bar. At a **brewpub,** beer is brewed and served right on the premises. The result: fresh, natural beers and ales, strong in flavor and aroma, with special seasonal offerings. Developed by small individual entrepreneurs and hobbyists, the beverage sets the theme of the restaurant. At least one shiny brew kettle is likely to be a major part of the decor, and the menu typically contains hearty, casual cuisine chosen to complement the beer. As popular as brewpubs are in many areas of the United States, they are not legal everywhere; some states still do not allow the manufacture and sale of alcoholic beverages on the same premises.

A popular type of food-beverage combination links a bar and a restaurant on an equal, semi-independent basis, with a common roof, theme, management team, and services that complement each other. The bar and restaurant areas are housed in separate portions of the building, and they may be open at slightly different hours to serve both the drop-in bar customer and the mealtime patron. The food/drink sales ratio is likely to reflect an equal status of food and drink, with bar and restaurant each doing better than it would without the other. In many cases neither side could make a go of it alone, but together the customer attraction and income are doubled, while the overhead costs are split between them.

Bars and the Smoking Debate

The **cigar bar** is another trendy addition to the beverage scene—and a profitable one, too. Customers who enjoy high-priced cigars also have the opportunity to order premium spirits, wines, beers, and after-dinner drinks to accompany them. The cigar boom is not legal in all venues since smoking is prohibited in many public places by local and/or state ordinance. But places that install heavy-duty ventilation systems and humidors—and offer extensive cigar selections, as well as single-malt Scotches, small-batch Bourbons, Cognacs, and Ports—are filling an interesting, upscale niche. Sometimes, in states or cities where smoking is illegal in foodservice establishments or public buildings, these businesses must be operated as private clubs that charge membership fees and restrict access to minors.

This brings up possibly the hottest issue in the bar and restaurant industry today: whether or not to allow smoking. In many cities and states it is no longer the prerogative of the business owner. At this writing more than 1,600 cities and a handful of states have passed laws that prohibit smoking in most public places. Some of the laws (in California, Delaware, Dallas, and New York City, for example) include bars in their smoking ban. Others (in Idaho and Florida, for instance) allow smoking in bars, but not in restaurants. Generally, although the individual laws are quite specific and worded very technically, a business is considered a "bar" if it earns most of its profit from alcohol sales and refuses entry to minors; it is considered a "restaurant" if it earns most of its profit from food sales and serves customers of all ages.

These laws are not being passed to harass smokers or put restaurateurs out of business, but to minimize workers' (and the general public's) exposure to secondhand smoke. Even the tobacco companies have agreed that cigarette smoke contains a variety of harmful chemicals, including Group A carcinogens. In past years these companies have suggested installing larger, more powerful ventilation systems to whisk the smoke away. However, multiple scientific studies have shown that while ventilation dilutes the smoke and helps with odor control, it does not rid the air of the chemicals. Further, state-of-the-art ventilation is expensive, and many small businesses (or those who rent instead of own the property) simply cannot afford it. It is easier to ask smokers to light up outdoors, or not at all.

The dilemma for businesses that are hospitality-oriented is how to make smokers feel welcome without allowing them to smoke. We'll discuss the options in greater detail in Chapter 3.

Hotel Beverage Operations

In hotels the beverage operation differs in many ways from the bar or the bar-restaurant combination. There might be three or four bars under one roof, each with a different purpose and a different ambience, say a lobby bar, a cocktail lounge, a restaurant bar, or a nightclub with dancing. In addition, there is room service, with a food menu that includes mixed drinks, beer, wine, and Champagne. Above all, there is banquet service, catering to conference, convention, and reception needs. Typically, the client makes beverage choices in advance of the event, which are served from portable bars by extra personnel hired for the occasion.

Individual rooms often have a **minibar**, a small refrigerator or cabinet stocked with a modest inventory of snacks and drinks, ostensibly for the convenience of hotel guests. Most business travelers find the unabashed price-gouging irritating. Who would willingly pay $6 for a bottle of water or $3 for a tiny bag of pretzels, fully triple what the same items would cost elsewhere on hotel property? Industry experts now suggest that nothing in the minibar be priced higher than a comparable item sold in the hotel's vending machines.

According to *Lodging* magazine, there are three keys to minibar profitability:

1. The unit must be installed so that it is easy to use and its contents must be clearly visible.
2. A reliable system must be in place for prompt restocking of cabinets and correct billing of guests.

3. Finally, guests must be enticed to somehow overlook the high prices of minibar goods!

In response to the last point, some hotels have begun packaging other types of items to sell, such as logo-emblazoned nightshirts, "intimacy kits," and grooming items, in addition to snack foods and mixed-drink ingredients. Even so, the minibar is not a major moneymaker for most hotels, and it does siphon some business away from the hotel's other food and beverage venues, especially room service. The item most likely to be purchased is not alcohol, but bottled water. However, food and beverage directors of large and/or luxury hotels say the minibar has become a necessary amenity, high prices and all, for its sheer convenience.

Perhaps the most daunting challenge of hotel beverage service is its diversity, coupled with the up-and-down nature of demand. Since a hotel's primary clientele is overnight guests, demand for beverages rises and falls according to the occupancy rate. This, too, is unpredictable: A hotel can be completely full for a convention and yet have very little bar trade, depending on the kind of convention it is hosting. On the other hand, a very low occupancy rate might net a lot of bar business. Again, it just depends on who the hotel guests are.

Resort and luxury hotels often have several bars and restaurants, with a variety of entertainment, food, and drink, to keep the hotel guests spending money on the premises, as well as to attract an outside clientele. On the other hand, a small commercial hotel in a big city might need only one bar with several stations to serve its lobby customers, a cocktail lounge, coffee shop, dining room, and room service.

Airline Beverage Service

Another type of beverage service that must adapt to special conditions is that on airline flights. The restrictions of space, time, weight, and equipment are formidable. (Cruise lines and passenger trains have similar storage limitations.) Of necessity, airelines' drink menus are limited. Liquors, beers, wines, and a few types of cocktail mixes are handed out in small, individual bottles or cans. The cups are nesting, plastic disposables, except in first- and business-class cabins. Flight attendants push a beverage cart down the aisle and, working from both ends, can garnish glasses and fill them with ice, pour beverages or hand out the individual-sized drink components, and collect the money. The process is a marvel of organization. Tight control systems follow the little bottles everywhere since they are extraordinarily tempting to both airline employees and customers. For higher-paying passengers, drinks are free and service typically includes real glassware, a choice of wines, Champagne for breakfast, and sometimes specialty drinks.

Similarities and Differences

Grouping types of beverage service into these rather arbitrary categories does not really adequately describe the character of individual enterprises. Many establishments do not fit handily into a specific category, and those within categories can be as different as day and night. Yet all categories have certain similarities. They all sell alcoholic beverages. They have similar staff structures, patterns of purchasing and inventory, and ways of controlling the merchandise. They all must meet certain government requirements and operate within certain government regulations. Even the prices charged for the same drinks are not wildly different from one type of place to another. Still, no two bar and beverage operations are alike unless they are part of a chain and are required to have uniform menus, décor, pricing, and other policies.

A successful business meets the needs and desires of a certain clientele and strives to be deliberately different from others serving a similar clientele in order to stand out in the competition for customers. Other major reasons for the wide variety of bar operations are simple: the special circumstances of each operation, as well as the personalities, desires, and budgets of their owners. But to be successful, the entrepreneur must put clientele above all else in shaping his or her enterprise.

SUMMING UP

Throughout history alcoholic beverages have played an important role in most cultures. People drank for many good reasons: for food and health, worship and celebration, pleasure and fellowship, wisdom and truth. As civilization developed, the inns, alehouses, and taverns were central to the growth of towns, travel, and the communication of ideas.

There have always been people who question the propriety of alcohol use and, in past centuries, they had plenty to complain about. Drunkenness and irresponsibility, illegal activity, and violent crime seemed to go hand in hand with alcohol abuse, and with a perception of decaying moral values that defied traditional religious beliefs. The pendulum of public opinion swung from acceptance, to fear and disgust, as women led the anti-drinking charge in many areas after seeing families destroyed by a father's alcoholism. First, the Temperance movement sought to shame people into giving up alcohol. Then came Prohibition, the passage of the Eighteenth Amendment to the U.S. Constitution that outlawed the manufacture and sale of alcohol except in certain, extremely limited circumstances.

Prohibition lasted about 14 years (from 1920 to 1933) and, ironically, created problems even more difficult to solve: a complex, illegal network of bootleg home distillers, secret bars known as speakeasies, and organized crime's entrance into the lucrative business of selling what people could not buy legally. Today's liquor laws still mirror some of the restrictions first created during Prohibition.

Alcohol use is still controversial, but an attitude of moderation and responsibility has enabled the beverage industry to grow and flourish once again in the United States. Today's consumer is likely to drink less but is interested in higher-quality products, even if they cost more. Establishments that specialize in wine sales, brewing and selling beer, full-bar service, and a variety of food-and-drink combinations often include some sort of entertainment. You can buy a drink on an airplane, in a hotel room, or in your favorite neighborhood restaurant, and no one threatens you with a hatchet or a baseball bat!

POINTS TO PONDER

1. What were the most important uses of alcohol in ancient civilizations? How has this changed?
2. Why did some cultures associate alcohol use with wisdom?
3. What was the food value of alcohol in early cultures? Why did people drink alcohol when they had other beverage choices?
4. What is distillation?
5. How has alcohol been used as currency in past centuries? Give two examples.
6. Name one positive and one negative aspect of Prohibition. (Your own opinion can, and should, color your answer.)
7. What are the reasons most Americans are drinking less alcohol?
8. Why is a beverage-only bar not often seen anymore?
9. What would you have to find out before selling wines by the case in a wine bar or opening your own brewpub?
10. What are some of the challenges specific to hotel beverage service?

TERMS OF THE TRADE

ale
amphorae
aqua vitae
Bacchus
bourbon
brewpub
brown goods
call brands
cigar bar
cover charge
distillation
distilled spirits
Dry and Wet
Eighteenth Amendment
lager
mash bill
minibar
moonshine
Ninkasi
pasteurization
pitching
Prohibition
pub
rectification
speakeasy
sports bar
Temperance
Twenty-first Amendment
viticulture
vitus vinifera
white goods
wine bar
wine flight

A CONVERSATION WITH...DALE DEGROFF

The King of Cocktails

Dale DeGroff came to New York City in the late 1960s. Like many aspiring actors, his first job was in the restaurant business—as a dishwasher at Howard Johnson's in Times Square. His next job, at an advertising agency, led him to work with an account called Restaurant Associates. Today it is still well known as one of the United States's most successful restaurant ownership groups, founded by Joe Baum.

"The ad agency team went to so many dinners and tastings with Joe," Dale recalls, "and I just fell in love with the bar business. I got my first bartending job at Charlie O's, and I was also a waiter there."

Today Dale's résumé includes the top bars and hotels on both East and West Coasts, and he is known worldwide as "The King of Cocktails." Dale has won numerous awards for his bartending skills and is the author of his own master bartending book, The Craft of the Cocktail, *published in 2002. He also teaches seminars on bartending and beverage history and does product evaluation and menu consulting.*

Q: What attracted you to bartending?
A: This group of advertising guys that I hung around with was so clever, so funny, so delightful, so intelligent, and their life was centered around bars. They'd have three-hour lunches, move their secretaries, forward their calls to the barroom at The Four Seasons! They worked from 6:00 A.M. to 7:00 P.M.; they worked hard, and they were intense! I got to go to all these great places with them, and the life and energy of the bar just overwhelmed me.

The bartending, I think, is an offshoot of being a performer, and I was good at it. I felt right at home at the bar, and I just seemed to fit. But it took me about three years as a bartender to figure out I was doing everything wrong.

Q: How so?
A: Because the cocktail wasn't a significant part of any restaurant in the 1970s and early 1980s. That generation was drinking jug wines and smoking pot, and there was nobody moving in to fill the shoes of the older generation in the bar scene. We had one kind of single-stem glass, and every drink was made in that style of glass. The service, the flair was really on the downside, and most people in the bar business were there only until they could do something else.

Well, in that environment, I went to Joe Baum in 1986 with the idea of creating a classic 1930s supper-club cocktail menu for his new place, the Rainbow Room. It took a lot of research, but I did it and he hired me. Joe was very high profile in the industry, and people paid attention to whatever he was doing. So as soon as I got behind that bar, it was a magnet for the press. And soon I saw these vintage drinks being prepared all over town. I was thrilled.

Q: What advice would you give to today's bar managers?
A: A good manager is just like a chef. When a dish goes out of a kitchen, he [or she] will test that sauce, look at that garnish, watch the portion size. There's got to be somebody doing the equivalent of that at the bar, and that should be the manager.

Of course you have to keep an eye on costs and portion control, but it is not necessary to always focus everything on the lowest common denominator. I see consultants who come in and suggest recipes and techniques simply because they are "bartender-proof," and that leaves no room for creativity. If you want to grow your place in a positive direction—really try to achieve excellence in a cocktail—it's all about management's attitude toward that. If there's a manager in place who shares the enthusiasm of the bartenders, then that kind of cocktail program is possible. But it does involve a tremendous amount of training, monitoring, equipment, week-to-week maintenance of ingredients, fresh fruit, correct price points for the drinks, analysis of your audience. It's not impossible; it's just hard.

Q: What are some no-nonsense service tips you would give new bartenders and servers?
A: When I teach, I tell servers, "The contract is this. Those customers have rented their table for two-and-a-half or three hours. That's their property, like real estate. You need to be there when they need something, but believe me, you are an interloper. You need to get in and out; no hanging around unless they want you to. It's private property."

At the bar, the contract is totally different. It's not private property, it's public property; customers are sharing the space. And, unfortunately, a customer has the right to break the contract with unpleasantness or rudeness. So the bartender's job is to turn enemies into friends. As soon as you become rude or unpleasant back to them, you've ruined the space for all the other customers. Then nobody wants to be there.

You're an actor behind the bar, and that makes you many things to many people: a conversationalist to one guy, a good listener for another, a protector to a woman who's not happy about the advances she's getting from the guy on the next stool. It is a complex job, but it never seems to be approached that way.

I also tell bartenders, "You are going to make some mistakes if you're busy, or if you're new. It's your job to monitor what is happening at the bar. If someone hasn't touched their drink, walk over and ask, "Is that drink a little too sweet or sour? I can fix that, no problem." That kind of attention is astonishing to a customer. Most people are used to bad bartenders. They will forgive a friendly bartender anything, just because he's friendly! There are so many of them who don't give you eye contact or the time of day.

Q: Are bars pressured by suppliers to use certain products?

A: Of course. But your attitude should always be, they work for you. You are providing a showcase for their products, so they should provide something for you, too, and that is support for your menus, tabletop, upcoming events. Ask them to help with your training program or print your menu for you. I want the distiller, when he [or she] comes to town, to visit my bar and talk with my staff. Everything they can provide me as a purveyor, I want. And when purveyors see your enthusiasm, they will rise to the occasion.

Q: How hard is it to deal with people who drink too much?

A: In New York we have it a little easier because 95 percent of the people take cabs, so there's not the issue of drunk driving as in other places. But the business of withholding service to a guest is a big, big issue that bartenders need to learn. Nobody's ever happy about this issue, and they never will be. The key is to do it so you don't lose the person as a customer. I'll say, "Okay, come back tomorrow and you're welcome here. I like you too much; I wanna see you here tomorrow night." Or suggest they eat something, in a friendly way. If they feel the warmth—I call it "the embrace of the house"—they'll respond. If they don't feel it, there are a million other joints. They don't need to drink here.

Q: What are some of the marketing ideas you've used to boost business at your bars over the years?

A: I think it's very important in a restaurant environment to have a great working relationship with the chef. I've sat down with my chef, tasted things together, and created a combination menu of food and cocktails. We called them "cocktail dinners" at the Rainbow Room and the Blackbird. They were delightful events, they were fun, they enhanced our bar business, and they sold out every time.

The other thing I did on a Monday night once a month was "celebrity bartenders." It was a slow night, so I asked professional athletes or actors to come in and tend bar with me; $2 of the price of every drink went to the charity of their choice. We'd make up drinks; ask four people in the room to each suggest an ingredient and make a drink on the spot, using those ingredients! It's the kind of thing you could do on a smaller, local scale, with a local newscaster or the coach of your football team.

Q: Let's talk about bar equipment. What is necessary and what is frivolous?

A: If you're gonna have a "real" bar, you need to teach your bartenders how to use a Boston shaker. It's like the chef's knife—once you know how to use that one, all the other knives are easier. It's what every bartender should be trained on and never is. The Boston shaker is a 16-ounce glass portion and a 30-ounce metal portion that fits on top to make a seal. I have four of those at every station because I shake all my drinks.

I think a glass chiller is a necessity. Each station should have a drainboard, and next to it a sink; a double-bin ice bin so that you can put bottles in one and one for drink use because every health department in America says you can't use the drink ice for the bottles. You've got to have both crushed ice and cube ice. I'm a fanatic about ice! For chilling, the crushed ice works well, but for drinks, I want big, whole, hard cube ice, like Mom makes at home. The other kinds melt too fast and weaken a good drink.

I also believe the cocktail glass should not be any bigger than 5 to 5½ ounces, no more. I mean, what is a cocktail? It's an aperitif, a shared experience before dinner. It's the beginning of your evening. It's not the end of your evening—at least, not unless you have an 11-ounce glass with 6 ounces of liquor in it! The whole sociability aspect of the cocktail is blown away by supersizing it. It seems to me that all the modern advances that are supposed to make bars so wonderfully fast and efficient—the bar guns, the premade mixes—conspire against a good drink. Sure, it's a little harder to make a "real" drink without all the shortcuts, but not with proper training and proper management.

CHAPTER 2
RESPONSIBLE ALCOHOL SERVICE

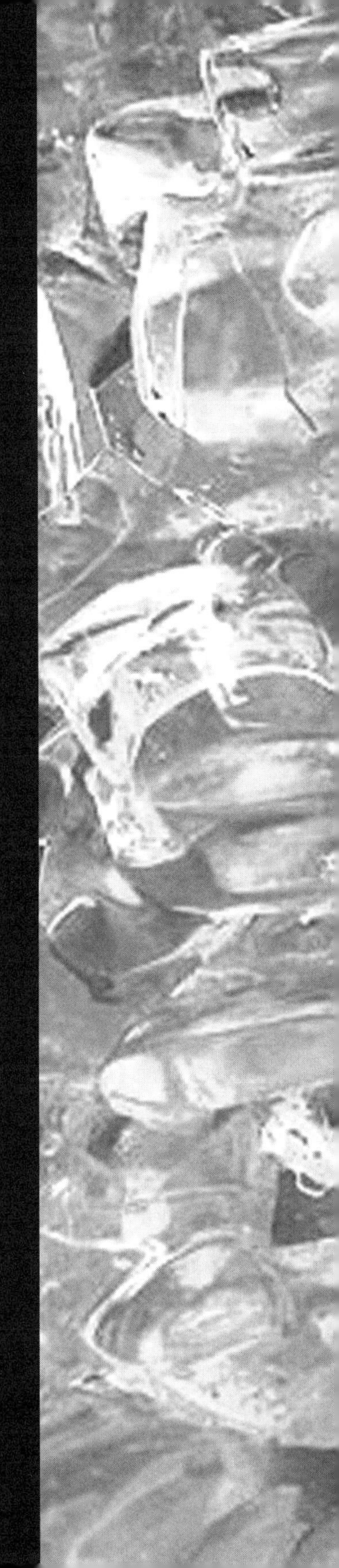

The positive attributes of alcohol have always existed alongside the potential for alcohol abuse. This negative side of alcohol, too, is as old as history. Today, however, there is more far-reaching awareness of the damage that alcohol can do, from the automobile accidents caused by drunk drivers, to the rising incidence of alcoholism. For the beverage operator, negative aspects of alcohol raise the risks of third-party liability and result in soaring insurance costs. Sellers and servers of alcoholic beverages must now stay fully informed not only about the beverages, but also the laws governing the sale of alcohol, which include how to deal with intoxicated customers.

The responsibility of a bar or restaurant is twofold. Offering alcohol is a pleasurable addition to the dining or entertainment experience: it can have a relaxing effect on people, it creates a sense of camaraderie among friends, and it whets the appetite and can enhance a meal by complementing the flavors of the foods being served. But just as important as encouraging their guests to enjoy their beverages, sellers and servers of alcohol are responsible for safeguarding their clientele from the unpleasant, and potentially dangerous, medical and legal effects of excessive alcohol consumption.

THIS CHAPTER WILL HELP YOU . . .

- Understand the effects of alcohol in the human body, both positive and negative, from health claims, to the latest hangover research.
- Understand the impact of alcoholism in today's society.

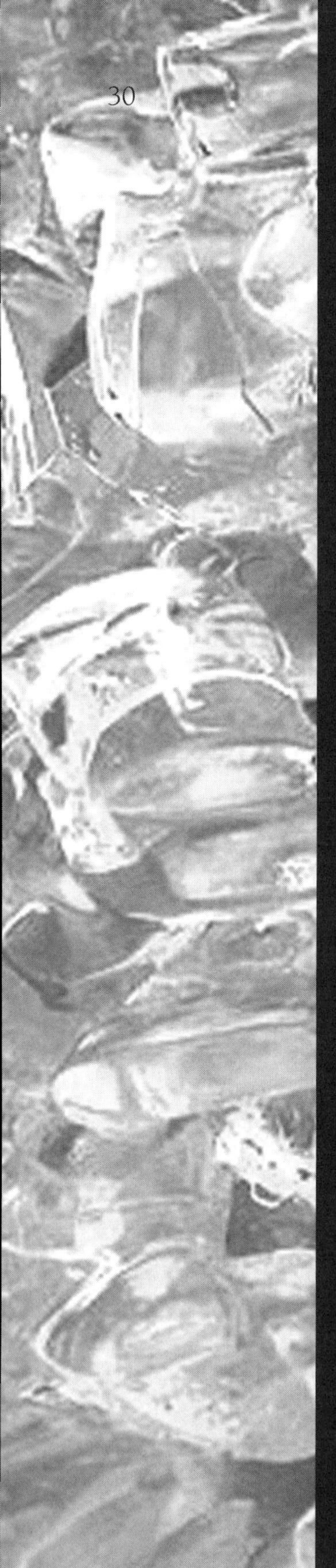

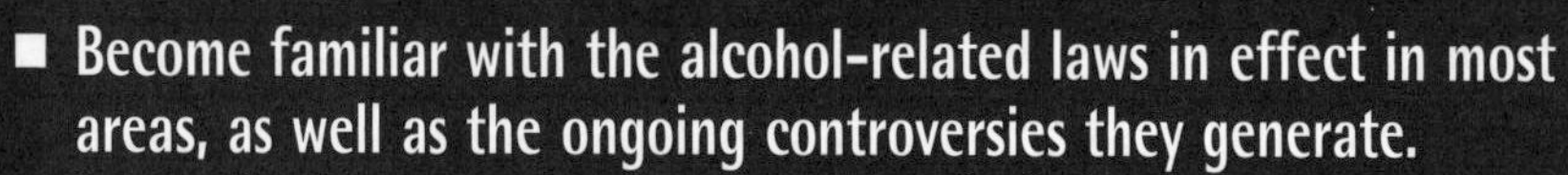

- Become familiar with the alcohol-related laws in effect in most areas, as well as the ongoing controversies they generate.
- Learn the importance of responsible alcohol service and how to spot and handle customers who may have had too much to drink.
- Set specific alcohol service policies and train staff members.
- Become proactive on behalf of the beverage service industry to educate consumers and uphold a reputation as a responsible business.

There are many good reasons to promote responsible alcohol service. First, we can help to reduce the number of deaths and injuries in automobile accidents caused by drunk drivers, which are all the more tragic because they are preventable. In this way we protect not only our customers, but also the entire community. In addition, we protect the reputation of our own business. A loud or belligerent drunk at the next table can have a permanent adverse effect on a guest's impression of a bar or restaurant, as can an employee who handles the situation badly. Finally, we protect each employee and the establishment itself from violating state liquor laws and, subsequently, from damaging and expensive lawsuits, which can ultimately mean the death of a business that cannot recover from the financial strain or the negative publicity. The bottom line? Responsible alcohol service means protection for our business. Before we can learn to offer responsible alcohol service, we need to take a closer look at how alcohol affects human health and behavior. As you'll soon see, research results on these topics are mixed . . . and often controversial.

HUMAN PHYSIOLOGY AND ALCOHOL

The form of alcohol found in liquor, beer, and wine is **ethanol,** which is a form of drug; it is a tranquilizer. In moderate doses ethanol can have beneficial effects, causing relaxation, stimulating the appetite, heightening pleasure, and providing a sense of euphoria. In larger doses, though, it becomes toxic, a form of poison.

Alcohol is not digested by the body in the same way that foods are. Instead of entering the digestive system, alcohol passes through the wall of the stomach or small intestine directly into the bloodstream. An alcoholic drink taken on an empty stomach empties itself into the bloodstream within about 20 minutes. If there is food in the stomach, the transfer is delayed, especially if the foods contain fats, such as cheese, meat, eggs, and milk. Carbonated beverages in the digestive system, on the other hand, speed the transfer. By way of the bloodstream, alcohol travels through the body wherever there is water to the brain, lungs, kidneys, heart, and liver until it is broken down by the liver into carbon dioxide and water (see Figure 2.1). The liver does this at the rate of one-third to one-half ounce per hour; the rest of the alcohol continues to circulate in the bloodstream. This amount is less than that contained in a typical 1½-ounce cocktail made with an 80-proof spirit. When this amount is multiplied by several drinks, it is clear that alcohol will still be circulating in the bloodstream several hours after it has been ingested. Consider that:

- The liver **metabolizes** about 90 percent of the alcohol consumed. The liver is the organ most often affected by **alcoholism** since it is the "first defense" organ (after the stomach) to attempt to disperse the alcohol. The remaining 10 percent is eliminated through the lungs and urine.
- Alcohol reaches the brain within a few minutes of entering the bloodstream.

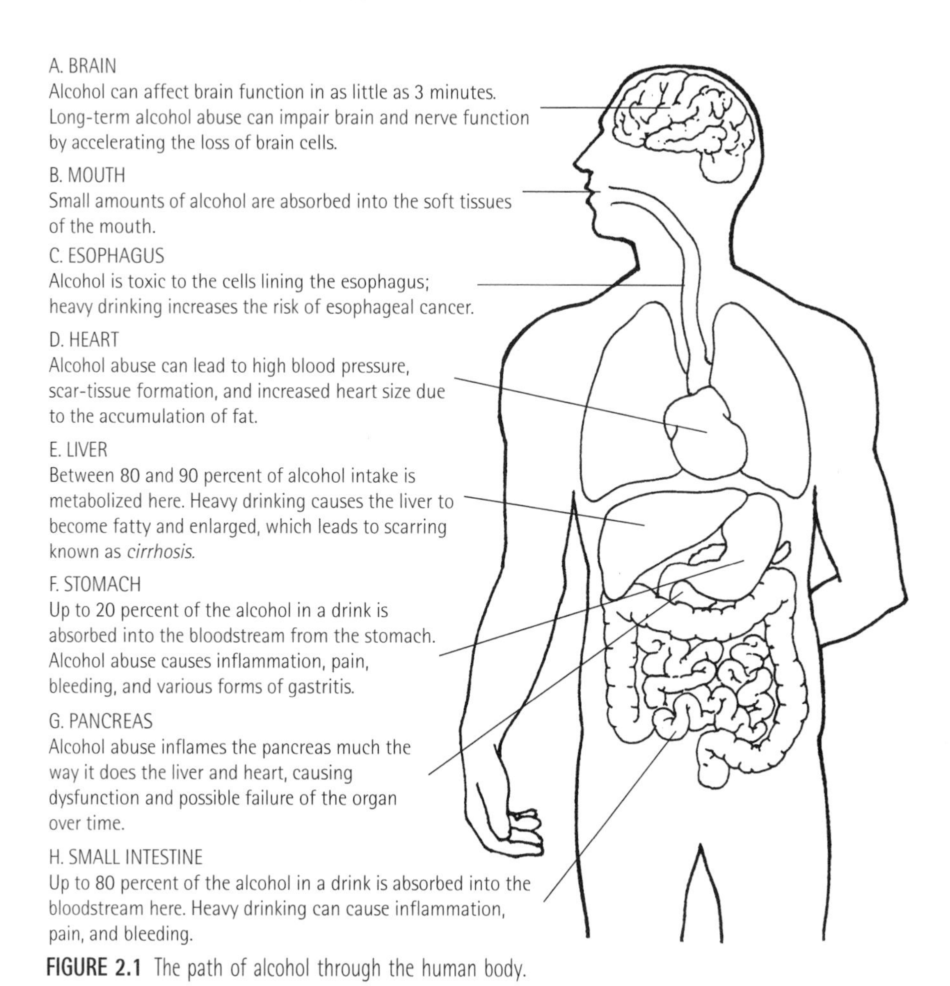

FIGURE 2.1 The path of alcohol through the human body.

Alcohol's effect on the brain is the key to both the pleasures and the problems with alcohol consumption. The first effect of alcohol is to stimulate pleasant feelings of well-being. As drinking continues, the concentration of alcohol in both the bloodstream and the brain increases, diminishing inhibitions and judgment, making the drinker more gregarious and expansive, but less able to accurately perceive reality. As intoxication takes over brain function, the alcohol impairs motor ability, muscle coordination, reaction time, eyesight, and night vision—all the normal skills that drivers need to get home safely. It does not take a great number of drinks to reach this point, and drinking coffee, walking around, and other efforts to "sober up" do not have an impact on blood-alcohol content. This is because nothing can prod the liver into breaking the alcohol down any faster. A drinker in this condition—that is, intoxicated—is unfit to drive.

Intoxication is measured by the percent of alcohol in the blood. The typical definition of intoxication used to be a **blood alcohol concentration (BAC)** of 0.10 percent, but in the first few years of this century, almost every state lowered the level to 0.08 percent as a condition of receiving federal highway-construction funding. (More about federal dollars in a moment.) To some extent, the size of the person affects his or her blood alcohol level: Assuming the same quantity of alcohol has been consumed, the heavier a person's body weight, the lower the percent of his or her blood alcohol. This is because alcohol mixes with the water in the body. This, in turn, is why women, who naturally have less water and a higher percentage of body fat than men, tend to have higher blood-alcohol contents than men of similar height and weight who have consumed the same amount of alcohol. The alcohol is more highly concentrated in the women's bodies than the men's.

How Much Do We Drink?

The most recent National Institutes of Health figures (2003) estimate that 62 percent of Americans drink alcohol. Ten percent say they "drink daily," and about 10 percent have problems with "excessive" alcohol consumption. However, the United States is nowhere near the top of the list for drinkers. In fact, we rank thirty-second in the world, with an overall consumption rate of 1.74 gallons per person per year. As a nation we have the strictest youth drinking laws of all the Western nations, and the highest minimum drinking age in the world (see Figure 2.2 for the Top Ten Alcohol-Consuming Countries).

In 1995 when the U.S. Department of Agriculture (USDA) revised its *Dietary Guidelines for Americans,* which the agency does routinely every five years, it made headlines by stating for the first time that "moderate drinking may lower the risk of heart disease," and that "alcoholic beverages have been used to enhance the enjoyment of meals by many societies throughout human history." How times change: In contrast the 1990 guidelines had stated unequivocally that "drinking has no net health benefits." Both the 1995 and 2000 guidelines balance those statements by warning that too much alcohol consumption can be harmful, raising one's risk of everything from high blood pressure to suicide. The guidelines also clearly state that alcohol should not be consumed by children or adolescents, women who are pregnant or trying to conceive, anyone taking medication of any kind, those who plan to drive or engage in an activity that requires alertness and skill, or anyone who cannot restrict his or her drinking to moderate levels.

THE TOP TEN ALCOHOL-CONSUMING COUNTRIES

	Per capita annual consumption (in gallons)
1. Portugal	2.98
2. Luxembourg	2.95
3. France	2.87
4. Hungary	2.66
5. Spain	2.66
6. Czech Republic	2.64
7. Denmark	2.61
8. Germany	2.50
9. Austria	2.50
10. Switzerland	2.43

FIGURE 2.2 Source: *The Top Ten of Everything* by Russell Ash, 1999, DK Publishing, Inc., New York.

The latest USDA guidelines, released in 2005, continue the agency's tone of cautious acceptance. An excerpt:

> The consumption of alcohol can have beneficial or harmful effects depending on the amount consumed, age and other characteristics of the person consuming the alcohol, and specifics of the situation . . . Alcohol may have beneficial effects when consumed in moderation. The lowest all-cause mortality occurs at an intake of one to two drinks per day. The lowest coronary heart disease mortality also occurs at an intake of one to two drinks per day. Morbidity and mortality are highest among those drinking large amounts of alcohol.

ALCOHOL'S IMPACT ON HUMAN HEALTH

Back in 1990 an editorial in the *American Journal of Public Health* stated that after 40 years of research into diet and health issues, only two conclusions could be drawn consistently from both laboratory and clinical studies: that exercise and drinking moderate amounts of alcohol are good for humans. Based on this statement, you might think that doctors would start prescribing a drink or two per day for their patients in the same way they prescribe regular physical activity as part of a healthy lifestyle. But it's not that simple. To determine what "moderate drinking" really is, we must look at it from a health perspective.

Generally an alcoholic drink contains the equivalent of one-half ounce of pure (ethanol) alcohol. In a glass this translates into:

- 12 ounces of beer, at 5 percent alcohol content
- 4 ounces of wine, at 12 percent alcohol content
- 1¼ ounces of distilled spirit, at 40 percent alcohol content ("80 proof")
- 1 ounce of distilled spirit, at 50 percent alcohol content ("100 proof")

Obviously the sizes of the glass and the serving can affect how strong a single drink actually is; moreover, many drinks are made with higher-proof alcohol, such as 151-proof rum, or cordials and liqueurs, which range in alcohol content from 20 to 40 percent. But based on the preceding list, health experts suggest that one drink for women and two drinks for men constitutes "moderation."

Scientists continue to study alcohol intake in relation to all kinds of medical conditions. Red wine, in particular, appears to show promise for reducing inflammation, and fighting bacteria and even cancer. The best news for the hospitality industry came in the 1980s, when multiple studies revealed that there seems to be a link between moderate drinking—again, especially of red wine—and a lower incidence of heart disease, which is the leading cause of death in North America. So this is where we'll begin our health discussion.

Wine contains **phenolic compounds,** part of what gives grapes their color and the acidity known as **tannins.** These compounds are **antioxidants.** Antioxidants break down "bad" cholesterol (LDL) and help prevent both clogging of arteries and blood clots that can lead to strokes. Antioxidants have also proven to be effective at inhibiting some types of cancer. **Resveratrol** is the primary antioxidant in wine. It is a **flavonoid** (a substance that gives fresh fruit and vegetables their colors), a component of grape skins that grapevines make naturally in response to stress, lack of nutrients, or fungal infections. Red wines contain more resveratrol than white wines simply because of the way they are made: The color of the grape skin gives the wine its color, so red wines have more "skin contact" than whites before the juice is strained off to make into wine. Sherry, a fortified wine, has also been found to have cholesterol-lowering capability.

Even the leftover skins and seeds from the crushed grapes, known as **pomace,** might have beneficial uses. A recent Turkish study indicates that these mashed-up leftovers inhibit the growth of more than a dozen different harmful bacteria, some of which cause foodborne illnesses. The researchers are experimenting with the idea of drying the pomace to use as a food preservative.

Gin has been found to have some of the same anti-inflammatory effects as red wine, but a 2004 study at Philadelphia's Thomas Jefferson University reported that wine is more effective.

Alcohol and Heart Disease. In 1991 a CBS television report on *60 Minutes* focused on the so-called **French Paradox.** R. Curtis Ellison and Serge Renaud, two medical doctors, discussed a longtime health irony: The French subsist on a diet rich in fatty foods, which are known to be bad for the heart, yet they have a low incidence of heart disease. Dr. Renaud claimed that their custom of mealtime wine consumption, particularly of red wines, was an important factor. In the United States sales of red wine rocketed 44 percent in the month following the report! Since the original news report, however, World Health Organization statistics show that heart disease is also the "Number One killer" in France, although at lower rates than those of the United States, and that the French die more often of cirrhosis of the liver and other alcohol-related causes than Americans.

To understand the correlation between alcohol and the heart, we must distinguish between "good" cholesterol, high-density lipoprotein (HDL), and "bad" cholesterol, low-density lipoprotein (LDL). To help prevent heart disease, people need to increase their HDL levels because this good cholesterol cleans fatty buildup from blood vessels. Ethanol, the alcohol in alcoholic beverages, raises HDL levels in the bloodstream. This does not happen immediately, but it can be seen over several weeks after moderate daily alcohol intake. Long-term, it might take a year to see significant HDL increases, depending on the person. In addition to resveratrol in wines, alcohol itself (ethanol) also contains a beneficial enzyme known as a **t-PA antigen.** This substance helps prevent chronic internal blood clots, and the anti-clotting benefits take effect within hours of alcohol consumption.

There is also interesting research for beer drinkers: The darker the beer, the better it might be for the heart. Darker brews contain more blood-clotting prevention than lighter beers, this is also a result of the flavonoids darker beers contain.

While these findings are encouraging to those who advocate responsible drinking, the same research emphasizes the dangers of alcohol abuse. Studies in both 1999 (United States) and 2000 (Finland) found that the heart attack and stroke protections from moderate drinking are relatively small, and they are offset by the greater risks of drinking too much. These include other types of heart disease, cancer, liver problems, and even a higher chance of violent death.

Alcohol/Drug Interactions. Brain cells are particularly sensitive to alcohol exposure. The first part of the brain to be affected by drinking is the frontal lobe, where judgment and reasoning functions take place. After more drinks, the vision and speech centers of the brain are sedated, along with voluntary muscle control. Breathing and heart action are the last to be affected, but by then the person would have imbibed so much as to risk death.

Some people drink alcoholic beverages as a kind of social anesthetic, to help them relax or relieve anxiety in social situations. Because alcohol relieves inhibitions, some have the mistaken opinion that it works as a stimulant. In fact, it works in the body as a depressant that sedates nerve cells. So a major concern for physicians is the use of alcohol by patients who are also taking medications, especially antidepressants. More than 2,800 prescription drugs and another 2,000 over-the-counter medications are available in the United States, and about 18 percent of the U.S. adult population takes three or more prescription drugs. At least 150 medications interact harmfully with alcohol, and the National Institute on Alcohol Abuse and Alcoholism (NIAAA) estimates adverse reactions might be a factor in 25 percent of emergency-room admissions.

Why? The simplest explanation is that, in the body, the alcohol "competes" with the drug for the same set of enzymes in the stomach and bloodstream that metabolize both substances. The drug can, therefore, remain in a person's system longer than it should, or it cannot be absorbed correctly because the alcohol is "taking up" all of the enzyme action. Drinking while taking prescription drugs can also increase the potency of either the alcohol or the drug, especially the sedative effect of some antidepressants and antihistamines. A chemical found in some types of wine and beer, called **tyramine,** interacts with some types of antidepressants, such as *monoamine oxidase inhibitors,* to increase blood pressure, possibly to dangerous levels.

Drinking alcohol may cause headaches, nausea, and/or dizziness when combined with everything from antidiabetic medications, to heart and circulatory system drugs, to antibiotics for treating infections. If there is a cautionary rule, it is ask your doctor and/or pharmacist about the impact of even a small, occasional amount of alcohol on the drugs—both prescription and nonprescription—that you are taking.

Alcohol and Women. You've already learned that alcohol is more concentrated in a woman's body than in a man's, even when their height and weight are similar.

We have also discussed the relationship between alcoholic beverages and heart disease. In women, heart disease is slightly less prevalent than in men, and when it occurs, it usually happens later in life. Therefore, it stands to reason that alcohol has more beneficial effects for women at midlife and older than it does for those in their childbearing years. For instance, an ongoing Canadian study that began in the 1990s has followed 3,300 women, all over age 40, and found that those who drank moderately (two to nine drinks per week), had less than half the cardiovascular risks of women who did not drink at all. Their heart health was assessed at the beginning of the study, then reassessed five years later. Interestingly the findings have not shown the same benefits for the 2,600 men in the study. Researchers have promised to continue the study in five-year increments for another two decades.

Scientifically speaking the jury is still out on the question of whether alcohol use contributes to higher breast-cancer levels in women. The figures seem to indicate an increased risk, even among moderate drinkers. But the researchers have been unable to pinpoint a conclusive medical reason why this is so, so they are hesitant to draw conclusions. Women who are moderate wine drinkers might have lower risks of developing ovarian cancer, but these benefits are not evident in women who drink beer or spirits in moderation.

The impact of alcohol on the female body seems to indicate that younger women—in particular those under age 40—should limit their alcohol intake and drink only in moderation. A woman who is trying to become pregnant should be aware that heavy alcohol use by either her or her partner may impair her ability to conceive at all. For moderate drinkers the evidence is less certain. Some clinical research suggests that alcohol may suppress the male reproductive hormone *testosterone* found in both men and women; however, a 2003 Danish study found that a woman who drinks one or two glasses of wine may find it easier to conceive than either beer drinkers or nondrinkers. The researchers cited wine's potential side benefit of protecting a woman from infections that can cause sterility.

The most controversial issue for women is whether to drink while pregnant. Science indicates that doing so is indeed risky. In the body of a pregnant woman, alcohol passes easily through the placenta into the body of the fetus, and drinking during pregnancy can cause a pattern of physical and mental defects in the child, known collectively as **Fetal Alcohol Syndrome (FAS)** or **Fetal Alcohol Effects (FAE).** Easch year as many as 12,000 children are born in the United States suffering to some degree from FAS symptoms, which include low birth weight, physical deformities, heart defects, mental retardation; or from FAE complications, which include low birth weight, mental retardation, cerebral palsy, neurobehavioral problems, and learning disorders. To counteract those alarming statistics, the federal government now requires all types of alcoholic beverages to carry on their labels the following message:

> *GOVERNMENT WARNING: (1) According to the Surgeon General, women should not drink alcoholic beverages during pregnancy because of the risk of birth defects. (2) Consumption of alcoholic beverages impairs your ability to drive a car or operate machinery, and may cause health problems.*

The topic of drinking while breastfeeding is also somewhat controversial. A nursing mother who is anxious and tired may find that an occasional drink helps her to relax. A common myth is that alcohol consumption promotes what is known as the "let-down reflex" in a nursing mother, prompting the release of stored milk in the breast to make feeding possible. However, the *American Dietetic Association* (*ADA*) says this is not true and, in fact, overconsumption of alcohol might actually inhibit the let-down reflex. The ADA guidelines suggest that if a mother wants to have a drink, she should either do so after her child is fed or postpone breastfeeding for at least one hour after consuming the drink. This allows her body to metabolize the alcohol before she nurses the infant.

Alcohol and Senior Citizens. Older adults metabolize alcohol more slowly than young people. As the body ages, it loses lean muscle mass and water content, so the alcohol reaches a higher concentration than in a younger person's body. Older stomachs do not secrete as many enzymes to start the breakdown of the alcohol, which leaves a bigger job for the liver. Blood flows slightly more slowly in older people, which means that alcohol is eliminated from their bodies more slowly. The result? Blood alcohol levels are 30 to 40 percent higher in a senior citizen than in a young person who consumes the identical amount of alcohol.

An added complication is that older adults tend to have myriad medical conditions that require prescription medications. An estimated 17 percent of adults over age 60 are alcohol abusers; however, they are sometimes harder to spot because the symptoms of alcoholism—e.g., trembling, sleeping problems, memory loss, unsteady gait—are not uncommon among older people. If they are retired or live alone, there are fewer people around to notice their behaviors.

On the other hand small amounts of alcohol have been found to have beneficial effects for seniors. Alcohol improves the blood lipid profile, decreases the risk of *thrombosis* (blood clotting), increases appetite, and improves digestion. Light and moderate drinkers in their seventies might be keeping their blood vessels healthier than their nondrinking peers. For healthy seniors, however, experts suggest that "moderate" drinking means no more than one drink per day.

Alcohol and Cancer. There is good news and bad news regarding alcohol and cancer. Medical research indicates that increased levels of liver, esophagus, breast, and mouth-related cancers in heavy drinkers. However, moderate drinkers have less likelihood of developing polyps in their bowels, which are a precursor to colon cancer. Since colorectal cancer is the third most common cancer in the United States, this is significant.

A study on peptic ulcers is a good way to summarize this section of the text. The research found that moderate drinking—one beer or glass of wine a day—curbed the formation of bacteria that are thought to cause ulcers in the stomach. But drinking twice that much, or consuming distilled spirits, actually increased the risk of getting an ulcer. The message? Moderation, moderation, moderation. If you require further evidence, read on.

ALCOHOL AND NUTRITION

The main nutrient components in alcohol are ethanol, simple carbohydrates, glucose, and fructose. Alcohol plays three main roles in human nutrition: as food, as an aid to the absorption of minerals, and as an appetite stimulant.

As food, it is generally agreed that drinking alcohol is ingesting "empty calories." Because alcohol is not full of vitamins and contains sugars, it is not especially good for you, but in moderation it's not particularly harmful either. In the stomach the alcohol in a glass of wine has the side benefits of helping to digest food and enhancing absorption of other nutrients from the food, particularly calcium, iron, magnesium, phosphorous, and zinc. But wine also contains about 25 calories per ounce and since it stimulates appetite, can prompt a person to eat more. Compare the "calorie counts" in Figure 2.3 to see how your favorites stack up.

Of course, Americans no longer need a stout mug of ale at lunch to give them the high-calorie boost that provided our colonial ancestors with the energy to do an afternoon of backbreaking work. So many modern-day nutrition experts contend that alcohol should be "counted" in the diet as fat instead of calories because of the metabolic interaction that occurs between fat and alcohol in the body.

For example, when presented with both fat and alcohol, the body does the "logical" thing: It uses the alcohol first to rid itself of the "toxic" substance, then stores the fat. This means that drinking might actually promote fat storage in the

CALORIE COUNTS OF COMMON BEVERAGES AND MIXERS

Beverage	Amount (in ounces)	Energy (in calories)
Beer	12	150
"Light" beer	12	100
Gin, rum, vodka, whiskey (86 proof)	1 1/2	105
Dessert wine	3 1/2	140
Table wine	3 1/2	85
Tonic, ginger ale	8	80
Cola, root beer	8	100
Fruit-flavored soda, Tom Collins mix	8	115
Club soda, plain seltzer, diet drinks	8	1

FIGURE 2.3 Source: *Nutrition Concepts and Controversies, 8th Edition,* Frances Sizer and Eleanor Noss Whitney, 1997, Wadsworth Publishing, New York.

body, particularly in the central abdominal cavity. As such, there is a medical explanation for that **beer belly,** which is noticeable even in many moderate drinkers! Recent studies have also shown that alcohol consumption slows down the body's overall fuel (fat) consumption by as much as one third, causing more fat to be stored. Thus, alcoholic beverages are fattening in two ways: They add at least seven calories per gram as you drink, and they affect your body's ability to metabolize fat.

Another more far-reaching side effect of drinking too much is malnutrition. The more alcohol a person drinks, the less likely he or she will be able to eat enough food to obtain adequate nutrients. When a body fills up with "empty" alcohol calories and volume, and so does not feel hunger, the alcohol is displacing food. Alcohol also directly interferes with the body's ability to use nutrients, making them count for less even if a person does manage to eat regular meals. The most dramatic impact is on *folate,* a vitamin that the body requires to make new cells. An excess of alcohol prompts the body to excrete folate. It dumps into the bloodstream, into the kidneys, and into other places it's not supposed to go. The result is a dangerous downward spiral: The more you drink, the more nutrient deficiencies your body will experience.

Anatomy of the Hangover. A grim reality of drinking comes as the result of overindulging. It is that awful combination of headache, nausea, stomach cramps, dehydration, and dizziness known as the **hangover.** A hangover indicates a chemical imbalance and a milder form of drug withdrawal. **Congeners** (from the verb *congeal,* meaning to thicken or solidify) are compounds found in alcoholic beverages that contribute to the hangover. Different types of alcohol (vodka, gin, scotch) have different congeners, and the more added flavoring and coloring in a beverage, the higher its congener content.

Lost workforce productivity due to hangovers costs U.S. companies an amazing $150 billion a year, so scientists are studying hangovers and how to cure them, and they've made some interesting findings about exactly what happens in the body when it's bombarded by alcohol:

- A byproduct of the overburdened liver, working hard to metabolize the alcohol, is a chemical called **acetaldehyde.** Some of it gets into the bloodstream, prompting inflammation. The stomach also gets into the action, secreting extra acid and histamines, which also cause inflammation.
- The acetaldehyde, along with the congeners, appears to stimulate the body's immune response, much as if it were fighting the flu or an infection.
- This triggers the release (by the white blood cells) of molecules called *cytokines.* These tiny culprits produce the flu-like feelings that come from drinking too much.

Laboratory research is now focused on how to prevent the release of the cytokines in the first place. Dehydration is, perhaps, the most serious of the hangover's side effects. Alcohol depresses the body's production of antidiuretic hormones and prompts greater urine output. With the "outgo," minerals like folate are lost that are vital to nerve function and muscle coordination. Intense thirst after drinking is a signal that your body needs water and, as you rehydrate, the common side effects are headache and nerve pain as the brain cells swell back to their normal size.

It is always smart, when imbibing, to drink at least twice as much water as you do alcohol to counterbalance its diuretic effects, and also to simply slow down your alcohol intake. For these reasons, servers should be taught to offer water and refill the glasses regularly.

For about a day after drinking too much, there are plenty of physiological reasons to feel awful. The heart works harder and beats faster. Blood pressure increases, brain-cell activity is suppressed, and the body has a more difficult time metabolizing glucose.

Folk remedies for hangovers abound: aspirin, vitamins, exercise, or eating specific types of food (for example, bread or pasta, or the traditional Mexican tripe soup called *menudo*). Unfortunately, they are all virtually useless and although the scientists are hard at work on it, there is no miracle cure. A couple of over-the-counter dietary supplements that claim to prevent the body's build-up of acetaldehyde are controversial and as of this writing, lack U.S. government testing and approval.

All you can do for a hangover besides vowing never to drink that much again is to give the body time and rest to process the excess alcohol intake and to replace the water you have lost.

ALCOHOLISM AND OTHER DRINKING PROBLEMS

It is estimated that 14 million adult Americans have alcohol abuse problems, and that 1 in 13 Americans is an *alcoholic*. According to the NIAAA, the four symptoms that signal this disease are:

1. A craving for the alcohol: A strong need or urge to drink
2. A lack of control: Not being able to stop drinking once the person has begun
3. Physical dependence: Withdrawal symptoms (shakiness, sweating, nausea, anxiety) when the person stops drinking
4. Increased tolerance: The need to drink greater amounts of alcohol to feel its effects

Alcoholics often drink as a coping mechanism, to relieve tension or escape from problems, only to find that soon they cannot control their cravings. Their insistence on drinking—despite worsening health, financial or legal problems, and despite attempted intervention by loved ones—may be characterized by denial. The alcoholic may lie, make excuses, drink secretly, and hide alcohol. The physiology of alcoholism in the human body is not entirely clear. It is not known precisely why one person becomes a compulsive drinker and another does not. Researchers use three different theories to explain this destructive behavior:

- The *genetic theory* defines alcoholism as the result of a predisposed reaction to alcohol due to chromosomes, genes, or hormonal deficiencies. It is medically and scientifically accepted that a low-threshold response to alcohol is genetic; so is a person's ability to drink a lot without showing the apparent effects and, in fact, the latter is a strong indicator of a genetic risk for alcoholism.
- The *psychological theory* defines alcoholism as a condition in people who have a preset disposition or personality that "sets off" a reaction to alcohol.
- The *sociological theory* defines alcoholism as a learned response, i.e., that addiction happens a result of the influences of society. This theory, as well as the genetic theory, may also apply to ethnic patterns of alcoholism, such as why problem drinking is prevalent on Native American reservations.

Whichever theory you ascribe to, one point is certain: Alcoholism is a type of addiction and the afflicted cannot be cured without some form of treatment. Over time alcoholism causes damage to the entire body, especially the liver, the heart, the digestive system, the central nervous system, and the brain. The disease also causes psychological damage, in the form of depression, low self-esteem, loss of concentration, insomnia, irritability, and violent behavior, among others. Alcoholics who do not seek help for their problem can shorten their lives by 10 to 15 years. More frightening is that many alcoholics also shorten the lives of others: 40 percent of all traffic fatalities occur in alcohol-related accidents. Moreover, alcohol-related crimes in this country account for 54 percent of murders and attempted murders, 52 percent of rapes and sexual assaults, and 48 percent of robberies.

Consider this: A liver transplant costs about $150,000 today—and it is the result of excessive drinking. On the other hand, it costs about $5,000 to undergo treatment for alcohol abuse before it gets that far.

Binge Drinking. Another type of problem drinking, not classified as alcoholism but potentially just as serious, is **binge drinking.** For men binge drinking is defined as the act of consuming five or more alcoholic beverages in a single, short time period, say, at a party or sporting event. For women four or more drinks qualify as a *binge*. In a 2002 study of college students' drinking habits, the NIAAA found that binges account for 70 percent of all alcohol consumed by students, and that 44 percent of them qualify as binge drinkers. One in three 18- to 24-year-olds admitted to hospital emergency rooms for serious injuries are intoxicated.

A 1999 study of the same college-age group revealed an interesting side effect: About 30 percent of the students surveyed reported engaging in "unplanned sexual activity" as a result of their drinking. It prompted at least one campus group, *Men Against Violence* at University of North Texas in Denton, Texas, to use this chilling slogan in its public awareness materials: "The Number One weapon used in campus rapes is alcohol." Clearly, binge drinking is a major concern on college campuses and among young adults.

HOW CAN YOU TELL IF SOMEONE HAS A DRINKING PROBLEM?

The NIAAA suggests asking these four questions, of yourself or the person you care about:

- Have you ever felt you should cut down on your drinking?
- Have people annoyed you by criticizing your drinking?
- Have you ever felt bad, or guilty, about your drinking?
- Have you ever had a drink first thing in the morning, to steady your nerves or to get rid of a hangover?

One "yes" answer suggests a possible alcohol problem. More than one "yes" answer means it is highly likely that a problem exists. However, you should see a doctor or health-care provider, who can help you determine if a drinking problem does exist, and plan the best course of action.

Some bars, and even colleges, have begun to distribute products that test drinks for the presence of so-called "date rape drugs," such as GHO or ketamine, colorless and odorless sedatives that impair judgment and induce sleep. There are now cocktail coasters treated so that they will change color when wet with only a few drops of mixed drink, as well as strips that can be placed into beverages to detect the presence of a drug. The newest do-it-yourself product is a similar type of strip that can be placed on the tongue; it changes color depending on how much a person has had to drink. These might be just intriguing enough to young drinkers for a bar to offer them regularly as an inducement to monitor alcohol intake.

As a seller and server of alcoholic beverages, you must learn to be especially vigilant about the signs of problem drinking. Later in this chapter we will discuss more fully how to identify problem drinkers, as well as how to handle them when they are your customers.

LEGAL CONSIDERATIONS

The surge of third-party litigation, the raising of the drinking age to 21, the placement of warning labels on liquor bottles, and the pressure to control media advertising of alcoholic beverages are all part of an ongoing national movement against alcohol abuse. Such efforts are dubbed by some as **neoprohibition**, a throwback to the disastrous nineteenth-century movement described in Chapter 1. But those who are involved in today's movement speak of it as **neotemperance,** aimed against the *abuse* of alcohol, not consumption of alcohol entirely.

The bar and beverage industry has seen its products and practices debated on national television talk shows, in newspapers, even in the halls of Congress. A number of related issues, including religious restrictions, health considerations, and alcoholism, tend to polarize people and create a turbulent climate for the industry. While most Americans do not support efforts to limit public access to alcohol, certain extremely vocal anti-alcohol groups are using the problem of drunken driving as a political agenda to push for stricter controls on alcohol sales and service.

Manufacturers and sellers of alcohol, who sometimes feel they are cast in the role of "the bad guys," worry that the concerns of both the public and the private sectors will adversely affect their profits long-term. Government at all levels tends to raise the tax on alcoholic-beverage sales whenever money is needed, referring to it (not entirely in jest) as a "sin tax." On the other hand the industry itself is also very much concerned about alcohol abuse. A number of industry organizations are developing ways to fight abuse through education, server-awareness programs, and new products suitable to a new market.

If you are going to be working in this facet of the hospitality industry, you must become familiar with the specific laws that affect your job. That is the purpose of this section: to introduce and explain laws that directly affect the bar and beverage industry. Like any other laws, those that apply to the sale and service of alcohol are impacted by the social and political climate, and can change accordingly. So it is important to stay up to date. The laws fall into four categories:

- Dramshop and third-party liability laws
- Blood-alcohol-content or blood-alcohol-concentration (BAC) laws
- Drunken-driving laws
- Drinking-age laws

First, we will define and discuss each type of law. Then we'll talk about ways that the food and hospitality industries are creating and promoting responsible alcohol-consumption policies.

No single federal agency or department establishes all of the rules and standards regarding the sale, service, or use or alcohol—nothing to compare, for instance, to the U.S. Food and Drug Administration, which sets safety and sanitation standards for foods and medicines. Consequently alcohol-related laws may vary drastically from state to state, and even between counties or voting precincts in "wet-dry" areas; and they might be enforced by a police or sheriff's department, a department of transportation, an alcoholic beverage commission, or another agency. This is one more reason that the first rule of responsible alcoholic-beverage service is to know your own state and local regulations.

Dramshop Laws and Third-Party Liability

In recent years attorneys have successfully argued that bars, as well as restaurants that serve alcoholic beverages, should be held at least partially responsible for how the beverages affect their guests. Such laws are generally known as **dramshop laws** (from *dram,* originally meaning a small drink of liquor, plus *shop,* the place where it is sold). The thrust of these laws is that the liability for the damages in a drunk-driving accident, for instance, should be shared by the driver who caused it and the server or alcoholic-beverage licensee who provided the intoxicating drinks. This concept is known as **third-party liability.**

The earliest dramshop laws were enacted in nineteenth-century England, to protect families of so-called habitual drunkards. The laws penalized tavern owners if they continued to serve a patron after being notified of his or her drunkenness by his or her spouse, children, or employees. Starting in the mid-1980s successful lawsuits resulted in millions of dollars in damages being awarded to victims of drunk drivers who had been served liquor by a third party. Furthermore, even when a state does not have a specific dramshop law on the books, courts in more than 20 states have chosen to recognize these third-party-liability lawsuits as legitimate "common law" causes of action. Part of their reasoning is that since the business profits from the sale of alcohol, it should be held accountable for the "social costs" of liquor sales as well.

Whether or not bar or restaurant owners agree that they should be held responsible for their customers' drinking, the fact is that today society is doing so. It is also generally agreed that without this "threat," licensees and servers would be less likely to establish service standards to prevent customers from becoming intoxicated, or to train their employees to recognize the problems. Other types of legal liability related to the dramshop laws apply to alcoholic-beverage service. **Criminal liability** allows the state to file a lawsuit against a licensed business, individuals employed by that business, or the social host of a private party where alcohol is served. Unlike a civil suit the criminal suit addresses the criminal aspects of serving alcohol irresponsibly. For example, when an intoxicated guest at a bar injures an innocent bystander (either inside the bar or after leaving the premises), the state sues both the guest and those who served that guest alcohol. A civil suit usually includes a financial penalty; a criminal suit can mean serving jail time. Sometimes both civil and criminal suits are filed simultaneously in separate courts, and the outcome of the criminal suit is not dependent on the outcome of the civil action. Both cases are decided independently, which means that the defendant can be held accountable by both courts, or in one and not the other.

Administrative liability applies to any liquor-license holder in a certain state. Liquor licenses are granted by state liquor-control agencies (you will learn much more about them in Chapter 16). If regulations are broken the state can mete out stiff penalties, including fines, license suspensions, and license revocations. As you might imagine this can cause financial harm or ruin to a bar or restaurant business.

In many court cases alcoholic-beverage servers have been held responsible for **foreseeability,** that is, the reasonable anticipation that a particular course of action will likely result in harm or injury. Furthermore, the most prosperous defendant in a third-party-liability suit (often the bar or restaurant owner) can be forced to pay most (or all) of the damage costs, especially if the codefendants are unable to pay. Some attorneys choose to sue only the wealthiest of the potential defendants, even if that party is not solely or even primarily responsible for what happened.

The term **reasonable care** is used to describe the degree of diligence or the standards of precaution that are expected in a particular set of circumstances. Reasonable care includes, but is not limited to, what an ordinary, prudent person would do to prevent harm or injury. The flip side of reasonable care is **negligence**, which means that the failure to act (that is, the failure to exercise reasonable care) resulted in harm or injury to someone. In other words a bar or restaurant has a basic duty to prevent any action that would cause injury or permit injury to occur as a result of the way it serves beverages on its premises. What does this mean to your serving staff? All employees should be aware that they can be held personally liable for serving alcohol to a minor or to an already intoxicated guest, or even by letting an intoxicated guest get behind the wheel of a vehicle. Conversely people have also sued bars or restaurants that refused to seat them or serve them, citing the embarrassment and emotional distress it caused. Fortunately these businesses, explaining that they had good reason to believe that these persons were already intoxicated, have been successfully found not liable on the grounds that they would have been negligent to serve these people, then let them drive away from the premises. With the advent of these lawsuits the third-party-liability issue caused a major crisis for insurance companies that offer coverage to the beverage-service industry. Insurance rates skyrocketed beyond the reach of many bars and restaurants, and many insurers refused outright to sell liability insurance to enterprises that served liquor on-premise. For a time in the mid-1980s the situation threatened the entire beverage industry. Luckily that is no longer the case. As long as a bar's business plan and financial backing are solid, it can obtain insurance as easily as any other type of business.

Blood Alcohol Content (BAC) Laws

You are considered legally intoxicated when your blood alcohol content is higher than what the law permits in your area. The legal level of intoxication varies from state to state, but it has been in flux because in 1999 Congress mandated that states adhere to the .08 BAC standard by the year 2004, or they would no longer receive millions of dollars in federal highway-improvement money. An interesting scramble resulted:

- In 2001 twenty-five states had BAC levels of .08, twenty-four states had BAC levels of .10, and only Massachusetts had not set a BAC *per se* level.
- By December 2003 only fourteen states still had BAC levels of .10, and Massachusetts decided on a .08 level, along with thirty-six other states.
- By May 2004 only Delaware had not approved a .08 BAC; Minnesota enacted its .08 BAC law with an effective date of August 2005.

Federal money talks. But what exactly does it *say?* The BAC figure is a percentage of the amount of alcohol in your bloodstream. For example, at a .10 BAC level you have one drop of alcohol in every 100 drops of blood. That may not sound like much, but remember how potent alcohol is and how long it takes your system to process and eliminate it. At a BAC level of .30, you could lapse into a coma; at a BAC level of .40, you risk death.

The debate in the United States over changing the BAC level from .10 to .08 was heated, and it centered around the amount of alcohol absorbed by the body. The beverage industry, with science on its side, pointed to the differences between potencies of beer, wine, and spirits, as well as to the fact that each individual has a different build, a different amount of fat, a different metabolic rate, and a different amount of food in his or her stomach at the time of a BAC test. In sum gender, age, weight, overall health, mental state, and whether a person is taking medication all affect the way that the body processes alcohol. This makes it difficult, if not impossible, to draw absolute conclusions about minimum BAC standards and, hence, to legislate them.

Since states began to adopt the more stringent .08 BAC level, public reaction has been mixed. Many people simply are determined to spare themselves the embarrassment of blowing into a breath-test machine or standing in a police lineup, and so have decided to drink less and/or not drive if they do choose to imbibe. Others view it as a mixed blessing, but one that causes everyone to behave more responsibly. Still others see it as the continuing effort of neoprohibitionists to slowly but surely legislate morality by forbidding consumption of alcoholic beverages. There have been suggestions to lower BAC standards to 0.05 or even 0.02, levels at which it would be impossible for most people to have even one drink and then drive without violating the law.

In spite of the fuss about lowering the BAC standard to .08, it might seem discouraging to its proponents that the results have not been as promising as they had hoped. In a Government Accounting Office study published in the September 1999 issue of *Restaurants USA* (the magazine of the National Restaurant Association), lowering the BAC level has not actually resulted in fewer alcohol-related fatalities. The study found that tougher alcohol law enforcement, drivers'-license revocation, and *Zero Tolerance* policies for minors who consume alcoholic beverages are the more effective methods of reducing the number and severity of alcohol-related driving accidents.

Drunken-Driving Laws

During the 1960s and 1970s people who were convicted of drunken driving were fined between $10 and $50 and admonished by a judge. The defendant would solemnly promise not to drive drunk again, pay the fine, and walk away, with car keys in hand. If the person had been unlucky enough to cause an accident resulting in serious injuries or even deaths, a fine of a few hundred dollars and a suspended sentence was regarded as sufficient for this "basically law-abiding citizen."

Today Americans are far less tolerant of people who drive drunk. Activist groups, such as Mothers Against Drunk Drivers (MADD), Students Against Driving Drunk (SADD), and Remove Intoxicated Drivers (RID), have spearheaded powerful national campaigns for stringent new legislation. Their efforts have changed forever the arrest, recording of charges, and penalties for an offense now commonly known as **"driving while intoxicated" (DWI)** or **"driving under the influence" (DUI).** This national reaction to drunken driving has resulted in the implementation of several different types of **per se laws.** Under a *per se* (Latin for *by itself*) law, a single piece of evidence—a breath test administered to a driver, a roadside sobriety test (e.g., walking in a straight line, standing on one leg), *or* the refusal of a driver to take such a test—is automatically presumed to indicate guilt, without regard to other possible circumstances. (See the interview with attorney Christopher Hooper of Texas for a defense lawyer's interesting viewpoint on these issues and the civil-rights questions they raise.)

The *per se laws* include:

- *Presumptive laws,* which allow an arresting officer's self-administered sobriety test to be the basis for proving a person guilty (in effect in 35 states).
- *Administrative license-suspension laws,* which empower an arresting officer to immediately revoke the driver's license of a person who refuses to take, or fails to pass, an alcohol breath test (in effect in 42 states and the District of Columbia). These are termed *administrative* because they are invoked on-site at the time of the arrest, and are not part of a criminal procedure.
- *Open-container laws,* which prohibit drivers and/or passengers to have open containers of alcohol in vehicles (in effect in 42 states).
- *Vehicle-forfeiture laws* that allow multiple offenders' vehicles to be impounded if the offenders are caught driving under the influence again (in effect in 29 states). These are among the most controversial laws since the drivers may not own their vehicles outright; they might be leasing them, or a bank or finance company technically owns the vehicles while they are being paid for.
- *Ignition-interlock laws* that require accused drunk drivers to install devices in their vehicles into which they must blow (proving that they are sober) in order to start the ignition and/or keep the vehicle running (in effect in 43 states)—even when they are awaiting court dates and have not been convicted.

The fines and penalties for drunken driving are being raised, too (see Figure 2.4, which lists just a few of them). Most states revoke drivers' licenses for three months for a first offense, and one to two years for second convictions. Some 30 states now mandate jail sentences for repeat drunk-driving offenses. Insurance companies also now penalize drunken drivers. Since 1984 in New York, for example, all insured drivers convicted of DUI can have their automobile-insurance coverage cancelled, or, at least, they run the risk of it not being renewed by their carrier. This forces the individual to seek coverage by the state's "assigned-risk plan," with insurance rates up to 75 percent higher than typical premiums.

Most drunken-driving legislation is passed and administered at the state and local levels. This is not to say that Congress has not gotten involved, however. In 1981 it voted to withhold federal highway funds from states that had not raised their legal drinking age from 18 to 21 by 1986. In 1999, as you just learned, the same strategy was used to force states to lower the *per se* BAC level from .10 to .08 for motorists. Congress also has established a grant program that awards federal

DUI/DWI LAWS BY STATE (AS OF MARCH 2004)

State	Fines for DUI/DWI First Offense	Admin. License Suspension for 1st Offense?	Can driving privileges be restored during the license suspension?
Alabama	$500-2000	90 days	No
Alaska	$250	90 days	Yes, after 30 days
Arizona	$250 minimum	90 days	Yes, after 30 days
Arkansas	$150-1000	120 days	Yes
California	$400-1000	4 months	Yes, after 30 days
Colorado	$300-1000+	3 months	Yes
Connecticut	$500-1000	90 days	Yes
Delaware	$230-1150+	3 months	No
District of Columbia	(Unavailable)	2 to 90 days	Yes
Florida	$250-500	6 months	Yes
Georgia	$500-1000+	1 year	Yes
Hawaii	$150-700	3 months	Yes, after 30 days
Idaho	Up to $1000	90 days	Yes, after 30 days
Illinois	Up to $1000	3 months	Yes, after 30 days
Indiana	$500	180 days	Yes, after 30 days
Iowa	$700-1200	180 days	Yes, after 90 days
Kansas	$250-500+	30 days	No
Kentucky	$250-900	(Unavailable)	(Unavailable)
Louisiana	$225-600	90 days	Yes, after 30 days
Maine	$400 minimum	90 days	Yes
Maryland	Up to $1000	45 days	Yes
Massachusetts	$500-5000	90 days	No
Michigan	$100-500	(Unavailable)	(Unavailable)
Minnesota	$700	90 days	Yes, after 15 days
Mississippi	$250-$1000	90 days	No
Missouri	Up to $500	30 days	No
Montana	$300-500	(Unavailable)	(Unavailable)
Nebraska	$200-500	90 days	Yes, after 30 days
Nevada	$200-1000	90 days	Yes, after 45 days
New Hampshire	$350-1000	6 months	No
New Jersey	$250-400	(Unavailable)	(Unavailable)
New Mexico	$500-800	90 days	Yes, after 30 days
New York	$300-1000	Variable	Yes
North Carolina	Up to $2000	30 days	Yes, after 10 days
North Dakota	$250 minimum	91 days	Yes, after 30 days
Ohio	Up to $1000	90 days	Yes, after 15 days
Oklahoma	Up to $1000	180 days	Yes
Oregon	$565-5000	90 days	Yes, after 30 days
Pennsylvania	$300 minimum	(Unavailable)	(Unavailable)
Rhode Island	$700-1000	(Unavailable)	(Unavailable)
South Carolina	$200 minimum	(Unavailable)	(Unavailable)
South Dakota	Up to $1000	(Unavailable)	(Unavailable)
Tennessee	$350-1000	(Unavailable)	(Unavailable)
Texas	Up to $2000	90 days	Yes
Utah	Up to $1000	90 days	No
Vermont	Up to $750	90 days	No
Virginia	Up to $2500	7 days	No
Washington	$350-500	90 days	Yes, after 30 days
West Virginia	$100-500	6 months	Yes, after 30 days
Wisconsin	$150-300	6 months	Yes
Wyoming	Up to $750	90 days	Yes

FIGURE 2.4 Sources: OHS Health and Safety Services, Inc. (Costa Mesa, California); The Insurance Institute for Highway Safety (Arlington, Virginia); and *What's Driving You?* Intervention Instruction Community Programs (Chicago, Illinois).

money for implementing safe-driving programs and aggressively enforcing drunken-driving laws. In 2004, for example, $22 million was paid to states for enforcing "Alcohol-Impaired Driving Countermeasures." These include:

- License-suspension programs
- Underage-drinking programs
- Sobriety checkpoints or other "similar intensive-enforcement" programs
- A graduated licensing law with nighttime-driving curfews and other restrictions
- Programs for drinking drivers ages 21 to 34
- Programs to increase testing of drivers in fatal crashes

The states might qualify for additional money if they enact "supplemental" programs, such as police videotaping drivers stopped for violations or using passive alcohol sensors.

Others who say alcohol-related laws have become too stringent, to the point of violating drivers' rights, suggest the need for better seat-belt-law enforcement instead. In the late 1990s, when the controversy about changing the BAC standard for drivers from .10 to .08 was raging, it was estimated that the measure would save about 600 lives per year. The National Transportation Safety Board estimated that there would be about 10,000 fewer deaths per year if everyone wore seat belts. It is ironic, then, that $11 million was paid to states to enforce "Occupant Protection" (seat-belt) programs in 2004—only half what was spent on drunk driving.

In the future we can expect more penalties to be suggested by consumer activists and passed by lawmakers. Unfortunately no matter what the laws, fines, penalties, or educational programs, approximately 10 percent of all drivers will continue to be problem drinkers, regardless of the cost to themselves and others. That makes it all the more important for everyone else to refuse to accept drunkenness, to learn how to recognize drunks in other vehicles and react defensively, and most of all, to drink responsibly themselves.

Drinking-Age Laws

The Twenty-sixth Amendment to the U.S. Constitution, the Age of Majority amendment, endows Americans who reach age 18 with nearly all the rights and privileges of adulthood. Eighteen-year-olds can vote, sign contracts, marry without their parents' consent, ignore curfews, and buy tickets to X-rated movies. However, society has determined that it will be three more years before these new "adults" are responsible enough to have a drink that contains alcohol.

This reasoning stems at least in part from the controversial contention that many in this segment of the population will end up as highway fatalities if allowed to drink. Motor-vehicle crashes are the leading cause of death in the 16-to-20-year age group; about 22 percent of them involve underage drivers and alcohol. Beverage-industry groups have countered with statistics that show that while 16-year-old drivers have far higher rates of traffic violations and fatalities than the rest of the population, those rates decrease dramatically once the young drivers reach age 18. In the 1990s the beverage industry lobbied to raise the driving age to either 18 or 21. This did not go over well with busy parents, but it caught the attention of lawmakers, who proposed a different and more stringent standard for teens caught drinking and driving. Today most states have **"Zero Tolerance"** laws for persons under age 21, with lower BAC levels (.01 or .02) than for adults, stiff fines, and license suspension. (For most teens, a .02 blood alcohol concentration can be achieved with a single drink.) The theory behind Zero Tolerance laws is that since it is illegal for persons underage to drink in the first place, it should also be illegal for them to drive with *any* alcohol in their system.

A diverse group of experts sociologists, psychologists, and beverage-industry representatives have suggested that the parents of the underage drinker be the primary influences and rule-makers, not the government. However, the news in 2003, from Columbia University's National Center on Addiction and Substance Abuse, indicated that underage drinkers were responsible for 19.7 percent of the alcohol consumed in the United States. (Other, government-sponsored surveys come up with a lower figure, just over 11 percent).

No matter what the numbers, the ongoing debate is a very personal one for anyone with children. Is it better for youngsters to learn about alcohol, and how to use it in a controlled way, in a family setting, or is it better for parents to demand that children abstain until they are of legal drinking age? Of course, teens who drink should not be allowed to drive, and families with a history of alcohol abuse should seriously consider the message they convey to their children each and every time they take a drink. If alcohol is treated with disregard as to its risks, the message will be the wrong one, no matter who delivers it first to a child.

Some of the responsibility for underage drinking must surely rest with the beverage manufacturers, for the wide variety of fizzy, fruit-flavored products they market to younger drinkers that, unintentionally but certainly, end up in the hands of minors and are perceived as "one step up" from their favorite soft drinks. This beverage category even has nicknames: *alco-pops* and *malternatives*. To their credit the manufacturers have also been progressive in creating community-relations programs to inform minors and parents about alcohol abuse. One of the oldest and best-respected is beer manufacturer Anheuser-Busch's program, called "Family Talk About Alcohol." The makers of Budweiser beer budget $250 million to provide speakers and print materials to high schools and colleges. Among the program's major points for parents:

- Always set a good example by drinking responsibly. Parents are the single most important factor in their children's decisions about alcohol.
- Talk openly with children about the law. Explain that it is illegal to purchase alcohol in any form, under the age of 21. Explain to them that the law is meant to protect people and that laws must be obeyed.
- Remind children that there are many other laws that also require people to be a certain age before they can do certain things. Tell them that the laws apply to all. It is not okay for adults to disobey them.

- Stick to the facts; avoid any scare tactics. Be truthful if you expect to continue to receive your children's trust.
- Be approachable and involved. Answer any questions your children ask about alcohol.

Parents may also want to discuss responsible drinking with other adults with whom their children come into contact (friends, teachers, coaches, relatives) and encourage these adults to reinforce the legal, responsible behavior they are trying to teach. The benefits of helping children learn the facts about alcohol use, and abuse, not only help in the fight against underage drinking, but also underscore the importance of personal responsibility in future generations of adult consumers.

SOLUTIONS FROM A CONCERNED INDUSTRY

In light of social and legal developments, the food-and-hospitality industry has been at the forefront in the effort to promote responsible consumption of alcoholic beverages. The Anheuser-Busch program you just read about is only one of many examples. Also, the term *legal developments* includes more than stringent *per se* laws. For example:

- In 2003 an Indiana jury ruled that the owners of an Outback Steakhouse pay $39 million when a man who had been drinking at the restaurant left in his car and struck two persons on a motorcycle.
- Also in 2003 a TGI Friday's restaurant in Kentucky agreed to pay $21 million to the parents of two teenagers killed by a drunk driver who had been served there.

These are just two of the third-party liability cases that are prompting bars, hotels, and restaurants to rethink their responsible-service policies. Obviously training both managers and employees is a key ingredient in the success of such a program. All staff members who come into contact with guests should be thoroughly trained in alcohol awareness, which is defined as the knowledge and skills to appropriately serve alcoholic beverages, monitor guest behavior, and deal decisively with any undesirable or illegal situations. Another commonsense training program, called *ServSafe Alcohol* has been developed by the National Restaurant Association Educational Foundation. Among the facts shared with workers in this program are:

- If wine is served in an 8-ounce glass, the net result is twice as much alcohol as if served in a 4-ounce glass and should be counted as two drinks instead of one. The use of oversized glasses is chic where wine aficionados dine, but try to limit each serving to four or five ounces.

- Since the liver can metabolize only approximately one drink per hour, consuming more than that naturally increases the amount of alcohol absorbed into the bloodstream. Alcohol will build up in the bloodstream and affect a person long after he or she has stopped drinking.
- A person's BAC level can continue to rise even after he or she has stopped drinking and left your establishment. The guest might appear to be acting normally, but the full impact of the alcohol might not be felt until he or she is driving home. Knowing this, a bar should never serve *doubles,* drinks containing twice the normal amount of alcohol, or drinks containing two or more spirits (e.g., Martinis, Manhattans, Long Island Ice Teas) at "last call."

Also extremely important in responsible beverage service is the practice of offering food when serving alcohol because food consumption slows the absorption of alcohol into the small intestine (see Figure 2.5). Also, guests who are relaxing and enjoying their food may not drink as much or as fast. The pace is slower when they are savoring the experience. As you monitor a guest's reactions, observe the type and amount of alcohol that he or she is drinking, as well as the physical size of the person, keeping in mind that women tend to become intoxicated more quickly than most men, even if they drink less.

FIGURE 2.5 Drinking an alcoholic beverage with food is a way to better savor both. Courtesy of PhotoDisc/Getty Images.

High-Risk Factors

It is also important to be aware of a number of factors that might predispose someone to be especially high-risk for the negative effects of consuming alcoholic beverages. For these people the usual BAC levels do not apply. It can be difficult to identify these individuals, although there are guidelines to follow, again from the ServSafe Alcohol program:

Stress or Depression. People who are feeling intensely stressed or depressed can show strong and sudden reactions when consuming alcoholic beverages. When the human body is under duress, it protects itself by coating the stomach to protect it from excess acid generated when the person is stressed, anxious, or depressed. Unfortunately this protective lining can trap alcohol in the stomach and prevent it from moving on to the small intestine to be absorbed. Consequently as the person consumes alcohol, he or she does not readily feel the effects of it and might need to drink more to induce the anticipated relaxation. Eventually the temporary stomach lining dissolves, and at that point the alcohol passes quickly into the intestines and bloodstream, causing a rapid rise in BAC level.

Diets and/or Fatigue. A guest who is dieting, purposely limiting his or her calorie intake, might not have eaten, or eaten much, for quite some time. This means that any alcoholic beverage consumed will be very quickly absorbed into the bloodstream. The same thing happens when an individual is tired. Fatigue also tends to affect overall judgment, thus compounding some of alcohol's side effects.

Altitude. People who live and/or work in high-altitude communities, such as ski resorts, typically react more quickly to alcohol. It takes fewer drinks to become tipsy. This is a result of lower atmospheric pressure, and it affects the way that the human body absorbs alcohol. People accustomed to living closer to sea level but vacationing in a high-altitude location might find that each drink seems twice as potent. This means that staff working in bars and restaurants in these locations must be more alert to clientele who are unfamiliar with this effect on their drinking.

Alcohol Tolerance. Have you ever known someone who seems to be able to drink a lot of alcohol without showing the typical signs of drunkenness? The human body and brain can build up a tolerance to alcohol. Long-term drinkers can sometimes consume large quantities without feeling or showing the effects. Conversely inexperienced drinkers might show symptoms before they are legally intoxicated because their bodies are unaccustomed to alcohol. It "hits" them harder and more quickly than it hits experienced drinkers. Bar staff need to be cognizant of these two extremes.

Medication. We've already discussed the dangers of mixing drugs and alcohol, whether they are over-the-counter, prescription, or illegal drugs. Drinking alcohol interferes with the body's ability to process, or break down, many medications, so they build up instead of being distributed in the system, thereby magnifying the impact of both the drug and the alcohol on the body. Certain combinations, like alcohol and tranquilizers, can even be fatal.

If you are a server and know that a guest is taking medication, monitor that person carefully to observe any behavioral changes. Curtail service to that person sooner than usual, and do not allow the guest to drive away from the premises if you feel he or she might be unsafe.

Pregnancy. Pregnant women automatically qualify as high-risk guests. We have already discussed the tragedies of fetal alcohol syndrome (FAS) and fetal alcohol effects (FAE). Although there is no legal prohibition against serving alcohol to a pregnant woman, bar staff should be trained to watch for potential problems, and even to be able to discuss the consequences of consuming alcoholic beverages with the guest.

Watching Behavior. You've read a lot so far about keeping an eye on guests, observing their behavior, and watching for signs of problems. But what exactly should you be looking for? Along with the obvious steps of counting the number of drinks that guests have ordered and monitoring how quickly they are finishing each drink, you can discern a great deal from most people's behavior about how much alcohol they can safely consume.

All of us have different ways of socializing that are part of our personalities. There is a difference between a guest who is loud and boisterous and one who *becomes* loud and boisterous after having a few drinks. As a server it's important to notice the changes in a person's natural style because experts tell us that a change in behavior is more revealing than the behavior itself. It is also essential for you to learn that certain disabilities or physical conditions might cause a person to stumble, slur speech, or have difficulty concentrating. These are not to be confused with drunkenness, and if you're observant enough, you'll learn the subtle differences.

Common signs of intoxication include:

- ***Relaxed inhibitions.*** When alcohol first enters the brain, it relaxes a person's normal sense of cautiousness and propriety. People say and do things they might not normally do or, at least, would think twice about. They might become very friendly or overly affectionate to employees or other guests, or they might become brooding or quiet. They might suddenly leave a group of friends and sit elsewhere, choosing to drink alone. They might annoy other guests by making loud and candid comments or by using foul language.
- ***Impaired judgment.*** Emotions and judgment are influenced by alcohol. Common sense doesn't seem quite as important when you've had too much to drink. The most powerful example is, of course, a person's refusal to hand over the car keys, insisting "I'm fine" and arguing with anyone who disagrees. Other signs of impaired judgment include drinking faster or switching to a stronger drink; showing extreme emotion, by becoming angry or tearful; making irrational claims or becoming argumentative; complaining about the last drink (after having had others that were of exactly the same type and strength); and being careless with money, which includes buying drinks for strangers or offering to buy "for the whole house."

- ***Slow reaction time.*** People who drink too much might report later that they felt they were moving "in slow motion." Indeed the more alcohol they consume, the slower their reaction and/or response times. They might exhibit a loss of concentration or memory, strain to finish sentences, not make sense, or slur their words. They also might be unable to focus their eyes or to maintain eye contact with others. They often look and act drowsy.
- ***Impaired physical condition.*** Alcohol consumption almost always impairs motor skills. This condition is known as **ataxia,** the inability to control voluntary muscle movements, which affects balance and coordination. People who experience ataxia spill drinks, stagger, stumble, sway or even doze off while seated, fall down or bump into things, and seem awkward when trying to retrieve change and bills left on the table or counter.

MAKING A PLAN

Now that you have some idea of what to look for when people overindulge in alcohol, you need to know the next step to take. It is management's responsibility to create and implement a complete responsible-alcoholic-beverage-service program that builds awareness throughout the organization.

Some beginning steps for creating a written plan have been suggested by the National Restaurant Association Educational Foundation:

1. Review any existing records your operation may have about this topic.
2. Identify the special needs of your operation.
3. Develop, review, and update written policies.
4. Manage the staff to ensure a successful program.
5. Promote the responsible service of alcoholic beverages.

Let's consider these steps one at a time.

Review Existing Records

First you should carefully examine the history of your establishment in **incident reports** or a current written policy, if available. Can a pattern be discerned from incidents, accidents, or related factors that contribute to problems? Then talk to employees. Ask what they have noticed, and solicit their suggestions. Set up a meeting with your insurance carrier and your attorney. Ask for up-to-date information about third-party liability, and for their suggestions about good prevention programs.

When you look at incidents that might have occurred, search for specifics: Exactly what happened and why? Was the bar or restaurant too crowded for adequate staff observation of all guests? Were the servers adequately prepared for this par-

AN OUNCE OF PREVENTION

Suggestions and recommendations to enhance a Responsible-Beverage-Service program include:

- "Advertise" your commitment to responsible alcohol service on the printed items used in your establishment: menus, coasters, table tents. Put up posters in your restrooms that mention alternate transportation modes that guests can use, as well as how to reach them.
- Put your responsible-alcohol-service-program pointers on cards that your waitstaff can carry with them and refer to if necessary.
- Pay a private company to do the weekly alcohol inventory instead of relying on your staff or having to do it yourself. Reconciling the number of drinks served with the amount of liquor poured can help with portion control (i.e., pouring too generously), as well as theft prevention.
- Set advance limits for particular types of drinks, for example, no more than three Martinis per customer, ever.
- For large parties or on such busy holidays as New Year's Eve, consider hiring outside security.
- Focus at least part of training on employees' attitudes toward customers. By smiling, making eye contact, and learning to chat a little instead of being strictly an order-taker, the server is better able to size up the customer; the customer, in turn, feels more comfortable. It makes for a smoother situation if the server eventually has to deliver the "cut-off" message.
- Teach the same observant friendliness to your door staffers and/or security staff members. If they approach a difficult customer with a calm voice and a handshake, for instance, they can diffuse the tension—even while the customer is being escorted out of the bar.
- Forge relationships with a limousine company or towing service in case it is needed to get a guest (and in some cases, his or her vehicle) safely home.

ticular incident? Were written policies in effect at the time to guide the staff? If so, were they inadequate or did no one bother to refer to them? Did managers and/or employees communicate well or poorly? Did they communicate at all?

With this detailed information you might be able to pinpoint a type of incident and even a frequency rate of occurrence. You also might be able to identify the types of guests who are typically involved in problem situations at your place of business. Were they, for example, minors who were upset about not being served? Were they intoxicated adults? Did verbal abuse and/or physical fighting make the situation worse? Was anyone armed with a weapon? Did the people involved in the fray drive away from the establishment?

Next, look closely at how each incident was handled. Ask: Were certain servers involved in more problem situations than others? Did the servers use good judgment and practice the skills that they had learned in training? Were managers called when needed? If so, how did they react? Was it necessary to call police? Was an incident report filled out completely? If so, is a copy of it on file? Following the incident, was additional training held for staff members to teach prevention or public-relations skills?

It is also important to realize that an incident doesn't end when the guests who caused it leave your premises. Was it investigated by the local police or the alcoholic-beverage commission in your area? Did your business receive unfavorable publicity in the news media? Were customer counts and sales affected that evening, or on an ongoing basis? Did your insurance rates increase as a result of the incident? Did you lose employees because of it?

The final aspect of this step is deciding what to do next. You need to assess the true readiness of your operation to handle a difficult customer, an armed customer, a suicidal customer, and a noisy and/or lewd customer who is annoying other patrons and who refuses to leave. In short there are as many potential problems as there are customers. Ask your employees to help you think through any possible kind of difficult situation, from the minor hassles, to the real crises. Adapt your written policies to deal with all of them. (For more on this, refer to Appendix A, which contains a comprehensive Responsible-Beverage-Alcohol-Service General Audit form.)

Identify Special Needs

Special needs refers to the differences inherent in the various types of alcohol service. A bar or restaurant, for example, has very different needs from those of a sports stadium, a hotel, a casino, or a banquet/party facility. Once an audit or survey has been completed and you have pinpointed areas of your business that might require special rules or attention, consider these differences and decide how you must compensate for them.

In bars, lounges, and restaurants, most guests come to enjoy the atmosphere and camaraderie as much as the beverages. But it is the alcohol that invites the scrutiny of law-enforcement agencies. Employees who interact with the customers should be polite and pleasant, not intimidating. One of their goals should be to encourage voluntary compliance with the laws, not to cause confrontations or be accusatory. When employees consistently exhibit a reasonable attitude and pleasant manner, they will gain the respect of all guests, as well as have an easier time dealing with troublesome ones.

Employees who serve as door staffers or hostesses are a wise addition to many venues serving alcohol. These employees are the first to greet incoming guests and to notice potential incoming problems. They are also responsible for checking identification (ID); today there is plenty of good information from law-enforcement agencies about how to spot increasingly sophisticated fake IDs. These employees should follow a specific ID-checking policy to prevent, among other legal infringements, a single form of ID being passed to multiple underage persons as individuals leave and return. No one should be "immune" from being checked for proper identification, including entertainers, their friends, or even regular guests.

Door staffers should also be able to deny entrance to anyone who appears to already be intoxicated, and even to ensure that the person who has been turned away does not get in a vehicle and drive off. Door employees can explain to the person that they will call the police if they see the person drive away, then they should be prepared to follow through with the threat. Servers should be both alert and pleasant: alert to the number of drinks consumed by each guest and continually mindful of signs of drunkenness. Having a manager walking around at all times as an additional, active observer is a necessity when a place is busy. A good manager can help servers communicate with each other, offer second opinions about questionable behavior, follow or divert suspicious guests, and generally alert employees to any potential trouble. If the facility is large and has partitioned areas, it's a good idea to consider purchasing handheld walkie-talkies so that employees can easily contact a manager, security guard, or other employees.

The manager should be able to forecast the volume of expected business, so that he or she can schedule sufficient numbers of servers for each time period. Being understaffed during busy times is an automatic invitation for trouble because both employees and guests suffer the frustration of long waits and inattentive service.

Banquet facilities and private-event centers face unique challenges. Here are a few examples: the 20-year-old bride who insists that all her guests should have Champagne at her wedding reception; the 65-year-old retiree who insists on celebrating at his party past the point of good judgment; the business banquet spread across several different rooms at a large hotel, where guests and crashers can move about and order drinks in each room. A well-prepared manager will take preventive steps *before* each of these events is booked. The manager will explain all applicable laws to the host, orally and in writing, to make the host an ally of the facility, thus helping to ensure that guests will adhere to these laws. In this contract the specific policies that govern responsible-alcoholic-beverage service will be spelled out, including a clause about the host's responsibilities and liabilities. The rules will be explicit; for example: You will not serve minors or intoxicated individuals; you will slow the beverage service to guests who appear to have had too much. The host should be asked if he or she would like to be personally involved if a difficult situation arises during the event. Finally, the manager will ask the host to sign this agreement.

If minors will be attending an event, be sure to have adequate supplies of nonalcoholic beverages. Consider using two different kinds of glasses, one for those underage and one for those over 21. Groups of college students are especially challenging because they might be of mixed age groups, making it difficult to tell who's 21 and who isn't. Some facilities that cater sorority or fraternity parties, for example, have simply made it their policy not to serve alcohol at these events. Nevertheless whenever alcohol is served, it's not unusual for a drink to be passed from adult to minor, and it is almost impossible to count drink consumption when people are moving about. This is why it is essential that all staff members be vigilant and communicate at all times, especially during shift changes.

Hotel and motel beverage directors have responsibilities similar to those of restaurant and bar managers. But hotel guests might also choose to consume alcohol in their rooms, which generates an additional challenge. When you are developing service policies for a hotel, consider:

- Whether to allow guests to take alcohol to their rooms, where staff members will not have control of the amount consumed
- How alcoholic beverage service is requested. If it is in-room, how will your staff members know how many people will be drinking or if they are of legal drinking age?
- Minimum and maximum quantities to stock in minibars
- Drinking to excess in the on-premise lounge or bar, assuming that the guest will be walking back to his or her room instead of driving

And don't forget that in hotels, housekeeping, security, and room-service employees must also be trained to note problems and to know whom to contact to report them when necessary.

Develop Written Policies

We've already discussed that for employee-training purposes, you should put in writing basic rules and guidelines for dealing with customers. In this section we explain why this is necessary for a broader purpose. In case there is an incident or accident on your premises or your establishment is named as a responsible party in a lawsuit, your attorney and insurance company will use these written documents to help you out of a potentially damaging and expensive situation.

One of the first things you should decide is who will approach the over-served customer with "the bad news" that he or she is being cut off. Some businesses leave this specifically to the manager on duty; others feel that the person who has already established some rapport with the guest—the server or bartender, perhaps—is the most logical choice. Decide in advance rather than wait for an incident. Either way, telling the customer must be done tactfully and respectfully, and should be role-played extensively in training so that all employees are fully aware of the policy and how to enforce it. Some establishments require each employee to be able to recite the policy because, sooner or later, a guest *will* ask. After the training each employee should sign and date a standard form stating that he or she understands and accepts the policies and procedures. Some businesses also require employees to pass a written test before they can join the serving staff.

You should also require that a standard incident-report form be filled out any time there is a problem. This includes when a server decides to stop serving alcoholic beverages to a guest. Why? You are covering yourself, your manager on duty, and your employee. What if this customer sobers up and calls his or her lawyer in the morning? What if the customer returns the next night, and the next, and starts harassing your waitstaff? You want a record of each incident.

Your insurance company, attorney, and local law-enforcement agencies can offer advice for creating and launching your training-and-documentation program. They might also have informational materials and/or boilerplate forms available for you to use. Ask your advisors such questions as, "If a customer, intoxicated or not, is harassing one of my servers, what are my rights? What are the server's rights? What is the best or safest way to ask such a customer to leave the premises?"

It is to your benefit in more ways than one to take advantage of the expertise of these professionals. Many insurance companies, for example, have agreed to sell liability insurance at reduced rates to enterprises that have trained all or a large percentage of their serving personnel in an insurer-approved program. Certain smaller insurance companies have formed insurance pools to spread their risks and are now offering affordable liability-insurance rates. If you shop around you can get the coverage you need to protect yourself from third-party liability. Be aware that the rates are likely to be *far* higher than you wish they were, so get your money's worth.

Manage the Staff

Total staff commitment to your responsible-service policies is essential to the success of their implementation, and this begins with the hiring process. In a prospective worker, look for the attitude and sense of responsibility necessary to enable someone to make a quick decision in a high-energy, high-pressure situation. Is this person, simply, a responsible and levelheaded individual? Keeping in mind that in third-party-liability cases, an employer can be held responsible for employees who were not properly screened, screen each job candidate carefully for histories of violence, criminal acts, sexual harassment, drug or alcohol abuse; also, examine the person's work history and call past employers for references. (Think for a moment about the news stories you've read or heard about elementary-school employees, for example, who have been accused of sexual impropriety with children, and whose past records were not checked. You can easily see how serious problems may arise.)

Develop a shift-change policy to ensure that incoming workers communicate with those who are ending their workdays. Also, as mentioned earlier, never understaff on days or evenings that are known to be busy periods. When enough servers are on the floor, each is better able to practice the essentials of customer service, which goes a long way to prevent problems. New employees should never be serving customers without supervision. Empower more experienced employees to guide trainees through their first days on the job; give trainees feedback and praise for a job well done. Encourage staff to help one another during busy periods. Back up any staff member who is being harassed by a customer. If the customer is not intoxicated, you are completely within your rights to ask a troublesome customer to leave the premises, remembering that the way you do so will affect all involved, as well as your business. But remember that if he or she is intoxicated, you might have to provide a means of transportation to avoid potential third-party liability later should the customer get into an accident after leaving your establishment.

You might want to consider implementing a salary structure that bases compensation on sales of combined food and beverage instead of only beverages, to motivate employees to further reduce the chances that customers will drink too much on their shifts. Teach staff how to use **suggestive selling** techniques, offering or recommending foods to customers who order drinks, or to *upsell*, which means suggesting drinks made with the more upscale, premium brands of liquor instead of *well brands*. Guests tend to consume the premium brands at a slower rate, presumably to enjoy the superior quality. You might want to give your waitstaff permission to offer small tastes of certain food items free of charge, as an enticement to buy. In addition to being methods of encouraging responsible-beverage service, all of these efforts will mean higher average checks and, therefore, greater tips for your employees.

Finally, as just mentioned, always give praise for a job well done, but realize that occasionally you will have to discipline an employee. When this situation arises, you'll find that the more concise your written policies, the easier it will be to back up your critique and justify any disciplinary action. Your policies will also make it easier to make even-handed decisions. Do not hesitate to remind your workers that if they willfully violate your state's liquor laws by, for example, serving alcohol to a minor, they will be dismissed immediately.

Promote Responsible Service

If you expect your employees to support your policies, *you* must support them. This means that you do not ask your staff to act irresponsibly, even one time. Don't ask them to bend the rules for your friends or relatives, so-called good customers, or regular guests. Doing so will undermine any credibility you might have built with them. Instead stress to staff that their working conditions (and probably their tips) will be better when they are serving people who are in control of themselves.

Communicate regularly with employees; this can be done in short meetings at regular intervals. At these meetings ask staff for ideas and address potential problems. Invite speakers from law-enforcement agencies or your alcoholic-beverage commission, or a counselor, to address, for example, the problems inherent with teen drinking, or alcoholism and related behavior. Provide examples and praise those who have exhibited good judgment in handling difficult situations.

As far as publicity is concerned, many formerly popular promotions are no longer in vogue; in fact today, some are actually illegal. Gone are the days of all-you-can-drink offers, two-for-one drink specials, ladies-drink-free nights, and even those so-called happy hours. Instead the focus of promotional activities has shifted toward events, themes, holidays, and entertainment and away from alcoholic enticements. Emphasize your food specials, however limited. Provide fun and entertainment that showcase your atmosphere. To do this, you'll need to know who your customers are, both regular and infrequent. Take the time to analyze why these individuals visit your business. What makes your establishment unique? What makes it appeal to "your" crowd? You'll learn more about researching your target market and building business in Chapter 3, but for the purpose of this discussion, remember that if you promote heavy alcoholic-beverage consumption, this practice could be used against you in court. Avoid advertising activity that fosters or glamorizes intoxication.

One good way to divert attention from alcohol is to plan an interesting, delicious menu that complements alcoholic-beverage sales. The food doesn't have to be gourmet, just appealing and satisfying. Be sure the choices include some fatty, high-protein snacks, which help absorb alcohol. Consider offering a free or moderately priced appetizer buffet in the early evening in lieu of the two-for-one happy hour. If you own a restaurant, consider the idea of **bundling,** or offering a food and drink in combination, for example, including a bottle of wine with two dinner entrées, or a free appetizer with an alcoholic beverage. Ask your wine or spirits supplier for help with these promotions; perhaps he or she will be willing to give you discounts on the cost of goods or help you pay for advertising costs.

CRISIS MANAGEMENT

Smart managers plan for the possibility of injuries, legal and insurance entanglements, and bad publicity, which are all consequences of alcoholic-beverage-related incidents. These events must be treated at least as seriously as a fire, flood, or armed robbery, and they should be part of your crisis management contingency plans. The Bar Code, quoted throughout this chapter, has some suggestions for crafting a crisis-management plan that will restore normalcy as soon as possible following an incident of this sort. It involves a three-pronged approach, each with a series of steps to follow. First, you must *address immediate needs,* in this sequence:

1. Contact the manager or owner.
2. Call police, ambulance, and/or emergency services as needed.
3. Safeguard guests and employees by cleaning up spills and breakage. (Ask police about specifics in case of a crime scene.)
4. Reassure guests while the incident is being resolved.

Second, you must *manage the crisis:*

1. Gather accurate information from as many sources as you can.
2. Contact attorneys and insurance agents.
3. Assign a trained spokesperson to handle information requests from the press or regulatory or law-enforcement agencies.
4. Decide whether to temporarily close or to immediately return to normal operation.

Third, you must *assess, then repair any damages:*

1. Determine the cause of the crisis.
2. Assess damages to the property, employee wages, and the flow of business.
3. Begin repairs.
4. Launch a marketing effort to offset damages to your public image.
5. Identify and reward employees who reacted quickly to minimize damages.
6. Deal with employees' reactions: guilt, fear, anger, depression.
7. Revise policies and training procedures to prevent a recurrence.

SUMMING UP

Practicing responsible alcohol service is the only way to ensure the safety of your guests, employees, and business. Much involved in this practice is common sense; but, in addition, you must educate yourself about alcohol and its impact on the human body, both positive and negative. It is important for sellers of alcoholic beverages to recognize and not minimize the negative effects of alcohol, and to develop written policies and training programs for staff members about how to deal with uncomfortable or potentially dangerous situations.

You might be forced to deal with numerous medical, social, and legal complications when someone drinks too much. Remember, that although the liver metabolizes most of the alcohol in the body, it does not do so quickly, complicating the question of exactly when a person has crossed the line and is "legally drunk." Everything from that person's natural tolerance, to his or her weight, mood, and any medications that he or she is taking, combined with the location of your establishment, can affect how hard alcohol hits him or her. Teach your staff members to recognize the signs and symptoms of problem drinkers, including alcoholics and binge drinkers.

Familiarize yourself with your local dramshop and third-party-liability laws, drunken-driving laws, blood-alcohol-content (BAC) laws, and the penalties for serving alcohol to minors, keeping in mind that states and counties have specific, and differing, laws, and any of several different agencies may be responsible for upholding them.

As the owner or manager of a business that serves alcohol, you should have written policies rules and guidelines for your establishment that cover alcoholic-beverage service, intelligent management of uncomfortable or dangerous situations, and penalties for staff members who break the rules or laws. Before hiring, screen potential employees carefully for behavior problems that may be alcohol- or drug-related. Following training, require every employee to sign a statement signifying that he or she understands your policies and is willing to abide by them. Implement a crisis-management plan to help all staff know how to cope with a serious incident; enlist the help of experts—attorneys, law-enforcement officers, and insurance agents—to stay current with the laws.

By taking these precautions, you will create a safe, pleasant, and friendly place with a good reputation, one to which people will keep coming back. You'll minimize property damage to the establishment, and reduce or eliminate conflicts between guests. Everyone benefits from well-considered and well-instituted preparedness programs.

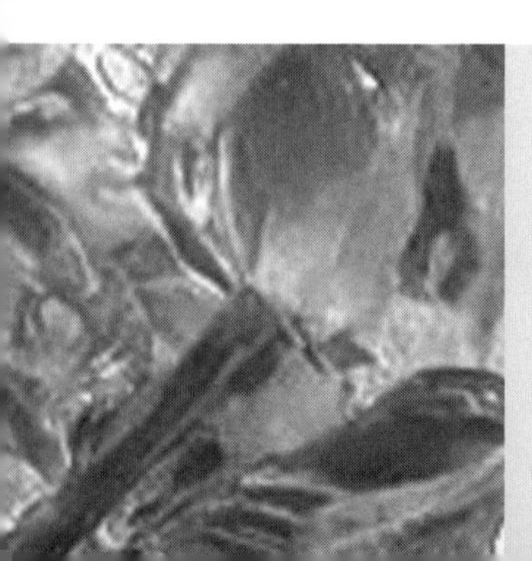

POINTS TO PONDER

1. Why does alcohol circulate in the bloodstream several hours after it was first ingested?
2. Name three effects that alcohol typically has on most people.

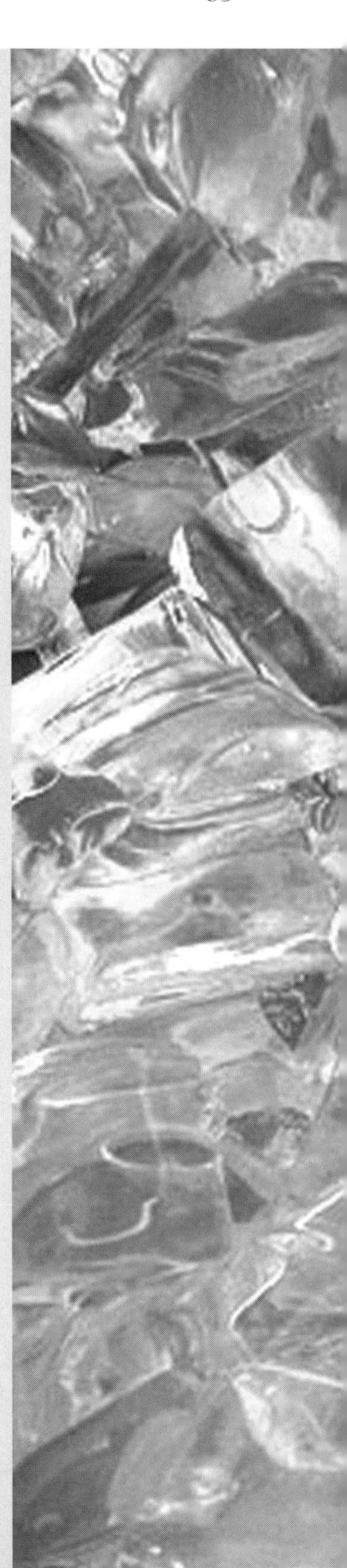

3. What distinguishes alcoholic behavior from the behavior of someone who drinks occasionally?
4. What is a *per se* law? Do you think the current *per se* laws in your state are fair? Why or why not?
5. As a waiter, how might you determine when a guest is starting to get drunk?
6. What are the responsibilities of the door staff at a nightclub?
7. Does your school have regulations about student drinking, or *binge drinking*, on or off campus? If so, who enforces them? If not, why not?
8. What types of documentation should a restaurant or bar have on file, that are directly related to the service of alcoholic beverages?
9. What are the unique challenges of in-room alcohol availability in hotels?

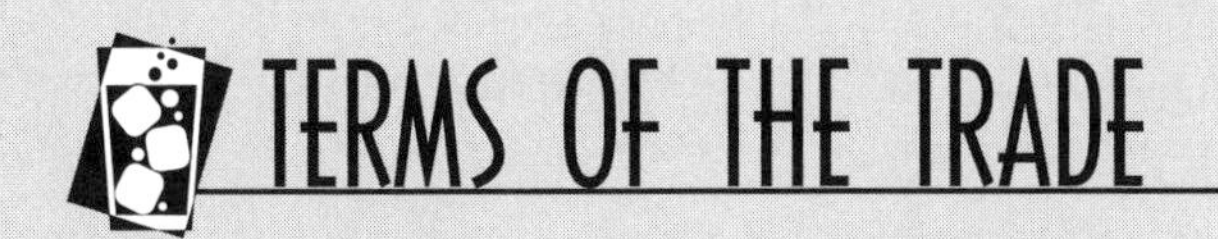

TERMS OF THE TRADE

acetaldehyde
administrative liability
alcoholism
antioxidant
ataxia
beer belly
binge drinking
blood alcohol content (BAC)
bundling
congener
criminal liability
dramshop law
DUI (or DWI)
ethanol
fetal alcohol effects (FAE)
fetal alcohol syndrome (FAS)
flavonoids
foreseeability
French Paradox
hangover
ignition-interlock law
incident report
metabolize
negligence
neoprohibition
neotemperance
per se law
phenolic compounds
pomace
reasonable care
resveratrol
suggestive selling
tannins
third-party liability
t-PA antigen
tyramine
Zero Tolerance

A CONVERSATION WITH...CHRIS HOOVER

This interview has a different slant from the others that you will read in this book. Chris Hoover is an attorney who specializes in defending people accused of drunken driving. He has some strongly held opinions about DWI laws and third-party liability, and about the clash of law enforcement and science in obtaining evidence and making arrests in these cases.

Hoover began as a general practice attorney in Texas in 1986, doing (as he puts it) "everything from probate to real estate to divorce cases." In 1991, he received a flyer inviting him to an informational course for defense attorneys, teaching them what police officers learn about making DWI arrests. He found it fascinating and began taking additional law courses focused on DWI-related topics. By 1997 he had shifted his practice strictly to DWI defense.

In his prelaw days, Hoover worked in the restaurant industry, as a waiter and trainer for the Steak & Ale chain.

Attorney at Law
Dallas, Texas

Q: When people come to your law office, what is the typical situation? What kinds of potential trouble are they in?

A: Their arrest can be the result of anything from overzealous police picking up young kids, which we have a lot of in some areas, to just regular law enforcement, to the "Home for the Holidays" special DWI task force, out to make extra money and finding someone who's weaving in and out of lanes. It doesn't even really have to be the result of real bad driving, to be honest with you. If it's 1:00 A.M. and in a bar-related area and you seem to be having trouble staying in your lane, you've got a 90-percent chance of getting stopped.

DWI transcends all socioeconomic boundaries. For the most part, my clients are pretty nice people that either made a mistake or got caught up in a net. What they have in common is that they are all scared because they've entered into a process that they have absolutely no experience with or knowledge about. And they're afraid every inch of the way. I never see 90 percent of them again—in my line of work, I discourage repeat business! But 10 percent come back on a regular basis until they go away for long periods of time because of big sentences; or they end up hurting or killing someone, and then they do go away for a long time.

Q: Tell us about the financial ramifications of DWI arrests, for individuals and for states.

A: Well, my practice is in Texas, so we'll use Texas as an example. The state has approximately 100,000 DWI arrests a year, and of those people, about 95,000 lose their driving privileges for either refusing to take a breath test or testing above the legal limit of .08. Each of those people has to pay a $125 reinstatement fee to the Texas Department of Public Safety—that's $11,875,000.

When their licenses are suspended, they're entitled to get an Occupational Driver's License to drive up to 12 hours during a 24-hour period for work, school, or household duties. That used to cost $10, but now it costs a minimum of $150, which is paid to the county. Let's say 82,000 of them apply for it; that's $12,300,000 to the counties.

And let's say that roughly 85,000 of them are actually convicted of DWI. In September 2003, the state started requiring them to pay a surcharge to get their licenses back, of $1,000 a year for three years. That's another $85 million a year.

We're still not including fines and court costs, which also vary by county. The average fine on a DWI in Texas is $500 to $700, and then they'll pay another $250 for court costs to prosecute the case. I could keep going, but the point is that DWI is a big, money-making racket.

Q: You walk an interesting line in this field. How do you see your role?

A: My job is to make sure that the criminal justice system doesn't break down somewhere. In other words, I don't want the system to go so low that a cop can arrest and convict you all by himself. In that respect, I think DWI defense is on the front line for criminal defense, because they have made so many "DWI exceptions." For instance, your conversation with a police officer at the roadside is not, unless you establish that you're in custody, subject to Miranda rights. Therefore, all of your statements, although incriminatory, are totally admissible against you. The questions—"How have you been drinking? How many? When was your first? When was your last?"—are all coming into court against you, and nobody's telling you this at the time they're gathering that information. It's not like if you were a suspect in a convenience store robbery, where a police officer says, "I'm here to talk to you, but you need to understand that you're considered a suspect in a criminal activity and you have the right to remain silent and talk to a lawyer before you say anything." DWI is an exception to that rule. And the courts, all the way up to the United States Supreme Court, have swung the pendulum that way.

Q: Are you seeing any trends in this type of law?

A: I've seen a considerable rise in the use of prescription antidepressants, which cause a whole different situation with the mix of chemicals and alcohol in the body. These are very powerful and serious drugs, and people are not necessarily being warned about the problems of combining them with alcohol.

Videotaping, both before and after arrests, is another controversial issue. They split that hair by saying it's not "testimonial" in nature; therefore, it's not protected by the Fifth Amendment—that's the one that says you have the right not to testify against yourself. So you're seeing more and more cameras in the squad cars, although the cops on the street don't like them either.

In the courtroom, the biggest battle we're fighting in DWI law right now is the admissibility of "scientific" evidence. This means using various types of technology—different types of breathalyzers, flashlights with sensors on them to detect alcohol on a person's breath—as well as administering the Standardized Field Sobriety Tests.

Q: Those are the things you do when you are asked by a police officer to step out of the car, right?

A: That's right. There are three of them: the walk-and-turn test, asking you to stand on one leg, and the horizontal nystagmus test, which is when the officer waves a pen horizontally across your eye, looking for a jerky motion. The National Highway Traffic Safety Administration, in forming these nationalized standards, had no control group in its study, and there is a lot of debate about the lack of actual peer-reviewed science involved in creating these standards that are now being used to make decisions about whether or not to arrest people.

Q: Can bars and restaurants do anything to keep their customers from having to deal with all this—and also save themselves the third-party liability hassles?

A: First you must develop a procedure for dealing with the guy or girl who is overconsuming, and it needs to be pretty airtight. If you're any good at being a waiter or bartender, you know what your customers are drinking and how fast they're ordering. It's not that hard to keep up with it, especially now, with all the computerized ordering systems.

Managers should understand that these types of customers put the servers in a tough spot. Servers are trying to make money by pleasing the guest, so it should be the manager's responsibility to handle the situation, talk with the guest, and have some options ready. I think the cost of having a relationship with a limousine service is well worth the money, for you to be able to say, "We're gonna keep your car here. We're gonna give you a free ride home, and you can come back tomorrow and get your keys and take your car."

For the customer, when he gets up the next day and knows he had too much to drink and was probably a jerk, it's embarrassing enough. But if someone treated you well, put you in the backseat of a nice Lincoln Town Car and took you home rather than calling a taxi, and paid for it, that's going to leave a favorable impression.

There are also saliva tests, which you might use if you could do it in a way that would not be offensive—like giving 'em to every one of your customers with their check, so no one feels singled out. They are strips that you can put on your tongue and see what color it changes to. It might be a nice little novelty. Everyone's awareness of alcohol use is very high now; they're not as likely to be offended as they would have been, say, ten years ago.

You also have to be especially watchful with private-party situations, things like wedding receptions and holiday parties. These should be discussed when the event is first being booked: "Have you arranged for transportation for the guests?" This is another instance when your partnership with the limo service can come in handy. For an extra charge, you could offer it as part of the package.

Q: Any final thoughts for would-be bar owners and managers?

A: I think the most important thing to note is that responsible social drinking is not against the law. I'm angry about our DWI laws because so many innocent people get caught up in them and are afraid to put another drop of liquor in their mouths, ever. That should upset anyone in the industry. I despise it.

The other thing I want to say is unfortunate—but unless somebody's violent or causing a major disruption of your bar or restaurant, you're better off getting a limo or a cab and taking the person out of there than calling a cop. The only way a cop can take them out of there is to arrest them, or take them to jail. When that happens, then the system has started. The paperwork begins, and it may change that customer's life forever. So I would think of every available alternative to get that person home safely before involving law enforcement.

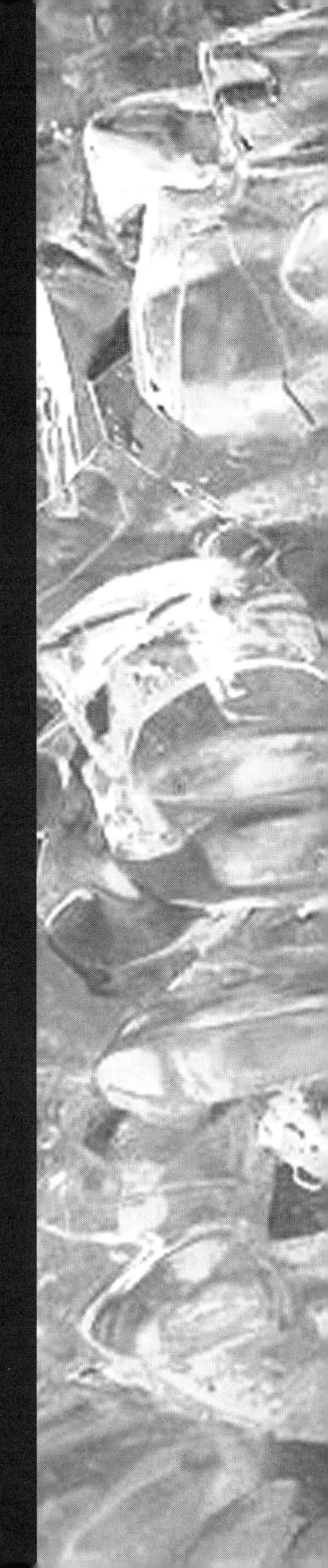

CHAPTER 3
CREATING AND MAINTAINING A BAR BUSINESS

Some things about the bar business will never change—but in other respects, this is the trendiest of industries. Twenty years from now what will American demographics look like, and what will it mean for a bar owner? The industry publication *Food Equipment Reports* hired a consulting company to do just such a projection (in this case, for the United States) in 2004. The results included the following information:

- The United States's population will continue to grow significantly (about 17 percent by 2020) and will include more Hispanic and Asian residents. By 2000 15 states had foreign-born populations of more than 10 percent.
- The Caucasian or non-Hispanic market will include many senior citizens, and just about one half of the U.S. population will be over age 50.
- Real income growth will be slower than it was in the decades between 1980 and 2000. The so-called middle class will make less money and will also shrink in size, with more people who are super rich, as well as more who are truly poor.

At first glance it appears that the hospitality industry will continue to find customers at both the highest and lowest price points, but that middle-income customers will generally have less money to spend on entertainment and may be hard-pressed to find bar and restaurant concepts that fit their niche. A more culturally diverse clientele is guaranteed, as well as a more culturally diverse waitstaff.

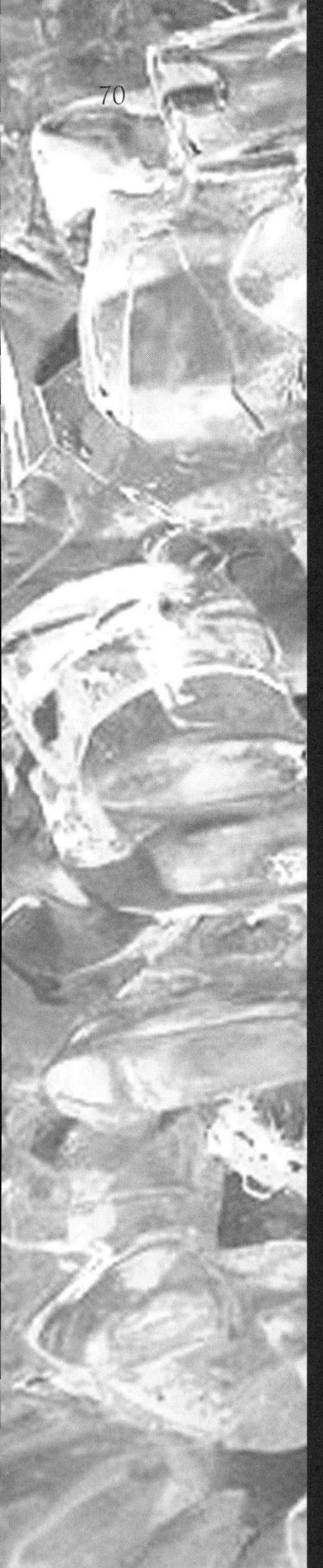

For the purposes of this chapter, we'll assume that you are going to open a new, or renovate an existing, bar to take these modern trends into account. Although this chapter discusses planning the actual physical facility in which you will serve beverages, we begin by addressing how to decide which types of customers you want to serve, which kinds of physical surroundings will appeal to them, and where you will locate your enterprise to serve them.

Many ingredients go into creating just the right environment: the atmosphere, the decor, the efficient use of space, the bar itself. Since every bar business is different, the discussion centers on basic questions and the principles and guidelines you can follow to find the answers for your specific situation.

THIS CHAPTER WILL HELP YOU . . .

- Develop an overall concept and tailor it to meet the needs and desires of a particular clientele.
- Study the market, choose an appropriate location, and determine financial feasibility.
- Plan an atmosphere and decor suitable to a concept and its intended clientele.
- Plan the efficient use of available space.
- Analyze the design and space needs of the bar itself.
- Weigh the pros and cons of hiring professional design consultants.
- Examine the major factors before investing in a specific location or building.

If you were to pick up a 10-year-old entertainment guide to almost any city in this country and compare it with a current guide, you would be astonished by the number of bars and restaurants listed in it that no longer exist, as well as the number of establishments flourishing today that were not in business 10 years ago. The food-and-beverage industry is famous for its volatility and, often, for the magnitude of individual failure. Sometimes, it doesn't seem to make sense: Why does one bar fail while another, directly across the street, is successful year after year?

The reasons for hits and misses in the bar-and-beverage industry are often complex. Like the entertainment business, food-and-beverage facilities are vulnerable to bad luck, the fickleness of music and fashion trends, location, even the weather. But more often, success or failure is a consequence of management and planning. Either can be good or poor, with the consequent results.

The elements that make up good planning and management are extraordinarily interdependent, and isolating them is a somewhat arbitrary task. In practice they are not separate, but highly interactive. Nevertheless, we'll take them one at a time. This chapter focuses on the space itself, and how to determine the types of customers who will want to frequent it.

As you will soon notice, today's bar business is often part of a larger operation that includes foodservice. Some of the discussion that follows, therefore, will apply to a total facility. You could not, for instance, plan the decor of a bar located in a restaurant without considering the restaurant, too. But for now, we will focus on only those physical aspects of the total facility that affect beverage service.

TARGETING YOUR CLIENTELE

The starting point for designing a successful bar is to identify its target clientele: the people you want to attract and serve, and who are going to pay your bills, generate your profit, and give you the pleasure of making them happy. They are the focal point around which everything else revolves: the atmosphere you create, decor, entertainment, sound, lighting, dress, as well as the drinks you serve—that is, the overall impact. The customers influence your location, your floor plan, your bar equipment, of the kind of staff you hire—in short, everything!

Many people dream of opening "a little place" that will be their idea of perfection, convincing themselves that the public will surely recognize it for its excellence and "when word gets around," will flock to its doors. Unfortunately, it doesn't often work that way. Everyone has his or her own idea of perfection, and it is impossible to please them all. People go to bars for various reasons, bringing with them different needs and expectations. Usually the drink is not the primary motive; after all they can buy any beverage they want at a package (liquor) store for much less money and do their drinking at home. Therefore, we must begin by exploring the different types of customers and their motives for patronizing bar businesses.

Types of Customers

We can divide customers into several different groups according to their reasons for choosing to imbibe in a public setting:

- ***Diners at restaurants where drinks are served.*** These diners come to enjoy a good meal *and* a drink, whether in the form of a cocktail, wine, an after-dinner drink, or all three. Each enhances the enjoyment of the total experience. Although the food may be the primary focus at a restaurant, people often want to drink an alcoholic beverage, too. Restaurants that do a flourishing business without alcohol are the exception rather than the rule.
- ***Drop-in customers who are on their way elsewhere.*** They usually want refreshment, a quick pick-me-up or a stress reliever after a day's work. In this case the drink is the focus; the customer has one or two at most, then is on the move again. People who are waiting to board a plane or a train or are meeting someone at the bar also belong to this group. Bars near office buildings or factories and in train or bus stations, airports, and hotel lobbies typically cater to this category of customer.
- ***Meet-and-go customers.*** These individuals are looking for a relationship connection, whether a date for the evening or a longer-term plan. They go to singles bars or "meet bars" that are attractive to others like themselves. They stay long enough to meet someone whom they would like to spend the evening with, and the two may or may not move on to a place where the food and/or the entertainment is more suitable for leisurely conversation and an evening together. Today most singles bars include dancing and very-late-night hours.
- ***Entertainment seekers looking for relaxation, stimulation, or a change of pace.*** They frequent bars, lounges, clubs, and restaurants where entertainment is offered, such as country-and-western music, games, and/or dancing. These individuals want to meet new people or keep up with social trends. They may visit several places or spend a whole evening in only one place if the entertainment, the drinks, and the company are to their liking.
- ***Sports fans.*** In almost every major city, you'll now find at least one sports bar, featuring big-screen television viewing from every angle and special promotions for championship games, boxing matches, and so on. Another newer trend is the cigar bar, where guests can puff away at high-priced cigars and enjoy high-end liquors to go with them. The idea is that people want to commune with individuals who share their interests, whether that means a great game or a great smoke. (Despite the growing number of states that make smoking in public places illegal, there are still cigar bars, as well as states in which bars [but not restaurants] are exempt from the no-smoking regulations.)
- ***Regular patrons of neighborhood bars and taverns.*** They are interested in enjoyment and relaxation, too, but their primary desire is for companionship: being with people whom they know and like, feeling comfortable, feeling that they belong.

Most customers fall into one or more of these groups. The moods, tastes, and interests of the groups differ, and the people tend to differ in background and lifestyle as well, although some individuals cross group lines at times. A diner or entertainment seeker at home might be a drop-in customer on a business trip because the mood and purpose have changed. Generally though, in spite of some crossover, these groups are not especially compatible. A customer from one group visiting a bar frequented by another group is prone to think of the others as "the wrong crowd" people who certainly are not dangerous, but different enough to make the "outsider" feel somewhat uneasy and out of place. In this case the outsider does not experience the venue as having a friendly atmosphere, even if the bar personnel are friendly and the drinks are great. The outsider will not stay long—or come back.

Within these broad groups, however, are many subgroups, divided loosely according to lifestyle, interests, age, income level, family status, occupation or social status, even gender. A few of the largest and most common subgroups are defined in the following subsections.

Women. As purchasers and consumers of alcoholic beverages, women exert a powerful influence, which is destined to become even greater in the years to come. More than 196 million women in the United States are of legal drinking age, representing a huge opportunity for the hospitality industry. Today's female customer is better educated and marries later in life or not at all. Women today also make up a large portion of the workforce, which means that they have discretionary income. They are responsible in large part for the increase in popularity of so-called *white goods*—the clear liquors, such as gin and vodka—and first claimed the Cosmopolitan (vodka and cranberry juice) as their own, wildly popular invention in the 1990s.

Many women form groups to share regular, informal dinners or drinks weekly or monthly at a favorite place. Still, for many women, going to a bar (especially alone) can be an uncomfortable experience, so the savvy bar owner will make an effort to put them at ease. Something as simple as acknowledging the customer within the first 30 seconds of her arrival in the establishment is a major factor in raising her overall comfort level. Cleanliness and unquestionable quality of ingredients also rank as higher priorities among female customers than male customers. For instance, surveys reveal that many women regard hanging glasses above the bar as unsanitary, particularly if smoking is allowed there. Servers should always offer clean napkins with a drink, a courteous touch that women expect and appreciate. In short a female clientele is observant and knowledgeable, awarding loyalty to places that earn it.

Latino Customers. More than 35 million Americans are of Hispanic origin. About 20 million of them are from Mexico—in the 1990s, the number of U.S. residents of Mexican ancestry jumped by 53 percent—but others are from Cuba, Puerto Rico, and the nations of Central and South America. Finally, many distillers and brewers have acknowledged this trend by advertising in Spanish, and more can be done to adequately address this customer category. To build lasting relationships with this broad and diverse group, we must develop an understanding of the intricate differences that distinguish one ethnicity from the next. In some communities there is little push to assimilate into the melting pot, with widespread Spanish-language media and generalized support for the various Hispanic cultures. Often they can continue to live and work within native-language environments.

But one thing is clear: community, family, and tradition are powerful Hispanic values. In October 1997, Paul Mediata, the Hispanic Marketing Coordinator for Coors Brewing Company, said in *Market Watch* magazine, "In the Anglo culture, a business relationship is developed first, then a friendship. In the Hispanic culture, it is the opposite." Words to the wise for anyone aiming to serve this fast-growing clientele.

Baby Boomers. Americans born between 1946 and 1964 are considered baby boomers, the last generation to grow up in an American society in which drinking was the norm. Members of this generation are now reaching their fifties and are in the prime of their careers. Unlike their parents, boomers refuse to think of themselves as old or even middle aged. According to the National Restaurant Association this age group spends more money dining out than any other demographic category: 23 percent more than the average person on restaurant dining. Although boomers might not be crazy about exercise, many work out to stay in shape, at least partly so they can continue to enjoy certain foods and beverages, including beef, pastries, eggs, and, yes, alcohol—in moderation. Boomers in general are relaxed and open about drinking, and they do not hesitate to take their children with them when they dine out; these attitudes have affected the dining industry. Today a whole group of casual but slightly upscale "adult-fast-food" eateries are designed to cater to boomer families; TGI Friday's, Applebee's, Chili's, to name just a few, appeal to these time-crunched, child-toting, beverage-savvy boomers, who enjoy relaxing over a fairly quick but well-prepared meal that features both drinks from the bar and a children's menu.

Baby boomers also tend to be partial to intense flavors in their foods and beverages, and they are willing to pay higher prices for specialty beers and premium wines and liquors. They are both knowledgeable and critical about their foods and beverages, so servers themselves need to know a lot about the wine, beer, and cocktails available because they will be asked.

Generations X and Y. No one knows quite how to describe the wave of legal-age customers who entered the market as the twenty-first century began. Simple definitions elude this group of nearly 33 million, raised with the Internet as a playmate. They have been dubbed either *Generation X* (ages 25 to 29) or *Generation Y* (ages 21 to 30). They constitute 21 percent of the workforce, quickly moving from college (many have at least Bachelor's degrees) into jobs and incomes that took their parents years to achieve. Web-based marketing is a critical component of any marketing plan for these technologically savvy consumers.

About 68 percent of this information-saturated group drinks alcohol: 50 percent prefer beer; 36 percent, distilled spirits; and 10 percent, wine. The rest drink all three. The group also represents some of the most frequent imbibers, with 13

FIGURE 3.1 Many bars and restaurants serving alcohol cater to families. Courtesy of PhotoDisc, Inc.

percent having a drink once a week, and 26 percent once a month. However, they have also grown up with the "Just say no" mentality, which includes a clear message to drink responsibly, by assigning a designated driver or accepting a cab ride if they have overindulged.

This group has grown up knowing about microbrewed beers and gourmet coffees, so they are adventurous and not especially brand-loyal—although this doesn't stop the beverage industry from trying. In recent years Kahlua has been an example of beverage-industry efforts to introduce cordials and liqueurs, with their sweetness and "mixability," to entry-level drinkers who shy away from the more traditional scotches and bourbons. The American sibling of Remy-Martin has introduced RemyRed, a line of cognac-base liqueurs for the Generation Y group. Similarly the logo on Beefeater's Gin has changed. The stodgy London guardsman is much younger: His beard is dark instead of gray!

Beer-makers are also vigorously courting Gen X and Gen Y customers because this age group is incredibly important to the industry. Traditional media outlets (network television, radio, print, and billboards) are being augmented by computer games, web sites, and cable television. The ads also appear on sports programs other than football games, including hockey, surfing, soccer, and snowboarding. When it comes to wine, this demographic appears to be more interested in the sensual aspects of the beverage and knows that it is not just for special occasions, but is an everyday beverage to be sipped with burgers, pizza, and gourmet meals. The Wine Brats, an organization founded in 1995 by the grown children of some of California's top wine producers, have attempted to spark interest in their age group, and it seems to be working. Today's young consumer doesn't mind paying $6 or more for a wine-by-the-glass program.

Connoisseurs and Sophisticates. You will always find a certain number of customers who are truly well informed, enjoy food and wine as a serious hobby or vocation, and often know more than most bartenders or servers. Offering these customers a wide selection of wines or spirits is simply not enough, so some bars and restaurants have decided to specialize in a particular area and use that as a hook to attract a specific, upscale clientele. They hire a sommelier, build a wine cellar, and stock an impressive selection of old-growth Bordeaux, for example. The trade press regularly covers events in bars populated by these lively, well-heeled crowds. The sophisticated customer is willing to pay for style, cleanliness, and a well-trained service staff. The bar must be stocked with wide selections of flavored vodkas, classic single-malt Scotches, cutting-edge single-barrel bourbons, and even some new gins, rums, and tequilas. We've also seen a renewed interest in bar professionalism, exemplified by people like Dale DeGroff and Tony Abou-Ganim, who pour and shake with pride, creativity, and dedication to the craft.

Catering to the high-end customer includes touches like V.I.P. memberships, such as the Altitude Club at Top of the Hub in Boston. Member perks include bypassing long wait lines at the door, assurance of a window seat once inside, and a subscription to the restaurant's quarterly newsletter.

Any bar manager who runs a premium-spirits program will tell you that the customers it attracts are worth having. They will return and bring friends along. However, while offering a selection of high-end beverages can bring both prestige and profit to the business, it also increases the cost of inventory and requires a serious commitment to education, both for the staff and the guests. This commitment comes in the form of tastings, classes, seminars, multiple-course wine dinners, and the related publicity for these types of events. Suppliers and distributors are usually willing to help with these efforts, and you'd be wise to take advantage of the guest speakers and sample bottles they can provide for these occasions. If your concept allows it, consider the benefits you may incur from selling high-end beverages.

PLANNING AND RESEARCH

So who will *your* customers be? You might choose to cater to any one group or subgroup; you cannot expect to please them all. In fact it is a mistake to attempt this—it just won't work. Part of the atmosphere of any bar is its customers, and if they don't have something in common—mood, attitude, reason for coming—the ambience will be found lacking. They won't have a good time and probably won't come back.

SELLING HIGH-END SPIRITS

Any bar manager who runs a premium-spirits program will tell you that often return customers bring their friends along and inevitably share with them the information that they learned on their previous visit.

Bar and restaurant owners have a love-hate relationship with high-end spirts: Offering a selection of such beverages can bring both prestige and profit to the business, but it also raises the cost of inventory and requires a serious commitment to education, both from the staff and the guests. This commitment comes in the form of tastings, classes, seminars, multicourse wine dinners, and publicity for public events. Suppliers and distributors are usually willing to help with these efforts, and you should take advantage of the guest speakers and sample bottles that they can provide for these occasions.

If your concept allows it consider the benefits that you may incur from selling high-end beverages. As of this writing, although they account for less than 12 percent of total distilled spirit volume, they account for 26 percent of the industry's sales dollars. That figure has grown steadily in the last five years in a market where distilled spirits as a whole have lost 6 percent of their total volume.

The experienced entrepreneur concentrates primarily on a single, definable customer group, or **market segment,** whose members will have similar reasons for visiting a bar, and shapes the entire enterprise to attract and please this group. No one group is an inherently better choice than another; you can make a profit with any type of clientele if you can satisfy their needs. One good way to help decide who will form your client base is to imagine your customers. How old are they? Where do they come from? How much money do they like to spend? Why do they go out? What kinds of drinks do they buy? What kind of atmosphere do they respond to? What appeals to them? To answer these questions, you have to do some homework: Visit the favorite places your target clientele is flocking to now. Talk to their customers. Watch their reactions. What do they like or dislike about the place? Your goal is to learn how *they* feel, not to decide what *you* like or dislike. Study everything about the operation: the decor, drinks, layout, ambience, food, entertainment or absence of it. Talk to the bartenders. Study the bottles behind the bar, the wine list, and the menu.

Conduct your research locally. Tastes and interests vary widely from locale to locale, even among the same age groups and income levels. Look at ads in local papers and read the restaurant reviews. Talk to local beverage wholesalers; they are some of the best-informed people around. They know who is buying which kind of liquor and which types of customers are drinking it; which places are raking in money and which ones are having trouble paying their bills on time.

Planning Services to Define Your Image

Much of what will set you apart from competitors is your overall **image,** which is difficult to define in the bar business. The mystique of some bars cannot be fully explained. Nevertheless you must make an effort to define whatever special character your bar exudes that will entice people to visit your establishment instead of your competitors'. Perhaps the best way to describe the necessary mindset is to think about what kind of energy you would like your bar business to exude. It is a combination of what springs to customers' minds when your place is mentioned, what they anticipate before they arrive, what lingers in their memory afterward as a special pleasure, and what will keep them coming back and bringing their friends. From this description, it should be clear that image is the most intriguing and elusive element of success and the one most worth striving for.

Luckily at least some components of image involve very practical decisions that must be made for this type of business, including the following:

- ***What services will you perform for your target market, and how?*** Will you offer drinks with an appetizer menu, with full meals, and/or with entertainment? The extent to which food will be emphasized is a critical decision, and the food and drink concepts must somehow be related. Is entertainment part of your plan? Music options include live bands, deejays, and "canned" sound packages. Wherever people are expected to be either listening or dancing, there are special space and sound considerations.
- ***What kind of bar do you envisage?*** A stand-up bar favored by crowds or those in a hurry? Table service in a cocktail lounge? Dining-room service from a service bar? A holding area for people waiting to eat in your restaurant? Sometimes the answer will be a combination of these.
- ***What kinds of drinks will you serve?*** Drinks for the casual light drinker or the connoisseur? Beer on tap or bottled? Wine by the glass or by the bottle? Mixed drinks? Fancy drinks? Frozen drinks? Flaming drinks? Coffee drinks? As in every other area you need to seek answers based on what appeals to your intended clientele, not necessarily what you yourself would buy as a customer. Specialty cocktails are to a bar what signature dishes are to a restaurant. They provide an important point of difference and an opportunity to promote the business.

Some bars favor a showy image, designing places where people like to "see and be seen," where new drinks are improvised, and where trends are born; others prefer the classic approach, serving cocktails in a more intimate or subdued atmosphere. In either setting an establishment offering inventive but tradition-based drinks, simple to prepare but executed with crispness and showmanship, will convey the image of what a bar should be. One trend is to put a modern spin on a classic drink recipe, using a product not typically available in a home setting to develop a signature drink. For example, at the elegant Bellagio Hotel and Casino in Las Vegas, the Presidential Martini is made with Belvedere vodka, Poire William liqueur, and Muscat d'Asti. It commands an impressive $11. The Outback Steakhouse chain upsells the ubiquitous Screwdriver by using Fuga Tangerine (a Hiram Walker product), giving the drink a fresh, new flavor profile. The Olive Garden chain offers its Venetian Sunset—sparkling Asti Spumante, pineapple juice, and Grenadine, served in a hurricane glass—as a light, refreshing, and low-alcohol specialty drink. Brennan's of Houston tops its spicy Creole Martini with crab-encrusted olives and rims the glass with a salt-and-pepper mix.

In today's most successful bars and restaurants uniqueness may begin with a signature drink, but it is carried through as a carefully planned total concept. In these venues the name of the establishment, drinks, decor, layout, service, uniforms, training program, and menu all fit into the total concept and reinforce it. Ironically individual customers might remember only one standout element, such as a creatively written menu full of puns, a perfect view of a giant television screen, a 1,500-bottle wine selection, or a revolving panorama of the city at night from atop a tall building. Each, however, is a symbol of the collective ambience, a crystallization of the concept.

The point is that to ensure success, you need an overall concept that can tie all of the elements of your bar together. A concept should begin with an idea that can be stated simply, for example, a neighborhood bar-restaurant with a family feeling, an upscale wine bar for wine enthusiasts, or a health-and-fitness bar-restaurant where the drinks are made with fresh juices and the food is low-fat, low-calorie, and memorably tasty. Decor, lighting, menu, and service will all be developed in keeping with the concept.

Your total concept will grow out of a thorough understanding of your chosen clientele and the careful planning you do to serve them. The concept will be shaped by your observations of the kinds of places your clientele favors. But it will not be a copy of these other places; its own personality, and identity will be the magnet that draws your target customer to your front door. Formulating this concept is a real challenge, so take some hints from the many examples mentioned in this chapter.

In certain cases the purpose of the bar will dictate its image. Customers of a sports bar, for example, have very clear expectations about what they will see, hear, and do when they arrive. In contrast in a bar attached to a restaurant that takes reservations, the lines blur; of course, you'll seat people in the bar while they wait to be seated at their tables, but this should not be the only purpose of a restaurant bar. The restaurant bar should also serve as a marketing tool for the dining room: Bar customers often look in advance at the food menu and notice other customers being escorted to their seats or waiters walking by with trays full of food. For this very reason, the Topaz Lounge in Washington, DC, and Encore in Chicago has revamped its old-fashioned "happy hours" with an amusing name, Liquid Therapy, using them as a chance to showcase the regular dinner menu. The point: If you can get people to come into the bar for a drink, sooner or later, they will stay for a meal.

The hotel bar also presents interesting image challenges. If you cater to only the travelers who are hotel guests, you'll miss out on a major source of revenue: the locals. Hotel bars and lounges have emerged as new hot spots for both groups, with an increasing number of small, so-called *boutique hotels* distinguishing themselves through their bar designs and themes in an attempt to woo both kinds of customers. The neighborhood regulars become part of an overall welcoming tone for the person who is away from home. For example, in New York City's Mark Hotel, Mark's Bar is a five-foot bar presided over by a tie-wearing bartender who specializes in classic drinks and local signatures, such as the "Big Apple," which is made with vodka, Calvados, and lemon juice. The room is reminiscent of a small, private club with dark green walls, black wooden trim, and comfortable chairs upholstered in green velvet.

In an attempt to define a new type of drinking experience—more satisfying than a bar or lounge, less formal than a restaurant—The Saint in Boston's Copley Square Hotel refers to itself as a *boutique nightery.* It is divided into three areas, each with its own décor and music: a room with stark, white patent leather features and a menu of infused vodkas, a second room with shorter tables reminiscent of home coffee tables rather than dining space, and a full-service restaurant. The smaller tables necessitate smaller serving plates, with such touches as presliced steaks and tiered food presentations that conserve space and keep things interesting.

Above all running a bar is a people business. An integral part of any bar's image is the bartender. Most of us view this role as being filled by someone at the pinnacle of creative salesmanship, a friendly face with an impressive repertoire. He or she knows how to mix dozens of different drinks quickly and well, yet still has time for a joke or a chat, and will remember your name, too, after you've been in a few times. Bartending is a profession steeped in nineteenth-century tradition and reinforced by images in books, movies, and television shows that portray bartenders as kind, observant, amusing, and competent. They are part mixologist, part comedian, and part psychologist. Never doubt the role that great bartenders and sommeliers can play in your success—and never underestimate the importance of giving yours the tools, equipment, and ongoing training to excel at their trade.

Another factor in creating an image for a hotel bar is the type of food you will serve. Simple, salty snacks, for example, mixed nuts, pretzels, and some form of trail mix, were once the norm in many hotel bars, but today that is simply inadequate in most cases. Guests will linger longer where there is good food, and even the smallest menu of appetizers (e.g., crowd-pleasing nachos, mini pizzas, or a great shrimp cocktail) will add new dimensions to your customers' enjoyment, as well as your profit picture. Offering food is also part of responsible alcohol service.

In Boston two James Beard Foundation award-winning chefs collaborate with their bartenders to create bar food that far surpasses casual snacking and elevates profit margins. Chef Lydia Shire's place, the Excelsior, packs two dozen items onto the menu of appetizer-sized dishes—spicy chorizo sausage, short ribs, and charbroiled eel, to name a few—with prices from $8 to $24. This chef's theories are that a bar menu should offer a wide variety of freshly prepared foods—no shortcuts or convenience items here—and that the drinks should be crafted to whet the appetite. It is obviously paying off, with food sales accounting for 30 percent of the Excelsior's profit.

Susan Regis's Upstairs at the Square is a restaurant/bar combination, and the goal with its downstairs "Monday Club Bar" is to woo the 21-to-30-year-old college crowd. (The area is home to about 250,000 students who, one would assume, occasionally need a break from their Ivy League studies!) Bar food is served on platters for group consumption along with smaller, appetizer plates. Chef Regis wisely coordinates the menus to utilize extras from the restaurant for the inventive bar menu: For example, unused scallops are sauteed and served with celery root chips, sweet potatoes are cut into thick fries and served with tasty purees for dipping, and pizzas are topped with whatever there is plenty of. The bar menu consists of about 10 main-dish items, 10 more appetizer-sized items, and four desserts. The items range in price from $6 to $16 and account for two-thirds of the bar sales.

LOCATION AND MARKET FEASIBILITY

The next question you need to answer is: Where will you establish your unique new beverage enterprise? You will want it to be convenient for your target customers. If you are going to serve meals as well, you will want to be accessible to a residential area, to places of work, or both. For people in search of entertainment or a companion for the evening, you will probably want a location in an area already known for its nightlife. To attract drop-ins, you will want to place yourself on the route to wherever they are going; to attract a more regular group of people, you'll want to be near the neighborhood in which they live.

Choosing an Area

Certain areas of cities tend to be lively places, where bars and restaurants are clustered and competition is intense. A crowded area has its advantages. Bright lights and crowds typically make for a festive atmosphere. People enjoy going where they've been before because familiar places are comfortable. Furthermore they know that if they can't get into one place, they can try another, so the competitive environment benefits everybody. On the other hand, such areas can become saturated when too many new ventures try to imitate the success of their predecessors. Therefore, if you are thinking of starting a business in such a location, take two precautions. First investigate the number of businesses that have opened and, especially, closed in the area during the past few years, to try to determine which kinds of places have staying power and which kinds have been overdone. Second study the competition carefully, and be very sure that you have something unique to offer. Can your business truly make a special contribution to the area?

The alternative is to open your enterprise in a new or isolated area. Of course this might be risky, but it can be also rewarding if your research uncovers a market demand that is going unmet. Once you have made a success in a new area, however, you probably will soon be joined by competitors, so think about building a following for the long-term, and don't expand too quickly on the basis of an initial high demand.

In general, it's a good idea to avoid declining areas; look instead at neighborhoods that are stable or growing. That said, be aware that in many cities once-neglected areas are being revived. It has become trendy and an expression of environmental conscientiousness to restore older buildings and rehabilitate dilapidated sections of town. Advantages of older properties include that they are often more spacious, are better built, and are generally more accessible than new facilities in the suburbs. Furthermore development money is often available for people who are willing to undertake these types of projects, especially if they agree to restore the building with historically correct details and materials.

Estimating Customer Potential

Once you have an area in mind you need to determine whether enough of your target-market customers live in or frequent the area to support your concept. There are a number of resources for answering these questions. In some cities you can get help free of charge from various state and local agencies that compile population demographics (e.g., who lives where, how much money they make, what their level of education is, what their eating and spending habits are) and maintain statistics about neighborhoods, urban planning, and area traffic. Chambers of Commerce have information on business growth, tourist and convention markets, and real-estate development. Banks, because they lend money to restaurants and bars, can tell you a great deal about the community in question; they can prevent you from opening the right facility in the wrong place, say a swinging singles bar in a retirement colony. Talk to real-estate agents, too; contact restaurant and club owners' associations; and pay a visit to local restaurant-equipment firms. All will usually know who is opening and where, as well as who is closing and why.

In some cities there are demographics firms that specialize in the foodservice field. They can run a computerized analysis of a specific area based on census figures, giving you data on population density, age, gender, occupation, size of household, income, ethnic makeup, money spent dining out, or whatever demographic information you specify. From such figures you can determine an area's overall customer potential for your type of business.

Sizing Up the Competition

As you explore the various areas of your town to determine customer potential, you must also closely examine potential competitors. How well are the customers' needs and desires already being served and, even more important, how could you serve the chosen clientele better? To determine this, visit all the bars and bar-restaurants in the area that serve your target customer. Count and classify them;

for each one, record its location and as much as possible of the following information: number of seats, hours, price range, average check, average number of patrons per day, number of days open per week/month/year, slow and busy days, slow and busy times of day, and annual gross volume (dollar sales per year). You can gather such data by talking to people connected with each operation, including bartenders, servers, and managers. Count the seats. How many are empty? How many people are waiting to get in? Estimate the same information for your proposed enterprise and compare. Check the total against your study of market potential.

If all of your competitors are busy all the time, chances are good that you will be, too. On the other hand, if business is slow and seats are empty everywhere, you can conclude that the area is saturated and that there probably is no room for you, no matter how delicious your food and drink or how charming your atmosphere—unless you are lucky enough to identify a void. For example, you discover there is no bar for the late-night theater crowd. Probably the quickest and most accurate method, but also the most expensive way, of learning about your competition is to hire a professional food-facilities consultant or a market-study specialist. This individual or firm will conduct a detailed investigation of a given area and the current competition, to determine whether there is a market in that area for your bar concept. Alternately if you already have a facility but want to revamp it, a consultant's market study can help you adapt your concept to be more up-to-date. But be aware that when you use a professional, you run the risk that you'll spend a few thousand dollars for bad news: The market you are aiming for is not there. Remember, however, that this knowledge will save you much more money and grief in the long run. The cash you spend on a professional market study at the beginning of a project will be minor compared to your total investment in your business.

Selecting a Site

Once you are satisfied that there are enough potential customers in your chosen area, you can begin to shop for a specific site. When you do this, it is important that you attempt to see each site through the customers' eyes. Does it have good visibility? Is there adequate public transportation nearby? Is there plenty of parking? Is it easy to reach? Watch out for one-way streets, planned future construction, and heavy traffic. Be alert to changing circumstances; talk to other retailers in the neighborhood. If you are thinking of taking over an existing facility, find out exactly why the last tenant(s) left and, if you should decide to convert a failed-restaurant site, plan to start with a clean slate; keep *nothing* reminiscent of the past concept or ownership.

Consider the Structure. You might choose a freestanding building, or one that is part of a complex, such as a shopping mall or a unit in a strip mall with street access and good visibility. In a strip mall the ideal location is the end unit because it has two visible walls, front and side. Depending on your concept and target clientele, you might even consider space in an office building or along an underground walkway where there are shops and pedestrian traffic. As mentioned earlier don't overlook the possibility of refurbishing an older building, whether a warehouse, a church, a school, or a gas station. Converting from a different use is usually less expensive than starting with an empty shell, and keep in mind that such a building might have historic value, or image potential, to bring to your concept.

Most important check out the licensing, zoning, and other restrictions of the area you are scouting because even different parts of the same city might have different licensing requirements. For example, a nearby church or school might prevent your getting a license to sell alcohol in the same area, even if your business is going to be a family-themed restaurant. Simply put zoning restrictions can make it impossible to open the kind of facility you want or to open at all in your chosen location. At the very least cutting through the red tape involved in the permit and licensing process can delay your opening for months. In relation to all this, consider the importance of a favorable community attitude. If you discover the community is hostile to the opening of your enterprise, it might be better to start over in another area.

Determine Financial Feasibility. Finally, be aware that even the most promising site might turn out to be unprofitable if costs and operating expenses are high in relation to potential sales volume. To determine this ratio you need to analyze the financial feasibility of your projected business for that site and market area. To begin draft a realistic financial plan for your intended facility in terms of your profit goal. Estimate the capital needed for land and buildings, furnishings and equipment, and opening expenses, as well as a reserve for operating at a loss in the beginning. Next, based on your market research for your site, make a detailed projection of sales and receipts against fixed and variable expenses. These projections should represent an operating budget, which is described in Chapter 14, with detailed plans for such items as drink menu, staff, and hours of operation.

Estimate sales conservatively and expenses liberally. If the income does not exceed expenses by the desired profit margin, your project is not feasible for that market and location.

ATMOSPHERE AND DÉCOR

The atmosphere of your place will determine who comes to buy drinks from you, how long they stay, how much they spend, and whether they come back and bring their friends. This is simple to understand. After all, why do people go to bars? They go to have a good time. They don't go just to drink; they go to relax, to socialize, to rendezvous with old friends or meet new ones, or perhaps to be alone with a special person; they go to escape their everyday mood and scene. If you can transport them from a world of problems, deadlines, and frustrations to a world of pleasure, you will have the first ingredient of success.

Successful Examples

Consider a few bar concepts that have thrived in recent years, in addition to those that we have already mentioned. Perhaps the most imitated restaurant/bar concept in the United States is TGI Friday's. The actual bar, which is corralled with brass rails and trimmed with stained glass, continues to be as central to the restaurant's business in the new millennium as it did in 1965, when the chain was founded in New York City. Quite literally, the bar is "central" to the restaurant: TGI Friday's was the first to locate its bar area prominently in the middle of the front-of-house restaurant space. For all its years of existence, TGI Friday's has continued to serve good drinks in an atmosphere that has remained consistent. It has a bustling, friendly, and casual ambience. The chain has its own 36-page beverage manual that contains standardized directions for making more than 140 cocktails.

Another good example of a successful casual atmosphere is Fado's, an Irish pub in Atlanta that was, literally, designed and built in Ireland, then shipped to the United States, where is was assembled and decorated by a team of Irish craftspeople. Although the building's shell was already in place, most fixtures, fittings, and furniture are Irish. Its dark, floor-to-ceiling wood interior is stuffed with all things Irish, from sports memorabilia to quotes from the Green Isle's literary greats. You can get a pint (20-ounce glass) of Guinness Stout or Harp Lager, Ireland's signature brews, or sample a microbrew from the Atlanta area (the latter being Fado's way of acknowledging the local scene). The bar also offers a list of famous Irish whiskies. And, as you would expect in a true Irish pub, conversation is the main attraction, so you won't find video games or big-screen television sets here.

The Continental in Philadelphia is a diner that has been converted into a Martini lounge. The design of everything, from menus to uniforms, is strictly controlled, created to appeal to an under-30 crowd. The combination of sweet, juice-spiked cocktails in distinctive Martini glasses enables even the most the inexperienced customer to feel sophisticated. The drinks are delivered in individual Martini shakers emblazoned with the Continental logo (which are available for sale) and poured at the table. A smart balance of modern twists to venerable Martini-making traditions has enabled the bar owners to make the transition from trendy hot spot to established classic, turning a new, younger crowd into loyal customers.

At the Flatiron Lounge in New York City owner/mixologist Julie Reiner believes that bartenders require their own domains, set up exactly as they wish, to create their own cocktail whims and build a loyal following. The Flatiron structure is designed to hold more bottles than most, including Reiner's trademark unique, fresh juices—liquid guava, passion fruit, hibiscus, and more. A nightly cocktail flight, changed regularly, includes three drinks of 3½ ounces each for $18. The bar is upstairs to reinforce the fact that Reiner's focus is on drinks; a quieter area, The Parlor at Flatiron, is located downstairs to serve upscale appetizers.

THE BLUE AGAVE CLUB

Do you want to know more about tequila? You can sample more than 200 different types and brands at the Blue Agave Club in Pleasanton, California. Restaurateurs Alexandro and Susi Garcia opened the 70-seat restaurant and bar in 1997 to showcase gourmet Mexican cuisine and the adaptability of Mexico's "national spirit." Tequila is part of the food menu, too: Chef Ramon Sepulveda uses it in the salad dressing, as a component of sauces, and to baste barbecued meats and flame elegant desserts. "The idea was not only to showcase the true flavors of Mexico," explains Alexandro, "but to dispel some of the myths about tequila. People here say, 'Tequila makes me crazy,' and 'Tequila gives me a headache, or a bad hangover.' Well, they need to know it's because they are not drinking the real tequila; they are drinking the more commercial, mixed spirits. Real tequila is every bit as sophisticated as wine." Some of the larger tequila producers, says Alexandro, ship tanker trucks of product from Mexico into the United States to be blended and bottled; but, technically, tequila is the only spirit made in a single nation. So if you're interested in taste-testing tequila, the Blue Agave is the place to go, and you'll find that the "tastes" are generous.

In villages of past centuries, tequila was poured into a bull's horn as measurement, and the resulting amount was about 2 ounces. Alexandro's grandfather told him long ago why the 2-ounce pour is called a *caballo,* the Spanish word for horse. "In Old Mexico, tequila was sold on the street corners, and people were on horseback. They'd work in the fields, then ride into the small towns for a drink. But the drink was so potent that they didn't dare get *off* their horses because they wouldn't be able to get back on! So my grandfather said you'd see groups of 10, 20, 30 men on the corner, all on horseback, drinking and talking."

Luckily at the Blue Agave Club you can also get *caballitos* ("little horses") of 1 ounce or ½ ounce. They also pour flights tastes of several different styles of tequila so you can compare *blanco, reposado,* and *anejo.* Despite tequila's availability by the shot, the most popular drinks at the Blue Agave Club are Margaritas. The restaurant has been distinguished with "Best Margarita" honors by its patrons and local food critics. Alexandro says the secret to making the perfect Margarita (more than 100 selections are on the menu) is his proprietary sweet-and-sour recipe, which is made fresh daily. The restaurant sponsors well-attended tequila dinners and tastings, featuring tequila producers as guest speakers. Word of mouth has been the restaurant's best form of advertising. "The customers love the idea of learning more," says Alexandro. "They sometimes comment on the prices, I mean, the high-dollar tequilas cost $45 to $75 for the 2-ounce pour, but I tell them, 'Just imagine if this was made in France! You'd be paying $200 a shot!' It's a completely natural, pure spirit with nothing artificial added in the distilling process. Showcasing it like this, in a high-end restaurant environment, has been a very good idea and a lot of fun."

FIGURE 3.2 Alexandro Garcia, owner of the Blue Agave Club in Pleasanton, California. Photo courtesy of Mats Bodin. Used with permission of Bodin Studio Photography, Livermore, California.

Hudson Bar and Books, in Manhattan's West Village, is a wonderful example of using atmosphere to blend into a neighborhood. In this case bar owners pay homage to its avant-garde past, when writers and poets lived and worked here and sometimes visited pubs until dawn. The intellectual heritage of the West Village is evident at this establishment, with its jammed floor-to-ceiling bookshelves. Intimate tables line a wall opposite the fully stocked bar, and the room converges into a back area with a U-shaped couch. The effect is comfortable, dark, and literary. Beer is served in frosted glasses, each pour of wine is served in a clean wineglass, and water glasses are continually replenished.

In Chicago's West Loop area, another good example of a successful atmosphere is Drink and Eat, Too!, a massive (25,000-square-foot) bar (see Figure 3.3). Larger-than-life salt shakers and lime-shaped lights grace the ceiling above its Tequila Bar, a chandelier made of Absolut Citron bottles is suspended above the Vodka Bar, and certain mixed drinks are served in buckets! There are no dark, quiet corners at Drink and Eat, Too!; the bright lighting and clean, vibrant decor promote a fun-filled environment, and the layout encourages social mingling.

Also in Chicago, Narcisse drips with decadence. Semicircular booths with curtains (that may be pulled for privacy) line the perimeter of a room full of artwork;

FIGURE 3.3 The tequila bar at Drink and Eat, Too! Note the above-bar lighting, cleverly designed as lime slices. Photo courtesy of Drink and Eat, Too!, Chicago, Illinois.

a separate room called the Boudoir features a palatial bed as its centerpiece and velvet draperies between booths. Top-of-the-line Champagnes and vodkas are available here, and *bottle service* is offered. This means that if you do not finish the bottle of liquor purchased that evening, the remainder will be held in your name for a return visit.

In the South Beach area of Miami, Florida, you'll find an East Indian–inspired bar. Ancient artwork, scented candles, and oversized pillows are part of the comfortable but exotic appeal of Tankard. Moroccan tents, low tables, and grass-carpeted floors prompt guests to sit on the floor; in another room fiber-optic stars twinkle in a faux sky; and the V.I.P. Room features a huge hammock and ample pillow-filled romping space for up to 30 people. Tankard also has a restaurant with booths, tables, and a mahogany and copper bar. Across the country in Seattle, Washington, the Palace Kitchen advertises itself as a "tavern with good food." The décor is simple; the central feature is an enormous, horseshoe-shaped bar that gives guests a clear view of the kitchen and the employees at work (see Figure 3.4). The owner's intent is to convey the idea of a friendly, unpretentious employee dining room. You can even see the dishroom employees at work. The bar is the primary focus here: the Palace Kitchen has twice as many appetizers as entrees.

FIGURE 3.4 The U-shaped bar at Seattle's Palace Kitchen allows maximum guest interaction. Photo courtesy of the Palace Kitchen, Seattle, Washington.

The sports bar has benefited greatly from technology—from bigger, better television sets, to satellite broadcasts that provide more than 100 channel choices. In New York City Manhattan's Park Avenue Country Club boasts 10 satellite receivers and the ability to tune in nearly every major college football game around the country. Team standings count, too; fans of the winners get the "best" seat selections! The friendly rivalry, mixing and noshing, and cheering, begins before noon and continues well after midnight.

DÉCOR REQUIREMENTS

Do the previous examples have anything in common? Sure they do! They prove that, indeed, anything goes when it comes to bar themes and décor. Whatever the specific attractions you decide on, they should be inviting from the very first moment. The atmosphere should convey a message of welcome, of festivity, of caring for customers. Some of this will come from you and your personnel, and some will come from your other customers—since, after all, most customers enjoy being among likeminded people who are having a good time. But the physical surroundings are equally important. They create the first impression, set the stage, and strike the keynote.

The kind of décor you choose for your facility will be the visual expression of its mood. Décor includes the furniture and its placement; the wall coverings and artwork; floor, ceiling, lighting, and window treatment; plants and other accessories; special displays; and the front and back of the bar itself. Each element should be planned in relation to the total concept. In effect it is the packaging of your concept; not only does it help to create mood, but it merchandises your product.

What kind of mood do you want to inspire? What does your research show about what is important to your target clientele? Do you want to impart a sense of spaciousness, relaxation, and restfulness—a place where people come to talk to each other without shouting; or are you after a noisy, crowded, stimulating atmosphere? Do you want to convey elegance, opulence, and luxury, or modest comfort and terrific value for the price of your food and drink?

Soft colors and rounded shapes are restful; bright colors and bold patterns are stimulating. Mind the *soundscape* as well. This is what you want the place to sound like, both when full and not-so-full. Carpets, drapes, upholstered chairs, and fabric-covered walls can mute noise of all sorts, but it bounces off and might be amplified or distorted by tile and concrete floors, plaster walls and ceilings, and glass. High ceilings give a sense of space; low ceilings make a room seem smaller and more intimate. Ceilings that are too low and rooms that are too small can make guests feel claustrophobic. Soft lights and candlelight send messages of intimacy, romance, and intrigue. Bright and/or flashing lights are appropriate to noise, crowds, action, and excitement. Firelight is restful, dreamy, romantic, but be aware that fireplaces must meet stringent local fire codes and might have special insurance-company requirements, too. Luxury can be conveyed by the use of:

- Expensive fabrics, furniture, and accessories
- Museum pieces and art objects
- Dramatic effects, such as waterfalls, magnificent views, and murals by accomplished artists
- Gleaming silver and crystal
- Fresh flower arrangements
- Ice sculptures
- An elaborate wine list
- Tuxedoed waiters
- Expensive food and drinks
- Valet parking
- Attentive and highly professional service.

Terrific value can be conveyed by simple, and inexpensive but imaginative decor, good drinks at moderate prices, and quick, friendly service.

Investors sometimes spend a fortune on decor to compete for certain types of customers or to build a certain image in a national or international market. If this is your situation, you'll probably want to hire a professional interior designer who specializes in the restaurant field. But not all decor involves spending a lot of money.

It does, however, always involve a great deal of thought and good taste. Paint, plants, posters, or art prints, for example, judiciously chosen and placed, to complement the furnishings and their groupings, the right lighting, and the right sound (or its absence)—all combine to create a mood. A few inexpensive conversation pieces can add to the fun. The trick to achieving a successful décor is to continually keep mood and clientele in mind, and pick colors, textures, shapes, furniture, and fixtures that mesh for a total, finished look.

Work toward a décor and a mood that are not copies of a competitor's and that are not built on a passing fad. Make sure to carry out your theme in your service, drinks, uniforms, and all of the small details. Otherwise you'll be sending your clientele a mixed message. Crystal chandeliers say one thing; shabby restrooms with no hot water say something else.

LAYOUT AND DESIGN

Whether you are starting from scratch or remodeling, your first step is to think through your layout carefully to ensure that it jibes with the critical factors: customers, services, and atmosphere. To these essentials, add a fourth one: efficiency. Designers of bars face the continuous challenge of providing employees with a functional space in which to work quickly and accurately. Practical, daily bartending concerns include the ability to take orders, mix and garnish drinks, wash and dry glasses, handle cash, and restock supplies with limited effort and maximum productivity, all the while ensuring that the bar space is clean and attractive, makes customers feel comfortable, fits in with the rest of the decor, and stimulates beverage sales. Today bars also often include at least limited foodservice. Not surprisingly then, some hard choices must be made to bring bar design in line with budgets and a confined space. Appendix A, which contains a sample Cocktail Lounge Design Questionnaire, should help immensely in this effort.

If you'll be working with professionals, such as an interior designer for the "look" and furnishings, and a facilities designer for the bar equipment, plumbing, and electrical requirements, you will find it helpful to understand what they are doing. The best way to accomplish this is to visit other facilities that they have designed. In addition, you can study several major trade publications that include articles about effective bar design to keep up on trends.

Trends in Bar Design

Increasingly hotels and restaurants are utilizing their bar space for meals. Even the bar itself has become *de facto* dining space: Bar tops are widened to accommodate table settings, and wait stations are set up to store dishes and flatware, both clean and soiled. An advantage of offering lunch or dinner at the bar is, of course, money;

tips are better for bartenders and servers, and the average check is higher. However, this arrangement, especially if not well designed, splinters the attention of the bartender, requiring more multitasking, trips to the kitchen, and extra work. Customers who want just a drink instead of a full meal might feel less important as they "compete" with diners for service and bar space.

From Europe comes the idea of the **gastro pub,** a bar that also offers world-class lunches and dinners. British pubs, with their picturesque settings and centuries of tradition, are remodeling for discriminating diners. No fish and chips here; instead they offer gourmet menus with crystal stemware, starched linens, fireplaces, and pretty outdoor-dining patios when weather permits.

The **concept bar,** where the goal of the décor is to whisk patrons away to new or exotic locales, became popular in the 1990s and continues to do well. The Elephant Bar, a California-based dining chain with its African-jungle theme, and Latin-themed bars that serve up salsa dance lessons as well as South American specialty drinks, are some examples. Another trend is **participatory bars,** where customers are part of the action, whether they play pool or video games or sing karaoke. On the nightclub scene design trends include lighter colors, to make the bar friendlier to women; more space for *cool-down areas,* where people can sit and talk if they prefer not to dance; and layouts that encourage eye contact and more social interaction between dancers and nondancers (this translates into fewer *terraced levels* to negotiate within the club.

Upscale bars have shown a new vigor, with all the elegant touches of yesteryear: dark woods; comfortable, overstuffed furniture; art-deco motifs; and other classic touches. Nightclub menus are being expanded to offer more food as part of the ongoing effort to encourage responsible alcohol consumption. In sum patrons are drinking less and demanding better quality—they want an experience, not just an evening out.

In a trend perhaps no one could have predicted, airport bars have received a boost in popularity since international terrorism reared its head in the September 11 attacks. Passengers have learned to cope with longer wait lines and late takeoffs, and they have more time to spend in on-site pubs and eateries at airports. What used to be a generic bar with tiny, overpriced drinks and inattentive service has become a genuine attempt to provide a brief, comfortable oasis from the stress of traveling. Brand-named national chains, such as Sam Adams's Pubs and Wolfgang Puck Express, are taking the lead. Beer-making powerhouse Anheuser-Busch also owns a chain of airport pubs and fills its spaces with memorabilia. At the Dallas/Fort Worth International Airport, La Bodega Winery is successful in a 500-square-foot retail space, selling 30 wines by the glass, gourmet snacks, and wines by the bottle to travelers passing through.

Games on the bar scene—other than pool, pinball, darts, and video poker (where permitted)—now include video golf. In particular Golden Tee is a realistic, simulated golf game that has in recent years become the most successful coin-operated, arcade-style game since PacMan. More than 100,000 Golden Tee games are featured, primarily in sports bars, and an online tournament for true enthusiasts has a monthly purse of $250,000. "Weather conditions," pin placement, and tee distance change daily in this three-dimensional game, and participants pay $3 to "play" 18 holes with computer-simulated cheering and even color commentary by golf "announcers." Bar owners, who typically rent space to individual owners of the Golden Tee machines, say the addition of this sophisticated game to their entertainment lineup can increase bar business as much as 25 percent. Now *that's* an upward trend!

Basic Elements of Layout

Certain facets of a bar start-up are universal: the amount of space available, the activities taking place in that space, the number of seats, the size of the bar (it must be large enough to hold equipment for the drink types you'll offer), and the relationship of the bar area to other aspects of a larger facility, such as a restaurant, hotel, or club. Other layout and design needs and issues come into play: plumbing, refrigeration, lighting and other electrical requirements, ventilation, heating and air conditioning, health and fire regulations, local codes, and state laws and regulations, such as separate smoking areas and restroom facilities for physically disabled patrons. Last but not least comes profit: How can you make the most profitable use of the space available? The final layout emerges from the decisions you make regarding all of these factors. We will discuss them one at a time to explain the impact of each.

Available Space. The amount of space available to you for your layout includes not only square footage, but also the shape of the area, the position of entry and exit(s), and whether you will be sharing space with dining, dancing, or live-entertainment facilities.

- The *square footage* will set an outside limit on the number of customers you can serve at a time. It may also determine whether you'll have seating at the bar or at tables, lounge style.
- The *shape of the room* is critical to the arrangement of the furniture and fixtures. Consider the three rooms shown in Figure 3.5. They are of the same square footage, but one is long and narrow, one is square, and one is L-shaped. The shape of the room also affects the number and arrangement of tables, the position of the bar itself for the best visual and psychological impact, and the bar's size and shape. Room shape also influences the traffic flow for entry and exit and for service. And it certainly affects how you'll share space with such activities like dining or dancing.
- *Entry and exit* require special attention because the relationship between the entrance and the bar will influence the movement of customers into the room and the way the room fills up. Do you want your customers to move immediately into noise and conviviality? Do you want them to stop at the bar before going on to dine and dance? Will a crowd around a bar near the entrance block access both visually and physically, leaving the room beyond it empty? If the bar is associated with a restaurant, should it have a separate entrance or be part

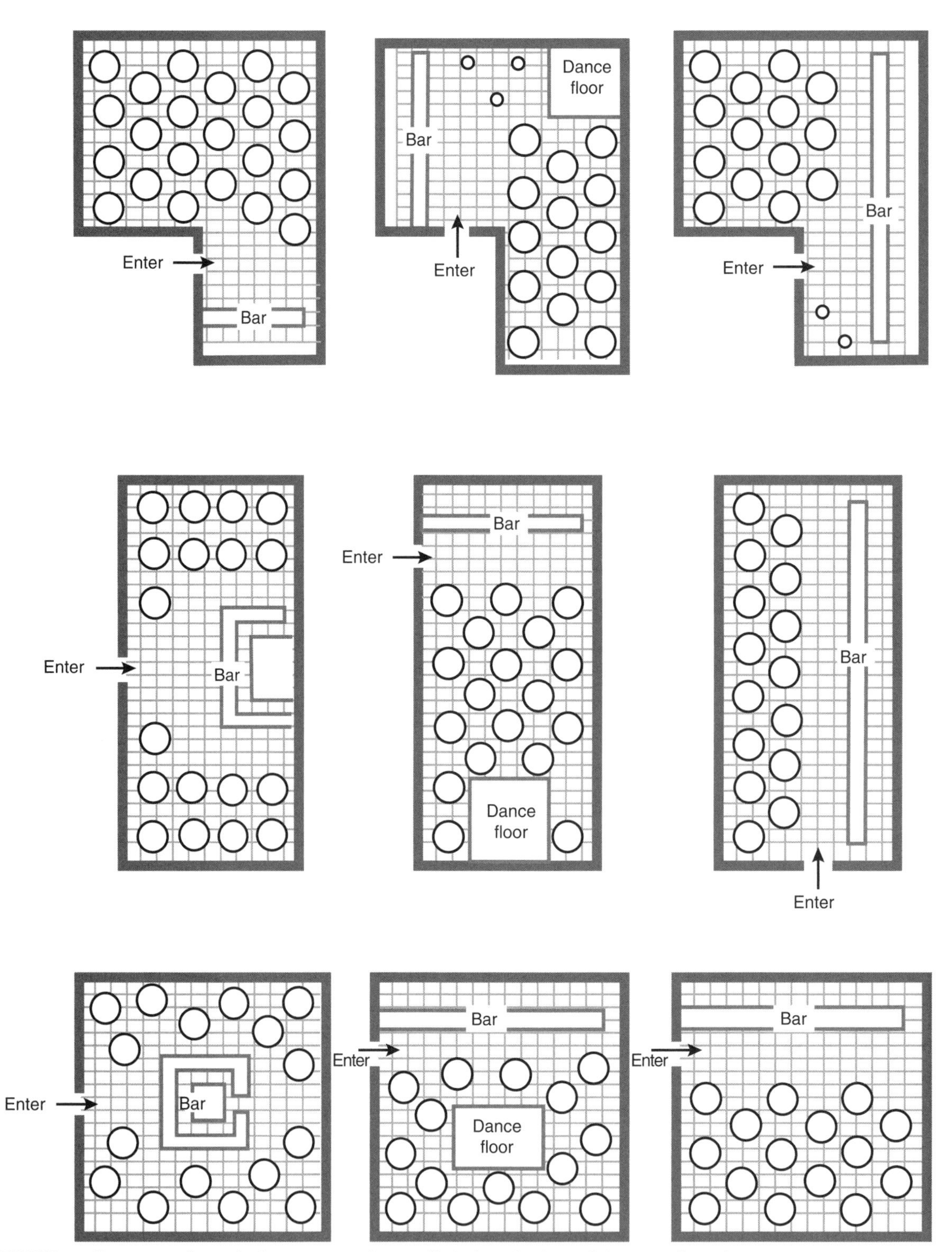

FIGURE 3.5 These rooms all contain the same square footage. Notice how the shape of the room affects the room arrangement.

of the restaurant? Will it serve only as a holding area for the restaurant, or do you want it to be its own destination, with its own patrons?

- *Sharing space* with other activities takes careful planning. You must consider the amount of space each element (the bar, the activities, the furniture and fixtures) requires. You will probably want to measure everything and plot it to scale on a floor plan. Estimating the sizes of objects and spaces simply by looking at them is very difficult. An empty room usually looks smaller than it is. A room with furniture already in it is very difficult to picture accurately in a different arrangement. Although most empty dance floors don't look big enough for more than three or four couples, "in action" they might accommodate many more. (People may bump into each other, but that's part of the fun.) Stage areas for musicians and their instruments take up a surprising amount of space. If you plan to have live entertainment, you need to determine whether the available space is big enough to accommodate the sound, the area for the entertainers, and enough customers to support the undertaking. Is the space too big? Can you fill it?

Consider how it feels to be in a half-filled room as opposed to being in a small place that is crowded with people having fun. You need to be sure that the space will function as you intend it to, while there is still time to change your plans. Set space priorities and guidelines. Then, whether you do the layout yourself or have a designer do it, there will be fewer problems and unwelcome surprises.

Activities and Traffic Patterns. Consider the movement of people in the room, as well as the reasons for their motion. In addition to bar service, you might need to accommodate dining, dancing, live entertainment, and/or the traffic of guests in a hotel lobby. You also must factor in the coming and going of the bar patrons themselves: entry and exit; visits to restrooms, telephones, and the coatroom; or just milling around. For an efficient layout, the space and direction of each activity must be accounted for, so that doors, furniture, and fixtures are placed for maximum efficiency.

In particular, a good layout will establish efficient traffic patterns to and from the bar for table service, to and from the kitchen and service areas for dining service, as well as for customer entry and exit. The goal is to achieve an orderly flow, minimizing potential collisions and general chaos. The bar must also have easy access to storage areas; you don't want the bartender sloshing a tub of ice through a throng of customers. Figure 3.6 shows good and poor traffic patterns for the same space.

A good layout will also consider clientele, mood, and ambience. The position of the bar itself can boost liquor service or intentionally understate it. In a family restaurant, for example, you might place a service bar discreetly in the background, whereas in a singles cocktail lounge you might position an island bar in the middle of the room.

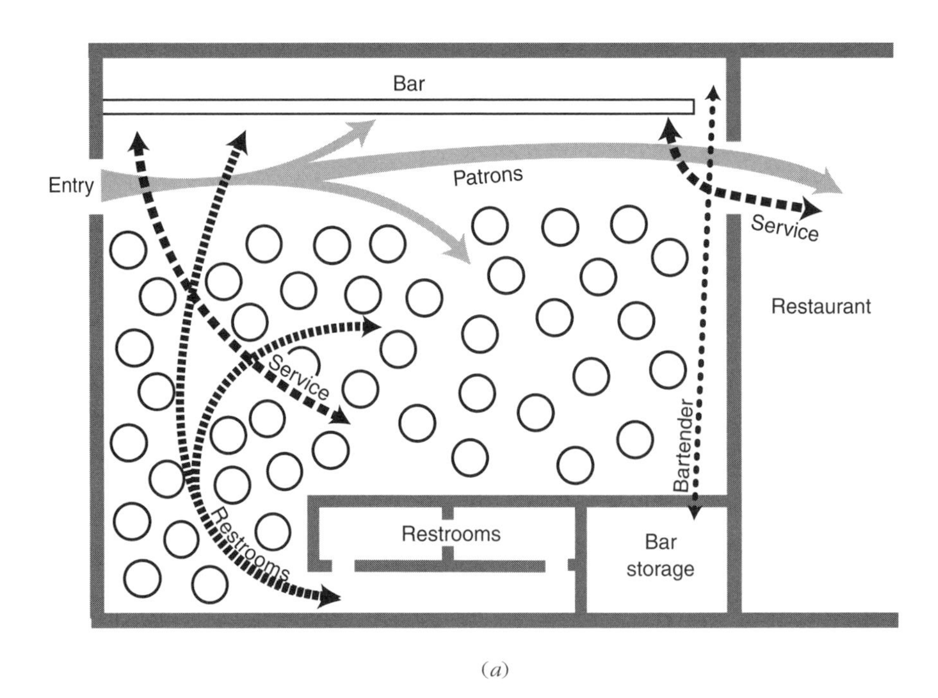

(*a*)

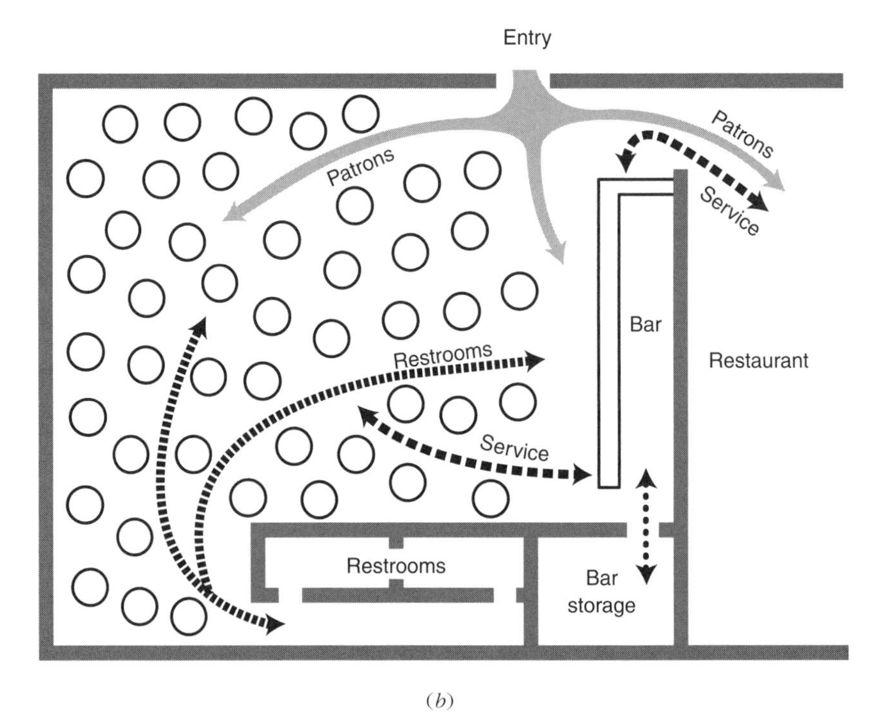

(*b*)

FIGURE 3.6 (*a*) A tangle of conflicting traffic patterns in a bar lounge. (*b*) The flow of traffic smoothed out by repositioning the entry and the bar.

Furniture. Choose all furniture, and lay it out in relation to the total bar concept. Barstools and lounge chairs should look inviting and be comfortable. Chair designers say they can control the rate of customer turnover simply by the degree of comfort of the seat cushion, and the claim certainly makes sense.

Today's barstools come in all types of decorative styles, but no matter which you select, be sure to allow 24 inches of linear bar space for every stool at the bar. Some bars allow up to 30 inches, measured from the center of one barstool to the outer edge of the next. Looks are important, but don't ignore the other functions that the barstools must support. Barstools work hard, and the home-use models are not sturdy enough to withstand the rigors of commercial use.

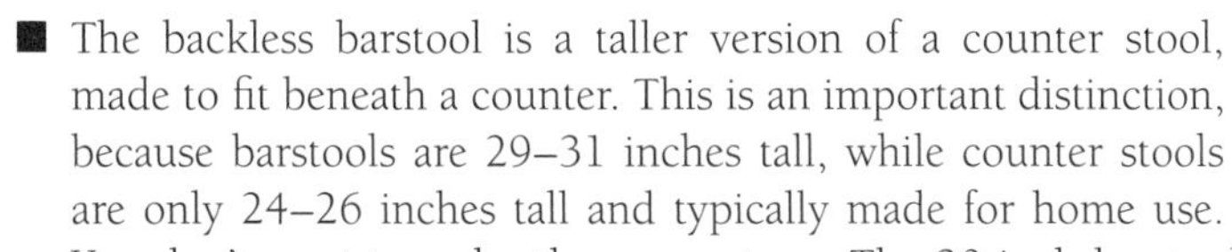

FIGURE 3.7 There are hundred of bar stools, but only three basic types: the backless stool, the stool with a back, and the stool with a back and arms. Images by Thomas Verdos, Tevalia Design, Seattle, Washington.

The basic barstool choices are shown in Figure 3.7. They are:

- The backless barstool is a taller version of a counter stool, made to fit beneath a counter. This is an important distinction, because barstools are 29–31 inches tall, while counter stools are only 24–26 inches tall and typically made for home use. You don't want to order the wrong type. The 30-inch barstool allows the guest to "pull up" to a bar that is either 36 inches or 42 inches high. For a bar the backless stool is the least comfortable option, even with an upholstered seat, but some bar owners consider this an advantage because in a busy nightclub atmosphere, it discourages customers from "parking" on the same stool for long time periods.
- The barstool with a back, which is mandatory if comfort is a primary concern.
- The barstool with both a back and arms, which is an option only if there is sufficient room for guests to comfortably place their arms on the armrests without knocking into other guests, other barstools, or the bar itself.

Barstools can be made of high-impact plastics, wood (of varying types and qualities) and metal; seats and backs can be upholstered with cloth, leather, or plastic. Choose upholstery that feels good and is easy to clean, and check for sturdy stitching of the fabric to the barstool. Look for a suitable, comfortable footrest height. Footrests are also available in multiple finishes, such as brass and chrome. Be sure the barstools swivel, too. This feature is important because it enables customers to turn with ease to talk with people beside them. Barstools with backs can also be ordered with memory-retaining swivel seats, which means that the seat returns to a certain, standard position when a person gets off the barstool. Finally, for barstools and chairs alike, be sure that the ends of their legs or feet are rubber-coated, so they stay put and don't scratch floors or snag carpets when they are moved.

Lounge chairs should fit well around cocktail tables. The tables themselves can be small if they are to be used for only drinks, and in a busy bar you can crowd them somewhat, adding to the conviviality. Both the size and shape of tables and chairs are important elements in layout.

Utilities, Codes, and Licensing Restrictions. When it comes to positioning the bar, plumbing is an important factor. Supply pipes and drains should not travel long distances because they are expensive to install. Also, the longer and more elaborate the plumbing connections, the more that can go wrong. If the space will include a kitchen, it is most efficient to coordinate plumbing for both.

You must also think carefully about electrical requirements in relation to layout. In addition to lighting designed for mood and decor, underbar equipment has numerous special electrical needs. If you offer live entertainment, you have to plan an electrical supply for such items as amplifiers and speakers. All of these considerations will affect your general layout, making you think twice, for example, about putting the bar or the musicians in the center of a room.

Heating and air-conditioning ducts and vents, "smoke eaters," and air circulators are also layout issues in terms of their output, the space they occupy, and their visual effect. A ceiling fan, for example, must have a certain visual relationship to the furniture and fixtures below it. Local health and fire regulations often impinge on layout, especially in respect to exits and aisles. Similarly, health-department requirements regarding glass washing can influence the space requirements inside the bar, as well as the plumbing and electrical requirements.

In some states and localities, requirements for liquor licensing can affect layout. Some prohibit open bars, so a restaurant must have a private club in a separate room in order to serve liquor. In other locales food must be served in the same room where liquor is being served. A few states require bar cabinets to be lockable, and require all liquor to be locked up at the moment that service is supposed to legally end for the night.

Finally remember that the room layout must accommodate persons with disabilities; they must be given equal access to public or commercial buildings, according to the Americans with Disabilities Act (ADA). It requires wheelchair-accessible entrances, doorways, and restrooms for patrons and employees alike who may be disabled. Be aware that in some cities, building codes include these provisions, but in others, they do not. As a result it is dangerous to assume that if you present your plans and receive a building permit, the plans have also been approved for ADA compliance. It is smart to have the plans checked first by an architect or contractor who is knowledgeable about the ADA. The U.S. Justice Department and Equal Employment Opportunity Commission (EEOC) enforce this law and can fine building owners for noncompliance. It is less expensive to design a building that is handicapped accessible than to retrofit one after a complaint has been filed.

THE BAR ITSELF

Determining the size, shape, and placement of the bar itself is a twofold design problem involving decor and function. The size and shape of the bar, its appearance, and its position in the room are typically planned by the owner, architect, or interior designer, whose primary concerns are layout and décor. The working areas, where the drinks are mixed and poured, are planned by a facilities-design consultant or by an equipment dealer. Sometimes these professionals work together from the beginning, but too often a facilities designer or equipment dealer is called in after the bar has been positioned and its dimensions set, and must do the best job possible within the allotted space.

Selecting a Bar

When you select your bar, avoid a straight-line, rectangular model in favor of one with corners and angles if possible. This automatically prompts guests to sit opposite each other and visit, instead of staring straight ahead at the backbar. Of course, although your imagination might be unlimited, in practice the layout possibilities are limited by your available space and your budget. Figures 3.8 and 3.9 show two bar designs by Sue Miller of Glastender, Inc., of Saginaw, Michigan; the latter for wine/beer service. Abbreviations refer to pieces of equipment.

Today's possibilities include modular bar designs, which may cost more to purchase but have some built-in advantages. They are already outfitted for plumbing and electrical needs, and they are easy to maintain, remodel, or upgrade if necessary. The companies that design these ready-made bar units will also provide design and installation assistance.

A common mistake in bar design is to assign space for it without factoring in the projected volume of drinks that will be served and how much space and equipment will be needed to meet that volume. Only after money has been spent building the bar and buying the equipment does the owner discover its inadequacies. A poorly-thought-out bar can cost more initially, limit profits, and cause daily frustration to those who work it. You will see why as we examine the bar in detail.

Parts of the Bar

A bar is made up of three parts: the **front bar**, the **backbar**, and the **underbar.** Each section has special functions. Figure 3.10 shows these parts in profile, as though they were sliced through the middle, from front to back. The dimensions given are those of a typical bar of good, workable design. The length of the bar will vary according to need.

The Front Bar. The front bar is the customer area, where drinks are ordered and served. The bar is typically 16 to 18 inches wide, with a surface that is alcohol-proof, usually of laminated plastic. An armrest along the front edge, often padded, adds another 8 inches to its width. The last few inches of the back edge are usually recessed, and it is here that the bartender pours the drinks, to demonstrate liquor

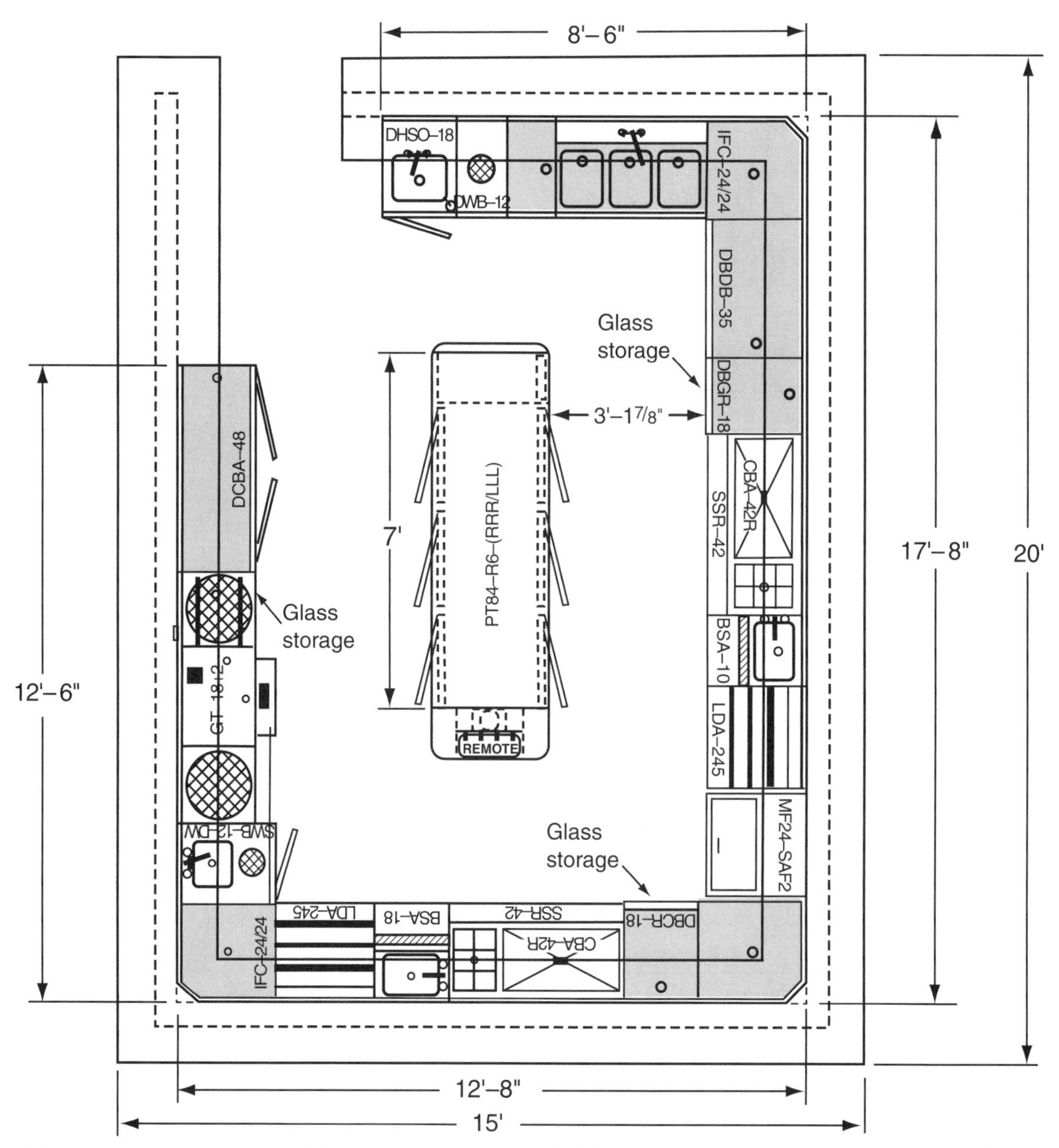

FIGURE 3.8 A sample bar design. The letters and numbers on this plan (and in Figure 3.9) represent certain equipment models to be ordered. Courtesy of Glastender, Inc., Saginaw, Michigan.

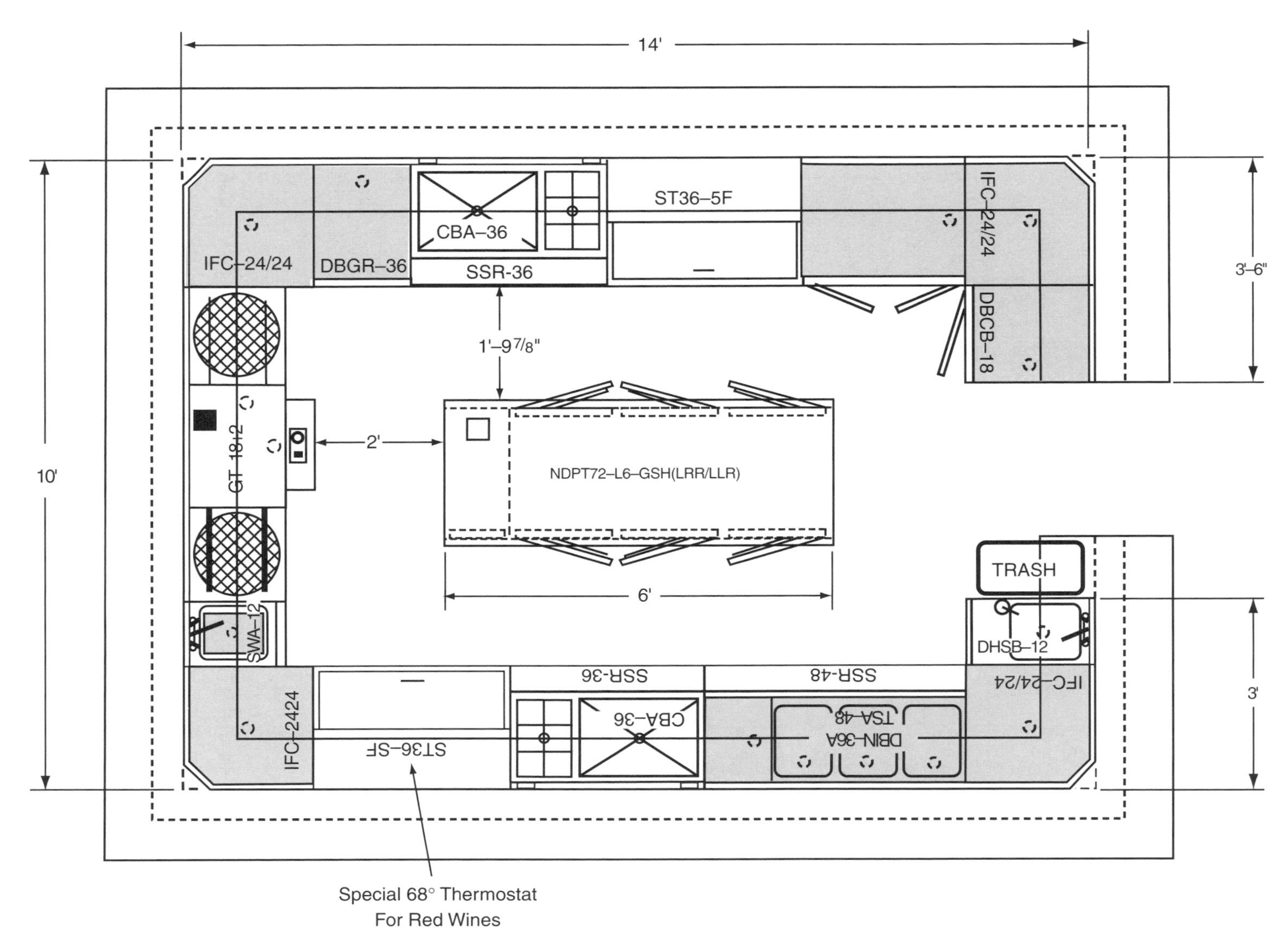

FIGURE 3.9 A layout for a wine and beer bar. Courtesy of Glastender, Inc., Saginaw, Michigan.

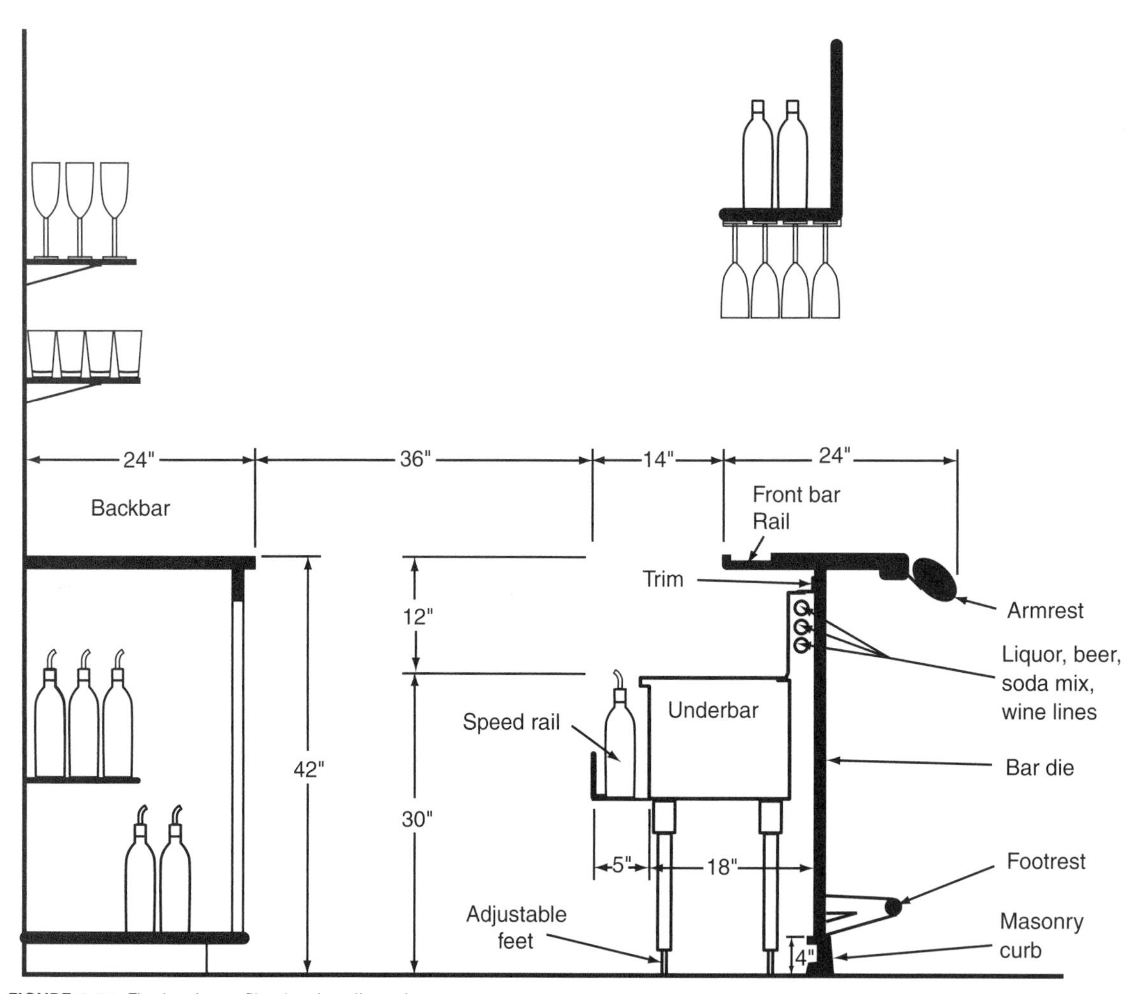

FIGURE 3.10 The bar in profile, showing dimensions.

brand and pouring skill. This part of the bar is known variously as the **rail, glass rail, drip rail,** or **spill trough.**

The vertical structure supporting the front bar, known as the **bar die,** is like a wall that separates customers from the working area. Seen in profile it forms a "T" with the bar, making a kind of table on the customer side, with the other side shielding the underbar from public view. A footrest usually runs the length of the die on the customer side, about a foot off the ground. On elegant mahogany bars of the 1800s the footrest was a brass rail, and underneath it every few feet were brass spittoons. The Prohibitionists made the brass rail a symbol of the wickedness of drink, along with swinging saloon doors and Demon Rum.

The height of the front bar is 42 to 48 inches because this is a good, basic working height for most bartenders. This height also makes the front bar just right for leaning against with one foot on the footrest, in the time-honored tradition of the nineteenth-century barroom. All underbar equipment is designed to fit beneath or behind a 42-inch bar. A sit-down bar will have barstools tall enough so that customers can use the top of the bar as a table. The length of the bar will determine how many stools you will need since each stool is allotted a 2-foot length of bar. Barstools are designed so that their seats are high off the ground, so they typically have rungs for footrests; or the footrest of the bar is within easy reach of the customers' feet. Even numbers of barstools make seating convenient for couples.

The elements of the front bar—the surface, die, armrest, footrest, and stools—are part of your public's perception of your establishment, so their look must be carefully planned in conjunction with the total decor.

The Backbar. The backbar has a dual function: as a decorative display area and as a hard-working storage space. No matter how tidy or cluttered, grand or humble, the backbar speaks volumes about a bar operation. Some people say it is the soul of the bar. It conveys an image of the establishment and showcases the kinds of beverages a patron can expect to be served there. It stimulates conversation, displays the wares, and can be used to post information, including prices, drink specials, the bar's logo, funny signs, neighborhood flyers, or sports pools. (It is always smart to insist that anything posted on the backbar fit in with your own decor and standards.)

The shiny splendor of bottles and glassware is usually reflected in a mirror, a tradition of the backbar. In the Old West, or at least in Old West movies, the mirror had another function: It showed customers at the bar whether anyone was coming up behind them, gun in hand. Today the mirror adds depth to the room; it also gives customers a view of others at the bar and elsewhere in the room. Bartenders sometimes use it, too, to observe customers without being noticed. The typical modern bar consists primarily of mirror, bottles, and glassware. Some people feel that a bar is just not a bar without these elements. There are functional reasons for the prominence of these elements, too: the liquor and glassware make up the bartender's working supplies, and the backbar is a good place to display call brands as a subtle form of merchandising. **Multiple facings** are often used, which means that three or four bottles of a known brand are displayed side by side, reinforcing its popularity. White and brown liquors are alternated for visual effect or the backbar stock is rotated occasionally to showcase different brands. Sometimes the bartender simply organizes the backbar based on what he or she will need to have handy at the busiest times. Whatever the system the merchandising power of the backbar should never be underestimated. Fashions in backbar decor include stained glass, paneled or textured walls, murals, paintings, posters, wine racks, mood pieces, and conversation starters. The base of the backbar is likely to be allocated as storage space, refrigerated or otherwise. Otherwise it might house special equipment, such as a glass froster, an ice machine, or a mechanical dishwasher. If specialty drinks are featured, the frozen-drink or espresso machine will probably be on the backbar. The cash register is usually there, too, in a recessed space. Whatever the backbar's uses, it must be visually pleasing from top to bottom since customers look at it, and it must coordinate visually with the decor of the room as a whole.

TIPS FOR MAINTAINING A PERFECT BACKBAR

- Keep the labels on your bottles facing out at all times.
- Replace any bottles with torn or crooked labels.
- Group your spirits by category: Scotch with Scotch, Bourbon with Bourbon, etc. Mixing up your inventory makes it more difficult for patrons to see what you offer, and makes bartenders less productive.
- Check your inventory on a regular basis. Spirits that aren't selling don't belong on your backbar—or in your bar at all for that matter.
- If you have space, highlight special selections, such as a collection of single-malt Scotches or high-end liqueurs.
- To create impact, use multiple facings of premium spirits where possible, especially if you feature a premium well. It shows your patrons that you believe in pouring the best.
- Use underlit glass shelving or bottle steps and spotlights to highlight your backbar display and create a bit of drama.
- Be sure that signage, promotional materials, and knick-knacks that you want to keep on your backbar all fit in with your decor and your image.
- Keep the backbar clean. Wipe down bottles, shelving, registers, and other equipment at least once a week, if not daily. If you keep open bottles on your backbar, make sure pourers are clean as well. Making sure that all your pourers match also creates a clean, consistent look.

Source: Mike Sherer for *Top Shelf Magazine*.

The Underbar. The underbar is usually the last section of the bar to be designed, after the front of the bar has been created. The underbar deserves the same degree of careful attention as the rest of the bar because it is where most of the equipment and supplies for the products you are selling must be arranged compactly and efficiently, to facilitate speed of service. Overall your goal should be to design an underbar and backbar area that makes wise use of space, is as sanitary as possible, and is able to respond to consumer tastes and trends in drink preparation. Consider your clientele, their demographics, and their personal preferences when planning your underbar.

The area where individual bartenders work is called a **pouring station.** It must have an individual supply of liquor, ice, mixes, glasses, blender, and garnishes, all within arm's reach. Each pouring station also must have an ice bin and one or more bottle racks for the most-used liquors and mixes. (You will learn more about bar-related equipment in Chapter 4.) A supply of glasses may be placed upside down on a glass rail, on drainboards near the ice bin, on special glass shelves, in glass racks stacked beside the station, on the backbar, in overhead racks, or in all of these places, grouped according to type and size. The blender, and probably a mixer, may be placed on a recessed shelf beside the ice bin, while the garnishes are typically located on the bar top in a special condiment tray.

Most operations use an automatic dispensing system for carbonated beverages. Such a system has lines running from bulk supplies (hidden within the underbar) to a dispensing head with multiple push-buttons. The system goes by several common nicknames: a **handgun** or **six-shooter** (it is aimed into the glass and buttons are pushed to dispense liquids), and a **cobra gun** (it has snaking lines that connect to the head). A cobra gun is needed at each pouring station. If the bar has an automated liquor dispensing system, the setup is similar.

Dispensing systems will vary drastically depending on the situation. The needs of a beer concession stand in an athletic stadium, for instance, are quite different from those of a bar in a fine restaurant. In the former, it may not matter that the beer lines from keg to tap are long. But in the latter it would because line length affects the quality of the beer, and a connoisseur will notice the difference.

The number of pouring stations at your bar will depend on the volume and flow of business. The bar should be designed with enough stations to handle the peak periods, and with the equipment needed to do it. Figure 3.11 shows the plan of a hotel bar (shown in greater detail in Chapter 4, Figures 4.2 and 4.3). Notice that three stations serve different areas: dining room, coffee shop, and bar lounge.

When drinks are served from the main bar for table service, the bar must always have a **pickup station,** a section of the front bar near the pouring station where serving personnel turn in and receive orders and return empty glasses. The pickup station must be separated somehow from where customers sit and order. Otherwise, servers must elbow their way through the customers, in which case confusion reigns and spills occur. Furthermore your profits might end up on the jacket of a celebrity who has just dropped in for a drink, or an ice cube might find its way down someone's neck. The pickup station should be near a pouring station and the cash register. In Figure 3.11 you can identify two of the pickup stations (top right and bottom left) by the railings (M) that set them apart from customer seating areas of the bar. Another area of the underbar contains glass-washing equipment—here a three- or four-compartment sink (I on the plan in Figure 3.11) with drainboards on both sides or, in some cases, a mechanical dishwasher. The underbar must also have provision for waste disposal and a hand sink (G on the plan). These are typical health-department requirements. Be aware that health departments are continually scrutinizing the sanitation procedures of bars. For example, rules may dictate where you store empty beer bottles if your operation recycles them.

Together the underbar and backbar must provide enough storage for the day's reserve supplies of liquor, mixes, wines, beers, ice, garnishes, and such non-beverage supplies as bar towels, cocktail napkins, picks, and stir sticks. All of these items must be arranged so that access to them requires a minimum of movement. Movement is time, and time, as we all know, is money.

Three feet is the customary distance between the backbar and the underbar because it accommodates the bartenders' movements and the opening of storage cabinet doors. Cabinet doors must not be so wide that they block passage when open. Storage areas must be available to each bartender without interfering with another's movements.

You can order underbar equipment three ways. You can choose stock designs from manufacturers' catalogs or web sites, you can have custom equipment con-

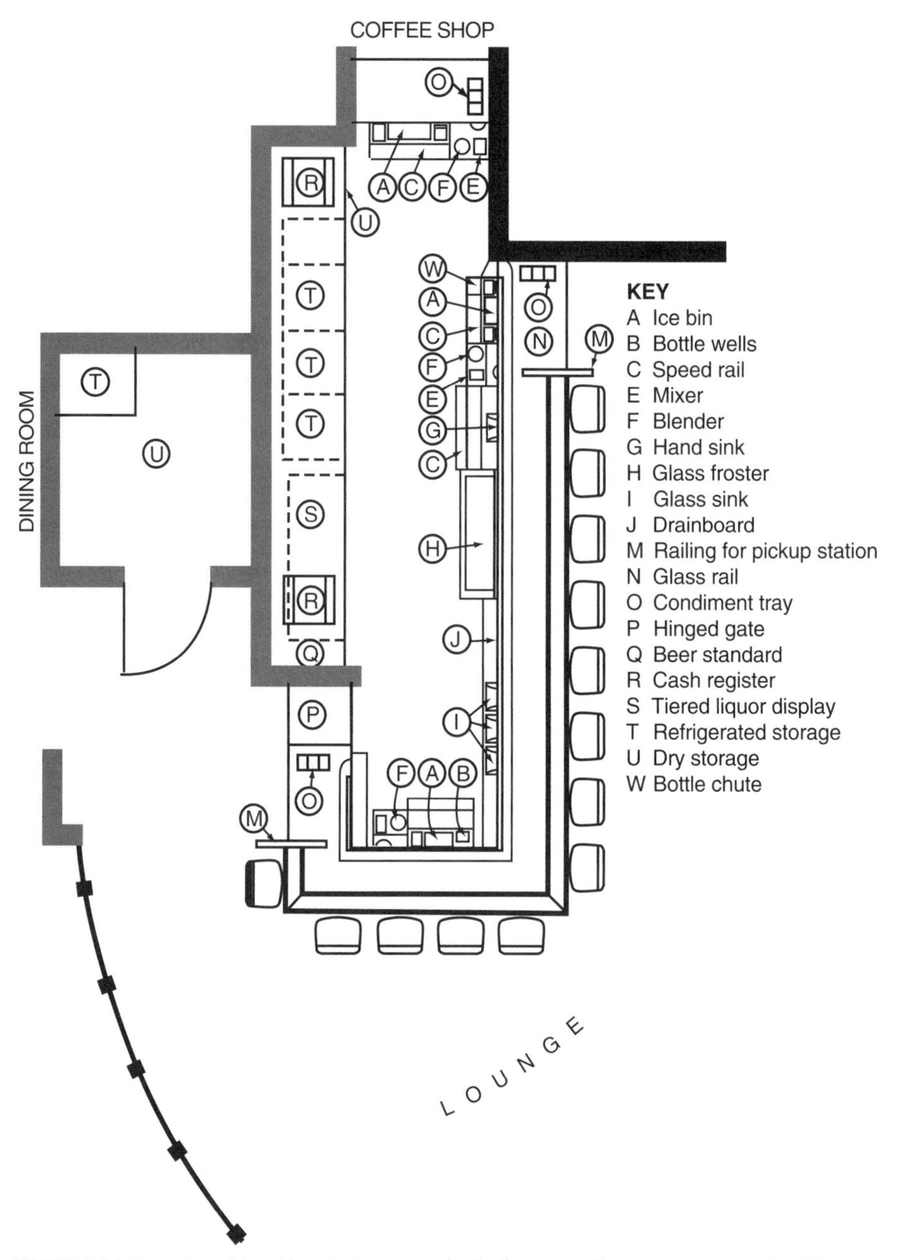

FIGURE 3.11 Floor plan of hotel bar. Station at top (A, C, O) serves coffee shop across corridor. Right-hand station (A, C, M, O) serves cocktail lounge and bar. Station at bottom (A, B) serves bar and pickup station (M, O) for dining room to left (U). Rear portions of underbar equipment are not visible in this view. Plan courtesy Norman Ackerman, Ackerman-Barnes Consulting.

structed to meet specific needs or spaces, or you can use a combination of both. In most cases a few stock components are ordered, and a few pieces are custom-made to fit precisely in the underbar area. The equipment is usually installed by a local equipment dealer. When you design the bar, make sure to get input from an equipment dealer or manufacturer. If you're planning on serving special drinks, you will need to plan for the equipment they require. If you intend to have beer on tap, for instance, you must know to place the "standards" (faucets; Q in Figure 3.11) so that they are easily accessible to the bartender (but not to the customer!) You must also have refrigerated storage space for each keg, either at the bar or in a nearby storage area with lines installed for bringing the beer to the bar. For obvious reasons, the latter arrangement is more sophisticated than having kegs at the bar, but it requires that you install custom-engineered equipment to maintain beer quality. Frozen-drink dispensers, ice-cream equipment, and glass frosters also have special space requirements that must be designed into the overall bar scheme.

You have plenty of design variations from which to choose: Your pouring station can be a bit larger and, as just mentioned, your beer kegs can be stored elsewhere with a system of remote lines and taps. If your local health department does not require a four-compartment bar sink, you can opt for a handy automatic glass-washer; you can also provide more room for bottle coolers if you decide to serve a wide selection of bottled beers. Whatever you choose to do, be sure to decide on your drink menu *before you design your bar space.* Give equal weight to form and function in the design process.

Hidden but essential factors in underbar and backbar design are the plumbing and electrical needs of the equipment. Faucets, icemakers, cobra guns, and dish-washers all need a water supply. Sinks, refrigerators, glass frosters, ice bins, ice-makers, dishwashers, and waste disposal need proper drainage. Some equipment may need special electrical wiring.

All equipment must be installed to enable ready access for repairs. To achieve this, the entrance to the bar is sometimes made large enough to accommodate the biggest piece of movable equipment, in case it has to be replaced or repaired. On the other hand the smaller the access, the more space you have available for equip-ment, so the bar entrance is usually designed as a hinged section of the bar top that lifts up (P on the plan). Repairs are made in place, or replacement equipment is lifted over the bar when necessary. Sometimes one end of the bar is left open, although this leaves the liquor supply more vulnerable to tampering and makes control more difficult. Another alternative is to install a doorway in the backbar.

The Bar Floor. Think about the bartenders' comfort and safety when you plan the bar floor. They are on their feet for hours, and you want them to look fresh and feel good. The floor under their feet must have a nonporous surface, such as tile or sealed concrete, to meet sanitary-code requirements. Wood and carpeting are not acceptable. A tile or concrete surface is cold, hard, and slippery when wet. Also, keep in mind that as an evening wears on, cubes ice, beer foam, soapy water, debris from empty glasses, and broken glass might accumulate.

There are ways to improve floor comfort and safety, but none is ideal. Slotted plastic panels allow spills to go down between the slats, to minimize hazards of slipping. But these panels must be taken up for cleaning, which is a nuisance, and if it isn't done often they become stale-smelling and unsanitary. They are also hard on the feet. Rubber or plastic mats minimize slippage and are easy on the feet, but they also must be cleaned frequently.

Materials and Upkeep. A consideration that often escapes newcomers to the bar business is the ease of care of the furnishings and finishes, especially, for example, surfaces of counters, bar tops, and tables. Some learn the hard way that aluminum and nickel can be damaged by salt, or that stylish slate countertops absorb juices and wines and require periodic resealing. Plastics discolor or turn foggy when exposed to direct sunlight or cleaned with glass cleaners, while stainless-steel surfaces scratch easily, show fingerprints, and must be polished or buffed frequently. A great deal of extra work may be avoided with attention early in the design process to materials that are as functional as they are attractive under hard-working bar conditions. There are plenty of interesting options, including an artificial slate product called *Fireslate,* fiberglass, sealed and stained concrete, acrylic, and marble and more—but not all of them are suited for all purposes. Making the right decisions during the design process will prevent the need for expensive replacement of fixtures and furnishings that don't perform as well as you had hoped.

Bar Size, Shape, and Position in the Room. From the front of the front bar to the back of the backbar, the overall depth of your bar should be about 8 feet (again, refer to Figure 3.11). Determine the minimum length of the bar from the inside, according to equipment needs. Then determine additional length and shape from the outside, according to the number of customers you want to seat (if there are seats), the size of the room, and the overall design requirements.

The inside factors are determined mainly by the kinds of drinks served and the number of pouring stations needed to meet peak volume. The outside factors involve your total concept, your clientele, your décor, and the available space.

Unfortunately the last consideration, the available space, is usually the tail that wags the dog. Often the available space is what is left over after everything else has been planned. Many times an inadequate bar space will limit what you can serve and how much, thereby decreasing your profits. Otherwise it might require expensive and complicated equipment solutions to problems that would be simple to solve in a larger space. The best way to proceed is to plan your drink menu first, with your clientele in mind. Figure carefully the volume you can expect at peak periods. Size your bar to accommodate space and equipment needs for those drinks in that volume, or have a specialist do it. Do not box yourself into a bar that is too small.

If your facility is already built and available space is predetermined, it becomes even more critical to think through your bar design and equipment to make the most profitable use of the space you have. Again, your clientele and your drink menu are the logical starting points. You may, for example, have to choose between beer on tap and ice-cream drinks in frosted glasses. If you know your clientele, it is much easier to make the most profitable choice.

Bars can be many different shapes: straight, curved, angled, horseshoe, round, square, or freeform. Shape, too, is a decision involving many factors: room size and shape, mood, décor, and function. Unusual shapes are tricky. Most underbar equipment is factory-made in standard sizes that might not fit an irregular shape. Custom work increases cost and sometimes does not work as well in action. It can also create maintenance and repair headaches. Usually a bar has its back to the wall; but in a large room, it might be the centerpiece or focal point: a freestanding square, round, oval, or irregular island, with stations facing in several directions and a backbar in the middle. Obviously an island bar will have special design considerations. The backbar will be smaller and the front bar larger, and the underbar will be visible to the patrons. There might be special plumbing and electrical problems. The bar's position in the room deserves as much consideration as its shape and size because it might affect both. Do you want it to be seen from the street? Do you want it to set the tone of your establishment or take second place to your foodservice, your bowling alley, or your dance floor?

Consider the customers' reactions as they enter the room. Crossing the room to get to the bar might be inhibiting. Some people may turn around and go back out rather than cross an empty room at 4 P.M. or, a couple of hours later, plow through crowds or thread their way through the lounge amid staring eyes. Usually the best place for the bar is near the door where customers can head straight for it. Make these kinds of decisions before you draw up any plans.

The Bar as Control Center. While a bar's major function is the dispensing of drinks, it also serves as your control center; it is where you keep records of the stock on hand, the types and quantities of drinks poured, and their sales value. After each serving period the sales record is checked against money received to verify that one equals the other. This leads to the most important piece of equipment in the bar: the cash register, or *point-of-sale (POS) terminal,* as it is often called in this technological age. It is at the core of the control system by which management ensures that its liquor is sold to the customer with little or no "evaporation" en route. In some operations the bartender also takes in the money; in others, this is done by a cashier at a separate register. In a large or busy establishment, each bartender may have a separate register, or bartenders may share a register that has a separate drawer for each one. In any case a register must be close to each pouring station and the pickup station, so that a minimum of time and motion is lost. Since the register is usually within full view of customers, its placement also becomes an important design element.

Smaller, Specialty Bars. The term **service bar** refers to a bar that pours for table service only, usually in conjunction with foodservice. It does not serve customers directly; it deals only with filling drink orders brought by wait staff. Usually a single service-bar station is enough to handle the volume, except in very large restaurants.

Sometimes a service bar is part of the dining room, but more often it is out of sight, in which case it is small and has a simple design. Instead of a backbar display, it has room for bulk supplies of beer, mixes, and liquor stock, and there is no need to camouflage or hide ugly or noisy equipment. Mechanical dispensing systems are often used here instead of hand pouring, to increase speed and reduce liquor loss; at a public bar, there may be customer resistance to such impersonal methods. In terms of basics, however, a service bar is like any other bar. It has the same functions, uses the same kinds of equipment, and performs the same tasks of recording and controlling the pouring and selling of drinks. As such, it needs the same forethought to plan as any other bar.

The same goes for the **portable bar,** a typical extension of a hotel's beverage service where banquets, meetings, receptions, conferences, and conventions are being held. Portable bars give the hotel the flexibility to serve beverages on short notice anywhere on the premises, indoors or out. The typical portable bar ranges in length from 4 to 8 feet. Larger models can accommodate two bartenders working side by side, and often can hold sealed-in cold-plate units for dispensing chilled beverages. Some portable bars fold into 2-foot widths for easy storage, and most have 5-inch casters for rolling them into place, as well as locking brakes on the casters. Ice bins on portable bar units should have both a water drain for the inevitable melting that occurs and a sufficient reservoir to hold the runoff. Underbar storage should consist of removable, adjustable shelves. Speed rails (to hold liquor bottles) and storage cabinets are other desirable options. Look for a portable bar with a stainless-steel backsplash and side splashes, and a laminated top that cannot be stained by water or alcohol.

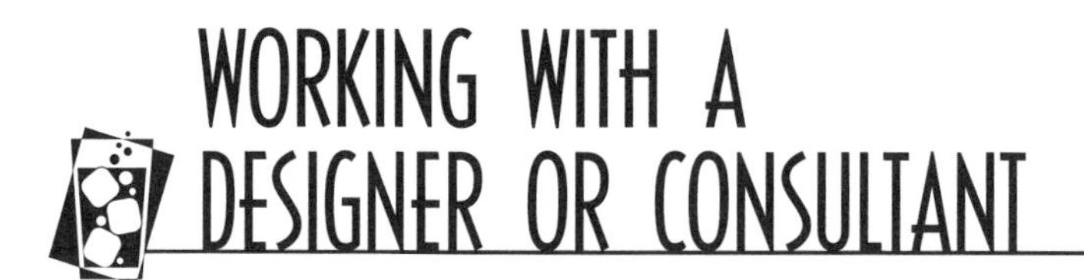

WORKING WITH A DESIGNER OR CONSULTANT

A new generation of bar designers is making a reputation for itself. The group is, perhaps, personified by Dodd Mitchell, a talented young designer who has created the ambience for about two dozen bars, restaurants, and hotels. Mitchell, who designs everything from airplane interiors to women's lingerie, learned his trade while working as a set designer in Hollywood. His hallmark in hospitality projects is the use of lighting and materials that flatter the customers—and who doesn't want to look prettier, thinner, or younger when they go out on the town? Mitchell has become somewhat controversial for his lack of formal design education and his tendency to borrow liberally from other designers' good ideas, but no one can argue with his success. As of this writing, recent Mitchell projects include Dolce in West Hollywood and Lotus, a New York City nightspot.

A wide range of expertise is available to help you plan the physical environment of your facility. Your first challenge is to sort out who you really need. Your options are described in the following sections.

Consultants. At one end of the range is the food-facilities consultant firm that will do the entire job for you, from carrying out detailed market and feasibility studies, to developing a concept that will sell to your clientele through completion of the job. These professionals can choose your glassware—and even design your matchbook covers! Many consultant firms offer a full spectrum of design services, including architects, interior designers, graphic artists, and foodservice-facilities designers who specialize in kitchens and bars. Other consultant firms have only some of those skills within their firms, but can put together a whole design team for you by subcontracting out to other specialists. Consultants are typically used on projects for which a sizable investment has been made. The right consultant will make you money in the long run by doing the most appropriate, efficient, and profitable job. Many food-facilities consultants also accept small jobs. You can find them listed in the Yellow Pages, or you can write to their professional organization, Foodservice Consultants Society International (FCSI), which offers planning, design, and management consulting services in this specialized field. Members must have 10 years of experience and must pass critical reviews of professional competence.

For bar design the most specialized service a consultant has to offer is the design of the space inside the bar by a facilities designer. This specialist will identify the equipment you need to serve your drink menu and lay it all out for maximum efficiency and economy. Facilities designers' knowledge is different from that of interior designers and architects, especially regarding code requirements, the equipment available, and typical problems and solutions. These designers often work closely with interior designers and architects, however, and should be brought into the picture before the size and shape of the bar are finalized. If a facilities designer puts your bar project out for bid, you'll be given a choice of equipment from several companies. You might get a better bar for less money than if you tried to put it together yourself or had a restaurant supply house do it using only the equipment lines it carries.

Interior Designers. The interior designer who specializes in restaurants is trained in the aesthetics of this particular type of design, and an experienced interior designer will be familiar with restaurant design trends and with the commercial furniture, fabrics, and other materials available. This type of designer will typically do your space planning (layout); select your furnishings; design your floors, ceilings, walls, window treatments; and plan your lighting, coordinating the entire design to fit your overall concept and supervising all installations. When choosing an interior designer, you must focus on the right kind of experience. Designers who have done only residential work or other types of commercial establishments might not understand the very specialized design needs of bars and restaurants.

Choosing Design Assistance

Before choosing a designer or consultant, shop around. Find a bar or restaurant that you think has been particularly well designed. It doesn't have to reflect your kind of concept or attract your kind of clientele; it simply has to be well done in terms of its own purpose and concept. Ask who designed it. Then find out what else that person has designed and visit as many of those places as possible. If they are all on target, go ahead. If not, do some additional exploring until you find someone who does the kind of job you are looking for, consistently well. As with any other profession, different designers will have reputations and preferences for different types of work.

Working Arrangements. Consultants and designers work on contract, which is adventageous to you and to them. Typically, you will pay a *retainer,* a standard "starting fee" or percentage, to begin the job. Some interior designers will work on the basis of a design fee plus a commission on the furniture and materials you buy. Others will do a design on an hourly fee basis and let you carry out parts or all of it yourself.

Whatever your investment, be sure the contract spells out clearly the scope of the job, the fees to be paid, and the various stages of the project at which payment is to be made.

Smaller-Scale or Remote Projects. What if you have only a limited budget or want to open in a small town or remote area where specialists are not available to you? Specialists will go anywhere for the right money, but you'll have to pay their travel expenses. You can also get help from dealers, restaurant supply houses, commercial furniture dealers, and the like. Investigate as many as you can. Some of the help will be good, because many facilities designers began their careers designing in restaurant supply houses. But some of the help will be no better than what you could do yourself if you planned carefully. Be aware that most, if not all, recommendations from these businesses will be limited to the brands and products they are selling. You might find a local interior designer who is willing to work with you on an hourly basis. Or you might consult an art teacher to help you with design and color coordination. Assistance might also be available through manufacturers' representatives. Of course, you yourself have a talent for design. More often, though, people who have the operational know-how focus on the product, the staff, and getting the money together, and they neglect the physical ambience. However you decide to cover this base, keep in mind that in today's market, the bar-restaurant is part of the entertainment business, and the physical setting is at least half the story; where competition is keen, it might be the whole story—your identity. If you do decide to go it alone, opt for a simple, clean look. Don't clutter it up or try for pseudosophistication. Today the clean line is sophisticated; it is currently one of the major design trends.

CHECKLIST OF BAR-DESIGN ESSENTIALS

Whether you hire a designer or design your bar yourself, define your needs and wants clearly. The more information you can give a designer and the clearer your own goals, the better the result and the easier the collaboration. The following is a checklist of basics you should decide on before you meet with a consultant or designer or take the important next steps on your own:

- Target clientele
- Services to be offered
- Overall concept
- The competition
- Projected volume of business (number of seats, turnover, drinks/patrons per day, days open, annual gross income)
- Types of beverages you'll serve
- Size and shape of bar area (an architect's plans for an existing structure if you have them)
- Activities to take place in bar area
- Relationship of bar to dining and service areas (kitchen, storage)
- Existing décor, equipment, furniture, and fixtures you expect to keep
- Licensing, zoning, health, fire, and building code requirements
- Time limitations
- Budget limitations (This is a must before you consult anyone else, unless you are hiring a consultant only to give cost estimates for the job.)

SUMMING UP

The first step for turning a building, room, or space into a popular and profitable bar is determining your target clientele. The next step involves choosing the products and services you will offer to this clientele, or *market segment.* The third step is defining a unifying concept with a special character or identity. This is more than a signature drink or clever advertising tagline; it is the components that, together, will create the bar's energy and mood. Next, you must study the market by visiting the other bar businesses in the neighborhoods you are considering, as well as other bars with similar clientele, prices, or concepts. Choose a location on the basis of the market study, then determine the feasibility of your project for that location. Only then will it be time to deal with the physical facility. The goal is to make it an environment that attracts the desired clientele, gives them pleasure, and makes them want to come again.

Décor is a large factor in creating this environment. Color, light, arrangement of furniture and fixtures, efficient use of space, and the sounds to be heard in the room all contribute to décor. The bar should be designed from the inside out, so to speak, beginning with the drink menu. Then, décor should be developed in partnership with functional needs. You will also need to accommodate disabled patrons and employees, to meet the requirements of the ADA.

The bar itself should be designed based on the types of drinks that you'll serve since some require special equipment, such as blenders. The overall appearance of the backbar area is another consideration. Will it be packed with bottles or sleek and uncluttered? Will it be used mostly for storage or for show? Try to make the most profitable use of the limited space at and behind the bar, and take care to choose fixtures and finishes that will be sturdy and stain-resistant. Bar furnishings work hard; cleaning them should be as easy as possible.

Enable traffic patterns of servers and customers to flow smoothly; people should not have to "cross paths" too often, for safety reasons. If entertainment is part of the concept, allow adequate room for it in the design for, perhaps, dance floors or a stage. Carefully plan the locations of utilities (water, power, air vents). In large rooms, where ancillary bars (portable bars or service bars) are part of the setup, hire a designer or consultant to help with the initial plans, or try it yourself.

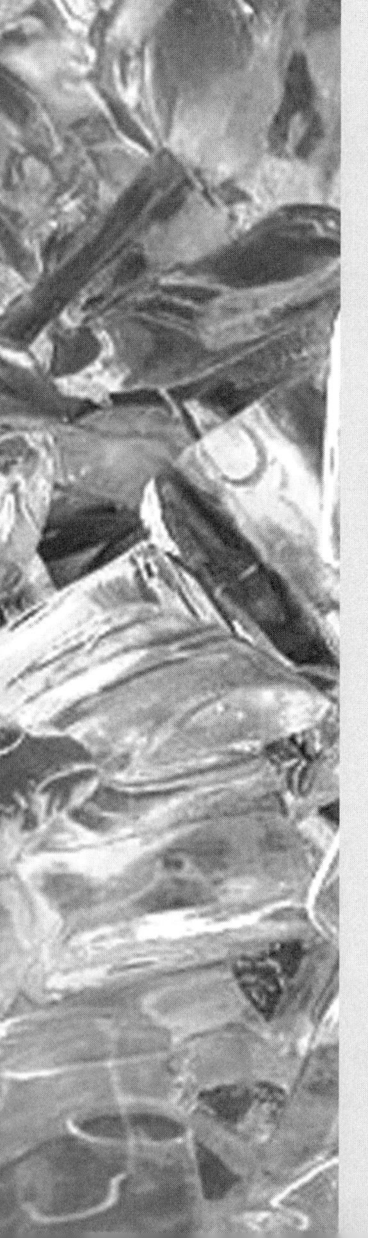

POINTS TO PONDER

1. Why is it so important to design the physical environment of a bar with a particular type of customer in mind?
2. In a few words describe the colors, lighting, sound level, and types of furnishings you might use to set the mood in a. a casual, family restaurant that includes liquor sales, b. a Latin dance club, and c. a cocktail lounge in a prestigious resort hotel.
3. What does the term *market segment* mean? Why is this concept important in developing a plan for a new bar?
4. What should you look for when making a detailed study of other bars in your market area?
5. Do singles bars still exist, or is this a long-dead generalization in your area? In your view, what would make a bar a singles bar?
6. Which of the successful bars described on pages 85–89 would be most successful in your local area? Which bars would not do especially well in your market? Explain why.
7. In Figure 3.5, how does the overall shape of the room affect a. arrangement of furniture and fixtures, b. number of people accommodated, and c. feasible activities? Can you improve the layout by changing the entry or the size, shape, or location of furniture and fixtures?
8. When designing the bar itself, why should you start with your drink menu?
9. In your particular bar, what do you think the backbar should "say" about your business?
10. What is the difference between an interior designer and a facilities designer? What are the particular skills and expertise of each? Do you need both?

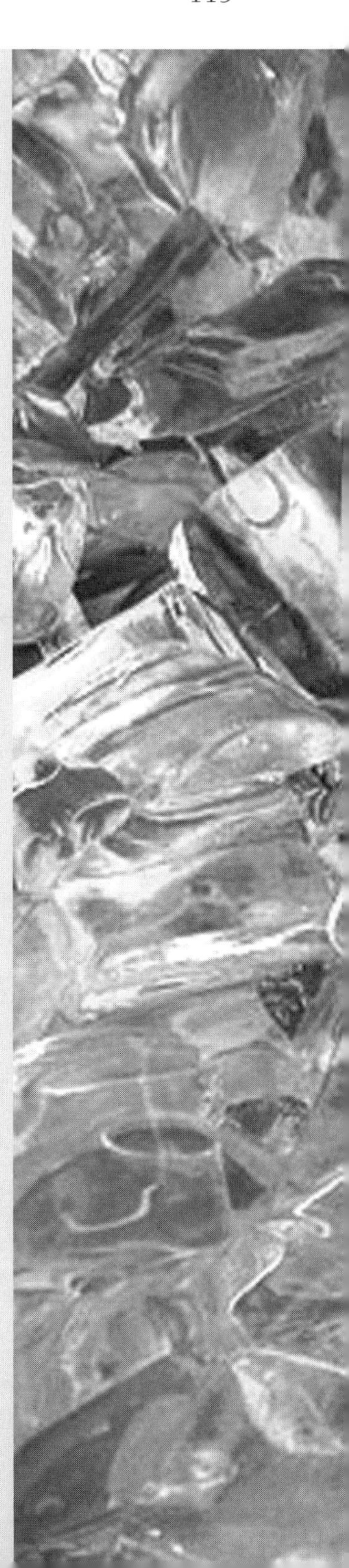

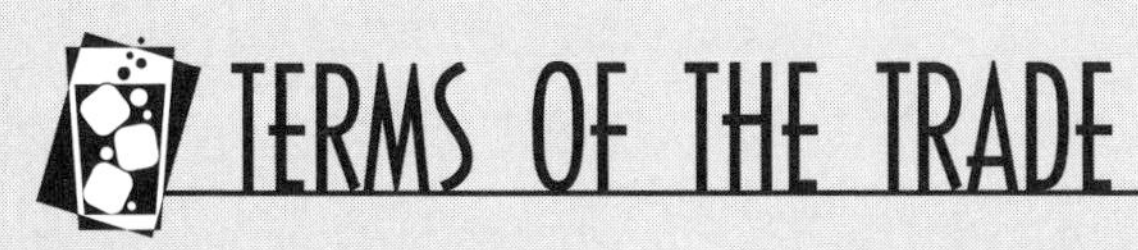

TERMS OF THE TRADE

Americans with Disabilities Act (ADA)
backbar
bar die
cobra gun (handgun, six-shooter)
concept bar
front bar
gastro pub
image
market segment
multiple facings
participatory bar
pickup station
portable bar
pouring station
rail (glass rail, drip rail, spill trough)
service bar
underbar

A CONVERSATION WITH...GEORGE MAJDALANI

After majoring in Business Information and Accounting in college George Majdalani was trained as a bar and restaurant manager by Robert Zimmerman, the former CEO of Rosewood Properties (a Texas-based company that owns upscale hotel properties). After a stint as executive operations manager for the M Crowd Restaurant Group in Dallas, Texas (with 19 locations and 8 dining concepts), Majdalani is now managing director of Stephan Pyles LLC, a fine dining company founded by the well-known Dallas-based chef Stephan Pyles.

Restaurant Operations Manager

Q: What does an operations manager do?

A: I have general managers, managers, chefs, and sous chefs who operate the restaurants. My main objective is to make sure that the managers and chefs are operating them the way that the owners and partners meant for each restaurant to be run—whether it's the style of the food, the service, the feel of the restaurant. I maintain that and I make sure they all focus on that. I focus on whatever the goals of each restaurant are—financial, marketing, or whatever—and I work with the chef and the general manager to achieve those goals.

Q: What have you learned about hiring people?

A: Mr. Zimmerman's theory was, "When you hire someone, always hire them with their management potential in mind. Never hire them to be an 'employee.'" So when you interview someone ask the questions as if they were being hired for a management position. You'll have more success with them, and they'll have more success with you.

They also have to be serious about the job, and not look at it as a job, but as a career. I always look at hourly employees as managers for the future. When I go to a restaurant, I don't think, "Which one of these employees would *like* to be a manager?" I think, "Which one of them really *wants* it?" I can teach anybody this business. But I can never teach them the desire, the attitude, to be truly successful.

Q: If you're in an entry-level position, what is the best kind of experience to get? Front of the house? Back of the house? Bartending?

A: I don't believe that you have to be a dishwasher before you can become a great chef, or a busboy to become a great manager. But I do believe that, in some way or other a person has to understand and accept any position in the restaurant in order to grow. If you become a manager, believe me, you have to know how to mop, wash dishes, how the ovens and grills work. You may not be able to execute a dish like the chef, but when anyone doesn't show up, the staff looks up to the manager to be able to do the job. If you don't know how, you are in trouble.

Q: How do you handle liquor storage, and how do you keep it secure?

A: We store enough liquor for our approximate weekly usage at the bar; that's our par stock. Then we have a small storeroom near the bar that does not hold more than a couple of cases and other bar-related supplies. We don't mix our bar storage and restaurant or food storage. There is too much access to food storage, and with liquor, I want only the manager or bartender to have access. The bartender is held to stricter standards, I'd say, than any other employee, for obvious reasons; this person handles not only a lot of cash, but liquor, beer, and wine as well.

In terms of inventory, things that you buy per piece and sell by the piece—like a bottle of beer or wine—are much easier to keep track of. We have a proportioned pour for wines by the glass; we know we're going to get exactly four glasses from each bottle. But I must control liquor access far more carefully. There are only a few keys: for the manager who opens, the manager who closes, and the chef if he [or she] opens or closes. The owner has one and I have one. And that's it. Managers only—no employees have keys.

Q: What do you think is the hardest part of managing a beverage operation?

A: Control of the product is one thing. First I believe you must have a computer system that does not allow the bartender or employees to verbally order and that everything being served must be recorded and charged to somebody. It's not just a trust factor; things get busy and people can't rely on their memories to ring things up later. And the second factor is, there is a lot of cash handled at a bar. As a manager, you have to keep your eyes open and make sure—if a certain bartender uses more cash than credit cards—that nothing is forgotten. Hire staff that you trust very, very much, and then create a system that supports them to be successful. If the system does not prompt their success, then they will find "ways" of making more money.

So we monitor very carefully. My philosophy is, if I see something I don't understand, I ask. There are so many ways you can interpret things, and you've got to let the staff be related and comfortable—it's not that you're watching them every minute. Nobody likes to work under those conditions. But theft is a reality, and there are hints and suspicious behaviors you must be aware of. Also, random drug testing is a policy in our company.

Q: What kinds of training do you give for dealing with customers who drink too much?

A: In Texas individual servers have to be certified to serve alcohol. The state provides a three-hour course for servers. One of the things they teach in that program is, don't serve more than three drinks to a person the first hour; don't serve more than two drinks the second hour; and don't serve more than two drinks the third hour. And they have to eat something during that time. In our restaurants, the manager is notified anytime a customer has had three drinks and orders a fourth, so that the manager can discuss it with the guest.

Q. You let the manager handle it, not the server?

A: That's right. The server just says, "I'm worried about Table 5; they've had a lot to drink, please go talk to them." It's simple. The manager observes the guests and may go up to them and say, "You are showing signs of intoxication and I can't serve you anymore." We give them their check and say, "Have a good night." And, immediately, we remove all the drinks from the table; we don't even serve a person sitting next to them at the same table because he or she could take a sip from that drink. We do offer complimentary cab rides if a guest shows any sign of intoxication.

Q. What trends are you noticing at the bar?

A: Classic drinks are coming back—the Martinis, Manhattans, Cuba Libres. Lately, vodkas, gins, and tequilas are "hot" on the market; also the different flavors of bottled waters and single-serving iced teas for people who want a nonalcoholic drink.

I also think today's bartender has to know more about the food side of our business. People now like to have an appetizer with their drinks or relax at the bar and ask for menu recommendations before they sit down to eat. Bartenders should know how to match foods and wines, more about fine dining touches, like Port and Cognac.

Q: I've noticed two things about your design: that your bar does not have a busy-looking backbar area stocked with liquor and supplies and that the bar is the first thing you walk into when you enter the restaurant. Are there reasons for this?

A: Absolutely. We describe our concepts as "neighborhood restaurants." I don't want people to come in and eat and leave. I want 'em to have a whole package: to come in, relax with a glass of wine or even water! It's a relaxing buffer zone between the outside and the restaurant. I don't like to rush the guest.

Q: What kind of education do you think a person should have to go into bar or restaurant management?

A: Personally I feel it is important for a person in a business environment to have a degree or some type of education from a business point of view—to understand how different industries combine and work together to be successful. My intention when I went to college was to have more than one business. I didn't know exactly what I was going to do, but I know that I was going to be able to do more than one aspect of a business. I was not going to restrict myself to only one area!

In a bar or restaurant, we are really a type of manufacturing business. We have raw products coming in and, at a certain time of day, we have to produce a finished product. That takes more than people to do. You need equipment, service experts, chemicals, produce, and they all have to be on hand and working correctly to produce what you need to produce. So I think business sense, financial sense, is mandatory to be in this business; and second is communication, to keep yourself in check and your employees in check.

Q: In a bar/restaurant operation, how important is the bar in the overall profit mix?

A: The beverage program, as a whole, can make or break a restaurant. It has the most profit margin of any product in the restaurant. The food may keep them coming back, but it is the liquor that pays the bills. So it is important to build a good bar crowd, of people who don't necessarily stay for dinner.

For every $100 I sell, I want liquor, beer, and wine to be $35 of that, and food to be $65. That is the ideal ratio. For a fine-dining restaurant with, say, $2 million in sales per year, that means at least $700,000 running through the bar, much of it in cash. It has to be correct; it has to balance at the end of the night. So you see how important security is.

I also regularly analyze how much of each—liquor, beer, wine—is being sold. There's sometimes a good reason for a change—it's hot outside, so people are drinking more beer or frozen drinks and less wine. Other times it points out a weakness you have to correct.

Then it is important to share this information with the staff. A good waitstaff is a good sales force, and salespeople can get bored if you never give them anything new or interesting to sell. So always keep them in the loop, with training and regular meetings. And make sure they know how important the bar business is to the restaurant's overall profitability.

CHAPTER 4
BAR EQUIPMENT

Complete familiarity with the bartender's working environment—the underbar, backbar, and equipment—is a requirement of good bar design because it is essential to profitable bar management. To produce the drinks ordered, of the quality desired, with the speed and efficiency needed to satisfy the customers and to meet the profit goal, the right equipment must be in place. One key to good bar design is known as the *one-step rule,* that is, the bartender at his or her pouring station should be able to make 90 percent of all drinks ordered by taking no more than one step from the central point of that station.

With the information in this chapter you will be able to accomplish this. You will also be "one step" ahead of many managers, who do not fully comprehend equipment needs, the effects of equipment on drink quality, and the limitations that equipment and space can impose on a drink menu. Furthermore managers talk more with interior designers and equipment dealers than with bartenders about how to set up this critical portion of their businesses.

The purpose of this chapter is to describe the basic equipment essential to any bar, as well as the alternatives that can be used to meet a wide variety of needs.

THIS CHAPTER WILL HELP YOU . . .

- Plan a complete pouring station.
- Choose among various methods of measuring and pouring liquors.
- Choose among various methods of pouring carbonated mixers.
- Determine the kind of ice needed for a given bar and the size of the ice machine.
- Install the required equipment for washing glasses.

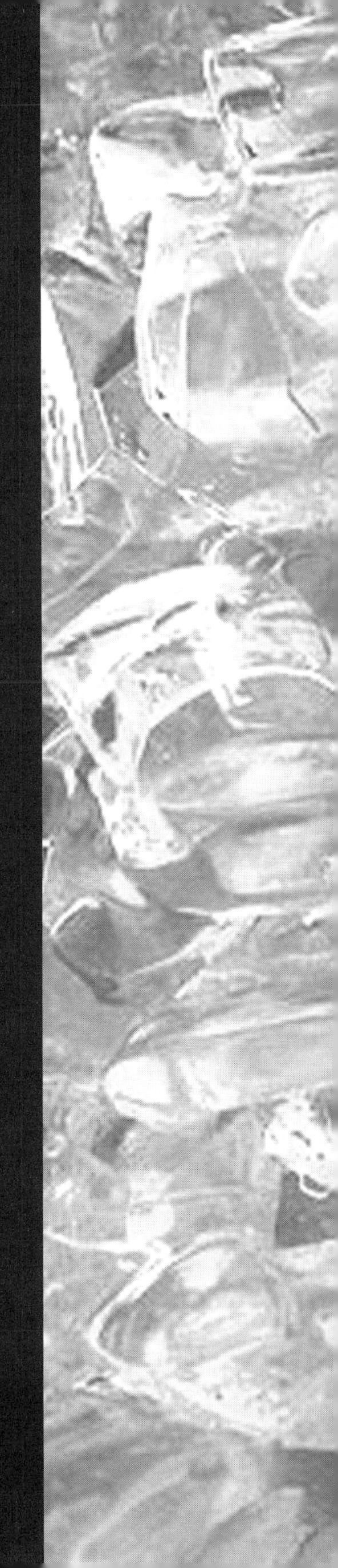

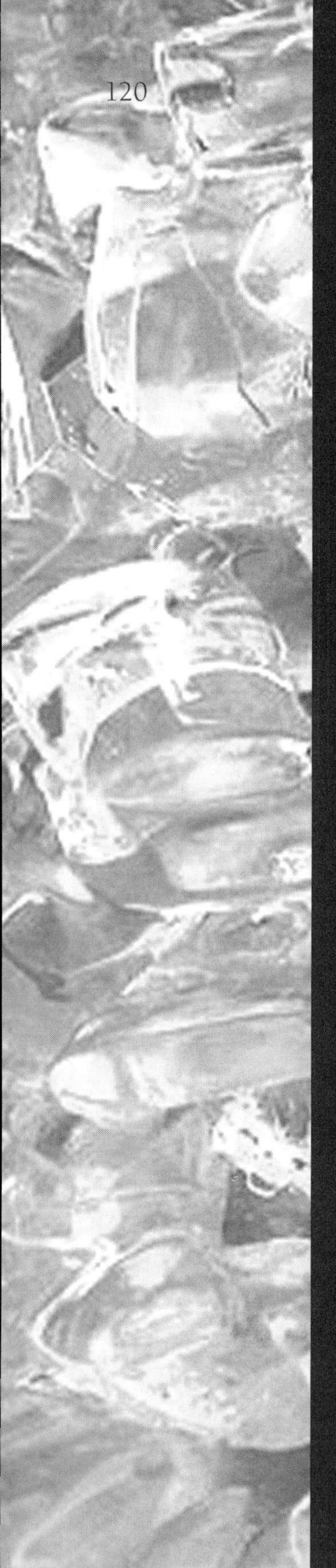

- Provide for the special needs of draft-beer service.
- Determine the space needed for refrigeration, dry storage, liquor stock, and glassware.
- Assemble the hand tools and equipment needed to mix and serve drinks and prepare garnishes.
- Select glassware appropriate to the drinks to be served.
- Choose a cash register or point-of-sale (POS) system that works well for your operation.

When Abe Lincoln was selling whiskey back in the 1830s, he did not use much equipment at all. In fact his customers often brought their own Mason jars into Abe's general store in New Salem, Illinois, and Abe would pour whiskey out of the barrel tap into the jars.

Earlier in colonial taverns drinks were poured from heavy glass decanters into tumblers, mugs, and tankards. Mixed drinks were stirred with a toddy stick (an early form of a **muddler**) or a loggerhead, a metal bar on a long handle, heated in the open fire, then thrust into the mug or punch bowl to stir a hot toddy or flip, an old-fashioned drink that usually contains an egg and/or cream. Along with the beverage equipment there might have been a *dice box;* people would roll dice to see who would pay for the drinks.

In the saloons of the Old West customers poured their own whiskey, neat, from the bottle set on the counter by the bartender. By the mid-1800s hotel bars were serving mixed drinks, often with ice that was scraped, chipped, or pounded from large cakes transported from frozen lakes or rivers. By 1890 a hotel might have had its own ice machine, which could make a large block of ice in 15 hours. Mixed drinks spawned tools for mixing: barspoons, measures, shakers, and seltzer bottles. The cash register was first used in a tavern in 1879. Most of today's bar equipment can be traced to post-Prohibition days. It fits handily into compact spaces and is designed for both high-speed individual service and easy manipulation by that master of dexterity and showmanship, the bartender. We will take a closer look at this equipment.

UNDERBAR AND BACKBAR EQUIPMENT

Several interrelated components of the pouring station each require some portion of square footage: beverage dispensing, beer dispensing and storage, ice making and storage, and glass washing and storage, as well as a blender, bar tools, a cash register, and a printer.

As a general rule plan to spend $1,000 per linear foot of bar to outfit it with equipment. With the exception of the cash register and printer, all equipment must meet local health-department requirements, which typically follow the sanitation standards set by National Sanitation Foundation International (NSFI). Equipment meeting these standards carries the NSFI seal, shown in Figure 4.1. The major pieces of underbar equipment have stainless-steel surfaces. This makes them durable and easy to clean and sanitize. Stainless steel stands up to the harshest chemicals yet looks good and can be polished to an attractive sheen.

FIGURE 4.1 The National Sanitation Foundation International seal of approval. Courtesy NSF International, Ann Arbor, Michigan.

Work surfaces supporting underbar equipment are a standard 30 inches high, with a depth of 16 inches to the backsplash at the rear. Units from the same manufacturer fit side by side and give the appearance of being continuous. Each piece of equipment either stands on legs that are 6 or more inches high, for access to plumbing and ease of cleaning, or is flush with the floor. The legs have *bullet feet* (tapered, to resemble bullets), again, for easy cleaning. All these features are NSFI standards. The feet are adjustable to accommodate uneven flooring.

Figures 4.2 and 4.3 show the underbar and backbar of the hotel bar shown in Chapter 3, Figure 3.11. They serve the hotel's cocktail lounge, dining room, and coffee shop from three stations. The station at the center of Figure 4.2, where you see ice bins, bottle wells, and condiment tray, is the pouring station used to serve customers seated or standing at the front bar; it also is used as the pickup station for cocktail waitresses serving the lounge. In the bottom right in this figure, where you see a second condiment tray on the counter, is the pickup station for the dining room, seen from the waiter's side. This station also is used to serve customers seated or standing at the bar. The third station, in the top left, serves the coffee shop. It is also shown from the waiter's side in the bottom right of Figure 4.3.

All three stations are set up in the morning, and a single bartender works from all three, according to where the calls for drinks come in. Two bartenders are on duty for the busy late-afternoon and evening periods. Serving personnel garnish the drinks at the pickup stations; notice the condiment trays on the bar top (O in both figures). A shelf below on the server's side holds ashtrays, napkins, and other server supplies. Railings (M) set these pickup stations off from customer use. There are also return stations for used glasses; notice the waste dumps below (L).

Equipment for Mixing Drinks

Each of the stations in Figures 4.2 and 4.3 is outfitted with the following equipment:

- Ice chest and ice bin (A)
- Containers for bottles: bottle wells (B)—and speed rails (C)
- Handgun for dispensing soft-drink mixes (D)
- Mixer (E) and blender (F) on recessed shelf
- Glasses: overhead, on the backbar, on drainboards, almost anywhere there is room

The centerpiece of any pouring station is an **ice chest** or **ice bin** (A), with or without **bottle wells** (B), usually with a **speed rail** (C) attached to the front. This piece of equipment is variously known as a **cocktail station, cocktail unit,** or **beverage center,** or colloquially, as a **jockey box.** Figure 4.4 shows a complete **cocktail station.** Its centerpiece is a 30-inch ice chest with a sliding or removable cover. The front of the unit is a 3½-foot bottle rail (speed rail), with a shorter hands-on rail on the front. On the left of the ice chest is a double row of condiment cups, used to hold garnishes, which are chilled by the ice. Often such equipment has bottle wells rather than condiment cups; they are used to keep juices and prepared mixes cold. On the right-hand side of the unit is a blender station, es-

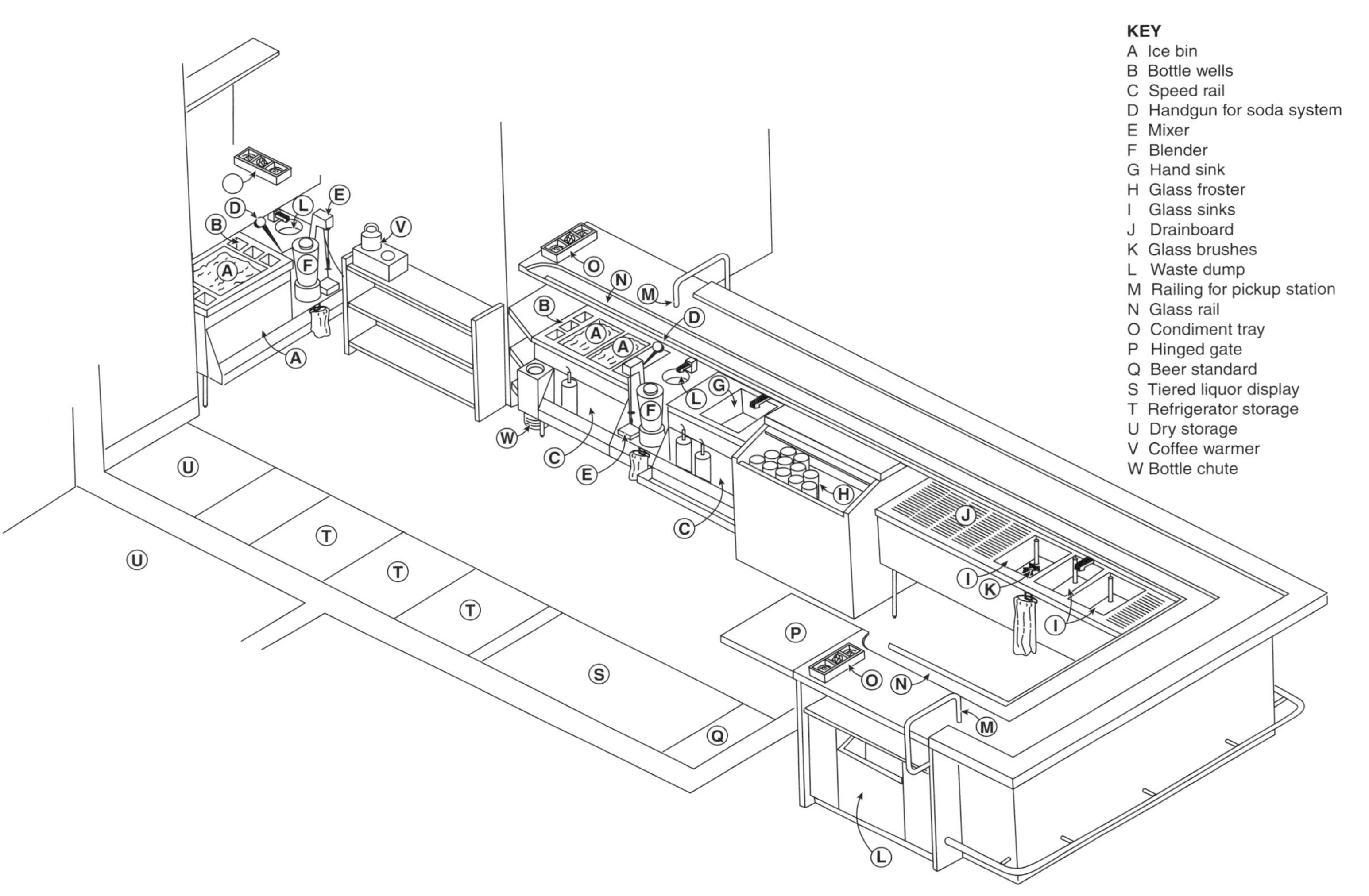

FIGURE 4.2 The underbar of hotel bar in Figure 3.11.

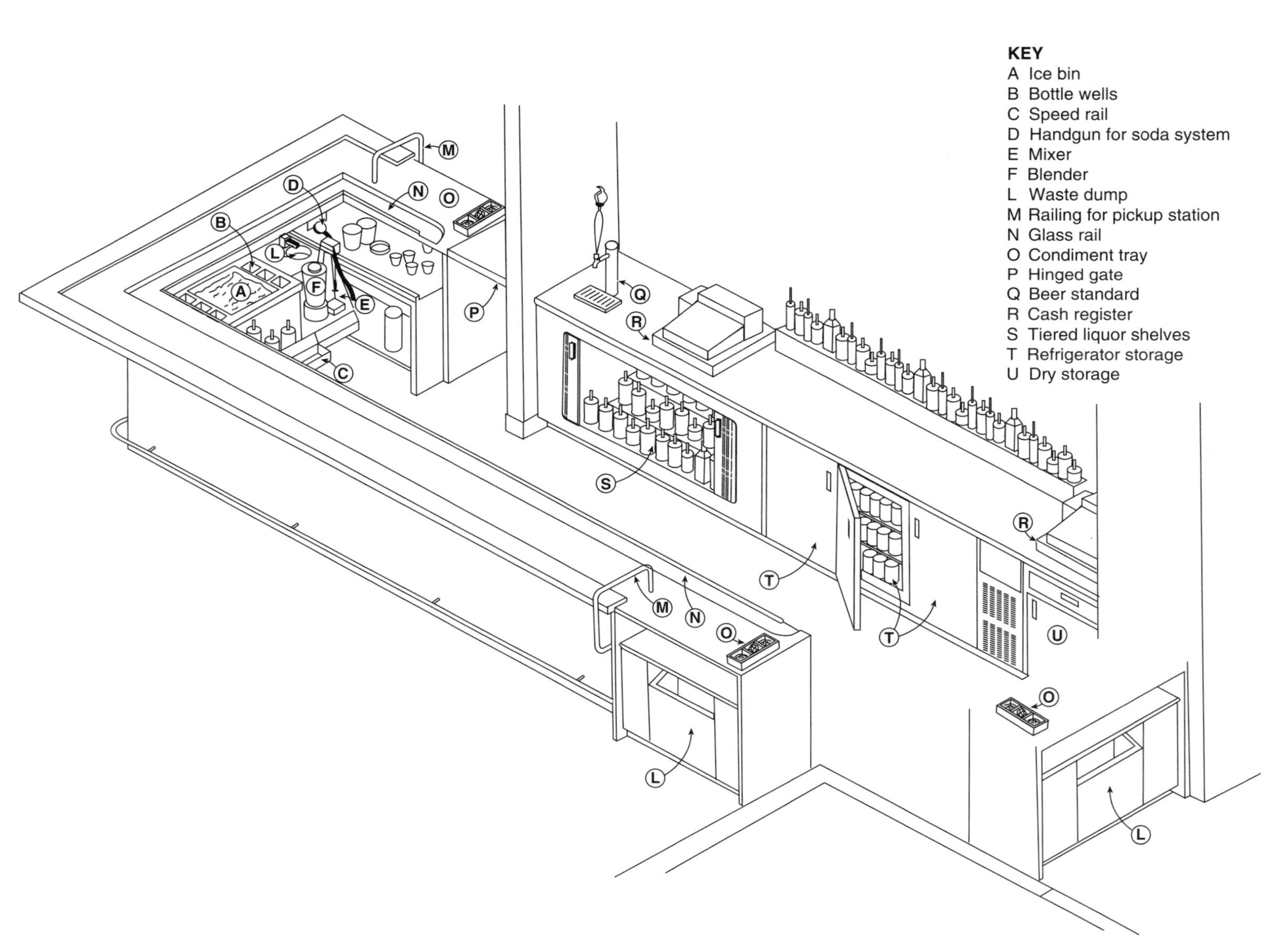

FIGURE 4.3 The backbar of hotel bar in Figure 3.11.

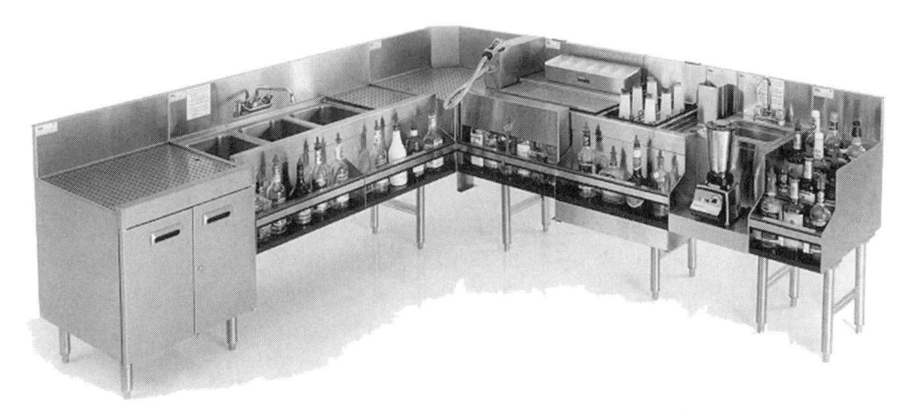

FIGURE 4.4 A complete cocktail station. Courtesy of Glastender, Inc., Saginaw, Michigan.

sentially a recessed shelf for the station's blender and mixer with a special dump sink and faucet (behind the machines). A glass shelf and a towel rack complete the unit. Figures 4.2 and 4.3 display all of these elements in slightly different configurations at the three pouring stations. In addition to bottle rails on the cocktail stations, there is a double rail on the hand sink. Not shown in any of these pictures is another type of ice chest with a divider, which enables a station to have both cubed and crushed ice.

A speed rail typically contains the most frequently poured liquors (usually Scotch, bourbon, or a blended whiskey, as well as gin, vodka, rum, tequila, and brandy). The standard variety changes with the area and the clientele. The liquor supply at a bartender's station is known collectively as the **well,** and the brands used there are called **well brands, house brands** or **pouring brands.** These are the brands that the house pours when a drink is ordered by type rather than by brand name. Popular **call brands,** brands customers "call for" by name, vermouths, a couple of bottles of house wines, and the current favorites in liqueurs are also set up within easy reach. Additional liquors—more call brands, liqueurs, premium brandies—are typically displayed on the backbar. Many bars have tiered liquor shelves containing reserve supplies as part of the backbar itself, such as (S) in Figure 4.3.

Dispensing Beverages

At each station of the bar is the **cobra gun** that dispenses the carbonated mixes (see Figure 4.5). It consists of a head with a nozzle and pushbuttons that deliver plain water and carbonated mixes (one per button), such as club soda, tonic water, soft drinks, and Collins mix—whatever half-dozen you choose. Behind the scenes are bulk supplies of concentrated syrups and a tank of carbon dioxide (CO_2) under pressure. Syrup lines run from each syrup supply to the underbar and through an ice-cold plate on the bottom of each ice chest, made especially to quick-chill them.

FIGURE 4.5 Handguns for a soda system. Photo courtesy of Wunder-Bar Automatic, Controls, Inc., Vacaville, California.

The CO_2 line goes to a motor-driven **carbonator** under the ice chest where the CO_2 is mixed with filtered water. A carbonated water line then runs from the carbonator through the cold plate, as does a line with plain filtered water. Finally all of the syrup and water lines run through a **flexhose**, which is flexible metal hose, to the head of the gun. Here, the syrup mixes with carbonated water in a 5:1 ratio at the touch of the proper button, or plain chilled, filtered water is dispensed. Together all of this is known as a **postmix** dispensing system because the soda is mixed at the time of service.

There are also **premix systems**, in which the complete beverage is supplied in bulk containers that have already been mixed at the manufacturing plant. In a premix system a separate supply of CO_2 is needed to propel the product from the container to the dispensing head. The premix lines from the bulk supplies are run through ice or a cold plate to cool the product. A good postmix or premix drink should be cooled to between 37°F to 42°F in order for it to maintain good carbonation. Premix systems are seldom used in today's bars, with the exception of portable bars for special-occasion use. Because postmix systems are far cheaper per drink (about two-fifths the cost) and are much more compact (about one fifth the size) than premix systems they are generally the better choice.

You will want to establish and maintain high-quality standards for your carbonated beverages. Doing so is a way to control their costs and to ensure that the drinks made with them will be satisfactory to customers. Four primary factors are involved in dispensing carbonated beverages:

- ***Water quality.*** Carbonated drinks are about 80 percent water, not even counting the ice that may be put into a mixed drink. If the water does not taste good, neither will your beverages. Filtered water is a requirement in most areas.
- ***Ingredient temperature.*** Water needs to be very cold to make good soda; otherwise, it melts the ice in the drink too quickly. The optimum temperature is close to the freezing point of water (32°F), and the chilling equipment in your system must be sufficient to provide this. Keep in mind that heat accelerates the aging process in carbonated drink syrups and mixes. As a result it is important that these items be stored in cool areas, ideally at temperatures that do not exceed 65°F, and where they are protected from direct sunlight.
- ***Mix ratio.*** Correctly proportioned drinks contain the right amounts of syrup, water, and CO_2—and no more. Any variation will affect the taste of the drink. You should regularly taste-test each and every liquid that comes out of your cobra gun. Amazingly few bartenders remember to do so until a customer complains, "My drink is flat!" Smell the liquid, as you would a fine wine; sip a bit of it, then hold it in your mouth to get the full impact of both flavor and carbonation.
- ***Carbonation.*** A good carbonator (the pump that takes the CO_2 from the tank and injects it into the water/syrup mix) provides just the right amount of fizz to the product. This piece of equipment must be sized to your bar's overall drink

volume, so there is no fluctuation in the amount of carbonation during peak demand periods. Also, liquids in improperly sealed or stored CO_2 containers can lose their effervescence; they should be stored at cool temperatures.

Neither a premix nor a postmix system comes ready-made. To assemble a postmix system, you must purchase the gun and carbonator from one manufacturer; the cold plate is part of the cocktail station; the syrups come from the individual beverage distributors; the CO_2 from a CO_2 supplier. Then all of these components are assembled on-site. Usually the purchase and assembly of supplies and refills can be arranged through a single soda distributor. Of course you can also use soft drinks and mixers in bottles, purchased and stored by the case. However, this is much more expensive than a postmix system—in terms of portion cost, labor, time, and storage space—both at the bar and in the storeroom. Nevertheless there are bars that use bottles by choice. Why? Chilled, bottled soda tastes better and keeps its carbonation longer (after all, the bubbles were put in at the factory), and discriminating customers know the difference and like to see the label. Bottled mixers are a specialty item used by bars in which a top-quality drink is part of the total concept.

Automated Pouring Systems

At many bars today you'll find that pouring is completely automated, not just for the soda system, but also for beer, wines, juices, and liquor. A number of electronic dispensing systems on the market pour preset amounts and count each drink. Different systems measure and pour anywhere from half a dozen well brands, for instance, to a complete spectrum of mixed drinks. Some systems use a handgun mounted on a flexhose that is similar to the gun for a soda system. Buttons on the gun activate the flow from 1.75-liter or 750-milliliter bottles mounted upside down on the walls of a remote storeroom. A preset amount of liquor is delivered, and counters keep track of each drink. A *long shot* and a *short shot* can also be poured.

Another kind of dispenser is composed of a series of faucets, each activated by touching a glass to a button under the faucet. Systems like these can dispense and control perhaps three-fourths of the volume of liquor poured. These systems, or **dispensing towers** as some are known, can portion between 12 and 32 different liquors, up to 16 per bar handgun. Beyond this the call brands, liqueurs, juices, cream, and other liquids can always be dispensed by hand in the usual way. In still another type of system, electronic dispensing equipment is integrated or interfaced with a computerized cash register. To operate this system the bartender or server must ring up a guest check before drinks can be poured. This offers high control, but the precheck function can slow down operations in a fast, high-volume operation. Systems can be connected to a printer for reports that detail each server or bartender's sales or output.

Automatic liquor-dispensing systems require a sizable investment, and not everybody reacts favorably to them. Some bartenders are unhappy with mechanical pouring, and some customers dislike them as well; the service seems less personal, and they suspect that liquor poured out of sight is inferior to the brands that they can see being poured at the bar rail. Another common problem is blocked lines. Still another is that liquors that are not ordered frequently sit in the lines for long periods of time and may acquire an off taste. On the plus side, automatic systems cut pouring costs in several ways. These include the savings that come from using large-size bottles; the savings of speed; the savings of getting the last ounce out of the bottle that, in hand-pouring, clings to the bottle's side; and the savings in labor thanks to faster pouring (it is often so much faster that you eliminate the need for an extra bartender at peak periods). One great advantage of an automatic system is the consistency of the drink served, which is a desirable goal that is hard to achieve with hand-pouring, even measured hand-pouring. The gun also makes for a smooth, swift operation, with less handling of glasses.

A major selling point of the automatic dispensing system is that it provides tighter liquor controls. This does not mean you automatically eliminate losses: There are still spills, mistakes, and pilferage in any bar operation. Drinks are measured and counted, but the count must still be checked daily against sales and inventory. It is far easier to spot a discrepancy with an automatic system, but the cause of it must still be removed to make this type of policing effective.

Each enterprise must weigh these and other savings against the cost of the equipment in relation to its volume of business. In a small operation an automatic system might not be worth its high price tag. In a high-volume bar it might be what makes that volume possible and pays for itself in just a couple of years—or less.

(a)

(b)

FIGURE 4.6 (*a*) A blender (*b*) and a spindle blender. Courtesy of Hamilton Beach /Proctor-Silex, Inc., Glen Allen, Virginia.

Mixers and Blenders

Referring to the illustrations of pouring stations again, you see a mixer (E) on the shelf next to the cocktail unit. It is like the machine that makes shakes at McDonald's, and in this book we refer to it as a **shake mixer** or **spindle blender** (see Figures 4.6*a* and *b*). The mixer has a shaft coming down from the top that agitates the contents of its cup. It is used for cocktails made with fruit juices, eggs, sugar, cream, or any other ingredient that does not blend readily with spirits. This mixer is one of today's mechanical substitutes for the hand shaker. Countertop models can make up to five drinks at once; hand-held models make individual drinks. Some models have three height settings to accommodate different sizes of stainless-steel mixing cups. A water source and/or drain will be necessary if you are using a multiple-head spindle blender.

The machine on the shelf beside the shake mixer is a **blender** (F) of a different type, which takes the mixing process one step further. Blades in the bottom of its cup can grind, puree, and otherwise refine ingredients that are put into it. Some drinks that incorporate food or ice, such as Banana Daiquiris and Frozen Margaritas, require such a blender (Figure 4.6*a*). Blenders used strictly for making drinks are called **bar mixers**, and are not to be confused with shake mixers. Many bars have both.

The typical commercial blender has two speeds, but you can purchase them with variable-speed controls or a *pulse* function. Some blenders can be preprogrammed to mix the most popular drink types unattended and shut off automatically, freeing up the bartender's time, however brief, for other duties. The body of the blender has sealed seams for sanitation reasons, and it usually rests on a heavy base with rubber feet to keep it stable. A toggle switch activates the motor, which turns a set of four or six blades attached to a clutch. Look for a blender with blades that are easy to remove for cleaning. Also look for sturdy containers in which to do the blending because they will be used a great deal. Containers can be made of glass, polycarbonate, or stainless steel, with a single handle or two handles. The container top can also be a single piece, usually rubber or vinyl, or a two-piece **filler cap**, so that you can add ingredients safely while the blender is in use.

Commercial bar mixers are larger than those made for home kitchens. They are identified by the capacity of their containers, from 24 ounces to 1 gallon. Their motors range in size from ¼ to 3 horsepower. When it comes to blenders, the lightest-duty commercial model has a one-fourth to one-third horsepower motor; if you mix more than 75 to 100 drinks in a day, you should purchase at least a medium-duty model with a 1 horsepower motor.

Bars that specialize in a particular frozen drink may have a **frozen drink dispenser**, also called a **slush freezer** or **cocktail freezer.** Similar to the soft-serve ice-cream machines at Dairy Queen, it soft-freezes a large quantity of premixed drinks. Commercial-machine capacities range from 8½ quarts to 72 quarts. You pour gallons of, for example, liquid Strawberry Daiquiri or Margarita Mix into the top of the machine, and in a few moments it is frozen to a slush. To serve an individual drink, you hold a glass under the tap and move a lever.

The frozen-drink dispenser pumps air into the liquid mix, increasing its volume and giving it a soft-frozen consistency. The percentage of air forced into the mix is called its **overrun.** For example, a 100-percent overrun produces exactly twice the volume of the mix that was put into the machine. Therefore, 16 ounces of mix with a 100-percent overrun produces a 32-ounce frozen drink, a 50-percent overrun produces a 24-ounce drink, and so on. In *gravity-feed machines,* the liquid mix is placed in a hopper and flows as needed into a cylinder below, where it is frozen, scraped out of the cylinder, and dispensed. These are inexpensive and easy to maintain and clean. More expensive pressurized machines which use an air pump to drive mix into the freezer chamber, then force it out through a spigot. Pressurized machines can control overrun percentages better than gravity-feed machines. With either type of machine the hopper should be kept fairly full of drink mix for the machine to do its job well.

At the end of the day you drain off the frozen-drink contents that are left and store them in the refrigerator for later use. Nightly cleaning of the machine is especially important, to prevent off-tasting drinks and to keep the cylinder and hoses from becoming gummy from the sweet, sticky ingredients. Regular maintenance might also include changing the blades inside the machine periodically, to prevent them from becoming too dull to scrape frozen product off the sides of the freezer chamber and to keep things well mixed.

Glassware

Elsewhere in this chapter you will find much more information about glassware trends, types, and styles, but let's begin with a brief discussion of what you will *do with* glasses at the bar, including washing, storing, and frosting, and so on. At a typical bar, glasses are everywhere, posing a significant storage problem that must be addressed in the design phase of the entire bar area. Think long and hard about exactly how many glasses you will need per bar shift, and plan accordingly for their storage, washing, drying, and clean landing space between uses.

Stemware is sometimes stored in overhead racks, arranged according to type, although this has fallen out of favor in recent years with health inspectors and may no longer be legal in some areas. When glasses are set upside down on drainboards, ridged shelves or heavy plastic netting are health-code requirements. These allow air to reach the insides of the glasses and keep bacteria from growing. You must resist the temptation to put towels under netting to catch the runoff from wet glasses because this cuts off the air, negating the effect and making the problem worse. Unused glasses must be kept dust-free, both for appearance and for sanitation reasons.

Bar Sinks and Glasswashers

Equipment for washing (both glasses and hands) is specified in great detail in local health codes. It typically includes these items, which are shown in Figure 4.2:

- A three- or four-compartment sink (I)
- Drainboards (J)
- Special glass-washing brushes (K)
- A hand sink (G) with a towel rack (attached to blender station)
- A waste dump (L)

A three-compartment sink with drainboards is usually a single piece of equipment placed near a bartending station or between two stations (see Figure 4.7). One compartment is for washing, one for rinsing, and one for *sanitizing,* or killing bacteria with a chemical solution. Dimensions will vary from 60 to 96 inches in length, with a foot-long drainboard on one side or both sides. Each sink compartment is 10 inches wide and about 14 inches from front to back, with a depth of 10 to 11 inches. In a four-compartment sink the fourth compartment is usually used as a waste dump, a netting is placed in the bottom to catch the debris from used glasses. You will need to decide if you want each sink to have its own faucet,

FIGURE 4.7 A three-compartment sink with drainboards. Courtesy of Glastender, Inc., Saginaw, Michigan.

or if two will suffice—each one can swivel to serve two sinks. Plumbing requirements are slightly different in either case.

Glass brushes stand up to the soapy water of the wash sink. Figure 4.8 shows a motorized model, which is highly recommended if glasses are washed by hand. The bartender places a glass over the center brush and presses a button to make the bristles spin. With hand models the bartender twists the glass around and between the brushes to clean the inside and the rim. Next the glass goes into the rinse sink, then into the sanitizing solution, and finally onto the drainboard, upside down, to air-dry. It is best to air-dry glassware becasue towel-drying is inefficient and can leave bits of towel fuzz on the clean glasses.

FIGURE 4.8 Motorized glass brushes. Courtesy of Hamilton Beach/Proctor-Silex, Inc., Glen Allen, Virginia.

Stricter sanitation laws and labor savings are two major reasons for the increased use of automatic **glasswashers** (seen in Figure 4.9). In fact more and more health departments are requiring them. This machine is a type of small dishwasher that fits neatly under the underbar or backbar. It washes and rinses glasses with tap water, provides a final high-temperature rinse to sanitize them, and blow-dries them. Wash temperatures range from 150°F to 212°F for quick drying. An advantage of higher temperatures is that the faster the glasses dry, the less likely they are to emerge with water spots. A full cycle of washing, rinsing, and drying takes about 20 minutes and uses about 3 gallons of water for each fill, at a water pressure of 20 pounds per square inch (psi). Some models have a variety of "cycles" for different types of glassware. You might also look for a glasswasher that provides a final rinse of cool water, which eliminates cool-down time and makes the glasses ready to use as soon as they are clean.

FIGURE 4.9 A rotary glasswasher. Courtesy of Glastender, Inc., Saginaw, Michigan.

Some models of glasswashers, like commercial dishwashers, require the ability to vent away the steam and heat created by the machine. Be sure to ask before you buy. There are so-called high-temperature (180°F) and low-temperature (140°F) machines. The high temps require ventilation; the low temps do not. It is usually impractical, if not downright impossible, to vent steam from glasswashers in a bar area, so some bar owners opt for a sanitizing system that uses chlorine or other chemicals instead of super-hot water during the rinse cycle. Detergent suppliers sell, install, and maintain them. Typically the sanitizing system is mounted under the bar, next to the dish machine. The system works by injecting a preset amount of chemical solution directly into the rinse water. Some cities require periodic testing of the system to make sure that the solution is strong enough to sanitize effectively. Figure 4.10 lists different guidelines for chemical concentrations and rinse-water temperatures. Some words of caution: No matter what the manufacturers claim about the cost-saving advantages of low-temperature units, there is nothing worse than that soapy taste on the rim of a glass that results when the types or amounts of chemicals used are incorrect. Also, if you put other utensils in your glasswasher, some of them, especially those made of aluminum, pewter, or silverplate, might react poorly to chemical sanitizing systems.

Another problem for bars where space is in short supply is that glasswashers require about 4 linear feet of underbar area. The machine itself takes up 2 feet,

Specifications for the Chemical Sanitizing Rinse

Sanitizing Solution Type	*Final Rise Temperature*	*Concentration*
Chlorine solution	min: 49°C (120°F)[a]	min: 50 ppm (as NaOCl)
Iodine solution	min: 24°C (75°F)	min: 12.5 ppm, max: 25 ppm
Quaternary ammonium solution	min: 24°C (75°F)	min: 150 ppm max: 400 ppm

[a]For glasswashing machines that use a chlorine sanatizing solution, the maximum final rinse temperature specified by the manufacturer shall be at least 24°C (75°F).

Source: NSF International, Ann Arbor, Michigan.

FIGURE 4.10 Data-plate specifications for the Chemical Sanitizing Rinse. Courtesy NSF International, Ann Arbor, Michigan.

and there should be a foot of drainboard space on either side of it, as well as a dump sink on the soiled-glass side. The advantage is that the machine can easily wash up to 500 glasses per hour, giving bartenders more time to prepare drinks. There are also conveyor-type washers, capable of cleaning up to 1,000 glasses per hour, for use in high-volume operations.

You might be wondering why not just wash bar glasses in a regular, kitchen dish machine, especially if the bar is located where food is also served. Doing so has several drawbacks. Glasses have to be carried back and forth, increasing the possibility of breakage. Different kinds of dishracks are required for glasses, also to prevent breakage. The other good reason to wash glasses separately from other dishes is that even a trace of grease on a glass can spoil a drink or the foamy head on a beer.

At the hotel bar pictured in Figures 4.2 and 4.3, each pickup station has a waste dump (L) on the server's side of the bar. Cocktail servers returning with dirty glasses dump the debris here. Behind the bar are removable trashcans.

A bottle chute (W on Figure 4.2) conveys empty beer and soda bottles to the basement below the bar for disposal. Empty liquor bottles are accumulated at the bar to be turned in to the storeroom in exchange for full bottles. In a bar with a storeroom below it, a bottle chute can convey the empties directly to the storeroom.

REFRIGERATION NEEDS

You will need a way to chill glasses for straight-up cocktails, frozen drinks, and ice-cream drinks. Some bars make a special promotional point of serving drinks in frosted glasses or beer in frosted mugs. This requires a **glass froster,** a top-opening freezer that chills glasses at temperatures around 0°F (H on Figure 4.2). When glasses are removed from the freezer, they sport refreshing coats of frost. Glasses and mugs placed in a glass froster must be dry to begin with; otherwise a thin coat of ice will form on them. Then, when a drink is poured into the glass or mug, it might stick to the lip of the drinker or the ice might dilute the drink.

If you do not have sufficient space for a glass froster, you must have another way to chill glasses for straight-up cocktails and frozen and ice-cream drinks. If you have refrigerator space, you can use it to frost a wet glass without making ice. The other alternative is to ice a glass by hand with cube ice just before the drink is poured.

A **bottle chiller** or **bottle cooler** is available for quick-chilling wines. There are reach-in or reach-down units, some wall-mounted with glass fronts that have the additional advantage of showing off the wines inside. The advantage of a bottle chiller is that a minimum inventory of white wines may be kept under refrigeration close to the bar area, while the rest can be stored elsewhere until needed. Bottle chillers can be used in wait stations, too.

Cold storage in the form of an underbar refrigerator is a requirement for most bars. These units, miniatures of standard commercial refrigerators, range in size from 60 to 90 inches in length, of the correct depth and height to fit in the underbar or backbar space. They provide from 5 to 15 cubic feet of storage space. Although this is not much, it is enough for common bar perishables, such as garnishes and dairy products.

It is not sufficient to purchase a mini-refrigerator for home use and expect it to do the hard work of an underbar unit. Health departments do not allow the enamel or porcelain exterior finishes of home units in a commercial setting, and the coveted NSFI seal will be required. Sturdy doors and handles, the ability to self-clean and drain wastewater away from the unit, and a warranty are among the desired features. Think about how the doors open and to what extent they will get in the way on busy nights. Consider a sliding door instead of one that opens out into the bartender's path. Look for the biggest internal cabinet capacity you can get for the size of refrigerator that your bar can accommodate.

Ice and Ice Machines

The debate among serious cocktail aficionados may never be settled: Does the use of ice interfere with the taste of spirits, or enhance it? Either way, a cocktail bar could not operate at all without a plentiful supply of ice. Furthermore the hotter the climate, the more important ice becomes as part of most drinks' appeal. The most inventive use of ice that we have heard recently is from an enterprising bar owner who arranged to have a chunk of an actual North Atlantic iceberg brought into the bar; customers were charged $1 extra for use of actual "iceberg ice" in their drinks!

Fortunately there are less complicated ways to chill a cocktail. Every bar operation has an **icemaker,** or ice machine; some have more than one. If the bar is large enough the icemaker can be part of the underbar or backbar but often this is not possible. If the ice maker must be installed elsewhere, be sure to design the bar space so that there is plenty of room for ice storage. The typical ice bin is 24 to 36 inches in length, and its capacity varies from 100 pounds (for a 24-inch bin) to 150 pounds (for a 36-inch bin).

Technology has resulted in terrific improvements for ice machines. Today you can either flip a switch on a modern icemaker and it cleans itself, or program the machine electronically to change its output based on daily or seasonal demands. Regardless of the technological capabilities you want, before you select an icemaker you must decide what size and shape of cube ice to use. Why? Because different sizes and shapes of cube ice serve different needs. Large cubes melt more slowly, smaller sizes stack better in the glass, round cubes fit the glass better at the edges; and rectangular cubes stack better than round ones, leaving fewer voids; and in a fast pour, liquor hitting a round cube can splash out of the glass. A medium-sized cube will suffice if you do not have any special needs. Otherwise your ice-size-and-shape decisions will be made based on your clientele, drink menu, glassware, type of pour, and speed of service. If you're using an ice dispenser, the cubes should also be small enough to fit into it and be dispensed easily without clogging or jamming the dispenser. If you are making a lot of blender drinks, large cubes will

KEEPING ICE CLEAN

Although not often thought of as a food item, cube ice is consumed by your customers, and it needs to stay as clean and sanitary as anything else you serve.

Clean ice starts with a clean machine. Cleaning and sanitizing your ice machine means removing built-up mineral deposits, algae, and slime from the machine's parts. According to Frank Murphy, the national training director for GCS Services, this process should be completed at least every six months.

"Cleaning and sanitizing is essential to make sure the very delicate cycle of making ice is not interrupted and that every cube looks the same as every other cube," Murphy says.

Use the following tips for keeping your machine and ice clean between big cleanings:

- Always have staff wash their hands before removing ice, and always have them use a plastic ice scoop.
- Keep the plastic ice scoop clean. Wash it frequently with a neutral cleaner and always rinse thoroughly.
- Do not store food and beverage items or containers in the ice bin. It is not a refrigerated storage space and should not act as one.
- Clean the bin liner frequently with a neutral cleaner, rinsing thoroughly.
- Prevent corrosion on the exterior of your machine by wiping it occasionally with a clean, soft cloth. To remove oil and dirt, use a damp cloth with a neutral cleaner.
- Check the air filter on air-cooled models at least twice per month. If the filter get clogged use warm water and a neutral cleaner to wash it out.
- Check the condenser (if your machine has one) once a year, and clean it with a brush or a vacuum cleaner. More frequent cleaning may be required depending on the location of your ice machine.

Source: Restaurants and Institutions, Cahners Business Information, A Division of Reed Elsevier, Inc.

make your blender blades work all that much harder, and possibly compromise the consistency of the drink. Consider these factors when deciding on the type and size of cube ice to use:

- ***Displacement.*** Cubes should "pack" well into the glass, but not appear to. You never want a customer to think he or she is paying for a drink that is mostly ice. The shape of the cube also determines how much of its surface touches the liquid and, therefore, how quickly it works to chill the drink. Cube ice should be used for pure spirits such as single-malt scotches and plain bourbon on the rocks. Cube ice chills the liquor without melting too quickly to water it down.
- ***Clarity.*** Ice should be completely clear, made with pure, sanitary drinking water that produces no off taste, color, or odor. (This includes not tasting or smelling

like water-purifying chemicals.) For this reason, distilled water makes the clearest and most neutral-tasting ice.

- ***Density.*** How "hard" or "soft" the ice is frozen determines how quickly it interacts with the drink. The cubes also should not be so soft that they stick together in the bin. Local temperature and humidity affect density, the location of the icemaker in your operation, and its temperature setting.

Ice quality is important enough to a bar business that if possible, ice should be dumped out at the end of a workday and fresh ice made for the next day. As you probably know from home ice-making in your own refrigerator, ice that is left to sit can quickly absorb odors and become stale. (A bartender's trick from *Sante* magazine: When faced with "old" ice and no time to make fresh, it can be quickly rinsed with warm water just before use.)

Ice-making machines are refrigeration units. A pump inside an ice-making machine circulates water from a tank. You will want a machine with a good filtration system to ensure pure water and minimal buildup of the minerals and chlorine found in most drinking water. The water runs through tubing to a freezer assembly, which freezes it into a single sheet of ice. The frozen sheet is then forced through a screen (to produce cube ice) or crushed (to produce crushed ice). Different types of screens produce different sizes and shapes of cube ice. Each machine makes only one type and size, but in some machines you can adjust the cube size. For example, a machine will make a ¾-inch × ¾-inch cube varying from ¼- to ½-inch thick with a simple adjustment you can make yourself. A different grid for the same machine will give you a big (1¼-inch × 1½-inch) cube, ½ to 1 inch thick. But no machine makes more than one cube size at a time.

After the ice is crushed or cubed, it is dumped into a storage bin. When the bin fills to capacity, a sensor inside the bin stops the ice-making process until there is room to make and store more ice. Since most of the icemaker's parts come into constant contact with water, it is important that they be made of rustproof materials, with storage bins of either stainless steel or heavy-duty plastic.

In addition to cube ice you can also opt to use crushed ice, cracked ice, flake ice, and shaved ice. Crushed ice can be made by running cube ice through an **ice crusher.** Another type of machine produces crushed or cracked ice from scratch instead of from cube ice. Both machines make small, random-size pieces of hard, clear ice. Some drinks call for crushed or cracked ice, which is also used in making frozen drinks.

A **flake-ice machine,** or **flaker,** produces a soft, snow-like ice that is used mostly for keeping beverages cold. In a wine bucket, for example, flake ice will assume the shape of the bottle. If you use cubes in a bucket they will slide to the bottom when you take the bottle out, and it will be hard to replace the bottle in the ice. This more or less defeats the purpose of the bucket, except as decoration.

Flake ice is suitable only for frozen drinks, not as standard bar ice, because in an ordinary mixed drink, it melts quickly, dilutes the drink, and tends to create a water cap on the surface, which makes the drink taste weak. Shaved ice, made by a machine that shaves ice off of large blocks, is similar to flake ice; it is soft and opaque and has the same uses.

Determining Icemaker Size and Other Factors. An ice machine's size refers to the number of pounds of ice it can produce in 24 hours. Today's underbar models are so compact that even a 22-inch-wide machine can make 500 pounds of ice per day. How much do you need? The general rule is 3 pounds of ice per customer; 1 pound of ice makes three drinks. Ice is used for things other than mixed drinks, and some melting, in transit and in storage, has been factored into these guidelines. However, this is a very broad average. Your needs will change based on daily traffic, seasonal business, and time of day, as well as whether you must share ice output with a kitchen or other parts of your operation. It is always smart to plan on making 20 to 25 percent more ice than you will actually need, to allow for spillage, staff use, and the overall growth of your business. To do a basic ice-needs calculation, try this:

1. Estimate ice usage for one full week by multiplying the number of guests to be served that week by 3 pounds per guest.
2. Divide the result by 7 (days per week). This is the daily number of pounds of ice you will need.
3. Multiply that figure by 1.25, to add a bit of extra output.
4. If your average is not constant—because, for example, you know that Fridays and Saturdays your place will be swamped—estimate an additional amount for those days and include it in the total. This way you know there will be enough ice, even for your busiest days.

Where you put the ice machine can drastically affect its production. The warmer the air around it and the warmer the water it is fed, the less ice it will produce. Other factors to consider are the available space, the noise it makes, and the heat it generates, along with whether you have to share the ice with a kitchen. Wherever you put the icemaker, make sure that it is well ventilated to ensure that it functions properly, and that the area meets the same sanitation standards as the bar itself.

If the incoming water supply is warm, you might consider adding an **inlet chiller** to the ice-making system. It collects cold water that would normally be drained away from the icemaker and recirculates it in a series of copper coils to chill fresh water on its way into the icemaker to be frozen. Inlet chillers are about the size of a household fire extinguisher. They have no moving parts and use no electricity, but their *prechill* function can save up to 30 percent of your electric costs and boost your icemaker's capacity. In the United States we consume more ice than bread—more than 100 million tons every year! Like any other type of food or drink we ingest, it can become contaminated, retain bacteria, and, therefore, cause illness. This is why cleanliness and sanitary handling practices are critical in your manufacture, storage, and use of ice.

Icemaker Maintenance. The most important maintenance task regarding icemaking machines is to clean the unit's compressor and condenser coils according to the manufacturer's directions. About 80 percent of service calls can be traced to dirty coils. Keeping them free of dirt and grease allows better air circulation. The coils hold refrigerant, which is pressurized and turns from liquid to vapor and back again during the cooling process. Since the 1990s the U.S. Environmental Protection Agency (EPA) has prompted a change from old-style refrigerants (that were thought to deplete the ozone layer in Earth's atmosphere) to newer ones, called **hydrofluorocarbons (HFCs)** and **hydrochlorofluorocarbons (HCFCs).** Even these are a stopgap measure, though. They are to be phased out of service between the years 2015 and 2030. What this means for bar or restaurant operators is that there are strict rules for any type of refrigeration repair. If you have an old model that still uses the *chlorofluorocarbons* (*CFCs*, or the old brand name, *Freon*) that have fallen out of favor, the EPA says that if the machine is leaking 35 percent or more of its refrigerant pressure per year, it must be fixed. You are required to keep records of when, and how much, refrigerant is added during servicing. (If you fail to do so, you will be in violation of the federal Clean Air Act and you can be fined.) Use only repair technicians who are EPA-certified since they know how to dispose of old refrigerant properly. In addition look for the Underwriters Laboratories (UL) label on any new, ozone-safe refrigerant that is added to your machine.

Other types of regular maintenance include cleaning and/or changing the water and air filters, wiping down the inside and outside of the unit and ice-storage bin, and checking for mineral buildup on switches and sensors. Some manufacturers offer an acid-based ice-machine cleaning solution. Your ice machine might stop working and need to be reset if a filter is clogged or if there has been a power outage. The warmer or dirtier the environment in which the icemaker must work, the more frequent its maintenance checks should be.

Essentials for Draft-Beer Service

A draft-beer serving system consists of a *keg* or *half-keg* of beer, the **beer box** where the keg is stored, the **standard** or **tap** (faucet), the *line* between the keg and the standard, and a CO_2 tank connected to the keg with another line. The beer box, also called a **tap box,** is a refrigerator designed especially to hold a keg or half-keg of beer at the proper serving temperature of 36°F to 38°F. Generally, a beer box is located right below the standard, which is mounted on the bar top, so that the line between keg and standard is as short as possible. If more than one brand of draft beer is served, each brand has its own system—keg, line, and standard—either in its own beer box or in a box shared with another brand.

The supply of beer at the bar should be sufficient to last the serving period because bringing in a new keg of beer and tapping it is a major operation. Sometimes several kegs are needed to provide enough beer for a high-volume bar. A beer system may be designed into either the front bar or the backbar. If there is no room at the bar, the beer boxes may be located in a nearby storage area with lines running into the standards. On the backbar of the hotel bar in Figure 4.3, you see the beer standard (Q), but the rest of the system is on the garage level below. The beer box consists of a large walk-in cooler; a beer line runs behind the liquor display up to the standard. Since a single beer keg takes up a precious 24 square inches of cold storage space, remote systems, even though they are more expensive than beer boxes, work best for bars where draft-beer service is popular.

Keep the lines as short as possible, and keep them as cold as possible, even if this means mechanical refrigeration.

Storage Equipment

You need enough storage space at the bar to take care of all your needs for one serving period. This means liquor, mixes, bottled drinks, wines, beers, garnishes, and miscellaneous supplies, such as cocktail napkins and stir sticks. Generally this storage forms the major part of the backbar, as in Figure 4.3. The day's reserve supplies of liquor (all of the unopened bottles as backups for those in use) are either stored in dry (unrefrigerated) storage cabinets with locks or displayed on the backbar. Also in dry storage are red house wines for pouring by the glass or carafe, and reserve supplies of napkins, bar towels, matches, picks, straws, stir sticks, and other nonfood, nonbeverage items. Undercounter and backbar refrigerators (see Figure 4.11) hold supplies of special mixes and juices, bottled beer, bottled mixes if used, white wines, fruits and condiments for garnishing, cream, eggs, and other perishables. These refrigerators may also be used to chill glasses. It is important not to overload the cabinet, however, since proper airflow is essential to chilling the contents properly.

FIGURE 4.11 A backbar refrigerator. Courtesy of Glastender, Inc., Saginaw, Michigan.

From the outside the backbar refrigerator looks just like the dry-storage cabinets. Some backbar units are half refrigerator and half dry storage. Bar-sized refrigerators are tested for sanitation and temperature control by the NSF International so you should look for the NSFI seal when making your selection. The refrigerator should be able to hold foods at a temperature of 40°F.

Looking again at Figure 4.3, you can see how this works. Backbar refrigerator cabinets (T) store supplies of perishables in one section, and bottled beers and soft drinks in another section. To the right at the backbar is a dry-storage cabinet (U) for bar towels, napkins, and other supplies. Reserve supplies of liquor are stored in locked overhead cabinets above the front bar.

How Refrigeration Works. In basic principle refrigerating a space means to transfer heat out of that space, extending the life of the food inside the refrigerator. The more heat you can remove from a product, the longer it can be held in usable condition. The refrigerator fights a constant battle: Its door is opened and closed to insert products that are not yet chilled, letting in outside air. Even when the door is closed there may be tiny leaks around the rubber door seals.

The **refrigeration cycle** is the process of removing heat from a refrigerated space. The **refrigeration circuit** is the system of equipment that makes the cycle possible. Successful refrigeration is a combination of temperature reduction, humidity, and air circulation. To keep most foods at their peak, you need a refrigerator capable of cooling them to 40°F. (In the past it was thought that 45°F was cold enough, but that is no longer the standard.)

Take a look at what happens when you open the refrigerator door of that little underbar unit. The components of the circuit are shown in Figure 4.12. First, opening the door immediately introduces warm air into the cooled space. The warm air rises and is drawn toward **evaporator coils** made of copper. Inside the sealed evaporator coils is liquid **refrigerant** (the HFCs and HCFCs mentioned earlier), which becomes vapor (gas) as it winds through the coils. It is pumped through a suction line by a **compressor** into another series of coils, called the **condenser.** There, it turns back into a liquid. The amount of refrigerant flowing through the system is determined by an **expansion valve,** which is a small opening between the evaporator and the condenser. The more the surrounding air needs to be cooled, the more often the refrigerant flows.

Depending on the size of the refrigerator, it will have a one-half to one horsepower compressor; some larger (four-door) units rely on two three-quarter horsepower compressors. Compressors can be mounted above or below the refrigerator. Bottom-mounted ones reduce interior space somewhat and require smaller doors. You can also have remote compressors that sit elsewhere in your building and are connected to the refrigerator by copper lines, so as not to take up scarce underbar space and to minimize the heat and noise generated by the compressor.

A cousin to the bar refrigerator is the *horizontal bottle cooler.* If you serve a lot of individual bottles or cans, this unit enables you to store them in chilled bins with sliding top lids. The bottle cooler has the same small refrigeration system discussed earlier. Like icemakers, bar refrigerators and bottle coolers require coil

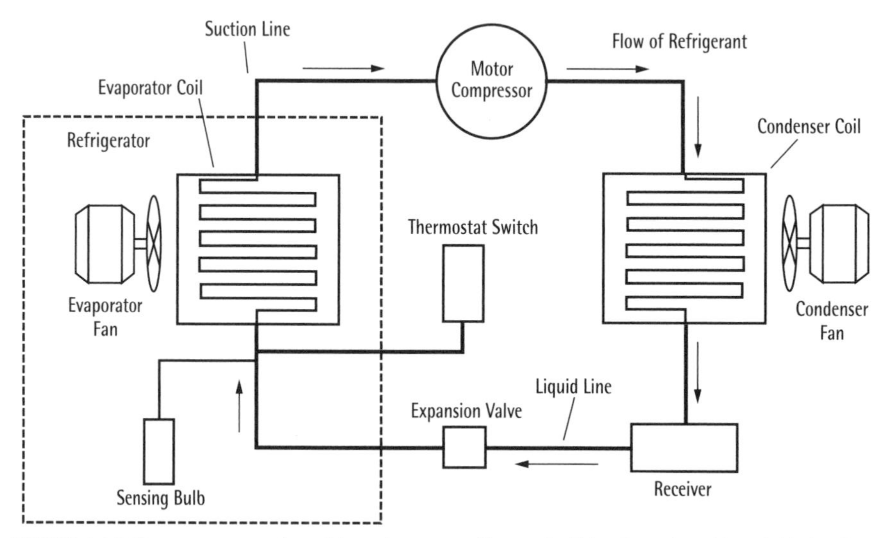

FIGURE 4.12 The components of a refrigeration system. Source: Facilities Operations Manual, National Restaurant Association, Washington, DC.

cleaning and periodic preventive maintenance. Servicing and recharging with new refrigerant should be done only by an EPA-certified repairperson.

Beverage Storage Considerations

The fictitious hotel bar we have been using as an example keeps its daily supply of wines by the bottle for dining-room service in a storeroom around the corner, which includes a large cooler set at 45°F to 50°F for the white wines. Some restaurants may store their daily wine stocks at their bars, display them in wine racks as part of the room décor, or store them under lock and key in a wine cellar.

Oxygen and sunlight are the enemies of both beer and wine. Leaving a wine bottle open for any length of time changes the taste of the remaining wine. Several devices have been invented to deal with the problem of storing open, partially empty bottles of wine, and you will learn about them Chapter 7.

In beer, oxygen reacts with the natural fatty acids in the brew to form compounds known as unsaturated *aldehydes*, leaving an off-taste that some describe as "wet cardboard." Partially used beer bottles, of course, aren't a storage problem.

Strong, direct sunlight can cause damage to both beer and wine quality. In wine, unnecessary warmth (either from sunlight or storage in, for instance, a warm vehicle) can heat the wine and damage the seal on the cork. Bottles that have messy labels—where wine has clearly leaked onto them—should not be accepted from suppliers because they might have suffered heat damage and the wine might be spoiled.

Light reacts with a naturally bitter substance in beer (from the use of hops) to produce another undesirable compound, an intense odor that is commonly referred to as "skunky." This is why many brewers use brown bottles. The ones that use clear or green bottles take an extra step, extracting the bitter compound from the hops and treating it so it is no longer light-susceptible. Treating this compound also results in better-quality beer foam.

Beer in aluminum cans is most often used for off-premise sales. These cans are an acceptable option only if your establishment is casual. They are easy to stack and unbreakable. Canned beer gets colder more quickly than bottled beer, but it also loses it chill quicker. Cans stay freshest when stored between 40°F and 70°F (4°C to 21°C). Warmer temperatures will destroy flavor and aroma.

Bottled beer storage temperatures are the same as those for canned beer. Both cans and bottles should be stored away from any light or heat source. Unlike wine, beer bottles should be stored upright to avoid contact of the beer with the bottle cap. The only exceptions are the Farmhouse Ales in large, wine-type bottles with corks, which should be stored lying down.

If beer gets cold enough to freeze, it is likely to precipitate its solids and form flakes that will not dissolve when thawed. Beer kept too cold for a long time may "gush" and spew out when opened. The same thing happens when bottles or cans are handled roughly. Beer that is too warm foams too much, which is just as wasteful.

Draft beer in kegs has the most stringent temperature requirements. It must be kept cold from brewer, to distributor, to storeroom, to bar, perferably at 35°F to 39°F (2°C to 4°C). Since draft beer is not pasteurized in the way that bottled beers are, it is much more susceptible to deterioration and might begin secondary fermentation if kept above 44°F (7°C), turning sour and cloudy and reducing its lifespan significantly. Stored at ideal temperatures, kegs have a life cycle. They start aging as soon as they are tapped, and last 30 days (optimistically, up to 45 days) after that.

Beer kegs should not share a walk-in cooler with food storage since frequent opening and closing of the door will make it impossible to keep the beer at a constant temperature. For the same reason, kegs in an underbar beer system should have their own special refrigerated storage space. The beer box or cooler should be maintained at a constant temperature between 36°F and 38°F (2°C to 3°C). Beer allowed to warm over 45°F (7°C) might become cloudy or turn sour. Beer allowed to chill below freezing might become unsalable; the water content of the beer freezes and separates from the alcohol. If allowed to thaw slowly at its normal temperature of 36°F to 38°F (2°C to 3°C), beer can sometimes be blended back together by gently rotating the kegs. (This is best done by your distributor.) But if the beer is cloudy after thawing and rotation, it is beyond salvaging.

There is more information in Chapter 8 on cleaning and caring for draft beer systems.

BAR TOOLS AND SMALL EQUIPMENT

Just as chefs have their favorite sets of kitchen knives that they guard zealously, bartenders have their favorite tools. Seasoned bartenders generally agree that the simpler the tool, the better. Gimmicks take up space and may not save any time, and a good bartender does not waste either. Buying high-quality tools is important because no one can afford to waste time at a busy bar struggling with poor-quality implements. Moreover, doing so can be dangerous or at least inefficient. An inexperienced bartender wielding a hand shaker with an ill-fitting lid can drench a customer. Stainless steel is the metal of choice for small equipment and utensils, just as it is for large underbar pieces, and for the same reasons. It looks good, it is durable, and it is easy to clean. Most small bar equipment is used for mixing and pouring. A second group of utensils is used in preparing condiments to garnish drinks. A third group is used for serving.

Smallware for Mixing and Pouring

The indispensable tools for mixing and pouring by hand are:

- Jiggers
- Pourers

- Mixing glass
- Hand shaker
- Bar strainer
- Barspoon
- Ice scoop
- Ice tongs
- Muddler
- Fruit squeezer
- Funnel
- Glass rimmer

A **jigger** (Figure 4.13) is a small container that measures ounces or fractions of ounces of liquors used for cocktails, highballs, and other mixed drinks. (Although these liquors are bought in bottles measured in metric terms—a liter, or 750 milliliters—they are measured in ounces when drinks are poured. One ounce of liquid equals approximately 30 milliliters.) There are two types of jiggers. The double-ended, stainless-steel jigger has a small cup on one end and a large cup on the other. It comes in several combinations of sizes, such as ½ ounce/1 ounce, ¾ ounce/1 ounce, and 1 ounce/1½ ounces. The most-used combinations are probably the ¾/1½ ounces and the 1 ounce/1½ ounces, but what you need depends on the size drink you serve.

FIGURE 4.13 Jiggers for measuring liquor. Courtesy of Co-Rect Products, Inc., Minneapolis, Minnesota.

The second jigger type is made of heavy glass with a plain or elevated base. It comes in several sizes, from ⅞ ounce to 3 ounces. This jigger also comes with or without a line marking off another measure, for example, a 1-ounce glass with a line at ½ or ⅝ ounce, or a 1½-ounce glass with a line at ½, ⅝, ¾, ⅞, or 1 ounce. A glass jigger may also be used as a **shot glass** when a customer orders a straight shot.

To measure using the steel jigger, the bartender fills the cup to the brim. To measure using the glass jigger, the bartender fills to the line. After pouring the drink the bartender turns the jigger upside down on the drainboard so that any residual liquor drains out and one drink's flavor will not be carried over to the next. If a jigger is used for something heavy, such as cream or a liqueur, it is rinsed with water before reuse.

A **pourer** (see Figure 4.14) is a device that fits into the neck of a beverage bottle and is constructed to reduce the rate of flow to a predictable, controllable amount. A pourer is used on every opened liquor bottle at the bar. There are three categories: slow, semi-fast, and fast.

Pourers are available in either stainless steel or plastic. The plastic pourers come in different colors and can be used to color-code different types of liquor. The stainless-steel pourers are better looking and last longer than the plastic versions,

FIGURE 4.14 A pourer, which fits on bottle tops. Courtesy of Metrokane Products and Pollen Design, New York, New York.

with the exception of corks that fit into the bottlenecks; these wear out and must be replaced from time to time.

Some pourers that measure the liquor poured, then cut off automatically when a preset amount is reached. They are expensive and most bartenders don't like them, but they are a form of control not to be overlooked if they will save more money and aggravation than they cost.

A **mixing glass** (see Figure 4.15) is a heavy glass container in which drink ingredients are stirred together with ice. A typical mixing glass has a capacity of 16 to 17 ounces. It is used to make Martinis, Manhattans, and other drinks whose ingredients blend together readily. It is rinsed after each use. Mixing glasses should be heat-treated and chip-proof.

A **hand shaker** or **cocktail shaker** (see Figure 4.16) is a versatile favorite of bartenders. It is a combination of a mixing glass and a stainless-steel container that fits on top of it, in which drink ingredients are shaken together with ice. The stainless-steel container is known variously as a **mixing cup, mixing steel**, or **mix can.** Ingredients and ice are measured into the mixing glass, then the cup is placed firmly on top, angled so that one edge is flush with the side of the glass. The two are held tightly together and shaken. The cup must be of heavy-gauge, high-quality stainless steel; if it loses its shape it will not fit tightly over the glass. Usually a shaker comes in a set with its own strainer. The strainer and shaker cup should have an overhang of about 1½ inches to seal properly. A shaker is used for cocktails made with fruit juices, egg, sugar, cream, or any other ingredient that does not mix readily with spirits. A shaker is rinsed after each use.

FIGURE 4.15 A mixing glass. Courtesy of Co-Rect Products, Inc., Minneapolis, Minnesota.

The mixing container of the shake mixer (mentioned earlier in the section on blenders) is also called a *mixing cup, steel,* or *can.* This machine has supplanted the hand shakers at some bars. It is faster and more efficient. It can even make ice-cream drinks, which is something hand shakers can not do. A **bar strainer** (see Figure 4.17) is a round wire coil on a handle, which fits over the top of a shaker or mixing glass; it has "ears" that fit over the rim to keep it in position. The strainer keeps ice and fruit pulp from going into the glass when the drink is poured. A bar strainer is used with mixing glasses and shaker and blender cups. An elongated strainer, for 19-ounce bar glasses and shakers, is a modern addition.

A **barspoon** (see Figure 4.18) is a shallow spoon with a long handle, often with a bead on the end. The spoon and handle are stainless steel, typically 10 or 11 inches long. The bowl equals one teaspoon. Barspoons are used for stirring drinks, either in a drink glass or in a mixing glass or cup. During Prohibition humorist George Ade, writing nostalgically in *The Old-Time Saloon,* described the use of the barspoon in pre-Prohibition days when, he said, a good bartender would have died of shame if compelled to use a shaker: "The supreme art of the mixing process was to place the thumb lightly on top of the long spoon and then revolve the spoon at incredible speed by twiddling the fingers . . . a knack acquired by the maestros only." Perhaps this mixing method explains the traditional bead on the end of the handle.

FIGURE 4.16 The shaker cup fits tightly over the mixing glass for hand shaking. Courtesy of Co-Rect Products, Inc., Minneapolis, Minnesota.

An **ice scoop** (see Figure 4.19) is, as its name implies, an implement for scooping ice from an ice bin. It usually has a 6- or 8-ounce capacity. A standard size makes it easy to get just the right amount of ice with a single scoop. Bartenders who scoop ice out of bins directly with a glass are asking for trouble, which they will realize the first time that they break or chip a glass, leaving broken glass in the ice bin and a razor-sharp rim on the glass. Use the scoop!

Ice tongs (see Figure 4.20) are designed to handle one cube of ice at a time. One of the less popular bar tools, tongs are a relic from the days when all cube ice were large. Nevertheless they are still used, for example, in airline service. They serve an important function because ice that goes into a drink should not be touched by human hands.

A **muddler,** or **muddling stick** (see Figure 4.21), is making a comeback with the renewed popularity of classic drinks, such as the Old-Fashioned. A muddler is a wooden tool that looks like a little baseball bat. One end is flat for *muddling* (crushing) one substance into another, such as sugar into bitters in an Old-Fashioned. The other end is rounded and can be used to crack ice. The muddler,

FIGURE 4.17 Bar strainers. Courtesy of Co-Rect Products, Inc., Minneapolis, Minnesota.

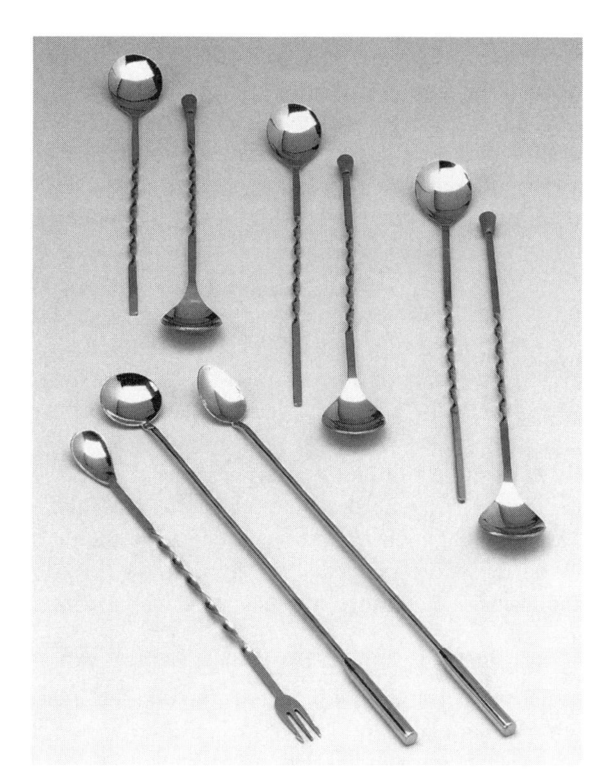

FIGURE 4.18 Barspoons. Courtesy of Co-Rect Products, Inc., Minneapolis, Minnesota.

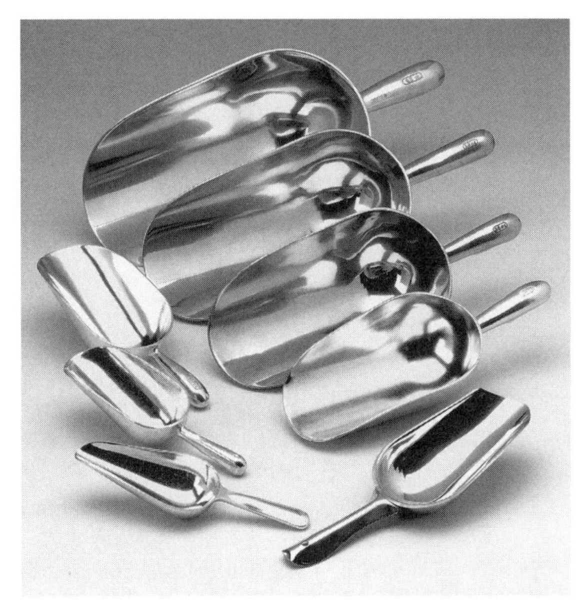

FIGURE 4.19 Ice scoops. Courtesy of Co-Rect Products, Inc., Minneapolis, Minnesota.

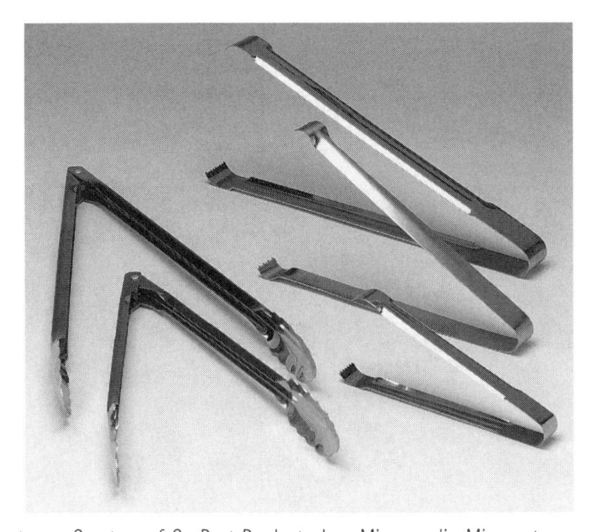

FIGURE 4.20 Ice tongs. Courtesy of Co-Rect Products, Inc., Minneapolis, Minnesota.

FIGURE 4.21 Muddling sticks. Courtesy of Co-Rect Products, Inc., Minneapolis, Minnesota.

too, is a relic from another day; now simple syrup instead of lump sugar is used, and ice rarely needs to be cracked.

FIGURE 4.22 Fruit squeezers. Courtesy of Co-Rect Products, Inc., Minneapolis, Minnesota.

A bar-type **fruit squeezer** (see Figure 4.22) is a hand-powered gadget that squeezes half a lemon or lime for a single drink, straining pits and pulp.

Funnels (see Figure 4.23) are needed in several sizes for pouring from large containers into small ones, such as transferring special mixes from bulk containers into plastic bottles for bar use. Some funnels have a screen at the wide end to strain pulp.

A **glass rimmer** (see Figure 4.24) is a handy gadget used to rim a glass with salt or sugar. It is made up of three trays. One tray contains a sponge that is saturated with lemon or lime juice, the second contains a layer of salt, and the third a layer of sugar. The glass rim is pressed on the sponge, then dipped in salt (for a Margarita or a Bloody Mary) or sugar (for a Side Car).

FIGURE 4.23 Funnels. Courtesy of Co-Rect Products, Inc., Minneapolis, Minnesota.

FIGURE 4.24 A glass rimmer. Courtesy of Co-Rect Products, Inc., Minneapolis, Minnesota.

A BARTENDER'S TOOLKIT

Little things matter to good bartenders, and this means attention to details that require specific tools and products. The top bartenders have their own toolkits, just like other types of hard-working professionals have their toolboxes. Use an easy-to-clean, lightweight, portable container with a handle. You can bring your kit to work, use it, keep an eye on its contents, and take it home with you when your shift is over. A toolkit can also come in handy when you are asked to tend bar at an off-site, catered event. Over time you add your own touches to the kit based on, for example, your own drink recipes and favorite tools. The following is a good starter list:

- Bar spillage mats
- Cigar slicer
- Cocktail shaker
- Cocktail strainer
- Small cutting board(s)
- Long-stemmed barspoon
- Muddler(s)
- Pourer tops
- Swiss Army knife
- Can and bottle opener
- Clean bar towels
- 16-ounce mixing glass
- Fruit paring knife
- Lighter
- Jigger(s)
- 24-inch stainless-steel ice scoop
- Wine corkscrew

Tools and Equipment for Garnishing

FIGURE 4.25 A plastic condiment tray. Courtesy of Co-Rect Products, Inc., Minneapolis, Minnesota.

Usually part of the bartender's job is to set up the fruits and other foods used to enhance or garnish a drink. These are typically lined up, ready to go, in a multicompartment **condiment tray.** Often the tray is mounted on some part of the underbar at the serving station. The tray should never be located directly above the ice bin. Many health codes define this as a potential hazard because of the likelihood of dropping food into the ice.

An alternative to the installed condiment tray is a plastic tray on the bar top or glass rail. Such a tray can be moved around at the bartender's convenience, and can be cleaned more easily than one fixed to the underbar. If servers garnish the drinks, which is often the case, the garnishes must be on the bar top at the pickup station, as shown in Figures 4.2 and 4.3. A plastic condiment tray is shown in Figure 4.25.

The tools for preparing condiments are few but important (Figure 4.26):

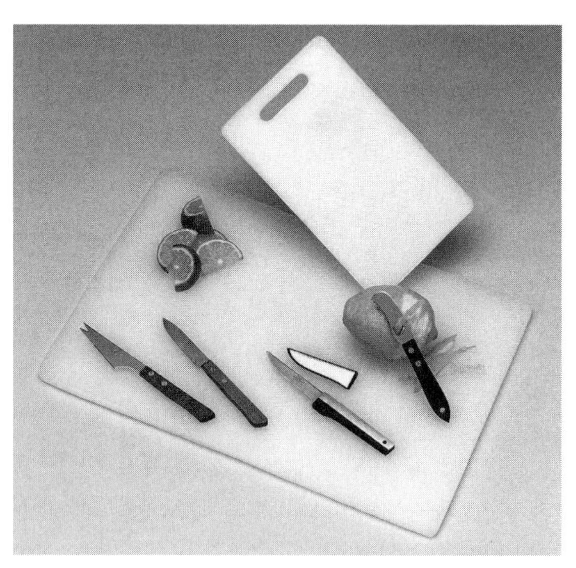

FIGURE 4.26 Cutting boards, bar knives, and zester. Courtesy of Co-Rect Products, Inc., Minneapolis, Minnesota.

- Cutting board
- Bar knife
- Relish fork
- Peelers: zester, router, or stripper

A cutting board for the bar can be made of any surface material that will not dull knives, though rubber or plastic is usually best. Wood is the most pleasant surface to work on, but most health codes rate it a health hazard because it is hard to keep bacteria-free. A small board is all you need—and all you will have room for.

A **bar knife** can be any small- to medium-size stainless-steel knife, such as a paring or utility knife. It is essential that it be stainless steel; carbon steel will discolor, and the color will transfer to the fruit being cut. The blade must be kept sharp, not only to do a neater, quicker job, but because it will not slip—and will be safer. The bar knife in the picture has a serrated blade, which is especially good for cutting fruit. Knife handles should be made of heavy-duty rubber or plastic for sanitary reasons.

A **relish fork** is a long (10-inch), thin, two-tined, stainless-steel fork designed for reaching into narrow-necked bottles for onions and olives. Some have a spring device that helps to secure the olive or onion firmly. The **zester, router,** and **stripper** are special cutting tools for making the twist of lemon that some drinks call for. These three tools peel away the yellow part of the lemon skin, which contains the zesty oil, eliminating the white underskin, which is bitter.

Tools and Equipment for Serving

The tools in this category make up a short and somewhat miscellaneous list, but these are important items that no bar could do without:

- Bottle and can openers
- Corkscrews
- Serving trays (round)
- Folios (checks or forms for taking drink order, see Figure 11.9)

Any type of bottle or can opener that is of good quality and does the job is acceptable. Stainless steel is best; it is rust-free and easy to clean. These openers must be kept clean; however, this is an easy task to forget.

The first patent for a **corkscrew** was held by a British minister named Samuel Henshell. Today there are many different kinds of corkscrews, or wine openers, a few of which are pictured in Figure 4.27. Each one is designed for one purpose: to extract corks from wine bottles.

The screw, or **worm,** that penetrates the cork should be made of stainless steel and be 2¼ to 2½ inches long and about ⅜ inch in diameter, with a hollow core

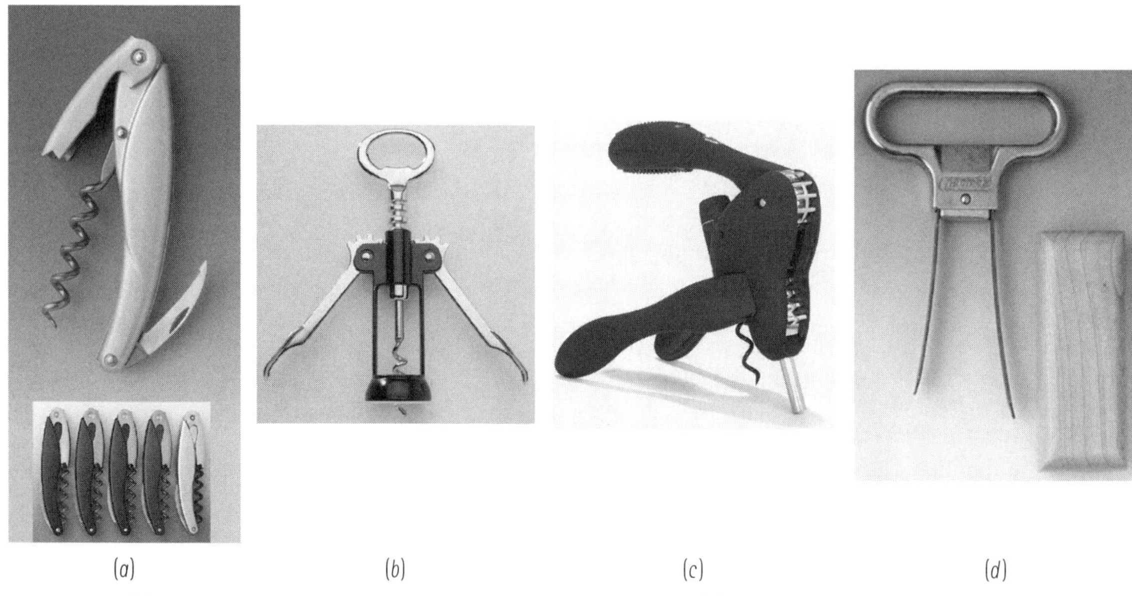

(*a*) (*b*) (*c*) (*d*)

FIGURE 4.27 (*a*) A waiter's corkscrew. Courtesy of Franmara, Inc., Salinas, California. (*b*) A wing corkscrew. Courtesy of PhotoDisc/Getty Images. (*c*) A Rabbit corkscrew. Courtesy of Metrokane Products and Pollen Design, New York, New York. (*d*) A two-prong or ah-so corkscrew with sheath. Courtesy of Franmara, Inc., Salinas, California.

in the middle. (A solid core would chew up the cork.) The screw should have enough spirals to take it completely through the cork. A corkscrew with an elongated spiral and a longer pitch (distance) between the twists of the screw makes for easier insertion into the cork. The screw's edges should be rounded, not sharp.

The **waiter's corkscrew** (several are shown in Figure 4.27*a*) is specifically designed for tucking into a pocket to open wines at tableside. This tool includes the corkscrew itself, a small knife for cutting the seal of the bottle, a fulcrum to grip the lip of the bottle, a lever to hold as you ease out the cork. Made of stainless steel, the waiter's corkscrew folds like a pocketknife.

In Figure 4.27*b*, the **wing corkscrew** commonly used in bars is so named because it has "wings" on either side that rise as the screw is twisted in. When the wings are pushed down again, the cork is pulled out. This corkscrew is fine for use at the bar, but it is probably too bulky for table service.

The Rabbit Corkscrew was introduced in 2000 and has won major design awards for its unique mechanical principles. It may look intimidating at first (see Figure 4.27*c*), with 31 separate parts, but it is easy to master the use of the Rabbit. Its two side handles grab the top of a wine bottle and hold it firmly, and a third handle on top drives the corkscrew into the cork. Push the third handle down quickly, then lift it up just as quickly. Metrokane, the company that owns the technology, says the Rabbit can eject any cork in three seconds. A new Rabbit kit includes a spare worm because repeated use through foil or bottle seals can dull this tool and compromise its effectiveness.

The device pictured in Figure 4.27*d* is nicknamed the **ah-so.** It is a simple pair of prongs that straddle the cork. You place the prongs on the side of a cork, then rock them side to side until they are wedged into the neck of the bottle, between glass and cork. Then the ah-so is twisted and pulled gently, to bring the cork out whole without a puncture in the middle. People who learn how to successfully use the ah-so swear by it, but it can be slow and frustrating for those who have not perfected the technique. For high-volume operations, you will want to invest in an uncorking machine. These machines are mounted on a countertop with a vise clamp and wingnut. The spiral cork is inserted into the cork, which is extracted from the bottle in a single downward stroke. Uncorking machines are between 12 and 22 inches in height. You will need *round serving trays* in two sizes: 14-inch and 16-inch (see Figure 4.28). Bar trays should have cork surfaces to keep the glasses from slipping.

FIGURE 4.28 Serving trays. Courtesy of Co-Rect Products, Inc., Minneapolis, Minnesota.

GLASSWARE

The glassware you use in your bar should be considered an element of your overall décor and concept. It has a subtle but clear impact on your customer's perception of the bar's style, quality, and personality. A great deal of tradition is involved in cocktail service. Using the proper size and shape of glass for a drink indicates that you know your business and signals a respect for that tradition to your guest. Glassware can be a merchandising tool, stimulating sales with subtle or flamboyant variations: tall, sleek, frosted pilsner glasses for beer; oversized glasses with thin, delicate rims for certain wines; colorful, whimsical, oversized goblets for Margaritas; attractive mugs for specialty coffee. The Four Seasons Hotel and Resort in Carlsbad, California, for instance, uses a different glass for every martini recipe! Glassware is not just used for drinks; you are likely to see gourmet appetizers such as shrimp cocktail or ceviche served in eye-catching, oversized martini glasses, or fresh fruit and ice cream looking especially elegant in a large brandy snifter.

As Americans become more sophisticated about their dining preferences, glassware manufacturers try to stay one step ahead of the trends. Wine service has seen the greatest impact. Riedel Crystal claims one of the company's forefathers was "the first to recognize the effect of the shape of a wineglass on the sipper's perspective and drinking pleasure." Riedel began in the 1970s to develop a "gourmet glass" series with the Association of Italian Sommeliers. The series began with ten glass sizes and has now grown to 32. Today the company has a total of four separate series of wineglasses at different price points. The latest is a deep, almost black shade of purple, which might shock purists at first! But Riedel's aim was to make a glass in which fine wine can be judged only by aroma and flavor, without peeking first at the color. Riedel's series are getting a fair amount of trade press and might just catch on.

One trend that probably has "legs," to use appropriate wine terminology, is the use of oversized glasses for serving wines. A large bowl, filled about halfway with wine, leaves plenty of room for swirling the wine without spilling to develop its aroma. Even the Olive Garden, very much a casual dining chain, now uses a $17\frac{1}{2}$-ounce, Italian crystal goblet for reds, and a 15-ounce glass for whites. Some restaurants order two sets of stemware, one for wine-by-the-glass programs and bottles under $40; the other, for higher-dollar wine sales. Still others argue that more wine would be sold if the pretense and formality of stemware were eliminated altogether. For casual dining or other informal establishments, stemware has become strictly functional, or even optional. You must determine whether you will be gaining or losing wine sales by adopting the more informal attitude. The point: Your customers are driving today's glassware trends at both ends of the spectrum, and yours should match the overall mood of the establishment.

Martini glasses are another trendy family since a good martini has always been an equal combination of good spirits and great presentation. Its top-heavy style became popular in the 1940s; it was a little bit hard to drink from, but showy and distinctive in design. Just to give you an idea of what is available, Figure 4.29 shows a sample of available martini and margarita glasses. There are dozens more. Smart bar owners and bartenders know that drink presentation makes a pleasant experience more memorable and reflects both the mood and the personality of the bar itself.

FIGURE 4.29 Martini and margarita glasses. Courtesy of PhotoDisc, Inc.

As microbrewed beers have become more popular, connoisseurs also have come to expect a variety of beer glasses. Heavier lager beers are generally served in heavy glass mugs with handles; lighter pilsner beers have more carbonation and are best showcased in a tall, narrow glass that widens at the top. For ales, including stouts and porters, a straight-sided, traditional pint glass with a wide mouth enables guests to smell and sip. Customers who know their beers will appreciate the fact that you know how to serve them correctly.

Glass Terms and Types

Glasses have three characteristic features: the **bowl**, the **base** or **foot**, and the **stem** (see Figure 4.30). A glass may have one, two, or all three of these features. The three major types of glassware—tumblers, footed ware, and stemware—are classified according to which of these features they have.

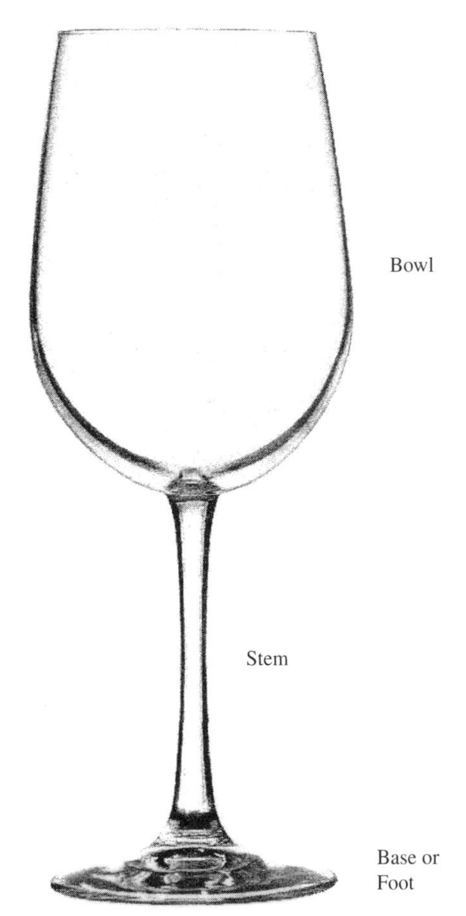

FIGURE 4.30 The parts of a glass.

A **tumbler** is a flat-bottomed, cylindrical glass that is basically a bowl without a stem or foot. Its sides may be straight, flared, or curved. Tumblers are used for shorter drinks, drinks served on the rocks, and generally for drinks that are stirred rather than shaken. Various sizes and shapes of tumblers are known by the names of the drinks they are commonly used for: Old-Fashioned, rocks glass (for cocktails served "on the rocks"), highball, Collins, cooler, Zombie, and pilsner (see Figure 4.31). The typical tumbler is an 8-ounce glass. Glass jiggers and shot glasses are miniature versions of tumblers.

Footed ware refers to a style of glass whose bowl sits directly on a base or foot. The bowl and base may have a variety of shapes. Traditional footed glasses include the short, rounded brandy **snifter,** the Pousse-Café glass, and certain styles of beer glass (see Figure 4.32). Today footed ware is also popular for on-the-rocks drinks

FIGURE 4.31 Tumblers: (*a*) Collins, (*b*) Highball glasses, (*c*) Double Old-Fashioned, (*d*) Old-Fashioned, (*e*) Rocks, and (*f*) Shot glasses.

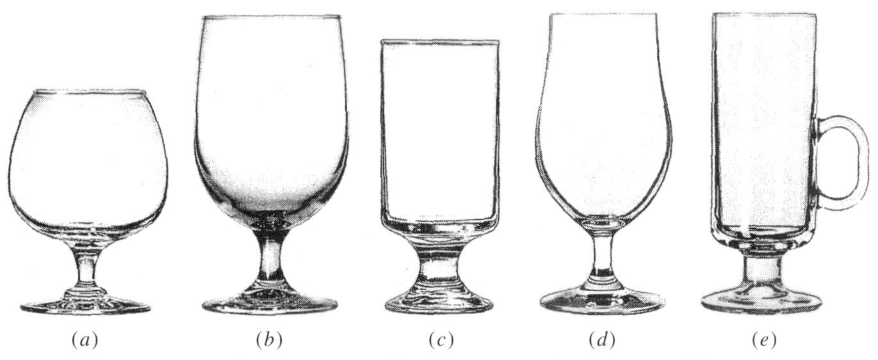

FIGURE 4.32 Footed ware: (*a*) Brandy snifter, (*b*) Iced-tea glass, (*c*) Highball glass, (*d*) Beer glass, and (*e*) Irish coffee mug.

and highballs. In fact any type of drink can be served in a footed glass of the right size.

Stemware includes any glass having all three features: a bowl, foot, and stem. Stemware, too, comes in a variety of shapes. Wine is always served in a stemmed glass, as is a straight-up cocktail or a straight liqueur, the latter in tiny, 2- or 3-ounce glasses. Certain shapes and sizes of stemware are typical of specific drinks, such as wine, sour, Margarita, and Champagne (see Figure 4.33). Stemware, for obvious reasons, is the type of glass most easily broken, and you might as well plan for this when you place your glassware order.

A fourth type of glass is the **mug** (see Figure 4.34). You can think of a mug as a tumbler with a handle or as a tall glass cup. The most common size (16 ounces) is usually used for serving beer, and smaller specialty mugs are used for coffee drinks. When used to serve beer, mugs are sometimes called **steins.** Mugs are appropriate for serving ales, but the lighter-style pilsner beers require a different type of glass, which is called a **pilsner glass.** This is a tall, footed glass designed to preserve beer's natural effervescence. You'll learn more about serving beer in Chapter 8.

How Glass Is Made

Glass is made of very fine sand, called **silica,** that is mixed with soda, lime, and **cullet,** which is reused broken glass bits, and heated to temperatures of nearly 1,500°F. When it is in this pliable, super-hot form, the molten glass is either blown into its final shape by introducing air into it or pressed into a mold to shape it. Most commercial glasses are pressed and are known as **pressware.** After the glass is shaped, it is put into a warm oven to cool slowly, which is called **annealing.** The slow cooling stabilizes and strengthens the glass and removes any stress points that may have developed during shaping.

After annealing some glass goes through another step called **tempering.** The cooled glass is reheated, almost to its original high temperature, then blasted with

FIGURE 4.33 Stemware: (*a*) Wine taster, (*b*) Wineglass, (*c*) Burgundy wineglass, (*d*) Tall flute, (*e*) Tulip flute, (*f*) Tall wineglass, (*g*) Liqueur glass, (*h*) Spirit glass, (*i*) Martini glass, and (*j*) Margarita glass.

cold air. The process "shocks" the glass and makes it more resistant to temperature extremes. If a glass is advertised as **fully tempered**, it means the entire glass underwent a tempering process; **rim tempered** means only the rim received this extra treatment. Most stemware is fully tempered; mugs or tumblers may be only rim tempered.

A curved or barrel-shaped glass is more durable than a straight-sided glass, and a short, thick stem is sturdier than a thin, delicate one. You will notice that manufacturers make glass a little thicker at possible stress points. A rolled edge at the rim of a glass, or swirled or ribbed patterns, all indicate extra thickness.

FIGURE 4.34 The frosty beer mug. When serving beer, try for a smaller frothy head, perhaps half the size of what is shown here.

Glass Names and Sizes

In bar terminology glasses are typically named after the drink most commonly served in them, and that drink is related to glass size. Thus, a highball glass is typically 8 to 10 ounces, and a Collins glass is typically 10 to 12 ounces. When mixing a drink the bartender relies to a certain extent on the glass size. For a highball, for example, the glass is a measure of the amount of ice to be used and the amount of mix to be added. If the bartender uses the wrong size glass, the drink might be too weak or too strong. Before you purchase glassware for your bar, you must decide how strong a drink you will serve—that is, how much spirit you will use as your standard drink: such as 1 ounce, 1¼ ounces or 1½ ounces. Then you can select glass sizes that will produce the drinks that look and taste right to your customers.

Tips on Glass Purchase

When you select glasses, size is a better guide than the name of the glass since a glass with a specific name will come in many sizes. Figure 4.35 gives the range of sizes offered by one manufacturer for various types of glasses in various styles. In addition, nearly all glass types come in giant sizes for promotional drinks.

Buy glass sizes that you will never have to fill to the brim, to avoid spills. As mentioned earlier in this chapter, wineglasses to be used in meal service should be filled only halfway so the drinker can swirl the wine around and appreciate its bouquet. A brandy snifter serves the same purpose: No matter how big the glass, only 1 to 2 ounces of brandy is served, so the customer can savor the aroma. Most bars buy only a few of the different types and sizes of glass. One type and size can

SELECTION OF GLASS SIZES

Glass	*Available Sizes (oz)*	*Recommended Size (oz)*
Beer	6 to 23	10 to 12
Brandy, snifter	$5\frac{1}{2}$ to 34	Your choice from middle range
Brandy, straight up	2	2
Champagne	$3\frac{1}{2}$ to $8\frac{1}{2}$	$4\frac{1}{2}$ or larger[a]
Cocktail	$2\frac{1}{2}$ to 6	$4\frac{1}{2}$ for 3-oz drink
Collins	10 to 12	10 to 12
Cooler	15 to $16\frac{1}{2}$	15 to $16\frac{1}{2}$
Cordial	$\frac{3}{4}$ to 1	$1\frac{3}{4}$, or use 2-oz brandy glass
Highball	7 to $10\frac{1}{2}$	8 to 10
Hurricane	8 to $23\frac{1}{2}$	Your choice for specialty drinks
Margarita	5 to 6	5 to 6
Old-fashioned	5 to 15 (double)	7
Rocks	5 to 12	5 to 7
Sherry	2 to 3	3 for 2-oz serving
Sour	$4\frac{1}{2}$ to 6	$4\frac{1}{2}$ for 3-oz drink
Whisky, straight shot	$\frac{5}{8}$ to 3	$1\frac{1}{2}$ to 3 depending on shot size
Wine	3 to $17\frac{1}{2}$	8 to 9 for 4-oz serving; larger sizes OK
Zombie	12 to $13\frac{1}{2}$	Your choice

[a]The tall flute is recommended over the broad shallow bowl

FIGURE 4.35

work for Old-Fashioneds, rocks drinks, and highballs; similarly, one cocktail glass can serve for straight-up cocktails including sours, and for sherry and other fortified wines. On the other hand, if you are building a connoisseur's image, you will probably want the traditionally correct glass for each type of drink, and you will want several different types of wineglasses, to serve different wines with each course of an elaborate dinner, including tall, thin Champagne flutes. Keep in mind that the flat, coupe-style Champagne glass—said to be modeled after the shape of Marie Antoinette's left breast—is back in style in some bars. It had fallen into disfavor in the 1980s for exposing too much bubbly to the air too quickly, causing the wine to lose its effervescence too soon. Trendsetters say that the solution is to down the Champagne like a shooter rather than sipping it!

How many glasses should you buy? For each type of drink, you may want two to four times as many glasses as the number of drinks you expect to serve in a rush period. Four times would be ample; two times would probably be enough for restaurant-table service only. Because there are so many variables, you have to be your own judge, based on your clientele and rate of use.

When making your glass selection, remember that glassware is among the most fragile equipment you will be using. Consider the following: weight and durability; heat-treated glass, if you use a mechanical dishwasher; design (buy glasses that do not need special handling—flared rims break easily; rounded edges are easier to clean). Of course consider the breakage factor in figuring the quantity you need. Remember to choose existing styles and patterns so that they will continue to be available for replacements in months and years to come.

If your bar is in a trendy neighborhood or tourist area, you might also consider take-home glassware. In cities like New Orleans and Las Vegas, sometimes the glassware is included in the price of the drink, emblazoned with the logo of the bar or restaurant as a keepsake for visitors. Souvenir beer mugs and glasses are also popular in brewpubs.

Glassware Care

Glasses break for two main reasons: *mechanical impact* (when glass hits another object, causing it to crack, chip, or shatter) and *thermal shock* (when a quick, intense temperature change cracks or shatters the glass). Obviously you can not prevent breakage entirely, but you can reduce it significantly by implementing a few commonsense handling practices:

- Train your staff members to never *stack,* or *nest,* glasses one inside the other, and not to pick up multiple glasses at the same time, for example, putting one on each finger.
- Do not mix glasses with plates and silverware, either in bus tubs or on dishracks to be washed in a dish machine. Use separate bus tubs, as well as special dishracks made for glassware.
- Never use a glass for scooping ice. Always use a plastic scoop in the ice bin; metal scoops are more likely to chip a glass rim.

- Be aware of sudden temperature changes and their impact on the glass. Do not pour hot water into an ice-cold glass, or vice versa. Keep enough inventory on hand so that you're not forced to use hot glasses directly from the dish machine. Give them time to cool off first.

Finally, keep in mind that a chipped or cracked glass is a broken glass. A crack or chip might cut a customer's lip or cause a drink to spill. Throw it out.

CASH REGISTERS

Since its invention more than a century ago by a tavern owner, the *cash register* has been a "Rock of Gibraltar" at the bar. The first version, known as "Ritty's Incorruptible Cashier," was a slow, noisy, hand-operated machine with a pot belly and a shrill bell that rang when a crank was turned to total the sale and open the cash drawer. In contrast today's computerized register, also called an **electronic cash register** or **ECR**, or a **point-of-sale terminal**, or **POS**, is slim, quiet, and lightning-fast.

In a small enterprise a single register at the bar may be all that is necessary, although its data-processing capability and its *storage capacity, memory,* will be limited. In a large system the POS terminal at the bar feeds the data it gathers into a **central processing unit (CPU)**, which runs the entire system (see Figure 4.36). This system is suitable for a medium-size or large enterprise with several different registers at various locations. In a chain the registers at every bar may feed into a company-wide computer network that can collect and analyze sales and inventory data from all over the country at the touch of just a few computer keys. A computerized system can also make the bar more efficient by sending drink orders electronically. An order can be transmitted from a station in the dining room to a screen at the bar so the drinks can be ready by the time the server reaches the bar. At the same time the guest check is output by a printer at the bar for pickup with the drinks. Orders can even be transmitted to the bar from an order pad held in the server's hand. However, such devices are expensive and require a certain amount of maintenance.

In some places the bar's cash register does not always handle cash; instead, the customer pays a cashier rather than the bartender or cocktail waitress, and credit cards have become as common, if not more so, as cash. Still the function of recording each bar sale remains at the bar, no matter how or where payment is made. This record of the type and cash value of liquor sold is the starting point of the control system by which the bar tracks its sales, costs, and liquor inventory to determine whether everything adds up.

Cash registers have always performed two basic functions: to record sales and to add and total them on a report that becomes a master record. Each register has

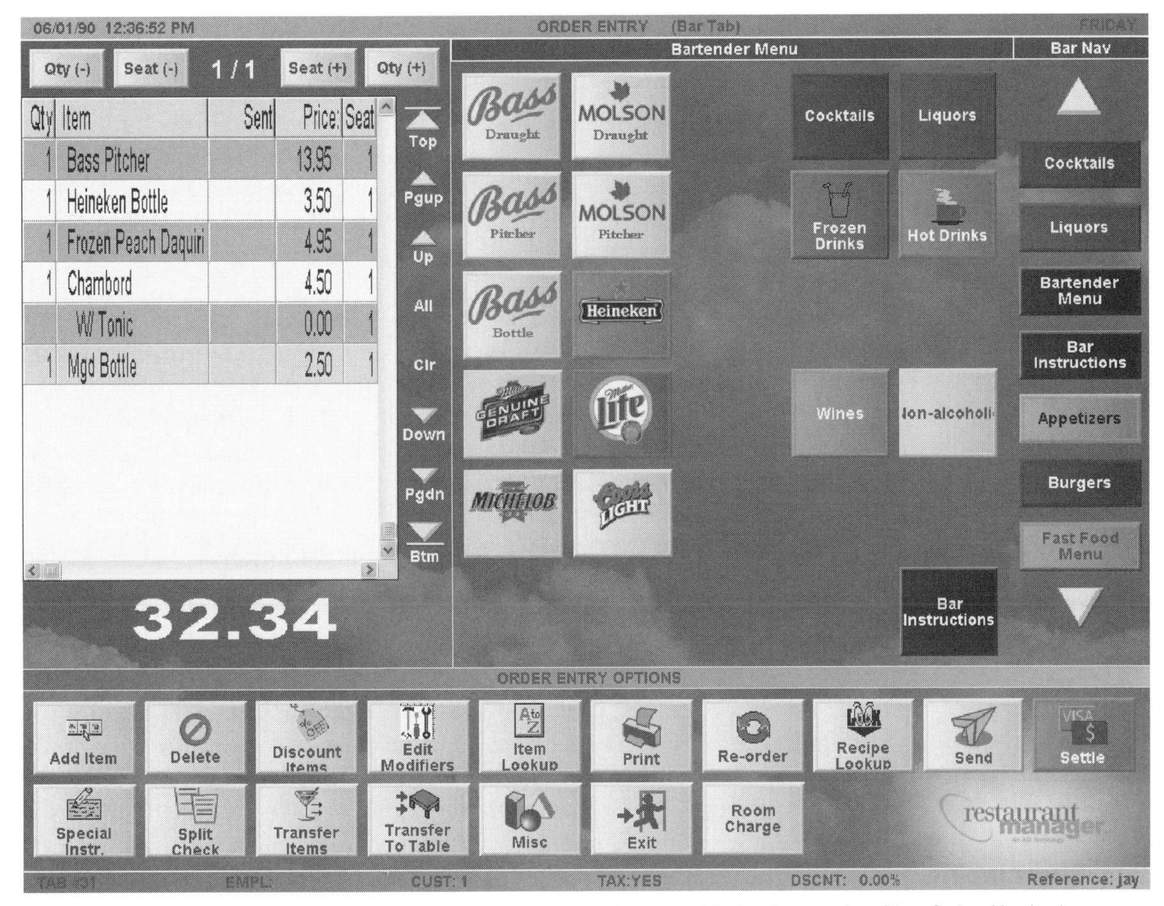

FIGURE 4.36 The screen of a POS system is programmed for easy use. Courtesy of Action Systems, Inc., Silver Spring, Maryland.

a set of keys used to record sales in dollars and cents. Another set of keys represents sales categories, such as spirits, wine, beer, soft drinks, food, tax, or anything else the operation needs or wants to figure separately. There may be a third set of keys representing different bartenders or serving personnel. On some registers each of these keys controls a cash drawer, so that each person is responsible for his or her own take. Each register prints an item-by-item record, plus the totals, category by category. This becomes the daily sales tally. It also forms the source document for all of the reports sent to the state liquor control board. The kind of information required varies from state to state and will determine the basic key categories needed on the register.

Some registers are designed to prerecord each order on a guest check. This **precheck system** acts as a double control against losses when the printed order is checked against the sale, then both totals are checked against receipts at the end of the serving period.

A more elaborate register may have single keys representing specific drinks with their prices. These keys are known as **presets.** They may be code numbers or they may name the drink on the keys. Each key will print out the name of the drink and its price and make the correct extensions both on the record and on the guest check. When the "Total" key is pressed, the register will add up the check, figure the tax, print the total on the guest check, and record everything on the day's master record.

POS terminals can also gather and tabulate sales-related data in many other useful ways. They can record the time of the sale and the server involved, along with the drink served. They can compare the liquor used in a given period with the liquor remaining in inventory. They can even function as a time clock on which employees punch in and out. In short they are more accurate and more efficient, and people need far less training to operate them. POS systems also provide tighter controls over losses and supply data to watch and analyze operations daily, instead of weekly or monthly. On the other hand the more sophisticated the system, the higher its initial cost. For large operations and chains, the cost savings and the "instant" processing of vital data make a large investment well worth the money. A central computer system can also manage administrative functions, including payroll and accounting.

No matter the complexity of your cash-register system, you might be surprised to learn how easily it can be outwitted. The time-honored saying, "Make a drink, enter a sale," should be a mandatory part of bar employee training. Each and every sale must be accounted for. Each and every drink must be accounted for. This is the only way that "free drinks" and the resulting cost control problems can be avoided.

Here's a suggestion: Go into the bar and sit at any of the various places your guests would sit. From each location ask yourself: "Can I view the full register system?" If not, there are blind spots that could be used by dishonest employees to manipulate sales. The *register screen,* or *computer monitor,* should be visible to all guests at the bar—not set at such a low angle that only the bartender can see it. Select POS software that keeps the last transaction on the screen until the next sale is entered. Choose a *pole display option,* where the sale is seen on both sides of the bar. At the very least be sure your sales policy requires a cash-register receipt for all cash transactions and those that require change be made to a guest.

GENERAL EQUIPMENT GUIDELINES

Finally consider the following general equipment guidelines.

Look for Quality

It is very good business sense to invest in high-quality equipment for your bar. This is true across the board, from the large underbar units, to the jiggers, pourers, and wine and cocktail glasses. There are a number of reasons why:

- ***Durability.*** Quality equipment will last longer and will better withstand the wear and tear of a high-speed operation. For example, heavy-gauge surfaces will resist dents, scratches, and warping. Heavy-duty blenders will better survive the demands of mixing frozen drinks. Quality glasses will break less easily than thin, brittle ones.
- ***Function.*** High-quality products are less likely to break down. Breakdowns of any kind hamper service and give a poor impression of your operation. If your pourer sticks, you have to stop and change it. If your corkscrew bends, you may crumble the cork and lose your cool as you present the wine, or the customer may refuse it. If your icemaker quits, you are in real trouble. Repairs or replacements can be frustrating, time-consuming, and costly. Quality products, moreover, usually come with guarantees.
- ***Appearance.*** High-quality products are usually more pleasing to the eye and are likely to maintain their good looks longer. Cheap glassware becomes scratched and loses its gleam. Cheap blender containers get dingy looking, as do work surfaces. Since much of your equipment is seen by your customers, it is important that it project an image of quality, cleanliness, and care.
- ***Ease of care.*** High-quality equipment is likely to be better designed, as well as better made. This means smooth corners, no dirt-catching crevices, and dent-resistant surfaces that clean easily. All together this makes for better sanitation and better appearance.

Like everything else in life, quality cannot always be judged by price. This discussion is not to imply that you should go "top shelf" all the way; you will certainly not buy lead-crystal glassware unless your entire operation sustains this level of luxury. For equipment quality examine weights or gauges of metals (the lower the gauge, the thicker the metal); at energy requirements, the horsepower of generators; the insulation of ice bins and refrigerated storage; and manufacturer's warranties and services. Consider the design features of each item in relation to its function, size, shape, and capacity, as well as to needs.

Keep It Simple

The number of bar gadgets available today, both large and small, is mind-boggling. They range from trick bottle openers to computerized drink-pouring systems that cost many thousands of dollars. Each has its bona-fide uses, and some are highly desirable for certain operations. But the wise buyer will measure his or her purchases by these criteria:

- Does it save time or money or do a better job?
- Is it worth the time and money it saves?
- Is it maintenance-free? If not, how upsetting will it be to the operation if it malfunctions? If it needs repairs, is local service available?

It is easy to go overboard on hand tools; there is a gadget on the market for every little thing you do. It is better not to clutter up your bar with tools that you seldom use. On the other hand it is wise to have a spare of every tool that is really essential, from blenders to ice scoops. This way no time will be lost if something breaks or malfunctions. Keep the spares handy in a place that is easily accessible in emergencies.

SUMMING UP

Bar equipment must be suited to the drink menu of an enterprise, just as kitchen equipment must appropriately service a food menu. All equipment must meet health-department sanitation requirements and must be kept in top condition, with special attention to temperatures and pressures and the right conditions for proper functioning. It is easy to forget that these small details affect such issues as the taste and the head on a glass of draft beer, the loss of bubbles in carbonated mixes, and the rate of production of an icemaker, but they matter as much as the initial selection of equipment.

Typical questions bar owners must answer include: Should my bartenders pour by hand or use an automatic liquor-dispensing system? What types of, and how many, blenders do I need, or should I buy or rent a frozen-drink dispenser? Should bartenders or barbacks wash glasses by hand or use a glasswasher? What types of cube ice will best suit the types of drinks on the menu? What should the capacity of the ice machine be, and where will I place it? Do I understand how a basic refrigeration system works? (This is important to know because beer and some other items require constant refrigeration.)

At least a dozen tools, called *smallware,* make up the bartender's arsenal. These enable him or her to make garnishes, measure, pour, stir, strain, and complete other necessary tasks. Bottle and can openers and good corkscrews are also critical, as are cutting boards that are easy to sanitize between uses. The right equipment, arranged for maximum efficiency and used and maintained with respect for its function, can be one of the best investments a bar owner can make. Three additional major considerations are: the proper types of glassware to complement the drink menu, and how to wash and store them. Finally, choose and use an ECR or POS system (the modern-day cash register) to accurately record all sales.

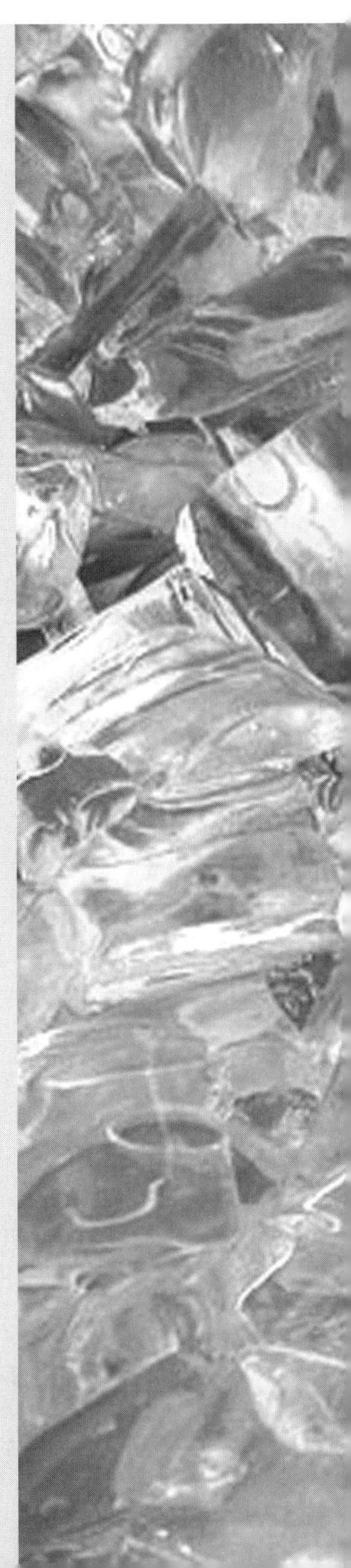

POINTS TO PONDER

1. For what types of beverage service would an electronic pouring system be considered appropriate? Where would it be inappropriate? Give reasons for your answers.
2. What are the essential pieces of equipment that make up a pouring station?
3. What questions would you ask before buying an electronic cash register? What would you want it to do?
4. Why is the type of ice so important to the taste of a drink? When might you need more than one type of ice?
5. In what situation would you buy *fully tempered* glasses? What about *rim-tempered* glasses?
6. Why is the glass in which a drink is served important to the taste?
7. Add your own flair to your personal Bartender's Toolkit. What is in it, other than the starter list on page 149? Why?
8. Explain the difference between a *premix* and a *postmix* soda-dispensing system, and cite the advantages of each.
9. Where does the term *well brand* come from and how does it differ from a *call brand*?
10. What guidelines would you use in deciding what equipment to buy for a brand-new bar?

TERMS OF THE TRADE

ah-so
annealing
bar knife
barspoon
bar strainer
base (foot)
beer box (tap box)
blender (bar mixer)
bottle chiller
bottle wells
bowl
call brands
central processing unit (CPU)
cocktail station (cocktail unit, beverage center)
compressor
condenser
condiment tray
cullet
detail tape
dispensing tower
electronic cash register (ECR)
evaporator
expansion valve
filler cap
fins

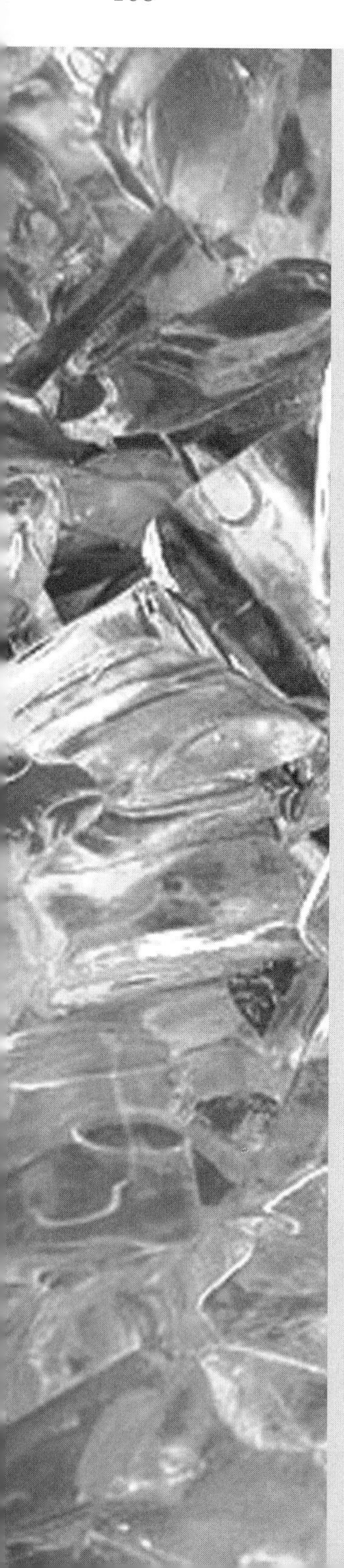

flaker (flake-ice machine)
flexhose
footed ware
funnel
frozen-drink dispenser
fruit squeezer
glass brushes
glass froster
glass rimmer
glasswasher
hand shaker (cocktail shaker)
hydrochlorofluorocarbons (HCFCs)
hydrofluorocarbons (HFCs)
ice chest (ice bin)
ice crusher
icemaker
ice scoop
ice tongs
inlet chiller
jigger
jockey box
mixing cup (mixing steel, mix can)
mixing glass
muddler (muddling stick)
overrun
point-of-sale (POS) system
postmix system
pourer
premix system
preset keys
pressware
refrigerant
refrigeration circuit
refrigeration cycle
relish fork
router
shake mixer (spindle blender)
shotglass
silica
speed rail
standard (tap)
stein
stem
stemware
stripper
tempering (fully tempered, rim-tempered)
tumbler
waiter's corkscrew
well brands (house brands, pouring brands)
worm
zester (router)

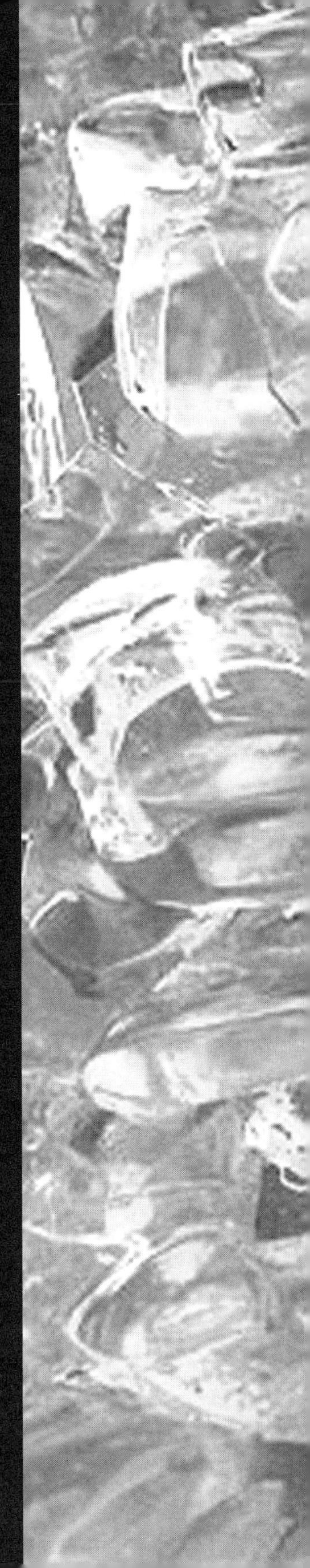

CHAPTER 5
THE BEVERAGES: SPIRITS

Premium spirits represent one of the fastest-growing components of beverage sales, which is a result of both the maturing American palate and an unprecedented surge in marketing. People who once may have asked for a shot of tequila or a Vodka Martini now order a snifter of *Commemorativo* or a *Grey Goose* Martini, straight up and chilled. Yet, although they might know the contents of liquor bottles by linking names to tastes, most do not have a clue about the basic ingredients of liquors and liqueurs or how they are made.

For a bartender or beverage manager, the question goes beyond, "What makes them different from one another?" to "How can I use them to their full advantage behind the bar?" This chapter examines the various kinds of spirits: how they are crafted and how they differ, why some spirits cost more than others, which ones are most intoxicating, where they come from, and all sorts of incidental information that makes this industry so interesting. All of this information is important in helping you to understand what you are buying and selling.

THIS CHAPTER WILL HELP YOU . . .

- Distinguish between fermented and distilled beverages and identify them on your shelves.
- Select the types and price ranges of spirits that fit your clientele.
- Define *proof* and relate it correctly to alcohol content.
- Understand the variables in distillation and their importance to the finished product.
- Become familiar with each of the spirit types commonly served from today's bar.

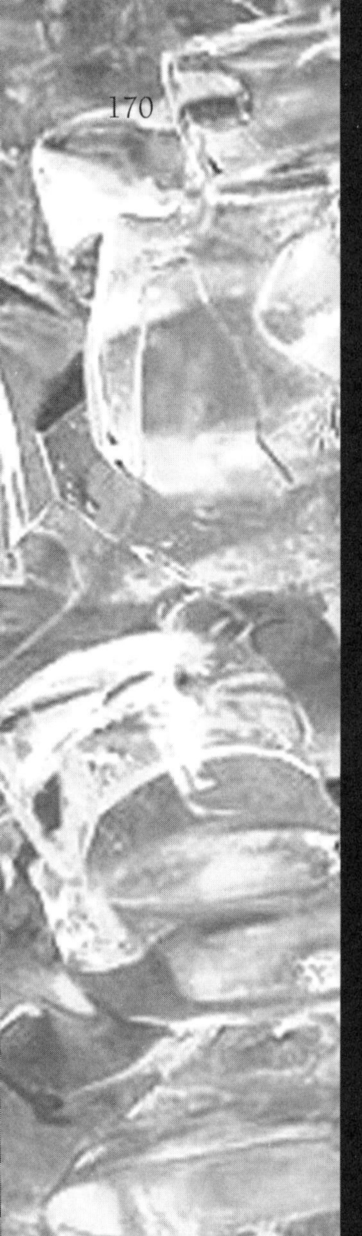

- Define and explain such familiar but mysterious terms as bottled in bond, aged in wood, sour mash, single malt, London dry, neutral spirits, VSOP, and more.
- Serve each type of spirit correctly and profitably.
- Increase sales of after-dinner drinks.

Consider this question: Which of the following well-known beverages are spirits: rum, brandy, Champagne, **Scotch**, sherry, **bourbon,** vermouth, gin, ale, or vodka? Many people incorrectly use the term *spirits* to include any type of beverage that contains alcohol. On the aforementioned list rum, brandy, Scotch, bourbon, gin, and vodka are spirits. So are the other whiskies, tequila, and all liqueurs and cordials. Champagne, sherry, and vermouth are not spirits; they are wines. Ale is a beer, not a spirit. What is the difference—and what difference does it make?

Beers, wines, and spirits taste different, have different alcoholic contents, are served differently, and tend to have different uses. In order to provide for your customers properly you need to know about these differences and how to handle each kind of beverage, from purchase to pouring.

TYPES OF ALCOHOLIC BEVERAGES

All beers, wines, and spirits are alcoholic beverages. An alcoholic beverage is any *potable,* or drinkable, liquid containing ethyl alcohol. It might have as little as ½-percent alcohol by volume, or as much as 95 percent. (The ½ percent was a figure chosen by the federal government at the time of the Prohibition Amendment, as it was groping to define an *intoxicating* beverage. At ½ percent you would have to drink 4 to 5 gallons of a beverage to become intoxicated, but the figure remains in the government's definition.)

Fermented Beverages

All alcoholic beverages begin with the fermentation of a liquid food product containing sugar. **Fermentation** is the action of yeast upon sugar in solution, which breaks down the sugar into carbon dioxide (CO_2) and alcohol. The CO_2 gas escapes into the air. The alcohol, a liquid, remains behind in the original liquid, which then becomes a *fermented beverage.*

Beers and wines are fermented beverages. Beer and ale are made from fermented grains. Wines are made from fermented grapes and other fruits. Our ancestors fermented honey, dates, rice, milk, sugarcane, molasses, palms, peppers, berries, seeds, and pomegranates, all to create alcoholic beverages. Any liquid with sugar in it could be fermented if yeast were available to start the action. When the sugar was converted to alcohol and carbon dioxide, the result was a beverage with an alcohol content of about 4 to 14 percent, depending on the amount of sugar in the original liquid.

Distilled Spirits

If you can separate the alcohol from a fermented liquid, you will have what you might think of as the essence, or the spirit, of the liquid. This is exactly what spirits are and how they are made. The process of separation is called **distillation.** The liquid is heated in an enclosed container, called a **still,** to a temperature of at least 173°F (78.5° Celsius [78.5°C]). At this temperature the alcohol changes from a liquid to a gas, which rises. Most of the water of the liquid remains behind; water does not vaporize until it reaches its boiling point of 212°F (100°C). The gas is channeled off and cooled to condense it back into a liquid. The result is a *distilled spirit,* or simply a *spirit.*

All of the spirits we use today are made by this basic process, diagrammed in Figures 5.1 and 5.2. It is not known for sure how long the distillation process has been in use, but historians credit the Chinese with distilling spirits as far back as 1000 B.C. In addition although the Greeks and Romans did not use the process, they at least knew about it. If we limit our discussion to the Western (mainly European) experience, we must credit the Arabic people for introducing distillation to Europe through the Iberian Peninsula and into the area that is now Spain. Ironically the Arabs were forbidden to drink alcohol for religious reasons. Instead

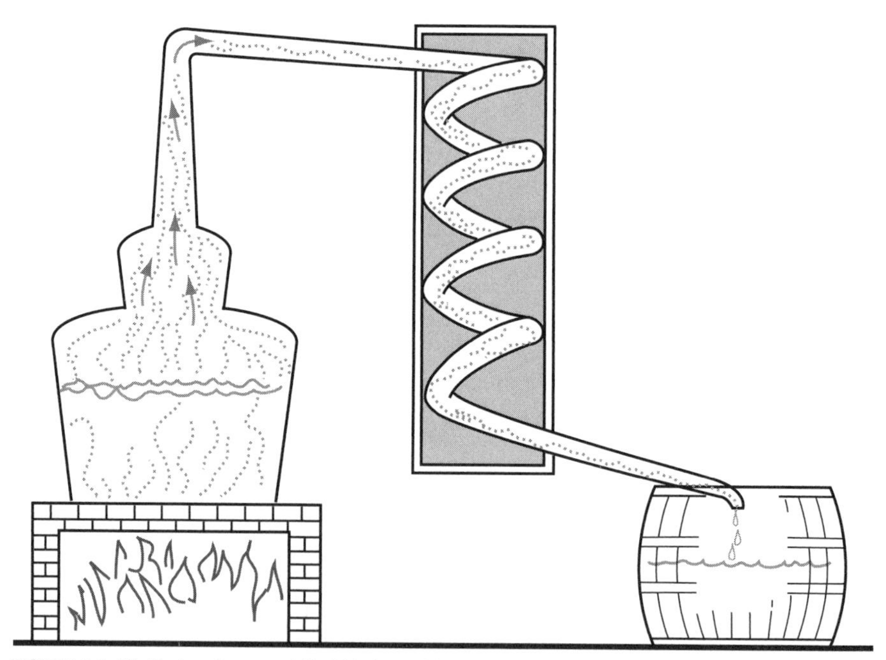

FIGURE 5.1 Distillation: Fermented liquid is heated in a still. Alcohol vapors rise and are carried off through a coil that passes through cold water, condensing them into liquid spirit.

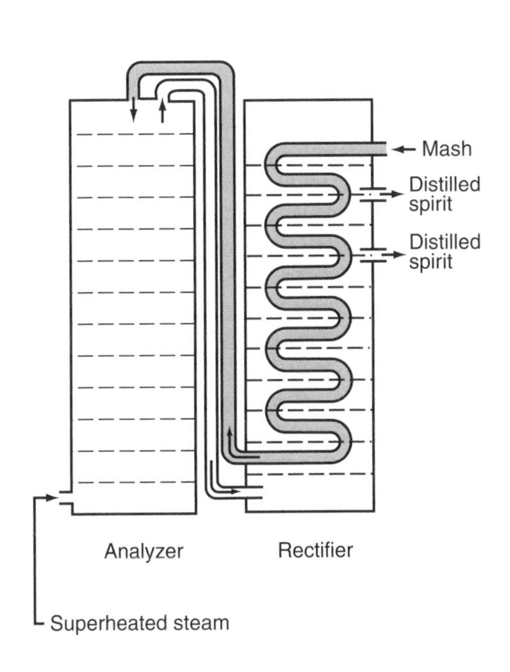

FIGURE 5.2 A continuous column still. In the version shown here, fermented mash (gray) enters the rectifier column and flows downward through a twisting pipe surrounded by superheated steam. This hot mash is then pumped to the top of the analyzer column. Here it steeps down through perforated plates, meeting superheated steam entering from the bottom of the rectifier. There they rise again through perforated plates condensing as they are cooled by the mash descending in the twisting pipe. Then the condensed spirits are drawn off at their desired degree of alcohol content. Photo courtesy of Clear Creek Distillery, Portland, Oregon.

they distilled perfume from flowers and used the process to produce a powdered cosmetic for eyes that they called *al kuhl,* from the word *kohl.* It is the word from which *alcohol* is derived.

In Europe in the Middle Ages alchemists experimented with distillation in an attempt to cure diseases or prolong life. These practitioners were equal parts scientist, philosopher, magician, and, some say, charlatan, who sold elixirs and potions about which great promises were made. Although their *aqua vitae,* which means water of life, was not quite the miracle drug they were looking for, it did gain respect as a medicine. When it was flavored to make it more palatable, people discovered that they liked it. Soon the technique of distilling was applied to all kinds of fermented products to produce much stronger beverages.

Classifying Beverages

Which of those bottles at the bar are fermented and which are distilled? You can put the familiar names into place by examining Figure 5.3.

The U.S. government has established **Standards of Identity** for the various classes of alcoholic beverages, that is, the types of spirits (gin, vodka, brandy, rum, tequila, the various whiskeys), types of wine, and types of malt beverages (beer and ale). For example if a bottle contains bourbon and is labeled as such, there is a Standard of Identity stating certain requirements for that type of product: what it is made of, how it is made, the type of container it is aged in, and its alcoholic content. These standards, rigidly enforced, produce a beverage with the distinctive characteristics that everyone recognizes as bourbon. If the name is on the bottle, you will know what is inside because a federal inspector makes periodic compliance investigations at each distillery in the country. Imported products must meet similar standards in order to enter the country.

These Standards of Identity were developed after the repeal of Prohibition as part of the strict control system imposed on the new beverage industry to avoid the chaos of the Prohibition era. The purpose of the standards is twofold: to provide the base for assessing and collecting federal taxes, and to protect the consumer. Beyond this the standards can help you to learn to read bottle labels so that you know what you are buying, and to understand the differences between similar products. The three beverage chapters in this book draw heavily on Standards of Identity.

Alcohol Content

There are other differences between fermented and distilled beverages in addition to the way they are made. One is their alcoholic content. Beers and ales contain 2½ to 8 percent alcohol by weight (3.1 to 10 percent by volume). Table wines may be 7 to 14 percent by volume; aperitif and dessert wines, 14 to 24 percent since they have a small percentage of added spirits. Spirits usually range from 35- to 50-percent alcohol by volume, with a few liqueurs as low as 18 to 20 percent and one or two rums as high as 75½ percent. (There are even neutral spirits available at 95 percent, but they are never used as bar liquors.)

For spirits you will see a number on the label and the word **proof.** Proof is a system of determining the alcohol content and, therefore, the relative strength of the beverage. It is also used as a base for collecting federal taxes on alcoholic beverages.

The history of the term is rather colorful. It comes from the early days of distilling, when the distiller tested, or *proved,* the product by mixing it with gunpowder and setting it on fire! If the liquid didn't burn, it was too weak. If it burned fiercely, it was too strong. The spirit that was "just right" for drinking (without the gunpowder) burned with a steady blue flame and turned out to be 50-percent alcohol,

ALCOHOLIC BEVERAGES

Fermented		Distilled							
Beers and ales	*Wines*	*Whiskies*	*Gins*	*Vodka*	*Rum*	*Tequila*	*Brandies*	*Liqueurs*	*Others*
Lager beers	Table	Scotch	London dry		Arrack	Mescal	Cognac	Amaretto	Aquavit
Light beers	Reds	Irish	Hollands		Cachaca	Mixto	Armagnac	Anisette	Bitters
Ales	Whites	Bourbon	Plymouth gin				Calvados	Bailey's Irish Cream	Neutral spirits
Porter	Rosé	Rye					Kirsch	Bénédictine	
Stout	Aperitif	Blends					Brandy (U.S.)	Chambord	
Bock beer	Vermouth	Canadian					Applejack	Chartreuse	
Steam beer	Dubonnet	Light					Slivovitz	Chéri-Suisse	
	Lillet						Pear William	Cointreau	
	Byrrh						Metaxa	Crèmes	
	Dessert						Pisco	Curaçao	
	Sherry[a]						Weinbrand	Drambuie	
	Port						Singani	Frangelico	
	Madeira						Grappa	Galliano	
	Marsala						Pomace	Grand Marnier	
	Muscatel						Brandies	Irish Mist	
	Sparkling						Marc	Kahlúa	
	Champagne							Limoncello	
	Sekt							Noisette	
	Sparkling burgundy							Ouzo	
	Spumante							Peter Heering	
	Saké							Pernod	
								Sabra	
								Sambuca	
								Schnapps	
								Sloe gin	
								Southern Comfort	
								Tia Maria	
								Triple sec	
								Tuaca	
								Van der Hum	
								Fruit liqueurs	

[a]Often served also as an aperitif

FIGURE 5.3 These lists are by no means comprehensive; they are meant only to familiarize you with the various types of products.

more or less. The other 50 percent of the liquid was water. Thus the American proof standard was born: A *100 proof* whiskey contains 50-percent alcohol by volume. (Take the percentage of alcohol, double it, and you get the correct proof number for that spirit.) As you might imagine this was a less than exact science. Today there are also very specific legal definitions of proof; for instance, a Proof Spirit is one that at 58°F weighs $^{12}/_{13}$ of an equal measure of distilled water. At 58°F this spirit has a specific gravity of .92308. It is a mixture of about 57-percent pure alcohol and 43-percent water. An instrument called a *hydrometer* is used to measure spirit strength.

In the past proof was indicated by the same symbol used for degrees of temperature—80°, for example. Today U.S. law requires that the label on a liquor bottle list both alcohol content and proof, with the alcohol percentage by volume stated first, and the proof following in parentheses with the word *proof* spelled out—for example, "Alc. 40% by vol. (80 proof)." This labeling system is not as clear-cut as it might appear, however, because other nations have adopted their own proof systems. The other common ones are the British/Canadian proof system. The Gay-Lussac (G-L) proof system used elsewhere in Europe is simply a statement of the percentage of alcohol by volume.

To convert from one system to another, start with the G-L value (the percentage-of-alcohol figure). To convert to the American system, multiply the G-L value by 2; to convert to the British system, multiply the G-L value by 7, then divide that answer by 4. Figure 5.4 compares the three systems of measure.

G-L System	American Proof	British/Canadian Proof
100%	200	175.2
50%	100	87.6
40%	80	70.0
10%	20	17.7

FIGURE 5.4 Three systems of measuring proof.

It is the alcohol in any beverage that causes the intoxicating effect as it runs through human veins. Looking at the percentage figures, you might conclude that a 90-proof gin is 10 times as intoxicating as beer. Ounce for ounce this is true. But comparing percentages gives a statistical picture with very little meaning since the typical serving size varies widely from one beverage to another.

We will translate the statistics into the drinks you might be serving at the bar. A 12-ounce bottle of 4-percent beer would contain 0.48 ounces of alcohol. A 5-ounce serving of 12-percent wine would have 0.6 ounces of alcohol, or 25 percent more than the bottle of beer. A Gin and Tonic made with 1½ ounces of 80-proof gin would have 0.6 ounces of alcohol, which is the same amount as the glass of wine and 25 percent more than the beer. A Martini made with 2 ounces of the same gin and ½ ounce of 18-percent vermouth would contain 0.89 ounces of alcohol, which is 33 percent more than the Gin and Tonic and the wine and 85 percent more than the beer. Figure 5.5 condenses all this information.

Comparing these beverage types you can see that alcohol content has a lot to do with the size of a serving. Imagine the consequences of pouring gin in 5-ounce servings as though it were wine. Obviously more than tradition dictates a certain glass for a certain type of beverage—for example, why beer is served in tall glasses and Martinis are served in small ones (it still takes almost two beers to equal the

A COMPARISON OF ALCOHOLIC CONTENT

Drink	Alcoholic Content (oz)	More than Beer (%)	More than Wine (%)	More than Gin-and-Tonic (%)
12 oz of 4% beer	0.48			
5 oz of 12% wine	0.6	25		
Gin-and-Tonic with 1½ oz of 80-proof gin	0.6	25	same	
Martini with 2 oz of 80-proof gin, ½ oz of 18% vermouth	0.89	85	33	33

FIGURE 5.5 Alcoholic content of drinks compared.

alcohol in one Martini). You can also understand why a customer who is gulping Martinis will need to be watched more closely for signs of intoxication than someone having a leisurely glass of wine or a bottle of beer with dinner.

Mixed Drinks

A **mixed drink** is a single serving of two or more beverage types mixed together, or of one beverage type mixed with a nonalcoholic mixer. The cocktail and the highball are the two most common types of mixed drinks, but there are many others, such as coffee drinks, Collinses, and cream drinks.

Most mixed drinks are made with spirits, although a few wines are used in **wine spritzers** and as cocktail ingredients, notably the vermouths. The most common use of spirits is in mixed drinks. The rest of this chapter takes an in-depth look at spirits, those inviting and expensive bottles that are so important to your profit that you have to keep track of every ounce.

SELECTING SPIRITS FOR THE BAR

From casual family restaurants, to fancy hotel bars, the hospitality industry is serving expensive libations to guests who are opening their wallets to pay the prices. Much like paying $3 to $4 for what once was "just a cup of coffee" by going to

Starbucks (which has introduced a coffee liqueur) or one of its many competitors, paying for an upscale drink is still an affordable indulgence for many Americans. It is a status symbol, of sorts, to order a *superpremium* spirit, and consumers' perceptions of what constitutes superpremium has been skillfully massaged by multimillion-dollar advertising campaigns.

The lack of consumer loyalty to any one drink or spirit category also provides companies with plenty of opportunities for introducing new products. An amazing number of new labels have flooded the market, each trying to claim its part of the open landscape. Often clever packaging is the prime marketing ploy; as of this writing, we have witnessed about a decade now of new, flavored vodkas in sleek, tall, frosted bottles, but the trend is getting a bit tiresome. Bartenders have to accomodate interesting new bottle designs that may be unwieldy, taking up more space on an already-packed backbar. The rectangular Boodles Gin bottle, which is awkward to pour and store, is a good example.

All the new spirit brands revolve around one principal character: the bartender. His or her role in determining which brands to use and which to ignore is more important than ever before. Every time a bartender asks, "What are you in the mood for?" and a guest replies, "I don't know. Surprise me!" there is an opportunity to recommend a new brand.

Stocking Your Well

Affordable, generic brands have been traditions in most bars and restaurants. 'Why spend more for that fancy bottle?' their owners thought. But there is a downside to pouring only bargain brands, especially if price is the bar manager's sole consideration. It might be possible to cover up an inferior spirit in a mixed drink, but it will be exposed for what it is when it is served neat, straight up. Marketing muscle and creative advertising have convinced younger customers to focus on brand names and view generic labels with suspicion. Do the pennies you save make your bar more profitable if it cannot attract your target clientele and earn their return patronage? This is a tradeoff that every bar owner must consider carefully.

The bar well can be viewed as its own three-tier system. At the highly competitive low tier, price is everything; there is little loyalty and almost no marketing influence on customers. The middle tier offers midpriced establishments (primarily casual restaurant and hotel chains) a chance to keep patrons happy while making the bottom line look good with reliable products that are priced right. The high tier is today's hottest market; it is the home of premium and superpremium brands with a sense of exclusivity in their use, pricing, and marketing.

No matter what type of bar you run, smart well management that harmonizes with your target market should be part of your plan. The following three situations offer some insight:

1. You own a neighborhood bar with value-conscious patrons. You have 50 calls a night for bourbon and water, for which you charge $1 less than for a call

brand. Your liquor sales rep convinces you to switch to Jim Beam as your well brand, but this upgrade clearly does not match your needs. Only about 5 guests per night order Jim Beam by name and are willing to pay extra for it—and now, here they are, getting the same product as everyone else. The appeal of ordering something "special" is gone. To them the lower cost of a well drink is of no importance, but you have written off the extra profit from pouring a lesser-priced well bourbon.

2. You own a nightclub with lines of "beautiful people" at the door. You would like to keep drink prices reasonable to continue to attract the trendy younger crowd, but you decide you want to offer a high-end well. Unfortunately most of your patrons will neither notice nor appreciate this effort. In the crowd they rarely get near the bar to even see what you are pouring. Honestly they do not care; they come for the scene and good drinks, not necessarily high-end "designer drinks." Without a lower tier well, your profits will take a beating on two-for-one specials, Ladies' Nights, and other promotions.
3. You own a three-star restaurant in New York City, with a speed rail full of premium brands that are identical in price or quality to the special backbar pours asked for by name. If you offer the highest quality food and service, wine service, ambience, and so forth, why would you cut corners and stock a low-tier well?

In short, the well is an important profit center that should reflect the bar's image and respond to the desires of its clientele. If that clientele knows what they want and can ask for it, the bartender should be able to pour it for them, exactly the way they want it.

Trading up to premium spirits does not have to be an expensive transition if the change is planned to generate profits and increase sales volume. The extra expense can be covered either by slightly increasing the price of a well drink or by charging more for the competitive backbar name brands. An incremental price hike across the board can help you keep pace because some spirits categories spiral up in cost faster than others. Servers and bartenders take a little more pride in offering better-quality brands, and moving established brands to the well opens up backbar shelf space and inventory dollars for a few new products and high-end items. Spirits distributors are usually happy to train the staff as part of the upgrade.

To determine whether or not to upgrade your house pours to premium pours, ask yourself these questions:

- ***Are my customers label-conscious?*** How hip are they? If they wear brand-name fashions and drive luxury cars, you have got your answer.
- ***Would an upgrade improve my best-selling drinks?*** If you sell mostly draft beer or your signature drink is the Frozen Strawberry Daiquiri, it's probably not necessary to load the speed rack with premium liquors.
- ***Are the current house pours a liability?*** It's a fact that most bar owners stock their wells and don't think much about it after that. But now and then, sit down and taste-test the well brands against the most affordable premium brands. How do they compare? What do they say about your bar's image?

Well brands are the workhorses of a bar, bringing home regular, reliable profits. Without low-tier spirits, high-volume clubs and neighborhood bars would have to raise prices and face the possibility of alienating their core clientele. For mid-tier and high-tier operations, the challenge is different but the outcome is the same: to cut costs by downgrading premium well selections to low-tier spirits risks running off spirit-savvy patrons.

HOW SPIRITS ARE MADE

All spirits are alike in several ways. They are all distilled from a fermented liquid. They all contain a high percentage of alcohol in comparison to other alcoholic beverages: Most spirits are nearly half alcohol and half water, and 80 to 100 proof, with the exception of some liqueurs.

There are several distinct and familiar categories of spirits. The primary differences between them are flavor and body. Each type has a characteristic taste: for example, whiskeys have a whiskey taste; gins, a gin taste; and rums, a rum taste. Categories of spirits have other taste variations, too: bourbon whiskey, for instance, tastes very different from Scotch, and Irish whiskey tastes different from both. There are also taste differences between brands, and there are variations in body: full-bodied spirits and lighter ones. While federal law regulates what is put on a liquor bottle's label, it requires almost no information about how the product was made or aged. What are the differences, and how do they affect the taste of the finished product?

Three main factors determine flavor and body: the ingredients in the original fermented liquid, the proof at which it is distilled, and what is done with the spirit after distillation. To understand these factors, we need to look at the distillation process more closely.

Congeners

At lower proofs there are more **congeners** and **fusel oils** in the spirit. Do not consider these detrimental to the quality of the product; they give some liquors (particularly whiskeys and brandies) their character. The core of the distillation process, as explained, is evaporating the alcohol by heating it until it separates itself from the fermented liquid by vaporizing. If this were the only element that vaporized at distilling temperatures, we would have 100-percent pure ethyl alcohol—a 200-proof spirit. It would be colorless and have a raw, sharp taste with no hint of its origin. The taste would be the same no matter what it was distilled from: for example, wine, grain, or molasses.

But other substances may join the alcohol as it vaporizes. In addition to water, minute amounts of other volatile substances provide flavor, body, and aroma in the beverage. These *congeners* come from ingredients in the original fermented liquid.

WHICH NEW SPIRITS SHOULD YOU STOCK?

You can not carry every new spirit out there, and if you buy only those that your customers ask for, you will be at least one year behind your competition. Here is a step-by-step guide for sorting out the winners from the also-rans:

1. **Be open-minded and critical.** Taste everything that salespeople offer you. But taste every new spirit blind against one of your favorites in the given category, and taste them both at room temperature in a wineglass, without any mix or ice. During the comparison tasting look for elements of smoothness and length of finish. Be aware that many distillers think you will be fooled by the addition of sugar or syrup. Sweetness can mask a poorly made spirit, but it leaves a cloying feeling in the mouth that is the opposite of the refreshing character of a great spirit.
2. **Decide whether the new spirit is both different from and as interesting as your standard.** If you're convinced of the high quality of a new spirit, show it to your colleagues and staff, then take them through a blind tasting to test it.
3. **Before introducing a new spirit, discuss with your key personnel its style and what drinks might bring out its best attributes.** This process will help you to make the final decision. Adding a new spirit to your current offerings can be tricky. If you've already taken on two or three new flavored rums and vodkas, is there any point in pushing another one onto your backbar? Your core staff must be enthusiastic about promoting the new spirit.
4. **Develop specialty drinks for the new spirit and promote them.** Remember that balance in a specialty drink list is as important as balance in a great drink. Don't try to promote more than four to eight special drinks at a time.

Source: Doug Frost, MS, MW, in *Santé,* the Magazine for Restaurant Professionals, Bennington, Vermont, October 2002.

Chemically they have such identities as acids, other alcohols, esters, aldehydes, and trace minerals. In the product they translate into, for example, the smoky malt taste in Scotch, the full-bodied pungency of bourbon, a hint of molasses in rum, and the rich aroma of fine brandy, and so on.

One congener is amyl alcohol, commonly known as fusel oil. The dictionary defines it as an "oily, acrid and poisonous" mixture. But in alcohol a very small amount of fusel oil imparts a distinctive flavor to whiskey.

Distillation Proof

When the distillation temperature, the length of distilling time, the type of still, and other factors are varied, the amounts of water and congeners can be controlled. The higher the distillation proof and the less water used, the fewer the congeners

COCKTAILS AND FOOD

In past decades spirits were almost always served before or after dinner rather than with a meal. The prevailing opinion was that alcohol "kills" the taste of the food by overpowering it. However, this mindset is changing. A small, feisty group of consumers would just as soon sip bourbon with their steak as a pedigreed Cabernet Sauvignon. As highly spiced Asian fusion and Latino cuisines increase in popularity, the libations from those cultures are being served to accompany them, such as the Sake Martini with Asian foods, and the Margarita and other tequila-based drinks with Mexican foods.

Beginning in the 1990s bartenders, including Dale DeGroff, helped to blast the stereotypes by marketing such events as "Cocktail Dinners" at a beloved (but now defunct) New York City bar called The Rainbow Room. For example, he matched a juniper-roasted venison chop and black-olive mashed potatoes with a cocktail he called *Blood and Sand,* made with J&B Select Scotch, Cherry Heering liqueur, sweet vermouth, and orange juice.

Scotch may be matched with smoked salmon, steak, burgers, and wild mushrooms. While a Gin Martini may be too complex for food-matching, a Vodka Martini with a splash of vermouth pairs well with light fish, such as sole.

So-called **edible cocktails** are another interesting development; they use alcohol to create or enhance a dessert. They may be as simple as a peach cobbler laced with peach-flavored liqueur or as decadent as frozen drinks blended from specially made gelatin and spiked whipped cream. At Karu & Y, a Miami, Florida, lounge, the venerable Bourbon Street Milk Punch begins with the basics—half-and-half, vanilla, powdered sugar, and bourbon—but takes on a whole new personality with the Spanish *alta cucina* trend of deconstructing "normal" recipes into new, surprising forms. In the "new" milk punch, Maker's Mark Bourbon is used to make a gelatin, which is finely diced and added to a granita made with milk and ice. The vanilla and half-and-half are whipped into an aromatic foam to top the drink, which is garnished with powdered sugar. At the same bar the Mojito is made with mint granita, Bacardi-based gelatin, and lime-flavored foam. Sangria is made by extracting green apple juice to make a fruity gelatin, which then becomes part of a refreshing wine-based drink. These edible cocktails are priced from $8 to $10 and are promoted with a tapas menu at Karu & Y.

and the purer the alcohol. Since the congeners are the flavorers, the flavor is less pronounced and the body of the spirit is lighter. Conversely the lower the distillation proof, the more distinctive and pronounced the flavor of the spirit. To experience the difference, taste a vodka and a bourbon: vodkas are distilled at 190 proof or above; bourbons are usually distilled at 110 to 130 proof.

The ideal in the world of liquor manufacture is to hit on the right combination of low distillation proof (with more flavor from congeners and fusel oils) and high bottled proof (not overly diluted with water). Spirits distilled from any material at

190 proof or above show almost no distinct characteristics. Therefore, they are known as **neutral spirits** or *neutral alcohol,* and are almost pure alcohol. If bottled, neutral spirits must be bottled at 80 proof or higher. These are used to make vodka and gin and to blend with spirits distilled at lower proofs.

All neutral spirits, as well as many lower-proof spirits, are distilled in *column stills* (see Figure 5.2). It is also called a **Coffey still** (after Aeneas Coffey, its Irish creator who developed the process in 1832), or a **continuous** or **patent still,** and it is the type of still used to make most spirits in this country. The column still can be controlled to produce spirits at a wide range of strengths, up to about 196 proof. It consists of a tall column or a series of columns, in which the fermented liquid is heated by steam inside the still instead of heat from below. The alcohol vapors can be drawn off at various heights and redistilled in a continuous process. This makes it possible to separate nearly all of the water and congeners from the alcohol if neutral spirits are the goal, or to produce spirits at almost any lower proof. Another advantage of the column still is that it operates without stopping (hence the term *continuous*), thereby producing significantly larger amounts of product than its smaller cousin, the short, rounded *pot still.*

Cognac, malt scotch, Irish whiskey, tequila, and some rums, gins, and liqueurs are made in **pot stills** that have not changed much in design since the early days of distilling. Pot stills with copper pots are called **alambic stills.** (The ancient Moorish word for still was *al-ambiq.*) Pot stills are limited in the degree of proof they can achieve; consequently, the liquor they produce always has a great deal of flavor, body, and aroma. With the pot still, only one batch at a time can be made, and the pot must be cleaned after every use. This type of still is associated with high quality and exclusivity, creating the "microbrews," if you will, of spirits.

Aging, Blending, and Bottling

A newly distilled spirit is raw, sharp, and biting. How is it turned into the mellow and flavorful product we sell at the bar? Our less sophisticated ancestors drank the spirit as it came from the still. The story goes that someone noticed that a batch of spirits shipped a long distance in wooden barrels tasted better on arrival than it did when it left the still. However the discovery was made, most of today's spirits distilled at less than 190 proof are aged in wooden (usually oak) barrels for periods ranging from one year for some light rums to 20 or so years for choice brandies. The age on the label is the length in years that the distiller kept the product in the barrel. Longer time periods do not necessarily indicate a better-quality product; it's all relative. Some Cognacs can improve for 25 years, while other spirits turn woody and bitter after only three years.

Two things happen in the barrels. First the spirit undergoes changes as the congeners interact with air filtering through the porous wooden casks. Then new congeners are absorbed from the wood itself, adding other flavoring agents. In due course all of the flavors are "married," or blended, and mellowed to the desired final taste. Aging in wood adds color as well as flavor to the spirit. (We also discuss barrel-aging in the following section on Brown Goods: Whiskey and Scotch.)

Not all spirits are aged. Sometimes the sharp bite of a raw but flavorful spirit is part of its appeal, such as gin, or kirsch. There are other means of producing or modifying flavors after distillation. One is by introducing new flavors, as is done with gin and liqueurs. Another is by blending two or more distillates, as is done with many whiskeys. A spirit taste may also be modified by filtering through charcoal, as is done in making vodka, or by other special ways of removing certain congeners. At bottling time spirits are diluted to drinking levels of taste, usually 80 to 100 proof, by adding distilled water. This lessens the intensity of the flavor but does not change it. When the term **cask strength** is used on a whiskey label, it means that no water was added to the spirit during bottling. It does not mean that the product was never diluted, just that it was not diluted during the bottling process. The term is a good sign that the whiskey will be flavorful. Once in the bottle a spirit does not undergo any further change. No matter how old it gets sitting on a shelf, it does not age since it is not exposed to air or wood.

Consumers in the United States used to purchase their spirits, mostly whiskey, by filling their own jugs from a retailer's or vendor's casks. This practice kept packaging costs down, but it also enabled dishonest vendors to dilute the product. In the early 1800s the reputation of a liquor was made by its vendor, not by the distiller who created the product. This changed in 1870 when George Carvin Brown became the first distiller to bottle, label, and market his own bourbon, known as *Old Forester.* Brown put it in clear, sealed bottles that were not easily tampered with. The idea caught on, and soon other distillers began bottling, sealing, and labeling their wares instead of selling casks to retailers.

Today all of the spirits produced in the United States are stored and bottled in bonded warehouses. At bottling time the bottler checks for full bottles, correct proof, accurate labeling, and purity. If everything complies with all federal standards, the federal tax is paid and the bottle is sealed with a federal revenue stamp or, more often, with a tamper-evident closure of metal or plastic. This does not mean that the government guarantees the quality of the product. Many people mistakenly think the phrase **Bottled in Bond** on a label is a guarantee of quality conferred by the government. What it really means is that a given spirit meets certain conditions: It is straight (unblended), distilled at 160 proof or less at one plant by one distiller, aged at least four years, and bottled at 100 proof in a bonded warehouse. Since all spirits are now bottled in bonded warehouses, the phrase has lost much of its meaning.

You can see that there are literally hundreds of ways in which a beverage that is roughly half alcohol and half water can be made in thousands of different varieties. Every ingredient, from the grape or grain, to the water and yeast, can make a difference in taste. Distillation methods are critical. Different aging times and conditions produce different tastes. The type of wood in the barrel, and whether the barrel is new or used, charred or uncharred, has a definite effect on flavor. Blending and flavoring can produce an almost infinite number of products. All of these factors explain why each brand of each spirit is unique.

Fortunately there are only a few basic spirit types, and they are easily recognizable by general taste, aroma, and character. Let's look at them in greater detail.

BROWN GOODS: WHISKEY AND SCOTCH

The term **brown goods** is commonly used to describe spirits like whiskey, Scotch, and brandy because of their rich, earth-tone colors. In general brown-goods sales have gradually declined over the years, perhaps because their hearty flavors and dark colors give the impression of a strong, high-proof drink. But they are no higher in alcohol content than other spirits, and brown goods are mainstays of any bar and the backbone of many traditional drinks. In addition, the single-malt scotches and **BMSWs** (a term you will soon learn) are among the most cutting-edge contemporary adult beverages.

(An important note: You will see whiskey spelled with the "e" and without, in this book and on product labels. Both spellings are correct, but whiskey with an "e" is the American and Irish spelling (plural *whiskeys*); products without the "e" (whisky, plural *whiskies*) are most often from Scotland or Canada. There are a couple of exceptions: Old Times and Old Forester are American whiskeys that spell their name *whisky,* to pay homage to their Scottish roots.

The four major whiskey-producing countries of the world are Canada, Ireland, Scotland, and the United States. Ireland was the first of these four to export its whiskey. After a root-rotting disease called *phylloxera* destroyed many French vineyards in the 1870s (and reduced wine and Cognac production), Scotland began exporting also. Scotch whisky has been the dominant product in this category ever since.

The earliest spirit makers started with whatever fermentable product was readily available. In the southern European nations it was wine, already fermented and available. In such northern climates as Scotland and Ireland, grapes did not grow well, but grain did, and beer and ale were plentiful. As a result the first distillers started with a fermented mash of grain, similar to the early stages of making beer, and distilled that. They produced a raw, biting drink called *uisgebeatha* in Scotland and *uisegebaugh* in Ireland, Celtic translations of *aqua vitae, water of life.* Later the last syllables were dropped and the name became *uisge* and, eventually, "whiskey," with or without the "e" depending on origin.

To get a grain product to ferment, an extra step is required to begin the whiskey-making process: the starch in the grain must be converted to sugar. This is done by adding a malt. **Malt** is sprouted grain, usually barley. It contains an enzyme called **diastase,** which changes the starch to sugars. Malt, grain, and hot water are mixed together until conversion takes place. This is the *mash.* The liquid is then fermented by adding yeast. After fermentation it is distilled. Figure 5.6 shows the sequence of steps.

Master distillers say the quality of the water and barley, as well as the locations of their distilleries, all make a difference in overall taste of the final product. (Location affects the flavors of the raw materials.) They also say the size of the still

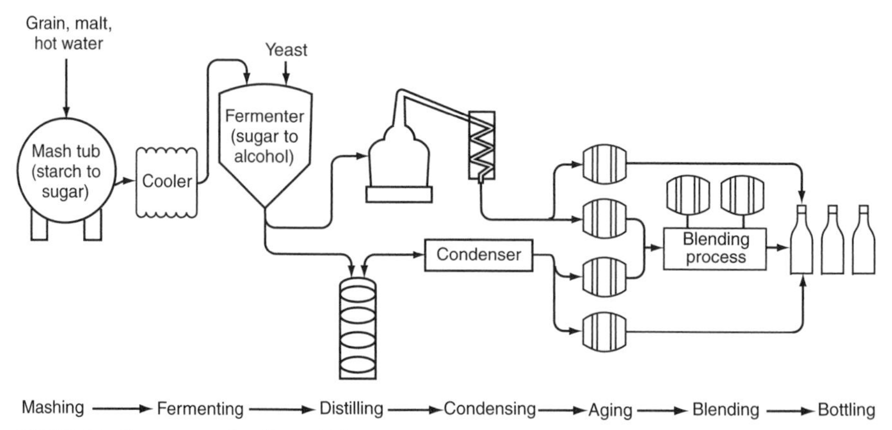

FIGURE 5.6 The process of making whiskey.

has a flavor impact: the smaller the pot, the more intense the whiskey that comes from it; the taller the still, the more delicate the whiskey. As with any other handcrafted product, dozens of variables are all points of individual opinion, professional pride, and heated debate!

After distilling, the raw whiskey is stored in barrels (usually made of oak) for at least two years. (By Scottish law, Scotch whisky must be in barrels for a minimum of three years.) Again, the type and age of barrel affects the flavor. Whiskies stored in former sherry casks have a sweet, fruity aroma; those stored in bourbon casks have a smoky aroma, sometimes reminiscent of vanilla or caramel. New barrels give off sharper, more pronounced aromas than older, well-seasoned ones. Theories about **wood management,** as it's called, abound. Modern-day whiskey makers have strong preferences about the origin of their oak—American, French, Spanish—as well as what the barrels originally contained. Port, Madeira, bourbon, and sherry casks impart their own specific nuances to the spirit, as does the type of oak itself. Some distillers age their wares in one type of barrel, then transfer the spirits to another type for the final 6 to 12 months of aging. Of course the length of time for barrel-aging depends on the character of the raw product; some spirits take longer to mellow than others. For this reason, a 12-year-old whiskey is not necessarily better quality than, say, a five-year-old or one whose age is not given on the label. It all depends.

For straight whiskies, the product manufacture ends at this point. The most common straight whiskeys include bourbon, **rye,** and corn, each containing 51 percent or more of a single grain type. But the majority of whiskeys marketed in the United States (this includes imports) undergo yet another process, known as **blending.** Whiskeys of different grains or different batches, different stills, or different ages are blended together, sometimes with neutral spirits, to produce the standard of flavor and quality that represents a particular brand. In short a blend is labeled with a brand name, not a distillery name. The use of neutral spirits in the blends (a common practice in the United States and Canada) is frowned upon by purists, who consider it an inexpensive way of diluting the true spirit. Usually the formula is a house secret, and the final blend is perfected by skilled master blenders. This person, responsible for making an appealing and consistent mix, is often referred to as a *nose* because he or she smells the whiskey's aroma but rarely actually tastes it. The alcohol content of the spirit would overpower the taste buds after only a few sips.

We will examine the different types of whiskey/whisky available for your bar by starting with a primer on Scotch.

Scotch

Scotch is short for *Scottish whisky*—although Americans are just about the only people who use the shortened term for whisky made in Scotland. There are a number of categories of Scottish or Scotch whisky, and we defer to the Scotch Whisky Association's definitions, proposed in June 2004, to help you decipher the various product labels. These are reprinted with permission of *Wine Enthusiast* magazine, where they appeared in the March 2005 issue:

- ***Single Malt Scotch Whisky:*** A Scotch whisky distilled at a single distillery from water and malted barley, without the addition of any other cereals and by batch distillation in pot stills.
- ***Single Grain Scotch Whisky:*** A Scotch whisky distilled at a single distillery from water and malted barley, with or without whole grains of other malted or unmalted cereals, that does not comply with the definition of single malt Scotch whisky.
- ***Blended Scotch Whisky:*** A blend of one or more single malt Scotch whiskies with one or more single grain Scotch whiskies.
- ***Blended Malt Scotch Whisky (BMSW):*** A blend of single malt Scotch whiskies that have been distilled at more than one distillery. These may be known as **vatted malts** or **pure malts.**
- ***Blended Grain Scotch Whisky:*** A blend of single grain Scotch whiskies that have been distilled at more than one distillery.

The difference between malt whiskies and grain whiskies is much like the difference between ales and lagers, which you will learn more about in Chapter 8's discussion of beer-making—that is, different ingredients are used to produce the end result, with slightly different methods and equipment as well.

The **malt whiskies** are made in pot stills, mainly from sprouted barley that has been dried over peat fires, giving it a smoky flavor and aroma that carries over into the final product. *Peat* is a natural fuel made of decomposed vegetation; its rich organic content (and, therefore, the aroma it imparts when burning) may be moss and seaweed, or wood and heather, depending on where it was harvested. There is an ongoing debate in Europe about the peat-harvesting practices, specifically whether they are damaging the ecosystem (see Figure 5.7) When Scotch is de-

FIGURE 5.7 Peat harvesting is controversial because of the environmental damage it can cause. This photo is of a moor in Germany used for peat production. Photo courtesy of Christian Fischer.

scribed as **"peaty"** or having a "peat reek," it refers to the smoky or ash-like character imparted either by the use of peat fires to dry the grain, or by the water from which the Scotch is made coming into contact with peat fields. The barley may be exposed to as few as 15 hours of peat smoke or as many as 40 hours. A few Scotch whiskies do not use peated barley.

Malt whisky was born well before the fifteenth century, which is the first time Scottish records mention it. An old Scottish quip says that it was created to reward the Scots for having to endure the cold, wet climate of their homeland. The 1600s and 1700s were marked by continuous disagreements between distillers and the government over taxation of spirits, and laws were enacted with the intent of putting the smaller (fewer than 200 gallons) home producers out of business. This only ensured a lively smuggling market for their product. Finally in 1823 Scotland's Parliament enacted more lenient laws.

About 130 years ago a Scotsman named Andrew Usher is credited with being the first to blend malt whisky and grain whisky to reduce its pungency. The **grain whiskies** are made chiefly from corn (or corn and wheat) and are distilled in column stills at around 180 proof, which is somewhat below neutral spirits but very light in flavor. Malt and grain whiskies are aged separately for several years and then blended, with as many as 30 or 40 (or more) different malt and grain whiskies in a given brand.

Scotch became popular in the United States during the Prohibition years, when it was smuggled into the country from Canada, the Caribbean, and ships at sea. The earliest brands were dark, peaty, and strong. After the repeal of Prohibition, Scotland's distillers began tailoring their products to the lighter American palate. Scotch got another boost in popularity when American soldiers returned from the World Wars having acquired a taste for it. A light-bodied Scotch is not necessarily light colored since all Scotches have caramel (burnt sugar) added to ensure color uniformity, nor does light body mean low alcohol content. All Scotches are bottled at a minimum of 80 proof; most are 86 proof.

Scotch and the American Consumer

Now that you are familiar with the categories of Scotch whisky, we can describe the role of each on the American bar scene. Interestingly, although the popularity of Scotch has waxed and waned over the years, this spirit has never lost its perceived prestige. The true Scotch drinker will not be satisfied with anything else, except perhaps a good Cognac.

More than 95 percent of the Scotch whisky produced is blended Scotch whisky, identified by popular brand names with which any bartender should be familiar:

Chivas Regal, Cutty Sark, Dewars, J&B, Johnnie Walker Red or Black, and White Horse. Scotch whisky's appeal is subtlety—no sharp, distinguishing characteristics, just smoothness and consistency for a good drink.

Grain Scotch whisky is not often sold in the United States, although Compass Box has an all-grain blend called Hedonism and Invergordon's 7-Year-Old is a single-grain. Usually, though, grain scotch is used in blending with malt scotches.

Single-malt scotch is the only segment of the overall Scotch category that is showing growth, partly because of clever marketing that capitalizes on its super-premium, artisan's image—tiny batches, third- and fourth-generation distillers, aging for a decade or more, and so on—and partly because Americans are drinking less but seeking higher-quality spirits. Single-malt Scotch drinkers are as enthusiastic as wine buffs about finding and tasting the rare and unusual brands, each named for the distillery where it is born. There are fewer than 100 single-malt distillers operating in Scotland today, and these can be grouped into several distinct regions:

- *Lowlands malts* are big and soft in body and aroma, perhaps a reflection of the region's gentle terrain.
- *Highland whiskies* are as diverse as the area's rugged geography, so it is impossible to characterize a single style. About half of Scotland's single-malt distilleries are located in the area around Speyside, and their products are known for delicacy and elegance. Western Highland malts have light exposure to peat and a plummy aroma; Northern Highland malts are smokier and spicier in character.
- *Island malts* are from three islands: Isley, Orkney, and Skye. They are characterized as intensely smoky, with lots of *peat reek,* which means heavy wood flavors and an alcoholic bite. Distilleries near the sea also produce whiskeys with a briny (salty) flavor or aroma. Laphroaig is among the best known of the Isley malt Scotches.
- *Campbeltown malts* also feature the briny characteristic, along with a hint of sweetness. This region contains distilleries that have three stills but stop the distillation process after "two-and-a-half." Campbeltown brands are rare since there are only two distilleries where there once were dozens.

Remember that these are the bare basics of a very complex and proud industry. Within each region, finer distinctions exist. Taste-test them and you will soon see!

Finally the BMSWs (vatted malts) are enjoying a first blush of attention from American consumers. The idea is not really new—these are blended malt Scotches—but their distinctiveness comes from the marriage of two or more of the prestigious single malts from different distilleries. The appeal is clear for consumers who might be interested in Scotch whisky but put off by the snobbishness that surrounds the passionate single-malt crowd. If you are convinced that you will never be able to tell a Glenfiddich from a Glenfarclas from a Glenlivet, perhaps a BMSW is for you. Some of the names you may encounter are Johnnie Walker Green Label, The Famous Grouse 10-Year-Old Malt Whisky, Compass Box Eleuthera, and Michel Couvreur Unfiltered 12-Year-Old.

The graying of the demographic base for Scotch whisky is well known, but single-malt offerings can provide a bar with the chance to grow product acceptance by engaging a new generation of consumers: people ages 25 to 40, with disposable income, sophisticated palates, and a desire to learn more. The recent revival of classic cocktails and the increased availability of products from around the world are helpful trends. The Johnnie Walker brand reports that 20 to 30 percent of its consumer base is now female. Scotch whisky producers also have launched promotional campaigns aimed directly at Latino and Asian consumers, who see this spirit in particular as a symbol of economic success in America.

For the bar the social aspects of Scotch can be used in marketing events. In almost every city at least one bar prides itself on having the area's largest variety of single malts; some bars have Scotch tastings, seminars, and dinners for hobbyists. For example, Piper Pub Bar & Grill in Boise, Idaho, has turned typically slow Tuesday nights into an informative social event called "Scotch Club." For $25 participants taste three or four single-malt Scotches (which normally retail for $7 to $11 per shot). Hors d'oeuvres and a cigar are included in the price, with other premium beverages and cigars available for purchase. Sometimes there's a brief talk or slide show by a beverage distributor; other events just offer patrons a fun chance to swirl, puff, and chat with other Scotch lovers. "Scotch Club" evenings take place twice a month.

Irish Whiskey

Generally Irish whiskeys are smooth alternatives to the heavier-flavored Scotches. In terms of liquor craftsmanship, Irish whiskey is in the same league as single-malt Scotches and single-barrel Bourbons. It has an ancestry going back to the twelfth century, when King Henry II's troops invaded and found a well-established whiskey trade, begun by monks who had settled in the area in the Dark Ages.

Today's production techniques for Scotch whisky and Irish whiskey are similar, but with some differences that affect the flavor. The main difference is that the freshly malted barley in Irish whiskey is not exposed to peat smoke when it is dried, so there is none of the smoky taste of Scotch. Another difference is that Irish whiskey is made from a mixture of several grains, not just malted barley. A third is a triple distillation process that takes some of the Irish product through three separate stills (most pot-still whiskies go through two). Of course whiskey-making being the art form that it is, there are exceptions to each and every one of the statements just made. For example, in some Irish whiskeys, a small portion of the malt is either peat-smoked or distilled only twice, or the formula uses some malted and some unmalted barley.

Like the one in Scotland, the legal requirement in Ireland is that whiskey be aged for three years, although most is kept in wooden barrels for 5 to 8 years, and some up to 20 years. The result is a particularly smooth, mellow whiskey of medium body. The traditional unblended Irish whiskey is seldom called for in America. The more familiar Irish brands are blended with high-proof grain whiskey, as in making Scotch, to create a lighter drink for today's market.

In the United States, Irish whiskey is the smallest category of distilled spirits, with less than 1 percent of the total market. However, it is a fast-growing category.

The Atlanta-based chain Fado Pubs, Inc., has erected more than 150 Irish pubs in the United States in the past decade, all with interiors built in the Emerald Isle and transported overseas. A younger crowd is learning that Irish whiskey's triple distillation often makes it a smoother sip than the more assertive bourbons and Scotches.

Although whiskey-making is big business in Ireland with dozens of brand names, there are only three distilleries: Bushmills in Northern Ireland, and the Cooley and Midleton facilities in the Republic of Ireland. A single company, Irish Distillers, owns two of them (Bushmills and Midleton)—and Irish Distillers is owned by Pernod-Ricard of France.

The Irish distillers have capitalized on the single-malt-Scotch craze by introducing single-malt Irish whiskeys (labeled *pure pot still whiskey*) as "lighter" alternatives. This has proven to be a smart move; after almost 20 years of slowly declining sales, Irish whiskeys are now on the increase again. As many as 20 brands are available in the United States, and the pack is led by Jameson's Irish Whiskey, a Midleton-made brand with double-digit sales growth in the 2000s.

Bourbon

Bourbon is the best-known straight (unblended) American whiskey. Unlike the way bourbon makers regard the other brown goods in this category, they prefer to think of their product as "the golden spirit," a palatable drink and versatile cocktail ingredient. To be called bourbon it must be:

- Made in the United States
- Unblended
- Distilled at 160 proof or less from a fermented mash of at least 51-percent corn (although most bourbons contain more, up to 79 percent)
- Aged at least two years in charred (burned), new-oak containers

These requirements are spelled out in the federal government's Standards of Identity. Most bourbons are aged for four to six years, or for however long it takes to reach their desired mellowness. At the usual distillation proofs of 110 to 130, the whiskey produced has a strong flavor component and a full body. Also by law bourbon does not have to be distilled in Kentucky, as long as it is made according to the federal regulations. But if it is called *Kentucky whiskey,* it must be distilled there. The same law applies to **Tennessee whiskey.**

The bourbon-making business is replete with legend and colorful history. In 1776, patriot Patrick Henry helped craft and pass a "Corn Patch and Cabin Rights" law that gave settlers 400 acres of free land (in what is now Kentucky) if they would use it to build a house and grow grain. Corn was the easiest grain to grow and, as luck would have it, when combined with the mineral-free water that emerged from the area's underground springs filtered through natural limestone, it made very good whiskey. This bourbon was lighter than what had been produced in the Northeast.

TASTING AND APPRECIATING BROWN GOODS

Most consumers are surprised to learn that almost anyone can cultivate a taste for whiskey/whisky and bourbon. Like wines, these spirits have a broad spectrum of aromas, textures, flavors, and complexities. By learning to synchronize your senses, you can increase your spirits appreciation considerably. Begin by pouring 1½ ounces of the liquor into a 6- to 8-ounce Old-Fashioned glass or a snifter; then examine it as follows:

- **Sight:** For Scotch whisky, the appearance of the liquid is perhaps the least important attribute, indicating neither quality nor age. It may be pale yellow, gold, amber, or chestnut brown. The pivotal element here is clarity. The liquid should be clean, almost glistening, and appealing to the eye.
- **Smell:** Your sense of smell accounts for at least 90 percent of your sense of taste. The best way to smell whiskey is to aerate it by swirling it around in the glass, an action that, as with wine, releases aroma. Stick your nose into the bowl of the glass and, with your lips parted, inhale deeply, filling your nose with the spirit's fragrance. Try to pinpoint what you smell by comparing it to everyday foods or odors with which you are familiar—yes, *everything,* from paint, to seawater, herbs, grasses, fruits, nuts, candies, smoke, and so on. Think about whether the liquid smells sweet, bitter, salty, or acidic. Master Scotch distillers even suggest adding a few drops of mineral water to whiskey before smelling it, which further "opens" its aroma.
- **Taste:** Take a small amount (no more than ¼ ounce) onto the tongue and allow it to rest there for 10 to 15 seconds before swallowing. What do your taste buds experience? You may identify the sensations as sweet, bitter, salty, hot, smoky, or biting, to name a few. Does the liquid gently warm the palate and throat, or is it harsh?
- **Touch:** In this case the correct term is *mouthfeel,* and it works to unite the rest of your impressions. Try to describe the liquid in terms of its "weight"—light, medium, or full-bodied. Is it syrupy or delicate? Does its texture complement the aroma and flavors you picked up? In cold-weather months some bartenders rinse the outside of the snifter briefly in hot water to warm it. The slight bit of warmth, which increases when you rest the snifter in the palm of your hand, helps release the whiskey's aroma and flavor nuances.

Bourbon was named for Bourbon County, Kentucky, which, in turn, was named for the royal Bourbon family of France that had supported American colonists during the Revolutionary War. The man credited for discovering the bourbon style of whiskey-making was Reverend Elijah Craig, a Baptist preacher, in the late 1700s. He was the first to burn the insides of his oak barrels—whether intentionally or accidentally is unclear—and found that the charred wood added a beautiful, amber color and distinctive taste to his whiskey. Bourbon makers have been burning the insides of the barrels ever since. In those days having whiskey on hand was an ordinary part of life, and many a farmer had his own still or raised grain for his neighbor's still. Today most bourbons are made in Kentucky, though as of this writing there is no working distillery in Bourbon County.

The other historical event that sets bourbon apart from other spirits is the discovery of the **sour-mash** yeast process. In the 1820s Dr. James C. Crow went to work at a Kentucky distillery, determined to use science to make the often rough-tasting spirit better. He found that, along with the fresh yeast, a portion of the leftovers (the "soured" mash) from a previous distilling could be added to the mash. This encourages yeast growth, inhibits bacterial contamination, and provides a certain continuity of flavor. There's nothing "sour" about the taste, either.

By the 1860s bourbon was used as much as a medicine and anesthetic as it was a beverage. It was prescribed for at least a dozen ailments. Its quality became more consistent with George Carvin Brown's decision to sell his bourbon in sealed bottles in 1870. President Abraham Lincoln wondered aloud which brand of bourbon General Ulysses S. Grant drank. Since Grant was so successful leading the Union army (and quaffed quite a bit of bourbon) Lincoln thought perhaps he should send some of the same brand to his less-motivated military leaders. Lincoln also taxed alcohol after the Civil War in an attempt to raise quick cash for the government, a move that inadvertently put the small owners out of business and began a steady consolidation of the industry that continued for the next century.

A hundred years later bourbon had fallen out of favor with the public. Scotch became the drink of choice, and *white goods* (gin and vodka) also cut into its market share in the 1970s and 1980s. Today, however, smart bartenders are reintroducing bourbon as the versatile spirit it can be, both in "retro" cocktails and higher-end small-batch and single-barrel bourbons. In bourbon terminology *single-barrel* means just that: The bottle comes from one particular barrel. *Small-batch* means that the bourbon is blended from a number of barrels that show the finest characteristics. Variables in the bourbon-making process are the water, the grain (based on ripeness and moisture content), the yeast (a special "secret" mix known only to the distiller), the type of barrel and amount of charring, the time of year it is put into barrels (summer heat adds intensity of flavor and color, while in winter the liquid "rests"), and even placement of the barrel within the storage area, called a **barrel house.** Barrels are stacked on racks up to nine stories high; the ones closest to the top get more heat, which speeds the aging process and intensifies their alcohol content. Barrel contents are either bottled directly or blended first, but not until at least two years have passed. Master distillers must think multidimensionally, knowing how the spirit ages in each part of the barrel house and sensing when to rotate barrels for consistent maturation of the spirits inside.

As might be expected from such a competitive industry, clever marketers have taken the term *small-batch* and adapted it for their own sales gains, taking a few barrels from large-batch production and bottling them separately, then creating ad campaigns that appear to endow these technically "smaller batches" with prestige of exclusivity. Used in this way, the term is a bit misleading.

A sour-mash whiskey similar to bourbon is Jack Daniel's, a Tennessee product. Made in Lynchburg, a town of fewer than 400 people where liquor has not been sold since Prohibition, the distillery has been allowed, since 1995, to sell commemorative bottles on-site, but no one can buy and consume alcohol on the premises. While Tennessee whiskey meets the grain requirements of bourbon, it has a special twist to its production: The distillate is filtered through maple charcoal before it is barreled for aging. This bit of regional tradition eliminates some harsher elements in the whiskey and adds its own touch of flavor and romance. George Dickel and Jack Daniel's are the only two legal distilleries in the state of Tennessee.

Jack Daniel's (owned by Brown-Forman) and Jim Beam (owned by Fortune Brands, in partnership with Pernod-Ricard) compete for supremacy in the brown-goods market, each with a loyal market share of more than 20 percent. Other familiar bourbon brand names include Ancient Age, Early Times, Evan Williams, Old Crow, Old Forester, Old Grand Dad, Maker's Mark, Ten High, and Wild Turkey.

Canadian Whisky

Canadian whiskies are mostly blended whiskies, light in body, and delicate and mellow in flavor. Canadian brands provide "imported" status to consumers at less expensive prices than fine Scotches. Canadian law requires only that the whiskies be made from cereal grains and be aged at least three years, leaving the rest up to the distiller. The grains usually used are corn, rye, barley malt, and wheat, and each brand's formula is a trade secret. The whiskies are distilled at 140 to 180 proof, and most are aged six years or more. Their lightness keeps them popular in the current "light-minded" market.

Here's a perplexing question: Which Canadian whiskies are actually Canadian products? In a conundrum that has also overtaken the wine world, a couple of large multibrand corporations control much of the Canadian whisky production. Pernod-Ricard acquired Seagram's in 2001 and Allied Domecq in 2005, which means that Pernod-Ricard now owns Toronto's Corby Distilleries, McGuinness, the Seagram's brands (Seagrams and Crown Royal), and Hiram Walker (makers of Canadian Club and Hiram Walker). Brown-Forman of Louisville, Kentucky, owns Canadian Mist, as well as Old Forester and Jack Daniel's.

Taking a cue from their bourbon-making cousins, Canadian brand lineups include a variety of superpremium aged whiskies. Canada also has one independent distillery, Glenora in Nova Scotia, that makes unblended malt whisky in the Scottish style.

Other Whiskey Categories

A *straight whiskey* is a whiskey made from a mash in which one grain makes up the majority (51 percent or more) of the total grain content. It may be rye, wheat, or barley.

A *blended straight whiskey* is a blend of two or more straight whiskeys of the same type, for example, blended straight bourbon.

A *blended American whiskey* is made by blending at least 20 percent straight whiskey with neutral spirits or light (lower alcohol content) whiskey. It may also contain a blending agent (no more than 2½ percent), such as sherry, peach juice, or prune juice, for added flavor or color. Often the neutral spirits are aged in used oak barrels to remove harshness. The blending process produces a whiskey that is lighter in flavor and body than the original unblended whiskeys, though not lower in proof. Blended whiskeys made in this country have the words "American Whiskey" on the label. Many of the U.S. whiskeys are blends, for example, Seagram's 7 Crown or Schenley Reserve. There is no aging requirement for blended American whiskey, which means that the cheapest brands can be harsh—and definitely unsuitable as bar whiskeys.

A **rye whiskey** is one that is distilled at 160 proof or less from a fermented mash of at least 51-percent rye and 49-percent corn grain, aged in charred, new-oak containers at least two years. Notice that this description is almost the same as bourbon except for the percentages of grain. The difference in mash content results in rye whiskey's characteristic spicy or peppery overtone. In the early days of American whiskey-making rye was the grain of choice. As America expanded westward corn and other grains took the place of rye. Today few people drink straight rye whiskey, although many classic cocktail recipes called for straight rye. Mount Vernon, Old Overholt, and Sazerac 18-Year-Old are among the best-known brands of straight rye.

A confusing but necessary note: Along parts of the East Coast blended whiskeys are referred to as "rye," but this is a nickname; these are not ryes. Straight rye is a full-bodied spirit with the strong flavor of its parent grain, whereas most blended rye whiskeys are lighter and less defined.

Corn whiskey is a cousin to bourbon; the difference is that corn whiskey (also called **corn liquor**) has a higher corn content, a minimum of 81 percent in the mash. It is aged in uncharred barrels and has a relatively high alcohol content (80 percent by volume). A single U.S. distillery, Heaven Hill in Bardstown, Kentucky, makes corn liquor today under several brand names, including Dixie Dew, Georgia Moon, and Mellow Corn.

"Made-in-USA" **light whiskey** came into being in order to let American distillers compete with the lighter Canadian imports, which are distilled at higher proofs than those allowed in the United States. In 1972 the federal government created a new category for whiskeys distilled at above 160 proof but below 190 proof. These whiskeys may be stored in used or uncharred new oak. Aging in seasoned (used) wood permits good development of the lighter flavor, without the intensity of the high-proof spirits. There are several light whiskeys on the market, but none has caught on with the drinking public. Today they are generally used in blending.

International Whiskeys

Kentucky and Tennessee do not have exclusive rights to the brown-goods business. California boasts some thriving distilleries, including Peregrine Rock in Southern California and Anchor's Old Potrero in the San Francisco area. McCarthy's Oregon Single-Malt is getting good reviews, too.

In almost every country you will find someone making and selling whiskey, or at least what he or she calls whiskey. France has more distilleries than Ireland; its products are often labeled "Whisky de Breton" (or Bretagne) for the Northwestern region where they are located.

India (Ponda, McDowell's, Sikkim), Australia (Lark), and Germany (Blue Maus) are among the countries with whiskey products that occasionally make their way to the United States. Respectable brands from other countries include DYC from Spain, Yamakazi and Yoichi from Japan (which have been in business since the 1920s and 1940s, respectively), and Tesetice from the Czech Republic. The latter's colorful names for its exported products are Gold Cock and King Barleycorn.

Serving Whiskey

Whiskey drinks are served before, after, or between meals, but they are usually not offered with the meal. They may be ordered by type ("Give me a Scotch . . .") or by brand name ("May I have a Dewars and water?"), and sometimes in cocktails. Common ways that you will serve them are:

- ***Neat:*** Undiluted, at room temperature. Serve it in a shot glass or other small glass, with a separate glass of ice water beside it.
- ***Straight:*** Same as "neat." Also called *up* or *straight up.*
- ***On the rocks:*** Poured over ice in a 5- to 7-ounce rocks glass. Use fresh ice, preferably made from distilled or filtered water.
- ***With a splash:*** Mixed with water, preferably bottled spring water.
- ***With soda:*** Mixed with club soda, or high-quality sparkling spring water. People who know their liquor will often want it mixed with water or soda, not "straight." They know that subtler flavors may come to their attention more readily when the alcohol is somewhat diluted. When served with soda or another mixer, a whiskey drink is served in a highball glass. Fill it first with ice, then pour in the whiskey, and fill with the mixer. Swirl it with a barspoon before serving. (The "Branch" in "Bourbon and Branch," by the way, refers to clear spring water: old-timers felt bourbon was too good to mix with ordinary tap water.)

WHITE GOODS: VODKA, GIN, RUM, AND TEQUILA

Vodka, gin, rum, and tequila are known as **white goods** because they are similar in color, or more accurately lack of color, and are lighter in body and taste than the brown goods, such as whiskey and brandy. The key to the enduring popularity of white goods rests on an interesting public misconception: they are "lighter" in alcohol than brown goods. When it comes to alcohol content, white goods pack just as powerful a punch as whiskeys or other spirits, at 80 proof or higher. However, many of today's consumers, intent on a moderate alcohol intake, often assume that spirits lighter in color and flavor are not as "strong" as the darker, richer-tasting ones. This misconception has done wonders for the sales of white goods.

The major trend in white-goods marketing in the 2000s has been the emergence of dozens of new products, a practice known as creating **line extensions,** in order to gain attention and innovate in what have long been rather conventional product categories. In the discussions of individual spirits that follow, you will notice the trend toward flavored and infused spirits. But numerous liquor hybrids on the market almost defy classification. These products include Hpnotiq, a French import that mixes vodka, Cognac, and fruit juices; and Bacardi's Ciclon, a blend of rum, tequila, and lime. Perhaps you will appreciate these hybrids more after you learn about the origins of their base spirits.

Vodka

Vodka is the top seller of all distilled spirits, accounting for more than one-fourth of the liquor sold in the United States. Its exact origin is questionable. While most purists argue over whether it was created in Poland or Russia, writings from the early eleventh century suggest that this spirit first appeared in Persia, now Iran, and was transported through Turkey and Spain to Poland. The word *vodka* is derived from the Russian phrase *zhizenniz voda,* which means "water of life." It later evolved to *wodka,* an endearment that roughly means "dear little water."

The earliest vodkas were made from grain or sometimes potatoes, distilled at fairly high proof but not aged, and so strongly flavored that they were often spiced to mask the raw grain taste. In the early 1800s it was discovered that charcoal absorbed the congeners, and modern-day vodka was born. It is clear, odorless, and, oddly enough, flavorless. Drunk neat, chilled, usually with spicy foods—caviar, smoked salmon, anchovies, at least by the upper classes—it became the rage in Russia. Peasants drank it, too. Everyone did.

In 1914 the Smirnov family was producing a million bottles a day and exporting vodka to Europe, parts of Asia, and the United States. Three years later everyone in the family of more than 100 members was wiped out by the Russian Revolution, except one: Vladimir Smirnov, who escaped to France with the family formula. He tried to reestablish the business in other European cities but did not have sufficient funds. Eventually he sold the rights to the vodka business to another man, who brought the formula to the United States, began distilling in 1934 as "Pierre Smirnoff & Fils," then sold the license to the Heublein corporation in 1937. Years later a legal battle was being waged between descendants of the Smirnov family and Heublein, which sold the brand name Smirnoff Vodka (half a million bottles a day in 150 countries), over the rights to the family name and product portfolio. As of this writing the Smirnoff brand is owned by London-based beverage giant Diageo, and is still by far the best-selling U.S.-made brand, with a market share of 40 percent and a brand lineup that now includes seven flavored vodkas.

Another famous Russian brand also has landed in court. Allied Domecq, the current owner of Stolichnaya, is being sued by the Russian government in a U.S. court. The government alleges that when the Soviet Union was dismantling and privatizing state-owned businesses (including Stolichnaya) in the early 1990s, the trademarked name was missappropriated by wily business managers who illegally sold it to its current owner.

Vodka got a slow start in the United States until 1946, when the owner of the Cock 'N Bull restaurant in Hollywood put together a drink made from vodka, which was not selling, and ginger beer, which wasn't selling either, added half a lime, served it in a copper mug, and christened it the "Moscow Mule." With skillful promotion the drink and the spirit caught on. Vodka was "discovered" as a perfect partner for all sorts of juices and mixers since it has almost no taste of its own but adds a definite alcohol kick. Soon came the Screwdriver, the Bloody Mary, and a host of others, including the Vodka Martini, which is every bit as popular as its gin-based counterpart. In 1976 vodka sales surpassed those of whiskey sales.

Vodka is defined in the U.S. Standards of Identity as "neutral spirits so distilled, or so treated after distillation with charcoal or other materials, as to be without distinctive character, aroma, taste, or color." Vodka can be distilled from any fermented materials because neutral spirits from any source taste pretty much alike, which is to say, they do not *have* a taste. Experts say the differences between vodkas are largely based on the water used to make them.

Any agricultural product that contains fermentable carbohydrates may be used in the vodka-making process. American vodkas are made from grain, although Idaho distillers, including Teton Glacier, use that state's bumper crop of potatoes; Oregon has Spudka brand potato vodka. Scandinavian vodkas are usually made from wheat mash, giving them a lightly sweet flavor. The Dutch use winter wheat, high in glucose, which adds complexity. Poland's Belvedere brand and American-made Shaker's Rye are distilled from rye. No matter what the base ingredient, the final product is 70 to 100 proof, a smooth, adaptable form of alcohol that can be used in a variety of mixed drinks. In the United States, the Standard of Identity for flavored vodka requires that the name of the predominant flavor appear as part of the designation.

Many vodka producers buy neutral spirits from distillers who specialize in making them, then continue processing them to selectively remove impurities, congeners, and undesirable flavors, while improving clarity and smoothness. There are several ways to do this, including:

- Filter the spirits through charcoal, bark, sand, seashells, and even diamond dust! (Filtration methods are the trade secrets of the vodka producers. Fashion designer Roberto Cavalli, for instance, puts his name on a trendy vodka product filtered through layers of crushed Italian marble.)
- Inject oxygen bubbles into the spirit to catch impurities.
- Use *extractive distillation*, boiling the spirit and "bathing" it in water. Impurities attach to the water molecules and are extracted.

- Spin the liquid in high-speed centrifugal purifiers that separate the congeners from the spirit.

Vodka is not aged. Many people assume that all vodkas are alike simply because they are neutral, but this is not the case. Quality, or lack of it, is definitely perceptible, and vodka is emerging as a much more complex and sophisticated product. Some vodkas are triple- and quadruple-distilled, and the people who choose one over the other swear that there are subtle differences.

It is, perhaps, ironic that the most successful ongoing trend in the production of this flavorless spirit has been to flavor it. Flavored vodkas might originally have been produced to mask the intensity of the unflavored spirit, but some are made to showcase the distiller's skill. Vodka production guidelines allow for up to 2½ percent sugar in the formula to help carry the flavoring agent; that is quite a challenge to distillers, and citrus flavors provide the biggest "blast" of taste within this limit. Today's bartender has a variety of good reasons for using a flavored product, including complexity, mixability, and convenience. Swedish-made Absolut has several vodka flavors, including Absolut Peppar, a peppery vodka for spicy Bloody Marys and Cajun Martinis, and Absolut Citron, a lemon-flavored vodka with mandarin orange and grapefruit accents. Stolichnaya from Russia has countered with vanilla-, strawberry-, peach-, cinnamon-, and coffee-flavored vodkas; American-made Skyy now boasts half a dozen flavors, including a raspberry "Cosmo Mix" for making Cosmopolitans. A Canadian-made vodka from independent distiller Kittling Ridge of Ontario called Inferno Pepper-Pot has been infused with hot peppers nicknamed "9-1-1 chiles," or Flamingo Reds, that are left in the bottle (Figure 5.8). A hot trend, indeed!

FIGURE 5.8 Inferno Pepper Pot Vodka, a Canadian vodka infused with hot peppers. Photo courtesy of Boschler Studios.

Like all popularity contests, however, the flavored-vodka showdown has had its critics, and bartenders are chief among them. They claim that the profusion of products takes up too much backbar room, and takes some of the flair out of bartending. When mixing a drink becomes as simple as pouring an already-flavored spirit into a glass, the element of fun disappears. Other mixologists feel that vodka's beauty is its simplicity as a colorless, odorless, and flavorless liquid that makes a wonderful base upon which to build and experiment.

In recent years Americans have fallen in love with imported vodka. This trend is the result of a couple of factors: the persistent misperceptions about it as a "light" spirit, and the association of an imported label with financial success and social status. Although Smirnoff remains the market-share leader, there are plenty of upscale fans of Grey Goose (from France), Ketel One and Belvedere (both from Poland), and Svedka (from Sweden). In fact all four vodkas were on the 2004 Impact Databank list of "Hot Brands" for double-digit U.S. sales increases in 2002 and 2003. In addition Sweden's Absolut line does well at premium prices, as does Finlandia, Finland's entry into the upscale import market. In many cases you pay for the brand name and amazing advertising budgets of these formidable competitors. Keep in mind that you can find excellent values in imported vodka at less than $25 per bottle.

Aquavit

The Scandinavian version of vodka is often called **schnapps** (not to be confused with the liqueur of the same name), but its official names are **aquavit** (from Norway) and **akvavit** (from Denmark). The word *schnapps* is from an ancient Norwegian word meaning "to snap up or gulp," and, not surprisingly, the traditional way to drink this bracing spirit is ice cold, in a single gulp, sometimes followed by a swig of beer. Aquavit is stored in the freezer in Scandinavian homes, and drinking it is a special tradition at Christmas and on May 17, the anniversary of the drafting of Norway's constitution.

Aquavit is most often produced from distilling potatoes. It is distilled at 190 proof and then redistilled (like gin) with flavorings; caraway seed is the classic, but you may also find hints of cumin, fennel, dill, coriander, clove, and orange peel. It is aged in oak sherry casks and bottled at 86 to 90 proof, and makes an interesting substitute in some cocktail recipes that normally call for vodka. On the Internet you can find numerous recipes that use vodka as the base for homemade aquavit.

In the United States, Minnesota, with its large numbers of Scandinavian descendants, leads the nation in aquavit consumption. Exported brands sometimes seen here include Aalborg from Denmark and Loiten Export or Lyshold Linie from Norway. The term *Linie* (pronounced LINN-yuh) on the label means "line" and refers to the practice of shipping the aquavit, still in its oak casks, across the equator from Norway to Australia in a round-trip journey, a tradition that dates from the 1800s. The theory is that aquavit gains a richer flavor by spending several weeks at sea, gently sloshing around in the barrels. The label may even designate the ship and the date that it sailed.

Germany makes a similar product, known as **korn** because it is made using corn, not potatoes. German korn liquor is sometimes flavored with fruit and does not make the trip to Australia—except perhaps to be sold there.

Gin

Gin makers have probably looked enviously at vodka's popularity in recent years since their own fortunes have been down slightly. But gin was a flavored spirit long before vodkas were infused with lemons, berries, and hot peppers. Gin's hallmark is the distinctive, predominant flavor of the juniper berry. Juniper berries (Latin name *ginepro*) was made into medicinal potions by monks in the fourteenth century as protection against bubonic plague, and as cures for kidney and bladder ailments and indigestion.

MAKE YOUR OWN FLAVORS: INFUSING SPIRITS

Some bartenders make their own signature vodka flavors, using such ingredients as horseradish, currant, mango, kiwi, cranberry, rosemary, and many others, then charge premium prices for the exclusive concoctions. Flavoring vodka or any other type of spirit is not difficult. It requires a simple *infusion,* meaning that you immerse the fruit (peeled, dried, or not), herb, or vegetable in the spirit and let it marinate at room temperature in a clean container for a couple of days or a few weeks, depending on the intensity of flavor you wish to achieve. Displaying the infusions in large, clear glass containers on the backbar will add lively color to your bar setup, and will probably also spark customers' questions and interest. Just make sure that the containers are always clean and well sealed.

The possible combinations are as limitless as the list of ingredients and your liquor inventory. Consider for instance the Beefeaters' brand "Deli Gin," which contains sun-dried tomatoes, large olives, fresh garlic, dill, and red onions. There are also infusions made from tequila, rum, gin, vodka, and some liqueurs.

Before you start making your own, however, check with your state's liquor-control agency because in some areas these blends are regarded as "tampered" spirits, and it may be illegal to sell them.

Gin as we know it was invented in the 1500s by Franciscus Sylvius, a Dutch professor of medicine who made an *aqua vitae* from grain flavored with juniper berries. Dr. Sylvius also had medicinal benefits in mind, but his concoction was so potable that it swept the country as a liquor, under the name **Geneva** or **Genever** (from the French *genievre,* which means juniper). It crossed the English Channel via British soldiers, who called it *Dutch courage* and shortened its name to *gin.* In England it was also sometimes known as **Hollands.**

Cheap gin was soon being made in London from almost anything—"Make it in the morning and drink it at night"—and sold in hole-in-the-wall dramshops all over London. To become a distiller all you had to do was display a "Notice of Intent" in a public place for 10 days, and then start selling. William of Orange, the King of England at the time, was from Holland, which made all things Dutch suddenly fashionable. (His own gin consumption became somewhat legendary; the royal banquet hall was nicknamed *The Gin Palace.*) But it was not just the elite who succumbed. England's desperately impoverished population drank gin on a national scale to the point of disaster: 20 million gallons at its peak in 1750.

The pattern repeated itself in the United States during Prohibition, when so-called *bathtub gin* was made at home from alcohol, juniper, and glycerin. Bathtub gin, too, was a poor and sometimes lethal product, and the custom arose of mixing it with something else to kill the taste, thus popularizing the cocktail. It took gin some years to outlive its tacky history, but today it is a highly respected favorite. The British officer's Gin and Tonic (consumed in an effort to prevent malaria) and the post-repeal adoption of the Martini as a fashionable cocktail had a lot to do with changing gin's image.

The U.S. Standard of Identity for gin spells out the many ways in which gins are made: It is "a product obtained by original distillation from mash, or by redistillation of distilled spirits, or by mixing neutral spirits, with or over juniper berries and other aromatics, or with or over extracts derived from **infusions**, percolations, or maceration of such materials, and includes mixtures of gin and neutral spirits. It shall derive its main characteristic flavor from juniper berries and be bottled at not less than 80 proof. Gin produced exclusively by original distillation or by redistillation may be further designated as 'distilled.'"

Confusing? The main point is that the essential characteristic of all gins is the flavor of juniper berries. The remainder of the standard simply mentions all the various ways by which a spirit with such flavor may be produced. The juniper flavor is typically enhanced by adding the undertones and flavors of other aromatics, often referred to as *botanicals.* These are parts of plants (leaves, roots, bark, seeds, berries, and peels) that yield aromatic oils. The list includes angelica, coriander, cardamom, cassia bark, fennel, anise seed, nutmeg, caraway, and lemon. The precise mix and method are the secret of each producer, and these account for the subtle flavor variations from one brand of gin to another.

There are two types of gin: Dutch and English style. Dutch gin is obtained by "original distillation from mash," and English-style gin is made by any of the other methods. The two types are quite different, and only the English style, whether imported from England or made in the United States, is used in mixing drinks.

Dutch gin is a product of the Netherlands and is known as *Hollands, Genever,* or (rarely) *Schiedam.* It is made beginning with a mash of barley malt, corn, and rye, which is fermented to make a beer, then distilled and redistilled in pot stills at low proof, with the juniper berries and other aromatics included in the final distillation. The result is a full-bodied gin with a definite flavor of malt along with the juniper. This flavor would overpower almost anything it might be mixed with. This is not a bar gin. It is drunk straight and icy cold. Bols, in a stone crock, is probably the only brand you will find in the United States.

English-style gin is made in both England and the United States. It is usually called *London Dry,* wherever it is made. The historical tidbit behind this name is interesting. In the past some gins were sweetened with sugar, and these were known as *Old Tom gins.* The unsweetened gins were labeled *Dry* or *London Dry* to distinguish them from Old Tom gins, and the names stuck. Today some are labeled *Very Dry* or *Extra Dry,* but they are no drier than the others. **Plymouth gin** is a lighter product (at 82.4 proof) also made in England; it has the distinction of being a favorite of Franklin Roosevelt and Winston Churchill, both Martini drinkers.

In England gin is made from nearly neutral grain spirits distilled in column stills at 180 to 188 proof. These are reduced to 120 proof with distilled water, then redistilled in tall pot stills with juniper berries and other aromatics either in the spirits (see Figure 5.9*a*) or suspended above them on mesh trays so that the rising vapors pass through and around the berries (see Figure 5.9*b*). Some gin is made by steeping the botanicals in the liquid.

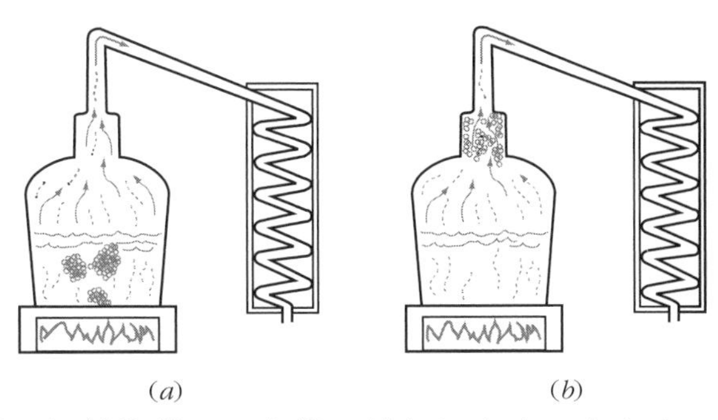

FIGURE 5.9 Making gin: (*a*) Distilling or redistilling with juniper berries and other botanicals. (*b*) Redistilling to pass vapors through juniper berries and other botanicals.

American gins are made in two ways: distilling and compounding. Distilled gins are made in much the same way as the English gins: by redistilling neutral spirits with juniper berries and other aromatics. **Compound gins** are made by simply mixing high-proof spirits with extracts from juniper berries and other botanicals. Like vodka makers many U.S. producers of gin buy their neutral spirits from distillers in the Midwest who specialize in these spirits. Distilled gins are allowed to use the word *distilled* on the label; compound gins are not identified as such on the label.

Gin is also made in Spain, France, Lithuania, the Philippines, and Africa. Gin does not need to be aged, and it is usually stored in stainless-steel or glass-lined tanks until bottled. One type known as *golden gin* is aged briefly for color. **Sloe gin,** by the way, is not a gin at all; it is a liqueur made from sloe berries, which are not berries but small wild plums. Sloe gin is used at the bar to add color to drinks and, at other venues, as desserts.

While there are some flavor-infused gins (lime, grapefruit, mint, green olive) and a few premade, gin-and-juice drinks, the juniper taste does not lend itself as well to the creation of line extensions as vodka does—with a few striking exceptions. One that comes to mind is Magellan, a French-made gin infused with botanicals and iris petals, which give the spirit an unusual, light blue color. Another is Hendrick's, made in Scotland, that bills itself as "the world's most peculiar gin," adding rose petals, citrus, and cucumber along with the juniper berries. Sales of super-premium imported brands like these are the only real bright spots in a category that, as a whole, has been flat.

The best-selling premium bar brands are currently British-made Bombay Sapphire and Tanqueray; other reliable names include Seagram's, Gordon's, Gilbey's, and Beefeater. A good bartender will know enough about gin's colorful history to intrigue his or her customers and make some recommendations.

Gin is almost never consumed straight, except in the very dry Martini. Martini-making is practically an art form: Every bartender and every serious Martini drinker has preferences and opinions as strong as the gin itself. There is a definite difference between the classic, traditional gin Martini—gin, Vermouth, and a twist, garnished with stuffed olives or cocktail onions—and the trendy recipes that younger consumers enjoy. Chocolate liqueur, cranberry juice, and maraschino cherries have all been Martini ingredients. Along with the venerable Martini other popular gin-based drinks are the Gin and Tonic, Tom Collins, and Singapore Sling. The resurgence of the classic cocktail might eventually mean a boost for gin sales—but it hasn't happened yet.

Rum

Vodka might be the best-selling spirit overall, but rum is the spirit with the fastest-growing sales, especially among the under-30 crowd. The category leader in the United States is Bacardi, with a line that includes several premium and superpremium brands, six flavored rums, and a few low-calorie, flavored rums under the Bacardi Breeze label. But Diageo's Captain Morgan Rum is coming on strong in the second spot, with the largest sales increases of *any* spirit in *any* category in recent years. Diageo also owns Jamaican rum-maker Myers's and a secondary label, Parrot Bay, which comes in tropical flavors from pineapple to passion fruit.

Rum, according to its Standard of Identity, is an alcoholic distillate from the fermented juice of sugarcane—in the form of syrup, molasses, or other sugarcane by-products—produced at less than 190 proof and bottled at not less than 80 proof. It has a long and somewhat unsavory history. It was first made in the East Indies in the seventeenth century, then spread to other areas where sugarcane was grown: China, India, and North Africa. The Spanish and Portuguese explorers transplanted sugarcane to the New World when they saw that the Caribbean and South American climates were perfect for this valuable crop. A writer reported in 1660s that "the chief fuddling" (intoxicant) made on the island of Barbados was "rum-bullion, alias 'kill-devil,' and this is made from sugarcanes distilled, a hot, hellish, and terrible liquor." No matter how harsh the taste, rum was given as payment to slaves, drunk by pirates who scourged the shores of the Spanish Main and the Caribbean islands, and consumed by the British Navy, with lime juice added to prevent scurvy. (Hence the nickname *limeys* for the British.) Rum was also popular in seventeenth-century Europe and the eighteenth-century American colonies.

Rum-making became a flourishing industry in New England at this time, which marked one of the darkest periods of rum's history. For years rum manufacturers and New England ship captains carried on a highly profitable triangular trade with Africa and the West Indies. They exchanged New England rum for slaves in Africa, as well as slaves for molasses in the West Indies, and turned the molasses into rum for the next go-round. British taxes and restrictions on the rum trade were as much a cause of the American Revolution as were the taxes on tea.

Unsurprisingly, in the nineteenth century Temperance leaders made "Demon Rum" the symbol of the evils of alcohol. The image remained through Prohibition when smugglers were called *rumrunners* and the offshore ships were known as *Rum Rows,* even though they sold as much Scotch as rum. The name *rum* (or *rhum,* the spelling that still appears on French-influenced labels) may come from the name for Dutch drinking cups of the time (*roemers* or *rummers*); or it may be either a derivation of the islanders' word *brum,* which means "a sugarcane drink" or a shortening of the word *rumbullion,* an antiquated term for a disturbance or uproar.

Rum is made from molasses or sugarcane juice, fermented to create a liquid (known at this stage as *wash*) with water and yeast. The wash is boiled in the distillation procees to 160 proof or higher. Some distillers use pot stills; others use column stills. The spirit comes out of the still as a clear liquid, which takes on both its color and much of its character from barrel aging. White (clear) rum is often not put in barrels at all, but in tanks until bottling. For aged rums casks that once held bourbon, Cognac, wine, and whiskey are redeployed as storage (see Figure 5.10). The Caribbean climate is so hot and humid that aging happens rather quickly, and some of the liquid is lost to evaporation. A few distillers ship their barrels elsewhere, to cooler climates, for long-term storage. There are three basic types of rum, which differ somewhat in flavor according to the amount of aging. These are:

- ***White or Silver:*** Aged only a year or two. These are the lightest in color, although they have the highest alcohol content (and are sometimes referred to as **overproof**) and the least-refined flavors.
- ***Amber or Gold:*** Aged at least three years. These are sometimes colored with caramel and take on a richer hue from spending more time in barrels than other rums. Amber rums have somewhat more flavor and are a bit mellower than the Whites and Silvers.
- ***Red Label or Dark:*** Aged six years or more. These feature a dry, mellow, full-bodied flavor and bouquet; a deep golden color; and a slightly lower alcohol content.

FIGURE 5.10 A barrel house. Photo courtesy of Cruzan Rum Distillery, St. Croix, United States Virgin Islands

- ***Rum Vieux:*** Aged ten years or more, these rums often are compared to fine Cognacs, but with less acidity.

It is important not to judge rum strictly by its color. Some of the clear rums are the sharpest in flavor because they have not spent much, if any, time in barrels; the milder and mellower ones may be the darkest in color.

Much of the rum consumed in the United States (the Ronrico brand, for example) is made in Puerto Rico, but Jamaican rum is also popular. The Jamaican style is full bodied and pungent, with a dark mahogany color that it owes mainly to caramel. Jamaican rum begins with molasses that is fermented by yeasts from the air, a process (also used in making some beers) called *natural, wild,* or *spontaneous fermentation.* It is distilled at 140 to 160 proof, producing a spirit with full flavor and body. This is aged five to seven years. It is bottled usually at 80 and 87 proof, and occasionally at 151 proof, for flavoring and flaming. Myers's rum is the familiar Jamaican brand; its label proclaims it to be "the Planter's Punch brand." Cruzan rums are distilled in St. Croix, in eight flavors today. A few U.S.-made rums are making names for themselves in this competitive field, including Aristocrat and Monarch.

A good place to gaze into the future of specialty drinks is at the bar of a smart new Latin or Caribbean restaurant. These cultures represent fast-rising demographic groups in the United States, and rum is as traditional to them as Scotch is to the Scottish and whiskey is to Americans. The soaring popularity of "retro" classic cocktails—the Mojito, the Zombie, Planter's Punch, and the Pina Colada—among hip young consumers is one reason for rum's sudden popularity, but the other is strictly economic. Some of the smaller rum producers have been absorbed into larger beverage companies that can afford to advertise and build brand awareness among the impressionable younger crowd.

Yet another style of run, Demerara rum, is made in Guyana along the Demerara River. Darker in color but lighter in flavor than Jamaican rum, it is bottled at 80, 86, and 151 proof. Until the Zombie cocktail was invented, the chief market for 151-proof Demerara rum was among lumbermen and fishermen in far northern climates, who drink it half-and-half with hot water as a grog to warm the bloodstream. High-proof Demerara is often used to flame drinks. You may also encounter Barbados rum or medium-bodied rums from Haiti, Martinique, and Guadeloupe that are made from sugarcane juice instead of molasses.

Arrack (or **arak**) rum is distilled in the East Indies, Middle East, North Africa, and India from rice, molasses, coconut milk, figs, dates, or even sap from palm trees, depending on the country and the raw ingredients at hand. This broad category of small-volume liquors takes its name from an Arabic word, *araq,* which means "juice" or "sap." Some of the results yield rum or brandy-like spirits with quite a kick.

Puerto Rico, Nicaragua, and Jamaica also make "liqueur" rums, aged up to 15 years like fine brandies. Brazil's national liquor is a cousin to rum called **cachaca,** which is poised to be the "next big thing" among rum aficionados in the United States. While rum is distilled from molasses, cachaca is distilled from unrefined sugarcane juice. After fermentation the liquid is boiled until it becomes a concentrate. The finer-quality cachacas are barrel-aged, and the liquor emerges with the rich flavor of rum and a unique, pleasant sugarcane scent. Cachaca is used to make the wildly popular *caipirinha* and the less-well-known sweet, fruity *batidas cocktails*, which are traditional pre-Lenten carnival libations in South America.

The Brazilian government is waging a campaign to reserve the name *cachaca* exclusively for Brazilian-made products, and has brought the issue to the attention of the World Trade Ogranization (WTO). Brazil's cachaca exports rose from $7.3 million in 1999 to $14 million in 2004, so the nation has an economic stake in protecting its output from would-be rivals, such as Caribbean nations, where sugarcane also is grown.

In Mexico rum (and any other liquor made with more than 50-percent cane-based spirits) is labeled **aguardiente**, which is Spanish for "burning water." In that country as much aguardiente as tequila is consumed, which brings us to our next topic.

Tequila

Today about three fourths of the tequila poured in the United States goes into making the Margarita, and the more flavor variations bartenders create, the better for tequila sales. But this Mexican spirit has its own unique history, identity, romance, and flavor profile, and it is also gaining popularity as a high-end product with America's liquor customers, especially those in their 20s and early 30s. Superpremium tequilas are commanding the same respect as single-malt Scotches and single-barrel bourbons. Bars hold tequila tastings and dinners, pairing the spirit with multiple courses to show its adaptability to food. Tequila makers are creating a smoother and more refined product for the international palate and to use in cooking. There is no longer a need, as is the custom in Mexico, to "slam" or "shoot" (i.e., gulp) a straight shot of tequila followed by jolts of salt and lime; gourmands say that would be wasting a truly fine product, which some even compare to Cognac.

Tequila is defined as an alcoholic distillate from a fermented mash derived principally (51 percent or more) from the Agave Tequilana Weber, commonly known as the **blue agave** plant. There are more than 200 strains of agave, a desert relative of lilies, but only the blue variety is used to make tequila, and it must be grown and harvested in one of five regions authorized by the Mexican government.

The agave plant has had mystical meaning to the Mexican people for centuries. It is said to be the incarnation of Mayahuel, a goddess, and the earliest spirit made from the plant, called *pulque* (PUHL-kay), was used in celebrations and religious ceremonies to bless land, and crops. Its power as an intoxicant was also well known, even to the ancient Aztecs. The agave distilling industry started to spring up around the town of Tequila in the mid-1700s (until these plantings were legally permitted by the King of Spain, all the agave had been harvested wild). The first official, commercial agave farmers and distillers were the Don Jose Antonio Cuervo family, now the familiar Jose Cuervo brand name. Tequila was not routinely exported, however, until after World War II.

Some production details: The heart of the agave plant is called a *pina,* which means pineapple, because this is what it looks like. Growing a pina large enough to be harvested takes about nine years. It weighs 50 to 200 pounds and is harvested by hand by workers called *juiadores.* The pinas are filled with a sweet sap that emerges as they are baked or steamed and crushed into juice. The juice is then fermented and distilled twice at about 110 proof, producing a strongly flavored spirit with a sharp bite. A spirit light in appearance but definitely not light in taste, it is bottled at not less than 80 proof. It is a distinctive product of Mexico: It is manufactured in Mexico in compliance with Mexican regulations.

In the 1970s the Mexican government changed the rules to allow up to 49 percent of spirits other than blue agave in the mixture—that is to say, neutral spirits, or distillates of sugarcane or corn. This half-agave, half-other-sugars blend is commonly known as **mixto,** and it accounts for about 80 percent of Mexico's total tequila production. While it is not the high-end tequila, it is what most Americans drink when they order tequila in a cocktail, and it is lighter and less intense than the pure, 100-percent blue agave tequilas. Large producers send their mixto, often fruit-flavored, from Mexico in tanker trucks to be bottled in the United States.

At the turn of this century tequila production suffered a major setback due to an agave shortage that resulted in fewer producers and higher prices (an astonishing 800-percent increase in 1999). However, in 2005 producers reported a glut of blue agave and complained that their harvests net only pennies per pound. The Mexican government has mandated that beginning in 2006, every newly planted plot of blue agave must be registered with a Tequila Regulatory Council, and that distillers will be allowed to buy pinas from only registered plots.

The smart distillers also produce small quantities of 100-percent blue-agave tequila, aging it in barrels for smoother and more complex flavors to satisfy the connoisseur. This type of tequila is known as **tequila puro.** So how do you know what you're getting? Label designations, which explain the bottle contents, are as follows:

Mixtos

- ***White tequila:*** Colorless and unaged. On labels, it is identified with the term *blanco* (white) or *plata* (silver). Some aficionados prefer white tequila because it showcases the true agave flavor without the barrel influence.
- ***Gold tequila:*** Also unaged. Its golden color refers to the addition of caramel or cane sugar; it is not a designation of quality. This is the tequila type most popular in the United States. Another common term for it is *joven abogado,* which means "young and smooth."

Tequila Puros

- ***Reposado tequila:*** Made in small batches and, by Mexican law, must be barrel-aged from 2 to 11 months before bottling. *Reposado* means *resting* or *rested.* In Mexico these are the best-selling tequilas.
- ***Anejo tequila:*** Aged in wood for more than one year. It is the closest thing to Cognac, with an amber or golden color, but it does tend to lose flavor when it has been aged more than four years. *Anejo* means "aged." Recent standouts in

this category include distillers that use sherry pipes (Del Dueno) or cognac casks (El Tesoro) to impart the character of the other spirits to their Tequila puros. After more than three years of aging, some distillers label their products *muy anejos* or *tres anejos,* not official terminology but indicative of the spirit's additional time in barrels.

Another unofficial but common term used to identify premium or limited-production tequila is *reserva de casa* (which means "house reserve").

The Jose Cuervo brand, now owned by Diageo, is the dominant tequila in U.S. sales, but Sauza and Montezuma are hot competitors. In the late 1990s Anheuser-Busch began to capitalize on tequila's popularity by creating **Tequiza,** a beer product that contains tequila (described as "blue agave nectar") and lime touted as having only 128 calories per serving. It is aimed at people who drink Mexican beer (adding a lime wedge is customary) or non-beer drinkers who might be willing to experiment. As of this writing it is still on the market.

A new generation of **tequillarias** has sprung up in Mexico City and in other urban markets in addition to those in Mexico. Tequillaries are popular at upscale restaurants with the tequila mystique as part of their theme, in both food and drink.

Mescal

There is another Mexican-made liquor that some insist is tequila's "poor cousin," while others argue that it is a "rare and high-end sibling." Either way it's called **mescal** or **mezcal,** and it is the spirit made from agave plants that are not necessarily blue agave, and/or not located in the five designated tequila regions. (Other types of plants are called **maguey, spading, sotol,** and **tobola.**) Spanish explorers of past centuries referred to the spirit as *Vino de Mescal.* The center of mescal production is the state of Oaxaca. The mescal-making process is also a bit different from that of tequila. The agave hearts are slow-roasted for three days in adobe or gas ovens or in deep, stone-lined pits in the ground. This imparts a smoky flavor that is different than that of tequila. Then the cooked hearts are left to ferment naturally, from four or five days to a full month, before being crushed and distilled—once or twice—in clay or copper pot stills. The final product is about 80 proof, with a flavor that might be described as nutty and more herbaceous than tequila.

Mescal is guaranteed by Mexican law to be 100-percent agave, which purists say indicates its overall fine quality. They call it "the Cognac of Mexico," and order it very slightly chilled in a brandy snifter. A couple of companies do export their mescal products, notably the del Maguey and Hacienda Sotol distilleries, but most of it is locally made for use within Mexico's rural communities and flavored with herbs, bark, or fruit.

You will note that, quite often, a bottle of mescal contains a worm. Yes, a worm. It's called a **gusano,** and lives in the agave plant. Part of the lore and legend of the drink is that the worm contains some of the mythic power of the plant, and that he or she who eats the worm acquires that power. What do you think? Scorpion Mezcal, a high-end, triple-distilled 100-percent agave spirit, has even been bottled with a whole scorpion inside!

AFTER-DINNER DRINKS

This wide-ranging category will prove, if nothing else, how creative the world's distillers have become in satisfying just about every taste and whim. Very often while the traditional brown goods and white goods are imbibed before meals to whet the appetite, the idea behind after-dinner drinks—brandies, liqueurs, **cordials,** digestifs—is to enjoy something smooth and satisfying that promotes good digestion of the meal. Of course some after-dinner drinks are also used in cocktails. Today's restaurateurs generally agree that not enough has been done to develop the after-dinner drink market, although customers seem to enjoy the "luxury" experience of relaxing after a meal to enjoy an interesting liqueur. Obviously the profit opportunity is huge for anyone who implements a well-executed after-dinner-drink program that is both classy and consistent.

You will notice that not all bars or restaurants offer extensive after-dinner-drink choices. As you will soon see, there are so many to choose from that it can be confusing. Your clientele and your budget will help you decide which to have on hand, as well as your bartenders, who will also use some of the ingredients in cocktail recipes.

Generally guests are looking for certain things from their after-dinner libations: a soothing spirit that gently warms the drinker all the way from tongue to stomach; a frothy, spiked coffee drink; a celebratory glass of Champagne; or a sweet, creamy beverage that substitutes for a traditional dessert. Make sure to offer a good (but not overwhelming) range as you compile your after-dinner list, which *should* be presented in list form, whether as a separate list, on the regular dinner menu, or as part of a separate dessert menu, depending on the type of establishment. Staff members must be trained to suggest end-of-meal or end-of-evening nightcaps, just as they would suggest coffee or dessert.

Brandies

Brandy began as an *eau de vie,* the French version of *aqua vitae* that in other countries became whiskey, vodka, and gin. In France brandy was thought of as the spirit or soul of the wine. Italian monks and Moorish scholars probably began distilling in the sixteenth century, and brandy was one of the first results of their efforts. The process was used even earlier in Spain to transform grapes and their juices into a more potent, but still sophisticated, spirit. At the time the Netherlands ruled the seas as merchants. Dutch ship captains used the powerful, distilled wine to fortify the regular table wines on their journeys and to add to drinking water stored on board to kill parasites. They called it *brandewijn,* which means *burned wine,* and was shortened in time to brandy.

Today most brandy drinkers are over age 30. Brandy is perceived to be a healthy, classy spirit that fits an upscale lifestyle. The U.S. Standards of Identity define brandy as the distilled product of any fruit, but what we call brandy must be made from grapes. Other fruit brandies must carry the name of the fruit. All brandies must be bottled at 80 proof or higher. Most bars use two types: a good domestic brandy in the well for mixed drinks, and premium brands, usually imported, for after-dinner service. Brandy-based cocktails include the Stinger, the Sidecar, the Brandy Alexander, and the Brandy Manhattan.

American Brandies. Most brandy consumed in the United States is made in California. It is made in column stills at up to 170 proof and is aged in white-oak barrels at least two years, but usually longer. Most of these brandies are blends—smooth and fruity, with a touch of sweetness—that may contain up to 2½ percent of added flavoring. There are also straight brandies that contain caramel coloring and no other additives, some premium brands that qualify as after-dinner brandies, and lower-end products that actually are blends of brandy and 20-percent (or more) neutral spirit alcohol. Quality differences account for the incredible price differences—from $7 or $8 for a bargain blend, to $35 for a mid-priced brandy, to $350 for Germain Robin's top-shelf *Anno Domini* brand.

Christian Brothers and E & J Gallo have been competing for years as the two top brandy producers in the United States. Recently these companies have faced stiff competition from French imports, in bottles that make them look more expensive than they are. Some U.S.-based producers, including Germain Robin, St. George, and RMS, make their brandies the European way, the same as Cognac, by crushing the grapes at the peak of ripeness, not adding sugar during fermentation, and distilling in pot stills. Brandy is most popular in three markets—African Americans, people over age 50, and in the so-called "Brandy Belt" of Wisconsin, Minnesota, and Northern Michigan, where German and Scandinvian immigrants from past generations settled and remained loyal to this spirit that was popular in their native countries. Marketers are attempting to widen the audience for brandy with upscale releases, flavored products (for example, Korbel Extra Smooth contains orange, vanilla, and nutmeg) and brandy-based cocktails, such as the Brandy Martini (brandy, Amaretto, and a splash of cherry juice) and Brandy Sunburst (brandy, Triple Sec, sweet and sour mix, grenadine, orange juice, and a splash of 7UP).

American brandies from other fruits, such as apple, apricot, blackberry, and pineapple, must always include the name of the fruit on the label. These brandies may or may not be aged. Apple brandy, also called **applejack,** was one of the earliest and favorite spirits of early New Englanders. Applejack may be distilled from **hard cider** (fermented apple juice) or from apple pomace, the leftover skins and pulp after cider has been pressed from them. Today federal law requires that to be called applejack, the spirit be aged fours years in used bourbon barrels. It is bottled at 100 proof as a straight brandy or blended with neutral spirits and bottled at 80 proof. There is only one applejack distiller, Laird's of New Jersey, which has been producing applejack since colonial times. However, numerous orchard owners make and sell apple brandy.

Cognac. Of all the brandies in the world, Cognac is the most famous and prestigious. It has been called the *king of brandies*, and also the *brandy of kings*, and has a somewhat stuffy reputation. In recent years an oversupply in French warehouses has driven prices down, and the government has even paid vintners to remove some of their grape acreage from Cognac production. Still, some people think that there is no better way to end an evening than with a glass of fine Cognac (today a good cigar to accompany it is optional).

Like Champagne you can call it "Cognac" only if it is made in the Cognac area of France, made up of six specific areas, where chalky soil, a humid climate, and special distillation techniques produce brandy under strict government control. Only certain kinds of white grapes may be used (primarily a variety called **Ugni Blanc**, although *Colombard* and *Folle Blanche* are also used), and specific distillation procedures must be followed, including two distillations in traditional copper pot stills (*alambics*) and precise control of temperatures and quantities. The farmers sell their freshly distilled spirits to shipper-producers, who age and blend them to meet the standards of their particular brands. Cognac is aged in special oak casks at least 1½ years. Most are aged 2 to 4 years, and some even longer. Caramel may be added for uniform color.

During aging the alcohol evaporates through the porous casks at an average of 2 percent per year. In the warehouses the escaping vapors—known as "the angels' share"—are noticeable.

A Cognac label may carry cryptic letters, special words, and varying numbers of stars. The stars may mean somewhat different things for different brands. By French law a three-star Cognac must be at least 1½ years old; most are around 4 years old. Since Cognacs are blends of brandies of various ages, no age is allowed to appear on the label. The cryptic letters are symbols of relative age and quality, as follows:

V = Very
S = Superior or Special
O = Old
P = Pale
E = Extra or Especial
F = Fine
X = Extra

Generally a Cognac specified VS (very superior) is similar to a three-star Cognac. A VSOP (very superior old pale) has been aged in wood at least 4½ years, and probably 7 to 10. An XO (extra old) means the youngest spirit in the blend has been aged more than 6 years, although the average age for this type of high-end Cognac may be 20 years. The designations *Extra, Vieille Reserve,* and *Napoleon* may not appear on the label unless the Cognac is at least 5½ years old. (Contrary to legend, there is no Cognac around dating from Napoleon's day, though some shippers have stocks of 50 years old and more to use in blending their finest Cognacs.)

The top-of-the-line designation is the term *Luxury*, as in "Luxury XO." For all the work put into the labeling system, it is a voluntary set of guidelines, not enforced by law. Cognac shippers can put whatever designations they want on their labels.

A Cognac labeled *Grande Champagne* or *Fine Champagne* has nothing to do with the bubbly beverage. The French word *champagne* means field, and the French bubbly and the Champagne Cognac both take the name from the common word.

Grande Champagne is one of seven Cognac appellations and generally, the more Grande Champagne grape content, the better the Cognac. The appellations are as follows:

- ***Grande Champagne:*** The heart of the Cognac district, its grapes are considered best of all. Grande Champagne on the label means that the Cognac was made from these grapes, and about 18 percent of Cognac production fits this description.
- ***Petite Champagne:*** The "next-best" grapes, coming from the area that almost surrounds Grande Champagne. Petite Champagnes account for about 20 percent of Cognac production.
- ***Borderies:*** This area also borders Grande Champagne and is the smallest Cognac appellation. Its output is highly valued for use in blending.
- ***Fin Bois:*** The largest (and largest-producing) appellation, with 40 percent of the Cognac output. Much of it is used for blending.
- ***Bons Bois:*** On the outskirts of the Cognac region, this area produces less desirable blending grapes.
- ***Bois Communes:*** Also on the outskirts, this large area produces average Cognac products. The appellation also is known as *Bois Ordinaires*.
- ***Fine Champagne:*** An appellation, but not a geographic area, this means that 50 percent or more of the product's grapes came from Grande Champagne and the balance came from Petite Champagne.

In addition to single-district Cognacs made only from grapes in a certain appellation, there are blended Cognacs, single-distillery Cognacs, single-estate Cognacs, and a few high-end Cognacs that are both single-distillery and single-estate.

The best-known brands of Cognac are Courvoisier, Hennessy, Martell, and Rémy-Martin; of these Hennessy is by far the market leader in U.S. sales. Grand Marnier is also considered a Cognac although it is a blend of Cognac and Curacao; the latest "flavor," Grand Marnier Navan, blends Cognac with black vanilla from Madagascar.

Clearly Cognac producers are creating line extensions in an effort to market their products in new ways. Rémy-Martin has had notable success with its RémyRed line, infusions of fruit juices with Cognac. The attempt, of course, is to erase Cognac's image as an old person's drink. Cognac can also be served with a simple lemon twist in a sugar-rimmed glass.

Armagnac. **Armagnac** (ARM-un-yak) is another French spirit familiar to Americans, distilled from white-grape brandy and with much the same upscale appeal as Cognac. Armagnac comes from its own restricted region of Southwest France (Gascony home of "The Three Musketeers"), which is divided into three districts. There are several major differences between Armagnac and Cognac: Armagnac makers are allowed to use any of a dozen grape varietals; their product is distilled only once, not twice like Cognac; and Armagnac is distilled more often in a column still than a pot still. These particular column stills, called *alambic Armagnacias,* are very small and made of copper; they are almost a hybrid of the column still and pot still. Armagnac is also aged in oak, and typically it is aged longer than Cognac. On the label you'll see some of the same jargon and abbreviations, although Armagnac is permitted to have its age printed on the label. If the product is a blend, the age of the youngest component of the blend is used; the oldest blends (10 years or more) may be vintage-dated or labeled *Hors d'age.*

Armagnac is traditionally served at the end of a meal and can be paired with fresh fruit or chocolate. However, the Armagnac National Association Bureau also suggests serving it in the following ways:

- *Trou Gascon,* which means ice cold, as a palate cleanser between courses.
- With foie gras, smoked salmon, or other meat-based hors d'oeuvres.
- *Floc de Gascogne,* half-and-half with grape juice. This can be an aperitif with melon or cheeses, or as a dessert.

The various Armagnacs are more different from one another than the Cognacs are, and typically less expensive. Most Armagnac producers make such small quantities that no one has a corner on the American market, but among the brands you may see are Domaine de Papolle, de Caussade, Janneau, Chateau Laubade, Chateau du Tariquet, Napoleon, and Vielle Reserve.

Brandies Around the World. When you start looking you will be surprised at how many countries have brandy-making industries. The next few paragraphs can offer only brief introductions to a few of them.

In the United States, brandy production dates back to the Spanish missions of 1800s California, although in the 1920s a combination of phylloxera and Prohibition proved almost lethal for the booming industry. Today's market is fairly well cornered by the major producers (Christian Brothers, E & J Gallo, and Paul Masson) that use such table-grape varieties as Flame Tokay and Thompson Seedless to make their wares. But a small number of specialty distillers have sprung up, using pot stills and **solera systems** (see the following section on Spanish brandy) for production of finer-quality brandies.

The earliest brandies of Spain were not taken seriously or consumed on their own, however; they were made to fortify sherry, for which the country is famous. It was the Dutch traders who recognized the true worth of the Spanish brandy and prompted its export in the 1700s.

Today Spanish brandies have reputations as some of the world's finest. They come from two areas. In *Jerez,* the Southwestern town where the majority of brandy makers are congregated, distilling has been going on since 900 A.D.. The vineyards around Jerez are used for making sherry. For brandy the grapes are trucked in from the La Mancha region, a hot climate that produces grapes higher in alcohol and lower in acidity than those grown in France. After distillation in column stills, the new brandy goes into sherry butts (wooden casks) and is stored in **solera systems,** just like sherry—that is, the casks are stacked several barrels high, but each horizontal row contains brandy of about the same age. When some is taken out of a barrel (and no barrel is ever completely emptied) it is refilled with some from the next oldest row. This constant refilling and decanting is a way of gradually blending the new with the old, for smooth, consistent flavors. Depending on the length of aging (a minimum of 6 months), the brandy may be labeled *Reserva* (aged 1 year) or *Gran Reserva* (aged a minimum of 3 years), although many are aged for more than a decade.

The other Spanish brandy-making region is *Penedes,* which is not far from Barcelona in Northeastern Spain; however, there are only two producers in this area, Mascaro and Torres. Pot stills are used here, and the soleras are made from French oak instead of sherry butts, creating a hearty spirit with a different, drier character than *Brandy de Jerez.* Today in Spain brandy is considered somewhat an "old folks' drink," but the industry is doing some marketing to bring young customers into the fold. Cardenal Mendoza and Domecq are some recognizable brand names in the United States.

German brandies are called **weinbrand** (VINE-brond), produced in pot stills, and aged for a minimum of 6 months in oak. Those aged a year or more are designated as *uralt* or *alter,* which means older. These brandies are usually made of imported grapes from France, and the German style is somewhat lighter and sweeter than traditional cognac.

Mexico does not come to mind as a wine-producing country, and perhaps that is because most of the wine produced there is distilled to make brandy, which now outsells both rum and tequila in that country. Mexican brandies are made in both column and pot stills and aged in solera systems. Pedro Domecq and Presidente are among the Mexican brand names exported to the United States.

Pisco (PEES-koh) is a strong brandy that originated in Peru (Pisco is the name of a local tribe that created the drink from sweet, wild Muscat or Quebranta grapes) but is now a major product of Chile and Bolivia as well. If made in Bolivia, it may be called *Singani.* Pisco was popular in California during the Gold Rush and is still the base for a refreshing summer cocktail called the Pisco Sour, although Pisco is not easy to find in the United States.

Metaxa is the well-known after-dinner spirit from Greece. Made in pot stills, slightly sweetened, and infused with herbs and spices, it is technically a liqueur but is generally thought of and marketed as brandy.

South Africa has a well-established brandy industry that dates back to the arrival of Dutch colonists in the 1700s. South African brandies must be aged 3 years in oak, by law. About 25 percent of the production is premium spirits; the rest is often used to mix with cola, a drink that is popular there. KWV and Backsberg are brands sometimes seen in America, but there are at least 50 made in South Africa. A South African Brandy Foundation was formed in 1984, and a "Brandy Route" enables tourists to visit multiple distillers and sample the products.

Pomace Brandies and Grappa. There is one more spirit that, although it is not a brandy, is made in much the same way—in this case, by distilling the leftover skins, stems, and seeds from winemaking. These leftover grape pressings are known in Italy as *vinaccia,* in France as **marc**, and elsewhere as *pomace.*

Although sometimes called a **pomace brandy**, the spirit is more often labeled **Grappa** (GRAWP-ah). This has been a source of contention since 1989 when the European Union (EU) granted Italy the exclusive rights to use the word *Grappa* as an official designation. (The name comes from the area of Italy where the spirit originated, near Mount Grappa.) Technically the EU edict means that if this particular spirit is made anywhere other than Italy, it should be called *pomace brandy*. (Alternately France labels its products **Marc.**) In the 1990s South Africa and the EU had quite a legal squabble over this issue.

No matter what the label on the bottle says, when you taste this product, you will know instantly why people either love it or hate it. Grappa used to be inexpensive, made just out of being thrifty rather than throwing anything away. It had an awful reputation and an even worse taste. Today, however, grappa producers have learned how to create smooth-sipping products that are more brandy-like—and connoisseurs are paying $15 to $30 per shot to try them! As many as 1,000 Italian vintners make their own brands of grappa, and a few American and Canadian wineries have jumped on the bandwagon, too. The top destinations for the imported Italian products are Germany, France, and the United States.

The quality of the spirit is determined in large measure by how fresh the batch of pomace is at the time of distillation. Premium grappa makers have recognized this importance, and they are also experimenting with using whole grapes (not the leftover crushed ones), using single varietals instead of blends, and aging them in wood. The grappas made from sweeter grape varietals seem to be the most flavorful, but grappa comes in a wide variety of styles, and many are sold in different types of collectable, hand-blown bottles—another marketing tool.

Grappa is best consumed cool, not ice cold, in shot glasses. In Italy it is also used to make Caffe Corretto, a bracing after-meal drink that is one part grappa, two parts espresso. Italian brands you may see in the United States include Nonino, Bertagnoli, Maschio, and Jacopo; Bonny Doon, from California; and Clear Creek, from Oregon.

Imported Fruit Brandies. **Fruit brandy** is the general term for the category of brandies made from fruits other than grapes. To further confuse the novice, there are also *fruit-flavored brandies,* which are grape-based brandies with fruit extracts added. Fruit-flavored brandies are not true brandies, but sweetened liqueurs of lower proof with a brandy base. In Europe the word *flavored* is omitted from these spirits, so do not be fooled: An imported strawberry brandy is not a brandy but a strawberry-flavored liqueur of considerable sweetness. The word *flavored* is required on the labels of the comparable American products.

A fine apple brandy known as **Calvados** comes from France. By law it can bear the Calvados name only if it is made in the province of Normandy, where since it was too cold to grow grapes, early settlers grew tart apples instead. Calvados begins as cider (the juice pressed out of apples) and is distilled and aged in wooden barrels. The juices of several different apple types and ages are blended to make the final mix, which is 40 to 45 percent alcohol. All varieties of Calvados are aged at least two years in oak, but many are aged 5 to 10 years. The cognac label designations, traditional but not required by law, are also found on Calvados labels. The best known appellation for Calvados is *Pays d'Auge*.

Numerous distillers make apricot brandies as well. Cherry brandy is also popular. This is called **kir** (made in the Alsace area of France), **kirsch,** or *kirschwasser* (made in the Bavarian region of Germany). It is a colorless liquid made from the wild black cherry that grows in these areas. Often called a white brandy, it is made in pot stills from a mash that includes the cherry pits and skins. A low distillation proof of 100 or less allows the bitter almond flavor of the pits to be carried into the final spirit. It is bottled immediately to retain the maximum flavor and aroma of the fruit. Although production is relatively simple, the cost is high because of the large amounts of wild fruit needed. A liqueur of the same name is also made; it is sweetened and includes the word *liqueur* on the label. France and Germany also produce raspberry brandies, called *Framboise* and *Himbeergeist,* respectively.

Another fruit brandy familiar to many is *Slivovitz,* a plum brandy made in central Europe. It is distilled in the same way as kirsch but is aged in wood to a golden color. Other popular brand names in the world of plum brandy are Mirabelle (made from a type of yellow plum) and Questch (made from a large, mauve-colored plum variety). A colorless, unaged brandy called *Poire William* is made from pears in Switzerland and France; elsewhere, pear-flavored liqueurs (made from neutral spirits and crushed pears) carry the similar name *Pear William* although they are not the same product. In both cases you may see a preserved pear inside the bottle (see Figure 5.11).

FIGURE 5.11 A bottle of Poire William. Photo courtesy of Clear Creek Distillery.

LIQUEURS, CORDIALS, AND MORE

Liqueur and *cordial* are two terms for the same thing: a distilled spirit flavored or redistilled with fruits, flowers, plants, their juices or extracts, or other natural flavoring materials, and sweetened with 2½ percent or more of sugar. To simplify matters we will use the word *liqueur.* In addition to mixing into a wide and wild variety of cocktails, liquers have two main functions: to begin and end a meal.

Great Beginnings: Aperitifs

An **aperitif** is served before dinner to whet the appetite. The name has its roots in the Latin word *apeio,* which means "to open." In Europe, where aperitifs are popular, they usually are wine-based drinks served at room temperature. The list includes crisp, dry wines, such as Champagne, manzanilla, and fino sherries, Muscat and Alligote; or aromatized wines, fortified and steeped in herbs, such as Byrrh, Campari, Dubonnet, Lillet, Pastis, Ouzo, and Vermouth. Relatively low in alcohol (from 16 percent to 24 percent by volume) and with distinctive bittersweet flavors, they promote conviviality without dulling the palate for the food to come.

In the United States, the definition of aperitif has broadened to include almost any before-dinner cocktail.

SERVING BRANDY

When it is not an ingredient in a cocktail, dessert drink (Brandy Alexander, Stinger, American Beauty) or coffee drink, brandy served straight as an after-dinner drink is presented according to custom in a large, rounded brandy glass called a *snifter* (see Figure 5.12). The glass is cupped in the palm of the hand, which warms the liquid slightly, and swirled slightly to release the brandy's rich aroma, an important part of the sensual pleasure of the drink.

However, like any tradition, not everyone agrees with it. The tulip-shaped, footed glass or the two-ounce "pony" or liqueur glasses also are acceptable. White brandies ordered straight should be served icy cold in a pony or liqueur glass. Fruit-flavored brandies should be served either cold or over ice in a chilled glass.

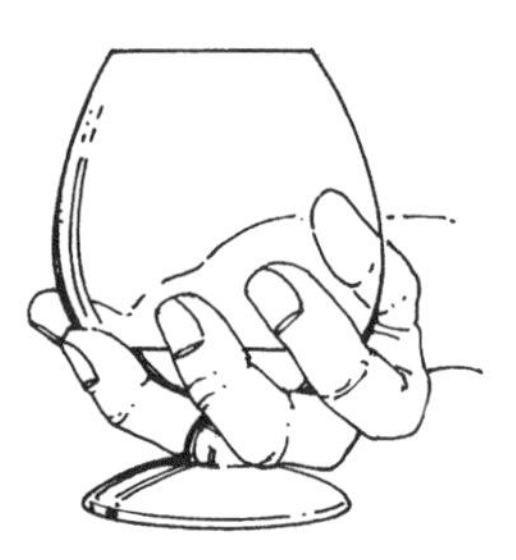

FIGURE 5.12 Traditionally brandy is served in a footed, wide-based glass called a *snifter*.

Getting U.S. consumers to try the more traditional aperitifs will be difficult unless your staff has tasted them and can make recommendations. Beautiful glassware and eye-catching drink menus will help. Alternately bartenders can use them to prepare premium cocktails.

Satisfying Endings: Digestifs

Liqueurs are natural after-dinner drinks, often sweet and flavorful; the category known as **digestifs** was created centuries ago for less-than-glamorous task of aiding digestion. Digestifs are spirits distilled from fruits, herbs, and spices, and roots. Artisan distillers in the United States are producing *eaux de vie,* a category of fruity, aromatic young brandies to cleanse the palate after mealtimes. In addition to liqueurs, aquavit, grappa, and marc, Cognac, Armagnac, and Calvados all are considered end-of-meal spirits.

These products can be difficult to sell to U.S. consumers who feel, after a meal that includes wines, that another dose of alcohol is superfluous. Restaurateurs who are pressed to turn tables realize that diners who order after-dinner drinks are planning to stay a while, thus causing delays. However, a good digestif can be warming and elegant; some can be used to concoct premium coffee drinks. A bonus: these products, unlike wines, do not easily spoil, even after the bottle has been opened. The usual care should be taken to protect them from sunlight and heat.

The Making of Liqueurs

The makers of liqueurs are today's alchemists, with their secret formulas of herbs, spices, flowers, fruits, and exotic flavorings. No longer looking for the elixir of life, they deal in flavor, color, romance, and profits. New liqueurs are continually being developed, and both old and new are promoted with recipes for new drinks in the hope that something like the Moscow Mule miracle will happen again. And it does happen now and then: the oddly named Harvey Wallbanger cocktail put Galliano in every bar!

Any liqueur begins as a distilled spirit; it might be brandy, whiskey, rum, neutral spirits, or others. The distinctive flavorings may be any natural substance, such as fruits, seeds, spices, herbs, flowers, bark. Many of them are complex formulas containing as many as 50 ingredients. For example, Cointreau claims to use oranges from five different countries. The flavorings may be combined with the spirit in different ways. One method is **steeping** (soaking) the flavoring substances in the spirit; this is called **maceration.** Another is pumping the spirit over and over the flavoring substances suspended above it (as in a coffee pot) called **percolation.** Alternately the flavoring substances may be added when the spirit is redistilled.

The sugar may be any of several forms, including honey, maple syrup, and corn syrup. The sugar content is the main element that distinguishes liqueurs from all other types of spirit. It varies from 2½ percent to as much as 35 percent by weight from one liqueur to another. A liqueur with 10 percent or less sugar may be labeled *Dry.*

Color is often added to colorless spirits, as in the cases of green Crème de Menthe and blue Curacao. Colors must be natural vegetable coloring agents or approved food dyes.

A liqueur can be consumed as a *shooter,* served in a shot glass and quickly hoisted and downed as part of a celebration, or as a cocktail ingredient: liqueurs are integral parts of the Cosmopolitan, Margarita, and Rusty Nail. A liqueur can be sipped straight (undiluted) after dinner in an elegant stemmed glass or snifter, added to coffee, or mixed with cream to play the role of dessert. An easy way to make ice cream more elegant is to pour a bit of liqueur over it just before serving. Another option is to drizzle a teaspoonful of liqueur into a flute of Champagne.

It is impossible to include the names and uses of every liqueur here, but we will attempt to list and describe a few of the most common ones—some generic types, some brand names—alphabetically (see Figure 5.13).

Absinthe (AB-santh): This nineteenth-century French liqueur is a distillate of a variety of herbs which in past centuries included aniseseed and wormwood. Absinthe in its strongest forms caused convulsions and hallucinations, so today it is strictly regulated in Europe to contain no more than 10 parts per

LIQUEURS

Liqueur	*Spirit Base*	*Flavor*	*Brand or Generic*	*Color*	*Proof*
Amaretto	Neutral spirits	Almond-apricot	Generic	Amber	48–56
Anisette	Neutral spirits	Anise, licorice	Generic	Red, clear[a]	40–60
Apricot liqueur or cordial	Neutral spirits	Apricot	Generic	Orange-amber	60–70
Bailey's Irish Cream	Irish whiskey	Irish-chocolate	Brand	Pale café au lait	34
Bénédictine	Neutral spirits	Herb-spice	Brand	Dark gold	86
B & B	Neutral spirits, Cognac	Herb-spice	Brand	Dark gold	86
Blackberry liqueur or cordial	Neutral spirits or brandy	Blackberry	Generic	Red-purple	60
Chambord	Cognac	Raspberry	Brand	Raspberry	33
Chartreuse	Brandy and neutral spirits	Spicy herb	Brand	Yellow	80, 86
				Green	110
Chéri-Suisse	Neutral spirits	Chocolate-cherry	Brand	Red-pink	52, 60
Cherry liqueur or cordial	Neutral spirits or brandy	Cherry	Generic	Red	30–60
Cointreau	Neutral spirits	Orange	Brand	Clear	80
Cordial Médoc	Neutral spirits, Cognac, Armagnac	Brandy and fruit	Brand	Dark amber	80
Crème de bananes	Neutral spirits	Ripe banana	Generic	Yellow	50–60
Crème de cacao	Neutral spirits	Chocolate-vanilla	Generic	Clear, brown	50–60
Crème de cassis	Neutral spirits	Black currant	Generic	Red-black	30–50
Crème de Menthe	Neutral spirits	Mint	Generic	Clear, green	60
Crème de noyaux	Neutral spirits	Almond	Generic	Clear, red, cream	50–60
Crème d'Yvette	Neutral spirits	Violet, jellybean	Generic	Blue-violet	36–40
Curaçao	Neutral spirits (rum or brandy)	Orange peel	Generic	Clear, orange, blue	54–80
Drambuie	Scotch	Scotch-honey-herb	Brand	Gold	80
Forbidden Fruit	Brandy	Grapefruit	Brand	Red-brown	60–64
Galliano	Neutral spirits	Anise-vanilla, licorice	Brand	Bright yellow	80
Goldwasser	Neutral spirits	Orange-anise	Generic	Clear, gold-flecked	60–86
Grand Marnier	Cognac	Orange peel, Cognac	Brand	Light Amber	80
Irish Mist	Irish whiskey	Irish-honey-herb	Brand	Amber	80
Jeremiah Weed	Bourbon	Bourbon	Brand	Gold	100
Kahlúa	Neutral siprits	Coffee	Brand	Brown	53

FIGURE 5.13 Liqueurs.

LIQUEURS (continued)

Liqueur	*Spirit Base*	*Flavor*	*Brand or Generic*	*Color*	*Proof*
Kirsch liqueur	Kirsch	Sweetened kirsch	Generic	Clear	90–100
Kümmel	Neutral spirits	Caraway	Generic	Clear	70–100
Lochan Ora	Scotch	Scotch-honey-herb	Brand	Gold	70
Mandarine	Brandy	Tangerine	Generic	Bright orange	80
Maraschino	Neutral spirits	Cherry-almond	Generic	Clear	60–80
Midori	Neutral spirits	Honeydew	Brand	Ice green	46
Ouzo	Brandy	Anise, licorice	Generic	Clear	90–98
Peach liqueur or cordial	Neutral spirits	Peach	Generic	Amber	60–80
Peppermint schnapps	Neutral spirits	Mint	Generic	Clear	40–100
Pernod	Neutral spirits	Licorice, anise	Brand	Yellow-green	90
Peter Heering	Neutral spirits, brandy	Cherry	Brand	Dark red	49
Raspberry liqueur or cordial	Neutral spirits	Raspberry jam	Generic	Red-purple	50–60
Rock and rye	Rye and neutral spirits	Rye-fruit	Generic	Gold-brown	60–70
Sabra	Neutral spirits	Chocolate-orange	Brand	Deep brown	60
Sambuca	Neutral spirits	Licorice	Generic	Clear	40–84
Schnapps, peach, etc.	Neutral spirits	Peach, other	Generic	Clear	40–60
Sloe gin	Neutral spirits	Wild plum	Generic	Red	42–60
Southern Comfort	Bourbon	Bourbon-peach	Brand	Gold	80, 100
Strawberry liqueur	Neutral spirits	Strawberry	Generic	Red	44–60
Strega	Neutral spirits	Herb-spice	Brand	Gold	80
Tia Maria	Rum	Coffee	Brand	Brown	63
Triple sec	Neutral spirits	Orange peel	Generic	Clear	60–80
Tuaca	Brandy	Eggnog-cocoa	Brand	Yellow-brown	84
Vandermint	Neutral spirits	Chocolate-mint	Brand	Dark brown	52
Vieille Cure	Neutral spirits	Herb-vanilla	Brand	Green, yellow	60
Wild Turkey liqueur	Bourbon	Bourbon	Brand	Amber	80
Yukon Jack	Canadian whisky	Light whisky	Brand	Light golden	80, 100

[a] Often referred to as white.

FIGURE 5.13 *(Continued)*

million of *alpha thujone*, the nerve-damaging ingredient. (Absinthe of the 1800s contained as much as 260 parts per million.) Today absinthe is made in France, Bulgaria, and the Czech Republic, and is known for its incredibly high alcohol content (55 percent and higher). It is still illegal to purchase absinthe in the United States, although many other nations allow it. The liqueurs *Pernod Anise* and *Pastis* are similar in flavor, without the addictive component, as is a New Orleans-made liqueur called *Herbsaint*.

Amaretto (am-ah-RET-oh): Generic name for almond-flavored liqueur.

Anisette (ANN-ih-set): Generic name for a very sweet liqueur made with anise seed, an ingredient that got its start in Switzerland as a medicinal herb. At least a dozen other herbs and fruit peels are added.

Benedictine (ben-ah-DIK-teen): Made by Benedictine monks in France, this liqueur is among the world's most prestigious brands, and its formula is top secret. The monastery claims the distillation process includes five separate batches of 27 botanicals.

Chambord (sham-BORD): Brand name of a black-raspberry-flavored liqueur from France.

Chartreuse (shar-TROOS): Like Benedictine this brightly colored herbal liqueur's secret recipe has been handed down in a single monastery since the seventeenth century. The monks will admit only that every ingredient is natural, with no added coloring. Experts agree that the two formulas (Green, 110 proof, and Yellow, 80 proof) taste like a heavenly combination of honey, flowers, and fruit, and that Chartreuse is arguably the world's best liqueur.

Cointreau (KWON-troh): Brand name of a liqueur made of several types of citrus fruit, including bitter oranges. Cointreau is the name of the family that first produced it in the mid-1800s after visiting Curacao (see below) and discovering its orange liqueurs. Today Cointreau is made in both the United States and Spain.

Crème de Cacao (KREM dah KOH-koh): Generic name for a cream-based, chocolate liqueur. It may be brown or colorless.

Crème de Menthe (KREM dah MAW): Generic name for a cream-based, mint-flavored liqueur that may be green or colorless. This is important in some drink recipes: a Grasshopper requires green crème de menthe, while a Stinger requires the clear type.

Curacao (KYOOR-ah-sau): Generic name of a liqueur made from the peel of the bitter orange (not the same fruit as a typical orange) in Curacao, Haiti, and other Caribbean islands.

Drambuie (dram-BOO-ee): Brand name of an amber-colored liqueur that begins as scotch, with honey added for sweetness.

Frangelico (fran-JELL-ih-koh): Brand name of a sweet, hazelnut-flavored herbal liqueur made in Italy.

Galliano (GAL-ee-AH-noh): Brand name of a deep yellow, Italian-made, herb-based liqueur.

Grand Marnier (GRAN marn-YAY): Brand-name of a Cognac and Curacao blend aged in oak in the Cognac district of France. A bottle of original Grand

Marnier (from an 1880s recipe) is sold every two seconds; a newer, a upscale vintage version (called *Cuvee de Cent Cinquatenair*) retails for $225 per bottle.

Kahlua (kuh-LOO-ah): Brand name of a Mexican-made liqueur that combines coffee and vanilla with cane spirit. It is often mixed with milk or cream.

Limoncello (lim-un-CHEL-loh): Also called *Lemoncello,* this lemon-flavored liqueur is produced in Italy by immersing fresh lemon peel in distilled alcohol and syrup. Can be used as a digestif or a mixer, or over ice cream.

Noisette (nwah-SET): French brand of hazelnut-flavored liqueur.

Ouzo (OO-zoh): Thick, clear Greek aperitif distilled from grapes, and flavored with aniseseed, fennel, and herbs, along with *mastic* (the resin of evergreen trees). The name comes from the inscription on crates of the liqueur that were exported from Greece to France in the late 1800s—*Uso di Massalia,* which means "for use in Marseilles."

Pastis (poss-TEESE): Category of European liqueurs made with licorice or aniseseed; the best known pastis is absinthe.

Sabra (SAHB-rah): Liqueur from Israel made with Jaffa oranges and chocolate. Very sweet; good in coffee or over ice cream.

Sambuca (sam-BOO-kuh): Generic name of a clear, plant-based liqueur with a spicy, licorice flavor, somewhat similar in flavor to Ouzo.

Schnapps (SHNOPS): In Europe, an herb-flavored dry spirit (see **Aquavit,** discussed earlier in this chapter); in the United States today, it is a sweet liqueur, fruit or mint-flavored. Some people like it because of its relatively low alcohol content, which is about 48 proof. Peach schnapps is a prime ingredient in the cocktails Woo Woo and Fuzzy Navel.

Southern Comfort: Liqueur that begins with American whiskey. A secret blend of ingredients, including peach juice, gives it a light sweetness and makes it a good substitute for bourbon. Its market share is growing at twice the rate of other cordials, and international sales comprise 40 percent of its sales.

Tia Maria (TEE-ah mah-REE-ah): Brand name of a Jamaican coffee-flavored liqueur. Tia Maria is sweeter than Kahlua and often used for mixing.

Triple Sec (TRIP-ul SEK): Generic name of white (no color added) Curacao.

Van der Hum (VAN-dur-HUM): South African equivalent of Curacao; a brandy-based liqueur with a citrus tinge from a local tangerine-type fruit called *naartjies.* This spirit's name means "What's His Name."

Figure 5.13 also lists the base, flavor, color, and bottling proof of these and other spirits. Notice how much the proof varies. Generic types are made by more than one producer and vary in flavor and proof. Remember, no category of beverage gets better customer response from servers' suggestions than liqueurs. There is almost no end to the flavors, textures, price spreads, and preparation options available to the smart bar owner. Liqueurs are a very trendy part of the industry. New products are released every year, as are new recipes to use existing products in new concoctions. As a result it is easy for a distiller's pride and joy to become the "flavor of the month." But a "flavor of the decade?" That's a true challenge.

Hard Ciders

Hard cider, the enduring term for fermented cider, was mentioned earlier in this chapter in the discussion of applejack. Hard cider dates back to the Roman Empire and is still a staple in many British pubs. In colonial America hard cider was a daily mealtime beverage until the late nineteenth century, when other immigrants brought their beer-making skills to the United States. Cider was replaced by lager beer, which was easier and cheaper to produce.

Small artisan-like producers have revived hard cider as a beverage option, and in 1997 the U.S. government even lowered the taxes on it. Cider's alcohol content is typically 4 to 8 percent by volume (which is the same as, or a little higher than, that of beer), although some blends can contain up to 14 percent. Brands imported to the United States from France, England, and Ireland have as little as $2\frac{1}{2}$ percent alcohol content by volume. These make nice counterparts to spicy foods, because they are not too filling and offer a crisp, complex type of refreshment that appeals to the same crowd interested in microbrewed beers The U.S. Food and Drug Administration (FDA) also requires hard cider to carry nutritional content labels, a boon for health-conscious drinkers who like the combination of a fruit-based drink with a lower alcohol level. An important note: the beverage known as **hard lemonade** is a mixture of beer and lemonade, and not at all kin to hard cider although they compete for the same customers.

Hard cider makers seem to have congregated in two areas of the United States: New England (Vermont's Flag Hill Farm, Massachusetts's West County Cider) and the Pacific Northwest (Oregon's Traditional Company, and Cyderworks; Washington's Blue Mountain and White Oak). The largest domestic cider maker is Green Mountain Beverage of Vermont, with Woodchuck, Cider Jack, and imported Strongbow brands. Canadian import Wyder's Cider has a wide product range and a respectable market share in this offbeat beverage category. There are also British and French brands of hard cider, seldom exported to America. The top British import in the category is Strongbow; French brands include vintage-dated Etienne du Pont, Lecompte, and Henri Bellot.

Bitters

Well, have we finally come to the bitter end of this lengthy discussion on spirits? Not without a quick rundown on **bitters.** These very unique spirits are flavored with herbs, roots, bark, fruits, and so on, like liqueurs. The difference is that bitters are unsweetened, so "bitter" is the right word for them. Once used primarily as medicines or for hangover cures, bitters come in two basic varieties: bitters that provide concentrated flavor and bitters for beverages. Most contain 30 or more different herbs and spices. On the list are Angostura from Trinidad (originally a malaria medicine), various orange bitters, and the lesser-known Peychaud's, a New Orleans product. They are used in minute amounts to flavor mixed drinks, for example, Angostura is used in the Old-Fashioned.

Among the best known of the beverage bitters is Campari, a 48-proof red Italian spirit that truly has a bitter flavor. It is usually quaffed with soda or tonic or in a cocktail, such as the Negroni. Campari is a fashionable drink all over Europe and has become well known in this country, especially among sophisticated drinkers.

The bitters category is also home to some of the more interesting libations for the intrepid drinker. Amer Picon, a 78-proof, quinine-laced French bitters with a brandy base, is said to have been what the French Foreign Legion in Algeria added to the water in their canteens. Amer Picon is served with ice and water or used in cocktails. From Italy, *Cynar* is the world's only spirit made from artichoke leaves. Its name is from cynarum, the Latin word for artichoke, and its reputation is as an aperitif that is good for the liver. It is brown, syrupy, and high in alcohol content; it is typically mixed with seltzer or tonic.

Perhaps the biggest surprise in the bitters market is the incredible popularity of Jägermeister (YAY-gur-MICE-tur), a German product with a stately stag on its label and high alcohol content. "Jager" has made the list of Hottest Brands in the liquor industry during the first several years of the 2000s, mostly for its reputation as a shooter in bars frequented by entry-level drinkers. The company works hard for its rowdy, sexy reputation with rock-concert-tour sponsorships, a traveling JagerBus full of gorgeous Jagerettes and hunky JagerDudes, and a Jäger Tap Machine that dispenses the spirit supercold.

Germany also exports Underberg, which is known primarily as a hangover cure and sold in small bottles wrapped in brown paper. Still another of these supposedly drinkable bitters is Fernet Branca, a 78-proof spirit, known chiefly as a hangover treatment (perhaps as a counterirritant?). Everyone agrees that its taste is terrible.

SUMMING UP

All of the alcoholic beverages you serve begin in the same way: by fermenting a liquid product containing sugar to break down the sugar into alcohol and carbon dioxide. This is the basic process by which beers and wines are made.

Distilled spirits take the procedure one step further: The fermented liquid is heated in an enclosed space to vaporize the alcohol, separating it from the remaining liquid. The vapors are drawn off in a closed container and condensed as a concentrated spirit. All distilled spirits are made in this way. The sensory characteristics (taste, aroma, color, body) of each finished product come from combinations of many factors: the original ingredients, the distillation proof, whether or not the spirit is aged (and for how long and in what type of container), whether it is blended or infused (and with what additional ingredients), whether and how flavorings are added, and the bottling proof.

Spirits fall into several basic categories, by which they were grouped in this chapter. Brown goods are the venerable Scotch whiskies and Irish whiskeys, American bourbons, and Tennessee sour mash. White goods are the (generally) colorless liquors: vodka, gin, rum, and tequila, although the latter two spirits are sometimes tinged brown by barrel-aging and/or the addition of caramel. Liqueurs are distilled spirits to which other, aromatic ingredients—herbs, nuts, fruit extracts, and so on—are added. In the past these were added for medicinal value; today they are added for consumer interest, uniqueness, and mixability. The uses of hard ciders and bitters were also discussed.

This chapter told you something about each bottle in your well and on your backbar, their interesting origins and histories, and how they differ from one another. Knowing all about them is an asset. It will help you in pouring, in purchasing, in answering customer questions, and in preventing or dealing with intoxicated guests. In fact this product knowledge will give you a better understanding of the information in the chapters to follow.

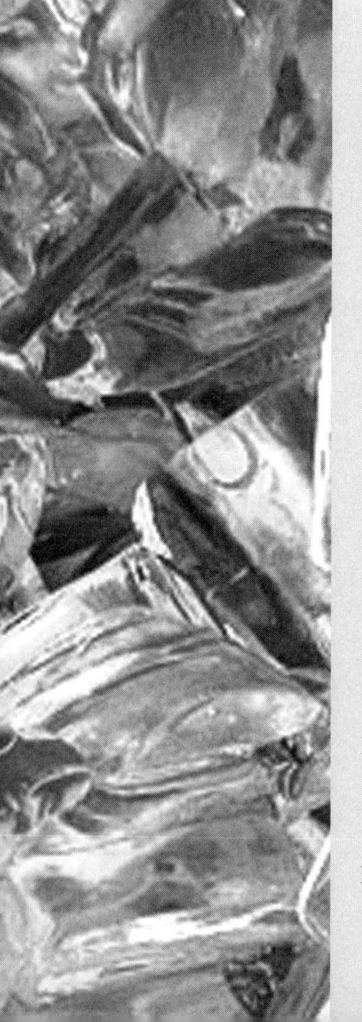

POINTS TO PONDER

1. You know now that white goods outsell brown goods. In your opinion what would it take for the brown-goods producers to change this long time trend?
2. Trace the history of the popularity of vodka in the U.S. market. How do you explain it?
3. What is a neutral spirit, and how is it used?
4. Describe how tequila is produced. How does it differ from other white spirits?
5. Why are aged whiskies and brandies considered better than younger ones, and why are they more expensive?
6. Which of the following phrases indicate superior quality in a spirit: VSOP, bottled in bond, sour mash, London Dry, aged in wood, reposado? Briefly define each phrase, and explain how it applies to quality.
7. There are two different products commonly called schnapps. Describe each and explain how they differ.
8. What is the difference between a liqueur and a cordial?
9. If someone asked you for a mixed drink with very little alcohol in it, what would you suggest, and why?
10. If you were deciding on the liquor inventory for a bar and you knew that your budget wouldn't stretch to include *every* possible choice, how would you approach the challenge of what to buy?

Extra Credit

11. Would you eat the worm in the mescal bottle? Why or why not?

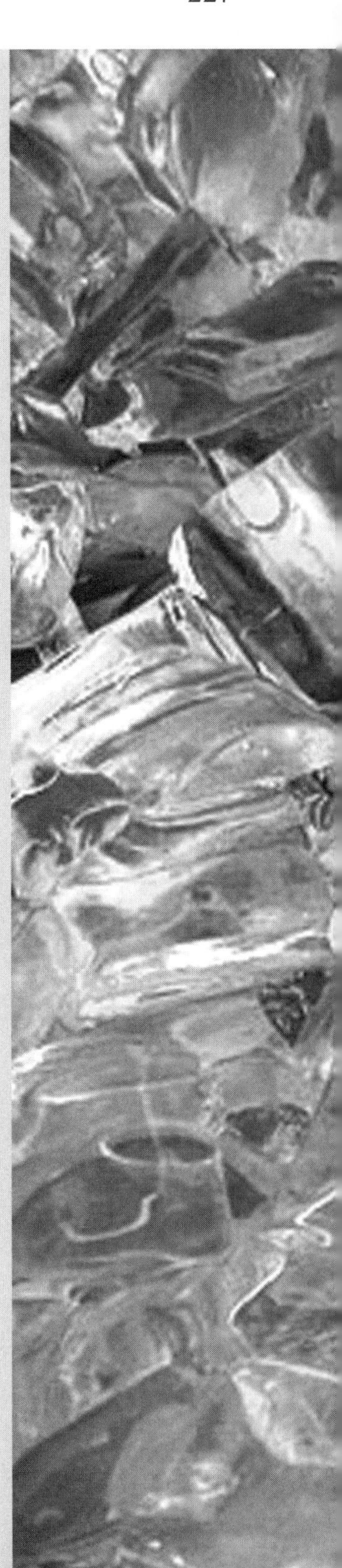

TERMS OF THE TRADE

aguardiente
alambic (alembic) still
anejo (tequila)
aperitif
applejack
Aquavit
Armagnac
arrack (arak)
barrel house
bitters
blending
blue agave
BMSW
Bottled in Bond
bourbon
brown goods
cachaca
cask strength
Coffey still
compound gin
congener
continuous (patent) still
cordial
corn liquor
diastase
digestif
distillation
edible cocktail
fermentation
fruit brandy
fusel oil
Genever
grappa
gusano
hard cider
hard lemonade
Hollands
infusion
kir (kirsch)
korn
line extension
maceration
maguey
malt
marc
Mescal (Mezcal)
metaxa
mixed drink
mixto
neutral spirits
overproof
peaty (peat-reek)
percolation
Plymouth gin
pomace brandy
pot still
proof
pure malt
reposado (tequila)
rye
Scotch
single malt
sloe gin
solera system
sour mash
Standards of Identity
steeping
Tennessee whiskey
Tequila Puro
tequillarias
Ugni Blanc
vatted malt
weinbrand
white goods
wood management

A CONVERSATION WITH...F. PAUL PACULT

Paul Pacult (his byline is F. Paul Pacult) began his career in the wine-and-spirits industry like so many others—quite by accident! Working as a landscaper in the early 1970s he was hired to beautify a new Sonoma County winery, Rodney Strong Vineyards. When the landscaping was finished Strong asked if Pacult would be interested in staying on to help in the vineyard. He spent the next decade there, learning and participating in every facet of winemaking.

Pacult had always known that he wanted to be a writer and began penning wine-related articles for various magazines. That led to other writing jobs, relocation to New York City, and a retail manager's job at a prestigious liquor store. He also opened a wine-appreciation school.

Today Pacult writes regularly about wine and spirits for The New York Times, Wine Enthusiast *magazine, and Delta Air Lines's* Sky *magazine. He lives in the Hudson Valley area of New York, where he, his wife, Sue, and brother Rick, write and publish* Spirit Journal, *with subscribers in 31 countries. They also conduct educational seminars and tastings of wines and spirits.*

Editor, *The Spirit Journal* Wine-and-Spirits Writer

Q: What made you decide to branch out and write about spirits instead of just doing wine writing?

A: Well, when *The New York Times* called and ask me to write an article about Scotch for its Sunday magazine, I didn't know what to say. I didn't know a thing about Scotch! But I was a good writer; and how do you turn down an offer from a paper like that? It turned out to be 28 pages, and just fascinating to research. It got tremendous reader response—I don't think we ever imagined it would get that kind of response. And it soon became apparent to me that all of my peers were writing about wine, but nobody was really writing much about spirits. So I decided to put part of my creative thrust into that area. Spirits were still, in the late '80s, kind of impolitic. They were mostly brown, and people still had some misgivings about them.

Then I decided—since I was tasting so much product coming from all over the world to my office—to start a newsletter [and] not to accept any advertising, but to exist on subscriptions only and maintain complete objectivity. That's when *Spirit Journal* was born, and we just passed our eleventh year. We review spirits and we have since 1991.

Q: I guess the point your career makes for students is that with the knowledge you can take it many different directions.

A: Yes. You really need to be open and never say, "No, I can't do that." When the [New York] *Times* came to me and said, "We want you to write a 10,000-word piece on Scotch whiskey,"—after I regained consciousness—I said, "I don't know a thing about it! But of course I'll do it!"

I've always been really open to opportunities, and I've never allowed myself to get into a rut. All the things I'm doing now are the sum-total of working in a winery, working in a retail store, teaching class, learning how to cook. It's important for young men and women to have a sense of adventure, a willingness to try new things. Don't ever feel that any job is "beneath" you. You will gain something from everything even if it doesn't end up working out.

Q: What are the trends in spirit consumption that you see today?

A: I think certain areas of spirits that were very hot in the 1990s have plateaued. Cognac—which was very quiet in the '90s—is now staging what I think is a significant comeback.

Tequila, for lots of reasons, is stagnant. The agave shortage is part myth and part reality. The industry-funded board in Mexico that tries to project trends for tequila has said that it was part disease, part frost, part El Nino. What they're not saying is that they miscalculated horribly in the early '90s as to where tequila consumption was heading, and that they were recommending steady growth but got explosive growth, particularly from 1995 to 2000. Taking that miscalculation, the agave growers in the 1990s didn't cultivate new areas. They just kept plodding along, planning for steady growth but nothing dramatic. But a few companies—mostly Cuervo—saw it coming and sewed up a lot of the agave futures through very astute contracts with growers.

One out of every four bottles of booze sold in the world is vodka, but sales have slowed and that's why you're seeing the introduction of so many flavored vodkas—they're trying to stimulate it. Gin is making a small comeback, mostly because many consumers think of vodka as bland and are looking for something a bit more challenging as their palates become more sophisticated. Gin certainly offers that so it's on the upswing.

Brandies are all plenty static right now, not much growth. But pot-still brandy from California is really coming on strong.

Q: What about whiskey?
A: Bourbon continues to be driven by sales of Jim Beam, and Tennessee spirits sales driven by Jack Daniel's. There's some minor growth in the high-end products, small-batch and single-barrel. But people are so smitten with single-malt Scotch and the caché that it carries that it's making it hard for the superpremium bourbons to make inroads.

Q: What do you think makes a liquor product successful, not just a "flash in the pan"?
A: A marketer who is able to discern what direction an average consumer—not a "status" consumer; but an average consumer—will take in buying a beverage in the next one to three years. Then to develop a product that will appeal to that person and put the money behind it to market and promote it.

I see so many brands flooding into our office at *Spirit Journal*. Sometimes they're good, sometimes they're bad, but six months later, they're off the shelves. That often happens when they are simply underfunded. Money does make a difference.

Q: What about the sexy campaign? Surely you've seen cases where you didn't think the product was good, but the ads were really a hit with younger consumers.
A: I often think, because I'm 52 years old, it's like I'm on Pluto compared to what's happening with people in their 20s! But again, it's a good marketer who can gauge the gas tank of the industry; and that person is not the connoisseur, or even someone who is relatively savvy about beverage alcohol. The marketer must look at the person who's in his or her early 20s, fresh out of college, got his or her first or second job, and finally has a little disposable income, living away from home or newly married. This person wants to learn, and part of the learning experience is social grace. Part of that, today, means learning about wines and spirits and beers, and you have to start somewhere.

All the big hits in spirits and wine are associated with that entry-level customer. For instance in the wine business, Sutter Home put White Zinfandel on the map. Why? Because Sutter Home looked at the market and said, "What can we do to appeal to a mass audience, keep it affordable, keep it slightly sweet?" They understood that you need to get into that younger, mass audience, who is willing to be adventurous.

Q: What do you think about the state-run liquor-store system?
A: I consider the control states a ripple from the tidal wave of Prohibition that is still with us today. In some sense there is a restriction of product in control states, which is another form of Prohibition. The people who control liquor in these states, and the distributors, are extremely powerful. And they are dictating the rules—it is not a truly free and open market in those states. To me it's absolutely appalling. In my experience the pricing is outrageous, at least 10 to 15 percent higher than the noncontrol states. Each state in the control system is making a fortune off of liquor sales.

Q: Any advice for students about what they should study?
A: Mine was all on-the-job training, but I think one of the best ways to break into the wine or spirits industry at some level is to first take some food courses—train as a chef or an assistant chef. There is no wine or liquor school in the world that can teach you about taste and "tune you in" to the sensitivity of your plate. But cooking is where you can learn to hone and refine your sense of taste, as well as learn to match foods and beverages. All of our wonderful beverages just about always work best with food. So to understand on a sensory level what you are doing and to learn the history behind it, is an excellent place to start.

CHAPTER 6
WINE APPRECIATION

The more you know about wine, it seems the more there is to know. Like any other multifaceted subject, the trends, players, and etiquette change over time and can be difficult to keep up with. Luckily you don't have to be an expert to enjoy good wines, match them with foods, and recommend them to customers. There are excellent magazines, newsletters, and Internet web sites for wine lovers, and any good bookstore will have dozens, if not hundreds, of books about the world's various wine regions and their histories, heroes, and wares.

The problem is that for a bartender, server, or manager written information is simply not enough. Useful wine knowledge begins with experimentation, which means tasting and comparing wines from different countries and trying them with foods as you learn more about their origins. Don't think of it as a mystery or a daunting task. Think of it as an adventure, and one on which your customers have already embarked. In 2004, the most recent year for which figures were available for this edition, wine sales in the United States were up 4 percent in volume and 7 percent in value over the previous year. The U.S. Department of Agriculture says that wine consumption in the United States has grown steadily in the past decade, and 25 percent of Americans now drink wine. About half of this group says they drink it at least once a week.

In today's beverage-service industry wine is often ordered in lieu of cocktails. It is such a potentially important and profitable part of your business that the next two chapters are devoted to wine appreciation and wine sales.

THIS CHAPTER WILL HELP YOU . . .

- Classify wines according to type and recognize some of their distin-

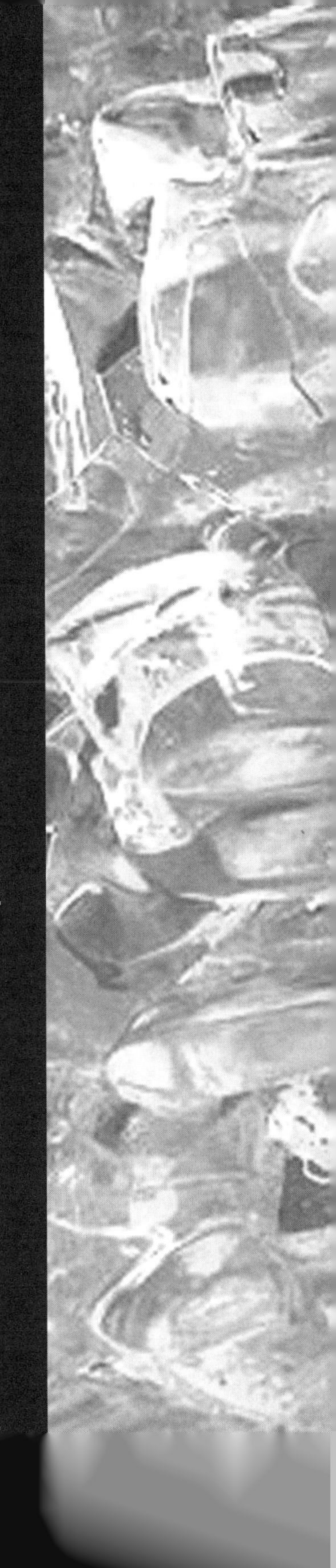

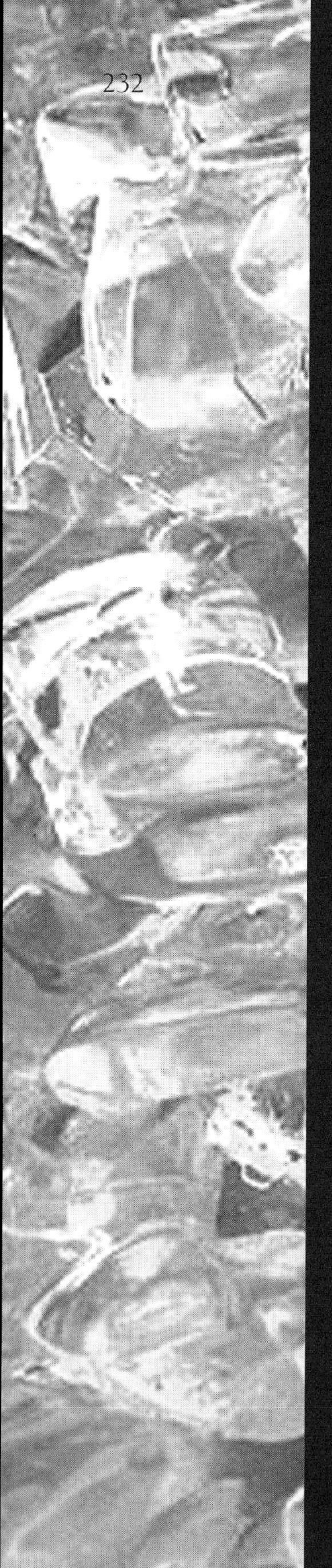

- Learn about the grapes used to make wine, and the winemaking process.
- Learn how to taste a wine so you can adequately assess its characteristics and describe them to customers.
- Familiarize yourself with the world's leading wine regions and the types of wine they produce.
- Understand how to read wine labels.

A BRIEF HISTORY OF WINE IN THE UNITED STATES

Making wine is as ancient as history itself; it is referred to in the Bible, in hieroglyphics, and in Greek and Roman literature. Winemaking is the process of fermenting the juices of ripe grapes. The chemical reactions in this process are as follows: Yeast converts the sugar found naturally in the fruit into alcohol and carbon dioxide. The carbon dioxide (CO_2) escapes into the air, leaving the juice and alcohol behind to be stored, bottled, and eventually consumed. The quality of the fruit has a great deal to do with whether or not the wine is worth drinking. When Europeans first came to the New World, they did their best to grow grapes from cuttings they brought with them. But the grapevines did not flourish in the cold northeastern climate, so most alcoholic fruit concoctions were made from berries or apples.

In 1769 a priest named Padre Junipero Serra traveled to California from Mexico, bringing with him some European grapevine cuttings. Others followed and by the mid-1800s, European grapes were flourishing in the temperate California climate. By the late 1800s some California wines were winning medals in international winemaking competitions.

Of course Prohibition slowed things down significantly. Grape growers could only make small quantities of home-produced wines, sell table grapes, or make sacramental wines for churches. Some growers also sold grape-juice concentrate, to which enterprising folks added their own yeast and sugar to make their own wine. But most of California's 188,000 acres of vineyards (the 1933 figure) languished from the 1930s to the 1960s. In the 1970s wine finally became trendy again in this country, as health-conscious consumers looked for lighter drinks and California winemakers received international acclaim for some of their wares.

Today there are more than 3,000 wineries in the United States producing wines with a total retail value of over $21 billion annually. About two out of every three bottles of wine consumed in America are from California, but wines imported from other nations account for 25 percent of U.S. consumption. Wines from states other than California make up the remaining 8 percent.

TYPES OF WINE

No matter where a wine comes from, it is identified by a combination of these elements: its producer, its vintage, and its varietal. The *producer* is most often a winery, but wines are also made by blending together grapes from many different small vineyards. This is common in Europe, and wine made this way is labeled with the name of the cooperative or exporter, not an individual winery. The **vintage** is the year in which the grapes were picked and the winemaking process began for that particular bottle. The **varietal** is the type of grape used. It is very common to blend different varietals in a single bottle, but unless the second grape type makes up a significant percentage of the wine, the bottle is usually labeled with the name of the predominant grape. There are laws (that vary in the United States and in other nations) about how to label these blends, depending on the percentages of the varietals used. (You will learn more about how to read a wine label later in this chapter.)

There are three different types of *table wines:* red, white, and rosé. A table wine is simply a wine that is served at a dining table; this is the term used by the Federal Standard of Identity for wines that have an alcohol content of "not in excess of 14 percent by volume." The percentage of alcohol (usually from 10 to 14 percent) must be stated by law on the wine label. Here are a few very general comments about each type of wine:

- Red wines tend to be hearty, full-bodied, and nearly always dry. Their color can range from a deep crimson, to purple, to reddish-orange or rust, depending on the type of grape used and the age of the wine. The term *dry* in the wine business means "lacking in sweetness." Dryness is one of the qualities that makes red wine a suitable accompaniment to hearty dishes like steak, game, and lasagna. Red wines are not refrigerated, but served at a slightly cool room temperature of 60°F to 65°F, or very lightly chilled. (An important note: This serving temperature range is 5°F cooler than suggested in previous editions of this textbook. The newest theory is that at room temperature the alcohol is more predominant in the wine, making it taste "hotter," or harsher and not as pleasant as with a light chill.)
- White wines range in color from pale straw, to bright yellow, to gold. They are generally more delicate in flavor than reds, and they range in flavor from very dry to very sweet. Many people begin a meal with appetizers, soup or salad, and a white wine, then switch to red if they will be having a hearty main course. The drier whites also complement fish, veal, and pasta dishes in light (butter or cream-based) sauces. The sweetest white wines usually are made to be served as dessert or with desserts. White wines are always served chilled, sometimes lightly, sometimes fully refrigerated.
- Rosé wines are various, attractive shades of pale red, pink, or salmon, and they are sometimes referred to as **blush wines.** They are made from red grapes, but in character and taste they are lighter and more like white wines. After years of being lumped in with such "starter wines" as White Zinfandel, rosés are now gaining new respect from wine aficionados who once considered them somewhat unsophisticated. These wines are generally fresh and fruity, and many have a touch of sweetness, making them lovely complements to ham, turkey, or lighter styles of food. The best rosé wines from France are very dry, called *Tavel,* made from the Grenache grape. Chile also makes some fine, well-priced rosés.

As mentioned, novice wine drinkers often begin with White Zinfandel or White Pinot Noir since they provide a nice transition from soft drinks to the world of wine. However, it is probably unfair to label blush-wine drinkers as inexperienced. Just remember, to the bar owner, they are customers, and they are often eager to learn about and try new wines.

Sparkling Wines

Up to this point, the types of wines that we have discussed have been so-called *still wines,* or wines that do not contain bubbles. But there are also sparkling wines, which come in red, white, and blush. Sparkling wines are often referred to as "champagne," but the French will tell you that *only* wines made in the Champagne region of France can truly be called *Champagne* (with a capital "C"). Indeed most winemakers respect this designation, and although there is no law governing this, you will find that most non-French bubbly is labeled "sparkling wine." If these products are made in exactly the same way as French Champagnes, their label will also say **Methode Champenoise.** Sparkling wines are also known as **Sekt** in Germany and **Spumante** in Italy.

Champagne is the classic wine of celebration. Sparkling wines should always be served well chilled. They complement almost any food and are also good to drink by themselves. Usually sparkling wine is sold by the bottle, but some bars and restaurants also serve it by the glass or as an ingredient in a mixed drink, such as the Mimosa. This drink combines Champagne and orange juice and is popular for breakfast or brunch.

(You will learn later in this chapter what puts the bubbles in sparkling wine.)

Fortified Wines

Another wine category consists of wine that has extra alcohol or brandy added to it. This process is known as *fortifying* the wine, but the government does not allow the word *fortified* to be used on the label to prevent consumers from mistakenly thinking that it is of some health benefit. The percentage of alcohol listed on the label is your first clue: Generally anything with an alcohol content of over 14 percent has been fortified. Most fortified wines have an alcohol content of 17 to 19 percent. The legal limit is 24 percent. The most famous fortified wine is probably Port, which is made for the most part in Portugal.

Federal Standards of Identity divide fortified wines into two categories: **aperitif wines** and *dessert wines.* Aperitifs are also **aromatized,** which means that they are flavored with aromatic herbs and spices. Traditionally they are sipped before dinner to stimulate the appetite or aid digestion of the upcoming meal. The word *aperitif* comes from a Latin word meaning "to open."

The best-known aromatized wine is vermouth, which most folks probably associate with bar liquor, not wine. Dry French vermouth is put to good use in Martinis, while sweet, Italian vermouth goes into Manhattans. Vermouths and other aromatized wines, including Dubonnet and Lillet from France, can be served straight up and well chilled, on ice, or mixed with soda and a twist of lemon. It is also popular to drink them half-and-half, i.e., mixing equal parts of dry vermouth and sweet. Sherry, another aperitif, is often associated with cooking, but it has made a real comeback in recent years as an after-dinner drink. (Sherry is discussed later in this chapter in the section on Spanish wines.)

The other group of fortified wines, the *dessert wines,* are designed to end the meal. They are rich, sweet, and heavy, and imbibed in small quantities like liqueurs. Dessert wines include Madeira (from the island of the same name off the African West coast), marsala, angelica, and muscatel. There are also *late harvest wines,* usually white, made from grapes that have been allowed to overripen on the vines, almost to spoilage, for maximum sugar content. These wines are not fortified, but they are included in the dessert-wine category. Any dessert wine may be served either chilled or at room temperature.

Sake

One kind of wine served in restaurants is not made from grapes at all. In Japan, **sake** (pronounced SAH-kay) is a beverage made from rice, referred to as the "drink of the gods" and indeed, once was used as an offering to Shinto gods.

Although the sake-making process has more in common with beer brewing than it does with winemaking (because the grain is fermented with water), the finished product often has the characteristics of a delicate white wine. Its flavor profile can range from dry to sweet and fruity. With a 14- to 16-percent alcohol content, sake is a bit more potent than wine and a great deal more potent than beer.

Before the rice is fermented, it is polished to remove the proteins and fats in the hull that surrounds each kernel's starchy core. If the polishing is not sufficient, the resulting product is inferior. After polishing, workers soak and steam the rice, then spread it on large tables to cool. Mold (called *koji*) is folded into the rice, converting the remaining starches into sugar in a climate-controlled setting. The wild spores interact with the cultivated spores, giving the sake a flavor unique to each brewery.

Water is added to the moto (rice seed and yeast mash), which helps with continued fermentation and adds more bouquet and flavor. After about four weeks, when the mixture is soupy and very slightly carbonated, it is strained and bottled. Sake is not aged, and experts recommend consuming an open bottle within six months. Release dates are printed on most labels.

Premium sake products fall into two major categories: a small amount of additional alcohol is added to *honjozo* sakes to give them a smoother taste, while *junmai* is pure rice sake. To aficionados, the latter has greater depth and complexity. Junmai sakes are further classified depending on the percentage of rice hull that is originally removed in the polishing process—theoretically, the higher the percentage removed, the finer the sake. A third category, *futsuu-shu,* is the "house wine" category of inexpensive sake.

The tradition of slightly heating sake before serving is done to make the cheaper products more palatable. In fact sake is a somewhat fragile beverage that should be refrigerated, and the finer-quality products should be served lightly chilled. Some suggest that the type of rice used to brew and the polishing process should determine the ultimate serving temperature—but with 25 varieties of brewing rice, it's simpler to plan on chilling the expensive bottles. Sake is also becoming increasingly popular as a sophisticated cocktail ingredient in trendy Martini and Margarita recipes.

In addition to Japan's 1,500 sake breweries, some of which have U.S.-based facilities, there are fledgling domestic U.S. sake producers in Hawaii, California, Colorado, and Oregon. The iron-free water in these states is reportedly key to successful sake brewing.

THE GRAPES

It all starts with the grapes. The grape contains the natural sugar, the fruit, the liquid, and the acidity that gives the wine its taste and balance; as well as the tannins (in red wines) that provide taste and longevity. From the grape's skin comes the color of the wine. Different types of grapes exhibit different characteristics and, therefore, become different-tasting wines.

There are red grapes and white grapes. Whether the red grape is actually red or blackish or purple, it is still considered a red grape. Red wines are made when red grapes are crushed and fermented (soaked) along with their skins and stems. The color leeches out of the skin into the juice. (Rosé wines are made when the skin has limited contact with the juice, imparting only some of its color.)

During the fermentation process the red wine gets its **tannin.** (Tannin is the same type of substance that is used to tan animal hides into leather. It's found naturally in coffee and tea, too.) In wine tannin comes from the skins and stems of the grapes, and it acts as a preservative that enables red wine to age without going stale. If you've ever bitten into a grape stem, you know how bitter it can taste. Tannins impart some of this bitterness to the wine and can taste unpleasant when the wine is young. But they mellow with age and are considered an important component of good, long-lasting red wine.

White grapes are fermented without their skins. They are lighter in color and flavor than red grapes and lack the tannins of red wines. White wines can be made from red grapes since the juice is separated from the skin: The color does not leech into the juice. But because the tannins are missing, white wines generally do not last as long (age as well) as red wines.

We will briefly discuss some of the most popular wine grapes. You will see these names on most wine labels today, so you should be familiar with their pronunciations and the types of wine they produce.

Red Grape Varietals

Cabernet Sauvignon (cab-er-NAY so-vin-YON) is possibly the most important and widely planted grape varietal in the world. It produces the greatest red wines of Bordeaux and the best reds in both California and Australia. This grape is often called simply *Cabernet.* The sharp tannins in young Cabernet give it the ability to last a long time in the bottle, slowly mellowing with age. *Cabernet Franc* (cab-er-NAY FRONK) is a close, but lower-quality, relative.

The great Burgundy wines of France are made from **Pinot Noir** (pee-no NWAHR). This grape is also used to make some of the world's finest Champagnes, when the juice is separated from its red skin. Interesting red wines, lighter in body than Cabernets, are made from Pinot Noir in Oregon and California. Winemakers seem to love the challenge of growing Pinot Noir; it requires a cool climate, and needs to be babied and pruned more than other types of grape vines.

Merlot (mair-LOW or mur-LOW) is an important red grape in Bordeaux, Italy, and California. At one time it was used mostly to blend with Cabernets since it is smoother and less tannic. But now you'll find just as many Merlots as Cabernets on wine-store shelves, and they are a favorite red wine of American consumers because they are mellow and easy to drink, and can be enjoyed younger than Cabernets because of their softer tannins.

Zinfandel (ZIN-fun-dell) is a red grape grown almost exclusively in California. It was once used to make inexpensive bulk wines, but it has developed its own following and there are now some exceptional California "Zins" being bottled. Zinfandel is a very adaptable grape; it can be used to make everything from sweet, pink, fruity White Zinfandels, to thick, dark, full-flavored reds best served with steaks or hearty pastas.

The next hearty red wine grape is known by two names: **Syrah** (sir-AH) in France and California, and **Shiraz** (shur-OZ) in Australia. South Australia is the home of some of the world's oldest Shiraz vines. In California Syrah plantings rank fourth behind Cabernet Sauvignon, Merlot, and Zinfandel. In France this intensely tannic, full-bodied wine is often blended with other grapes in such well-known wines as Hermitage and Coté Rotie.

The **Grenache Noir** (gren-OSH n'wahr) grape is not one of the best known, but it might be the most widely planted red grape in the world. Usually known simply as **Grenache,** it produces an elegant, lightly colored wine. You read earlier about the Tavel Rosé of France; Grenache is also a major component of the Rioja wines of Spain, of California rosés, and of some brands of port. (Do not confuse it with the white **Grenache Blanc,** which is most often used to blend Chateuneuf-du-Pape and Roussanne wines.)

Gamay Beaujolais (gam-AY BO-zha-lay) is the name of the light, fresh, and fruity red wine made from the Gamay grape. This wine was first produced in the Beaujolais region of France, but now California wineries make similar wines and call them either *Gamay Beaujolais* or *Napa Gamay.* Scientists discovered that Gamay is a clone of the Pinot Noir grape. These wines are not meant to be aged, but to be consumed young.

Mourvedre (moo-VED-rah) was probably originally native to Spain, where it is also known as *monastrell.* California wineries may call it *mataro.* No matter what the moniker, this red grape produces sturdy wines that are most often used in blending. In France Mourvedre is the primary grape used in Bandol wines, both red and rosé.

Tempranillo (TEMP-rah-NEE-yo) is the main red wine grape of Spain, blended with Grenache to make award-winning Rioja wines. With its softer tannins, Tempranillo has developed a kind of cult following among wine lovers. Some Spanish wineries are now bottling 100-percent Tempranillo instead of blending it. California winemakers have tried to grow this varietal, but without as much success.

In the Tuscany area of Italy the **Sangiovese** (SAN-gee-oh-VAY-zee) grape makes the well-known **Chianti** (kee-ON-tee), a red wine with a slightly lighter color and earthy, sometimes strong, tannins. When blended with Cabernet, it is the base for a trendy group of wines that were first dubbed the *super Tuscans* in the 1990s. Sangiovese is also becoming more popular in California. In Italy's Piedmont region the **Nebbiolo** (neb-ee-OH-loh) grape is blended with others to make **Barolo** (bah-RO-loe) and *Barbaresco* (BAR-bah-RESS-koe) wines. *Barbera* (bar-BAHR-ah) is another Italian red grape that has transplanted well in California, where it is used for blending and for making a variety of wine styles.

Finally there is **Lambrusco** (lam-BROOS-koe), a grape grown in Northern Italy that produces a very fruity, rather sweet red wine with a fizzy characteristic (in Italian, *frizzante*). Some people think it tastes more like a soft drink than a wine, but it is popular nonetheless.

White Grape Varietals

Chardonnay (SHAR-den-NAY) is the white wine grape most Americans are familiar with. In fact it is the world's most popular wine grape because it can be grown almost anywhere and develops characteristics based on the soil and climate in which the vines are planted. It also adapts well to a variety of winemaking styles. The grape produces mostly dry wines of strong body and distinctive flavor. Chardonnay is the best-selling wine in California and is the base for all French **Chablis** (shah-BLEE) wines, as well as the famous white *Burgundies* of France. Chardonnay grapes are grown all over Europe, in Australia, and in New Zealand.

In California the grape second only to Chardonnay is **Sauvignon Blanc** (SO-vin-yon BLONK). In France it is the predominant white grape of Bordeaux. It is used to make the dry, fruity wines of the **Graves** (GRAHVZ) district; the rich, golden **Sauternes** (saw-TURN); and the fresh, crisp Loire Valley whites called **Sancerre** (san-SAIR) and **Pouilly Fumé** (POO-ee foo-MAY). New Zealand is developing an excellent reputation for its intense, acidic Sauvignon Blanc wines. In California a few wineries label their products **Fumé Blanc** (FOO-may BLONK).

Semillon (SEM-ee-YON) used to be a grape used primarily for blending with Chardonnay, Graves, and Sauternes wines, but it has developed a loyal following and is now bottled separately by many wineries. Semillon makes a dry wine known for its rich fruit flavor. It is high in acidity when young, but it can mellow in the bottle with age. Like Semillon, **Viognier** (VEE-ohn-YAY) is another white grape that has garnered recent attention on its own merits. It produces a lightly sweet, intensely fruity wine that was once used primarily in blending other wines—until adventurous winemakers saw its potential as an alternative to Sauvignon Blancs and Rieslings and began bottling it separately. Viognier can be expensive because not much of it is planted anywhere in the world; it is considered a temperamental grape to grow.

Riesling (REES-ling) is the fruity white grape used to make many German wines, including sweet, late-harvest or dessert wines. In the past, it got a reputation for being sweet, but some of the best Rieslings are sophisticated wines, fully fermented and intensely fruity but also very dry. Although this varietal is also widely grown in California, it requires a cooler climate to do well.

Chenin Blanc (SHEN-in BLONK) grapes make tasty white wines, such as Vouvray, in the Loire Valley region of France. Some of them are sparkling wines. Chenin Blanc is also a widely planted white grape in California, where it is made in a variety of styles ranging from dry to sweet. In South African winemaking, Chenin Blanc is called *Steen.*

Gewurztraminer (ge-VURTZ-tra-mee-ner) is the spicy white (actually pink) grape of the French Alsace region and parts of Germany. (*Gewurz* means *spice* in German.) This grape typically makes a flavorful dry white wine but like the Riesling, it can produce late-harvest sweet wines. In California this grape produces both dry and sweet wines. It is also grown in Australia and New Zealand.

Alberino (al-behr-EEN-yoh) is an increasingly popular Spanish white grape. It makes a wine similar to Viognier, but with the strong body of a Riesling. Enologists have traced it to the Riesling grape family. In Portugal it is known as Alvarinho.

Pinot Blanc (PEE-no BLONK) is a white grape grown in Alsace, northern Italy, and along the West Coast of the United States, in Washington, Oregon, and California. It is an especially good grape for making sparkling wine, and is occasionally bottled as a still, varietal wine in California. Pinot Blanc is often confused with **Pinot Grigio** (PEE-no GREE-zhee-oh), a completely different white grape grown primarily in Italy, France, and Oregon that is quickly increasing in popularity. Pinot Grigio grapes can be made into two different styles of wines: The Italians are known for being light and crisp; the French are deeper and richer in flavor. Pinot Grigio is sometimes known simply as **Pinot Gris** (PEE-no GREE).

Marsanne (mar-SOHN) is a hardy white grape from Southern France that is a component of many Rhone wines, some just as good as higher-priced Chardonnays. It is also widely grown in Australia.

A **Muscat** (MUS-kat) grape can be either red or white, and the wines made from it, all over the world, are usually sweet. One made from a white Muscat, Asti Spumante (OSS-tee spoo-MON-tee), is Italy's popular sweet, sparkling wine.

Among Italy's white grapes is the **Trebbiano** (treb-ee-AH-no), which makes such varied wines as the light, dry Soave in northeast Italy and sparkling wines in the Po valley.

Muller-Thurgau (MYOOL-ur TUR-gau) is the most widely grown grape in Germany. It makes many soft, aromatic white wines of varying degrees of sweetness, but experts generally feel it cannot compare with the Riesling for quality.

All of these grapes, and others, are listed alphabetically in Figure 6.1. No one can possibly remember them all, so this is material you should plan to return to periodically as you learn more about wines.

HOW WINES ARE MADE

All wines begin in the same way, with the grapes, the soil, the weather, and the winemaker combining to turn the same basic product into an infinite variety of forms. It is a process in which nature plays a large part. The climate in which grapes grow is a very important influence on how they taste. Warm climates yield ripe grapes and rich wines: The riper and sweeter the grapes at harvest, the more alcoholic the wine. Australia, parts of California, and southern France, for example, have this potential. Cool climates, including those of Germany, northern Italy, and the Champagne region in France, typically produce "greener" (less ripe) grapes and lighter wines. Year after year in any given district, the ripeness and quality of the grapes at harvest will vary according to the weather, which means that the wines will vary in quality, too. This is why the vintage of a fine wine is important. As you've learned, *vintage* refers to the year the grapes were harvested and the winemaking process began.

Three factors—the grapes, the climate in a given location, and the weather in a given year—combine to determine the character of an individual wine. Each wine will be different from any other.

It's ironic that grapes grow best in gravelly soil that is considered poor for other types of crops, on well-drained land (such as hillsides), in a temperate climate with enough sun and warmth to develop their sugar, and a little rain at the right times. As the grapes mature, they increase in sugar content and decrease in acidity. It takes about 100 days of sunshine from blossom to harvest before the grapes ripen to the precise balance of sugar and acid that makes the best possible wine. The moment of harvest is determined by frequent taste-testing for sugar content and by keeping an eye on the weather forecast. A heavy rain on ripe grapes can be a disaster.

GRAPE VARIETIES

Grape	Color	Body	Sweetness	Flavor Intensity	Region/Country of Use
Barbera	red	medium to full	dry	medium to intense	California, Italy
Cabernet Sauvignon	red	medium to full	dry	medium to full	California, Bordeaux, Australia
Chardonnay	white	medium to full	dry	medium to full	California, Burgundy, Chablis, Champagne, Italy, Spain, Bulgaria, Australia, New Zealand
Chenin Blanc	white	medium	slightly sweet	medium	California, Loire
Gamay	red	light to medium	dry	delicate	Beaujolais
Gewürztraminer	white	medium	dry	spicy, full	California, Alsace, Australia, New Zealand
Grenache	red	light to medium	dry	light to medium	California, Rhône, Spain, Australia
Merlot	red	light to medium	dry	soft, delicate	California, Italy, Bordeaux
Müller-Thurgau	white	soft to medium	sweet	mild to medium	Germany
Muscat	black or white		medium to sweet	medium to full	Italy, Alsace, Bulgaria
Nebbiolo	red	full	dry	intense	Italy
Pinot Blanc	white	light to medium	dry	light	California, Italy, Alsace, Champagne
Pinot Noir	red	medium to full	dry	medium to full	California, Burgundy, Oregon, Champagne, Australia
Riesling	white	light to medium	slightly sweet	delicate	Germany, Alsace, Australia, California, Washington, Oregon
Sangiovese	red	medium to full	dry	medium to full	Italy
Sauvignon Blanc	white	medium	dry	medium	California, Bordeaux, Loire, Chile
Sémillon	white	light to medium	dry	medium	California, Bordeaux
Silvaner	white	light	dry	light	Alsace, Germany
Syrah, Shiraz	red	medium to full	dry	intense	Rhône, Australia
Trebbiano	white	light to medium	dry	light to medium	Italy
Zinfandel	red	medium to full	dry	medium to intense	California

FIGURE 6.1 Grape varieties. (21 of hundreds)

The Winemaking Process

Within 12 hours, or as soon as possible after being picked from their vines, the whole, ripened grapes begin their journey (see Figure 6.2). If a white wine is being made, the grapes, no matter what their color, go through a crusher/stemmer that removes the stalks and breaks the skins. Then the grapes are pressed to extract their juices. The skins are discarded, and the juice, now called *must,* is channeled into a fermentation tank.

For a red wine or a rosé, dark-skinned grapes are crushed, then both must and skins go into a fermentation tank. It is the red or black or purple skins that yield the color, as well as much of the character, of a red wine. For a rosé, the skins are left in the fermenting must briefly (12 to 24 hours), which is just long enough to achieve the color desired. The must is then pumped into another tank, leaving the skins behind.

For any type of wine, before fermentation begins special strains of yeast are added. Traditionally winemakers depended on the wild yeasts found naturally on grape skins, but today American winemakers use laboratory-produced yeast cultures to ensure a more predictable result. The wild yeasts are killed off, either by the special yeasts or by the addition of sulfur dioxide. In some parts of the world, when the climate or the weather has not produced enough sugar in the grapes, extra sugar—fine-grain "powdered sunshine"—is added before fermentation begins. This is called **chapitalization.**

In the fermentation tank the yeasts feed on the sugar and break it down: One molecule of sugar yields two molecules of alcohol and two molecules of carbon dioxide. Fermentation continues for one to two weeks, or even longer, until the sugar is consumed or the alcohol content becomes high enough (around 14 percent) to kill the yeast. The process stops automatically unless the winemaker intervenes. If the sugar has been completely consumed by the yeast, the wine is dry. If sugar remains, there is sweetness in the wine. When fermentation stops, the wine is placed in large casks or vats. During the making of red wines, the skins are pressed out in the transfer. The wine pressed from the skins is rich in such extracts as tannin, which give the wine more character.

Each wine is stored until residues (the **lees**) settle out and the wine stabilizes. Periodically the wine is drawn off the residues and placed in a fresh cask to settle further. This is known as *racking.* When the wine *falls bright* (becomes clear) it is moved to other vats or casks for maturing.

White wines and rosés are often matured in vats lined with plastic or glass or in stainless-steel containers. These wines are usually ready for bottling in a few months. Most red wines and certain whites are aged in wood casks (usually oak) from six months, to two years or more. Here they undergo changes that mellow and smooth them and develop their special character. Some elements of flavor are absorbed from the wood. Some changes come from slight evaporation of the wine in the casks. Other mysterious chemistry occurs within the wine itself, contributing complexities of flavor, especially to wines that age slowly.

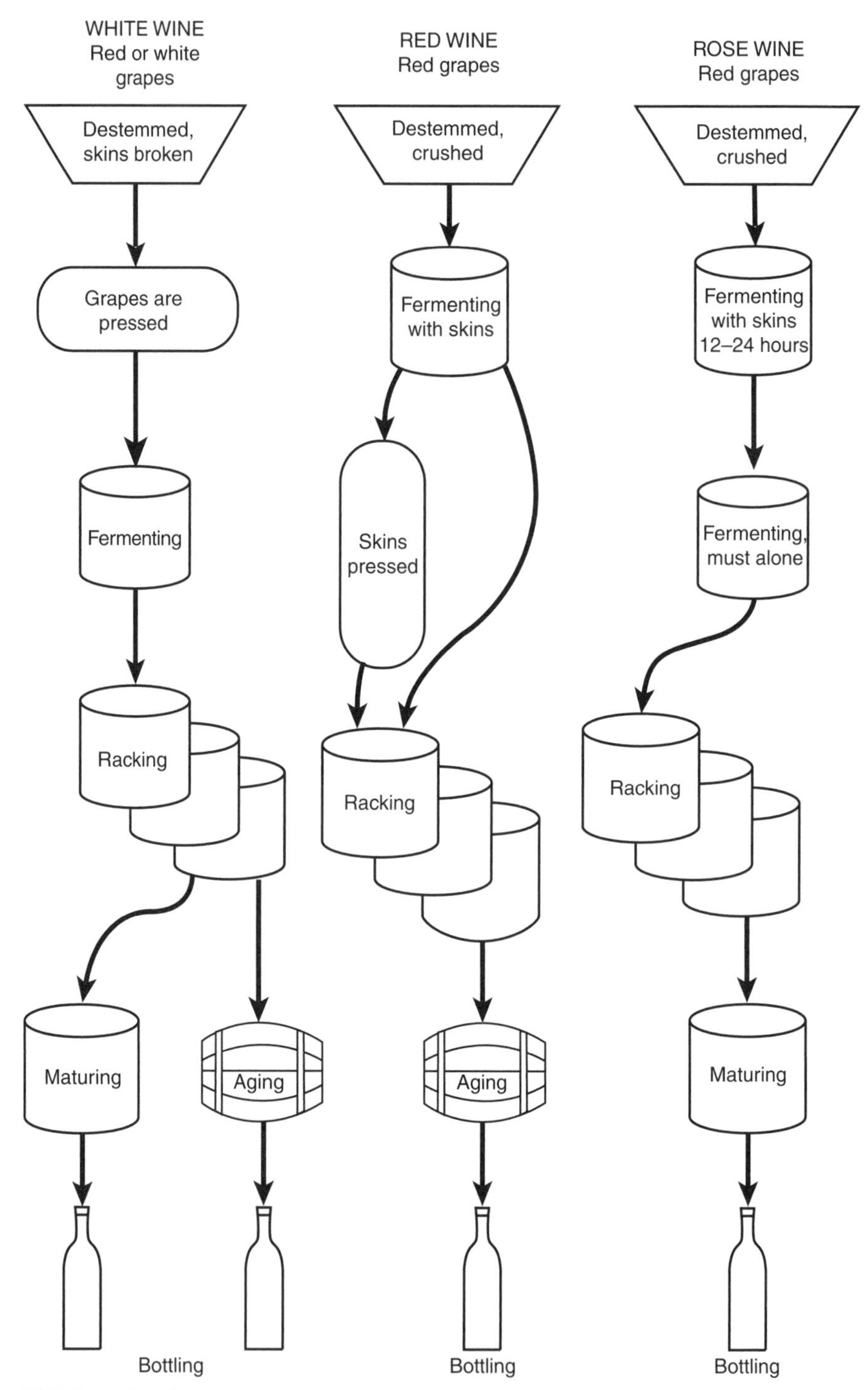

FIGURE 6.2 The winemaking process varies slightly depending on the type of wine being produced: white, red, or rosé (blush).

A winemaker's decisions about how long to age a wine and in which type of container—tanks or wood, old or new wood (the newer the barrel, the more intense the wood character it imparts), large casks or small barrels (small ones yield more intense wood character than big ones)—are significant in deciding the wine's quality and price.

The moment when the wine is ready for bottling is determined by the winemaker's taste. When tannins and acids soften and become more agreeable, the wine is moved from the cask to the bottle. Before the bottling process, the fine particles that remain in the wine are filtered out or spun out by centrifuge. The wine is then bottled, and the bottles are individually sealed.

The Great Cork Controversy

We will depart from the winemaking process just briefly to explain one of the most controversial ongoing issues in the wine world: how to seal the bottles. A bit of history: over the centuries and in various countries, bottles have been sealed with pitch, gypsum, or plugs (called *stoppels*) made of ground-up glass. Bottles have even been stuffed with leather or cloth and coated with wax. Sealing bottles was an inexact process because the bottles and, therefore, their openings were not uniformly made until the last 100 years or so. Cork is a successful closure because it can fit snugly into the neck of almost any type of bottle. Cork's flexibility enables it to be compressed. It is light, moisture-resistant, and doesn't deteriorate, even under extreme temperatures. All of these qualities, which modern winemakers still value, allowed greater freedom of trade in the past. Wine no longer had to be shipped in bulk in casks or barrels to keep it from spoiling. In today's wine bottling process, a *capsule*—a cap of foil or plastic—is placed over the cork for additional protection.

FIGURE 6.3 Although it doesn't look like it will survive being stripped of cork, the suberin oak tree will regrow its outer layer in eight or nine years. Photo copyright Armstrong World Industries; used with permission.

Corks are pieces of bark from the **suberin oak** tree that grows mostly in Portugal and Spain (see Figure 6.3). (Other nations have tried unsuccessfully to plant them.) The tree has two layers of bark: the inner layer is alive; the outer layer is the one that is stripped and used to make not only wine corks, but also insulating tiles for floors and walls. The harvesting process is very interesting, but too long to detail here. It does not harm the tree; Portugese laws are strict about ensuring protection of the cork oak forests. However, each tree requires almost a decade of growth to replace its stripped outer bark layer. In the mid-1990s several factors combined to send the wine world frantically looking for synthetic alternatives to cork. In addition to a climate of environmental activism and rumors about a possible cork shortage after a drought in Portugal, there were complaints that the overall quality of wine corks had deteriorated. Experts and studies suggested from 1 to 8 percent of wines were contaminated by **2, 4, 6-Trichloroanisole (TCA),** a harmless but smelly combination of mold, chlorine, and moisture that sometimes forms on natural cork, permeating the wine inside the bottle and tainting it with an off-putting, musty odor. (When wine is referred to as *corked,* TCA is often the culprit. However, TCA can also form on other surfaces, such as barrels, bottles, and pallets.)

In the United Kingdom some supermarket chains decided to boycott wines with corks. New Zealand was among the first countries to adopt a policy promoting the use of screwtops or screw caps, which until then had been associated with wines of lower price and quality. Australia and California soon followed. The cork producers accused the synthetic stopper-makers of circulating the rumors. Then they began questioning the safety and longevity of plastic stoppers and screwtops and touting the fact that corks are recyclable and biodegradable. The plastics manufacturers countered with their own points: that wines with stoppers or screwtops don't have to be stored on their sides, and that plastic stoppers don't break or crumble like corks. This rash of finger-pointing, and in some cases misinformation, resulted in the first World Cork Congress, held in Lisbon in 2000, where attendees from the various factions may not have agreed on much except to call off the public-relations war—for a while.

Today some wineries now use synthetic plastic bottle stoppers (with such names as SupremeCorq), some use screwtops (the best-known is probably the French-made Stelvin), some are trying cap-like closures similar to those on liquor bottles (called *Torqued On Pilfer-Proof* [TOPP] caps), and still others continue to use corks. Many wineries are studying different types of closures long-term, bottling identical varietals and vintages and holding them for later inspection to determine how the reds will age. In making these various decisions, wineries cite availability, cost, environmental sensitivity, and/or tradition. No doubt the debate will rage on. What do consumers think? In 2003 an independent opinion poll (released by the Portugese Cork Association) said 73 percent of consumers "have a preference for cork," and 54 percent still believe screw caps indicate a "cheap wine," even if they are effective at sealing the bottle.

Aging and Blending

Financially winemaking is a tough business, and many wineries cannot afford to have their products sit in inventory, whether in vats, barrels, or bottles. As a result many of today's pleasant, easy-to-drink wines are not made for longevity, but to be enjoyed within a year or two of being bottled. However, others must undergo further aging in the bottle. When people talk about *aging* a wine, they refer to the flavors and complexity of the wine that can develop in the bottle if the wine sits for a few years before being consumed. For aging, the bottles are usually stored on their sides in a cool dark place. These are the types of bottles with traditional cork closures, and laying them on their sides keeps the cork moist so that it does not shrink and become loose, which can ruin the wine by allowing air into the bottle. Fine wines are often sold before they are ready to drink, to merchants or collectors who are willing to store the wine for an additional period of time. A vintage date identifying the year the grapes were harvested is essential to wines that mature slowly.

Most wines are blends of different grape varieties, grapes from different vineyards, or wines of different vintages or degrees of maturity. Blended wines are sometimes known as *meritage* (MAIR-ih-tij) *wines*. The blending may be done at different points of the winemaking process (which is why you don't see it in Figure 6.2). Sometimes the grapes themselves are blended before crushing. Sometimes the new wines are blended during racking. Sometimes wines are blended after they mature. Blending serves several purposes. It may be done to produce the finest wine possible, to maintain product consistency from one year to the next, to tailor a wine to a special market, to make more wine for less money, or to make the best of a bad year by combining some mediocre grapes with some better ones.

In the bottle wine continues to change. In fact wine is a living substance that evolves more or less quickly from youth, to maturity, to senility, and each wine has its own rate of maturity and its own life span. White wines and rosés mature most quickly. Most moderately priced whites and rosés mature early and are put on the market ready to drink within a few months after harvest. They have a life span of two to five years, depending on the wine. Premium whites are not ready to drink quite as early, but they can last longer. Generally the better the wine to begin with, the longer the life span.

Red wines mature more slowly than whites, but the rate of maturity varies greatly from one red wine to another. Light-bodied reds, for example, Beaujolais, Valpolicella, and inexpensive light Cabernets, are generally best within three years of their vintage. Fuller, richer reds can generally live many more years, thanks to the tannins and acidity that preserve them. Some of the finest wines may take 8 to 10 years or even longer to reach their peak, and may be drinkable for decades thereafter. Most wines today list their vintage on the bottle. In addition to telling how old the wine is, it can be a clue to quality for the better wines. There are great, poor, and average years for wines, depending on the weather. A great vintage year produces a wine of finer taste and longer life span than an ordinary year. But a great year in one region may be a poor year in another. A vintage date must always be evaluated in terms of the specific district and the specific wine.

Before we leave the subject of winemaking, a note on **sulfites** is in order. Sulfur dioxide exists naturally in wines in small quantities as a by-product of fermentation. It is also an invaluable tool of winemakers at every stage. It protects wine from spoilage due to contact with air, kills bacteria, inhibits "bad" yeasts while stimulating "good" yeasts, helps preserve **aroma,** purifies used barrels, and keeps the finished wine fresh and stable. The phrase *contains sulfites* on a wine label points out a fact that has always been true. But there are a few people—a very small percentage—who develop serious allergic reactions to sulfites. The government requires the label statement for their protection.

The Making of a Sparkling Wine

Sparkling wines and fortified wines are made by adding something to the process described above. To make a sparkling wine, winemakers add yeast and sugar to still wine to prompt a second fermentation. This is done in closed containers, so that the carbon dioxide produced cannot escape and thus becomes part of the wine. In the French Champagne method mentioned earlier (*Methode Champenoise,* pronounced "meth-ODE SHAMP-en-WAHZ"), the closed containers are the heavy glass bottles in which the still wine was first bottled. This is a long, complicated process involving handling each bottle many times, removing sediment bottle by bottle, and other refinements. All of this makes the Champagne very expensive and very good. A wine made in the United States using the Champagne method may legally be called *Champagne*. It may mention the Champagne process on the label or it may say "Fermented in this bottle."

Two other methods have been developed to shorten the more time-consuming process. In the **Charmat** (shar-MOT) or **bulk process** refermentation is carried out in large, closed pressurized tanks, then the wine is bottled under pressure. Such wines can be very modestly priced, but they do not begin to approach the quality of those made by the Champagne method. For example, they lose their bubbles quickly. In the United States the label must refer to this type of wine as a *sparkling wine* rather than Champagne. The label may contain the words *champagne style* or *champagne type,* or may call it *American* (or *New York State, California,* etc.) *champagne-bulk process.*

The other alternate method referments the still wine in bottles but then transfers it under pressure to other bottles, filtering it during the transfer. This results in a moderately priced product of a quality that might satisfy many consumers, but not wine buffs. Sparkling wines made in this way are labeled *fermented in the bottle.* Figure 6.4 shows a Spanish sparkling wine label. It is indicative of the trend toward a cleaner, less cluttered look for the bottle by squeezing most of the information onto a back label.

TASTING WINES

Wine can be an extremely complex beverage. It fascinates some people and bewilders others. No matter what your level of wine understanding or appreciation, you can read only so much about the subject. The only way to truly learn more is to taste the stuff! Drinking wine and tasting wine are two distinctly different pursuits,

FIGURE 6.4 A sparkling wine label from Spain. Wine can't be called "Champagne" if it is not made in the Champagne district of France. Courtesy of Classical Wines of Spain, Seattle, Washington.

and tasting comes first. Tasting can help you to understand your own preferences and why a good wine is good, which can give you pleasure and confidence. More important for the restaurateur or bar owner is what that confidence and understanding can do to increase business: It can enable you to buy the most suitable wines for your clientele; to develop a wine list; and most critical, to train your serving staff about the wines on your list so that they can describe and sell these wines to your customers. So let's learn some wine-tasting basics.

When you taste a wine, pour it in a thin, clear glass with a stem. Hold the glass by the foot or the stem, never by the bowl, which would convey the heat of your hand to the wine. Whenever you taste wines, use the same size glass and the same amount of wine so that you can make valid comparisons. Comparison tastings—tastings of the same varietal by different producers, or the same varietal from different years—are terrific ways to learn more about the subtle differences between wines.

Tasting a wine really begins with appraising its appearance. Pour a small amount, then hold it up to the light or look at it against a white background, like a white tablecloth. The wine should be clear and bright. A wine that looks cloudy or hazy has a problem. Don't buy it, and don't serve it. Note that sediment in a bottle of aging wine is not a problem; this will settle out when the bottle is left to sit a while.

Next, focus on the wine's color. Color will tell you if the wine is light-, medium-, or full-bodied. Many white wines have a pale, straw color. Young whites, especially those from cooler climates, might have a tinge of green. Wines from warmer climates and sweet dessert wines are often a beautiful golden hue. White wines darken, turning brownish as they age, so any tinge of brown or amber might signal a problem.

Red wines range from purple in a young wine, to reddish-brown in a mature wine. Too much rust or amber color is a warning signal that the wine may have been stored incorrectly or not sealed properly. *Oxidation,* which occurs when oxygen comes into contact with the wine, can cause this discoloration, a sign of spoilage.

Rosé wines are pink to pale orange; too pink or too orange is not good, and again, any touch of amber is a warning.

The next step is to smell the wine, and to do that most effectively, you must learn to swirl it around inside the wineglass. The best way for a novice to manage this is to keep the glass on the table, hold the bottom of the stem between your fingers, and move the base of the glass around in a small, clockwise circle, which will cause the wine inside the bowl to move in a circular manner, too. You do not have to swirl too hard to get the wine moving around. When you are confident doing this with the glass still sitting on the table, you can pick up the glass and try swirling it.

Why swirl? Swirling allows some of the alcohol in the wine to vaporize. As the alcohol rises it brings with it the scent of the wine. If you doubt this sniff two glasses of the same wine, one sitting still and one just after you have swirled it. The scent will be more intense from the swirled wine. Some people put one hand over the bowl of the wineglass as they swirl in order to hold the aroma inside until they sniff.

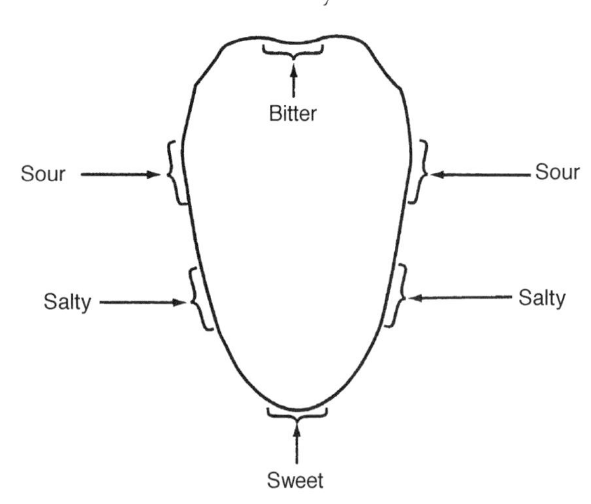

FIGURE 6.5 Taste buds on different parts of the human tongue taste different flavors.

Aroma is the term used if the scent is fruity or flowery; it will give you some important clues about the grapes and winemaking methods used. The scent of a more complex and mature wine is called its *bouquet.* Bouquet may include aroma, but aroma does not include bouquet, an essential distinction in learning to describe wines.

When sniffing the wine, don't be shy. Put your nose right inside the glass so that the bridge of your nose touches the far side of the glass, then inhale. Try to describe the fragrance to yourself. A wine's bouquet reflects the changes that have slowly taken place inside the bottle. The bouquet of a good mature wine is a significant part of the pleasure it gives. There are also "off" odors to check for: vinegar, sulfur, or an inappropriate smell of sherry or Madeira in an ordinary table wine. Do not serve such wines.

Finally taste the wine. Take a small sip, and roll it over your tongue. Hold it in your mouth for 10 seconds or so. The key to the taste of the wine is on your tongue; your taste buds are arranged so that they detect certain flavors on certain parts (see Figure 6.5). As you taste the wine you will perceive its sweetness first, then its sourness or acidity, then any bitterness at the back of your mouth as you swallow the wine.

These tastes represent four components of the wine's *structure,* a term used to describe the nature of a wine apart from its scent and flavors. The components that make up structure are:

- ***Sugar.*** Sweetness is sensed as the wine first enters your mouth.
- ***Acid.*** This is perceived mainly on the sides of your tongue as a tartness or sharpness.
- ***Tannins.*** A bitterness or astringency sensed on the rear of the tongue, tannins pucker the mouth, as strong tea does. Tannins are found mainly in red wines.
- ***Alcohol.*** Alcohol has a sweet flavor that enhances any other sweetness. Alcohol makes a wine seem round and full, although in high quantities it can cause a slight burning sensation in the mouth.

The way in which these four components relate to each other determines the **balance** of a given wine. Balance is the dynamic of the structure, that is, the way the components relate. Ideally the richness created by the sweetness-plus-alcohol will counterbalance the harshness of the tannin-plus-acid, creating an impression of harmony. To the degree that this occurs in a wine, we say that the wine is balanced. More than any other factor, balance determines wine quality.

When you first taste a wine you are trying to find specific elements. The following are some of the common terms and characteristics:

- ***Body.*** This is the feel of the wine in the mouth. Body comes from the amount of alcohol, sugar, **glycerin** (a soluble substance formed during fermentation), and extracts from the grapes, such as tannin. A wine is referred to as *light* or *light-bodied* if it is low in one or more of the body components. A full-bodied wine is typically high in body components. It will cling to the sides of the glass if you swirl it. (The glycerin content causes small streams of wine to run down the sides of the glass after you swirl; aficionados refer to these streams as the **legs** of the wine.) When you taste a full-bodied wine, it has a texture all its own, filling your mouth in a sensuous way.
- ***Degree of sweetness.*** If the grape sugar has been entirely consumed during fermentation, and none has been added, a wine will be totally lacking in sweetness, or *dry.* This is an important characteristic for your servers to know about each wine on your list since the most often-asked questions involve wine dryness. Generally a dry wine or one with only a little sweetness is preferred with the meal, while a sweet wine is an appropriate "beginning" with lighter appetizers or as a finish to a meal. Many Americans brought up on carbonated soft drinks prefer a wine with some sweetness.
- ***Flavor intensity.*** This refers to whether a wine is light and delicate in flavor, full and concentrated, or somewhere in between. Again, your servers should have this information for each wine on your list. It is important in terms of matching wines with food.

- ***Tartness, acidity.*** This is a sharp, acid taste, like green fruit. In a balanced wine tartness is a crucial quality: It gives life to the wine.
- ***Softness.*** This is the opposite of tartness. The term is also used for an overaged wine when its tannin is gone.
- ***Astringency.*** A taste that the beginner may mistake for dryness or acidity; astringency puckers the mouth. You will find it in young red wines that are not quite ready to drink. It comes from the tannin derived from the grape skins and will disappear as wines mature and mellow.
- ***Mellowness.*** The opposite of astringency, this term means "softened with age, ripe."
- ***Finish.*** This is the aftertaste. A good wine should have a pleasant aftertaste in keeping with the wine itself.
- ***Character.*** This comprises positive, distinctive taste characteristics that show that a wine is truly representative of the grape varietal(s) from which it was made. As to taste preferences the customer is always right. There are no longer rigid rules about what kind or color of wine to drink with what type of food. In the end taste is an individual matter. The Romans, for example, sometimes mixed their wines with seawater. Who's to say they were right or wrong?

Many customers know very little about wines, are intimidated by a printed wine list, and might not order wine at all unless they are encouraged by a friendly server who knows how each wine on the list tastes and which wine goes well with which food. We will discuss this subject further in Chapter 7.

HOW WINES ARE NAMED

The bewildering variety of table wines on the market is enough to confuse anyone, whether the person is a restaurateur introducing wines for the first time or a customer struggling to make a selection in a supermarket wine aisle. The picture may become simpler when we examine why wines are named the way they are. Every label must carry a name to identify the product inside the bottle. In the United States wines are named three ways: by the predominant variety of grape used (varietal), by broad general type (generic), or by brand name. Imported wines may also be named by these methods, but a fourth method is more common: by place of origin.

Varietal Names

A *varietal wine* is one in which a single grape variety predominates. The name of the grape is the name of the wine, and that grape gives the wine its predominant flavor and aroma. Well-known examples are Cabernet Sauvignon, Chardonnay,

Chenin Blanc, and Zinfandel. In the United States, to be named for a particular grape the wine must contain at least 75 percent of that grape. Within the European Economic Community the minimum is 85 percent, and some countries or districts have raised that requirement to 100 percent. In France the figure has been 100 percent for some time.

Varietals are very popular in the United States, and they are well worth exploring for your wine list. The names, once learned, are quickly recognized, and the better-known varietals almost sell themselves. Varietals range in price from moderate to high, depending to some extent on the wine quality. You should taste them before buying because they can vary greatly from one producer to another and one vintage to another. (Of course this is true of all wines.) The name and fame of the grape alone do not guarantee the quality of a wine.

Generic Names

A *generic wine* is a U.S. wine of a broad general style or type, such as Burgundy or Chablis. Their names are borrowed from European wines that come from well-known wine districts, but their resemblance to these European wines is slight to nonexistent. Federal law requires all U.S. generics (the law refers to them as *semi-generics*) to include a place of origin on the label (such as California, Washington State, Napa Valley, or even America). The idea is to distinguish them clearly from the grapes of European wines whose names they have borrowed.

The best of the generics are pleasant, uncomplicated, affordable wines that restaurants can serve as house wines. If you are exploring generics to serve at your bar or restaurant, the only way to determine reliable character and quality is to taste them: The name will not necessarily provide any clues. Those that come in large-size bottles, $1\frac{1}{2}$ to 3 liters or even 4 liters, are sometimes called *jug wines,* although the industry prefers the term *extreme-value wines* for any of the lower-cost product. Some come in bag-in-a-box form, a sturdy cardboard box lined with a heavy plastic bag that holds 10 to 15 gallons of wine. The wine is dispensed through a spigot in the side of the box, and the bag shrinks as wine is removed so that the wine remaining in the bag is unspoiled by contact with air. Many wineries have begun to use the names *Red Table Wine* and *White Table Wine* instead of the old generic names. These are inexpensive blends like the generics and can be used as house wines if they pass your own taste test.

Brand Names

A brand-name wine may be anything from an inexpensive blend, to a very fine wine with a prestigious pedigree. A brand name, also called a *proprietary name* (in France, a **monopole**) is one that belongs exclusively to a vineyard or a shipper who produces and/or bottles the wine and takes responsibility for its quality. A brand name distinguishes a wine from others of the same class or type. It is a means of building an identity in the mind of a customer who is used to choosing liquors and beers by brand, is confused by the profusion of wines from which to choose, and would rather pick one and stay with it, as he or she would select a favorite beer.

Winemakers, who for the most part are feisty nonconformists, have released a host of high-quality blends with clever brand names to add personality and marketing panache to their products. The wines of California's Bonny Doon Vineyard are perfect examples. Eccentric winemaker Randall Grahm (who believes, according to his web site, that "wine should be as much fun as government regulations allow") has a fiercely loyal following among connoisseurs for both his humor and his winemaking skills. Grahm gives his wines such names as *Le Cigare Volant* ("The Flying Cigar," both red and white blends), *Cardinal Zin* (a Zinfandel, of course); and *Big House* (yes, there's a prison on the label) *Red, White,* and *Pink.*

Remember, a brand name alone does not tell you anything definitive about the wine. The reputation of the producer and the taste of the wine are better clues.

Place-of-Origin Names

Many imported wines use their place of origin as the name on their label. The place of origin is usually a rigidly controlled area that produces superior wines of a certain character because of its special soil, climate, grapes, and production methods. Wines from such an area must meet stringent government regulations and standards of that nation in order to use the name. The defined area may be large (e.g., a district or a region) or small (e.g., a commune, a parish, a village, or a vineyard). Generally the smaller the subdivision, the more rigorous the standards and the more famous the wine.

Along with the area name on the label is a phrase meaning "controlled name of origin." It may be, for example, *Appellation Controlee* in France or *Denominazione di Origine Controllata* (*DOC*) in Italy. Other countries have similar requirements for using the name of a particular place of origin. Figures 6.6 and 6.7 show an Italian wine label and a Spanish sherry label, respectively. Wine exporters are trying harder to make their products' labels easier to decipher.

Generally a wine from a controlled area has a certain claim to quality, and the best wine-growing areas have the strongest claim. But the name is not a guarantee, and all wines from the same area are not the same. Picking the right wines from the right places is a job for an expert. Ultimately a good producer is the only assurance of quality.

In recent decades in the United States, a system called *Approved Viticultural Appellations* (*AVA*) has been in force. Through this system the names of unique vineyard areas (for instance, Napa Valley, Russian River Valley, and Sonoma County) are officially defined and their use is controlled. New AVAs are continually being approved. These geographic names are generally coupled with a varietal name, and there is no indication on the wine label as to whether a geographic name is an approved AVA or not.

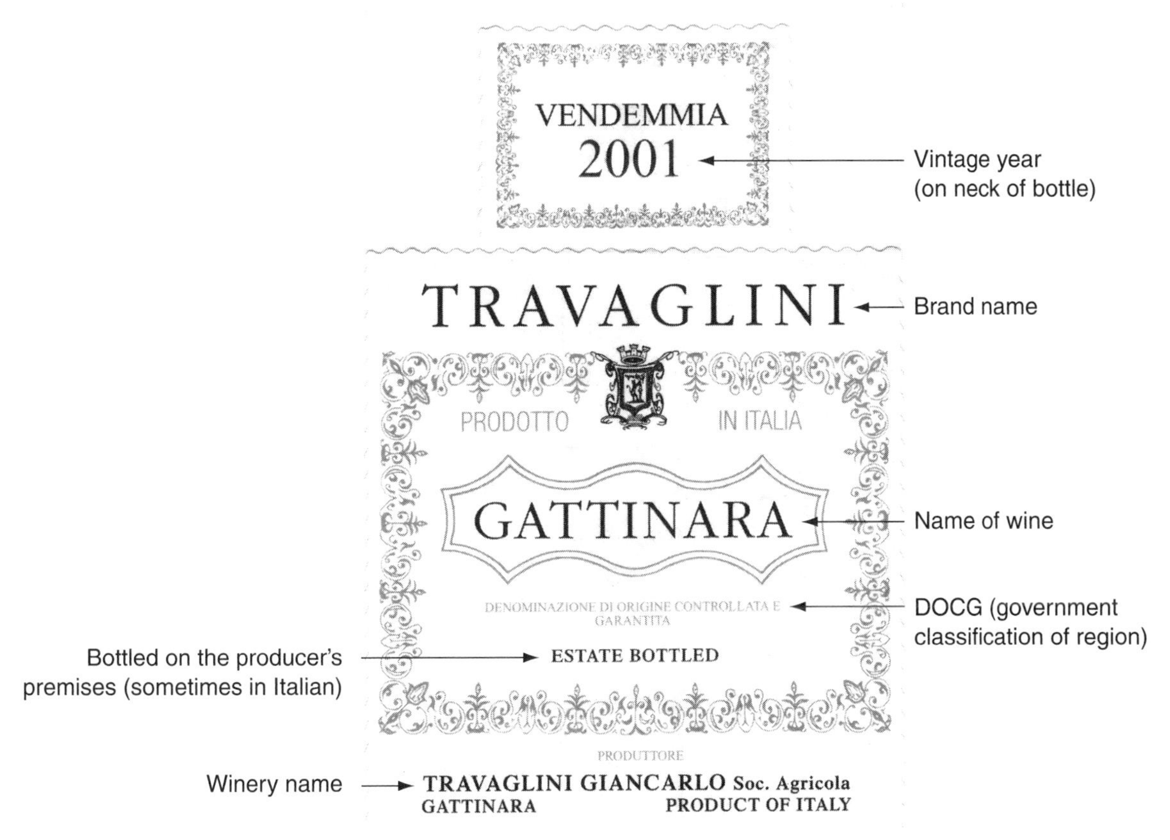

FIGURE 6.6 Italian wine labels are not so daunting when you know what to look for! Courtesy of Palm Bay Imports, Boca Raton, Florida.

A QUICK WORLD WINE TOUR

Like the rest of the business world the wine industry has gone global, with so much import and export trade between nations that anyone, anywhere, can cultivate an international palate. The five winemaking powerhouses of the European Union (EU) are responsible for two-thirds of the wine imported in the world; the United States has managed to command only 6 percent of the import market; and a variety of other, smaller-producing countries share the remaining 27 percent. Listed by volume of wine produced, the world's top ten wine countries are as follows:

1. France
2. Italy
3. Spain
4. United States

FIGURE 6.7 A Spanish sherry label is representative of a worldwide trend to keep front labels relatively uncluttered. Many wines now include a back label with information and the required U.S. government warning. Courtesty of Classical Wines of Spain, Seattle, Washington.

5. Argentina
6. Australia
7. South Africa
8. Germany
9. Portugal
10. Chile

Most of the non-European or so-called "New World" competition is from Australia, where grape production is soaring and the government aggressively promotes wine exportation by helping wineries with overseas advertisement and shipping costs.

Let's take a quick spin around the globe and find out more about the top ten countries. World politics and individual preferences aside, we've arranged them in descending order based on their volume of production. At the end we've added a section to mention a few other nations' wines.

Wines from France

France has an interesting dilemma. Despite being the world's most prolific wine producer, its own people are drinking less. Wine consumption has decreased slowly but steadily in France to almost half of what it was in 1980. That said, the French still drink much more wine per year (56 liters per person) than Americans (12 liters per person), citing 2003 estimates based on U.S. Census figures and Wine Institute data.

No matter who consumes fine French wines, they lead the world in prestige, and no wine list in any upscale restaurant or fashionable hotel would be complete without these choices. Patrons who know wines may expect to see several well-known French wines at very high prices on the wine list, even if they do not order any of them, along with several wines at lower prices that they would be glad to buy. The label on the bottle will carry the name of a well-known vineyard or commune, a district or shipper, a vintage date, and the phrase *Appellation Controlee,* indicating that all of the government requirements have been met. Rarely will a French wine be identified by the name of the grape. However, as you will see, the same outstanding wine grapes are used all over the world to produce quality wines.

In France the major wine producing regions are Bordeaux, Burgundy, the Rhone Valley (Côtes du Rhône), the Loire Valley, Champagne, and Alsace. The wines of the Bordeaux region have been famous since Roman times. Bordeaux wines come in a high-shouldered bottle (see Figure 6.8a). A wine spoken of as "a Bordeaux" means a red wine from Bordeaux; it is also referred to by the British term **claret.**

Bordeaux produces a range of wines, from connoisseurs' dreams, to everyday table wines, from more than 50 distinct regions within the Bordeaux area. Nearly all red Bordeaux is made by blending grapes, mainly Cabernet Sauvignon, Merlot, and Cabernet Franc. The style of the wine depends on the blend, which varies from one producer to another. There are two distinct production areas, divided by the Gironde River. On one side, in the Medoc and Graves districts, Cabernet is the main grape. On the other side of the river, in Pomerol and St. Emilion and numerous satellite zones, Merlot and Cabernet Franc tend to dominate the grape blend.

Most prestigious are the Bordeaux wines named for the chateau (vineyard) that produces them. The best wine from each vintage is usually bottled at the vineyard and carries the phrase *Mis en bouteille au château* (literally, "placed in the bottle at the vineyard") or the phrase *Mise du château.* The rest of a vintage may be sold to a shipper, or a *negociant,* who blends wines from various vineyards to sell under the shipper's label or under a *monopole,* which is a registered brand name.

At the top of the Bordeaux-quality pyramid are the **classified growths,** chateau wines that were recognized as the leaders as long ago as 1855 when Napoleon III

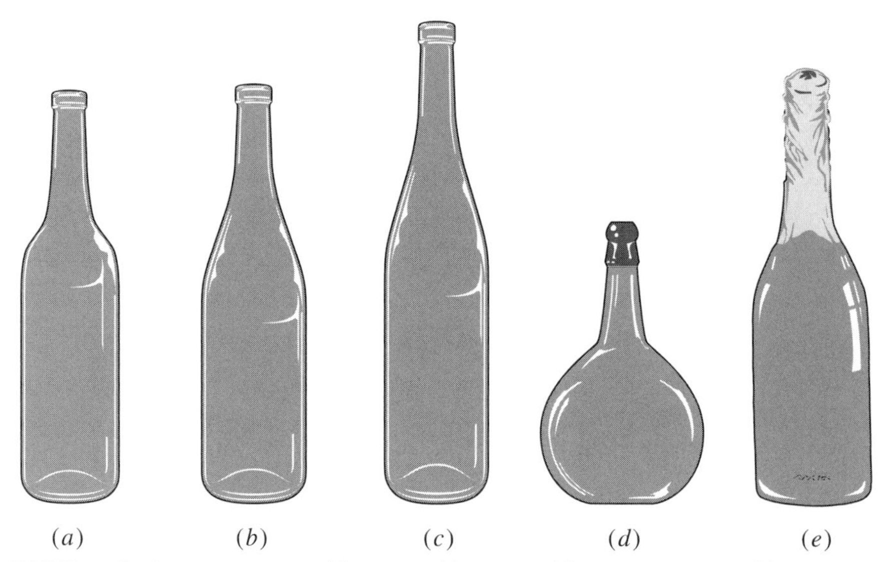

FIGURE 6.8 Traditional bottle shapes: (a) Bordeaux, (b) Burgundy, (c) Rhine, Mosel, Alsace, (d) Bocksbeutel (German Franken, Chile, Portugal), (e) Champagne and other sparkling wines (heavy, with a wired cork).

ordered an official classification of French wines. Such chateau wines as Lafite-Rothschild, Latour, Margaux, Mouton-Rothschild, and Haut-Brion are known as the *first growths* and are the most prestigious. There are 65 classified growths in the Medoc and Graves, ranging from first growths to fifth growths. In St. Emilion 74 chateaux are classified as *Premiers Grand Crus Classes* or *Grand Crus Classes,* but they are little known because most are too small to produce much.

There are also plenty of Bordeaux reds, either generic or monopole, blended from wines produced anywhere in the large Bordeaux zone or from vineyards in a specific commune, such as St. Julien and St. Estephe. Some of these wines are outstanding.

In addition to the reds for which it is famous, Bordeaux produces white wines from the Semillon and Sauvignon grapes. Those from the Graves district are fresh, dry, full-bodied, and fruity. Those from the Sauternes district to the south, although made from the same grapes as the Graves wines, are very different; they are extraordinarily sweet and rich. These qualities come from the warm climate and especially from the harvesting method. The grapes are left on the vines until they are overripe and develop *Botrytis cinerea,* a special mold known as *noble rot* (*pourriture noble* in French, *Edelfaule* in German). This mold dries the grapes, concentrating their sugar and flavor. Each bunch is individually selected at its peak of desirability; a vineyard may be handpicked in this way as many as eight times. The wines from Sauternes are served at the end of a meal, either with dessert or as dessert. Of the Sauternes wines, Chateau d'Yquem is the ultimate in terms of fame and fortune.

Burgundy wines also belong on a fine-wine list. The French wines referred to as *Burgundy* are the classical reds made from the Pinot Noir grape in the Côte d'Or region. Like the Bordeaux, they are wines of great character and long life. They are shipped in a Burgundy bottle (see Figure 6.8b.) Burgundy vineyards are also classified for quality; the magic phrase here is **Grand Cru,** which means "great growth." Of the Grand Cru vineyards, the most famous are Romanee-Conti, Clos de Vougeot, and Chambertin, followed by certain hyphenated Chambertins (from villages with hyphenated names, such as Gevrey-Chambertin) and Musigny.

Knowing what sort of wine lies beneath the label of a Burgundy wine is a far more complicated business than it is for a Bordeaux wine. In Bordeaux each vineyard (chateau) is owned by a single family or corporation, but in Burgundy a single vineyard might be owned by many individuals, each with a few acres or perhaps just a few rows of vines. Each vineyard is an *Appellation Controlee,* and each owner/grower is, therefore, entitled to make an individual wine with the name of the vineyard on the label. As such there might be great variation in quality depending on the skill of the grower, and conceivably as many as 5 to 50 different wines of the same name and vintage could come from a single vineyard. Similarly the phrase *Mis en bouteille au domaine* which means "bottled at the vineyard," does not guarantee quality or consistency: This is because there is no uniformity among growers' products even when they *are* bottled at the vineyard. For this reason it has become the practice for Burgundy shippers to buy wines from several growers in a vineyard and make a wine carrying the vineyard label on which they stake their own reputation.

What a shipper's wine offers is consistency, but often at the expense of individual vineyard character. Many shippers make wines that tend to taste almost like each other, in the shipper's "house style," regardless of the commune from which the grapes come. As a result shippers play a valuable role in providing readily available, fairly predictable, decent wine—just not the very best. The best Burgundies come from individual growers and are made in miniscule quantities, and knowing one's way around among them is one of the most challenging tasks that any wine expert can face.

The district of Beaujolais is also part of the Burgundy region, but it produces a very different wine from the classical Burgundy. The wine called *Beaujolais,* made from the Gamay grape, is a fresh, light red with a short life span of two to three years. It, too, is shipped in the Burgundy-shaped bottle shown in Figure 6.8b. Unlike most red wines it is often served at a cool cellar temperature. The best Beaujolais is identified on its label as *Cru Beaujolais,* along with the appellation of the commune it comes from. Next in rank is the Appellation Beaujolais-Villages.

The arrival of Nouveau Beaujolais (or Beaujolais Noveau) in the United States on the third Thursday of every November is one of wine's charming celebratory traditions. The young wine, barely two months old, is the first wine of the new harvest; it is meant to be uncorked and consumed immediately. Always served chilled, it is grapey, refreshing, and fun. It has a very short life span of only about four months.

Although Burgundy is probably best known for its red wines, the whites, made from the Chardonnay grape, can be magnificent. They are among the best white wines in the world. One of the reasons Chardonnay has become so desirable all over the world is the success of the Burgundian prototype. The term *white Burgundy* encompasses several rather different wines, even though all are made from Chardonnay grapes. The vineyard of Montrachet and its neighbors are one group, Macon wines are another, and Chablis wines are a third.

Montrachet is a small vineyard that produces a white wine of great prestige and excellence. The vineyard is so famous that its neighbors have hyphenated its name to theirs. Other well-known white Burgundies from this region are Meursault and Corton-Charlemagne. It is said that Charlemagne himself planted this latter vineyard. As with the red Burgundies, there are many small growers in these vineyards, and a reliable producer/shipper rather than estate bottling is often the key to quality.

Of the white wines of the Macon region, the best known in the United States is **Pouilly-Fuissé** (POO-ee fweh-SAY). Other Macon wines with a district or village appellation are also imported and are often better values. Chablis is a Burgundy region that produces an entirely different white wine from the others, although it is made from the same Chardonnay grape. In fact it is seldom called a *white Burgundy;* it is simply called *Chablis.* It is pale, greenish, light, and very dry, with a taste described as "flinty"; it is most definitely different from the typical, sweet American "chablis." There are several classifications: Grand Cru, **Premier Cru**, and Chablis, in descending order. Quality varies greatly from one vintage to another because of the weather. This cool northern climate does not often give the grapes a chance to ripen fully, resulting in a light, crisp personality in the wines.

Red wines from the Côtes du Rhône district in the Rhone Valley have recently become very interesting to Americans, especially that adventurous group who likes to try something new and different. These wines are far from "new." The best-known Chateauneuf-du-Pape vineyard is said to have been planted in the fourteenth century by Pope Clement V, the first of the French popes who moved the papacy temporarily from Rome to Avignon; hence the name, which means "New Chateau of the Pope." But these wines are different in several ways. They are made from blends of many different, mostly unfamiliar grapes; a single bottle of Chateauneuf-du-Pape may contain as many as 13 grape varieties. They are big, deep-red, full-bodied, alcoholic wines that must be aged many years before they are ready to drink. They have a richness that derives from the grapes ripening in the long, hot growing season of southern France.

Other fine Rhone reds, such as Hermitage and Côte Rotie, are similar in style and pedigree. The district is also the home of Tavel, a fresh, dry, but fruity rosé wine.

Another group of white wines comes from the Loire Valley. The best known are **Pouilly-Fumé** (POO-ee fyoo-MAY), often confused with Pouilly-Fuissé but very different, as well as Sancerre and Vouvray. Both Sancerre and Pouilly-Fumé come from the Sauvignon Blanc grape so popular in the United States today. Although this is also the grape of white Bordeaux, these Loire wines have a crisper, fruitier style. Vouvray is made in several styles, from bone-dry and fruity, to sweet, to sparkling.

Rosé d'Anjou is also from the Loire Valley. One of the most popular Rosés until the advent of White Zinfandel, it is made primarily from Gamay grapes. It has a charming pink color and a touch of sweetness. The Champagne district of France produces the sparkling white wine that bears its name. All French Champagnes are blends of wines from several vineyards and carry the name of the shipper/producer rather than that of a vineyard. They are made from both white and dark grapes unless they are labeled *Blanc de Blancs,* literally, *white from whites.* A French Champagne carries a vintage date only if it is from an exceptionally good year. A Champagne label indicates its degree of sweetness. The French terms might confuse the novice. They range from:

- Brut or Nature (the driest)
- Extra Sec (extra dry, which means that it contains a small amount of added sugar)
- Sec (dry, which actually indicates slight sweetness)
- Demi-Sec (semi-dry, which actually is quite sweet)
- Doux (very sweet; a seldom-made style, so this label designation is seldom used)

These French terms should appear on a wine-list entry, and servers should be familiar with them. Most of today's Champagnes are Brut or Extra Dry. Nearly every Champagne house, besides making a nonvintage Champagne, also makes vintage-dated Champagnes (in good years only) and a superpremium wine that is tremendously prestigious, not to mention expensive. Dom Perignon and Cristal are two of the best known.

The wine region of Alsace lies across the Rhine from Germany and grows many of the same grape varietals. Because of the district's cool climate most of the wines are white. Chief among the grapes are Riesling (full-bodied, fruity, and slightly sweet) and Gewurztraminer (spicy and full-flavored). Unlike the wines of the rest of France, most of the Alsatian wines are varietals. Alsace wines are big, firm, flavorful, and dry. They are unlike any other wines in the world, and they have a small but loyal following of fans. Because they are not especially stylish, they are also excellent values. You will find them in the distinctive tall, slender green bottle required by law (see Figure 6.8c). It is similar to the bottle shape for German wines and looks more German than French.

Wines from Italy

Italy vies with France as the world's largest wine producer, and it exports more wine to the United States than France does. Most Italian wines come from native Italian grapes that are not grown anywhere else in the world, and they can be excellent values. Italy also makes plenty of wines from such well-known grapes as Chardonnay and Cabernet, and these wines are often varietally labeled. The style and character of Italian wines vary tremendously from one region to another, depending on climate, grape variety, and local custom.

It is really not a mystery why Italian wines are not as popular as French wines. Their names are not as familiar to U.S. consumers, and there is no specific government program to help winemakers promote their exported products. Add to that the undeniable fact that Italian wine labels can be difficult to read. Knowing three label designations might be helpful in determining overall quality:

- *Riserva* means "reserve," and in Italy it legally means that the winery has aged the wine longer than the standard minimums. It sometimes means the wine has a slightly greater alcohol content than nonreserve wines of the same type.
- *Classico* means the wine comes directly from a particular wine-producing region. If a wine is a Chianti Classico, for example, it comes straight from Chianti, not a neighboring area.
- *Classico Superiore* means both of the above: The wine is from the "classico" part of the region *and* it has a higher alcohol content.

Most of Italy's quality wine production is governed by the DOC appellation system. This system recognizes and defines more than 200 types of Italian wine from specific geographic areas. However, unlike France's appellation system, which actually classifies individual vineyards, DOC does not classify wines by quality. A high level of DOC status is DOCG; the "G" stands for *garantita,* which means *guaranteed,* because every wine must pass an official taste test before being sold. The DOCG system builds in incentives and risks that encourage producers to make quality wine. There are currently six DOCG wines: Barolo, Barbaresco, Chianti, Brunello di Montalcino, Vino Nobile di Montepulciano, and Albana di Romagna, a white wine.

The DOC classifications took effect beginning in 1963; the DOCG system followed in 1992. A third designation, *Indicazione Geografica Tipica* (which means "Typical Geographical Indication"), was created in 1996 to account for wines that are typical to their region but not quite prestigious enough to fit into the DOC and DOCG categories. Wines that meet IGT standards for five years are able to move up to the DOC category.

Some of Italy's best wines, however, exist outside the DOC framework, often because their producers have chosen not to participate in the system. They are technically merely *vini da tavola, table wines,* but their high prices are clues that these are serious wines, and not to be taken lightly. Of the many wine regions in Italy, three are of particular importance to American restaurateurs. Piedmont and Veneto in northern Italy, and Tuscany farther south.

In northwest Italy Piedmont borders on France and produces two of Italy's greatest reds, Barolo and Barbaresco. These wines come from the native Nebbiolo grape. They are big, robust reds of great distinction, Barbaresco being somewhat more delicate than Barolo. In this part of Italy it is common to label wines with individual vineyard names in addition to the name of the wine itself.

Piedmont is also home to Asti Spumante, a delicious, sparkling white wine made by the Charmat (bulk) method from Muscat grapes. It captures the fruity freshness of the grapes and is sweet, making it more appropriate with dessert than other sparkling wines.

In northeastern Italy Veneto is famous for the trio of wines from Verona: Soave, a white; Bardolino, a light red; and Valpolicella, a medium-bodied red. They are all made from blends of local native Italian grapes. Along with its two neighboring regions, Friuli and Trentino, Veneto also makes many varietally labeled Cabernets and Chardonnays. Because the weather is relatively cool and Italians prefer their wines slightly on the acidic side to accompany food better, these wines will usually be lighter than their counterparts from other parts of the world. Pinot Grigio is a popular white wine from these areas.

Tuscany is Italy's other great red-wine region. It is the home of Chianti, a DOCG wine that has been improving its quality and image since the mid-1970s. Chianti is a blend of four grapes, predominantly Sangiovese, a native grape grown throughout central Italy. Once known as a rough young wine in a cute, straw-covered bottle, it is now taken more seriously in the wine community and is aged in a Bordeaux-shaped bottle. Chianti Riserva, for example, is aged at least three years. The best Chianti is from the Chianti Classico district, often identified by a black rooster on the neck of the bottle. Another DOCG wine from Tuscany is the red Brunello di Montalcino, made from a type of Sangiovese called *Brunello.* It is considered Italy's most expensive red.

Many producers in Tuscany are now making premium-quality reds and whites that are not DOC, in the manner mentioned earlier. These wines are often made with Cabernet and Chardonnay, using the most sophisticated winemaking techniques. As a result they are richer and fuller than the Cabernets and Chardonnays from the northeast, and considerably more expensive. You will often find enough information for two labels on an imported wine.

Of the many wines made in other Italian wine districts, Orvieto, Verdicchio, and Frascati (all made from native grape varieties) are popular in the United States. All three are light, crisp whites. There are also good white varietals made from Verdicchio, Pinot Bianco (Pinot Blanc), and Pinot Grigio grapes. A varietal of a different sort is Lambrusco, which is easy to drink and reminiscent of sparkling grape juice.

Wines from Spain

Spain has its own wine appellation system, with more than 50 *Denominacion de Origen* (*DO*s). Wineries in Spain are called *bodegas* (bo-DAY-guss), so you will see that word as part of the name on some labels (see Figure 6.7). Several other label designations indicate clues about the quality of a Spanish wine, and they are based on the amount of time the wine is aged:

- An ordinary table wine that has not been aged may have no designation at all.
- Wines that are described as *Tinto* (TEEN-toh) or *Jovan* (ho-VON) have not been aged in wood.
- *Crianza* (kree-ON-zah) wines have been aged a minimum of 18 months, in any combination of barrel or cask and bottle.

- Riserva wines are of slightly better quality, aged a minimum of 3 years.
- The best quality wines are labeled *Gran Riserva*. They must be aged at least 5 years before being released for sale, and 3 of those years must be in oak. Gran Reservas are selected in only exceptional grape-growing years.

A caveat: The new breed of Spanish winemakers, known as *expressionists*, feels strongly that wine doesn't always need such a long time "on oak" to be considered great. They proudly market their own unoaked or lightly oaked products as Tintos or Crianzas, and are making some exceptional wines. The world market is taking notice, although less than 3 percent of Spain's exported wines come to the United States. Instead Spain's biggest customers are other EU members.

The most famous red Spanish wine is *Rioja* (ree-OH-hah), a smooth and elegant wine, most often a blend of the Tempranillo and *Grenache grapes*, which are called *Garnacha* in Spain. With flavors reminiscent of Cabernet and Pinot Noir, Tempranillo has become popular enough with wine aficionados that some Spanish wineries also now bottle 100-percent Tempranillo. Although prices have been on the rise Rioja continues to deliver exceptional quality for a low price. There is also white Rioja.

From the same grapes *Ribera del Duero* (rih-BEAR-ah dell DWAIR-oh) is similar to Rioja, but "bigger" and more intensely flavored. The Tempranillo is sometimes blended with Cabernet Sauvignon grapes for this hearty wine. The Penedes region near Barcelona is becoming increasingly important as a source of red and white table wines, sometimes made from world-class grapes, such as Cabernet and Chardonnay. Its *Methode Champenoise* sparkling wines, called *Cava* (KAH-vuh), are extremely good values. The names Codorniu and Freixenet are found on many a moderately priced American wine list. In the Navarra region (where people run with the bulls at Pamplona) there are some excellent varietals made, as well as a rosé wine known as *Rosado*.

Spain is the original home of *sherry*, a fortified wine made for centuries in the Jerez district using time-honored methods and strict controls that yield a connoisseur's product. Its style ranges from crisp and lean to rich and sweet depending on production methods. It is one of the world's top aperitif wines.

By law only three grape varietals may be used in making sherries. The **palomino** grape makes up the bulk of the bottle, with *moscatel* and *Pedro Ximenez* sometimes added to impart sweetness and color. Sherries are fermented dry and put into barrels, where they form a natural yeast called **flor** that is native to this area and helps give the wine its unique complexity. (In the barrels, they also grow slow-forming sediment known as *madre* that is believed to contribute to the smoothness of the wine.) The various barrels are arranged in what is called a **solera** system: The rows, or tiers, at the bottom contain the oldest vintages, and the ones at the top contain the youngest. As the winemaker draws wine from the bottom barrels, they are refilled from the next row up, and so on, ensuring a consistent style and flavor over years of time, as well as continually replenishing the flor. A solera may have as few as 5 tiers or as many as 14.

There are several categories of Spanish sherry:

- *Fino:* Pale, dry, and delicate, with an alcohol content of about 15 percent. Fino may have been barrel-aged for as few as 3 years or as many as 10.
- *Manzanilla:* The driest fino, with a slightly higher alcohol content.
- *Amontillado:* Fuller-flavored and darker in color than the finos. It is aged only 2 to 5 years and contains more alcohol, 16 to 18 percent.
- *Olorosso:* Fortified by adding grape spirits that stop the flor from forming and raise the alcohol content, which can be as high as 20 percent. These wines are not sweet, but they are rich in flavor and dark in color.
- *Palo Cortado:* A sherry that began as a fino but lost its flor quickly. Alcohol content is 18 to 21 percent.
- *Cream sherry:* Considered the most "inferior" in quality, with the highest content of the sweet grape varietals.

Sherries will last longer after being opened than ordinary table wines because of their higher alcohol content, but they should be kept corked and used within 7 to 10 days.

Wines from the United States

Although many states nurture their own wine industries, California is by far the leading producer of U.S. wine, accounting for 90 percent of the nation's overall grape production. For the remaining 10 percent, rounding out the "top five" are Washington and New York (30,000 acres each), Oregon (14,000 acres), and New Jersey (less than 1,000 acres).

Wine grapes are grown in 46 of California's 58 counties and, in 2004, vineyards covered more than half a million acres. The California wine country can be divded roughly into five geographic regions, and further into 12 *Appellations of Origin,* which are divided into 93 smaller *American Viticultural Areas* (*AVA*). Dozens of books already have been written about winemaking in California, so the following list can be considered a very brief summary.

- *North Coast:* The prestigious Napa Valley is located here, where an acre of vineyard land can sell for as much as $350,000. Located north of San Francisco, Napa doesn't produce large quantities of wine, only about 3 percent of California's total, but most is top quality. It contains a dozen subappellations with diverse climates. Sonoma County is twice as large as Napa Valley. The North Coast AVAs are strongly identified with cultivation of certain grapes: Russian River with Chardonnay and Pinot Noir; Alexander Valley with Cabernet and single-vineyard Chrdonnays; the Dry Creek area with Zinfandel. Mendocino and Lake Counties are the farthest north appellations of the North Coast, with plentiful Chardonnay, Riesling, Gewurztraminer, and Pinot Noir plantings.
- *Central Coast:* This enormous region is its own AVA. It lies between San Francisco and Santa Barbara and produces about 15 percent of the state's wine grapes.

Moneterey, home of the famous Monterey Wine Festival, is here, as is the Paso Robles AVA. Investors in the Monterey area risked millions of dollars in early attempts to compete with Napa and Sonoma before settling on the white grapes that grow best in the region: Chardonnay, Gewurztraminer, and Riesling. More than 40 percent of the the vineyards are Chardonnay. Today, this region is home to more than 350 wineries. The counties of San Luis Obispo and Santa Barbara are included in the southernmost portion of the area, where the first California winemakers planted vines in the early 1800s.

- ***Central Valley:*** This inland area stretches 450 miles in length, with the Sacramento Valley to the north and the San Joaquin Valley to the south. Its 18 counties supply about one-fourth of the United States's food supply. The San Joaquin Valley produces 70 percent of all California wines with table grapes for inexpensive wines. Located between two mountain ranges, the Central Valley's relative isolation spared the area from the early ravages of *phylloxera,* so today it contains some of the oldest vines in the state. The towns of Modesto and Fresno are located in the Cental Valley; winemakers around the town of Lodi are raising the bar by creating some premium wines.
- ***Sierra Foothills:*** About 100 wineries are producing in the area between Sacramento (to the west) and Lake Tahoe (to the east) in Amador, Calaveras, and Eldorado counties. Most wineries are smaller, family-owned propeties. At elevations of 1,500 to 3,000 feet above sea level, the soil is granite and/or volcanic material, and typically the vineyards are not irrigated. This puts stress on the vines and creates excellent conditions for the "big reds" for which this area is known: Cabernet, Syrah, and Zinfandel.
- ***Southern Coast:*** The area between Los Angeles and San Diego includes five AVAs that cover 267,500 acres in Los Angeles, Orange, Riverside, San Bernardino, and San Diego counties. The region contains fewer than 50 wineries and is known primarily for a mix of offbeat varietals, such as Cabernet Franc, Cinsault, Primitivo, Montepulciano, and Sangiovese. The largest grape-growing areas are Temecula and the Cucamonga Valley, but the turn of the new century saw a major setback to the wine industry here with an infestation of *Pierce's Disease,* a bacterium (*Xylella fastidiosa*) that chokes vines by preventing them from absorbing water and soil nutrients. Today the Southern Coast wine industry is recovering from this infestation.

Before moving on, a final word about Pierce's Disease. The bacterium is spread by a large, leaf-eating insect known as the *glassy-winged sharpshooter* (GWSS; Latin name *Homalodisca coagulata*). It has been a serious enough threat that the California Department of Agriculture has imported tiny wasps that seek out the sharpshooter's eggs and prevent them from hatching. In 2004, 14 California counties reported outbreaks of Pierce's Disease. It has not had an impact on humans or pets, but it is fatal to grapevines and dozens of other plants, including citrus crops.

New York produced more than 142,000 tons of grapes in 2004. Of the five AVAs, the largest in terms of size and output is the Lake Erie region of Western New York. However, as the home of the National Grape Cooperative (better known as Welch's), most of the Lake Erie grapes are used for making grape juice instead of wine. The largest wine-producing region is Finger Lakes, which accounts for one-third of the grape-growing but 85 percent of the wine bottled in New York State. Classic white grape varieties do well here, such as Chardonnay, Riesling, and Gewurztraminer. There are about 215 wineries statewide.

New York's role as a wine industry powerhouse is partly due to its influence as a distribution center. About 10 percent of all licensed importers ship their wines to New York City on their way to other U.S. destinations, and almost every food and wine publication has an office here, too.

In the Pacific Northwest, the state of Washington has long been known for its fruit crops of apples, pears, and cherries, so its seems only natural that grapes would be an additional economic boon. The state is located on the same latitude as the Bordeaux and Burgundy regions of France, and about 360 wineries are making the most of this fortunate fact. Today Washington harvests almost 120,000 tons of grapes annually, volume that is second only to California in the United States.

New AVAs are always being proposed and considered, so the numbers may have changed by the time you read this, but Washington has at least seven AVAs. Most are in the warm, dry climates of Central and Eastern Washington. These areas receive more sunlight than their California counterparts, by as much as two hours at some times of the year, making conditions ideal for grape-growing. The state has been recognized for its Cabernet Sauvignon, Merlot, Chardonnay, and Sauvignon Blanc production, although at least 30 grape varieties are being cultivated. The largest AVAs are the Columbia Valley (along the Columbia River, which borders Oregon to the south), and the Yakima Valley (in the South Central portion of the state).

Neighboring Oregon shares three AVAs with Washington (Columbia Gorge, Columbia Valley, and Walla Walla Valley). The largest Oregon appellation, Willamette Valley, is also the home to the largest number of wineries in the state and has been subdivided into numerous, smaller microclimates to more accurately label the wines from each unique area.

When it comes to winemaking, the state's soil and climate have been favorably compared to the Rhone, Alsace, and Bordeaux regions of France. Oregon has had enormous success growing the temperamental Pinot Noir grape because its valleys are cooler than those of California. Pinot Noir is the leading varietal grown in Oregon, followed by Pinot Gris, Chardonnay, and Riesling. Merlot rounds out the top five. The state's 314 wineries grow 14,000 acres of grapes.

Oregon law requires that in order for a wine to be named after its grape varietal, 90 percent of the wine must be made from that particular grape. The sole exception is Cabernet Sauvignon, which must be at least 75 percent Cabernet.

Numerous other states have made very creditable wines, including Ohio, Vermont, Virginia, Idaho, and Texas. These wines are generally in small production, however, and seldom become well known enough to land themselves on restaurant wine lists, except in their own home state or region.

Wines from Argentina

Argentina has long been known for its value-priced red-wine products, but when it comes to the successful exportation of wine, Chile started before Argentina. Argentine winemakers mobilized when they saw how well other South Americans were doing and, in recent years, have even replanted up to one-third of their existing vineyards in their bid to craft and market better-quality varietals. The country has an ambitious strategic plan for its wine industry, aiming for a 10-percent international market share by the year 2020. (It is currently 2 percent.) Interestingly Argentina's top customers are, in order: Paraguay, the United States, the United Kingdom, Russia, and Brazil. In 2004 American imports of Argentine wines increased by almost one-third.

Argentina has a couple of advantages. First the land prices are low, which has already started to spur foreign investment in its vineyards. The country also has two unique grape varietals: Malbec is the primary grape in top-quality reds, and Torrontés produces a sweet, aromatic white wine. Chardonnay, Cabernet, and Tempranillo are also grown.

The best-known grape-growing area of Argentina is Mendoza, which borders Chile. Vineyards are planted straight up mountainsides, thousands of feet above sea level.

Wines from Australia

Australia seems to have sprung up somewhat suddenly as a winemaking giant, with shelf after shelf of bargain-priced products in U.S. supermarkets. About one-third of Aussie imports come to the United States. Australia also sells more wine to the United Kingdom than any other nation. For the most part this is the work of Southcorp, a single conglomerate that owns at least six of the largest and best-known Australian wineries, including Lindemans, Penfolds, and Rosemount Estates. The flood of Australian wines into the United States is expected to continue, especially since export tariffs are being eliminated over an 11-year period that began in 2005.

The seven major wine-producing regions in Australia are further divided into subregions, for a total of 50 areas where wine is made. All except one of the major regions (Margaret River, in Southwest Australia) are located in the southeastern portion of the country. Harvest time here is opposite that of the United States, from February to April. For an Australian wine to be labeled a particular varietal, area, or vintage year, it must contain at least 85 percent of that grape type, from that specific area or year. If the wine is a blend, the names of each grape used must be listed on the label in descending order based on volume. Australia's Label Integrity Programme (LIP) does not permit the use of generic labels.

The oldest winemaking region in Australia is the Hunter Valley, where commercial production began in the early 1800s. It is known for excellent Chardonnay,

Semillon, and Shiraz. An unusual name seen on some Australian labels, Coonawarra, probably deserves an explanation. Only 1 mile wide and 9 miles long, it is among the nation's smallest wine-producing regions. Known for its fruit orchards in the past, Coonawarra's vineyards are planted in a deep layer of dark red clay that the locals call *Terra Rossa,* which stresses the grapevines and results in the production of low-yield but highly concentrated fruit, both red and white grapes. The region is getting a reputation as the "Bordeaux of Australia," and there is an ongoing effort to restrict the use of the Coonawarra name to only those wines produced from grapevines planted in the famous red soil.

Wines from South Africa

In the past some people would not stock or purchase South African wines—no matter how good—because of the repressive political climate of apartheid. A United Nations embargo on all commerce was lifted in 1994, and since then the nation is slowly emerging from that stigma and its wines are once again gaining popularity. South Africa's biggest wine customers are the United Kingdom, the Netherlands, and Germany. The United States receives less than 3 percent of South African wine exports, but that is twice as much as in past years. Under the African Growth and Opportunity Act (AGOA), the incoming wines pay no duty, which helps keep prices low for consumers.

Instead of small, individual wineries, most of the grapes are grown by large cooperatives. Red wines from South Africa include Cabernet, Syrah or Shiraz, and Pinotage, the latter from a grape that is native to the area. It was created in the 1920s by a university professor who crossed Pinot Noir with another red grape, *Cinsault* (sin-SO), which thrives in hot weather and is known for its spicy characteristic. Wines that are labeled *Cape blends* have Pinotage as an integral component. South African white wines made from Chenin Blanc may be labeled *Steen,* which is what the grape is called there. The country is also known for its dessert wines.

Prime winemaking regions include Stellenbosch, known as the *Napa Valley of the Cape,* and Paarl, the largest wine district, which is known for distinctive sherries and Port-style wines.

Wines from Germany

About two-thirds of the grapes grown in Germany for winemaking are white because they flourish in the cool climate. Although recent years have seen an increase in plantings of red grapes, whites, such as Riesling and Silvaner, form the backbone of Germany's production, along with Muller-Thurgau, a hybrid of the two that the Germans developed to suit their climate. But all of the great wines derive from the noble Riesling.

The prototype German wine for many years was a fruity but acidic white, light in body and low in alcohol (about 9 to 10 percent), which combined a pleasant sweetness with a naturally high level of crispness. Today there is a movement in Germany toward dry and somewhat dry wines. (On the label, *trocken* means dry; *halb-trocken* means off-dry.) These have been slow to make headway in the U.S. market, where we still expect German wines to be at least slightly sweet; however, the United States is still Germany's second-largest export market.

This is one area of the world in which climate and geography can combine to affect wines greatly, both in quantity and quality. Germany's range extends from ordinary, inexpensive wines to some of the greatest white wines in the world. There are three basic categories in the country's rigorous system of quality classification and control:

- ***Tafelwein*** (table wine): the most ordinary wine. Sugar is added to these wines for fermentation to make up for inadequate ripeness of the grapes. It is seldom exported.
- ***Qualitatswein*** (QbA): translated as "Quality wine from a designated region." This may mean a single vineyard, a group of vineyards, or a group of villages. These wines also have had sugar added for fermentation.
- ***Qualitatswein mit Pradikat*** (QmP): translated as "Quality wine with special attributes." The major attribute is the ripeness of the grape.

In addition, there are five subcategories, called *pradikats,* being hotly debated among German winemakers, who correctly assert that the ripeness of the grape at the time they are picked is not an automatic indication of quality—that what the winemaker *does* with the grapes ultimately determines the quality of the wine. The top German winemakers are fermenting drier, more elegant wines and if they disagree with the pradikat system, refusing to include it on their labels. The five pradikats are listed in ascending order according to the natural sugar level of the grapes at harvest:

- ***Kabinett.*** This light, fruity wine is made from grapes ripened in the ordinary manner, but sweet enough to ferment without adding sugar.
- ***Spatlese.*** This wine is made from fully ripened grapes late-picked after the official harvest date.
- ***Auslese.*** This wine is made from particularly ripe grapes picked selectively in bunches at any time during the harvest. Auslese wines can be very sweet (dessert-style) or only somewhat sweet.
- ***Beerenauslese.*** This rich, top-quality wine is made from perfectly ripened grapes chosen one by one.
- ***Trockenbeerenauslese.*** This wine is the German equivalent of French Sauternes, made from individually selected overripe grapes that have shriveled with the "noble rot" that, as you have learned, the Germans call *Edelfaule*. The term *trocken* (dry) refers to the fact that the grapes have dried, not that the wine is dry.

A special category of wine is eiswein, a very rare and expensive wine made from grapes that have actually been allowed to freeze on the vine, concentrating their sweetness and richness.

There are 11 wine regions in Germany, all of them surrounding rivers that moderate the climate. Several regions are named for the Rhine River: Rheingau, Rheinhessen, and Rheinpfalz. The most famous is the Rheingau, Germany's smallest region, which abounds with top vineyards. Its wines are riper and fuller than Mosels, yet steely and firm. Among the famous vineyards here are Schloss Johannisberger and Schloss Vollrads. Together the wines from the Rhine and Mosel Valleys account for most U.S. imports of German wines. You can tell them apart at a glance by the color of the bottle: brown for Rhine and green for Mosel. Both bottles have a typical tall tapered shape, like a stretched-out Burgundy bottle, seen in Figure 6.8c. A green Bocksbeutel (Figure 6.8d) is used for wines from the Franken region.

Wines from Portugal

Portugal is famous for great fortified wines, and U.S. consumers are turning on to Port as a sophisticated after-dinner treat. Portugal exports more wine than either South Africa or Argentina, and as much wine as Germany.

The *Port makers,* called *Port houses,* harvest grapes annually, but declare their products *Vintage Port* only in years that they consider the best for long-term aging of the wine. The finest-quality Vintage Ports are stored in oak for up to two years, then bottled and aged for a decade or more before being sold. The year 2000 was declared a Vintage Port year. Another option for a top-quality wine is a Single Quinta Port. The designation *Quinta* on a wine label means "vineyard," the same as a chateau or domain in France. In non-Vintage years, bottling fruit from a single vineyard makes it a bit more exclusive, so Single Quinta Ports can be excellent buys, both in quality and value.

For years the only non-Port wines to cross the ocean for sale in the United States were a few brand-name rosés, pleasant but undistinguished. More recently this has changed, and you will find some great values for by-the-glass pouring. You may see *Touriga Nacional* on Portugese wine labels, which is the name of a red grape native to the country. The table wines from the Minho region, labeled *Vinho Verde* whether they are red or white, are particular bargains. The name literally means "green wine," but it refers to the fact that these wines should be enjoyed young and are not meant to be aged.

Portugal has its own appellation system, called *Indicacao da Proveniencia Regulamentada* (*IPR;* which means "Indication of Regulated Provenance," with four classifications that apply to all wines except Port:

- ***Vinho de Mesa:*** Ordinary or table wine.
- ***Vinho Regional*** (VR): At least 85 percent of the grapes used to make this wine are of the same varietal and harvested in the same year from the same region.
- ***Vinho de Qualidade Produzi en Regiao Detterminada*** (VQPRD): An intermediate classification, indicating a fine wine that is "just beneath" the top level.
- ***Denominacao de Origem Controlada*** (DOC): The top classification for Portuguese wines, indicated by a printed seal across the bottleneck (much like a *strip stamp*).

Portugal also classifies its winemaking regions much like the rest of Europe. The top wine-producing regions are the Douro (named for the Douro River, which in neighboring Spain is called the *Duero*), the Dao of Central Portugal (known for its reds), and the Minho (the largest region, known for white wines). The newest wine region, called both *Setubal* and *Terras de Sado,* has led the way in modernization of the wine industry. More than 30 varietals are grown there.

Wines from Chile

Rounding out the top-ten list of wine-producing countries is Chile, which exports 60 percent of the wine it makes even though the Chilean government does not cover any of the marketing or exporting fees.

For the most part Chile grows the same varietals as the United States, including Sauvignon Blanc, Chardonnay, Cabernet Sauvignon, and Merlot. Chile also has a beautiful blending grape, Carmenere, a rare varietal that was probably transplanted from Bordeaux. Some excellent and extremely low-priced varietals are Chilean.

The wineries have been busy in the last decade, ripping out unproductive vines and planting new, more marketable grape varieties—so much so that now the worry is when these new areas come into production, there will not be enough processing or storage facilities to handle the volume. Foreign investors have taken notice and are making deals. Concha y Toro, one of the largest and best-known Chilean wine corporations, teamed up with France's famous Bordeaux producer Mouton Rothschild under the label *Almaviva.*

Wines from Other Countries

You may have to look a little harder to find them, but wines from many other countries make it onto ethnic wine lists or the shelves of savvy wine merchants. New Zealand, with a climate considerably cooler than that of its neighbor Australia, has released some crisp Sauvignon Blancs to world acclaim in recent years; its Chardonnay and Pinot Noir are also worth trying. At least four Canadian provinces have wineries; Canada's best-known viticulture region is British Columbia, which has many of the same attributes as its Pacific Northwest neighbors.

These are just two examples. In the past few years the EU has added six wine-growing nations to its roster of member-states: the Czech Republic, Cyprus, Hungary, Malta, Slovenia, and Slovakia. Chances are that you have never tasted a Slovakian wine, but you might have seen the hearty Egri Bikaver, or "Bulls Blood," a first-rate, bargain-priced Hungarian red wine that occasionally makes it to the supermarket shelf. If you're curious about these wines, first-hand knowledge is as close as the bottle and your corkscrew.

In the following chapter you will continue your quest for wine knowledge by learning to create a profitable wine list and by-the-glass program, and to correctly serve wine to your guests for their enjoyment.

SUMMING UP

Wine appreciation begins with tasting the product and learning to distinguish what flavors and winemaking styles you enjoy. There are no rights or wrongs when it comes to wine preferences. This chapter introduced the major grape varietals used around the world and to the winemaking process. Grapes are picked, crushed, and fermented. Yeast is added to the crushed grapes, and as it feeds on the sugar in the grapes, it creates alcohol and carbon dioxide. When fermentation stops, the wine is stored until it stabilizes and settles, then the storage process continues in stainless-steel or oak casks, depending on the type of wine and the desired results. In sparkling wine or Champagne the carbon dioxide is captured in the wine bottle instead of being released into the air, making the wine naturally bubbly. The chapter also summarized an ongoing controversy about the use of natural-cork and synthetic bottle closures.

No matter where wines are made, all wine labels identify the producer, the year in which the grapes were picked (the vintage), and the type of grapes used (the varietal). The percentage of alcohol must also be included on the label. However, a label can reveal only so much. You have to open the bottle and taste the wine. Tasting wine involves much more than sipping it. You should look at the wine, swirl it around inside the glass, and smell it. The swirling motion enables a bit of the alcohol to dissipate, making the aromas inside the glass more intense.

Wines are named for their grape varietal (Chardonnay or Sauvignon Blanc); given a generic name (such as Meritage or Table Wine) that signifies a blend of several different types of grapes; or labeled with the name of a prestigious producer (such as Opus One or Tinto Pesquera). In some countries, a wine's place of origin is used on the label (such as Condrieu or Chateau Margaux); this might be a town or the winery name.

The chapter ended with descriptions of the wine industries, primary growing regions, and most popular grape varietals in the top-ten wine-producing countries in the world.

POINTS TO PONDER

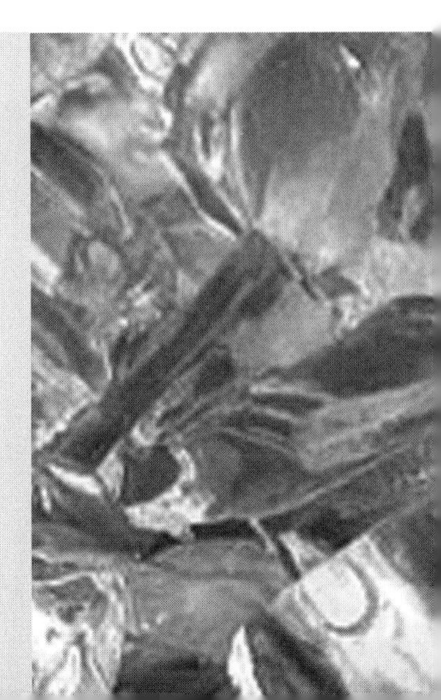

1. What are the four basic factors that go into making any type of wine? (Discussion questions: Which of these four factors do you think is the most important, and why? Which is the least important, and why?)
2. What does a wine's vintage tell you? Is the vintage date related to the quality of the wine? If so, how?
3. What do the skins of the grape have to do with the final wine product?

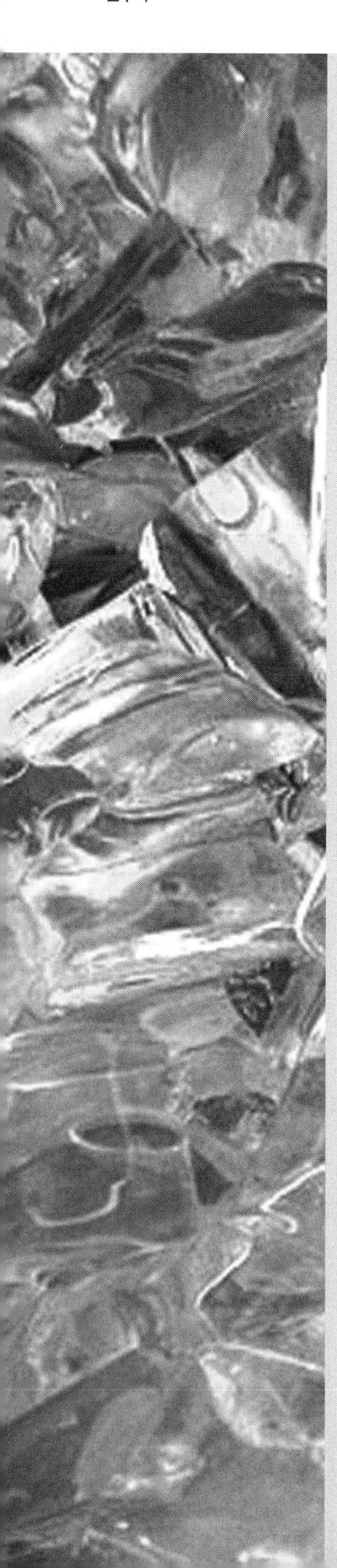

4. How does Champagne production differ from still-wine production?
5. Why do winemakers sometimes blend different types of grapes?
6. Why do you swirl a wine before tasting it?
7. List two things that you can learn from the color of a wine.
8. Name and briefly describe four wine characteristics that you examine when you taste it.
9. Where do you stand on the controversy about natural corks versus screwtops and synthetic plastic closures?
10. What information should you be able to learn from most wine labels, no matter what the wines' country of origin?

TERMS OF THE TRADE

Alberino
aperitif wine
aroma
aromatized
balance
Barolo
blush wine
Chablis
chapitalization
Chardonnay
Charmat bulk process
Chenin Blanc
Chianti
claret
classified growth
Cream sherry dessert wine
Fino
Flor
Fumé Blanc
Gamay Beaujolais
Gewurztraminer
glycerin
Grand Cru
Graves
Grenache
Lambrusco
lees
legs
Marsanne
Merlot
Methode Champenoise
monopole
Mourvedre
Muller-Thurgau
Muscat
Nebbiolo
palomino
Pinot Blanc
Pinot Grigio
Pinot Gris
Pinot Noir
Pouilly-Fuissé
Pouilly-Fumé
Premier Cru
Riesling
sake
Sancerre
Sangiovese
Sauternes
Sauvignon Blanc
Sekt
Semillon
Shiraz
Solera
Spumante
suberin oak
sulfites
Syrah
tannins
Tempranillo
2, 4, 6 Trichloroanisole (TCA)
varietal
vintage
Viognier
Zinfandel

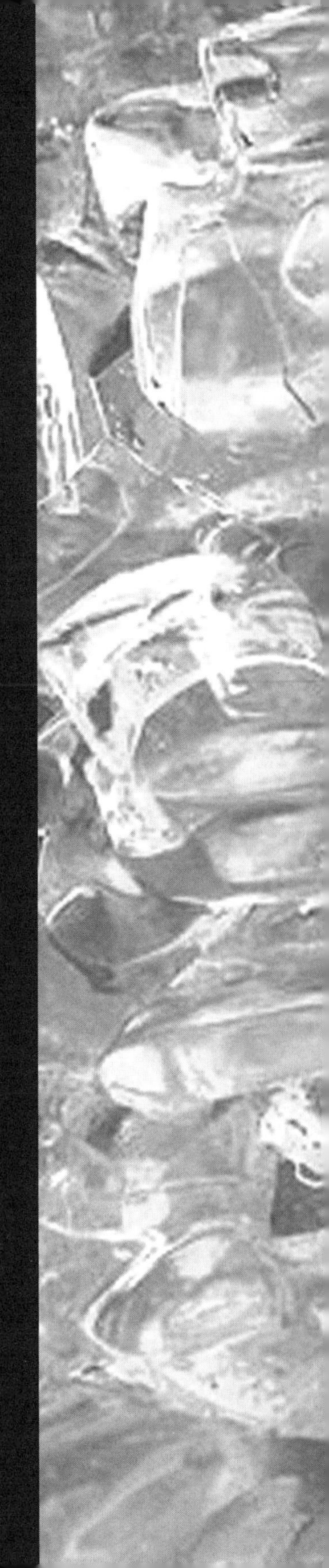

CHAPTER 7
WINE SALES AND SERVICE

Now that you have been introduced to the world of wine, the fun is just beginning. Many bar businesses focus primarily on liquor and draft-beer sales, but that's like leaving money on the table. By adding an interesting variety of wines to your lineup and training staff members to suggest, serve, and store them, you can create a wine program that can become a lucrative part of your business.

You've already learned that while most people are not wine connoisseurs, they expect wine to taste good, to complement their food choices, and to be a good value. In addition, today people do not buy only wines with which they are already familiar. They just need a bit of information and encouragement to try something new. Creating an interesting and profitable wine-sales program begins with understanding your designated clientele and market.

THIS CHAPTER WILL HELP YOU . . .

- Create a wine list by selecting and pricing the wines you want to sell.
- Train your service staff to recommend and serve wines.
- Increase your wine sales.
- Open and store wine properly.

CREATING A WINE LIST

Of course we are suggesting that you include wines as part of your beverage line-up! But when it comes to creating a wine list, a bar owner should first ask, "Do I *need* a wine list at all for my establishment?" Naturally we suggest that you include wines in your beverage lineup. Many casual and midpriced bars and restaurants serve only a few house wines by the glass or carafe and make a very good profit in this uncomplicated and inexpensive way. Usually they offer four to six wine choices with familiar names and general appeal—a short enough list to print on a table tent. This simple selection, typically offered along with an assortment of beer and soft drinks, is very appropriate for certain types of dining situations.

If you are going to sell wines by the bottle, you have four initial considerations: clientele, concept, cuisine, and price compatibility. Let's examine them individually.

- The bar's clientele will dictate the overall character of the wine list. You can keep it short, simple, and inexpensive; make it extensive, expensive, and loaded with prestigious choices; or settle somewhere in between. Will you sell by the bottle, by the carafe, by the glass? You have to know your target customers before you can make the basic decisions about what they will expect and how much they are willing to pay for it.
- The concept will set the tone for many critical details: how much of the wine is domestic versus imported and how esoteric the choices are; whether the list is a book, a sheet, a chalkboard, a table tent, and how it is worded; what types of glassware are required; and how extensively the servers must be trained, to name a few.
- Concept and cuisine go hand in hand. Consider the restaurant business: If fine French cuisine is served, clearly fine French wines are appropriate, although a few additional choices will make for a well-rounded and more interesting list. A steak house would list mostly red wines, with a few hearty whites and a couple of rosés for people who want alternatives. If seafood is the specialty, you'd feature white wines, with perhaps one or two light reds to go with salmon, perhaps a Beaujolais from France or a Pinot Noir from Oregon. A sparkling wine or two is always appropriate for special occasions. In a bar the focus may or may not be on food—but you certainly will serve *some* food, and the wine selection should complement it.
- Price compatibility means that the wine choices should suit not only the types of food you will serve, but also the other components of concept, the average check, and the price ranges of other food and beverage items. If each and every wine by the glass costs $2 more than the most popular mixed drinks or any of the appetizers, don't be surprised if you don't sell much wine. In restaurants optimal sales result when the wine costs make up approximately one-fourth of the average check. This does not mean that every wine must fall into a specific price range; you can safely offer wines in several price ranges.

Another point to consider is availability. Will you invest in a large stock that "sits on cash" in the cellar until it is sold or will you get regular selections in small quantities from your supplier? You don't want to print a list that will soon be full of wines you can no longer obtain. If you are just beginning to offer wine as part of your service, it is better to start with a short list of readily available wines, including a sparkling wine—say, 15 to 20 brands altogether—and to buy frequently, a little at a time, until you find out what sells. A long wine list does not necessarily generate more sales than a short one, and it requires more training and teamwork on the part of your staff. It is easy to add to your list but difficult to get rid of a wine that customers don't seem to care for. For most bar businesses, a limited, moderately priced wine list ensures favorable sales and regular inventory turnover.

Speaking of inventory, your final consideration—and a major one—will be storage. No matter how small your selection, you will need to have a separate room (ideally, a cellar) to stock cases of it, depending on your needs. Wines should never be stored in a restaurant kitchen, where the average temperature is too hot: They can age too quickly, and wines served too warm are a turnoff for most customers.

If you want a wine list befitting an upscale image and a knowledgeable clientele, it is essential that you find an expert to help you develop your list and advise you on purchasing. Critical factors to consider are the cellar space needed and the capital that must be invested. If space and funds are limited, wines that mature early and are ready to drink right now are the best choices. Taste the wines you are considering for your list, and ask your servers to taste them, too. This will greatly increase your servers' interest in selling wines if they have been included in the selection process. Most suppliers will arrange comparative tastings, at least of moderately priced wines. You might hold a wine tasting for a group of regular customers to seek their opinions on new items. In short use more than just your own tastes and preferences as you decide which wines to sell.

List Mapping

Greg Harrington is a Master Sommelier who has held wine director positions with B. R. Guest Restaurants, Wolfgang Puck Fine Dining, Emeril Lagasse Restaurants, and Square One. Harrington sought to make the wine-buying process more objective by creating a concept that he calls *list mapping* to develop a pricing structure for a wine list.

"When I hear guests say a list is 'expensive,' " says Harrington, "most are referring not to the restaurant's markup but to the wine prices in relation to the restaurant's concept and average check. List mapping is the system I use to counter this perception." He uses restaurants in his explanation of the system, but the concept would also work for a bar and makes a great deal of sense. Now a winemaker at Gramercy Cellars in Walla Walla, Washington, Harrington gave us permission to share his system for balancing a wine list by price and style, as he explained it in the June 2004 issue of *Santé* magazine.

Step 1: Develop the Average Bottle Price Range. Begin with the average price of the entrees on the menu. Let's use $20 as an example. Multiply the average entrée price by two. This number ($40) represents the lowest price range, by the bottle, of the wines that should dominate the list. Next, add the average price of the entrée to this number for the higher price range of the wines that should dominate the list. For this hypothetical restaurant, the bulk of the wine list should be between the $40 to $60 (per bottle) range. Of course the list should have selections lower and higher, but at least 35 to 45 percent of the selections should be in this range. And the majority of the list should be in the "sweet spot," which is about $20 lower to $20 higher than the calculated range. The allocation would look something like this:

Price	*Percentage of List*
$20–$40	20%
$40–$60	45%
$60–$80	15%
$80–$100	15%
$100+	5%

Step 2: Split the List Between White and Red Selections. This is a very subjective calculation, which will change with the concept. I try to split the list between 35 percent white and 65 percent red with most of my programs. Seafood-dominant restaurants may be as high as 50/50 white to read, while steak houses may trend toward 25/75 white to red.

Step 3: Select Each Wine Type and Price, Creating a Map of the Program. I find that the smaller the list, the more important mapping it becomes. As an example, let's use a casual concept restaurant with a 100-bottle wine list and a $20 average entrée price. We'll plan to purchase 35 white wines and 65 red wines. This is how I would map out the white wine section:

Price	*Percentage of List*	*Selection*
$20–$40	20%	7
$40–$60	45%	16
$60–$80	15%	5
$80–$100	15%	5
$100+	5%	2

Once the mapping is complete, I select the types of white wine for the list. An example:

California Chardonnay (7)	Sauvignon Blanc (5)	White Burgundy (6)	Riesling (5)
_____ $20–$40	_____ $20–$40	_____ $40–$60	_____ $20–$40
_____ $20–$40	_____ $40–$60	_____ $40–$60	_____ $40–$60
_____ $40–$60	_____ $40–$60	_____ $60–$80	_____ $40–$60
_____ $40–$60	_____ $60–$80	_____ $80–$100	_____ $60–$80
_____ $60–$80	_____ $80–$100	_____ $100+	
_____ $80–$100			
_____ $100+			

Italian White (4)	Miscellaneous (4)	Spanish White (2)	Rhone Varietals (2)
_____ $20–$40	_____ $20–$40	_____ $20–$40	_____ $40–$60
_____ $40–$60	_____ $40–$60	_____ $40–$60	_____ $40–$60
_____ $40–$60	_____ $40–$60		
_____ $60–$80	_____ $40–$60		

Step 4: Select the Actual Wines from Your Suppliers. Note that list mapping forces you to consider the entire list. Make sure that you are also balancing the price selection in each price category. For example, in the $40 to $60 category, don't select wines that will all sell for $58.

List mapping provides the wine buyer with a solid plan and ensures a balanced, well-priced list. After the initial lists are developed I provide wine-list maps for my buyers at each B. R. Guest restaurant. When a restaurant runs out of a wine the buyer may replace it with a selection of the same category, which allows for buyer input and creativity while still adhering to the structure imposed by the list map.

Matching Wine with Food

Andrea Immer, a Master Sommelier, as well as an author and longtime beverage director, calls wine "a love letter to food." Why? Acidity, which is a natural characteristic of wine, primes the customer's taste buds for food. In cooking, this is why so many chefs use acidic ingredients, such as mustard, lemon, tomato, and vinegar. They enhance other flavors and work well to increase our enjoyment of food.

Food and wine consumed together should "marry" well. This means that the two should be in balance; neither should dominate the other. Each should bring out different flavors in the other, and the combination should taste better than either one alone, thereby multiplying the total enjoyment. The wrong combination can diminish the food or the wine or both.

Figure 7.1 lists traditional guidelines for serving wine with food. Overall they are sound, but it is hard to apply them in individual situations because today's menu items often blend so many different spices, flavors, and ethnic styles that rules are hard to make—and even harder to follow. Furthermore one dry white wine or one hearty red wine might differ widely from another. The next step is to provide the necessary balance.

WHICH WINE WITH WHICH FOOD? STARTING POINTS

Menu Item	Wine Suggestion[a]
Appetizer	Champagne, dry white wine, dry sherry
Salad	No wine
Fish or seafood	Dry or medium-dry white
Beef	Hearty red
Lamb	Hearty red
Veal	Light red or full-bodied white
Ham or pork	Dry or medium-dry white or rosé
Turkey, duck, chicken	Full-bodied white or light red
Game (venison, pheasant, wild duck)	Hearty red
Lasagna, spaghetti, pizza	Hearty red
Cheeses, full-flavored	Hearty red,[b] sweet white (with roquefort)
Cheeses, mild	Sherry, port, madeira, mild table wines of any type
Desserts, pastries, fruits, mousses	Semisweet sparkling wine, sweet white table wine

[a]The diner's choice takes precedence. If more than one wine is to be served, the general rules are white before red, light before hearty, and dry before sweet.

[b]Some experts disagree.

FIGURE 7.1

The only way to determine how to match a wine to a given menu item is to taste the two together. If possible, from the beginning, plan your wine list with the food choices for your bar business, even if they are all appetizers rather than traditional main courses and side dishes. Sit down with your wine expert and taste each item on your menu with wines that the expert suggests. Include your kitchen staff and servers, too. They are part of your sales team, whether they are behind the scenes or interacting with customers.

If you already have a wine list you can pick the best matches from what you have, adding new wines if you discover that you need to.

Presenting Wine Selections

The wine list is a silent salesperson for your wine, just as your menu is for your food. There are several formats for presenting wine choices to customers. The chalkboard is the simplest; it is typically used in wine bars, especially for wines by the glass. It has a nice air of continental informality and gives the impression that you pay daily personal attention to the wine menu. The advantage of the chalkboard is that you don't have to make long-range commitments in print. You can take full advantage of your wine suppliers' sales and discounts and feature these wines on your board.

The **table tent** has similar advantages. It is appropriate in informal restaurants serving only a few wines. It can also be used to promote specials or new offerings. Just be sure that your servers are familiar with the selections, no matter how quickly they change.

For larger wine selections, a printed list should be available. It is given to one person at the table, usually the host, since wine by the bottle is typically ordered for the whole party. A printed list comes in two common formats: a printed card, or *carte,* similar to a menu, or pages folded inside a nice-looking cover. The latter format has several advantages: You can change the inside pages easily as your offerings change, reusing the more expensive cover. This type of list is often easier for the diner to handle than a single, oversized card. Also, depending on your state laws, your wine supplier might provide you with the permanent cover or even pay for the printing of the inner pages. We don't recommend this cozy arrangement, which normally comes with a promise (from you) to give the supplier a certain (substantial) percentage of your business. Today's computers and printers make it extremely easy to print your own lists, changing them as often as you need to, or to highlight daily specials or food/wine pairings.

What your wine list says about your wines should be clear, honest, and useful. It should include key information relevant to making a choice, and this is where opinions differ among enophiles. Historically wine lists have been grouped by varietal, by country or region, and/or by type, including reds, whites, rosés, sparkling wines, and dessert wines. "California Whites," for example, might further be listed in descending order from the driest to the sweetest. But today's trend is to be brief, clever, and descriptive, using the wine list—both the way it is arranged and the way individual wines are described—to represent in simple terms how a server might respond if someone asked, "What's this wine like?"

In short the idea is to impart a very brief description of each wine's chief characteristics. In addition to the category names, a single line on the list can instantly inform anyone who reads it. Is it dry, slightly sweet, or truly sweet; delicate, medium, or intense in flavor; light-, medium-, or full-bodied? Today, there's no reason the wording should be pretentious. Your wine list should show imagination and enthusiasm; it should make the whole subject of wine simple and inviting, not formidable and exclusive. The categories can be as fun or daring as your clientele and concept will allow. The following are some examples that we've noted recently:

- At Ten Steak and Sushi, a Providence, Rhode Island, restaurant, headings for each wine category are amusingly based on stereotypical women: "Crazy Mixed-Up Redheads" are blended wines and red Bordeaux; "Voluptuous Blondes" are big, fruity, oaky California Chardonnays; and wine flights are known as "Menage à Trois."

- Commune, a restaurant in Manhattan, has four basic headings on its list: "White," "Rose," "Red," and "Champagne & Sparkling"; they are further categorized, for example, as "Aromatic & Floral" and "Savory & Exotic" (for whites), and "Deep & Lavish" and "Soft & Sumptuous" (for reds).
- Tribeca Grill, also in New York City, includes a page of "Dave's Picks," sommelier David Gordon's personal favorites, on its wine list. (You could ask each of your servers to choose a favorite wine and list all of them with brief explanations for their choices.) There is also a page called "Wines of the Century," listing some of the world's great wines. Because these wines are incredibly expensive and would be attractive only to the most wine-knowledgeable customers, this page contains a full paragraph of explanation about each wine.

Hire a writer with some wine knowledge (and, perhaps, a sense of humor), research the wine publications and experts' descriptions, and ask your suppliers to help create wording that will make the wines sound as good as they taste. Mention the foods that each wine complements. You must include all of the essential information that will establish a wine's pedigree only if you are catering to connoisseurs.

Even if your wine list is relatively small, a **bin number** for each wine can precede its name on the list. Numbering the wines serves three important purposes. First it makes it easier to organize and inventory the wines in your storage area. Bartenders and servers can locate wines more quickly. Also it spares customers embarrassment if the wine is unfamiliar to them or if its name is hard to pronounce. Figure 7.2 is a simple but nicely developed wine list, with the wines chosen, annotated, numbered, and priced with customers in mind.

Before you print your wine list check everything carefully and be sure that all items on it are spelled correctly. Your computer's spell-checking program is almost worthless in the world of wine. When you're in doubt look at the labels! If your list contains misspellings your credibility is shot, especially with knowledgeable customers.

By-the-Glass Programs

We believe that it is mandatory for bars and restaurants to offer some wines by the glass (BTG), as well as by the bottle. Often one customer or a couple would rather buy one or two glasses of wine than a full bottle they might not finish. Wine by the glass is also a good option for people eating together but who prefer different wines. Perhaps most important, BTG sales can prompt people to experiment, to try new and perhaps more expensive wines than they would usually buy. If they like it, they will buy it again, perhaps by the bottle. Wines by the glass can also be very profitable (see the next section on pricing wines).

A good, basic BTG program should be diverse. The whole point of it is to be able to change it frequently in order to take advantage of sale items offered by wine distributors and to control your inventory, which means to introduce new wines or move wines that, by the bottle, have not been selling very well. You can also

WHITES

BIN #		Bottle
101	**Kenwood Sauvignon Blanc** Assertive citric flavors make this a great accompaniment for most foods.	24.00
102	**DeLoach Chardonnay** Dry, with soft, fruit flavors and a lingering finish.	26.00
103	**Penfold's Chardonnay** Light and fruity, with tropical undertones and a flowery bouquet.	28.00
104	**Dr. Burklin-Wolf Estate Riesling** Ripe apple flavors; a white with depth and a strong finish.	30.00
105	**R.H. Phillips Viognier** Smell this wine! Fresh, vibrant bouquet and strong fruit flavors set it apart.	26.00
106	**Clerget Pouilly Fuisse** A classic French-style Chardonnay; austere and rich.	35.00
107	**Cavit Pinot Grigio** Fresh, light, and palate-pleasing; a "summer-style" white.	22.00

BLUSH WINES

201	**Sutter Home White Zinfandel** Fruity, pretty salmon color; perfect with lighter dishes.	17.00
202	**Bonny Doon Vin Gris ("Pink Wine")** A dry, food-style Rosé with a whimsical finish.	22.00

RED WINES

301	**Hess Select Cabernet Sauvignon** Rich Flavors with cedar overtones; classic Napa style.	24.00
302	**Newlan Merlot** A subtle red wine with finesse; layers of flavor.	37.00

RED WINES (continued)

BIN #		Bottle
303	**Ravenswood Vintner's Blend Zinfandel** Good body and nice raspberry flavors; strong finish.	28.00
304	**Saintsbury Pinot Noir Garnet** Soft, earthy flavors; great choice for wild game or fish.	32.00
305	**Chateau Bel Air (Haut Medoc)** A classic French Claret; soft, rich, and flavorful.	32.00
306	**Georges du Boeuf Beaujolais Villages** A light, fruity, good-natured, all-purpose red.	22.00
307	**Rosemount Shiraz** A full-bodied but soft red from Australia.	26.00
308	**Lorinon Crianza Rioja** Spain's classic Tempranillo grape; spicy and earthy.	24.00
309	**Antinori Chianti** An Italian standard; peppery and tangy; lingering finish.	27.00

SPARKLING WINES

401	**Mont Marcal Cava NV** Spain's Methode Champenoise sparkler; bright and fun.	20.00
402	**Korbel Brut NV** California's most popular sparkling wine.	24.00
403	**Moet & Chandon White Star** An elegant, semi-dry French Champagne.	37.00

HOUSE WINES

By the glass		*By the bottle*
$7	**Leaping Lizard (Sonoma, CA)** Chardonnay, Merlot, Cabernet	20

FIGURE 7.2 A wine list for a moderately priced restaurant.

WHAT MAKES A WINNING WINE LIST?

Restaurant Hospitality magazine conducts an annual "Best Wine List in America" competition. Entries are sorted by size and category, and they are eliminated immediately if poorly written or contain what the judges term "serious technical flaws." The 2003 panel of judges explained what they look for in a great wine list as follows:

- ***Overall wine selection.*** "We were looking for lists that chose the best examples in any given style and price point. We wanted to see a thoughtful selection of quality wines, and not a wine list driven by price point and category decisions."
- ***Variety in style and brands.*** "We were looking for diverse lists with a wide selection of styles, producers, and regions. (One restaurant had a large selection of wines by the glass—all from one winery and its "family" of imported wines. Sweetheart deals with one supplier are not in the interest of the consumer.)"
- ***Fair pricing and value options.*** "We looked at each list to see if the pricing was fair for the consumer, with reasonable markups taken. (We took into consideration the higher prices and excessive taxes that restaurants face in some states.) We also looked at each list to see if there were a few inexpensive but decent alternatives for price-conscious diners."
- ***Compatibility with the menu.*** "A wine list with a focus on great big Cabernets can be awe-inspiring, but it is strangely out of place in a fish house. No matter how large the list, each and every wine should be chosen because it complements the restaurant's food, and for no other reason."
- ***Presentation.*** "Your wine list speaks for your restaurant. Make sure that it is neat, well organized, and readable."
- ***Extras.*** "Wines from unique regions, availability of half-bottles, tasting notes, and other well-thought-out extras were noted and awarded points."
- ***Overall impression.*** "A good wine list should encourage consumers to explore new wines. It should be interesting to read. Ultimately, we were looking for creativity and imagination. A boring wine list is not a great wine list."

Judges on the 2003 panel also noted that large wine suppliers had an all-too-obvious role in influencing or co-writing many of the lists: "Many lists offered wines from only two or three major importers or companies," they observed. "Limiting . . . wine selections from just a few sources deprives consumers of the myriad choices and experiences the highly diverse U.S. wine market provides."

Source: "Class in a Glass," *Restaurant Hospitality* magazine, © Penton Media, Inc., Cleveland, Ohio, May 2003.

pair the wines with daily food specials. The selection does not have to be extensive: four reds, three whites, two rosés (a dry and a sweet), and one Champagne or sparkling wine might be sufficient. You can build from there depending on your customers' wine knowledge and budget.

Upscale bars and restaurants have fun with some inventive BTG ideas. Some stock a small number of very prestigious vintages to sell by the glass, with the theory that their customers would love to try a glass, even at $20 or more, but probably would not splurge on a full bottle that costs $100 or more. Another way to acquaint customers with your full-bottle choices (or to test wines before you put them on the regular list) is to offer *wine flights*. These are two-ounce "tastes" of three or four different wines, priced from, say, $9 to $15, depending on the wines. Wine flights create a little more work for servers, but they are an excellent educational tool, both for the customer and the bar.

Plan the program so that all BTG pours are used within two days. If you can't use a bottle within two days, your servers are not doing enough to sell it. Partially used bottles should be refrigerated at the end of the day and, if your BTG business is brisk enough to warrant it, the bar should most definitely invest in wine-storage tools that keep wines fresh by displacing the oxygen in partially used bottles. (These are discussed later in this chapter.)

Pricing Wines

For years the standard wine markup in the industry for bars and restaurants has been "2.5," which means that you can charge 2½ times what you paid to purchase the bottle from the supplier. For example, you would charge $15 for a bottle that cost you $6. Some establishments, including country clubs, private clubs, and fancy restaurants in big cities, have gotten away with charging three times the wholesale cost, or even a bit more. That $6 bottle of wine would cost $18 or $20 at such places. These businesses have justified the percentages by citing their additional inventory and labor costs for storing and serving the wines, glassware, and so on.

Today the "automatic 2.5" tradition is changing, albeit slowly. Most customers know enough about wines to be well aware that when they dine out, they pay far more than the price of the same wine at their local supermarket or warehouse-club store. They are also starting to ask, "Why is this necessary?" Indeed the practice can seem like price-gouging. So a few forward-thinking restaurants and bars are striving to make wines a better value by simply doubling each bottle's wholesale cost. This amounts to a 100-percent profit per bottle, which is still a healthy figure. We know of at least one restaurant that makes things even simpler, adding a flat $15 to the wholesale cost. These establishments claim that the increased volume of wine sold more than makes up for the slightly lower prices.

For wines sold BTG the simplest way to price is to divide the price that you are charging for the bottle on your wine list by four, since you will pour four glasses from each bottle. However, some bar owners and restaurateurs feel that it is only fair to charge a bit more for the general hassle of offering individual glasses. Their aim is to pay for the entire bottle with the sale of the first glass. The other three glasses are pure profit. Of course wine sales improve tremendously when prices are reasonable. There should be a few BTG bargains (under $6), although today's upscale bars have no trouble selling $7 to $9 glasses of wine. The whole idea is to prompt the guest to try it.

Pricing for a higher-end wine list might not be so closely tied to menu pricing since wine enthusiasts are more likely to tolerate, and even expect, higher markups on rare and coveted vintages. Then again, pricing wines at markups below the norm will surprise and delight people who know enough to understand the excellent value they are getting, thereby earning you some true customer loyalty.

Finally don't forget to use pricing as a tool to promote your wines. For example, Lambertville Station in Lambertville, New Jersey, makes its slowest night "Wine Appreciation Night." On that night only, wines by the bottle are available at only $1 or $2 more than the wholesale price. This promotion has increased Lambertville Station's Monday-night business by 15 to 20 percent.

THE ROLE OF THE SERVER

Even a great wine list does not sell a great deal of wine by itself. No matter what their level of wine knowledge, most people depend on their server for some guidance. Many customers worry about wasting their money choosing a wine that they might not enjoy, mispronouncing the name, showing their ignorance, and so on. Rather than risk it, they simply avoid it.

If, instead, customers felt that they could comfortably discuss the choices with their server, they might be interested in trying a bottle or, at least, a glass. Unfortunately most servers have their own concerns. They also might be somewhat intimidated by the wine list, or feel uncomfortable opening the bottle at the table, or wonder if they'll know how to answer guests' questions. It all sounds a little like a first date, doesn't it? But for the proprietor, if these concerns go unaddressed, countless opportunities to increase wine sales—and servers' tips—will go unmet.

The solution is to educate bartenders and serving staff about each wine on your list, a process that begins during the hiring process. Include questions about wine knowledge in your employment interviews, and develop a well-organized and ongoing wine-sales training program for your staff. It will enable them to answer customer questions, build their own enthusiasm for selling wine, assist in team-building efforts, and give them a sense of professionalism. When they realize that wine knowledge and sales techniques can increase their tips by $5, $25, or more per shift, they will be eager to know more.

A good training program is carefully planned, scheduled regularly in short sessions (15 or 20 minutes a week), and consistently carried out. It must include tastings and retastings of every wine, as well as wine comparisons. Taste training should include learning to describe each wine in terms of color, degree of sweetness, body, flavor intensity, and other aspects of tasting discussed in Chapter 6. Most wine suppliers are happy to provide both wine samples and instruction—as long as they are given adequate advance notice. You should be involved, too, either as an instructor or as a trainee. Your training sessions should also cover the region of origin of each wine; the meaning of the information on the wine label, especially the vintage date and specific quality category; and the name and characteristics of the grapes from which the wine is made. Talk about which menu items each wine complements and serve sample-sized food portions at the training session. Keep each lesson simple, focusing on no more than two or three wines and a few key points. There is much to be learned, and presenting too much information at a time is discouraging. In addition wine lessons should occasionally cover the very practical business of wine etiquette, including knowing how to open bottles, what to do if a cork breaks, and what to say if a customer rejects a wine. Allow the servers to role-play and practice.

One restaurateur quizzes his staff about what they have learned during their wine sessions and rewards correct answers with scratch-off lottery tickets. The tickets cost him only $1 apiece, but they add a dimension of fun to the learning process.

Increasing Wine Sales

Take wine education another step by adding sales techniques. Any kind of special occasion—a birthday, retirement, engagement, anniversary—calls for the server to suggest a sparkling wine or Champagne. An attentive server who notices the wine levels in customers' glasses, continues to refill them, mentions promptly that the bottle is empty, and says, "Would you care for another bottle, or a glass?" is providing good service and probably boosting sales as well. Selecting a couple of featured wines and mentioning them to just-seated guests will implant a sales suggestion. ("Featured" doesn't necessarily mean lowering prices, just that the wines are of special focus.) If guests decline dessert, your servers should be trained to ask, "Well, then, how about a dessert wine or nice glass of Port?" Consider splitting the staff into teams and running a contest to boost wine sales, with a specific percentage and time frame in mind. Ask the waitstaff to brainstorm with you for new wine-sales ideas.

Many wine suppliers feel that when wine-sales potential goes unrealized in a bar or restaurant, the problem is usually a training issue. Suppliers cite a growing market of customers who are interested in exploring wines, expanding their knowledge about wines, and sampling good food/wine matches. Customers might be drinking less, but they're drinking better—and these are candidates for food-and-wine tasting events, interesting BTG programs, monthly tasting groups, and so on. Events may focus on the food or wine of a particular region, celebrate a special occasion, introduce wines from all over the world, or compare several bottles from a specific winery. Not only can such events be very profitable, they can build customer interest in wine that can pay off in future sales.

These customers might also be intrigued by special wine tastings, which enhance your reputation as a place to enjoy wines. Your suppliers will be happy to help organize a tasting event if there's a visiting winemaker in town, who can preside and instruct. Invite your own customers and entice the general public by contacting your local newspaper and radio stations a couple of weeks in advance of the event. Again, give a theme to the tasting: regional wines, varietal wines, wines from Spain, wines for the holidays. Serve light foods—baguettes, crackers, fruit and cheese—in conjunction with the tasting, with a delicious food-and-wine match as a finale. A "taste" of wine is 1 to 3 ounces per guest per taste, so you should be able to serve 8 to 10 people per 750-ml bottle. Wine by the glass also appeals to this customer group because it enables them to sample a variety of wines in a single evening.

The best way to increase wine sales to all types of customers is to develop your sales personnel. When you train them to know the wines on your list and the foods they accompany, you increase their enjoyment, their professionalism, their enthusiasm, and their value to you as employees—and ultimately your profit margin.

SERVING WINES

Few aspects of the gastronomic experience are as steeped in tradition as wine service. Part of the pomp and circumstance is necessary to present certain wines at their physical best; other parts are strictly showmanship, done for fun or out of respect for tradition. Even the mavericks in the industry, who decry the **decanting** and cork-sniffing that have given formal wine service its stuffy reputation, agree that some wines and occasions warrant special treatment. Also, whether the wine that customers have chosen is an inexpensive BTG wine at the bar or the finest wine in the finest restaurant, they generally expect and appreciate proper wine service.

Wineglasses

One of the "policy decisions" you must make as a bar owner or restaurateur is whether to bring the wineglass to the customer already poured or to place an empty glass in front of the customer and pour as he or she watches. When a wine is brought already poured to the guest, the glass should hold 6 or 7 ounces of wine. The customer might feel cheated if the glass contains less than that because it looks less than full. Ironically, when the wine is poured in the presence of the guest, it is traditional to pour a little less, perhaps 5 ounces, since it is assumed that the customer will want to swirl the wine in the glass.

The basic all-purpose wineglass has an 8- or 9-ounce **bowl,** and is made of clear glass with a long, thin stem and a base. If, however, wine service is going to be a priority in your business, you will probably want to invest in glasses with slightly larger 12-ounce bowls. Even bigger bowls are available—20- to 24-ounces. These

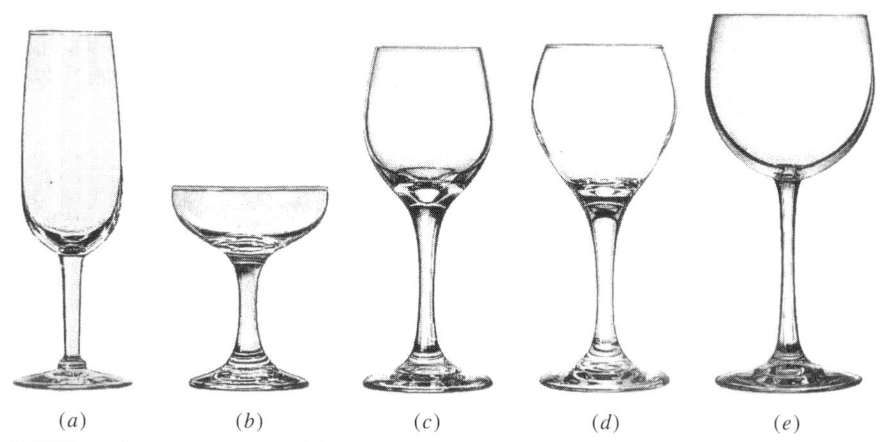

FIGURE 7.3 Types of wine glasses: (*a*) fluted sparkling wineglass, (*b*) champagne bowl, (*c*) white wineglass, (*d*) red wineglass, and (*e*) balloon wineglass.

glasses are showy and expensive, and can be awkward to drink from—but if your concept is upscale, they certainly are distinctive. The reason for a larger glass is *not* to pour more wine per serving, but to allow for better swirling inside the bowl.

You should also consider having at least three different, but very basic, types of wineglasses: for reds, whites, and sparklers. Figure 7.3 shows the difference.

Glasses for reds have larger very rounded bowls to facilitate better swirling and sniffing of the wine. Glasses for whites are narrower at the top, which helps "hold in" their more delicate bouquets. Rosé wines are also usually served in white wineglasses. Tall, thin glasses called **flutes** are appropriate for Champagnes and other sparklers. Their very narrow openings keep them colder longer (sometimes called "saucers") and help to keep the bubbles from dissipating. The wide, flat Champagne goblets that used to be so popular at weddings fell out of favor years ago, but they are making a fun, kitschy comeback in some bars. Our problem with them is that the wine goes flat too quickly.

In addition to the three basic wineglass designs there are many specialty glasses for different types of wine. Dessert wines are served in small after-dinner glasses. These are larger than a liqueur glass but much smaller than an ordinary wineglass, and generally don't have a stem. These glasses hold 4 to 6 ounces, but the serving size is half that. Ports and sherries are served in simple glasses—again, a 4- to 6-ounce size, for a 2- to 3-ounce serving (see Figure 7.4).

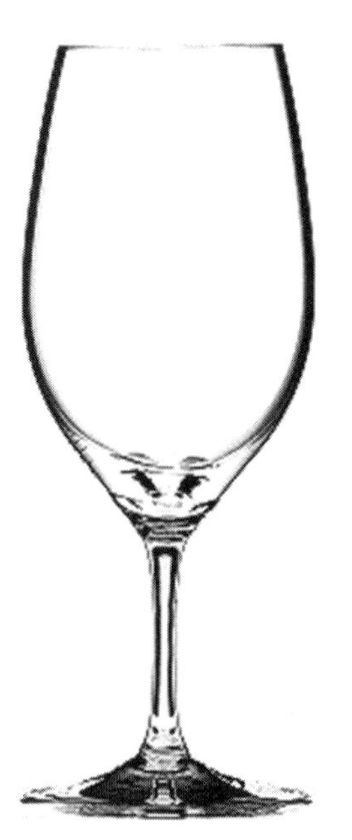

FIGURE 7.4 A port glass.

Serving Wine at Table

Proper table setting for wine service is important, even in a bar, both for etiquette and for efficiency of service. To begin, your glassware should be kept sparkling clean, and staff should hold it by the stem and set it down before the customer in a manner that dignifies wine as the graceful drink it is. The wineglass belongs to

(*a*) (*b*) (*c*)

FIGURE 7.5 Table setting with wineglasses: (*a*) One wine: a single, all-purpose glass. (*b*) Two wines: the white-wineglass at the bottom, to be served first. (*c*) Three wines: an apertif (white) at the bottom right, a white above it for the fish course, a red at left for the entree. If more than three wines are to be served each additional glass is set in place at time of service. Empty glasses are removed. The extra glass at each setting is for water.

the right of the water glass, as shown in Figure 7.5. If setting tables with wineglasses in advance does not fit your image or your clientele, servers should place the glasses in the correct position when the wine is brought to the table. If more than one wine is to be served, for instance, at a formal, multicourse banquet, the wineglasses are arranged in order of service, with the first wine at the right, and each glass is removed at the end of the course that the wine accompanied. Although, as just stated, a wineglass should generally be handled by its stem, a more informal way of carrying it is to hold it upside down by the base, with the stem between the fingers. You can carry as many as four wineglasses in one hand this way. In either case the server should never touch the bowl. In formal service the glasses are brought to the table on a tray held at waist level.

Serving Temperatures

Wine must be served at the right temperature: 45°F to 55°F for white wines and rosés, and 60°F to 65°F for reds. Wines served by the glass or carafe should be prechilled to the proper temperatures. White wines by the bottle should be kept in a cool place and chilled as ordered. This takes 10 to 20 minutes in a **wine chiller.** The most efficient procedure is to place some crushed ice in the bottom of the chiller, put the bottle in, surround it with crushed ice, and add a little water (and some table salt for faster melting if you wish). If you don't have crushed ice, place a layer of cubes in the bottom of the chiller, put the bottle in, add more cubes until the chiller is two thirds full and add cold water. Bring the wine to the table in the chiller. Figure 7.6 shows one of the latest styles in chillers for the table. Some chillers have a separate ice compartment, which prevents the problem of pouring from a wet, and dripping bottle. For truly elegant service, a fine Cham-

FIGURE 7.6 Techonolgy has allowed the sleek tabletop wine chiller to replace the messier ice bucket in most restaurants. Courtesy of Co-Rect Products, Inc., Minneapolis, Minnesota.

pagne or sweet white wine is often served from a tall, silver wine chiller placed beside the host's chair.

It is rare, but not unheard of, for wine to be ordered on the rocks, usually for refreshing wine coolers or wine spritzers. In these cases, the wine may still be served in a wineglass. Fill the glass one third full with ice, then pour the wine over the ice to within about half an inch of the top. If you offer a white wine that sells at a steady, predictable rate, you can keep a one- or two-day supply in the refrigerator, but no wine should be kept chilled for more than a week, and no wine should be put into a freezer. Overly quick chilling might cause it to **throw sediment,** which means to precipitate solids that are in solution. These solids are tiny crystals that drift to the bottom of the bottle and stick to the surface of the cork. The crystals are completely harmless, but some people, aghast that there is something crunchy in their wine, assume that it is shards of glass and, understandably, will refuse to drink the wine. You can try to explain and reassure them, but the customer is within his or her right to refuse a bottle that contains sediment. (We'll discuss the decanting process for older wines that also contain sediment later in this chapter.)

Red wines should never be served at more than 70°F. A fine, expensive red wine should be served at 65°F; younger wines, such as the fruity Beaujolais, can be served a few degrees colder. Sometimes a bit of chilling takes the harsh edge off a thin or rough wine. Sparkling wines should be served well chilled. Sweet white wines should also be served very cold, except for certain German wines, which should not be served below 55°.

The process of opening a bottle of red wine and allowing it to "breathe" a few minutes before pouring is the subject of much wine-snob-related humor. **Breathing** means **aeration,** the act of exposing the wine to air. Red wines do change slightly when exposed to air, and some people feel that giving the wine a minute or two after opening enables these delicate chemical changes to rid the wine of any aroma of mustiness that it might have developed in storage. In fact the wine gets plenty of air as it is poured and while it sits in a wide-mouthed red wineglass, so an extra "breathing" ritual is not necessary.

Presenting the Wine

The ceremony of wine service is one part efficiency and one part showmanship. Seasoned wine drinkers expect a ritual, each of whose steps has a practical reason. These steps are shown in Figure 7.7. With the glasses in place on the table, the server stands near the host (to the right of the host whenever possible) with the bottle of wine. If the bottle is in a chiller, the server removes it from the chiller and wipes it off with a clean napkin. Your server should have a clean, white **service**

(*a*) Showing the bottle to the host.

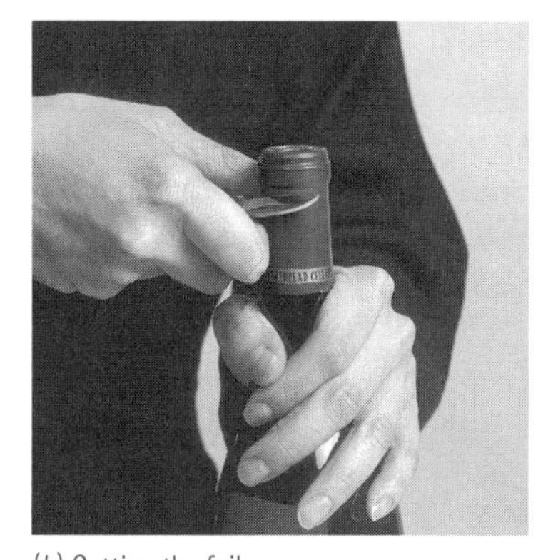

(*b*) Cutting the foil.

(*c*) Removing the top of the foil capsule.

(*d*) Inserting the corkscrew.

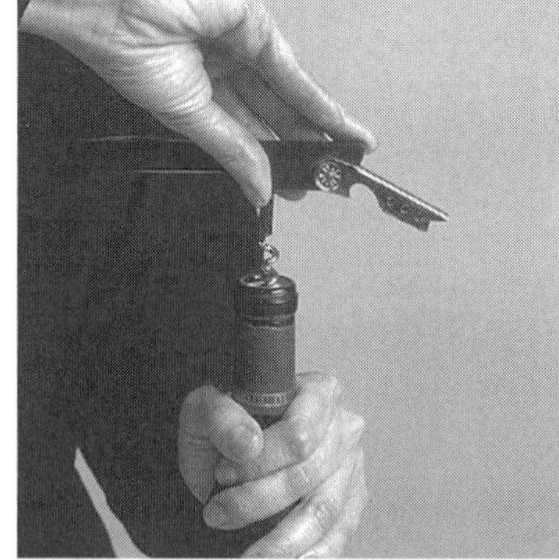

(*e*) Turning the corkscrew.

(*f*) Positioning the corkscrew prongs.

FIGURE 7.7 Wine service. Courtesy of the Culinary Institute of America, Hyde Park, New York.

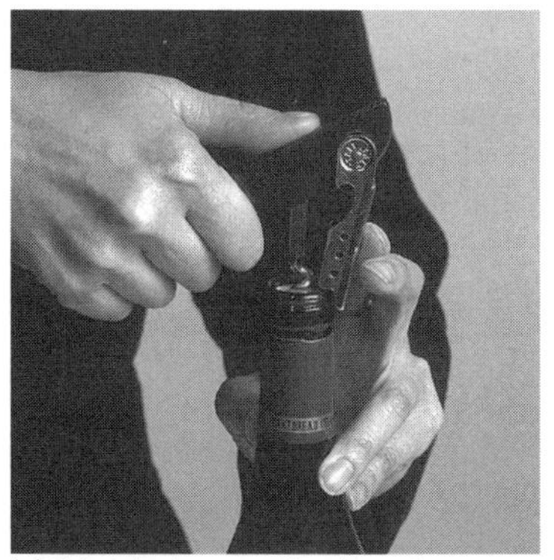
(*g*) Using the lever to raise the cork.

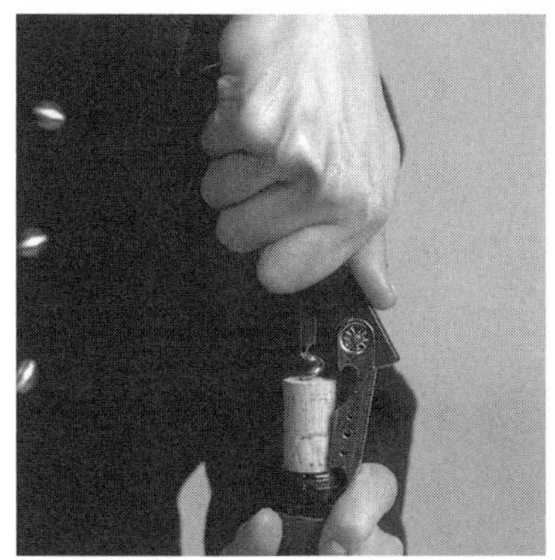
(*h*) Lifting the cork out of the bottle.

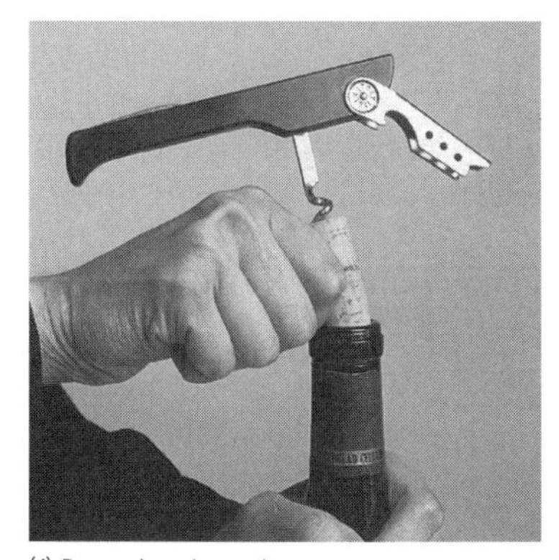
(*i*) Removing the cork.

(*j*) Pouring the wine.

FIGURE 7.7 (*Continued*)

napkin or **serviette** (French for "napkin" or towel) on hand whenever he or she serves wine. The napkin serves several purposes as you'll soon see. The other item that every server should bring to the table is an additional wineglass. You'll learn why in a moment.

Holding the body of the bottle from underneath, with the label toward the host, the server shows the bottle to the host for his or her approval (see Figure 7.7a). (Of course before the server even got to the table, he or she looked carefully at the label to be sure that the wine is indeed what the customer ordered.) Now it's time to open the bottle. With a screwcap closure, of course, the following instructions do not apply; they are only for wines with natural corks or synthetic cork-shaped closures.

The most practical opener is the flat jackknife type, known as a **waiter's friend** or *waiter's corkscrew,* which fits easily into the pocket. Using the blade of the small knife on one side of the opener, the server cuts through the *capsule,* the piece of foil that covers the neck of the bottle (see Figure 7.7b). The server does not remove the entire capsule, just the top part, using the ridge near the lip of the bottle as a guide (see Figure 7.7c). (Note: Some wineries now skip the capsule and use a little circle of plastic or wax instead to seal the very top of the bottle. If that's the case, there is no need to remove it; the server should leave it in place and let the corkscrew go right through it.)

If there is mold around the top of the bottle, the server should simply wipe the cork and the lip of the bottle with his or her napkin; the mold won't hurt the wine. The server then closes the blade, extends the lever at the other end of the corkscrew, and pulls down the corkscrew to form a "T." He or she then inserts the corkscrew with the point slightly off center (see Figure 7.7d) so that the screw, also called an **augur** or **worm**, is directly over the middle of the cork. Keeping the augur completely vertical, the server turns it clockwise until all of it has disappeared into the cork up to the shaft (see Figure 7.7e). Next the server moves the prongs of the lever into position on the rim of the bottle (see Figure 7.7f) and holds the lever firmly in place with his or her thumb. The lever is designed to catch the lip of the bottle, but the server really does need to hold it or it might slip. The server holds the bottle and lever together with a firm, steady pressure and slowly raises the opposite end of the opener (see Figure 7.7g). This brings the cork out of the bottle (see Figures 7.7h and 7.7i). The steady pressure on the lever is most important. Without it, a stubborn cork could cause the lip of the bottle to break. Photos and descriptions of other types of corkscrews are found in Chapter 4.

Now that you know how the wine-serving process is *supposed* to go, let's address potential problems that may occur during the procedure:

- ***What if the cork (or closure) just won't budge?*** To dislodge the cork, the server might need to twist the whole corkscrew back and forth, which should help to loosen a cork with a tight seal.
- ***What if the cork breaks?*** The server removes the top half of the cork, then gently places the screw back inside the bottle and removes the rest of the cork just like he or she did the top half. Working gently prevents pushing the other half of the cork down into the bottle. Some waiters prefer to handle a broken cork away from the table. They apologize, take the bottle away, extract the cork, and bring the bottle back. Servers should handle this as discreetly as possible, remedying the problem and returning quickly with the wine.
- ***What if the server pushes the cork into the bottle?*** This certainly won't hurt the wine, but it's not good form and the wine should not be served that way unless the customers insist that it is acceptable. Most bars and restaurants should have a **cork retriever** on hand (see Figure 7.8). Its long wires are designed to be inserted into the bottle to grab the cork and tighten around it. The idea is to turn the floating cork upright and use the wires to pull it out of the bottle. This process takes some practice, but it works very well. Again, servers should not do this in front of guests! They should apologize and take the bottle away, promising to have it back promptly.

Most of the time, the cork or other closure will come out without any trouble. After removing it the server should wipe the lip of the bottle inside and out with a clean corner of the napkin, remove the augur from the cork, and set the cork down on the table near the host. There is usually no need to present the cork for

FIGURE 7.8 Wine-service tools (counterclockwise from top right): basket or cradle, candle used for decanting wine, wine chiller, decanting funnel, thermometer, sparkling-wine pliers, cork retriever, sparkling-wine cap or preserver, cork retriever, tastevin, thermometer. Courtesy of the Culinary Institute of America, Hyde Park, New York.

an elaborate inspection. Wine lore suggests sniffing the cork to see if the wine has gone bad, but today's experts agree that doing so will not tell you much of anything—except how cork smells. Wine has to be looked at and tasted to determine its quality and condition. The tradition of presenting the cork can be traced to the first half of the twentieth century, when enterprising con artists tried to make money off great European wineries. The empty bottles with their prestigious labels were reused: They were refilled with inferior products and recorked. One way of ensuring the wine was not counterfeit was to check for an original cork, which was always stamped with the winery name or logo.

The next step in the wine-presentation process is to pour about an ounce of wine into the host's glass for tasting and approval (see Figure 7.7j). If a bit of cork falls into this glass, the server should use the spare glass that he or she brought to the table to pour another taste for the host, removing the wine with the cork in it when he or she leaves the table. To prevent drips, the server should twist his or her wrist slightly as the pour is ended and raise the neck of the bottle. When the host has approved the wine, the server pours wine for the other guests first, serving the host last. It is permissible to move counterclockwise around the table, serving from the right if possible. Etiquette suggests pouring women's glasses first, then men's, then the host's—whether the host is male or female. Each glass should not be poured more than half full. The best way to hold the bottle is by the middle of the body, not by the neck. When everyone is served, the wine should be placed on the table near the host or returned to the chiller if it is being served cold. Then the server should take the capsule, the spare glass, and the napkin when leaving the table. As the meal progresses the server should keep an eye on the wineglasses, replenishing them as they are emptied. When white wine is gone, it is customary to put the bottle upside down in the chiller to signal the host that it is empty. Suggestive selling would include a polite question to the host: "May I bring you another bottle?"

Serving Champagne

Because Champagne and other sparkling wines are under great pressure (about 90 pounds per square inch) and the bottles are sealed with special mushroom-shaped corks, they have to be opened and served in a special manner. Champagne is always served well chilled, partly to dull the pressure a bit. The warmer the wine, the more it will fizz and the faster it will lose its effervescence. It is important to handle these bottles gently so as not to agitate the wine. Shaking the bottles only makes them messier to open, which looks fun in the movies but wastes half the contents and flattens the rest of the wine. Figure 7.9 shows how to open a Champagne bottle. First present the bottle for the host's approval (Figure 7.9a). When you remove the foil capsule that covers the top of the bottle, you will find a wire hood called a **cage.** You can remove the foil with the blade on your corkscrew or with your hands. Keep one thumb on the top of the cork (Figure 7.9b) while you untwist the wire fastener that holds the cage on. You can remove the cage (Figure 7.9c), or just loosen it. You don't need a corkscrew to open a Champagne bottle. Keep one hand on the cork. (Some people cover this hand loosely with a clean towel or napkin to prevent the cork from hitting anything if it pops out with force.) With the other hand, hold the bottle at about a 45° angle, pointing it away from the guests—and anything breakable. The reason you tilt the bottle is to give the wine inside as much airspace as possible. This eases pressure and prevents the wine from "exploding" out of the bottle.

Hold the cork steady, and slowly twist the bottle in one direction only, about a quarter turn at a time (see Figure 7.9d). Don't pull on the cork; just hold it firmly and rotate the bottle. The pressure inside the bottle, plus the twisting motion, will ease the cork out gently. It should make a nice "thunk," not an enormous pop-and-spray!

When the cork comes out, hold it close to the bottle and keep the bottle at an angle for at least five seconds before pouring (Figure 7.9e). This equalizes the pressure, letting gas escape without taking the Champagne along with it. But just in case, have a towel and an empty Champagne flute with you. If you happen to have a wild bottle, immediately pour some Champagne and the bottle will stop gushing.

You serve Champagne the way you do other wines: by setting the cork near the host and pouring a taste for the host first. Bubbly is poured in two motions. The first motion brings mostly frothy effervescence (Figure 7.9f). Let the bubbles settle.

(*a*) Presenting the bottle to the host.

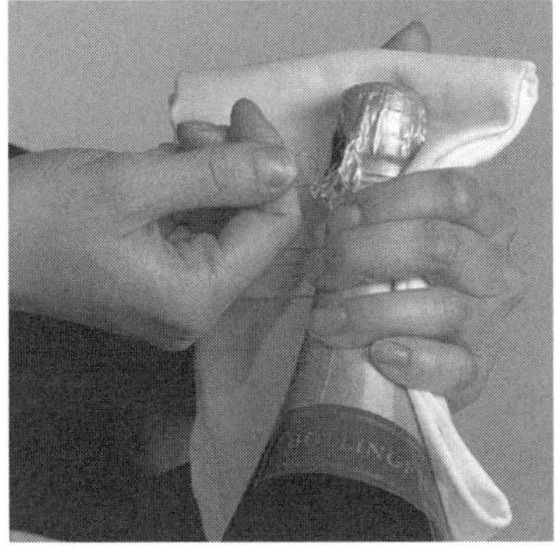

(*b*) Removing the foil capsule.

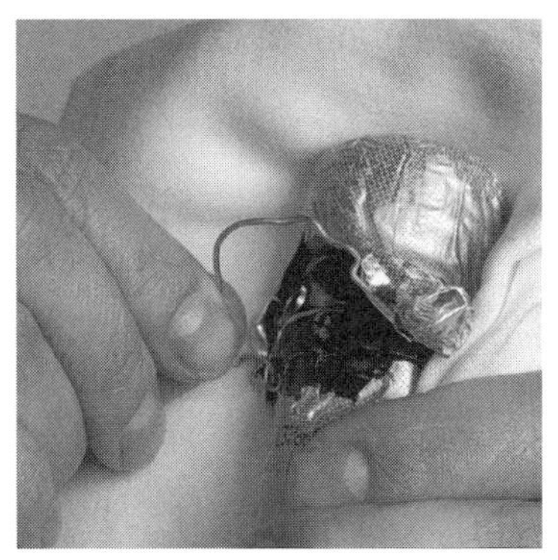

(*c*) Removing the wire cage with one hand on the cork.

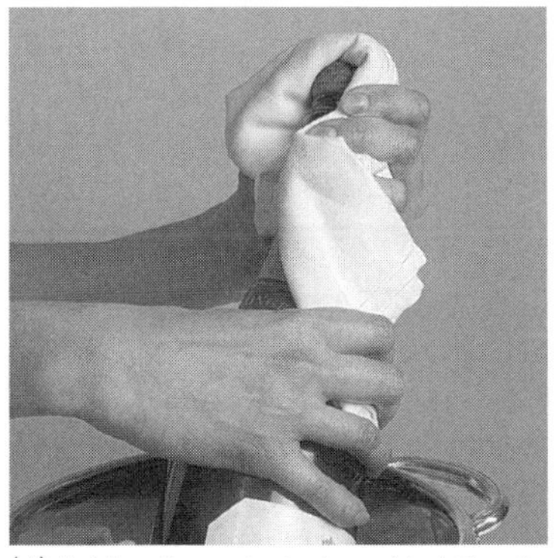

(*d*) Holding the cork steady and twisting the bottle.

(*e*) Holding the bottle at an angle.

(*f*) The first step of pouring, mostly froth.

(*g*) The second step of pouring, more wine than froth.

FIGURE 7.9 Champagne service. Courtesy of the Culinary Institute of America, Hyde Park, New York.

The second pour should slowly fill the glass about two thirds full (Figure 7.9g). When everyone is served, the bottle is put back into the chiller to conserve the bubbles. Remember, sparkling wine should be served to a discerning clientele in a tall, thin, tulip-shaped flute, to better conserve the effervescence and aroma. Do not chill these glasses in advance. The condensation on a chilled glass dilutes the Champagne and dissipates the bubbles more quickly.

Decanting Wines

To **decant** a wine means to pour it out of the bottle and into another container. This is done so that sediment that may have formed inside the bottle stays in the bottle, and so that the wine poured for guests is clear and not clouded by the sediment.

You might be surprised at how many wines benefit from decanting. Generally these include reds that are 10 years or older; rare, older white wines; and vintage-dated Ports. The latter almost always contain sediment; the older the Port, the more sediment it has thrown. "Big" young reds and whites may also be decanted, not because of sediment, but to aerate them before serving.

In case you have not seen the decanting process, you will discover that it involves a bit of romance and tradition. Here's how to do it: First handle the bottle to be decanted very gently. You want to keep the sediment all in one place in the bottle and keep it from mixing with the wine. You can do this in two ways: by standing the bottle up for a day or two before opening it so the sediment all falls to the bottom, or by keeping the bottle on its side, just as it was stored, so the sediment settles on one side of the bottle. (If you remember to store the wine with the label face up, the sediment will fall to the back of the bottle. This is the best position because the customer can see the label when it is time to decant and serve the wine.)

Sometimes the bottle is carried to the table in a special decanting cradle or wine basket, as shown in Figure 7.10. These carriers keep the wine in an almost horizontal position. The wine is not removed from the cradle or basket; you present, open, and decant the while it is still on its side.

You'll need a *decanter,* a clear glass container in which to put the wine, and a lighted candle (see Figure 7.10a). Place the candle just behind the shoulder of the bottle. This bit of extra light is used to see the wine clearly as it passes through the neck. Open the bottle, then pour the wine slowly and steadily in a single motion without stopping, until the candlelight shows sediment approaching the neck of the bottle (Figure 7.10b). The remainder of the wine—only a small amount—is not served, and the clear wine is served from the decanter. Leave both the decanter and the bottle with the guests so that they can still look at the label.

Since only a small proportion of wines served will require decanting, only the **sommelier**, or *wine steward,* or one or two experienced servers need this special training. However, your entire serving staff should at least be familiar with the process and the reason for it, as well as the other routines of wine service.

(*a*)

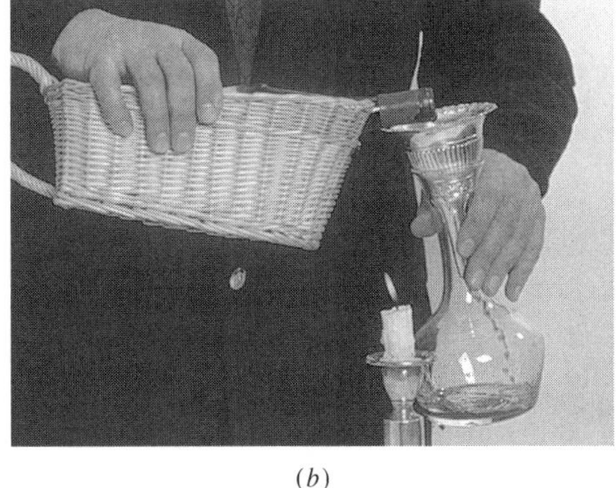

(*b*)

FIGURE 7.10 Decanting wine. The flame is behind the bottle, not touching it. Courtesy of the Culinary Institute of America, Hyde Park, New York.

"Bad" Wine

It's bound to happen; sooner or later, someone will refuse a bottle of wine, claiming even before they taste it that it has an "off" odor or color; or they might send back the wine and not want to pay for it because they tasted it and do not like it. You might as well have a policy that addresses this rare instance. It is customary to replace the bottle of wine with the customer's choice: another bottle of the same wine or a different wine altogether in a similar price range.

The difficult part is just because a customer doesn't happen to like a wine does not make it a "bad" wine. Wine that contains sediment or crystals is not bad, although you might have to explain to some customers that the sediment is a perfectly natural, and harmless, by-product of the wine. In the world of wine service, "bad" usually means that the wine is:

- ***Oxidized.*** Oxygen has gotten into the bottle, and the wine has become musty or even vinegary. **Oxidized** wine looks like air has gotten to it. The color appears dull or brownish, and sometimes the wine smells like dried apples or prunes instead of fresh grapes. This is different from wine that is "old." Oxidized wine is going bad or has already gone bad.
- ***Corked.*** When a wine is **corked,** it contains trichloroanisole (TCA), a harmless but smelly combination of mold, chlorine, and moisture (see Chapter 6, page 246). TCA can impart a moldy, unpleasant taste to the wine. Some people describe it as "wet cardboard," "wet newspaper," or worse.
- ***Maderized.*** This term is not heard as often, but it refers to the fact that a wine smells overly sweet, like a Madeira (hence the name) or Port, when it is not supposed to. Wine that has been exposed to heat or otherwise improperly stored can become **maderized**.

In these cases the wine can taste "just a little bit off" or be absolutely terrible. If the customer is insistent, you might as well offer to replace the bottle. If the customer mentions a possible problem but isn't quite sure, the bar or restaurant owner, the manager, or the sommelier should be summoned to taste the wine and to resolve the problem.

WINE STORAGE

We've already discussed not storing wine in a kitchen or other warm area. Unless it is sake, the Japanese rice wine, you don't want to serve wine warm. In addition high temperatures can prompt wine to mature faster or cause the problems that you just read about. The idea is to keep the wine at a steady, somewhat cool temperature, and away from sunlight or ultraviolet light, which also ages it more quickly.

Depending on your storage capacity and the size and value of your wine inventory (rare wines versus jug wines), it might be sufficient to store the wine in the cardboard case it comes in. If you do not stack the cases very high on top of each other, you can lay them on their sides. Otherwise, you can store them with the bottles upside down. This keeps the corks moist and well sealed. Use a thick marking pen to label each case with the bin number, and try to keep the cases stored in numerical order so that it will be easy for servers to find them quickly.

Unless your establishment is an elegant, fine-dining place or a wine bar known for its wide and exotic selection, you won't need long-term, temperature- and humidity-controlled wine-cellar capacity. (If you do have these special storage needs, you should consult with a wine expert before building or equipping such a space.) More likely your goal is to turn over your inventory regularly and not tie up thousands of dollars of capital in a back room.

Do you want customers to be able to see your wine investment? If so, you might think of ways to incorporate wine storage into your décor, such as placing a floor-to-ceiling wine rack along one wall, with a sturdy, attractive, and movable ladder for fetching bottles near the top; or building a wine cellar that is also a private dining area for special parties and tastings. You could also have a room specially insulated and air conditioned by a contractor who has experience building such spaces. Commercially made wine-storage cabinets are also available, from those with capacities that hold a dozen bottles, to those that look like rooms themselves, with separate temperature and humidity controls, as in cigar humidors. Bar- and restaurant-supply houses sometimes sell these cabinets; there are also a number of well-known wine accessory companies with web sites and mail-order catalogs from which you can order. These cabinets come with lots of attractive options, including locking doors, movable shelves, and decorative finishes. Just be sure to check with professionals about your electrical capacity and venting requirements before you buy.

By-the-Glass Storage

The more wines you serve by the glass (BTG), the greater your need for individual bottle storage. The goal is to keep oxygen out of the bottle between pours, even when it is partially empty. Here is a brief summary of how they work:

- For just a few bottles, it is easy to purchase rubber stoppers that have a one-way valve on the top. Place the stopper on the bottle, then use a hand-pump vacuum sealer to get the air out. The vacuum sealer is made of plastic and fits on top of the stopper. You pump the sealer up and down a few times, until it starts to resist your hand pressure. This means that the oxygen has been removed from the bottle and that it is sealed until you remove the stopper again. These stoppers enable you to keep wine for two or three days after opening with no loss of quality. Vacuvin (VAK-yoo-van), the most popular brand, also has stoppers designed for sparkling wines (see Figure 7.11). These stoppers are secure enough to store the wines lying down instead of upright. You can buy these stoppers at kitchen stores, department stores, in wine shops, and by mail order.
- Wine specialty catalogs sell cans of inert gas that can be used in a similar fashion. No need for a stopper; simply insert the tiny nozzle into the open wine bottle, squirt the nozzle for one second, and immediately reseal the bottle with its original cork. The gas displaces any oxygen in the bottle. For more expensive BTG wines, the inert gas is a little more effective than the vacuum-sealer method. WineSaver and Private Preserve are a couple of the popular brand names.
- *Cruvinet* (CROO-vin-ay) is the best-known brand of refrigerated cabinet for storing and dispensing BTG wines. Stainless-steel tubing connects the bottles to faucets (taps), and inert gas instantly replaces the wine that is dispensed from the bottle. The cabinets come in a variety of sizes and designs and can be incorporated into backbar décor.

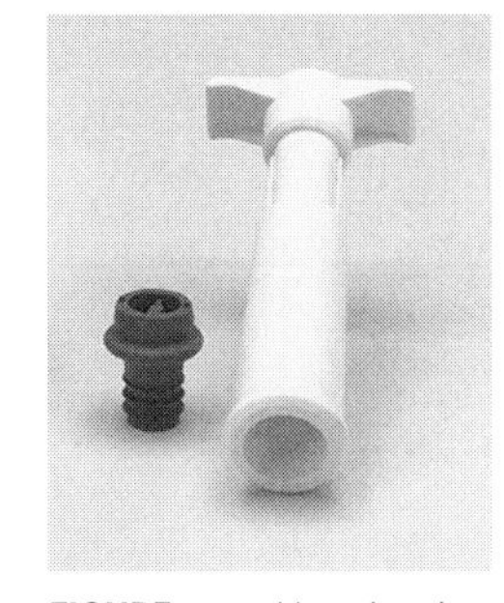

FIGURE 7.11 Vacuvin wine saver. Courtesy of Co-Rect Products, Inc., Minneapolis, Minnesota.

WINE LIST FOLLOW-UP

A book of this scope cannot hope to treat wines in any depth. Similarly a restaurant or bar that is just beginning to add wine service should not attempt to handle wines for connoisseurs. But by all means—serve wines!

Wine by the glass or carafe is easy to sell and can be very profitable. A modest wine list of two or three wines of each type can also be very successful if the wines are of general appeal, the list is informative, the servers are well informed and helpful, and the whole endeavor is well organized.

The most important effort you can make to boost your profit and satisfy your customers is to commit to regularly researching and revising your wine-sales program. It is not difficult to track wine sales, but you must keep up with them. Find out how much wine is sold per person: divide the total number of customers by the total number of bottles sold. This includes bottles used for BTG sales. For the number of glasses sold, divide this total by 4 (since, as you now know, there are four glasses in the average 750-ml wine bottle).

Track wine sales by color or type: Do you sell more red or white? If so, by how much? Do you sell more Californian or European wines? Perhaps you need to adjust your list accordingly. Ask servers or bartenders to make a note of any wines that customers request but that you don't have; you might notice a pattern. Inventory the wines regularly to see what sells the most and what just sits around. Close out the slow-moving wines by putting them on special or selling them BTG. Finally keep track of the wines by price. What is the average price of a bottle sold in a given time period? If your customers seem to order mostly the bargains, you'll want to expand that part of the list and stock fewer of the high-dollar bottles.

SUMMING UP

Any bar or restaurant business should decide whether to serve wine and how extensive to make its selection with four major factors in mind: clientele, concept, cuisine, and price compatibility. Dozens of other decisions, from how extensively the staff must be trained in wine service, to which types of glasses to buy, to how the wines are priced, will be based on at least one of these four factors. Additionally, the business owner must decide how much inventory must be held in storage. This is not only a financial decision, but also a matter of available space for storing wines at the correct (cool) temperatures.

There are a number of good ways to publicize the bar's wine sales. Your wine list will do as much as anything to sell the products that appear on it, so this chapter contains guidelines for making a wine list interesting and informative. The list itself can be as formal as a leather-bound book or as casual as a chalkboard of daily BTG selections. Again, this depends on your concept and clientele. Wines sell better when the list contains a brief description of each and, perhaps, a suggestion of which foods it complements.

For pricing wines, there are standard markups in the industry, and there are also good reasons to ignore them, as some bars and restaurants do. Their theory is that they sell more wine when they offer it at prices that are slightly below market. Of course rare or prestigious vintages warrant a higher profit margin and the norms do not always apply to them. There are a lot of good reasons to incorporate an innovative BTG program. These can be excellent tools to test new wines for your by-the-bottle list, to serve some of the more expensive ones or close out slow-selling bottles, and to prompt people to buy wine or try a new product without having to purchase a full bottle.

Most customers will depend on their servers to be able to make a wine recommendation, so be sure that your staff members are well trained. Schedule regular training that includes tasting, comparisons, and discussion. Enlist the help of your suppliers, but don't depend on them too heavily—and don't use one supplier's products exclusively. Every server should also know how to correctly open a wine bottle, as well as what to do if a cork breaks, if there is sediment in the wine, or if a customer sends back a "bad" bottle.

There is a growing customer base of wine-knowledgeable people. Impress them with correct wine-name spellings, proper glassware, and table service that follows the rules of wine etiquette.

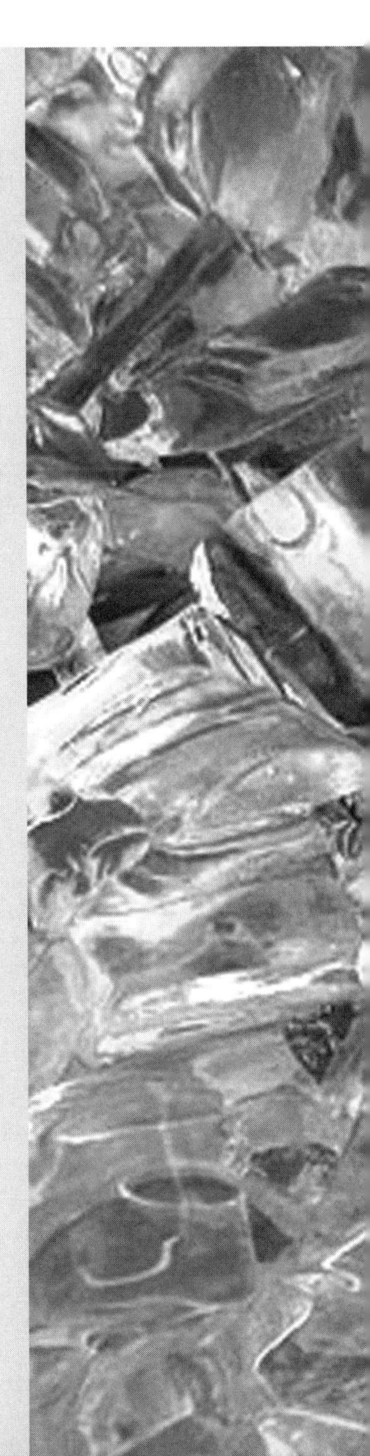

POINTS TO PONDER

1. List five major considerations you would address as a bar owner who decided that he or she needs to create a wine list. Include a brief description of their importance to your business.
2. Try writing a list of BTG wines for a local upscale bar. Explain your selections, including the number of wines you chose to put on the list.
3. What kinds of information, besides their names, should be included on a wine list to help sell the wines?
4. List five topics you should include when you have wine-training sessions for your servers.
5. What is the single most important piece of information that a server must have about wines to ensure greater sales?
6. Why do you need different types of glasses to serve different types of wines?
7. What do you do when you have broken a cork as you open a bottle of wine for guests?
8. What is the purpose of the cage on a Champagne bottle?
9. How do you decide when to decant a wine?
10. How do you determine how much wine your bar sells per customer, both by the bottle and by the glass?

TERMS OF THE TRADE

aeration
ah-so
augur
bin
number
bowl
breathing
cage
cork retriever
corked
decanting
flute
maderized
oxidized (oxidation)
screw-pull (lever-pull)
service napkin (*serviette*)
sommelier
table tent
throw sediment
waiter's friend
wine chiller
wing
corkscrew
worm

A CONVERSATION WITH...SHARON GOLDMAN

Director of Marketing, Luxury Division Beringer Blass Wine Estates

Sharon Goldman is the Director of Marketing for Beringer Blass Wine Estates' Luxury Division, which includes Beringer, Chateau St. Jean, and Chateau Souverain wine products. Her responsibilities include profit-and-loss metrics, designing wine packaging and labels, pricing the wines, deciding where they are sold and how they are publicized, and creating wine education programs for trade customers.

Sharon's résumé is an impressive list of marketing and management positions, from Lawry's Foods, to Universal Studios. She took her marketing skills to the wine industry in 1990, first with Fetzer Vineyards, then as the marketing manager for Kendall-Jackson Vineyards and Winery. In 1997 she was hired by Beringer. Today the company produces wines at six California wineries and imports wines from Australia, Italy, and Chile, with annual sales of $100 million.

Sharon received her bachelor's degree at the University of California, Los Angeles, and did graduate work at the University of California, Berkeley.

Q: What is the most important type of background to have to succeed in your industry, and what kinds of classes should you take to get it?

A: A diverse background is probably one of the strongest things you can have, and it is actually far preferable to coming into this business with a single area of focus. It is important to understand that the nature of the jobs will vary depending upon the size of the winery. There is a fairly small handful of large wineries that have more specialized jobs, versus the smaller wineries, where you can expect to wear multiple hats—one day you may be doing PR, one day you may be marketing, and the next day you may be in charge of sales—and that's all in the same position!

If your goal is to be in the restaurant side of the wine business, it helps to have experience outside of it, too. Numbers-crunching courses can be a real asset. Art classes will help with the more artistic and creative side of the business. In marketing we design labels and packaging, brochures, and other elements that use aesthetics. Naturally learning about the hospitality industry will be an asset. And the fact that the wine business is also an agricultural enterprise gives you another course of study. As you can see it just helps to be well rounded!

Q: What are the growth and consumption trends for wine, and how do they impact you?

A: The overall size of the business has not changed significantly, but people are paying considerably more for wine now than they were 10 years ago. One issue about wine that needs to be understood is that whether you're dealing with a coffee-shop style establishment or a high-end hotel bar, you're still dealing with price points that exclude a lot of people who are just not willing to spend the money on wine. They don't see that as where they should be spending their disposable dollars. So there is a finite population that is interested in your product, and as the price goes up the group becomes even more finite. It is also a relatively sophisticated audience, even at lower price points like White Zinfandel, which actually constitutes a good portion of the wine-drinking population. Wine is also a product that is very confusing because of the huge variety of wines that are out there—not just the grapes, but also the proliferation of labels.

Q: How much of an impact do nature's "curve balls," like rain or hail or diseases, really have on the price of wine?

A: Well, you're already talking about a considerable investment under the best of circumstances. To develop a wineyard in Napa (presuming you could buy a raw piece of land there) you need to figure on anywhere from $30,000 to $100,000 an acre to get it ready to produce grapes, and that's not including the purchase price of the land itself! It then takes three to five years to grow grapes that you can actually make into wine. Once you add the effects of Mother Nature, there is even more impact. A big heat wave may cause the grapes to be ready to be picked a month or so earlier than normal. It doesn't mean the grapes have full flavor, but it will mean they have to be picked. You get one crop a year and that's it. If Mother Nature is not nice to you or if you're not nice to the grape, you're in big trouble. And that, eventually, can impact the price.

Q: How can a bar, restaurant, or store manager help educate the public to assist them in making the right wine choices—and ideally increase sales by doing so?

A: It is up to the store or bar manager to educate the public, whether it's by providing good descriptions on the shelf tag or on the menu or by ensuring that the staff is well informed and make patrons feel comfortable when they ask questions.

There are three primary reasons why someone will choose a wine: 1. someone has recommended it (usually a family member or a friend), 2. the server or store clerk recommends it and explains why they like it, and 3. price—in that order. If someone you trust suggests that you try the wine and says you're likely to enjoy it, most people follow through on that recommendation. Wine by its very nature is somewhat experimental. At the same time it is often bought for a party or as a gift, so consumers or patrons want some assurance that they've made a good selection.

If you start developing a trust relationship with your clientele, your sales will grow. Remember that most people are too embarrassed to ask questions, so if your menu provides additional descriptive information or you have an informed staff person willing to assist, you are likely to get additional, incremental sales.

Q: What are some of the elements that go into making wine selections for a bar or restaurant wine list?

A: Just knowing that *The Wine Spectator* has rated a wine highly at a 90 or above is helpful, but it is often not sufficient to make a buying decision. Some wine buyers, bar managers, or restaurant managers say they create their wine lists because of their own palates (what they like and don't like). You also hear some say they won't put anything on the list that is readily available at retail down the street. On the other hand, if a wine is hugely popular and is widely available, it also may mean that people will look to order it, as they know it will be good.

A good range of wines by the glass is an easy and relatively affordable way for people to sample. I would suggest the wine list be balanced with some "safe" wines, and some lessser-known wines that you think are terrific. That can make it fun for you and the customer, if you can "hand-sell" it. This entails you getting to know your customers or ensuring that your waitstaff is sufficiently trained to describe each bottle of wine.

If you offer wine dinners or wine tastings, the actual winemaker doesn't have to be there. You can run the dinner yourself or ask the local sales rep, who truly knows the product, to show up, and it can be a good experience that increases sales.

Q: Which kinds of distribution issues do you face that might affect a bar or restaurant?

A: There are certain states that make it difficult for smaller wineries to get their wines into that market. In some states you just can't ship directly from a winery to a restaurant; the wine must go through a distributor, such as Florida, Kentucky, New York, Texas, or Connecticut. Each state creates its own rules. If you have a restaurant in Florida and you want to buy a wine that was highly rated [99 in *The Wine Spectator*], unless you hook up with a distributor who takes its margin off the top, the wine can't get to you—it's illegal.

Q: How can a bar manager become more effective at dealing with distributors?

A: By making lots of noise! Seriously if you are small and there are certain wines that you want, you may need to work a little harder at relationships with distributors. If you are small you may not be called on by that distributor salesperson regularly and you're just not "on the radar screen." If you can't make an impact with your buying power, you are immediately at a disadvantage and you have to do it instead by personal contact. You need to let it be known that you want the "good stuff," but also let it be known that you're not going to be a "cherry picker." If you are knowledgeable and are willing to buy multiple products, they are more likely to want to assist you and supply you when the supply is tight. So you need to be somewhat of a partner with your vendors, and understand what sales mix they need to maintain. They can always sell the high-demand items.

Q: Is it important to have a mentor in this industry?

A: I actually think your network of connections within your peer group is more important than having a mentor, although I don't wish to discount the importance of having a knowledgeable person who knows the ropes. But when it's time to get a job or change jobs, it is your network that can help you. Many of the best positions are filled before the general public hears about them, and having an inside track will help you.

One good technique for learning about the wineries is to request "information interviews," where you make it clear that you are just trying to learn rather than "hit on them" for a job. Always close those interviews with a query about who to talk with next. Your contacts are very likely to assist you in getting where you want to go later on. If they have a job available or they know of one, they are likely to mention that. If you ask for a reference for someone else to talk to, they will know you're looking for a job anyway—it's just a softer approach.

CHAPTER 8
BEER

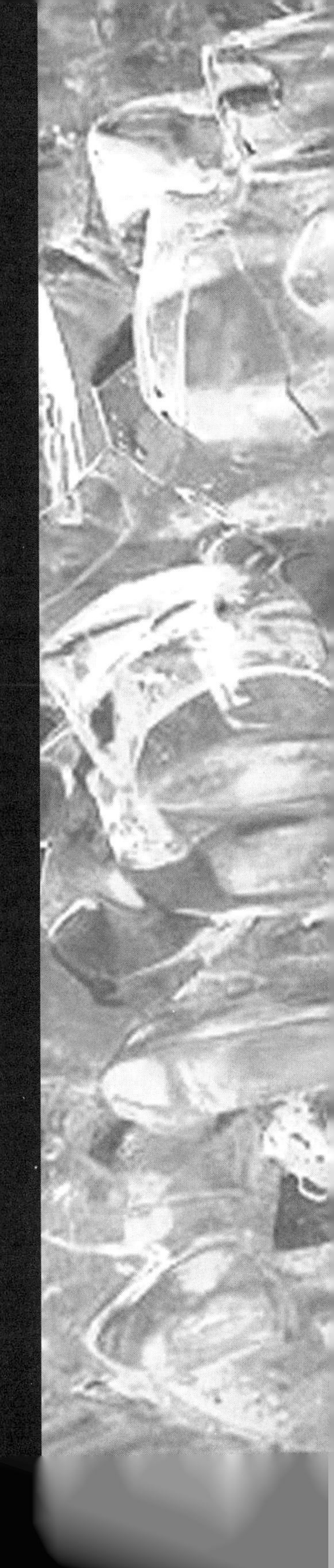

The brewing industry in the United States is a combination of successes and disappointments, innovations and setbacks. Despite these ups and downs, Americans love their beer. It is the alcohol we choose to drink most often, and our fourth most popular beverage (behind water, nilk, and soft drinks). The beer-making business has grown impressively, changing considerably in the last 50 years. In 1977 there were 50 brewers in America; today there are close to 1,400. Add the imports from dozens of other beer-producing nations and thirsty U.S. customers have thousands of brands and brews to choose from.

Despite the multimillion-dollar advertising blitzes of the big brewers, most U.S. breweries are small businesses with an average production of about 1,200 barrels a year. The ones that have done well financially are generally those that have found their own regional niches and/or have been willing to adapt to formidable market trends. For example, beer is subject to the same global forces that are changing the wine and spirits industries. More expensive raw materials and transportation are driving up the costs of manufacturing and delivery. Large brewers face an onslaught of foreign competition and in some cases, as you will see, U.S. breweries have joined forces with former competitors to create international brewing and import/export conglomerates. And let's not forget consumers, whose tastes are becoming more sophisticated. They are frequenting brewpubs and even making their own beers. They are looking for quality, for an interesting experience, for a more distinctive style—and for the most part they're willing to pay more for it.

All of this can be exciting news for bar owners, but the question is, how do you capitalize on these trends in your own bar? Developing a plan for selling and serving beer is not as simple as it may seem initially. As with wine, to give the customers what they want, you have

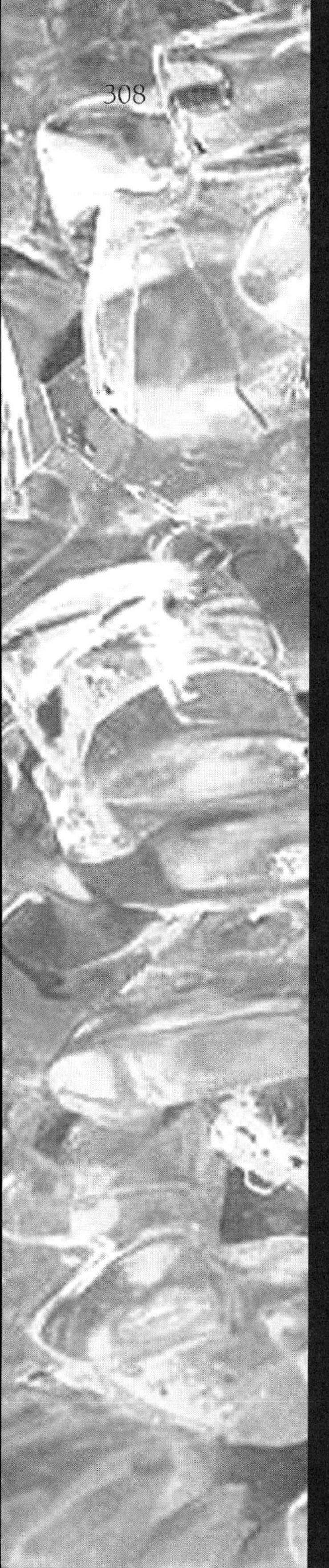

to learn a great deal more about the broad topic of beer, including lagers, ales, porters, stouts, microbrews, and so on. You'll have to know how beer is made and stored and the right way to serve it. Many bars and restaurants have beer lists as well as wine lists, so how do you decide which ones to stock? This chapter answers questions about almost every facet of brewing, including the various styles of beer and how to sell and serve them.

THIS CHAPTER WILL HELP YOU . . .

- Understand the market trends affecting today's brewing industry.
- Learn how beer is made and the role of each of its ingredients.
- Recognize and describe the various types and styles of beer.
- Learn how to take proper care of a draft-beer system and why each step is important.
- Learn to properly store canned and bottled beer.
- Correctly choose and clean beer glasses.
- Sell beer profitably in a bar or restaurant setting.
- Train and motivate staff members to sell beer.

A BRIEF HISTORY OF BEER

Human beings might have been making grain into beer even before they were baking it into bread. But whichever came first, beer and bread together constituted the principal items of the ordinary family diet for centuries. Noah took beer onto the ark. The Egyptians were the first to record their brewing process; they made beer from corn and passed their techniques on to the Greeks. Beer played an important role in these ancient cultures. It was thought to have medicinal properties, and many "prescriptions" included beer. Its use was taken seriously enough that a young Egyptian man would not offer a young woman a sip of his beer unless he intended to marry her!

By the late 1300s beer was the national drink of England. Both nobility and common folk enjoyed its refreshing qualities, and Queen Elizabeth I reportedly had a potent ale for breakfast instead of juice.

Primitive peoples derived much of their body fuel from the carbohydrates and alcohol in beer. Columbus found Native Americans making a beer from corn and the sap of the black birch tree. Hard-working English and Dutch colonists could not have survived without beer and made their own. The first colony to mount a regular brewing operation was Sir Walter Raleigh's Roanoke, Virginia, in 1587. But requests were made for imports from England, and in 1607 the first shipment was exported to the colonies. Unfortunately for those who ordered it the crew drank most of the beer before it arrived, so it is perhaps not surprising that in 1609 colonists placed the first "Help Wanted" advertisement in a London newspaper, looking for brewers to relocate to the America.

Brewers were considered artisans. Many of our famous forefathers had their own special beer recipes. George Washington had a private brewhouse; both Samuel Adams and William Penn operated commercial breweries. Thomas Jefferson was a beer aficionado, brewing at Monticello and collecting every book that he could find on the subject. Each soldier in Washington's army received a quart of beer a day. It was often safer to drink beer than water, and it offered nutrients and carbohydrates. In 1789 the Massachusetts legislature passed an act to encourage the manufacture of "strong beer, ale, and other malted liquors . . . (their) wholesome qualities greatly recommend them to general use as an important means of preserving the health of the citizens of the commonwealth."

It was not until the nineteenth century that the U.S. brewing industry began in earnest, when German immigrants brought European brewing techniques and beer-drinking customs to the United States. The art of brewing beer had made a major leap forward as a result of Louis Pasteur's experiments with yeasts. Not only did he unravel the mysteries of fermentation, he developed the technique of sterilizing through pasteurization. The process was used to stabilize beer 22 years before it was applied to milk. Before that time beer could not be stored safely for long periods of time before showing signs of spoilage.

By the late nineteenth century beer was sharing the limelight with bourbon in the old-time saloons. The excesses of both the beverage industry and the individual drinker during this time brought about Prohibition. Today the United States is undergoing a beer renaissance of sorts, which recaptures the period in European history when local breweries were valued community businesses and the corner tavern was the favorite gathering place for news, dinner, entertainment, and spirited political debate. Whether beer is shared with friends, good food, and/or good conversation, Americans today are not only drinking beer more responsibly, they are learning (and caring) more about what they are drinking. A growing population is experimenting with home brewing, and buying, sampling, and cooking with beers.

Two terms you will hear in conjunction with beer sales today are **on-premise** and **off-premise.** *On-premise sale* means beer that is sold and consumed on the same site. When you buy a beer at a bar or restaurant, this is an on-premise sale. When you buy beer at a grocery or convenience store to drink someplace else, this is an *off-premise sale.*

Starting Small: Craft Beers

Although the giant commercial breweries still control a lion's share of the beer market in the United States, the craft-brewing aspect of the industry is booming. Today's consumer is willing to experiment with new and different products, is willing to pay a higher price for them, and may well be more sophisticated than the prototypical beer drinker of years past. In contrast to the standard U.S. beers and many of the imports, *hand-crafted* brands are typically rich, hearty, colorful, aromatic brews that range from European-style beers, to specialties developed by the individual brewer. While the national giants are locked into their own formulas and images, most craft brewers have tried to capitalize on niche markets, by introducing fuller-flavored products or purchasing or contracting with smaller breweries to sell their specialty beers. Craft beers make up only 3.2 percent of the total beer industry, but their sales figures increase as they continue to receive media attention.

The Brewers Association defines the **craft-brewer** category as a combination of specialty brewers, brewpubs, and microbreweries. A **microbrewery** is defined as one that produces fewer than 15,000 barrels of beer per year. (In the beer business a **barrel,** contains 31 gallons.) A **brewpub** is a combination restaurant and brewery that sells the majority of its own beer on-premise, with food. The typical sales split is 70 percent food/30 percent beer. Some brewpubs make enough beer to package it for sale elsewhere, such as in regional supermarkets, to build the brand name. In these cases if a brewpub's off-premise sales exceed 50 percent of its total sales, it is classified as a *microbrewery.*

There will always be room for the small, specialty brewpub in the casual-restaurant segment, but brewpubs face some unique business challenges. To begin with they are part restaurant and part small manufacturing plant. Storage space for grain, yeast, and hops is needed, as are room for lagering and bottling. There are bulky tanks to clean and heavy barrels to move around. The environment must be

FIGURE 8.1 Toasting the success of the microbrew industry at a Denver brewpub. Photo by Richard Grant; courtesy of Denver Metro Conventions and Visitors Bureau.

absolutely sanitary along every step of the brewing process, to eliminate bacteria that will spoil the beer. Also, because 10 gallons of water are required for every gallon of beer brewed, provisions must be made for the disposal or recycling of water and used grains. The latter can be used as livestock feed, but someone has to store it and haul it away. In addition licenses and bonds must be obtained, inspections must be undergone, and fees must be paid, even more than those for a restaurant. Brewpubs must be registered with the U.S. Alcohol and Tobacco Tax and Trade Bureau (TTB). Their owners must be bonded, and they must pay a yearly $500 occupational tax (which as we explained in Chapter 16, this tax has temporarily been suspended until June 30, 2008). Each state's alcoholic-beverage authorities have a separate set of regulations and licenses, and counties or cities have health- and safety-related rules that must be followed.

The craft-brewing market experienced its largest growth in the early to mid-1990s. More brewpubs opened in 1996 than any other single year. Soon after, in 1998, more brewpubs closed than in any other year. Industry observers cite their fad-like popularity for people jumping into the brewpub business unprepared for the financial rigors of building a regional following. The purge appears to have eliminated the weaker operators, and the remaining successful brewpubs are fueling a whole new growth spurt—this time, in terms of volume of beer produced and sold. Sales by all craft brewers in 2004 were almost 6.6 million barrels, up from

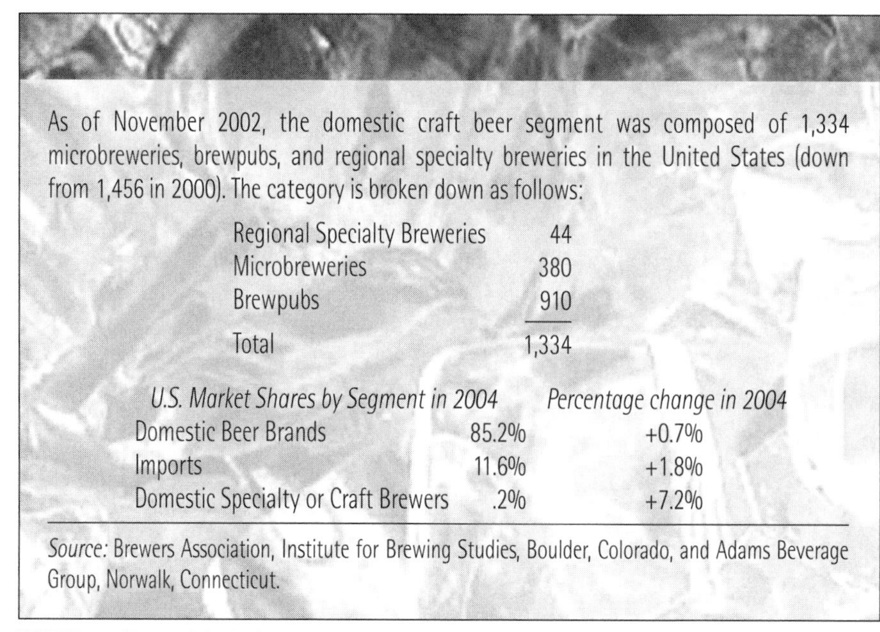

As of November 2002, the domestic craft beer segment was composed of 1,334 microbreweries, brewpubs, and regional specialty breweries in the United States (down from 1,456 in 2000). The category is broken down as follows:

Regional Specialty Breweries	44
Microbreweries	380
Brewpubs	910
Total	1,334

U.S. Market Shares by Segment in 2004		*Percentage change in 2004*
Domestic Beer Brands	85.2%	+0.7%
Imports	11.6%	+1.8%
Domestic Specialty or Craft Brewers	.2%	+7.2%

Source: Brewers Association, Institute for Brewing Studies, Boulder, Colorado, and Adams Beverage Group, Norwalk, Connecticut.

FIGURE 8.2 The statistics indicate that while craft-beer volume is still comparatively small, sales in this category are growing at a much faster rate than other types of beer sales. 2004 was the second year in a row that craft beers outpaced imports.

6.1 million barrels in 2003, and the Brewers Association reported that 66 craft-brewing companies boasted double-digit sales growth for three straight years: 2002, 2003, and 2004.

Next in terms of volume is the *regional brewery,* which can produce from 15,000 to 500,000 barrels per year. *Regional,* in this case, refers only to its overall output, not its area of distribution. Some regional breweries are hired as **contract brewers** to make and market other private-label brands for brewpubs. The regional brewery becomes known as a *regional specialty brewery* when, although its output is fairly large, the brewery's primary or largest-selling product is a specialty beer that is generally considered a microbrew.

Beer-Making Giants: The Macrobreweries

A **macrobrewery** is a large, national or international beer-manufacturing conglomerate with multiple locations and an output of more than 500,000 barrels annually. Anheuser-Busch, for instance, makes 103 million barrels a year. These companies are also called *mass-market brewers.*

Consolidation has been the keyword for major breweries. Following in the footsteps of their counterparts in many other industries, these breweries have snapped up smaller ones or forged partnerships in other countries to create global beer-making empires. Some of the biggest acquisitions took place in 2002, with Colorado-based Coors Brewing Company purchasing Britain's Carlin Brewing Company for $1.7 billion. A few months later South African Breweries, Ltd., spent $5.6 million to buy Miller Brewing Company, makers of Miller and Miller Lite beers. SABMiller, PLC, as the new company is now known, rocketed to the Number-2 spot in terms of sales volume with well over 100 brands. (Anheuser-Busch is still the sales leader, although not the volume leader.) In 2003 SABMiller also acquired Peroni, which controls about 25 percent of the Italian beer market. Outside the U.S., SABMiller is best known as a major bottler of both Coca-Cola and beer.

In 2004 Coors was on the move again, announcing a joint venture with Canada's Molson, Inc. The resulting Molson-Coors Brewing Company is the fifth-largest macrobrewery in the world. The products of both companies have been handled by the same distributors in most markets, and this "merger of equals" opens a new door for Coors because Molson, Inc., owns 80 percent of Cervejaria Kaiser, Brazil's third-largest brewer. Brazil is a hot market and is expected to replace Germany within the next few years as the third-largest beer-drinking market, after the United States and China. Brahma Chopp, the top Brazilian beer, is Number 9 on the list of the world's best-selling brands.

As their empires grow, expect these multinational brewers to challenge each other time and again. In China for example, SABMiller owned a portion of Harbin Brewery Group (China's fourth largest), but gave it up less than a year later when Anheuser-Busch offered to pay more for it. SABMiller already owns 32 other Chinese breweries through China Resources Breweries, a sister company; Anheuser-Busch also owns a small percentage of China's Tsingtao Brewery. With its enormous population China is considered a hot spot for brewers who want to increase their sales volume, although the U.S. Commerce Department notes that Chinese consumers are very price-conscious and seem most interested in the bargain macrobrews. Neighboring Japan has chosen to cultivate Russia as an export market instead, where the lighter style (with fewer calories than vodka) has become popular.

Even more foreign intrigue is underway. Belgium's Interbrew purchased Brazil's AmBev to create the world's largest brewing company in terms of volume produced in 2004. The new giant, called InBev, was created in a complex stock swap worth about $12 billion and now controls more than 14 percent of the global beer market, with about 200 brands. InBev recently purchased popular German beer-makers Beck's and Lowenbrau.

By the time you read this a dozen other chess-style moves may have been completed. In today's world of big beer business, the mergers and rifts can be as messy and hard to keep up with as the plot twists of a soap opera.

Trends in the Domestic Beer Market

Until globalization began in earnest the chief difference between the giant U.S. beer-makers and their foreign counterparts is that the Americans sold mostly domestically earning only a fraction of their income from overseas sales. Their international competitors were busy exporting their products. For example, Heineken, which is from the Netherlands, is sold in more than 170 markets worldwide, with international sales accounting for 90 percent of its total volume. Similarily Guinness sells 84 percent of its beer outside Ireland and has licensed bottlers in 51 countries to make it.

U.S.-based breweries have spent their time and effort building and maintaining strong brand loyalty among American consumers. They've focused on light beers and low-carb beers, courting the calorie-counting customer and turning out clever advertising campaigns. (Later in this chapter, we'll explain what makes beers *light* and/or *low-carb*.) The segments that continue to experience growth in an otherwise flat industry are the light beers and craft beers, a testament to the following consumer trends:

- Light beers now make up 47 percent of all beers consumed in the United States, and six of the top-ten best-selling beers in America are light brands. Health consciousness and an increased desire for physical fitness has prompted beer drinkers to choose a brew with fewer calories rather than to skip the beer altogether. (Ironically the healthy image of light beer might encourage people to drink more of it—e.g., two light beers instead of a single, regular beer, which negates its lower-calorie advantage.) The top imported light beers in 2005 were Amstel Light, Corona Light, and Labatt Blue Light.
- The generation of 21-to-30-year-olds has grown up with good beer and is interesting in trying new things. For these customers imported beers fit their image-conscious profile: no boring "mainstream" brews for them. The U.S.-made beers that are showing the hottest sales growth as of this writing include three regional success stories: Yuengling Traditional Lager (made in Pennsylvania at the oldest continuously operating brewery in the United States), Fat Tire Amber Ale (from Colorado's state-of-the-art New Belgium Brewing Company), and Samuel Adams Light (from Boston Beer Company, which makes 17 seasonal beers in Boston and Cincinnati and at five other contract breweries).
- Beer is getting stiff competition from wine and spirits producers, especially in terms of advertising to younger consumers. Health headlines touting the benefits of moderate wine consumption have prompted more middle- and upper-income consumers to buy wine instead of beer. A 2005 survey by investment firm Morgan Stanley suggests that wine sales will increase as much as 3.5 percent annually through 2010, spirits sales will be up 2 percent per year, and beer sales will be up only 0.5 percent per year.

Americans' beer-drinking habits also show a distinct seasonal pattern, picking up in June, July, and August. Three holidays, Memorial Day, Independence Day, and Labor Day, account for almost 20 percent of all U.S. beer consumption. An amusing term for macrobrewers' mainstream product lines now appears on brewpub menus: **lawnmower beers** (as in, the type of beer you'd quaff strictly for thirst-quenching while mowing the yard!)

Perhaps the most remarkable macrobrewed success story is that of Bud Light, the light-beer brand of Anheuser-Busch. In 2001 Bud Light surpassed sales of Budweiser, its "parent" beer, for the first time, with volumes of 33.6 billion barrels and 32.5 billion barrels respectively. Bud Light sells more than twice as much as Miller Lite, its nearest mega-brewer competitor; Coors Light is a distant third. The key to Bud Light's success, other than having fewer calories, has been its advertising team's ability to consistently portray the brand as fun, young, and social. Years of double-digit sales increases for Bud Light now mean that more people drink it than drink all wines, all distilled spirits, and all **malternatives** (other malt-based beverages) and hard ciders combined.

Generally beer advertising implies that brewers believe that there is no better way to get a customer excited about their product than to show people having a good time while drinking it. To reinforce their fun and lively brand images, U.S. macrobreweries spend millions of dollars for sponsorships to align themselves closely with big events, which is called **event marketing,** in sports, comedy, music, and other forms of entertainment. In particular there are longstanding connections to sporting events, especially football and baseball. Almost 80 percent of all beer sold at major sports stadiums and arenas is made by either Anheuser-Busch or SABMiller, but in some markets concessionaires are presenting a greater variety of crowd-pleasing alternatives. For example, Cleveland Browns fans can sample a selection of "Beers of the World" at Municipal Stadium. The lineup includes Rolling Rock, Harper Lager, Kirin, and Bass Ale.

The trend toward responsible-service training now includes sports-stadium employees. Anheuser-Busch's "Good Sport" program helps stadium operators and concessionaires to address crowd control and disruptive behavior issues. Coors teamed up with the Denver Police Department to start a "Designated Winners" program at Denver's Pepsi Center, offering free nonalcoholic beverages to designated drivers and a free cab ride home for any fan who imbibes too much.

There is a proliferation of imported beers to the United States, and they continue to arrive from distant shores and from just across the borders. Mexico's Corona Extra has been the top-selling import since 1997, when it outsold Heineken for that coveted spot. The Corona boom has paved the way for increased sales of other Mexican brands (Modelo Especiale, Tecate, Dos Equis, and others) and reflects in part the growing Hispanic population. Overall Mexican beer exports to the U.S. grew from 21.5 million cases in 1990 to 120.7 million cases in 2002. There are two giant brewing empires in Mexico: Grupo Modelo, which exports the Corona, Negra Modelo, and Pacifico brands, and Femsa Cerveza, which exports Tecate and Dos Equis. In 1998 Femsa Cerveza introduced another brand to the U.S. market. Sol resembles Corona in taste, color, and appearance, with its clear, longneck bottle.

Canadian beers also have loyal U.S. fans. About 16 percent of the beer made in Canada is exported, much of it to America, although export sales were down 6.4 percent in 2004 compared to 2003 figures. The top Canadian sellers in the U.S. are beers from Labatt, Molson, and Moosehead. (Labatt brews 60 beers and is the contract brewer for Budweiser in Canada.) On their home turf, Canadian brewers contend with the same challenges as American brewers, with an influx of upscale imported beers and more brands vying for consumers' attention.

You might not associate Asia with beer, but brews from half a dozen Asian countries are being poured and enjoyed with the foods of their native lands in many ethnic restaurants in the United States. Perhaps you will recognize one or more of their names: Sapporo (Japan), Tsingtao (China), Singha (Thailand), San Miguel (Phillipines), OB (South Korea), and Hue Lager (Vietnam). They are listed in order of their sales success; at this time, Sapporo leads the pack, but the top three Japanese imports to the United States—Sapporo, Kirin, and Asahi—are extremely competitive, partnering with North American macrobreweries to make their products more readily available. Today, Kirin is brewed by Anheuser-Busch, and SABMiller brews Asahi.

American consumers are also showing some preliminary interest in Spanish beers, which were seldom seen in the United States until recently. Spain is the European Union's third-largest beer producer (behind England and Germany), with 20 national brands. The major Spanish breweries are Cruzcampo, Damm, El Aquila, Mahoo, and San Miguel.

The Global Import/Export Market

You'll learn more elsewhere in this chapter about the imported beers available from a variety of nations, as well as how to sell them. But we're discussing importing and exporting, let's take a look at the future of the beer industry in light (or is it "lite"?) of globalization.

First it is becoming more and more difficult to determine which beers are truly imports. After all, if a Japanese brewery purchases or licenses a brewery in Los Angeles to make its product overseas, is the beer Japanese or American? Furthermore, does it really matter to the consumer? The alliances between large breweries to make each other's products in different countries makes it less expensive to transport the finished products. This is no small matter since beer is heavy, at least somewhat fragile and perishable, and expensive to ship. In addition the alcohol-related laws that govern shipping vary drastically between countries.

The U.S. Commerce Department says that the global beer trade reached $6.6 billion in 2003 (the most recent year for which figures have been released as of this writing) and that the international market grew about 7 percent annually from 1997 to 2003. The largest beer exporters in the world are the Netherlands ($1.5 billion), Mexico ($1.2 billion), and Germany ($886 million).

By 2003 the United States was exporting 45 percent less beer and importing 80 percent more beer than it was in 1997. The U.S. Commerce Department cites the following international-market factors at work:

- The major U.S. brewers are either brewing overseas themselves or licensing their products to local brewers to cut shipping costs.
- International currency fluctuations affect the competitiveness of the U.S.-made products.
- Most of the exports are currently macrobreweries' light products, which are going to China and Russia, two large (and still relatively unsophisticated) beer markets.

- The more developed beer markets—other North American countries, Western Europe, Japan, and Australia—are indicating a real interest in American-made craft beers. These premium-priced and niche-market beers are the only ones showing growth in the export market, and this trend is expected to continue.

The areas to which U.S. breweries export the most beer are Mexico (30 percent) and Canada (25 percent); the Number-3 spot is shared by the Dominican Republic, Hong Kong, and Taiwan, with 6 percent each.

BEER-MAKING BASICS

The term *beer* refers generically to ales, **lagers**, pilsners, and stouts, all of which are made from water, malted grain (usually barley), hops, and yeast. In fact, the U.S. Standard of Identity uses the term *malt beverage* rather than beer, defining it as "a beverage made by the alcoholic fermentation . . . in potable brewing water, of malted barley with hops," with or without various commonly used ingredients, such as malted or unmated cereals and carbon dioxide (CO_2). Federal regulations also define beer's minimum alcohol content as one-half of 1 percent by volume. The maximum content is not defined; this is a matter for state law, which varies from state to state. It may seem ironic that while federal regulations require alcohol content to be shown on a wine label, they *prohibit* this information from appearing on beer labels, except where state laws require it. This is why some brewers make the same beer in different "strengths," to meet different state requirements.

In the United States a beer's alcohol content is usually quoted as a percentage by weight; in Canada, it is shown as a percentage by volume. Therefore, a 3.2-percent beer and a 5-percent beer cannot be compared unless they are expressed in the same terms. For example a 4-percent beer by weight is 5-percent alcohol by volume, while a 4-percent beer by volume is 3.2-percent alcohol by weight. These differences are small and probably would not affect taste, but you would be able to taste the difference between a 3.2-percent beer and a 5-percent beer by weight (4 and 6.25 percent by volume, respectively). The alcohol content of beers is roughly one third to one-half that of wine, but when average servings of the two beverages are compared, the content is not very different (as you can see by referring back to Figure 5.5).

Raw Ingredients

Depending on the type or style of beer being made, the brewer will use different strains of yeast, as well as somewhat different methods of fermentation. In spite of these differences, which you will learn about in this chapter, the basics of production are the same for both beers and ales. First consider each of the raw ingredients in beer: water, malt, hops, and yeast. In the United States there is often a fifth ingredient: another cereal in addition to the malt, called a **malt adjunct** or **grain adjunct.** Variations in the character of each ingredient are important to the final product.

Water. Beer is nine-tenths water, so water quality is a critical factor in beer production. The various beer styles were originally derived from the rock on which their breweries sat. Molson-Coors emphasizes its use of "Rocky Mountain spring water," for instance, and this is not just advertising hype: It is essential to the taste of Coors brand beer. Some waters are suitable for ale but not for beer, and vice versa. Standard American tap water, for instance, is treated with chlorine or fluoride, hence is not suitable for brewing without being boiled or filtered first. Hard water is not good for making certain styles of beer, so brewers must know the characteristics of their water supply in advance.

The term *pH* is used to describe the amount of acidity in water, expressed on a scale of 1 to 14. A low number indicates high acidity, 7 is "neutral," and numbers higher than 7 indicate low acidity. The best brewing conditions for beer include water at a pH level between 5.0 and 5.8. Lower pH levels are good for beer of lighter colors.

The minerals in water, of course, also contribute to the taste of the beer. Many brewers modify their water—by adding mineral salts, for instance—to create a successful, standardized product.

FIGURE 8.3 Six-row barley. Courtesy of US Department of Agriculture. Photo by Jack Dykinga.

Malt. Malt is the word for *barley* that has been placed in water, allowed to begin to sprout, then dried to stop germination. Barley is the third major feed-grain crop grown in the United States, and there are three types: two-row, four-row, and six-row, referring to the numbers of kernel rows on the head of the stalk. *Six-row barley* is the type used by most mass-market brewers. It is less expensive and generally not as flavorful as two-row barley. *Two-row barley* is lower in protein, and higher in enzymes, and produces a higher percentage of plump grains than six-row (see Figure 8.3 for a closeup of six-row barley).

Except for a few beer malts made from wheat (and so-called **wheat malts,** which are made from half barley and half wheat), all are barley malts. The sprouted grain creates enzymes that break down the grain's starch molecules into simpler sugar molecules; these, in turn, break down into alcohol and CO_2 when attacked by the yeast. The drying process is called **kilning** because it takes place in a kiln.

WATER QUALITY AND BEER QUALITY: A QUICK EUROPEAN TOUR

Knowledge of water quality—including such factors as pH values and mineral content—is essential in beer-making. It allows brewers to enhance, or overcome, these factors as needed. It also enables brewers to compensate for year-to-year variations in barley and hops crops, to ensure production of consistent beers.

- In nineteenth-century commercial brewing operations in Europe, brewmasters discovered that their products spoiled easily, with notable exceptions. One of these, the British town of Burton-on-Trent, had 30 breweries producing pale ale (also called *English bitter*). The area soil was rich in minerals, including gypsum, and the water had a pH of 5 to 5.5, ideal for *mashing*, which is the step that extracts natural sugars from malting barley. The Burton-on-Trent water supply was also high in *sulfates*, which act as preservatives. The resulting brew could be shipped to distant locations, including colonial India. Thus, the Burton-on-Trent beers became known as **India Pale Ales,** or **IPA** for short. Today any brewer can produce an IPA-style beer by adding minerals, a step sometimes known as *burtonizing* the water.
- The Czech Republic town of Pilsen became a noted producer of lagers, and again geology played a central role. Pilsen well water is drawn from underground deposits of metamorphic rocks, which are created by high pressure and heat and are almost impermeable. The water is in constant contact with these rocks but draws no minerals from them. Although the water's pH is in the desired range for effective mashing of barley, its lack of mineral content is what distinguishes the finished Pilsen beer, giving it a clean, light taste.
- The story is different in Munich, Germany, where the natural water supply is overly alkaline and German law forbids brewers from chemically altering it. Instead they roast the malt a little before mashing. This releases natural phosphates from the barley. The phosphates increase its acidity that, combined with water, result in a mash that is in the correct pH range. It also results in a dark beer with a distinctly different taste because of this process.
- In Ireland groundwater in the Dublin area sits on limestone, which is even more alkaline than Munich's water. This requires even more roasting of the barley, which produces a beer known as *black malt*. It is very dark in color and has a grainy flavor. The distinctive taste of Guinness and other Irish stouts is a result of the unique properties of the water.

After drying, the malt is roasted, which gives the final brew much of its character. This can be compared to another grain product: bread. If you toast bread at a low temperature for a short time, it looks and tastes different than it does when you burn it. Malt is made in every possible gradient, from barely toasted to burnt. The lightest malts give beer a golden color and slightly sweet flavor; higher roasting temperatures enable malt to take on rich, dark colors, and such flavors as caramel, coffee, chocolate, and, yes, even toast. Most brewers buy their malt in the form of dried or roasted malt or malt extract; many cheaper beers use malt extract. Anheuser-Busch, Coors, and some small regional breweries malt their own barley. The malt and the adjuncts provide the sugars to be fermented. In addition to flavor and color, they contribute the body of the beer and the type of **head,** or foam, on top when it is poured. The body of the beer contains its nutrients: carbohydrates, proteins, and traces of the vitamins riboflavin, niacin, and thiamine.

Hops. **Hops** look like tiny pinecones waiting to open and grow on tall, thin vines. The hops that give beer its characteristic suggestion of bitterness are the blossoms of the female hop vine. The best are Bohemian hops, imported from Czechoslovakia, but high-quality hops are also grown in the Pacific Northwest; their names, including Willamette and Cascade, reflect their heritage. California's Sonoma Valley was a prime hop-growing region until winemaking became popular in the 1950s. The blossoms are picked, dried, and refrigerated until used. In brewing they might also add aroma, depending on how and when they are added.

Yeast. Yeast causes fermentation, a process that converts sugar into alcohol. There are two categories of **brewer's yeast**—*ale yeast* and *lager yeast*—and many individual variations within each category. The yeast may impart flavor to the beer. In a bottle-conditioned beer (which you will learn more about later), yeast is added just before the beer is sealed in bottles, allowing it to continue to "grow." The freshness and ripe flavors make this a favorite type of beer, but it does look oddly cloudy when first poured into a glass. The brewer's yeast is the special laboratory product of each brewer, and its behavior—it is constantly active—is closely watched. Erratic behavior or stray yeast from the air getting into the brew could cause a disaster, requiring the shutdown of a brewery, cleaning and sterilizing the equipment, and starting all over again.

Adjuncts and Additives. The most commonly used adjuncts are rice and corn, and they are very prevalent in American brewing. They give beer a light color and mild flavor, and cost less to use than barley malt. Rice imparts the lightest color to the beer. In general the higher the proportion of barley to adjunct, the more flavor and body in the beer and the better the head.

Superpremium beers typically use a higher proportion of barley malt: Anheuser-Busch's Michelob, for example, uses 95-percent barley malt and 5-percent rice, while its premium beer, Budweiser, uses 65-percent barley malt and 35-percent rice. In some European countries, including Germany, Switzerland, and Norway, adjuncts are prohibited by law. Beers are made entirely with barley malt in these countries.

Another type of ingredient has become more common in recent years. **Additives** are used to stabilize beer foam, prevent cloudiness, facilitate conversion of starch to sugar, prolong shelf life, and/or adjust color. All additives must be substances approved by the U.S. Food and Drug Administration (FDA). Many brewers, however, continue to produce beers without additives, relying on quality ingredients, efficient production methods, and their own experience to prevent the problems that additives are intended to solve.

The Beer-Making Process

Combining the raw ingredients to make beer is a four-step process: mashing, brewing, fermenting, and **lagering**, or *storing*, which involves maturing, aging, and conditioning. The first three steps are very similar to the first stages of making whiskey. Figure 8.4 diagrams the whole sequence.

Mashing, the first step, converts starches into sugars. The barley malt is ground into grist, which is fed into a container called a **mash tun** along with hot water. Adjuncts, usually corn or rice are precooked and added to the mash tun. Everything is mixed and cooked together at low temperatures (up to 169°F or 76°C) for one to six hours. During the process the malt enzymes are activated and turn starches to sugars. Then the grain residue is strained out and the remaining liquid, now called **wort**, is conveyed to the brew kettle.

Brewing, the second step, is the process of boiling the wort with hops. This step extracts the distinctive hops bitterness that makes beer taste like beer. In huge copper or stainless-steel brew kettles, the wort-plus-hops is kept at a rolling boil for 1 to 2½ hours. The boiling also sterilizes the wort and draws out the natural antiseptic elements in the hops that protect beer from spoilage.

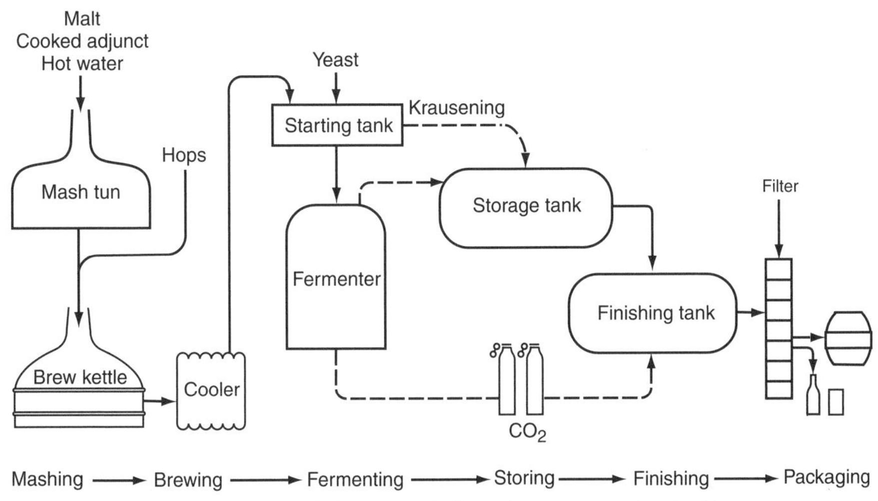

FIGURE 8.4 Making beers and ales. Broken arrows indicate alternate ways of carbonizing.

After brewing, the hops are strained out and the wort is cooled. At this point the techniques vary according to whether a lager beer or ale is being made. For ales the wort is cooled to a range of 50°F to 70°F (10°C to 21°C). For lager beers the wort is chilled to a range of 37°F to 49°F (3°C to 10°C).

The third step, *fermenting,* or converting the sugars into alcohol and CO_2, begins when yeast is added. If a lager beer is being made the yeast settles to the bottom of the fermentation tank, and the action proceeds from the bottom. In beer-making terminology, lager is referred to as **bottom-fermented.** The yeasts for ales are different strains that work at warmer temperatures; they rise to the surface and work from the top. Ale, therefore, is referred to as **top-fermented.** The usual fermentation period is a week or more, depending on the type of beer being made. During fermentation the CO_2 given off may be collected and stored under pressure, to be added again at a later stage.

Carbon dioxide creates the effervescence in beer. As a beer can or bottle is opened or beer is poured from a tap, the bubbles essentially bounce against the glass and break up, creating the beer's foamy head. These bubbles are relatively large, and they cause what some people describe as a full or gassy feeling from drinking beer or soft drinks. In the late 1960s Guinness brewers began using nitrogen in addition to CO_2. Nitrogen is an inert gas, colorless and odorless, that creates smaller bubbles and, therefore, less "gassiness" in the beer. **Nitrogenated beer** is known for its smooth, creamy consistency. The nitrogen is forced out of the beer just before pouring by a special restrictor disk in the tap.

Lagering (from the German word *lagern,* which means "to be stored"), the fourth step, means storing or conditioning. This step matures or ripens the beer, mellowing its flavor. Some further slow fermentation may also take place and impurities may settle out. Lagering of beer takes place at near-freezing temperatures and may last several weeks or several months. Ales are ripened, too, but for a much shorter time at warmer temperatures. Both beer and ale are matured in stainless-steel or glass-lined tanks. These tanks are commonly called *barrels,* but they are nothing like the wooden casks in which spirits are aged. A wooden barrel would spoil the beer taste. (Anheuser-Busch uses beechwood chips in its lagering tanks to clarify the beer, but since these are specially cooked and sterilized, they impart no taste.)

During lagering some beers are given a small additional amount of newly fermenting wort, to add zest and carbonation by prompting a little further fermentation. This process is called **krausening** (from the German word *krausen,* which refers to the froth that forms in fermenting wort at a certain stage), and is sometimes referred to as *natural carbonation*. If a beer is not krausened, it may be carbonated instead by adding the stored CO_2 at the end of the lagering period. Of the three major types of alcoholic beverages, beer alone retains the carbonation of its fermentation as an essential characteristic—that distinctive head of foam in the glass.

Beer Packaging

After storage the beer is filtered and then kegged, bottled, or canned. **Kegs** or half barrels (15½ gallons), provide bar supplies of **draft beer** (the British, and many purists and craft brewers, spell it *draught*).

Draft beer comes straight from the keg and is dispensed through a line and tap into a glass. (You will learn more about the care and correct use of beer kegs later in this chapter.) The latest innovation in keg design is a 1/6-th-barrel keg that holds 4.75 liters, or about 20 servings. It was introduced by Heineken as a spacesaver and includes its own CO_2 cartridge. Proponents claim that this keg can keep beer fresh for three weeks and can be placed between regular-sized kegs, thereby enabling bars to offer more beers on tap without requiring extra cooler space. The smallest keg is now being used by many microbreweries. A full-sized (15½-gallon) keg should yield about 200 pint glasses of beer; the smaller kegs' output can be estimated accordingly. Buying in small quantities costs more, which means that you will have to charge more for the beer, but the low-volume keg should guarantee higher-quality beer.

Draft beer's remarkable revival is a combination of new brands, microbreweries, packaging innovations, mandatory bottle-deposit legislation in some states, and old-fashioned merchandising efforts in taverns and restaurants. While most bars still serve more bottled beer—people like to see the label, and want other people to see the label and admire their taste in beer—draft beer has a much greater markup, ounce for ounce, than bottled or canned beer.

Variety, selection, and freshness are the buzzwords that bartenders use to push draft beer. They say that the most flavorful brews are best served fresh and unpasteurized. Bars that have a greater number of beers on tap sell more beer overall. The latest trend is to serve beer straight from the keg it was brewed in; this is called **cask-conditioned** beer. Cask conditioning is a secondary fermentation of the beer that involves adding some yeast and priming wort to the wooden cask. The beer is served directly from the cask, called a **firkin,** that sits on the bar and is hand-pumped. But most often draft beer is stored in stainless-steel kegs.

America's favorite beer container appears to be the can—we emptied more than 35 billion of them in 2004. The standard-size aluminum can contains 12 ounces, but some beers sell well in the oversized 25-ounce "oil can." Beer has been canned since 1935 when Gottfried Krueger, a New Jersey brewer, tried it and was rewarded with sales of more than five times the previous year! Can openers were required until 1962, when the first pull-tabs were introduced.

Today's featherweight aluminum cans are quite different from the first chunky steel cans that debuted in the 1930s. The aluminum cans protect their contents from sunlight and oxygen, and the insides and lids are coated with a water-based epoxy to prevent any "tinny" taste. Anheuser-Busch has experimented with an *aluminum bottle,* first introduced late in 2004 in single-serving and four-pack sizes that have been well received by consumers, according to the company.

Bottles now come in a variety of sizes. The 12-ounce glass bottle accounts for the bulk of packaged beer sales, but there are also 16-, 20-, and 40-ounce sizes, some with wider mouths. Consumer research shows that female customers like the wider-mouth bottles, finding them easier to drink from. Early in 2000 Miller became the first brewery to sell beer in plastic bottles. After a year of test marketing the company released 16- and 20-ounce plastic bottles, which are convenient for places where glass containers are often forbidden, like beaches, swimming pools, and stadiums. These bottles are resealable, and one-seventh the weight of a comparably sized glass bottle. Concessionaires at sporting events say plastic bottles are a big hit, keeping the product cooler than in Styrofoam cups and less likely to spill.

The plethora of beer-packaging options means that bar managers must do careful research to decide what to stock. Your decision will depend on your storage space and what size, style, or shape of container your customers like best. Market research indicates, for example, that Latino customers prefer beer in bottles. Strong, aromatic brews, such as stouts and porters, are available in cans and bottles, but serving them from anything but a tap might be a disservice to the true beer aficionado. Some of the cans and bottles contain a marble-sized *widget,* which releases a squirt of CO_2 into the beer when first opened. This in turn creates a rush of foam that is supposed to replicate what would happen if the beer were drawn from a tap. Whether this is an option for your bar depends entirely on the sophistication level and expectations of your customers. The recycling program in your area also may impact your decision because a bar creates a lot of solid waste with cans and bottles.

Pasteurization

Most canned and bottled beers are stabilized by *pasteurizing,* which means exposing them in the container to temperatures of 140°F to 150°F (60°C to 66°C) for 20 minutes to an hour. This heating process kills bacteria and any remaining yeast cells. Some draft beers might be flash-pasteurized with steam, but most are not pasteurized at all. This is why they taste better than canned or bottled beer. It is also why they are packaged in metal kegs that will withstand the increased pressure that may come from slight continuing fermentation, and why they are kept refrigerated constantly from brewery to bar. The constant cold temperature is essential to maintaining the quality of an unpasteurized beer. A beer that has been warmed and cooled again is known as a **bruised beer;** it suffers a loss in quality.

Some canned and bottled beers are not pasteurized. Instead the beers are passed through ultrafine filters that remove yeast cells and other impurities. Thus it retains many of the characteristics of draft beers and may be labeled and advertised as draft beer. Coors (now Molson-Coors) brands are the best-known examples of unpasteurized beers. They are made under hospital-clean conditions, and not only kegs, but cans and bottles are shipped and stored under refrigeration. Unpasteurized beers must be kept cold every step of the way until they are consumed. However, many people, including some delivery personnel, are not aware of this and store the bottles and cans at room temperature. Unpasteurized beer should not be accepted on delivery if it is not cold.

Under federal regulations, pasteurized beers in cans or bottles may refer in advertising to *draft flavor* or *on-tap taste* only if the label clearly states that they have been pasteurized; they may not be called *draft beer.* The difference is subtle, and although most consumers probably are not aware of these label nuances, anyone running a bar should be.

TYPES OF BEER

There are at least 5,000 breweries in the world producing some 15,000 brands of beer, which (as mentioned earlier) are categorized into two basic types: lagers (bottom-fermented) and ales (top-fermented). Within these two broad categories are many different styles. We discuss the major ones here.

Lager-Beer Styles and Products

As you have already learned *lagern* is German for "to store" or "to stock." The term refers to the long period of time during which the beverage is stored as it undergoes its slow second fermentation. This process produces a beer with a thinner body and dry, subtle flavors. Before the invention of refrigeration lager beers were very unstable in warm weather. German brewers did not make them in the summer and stored their beer in the caves of the Bavarian Alps. The brewers noticed that after some months in cold storage, the beer gained a permanent stability because the yeast had sunk to the bottom. Some beers are simply labeled *lagers,* but there are several major subclassifications, including *Pilsner-style beer, light beer, malt liquor,* **bock beer, steam beer,** and a few seasonal beers. You can glimpse the whole family in Figure 8.5. With the assistance of the Beer Judge Certification Program guidelines we will attempt to describe each type of beer (although tasting them will provide additional insight)!

Lagers made by macrobreweries are generally either *standard* or *premium.* The difference is the amount of *adjuncts,* or filler-type grains, used in the blend: up to 40 percent rice or corn in standard lagers, and up to 25 percent rice or corn in premium lagers. Lagers are highly carbonated and pale in color, and their white, frothy head dissipates quickly in the glass. Examples of standard American-style lagers are Budweiser and Miller High Life. Brewers in other countries also use this style, in such products as Corona Extra, Kirin Lager, and Foster's Lager. Premium lager examples include Beck's, Heineken, Michelob, Miller Genuine Draft, and Stella Artois. Generally they contain 3.2 to 4.5 percent alcohol by weight (4 to 5 percent by volume).

Light beers are variants of the crisp, dry American lager style. These beers were practically dismissed as a fad when Miller acquired the rights to the name *Lite* in 1972, but today four of the five top-selling brews in the United States are low-calorie products. How low? Figure 8.6 shows the difference in calories between a typical regular beer and a typical light beer. Fewer calories and less alcohol mean a higher proportion of water, and the brewer's challenge is to be sure that its beers are still flavorful. As popular as light beer is, the style will always be controversial; "serious" brewers and consumers scoff at these "watered-down" options. The best commercial examples of this genre are Amstel Light, Bud Light, Coors Light, and Miller Lite.

FIGURE 8.5 Courtesy of Glazer's Family of Companies, Dallas, Texas.

When it comes to the sale of light beers, the marketing focus is on lifestyle and health. You will see advertisments that tout these beers as *less filling* than the heavier microbrews and imports. The campaigns also focus on flavor, promising that a person who chooses a light alternative doesn't have to bypass taste and quality, in an effort to attract more upscale beer drinkers. The most recent addition to the trend is the introduction of *low-carbohydrate beer,* with Anheuser-Busch's Michelob Ultra in 2003. Coors soon followed with Aspen Edge, and Labatt debuted Rock Green Light. In truth light beers *are* low-carbohydrate beers.

There is also a *Dark American Lager* style of beer, so named for its darker color, which is obtained by roasting a darker malt variety or by adding coloring agents. These beers have a little more body and flavor than standard lagers (and certainly more than the *light* versions), but they are still highly carbonated in the American-lager style. Beck's Dark, Saint Pauli Girl Dark, Shiner Bock, and San Miguel Dark are examples.

Pilsner, which is also spelled *pilsener* and sometimes shortened to **pils,** beer is named after the village of Pilsen in the Czech Republic. This is the brew that we typically think of as "beer" in the United States: a lively, mild, dry, light-bodied, amber-colored, thirst-quenching liquid. Pilsner beer benefits from the use of extremely soft water and has a noticeable hops aroma and flavor. The best-selling U.S.-made lagers are often referred to as *Pilsner-style beers*—although they bear little resemblance to what is actually brewed in Pilsen. True German pilsners are made with Pilsner malt, German hop varieties and yeast, and water that contains sulfates.

REGULAR BEER (12 OZ)		LIGHT BEER (12 OZ)	
Calories	146	Calories	99
Protein	1 gram	Protein	0.7 gram
Fat	0 grams	Fat	0 grams
Carbo	13 grams	Carbo	5 grams
Fiber	< 1 gram	Fiber	0 grams
Minerals:		*Minerals:*	
Calcium	18 mg	Calcium	18 mg
Iron	<1 mg	Iron	<1 mg
Magnesium	21 mg	Magnesium	21 mg
Phosphorus	43 mg	Phosphorus	42 mg
Potassium	89 mg	Potassium	64 mg
Sodium	18 mg	Sodium	1 mg
Vitamins:		*Vitamins:*	
Thiamin	0.0 mg	Thiamin	0.0 mg
Riboflavin	0.1 mg	Riboflavin	0.1 mg
Niacin	1.6 mg	Niacin	1.4 mg
Pant. Acid	0.2 mg	Pant. Acid	0.2 mg
Vitamin B-6	0.2 mg	Vitamin B-6	0.1 mg
Folate	21.4 mcg	Folate	14.2 mcg
Vitamin B-12	0.1 mcg	Vitamin B-12	0.0 mcg

Source: USDA; Nutrient Database for Standard Reference.

FIGURE 8.6 The differences between regular and light beer.

Examples that you might see in bars are Bitburger, Konig Pilsener, Pilsner Urquell, and Warsteiner.

Dortmunder Export is a medium-bodied beer made with native German or Czech ingredients and high natural-sulfate levels in the water. This beer originated in the highly industrial Dortmunder region of Germany. The term *export* is a category of beer strength under German law; other German beers may also be labeled *export* if their alcohol level is 4.8 to 6 percent, which is slightly higher than the norm. The ideal Dortmunder is a balanced blend of malt and hops flavors with a slight edge to its flavor due to the hard water. Commercial examples are DAB Export, Dortmunder Union Export, Dortmunder Kronen, and Dominion Lager.

Malt liquors are lager beers with higher alcohol contents than pilsners (generally 5.5 to 6 percent or more by weight); these levels are frequently produced by adding extra enzymes to increase fermentation. The name of this beer style is misleading:

It is not very malty, and it is not a liquor. It has a small share of the market and tends to be chosen for its modest price and alcohol content. Colt 45, which has been on the market since 1963, remains today's leading seller.

Malternatives is the catchphrase for a subcategory of flavored, malt-based alcoholic beverages, sometimes also known (somewhat disparagingly) as *alcopops* for their sweet fruit flavors and their appeal to a young crowd raised on soft drinks. Another moniker is **ready-to-drink (RTD)** since they are presented as prepackaged "cocktails" that can be consumed as is, without mixing in other liquids. The first malternative was California Cooler, a grape-based wine cooler introduced in the 1980s that fizzled a few years later, almost as quickly as it took hold of the market. In 1998 small, independent brands, including Two Dogs and Mike's Hard Lemonade, received a phenomenal reception with their sweet but refreshing flavors, nontraditional advertising campaigns, and availability in sixpacks.

Soon the macrobreweries rushed to seize this opportunity to sell to young customers. Their entries into the category include Smirnoff Ice (Diago), Bacardi Silver (Anheuser-Busch and Bacardi, Inc.), Zima (Coors), Skyy Blue (Miller Brewing and Skyy Spirits, LLC), Cirtona (Miller and Allied Domecq), and Jack Daniel's Original Hot Cola (Miller and Brown-Forman Beverage Worldwide).

The target malternative consumer is aged 21 to 29, a person who wants a refreshing drink but doesn't especially like the taste of beer or the kick of higher-alcohol spirits. Young women and men are equally enthused about these brands after seeing their quirky, irreverent advertising. The popularity of most malternatives appears to be seasonal, with sales perking along in the summer and slowing in cooler months. Flavor innovations will be the key to this category's future success.

As you might imagine, malternatives also generate the constant criticism of people who cite their natural appeal to underage youths. After all kids listen to the latest music on the hottest radio stations, which is where malternatives are heavily advertised. Some critics charge that these brands provide an "end run" for spirits makers, who have been frustrated by network television's reluctance to air advertisements for hard liquor but will run ads for lower-alcohol beverages. (The typical malternative beverage has an alcohol content similar to beer, 4 to 6 percent by volume.)

Vienna lagers are named for their area of origin in Austria. Often a rich amber or coppery red color, they are noted for their distinctive, toasted malt aroma and a light-to-medium body. Brooklyn Lager, Negra Modelo, and Michael Shea's Irish Amber are popular examples. *Seasonal beers* labeled *Marzenbier,* which means March beer, and/or *Oktoberfest* beers are also made in the Vienna style, perhaps with slightly deeper colors and more intense flavors. Centuries ago European brewers adapted their styles to create different beers for different times of year, depending on what might fit a particular holiday or type of weather. The tradition makes sense and has been adapted by brewers in other countries. Fruit beers, for example, are usually made during the months in which the particular fruit is harvested.

Today seasonal beers are brewers' ways of keeping customers interested year-round with special formulas—slight variations in flavor, color, and/or alcohol content—and a specialty label. Much anticipated by loyal customers, they are usually timed to sell during spring or fall, or during the winter holidays, and generally are

MALT LIQUOR: A CATEGORY PLAGUED WITH PROBLEMS

In the 1980s malt-liquor producers changed their marketing pitches significantly in a move that has continued to prove controversial. When their market research indicated that black Americans drank proportionately more malt liquor than their white counterparts, the producers shifted their focus to create and place advertising to capture a greater share of the African-American market. But when basketball star Wilt Chamberlain appeared in ads holding a swooning beauty with such slogans as "High Performance Pleasure" and "Nobody Does It Better," or a woman sipped malt liquor through a straw and pronounced, "I Could Suck This All Night," people of all races were understandably taken aback.

Native Americans joined the outcry at the 1992 debut of Crazy Horse Malt Liquor. (In 2004 the estate of the famous Sioux chief Crazy Horse received $150,000 from Hornell Brewing Company along with a promise to stop using the name.) Most recently the makers of Steele Reserve (which terms itself a *high-gravity beer*) were criticized for a logo that, although the company insists it is a medieval symbol for steel, looks like the numbers "211," the California penal code for robbery and gang slang for "Blood Killers."

As of this writing, the nonprofit Center for Science in the Public Interest has asked for federal legislation to restrict the alcohol content of all malt beverages to 5 percent by volume. The hue and cry over malt liquor would, unfortunately, also impact many other beverage styles: barley wine, winter warmers, strong lagers, bock beers, imperial stouts, and some India Pale Ales, all of which contain more than the suggested maximum amount of alcohol by volume. This is a debate worth watching.

available for no more than a three-month period. Examples of seasonal lagers include Samuel Adams's Winter Lager, Thomas Hooker's Oktoberfest Seasonal Lager, and a variety of Pumpkin Lagers that hit the market in fall.

Munich Pale (in German, *Helles*) is a medium-bodied lager with a smooth, malty character. Some people who taste it find it slightly sweet. The style was created in the late 1890s in Munich to compete with Pilsner-style beers. Commercial examples include Paulaner Premium Lager, Spaten Premium Lager, and Stoudt's Gold Lager.

Munich Dark (in German, *Dunkel*) is dominated by the rich, complex flavor of Munich malt. Some say its sweet aroma reminds them of bread or toast. If the beer is unfiltered this aroma is even more pronounced. This beer has a deep brown color and a creamy head. Commercial examples include Capital Munich Dark, Penn Dark Lager, Harpoon Munich-Type Dark Beer, and Ayinger Altbairish Dunkel.

Bock beers are traditionally strong, usually dark lagers with a high alcohol content and a full, malty, sweet flavor. They are mainly German beers, but some small U.S. brewers produce their own bocks. Bock is one of the few types of beers

MALTERNATIVES AND ALCOHOLIC BEVERAGE LAWS

Federal and state authorities have wrangled in recent years with exactly how to classify the beverages in the hybrid world of alcopops—not quite booze and not quite beer. This is an important distinction because federal law acknowledges that beer and malt beverages are made differently than distilled spirits and taxes the two categories differently. A March 2003 report by the U.S. Treasury Department's Alcohol and Tobacco Tax and Trade Bureau (TTB) alleged that as much as 99 percent of the alcohol in some malternative brands comes from the distilled spirits found in the added flavorings, not from brewing the beverage itself.

After receiving more than 16,500 public comments on the proposed regulation, the TTB decided to tax malternative-type beverages according to the way their alcohol content is obtained. If a majority (51 percent or more) of the alcohol is the product of the brewing process, the product is taxed like beer, as a malt beverage. Malternative makers will have to change their product formulas accordingly or, by 2006, their products will be taxed at higher rates as spirits. In these cases some states will allow malternatives to be carried only in liquor stores.

that improves with age. You will often see a goat on traditional bock labels; it is the zodiac symbol for Capricorn. In addition to ordinary bocks are **doppelbocks ("double bocks");** the goal of their brewers seems to be to produce the strongest, richest beer possible, with an alcohol content of about 7 to 10 percent by volume. Bock beer was nicknamed *liquid bread* by monks of past centuries, who relied on it for sustenance during their fasts. Bavarian bocks and doppelbocks are traditionally served as *warming beers* in stone mugs at a temperature between 48°F to 50°F (9°C to 10°C). On the market today you may find imported examples, such as Ayinger Celebrator, Spaten Optimator, and Paulaner Salvator.

Bock beer is among the seasonal beers and is generally brewed in the fall to be consumed in the spring. Some bock beers are even called *Maibock,* which is German for "May bock." Once in a while you will see an **eisbock,** which is made by freezing the beer during the brewing process, then removing the ice crystals and lagering the beer before bottling. The process creates a highly concentrated, highly alcoholic (9 to 14 percent by volume) beer.

Steam beer is a truly American invention; it's the only kind of beer not borrowed from Europe. Its method of production developed in California during the Gold Rush days, when ice was hard to come by. It combines the bottom fermentation of lager beer with the higher-fermenting temperatures of ale. This process makes a beer with a lively head and the body and taste of ale, but with the same alcohol content as regular beer: 4 percent by weight (5 percent by volume). The beer's name has nothing to do with brewing; it comes from the "steam" released when the barrels are tapped. San Francisco's Anchor Steam Brewery makes the most famous steam beers; German steam beers are called *dampfbiers*.

Ale Styles and Products

Compared to lagers, *ales* have a characteristic fruity flavor that comes from the quicker, warmer top-fermentation process, at 60°F to 77°F (15.5°C to 25°C). Most styles of ales also have more body and more hops flavor and tartness than lagers, and some have more alcohol. In fact some states have laws requiring that any beer with more than 4 percent alcohol by weight must be labeled as ale even if it is not a true ale (which is somewhat confusing). The impressively large "Ale Family Tree" is shown in Figure 8.7. This category also includes the popular wheat-based beers, which have German and Belgian roots. We will begin our family-tree discussion.

Wheat-beer flavors are affected partly by the malted barley and hops used, and partly by the addition of two unique ingredients: malted wheat, and the yeast used in fermentation, which has a spicy, fruity character. Sometimes you will notice hints of banana, clove, and vanilla in the aroma of a wheat beer, and you will definitely taste the yeast when you sip it.

Wheat is ideal for bread-making, but problematic for beer-making. Its sticky gluten and soft husks result in a somewhat messy operation, and the yeast shows up as sediment that leaves the beer cloudy. Ironically the cloudy "homemade" look is one of its selling points. The brew is actually pale in color, light-bodied, and very refreshing. (A few imported wheat beers, labeled **krystal**, have been filtered for clarity.)

The first column on our "Ale Family Tree" is listed in descending order from the lightest to the darkest brews. The first, *Witbier,* which is Dutch for "white beer," is Belgian in origin. The Belgians are known for adding cane sugar during the brewing process to produce a complex and refreshing beer, and this milky-looking ale is no exception. Witbier usually also contains ground coriander and bitter orange peel, which is a very interesting mix. American-made examples include Lost Coast Brewery Great White, Blue Moon Belgian White, and Rogue Ales' Half-a-Weizen; also look for the Belgian-made Hoegaarden and Canadian-made Unibroue Blanche de Chambly.

Weizen or *Weissbier,* which is German for "white beer," is a pale, highly carbonated brew that originated in Southern Germany for summer consumption. Like most other wheat beers it is meant to be drunk when it is young and fresh. The variation most popular in the United States is the unfiltered *Hefeweisen,* which means "yeast wheat." (It is also spelled as two words, *Hefe Weizen,* and with either "z" or "s.") The name that you are most likely to see on the label is *U.S. craft brews.* There seem to be hundreds on the market, too many to list here.

Dunkelweisen and *Weisenbock* are the more traditional Bavarian-style wheat beers. These are fuller-bodied and deeper in color than other wheat beers, and have creamy, fruity flavors and a yeast content that requires the bottles to be gently swirled or rolled before serving. Dunkelweisens have a typical beer alcohol content

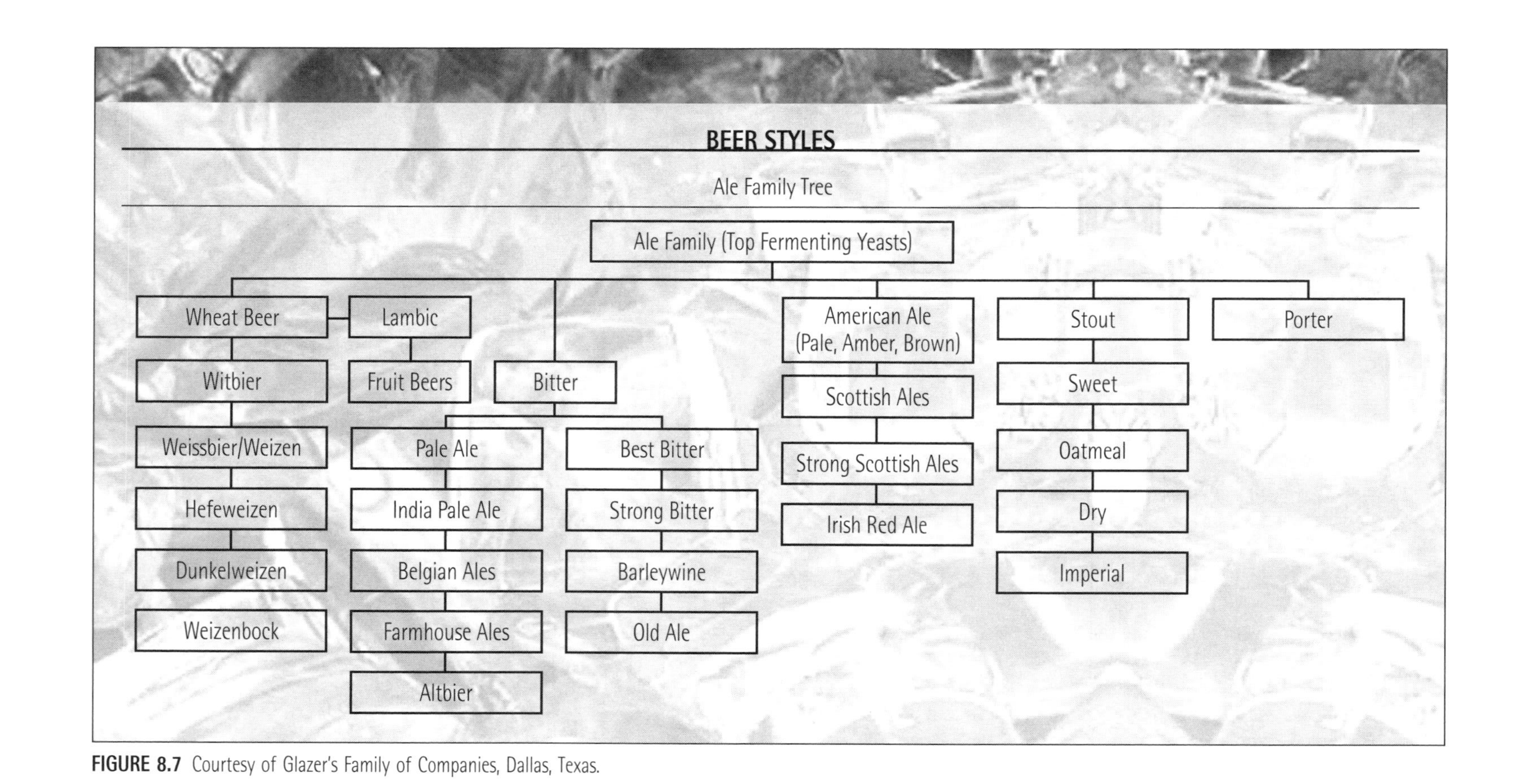

FIGURE 8.7 Courtesy of Glazer's Family of Companies, Dallas, Texas.

by volume (4.3 to 5.6 percent), but Weisenbocks are significantly stronger (6.5 to 8 percent). These beers have fallen out of favor because of the light-beer craze, but they are making a comeback in craft breweries. Spencer's and Brew Brothers make Dunkelweisens, as do major European exporters like Paulaner; Weisenbocks are made by Avenitus, Baltimore Brewing Company, and Emmetts, to name a few.

The beverages we typically think of as ales are best enjoyed without being thoroughly chilled. They were made to be consumed at room temperature or with only a very light chill; fully refrigerating them before serving only brings out the bitterness of their otherwise complex flavors. U.S. ales are descended from the beverages of the British colonists, and today most ales are mild reflections of colonial brews. Ales are often categorized by the terms *pale, amber* (or *red*), and *brown* based on the depth of color and richness of flavor. Because there are so many common subclassifications, we will not linger long on any of them.

First a *pale ale* is a type of **bitter**—in this case, "bitter" is a name, not a description. The term "pale" applied to an ale means translucent, not light in color. Bitters originally were draught ales served at cellar temperatures (cool but not refrigerated), although now they are widely available in bottles and cans. They are low in carbonation and not cloudy. They range in *grades,* of sorts, from *standard* (also called *ordinary*), to *best* (or *premium*), to *strong* (or *extra-special*). The higher the grade, the higher the alcohol content, although a brewer's "best" brand is considered his or her top-of-the-line ale.

In recent years the prevailing American-made bitter is a hearty, hoppy brew often labeled **India Pale Ale (IPA)**, although purists argue that if the ingredients come from the United States, the correct name should be *American IPA* or *American Pale Ale,* depending on the brewing style. The original IPAs were brewed strong enough in England to to survive the long sea voyage to India. The use of American yeasts and hops imparts a clean, slightly fruity flavor and an intense aroma to the stateside brews, which include Anderson Valley Hop Ottin', Stone IPA, Avery IPA, and Sierra Nevada Celebration Ale. American Pale Ales include Full Sail Pale Ale, Pyramid Pale Ale, and Deschutes Mirror Pond.

Americans have also pioneered a new category of so-called *Imperial IPAs,* high in alcohol (7.5 to 10 percent) and with a high percentage of hops in the mash. The names are as colorful as the brew itself: Stone Ruination IPA, Three Floyd's Dreadnaught, and Russian River Pliny the Elder.

For high quality and a single-minded sense of devotion to tradition, it's hard to beat the Trappist monks of Belgium. Today the term *Trappist* describes the source of these *Belgian ales* rather than a particular style. Only six breweries in the world are permitted to use the hexagonal seal of an "Authentic Trappist Product," which guarantees that the beer is brewed in an abbey under the supervision of the religious order (although the brewery employees themselves might not be monks). To further confuse the beer-drinking novice, dozens of Belgian breweries make their own excellent versions of the Trappist-made ales. Collectively these are known as **abbey beers** or **abbey ales;** some have even obtained licenses to use the monastery names.

A subcategory of Belgian ales is **Farmhouse ale.** In the days before refrigeration farmers in the French-speaking part of Belgium (and in France) made beer in the winter and spring to store for summer consumption. Also known as *saisons* ("seasons") or *bieres de garde* ("beers for keeping") the Belgian-style brews were tart and light-bodied, and sometimes flavored with pepper or orange rind, while the French-style brews were dark, earthy, and herbal in flavor. Farmhouse ales are bottled in 750-milliliter bottles with corks, just like wines. Centuries ago the ales were not brewed commercially so recipes are practically nonexistent, which gives today's U.S. microbrewers exciting leeway for experimentation. Examples include Brewery Ommegang Hennepin Farmhouse Saison, Flying Fish Brewery Farmhouse Summer Ale, New Glarus Spotted Cow Farmhouse Ale, and Three Floyd's Rabbid Rabbit.

Altbier, which means "old beer" in German is a beer made with traditional German Rhineland brewing methods, making this beer a cross between an ale and a lager, with a lovely copper color and a very hoppy flavor. Both Pilsner malt and Munich malt are used, but the beer is top-fermented and lagered (put in cold storage) to mellow its flavors. The town of Dusseldorf is the altbier-making capital of the world. Zum Uerige, the top brewpub there, makes its own Uerige Alt. Grolsch Amber, Frankenheim Alt, and U.S.-made Widmer Alt are other examples of the style.

Barleywine, both English and American versions, has a strong, intense malt flavor and noticeable bitterness. It is the thickest, richest, strongest type of ale, with an alcohol content of 8 to 12 percent by volume; it might taste or smell like caramel or toast, but it is not supposed to be syrupy. Barleywine is aged after brewing and may even be vintage-dated. British examples are Thomas Hardy's Ale and Fuller's Golden Pride; U.S. brewers tend to choose more colorful monikers, such as Weyerbacher Blithering Idiot, Bridgeport Old Knucklehead, Rogue Ales Old Crustacean, and Avery Hog Heaven Barleywine.

Beers labeled *Old Ale* are just a bit less intense than barleywine, with a touch more sweetness and a molasses, chocolate, or toffee aroma. They are also aged after primary fermentation and have alcohol levels from 6 to 9 percent by volume. Sometimes old ales are used to blend with other, newer "vintages," or they are released as cold-weather seasonal beers (and, therefore, labeled *winter warmers*). Examples include Harviestoun Old Engine Oil, Young's Winter Warmer, Great Divide Hibernation Ale, Hudson Valley Old Man Ale, and Samuel Smith's Winter Welcome.

Not to be outdone by England, Scotland and Ireland have their own ale subcategories. (Ireland's entry into the field is covered in the section on hybrids.) *Scottish Ales* are identified as light, heavy, and *export* which means the strongest ale of its type, just as it does in Germany. Interestingly these deep amber and reddish-colored brews are low in alcohol, ranging from 2½ percent to 4 or 5 percent for the "strongest" exports. Scottish-style beers contain fewer hops than their English counterparts because hops are not native to Scotland and must be imported. The labels on Scottish beers contain the designations *60/* (for light ales), *70/* (for heavy ales), and *80/* (for exports). Brewers who make Scottish ales include Belhaven, Caledonian, Orkney, and McEwan's.

A fourth category from Scotland is *Strong Scotch Ale*. This is another thick, almost chewy type of beer that may have hints of nuts, smoke, fruit, and caramel in the aroma. These ales are fermented at colder temperatures than most other ales, and aged before bottling. The high (6½ to 10 percent) alcohol level has prompted another round of creative brand names: Orkney Skull Splitter, Broughton Old Jock, Founders Dirty Bastard, and Belhaven Wee Heavy. (*Wee heavy* is a slang term for a pint of Strong Scotch Ale.)

Porter, a dark, bittersweet brew, got its name in the 1700s as a favorite of porters, the hard-working men who moved and delivered goods in London. Porter is an acquired taste, made in the United States as a specialty brew. Its dark brown color and distinctive bitterness comes from the use of roasted, unmalted barley. America's oldest existing brewery, Yuengling's in Pottsville, Pennsylvania, makes a "Celebrated Pottsville Porter," among other specialties. Other "big name" porters are produced by Anchor, Sierra Nevada, and Red Hook Brewing Company, and small craft brewers are also making their mark with these rich, malty brews.

When traditional porter fell out of favor in England, **stout** was its successor—literally, a "stouter" porter, fuller-flavored, aromatic, creamy, and dark brown to almost black in color. Also made with roasted and unmalted barley, it ranges from 4 to 8 percent alcohol (with some notable exceptions, as you will learn in a moment). As listed on our Ale Family Tree, there are four basic types of stout: sweet, oatmeal, dry, and imperial. In *oatmeal stout,* 5 to 10 percent of the grain content is oatmeal, which imparts a character that some describe as "silky" or "slick." (In the 1800s oatmeal stout was used to provide extra nourishment to nursing mothers.) The difference between *sweet stout* and *dry stout* is the use in sweet stout of milk, or *lactic,* sugar, and fewer hops; this results in a less bitter flavor that some compare to sweetened espresso. The famous Guinness Draught of Ireland is an example of a dry stout, and the Guinness formula is unique in its addition of up to 3-percent soured beer.

Imperial stout was originally brewed in England and exported to Russia for the czars. This style was almost extinct in England until it was revived in the 1980s by brewer Samuel Smith. Beloved by craft brewers, it has the highest alcohol content, 7 to 12 percent by volume.

Stout has experienced a popularity surge in recent years, which is a natural extension of consumer interest in specialty products—from beer and wine, to breads, cheeses, coffees, and so on. Specialty stouts are made with chocolate malt, coffee, dark berries, and dried fruit. Beer experts suggest linking stout to different types of cuisine. Stout can be overwhelming on its own, but with a good steak or even a rich chocolate dessert, a pint of stout can be wonderful. Aficionados insist it is the perfect complement to oysters, and a few brands label themselves *Oyster Stout.* Later in this chapter, you'll learn about using stouts and other strong brews to make **mixed pints**.

Hybrids and Specialty Beers

Some types of beer can be made using either the lager or the ale process. Wheat beers, such as *Weisenbier* and *hefeweizen,* are among them.

Lambic beer is one of the best-known wheats. Dry and sharply acidic, it is used as the base for adding fruit to make refreshing summer beers laced with peaches, cherries, apricots, raspberries, or honey. Also spelled *Lambiek,* the name comes from the Belgian town of Lembeek, where it has been made since the 1500s. The United States imports lambic *Witbiers* from Belgium and Germany, and produces many microbrewed, fruit-flavored versions of its own. The European imports sometimes use strains of yeast that impart spicy or fruity flavors, and are **wild-fermented**—that is, exposed for long time periods to natural ("wild") yeasts in the air. One popular lambic product is *Framboise,* a concentrated beer made from raspberries, which shares its name with similar products from wineries and distillers.

Irish Red Ale falls between the Scottish export and the "wee heavy" in terms of strength and flavor, and can be made using the lager process. Although the focus of its flavor is on traditional malt, part of the barley may be roasted to add to its red color and to give the beer an overall dry finish. The ale's alcohol content is average, 4 to 6 percent. The beer may be labeled Irish Red Ale, Irish Beer, Irish Ale, or Red Ale: Its deep red color is its signature.

Blonde beers, both lagers and ales, are so named because of their light color. The term is used somewhat loosely, but it has been around since the mid-1800s when, after years of dark, cloudy beers, the first clear, golden lager was created in Pilsen. Blonde beers are light- to medium-bodied, and contain less alcohol and less hop bitterness than true pilsners and ales. Blonde beers are all-malt products, made only with barley and very little wheat. They are viewed as *starter beers* by beer aficionados, but they have two side benefits: a very low alcohol content (2½ percent by volume) and only about 86 calories per bottle, fewer than so-called light beers. Whether the current popularity of blonde beers is just a fad remains to be seen.

Anheuser-Busch is making a run directly at the spirits producers with the introduction of malt-beverage products that appear to be crosses between beer and energy drinks, called *Tilt* and *BE.* The latter stands for *Budweiser Extra,* but the company also refers to it as *B to the E.* These products are sold in slim 10-ounce cans. Anheuser-Busch suggests serving them on the rocks, almost as cocktails, thereby making them suitable for stylish lounges and nightclubs. In an era when people are drinking 3½ percent more spirits and mainstream beer sales are almost flat, it makes sense to try a new approach. The Boston Brewing Company, best known for its Samuel Adams brands, has introduced *Utopia.* Billed as an *extreme beer,* it contains 25-percent alcohol, is packaged in a copper-colored decanter, and is being marketed as an after-dinner drink.

Nonalcoholic Beer

Nonalcoholic beer is in a class by itself. It cannot be labeled *beer* because of the federal regulations; it must be labeled a *nonalcoholic malt beverage containing less than ½ percent alcohol.* At first this type of beverage was targeted toward the health-and-fitness enthusiast and the non-drinking driver, but today's market approach is to emphasize flavor and satisfaction as well. Currently there are about two dozen no-alcohol beers, ranging from the Swiss imports Moussy and Kaliber to Sharp's (made by Miller) and O'Doul's (made by Anheuser-Busch).

These "beers" are made either by removing the alcohol after brewing or by stopping the fermentation process before alcohol forms. An added attraction for many customers is their low-calorie count, which is about half as high as that of a regular beer and a third less than that of a light beer. Although sales have risen, sales of these "beers" still make up only a tiny percentage of the beer market. But at least one expert compares this healthy niche market to that of decaffeinated coffee: There will always be a demand for it, so it will always exist.

SELLING BEER

With all the styles, and names, and ingredients, and brewing methods, it is probably a relief to know you don't have to brew beer yourself to be able to offer an interesting assortment to customers. If you're not up to the challenge of opening a brewpub, how about a *beer bar?* A certain percentage of beer drinkers are similar to the consumers of fine wines and spirits who want to be offered a wide selection of products, and beer bars specialize in ever-changing and ever-expanding lists of beers. Customers who like to experiment can sample beers by the taste or by the glass to find new favorites.

The obvious challenges for the beer bar include storage space and maintaining freshness and quality. Some beer bars, including Boston's Sunset Tap & Grill, have a "13-day pledge"; that is, all kegs will be disposed of 13 days after being tapped to ensure freshness. Sunset returns leftover brew for credit if possible or simply disposes of it. Careful tracking of sales indicates the slow-sellers and since many beers can now be packaged in one-sixth or one-fourth kegs, reordering is done accordingly.

BeerAdvocate.com does an annual survey to select the Top 20 Beer Bars in America. The 2005 list is a compilation of 7,000 consumer reviews of 2,500 bars. You can get the full list at *beeradvocate.com,* but we'll share the top five bars with you here. It's unfortunate (except for Northeasterners) that all five are located in either Massachusetts or New York. In case you don't happen to live nearby, we've listed their web site addresses:

1. **The Publick House,** Brookline, Massachusetts (*thepublickhousebrookline.com*). More than two dozen beers are on tap and even more are listed by the bottle, and the food menu is impressively upscale. The beers are used in cooking almost every dish, from Whale's Tale Pale Ale Battered Shrimp, to the Arrogant Bastard Meatloaf (named for a Stone Imperial IPA), to barbecue sauce made with Dogfish Head Indian Brown Ale.
2. **Spuyten Duyvil,** Brooklyn, New York (*spuytenduyvilnyc.com*). This pub has a loyal following for its love affair with rare Belgian beers. The bar offers so many that they are listed by style (Lambic, Flemish, and Wallonian). Of course you can also sample bottled beers from 10 other nations, as well as mead, wine, and

hot chocolate. Food offerings consist of cheese, meats, and locally made pickles on a mix-and-match menu, three selections for $10. The name takes liberty with a Dutch phrase that means "in spite of the devil."

3. **The Moan and Dove,** Amherst, Massachusetts (*themoananddove.com*). The draught selections are crowded onto an enormous, colorful chalkboard, and the list of bottled beers is two single-spaced pages at this casual campus hangout located between two colleges.
4. **RedBones Barbeque,** Somerville, Massachusetts (*redbonesbbq.com*). It is interesting that this family restaurant and catering company made the list of top beer bars. You would think it would be touted for its traveling meat smoker or its valet parking for bicycles. But RedBones Barbeque has well-attended monthly beer dinners, and a full bar that features 28 draught beers, at least 24 bottled imports, and 12 bottled domestic beers. There's even ginger beer and root beer for the kids.
5. **Blind Tiger Ale House,** New York City (*blindtigeralehouse.com*). The availability of 25 draught beers and 30 bottled beers is only the beginning at this casual pub, which is known for its clever promotions. For example on "You Cut the Cheese Wednesdays," artisan cheeses and beers are matched and customers who buy the beer get to snack on the cheese for free. There is also a "Connoisseur's Club"—drink 51 different beers there (not all at once, the bar cautions), and your name will be engraved on a brass plaque and placed on the wall.

Take a look at the web sites, all of which have plenty of photos, you'll get an idea of how much fun the beer-bar business can be. A good beer bar is a destination: You go there specifically to taste, to experiment, and to enjoy the wide variety, the knowledgeable servers and bartenders, and the company of other beer lovers.

Creating a Beer List

Beer enhances the enjoyment of food, and even if a beer bar is not what you have in mind for your own establishment, any bar or restaurant can create a beer list that exploits the opportunities to pair beers with foods, just as you match wines with foods. It is not necessary to install 30 taps for draft beers or an extra walk-in cooler in order to offer a diverse and food-friendly beer selection.

The family trees of lagers and ales presented earlier in this chapter can be somewhat intimidating, so we will distill the beer basics in terms of food:

- Lagers are smooth, often light or golden-colored beers that do not possess the fruity complexities of ales. U.S. lagers tend to have light, easy-drinking, neutral flavor profiles, while European, Asian, and South American beers may exhibit heady malt and/or herbal hop flavors and aromas. Most lagers offer a crisp finish with little or no lingering aftertaste. Like white wines, lagers pair well with chicken, seafood, salads, and potatoes.

- Ales are "bigger" beers than lagers. They have more body, deeper colors, and more pronounced aromas and flavors, and offer greater complexity because of their ingredients. Brown ales, such as porters and abbey beers, marry well with grilled and braised meats. These ales are more like red wines and adapt well to red meats, cheeses, sauces, and fruity or chocolate desserts.

Today's beer list should have a *minimum* of ten selections, and it's fine to change it every few months to introduce some variety and weed out the slow-sellers. Just remember, a bigger list is not necessarily a better list. It is expensive to add every brew that any distributor tries to sell you. Ask yourself the following questions instead:

- What do my customers want to see on a beer list? How beer-savvy are they?
- Which beers will boost my sales and increase customer satisfaction?
- How many selections can I safely afford to stock and serve based on my budget and available space?
- How extensive do I want the training program for my waitstaff and bartenders to be?
- When does a beer list cross the line from informative to ridiculous? In other words, how much information is enough? How much is excessive? A snobby list might turn customers off.

Your beer list should have a "point of view." It should represent major beer styles, as well as novelties, and contain something interesting for both "hopheads" and mainstream beer drinkers. In a casual-dining or sports-bar atmosphere, four or five of the ten beers should be specialty beers; in a more upscale environment, as many as seven of the beers should be imports or microbrews. Location also plays a role: If there are local breweries with solid reputations, their wares should be offered. Type of cuisine is a natural key to beer selection: for example serve Mexican beers with Mexican food, Spanish beers with tapas, and Japanese beers with sushi.

It's okay to start slowly. Carefully select seasonal offerings, and don't overbuy. Begin with a case or two, and gauge customers' interest. The goal is to rotate from 20 to 25 percent of your inventory every 30 days, to keep things interesting and to keep your stock fresh. Stay in close contact with your beer distributors (wholesalers), and let them know that you are interested in sampling new brews as they become available.

The menu of The Publick House, which is shown on its web site, is worth a close look for its masterful use of beer in cooking. Bars are offering more than burgers, hot wings, and nachos, knowing that people linger longer when they have something good to eat. Seasonal foods with seasonal beers are not only great match-ups, but also great promotion opportunities and a chance to stand out from competitors.

TOP-TEN BEER SELECTIONS (FOR CASUAL DINING)

4 light and low-carbohydrate North American lagers
1 wheat beer
1 fruit beer or malternative beverage
1 Irish stout
1 classic British ale
1 local or regional "hoppy" ale
1 foreign specialty beer (e.g., Asian, Belgian, Danish, German)

Source: *Restaurant Hospitality* magazine, May 2004.

On-Premise Beer Promotions

Bars have an advantage over many off-premise locations when it comes to beer sales, in that the bar sells one serving at a time. The customer doesn't have to make the commitment to a full six-pack or case and might be willing to sample new products. At a bar the guest is more likely to try something at the suggestion of the server or bartender. Image also plays an important role. Customers will often migrate to a higher-image (and usually higher-priced) beer if they want to impress the people they are with. Other guests do so to "treat" themselves to something more upscale than they would select at a supermarket or convenience store.

All of this gives a bar a chance to increase profit, brand awareness, and loyalty, but only if the product is visible at the point of purchase. Common ways that bars advertise their wares on-premise are as follows:

- ***Tap handles.*** Beer distributors will provide tap handles, or you can hire such companies as Taphandles, Inc. (*taphandles.com*) to design them. They can be made of aluminum, ceramic, plastic, resin, or wood, but the result should be attractive, colorful, and attention-getting. A profusion of interesting, creative tap handles is the hallmark of a true beer bar (see Figure 8.8).
- ***Lists and menus.*** Computers make it incredibly easy to create and regularly update your beer list. Like wine lists, beer lists are best organized by style or flavor profile and may include a short description of each beer and recommendations for food pairings. Merchant Du Vin Corporation (*merchantduvin.com*) of Tukwila, Washington, is a beer importer that offers an "Authentic Beer List Kit" with plenty of suggestions. One idea is to begin the list with the (more profitable) specialty and import beers, followed by the lower-priced domestics.
- ***Table tents.*** Beer-and-food pairings, special events, or nightly specials can be advertised on tabletop cards. Many breweries and beer distributors have them

FIGURE 8.8 Tap handles. Photo courtesy of Wunder-Bar Automatic Controls, Inc., Vacaville, California.

printed for bars, but you can also make your own on a computer and use clear-plastic holders to change them regularly.

- ***Beer coasters.*** The biggest decision here beer coaster is whether to advertise your bar or individual beers on them. They are a tradition in many bars and a colorful, collectible addition to your point-of-sale (POS) materials. Usually made of sturdy, recyclable pulpboard, they can be ordered in batches as small as 500 or as large as 10,000. Check out the web sites of two manufacturers, American Coaster Company (*americancoaster.com*) and Absorbent, Ink. (*absorbentprinting.com*), to explore some of the many options.
- ***Neon signs and logos.*** Another traditional beer-advertising medium, the major macrobreweries have turned out some impressive neon signage for distributors to share with bar owners. Some of these have become collectibles over the years. What you must decide in terms of décor is, How much is *too much* neon, and where and how will you plug it all in?

There are plenty of ways to create interest in your bar's beer program. *Beer flights* give customers an opportunity to try smaller-sized samples of several different beers for a fixed price. There are endless themes for beer-lovers dinners: craft beers, Mexican beers for the Cinco de Mayo holiday, German brews for Oktoberfest, perhaps a visiting brewer pouring and discussing his or her own products. You can have periodic tastings of new products, to ask customers to give their feedback—i.e., Do we put this product on the beer list or not? For example, the Four Points Sheraton Hotel in Los Angeles holds a weekly *prix fixe* dinner that includes foods cooked with beer and complementary brews. New York's Blind Tiger Ale House takes reservations for parties of 20 or more at a fixed price, $35 a person for a three-hour open bar.

Private-Label Beers

Although the beer market is crowded, there is no reason why you can't have your own beer with your own label to serve at your bar or restaurant—and you don't even have to brew it yourself. *Contract brewing* enables you to hire an established brewery or microbrewery to make and label beer for you. TGI Friday's was among the first to try this, offering a TGI Friday's Premium Amber on its menu.

The first step in creating a private label is to decide which type of beer is acceptable to your customers. This is no time for experimentation; you want something reliable, that is going to sell well and complements your food menu. You should also be able to estimate fairly accurately how much beer you will need. Then find a local or regional brewery (customers seem to think there's something more "genuine" about a local company doing the beer-making) and approach the brewery about making a private-label product. You might have to get your beer wholesaler or distributor involved since your state's liquor laws may require that you get beer only from them. Usually, though, they are happy to pick up the beer at the brewery and deliver it to you. Any new bottling requires federal approval of the label (the brewery can advise you or handle this paperwork), and you must choose a style of bottle and size of label that are compatible with the bottling equipment. Alternately you can choose to buy kegs from the brewery, which is faster and less expensive than bottles.

Mixing Beers

For many consumers, the thought of a big, dark, somewhat bitter brew is just not appetizing, especially when they are not accustomed to drinking or appreciating them. So bartenders have found interesting ways to present what is called the **mixed pint**—a blend of one beer with another beer or even with some other type of drink—to create a unique flavor. Mixing beers is a skill and a balancing act, much like successfully mixing a cocktail. You will find that the different brews and other liquids each have different densities, or specific gravity. They will layer one on top of another, creating a fun and dramatic appearance. The layers remain intact when the glass is sitting still; when it is tilted, the heavier liquid slices along the angle of the glass in such a way that the liquids can be consumed together. Some possibilities include:

- Black and Tan: A blend of Guinness Stout and Bass Ale
- Midnight Oil: Half stout and half port (not porter). Also called a *Dark and Smooth.*
- Irish American: Half Budweiser and half Guinness Stout
- Half and Half: A bitter ale draught and a pilsner
- Black Velvet: A stout mixed with Champagne
- Black Velveteen: A stout mixed with hard cider

BEER COCKTAILS

Whether you call them beer cocktails or beertails, they're quirky and fun to make and serve.

BUD LIGHT BERRY BLAST

Ice
12 ounces Bud Light (divided use)
1 1/2 ounces Strawberry Daiquiri mix
1/2 ounce simple syrup
Chilled pilsner glass
Strawberry and lemon slices

In a shaker with ice, pour 6 ounces of the beer, the daiquiri mix, and the simple syrup. Shake. Strain into the chilled pilsner glass. Add the remaining beer. Garnish with strawberry and lemon slices.

MICHELADA

Ice
Highball glass, rimmed with coarse salt
Juice of 1 lemon
2 dashes Worcestershire sauce
1 dash soy sauce
1 dash Tabasco sauce
1 pinch black pepper
12 ounces beer

Mix all ingredients except the beer in a tall (highball) glass with lots of ice. Add the beer, mix, and serve.

THE BALTIMORE ZOO

Ice
Highball glass
1 shot vodka
1 shot light rum
1 shot gin
1 shot Triple Sec
1 shot Southern Comfort brand peach liqueur
1 shot amaretto almond liqueur
1 shot grenadine syrup
1 dash sweet-and-sour mix
1 splash beer

Add the liquors and grenadine to a highball glass with ice. Top with the sweet-and-sour mix. Add the beer and stir.

THE BROOKLYN ZOO

Ice
Red wineglass
1 ounce rum
1 ounce vodka
1 ounce gin
1 splash pineapple juice
1 splash DeKuyper brand Razzmatazz liqueur
1 splash sweet-and-sour mix
1 to 2 ounces beer

Fill the glass with ice. Mix the rum, vodka, and gin. Add the pineapple juice, Razzmatazz, and sweet-and-sour mix. Serve with a separate side shot of beer, poured into the glass by the server or drinker.

THE "BEATCH"

Ice
Highball glass
1 can (10 ounces) Budweiser BE
1 ounce Chambord (raspberry) liqueur
Maraschino cherry and lemon twist

Pour BE into the glass with ice. Tilt the glass, and pour the liqueur down the side to layer on the bottom of the glass. Garnish with cherry and lemon twist.

Sources: Anheuser-Busch; drinksmixer.com

- Shandy Gaff: Draught beer and ginger ale
- Rock 'n' Bock: Rolling Rock beer and Shiner Double Bock
- Snake Bite: Lager and hard cider
- Purple Death: Bass Ale, Chambord, and hard cider
- Black Death: Guinness Stout and hard cider
- Bumble Bee: Half honey lager and half Guinness Stout
- Bloody Bastard: Bass Ale, Bloody Mary mix, and horseradish, with a peeled shrimp as garnish
- Bloody Russian: A Bloody Bastard with Russian vodka added

When you learn to make these, or create your own combinations, their names alone will spark some interesting conversations at your bar.

STORING BEER

Beer has the shortest shelf-life of any alcoholic beverage. Even pasteurization does not give it an indefinite shelf-life. All beers should be kept cool and used promptly. Beers kept too long will lose both flavor and aroma. Although canned and bottled beers are either pasteurized or specially filtered, they also have a limited shelf-life and should be used within three to four months of the date of packaging.

Freshness Dating

The competitiveness of the macrobreweries extends even to their freshness dating systems. Molson Coors and many other brewers mark each package with a **pull date,** which indicates the date you should pull it off your shelves if you have not served it yet. Budweiser countered with a **born-on date (BOD),** the date on which it was packaged, and states that the beer is at its peak of freshness 110 days from the BOD. SABMiller is sticking to its "don't-sell date," its own version of the pull date. All brewers note that regardless of labeling, proper handling by distributors and retailers pretty much guarantees that consumers will receive the best quality and the freshest possible beer—and they have strict quality-control standards for their wholesalers. To avoid serving over-age beers, rotate your stock, using the oldest first and putting new supplies behind existing stock.

Technological advances have helped beer makers maintain consistency. The art of brewing is scientific enough that brewers know, for example, that beer brewed in a short, squat vat tastes fruitier than beer brewed in a tall, slim vat because of the difference in water pressure pushing down on the yeast. As you learned in Chapter 4, the chief enemies of beer are oxygen and light.

Draft-Beer Systems

Another critical component of draft-beer quality is the proper use and care of the **beer system**. There are several factors to consider when selecting a system:

- How many different types of draft beer will you be serving?
- What is the potential beer volume of your bar on its busiest days or shifts?
- What is the distance between the taps and the refrigerated storage area where the kegs will be kept?

All three of these questions determine how much storage space you will need for the kegs and where to locate it—that is, how far the kegs will be from the service area where the beer is dispensed. **Direct draw** is the term for serving the beer directly from the keg, with a line of six feet or less in length. Figure 8.9 is an example of an underbar direct-draw setup.

Underbar beer dispensers take up a lot of room, and changing kegs at the bar can be disruptive. The hotel bar described in Chapter 3 stores its beer in its own

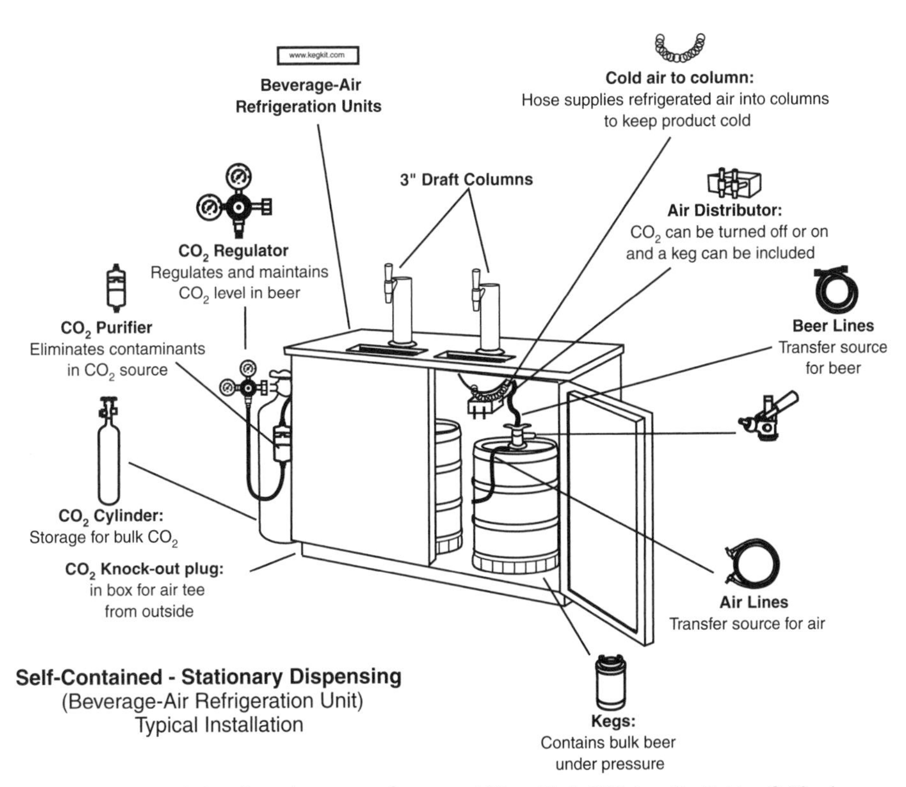

FIGURE 8.9 An underbar direct-draw setup. Courtesy of Micro Matic USA, Inc., Northridge, California.

walk-in cooler in the garage below the bar. With this type of remote system, which is also known as a **long-draw** system, the beer is piped up to the faucets at the bar; it is critical to keep the beer cold as it makes this journey. The beer lines are encased in a heavily insulated trunk line cooled with *glycol*. The longer the draft lines, the more expensive it is to install and maintain the system. Glycol systems require small electric pumps to keep the glycol cold and flowing, which is an extra expense and also raises utility costs, but they are recommended for beer lines of more than 25 feet or, if your bar doesn't store kegs in a walk-in cooler, lines of more than 14 feet.

Of course the best configuration would be to locate the cooler directly behind the bar so draft lines could be run through the wall and wouldn't have to snake very far from keg to tap. Figure 8.10 shows such a behind-bar system.

The other issue bar owners and their beer distributors must agree on is the type of gas used to propel the beer through the lines while maintaining the natural carbonation of the beer. Again, several options are available and you'll understand them better if you know more about how an individual keg is tapped.

The traditional beer system includes one or more kegs of beer, a cylinder of CO_2 with a *pressure gauge* (also called a *regulator*), a tap (faucet), heavy-duty lines (nylon or vinyl hoses) running from the **CO_2 cylinder** to the keg and from the keg to the tap, and a refrigerated **beer box** or remote cooler to store the keg. Figure 8.11 shows a keg as part of a basic system. The carbon dioxide gas in the CO_2 cylinder is under pressure of 1,000 pounds per square inch (psi) at room temperature. It has a pressure regulator that reduces the pressure of the gas between cylinder and keg, which is generally from 12 to 15 psi depending on the brand of beer. The CO_2 cylinder should be kept at room temperature. It should not be in the beer box with the keg.

The gas and beer lines are connected to the beer keg by couplings that fit into valves in the keg. Connecting the lines to the kegs is called **tapping.** There are two commonly used connection types:

- In one system the CO_2 line coupling fits into a valve in the top of the keg, and the beer line coupling fits into a valve at the bottom (Figure 8.12-a).
- In the other system a single coupling with two branches connects both the CO_2 and the beer lines through a valve in the top of the keg. CO_2 pressure forces the beer to rise through a long, hollow rod reaching up from the bottom of the keg to the beer line (Figure 8.12-b).

A popular alternative to the use of straight CO_2 is a **blended-gas** or **mixed-gas system,** which collects nitrogen (N_2) from the air and mixes it in a preset ratio with CO_2. This requires some additional equipment: a *nitrogen generator* to gather the nitrogen, a separate *regulator* for the nitrogen tank, and a *gas blender,* a chamber in which the N_2 and CO_2 are combined—or you can purchase mixed-gas canisters that already contain both N_2 and CO_2 in preset amounts. (**Blended gas** made for this purpose is also called **beer gas**.) Proponents of blended-gas systems say that it is more economical to use a gas blender than to purchase the mixed-gas canisters.

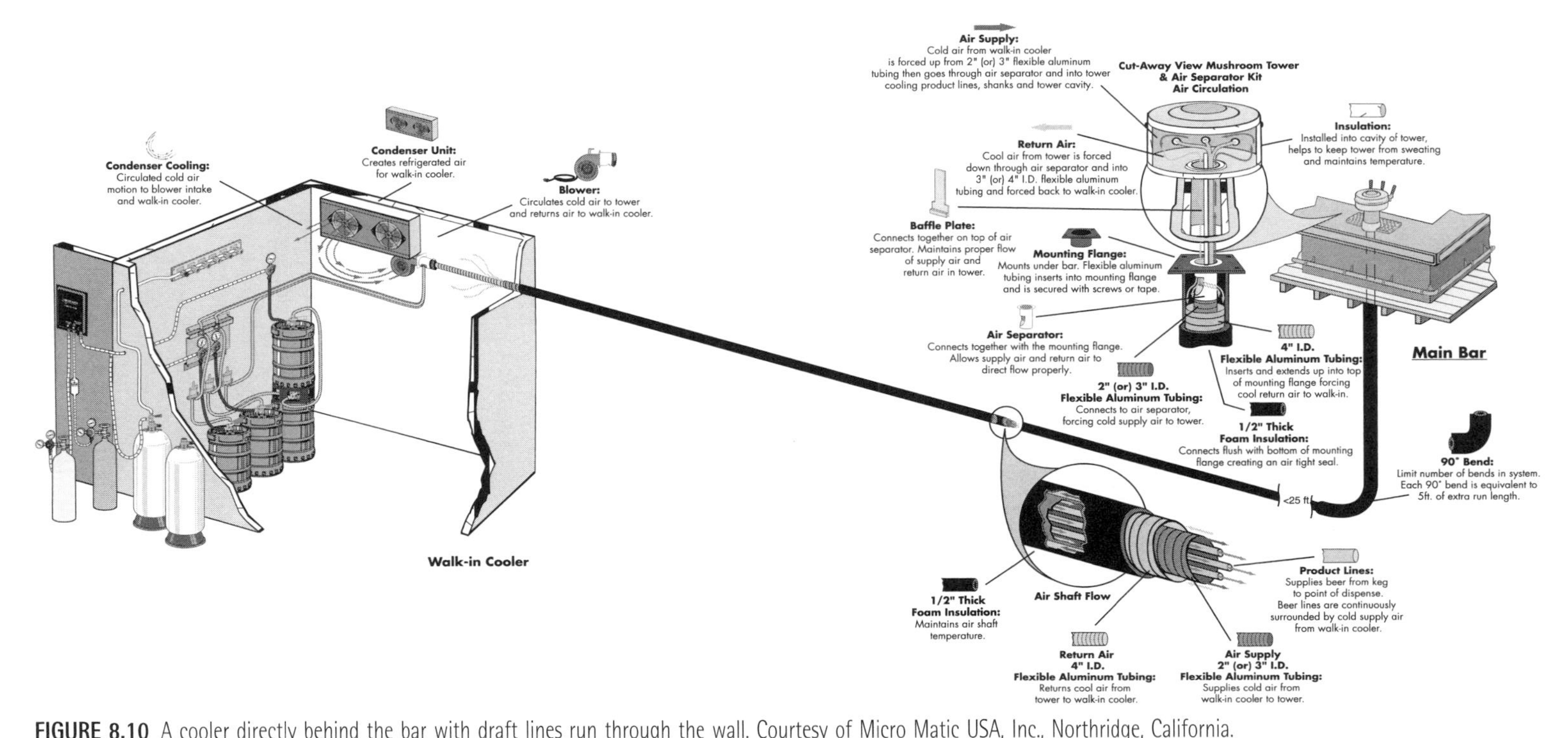

FIGURE 8.10 A cooler directly behind the bar with draft lines run through the wall. Courtesy of Micro Matic USA, Inc., Northridge, California.

FIGURE 8.11 A self-contained system. Dark lines carry beer from keg to tap. Light lines carry carbon dioxide to keg. Cylinder (not shown) is outside refrigerator at room temperature. Courtesy of Glastender, Inc., Saginaw, Michigan.

They also point to the fact that different types of beers require different CO_2 levels: 50-to-80-percent CO_2 is necessary for "fizzier" American beers, while the thicker, darker ales require only 25 percent CO_2 because they are not as highly carbonated. Different canisters with different percentages of gas mixtures enable each beer to be served at the appropriate CO_2 level.

With either system a separate pressure gauge indicates the pressure in the keg. When beer is sitting in the keg at a temperature of 38°F (2°C), its natural pressure is 12 to 15 psi. When a similar amount of gauge pressure is applied to the keg, it is enough to keep the natural carbonation in the beer and let it flow freely through the lines to the tap. If the pressure is too low (less than the natural pressure of the beer) the beer will lose carbonation and taste flat and stale. If the pressure is too high the beer will absorb too much carbonation from the CO_2 and it will foam too much upon pouring or will squirt wildly from the tap. The correct pressure, constantly maintained, will keep the beer in the keg lively and tasty.

Providing staff training about your bar's beer system is extremely important so that bartenders and servers can recognize and report problems. If the beer is too foamy, pours out too fast, or doesn't seem to taste right (according to customers), the system might not be working properly. A common mistake that decreases profitability is the unnecessary spillage that comes with drawing draft beer. For some reason people think it is necessary to open the spigot for a couple of seconds and let the foam spill out before putting a glass under the tap. If the taps are properly pressure-regulated, there is no need to do this. Never partially open a spigot: This automatically creates more foam!

In either system kegs may be connected in series, giving high-volume operations a continuous supply of beer without having to change kegs frequently (see Figure 8.13). Completely stainless-steel draft systems—storage keg, lines, and taps—are more sanitary and less susceptible to buildups in the lines. Your beer supplier can help you determine which tapping system is best for your bar and will supply the couplings that go with the type of kegs being delivered. Usually you must buy your gas cylinders from a different supplier. If you are serving more than one kind of draft beer, each beer type must have its own CO_2 and N_2 supply; as we've mentioned their pressure requirements may be different.

To care for your beer properly, you have to care for the whole beer system. The thermometer and the pressure gauge *should* be your allies, but if they are inaccurate, they can be your enemies. Check them frequently. If the arrow on the pressure gauge moves up or down from the pressure at which you set the regulator, either

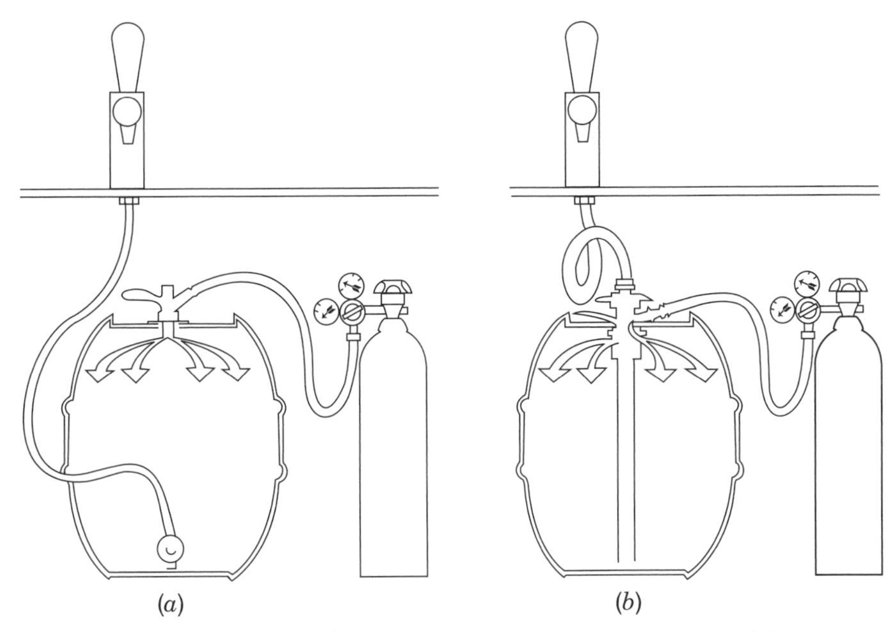

FIGURE 8.12 Two tapping systems. (*a*) Carbon dioxide enters at top of keg. Pressure sends beer up through line connected to keg at bottom. Keg must be tilted toward connection. (*b*) Carbon dioxide enters at top of keg. Pressure sends beer up through internal rod and into beer line. Both lines are attached to keg at top with single tapping device.

the regulator or the gauge is not doing its job properly. Check the thermometer by placing another thermometer in the cooler. Clean beer lines are essential to good beer taste. Dirty lines can cause pressure imbalances, as well as an eventual buildup of yeast and bacteria that will affect the beer's flavor. The beer may appear flat or cloudy and have an off-taste or odor that renders it unable to be sold. Beer lines should be thoroughly sanitized on a regular basis, usually once a week or at least once every two weeks. Your distributor may do this as part of the regular service in areas where it is allowed by law, you can do it yourself, or you can hire a professional beer-line cleaner. Since cleanliness is so vital to beer quality, the hired professional is often the best choice.

Short- and medium-length beer lines can usually be cleaned by your bar staff with simple, manually operated sterilizing equipment and special coil-cleaning compounds containing trisodium phosphate (TSP). The more sophisticated the beer system, the more technical the line-cleaning system process becomes. **Long draw** systems are cleaned with the same coil-cleaning compound, but an electric pump must be used for best results. Generally only professionals operate this type of equipment.

Never let your beer lines dry out. They should be kept full of beer at all times. If a line is left empty before a new keg is tapped, it will dry out, leaving dried beer residue and foam in the line, like a dirty beer glass. This will cause a bad taste and

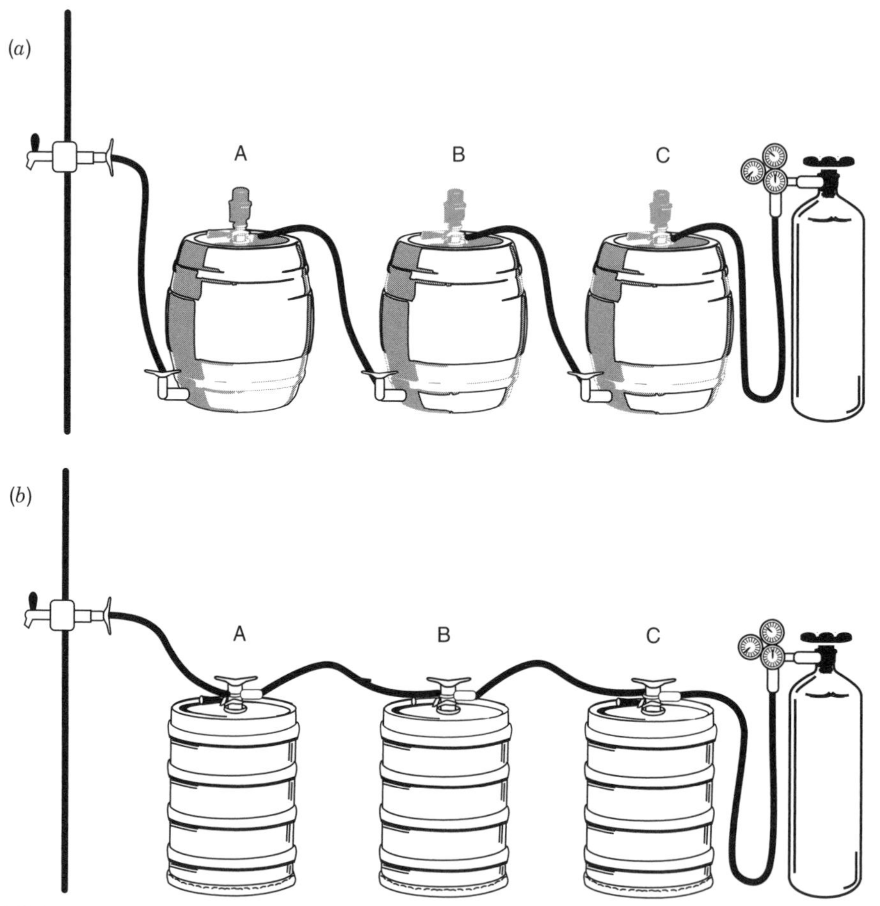

FIGURE 8.13 Kegs in series. Beer is drawn from keg nearest tap (*a*). Carbon dioxide enters keg (*c*), pushing beer flow from keg to keg. When fresh supplies are added, partly empty keg must be placed near carbon-dioxide cylinder.

is very unsanitary. In an emergency you can fill the beer line with water until a fresh keg is available. Then when the new keg is tapped, you must draw off all traces of water with the beer from the new keg.

Another housekeeping tip is to flush the drains below your beer taps with a pitcher of hot water and sanitizer when closing the bar for the night. Sometimes yeasts and bacteria can become active in the pipes overnight, clogging drains.

Since your distributor is the person you will call if your beer begins to taste funny, he or she may give you a list of troubleshooting suggestions, such as those listed in Figure 8.14. If you can figure out what is wrong, you will be able to give the distributor a clue, so the problem can be resolved faster. We suggest you make a copy of this table and post it at the bar. It also makes a good training guide.

TROUBLESHOOTING DRAFT-BEER PROBLEMS

Trouble	Causes
Flat beer	Greasy glasses Beer drawn too soon before serving Pressure: two low, leaky pressure line, sluggish regulator, pressure shut off overnight Obstruction in lines Loose connections (tap or vent) Long exposure to air instead of carbon dioxide pressure Precooler or coils too cold
Wild beer	Beer drawn improperly Too much pressure: faulty pressure valve or creeping gauge Beer too warm in keg or lines Lines: too long, poorly insulated, kinked or twisted Faucets in bad condition
Cloudy beer	Beer too warm at some time (storeroom or delivery) Beer frozen at some time Beer too cold Defective valves at keg Old beer (was stock properly rotated?) Lines: dirty, hot spots, poor condition
Bad taste	Keg too warm: 50°F and over at some time can cause secondary fermentation and sour beer Glasses: not beer-clean, not wet Dirty lines, dirty faucets Failure to clean beer lines Bad air in lines, oily air, greasy kitchen air Unsanitary conditions at bar
Unstable head	Beer drawn incorrectly (tilt of glass) Glasses not beer-clean Too short a collar Flat beer causes (see above)

FIGURE 8.14 Troubleshooting draft beer problems.

SERVING BEER

Serving a perfect glass of beer depends on three elements: the condition of the glass, the way the beer is poured, and the temperature of the beer. We will add a fourth, and more recent, priority for microbrews and premium imports: the type of glassware used.

Beer-Clean Glasses

This is absolutely critical! Have you ever had a beer that tasted flat or looked filmy? Chances are it was because of the glass it was poured into. A *beer-clean glass* is completely grease-free, film-free, and lint-free. Beer is incredibly susceptible to any type of grease, oil, fat, or foreign substance, visible or invisible, on the glass—including the detergents used for most other types of dishes. Any of these will spoil the foamy head on the beer, cause the CO_2 in the beer to dissipate immediately, and perhaps add an off-taste and unpleasant odor as well.

A beer-clean glass will support the original head and, as the glass is emptied, will leave the foam in rings on the sides of the glass. The taste will stay fresh and zesty all the way down to the bottom. The ideal way to achieve beer-clean glassware is to use a special glasswasher at the bar in which nothing but glasses are washed with a special fat-free washing agent. If you do not have a glasswasher you can produce a beer-clean glass by very carefully following the steps shown in Figure 8.15 and described here:

1. Using a special fat-free washing agent and hot water in the wash sink (a), submerge the whole glass and thoroughly brush the inside and rim with a glass brush designed for this purpose. Empty the glass of all wash water.

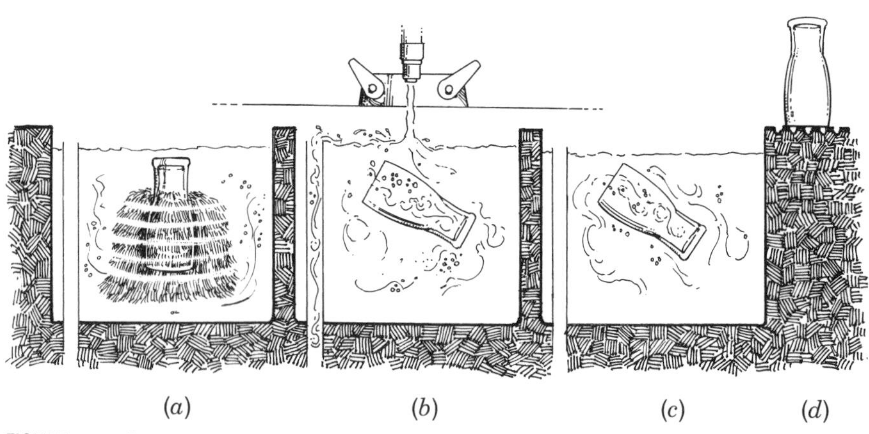

FIGURE 8.15 How to wash a glass "beer-clean."

2. In the rinse sink (b), in clean hot water (running water if possible) immerse the glass bottom end first, to be sure that you fill it completely. Swish it around or rotate it, then empty it.
3. In the sanitizing sink (c), repeat the rinsing procedure.
4. Turn the glass upside down on a clean rack or corrugated drainboard (d), and let it air-dry, inside and out. Do not place the glass on a towel or rubber mat or any flat surface; and do not dry it with a towel.

The bartender who polishes glasses until they sparkle does not exist anymore, if he or she ever did! There is a good reason for not polishing glasses: Bar towels and fingers can transmit grease, lint, chemicals, and bacteria to the glass.

A frosty beer glass or mug sounds especially appealing on a hot day, but even chilling beer glasses can be problematic. Moving a newly washed glass directly into a glass chiller before it is allowed to completely dry does not allow the sanitizing chemicals (used in the final rinse) to fully evaporate. This can leave an odd-tasting residue on the glass.

Pouring Beer

The second key to a perfect glass of beer is the way you pour it. A good, foamy head on a beer is a thing of beauty to a thirsty customer. The *head* is a collar of firm, dense foam reaching slightly above the top of the glass. It is the beer's natural way of releasing excess CO_2. The head is a total of ¾ to 1 inch thick and should be *tight,* made of tiny bubbles instead of large ones. If the head is scant the beer looks flat and lifeless, even when it is not. If the head is too thick the customer might feel cheated, and rightly so. The more foam, the less beer in the glass.

The size of the head depends on two factors: the angle at which you hold the glass while pouring and how long you hold the angle. Figure 8.16 shows you how. Rinse a beer-clean glass with fresh cold water and follow these steps:

1. Start by holding the glass upright (not angled), directly under (and about 1 inch below) the tap. Let the beer pour down into the middle of the glass, keeping the tap wide open (a).
2. When the glass is about half full, tilt it at a 45-degree angle and let the rest of the beer hit the side of the glass as it pours out of the tap. The foam that built in the first part of the "pour" is controlled during this second part. A tilted glass and steady stream of beer down the side stops the beer from foaming excessively (b).
3. When the head has risen a little higher than the rim of the glass (c), close the tap.

Notice that the draw is a single motion from beginning to end, not little spurts of opening and closing the tap. Some bartenders prefer to fill the glass three quarters full, then let it settle for a moment and put the head on last. This method

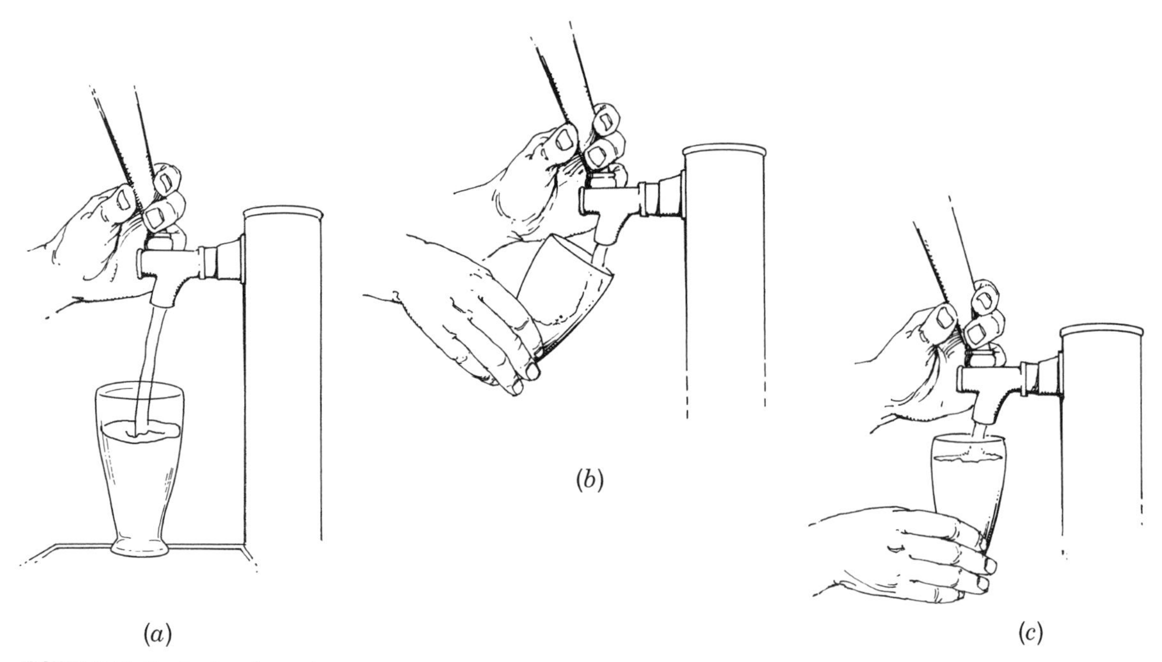

FIGURE 8.16 Pouring beer from a tap.

requires that you open and close the tap two times. A few practice draws will establish for you the angle of the glass and the time you should hold the angle to produce the head you want.

Sales representatives are fond of pointing out that your profit is in your head. But customer taste is your real criterion, and customers don't come back for little glasses that were mostly foam. When serving beer from a can or bottle you can produce a good head with the same tilting procedure, except that you place the glass upright and tilt the can or bottle instead, as shown in Figure 8.17. You should open the can or bottle in the customer's presence, to show that you are serving what the customer ordered, and proceed as follows:

1. Pour the beer straight into the center of the glass with the can or bottle at a steep angle (a) so that the beer gurgles out.
2. When it creates a fine-textured head of some substance, lower the angle (b) and fill the glass slowly until the foam rises to just above the lip.
3. Wipe the container and set it beside the glass on a coaster or napkin (c). Temperature is the third key to a perfect glass of beer. A lager-style beer that tastes "right" to the typical American customer is served at 40°F (4°C).

Ales may be served at 45°F (7°C). Stouts, porters, and bock beers are usually chilled only lightly, and other imports may have different serving temperatures. The glass the beer is served in has a big impact on its temperature.

FIGURE 8.17 How to serve beer from a bottle (or can).

Beer Glassware

The beer glass is part of the drinking experience, and just like fine wines, certain beer styles call for certain types of glassware. Figure 8.18 shows the two most common styles of beer glassware, mugs and pilsner glasses. Tall, thin pint glasses for stouts, ales, and porters have been in use for many years for a reason: They

FIGURE 8.18 Two of the most commonly used beer glasses, the pilsner and the mug.

help capture the full character of the beer. The traditional British 20-ounce pint glass is called a **nonik** or a *tulip pint,* which has slightly smoother sides than the nonik. All of these glasses are designed to allow the less-carbonated European ales and lagers to produce a decent-sized head.

The nonfooted pilsner glass is called a *pils,* a **vase,** or a *weizen glass*. Belgian ales and Scottish ales may be served in short-stemmed, wide-bottomed glasses that look like brandy snifters; they are also known as **thistles.**

The all-around beer glass most often seen in U.S. restaurants (but not pictured here) is called an **hourglass,** and is available in sizes from 10 to 16 ounces. Beer mugs or steins can hold up to 16 ounces. It is smart to stock two different glass sizes and price them accordingly. Not everyone wants a full pint.

Consider the thickness of the glass too. If beer is served in a thin glass at room temperature, its temperature will rise two degrees every couple of minutes. If served in a heavy glass, such as a thick mug, it may rise as much as five degrees. As such a 40°F beer served in a mug at room temperature may be 45°F by the time it hits the customer's mouth. This is one reason that frosted glasses or mugs for beer are in fashion, especially in warm climates. To some extent the freezer-frosted glasses are a merchandising gimmick: They spark interest and underscore beer's cooling, thirst-quenching character, and they do keep the beer cold longer. But some people don't like them. If the glasses make the beer too cold, the taste buds will perceive less flavor. Refrigerated glasses may be an alternative. Your beer distributor should have suggestions about which types of glasses to use, from German steins, to Trappist ale goblets, and whether to chill them before serving. Making the correct choices will impress knowledgeable beer customers and intrigue those who want to learn more.

SUMMING UP

This chapter provided an overview of the extremely competitive beer industry, including the trends now affecting U.S. brewers and customers in an increasingly global industry.

Beer rounds out the trio of alcoholic beverages found at every bar. Beer's four ingredients—malted grain, hops, water, and yeast—produce a lively, refreshing carbonated beverage that is as unique as the brewers that combine them. The two main types of beer are bottom-fermented lagers and top-fermenting ales, and within these categories are numerous subcategories, many of which were discussed in this chapter. Malternative beverages are among the most controversial, a cross between beer and spirits because of their brewing styles and ingredients. Nonalcoholic beers have also joined the beverage scene, although they are not technically beers.

Light beers, imports, and regional microbrews are the only beer categories that seem to be growing in an otherwise flat industry. When deciding on a beer list for a bar or restaurant, it is important to take these trends into consideration and to be savvy about promoting beer selections through on-premise events, menus, food-and-beer pairings, and the use of point-of-purchase reminders. Bars are in a unique

KNOW YOUR BREW: TRAINING YOUR STAFF TO SELL BEER

The more you know about beer, the easier it is to sell. Beer training involves two types of information—industry knowledge and product knowledge. Industry knowledge includes information on a beer's history, how it's made, and beer styles, origins, and ingredients. Product knowledge focuses more specifically on the brands available, what they taste like, what foods they go well with, and how to serve them.

"Training is a huge focal point for us," says Robert White, owner of the BrewHouse Pub in Helena, Montana. "It is important in brewpubs because guests often are trying these beers for the first time. Montana is still a domestic premium beer state. We're still far behind in terms of exposure to micros, so our guests can be intimidated by our beer list. The staff needs to be able to make them feel comfortable."

BrewHouse servers go through two weeks of initial training, with beer playing a big part of each day's session. They tour the brewery, study schematics of the brewing operation, and learn the smells and tastes of hops and malt, in addition to gathering general beer knowledge.

Some restaurateurs want their staff to focus on product knowledge. Beer training at the 19 units of Champps American (headquartered in Wayzata, Minnesota) concentrates on the chain's eight draft and 20 bottled beers. The staff attends formalized training sessions that teach information on characteristics of the draft beers, serving sizes, price points, and other specifics. Servers are tested on their knowledge before being allowed on the floor.

"In a new store environment, especially, distributors and vendors are eager to showcase their products," says Scott Dyke, director of beverage operations. "They'll come out and help with training and talk about the comparative nature of different beers."

To help servers memorize the range of 110 beers sold, Old Chicago Restaurants in Englewood, Colorado, provide flash cards with the name of each beer, its brewery and country of origin, and specific style. The chain also distributes training booklets with information describing the proper head, how to pour beer and other specifics.

"Servers need to understand the basics of how beer is made," agreed Larry Dwyer, general manager of the Hudson Club in Chicago. Known more for its 100+ wines sold by the glass, restaurant management takes beer just as seriously. With 20 draft beers and 70 more in bottles, the Hudson Club tries to represent every beer style with a couple of excellent examples.

The Hudson Club holds general training sessions every Saturday, with additional beer training sessions scheduled whenever the beer list changes every six to eight weeks. At each beer session, Dwyer offers a general beer refresher, and then concentrates on tasting products, discussing production methods, pairing beers with menu items, and discussing serving and sales techniques. Servers are quizzed the following Thursday about the information.

Beer training has obvious benefits. Servers who sell more beer or persuade customers to trade up or try a menu item as a result of suggestive selling make more money for the house and usually a bigger tip. Servers who help customers find the right beer or the right menu item to go with it are providing the kind of service that brings customers back. That's another win for both the restaurant and the server.

(continued)

Another way to motivate the troops and make beer training stick is through incentives. The Hudson Club gives prizes, such as a magnum of Spaten Oktoberfest, to those who score highest on the Thursday quizzes. At Old Chicago Restaurants, servers play "Beer Jeopardy" for "staff cash," money that can be spent in the restaurants on food and merchandise. During special promotions, servers are given incentives, usually cash, tied to sales of certain brands.

Champps relies heavily on suppliers for incentives, particularly for promotions tied to their brands. Recently, servers in the Denver unit of Old Chicago had the chance to win a Sam Adams leather jacket to help improve brand sales. Other staff contest awards have included trips to California's wine country, cash, and merchandise.

"It helps to give incentives to managers and bartenders, too," Dyke adds, "because if you do not have them follow up, you will not meet your objectives."

Six Selling Strategies

Hundreds of sales technique books have been published. Your area's wholesale beer distributors and local craft brewers can help with training, and most major breweries offer pamphlets, videos, posters, and more. When it comes to selling beer or food, here are six strategies that operators rely on.

Use descriptive language.
Describe how a beer is made and how it tastes. Involve customers by telling a story about where it comes from or how it originated.

Ask open-ended questions.
Get customers to tell you what kind of beer they like, then guide them to one or two on your list that fit their tastes.

Suggest sharing.
If two guests order the same beer, suggest a pitcher for the table.

Suggest the larger size.
Many operations offer two sizes, such as a glass and a pint. When guests don't indicate which they want, servers should confirm their order by asking, "A pint, ma'am?"

Sell your favorites.
The more enthusiastic you are about an item, the more likely a customer will order it. When customers ask for recommendations, suggest what you like best.

Suggest natural complements.
When a customer makes a beer selection, suggest an appetizer or entree that goes particularly well with that brand or style of beer.

Source: Condensed from an article by Mike Sherer, *"World champion beer sellers train their staffs into tip-top brew shape,"* in *Cheers,* a publication of Adams Beverage Group, Norwalk, Connecticut, June 1999.

position to offer customers a chance to try new things—but only if customers know about them.

Beer is a product with a short lifespan and a need for special care. For certain clienteles draft beer is a big attraction, and is worth the space it takes, the added cost of constant refrigeration, and the care required in keeping it at its best. This chapter included every consideration for correct storing and serving of beer, from ideal temperature ranges, to selection of a draft-beer system, to cleaning glassware and pouring beer correctly. Employees should be well trained, not only in beer-making techniques and flavor profiles, but in the mechanics of pouring a consistently top-quality product. This involves how to operate and care for a beer system, how to wash and chill glasses, how to rotate stock, how to pour beer, and how to use beer in cooking and beer-based cocktails.

POINTS TO PONDER

1. Select a major multinational brewing company and trace its history of growth and acquisitions. Describe the possible reasons that the company has for acquiring and/or selling the properties it has bought and/or sold, and predict its future for the next five years based on the sources of your research.
2. Where do you stand on the controversy about malt liquor? Would you work to change its reputation, or keep the public stir "brewing," so to speak? Explain what you would do and why.
3. What does beer have in common with Champagne and soft drinks? How do the care and service of beer resemble the care and service of these other beverages?
4. Explain which conditions you would want if you were installing a remote beer system because you did not have room to put it at the bar.
5. Your customers have been complaining that their beer "tastes flat." What might the possible causes be? How would you analyze and correct this problem?
6. Who determines whether or not the alcohol content of a beer appears on the label? How does this differ from the labeling of wines and spirits?
7. In what way is each of the following related to beer quality in the glass: Temperature? Pressure? Care of the beer lines? Age? The glass itself?
8. Describe three current trends in beer consumption, and comment on their significance to a bar or restaurant. Use this knowledge to create a beer list using the suggested ten-beer format.
9. List three ways that you can increase beer sales in a restaurant.
10. How is the alcohol taken out of nonalcoholic beer? Why should a bar stock this type of product?

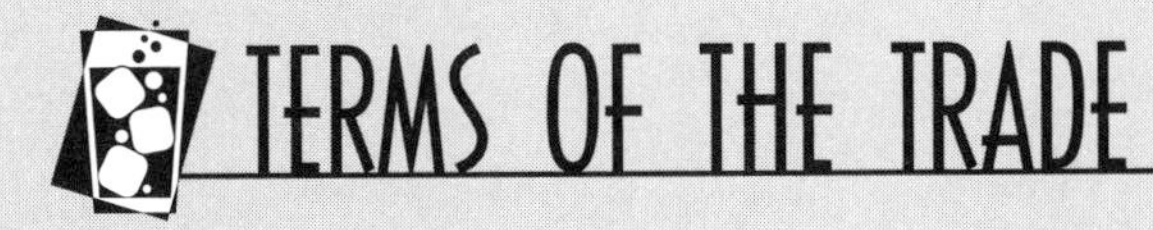

TERMS OF THE TRADE

abbey ales, abbey beers	barrel	blended gas
additives	beer box	blonde beer
adjuncts	beer gas	bock
altbier	beer system	born-on date (BOD)
barley wine	bitter (ale)	bottom-fermented

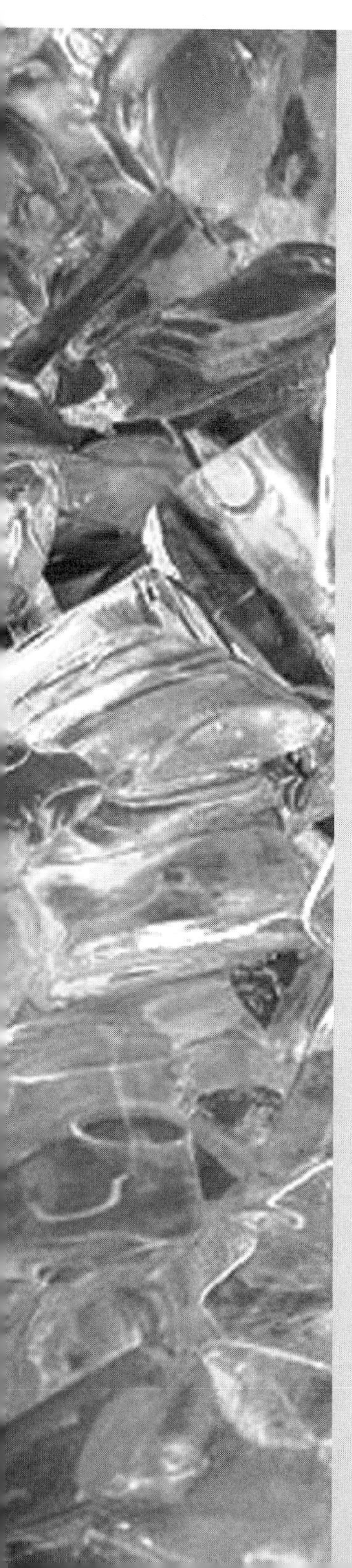

brewer's yeast
brewpub
bruised beer
cask-conditioned
chalice
CO_2 cylinder
contract brewery
craft brewery
direct draw
doppelbock
draft beer
eisbock
event marketing
firkin
head
hops
hourglass
India Pale Ale (IPA)
keg
kilning
krausening
krystal
lager
lagering
lambic
lawnmower beer
long draw
macrobrewery
malt
malt liquor
malternative
mash tun
microbrewery
mixed pint
N_2 canister
nitrogenated
nonik
off-premise
on-premise
pils
Pilsner (Pilsener)
porter
pull date
ready-to-drink (RTD)
steam beer
stout
tapping
thistle
top-fermented
vase
wheat malt
wild-fermented
wort

CHAPTER 9
SANITATION AND BAR SETUP

The design of the bar workspace requires using every inch as efficiently as possible, but setting up the bar means organizing it for smooth operation each day. This entails two elements: organization, or creating the correct routine for the setup, which is a management responsibility; and the actual setup tasks, which bar personnel perform. The manager should see to it that every bartender and barback is trained to clearly understand the setup routines and carry them out with precision and care. The correct procedures for closing the bar, at the end of the day or the end of a work shift, are equally important.

In addition to organization this chapter stresses the need for sanitation routines, which have always been critical but take on even more importance with the increase in major food-safety scares and the resulting liability claims of recent years. The discussion of sanitation will be useful for you in terms of ensuring quality and establishing sanitation standards, training employees, giving meaningful follow-up and feedback, and substituting at the bar in emergencies. The manager also has ultimate responsibility for correcting sanitation issues, no matter who is careless.

THIS CHAPTER WILL HELP YOU . . .

- Set, teach, and maintain sanitation standards and routines.
- Set up and maintain bar stock.
- Arrange liquor supplies for efficient pouring.
- Determine the mixes, garnishes, condiments, and accessories needed, and train employees to prepare and set them up.

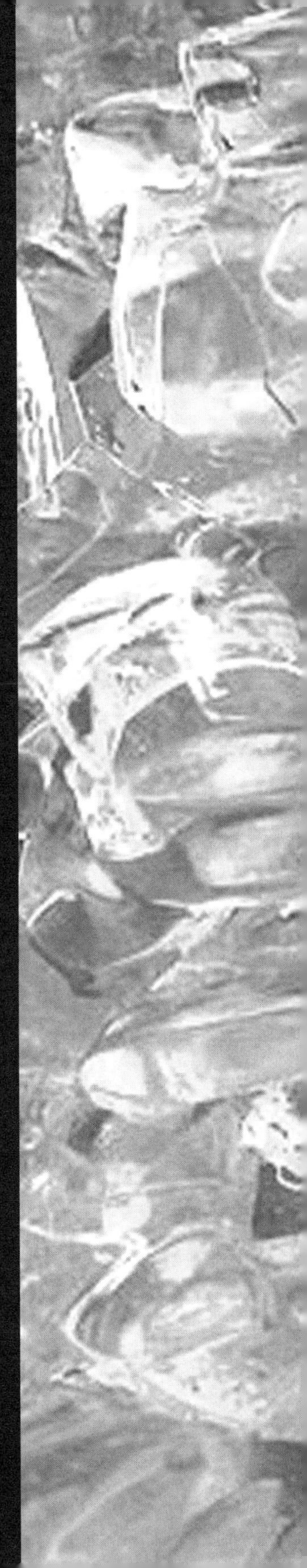

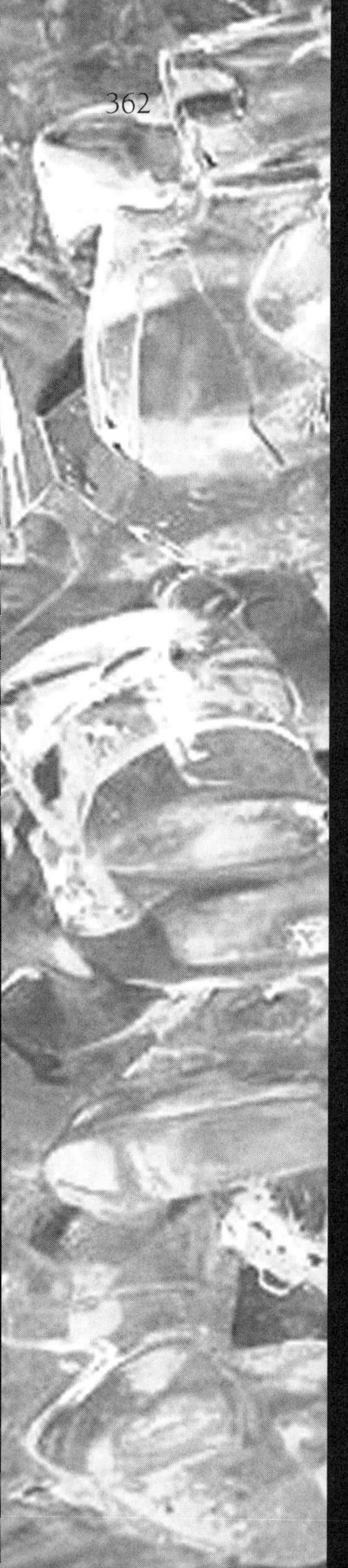

- Train employees to handle glasses and ice properly.
- Set up and close the cash register and train employees to do so.
- Coach employees in behind-the-bar behavior.
- Close down the bar correctly, and train employees in closing procedures.

Usually your bartender sets up the bar. You will have scheduled his or her shift to begin half an hour or so before you open your doors so that everything will be ready. There is nothing very complicated about being ready; it involves a series of routines, a few rules, and good organization. Efficient organization is the ingredient that you supply by clearly communicating the way you want things done and the way you have trained your employees. If you have everything organized, the day will flow smoothly. If something is overlooked or left undone, customers will have to wait for their drinks and your bartenders will be playing catch-up all day.

The essentials of setting up are few. Everything must be superclean. The day's supplies of everything you need must be on hand and in position. Most bars have a diagram of liquor and mixer locations for a workstation, as shown in Figure 9.1. The list also includes beer, wine, ice, glasses, garnishes, condiments, utensils, bar towels, napkins, snack foods, ashtrays, matches, and money in the register. That's it! Now, let's take a closer look at how to get it all ready.

SANITATION

Cleanliness is essential for two equally important reasons: customer appeal and customer health. Your local health department comes into the picture, too, and its inspectors are the guardians of customer health. If you don't meet the health-department standards you can be fined or even lose your permit to operate. But most health regulations establish only minimum standards for cleanliness and safety so your goal should be to exceed them.

A clean bar is an attractive bar. It has sparkling glassware, gleaming countertops, clean ashtrays, and fresh-looking garnishes, and everything is neatly arranged. The underbar should be in the same condition, with shiny-clean stainless steel, all bottles in order, and ice bins full to the brim with fresh ice. Remember, this is *all* visible to customers, if not directly, then in the mirror. Even though the underbar functions as the "kitchen area" of the bar, in a real kitchen, the chef can make a mess and clean up later since he or she is working behind the scenes. The bartender has no such luxury. Train your bartenders to start clean and work clean.

Bacterial Hazards

Fortunately a bar does not present nearly as many potential health hazards as a commercial kitchen. Very few things that you serve from the bar are potential vehicles for illness or disease. In fact in most cases alcohol kills bacteria. However, most bars now include some type of foodservice and, even if yours is the rare exception, there will be a few items on hand that may harbor unhealthful types of

Work Station With Soda Gun

Front Counter Top

DRINK RAIL	Gun	DRINK RAIL	
Laminated work counter	TOM CR GR OJ	Ice storage (Jockey box)	Drain board

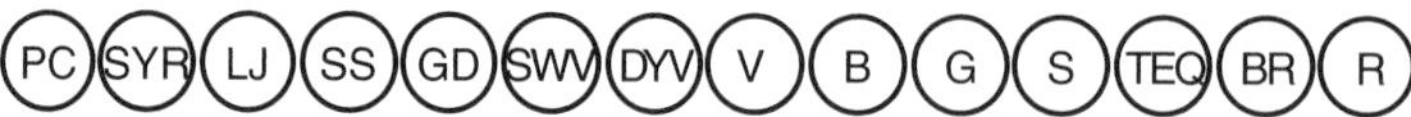

Definition of Abbreviations

Bottled Mixes in the Speed Rack		Bottled Juices		Well Alcohol	
PC	Pina colada	TOM	Tomato	TEQ	Tequila
GD	Grenadine	CR	Cranberry	TS	Triple sec
LJ	Lime juice	GR	Grapefruit	B	Bourbon
S/S	Sweet & sour	OJ	Orange	G	Gin
SWV	Sweet vermouth			V	Vodka
DYV	Dry vermouth			SC	Scotch
SYR	Simple syrup			BR	Brandy
				R	Rum

FIGURE 9.1 A diagram of a well-organized workstation.

bacteria. Your employees should know about these and be aware of the nature and habits of bacteria in order to understand why it is important to treat cleanliness very seriously. If the business includes a kitchen the health department may require workers who prepare and serve food to pass a food-safety-and-sanitation class. (If the health department does not do this you should make it your own requirement—and take the class yourself as well.) This training will be based on the popular *Hazard Analysis of Critical Control Points* **(HACCP)** system, a seven-step program designed to find and eliminate potential problem areas for contamination and sanitation, as well as for correct food-storage, cooking, and serving temperatures.

Bacteria that cause disease in humans have two characteristics that of particular importance to food-and-beverage enterprises. First bacteria multiply at room and body temperatures, and second they multiply very quickly. They do this by splitting in half. If conditions are right they can double themselves every 20 minutes or so. This means that one bacterium can become 4,000 bacteria in four hours. To do this a bacterium needs three things: moisture, warmth, and food.

Luckily, few foods at the bar make good nourishment for bacteria. Potentially hazardous foods include:

Dairy products: eggs, milk, and cream
Meat products: beef, pork, fish, poultry, and stock
Sauces: especially those that need to be heated or refrigerated
Hors d'oeuvres or **appetizers:** containing any of the items listed above

A single episode of foodborne illness can be devastating to your establishment's reputation as a business that serves the public. Hundreds of outbreaks of disease occur every year, through ingesting either contaminated food or drinking water, and health officials believe that many more go unreported. The way to avoid such disasters in your business is to keep your hot foods hot and your cold foods cold. The danger range for bacterial growth is 40°F to 140°F (7°C to 60°C), as shown in Figure 9.2. Bring your hot foods *hot* from the kitchen, and keep them above 140°F (60°C) until they are served. Holding equipment for maintaining foods at this temperature should be set at 165°F to 180°F (74°C to 82°C). Keep your hazard-prone cold foods at 40°F (4°C) until they are about to be served. Check your refrigerator temperatures daily and make sure that they are at the correct temperature.

Preventing the Spread of Bacteria. Most bacteria spread when germs brought in by people are transmitted to other people. Your health department may require your employees to get routine doctors' examinations to help prevent the introduction of chronic diseases into the workplace. But *everyone* carries bacteria and viruses of various sorts in the nose, mouth, and throat, on the hands, skin, and hair *all the time,* so of course it is impossible to prevent all occurrences. We all know how colds, flu, and other viruses can spread when people sneeze or cough, sending viruses catapulting into the open air where others can inhale them. Germs can also be transmitted more directly, by touching, and indirectly, on glasses, towels, or napkins.

To fight all of this "undercover" bacterial action, all bar equipment must be kept sanitary and scrupulous personal cleanliness is necessary. Each staff member must have clean hands, clean nails, clean clothing, and clean hair at all times. Each employee must wash his or her hands as a matter of course before beginning work, before handling equipment and supplies, after using the bathroom, after blowing the nose or covering a sneeze, after smoking, and as necessary during the workday. Many health codes require a separate hand sink at the bar for this purpose. Soap, hot water, and thoroughness are essentials. Effective hand-washing for handling foods and beverages takes a minimum of 20 seconds and includes a prerinse, the use of soap, and a complete final rinse-and-dry. Paper towels from a dispenser, not cloth towels, are used for hand-drying. The U.S. Food and Drug Administration (USFDA) also recommends a thorough scrubbing of the fingernails with a nail brush.

The consequences of lax hand-washing in foodservice make news headlines in numerous communities. Poor personal hygiene is the second cause of all foodborne illness, topped only by improper holding temperatures of food, and is responsible for as many as 30 percent of disease outbreaks according to the U.S. Centers for Disease Control (CDC). A number of companies now market high-tech hand-washing and monitoring systems. This noncontact "touchless" (which means that the employee can not spread germs by touching the faucets, soap, or towel dispenser) equipment automatically delivers hot water, soap, and a sanitizing solution, and even has the capacity to track hand-washing data and download it to a com-

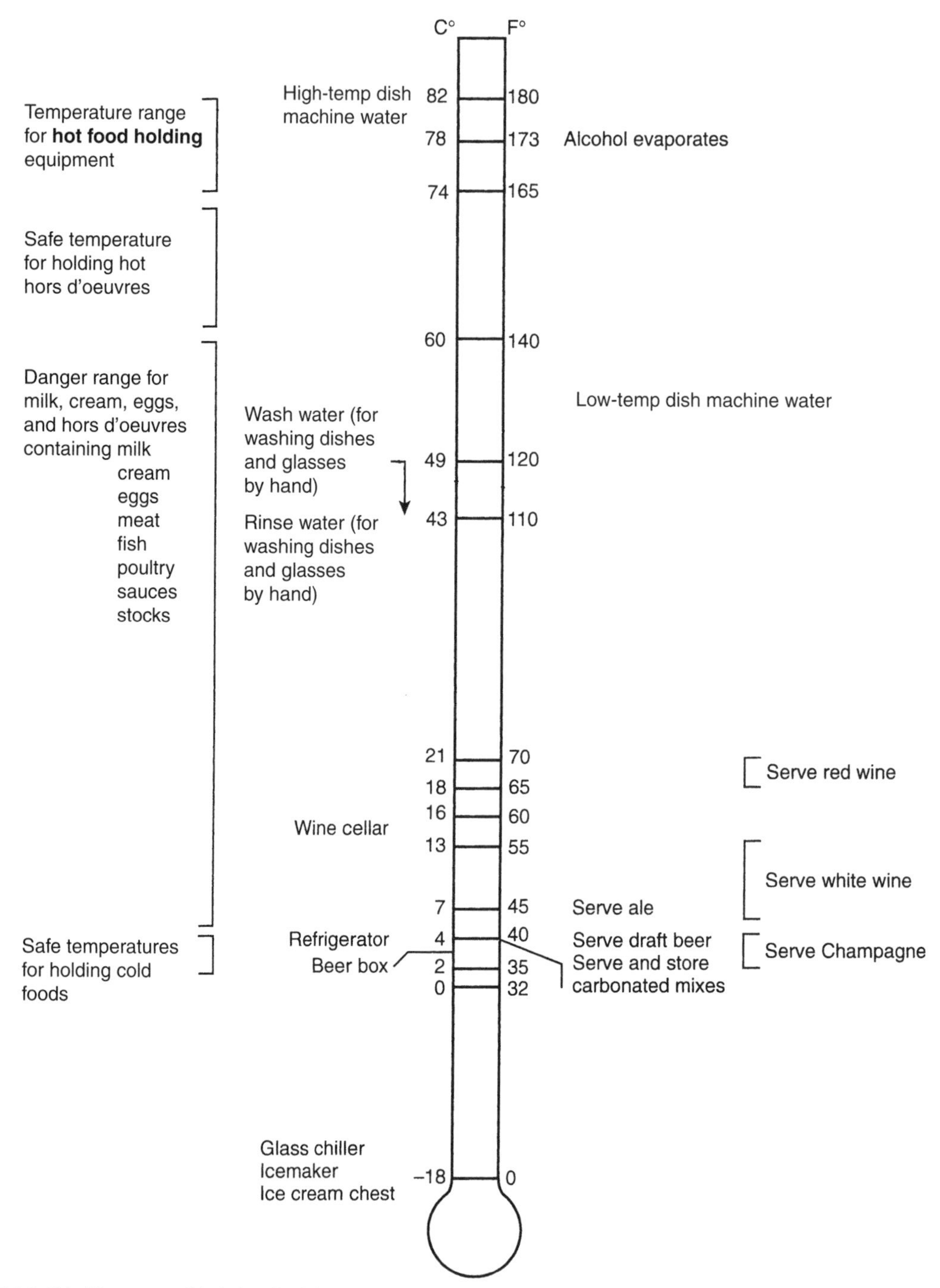

FIGURE 9.2 This "thermometer" includes all of the temperature ranges necessary for food-and-drink safety and sanitation.

puter. Other machines sanitize hands with infrared or ozone technology: All you do is stick your hands in the machine past the wrist. For off-premise caterers waterless hand-sanitizing products are available.

Although technology has made some very useful advances in sanitation, none will replace your own vigilant training and monitoring of employees, to create a sanitation culture in which safety is always a top priority, without exceptions. You should insist that employees stay home if they have colds or other illnesses. A cut, sore, or lesion of any kind should be securely covered. If a cut occurs on the job, it must be bandaged immediately and covered with a plastic glove. Any food, liquid, or ice on which blood is spilled must be discarded, and any glassware or equipment that blood touches must be washed and sanitized using whatever sanitizer your local health department requires. There should be no hand contact with ice. If your employees use plastic gloves in any aspect of serving, which is often a health-department requirement today, these gloves should be disposable. Employees must be taught to remove the gloves correctly (inside out) and to change them frequently because glove surfaces can harbor bacteria as readily as the hands themselves.

Spills should be wiped up promptly. Warm and moist, they can be ideal breeding grounds for bacteria. Used bar towels should be relegated to the laundry, *never* just rinsed in the bar sinks for reuse. Towels are among the worst offenders in spreading disease. A common habit among service personnel is to carry a towel on the shoulder or tucked in the belt. Doing so is unsanitary and should not be allowed.

Washing Glassware and Utensils. Glassware and utensils should be washed as soon as possible after use; dirty glasses are bacteria breeding grounds. The same method that produces a beer-clean glass (see Chapter 8) produces a bacteria-free glass. In case you don't have a glasswashing machine, you must teach employees to use the triple sink correctly. The water in the wash sink should be 120°F (49°C); do not let it cool below 110°F (43.3°C).

It is important to use the right amount of detergent. The package instructions indicate a specific amount of detergent per gallon of water, so to measure correctly you must know how many gallons your sink holds. The nonfat detergent you use for your beer-clean glasses is suitable for all of your other glasses. Brushing the glass thoroughly is particularly important; pay special attention to the rim for traces of lipstick, as well as the invisible residues of use. The rinse water in your middle sink should be 110°F (43.3°C). The water should be changed often, or you can let the faucet run slowly and the overflow drain take away sudsy or cloudy water.

The third sink is for sanitizing, the most important of the three steps because it kills bacteria and makes the glasses truly clean. Very often your health department will recommend or specify a particular sanitizing compound. Again follow the package instructions carefully to mix the right amount per gallon of water. Use too much compound and it might linger on the glass; use too little and it won't do the job. The water temperature should be at least 75°F (24°C) but not more than 120°F (49°C) to produce the right chemical reaction. Glasses should be submerged for 60 seconds, and the solution should be changed if it starts to look cloudy.

Functional Water. If you can call research about water exciting, then the development of so-called **functional water** for sanitizing and disinfecting is certainly that. Also known as **electronically altered water (EAW)** or **structured water**, the end product is created by adding a small amount of salt to water and then electrolyzing it. The results can be either acidic (low pH) water with the same disinfecting power as if chlorine had been added, or alkaline (high pH) water with extra cleaning power for tough grease and protein stains. An advantage of functional water is its safety in case of accidental ingestion or contact with skin and eyes. Another benefit is environmental: No harsh chemicals go into the drainage system.

Of course this new technology is controversial and has its critics. After all how would anyone but an expert with a laboratory be able to tell if the water had been altered, or altered correctly, to produce the desired benefits? But the proliferation of foodborne-illness scares has spawned a small army of companies that sell the electrolyzing machines. Sizes range from countertop units that weigh 6 or 7 pounds and are capable of making 2 liters of acidic or alkaline EAW in 15 minutes, to huge commercial units that can turn out 10 gallons of acidic or 25 gallons of alkaline EAW per minute. Other industries are experimenting with water-altering technology as well, including beverage-bottling companies. Proponents of EAW say that it produces a smoother-tasting, more flavorful soft drink.

Handling Glassware and Utensils. All glasses should be air-dried by inverting them onto a deeply corrugated drainboard, a wire rack, or a thick plastic netting made for the purpose. These surfaces should, of course, also be clean. Air-drying avoids recontamination by fingers and towels. The rack, netting, or corrugated surface allows air to circulate inside the glass as well as outside, removing the moisture that germs love—if any have survived the rigors of the thorough washing routine.

As part of their initial training, your service personnel should be coached about how to handle glassware. Fingers should never touch the inside of a glass even if it is empty and whether it is clean or dirty. Fingers should stay off the rim and should not touch the outside of the glass anywhere below the rim where a person's lips may touch it while taking a drink. Similarly the insides of mixing glasses, cups, and plastic containers; the bowls of spoons; and the "business end" of any utensil should not be touched. *Anything* that touches food or drink should be untouched by human hands. This includes the actual food or drink, as well as ice. NSF International says that sanitation should be a way of life. If this is to be true in your enterprise your own attitude, plus the training you provide, must set the tone.

LIQUOR SUPPLIES

One of the first things the bartender does in setting up is to replenish the supplies of liquor used the day before. Each bar should have a standard brand-by-brand list of liquors, beers, and wines that should be in stock at the bar to begin the workday, with specified quantities of each brand. This is known as **par stock.** The primary purpose of par stock is to ensure an adequate working supply, one day at a time. When setting up the bar the bartender checks the bottles in stock against the list and adds from the storeroom whatever is needed to bring the stock "up to par." Figure 9.3 is a typical par stock form.

Getting the liquor from the storeroom typically involves filling out a requisition slip or some other form to record what is being withdrawn, signed by the person withdrawing it. In a small enterprise only the manager and perhaps one other person, such as the assistant manager or head bartender, have access to the store-

BAR PAR STOCK FORM

Bar Name
Address

Effective as of (date): ____________ Bar Outlet: ________
Page _____ of _______ (total pages)

Item Number	Item Name	Size	Bar	Par	Item Number	Item Name	Size	Bar	Par

FIGURE 9.3

room. In a large operation there is a storeroom staff and no one else is allowed in. A requisition slip requesting the liquor is presented to the person in charge, who issues the liquor and signs the slip. In this way the amount is recorded as the liquor leaves the storeroom and responsibility is pinpointed for issuing it. This amount now becomes the responsibility of the person withdrawing it, who has also signed the slip. (Requisitioning and issuing processes are described in greater detail in Chapter 13.)

Next the beverages must be arranged for efficient use. Bottled beer, white wine, and sparkling wine must be chilled; the stock in the refrigerator must be rotated to bring forward the cold bottles from the day before. The speed rail at each station must be checked to be sure that there is a starting supply in every bottle, and reserves must be set up, with pourers in place, for those that are almost empty. The arrangement of bottles in the well must also be checked and arranged in a standard order, with the most-used liquors in front of the ice bin. Having every bar staff member adhere to an arrangement ensures that every bartender knows where every bottle is and can reach it with speed and accuracy. If one bottle is out of place another will be, too, and a guest might end up with tequila in a Vodka Martini.

Pourers should be checked daily. If corks on stainless-steel pourers are wearing and becoming loose, replace them. All pourers should be positioned at right angles to the label and the bottles should all face the same way, so that the bartender can use each one quickly without having to check the direction of the pour.

Setup is also the time to check the draft-beer system to prepare for the first draw of the day. If the beer lines in your system are not properly cooled all the way to the faucet, there may be some warm beer in the dispensing head that will foam when the faucet is opened. Draw beer until a clear, solid stream of beer is present in the line, with no water or excessive foam; then it is ready to go.

MIXES

During setup the supply of mixes must be checked and replenished, and any that you make fresh must be prepared. It is advisable to have a list of quantities needed daily—essentially "par stock" for mixes—based on records of past sales. Amounts may vary according to the day of the week, with some quantities rising on weekends. You do not want an oversupply of fresh-made mixes since they won't stay fresh indefinitely. More about that in a moment.

There are several mixes for specific drinks: Bloody Mary, Daiquiri, Margarita, Mai Tai, and Pina Colada. All you do is add the liquor. Of these the frozen concentrates are likely to be best. Commercial mixes are handiest for bars in which demand for some types of drinks is low. If there's not much call for Pina Coladas, why stock coconut cream and pineapple juice if a good mix is available or if one that can be "doctored" slightly to fit your needs? To a Bloody Mary mix, for example, you might add your own splash of lime juice, cumin, horseradish, olive juice, roasted garlic, or spicy salsa. A splash of lemon juice can enliven a sweet-and-sour mix.

When selecting mixes look for consistency of product. Taste each contender straight, then taste it again on the rocks. Instruct the bartender to taste each mix for freshness before each shift. The management staff at Chicago's Alligator Alley tried five different brands of Margarita mix before settling on one brand. They sell a lot of by-the-pitcher cocktails, so a prepared sweet-and-sour mix provided the necessary volume and consistency. The Iron Cactus restaurant in Austin, Texas, evaluated a variety of commercially made sweet-and-sour mixes and ended up creating a proprietary brand when managers were not satisfied with the others. The mix is used only for Frozen Margaritas; fresh lime juice is used for other tequila-based drinks.

Water Safety and Potability

One of the mixers that you will use the most is the one that you probably take for granted: water. Americans drink nearly 2 gallons of water per person per day, and yet there are serious water-quality problems in many cities and towns. Because you will use water to make ice, to mix drinks, to brew coffee, to serve on its own, and to wash glasses and dishes, you should be keenly aware of the water quality in your area.

In the United States the Environmental Protection Agency (EPA) is responsible for setting, implementing, and monitoring water-quality standards. The EPA's critics say that hundreds of toxic substances have been found in random samples of drinking water, and they decry the minimal standards that water suppliers are required to meet. How safe is your drinking water? It depends on where you live and when you check it. Water quality varies from city to city, season, and even from day to day within a single water system. Common problems that might affect the water that a bar business uses include odd taste, color, or *turbidity* (cloudiness), possibly caused by a substance, such as chlorine or fluoride, that your city uses to treat water. The most common waterborne parasites include **Cryptosporidium** and **Giardia lamblia,** which both cause flu-like symptoms: e.g., diarrhea and vomiting. With that in mind you might want to consider filtering your tap water.

A number of commercial filters are available, depending on what you are filtering out. You can get systems that, for example, kill viruses, remove particles or heavy metals, counteract taste or odor problems, and absorb chemicals. For commercial use the **micron rating** of a water filter is an important consideration. It refers to the size of particles the filter can remove: A lower micron rating means greater filtration. To remove the parasites mentioned above NSF International requires a **submicron rated filter** that removes at least half-micron-sized (1/50,000 inch) particles. Compare that to a system designed to filter only chlorine, which has a rating of 5 to 10 microns. NSF International also recommends a submicron filter that carries a 99-percent particle-reduction rating; an ordinary water filter has an

85-percent rating. (NSF International is an objective third-party organization that tests equipment for safety and sanitation standards, so you should look for its certification on any system you are considering.) The specific standards that a system must meet are Standard 42, which means the filter complies with taste and odor guidelines, and Standard 53, which means the filter complies with health guidelines, including the reduction of *Giardia* and *Cryptosporidium*.

To keep a water filtration system in top shape, you must replace the filter cartridges at least every six months or as instructed by the manufacturer. Cartridges are rated by the number of gallons that can pass through them before they need to be replaced—say 9,000 gallons. Use only the brand of cartridge intended for the system, otherwise you will void any warranty that was part of the sale.

Bottled Water. In 2003 Americans consumed 6.4 million gallons of bottled water, a 7.5-percent increase over the 2002 figure and one that marketers of other beverages can only dream about. Bottled water gains additional market appeal as consumers become more interested in fitness and nutrition. But what about bottlers' claims of purity? In 2000—when U.S. consumption of bottled water had already topped 17 gallons per person—a survey released by the National Resource Defense Council concluded that bottled water is not necessarily any purer or safer than ordinary tap water. This environmental advocacy group also asserted that one in four gallons sold is nothing more than smartly packaged water from a municipal system. The truth is that tap water receives more health-related scrutiny than bottled water, and about two-thirds of bottled water sold in the United States is exempt from federal regulations because it never crosses state lines.

What exactly is in bottled water? France and Italy, the world's two major bottled-water exporters, produce it in an untreated state. It is truly *ground water,* collected from protected underground sources that have not come in contact with animals, people, or the pathogens they might carry. U.S.-made bottled water is often *surface water,* but what is labeled *spring water* must (according to the USFDA) originate underground and flow naturally to the surface. This applies to *artesian* and *well water* also. But much of the U.S.-bottled water is simply, as it states on the label, *purified drinking water* with no special attributes. The USFDA also says that bottled water must be calorie-free and contain no added sweeteners or chemicals; flavors, extracts, or essences may be added if they compose less than 1 percent of the weight of the final product, which allows a few of the fruit-flavored sparkling waters. As with wines, the term **sparkling** is used to identify waters to which carbon dioxide (CO_2) has been artificially added to create bubbles. Some waters are naturally carbonated; light carbonation (effervescence) is up to 3 grams of CO_2 per liter; moderate carbonation is 3 to 6 grams per liter; and 6 to 9 grams of CO_2 is considered highly carbonated water.

Mineral water has its own mystique and can be marketed and upsold just like wine. For the most part, it is rainwater and melted snow that has percolated over the years through permeable soil and rock, soaking up minerals that endow it with (sometimes distinctly) different tastes. Actual mineral content varies by source, but a water is considered lightly mineralized at less than 500 milligrams per liter, and highly mineralized at more than 1,000 milligrams per liter. The source of most mineral water is deep subterranean aquifers, where a constant temperature and the

BOTTLED-WATER MOCKTAILS

Perrier from France was the first bottled-water product to break into the U.S. market. The company even created nonalcoholic-drink recipes to complement its sparkling water. They seem like a refreshing change of pace but are probably not drinks that people will ask for by name.

KIWI COOLER

BLEND

1 kiwi fruit, peeled and sliced

2 Tbsp coconut cream

Juice of one lime

6.5 oz Perrier, chilled

Garnish: Kiwi Slice

SUNDOWN SPRITZER

BUILD

1 cup white grape juice

6.5 oz Perrier, chilled

Garnish: Mint Sprig

LE FRENCH OPEN

BUILD

4 parts Perrier

2 parts orange juice

2 parts grapefruit juice

2 parts strawberry syrup

Garnish: Fresh Strawberry

chemical composition of the water ensure its purity. Bottlers cap the source to prevent external contamination.

No matter where the water in the bottle comes from or what its special properties are there is another point of view for the bar owner: Bottled water is too popular to ignore. It has every bit the profit potential of beer, wine, and coffee, as shown in Figure 9.4 and is a way to make money on a product that, when coming out of a faucet, is otherwise given away. For the slimmed-down, pumped-up generation water is seen as a healthy alternative to soft drinks. The caveat is that if you are serious about marketing to "water snobs" (can't really call them "purists" under the circumstances, can we?), you'll need to pay extra attention to the vendors whose products you select. Also, as with any other beverage, it is smart to have a sales program for your bottled-water products. Start with the following basic steps:

- Offer at least three or four types of water, with both *still* (noncarbonated) and carbonated water on the list. The still waters should include a local brand and a regional or nationally recognized brand.
- Include internationally known brands, such as San Pellegrino, Perrier, and Evian, if your menu or drink list includes items from those countries.
- List your bottled waters on drink lists and menus.

500 Glasses	(Number of glasses of tap water an operator serves each day)
× 10%	(Convert 10% of these to bottled water sales)
= 50 bottles	(Number of servings of bottled water per day)
$2 × 50 bottles	(Multiply by selling price per serving of bottled spring water)
= $100	(Added daily revenue)
× 7	(7 days, or weekly revenue from one unit)
= $700	(one unit)
× 52	(× 52 weeks = yearly revenue from one unit)
= $36,400	(one unit)

FIGURE 9.4 Calculations of the profit potential for serving bottled water in a bar or restaurant. Source: *Restaurant Hospitality*, May 1999.

- Train servers to point out the water selections and to routinely suggest them to customers along with other beverages: including soft drinks, beer, wine, cocktails, and coffee. The key to upselling here is a nonaggressive approach that informs without disparaging the local municipal-water system.
- Offer liter-sized bottles for groups and serving-sized bottles for individuals. All bottled water should be kept in the refrigerator and served chilled, in the opened bottle with an empty glass.
- A wedge of lime or lemon may be added if the customer wishes, but never add ice unless the customer requests it. Most customers are annoyed if they purchase an expensive glass of bottled water, then have it diluted with the local tap water of your cube ice. This is why you chill an adequate stock of mineral water in advance, making cube ice unnecessary.
- Serve bottled water in a different type of glass than you do regular tap water, such as a stemmed glass. This lessens the chance that a server will come around and refill the half-empty glass with tap water.
- People are not going to buy bottled water if they feel that it is overpriced. It's fine to make a profit, but don't gouge your customers. Some restaurants charge a flat $4 per person for unlimited pours of bottled water, just as they do for coffee and iced tea.

Carbonated Mixes

The indispensable carbonated mixes are club soda, tonic water, ginger ale, cola, and 7UP. In addition you may use Collins mix, diet drinks, root beer, and other soft drinks depending on your part of the country, your type of operation, and the preferences of your clientele. There are two criteria for setting up carbonated bev-

WATER SALES SPARKLE IN NEW YORK CITY

The Ritz-Carlton Hotel in Battery Park in New York City is an example of the ultimate bottled-water sales program. The hotel's dining room contains a separate menu of high-end waters, and a water sommelier advises guests about the choices. Three still and three sparkling waters are on the list, at prices ranging from $5 for a 500-milliliter bottle to $10 for a full-liter bottle. The sommelier recommends carbonated waters with grilled fish, particularly oily types of fish, and still waters with lamb and beef. He or she can discuss the types of minerals, the acidity and alkalinity of the waters, and the amount of effervescence in the sparklers. Packaging plays a big role in the appeal of fancy bottled waters. Guests are permitted to take the empty bottles if they want to, from the sleek, glass Voss bottle, to the Aqua Delta Madonna.

erages: an *adequate supply* and a *cold supply.* A carbonated beverage at room temperature will lose all of its bubbles as soon as you pour it, filling the glass with fizz and then leaving a flat and scanty drink. It is critical to have your mixes as cold as possible.

Three kinds of carbonated mixers are available: bottled, premix, and postmix. As explained earlier in Chapter 4 both premix and postmix come in bulk containers and are chilled and carbonated automatically at the time that they are dispensed. Setting up these systems consists simply of having the right number of containers, at least one in reserve for each mix, and checking the pressure gauge on each CO_2 cylinder. This gauge should read 60 pounds per squre inch (psi), which is the amount of pressure needed to carbonate the beverage and deliver it to the dispenser. If the indicator gives a different reading, the pressure should be adjusted accordingly.

If you use bottled mixes the small bottles are the only way to go. They stay fresh since they are used up more quickly, but they must be thoroughly chilled and opened only as needed. If an opened bottle sits more than half an hour it should be discarded: Your next customer wants a sparkling drink. A 12-ounce bottle will make three highballs.

So-called *microsodas* have been introduced every year since the late 1990s as an incredibly competitive but long-stagnant soft-drink industry attempts to launch new trends. Most new brands are simply *line extensions*—a new flavor or a diet version of an already-popular existing brand, but occasionally there will be an interesting, premium noncola in a world dominated by colas. The National Soft Drink Association estimates that there are 450 different soft drinks, many of them "microbrewed" with nostalgic ingredients, such as herbs, roots, and spices, or spiked with caffeine or nutrients. Beer breweries also turn out some amazing, handcrafted root beers. In short the hot new beverage image is often upscale, and the packaging usually reflects this. They may make a unique offering for the nondrinker or serve as a base for your own signature cocktail creations.

Juices and Juice-Based Mixes

Bartenders have learned a lot from chefs—in this case, about the use of the finest and freshest ingredients. Some mixologists pride themselves in making their own Bloody Mary mixes, squeezing their own fruit juices, and even pressing juice out of fresh apples, blueberries, and watermelon to enliven such drinks as Apple Martinis, Bluetinis, and Watermelon Martinis, respectively. However, the fresh-squeezed trend is not clear-cut. Much depends on the speed and volume with which drinks must be delivered to a waiting clientele, as well as, of course, the standards that clientele expects. In 2003 Sofitel Hotels undertook a chain-wide campaign to use only juices from fresh fruits in its bars. One of its most popular drinks is Le Orgie, which is made with Skyy brand vanilla vodka, freshly squeezed tangerine and orange juices, and raspberry puree, served in a chilled Martini glass.

Fruit juices are some of your most popular mixes. Besides the most common—orange, lime, lemon, tomato, and grapefruit—cranberry-juice cocktail rocketed to instant popularity in the Cosmopolitan. You may also need to stock V-8 (vegetable) juice, pineapple, and sweet-and-sour mixes depending on your type of bar, your drink menu, clientele, and regional preferences. Let's use cranberry-juice cocktail as an example of how versatile a single mix can be by listing a few drinks in which it is featured. We have already mentioned the Cosmopolitan (made with vodka, Triple Sec, lime juice, and a lemon twist); but here are some of its cousins:

BLOODY MARY MIX

- 2 46-oz cans tomato juice
- 2 6-oz cans Bullshot
- 2 lemons (from 135–165 count batch), juice only
- 1/2 cup Worcestershire sauce
- 5 dashes Tabasco sauce
- 2 Tbsp celery salt
- 2 Tbsp coarsely ground black pepper

- ***Metropolitan:*** a Cosmopolitan made with currant-flavored vodka
- ***Bay Breeze:*** made with rum and pineapple juice
- ***Sea Breeze:*** made with rum, grapefruit juice, and a lime wedge
- ***Cape Codder:*** made with vodka and a lime wedge
- ***Woo-Woo:*** made with peach schnapps
- ***Sex on the Beach:*** made with peach schnapps and orange juice
- ***Madras:*** made with vodka and orange juice

Just about any of the juices commonly found at a bar are at least as adaptable. How you prepare your juices depends a great deal on your location, the time of year, access to (and cost of) fresh fruits varies in many places, and there will be cost differences when using fresh juices versus premade mixes. For example it may cost 7 cents per ounce to use a sour mix and 10 cents per ounce to use fresh lemon juice—but this may be offset by the relative strength of the product. You will need 2½ ounces of mix, but only three quarters of an ounce of fresh juice.

As of this writing citrus is the trendiest flavor. Orange juice may be bought fresh in cartons, in cans, and frozen as concentrate. Canned orange juice, even the best of it, tastes unmistakably canned. Frozen, unsweetened orange-juice concentrate is the most consistent in flavor, keeps for months unopened in the freezer, and is quickly prepared. Some proprietors find that drinks made with fresh orange juice squeezed to order are a great house specialty even when they carry the high price tag of a labor-intensive product. You can buy oranges and squeeze your own juice, but the taste will vary depending on the season and the types of fruit available. The juice should be strained through a coarse strainer to exclude pith and seeds, but a little fine pulp gives authenticity.

Grapefruit juice is receiving considerable attention as a drink base, with the states of Texas and Florida marketing their wares specifically to bar owners. Examples include the following colorfully named juice drinks:

- ***Indian River Sunset:*** Vodka, Triple Sec, grapefruit juice, and cranberry juice
- ***Swamp Water:*** Vodka, Midori melon liqueur, grapefruit juice, and pineapple juice
- ***Puckering Grandma:*** Amaretto, vodka, and grapefruit juice

Texas's famous Ruby Red grapefruit is teamed up with citrus-flavored vodka, served in a Martini glass and garnished with a Ruby Red wedge, in the popular television series *Sex and the City*. Grapefruit juice is available in liquid form or as frozen concentrate, as well as fresh in the grapefruit itself. Each form has the same advantages and drawbacks as the comparable form of orange juice, except that there may be less flavor variation in fresh grapefruit juice.

Tomato, V-8, and pineapple juices come only in cans; cranberry juice comes in bottles, cans, or as a frozen concentrate. Lemon and lime juices may be freshly squeezed in quantity and kept in glass or plastic containers. Lemon and lime granules are also available, both sweetened and unsweetened. They leave much to be desired. Frozen, concentrated, unsweetened lemon and lime juices make the best drinks.

Not to be outdone by the freshly squeezed craze, the mixer makers have been busy creating some wild alternatives to their venerable favorites. The makers of Rose's Lime Juice also have Blue Raspberry, Sour Apple, and Cranberry Twist "Cocktail Infusions" for making easy variations on Martinis. These infusions also work well to flavor lemonade, tonic, and sparkling cider.

The "granddaddy" of bottled fruit juices is probably Rose's Lime Juice although it is not a juice per se, but a syrup made of lime juice and sugar. Rose's is named for a Scotsman, Lauchlin Rose, who developed and patented a process in the 1860s to preserve fresh fruit juices by stopping the fermentation process. (This is somewhat ironic, coming at a time when most of Europe was trying to *get* things to ferment, to make liquor.) Rose's fortunes were made when the Merchant Shipping Act of 1867 was passed by the British Parliament, requiring all British military ships to carry lime juice onboard for a daily ration. The juice contained a dose of vitamin C, which prevented scurvy. Today Rose's Lime Juice sports almost the same label it did back then. Most bartenders agree that there is no substitute for this sweet but pungent combination of lime and sugar. A sweet-and-sour mix of fresh lemon juice and sugar can be made ahead of time. Sweet-and-sour mixes can also be bought bottled, as frozen concentrate, or in powdered form. Some have a foaming agent, called *frothee,* that simulates egg white. Some mixes are better than others, so give them a try in small quantities first.

Interestingly just plain juices are making a comeback at the bar. At trendy Tru restaurant in Chicago, you can purchase a flight of six juices served in mini cordial glasses for $10 to $12. Blends sound exotic and enticing, and they vary according to what is fresh and creative that day: e.g., carrot-passion fruit, apple-rosemary, beet, pomegranate, cucumber-mint, and so on. The savvy bar owner soon realizes that freshly made juices can be used in a variety of ways, including mixing them with lemonade, iced tea, sparkling water, or seltzer to make light, refreshing combinations. These can be further promoted by giving them eye appeal, served in stylish glassware with the appropriate garnishes.

All fresh juices and bottled mixes keep for at least a day or two. Some keep a week or more, for example cranberry, tomato, and pineapple. As soon as they are opened canned juices should be transferred to glass or plastic containers. All should be refrigerated until just before you open your doors. Although juices are not subject to bacterial contamination they will lose their flavor at room temperature and will melt the ice in the drink too fast, thereby diluting its fresh, tart flavor. A new batch of juice should never be added to an old batch. It is a good idea to tape the date of preparation on the container.

Setting up juices and mixes is a matter of checking supplies, tasting leftover supplies for freshness, making new batches as necessary, and arranging them in place for efficiency and speed. If you have a frozen-drink machine, making a recipe for the day ahead is part of setting up. Remember, though, to first use anything left from the day before.

Other Liquids for Mixing

Another mix that you should have in constant supply is **simple syrup.** This is a labor-saving substitute for sugar in other forms; it blends more quickly than regular or superfine sugar or the traditional lump of sugar muddled with bitters in an Old Fashioned. To make simple syrup you use equal parts by volume of sugar and water, then boil the mixture for one minute, blend it for 30 seconds, or shake until thoroughly mixed. For 1 teaspoon of sugar in a recipe use ½ ounce of simple syrup (1 tablespoon). Keep simple syrup in a bottle or plastic container; it is safe at room temperature.

Of course even simple syrup is not so simple anymore! At Philadelphia's Cuba Libre restaurant and bar, the owner purchased a special machine that crushes and presses fresh sugar-cane stalks to make *guarapo,* or sugar-cane juice, which now replaces simple syrup in many cocktails.

There are a few other, common nonalcoholic liquid ingredients. Technically Rose's Lime Juice belongs in this category. Others are grenadine, beef bouillon, and cream of coconut. Grenadine is sweet, red syrup that is flavored with pomegranates, used as much for color and sweetness as for its special flavor. Beef bouillon is an ingredient of the Bullshot and is best purchased in single-serving cans. Cream of coconut comes in cans or bottles and is used in tropical drinks. Passion-fruit syrup is a bottled mix of tropical juices, sugars, and additives.

Less common are **orgeat** (pronounced OR-zhat), a sweet almond-flavored syrup made from barley; **falernum,** a slightly alcoholic (6 percent) sweet syrup with an almond-ginger-lime flavor and a milky color; and orange-flower water, a flavoring extract. All of these syrups can be safely stored at room temperature.

Milk and cream are often called for in drink recipes. Cream is usually half-and-half, but it may be heavy cream for a well-to-do clientele. Whipped cream is especially popular as a topping for dessert/coffee drinks. Milk and cream must be kept refrigerated, for health reasons and because they quickly turn sour at room temperature. Cream substitutes are sometimes used, but the drinks made with them are not as good as those made with fresh cream. In addition these substitutes spoil easily so you should keep them cold in the refrigerator, too. Cream whipped ahead with a little fine sugar will hold well. Consistency should be just short of stiff for most drinks. Whipped cream is also available in aerosol cans. It must be kept below 40°F (4.4°C). If coffee drinks are on your menu, customers will not want to wait until you brew a pot of coffee to deliver their drinks. However, coffee held for longer than an hour changes flavor and will spoil the finest recipe. Fresh coffee is essential, and in today's market people are as knowledgeable and particular about their coffee as their liquor, wine, or beer.

GARNISHES AND CONDIMENTS

Fun, fresh, and inventive garnishes sell drinks. Heads turn when people see a pair of orange "eyeglasses" perched atop a tropical cocktail, or the steam (from dry ice) rising from a pitcher of Long Island Iced Tea. Even lemonade rises a few notches in sophistication with a triple garnish of orange, lemon, and lime slices. Anyone can pour a drink at home—but you can bet they do not bother to embellish it with that kitschy little paper umbrella. Garnishes are part of the entertainment of going out for a cocktail and, to that end, your options are as limitless as your imagination. You can choose from exotic cocktail olives, stuffed with almonds or bleu cheese; pickled green beans, onions, brussels sprouts, and asparagus spears; fresh shrimp; skewers of golden kumquats; and fresh lemon twists wrapped around a coffee bean. The following are just a few examples of creative garnishes:

- Dylan Prime, a steakhouse in New York City, offers The Ultimate Martini for parties of four. A 48-ounce glass container on a revolving, "Lazy Susan" style tray arrives at the table with four glasses and a whole array of serve-yourself garnishes, from stuffed olives, to quail eggs. This grand entrance comes with a grand price tag of $48. The same bar garnishes its Bloody Marys with grated celery instead of the traditional celery stick.

- Brendan Crocker's Wild Horse Café in Beverly, Massachusetts, mixes Stolichnaya vodka, crème de menthe, Kahlua, and cream for its Girl Scout Cookie Martini, which is topped with a frozen Thin Mint Girl Scout cookie, of course.
- Barcelona, a Spanish restaurant in Duluth, Georgia, garnishes Martinis with fruit-infused gelatin cubes, which are a combination of fresh fruit juice and gelatin.
- The Martini Ranch in Chicago makes a martini with Absolut vodka, Frangelico, and Godiva liqueur and wedges a whole Reese's peanut butter cup onto the rim.

Each garnish—tasteful, goofy, or outrageous—has a niche in every style of bar operation. They all contribute something: a flavor, a texture, a contrast, or eye appeal. You should view garnishes (as TGI Friday's does) as drink ingredients. Garnishes are part of the presentation, and the unique appeal, of that particular cocktail.

Fruit Garnishes

Fruits are among the most popular garnishes, and preparing them for bar use is one of the most important aspects of setting up. The standard items include lemon wedges and lemon twists, lime wedges, orange and lemon slices, cherries, olives, and cocktail onions (not a fruit, but used like a fruit in some cocktails). Other fruits and vegetables sometimes used for eye and taste appeal are pineapple spears or chunks, cucumber spears, celery sticks, fresh mint, and stick cinnamon for hot drinks. Of course you can anything of your own inspiration.

Preparing Citrus Fruits. Lemon wedges are used for appearance and for squeezing juice into individual drinks. Lemon twists are used for the tart, unique flavor of the rind; they are rubbed along the rim of a glass and twisted to squeeze the oil into the drink. Whole lemons are also squeezed for fresh lemon juice in quantity.

All citrus fruits should be washed thoroughly before cutting, and so should the hands. For cutting, use a sharp knife and cut on a cutting board, not in midair. Always cut down and away from yourself, keeping the fingers and thumb of your other hand curled out of the way. The best lemons are medium in size, with medium-thick skin (too thick is wasteful; too thin is hard to work with and not as nice to look at). A good size of lemon is 165 **count,** which means 165 lemons to the case. You can increase the juice yield of lemons by soaking them in warm water and rolling them back and forth on a hard surface while exerting pressure with the flat of the hand.

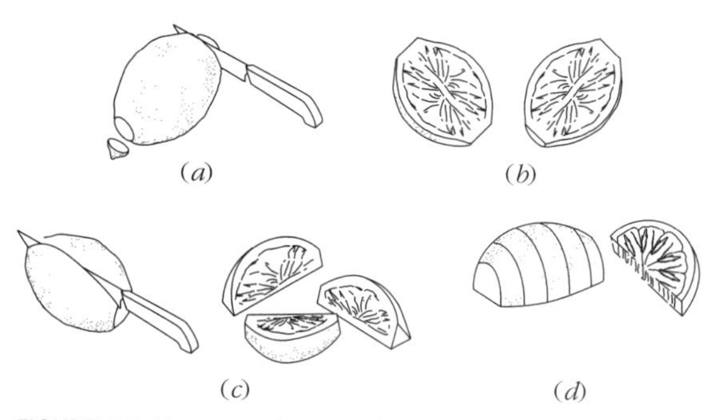

FIGURE 9.5 How to cut lemon wedges.

To cut *lemon wedges* (see Figure 9.5), first cut a small piece off each end—just skin, not pulp (a). Cut the lemon in half lengthwise (b) and with the cut side

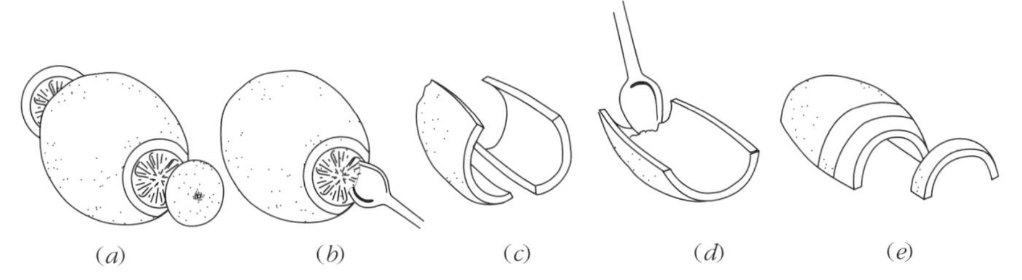

FIGURE 9.6 How to cut twists.

down, cut each half lengthwise into wedges of the size you want (c). An alternate way of cutting wedges is to cut the lemon in half lengthwise, then, with the cut side down, slice each half crosswise into half-inch slices (d). These smaller wedges fit nicely into a hand squeezer or are easy to squeeze between the fingers. If you want a wedge that will hook onto the rim of a glass, make a cut lengthwise down the middle of the half-lemon before slicing.

To make *lemon or lime* **twists** use a zester or stripper. These tools strip off just the yellow part of the skin, the zest. Cut pieces about 1½ inches long. To produce twists without a special tool (see Figure 9.6), first cut off both ends of the fruit (a), then scoop out the pulp with a barspoon (b), saving it for juice if you want it. Next cut through the rind (c) and lay it flat. Scrape away the white pith (d) and discard it, leaving about ⅛-inch thickness of yellow skin. Slice this in half-inch wide strips (e).

If you want *lemon or lime* **wheels** for garnishes (see Figure 9.7), simply cut crosswise slices beginning at one end of the fruit (a). Discard all end pieces with skin or pith on only one side. The slices should be thin, yet thick enough to stand up on the edge of the glass. Make slits halfway across the slices for this purpose (b). The best limes are deep green, seedless, and on the small-to-medium side (54 count, since the cases are smaller than lemon or orange cases), but the bar manager is often at the mercy of the market, taking what is seasonally available. The ideal size lime will make eight neat wedges (see Figure 9.8). First you cut off the tips, then cut the lime crosswise (a). Put the cut sides down (b), then cut each half into four equal wedges (c). Lime wheels are made the same way as lemon wheels.

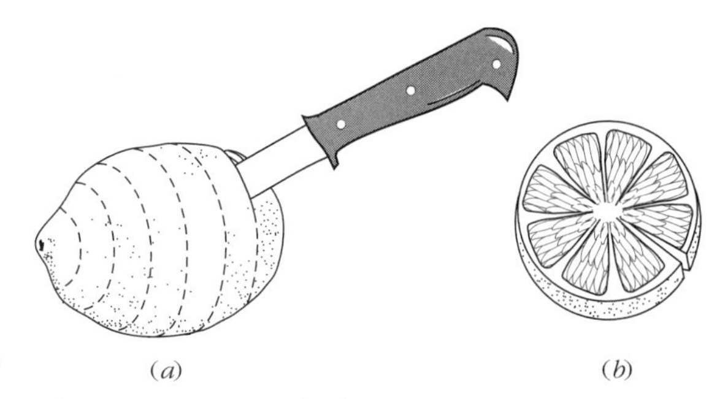

FIGURE 9.7 How to cut wheels.

Orange slices are made by slicing an orange crosswise as you do a lemon. Make the slices ¼-inch thick; if they are any thinner, they do not handle well and tend to dry out. Orange slices can be used whole, as wheels, or quartered and impaled on a pick, which is called *flagged,* with or without a cherry as in Figure 9.9 (a) and (b). The best-looking oranges are the California varieties; navel oranges are ideal because they have no seeds. A case count of 80 gives you fruit of a good size for slicing.

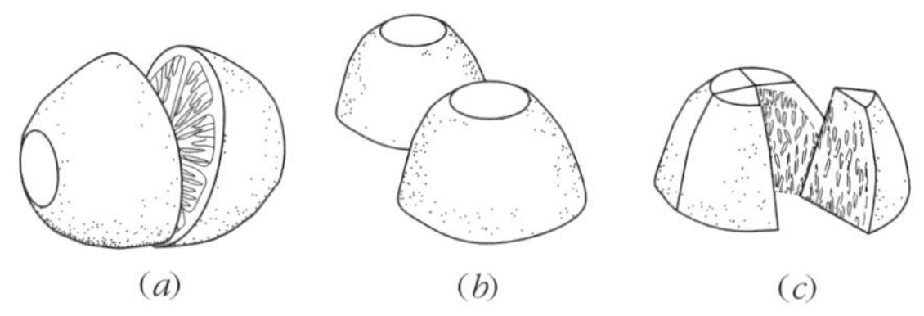

FIGURE 9.8 One method of cutting lime wedges.

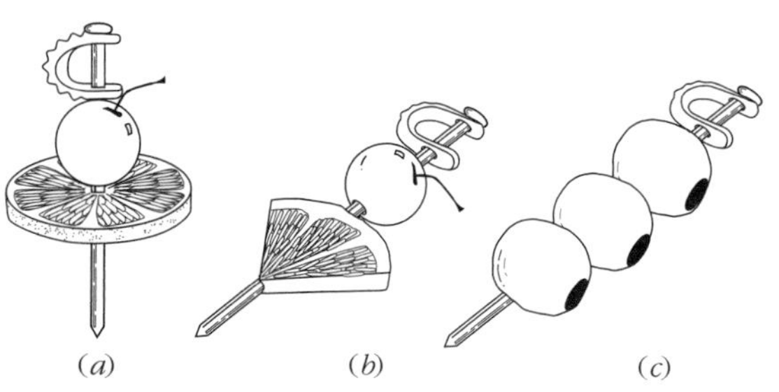

FIGURE 9.9 Simple garnishes on picks.

All citrus garnishes should be kept moist. They keep best if you can form each fruit back together again, but often there are too many pieces. Covering garnishes with a damp bar towel helps to retain moisture and appearance. So does refrigeration: You can bring them out in small batches. Often you can prolong their freshness by spraying them with 7UP. Twists dry out especially quickly and should not be made too far ahead.

Other Garnishes

Cherries, olives, onions, and pineapple chunks come in jars or cans and need no special preparation. Cherries used as garnish are maraschino cherries, pitted, both with and without stems, depending on the drink. Cocktail olives are small, pitted green olives of the manzanilla type. They are available plain or stuffed with anchovies, nuts, pimientos, or bleu cheese. They are often used on picks as flags (as in Figure 9.9c). If you're going to use a stuffed olive, be sure to mention it on the drink menu or mention it to the customer because some customers prefer the traditional, "unstuffed" olives. Cocktail onions are little onions pickled in brine.

Pineapple chunks can be purchased canned, but when pineapples are in season, it's better to use fresh. To prepare them, cut an untrimmed pineapple into half-inch slices, as seen in Figure 9.10 (a). Trim the skin from each slice and cut it in half (b). Cut out the hard center core of the slice (c), then cut the fully trimmed slice into wedges (d). You can use these on a cocktail pick with a bright cherry to contrast their pale yellow color. Canned garnishes are removed from their juices, set up in glasses or cups or on a condiment tray, and kept moist until it is time to serve them. The damp-towel covering is good for them, too.

Other fresh-cut garnishes, such as fresh pineapple spears, cucumber sticks, and celery sticks, should be cut to size and shape with an eye to appearance in the drink. They, too, should be kept chilled and moist. For added crispness celery and cucumbers can be kept in ice water in the refrigerator until needed. Just before serving time all perishable garnishes are set up on the bar in an arrangement that is both efficient and attractive, often in a condiment tray, such as the one shown in Figure 4.25. If the bartender does the garnishing, everything should be within

THE SKYY'S THE LIMIT WITH GARNISHES!

- "A garnish symbolizes the drink and what's in it," says Bryan Feigenbaum of the Four Seasons Hotel San Francisco. "Our Vanilla Colada has a vanilla pod accent, and Monkey Business (dark rum, banana liqueur, pureed bananas) is topped with shaved coconut and served with banana chips." He suggests pairing drinks with bar food. The hotel's Lemongrass Gingertini (lemongrass-infused vodka, lemon and lime juices) is featured with sushi.
- Flirt with fantasy. Whimsical garnishes lighten the mood and stimulate sales, says J. Ruth, the director of beverage development for ShowTenders. "The Cheeseburger in Paradise chain enjoys phenomenal success with tropical drink 'garanimals' (garnishes in the shapes of animals) wearing sunglasses. The menagerie includes Penelope Parrot (pineapple wedge, strawberry head, pineapple leaf tail), Lizard Lips (orange mouth, lime lips), Berry Beth (strawberry), and Red-Nosed Bill (pimiento-stuffed olive.)"
- Ophelia Santos, the owner of Ali-Oli in Atlanta, says: "Our fun poblano chile grasshopper garnishes perch on the sides of Bloody Maria drinks. These are time-consuming to make, so we only use them when we know about 10 of these specialty drinks will be served, not in a busy bar."
- Create seasonal garnishes and drinks, says Tim Halbert, the bar manager of Brasserie in New York City. "I ask bartenders to create a seasonal drink, for which they get credit on the menu. Staff recognition motivates them to promote their creations. My Big Tim's Hot Buttered Rum is garnished with a spiced butter pat, which melts into the hot drink."
- When making his Hot Taffy drink, Paul Saliba, beverage manager of the Ritz-Carlton Chicago, places an apple wedge in the mug before adding warm spiced cider, butterscotch schnapps, and sour-apple liqueur. "To create a balanced drink menu with wider appeal, invite staff members to evaluate new, garnished drinks," he suggests. "Work with the bartenders, making each drink and taking photos for the staff. Tasting the drinks helps them sell their favorites."

(**Source:** *Restaurants and Institutions* magazine, October 1, 2004.)

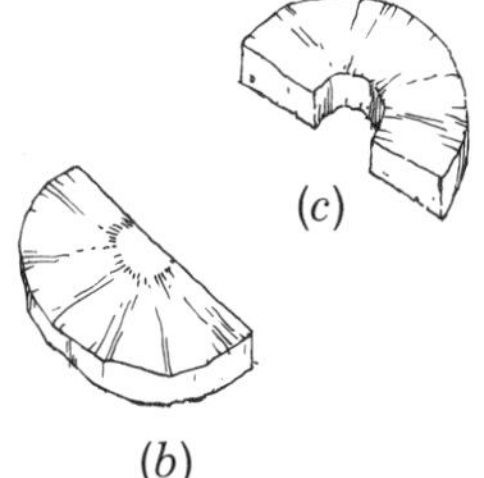

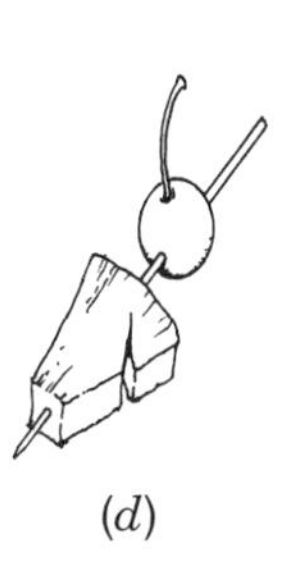

FIGURE 9.10 How to cut pineapple garnishes.

easy reach; there should be a separate setup for each station. If servers garnish the drinks, the garnishes should be at the pickup station. Each set of garnishes must have a supply of picks for spearing the garnishes to go into the glasses. If you don't want to serve picks in your drinks, have tongs handy for placing the garnish. Don't allow fingers for this step because it is both unsanitary and unsightly.

Condiments for Flavor

The term *condiments* is used for those garnishes prepared for eye appeal in a bar setting. In more general terms the word applies to a spicy or pungent food used to add a special flavor or to enhance the total flavor of a drink or dish. Condiments are also part of a well-stocked bar, and they include Tabasco and Worcestershire sauces, bitters, salt, sugar, and spices. Tabasco is liquid hot pepper, an integral part of most Bloody Marys. Other brands are available, but Tabasco is the one your customers traditionally expect in their drinks. It is dispensed drop by drop, from the dispenser that comes with the bottle.

Bar *bitters* are actually nonbeverage spirits, and undrinkable by themselves. They are like liqueurs without sugar, and are made by distilling or infusing alcohol with secret formulas of bitter herbs, spices, and other flavoring agents. You'll use bitters in everything from cocktails to sparkling mineral water as an aperitif. There originally were two kinds of bitters: those used for medicinal purposes, such as digestive ailments, and aromatic bitters used for flavoring cocktails. Today Italy makes the most brands of bitters, known there as *amaro*. The best-known Italian bitters are Campari and Fernet Branca.

You might need several kinds of bitters at the bar, each for the slight complexity it adds to a good cocktail: Angostura bitters from Trinidad (a venerable brand originally made in Venezuela as a malaria medicine), orange bitters for use in tropical drinks, and mint bitters for Mojitos. Peychaud's, a truly "bitter" bitters formula from New Orleans, is also called for in some drinks. Bitters are dispensed by the **dash**, which is the equivalent of ⅙ teaspoon. The dispenser built into the neck of the bottle is called a **dasher.** If you want only a drop you can hold the bottle level and tap it with one finger. For designated drivers you can add bitters to plain seltzer water, a combination that was popular during Prohibition.

Worcestershire sauce is a sharp, savory, nonalcoholic kitchen condiment that found its way to the bar to season some versions of the Bloody Mary. Worcestershire sauce comes with a handy built-in dasher/pourer: Turn it horizontally, and it is a dasher; turn it vertically, and you can pour from the bottle.

You will need salt at the bar in two forms: ordinary table salt and **coarse salt,** which is called *kosher salt* or *Margarita salt* (probably at a higher price). You'll use table salt in Bloody Mary mixes; coarse salt is for **rimming** (applying to the wet rim of) glasses for such drinks as the Margarita and the Salty Dog. You should stock sugar at the bar in several forms. Simple syrup blends best in drinks. Superfine sugar, often called **bar sugar,** is the best granulated type, but you can use ordinary sugar if you mix longer. Sugar cubes are not altogether obsolete; they are used in bars that make Old Fashioneds in the traditional manner, soaking the sugar cube that is part of the recipe with a couple of dashes of bitters. Sugar cubes are also an excellent means of making flambéed drinks: Soak a cube in 151-proof rum and set it aflame. Even honey figures in some recipes. You have to decide how far you want to go, how much room you have to store "extras" at the bar, and whether you can keep them well organized enough so you can find them when you need them. Certain ground spices should be on hand: nutmeg, cinnamon, pepper, and celery salt. Finally everything at each station, no matter how small or how seldom used, must be in its appointed place.

ICE

Shortly before opening time the ice bin at each station must be filled with fresh ice, and clean ice scoops must be placed in the bins. Some precautions are essential to keep the ice in the bins clean and fresh. All of your servers should observe the following rules:

- Never touch ice with the hands. Use a scoop.
- Never use a glass as a scoop. This is a common practice because it is fast but it is very dangerous. You can easily chip the glass or break it outright, then you will have glass mingled with your ice. You won't find the pieces of glass but some customer will. As soon as a glass breaks empty the ice bin and wash it out.
- Never put anything in the ice bin to cool—no wine bottles, no warm glasses. These might transmit dirt and germs. The sudden temperature change also might damage the warm glass.
- Do not position condiment trays over an ice bin; something might drop in.
- Never reuse ice, even if you wash it. Throw out all ice from used glasses. Start each drink with fresh ice in a fresh glass, even if it is the same kind of drink for the same person.
- Do not use your ice scoops for anything but ice. Keep them in the bins.

SERVICE ACCESSORIES

Accessories for garnishing are placed near the condiments at each station: the cocktail picks, straws, sip sticks, stir sticks, and cocktail napkins. You will have chosen them all as carefully as you planned your drink menu and garnishes so that the visual impression of each drink served carries out the total image of your enterprise.

Picks may be either the colored plastic kind, sword-shaped picks, or round wooden toothpicks. Picks are used to spear the olive, onion, or the cherry-plus-orange, and both spear and garnish go into the glass. Some establishments fill up the pick with three olives or onions, adding flare and an impression of generosity.

Straws are useful in two lengths: the 5-inch length for drinks in stemmed or rocks glasses and the 8-inch length for highballs and Collins-size drinks. Straws are essential for sipping frozen drinks, while customers use them as stirrers in highballs and rocks drinks.

You may prefer to use plastic stir sticks for highballs. These can be custom-made as souvenirs of your establishment for patrons to take home. Sip sticks are somewhere between straws and stir sticks; they are hollow but firmer than a straw and smaller in diameter. Usually only one sip stick is used per drink. Some places also use these for coffee drinks.

FIGURE 9.11 Keep serving accessories fully stocked for quick service. Courtesy of Co-Rect Products, Inc., Minneapolis, Minnesota.

The final essential is a supply of cocktail napkins, stacked with the folded edge toward the bartender or server for easy pickup, or arranged into a fan shape to prevent them from sticking together. Napkins should be two-ply; anything thinner disintegrates in no time. There should be a good stack at each station and plenty in reserve (see Figure 9.11). Where smoking is permitted, a good supply of sparkling-clean ashtrays should be stacked. Bartenders or servers should keep them emptied, frequently replacing a used ashtray with a clean one. (It is no longer considered proper etiquette to stand there and wipe the used ashtray clean at the bar or table; this should never be done in view of the guest.) Smoking tends to make people thirsty. Often the emptying of an ashtray will trigger a request for a second drink or another glass of wine. Where there are ashtrays, there must be plenty of matches available, imprinted with the bar's name, logo, address, and telephone number. Be sure to have "plenty" because they will go home with customers. You'll be amazed, even if few people smoke, how many will take the free matchbooks.

Any snacks you serve should be placed on the bar or on tables just before you open. These can be part of your image, or they can be subtle thirst promotion: small bowls of savory mixtures of peanuts, pretzels, popcorn, and cheese crackers. Some places opt to set up an old-fashioned popcorn maker, from which customers can fill their own bowls.

All the essentials for table service must be clean, in good supply, and ready at the pickup station. These include drink trays, folios for check presentation, guest checks for servers, drink or appetizer menus, wine lists, wine chillers, bottle openers, bar towels (or white table napkins), cocktail napkins, beer coasters, matches, and ashtrays.

OPENING THE CASH REGISTER

Most bar operations work with a standard amount of starting cash for the cash register, which is called the **bank.** The purpose of the bank is to have ample change in coins and small bills, primarily ones and fives. The amount of the bank will vary according to the sales volume and the policy of the bar.

When the bar is closed the bank is put into the safe, usually in a cashbox or a locked cash-register drawer. When you open the register, the first task is to count the bank to make sure there is adequate change, in the correct amount to start the day. In some systems the person closing the bar the night before has left a **bank-count slip** (see Figure 9.12), which lists the amounts of the various coins and bills. The opening bartender checks the opening count against this slip. If they agree the money goes into the register drawer, ready for business. If the register uses a paper tape the next step is to check to see that there is an ample supply for the day and that the printing on the tape is clear; it must be dark enough to be read easily. A clear tape is essential to the record-keeping of the bar. Then the register is cleared to ensure that no transactions have been recorded since the last shift. The next step is to ring up a "No Sales" transaction to obtain the first transaction number on the tape. This number must be recorded on the cashier's checkout slip (which is discussed later). This is a control procedure that gives management an audit trail when reconciling the register and the money at the end of the shift.

BANK COUNT SLIP

Total in drawer: $ 300.00

Bills: $ 250.00 Coins: 50.00

$1 Ones	$ 100.00	Pennies	$ 3.00
$5 Fives	$ 30.00	Nickels	$ 6.00
$10 Tens	$ 60.00	Dimes	$ 20.00
$20 Twenties	$ 60.00	Quarters	$ 20.00
		Halves	$ 1.00

Name C. Smith

Date 7/4/07

Shift: 11-3 3-7 7-close (circled)
(Circle one)

This form is to be used by cashier turning in the bank after sales have been accounted for. This slip should be left with the bank.

FIGURE 9.12

Finally the person opening the bar should make sure that the usual materials are available at the register: pencils, pens, paper clips, rubber bands, stapler, payout vouchers, credit-card forms, and guest checks.

Mise en Place

There is a fine tradition in the restaurant industry that is expressed in the French phrase **mise en place:** "everything in its place." This means that the setting up is complete and everything is in position and ready to go, right down to the last olive. The first customer has only to cross the threshold to set it all in motion.

Perfect *mise en place* is the result of careful planning and organization. It brings a moment of equilibrium between preparation and action that is important to start the action right. Not only is everything ready, but the bartender *knows* it. The resulting confidence influences all the action that follows: The readiness is both psychological and physical. A relaxed, confident bartender is a better host, makes fewer mistakes, and can cope with emergencies far more effectively than one who was not quite ready for that first customer and is still trying to catch up. A bartender who takes pride in *mise en place* is a real professional, and one to cherish. Part of *mise en place* is creating and adhering to a specific system for things like the underbar workstation. Overall, good *mise en place* is everything that you have learned about in this chapter, as well a few more points:

- Glasses of all the necessary kinds and sizes are clean and in place in the numbers needed.
- Bar implements are clean and in place at every station. These are jiggers, mixing glasses and cups, shakers, barspoons, strainers, squeezers, openers, zesters, scoops, and tongs.
- Equipment, including blenders, mixers, and ice crushers, is clean and in working order. The dispensing gun (or cobra head) and its system of hoses for dispensing liquids is used extensively (see Figure 4.5). Remove the tip of the nozzle and clean it in hot water to eliminate syrup deposits from soft drinks. The syrup and CO_2 canisters for carbonated drinks should also be checked and replaced if necessary. Figure 9.13 shows the line system of a typical cobra gun.
- A supply of guest checks and credit-card slips are in place, and the credit-card machine is in position and operating correctly.
- If coffee is part of your menu, it has been made.
- Money is in the cash register and has been counted and ready to go.

Figure 9.14 is a suggested checklist for a complete *mise en place*. This type of list can be useful for keeping procedures standardized and for orienting substitute bartenders and new personnel.

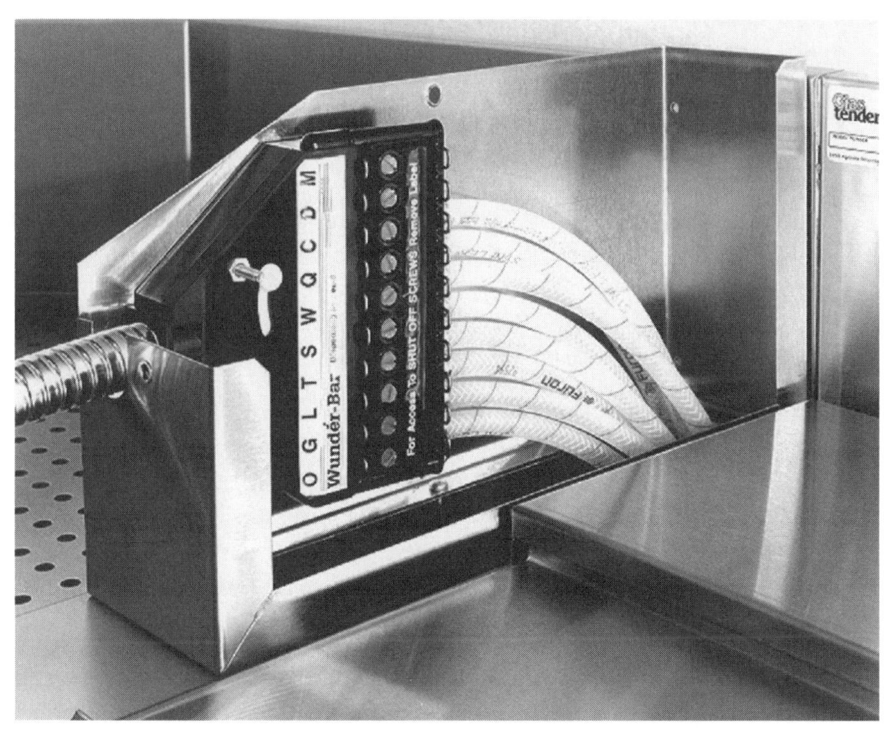

FIGURE 9.13 The series of hoses for a dispensing gun. Courtesy of Glastender, Inc., Saginaw, Michigan.

BEHIND-THE-BAR BEHAVIOR

Keep in mind that your bartender is the key person who conveys the image of your enterprise. You may have special requirements in personality, dress, and behavior if you are after a certain image. But some basic rules apply across the board.

Prompt, friendly, and courteous service is the overriding requirement. Greeting a new person immediately conveys a sense of welcome and belonging. Remembering a loyal customer's favorite drink makes that person feel appreciated. One warning applies here, however: If a regular customer comes in with a new companion, it is best not to give away that "regular" status. A genuine smile for everyone is a great sales asset—and a safe one.

If uniforms are not required your bartender should dress conservatively and appropriately for the general atmosphere. Blue jeans and T-shirts are out of place behind a hotel bar, just as a tuxedo would be at a truck stop. A white shirt, dark pants, and a conservative tie are safe apparel items anywhere. A bartender should never outdress the clientele. Clothing should be as neat and clean as the personal cleanliness you require.

Bartenders should not drink while working. Smoking, eating, and chewing gum are distasteful to many customers and should be confined to breaks away from the bar.

CHECKLIST FOR BAR SETUP

Liquor: Bring stock up to par. Turn in empties.

Well: Check supplies. Set up reserves. Check pourers. Line up bottles.

Bottled drinks: Replenish and rotate beers, wines, wine coolers, mixers, bottled waters in cooler. Check cooler temperature (40°F/4°C).

Draft beer: Check supply. Drain off excess foam, taste beer. Check pressure. Check beer-box temperature (36°F–38°F/2°C–3°C).

Soda system: Clean the (Cobra head) gun. Check soda supplies. Check CO_2 pressure.

Glasses: Wash used glasses. Check supplies. Arrange in order.

Implements: Check and set up blenders, mixers, mixing glasses, shakers, jiggers, barspoons, strainers, squeezers, openers, scoops, tongs.

Juices and mixes: Taste leftovers for acceptability. Prepare fresh juices, mixes; refrigerate. Prepare frozen drink mix; start machine. Check and replenish bottled-mix supplies. Make simple syrup.

Ice: Check and clean bins. Fill with ice. Be sure there is a clean scoop in each bin.

Garnishes: Prepare and set up lemon wheels, wedges, twists, lime wheels, wedges, orange wheels, flags, cherries, olives, onions, cucumber sticks, celery sticks, special garnishes.

Condiments: Set up salt and sugar for rimming, bar and cube sugar, bitters, Tabasco, Worcestershire, pepper, nutmeg, cinnamon, celery salt.

Serving accessories: Set up picks, straws, stir sticks, sip sticks, cocktail napkins, bat towels, coasters, bottle openers, wine carafes and chillers, ashtrays, matches, serving trays, folios.

Cash register: Count bank and set up register. Check register tape. Check and set up cashier supplies: guest checks, credit card forms, payout vouchers, pencils, pens, paper clips, rubber bands, stapler and staples.

Coffee: Make fresh. Set out sugar and cream, stirrers.

Snacks: Set out in clean containers.

FIGURE 9.14

The legendary bartender you "tell your troubles to" does not belong in most bars nowadays. It is best for bar personnel not to get too involved in conversations for simple reasons: They might neglect some customers or be perceived as playing favorites. This is especially true of personal conversations, especially those that include remarks about the bar, the boss, the other help, and the other customers. It makes a bad impression all around. It is also inappropriate to interrupt an ongoing conversation, whether it is about football, politics, men, women, or religion. Also it is disastrous for the bartender to get involved in an argument, even if he or she is asked to "settle a bet." For you, this is always a bad bet! Discretion is an absolute must. The bartender's lips should be sealed when a customer reappears

REPLACING BAR TANKS

To replace a carbonated mix tank, follow these steps:

1. Remove the incoming air hose and the outgoing syrup hose from the tank.
2. Replace the empty tank with a full tank.
3. Dip both hose fittings in hot water. This removes any syrup residue and ensures a clean connection.
4. Refit both hoses on the replacement tank.

To change a carbon-dioxide (CO_2) tank, follow these steps:

1. Turn the handle on top of the CO_2 tank to the "Off" setting.
2. Remove the regulator from the used tank.
3. Replace the empty tank with a full tank.
4. Use a new washer to attach the regulator to the new tank.
5. Tighten the regulator fitting as tightly as possible, using an open-ended wrench.
6. Turn the handle on top of the new tank to the "On" setting.
7. Take these additional precautions:
   - Don't lay CO_2 tanks flat on their sides.
   - Don't drop the tank—it could shatter.
   - Do not refrigerate or store CO_2 tanks in coolers.
   - Keep carbonated bottled mixes on hand in case your system malfunctions.
   - Keep the telephone number of the service company handy.
   - Never attempt to take apart a carbonated drink system by yourself. The system is usually leased to you and if you damage it, you are responsible for paying to fix it.

after having too much to drink the night before, brings in a different date, or brags about something that the bartender knows is not true. If a customer received a telephone call at the bar his or her presence should not be acknowledged without checking with that customer first.

Courtesy goes beyond the initial greeting. It extends to keeping one's cool under duress. There will always be that contentious customer who challenges everything, such as the drinks, the prices, and/or the change that you have carefully counted back. Only a cool, calm bartender can handle this situation. (Be sure that the change is right every time.) The list of tips that follows is a compilation of common sense and experience from real-life bartenders.

- Don't transfer your stress to your customers.
- Don't underestimate the economic power of fun. A bartender can positively affect how people enjoy themselves.
- Smile when you're not sure what to do or how to respond to a comment. A frown or deadpan expression is more easily misinterpreted.
- Put the "house" first. Never forget that the bar is a business. Run an honest till: do not steal or put up with others who do.
- Work smart, not hard. Learn how to complete tasks in the fewest number of steps possible, with the least amount of motion.

- After closing the bar just go home. Checking out the competition is fine once in a while, but having time at home enables you to save money and preserve brain cells; it also gives you a chance to enjoy the peace and quiet.
- Drink-making is an art. Every drink that you serve should reflect your artistry and pride of workmanship.
- Treat everyone as a guest, and remember that there are no "first-class" and "second-class" guests. To the bartender everyone is equal.
- Keep your bar clean. Otherwise, it will reflect poorly on the cleanliness level of the overall establishment.
- Don't fret about tips. If you make good drinks and provide great service, the tips will follow.
- Remember, every night is a new show. Appearance and demeanor should reflect this. Set professional standards and live by them.

If a customer begins to have too many drinks or shows clear signs of intoxication, the bartender or server has no choice but to stop serving alcohol to the customer, as well as to suggest coffee, a soft drink, or food—compliments of the house if necessary. If there is trouble, it is up to you as the manager to take over as discreetly and tactfully as possible, and to arrange a safe ride home for the guest. This might require enlisting the help of a sober friend, calling a taxi, or even getting a hotel room for the night. Your reputation is on the line and possibly your license, too: Third-party liability might be just around the corner if that customer gets into the driver's seat.

At this point in your studies you might find it useful to review the material on alcohol-related laws and server training elsewhere in this book.

CLOSING THE BAR

After standing on your feet for six or eight hours, or possibly even more, the prospect of cleaning up the bar is not thrilling. But clean you must. A good way to start is to safely lock up any wines that have been on temporary display. Next, put all perishables, such as cream and juices, into the refrigerator. Juices should be in covered plastic containers. If you have any opened cans of Bullshot, Coco Lopez, or other mixes, empty them into glass or clear plastic containers, label the contents, and refrigerate them.

Along with the juices tend to the cut-up fruits. Generally, cut limes will last for 24 hours. Place them in a jar with a lid, add some 7UP or Collins mix to keep them moist, put the lid on the jar, and place it in the refrigerator. Cut-up oranges do not keep well, so it really does not pay to keep them. Whole fruits go into the refrigerator. Olives and onions should be put back into their jars and submerged in their original brine, with the lid of the jar closed. The same goes for cherries: be sure they are covered with syrup, otherwise they will dry out and wrinkle. Anything that came from a can should be transferred to a clean, see-through plastic container with a lid. Everything goes into the refrigerator, where the cold, moist

WHAT'S ON YOUR RADAR?

Consider the modern bartender's behavior as a type of radar system, a beam of pulses that rotates a full 360 degrees from his or her station or, at least, over an assigned sector of the bar area. The bartender's job is to note the blips on his or her radar:

- When filling a glass with ice for a highball, you notice that you are running low on ice. BLIP! Get more ice.
- You scan the bar while delivering a cocktail to a guest, and notice the customers who have just seated themselves nearby. BLIP! Greet them and ask if they would like to see appetizer menus.
- You can see the other half of the bar en route to the cash register. BLIP! A new customer has joined a group already at the bar. Make eye contact, then ask what he or she would like to drink.

In short, visually break the bar into manageable sections and scan them regularly—even if you have a wait staff. You will find that in the few seconds it takes you to draw a draft beer, you can scan at least the two seats on either side of the standard. When you have a short break in action or when you are performing such routine tasks as glass-washing, make a full 360-degree sweep of the bar area. Work on honing your radar. It is the tool that will enable you to keep your customers satisfied and to keep the bar running smoothly during your shift.

air will preserve the quality of the product and help to ensure the health of your patrons.

Next, put away the bar snacks: the pretzels, chips, peanuts, crackers, and popcorn. Empty all leftovers into the trash. Never put anything touched by customers' hands back into a container with fresh items unless each one is individually wrapped. This is a health precaution to protect your clientele. Close all lids tightly to keep everything fresh.

At this point wash all the glasses and put them on the drainboard to air-dry. Wash all tools and equipment: blender, mixer cups, and utensils. Leave them upended on the drainboard to air-dry, too.

If you have a frozen-drink machine drain the contents into a plastic container and store them in the refrigerator. Turn off the machine and clean it out according to the manufacturer's instructions. The next step is to remove and soak all the pourers from the liquor bottles. This will prevent the sugars found in most spirits from building up and slowing the flow.

While the pourers are soaking clean the soda gun and the ring that holds it. Remove the nozzle parts and wash, rinse, and sanitize them. Wipe down the flex-hose with a damp cloth. After the pourers have soaked for about 10 minutes, dry them and replace them on the bottles at the standard angle. Bottles get sticky with use so wipe each one down with a damp cloth to remove any spills, then put them in back in their correct places on the pouring line.

When all of the supplies have been put away, the glasses washed, and the liquor bottles taken care of, it is time to clean out the ice bin. First scoop out all of the ice into the nearest compartment of the bar sink. Then run hot water into the bin to melt the remaining ice and wash down any debris left in the bin. Most of this debris will be trapped at the drain. Remove this with a towel and shake off the towel into the trash. With a clean towel scour the walls and bottom of the bin. If your bin has an old-style cold plate at the bottom (part of your dispensing system), pay particular attention to cleaning thoroughly under and around it. This is a great place for gunk to collect, which can make your bins smell stale and affect the taste of your ice, as well as being unsanitary.

After cleaning the ice bin proceed to the bar top. Remove everything and wipe down the surface with a damp cloth. A bar with a top of brass or another metal should be polished at this time. Empty the ashtrays, making sure all cigarettes are out before you dump them into the trash. Wipe the ashtrays clean. Replenish the supply of matches so that you are ready for the next day.

Now that everything has been washed, it is time to empty the sinks and scour them with a mild abrasive and very fine steel wool. It is also a good time to rinse the drains below the beer faucets with a pitcher of hot water and some sanitizer; this will prevent them from clogging overnight. It is also a good time to check the CO_2 pressure on each beer system.

After the sinks have been cleaned the bar floor must be swept and mopped. The nonskid floor mats must be removed and hosed down outside at least every other day. Emptying the trash is the next closing ritual. Hose down the receptacles and put a new plastic trash liner in each one.

Up to this point the cleanup has dealt with the sanitation and safety needs of the bar. The next step is to get the supplies replenished for tomorrow's business. If the storeroom is closed at this hour the stock can't actually be brought to the bar, but the accumulated empties (which you have been storing on a shelf of the backbar) can be counted and listed, and a requisition form can be completed for their replacement. Beer and wine supplies should be checked along with spirits, and necessary replacements added to the list.

Supplies of bottled mixes, fruits, and condiments should also be counted, and necessary replacements should be listed. The syrup supplies should be checked, too, as well as the pressure of the CO_2 cylinder. The entire closing-down procedure is designed to accomplish two things:

- Ensure that the sanitary practices essential to successful operation are carried out.
- Ensure that if anything happens to the person who opens up the next day, the bar will be ready to go with very little effort by a substitute. This is crucial: to be able to open at a moment's notice if you must.

In some enterprises closing the bar also includes closing down the register. This will differ from bar to bar, but here is a typical order of procedure:

1. If tickets or checks are used be sure that all have been rung up.
2. If a tape is to be used for checking out the register, remove the tape, sign it, and date it.
3. Read the register, and record the readings on the cashier's checkout slip (see Figure 9.15). This step, of course, will depend on the system used.
4. Remove the cash drawer with the cash and all supporting papers, such as credit-card charges, checks, and payout vouchers.
5. Reconcile the total register sales with the actual cash, plus house-credit slips, credit-card slips, checks, and payout vouchers. Record everything on the cashier's checkout slip.
6. Count out the bank and place this money in the cash-register drawer or cashbox. Write on a new bank count slip (see Figure 9.12) the amounts of the various coins and bills. This procedure is a continuous activity. It helps the person who opens the next shift to check the bank.
7. Turn over the money to the manager or lock it in the safe.
8. Leave the empty register drawer open. In case of a break-in, if the drawer is empty and open, it won't be pried open and ruined.

The closing process is almost complete. Check your refrigerators to be sure they are running and cold and that all their doors are tightly closed. Check your sinks to be sure they are clean. Make sure that your coffeemaker is turned off. Check to see that no lit cigarette butts, including your own, are left on the bar or anywhere else. Lock everything that should be locked, turn off the lights, check the thermostat if you are supposed to turn the room temperature up or down for the evening, and make sure that the Exit lights are on. Then you can go home.

SUMMING UP

Remember that a bartender is a liquid chef, working in a liquid kitchen. Therefore, it is essential to stock whatever specialty items are necessary to carry out the crafting of the cocktails in his or her drink repertoire—and to inspire the creation of new ones.

The smooth operation of a bar affects sales and profits in many ways. It influences the quality of the drinks, the quality of the service, the number of drinks that can be poured, and the number of people needed to serve them. Only if everything is in order at the start of business can the bar run efficiently and bartenders remain calm and sufficiently organized to serve customers with efficiency and good humor.

Safety and sanitation are critical in bar operations. This means everything from proper hand-washing, to storage of perishable foods at correct temperatures, to handling of glassware to minimize skin contact with it. City and state health codes set only minimum standards; your goal should be to exceed them.

Bar-setup procedures commonly include making any mixes from scratch, preparing garnishes, chilling mixers and bottled waters, filling ice bins, replenishing

CASHIER'S CHECKOUT SLIP

Date ______________ Opening transaction # ______________
Shift 11-3 3-7 7-2 (Circle appropriate shift)
Cashier ______________ Checked by ______________
Beginning bank ______________
Bills ______________
Coins ______________
Checks ______________ Number of checks ________
Charges: ______________
Amer Express ______________
Visa/MasterCard ______________
Other ______________
House credit ______________
Payouts ______________ (Itemize below)
TOTAL ______________
Less bank ______________
CASH ______________ (Include payouts and charges)
Total sales ______________ (From register tape)
OVER / SHORT ______________ (Circle one)
Overring/Underring ______________ Transaction # _____ Amount ________
ACTUAL OVER / SHORT ______________ Guest check # ________
Server ______________

ANALYSIS OF PAYOUTS

Name	Amount	Name	Amount

FIGURE 9.15 Record additional overrings or underrings on the back of the cashier's checkout slip.

supplies of accessories (straws, napkins, coasters), organizing the bar tools and equipment, and checking the draft-beer and carbonated-soft-drink canisters. The French term *mise en place*—which means *everything in its place*—is what you are striving to achieve.

The financial part of the setup means making sure that an accurate count and adequate supply of cash is in the register, as well as guest checks for the servers. At the end of the day, of course, it is time to count the money and reconcile it with the starting count, as well as to thoroughly clean everything to get it ready for the next day's business. Computerization of the point-of-sale (POS) system is only as good as the honesty of the people who input the data.

Good management plays an important role in efficient bar setup: by setting the standards and procedures and requiring that they are observed; by thoroughly training employees in the routines and clearly explaining what is expected; and by frequent follow-up on employee performance.

POINTS TO PONDER

1. What is wrong with tucking a towel in your belt or hanging it over your shoulder?
2. Why is it better to air-dry glasses than to polish them with a clean towel?
3. How do you determine what par stock should be?
4. What are the danger-zone temperatures for foods susceptible to bacterial growth? What kinds of bacteria are most prevalent and troublesome?
5. Find out more about functional water and write a few paragraphs about whether or not you believe it is a worthwhile expenditure for a bar business.
6. How do you make simple syrup? Why would you use it for mixing a drink?
7. What is the correct way to serve bottled water?
8. What is *mise en place,* and why is it important to bar operation?
9. Create two of your own unique garnishes for traditional cocktails. Show and explain them to the class.
10. Give two reasons why the cash register is balanced at night as part of the closing process.

TERMS OF THE TRADE

bank
bank-count slip
bar sugar
coarse salt
count
Cryptosporidium
dash
dasher
electronically altered water (EAW)
falernum
functional water
Giardia lamblia
HACCP
micron rating
mise en place
mocktail
orgeat
par stock
rimming
simple syrup
sparkling
structured water
submicron-rated filter
twist
wheel

A CONVERSATION WITH...GEORGE KIDDER

Imperial Club Bartender

George Kidder is a lifelong bartender. "The Great Kidder," as he is affectionately known in the Eastern Idaho farming community of Ashton, got his first job at age 21, working as a barback for his father, who was also a bartender. As of this writing George is 71 and celebrating 50 years behind the bar. He says that he did not plan to make a career of it, but has "always been able to make a good living this way."

George says that he has tended almost every bar in Fremont County, Idaho. It is an unusual career choice in a rural area known for its conservative political climate; the majority of residents are members of the Church of Jersus Christ of Latter-Day Saints (Mormons), who do not approve of drinking. At the moment he works at the Imperial Club, locally nicknamed "The Imp."

In addition to bartending George has a second career—as a cowboy poet of regional note. He performs at local fairs and poetry gatherings, and is often asked to deliver the eulogies of customers and friends.

Q: What is the hardest thing about tending bar in a small town?

A: When you have to be the bouncer, too! I have a bunch of steel and plastic in my left hip socket as the result of one of the bar fights.

Q: What happened?

A: I tried to break up a barroom brawl and after a while, they all ended up in a big pile. Guess who was at the bottom? Y'know that little knob on your hipbone? Well, mine busted off. They couldn't pin it back so they took it out; had to cut the bone off and stock a prosthesis thing in there.

Luckily bartending ain't near as tough as it used to be. Years ago this town was pretty wild. A lot of loggers and miners around here. Some nights we'd have four or five fights goin' on in one night. Now you might have one in a month.

Q: Do you call the police? What is the official procedure?

A: You call 'em if there's time, yeah. If not, you do it yourself.

Q: Do you keep a baseball bat behind the bar, or what?

A: (smiles broadly) Oh, we've got all kinds of accoutrements back here, yep.

Q: Do you have any advice for newcomers to the business?

A: First stay sober on the job. Some places you're not allowed to drink, but other places you are—and that can be a problem. Keep a smile on your face, and agree with everything the customers say whether you really agree or not. In a small town everybody that comes in the door is a friend . . . because they're a customer! Of course you do ocassionally have opinions about things. But a good bartender is noncommittal.

Q: Is there any fallout from selling alcohol in such a conservative and religious area?

A: Oh, we've got some pretty good Mormons who come in and drink. And some pretty good Catholics, and some pretty good Methodists, and all the rest of 'em. They don't drop their church-going tendencies, they just relax them a little bit when they come in here. It's the companionship they're look for. Of course, some come in lookin' for fights. But most come in just to be sociable. There are some who can be a little belligerent.

Q: What kinds of character traits do you think a bartender ought to have?

A: Patience is first. You've got to keep your cool if you can because people are just gonna rub you raw sometimes. You know that to begin with so patience should be your top priority. Then I'd say personality; and dependability and honesty, if you're gonna keep your job.

Q: Is your well or backbar set up differently from most bars because you like it a certain way?

A: Not really. Most bars have it described the way it's supposed to be set up. It just makes sense; the bottles you pour from the most, you set in front; those you don't pour too much of, you set in back. I have six bottles in the well. The backbar has a wooden panel that I can pull down and lock, and that's where I store most of the bottles. You can serve beer in Idaho at 7 A.M., but most people in the morning just come in for coffee. The backbar stays locked until 10 A.M., when you can serve booze.

Over the years you figure out an easy way to make just about any drink. And we have what we call a "bible" back there behind the bar, a book with our recipes and a lot of own own notes in it. It's always there.

Q: Do you have an automatic glasswasher?

A: (laughs) You're lookin' at him! Some places have a power brush, but I do it all by hand. We used to have one in the old Derby Club, but I don't think they work very well. The power brush requires the extra steps of turning it on, then turning it off. By the time you do that, you could have had 'em all done.

Q: What are the best things about your job?

A: I guess the companionship, the sociability of it. I was gonna quit when I started my cowboy poetry, but then I found out that some of my best material comes right out of this bar; the quips and quotes and profound things that people say. "The Sloppy Bartender," "The Lady Bartender," "The Honky-Tonk Angle"—all those poems I wrote based on people here at the "Imp."

The other advantage to bartending is you can always find a job. Working as a bartender has saved my bacon when it came time to start paying' child support and alimony and all that stuff! One job wasn't near enough!

Q: Does your bar have a policy about serving food?

A: Some of them do, but not this particular place. We do put out popcorn or pretzels, and we have pepperoni sticks and beef sticks for sale.

Q: Are there any trends here in Ashton? What are the "hot" drinks now?

A: Frozen Margaritas. Geez, I hate 'em! I make 'em in a blender, don't have a Margarita machine. It takes longer, so it's a hassle and they aren't worth that much more money, either.

Q: What's the oddest thing anybody's ever asked you to fix?

A: I don't dare tell you. But I will say that all those drinks—the ones called Skip and Go Naked, Sex on the Beach—they ain't new drinks! They're just some of the old drinks from years ago that have new names to make people blush.

Q: Well, what's your favorite kind of drink to mix?

A: Whiskey and water, because that's what I like to drink—but only when I'm not on the job!

CHAPTER 10
MIXOLOGY, PART ONE

The cocktail has catapulted back into the mainstream of American social life and in contrast to previous eras, its contemporary enjoyment crosses generations and market segments. The term *mixology* is not just a catchy phrase for bartending; it is a nod to bartending as a profession, which is typically defined as the art or skill of mixing drinks containing alcohol. Mixology encompasses the techniques of the bartender, which do indeed require skill and sometimes artistry, along with the knowledge to back up the skill. The bartender must know the drinks by name, their ingredients, their mixing methods, and the ways they are served. The bar manager must know even more, as the person responsible for setting the house standards for the drinks—e.g., drink size, glass size, types of ingredients (premix or fresh), and proportions—as well as developing drink menus and specialty drinks. A manager might not have a bartender's dexterity or know as many drink recipes, but it is the manager who makes decisions about how drinks are to be made and marketed, and who trains the bartenders in the ways of the house.

This chapter (and the next) are aimed at giving managers a thorough understanding of three topics: the structure of a good drink, the structure and essential ingredients of each type of drink, and the basic methods of mixing drinks. Illustrated step-by-step instructions will help you understand each method and will serve as training tools.

THIS CHAPTER WILL HELP YOU . . .

- Know what makes a "good drink" good.
- Understand the relationship between glass size and amounts of liquor, ice, and mix, and apply this knowledge in creating drinks.
- Decide on the method, equipment, ingredients, and garnish(es) to be used for each drink you serve.

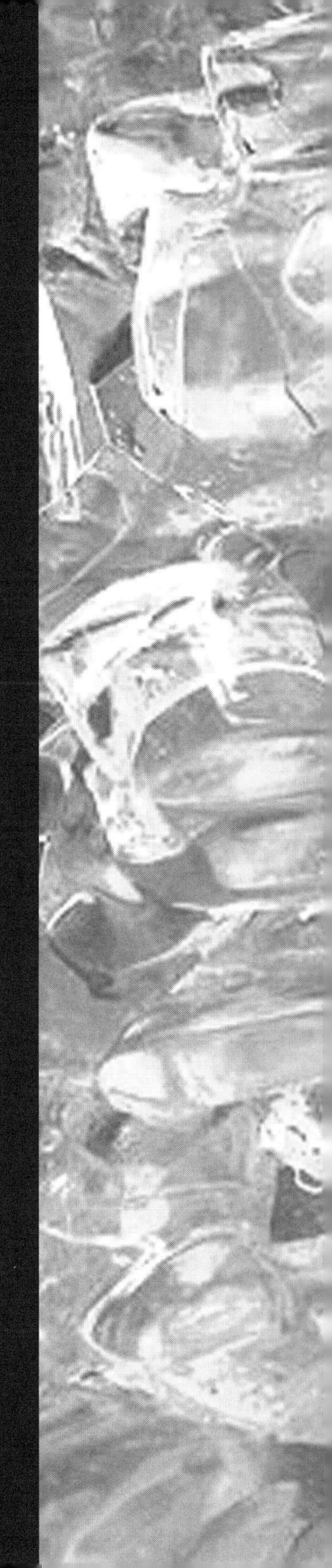

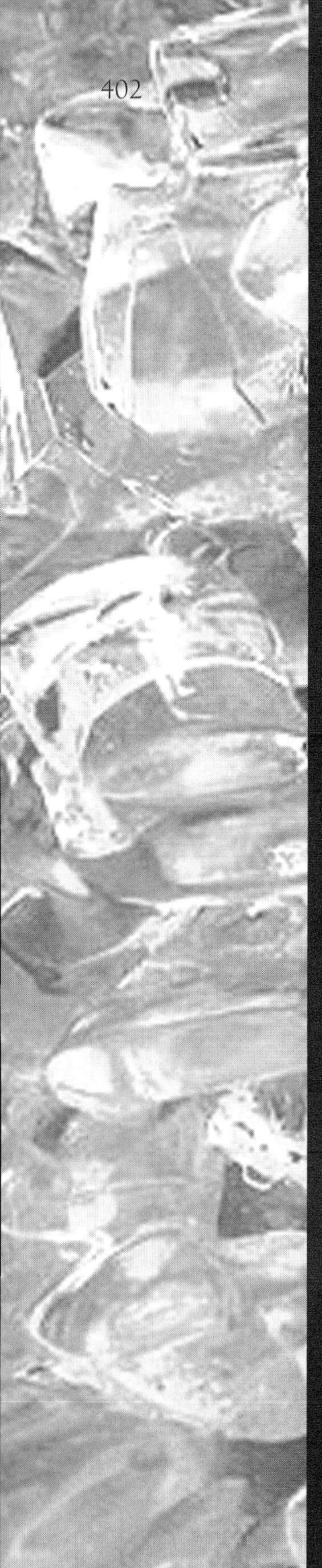

- Know how ingredients are measured and choose an appropriate method of measurement.
- Know how to use premixes and shortcuts appropriately.
- Explain and demonstrate the build method of drink mixing.
- Make highballs, juice drinks, liquor-on-ice drinks, Collinses (with mix), coolers, coffee drinks, pousse-cafés, and other build-in-glass drinks.

Sociologists cite several valid reasons for the modern-day mixed-drink resurgence. First is history: the cyclical nature of the bar business. From the 1950s to the 1970s people tended to choose a couple of favorite **drinks** and stick with them. Then in the 1970s and 1980s the bar scene practically became passe, other than the disco fad. Only in the 1990s did the sound of a cocktail shaker in motion once again become chic.

Second the beverage industry is more closely aligned than ever with the food industry, and in both, people are showing appreciation for creativity, presentation, and the use of top-quality ingredients. Consumers of all demographic segments have become more adventuresome in their tastes and willing to try new things, and culinary trendsetters are more than happy to accommodate. Chefs and bartenders work together to pair food and drinks on trendy menus, as well as to match malt scotches or small-batch bourbons with food, just as they do wines. Well-designed bars, clubs, and lounges have sprung up nationwide, offering "grazing menus" and serving superpremium spirits in response to customers' thirst for knowledge and social pleasures. Bookstores feature slick new volumes on how to make cocktails, how wine and beer is made, and how to pair beverages with food; magazines and newspapers regularly include articles on these lifestyle-related topics.

A third reason for the cocktail's renewed popularity is what might be termed its entertainment value. Chardonnay may have a lovely straw color and ale may be pale, but mixed drinks can be made in a kaleidoscope of festive hues that can enhance the mood of an evening. For example if the market is up there is reason to celebrate; if it's down there is reason to console one another. Either way, it's an occasion. The savvy bar owner creates a drink menu that includes a combination of classics and house specialties, and changes the repertory with the season, including holiday and special occasion drinks to suit a variety of tastes and moods.

A (Very) Brief History of Mixology

The origin of the word **cocktail** for a mixed drink is cloaked in mystery. There are about a dozen good stories about its history. The most persistent fixes its birth in 1779 at Betsy Flanagan's Inn, a rural New York tavern where American Revolutionary soldiers and their French allies mixed their gin and vermouth together as a token of brotherhood, stirring their concoction with the tail feathers of Flanagan's rooster. Another version claims that the Americans raided the British Army's commissary and stole several roosters, and that their favorite innkeeper (Betsy) stirred their drinks in celebration with the cocks' tail feathers. The accompanying toast, "Here's to the divine liquor which is as delicious to the palate as cocks' tails are beautiful to the eye!" was shortened by a toasting Frenchman to "Vive le Cocktail!"

In Joseph Lanza's book *The Cocktail: The Influence of Spirits in the American Psyche* (Picador USA, 1995) the author observes that cocktails became appealing in the twentieth century precisely when drinking them became a crime. Prohibition brought a new mystique to the same old drinks. A new breed of bartender developed to staff the speakeasies and later the elegant bars of the first half of the 1900s. He (the bartender was almost always a man) was splendidly dressed, wearing diamonds and gold, and could pour with such flourish that one contemporary proclaimed, "Such dexterity and sleight-of-hand is seldom seen off the conjurer's stage." It was these artists who began mixing the classic drinks we still know and love today. They were the first true mixologists.

More information is available now than ever before about the art of **mixology**, and it is an exciting time to be part of the industry. A new breed of bar owners and bartenders has put the emphasis on quality, not showmanship. Spirits and garnishes are readily available from all over the world, a real treasure trove with which to work. And in the hands of a great bartender even the most commonplace ingredients can become something extraordinary. Be sure to visit www.cocktailtimes.com and check the web site's extensive listings of recipes (by spirit, by style of drink, by temperature [e.g., hot drinks and frozen drinks) to enhance your own mixology experience.

Moderation and good sense are also part of the current trends. Today's three-ingredient drink may be only 4 ounces in size, not the jumbo libations of the disco era, but they are 4 ounces of first-rate components. The so-called "Happy Hour" that became known for bargain drink prices has been discouraged and is even outlawed in some areas. Instead smart establishments market their cocktail hours as a way to wind down from the pressures of the workday, offering a substantial snack and a drink that is too good to be gulped down when it can be sipped and savored in congenial surroundings.

ABOUT MIXED DRINKS

The term **mixed drink** includes any drink in which alcoholic beverages are mixed or added to one or more nonalcoholic ingredients. This includes cocktails, highballs, tall drinks, frozen drinks, coffee drinks, and almost every other bar product, with the exceptions of a glass of beer or wine or a straight shot of whiskey or brandy.

The Structure and Components of a Mixed Drink

Mixed drinks of all kinds share certain characteristics. One of these is a *structure* that is loosely typical of all drinks. Each drink has a major alcoholic ingredient, or **base,** usually a spirit, which determines its character and usually its predominant flavor; and one or more complementary ingredients, which modify or enhance that flavor. A Manhattan, for example, has whiskey as the major ingredient and sweet vermouth as the modifier or enhancer, while a highball has a carbonated mixer or water as the modifier. A drink may also have one or more minor ingredients that add a flavor or color accent, and one or more garnishes. For example a Manhattan sometimes has a dash of bitters or a drop of oil from a lemon twist added for a flavor accent, and a stemmed maraschino cherry is its standard garnish.

The major ingredient is the *base* of the drink. The modifiers and flavor accents make each drink different from all others with the same base. Some highly flavored mixes manage to reverse flavor roles with the major ingredients, as in a Bloody Mary (tomato juice) or a Cuba Libre (Coca-Cola). These types of drinks are often ordered by people who don't really like the taste of the spirit and expect the mix to cover it up. In this case, from the drinker's perspective, the mix is the major flavor ingredient and the liquor gives it the desired kick. But for the staff behind the bar the spirit is still considered the major ingredient in a cocktail.

Most drinks contain one jigger of the major ingredient, and the jigger size is a policy decision of the management—a basic cost-control factor, for obvious reasons. If the modifier is another liquor it is typically a smaller amount—anywhere from one half to one eighth the amount of the major ingredient—from half a jigger to a splash of vermouth in a Dry Martini. Even when several modifiers are added, the major ingredient typically comprises at least half the liquor in any drink. Accent ingredients are nearly always added in drops or dashes.

Many drinks have standard garnishes that customers expect and want. In many cases, garnishes have become as much a part of the drink as the liquid ingredients. Change the garnish on one of these you will have to change the name of the drink as well. Adding an onion to a Martini instead of an olive makes the drink a Gibson.

Some drinks have no prescribed garnish, but the showmanship of "dressing them up" is appreciated by guests in many different bar settings. It would be a serious mistake, however, to garnish such sacred standards as a Scotch and Soda, or indeed any drink that has been ordered by call brand, unless there is a standard garnish. Patrons who order such drinks usually want the unadulterated taste of the liquor itself.

Developing Drink Recipes

A successful mixed drink is based on carefully calculated relationships between the ingredients, as well as the relationship between the glass, the ice, and the drink ingredients. You should make these calculations when you plan your drink menu and before you buy your glasses and choose your size of cube ice. If you write down specific calculations for each drink that you serve you will have a set of standardized recipes for your bar. The idea is to train your bartenders to follow the recipes consistently so that customers are served a consistent product no matter who is tending bar. For each drink you establish the following:

MAKING A WELL-BALANCED DRINK

Professionals tell us that the well-made cocktail can be achieved by following these general rules:

- Taste with your brain as well as your taste buds, with the goal of understanding the interplay of flavors and ingredients.
- Search out interesting ingredients and use them to develop contemporary classics. This includes new, high-quality spirits, juices, and bar mixes. Don't neglect garnishes and glassware.
- Seek a balance of elements within the drink: acidity, sweetness, bitterness, and alcohol. A strong drink is not automatically a "better" drink; its alcohol content should complement the other ingredients.
- Involve all the senses. Remember, we "taste" first with our eyes, then with our nose, before we put a glass to our lips.
- Consider how the drink "finishes" when first swallowed. Clear and icy? The slight "heat" of the alcohol? A tinge of citrus or mint?

- The amount of major ingredient to be poured (1 ounce, 1¼ ounces, 1½ ounces, ⅞ ounce) or whatever. In metrics, the comparable amounts (rounded off) are 30 ml, 37 ml, 45 ml, and 27 ml, respectively. This standard amount becomes your jigger size.
- The other ingredients and their proportions to the major ingredient
- The size of glass to be used
- The amount of ice in the glass
- The garnish and its arrangement

The ice in the glass is a key ingredient in the taste of any drink made with a carbonated mix or fruit juice. While its primary function is to chill the drink, ice also controls the proportion of liquor to mix by taking the place of liquor in the glass. The ice goes into the glass before the mix, and the more ice, the less mix.

Suppose, for example, you want a highball to have 3 ounces of mix to 1 ounce of liquor in an 8-ounce glass. You put enough ice in the glass to take the place of 3 ounces of liquid, which will bring the finished drink up to a volume of 7 ounces, about half an inch below the rim. An 8-ounce glass filled three fourths of the way with small rectangular cubes will displace 3 to 4 ounces of liquid. (Different sizes and shapes of cubes will make a difference; with large, square cubes you have to fill the glass with more ice because the cubes have big spaces between them.) If you want a strong proportion of mix in relation to liquor you use less ice or a larger glass. If you want a stronger liquor taste, use more ice or a smaller glass.

Taste Complexity. In addition to the list of ingredients you should consider two other factors when creating a drink: its taste complexity, which means the overall sophistication (or lack thereof) of the drink, and the degree of difficulty that making the drink entails. Evaluate each drink you're thinking about pouring according to the following criteria:

Taste-Complexity Categories

- *Commonplace:* These drinks are simple, are ordered frequently, and are well received, although they are rarely "remembered" as anything exceptional.
- *Tasty but artless:* These drinks are for those who rarely order a cocktail; these customers generally enjoy wine or beer instead.
- *Inspiring:* These are truly classic cocktails. They are sophisticated and expertly mixed and will prove enticing to most guests. They can be served with pride.
- *Challenging and complex:* These drinks might require some explanation before being presented to guests, to prepare their taste buds for the experience.

Mixing-Difficulty Categories

- *Elementary:* Mixing drinks in this category is about as difficult as preparing a glass of ice water.
- *Basic:* These drinks are simple enough to be made well by anyone with a genuine interest or a little bartending experience.
- *Moderate:* These drinks can be made fairly easily, but require some skill.
- *Difficult:* These are not typical cocktails; they require extra steps in preparation.
- *Advanced:* In addition to being difficult, this category of drink complexity is compounded by a hard-to-find ingredient or a more challenging step in preparation.

Measuring. The only way to pour a drink that follows a recipe is to measure every ingredient. There are various ways of measuring liquor. There is the *metered pour,* in which at least the major ingredients are measured and dispensed through a handgun or through pourers that shut off at the proper measure. A second way is for the bartender to pour into a measured jigger of your chosen size—with lines along its side, like a tiny measuring cup—and to stop pouring at a predetermined line.

A third way is to **free-pour.** Free-pouring is a subjective form of measurement that involves turning the bottle with its pourer cap in place upside down for full-force flow while the bartender counts silently. There's a little bit of a trick to it. To pour an ounce, the bartender counts "one-two-three" or "ten-twenty-thirty." "One-two-three" will yield $^7/_8$ of an ounce. "One-two-three-four" will yield $1^1/_4$ ounces, and so on. Each bartender develops an individual way of counting that ensures the greatest accuracy for that person.

Free-pouring requires practice, experience, confidence, and good reliable pourers. It is the showiest but usually the least accurate way to pour since it is likely to vary from person to person and from day to day. Even the best bartender should check his or her pour every few days to see if it is still on target. If the free-pour is accurate and consistent it can have the advantages of speed and showmanship. But few bartenders can rival the accuracy and consistency of an objectively measured drink.

The typical manager tends to think of measured pour in terms of achieving the full value of each bottle in sales, which is certainly a major reason for measuring. But perhaps the best reason to measure is to ensure the best drink, consistently, every time. After all the proportions of the ingredients make a drink what it should be. If you pour an extra one-quarter ounce of gin in a Martini but only the usual amount of vermouth, that Martini is going to taste drier than usual. Perhaps the customer won't like that as well. Perhaps that customer thinks you made a great drink. That's terrific—until he or she returns and orders another Martini based on that standard and is disappointed.

Clearly measurement is important to keep the proportions right. We measure liquors in terms of jiggers or sometimes ounces. We measure ice in terms of how far to fill the glass. We measure condiments by drops or dashes, and sugar by teaspoonfuls (see Figure 10.1 for the standard measurements and their relationships).

Mixing Methods. The way you want a particular drink made in your bar is another aspect of mixology related to quality and consistency, as well as to speed and service. Many drinks are always made the same way; for others you have a choice. There are four basic mixing methods: build, stir, shake, and blend.

BAR MEASURES

dash = $\frac{1}{6}$ teaspoon or 10 drops
teaspoon (tsp) = $\frac{1}{6}$ ounce (oz, fluid ounce) or 5 milliliters (ml)
barspoon = 1 teaspoon
standard jigger = $1\frac{1}{2}$ ounces or 45 milliliters (or whatever amount you set as your basic drink)
pony = 1 ounce or 30 milliliters
scoop (of ice) = approximately 1 cup
splash (of syrup, lemon juice, etc.) = $\frac{1}{4}$ ounce
wineglass = 4 ounces or 120 milliliters
1 fluid ounce = 30 milliliters
1 ounce by weight = 28 grams
pinch = whatever you can get between your fingers and thumb

FIGURE 10.1

- To **build** a drink is to mix it step-by-step in the glass in which it will be served, adding ingredients one at a time. You typically build highballs, fruit-juice drinks, tall drinks, hot drinks, and drinks in which ingredients are "floated" one on another.
- To **stir** a drink is to mix the ingredients together by stirring them with ice in a mixing glass, then straining the mixture into a chilled serving glass. You stir a cocktail made with two or more spirits, or spirits plus wine—ingredients that blend together easily. The purpose of stirring is to mix and cool the ingredients quickly with a minimum of dilution.
- To **shake** a drink is to mix it by hand in a shaker or using a mechanical mixer (shake mixer). You shake a drink if it contains an ingredient that does not readily mix with spirits, such as sugar, cream, an egg, and sometimes fruit juice.
- To **blend** a drink is to mix it in an electric blender. You can blend any drink you would shake, and you *must* blend any drink that incorporates solid food or ice, such as a strawberry Daiquiri or a frozen Margarita. Some bars use a blender in place of a shaker or mixer, but it is not nearly as fast and easy as a mechanical mixer and doesn't make as good a drink as the hand shaker.

Before the days of electrical mixing equipment all drinks were built in the glass, stirred, or shaken in a hand shaker. In some establishments today, where the pace is leisurely and the emphasis is on excellence, drinks are still mixed by hand from scratch, without any premixed ingredients, shortcuts, or substitutes. This kind of bar might have a blender, but it is used only for newer drinks that cannot be made without it, and the shake mixer is never used. There is no question that the drinks are better.

At the other end of the spectrum is the high-speed, high-volume operation. This is the bar at the airport, the fairgrounds, or the baseball stadium, where the staff blends or shakes everything mechanically and stirs only in the serving glass—if the drink is stirred at all. The use of premixed products, shortcuts, and substitutes is absolutely necessary for speed and economy, and the drink selection is often limited. The drinks are not perfect; however, they have the right ingredients, they are cold, they are fast, and they are what the customer expects.

Between the two extremes are many enterprises that use some elements of both, with the majority near the simplified, mechanized end of the scale. Most bars have eliminated the mixing glass and hand shaker altogether and use at least some premixed products. They have valid reasons: speed, volume, cost, and suitability to the enterprise and the clientele. Many types of customers are not connoisseurs of premium drink quality and don't appreciate premium prices.

But as a bar manager you need to know how to make drinks from scratch and how to take advantage of all the shortcut options. You need to understand what if anything you will be compromising if you decide to use a shortcut. Only then can you tailor your drink menu to your type of enterprise and your clientele, choose your equipment and supplies, and train your personnel accordingly.

To this end, in describing how to make various types of drinks, this text will often give you both the original method of mixing (which is what most bartender manuals provide, although three-fourths of today's bars don't use it) and the "speed method" most commonly used now. Providing both methods will enable you to understand each drink type and to see how the shortcuts fit into it so you can work out what best suits your goals.

Common Mixology Terms

Like other types of recipes drink recipes use some jargon that you should become familiar with; they are useful terms, a sort of "bartender's shorthand." Here are the most common ones:

Add. To combine into the drink or container. "Build" is the more correct term.
Blend. To blend (as defined above) and pour unstrained.
Broken ice. Large cubes, chopped down to about one third their original size.
Dry. For a Martini, this means that the proportion of vermouth is very small compared to the proportion of gin, for example a teaspoon of vermouth to perhaps 3 ounces of gin (the teaspoon might be called a "splash" of vermouth).
Frosted. A glass chilled in the freezer or by filling with crushed ice so that a cool mist forms on the outside of the glass.
Garnish. To decorate or attach to the rim of a glass.
Ignite. To set on fire.
Long. A total of five measures or more of fluid.
Neat. A liquor poured as is: undiluted; not mixed with anything.
Pour. To add to the glass without straining, unless specified.
Rim. To coat the edge (rim) of the glass by moistening it, then dipping it into something like salt or sugar.
Short. Fewer than five measures of fluid in total.
Smooth. A mixture that when blended with ice has the thick consistency of a milkshake.
Spiral. A long, coiled, almost pith-free length of citrus peel.
Straight up. Undiluted; no ice or water added.
Strain. To filter out ice and other solids, leaving them behind when you pour out liquid. If the drink has been stirred a bar strainer is used for this purpose.
Twist. A piece of citrus peel, about 1½ to 2½ inches (3 to 6 centimeters) long, held over a drink and twisted to release a drop or two of oil from the fruit peel into the drink. The twist itself is usually dropped into the drink after its oil is released.

Mixed drinks are a lot like people: They have a structure, but within that structure are countless variations. Pick up any bartender's manual and unless you know your way around, you will find it mind-boggling; one manual contains 4,000 drink

THE BAR CHEF

Creating a cocktail involves a bit of chemistry, a bit of sensory excitement, and a lot of patience. We've alluded to the seriousness with which the "art of the cocktail" has been endowed, and the age of the celebrity bartender—a virtual "bar chef"—is fast approaching, fueled by the public's appetite for boldly flavored specialty drinks. Hotels, restaurants, and upscale bars hunt for mixologists who are able to gain media attention and customer loyalty for their expertise and passion for the craft of bartending.

This new generation of bar chef is a professional who operates much like a good chef or pastry chef. He or she may make television appearances, write a newsletter or book, and be a guest lecturer in local hospitality courses. The bar chef is likely to be as busy outside the pouring station as inside it, creating infusions, shopping for the freshest fruits and herbs, locating new sources for an obscure liqueur or ingredient. This is the person who actually thinks about the shapes and sizes of cube ice, the tartness of mint leaves, and the proper melting temperature of brown sugar.

There seem to be two categories of bar chef: the classicist and the avant-garde. The classicist lovingly recreates the venerable favorite cocktails of past decades, rediscovering bartending as it was in the late 1800s to 1950s with a nod to the profession's fascinating history. The avant-garde bar chef has the same quest for excellence, but on new frontiers: using his or her own imagination to blend unique ingredients and share new recipes with an enthusiastic following. There are, of course, some stylistic and philosophical differences between the members of the two camps. For one the classicist might place greater emphasis on the base spirits used in cocktails, while the avant-garde bar chef will prefer neutral spirits that are mixed or infused with unusual flavors. There is certainly room for both on the scene.

recipes, and the New York Bartenders Union lists 10,000. To confuse the issue even further new drinks are appearing all the time, proliferated by distillers, magazine writers, bartenders, and beverage managers.

Fortunately for a manager planning a drink menu and for a bartender learning dozens or even hundreds of drinks, these drinks evolved in families—again, like human beings do. The number of families is fairly small, so if you know the "family characteristics" you will have some basic knowledge about every family member. There are two keys to family character: the ingredients and the method of mixing the drink. A third element often comes into play, which is the size and type of glass. Whether the "glass determines character" or "character determines the glass" is an interesting point to ponder. In the rest of this chapter (and the next one), we will look at different drink families, with their characteristic ingredients and the mixing method that applies to each (see Figure 10.2 for summaries of the drink families).

DRINK FAMILIES

Drink Type	*Ingredients*[a]	*Method*	*Glass*
Buck	Liquor, lemon, ginger ale, cube ice	Build	Highball
Coffee	Liquor, (sugar), coffee, (whipped cream), (brandy float)	Build	Mug or wine glass
Collins	Liquor, lemon, sugar, soda, ice (cube or crushed), cherry	Shake/Build	Collins
Cooler	Liquor or wine, carbonated mix, (sweet, sour), (bitters), cube ice	Build	Collins
Cream	Cream, liquor, liqueur (or 2 liqueurs)	Shake	Cocktail or champagne
Daisy	Liquor, lemon, grenadine, crushed ice, (soda), fruit garnish	Shake	Mug, tankard, tall glass
Eggnog	Liquor, sugar, egg, milk, nutmeg	Shake	Mug
Fizz	Liquor, lemon, sugar, soda, cube ice	Shake/Build	Highball or wine
Flip	Liquor or fortified wine, sugar, egg, nutmeg	Shake	Wine
Flip, hot	Liquor, sugar, egg, hot milk, nutmeg	Shake	Mug
Frozen drink	Liquor, crushed ice, (any others)	Blend	8–12 oz, chilled
Highball	Liquor, carbonated mix or water, cube ice	Build	Highball
Hot Buttered Rum	Rum, sugar, hot water, butter, spices	Build	Mug
Hot lemonade	Liquor, sugar, lemon, hot water	Build	Mug
Hot toddy	Liquor, sugar, hot water	Build	Mug
Ice cream drink	Liquor, ice cream, (any others)	Shake-Mix or Blend	8–12 oz chilled
Juice drink	Liquor, juice, cube ice	Build	Highball
Liquor on rocks	Liquor, cube ice	Build	Rocks
Martini/Manhattan	Liquor, vermouth, garnish, (cube ice)	Stir	Cocktails (rocks)
Milk punch	Liquor, sugar, milk, cube ice, nutmeg	Shake	Collins
Milk punch, hot	Liquor, sugar, hot milk, nutmeg	Build	Mug
Mint Julep	Bourbon, mint, sugar, crushed ice	Build	Tall glass or mug
Mist	Liquor, crushed ice	Build	Rocks
Old-Fashioned	Bourbon (or other), sugar, bitters, cherry, orange, cube ice	Build	Old-fashioned

(continued)

FIGURE 10.2

DRINK FAMILIES (continued)

Drink Type	*Ingredients*[a]	*Method*	*Glass*
Pousse-café	Liqueurs, (cream), (brandy), floated	Build	Straight-sided cordial
Rickey	Liquor, lime, soda, cube ice	Build	Highball
Shooter	Liquors, (juice flavorers), straight up	Shake	Shot, rocks
Shot	One liquor straight up	Build	Shot
Sling	Liquor, liqueur, lemon or lime juice, soda, garnish, cube ice	Shake/Build	Highball or collins
Sling, hot	Liquor, sugar, lemon, hot water	Build	Mug
Smash (rocks)	Liquor, mint, sugar, cube ice	Build	Rocks
Smash (tall)	Liquor, mint, sugar, soda, cube ice	Build	Highball or collins
Sour	Liquor, lemon or lime juice, sugar	Shake	Sour or cocktail
Spritzer	Half win/half soda, cube ice, twist	Build	Highball or wine
Sweet-sour cocktail	Liquor, lemon or lime juice, sweetener, (cube ice)	Shake	Cocktail (rocks)
Swizzle	Liquor, sweet, sour, (soda), (bitters), crushed ice	Build	Highball or specialty
Tom and Jerry	Rum, whisky, or brandy, egg-sugar-spice batter, hot milk or water nutmeg	Build	Mug
Two-liquor	Base liquor, liqueur, cube ice	Build	Rocks
Tropical	Liquor (usually rum), fruit juices, liqueurs, syrups, ice, fruits, (mint) (flowers)	Shake	Specialty

[a]Ingredients in parentheses are optional.

FIGURE 10.2 *(Continued)*

The Highball Family

A **highball** is a mixture of a spirit and a carbonated mixer or water, served with ice in a highball glass. It is said to have gotten its name from the railroad signal for "full speed ahead" used in the late 1800s: a ball raised high on a pole. Legend has it that a St. Louis saloonkeeper invented the drink when his regular customers, mostly railroad engineers, asked him to "lighten up" their drinks so they wouldn't get in trouble on the job. The resulting whiskey-and-water combination, served in a tall glass, was probably speedy and satisfying enough, and has since become a classic combination. In the original method of building a highball, you use a small bottle of mixer and go through all the steps as they are given (see Figure 10.3). In the speed method you add the mixer from a handgun, and your stirring is probably limited to a couple of swirls with the stir stick; you count on the customer to finish the job. Next, we will look more closely at the whole procedure. First the sequence. Some people argue in favor of reversing steps 2 and 3, using an ice-mix-liquor sequence. The rationale for this sequence is that if you pour the wrong mix by mistake, you have wasted only the mix and not the liquor. If you use this sequence you must leave room for the liquor when you pour the mix; the exact depth depends on the width and shape of the glass.

The rationale for pouring the liquor first is that most mixes, which are heavier than the liquor, will filter down through the liquor. As a result you will probably need to stir less, which means less loss of sparkle from the carbonated mix. Also, it is more natural to "think" the drink this way: ice, liquor, mixer. Another point: If you free-pour you are more likely to pour a consistent amount of spirit if you are not looking at how much room there is left for it in the glass.

An important point about working with carbonated mixes comes up in step 4. Notice that you stir with the barspoon *very briefly,* just long enough to spread the liquor around in the mix. Like beer or Champagne, carbonated liquids should always be handled gently. Excessive stirring dissipates the bubbles. Vigorous stirring melts the ice, too, thereby diluting the drink. The customer can use a straw or stir stick if he or she wants to mix the drink more. The finished drink should always be the same size; that is, it should always reach an imaginary line half an inch (or some other distance you set) below the rim of the glass. Then each drink will be the same as the one before it and will have the same proportions and the same taste. A glass should never be filled to the brim, so as to avoid spillage. As to what is the "right" glass size, jigger size, and amount of ice, this is up to you. Highball glasses should hold no less than 6 ounces and no more than 10. An 8-ounce glass is a good all-around choice. It will make an excellent highball with 1 to 1½ ounces of base liquor. Any smaller glass is likely to look stingy and certainly won't work well for anything stronger than a 1-ounce drink.

SCOTCH AND SODA

BUILD

8-oz glass

¾ glass cube ice

1 jigger Scotch

Soda to fill

Now, let's look at some of the highballs most in demand. In this book we use an abbreviated recipe format, which is all you need. We give you the method, glass, ingredients, and garnish. Anything in parentheses is optional. You do not have to follow our choice of glass size, but it will give you a proportion of glass-to-ice to ingredients that you can adapt to your needs. You can use these prototypes for all similar drinks.

Any liquor called for with soda or water is prepared like a Scotch and Soda. A garnish may be added if the customer wishes; this is usually a twist of lemon. Many highballs, such as the Gin and Tonic, are served with a garnish of lemon or lime. This can be a wheel on the side of the glass or a wedge with juice squeezed in and the squeezed hull added to the drink.

GIN AND TONIC

BUILD

8-oz glass

¾ glass cube ice

1 jigger gin

Tonic to fill

Wedge of lime, squeezed

HOW TO BUILD A HIGHBALL

Ingredients

Liquor
Carbonated mix or plain water
Cube ice
Garnish, varying with the drink, sometimes none

Glass

Highball (6 to 10 ounces)

Mixing Method

Build

Equipment and Accessories

Jigger (standard house size)
Barspoon
Ice scoop
Fruit squeezer (for some drinks)
Stir stick or straws
Pick (sometimes)
Cocktail napkin

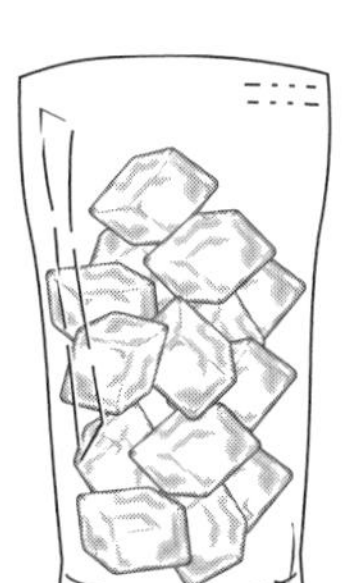

step 1: Using the ice scoop, fill the glass with the required amount of ice and place it on the rail.

step 2: Add 1 jigger of the liquor ordered.

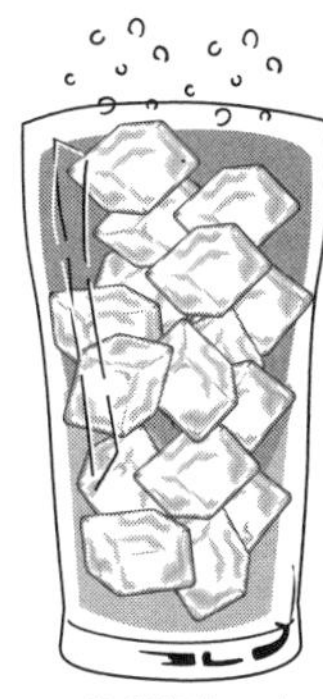

step 3: Fill the glass with mix to within 1/2 to 1 inch of the rim.

step 4: Stir with two or three strokes of the barspoon.

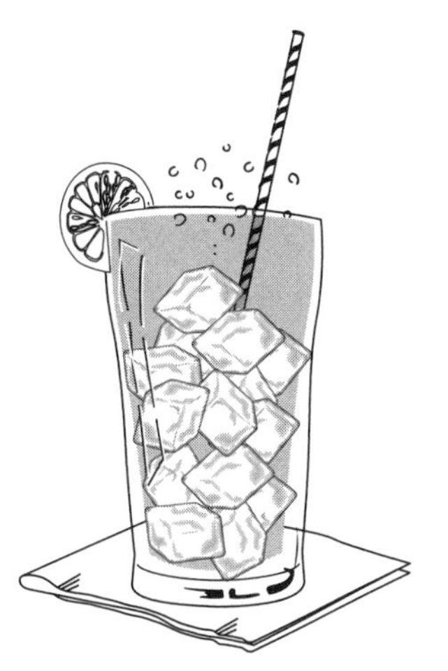

step 5: Add the garnish, if any, and a stir stick or straw. Serve on a cocktail napkin.

FIGURE 10.3

When making a Gin and Tonic and similar drinks, allow a bit more room for the garnish when pouring the mix, perhaps an extra 1/4 inch of glass rim. Squeeze the lime wedge with the hand squeezer (original method) directly into the glass. Then drop the squeezed wedge, minus the seeds, into the drink. Use your two or three strokes of the barspoon at this point. In the speed method you would probably squeeze the lime by hand or dispense with it altogether. When using a garnish whose flavor is added to the drink, standardize the garnish size so that your drinks will always have the same taste. The procedures given in these two recipes apply to any liquor-mixer combination, for example Rum and Coke, Brandy and Coke, Campari and Soda, Bourbon and 7UP, Vodka and Bitter Lemon, and Rye and Ginger. Some combinations have special names:

- ***Seven and Seven:*** Seagram's 7-Crown whiskey and 7UP
- ***Presbyterian:*** Customer's choice of liquor and half ginger ale and half club soda
- ***Cuba Libre:*** Light rum and cola, with a squeezed lime wedge (If dark rum is used, call it a *Cuba Libra*). Another, more modern drink of the same name that includes gin, bitters, and a splash of club soda.
- ***Mamie Taylor:*** Scotch and ginger ale, with a lemon twist or squeeze of lime.
- ***Moscow Mule:*** Vodka and ginger beer, with a squeezed lime half, served in an 8-ounce copper mug.

CLOSE-UP: The Mojito

Cocktails from Central and South America have blossomed alongside New World cuisine and have officially entered the mainstream of most bar businesses. Although the Mojito has become popular only recently in the United States, it has been around for decades. In Cuba in the mid-nineteenth century it was called the Draque, a name possibly taken from the English sea captain Sir Francis Drake, who is reputed to have fancied Cuban rum to excess. By the time writer Ernest Hemingway popularized the drink in the 1930s and 1940s (when he lived and worked in Havana), the name of this cocktail had already been changed to Mojito, which means *little wet one.*

The key to this refreshing Cuban cocktail is the use of fresh mint and fresh limes, muddled together in the bottom of a Collins glass. (The Mojitos of yesteryear were made with rum, sugar cane, and yerba buena, an indigenous, minty herb.) Muddling mint and lime extracts the lime juice without the zest and liberates the fresh smell and flavor of the mint. Simple syrup is added; the glass is filled with cube ice and a liberal pour of light rum, then finished with club soda and topped with a mint sprig or a stick of fresh sugar cane. A properly made Mojito balances both sweet and tangy flavors, but it is that time-consuming muddling step that has been a bit of a barrier to the drink's popularity. Fortunately this challenge has been met by a variety of marketplace innovations. Monin Mojito Syrup is a ready-made mix of lime and mint, and a new rum product called Marti is mint-and-lime flavored. At Loews' Ventana Canyon Resort in Tucson, Arizona, the kitchen staff has created a mint-lime sorbet, to which they add rum and garnish with mint.

The following is a time-saving Mojito version that skips both the lime pulp and the simple syrup:

Using the back of a wooden spoon, muddle 2 tablespoons roughly chopped mint leaves in the bottom of a 10-ounce cocktail glass. Add 1½ tablespoons fresh lime juice and 2 to 3 tablespoons sugar and stir until dissolved. Add 1½ ounces of white rum. Fill the glass with crushed ice and add club soda. Stir and garnish.

Because the Nuevo Latino cocktails are colorful as well as exotic, they are finding new fans on the U.S. bar scene. In addition to the Mojito try these:

- ***Conrico:*** Gin, lime juice, coconut milk, pineapple juice, and grapefruit soda, and served in a coconut shell.
- ***Roombatini:*** A rum Nuevo Latino martini (part light, part dark), peach schnapps, muddled lime, and sugar.
- ***Prickly Pear Margarita:*** Tequila infused with the sweet, red fruit of the prickly pear cactus.
- ***Rumba Tea:*** A hibiscus tea and juice drink made with Malibu and Bacardi Limon (lemon-flavored) rums and Cointreau.

Bartender Stefan Trummer of New York City's Citarella restaurant calls his Mojito "The Flaming Hemingway." He mixes fresh mint and lime with caramelized 160-proof rum and tops it off with nonvintage Moet & Chandon Rose Champagne instead of club soda. The dinner menu recommends pairing this Mojito variation with the breast of duck with figs and roasted shallots. *Delicioso!*

Fruit-Juice Drinks

As you'll note in the recipes that we've already shared, fruit-juice drinks are first cousins to the highball family. In fact many people consider them to be highballs since they are made in a similar way in the same type of glass. The major difference is that fruit juice takes the place of the carbonated mix as the body of the drink (see Figure 10.4). The original method and the speed method are identical here in most cases. One notable exception is making a Bloody Mary: in the original method it is made from scratch, ingredient by ingredient, and is sometimes shaken; in the speed method a prepared mix is poured from a bottle and stirred in the glass. (We will discuss this shortly.) Two points are worth noting in the basic method:

- In step 1 the amount of ice used is often less than that used in the highball to give a higher proportion of juice. The added juice is enough to retain the full flavor to the last drop even though the melting ice dilutes the drink somewhat.
- In step 4 the stirring is vigorous since juices and liquor do not blend as readily as mixers and liquor, and there are no bubbles to worry about.

Juice drinks are very popular, and there are many of them. Most have special, sort of cutesy names. The only real trick in making these drinks is to recall which

HOW TO BUILD A JUICE DRINK

Ingredients
Liquor
Fruit juice (sometime premix)
Accent ingredients (sometimes)
Cube ice
Garnish (sometimes)

Glass
Highball (6 to 10 ounces)

Mixing Method
Build

Equipment and Accessories
Jigger (standard house size)
Barspoon
Ice scoop
Fruit squeezer (sometimes)
Stir stick or straws
Pick (sometimes)
Cocktail napkin

step 1: Using the ice scoop, fill the glass with the required amount of ice and place it on the rail.

step 2: Add 1 jigger of the liquor ordered.

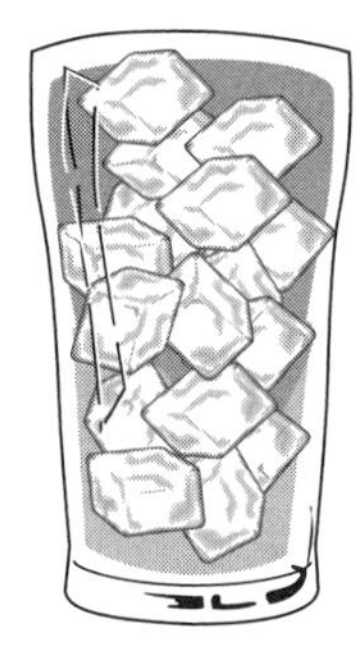

step 3: Fill the glass with juice to within 1/2 to 1 inch of the rim.

step 4: Stir vigorously with the barspoon.

step 5: Add the garnish, if any, and a stir stick or straw. Serve on a cocktail napkin.

FIGURE 10.4

name goes with which juice and which liquor. For instance, here are some variations of the Screwdriver:

- ***Left-handed Screwdriver:*** Gin and orange juice
- ***Kentucky Screwdriver*** or *Yellow Jacket:* Bourbon and orange juice
- ***Bocce Ball:*** amaretto and orange juice
- ***Persuader:*** half amaretto and half brandy, and orange juice
- ***Cobra or Hammer*** or *Sloe Screw:* Sloe gin and orange juice
- ***Southern Screwdriver*** or *Comfortable Screw:* Southern Comfort and orange juice
- ***Fuzzy Navel:*** peach schnapps and orange juice
- ***Golden Screw:*** Galliano and orange juice
- ***Madras:*** Vodka and half cranberry and half orange juice

In addition there is a whole series of Screwdrivers with "national names" made with the corresponding nation's liquor: Mexican Screwdriver (tequila and orange juice), Italian (Galliano), French (brandy), Greek (ouzo), Cuban (rum), Irish (Irish whiskey), Scotch Driver (Scotch), and Canadian Driver (Canadian whiskey). In other drinks the liquor is the same as in the Screwdriver but the juice changes:

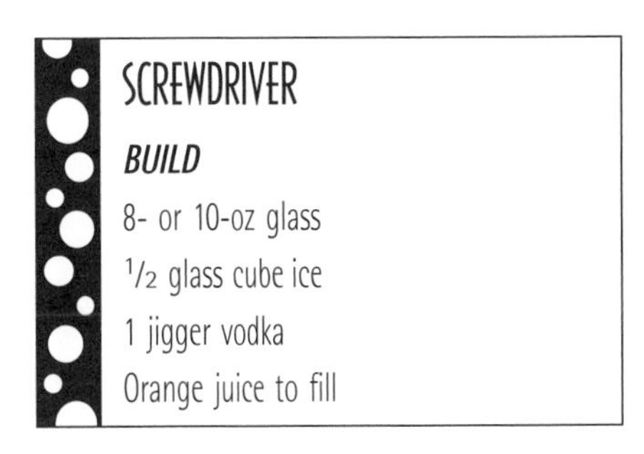
SCREWDRIVER
BUILD
8- or 10-oz glass
1/2 glass cube ice
1 jigger vodka
Orange juice to fill

- ***Seabreeze:*** Vodka, cranberry juice, and grapefruit juice
- ***Greyhound:*** Vodka and grapefruit juice
- ***Salty Dog:*** A Greyhound served in a salt-rimmed glass (usually a Collins glass, and sometimes made with gin)

Rimming a glass with salt is the first step in making a Salty Dog. To rim the glass use the rimmer described in Chapter 4. If you don't have a rimmer run a cut lemon or lime evenly around the rim (half a lemon will give you a firm, even surface). Dip the rim in a shallow dish of salt, then build the drink as usual, taking care to keep the rim intact. A crisp, even rim enhances the drink, but if the lemon is applied unevenly the rim will be uneven. Too much salt will spoil the taste of the drink. Also, remember to think creatively when rimming cocktail glasses. Today's bar chefs may mix peppers and other spices with their salt (or sugar), or use edible fruit granules and even finely chopped, edible flower petals!

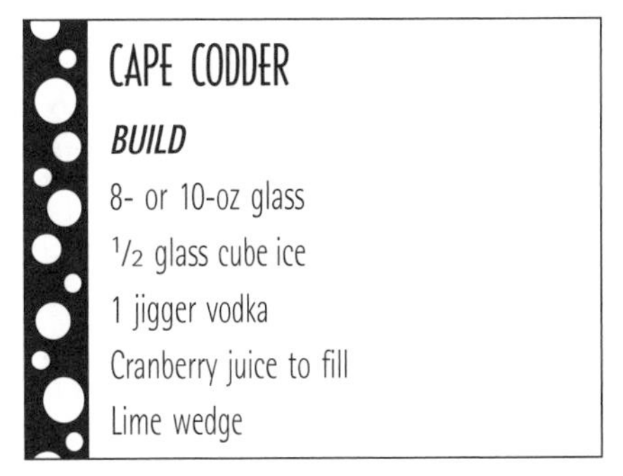
CAPE CODDER
BUILD
8- or 10-oz glass
1/2 glass cube ice
1 jigger vodka
Cranberry juice to fill
Lime wedge

Another series of drinks takes off from the Screwdriver by adding another ingredient as an accent and traveling under a fanciful name that is sometimes better than the drink, such as the Harvey Wallbanger and Tequila Sunrise. Legend has it that "Harvey the Wallbanger" was a surfer's nickname. Depending on who tells the story Harvey either won a surfing contest and celebrated with this drink, or lost a surfing contest and drowned his sorrows in it. Either way he had too many and "bounced from wall to wall" as he staggered out of the bar.

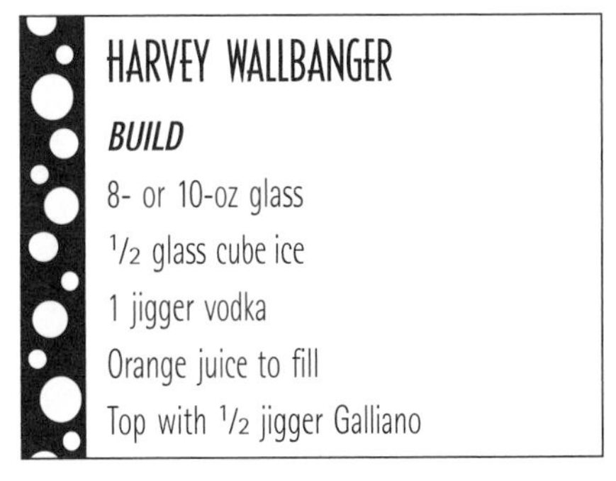
HARVEY WALLBANGER
BUILD
8- or 10-oz glass
1/2 glass cube ice
1 jigger vodka
Orange juice to fill
Top with 1/2 jigger Galliano

In both of these drinks when you pour the orange juice, you leave more room at the top for the last ingredient, and you do your stirring *before* you add it. The Galliano, poured carefully with a circular motion, will float on top of the Harvey Wallbanger. The grenadine in the Tequila Sunrise will sink to the bottom since it is heavier than everything else. Some Sunrise aficionados believe that in a true Sunrise the red color rises from the bottom. To create this effect you can pour the grenadine first and disperse it with a splash of soda, then add the ice, the tequila, and the orange juice, and eliminate the stirring.

> **TEQUILA SUNRISE**
>
> ***BUILD***
>
> 8- or 10-oz glass
>
> 1/2 glass cube ice
>
> 1 jigger tequila
>
> Orange juice to fill
>
> Top with 1/2 jigger Grenadine

A number of other drinks are variations of these two. When made with tequila a Harvey Wallbanger becomes a Freddy Fudpucker or a Charley Goodleg (or Goodlay). When made with rum a Harvey Wallbanger becomes a Jonkanov or Joe Canoe. When you keep the vodka but change the juice from orange to grapefruit, a Harvey Wallbanger becomes a Henrietta Wallbanger. When you use half orange juice and half heavy cream "Harvey" becomes "Jenny" (Wallbanger).

Variations on the Tequila Sunrise include the Russian Sunrise, which is made with vodka instead of tequila, and the Tijuana Sunrise, which uses a dash of Angostura bitters instead of grenadine.

To a certain extent you will find that drink recipes are like fashions: Everything old is, eventually, new again. One such example is the Hurricane, which was created in New Orleans in the 1940s and is reaching a new peak of popularity today. A shortage of alcohol during World War II forced New Orleans bartenders to get creative with whatever they could find, and rum happened to be the most plentiful liquor in the area. While most simply mixed rum with soft drinks Pat O'Brien, a bar owner on St. Pete Street, mixed it with lime and passionfruit juices and a little sugar, and poured it into a glass shaped like the cover of a hurricane lamp. The uniquely shaped glass is a must-have souvenir for New Orleans visitors—and you can still get it at Pat O'Brien's Bar. Today Island Oasis, a beverage-mixer-making company in Boston, sells a Hurricane mix.

CLOSE-UP: The Bloody Mary

Perhaps the most distinctive, classic fruit-juice drink is the Bloody Mary; it is robust, loaded with taste, and even nutritious. There are many versions, but the essentials are vodka and tomato juice with accents of lemon or lime and spices. Many different stories of its origin, but the drink's colorful history dates back to the roaring 1920s when bartender Fernard "Pete" Patiot combined tomato juice with gin at Harry's New York Bar in Paris, France, as a treat for his British and American clientele. (The patrons included Gertrude Stein, George Gershwin, and F. Scott Fitzgerald.) Patiot's drink was originally named the Red Snapper. Gin was its original base liquor because it was the most popular spirit of that period. Today a good bartender knows that the customer who orders a Red Snapper wants a Bloody Mary made with gin.

The drink's more sinister name is generally believed to be a reference to Mary Tudor, the Queen of England who was infamous during her brief reign for the savage persecution of Protestants. Others claim that the original Mary was either a frequent and popular guest at Chicago's Bucket of Blood Club in a bygone era or one of the characters in the Rodgers and Hammerstein musical *South Pacific.*

Whatever the Bloody Mary's origin its secret is the mix: whether it begins with tomato juice, V-8 juice, or Clamato juice. The next step includes the modifiers, which also vary radically, from Worcestershire sauce, to Tabasco sauce, to horseradish, to pureed salsa, to A-1 steak sauce, to clam juice. Spices include celery salt, garlic salt, coarse ground pepper, and chili powder. Daring bartenders experiment with such ingredients as anchovy paste, curry powder, crushed onions, basil, dill, and freshly pressed garlic, as well as chile-pepper-infused vodka as the base liquor.

BLOODY MARY (*FROM SCRATCH*)

BUILD

8- or 10-oz glass
1/2 glass cube ice
1 jigger vodka
3 oz tomato juice
Juice of 1/2 fresh lemon (1/2 oz)
2-3 dashes Worcestershire
2 drops Tabasco
Salt, pepper
Lemon wheel

In short there are as many Bloody Mary versions as there are bartenders. In a Dallas-newspaper-sponsored competition to create a new signature drink for a horseracing event, the "Tall Texan" was created. This Bloody Mary adaptation was made with Toto's vodka, Stubb's Smokey Mesquite Barbecue Sauce, and tomato juice, and garnished with a cilantro sprig and a lemon slice. The list goes on and on. The Bloody Mary has a host of close relatives that are, once again, made by substituting another liquor for the vodka or changing the mixer. They include:

BLOODY MARY (*SPEED*)

BUILD

8- or 10-oz glass
1/2 glass cube ice
1 jigger vodka
Bloody Mary mix to fill
Serve with celery stick "stirrer."

- ***Bloody Maria:*** substitutes tequila for vodka
- ***Danish Mary:*** Aquavit takes the place of vodka
- ***Virgin Mary:*** Everything except the liquor. Also called a Bloody Shame.
- ***Bleeding Clam*** or *Clamdigger:* 1 jigger of clam juice
- ***Bloody Bull:*** Substitute beef bouillon for half the tomato juice
- ***Bullshot:*** Substitute beef bouillon for all of the tomato juice

Sometimes the Bloody Mary glass is dressed up with a rim of celery salt, and sometimes the glass is special: a tulip shape or a balloon wineglass. The garnishes are many: favorite alternates to the lemon slice include a lime wedge, cooked and peeled shrimp, a cherry tomato, or stuffed Spanish olives on cocktail picks. Stirrer options include a celery stick, a marinated asparagus spear, or a cucumber spear.

You can have some fun with these versatile drinks by offering upscale presentations, such as a rolling cart to mix them tableside at Sunday brunch. Tomfooleries, a restaurant and bar in Kansas City, Missouri, is home to an impressive "Weekend Recovery Bloody Mary Bar," a buffet-style setup with more than 60 different items with which to embellish the drink basics. Guests receive a chilled glass, select their preferred brands of vodka and Bloody Mary mix, and can help themselves to pinches and dashes of various spices, peppers, fresh shrimp, crabmeat, garnishes, and so on.

Any of the highballs or juice drinks that we have discussed can become **"tall"** drinks if the customer specifies. To mix these you use a larger glass, such as a Collins or Zombie glass, and increase the amounts of everything in the same proportions—except for the liquor, which remains the same. What this customer wants is a long, cool drink that is not as strong as a highball.

Many fruit-juice drinks are easily dressed up to become house specialties. Use a specialty or larger size glass and garnish imaginatively, for promotional purposes and at a slightly higher price.

Liquor on Ice

Another type of drink built in the glass consists of a single liquor served over ice; nothing else is added. In today's drink market liquor on ice gets a lot of attention; it is the method often used for serving single-malt Scotches, small-batch bourbons, and a few of the superpremium whiskeys. These types of drinks appeal to the image-conscious consumer and, although they are no substitute for an after-dinner brandy, they are making inroads. Such drinks are typically served in rocks or Old-Fashioned glasses that, usually, hold 5 to 7 ounces. Strictly speaking these are not "mixed" drinks, but they are generally thought of as being related to the highball family. Often they contain more liquor, typically 1½ jiggers.

For example, the method used to build a Scotch on the Rocks or a Scotch Mist is so simple that it needs no explanation; you do not even stir the drink. However, keeping a few tips in mind may be helpful. A glass ¾ full of cube ice will leave plenty of room for the liquor without any danger of spilling. It will also make the glass look fuller than if you were to fill it completely with ice. Do not worry if the ice stands higher in the glass than the drink does. People who order this type of drink do not expect a glass filled with liquor. If your rocks drinks look too scant, you might try a different combination of glass size and cube ice. A 5-ounce footed glass with small cubes is often a good choice. Large square cubes do not fit well in small glasses; they leave spaces too large for the liquor to fill. Some establishments increase the jigger size for spirits served alone on the rocks.

SCOTCH ON THE ROCKS

BUILD

Old-Fashioned glass

¾ glass cube ice

1 to 1½ jiggers Scotch

Any kind of spirit can be served either on the rocks or as a "mist." Those most commonly requested are whiskies, brandy, and a few liqueurs ordered as after-dinner drinks, such as peach schnapps or other fruit liqueurs, Drambuie, and coffee liqueurs. If these are served over crushed ice in a cocktail glass or snifter instead of a rocks glass, they are known as **frappes.** If you do not have crushed ice or an ice crusher, you can wrap enough cubes for a mist or frappe in a towel and crack them with a mallet. You can also crack the wrapped ice by hitting the whole towelful on a hard surface, such as a stainless-steel countertop.

SCOTCH MIST

BUILD

Old-Fashioned glass

Full glass cracked or crushed ice

1 to 1½ jiggers Scotch

Lemon twist

Wines, especially white wines and aperitif wines, are rarely ordered on the rocks, but sometimes it happens. In this case they will be served in 4- to 6-ounce portions poured over cube ice in an 8- or 9-ounce wineglass.

Two-Liquor Drinks on Ice

Short, sweet drinks on the rocks have a special appeal to young drinkers and make good drinks to sip after dinner. They are too sweet to be true aperitifs, although people do order such drinks as a Black Russian or Stinger before dinner.

Two-liquor drinks typically combine a jigger of a major spirit (whiskey, gin, rum, brandy, vodka, tequila) with a smaller amount of a flavorful liqueur, such as coffee, mint, chocolate, almond, anise, licorice. Proportions vary from 3:1 to 1:1, depending on the drink and the house recipe. Even with a 3:1 ratio, the liqueur flavor often takes over the drink. Equal parts make a very sweet drink, although this varies with the particular liqueur. Since the two liquors blend readily these drinks are built in the glass and are among the easiest and fastest to make (see Figure 10.5).

Together the two liquors usually add up to a 2- to 3-ounce drink. Anything less would be noticeably scant in the glass. Notice that in steps 2 and 3 you add the base liquor first, then the liqueur. This is because the liqueur, with its higher sugar content, is heavier and will head for the bottom of the glass, filtering through the liquor and making it easier to blend the two. Few of these drinks call for a garnish (see step 5). If there is one, it is usually a lemon twist. Step 6 is necessary because the liqueur, with its sugar content, clings to the sides of the jigger and will flavor the next drink.

Two typical two-liquor drinks are the Black Russian and the Stinger, both of which have many variations and spinoffs. Twists on the Black Russian include the following:

- ***White Russian:*** A Black Russian made with a cream float; another version is made in a blender with ice cream.
- ***Black Magic:*** A Black Russian made with lemon juice and a twist
- ***Black Jamaican:*** Rum substituted for vodka
- ***Black Watch:*** Scotch substituted for vodka, with a twist
- ***Brave Bull:*** Tequila substituted for vodka
- ***Dirty Mother:*** Brandy substituted for vodka
- ***Siberian:*** A Black Russian with a brandy float

Similarly there are many variations on the Stinger, including the following:

- ***Cossack or White Spider:*** Made with vodka instead of brandy
- ***Irish Stinger:*** Green creme de menthe substituted for white creme de menthe
- ***International Stinger:*** A Stinger made with cognac as the brandy
- ***Greek Stinger:*** A Stinger made with Metaxa as the brandy

HOW TO BUILD A TWO-LIQUOR DRINK

Ingredients
A base liquor
A liqueur
Cube ice
Garnish

Glass
Rocks (5 to 7 ounces)

Mixing Method
Build

Equipment and Accessories
Jigger
Barspoon
Ice scoop
Stir stick or straws
Cocktail napkin

step 1: Using the ice scoop, fill the glass with ice to within 1/2 inch of rim and place on rail.

step 2: Add the base liquor.

step 3: Add the liqueur.

step 4: Stir with the barspoon.

step 5: Add the garnish, if any, and a stir stick or straw. Serve on a cocktail napkin.

step 6: Rinse the jigger.

FIGURE 10.5

- ***White Way:*** Gin substituted for brandy
- ***Smoothy:*** Bourbon substituted for brandy
- ***Galliano Stinger:*** Galliano substituted for creme de menthe

Other popular two-liquor drinks include the following:

- ***Rusty Nail*** or *Knucklehead:* Made with Scotch and Drambuie
- ***Godfather:*** Made with Scotch or bourbon and Amaretto, the bourbon version is also called The Boss.
- ***Godmother:*** Made with vodka and Amaretto
- ***Spanish Fly:*** Made with tequila and Amaretto

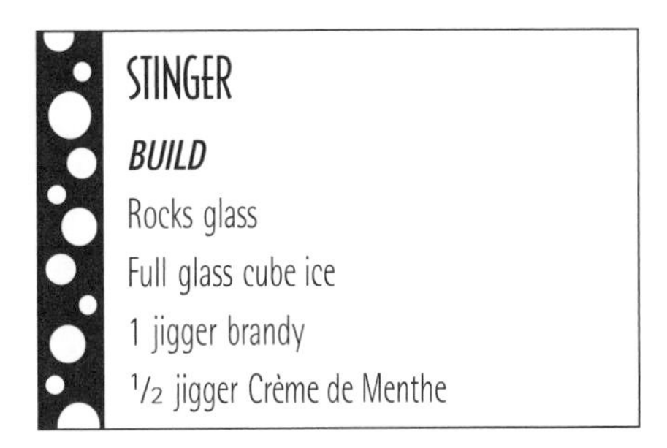

All of these two-liquor drinks may also be served straight up in a cocktail glass; they are stirred with ice in a mixing glass and strained into a chilled glass (see in Chapter 11).

Collinses, Rickeys, Bucks, Coolers, and Spritzers

Several other drink families are also built in the glass. Some of them take off from the highball and juice drinks by adding other characteristic ingredients. The best known of these is the Collins family.

Family Characteristics

- **Ingredients.** Liquor, lemon juice, sugar (or sweet-and-sour mix), soda, cube ice, maraschino-cherry garnish, optional orange slice. Today the lemon juice, sugar, and soda are typically combined in the *Collins mix.*
- **Glass.** Collins (12 to 14 ounces)
- **Mixing method (speed version).** Build with Collins mix.

The basic steps are those for making a highball. (We will discuss making a Collins from scratch in Chapter 11.) In the Collins family the first name of the drink changes with the liquor: Tom Collins for gin, John Collins for bourbon, Mike Collins for Irish whiskey, Sack for applejack, Pierre for cognac, and Pedro for rum. There are as many other Collinses as there are spirits, including vodka, Scotch, rye, and tequila.

Rickeys are cousins to the Collinses. They use lime instead of lemon and are a shorter, drier drink. They are served in a smaller glass and contain little or no sugar.

Family Characteristics

- **Ingredients.** Liquor, fresh lime, soda, cube ice
- **Glass.** Highball or Old-Fashioned
- **Mixing method (speed version).** Build with Collins mix.

The basic steps are similar to those for making a highball, but start off with half a fresh lime squeezed over ice. Do not use Rose's Lime Juice because it is much sweeter than regular, unsweetened juice, which is essential to the drink. A Rickey may be made with any liquor or liqueur. A liqueur makes a sweeter drink and cuts the extreme dryness of the lime. Rickeys made with nonsweet spirits may have a small amount of simple syrup or even grenadine added. When you change the soda of the Rickey to ginger ale and the lime to lemon, you have a Buck. It is made like a highball, usually in a highball glass. It is not as dry as a Rickey because the ginger ale is sweet. Today's Buck usually goes by another name, such as:

- ***Mamie Taylor:*** Made with scotch, with a lemon wedge or lime juice
- ***Mamie's Sister*** or *Fog Horn:* Made with gin
- ***Mamie's Southern Sister:*** Made with bourbon
- ***Susie Taylor:*** Made with rum

The original *cooler* was typically a long drink made with liquor and soda or ginger ale, and served over ice in a Collins glass decorated with a long spiral of lemon peel curling around inside the glass from bottom to top. One of the best-known coolers was the Horse's Neck with a Kick, which consisted of 2 ounces of liquor with ginger ale and the long lemon spiral. A plain Horse's Neck was a Prohibition drink without the liquor.

Today the term **wine cooler** brings to mind the familiar sweet combination of bottled wine plus fruit juice. But there is also a mixed-to-order wine cooler that is half wine and half soda, iced, and served in a Collins or highball glass. When it is made with white wine it is called a **spritzer.**

Another similar drink is the Vermouth Cassis, which combines 1½ to 2 ounces of dry vermouth with crème de cassis in a 4:1 to 6:1 ratio over cube ice, with soda to fill, and a twist or slice of lemon. A different but related drink is Kir (pronounced keer), a glass of chilled white wine with ½ ounce or less of cassis, no soda, and sometimes no ice. A Kir Royale is a variation of Kir, with chilled Champagne instead of white wine, and served without ice in a flute or tulip champagne glass.

WINE COOLER

BUILD

8- or 10-oz glass

¾ glass cube or crushed ice

Half fill with red wine

7UP to fill

Twist or flag

SPRITZER

BUILD

8- or 10-oz glass

¾ glass cube or crushed ice

Half fill with white wine

Club soda to fill

Twist, lemon slice, or lime wedge

Old-Fashioned Drinks

Some mixed drinks have been around since colonial times. Many others originated in the era of the grand hotel bars of the late 1800s, or during Prohibition, when new ways were devised to mask the awful taste of homemade gin. Some described here you may never encounter directly, but they may have potential as specialty drinks, dressed up with modern techniques, intriguing names, and the romance of the past. Two venerable drinks are still very much alive: the Old Fashioned and

TOP SUMMER COCKTAILS

The Food Network (www.foodtv.com) listed its "Top Ten Summer Cocktails" for 2004 which are shown below. Did your favorite make the cut?

1. Mojito
2. Sangria (a red-wine-and-club-soda punch spiked with cognac and orange liqueur)
3. Gin and Tonic
4. Cape Codder
5. Martini
6. Mai Tai
7. Long Island Iced Tea
8. Pina Colada
9. Cosmopolitan
10. Sea Breeze

the Mint Julep. In structure they are simply liquor-over-ice-drinks that are sweetened, accented, and garnished. However, both involve more mixing than many other cocktails.

Ironically the Old Fashioned is a cocktail that is never served in a cocktail glass. It is always built in the glass, like a highball, but it is not a highball because it contains little or no mixer. This drink is such a classic that its traditional glass bears its name—a sturdy, all-business tumbler of 5 to 7 ounces, just the right size to make the drink without adding more than a splash or two of water.

Family Characteristics

- **Ingredients.** Liquor, sugar, bitters, water, fruit cherry, orange, cube ice
- **Glass.** Old-Fashioned
- **Mixing method.** Build

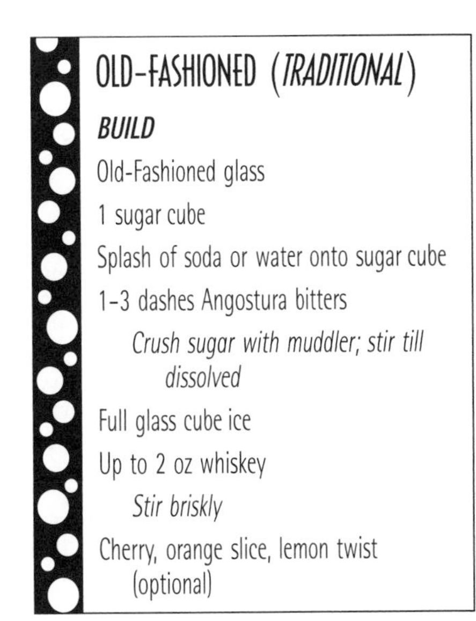

OLD-FASHIONED (*TRADITIONAL*)

BUILD

Old-Fashioned glass

1 sugar cube

Splash of soda or water onto sugar cube

1-3 dashes Angostura bitters

Crush sugar with muddler; stir till dissolved

Full glass cube ice

Up to 2 oz whiskey

Stir briskly

Cherry, orange slice, lemon twist (optional)

This drink came out of Old Kentucky and is full of tradition: the glass, the garnishes, and the tender loving care with which it is made. You certainly will not find this drink at a speed bar. Even less elaborate versions take several minutes to make. Older customers prefer it as it used to be; they want the rich taste of sweetened bourbon accented with bitters and fruit. If the undiluted drink does not fill the glass use smaller cube ice, more liquor, or a smaller glass. Today's younger customer with a taste for lighter drinks often prefers an Old Fashioned made with soda or water added. The customer should be queried as to preference.

An Old Fashioned can be made with any whiskey or with other liquors—brandy, applejack, rum, even gin—but unless the customer orders one of these, make it with bourbon in the South, a blended whiskey in the East, and most likely brandy in Wisconsin. Simple syrup really makes a better drink than lump sugar unless you are emphasizing ritual for the customer. Stir the drink very well in any case, and garnish it handsomely. If you want to gild the lily, you can add a dash of Curacao or sweet vermouth, or even a bit of the juice from the maraschino-cherry bottle. If you add these use less sugar accordingly. You can change the bitters (for example, use orange bitters with rum or gin) or you can float a teaspoonful of 151-proof rum on a Rum Old Fashioned. You can also elaborate on the fruit garnishes—pineapple is often used.

Someone in Old New Orleans elaborated on the Old Fashioned to create the Sazarac by coating the inside of the glass with absinthe. Today a substitute, such as Pernod, is used instead since absinthe is illegal in the United States. You roll a splash of Pernod around inside the glass until it is well coated, discard what is left, and proceed to make an Old Fashioned using Peychaud bitters, often with straight rye as the liquor. The Sazarac is served in New Orleans as prebrunch refreshment.

The Mint Julep, another Southern U.S. tradition, seems to have always represented southern elegance and leisure, and it's a must-have on the day that the Kentucky Derby horse race is run every year. The word *julep* is a modern adaptation of ancient words meaning "rosewater." There are said to be at least 32 different recipes for this classic, but they all have certain common elements:

OLD-FASHIONED (*CURRENT*)

BUILD

Old-Fashioned glass
Full glass cube ice
Up to 2 oz whiskey
1-2 teaspoons simple syrup
1-3 dashes Angostura bitters
Stir briskly
Soda or water to fill
Lemon twist (optional)

MINT JULEP

BUILD

16-oz glass, chilled
10-12 fresh mint leaves, bruised gently
1 tsp bar sugar with spash of soda (or 1 1/2 tsp simple syrup)
Muddle sugar and mint
Add 1/2 glass ice
1 jigger bourbon
Stir up and down until well mixed
Fill glass with ice
Add another jigger bourbon
Stir contents up and down until glass/mug is completely "frosted"
Insert straws
Garnish with mint sprigs, perhaps dipped in bar sugar or with fruit

Family Characteristics

- **Ingredients.** Liquor (traditionally bourbon), fresh mint, sugar, crushed or shaved ice
- **Glass.** 12- to 16-oz chilled glass or silver mug
- **Mixing method.** Build (ritual methods stir first, then build)

If the customer askes, you can make a Mint Julep with rye, rum, gin, brandy, or Southern Comfort, but the classic version is made with 100-proof, bottled-in-bond bourbon. Why else would you go to all this trouble? It makes a good premium-price specialty drink for some enterprises. A Smash is a cross between a Mint Julep and an Old Fashioned. A Smash is made with Mint Julep ingredients using the Old Fashioned method, in an Old Fashioned glass. You muddle a cube of sugar and some mint with a splash of water, add cube ice and a jigger of liquor, and garnish with mint sprigs. You can also make a Smash as a long drink in a tall glass by adding club soda.

Another old-timer is the Swizzle, a sweet-and-sour, liquor-and-soda drink served over crushed ice in a tall glass with a swizzle stick. A swizzle stick is a special stirrer (now rarely seen) with multiple tentacles at the bottom that are whirled about by rolling the top of the stick between the palms of the hands until the drink froths and the outside of the glass frosts. The handy old Caribbean recipe for such drinks is "one of sour, two of sweet, three of strong, and four of weak." The "sour" in a Swizzle is lemon or lime. The "sweet" may be sugar, simple syrup, a flavored syrup, or a liqueur. The "strong" can be any spirit, and the "weak" is melted ice or sometimes soda. Often a dash of bitters is added for accent. Fruit or mint garnishes are in order. This would make an interesting specialty drink if you can find some old-fashioned swizzle sticks.

New drink trends are often the result of improving on venerable recipes—by venerable bartenders! As long as you are stocking fresh mint leaves to make Juleps, you might try the "Alberto I," a specialty of La Caravelle, a New York City restaurant. This drink is named for Alabeto Alonso (nicknamed "Alberto"), its creator, who has been the bartender at La Caravelle for 38 years.

CLOSE-UP: Long Island Iced Tea

When pressed for a reason for the renewed popularity of the Long Island Iced Tea, bartenders will tell you that it is a hit with the artist-and-musician crowd: They're on a budget and want to get as much alcohol as possible for their dollar. Whether or not that is true the hallmark of this tall drink is the multiliquor punch that it packs while still managing to taste refreshing.

A typical Long Island Iced Tea recipe calls for equal parts of vodka, gin, white rum, and tequila, plus Triple Sec, orange juice, sour mix, and cola. (In some recipes, the tequila is omitted.) It's difficult to make this an upscale drink, because the multiple liquors practically eliminate the need to ask for anything other than the house pour, although some bars are making an attempt. Variations in glassware and presentation also help to showcase this durable libation.

The latest Long Island Iced Tea incarnations include the following, from the September 2002 issue of *Market Watch:*

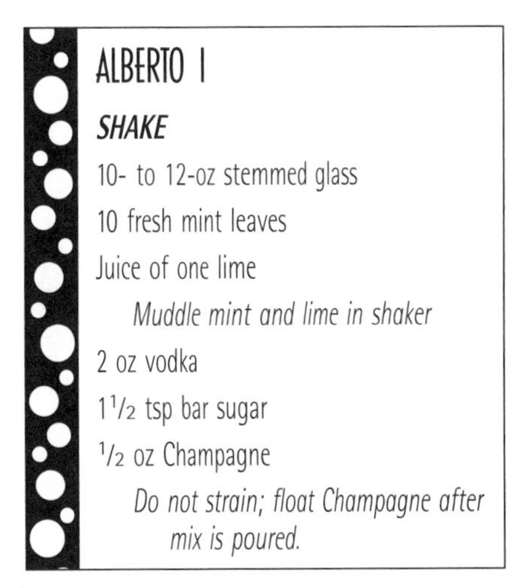
ALBERTO I

SHAKE

10- to 12-oz stemmed glass

10 fresh mint leaves

Juice of one lime

Muddle mint and lime in shaker

2 oz vodka

$1\frac{1}{2}$ tsp bar sugar

$\frac{1}{2}$ oz Champagne

Do not strain; float Champagne after mix is poured.

- ***Long Beach Iced Tea:*** Replace cola with cranberry juice
- ***Tokyo Tea:*** The four white spirits, melon liqueur, sour mix, and 7UP
- ***Florida Iced Tea:*** Replace the sour mix with orange juice
- ***Hawaiian Iced Tea:*** Replace the sour mix with pineapple juice
- ***Bimini Iced Tea:*** The four white spirits, plus Blue Curacao, and pineapple and orange juices
- ***Raspberry Iced Tea*** (or *Purple Haze*): A Long Island Iced Tea with a float of Chambord
- ***Spiced Tea:*** Use Captain Morgan's Spiced Rum (for the rum) and Absolute Peppar (for the vodka)

Pousse-Cafés

Okay, we admit it—you will rarely (if ever) receive an order for this drink of yesteryear, but we wanted to include it for the technique and showmanship it involves, as well as the light it sheds on some of the interesting properties of liquor. "Coffee-pusher" is the literal translation of the term **pousse-café.** In France it is a sweet liqueur drunk with or after coffee at the end of a meal. In the United States the drink first gained popularity in 1840s New Orleans as a show of bartending skills. It has taken on a very complex and elaborate personality, and you need a very steady hand to pour ribbons of different colored liquids into a liqueur or pony glass, layered so that each remains separate in a bright, beautiful rainbow. An added attraction is to make brandy the last ingredient, then flame it when served.

In Raymond Foley's *Ultimate Cocktail Book* (Foley Publishing, 1990) the author presents a list of 56 ingredients, any of which can be used in making a Pousse-Café.

Family Characteristics

- **Ingredients.** Liqueurs of different densities; sometimes nonalcoholic syrups, brandy, cream, or all of these
- **Glass.** Straight-sided liqueur or brandy glass
- **Mixing method.** Build (float)

Since so many different liqueur combinations can be used for a Pousse-Café there is no one formula. The secret of layering is to choose liqueurs of differing density and to "float" them in sequence from heaviest to lightest. Density depends a good deal on the sugar content of a liqueur; however, because there is no indication of sugar content on the bottle, we can only infer it from the alcohol content, or *proof*. In general the lower the proof, the higher the sugar content and density. For example a 36-proof Crème de Cassis is usually heavier than a 50-proof Triple Sec, which is usually heavier than a Curacao at 60 proof. At the top of the scale is green Chartreuse at 110 proof. Grenadine (which has no alcohol) is often used as a pousse-café base, while brandy (which has no sugar) is often used as the top layer. Cream will also float atop most liqueurs.

But proof is not an infallible guide. Neither is the generic name of a liqueur; products of different manufacturers often have different densities. The best system is to work out your own recipes, by trial and error if necessary, and to use the same brands of liqueurs every time. Tables that specify densities are available from liqueur manufacturers; ask your suppliers. (A partial list is given in Figure 10.6.) For best results, Foley says, use products that have at least five units of difference in terms of their specific

POUSSE-CAFÉ

BUILD

Straight-sided liqueur glass
1/6 Grenadine (red)
1/6 white Crème de Menthe
1/6 apricot brandy (oragne)
1/6 Chartreuse (green)
1/6 brandy (amber)

DENSITIES OF VARIOUS LIQUEURS

No.	Proof	Product	Specific Gravity	Color
1	40	Crème de Cassis	1.1833	Purple
2	25	Grenadine	1.1720	Red
3	54	Crème de Cacao	1.1561	Brown
11	56	Crème de Banana	1.1233	Yellow
12	54	Chocolate Mint Liqueur	1.1230	Brown
13	48	Blue Curacao	1.1215	Blue
16	60	Crème de Menthe–White	1.1088	White
17	60	Crème de Menthe–Green	1.1088	Green
44	70	Apricot Brandy	1.10548	Tawny
45	70	Peach Brandy	1.0547	Tawny
54	60	Sloe Gin	1.0241	Red
55	70	Ginger Brandy	0.9979	Light Brown
56	90	Kirschwasser	0.9410	Clear

FIGURE 10.6

gravities, and start with the product that has the highest specific gravity. The pousse-café is mainly a drink for show rather than taste: The object is to create a handsome sequence of colors and to show off the bartender's prowess. The technique is to pour each layer gently over the back of a spoon, into or over the glass, so that the liqueur spreads evenly on the layer below (see Figure 10.7). If you hold the tip of the spoon against the side of the glass, the liqueur will run slowly down the side and onto the layer below.

Like the Old Fashioned, the Pousse-Café is no drink for a speed bar. Because of the time and skill required, as well as the cost of the specialty liqueurs, a Pousse-Café commands a good price, even though there may be only 1 ounce of liqueur in it altogether. The Pousse-Café is never stirred. Instead the customer drinks the rainbow of colors layer by layer, as neatly as possible. Since the ingredients are chosen for color and density rather than for complementary tastes, some sequences of flavor can be rather odd. Keep this in mind as you develop your own Pousse-Café specialty—and contribute, perhaps, to its comeback as an after-dinner treat.

ANGEL'S KISS

BUILD

Straight-sided liqueur glass

1/4 dark Crème de Cacao (brown)

1/4 Crème d'Yvette (violet)

1/4 brandy (amber)

1/4 cream (white)

FIGURE 10.7 How to build a Pousse-Café.

COFFEE DRINKS AND HOT LIBATIONS

Mixed drinks are not limited to the chilled glass, as bartenders in ski lodges and other cold-weather establishments know well. Many of the mixed drinks in the early U.S. colonies were warmer-uppers heated in tankards by thrusting a red hot poker or loggerhead into the liquid. Today's hot drinks are not limited to cold climes: Coffee drinks are served just about anywhere. Many dinner restaurants have developed specialty coffee drinks that double as desserts, with the added benefit of ending the meal on a note of excitement or sophistication. Because these drinks are usually high-profit items they are a boon to the restaurateur in every way.

Undoubtedly people have been spiking their coffee with spirits for generations and finding it delicious. What you do to dramatize it makes it memorable. The Buena Vista Café in San Francisco started an Irish Coffee craze some 50 years ago when it put Irish whiskey, coffee, and sugar in a goblet and floated freshly whipped cream on top. People came from all over and fought their way through the crowds for a glass mug of it—and they still do. Today the proliferation of mochas, lattes, and cappuccinos provides a whole new set of coffee bases for specialty drinks. An International Cappuccino, for example, is a combination of espresso, Bailey's Irish Cream, Kahlua, Vandermint, Amaretto, and a layer of frothed milk. The Foreign Legion combines espresso with brandy, Benedictine, Frangelico, and Amaretto.

The basic hot coffee drink is very simple to make (see Figure 10.8). For a hot drink the decision about what to serve it in is especially important. The customer must be able to pick up the drink without it being too hot to grasp firmly. This means that a cup, mug, or stemmed glass is preferable. Stemware should be made

ADDING DRAMA TO COFFEE DRINKS

A touch of showmanship when serving coffee drinks is as simple as flaming a brandy float or liquor-soaked sugar cube as the coffee is served. Tony's Restaurant in Houston made Café Diablo into a dramatic tableside-brewing ceremony involving a long flaming spiral of orange peel that can be seen all over the dining room. At classy Commander's Palace in New Orleans (which reopened in summer 2006 after Hurrican Katrina) Café Brulo Diabolique begins with the waiter peeling both an orange and a lemon in two long, unbroken strips and studs the strips with whole cloves. He then breaks a cinnamon stick into a silver bowl placed over a warming fire, adds brandy and orange liqueurs, and ignites them. Using a silver ladle he lifts the flaming mixture and spoons it over the strips of citrus peel, which hang from a long-handled fork. Instantly the line of blue-gold flames climbs up the peels. The waiter then pours dark, chicory-laced coffee into the bowl, quenching the flames. Fresh orange juice is added to the coffee mixture, which is then spooned—hot and fragrant—into demitasse cups.

Also tableside at Commander's Palace, Café Pierre requires two preheated wineglasses, rimmed with lime juice and sugar. Brandy is poured into the glasses and flamed; the waiter pours the liquid back and forth, from one glass to the other. When Galliano is added to the brandy, the blue flame turns bright chartreuse. When the alcohol burns off and the fire goes out, dark coffee is added, along with a ladle of Kahlua and a dollop of whipped cream.

The collaboration of bartender and chef works well to end meals at Plate in Ardmore, Pennsylvania, where a charming trio of "Warm Drinks" is served as dessert. Diners receive three smaller-portion hot beverages: eggnog with peppermint schnapps, dark chocolate with pumpkin mousse, and hot cider with spiced rum and a cookie.

of tempered glass, which is better able to withstand heat without cracking. If your glass is not heat-treated, preheat it by rinsing in hot tap water. Thin glass is better than thick since it heats more evenly and quickly.

Ingredients are extremely important for these satisfying drinks. Use excellent, freshly brewed coffee, high-grade chocolate, and fresh whipping cream. For garnishes you can sprinkle nutmeg, cinnamon, shaved chocolate, or finely chopped nuts on top of the whipped cream, whatever is appropriate to the drink. A cinnamon stick can substitute for the stir stick or spoon in a shallow cup. It is certainly better to use brewed coffee when someone orders a decaffeinated drink, but in a pinch you can put an individual portion of instant decaffeinated coffee in the cup along with the sugar in step 1 and fill the cup with hot water in step 3.

Some drinks can also be made with hot chocolate instead of coffee. For example, the Peppermint Patty blends hot cocoa with peppermint schnapps; the Mounds Bar mixes cocoa with rum. When you mix hot cocoa with butterscotch-flavored schnapps you create a drink called Butterfingers.

HOW TO BUILD A HOT COFFEE DRINK

Ingredients
Hot coffee
Liquor
Sweetener
Whipped cream topping (or brandy float)

Glass
Coffee cup, mug, or preheated steam glass

Mixing Method
Build

Equipment and Accessories
Jigger
Barspoon
Coffee spoon or stir stick
Straws
Cocktail napkin

step 1: Add 1 spoonful sugar or other sweetener to cup, mug, or glass.

step 2: Add 1 jigger of the appropriate liquor.

step 3: Fill with hot coffee to within 1 inch of the rim.

step 4: Stir well with barspoon until sugar is dissolved.

step 5: Swirl whipped cream on top (or float brandy).

step 6: Add garnish if any, stirrer, and straws. Serve on a saucer or cocktail napkin.

FIGURE 10.8

A list of dozens of hot drinks would be excessive at most bars (except, perhaps, ski resorts), but a separate, small drink menu will showcase them and improve check averages during cold-weather months in your area. Here are just a few ideas, from classic to New Age, to get you started:

- ***Irish Coffee:*** Made with Irish whiskey
- ***Café Royale:*** Made with bourbon or brandy; another version is made with half Metaxa and half Galliano
- ***Dutch Coffee:*** Made with Vandermint, but no sugar
- ***Mexican Coffee:*** Made with tequila, and sweetened with Kahlua
- ***Bun Warmer:*** Made with apricot brandy and Southern Comfort
- ***Cherry Snowplow:*** Made with spiced rum, Amaretto, and B&B liqueur
- ***Nutty Irishman:*** Made with Frangelico and Irish cream liqueur
- ***Café Calypso*** or *Jamaican Coffee:* Made with rum and brown sugar. A "deluxe" version substitutes dark Crème de Cacao for sugar, and a "supreme" version uses Tia Maria in place of sugar
- ***Café Pucci:*** Made with half Trinidad rum and half amaretto
- ***Kioki*** (or *Keoke*) *Coffee:* Made with brandy and coffee liqueur for sugar; another version includes Irish whiskey
- ***Royal Street Coffee:*** Made with Amaretto, Kahlua, nutmeg, but no sugar

MOCHA RUM COOLER

SHAKE

Collins glass

8 oz black coffee

3 oz dark rum

$1\frac{1}{2}$ oz Crème de Cacao

Garnish (optional) $\frac{1}{4}$ cup rum-raisin ice cream

Many hot drinks can be traced back to the centuries when they supplied the only central heating available. The Hot Toddy is one example. It is made by mixing a jigger of liquor with sugar and hot water in a mug or Old-Fashioned glass. If the liquor is rum you might call the drink Grog. If you use dark rum and add butter and spices you might call it a Hot Buttered Rum. This drink is best if you premix the butter, sugar, and spices (cinnamon, nutmeg, cloves, salt) in quantity and stir in a teaspoonful per drink. Alternately you can use a packaged premix. In any case serve the drink with a cinnamon stick for stirring.

You can also add spices to any toddy and still call it a Hot Toddy or a Hot Sangaree. When you add an egg to a Toddy you make a Hot Flip or an Eggnog. When you use hot milk instead of water you make a Hot Milk Punch. Sprinkle nutmeg on the top. When you add lemon juice to a Toddy it becomes a Hot Lemonade or a Hot Sling, or a Hot Scotch, Gin, Rum, or Rye.

Of course the coffee does not have to be hot to make a good drink. There are a few interesting iced coffee drinks for summer. Feel free to make your own hot concoctions. Just about any flavorful spirit makes a good base, with the exception of vodka, which is not distinctive enough. Build your drink in a glass or mug, one ingredient at a time. Make it festive and if it is served hot, make sure that it smells good: Aroma is an important sales tool.

There is one more hot drink that makes a good specialty for the Christmas season. The Tom and Jerry was invented by "Professor" Jerry Thomas, a New York City bartender extraordinaire of the late 1800s, who is also credited with creating the original Martini and the Blue Blazer. The Tom and Jerry involves premixing a bowl of batter made of eggs, sugar, spices (allspice, cinnamon, cloves), and a little Jamaican rum (there are also packaged mixes and premade batters on the market). You put a ladleful of batter in a mug, add bourbon or brandy, as well as hot milk or water, and stir vigorously until everything foams. Dust it with nutmeg and serve it warm.

You can usually find some version of Jerry Thomas's Blue Blazer recipe in every bartending manual, but few people have ever seen one made. You put whiskey in one silver mug and hot water in another, set fire to the whiskey, and fling it with unerring accuracy into the hot water. Then you toss the flaming beverage back and forth between the two mugs to make a long streak of flame. "The novice in making this beverage should he careful not to scald himself," wrote Thomas in his 1862 treatise on mixing drinks. *That's* an understatement.

SUMMING UP

A *mixed drink* is any drink in which one alcoholic beverage is mixed with other ingredients. From that jumping-off point you can mix almost anything to create a new drink recipe. But it is important to understand the way a drink is structured: with a base (liquor), other complementary flavors to modify or enhance the base, minor ingredients (for color or a hint of additional flavor), and a garnish.

Drinks of similar structure and ingredients are known as *drink families*. Being aware of these "family relationships" makes it easy to learn a great many drinks using just a few fundamentals. It also makes it possible to recognize a drink type from a list of its ingredients and to make it even when no instructions are given. Beyond that a grasp of drink types and ingredient relationships makes it easy to invent drinks by substituting or adding appropriate ingredients to familiar drinks.

When creating a mixed drink take into account its taste complexity and the degree of mixing difficulty it requires. Drinks built in the glass are the simplest and fastest kinds to make. In this chapter you learned about the basic mixing techniques for highballs and juice drinks, two-liquor drinks, Pousse-Cafés and coffee drinks, with a closer view of the Bloody Mary and the Mojito. Chapter 12 presents drinks made by other methods that require mixing equipment beyond the barspoon and the handgun.

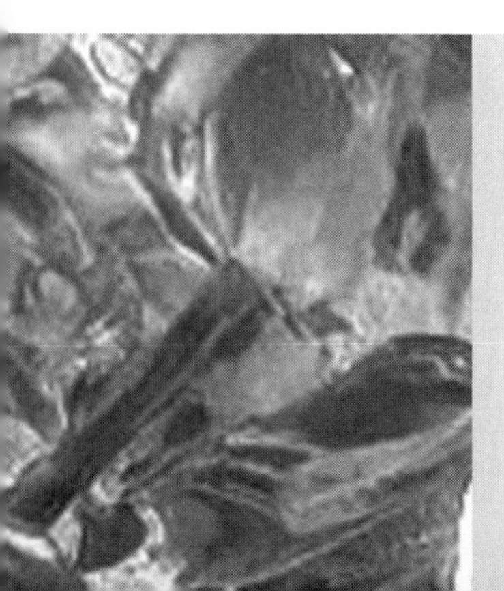

POINTS TO PONDER

1. What is meant by the following phrases: *drink structure, drink families, free-pouring,* and *building a drink?*
2. How do you measure the following drink ingredients: liquor, ice, mix?

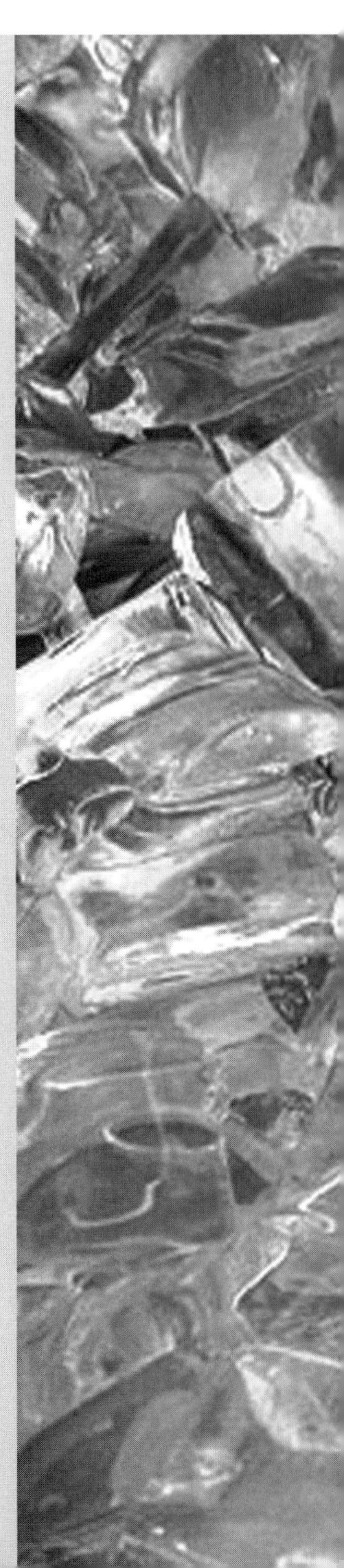

3. Why is it necessary always to use the same type and size of glass to make a given drink?
4. What are the advantages and disadvantages of free-pouring?
5. Explain why using premixed ingredients enables you to build certain drinks, such as the Collins, in the glass instead of shaking them.
6. What are the keys to making a good highball with a carbonated mixer?
7. Try your hand at devising a variation of a current drink by substituting or adding another ingredient. Explain why you chose this combination of ingredients.
8. Choose a drink from each family and write down the recipe from memory, including the glass type and size.
9. What is the difference between a wine spritzer and a wine cooler?
10. What type of bar chef would you prefer to be, classicist or avant-garde? Why?

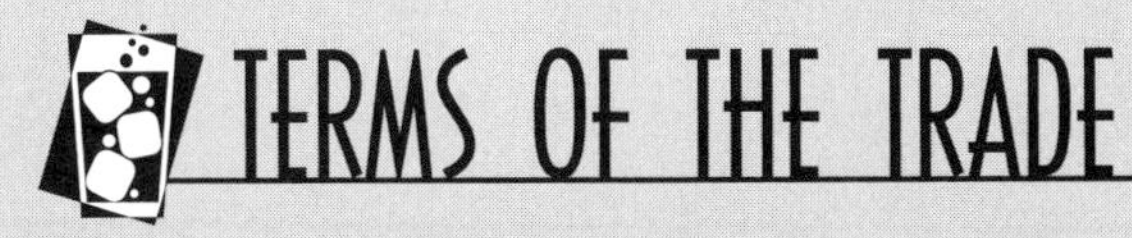

TERMS OF THE TRADE

base
blend
broken ice
build
cocktail
drink structure
frappe
free-pouring
highball
long
mixed drink
mixology
pour
Pousse-Café
rim (rimming)
shake
short
smooth
spiral
stir
straight up
strain
tall
twist
wine cooler
wine spritzer

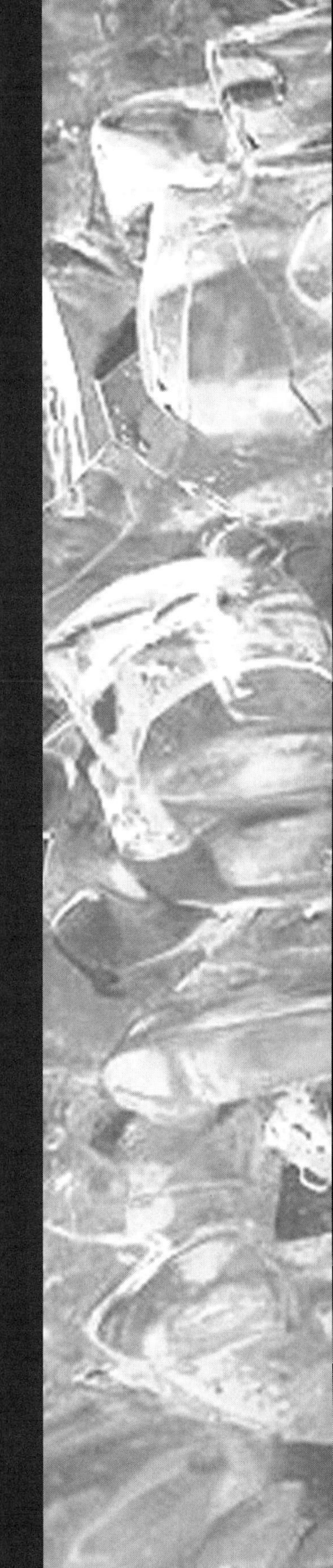

CHAPTER 11
MIXOLOGY, PART TWO

When the Martini began making its comeback in the 1990s it seemed that all a bartender had to do was throw together any cocktail ingredients, serve them in a Martini glass, and call it a "new" Martini. Purists might wince, but the use of sleek, stylish glasses helped elevate overall drink presentation to an art form, and experimentation has stimulated and improved many bar businesses. As you'll see in this chapter it is especially important to know how to make a classic Martini, as well as how to adapt it to your customers' tastes and special requests, and to your own whims as a bartender interested in *creating* trends instead of simply following them.

To continue our discussion of mixology this chapter presents the remaining methods of mixing drinks, including the original method of shaking by hand and the current methods of blending and mechanical mixing that make frozen drinks and ice-cream-based drinks possible. The chapter also explores additional drink families, as well as current methods and techniques for preparing and filling drink orders quickly and properly. Finally you will learn how the bar manager can use all of this knowledge to plan drink menus and create signature drinks that will increase profits and build a reputation for quality, creativity, and professionalism.

THIS CHAPTER WILL HELP YOU . . .

- Explain and demonstrate the stir, shake-by-hand, blend, and shake-mix methods of drink mixing.
- Explain and demonstrate how to make frozen and ice-cream-based drinks.
- Understand how to prepare cocktails from these families: sour, Collins (from scratch), sling, fizz, tropical, and cream drinks.

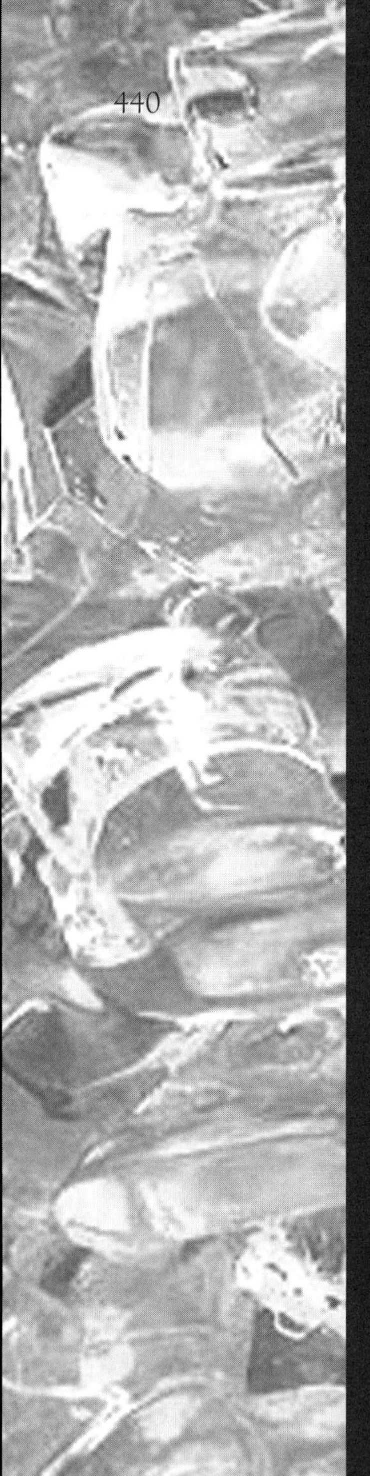

- Take drink orders accurately, fill them efficiently, and train others to do so.
- Develop a suitable drink menu for a limited-menu bar.
- Create signature (specialty) drinks.

Picking up the historical note on which we ended the last chapter, we find that Jerry Thomas of Blue Blazer fame was also a key figure in developing the art of mixology in general. When he wrote his first drink-making manual in 1862 the word *cocktail* referred to "composite beverages" that were generally bottled to take on picnics or hunting trips. As the world's most prestigious bartender of the day, Thomas's zeal and expertise turned the cocktail into a fashionable and desirable bar drink. His moniker, "the Professor," was bestowed out of respect for his dedicated research and experiments in mixology. Today people who know their beverages have much the same regard for such mixologists as Dale DeGroff and Tony Abou-Ganim, individuals who preserve time-honored bartending traditions while adding new drink recipes that surely will become classics.

More on creating signature drinks later. First, let's continue the discussion of drinks that are not built in the glass but are stirred, shaken, blended, or mechanically mixed with the shake machine. These drinks can also be grouped into families, with common ingredients and mixing methods as the family ties. It is important to be familiar with these drinks because they are making a big comeback among younger people, who may have only read about the glamour of the 1950s nightclub scene or seen it in the movies, but who are developing a taste for "venerable" cocktails, including the **Martini** and the **Manhattan.**

THE MARTINI/MANHATTAN FAMILY

It is hard to decide whether to call this group of drinks one family or two. Although today's Martinis and Manhattans are distinctly different from one another, in their second-generation variations and refinements lines cross and distinctions blur. Unlike that of the Martini, however, the lineage of the Manhattan is not in dispute: It was introduced at New York City's Manhattan Club by Winston Churchill's mother.

The basic characteristics of both branches of this drink family are very much the same—with some important caveats that follow:

Family Characteristics

- **Ingredients.** Liquor, vermouth (in a 4:1 to 8:1 ratio), and garnish
- **Glass.** Stemmed cocktail, chilled
- **Mixing method.** Stir

As to differences in a classic Martini the liquor is gin, the vermouth is dry, and the garnish is an olive or a lemon twist. In a classic Manhattan the liquor is whiskey, the vermouth is sweet, and the garnish is a cherry. The mixing method described in Figure 11.1 is for a **straight-up** drink, that is, one served in a chilled, stemmed cocktail glass with no ice in the drink itself. Today Martinis and Manhattans and all of their relatives are served more often on the rocks than they are straight up.

THE STIR METHOD: HOW TO MAKE A MARTINI OR MANHATTAN

Ingredients
Liquor, 4 to 8 parts
Vermouth, 1 part
Garnish

Glass
Stemmed cocktail glass, chilled

Mixing Method
Stir

Equipment and Accessories
16-ounce mixing glass with strainer
Jiggers
Barspoon
Ice scoop
Tongs, pick, or condiment fork
Cocktail napkin

step 1: Place a chilled cocktail glass on the rail, handling it by the stem.

step 2: With the scoop, fill the mixing glass 1/3 full of cube ice.

step 3: Measure liquor and vermouth and add to the mixing glass.

step 4: Stir briskly in one direction 8 to 12 times.

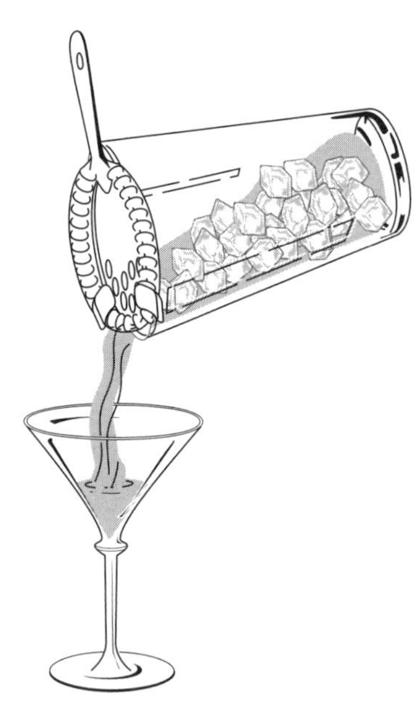

step 5: Strain the liquid into the cocktail glass.

step 6: Add the garnish, using tongs, pick, or a condiment fork. Serve on a cocktail napkin.

FIGURE 11.1

A more recent trend (and one that we believe is here to stay) is that young guests, those under age 35, cringe at the thought of putting vermouth in a Martini. They prefer sweeter drinks with the taste of alcohol softened by mixers or flavors. So unless otherwise specified many professionals now make the Martini without vermouth. Sensible or scandalous? You decide. Another major trend: The Martini used to always be made with gin unless the customer requested another liquor but a marketing push by vodka producers has changed that, too. In 2002 sales of super-premium vodkas rose 10 percent. The Vodka Martini has arrived, and it is just as popular as its classic, gin-based cousin.

There are several things to consider carefully in the mixing of Martinis and Manhattans. The first is a chilled glass. The cold glass is absolutely essential to the quality of the drink since there is no ice in the drink itself. Handle the chilled glass by the stem so that the heat of your fingers does not warm it or leave fingerprints on the frosty bowl. If you do not have a chilled glass to start with you must chill one. You do this by filling it with ice before you begin step 1. (Purists insist that prerefrigerating glasses simply does not have the same effect as the use of ice.) The cocktail glass chills while you are completing steps 2 through 4. Then you pick up the glass by the stem, empty the ice into your waste dump, and proceed with step 5.

The purpose of the stirring in step 4 is twofold: to mix the vermouth and liquor without producing a cloudy drink, and to chill them quickly without unduly diluting the mixture. If you vigorously stir or shake a drink containing vermouth it will look cloudy. If you stir too long melting ice will weaken the drink's flavor. (Dale DeGroff suggests 30 stirs with small cube ice, and 50 stirs with large cubes.) Stir just long enough to blend and chill these two easily combined ingredients and to add about an ounce of water—no more. Note that "ice" means cube ice; crushed ice would dilute the drink too quickly.

In step 5 you use the strainer to keep the ice out of the glass. In the "parent" drink recipe you will see a 6:1 ratio for both drinks. In terms of amounts it is commonly $1\frac{1}{4}$ ounces of liquor and $\frac{1}{4}$ ounce of vermouth. Allowing for a small amount of melted ice and the space taken up by the garnish, you will need a 4- to $4\frac{1}{2}$-ounce glass.

A 6:1 drink is fairly dry. The accepted standard used to be 4:1, but today's trend has been toward drier drinks. If a customer asks for a *dry* Martini you can decrease the vermouth in the recipe or increase the liquor, depending on house policy. For a *very dry* Martini, use only a dash of vermouth or none at all. Bartenders develop their own forms of showmanship about this: They may use an eyedropper or atomizer, or pass the glass over the vermouth bottle with great flourish—or face in the general direction of France and salute!

If you use equal parts of dry and sweet vermouth in either a Martini or a Manhattan it becomes a Perfect Martini or a Perfect Manhattan, respectively. The garnish usually becomes a lemon twist in each case. If you change the olive to a cocktail onion in the original Martini, you have made a Gibson.

There is also the Rum Martini, which will become the El Presidente if you add a dash of bitters or a little lime juice and sweeten the drink with grenadine and Curacao. There's a Tequila Martini, or Tequini; if this is made with Sauza Gold tequila, you might call it a Cold Gold. There is another variation, the Silver Bullet, which is made with gin but either substitutes Scotch for the vermouth or uses both Scotch and vermouth, floating the scotch.

Alternate modifiers to replace vermouth include dry sherry, Cognac, Lillet, Dubonnet with a dash of angostura bitters, Port, Madeira, and even sake. A Dirty Martini includes a splash of green olive juice. And don't neglect the garnish. For members of the Martini/Manhattan family, the garnish should be sophisticated and attractive. As discussed earlier these include olives stuffed with bleu cheese or prosciutto, or wrapped with anchovies; fresh strawberries; pickled green tomatoes; chunks of lobster meat; and peeled, cooked shrimp.

Clearly there are dozens of Martini variations. Each one substitutes ingredients, varies proportions, or adds flavor accents to the original recipe. You should be familiar with any that may be regional favorites in your area. Read on for more ideas.

Close-Up: THE MARTINI

The city of Martinez, California, hosts an annual Martini Festival to celebrate its heritage as the "birthplace of the Martini." Jerry Thomas ("the Professor") is said to have worked his magic and created it there. Of course there are other equally colorful claims. The British say that the Martini is their invention, named after the Martini & Henry, a renowned rifle known for its accuracy and its "kick." The Italians take issue with both of these stories. Italian vermouth maker Martini & Rossi says the drink was so named because it was first made with Martini & Rossi brand vermouth—and plenty of it. The controversy about whether this cocktail was named for a town, a gun, or a vintner will never be settled. This does not really matter for it has long been dwarfed by another controversy that has been brewing since there *were* Martinis: "How should a Martini truly be made?"

From the moment in the early 1800s when gin and vermouth were first blended the Martini has been a very special drink. The Martini prompted many Americans to sample a mixed drink instead of drinking whiskey straight. Many women enjoyed the Martini when social drinking standards relaxed in social and business circles that were previously "for men only."

In the White House President Franklin Roosevelt enjoyed his Martinis (4 parts gin, 1 part vermouth) nightly before dinner. President John F. Kennedy, while still a U.S. senator, singled out the Martini as a symbol of wealth or special privilege; he created the phrase *Martini lunch* to disparage business-related dining, especially at taxpayers' expense. Later President Jimmy Carter made headlines by proposing tax reform that would end the "three-Martini-lunch" wheeling and dealing of members of Congress and bureaucrats. But the cocktail's popularity did not wane.

By 1979 *The Perfect Martini Book* by Robert Herzbrum (Harcourt, Brace, Jovanovich, 1979) listed the ingredients for 286 different variations. Today the M Bar in

Miami, Florida's Mandarin Oriental Hotel features a menu of 250 Martinis in six broad categories: sweet, fruity, tangy, after-dinner, naughty-but-nice, and oddball. In short the Martini has become the mutant of the bartending world: It is continually redefined, reconstructed, and repositioned.

Fruit Martinis got a popularity boost in the late 1990s when the stars of the television show *Sex and the City*, a well-heeled group of 20-something girlfriends, were frequently shown sipping Apple Martinis in (where else?) the Big Apple. The basic drink recipe includes muddled or pureed apples, Calvados, vodka, and apple cider. Another version of the recipe is more specific: Granny Smith apples, DeKuyper Sour Apple Pucker liqueur, Ketel One vodka, and ice, garnished with a slice of green apple. You can muddle the apples with a bit of bourbon or rye, add apple schnapps, infuse the vodka with apples, use sparkling cider instead of still, and so on.

As Martini variations increase it is perhaps ironic that the sizes of the individual drinks are decreasing. The traditional $3\frac{1}{2}$-to-4-ounce drink served in a 5-ounce cocktail glass has returned to favor. The 1990s saw supersized Martinis served in 10-ounce glassware and, while these are still available in some bars, the smaller size better fits our mode of responsible alcohol consumption. Besides as Dale DeGroff so aptly puts it, "Cocktails were designed to stimulate the appetite, not knock someone out." New York City's Four Seasons restaurant features so-called "Weenie Martinis" in miniature sizes that can be ordered in combinations and paired with foods.

A Few Words about Manhattans

As the popularity of bourbon has surged there has been an equivalent renewal of interest in the Mahattan, the classic whiskey cocktail. The drink is smooth, aromatic, and satisfying. Unlike the classic Martini, which many agree is an acquired taste, the Manhattan possesses an almost universal appeal, the sophistication of the Martini without the snobbery.

Like any other traditional drink, the Manhattan has many variations, including the following:

- ***Dry Manhattan:*** Substitute dry vermouth for sweet vermouth, and a lemon twist for the maraschino cherry
- ***Perfect Manhattan:*** Use half dry vermouth and half sweet vermouth, and garnish with a lemon twist
- ***Sweet Manhattan:*** Add a dash of maraschino-cherry juice to the classic recipe.
- ***Rob Roy:*** Use Scotch whiskey, sweet vermouth, and a dash of bitters
- ***Latin Manhattan*** or ***Little Princess:*** Use rum instead of whiskey
- ***Quebec Manhattan:*** Use Canadian whiskey instead of bourbon
- ***Raspberry Manhattan:*** Add a splash of Chambord.
- ***Italian Manhattan:*** Add a splash of amaretto.
- ***Spanish Manhattan:*** Add a splash of sherry.
- ***Paddy:*** Made with Irish whiskey

FUN WITH FLAVORS: THE NEW MARTINIS

The trade press continually highlights the best, brightest, and/or oddest "new" Martini recipes. The following are just a few:

- ***Salmon Martini:*** At the Ca d'Zan Bar in the Ritz-Carlton Hotel in Sarasota, Florida, the inside of a Martini glass is lined with a thinly sliced filet of smoked salmon. Fries Vodka is used, and a teaspoon of farm-raised sturgeon caviar is floated as the garnish. This specialty drink costs $12.
- ***Tablatini:*** At Tabla, an East Indian fusion restaurant in New York City, the Martini is a chilled fruit soup with vodka, made with pineapple juice, Absolut Citron vodka, lime juice, and a lemongrass-stalk garnish. The kitchen preps the secondary ingredients.
- ***The Vesper:*** Pravda, a New York City restaurant, uses both gin and vodka in its best-selling Martini. Proportions are 3 parts gin, 1 part vodka, ¼ part Lillet; the garnish is a lemon twist.
- ***Godiva Diva Martini:*** At the Cool River Café in Irving, Texas, this dessert-like recipe mixes Smirnoff Vanilla Twist Vodka with Godiva Chocolate Liqueur and Amaretto.

A splash of liqueur will add a blast of flavor and an attractive color to the Martini. Liqueur recommendations include Frangelica, Godiva, Curacao, Chambord, Grand Marnier, Amaretto, B&B, and black Sambuca. The use of infused liquors can produce delicious results, from lemon-flavored gin, to chili-pepper-flavored tequila. There are also cherry-infused rums and pineapple-infused vodkas. Remember, the better the liquor, the better the Martini. Today's customer appreciates the top-quality, superpremium brands and will pay more for them.

You might also try presenting your guests with chilled cocktail glasses and a tray of all of the condiments and ingredients to build their own "perfect" Martini. Premeasure the liquor, of course, in a small carafe nestled into a bowl of ice; put vermouth and other modifiers in other carafes.

The names change with the ingredients. For example, when you use rum, the drink is traditionally called a *Little Princess,* but if you use equal parts rum and sweet vermouth, you will make a Poker. If you make a Manhattan with Southern Comfort as the whiskey, use dry vermouth to cut the sweetness of the liquor.

All versions of both the Martini and the Manhattan are made in the same way: stirred in a mixing glass, then strained into a chilled cocktail glass. Straight-up cocktails made with other fortified wines, such as sherry or Dubonnet, are made the same way.

As noted earlier all of these drinks may also be served on the rocks. In this case you have a choice of mixing methods. You can make a drink as you do the straight-up cocktail by simply straining the contents of the mixing glass into a rocks glass three-quarters full of cube ice. Or you can build the drink in the rocks glass as you do the two-liquor drinks on ice. The latter method (which was described in Chapter 10) is the easiest, the fastest, and by far the most common. If you build in the glass, it is wise to pour the vermouth first. Then, if the mingling of the ingredients is less than perfect, the customer will taste the liquor first.

If volume warrants Martinis and Manhattans can be premixed in quantity. Just follow these steps:

1. Fill a large, slender-necked funnel with cube ice and put it into the neck of a quart container.
2. Pour 4 ounces of the appropriate vermouth and a 750-millileter bottle of the appropriate liquor over the cube ice in the quart container.
3. Stir with a long-handled barspoon.
4. Keep chilled in the refrigerator until used.
5. To serve measure out $3\frac{1}{2}$ ounces per drink into a chilled cocktail glass.

Close-Up: THE COSMOPOLITAN

The other *Sex and the City* cocktail of choice is the Cosmopolitan, the rosy, refreshing Kool-Aid of young urbanites. Keep in mind that the Cosmopolitan is not, nor has it ever been, a variation of the Martini. The Cosmopolitan is a member of the sour family and a relative of the Gimlet, a British derivative that had its roots in colonial India. Like classic Martinis, the classic Gimlet used to be prepared with gin, but now vodka is also used. Rose's Lime Juice is the modifier.

A brief look at the family tree: The Gimlet was first adapted into the Kamikaze, which is a Gimlet with a shot of Cointreau, in the 1970s. Then the Kamikaze morphed into the Cosmopolitan by keeping the Rose's Lime Juice and Cointreau, switching to citrus-infused vodka and adding cranberry juice.

The proliferation of lemon, orange, and other fruit-infused vodkas makes experimentation fun and profitable. For example the Metropolitan is made with Absolut Kurant instead of Absolut Citron. The Purple Cosmo is made with Stolichnaya Limonaya, Blue Curacao, and Chambord.

THE COSMOPOLITAN

STIR OR SHAKE

Stemmed cocktail glass (6–8 ounces) or rocks glass, well chilled

$1\frac{1}{2}$ ounces Absolut Citron

$\frac{1}{2}$ ounce Cointreau

$\frac{1}{2}$ ounce fresh lime juice or Rose's Lime Juice

$1\frac{1}{2}$ ounces cranberry juice

Lime twist or orange twist

SOURS AND SWEET-AND-SOUR COCKTAILS

The idea of combining sweet-and-sour flavors with liquors has been around a long time. It is no accident that several of the drinks in the sweet-and-sour cocktail family originated in tropical climates, where lemons and limes grow in profusion.

Family Characteristics

- **Ingredients.** Liquor, lemon or lime juice, and a sweetener ("sweet, sour, and strong")
- **Glass.** Sour or cocktail, chilled
- **Mixing method.** Shake (or blend, or shake-mix)

The subgroup of drinks known as **sours** use lemon rather than lime, have a standard garnish of cherry and orange, and are traditionally served in a sour glass of about $4\frac{1}{2}$ ounces, whatever size and shape accommodates the garnish attractively. Sometimes a sour is made with egg white or a mix containing frothee, giving the drink an appetizing fizz topping. The other cocktails in this family, such as the **Daiquiri** or the Gimlet, are served in a standard cocktail glass of 4 to $4\frac{1}{2}$ ounces. Some use lime instead of lemon; some use a sweet liqueur or syrup in place of sugar. Most have no standard garnish. Any of these drinks may also be served over ice in a rocks glass if so specified. Some of them are also made in a frozen version or a fruit version.

Mixing Sours

The contents of these drinks, citrus juices and sugar, demand that they be shaken, blended, or mechanically mixed, whether you make them from scratch or use a sweet-and-sour mix. Neither the sugar nor the fruit juices can be smoothly combined with the liquor by stirring, and shaking adds air that lightens the drink and makes it a bit frothy.

The Shake Method. The cocktail shaker was a symbol of the joyous return to legal drinking after Prohibition. The shaking of a drink was a ceremony of skill that whetted the customer's appetite and simultaneously commanded admiration. When mechanical mixers were invented people quickly discovered that they made a smooth drink a great deal faster than with the hand shaker. Today most bars use shake mixers and blenders, and those that use hand shakers do so for reasons of tradition or showmanship. Ironically some bartenders do not even know how to shake a drink by hand. Figure 11.2 shows the making of a sour using a hand shaker. You will notice that the first three steps are essentially the same as those of the stir method. Since step 4 is the heart of the matter let's look at this technique more closely.

The cup of the shaker fits tightly over the glass because a certain amount of flex in the metal makes for a good fit. The cap should be put on at an angle with one

THE SHAKE METHOD: HOW TO MAKE A SOUR IN A HAND SHAKER

Ingredients

Liquor
Lemon juice } or sweet-sour mix
Sugar or simple syrup } or sweet-sour mix
Egg white (optional) } or sweet-sour mix
Cherry/orange garnish

Glass

Sour glass (4½ ounces), chilled

Mixing Method

Shake

Equipment and Accessories

Shaker: mixing glass with stainless-steel cup
Strainer
Jiggers
Barspoon
Ice scoop
Tongs or pick
Cocktail napkin

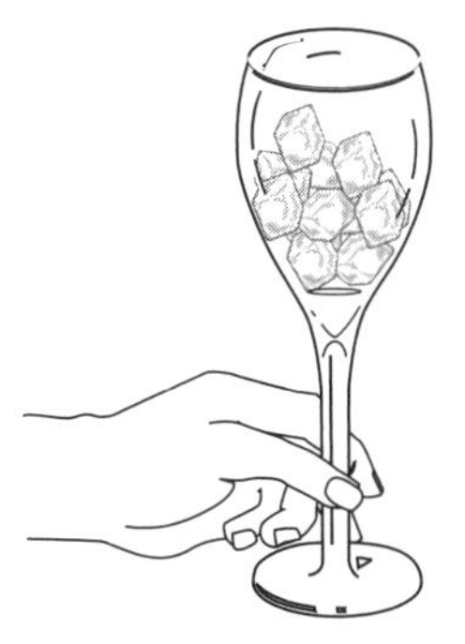

step 1: Place a chilled sour glass on the rail, handling it by the stem.

step 2: Fill the mixing glass 1/3 to 1/2 full of cube ice.

step 3: Measure liquor, lemon juice, and sugar (or mix) and add to the mixing glass.

step 4: Place the cup over the glass and shake 10 times.

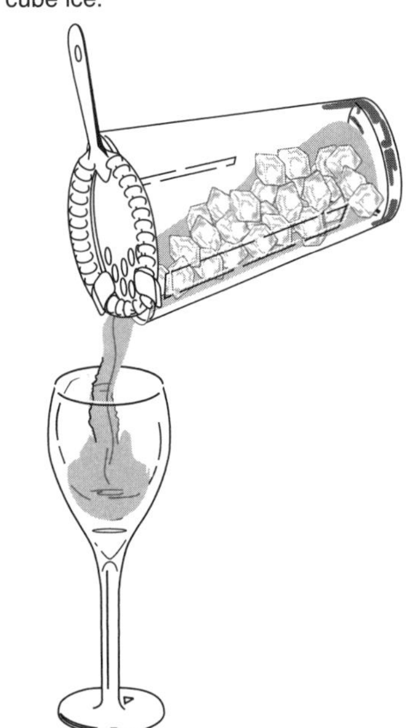

step 5: Remove the cup and strain the drink into the chilled glass.

step 6: Add the garnish, using tongs or a pick. Serve on a cocktail napkin.

step 7: Wash the mixing glass and cup and invert them on the drainboard.

FIGURE 11.2

of its sides running along the side of the glass. This makes it easier to separate the cup and glass again. (Sometimes shaking creates a vacuum, and the cup adheres to the glass.) Shake vigorously, using long strokes that send the contents from one end to the other. Some people shake up and down; others shake back and forth over the shoulder.

If you have trouble separating the glass from the cup do not yield to the temptation of banging the cup on the rail. You can easily break the glass this way. You might also dent the cup. Instead hit the cup with the heel of your hand halfway between the point where the cup touches the glass and the point where it is farthest away from the glass.

Washing, step 7, is necessary because sugar and fruit juices might cling to the sides of the containers after shaking.

The Shake-Mix Method. If you use a shake mixer to "shake" your cocktail, substitute the mixer can for the mixing glass and proceed as shown in Figure 11.3. As you can see the procedures are very similar, but there are some noteworthy differences. Notice that in step 2, you use only one-fourth can of ice. This is because the mixer can is bigger than the mixing glass. You need only enough ice to chill the drink. In step 4 you substitute the mixer can for the hand shaker. To estimate 10 seconds count "one-hundred-one, one-hundred-two," and so on up to "one-hundred-ten."

The Blend Method. To make the same drink using a blender substitute the blender cup for the shaker glass or mixer can. The mixing method is like that for the shake mixer, as you can see in Figure 11.4. Set the blender speed on high, but do not blend longer than the specified time. You do not want to incorporate bits of ice into the drink; you only want the ice to chill it. Blending too long will turn the drink into frozen slush.

A Whiskey Sour is usually made with bourbon or a blended whiskey. A Sour can be made with any other liquor, such as gin, brandy, Scotch, rum, tequila, and vodka. For speed production you can substitute a jigger of sweet-and-sour mix for the lemon juice and sugar—but at a considerable sacrifice in quality. In the other direction a special touch would be to add a teaspoon of egg white before blending the ingredients.

The Daiquiri dates back to the Spanish-American War and was named for the Daiquiri iron mines in Cuba. According to the story one of the mine's chief engineers, an American, developed the cooling, thirst-quenching drink using rum from the nearby Bacardi rum plant in lieu of drinking the malaria-tainted local water. The Daiquiri is the prototype for a number of other drinks made with different spirits. Most similar is the Bacardi; this is essentially a Daiquiri made with Bacardi rum, with a dash of grenadine replacing half the sugar. When you change the liquor or substitute a liqueur or a syrup for the sugar, you will find the following family members—some familiar, some passé but still occasionally called for:

THE SHAKE-MIX METHOD: HOW TO MAKE A SOUR IN A SHAKE MIXER

Ingredients

Liquor
Lemon juice } or
Sugar or simple syrup } sweet-sour
Egg white (optional) } mix
Cherry/orange garnish

Glass

Sour glass ($4^{1/2}$ ounces), chilled

Mixing Method

Shake-Mix

Equipment and Accessories

Shake mixer
Strainer
Jiggers
Barspoon
Ice scoop
Tongs or pick
Cocktail napkin

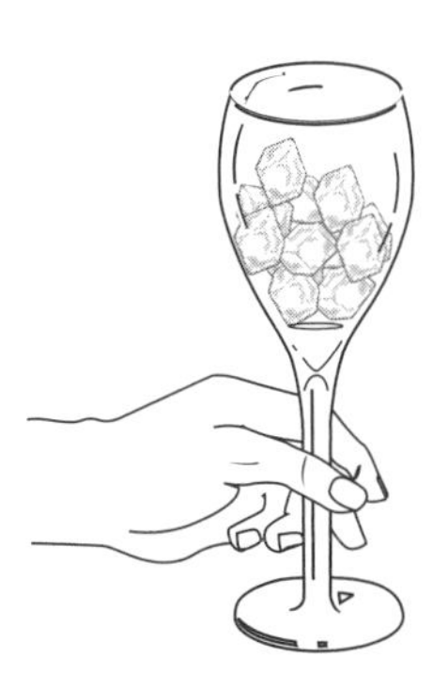

step 1: Place a chilled sour glass on the rail, handling it by the stem.

step 2: Fill the mixer can 1/4 full of cube ice.

step 3: Measure liquor, lemon juice, and sugar (or mix) and add to the mixer can.

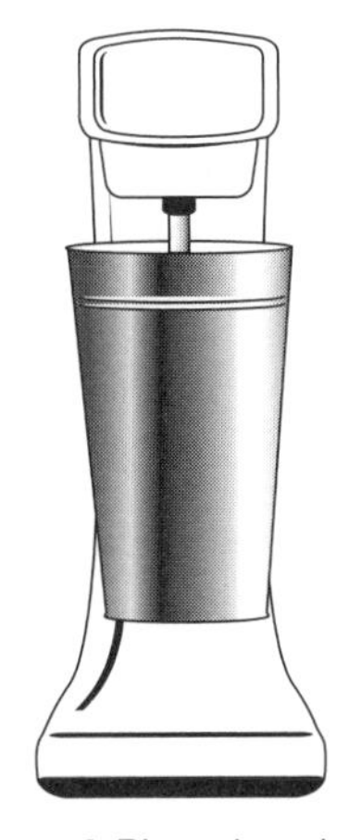

step 4: Place the mixer can on the mixer and mix for 10 seconds.

step 5: Remove the can and strain the drink into the chilled glass.

step 6: Add the garnish, using tongs or a pick. Serve on a cocktail napkin.

step 7: Wash the mixer can and invert it on the drainboard.

FIGURE 11.3

THE BLEND METHOD: HOW TO MAKE A SOUR IN A BLENDER

Ingredients

Liquor
Lemon juice } or
Sugar or simple syrup } sweet-sour
Egg white (optional) } mix
Cherry/orange garnish

Glass

Sour glass ($4\frac{1}{2}$ ounces), chilled

Mixing Method

Blend

Equipment and Accessories

Blender
Strainer
Jiggers
Barspoon
Ice scoop
Tongs or pick
Cocktail napkin

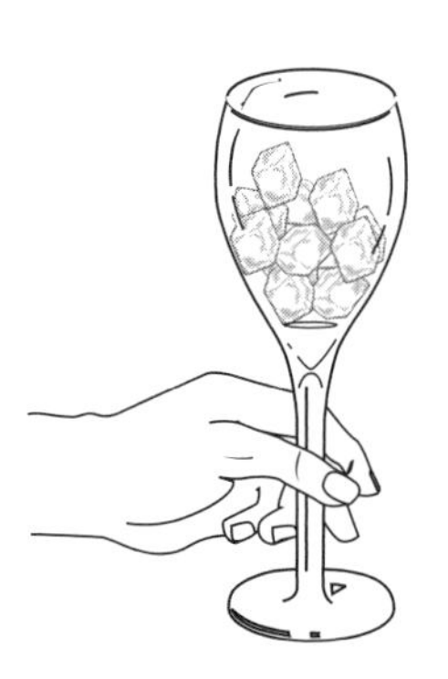

step 1: Place a chilled sour glass on the rail, handling it by the stem.

step 2: Fill the blender $\frac{1}{4}$ full of cube ice.

step 3: Measure liquor, lemon juice, and sugar (or mix) and add to the blender cup.

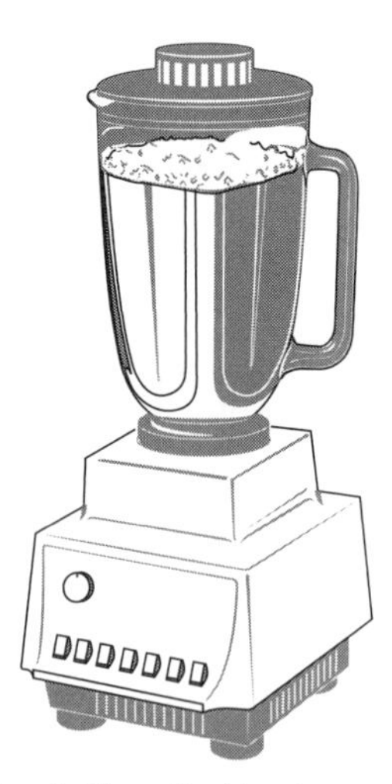

step 4: Place the blender cup on the electric blender and blend for 10 seconds.

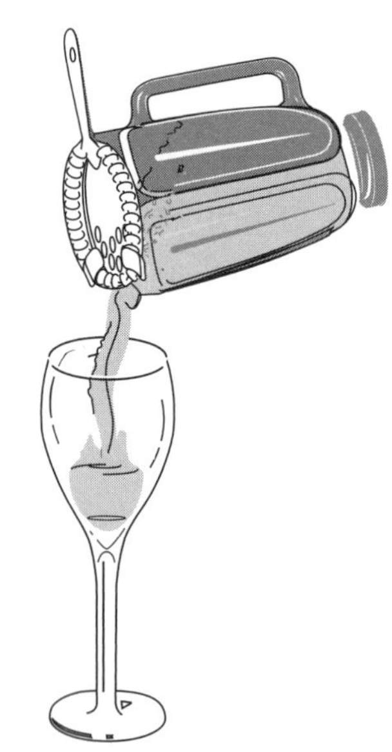

step 5: Remove the cup and strain the drink into the chilled glass.

step 6: Add the garnish, using tongs or a pick. Serve on a cocktail napkin.

step 7: Wash the blender cup and invert it on the drainboard.

FIGURE 11.4

- ***Ward 8:*** A Bourbon Sour with grenadine added
- ***Side Car:*** Brandy or cognac, lemon juice, and Cointreau, with a sugared rim. (This drink was invented by a World War I captain who rode to his favorite Paris bistro on a motorcycle with a sidecar.)
- ***Between the Sheets:*** Half brandy and half rum, lemon or lime juice, and Triple Sec. This is a variation of the Side Car.
- ***Jack Rose:*** Apple brandy, lemon or lime juice, and grenadine
- ***Clover Club:*** Gin, lemon or lime juice, grenadine, and egg white
- ***Tequila Rose:*** Tequila, lime juice, and grenadine
- ***Pink Lady*** *(yesterday's version):* Gin, apple brandy, lemon or lime juice, grenadine, and egg white. (The modern Pink Lady adds cream and often omits the juice and the brandy.)
- ***Gimlet:*** Gin, and Rose's Lime Juice (sweet) or fresh lime juice and sugar. (If you use Rose's Lime Juice, as nearly everyone does, you can stir it instead of blending or shaking.)
- ***Scarlett O'Hara:*** Southern Comfort, cranberry juice, and lime juice. In this dry version, the liqueur provides the sweetness. (A sweeter version is made with Southern Comfort, grenadine, and lime juice—a completely different drink, undoubtedly invented by a bartender who had no cranberry juice on hand.)

You can make other very popular versions of the Daiquiri by adding fresh fruit. For example you can blend in half a crushed banana for a Banana Daiquiri, garnishing it with a banana slice. Blend in crushed fresh or frozen strawberries for a Strawberry Daiquiri, using a whole fresh strawberry as a garnish. Fruit Daiquiris are often made as frozen drinks. You can serve any Sour on the rocks in a rocks glass. Shake, blend, or shake-mix the Sour the same way that you make a straight-up sour, then pour it over ice in a rocks glass.

WHISKEY SOUR

SHAKE, SHAKE-MIX, OR BLEND

$4\frac{1}{2}$-oz sour glass, chilled

1 jigger whiskey

Juice from $\frac{1}{2}$ lemon

1 tsp sugar or $\frac{1}{2}$ oz simple syrup

Lemon or orange slice, cherry

Close-Up: THE MARGARITA

One of the most popular drinks of the sour family is the **Margarita.** In fact it continues to be the most-requested cocktail in America. An exceptionally versatile offering, it can be classified as a shake- or blend-method drink and there are endless variations on its three simple ingredients: tequila, a flavorful liqueur, and citrus juice. Fruits—whatever is fresh and local: peaches, berries, melon, mango, pineapple, and even prickly pear cactus—are commonly used to add flavor and color. The liqueurs range from Triple Sec to Cointreau, and Grand Marnier to Chambord.

You can use either fresh lime or Rose's Lime Juice, depending on desired sweetness, or a nicely balanced base mix of both lemon and lime juices. Some bartenders add a tablespoon of simple syrup to the mix. You can also consider using more than one type of tequila in a single drink, such as half lively silver, and half mellow anejo.

Servers should also ask an all-important question when taking drink orders: "Frozen or on the rocks?" Many people think of Margaritas as adult snow cones; others insist that ice dilutes the drink and want it served with just a bit of ice. Customers also have strong preferences for rimming the Margarita glass; the tradition is salt, with a nod to "Los Tres Amigos" (the three friends): tequila, lime, and salt. But many folks don't like to sip a sweetish drink through salt and prefer an unrimmed glass. The Margarita's refreshing nature makes it a popular summer drink, but you'll sell them year-round. Frozen Margaritas offer the additional option of making two flavors in two different colors and layering them in a single glass. The casual Lone Star Steak House chain charges $6 for a three-layered frozen Margarita called Stars & Stripes, which is made with Blue Curacao on the bottom, Jose Cuervo Gold in the middle, and strawberry puree on top.

The watermelon and lemongrass margarita recipes are a couple of imaginative variations on this catchall tequila-based cocktail.

DAIQUIRI

SHAKE, SHAKE-MIX, OR BLEND

4½-oz cocktail glass, chilled
1 jigger light rum
1 jigger lime juice
1 tsp sugar or ½ oz simple syrup

WATERMELON MARGARITA

BLEND

14-ounce stemmed glass
1½ ounces tequila
¾ ounce Triple Sec
¾ ounces Midori melon liqueur
2 ounces sour mix
6 ounces cubed, seeded watermelon
8 ounces cube ice
Lime slice and watermelon wedge

LEMONGRASS MARGARITA

BLEND

14-ounce stemmed glass
Combine the following in a saucepan and heat until a syrup forms:
1 part sugar
2 parts water
Lemongrass stalks
Kaffir lime leaves
Grated fresh ginger
Lemon zest

Blend 3 ounces of syrup with:

2 ounces Sauza Commemorativo Tequila
1 ounce Triple Sec
Cube ice
Lemongrass-stalk garnish

Today's Margarita is certainly not confined to Mexican restaurants. It is a pleasing complement to seafood and chicken, and a refreshing alternative to wine.

Sour-Related Drinks

You can start with the ingredients of the Sour and make several other drink types by adding another basic ingredient. This results in another set of drink families that includes the Collins, Fizz, Sling, and Daisy. Like the cocktail, these drinks originated in the Victorian era and have changed to keep pace with the times. The **Collins** is simply a Sour with soda added, served over ice in a tall glass. We noted in Chapter 10 that today's Collins is usually a blend of liquor and mix, built in the glass. But if you break down the drink to its components, you can see that there are other ways to make it: from scratch with fresh ingredients or with a sweet-and-sour mix and soda. You will also see by looking at its structure that you can make other new drinks by changing or adding an ingredient or two.

Figure 11.5 shows a Collins being made from scratch using a hand shaker and freshly squeezed lemon juice. The essential point to grasp is that the drink is made by combining two methods: first shake, to mix together liquor, sugar, and fruit juice; then build, to incorporate the soda without losing its bubbles. You can also make a Collins from scratch using a shake mixer or a blender (see Figures 11.3 and 11.4) and adjusting the ice measurement in step 2. You can make this substitution in any drink that you can shake by hand. So when a recipe says "shake," you have your choice of three methods. If you substitute sweet-and-sour mix for the lemon and sugar in Figure 11.5, you will still make the drink the same way, although you will no longer be making a Collins from scratch.

A number of drinks take off from the Collins-with-soda by substituting or adding other ingredients:

- ***French 75:*** A Tom Collins (gin) with Champagne in place of soda
- ***French 95:*** A John Collins (bourbon) with Champagne in place of soda
- ***French 125:*** A Brandy Collins with Champagne in place of soda
- ***Skip and Go Naked*** or ***Strip and Go Naked:*** A Vodka Collins or Tom Collins with beer instead of (or in addition to) soda

A **Fizz** is much like a Collins except that it is a shorter drink, served in a highball glass or a stemmed glass of highball size. At one point in cocktail history the purpose of a Fizz was to be gulped down like an Alka-Seltzer, and for the same reasons. To make it as bubbly as possible, it was shaken long and hard with ice, the soda was added under pressure from a seltzer bottle, and the drink was served foaming in a small glass without ice.

HOW TO MAKE A COLLINS FROM SCRATCH

Ingredients
Liquor
Lemon
Sugar
Cube ice
Cherry, optional orange slice

Glass
Collins (10 to 12 ounces)

Mixing Method
Shake/Build

Equipment and Accessories
Shaker (for blender or shaker mixer)
Strainer
Jigger
Barspoon
Ice scoop
Fruit squeezer
Long straws
Pick
Cocktail napkin

step 1: Fill Collins glass 3/4 full of cube ice and place on rail.

step 2: Fill mixing glass 1/3 to 1/2 full of cube ice. Measure and add liquor, sugar, and lemon.

step 3: Shake the contents 10 times.

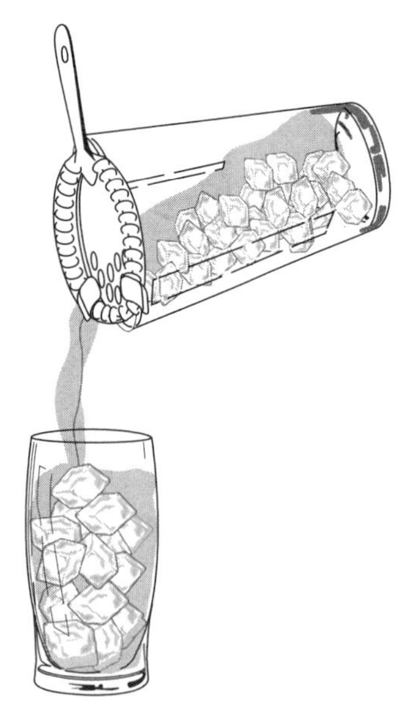

step 4: Strain shaker contents into Collins glass.

step 5: Add soda to within 1/2 to 1 inch of rim. Stir gently (2 or 3 strokes).

step 6: Garnish, add long straws, and serve on a cocktail napkin.

FIGURE 11.5

Today, because of our modern use of ice, a simple Fizz is more like a short Collins or a cross between a Sour and a highball. However, some of the elaborations on the basic Fizz make it a good deal more than a simple drink. The following is today's basic Fizz:

Family Characteristics

- **Ingredients.** Liquor, lemon, sugar, soda, and cube ice
- **Glass.** Highball or 8-ounce stem glass
- **Mixing method.** Shake-build

To make a Fizz follow the Collins-from-scratch method. The liquor can be any type. Gin is the most common, but rum, Scotch, brandy, or sloe gin are called for now and then. The Gin Fizz is the one most frequently elaborated on; others include:

- ***Silver Fizz:*** A Gin Fizz made with an egg white. If you add grenadine it will become a Bird of Paradise Fizz.
- ***Golden Fizz:*** A Gin Fizz made with an egg yolk
- ***Royal Fizz:*** A Gin Fizz made with a whole egg and sometimes cream
- ***New Orleans Fizz*** or ***Ramos Fizz:*** A Gin Fizz made with both lemon and lime, added egg white, cream, and a few dashes of orange-flower water, and served in a tall glass.

These more elaborate Gin Fizzes have undergone further transformation by being made with ice cream, which introduces new methods (see page TK). Other Fizzes include the Morning Glory Fizz, made with Scotch and a little Pernod, and the Sloe Gin Fizz. If you add cream to the Sloe Gin Fizz, it becomes a Slow Ride Fizz.

A Sling is like a Collins to which another ingredient, such as a liqueur or a special flavor or garnish, is added. A Sling is usually made by the Collins-from-scratch method and is served in a Collins glass with fruit garnishes. The most famous Sling, and probably the one made most often today, is the Singapore Sling. Notice that this drink is just like a Tom Collins except that it uses cherry liqueur, which is sweet, in place of sugar and has a different garnish. The Sling as a "species" has terrific potential as a springboard for creating your own specialty drinks.

A *Daisy* is nothing more than a Sour made with grenadine as the sweet, served in a larger glass over crushed ice and garnished lavishly with fruit. Sometimes a Daisy is served in a silver mug and stirred until the mug frosts, like a Julep.

SINGAPORE SLING

SHAKE/BUILD

12-oz glass

3/4 glass cube ice

1 jigger gin

1/2 jigger cherry-flavored brandy

1/2 jigger lemon juice

Soda to fill

Lemon or lime slice

SHOOTERS AND SHOTS

This group of drinks is only loosely considered a "family" because it is defined less by its pattern of ingredients and more by the size of the drink, its purpose, and the manner in which it is consumed. These are small, straight-up drinks, served in a shot glass, and their purpose is simple: pleasure and conviviality. Shooters and shots are generally gulped rather quickly in the company of friends. Creative bartenders are always coming up with new concoctions for this drink category, as they provide a good way to give a customer a taste of liquor without ordering a "whole" drink. Most shooters contain no more than 3/4 ounce of liquor; the exceptions are drinks made specifically to be shared. More about those in a moment. First, the basic shooter characteristics:

Family Characteristics

- **Ingredients.** Any of the following: liquors, liqueurs, fruit juice, soda, cola, sour mix, coffee, cream, and almost anything else—even black pepper with straight vodka, or Tabasco with cinnamon schnapps
- **Glass.** Shot or small rocks
- **Method.** Most are shaken briefly by hand with ice; a few are layered in the style of a Pousse-Café. The shaker is used for two reasons: to mix and to chill. A few vigorous shakes are enough; you don't want to dilute the drink. For a layered shooter the order of pouring is critical for visual effect (review the information about Pousse-Cafés), but the layered shooter is consumed in a gulp or two like any other shooter, not sipped.

Shooter recipes vary from year to year, from bar to bar, and from one part of the country to another. Here, for example, are three versions of the very popular Sex on the Beach:

- ***Original:*** Chambord or raspberry liqueur, Midori melon liqueur, and pineapple juice
- ***New York Style:*** Peach schnapps, vodka, and orange and cranberry juices
- ***Bennigan's:*** Vodka, Midori melon liqueur, Chambord, and pineapple juice

Other popular shooters include:

- ***Alabama Slammer:*** Southern Comfort, amaretto, orange juice, and grenadine. Another version adds sloe gin and vodka.
- ***No Name:*** Grenadine, Kahlua, and Bailey's
- ***Orgasm:*** Kahlua, Bailey's, Amaretto, and cream. If you add vodka, the Orgasm will become a Screaming Orgasm.
- ***Russian Quaalude:*** Stolichnaya vodka, Frangelico, and Bailey's
- ***Watermelon:*** Southern Comfort, Crème de Noya, vodka, pineapple and/or orange juice, and grenadine
- ***Woo Woo:*** Peach schnapps, vodka, and cranberry juice

Today's cocktails are for the most part drier and lighter and include more different kinds of flavors than their turn-of-the-last-century predecessors. Remember that additional splash, dash, or float of a juice or liqueur can be the "master stroke" that propels a drink to fame.

Although **shooters** are relatively new to the U.S. scene you can find their antecedents and counterparts in the use of straight spirits downed quickly for toasts, such as vodka in Russia, Dutch gin in Holland, and Aquavit in Scandinavian countries. These are straight **shots** of liquor, not mixed drinks. Another related drink is a straight shot of a spirit, such as whiskey, ordered with a **chaser**—something to drink immediately after the alcohol, such as beer or water. This jigger-size drink is served in a shot glass. If no chaser is ordered a glass of ice water is usually served anyway.

A confusing aspect of shooter recipes is that drinks with the same names and ingredients are often ordered on the rocks or as highballs, to be sipped and savored. In this style of drink the total liquor content may be at least twice the ¾-ounce limit suggested for shooters, but it will be diluted by longer mixing and melting ice, and consumed over a longer period of time. The person taking the order, for a Kamikaze, for example, should be careful to ask whether the customer wants a shooter, a rocks drink, or a highball. If a shooter is requested the server should monitor the patron's consumption and behavior carefully, keeping in mind that it is illegal everywhere to serve anyone "clearly" or "visibly" intoxicated.

KAMIKAZE

SHAKE

Shot glass

1/2 oz vodka

1/4 oz Rose's Lime Juice

Splash Triple Sec

Shake briefly in hand shaker with ice; strain

Many shooter recipes given today in books and magazines call for 2 ounces of liquor, and undoubtedly some bars pour shooters this size. But the prudent bar operation standardizes its shooter recipes on the safe side and trains its personnel to carefully monitor consumption.

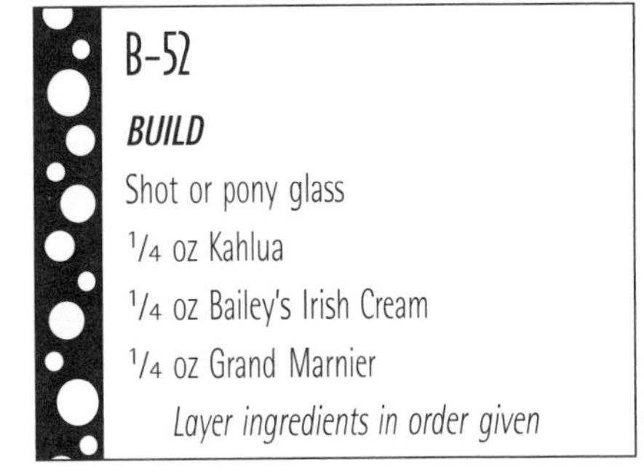
B-52

BUILD

Shot or pony glass

1/4 oz Kahlua

1/4 oz Bailey's Irish Cream

1/4 oz Grand Marnier

Layer ingredients in order given

In spite of the shooter vogue, you may see these drinks dwindling in popularity. They are characteristic of the old neighborhood bar where the primary focus is on drinking. This species of bar has, for the most part, been edged out by newcomers. The U.S. obsession with health, the neoProhibitionist movement, the crusade against drunk driving, and proprietors' fear of liability have combined to prompt a change of emphasis, which now links drinking with dining. Drinking for its own sake simply is no longer fashionable.

TROPICAL DRINKS

The collective term **tropical drinks** as used in the bar trade comprises a loose collection of drinks originating in resorts in the tropics and in restaurants with a tropical ambience. The family characteristics are diffuse: There are no indispensable ingredients that tie them all together. Generally they have various kinds of rum as their base and make lavish use of fruit juices, liqueurs, syrups, and flower and fruit garnishes. These drinks are showy, often expensive to make, and thus command a high price tag. Cheaper and easier versions of some can be made using bottled mixes.

Family Characteristics

- **Ingredients.** Rum (occasionally brandy and once in a while gin), fruit juices, liqueurs, syrups, coconut milk, fruit garnishes, flowers, and fresh mint
- **Glass.** Anything from a cocktail glass to a whole coconut or pineapple
- **Mixing method.** Shake (or blend, or shake-mix)

Among the fruit juices are pineapple and papaya, and such other exotics as kiwi and mango, in addition to the usual lemon, lime, and orange juices. Among the syrups, grenadine, orgeat, falernum, and passionfruit are popular. The liqueurs frequently called for are fruit-flavored brandies, cherry liqueur, Curacao, and Pernod or some other absinthe substitute. Coconut milk is another ingredient. Among the garnishes are pineapple cubes, coconut, mint leaves, the usual oranges, limes, and cherries, and orchids if available.

Both types of tropical drinks can also be made from prepared mixes, and usually are. The Mai Tai, like many other tropical drinks, was created by Trader Vic in the 1940s, and is still going strong. In Hawaii, where orchids grow on trees, your bountiful glass of Mai Tai will be topped with at least one flower. Pineapple used in the Pina Colada can be either fresh or canned. If you use the crushed fruit, be sure to blend at high speed until smooth. A variation of the Pina Colada is the Chi Chi, which is made with vodka instead of rum. Other classic tropical drinks are Planter's Punch, the Scorpion, and the Zombie. One story says that buckets of Planter's Punch were carried to workers in the sugarcane fields. Another story says the drink was a specialty of the famous Planter's Hotel in St. Louis. Both stories could be true. These three drinks are typically finished off with a float of 151-proof rum so that the customer's first sip is the "sting" of the scorpion, the "punch" of the planter, or the "kick" of the zombie. The Zombie made its fame with the kick, the name, the challenge of "only one to a customer," and in some cases the recipe: Some include four or five kinds of rum.

The Brazilian rum called *cachaca,* mentioned in Chapter 5, is the base for the Caipirinha, a very simple, tasty South American drink that has grown in popularity along with its Nuevo Latino cousins, such as the Mojito.

MAI TAI (FROM SCRATCH)

SHAKE, BLEND, OR SHAKE-MIX

12-oz glass

3/4 glass cubed or crushed ice

1 jigger light rum

1 jigger dark rum

1 lime (juice and peel)

1/2 oz orange Curacao

1/2 oz orgeat

Pineapple stick, cherry, mint sprig

PINA COLADA (FROM SCRATCH)

BLEND

12-oz glass

3/4 glass cubed or crushed ice

1 jigger light rum

1 jigger Cream of Coconut or coconut milk

1-2 jiggers pineapple juice or crushed pineapple

Cherry, pineapple, lim

CAIPIRINHA

SHAKE

6- to 8-oz Old-Fashioned glass

1/2 lime cut in four wedges

Muddle lime in bottom of glass

2 oz cachaca

3/4 oz simple syrup

CREAM DRINKS

Cream drinks are smooth, sweet, after-dinner drinks made with cream and usually served straight up in a cocktail or Champagne glass.

Family Characteristics

- **Ingredients.** Cream, and one or more liqueurs or a liquor-liqueur combination
- **Glass.** Cocktail or Champagne, chilled
- **Mixing method.** Shake (or blend or shake-mix)

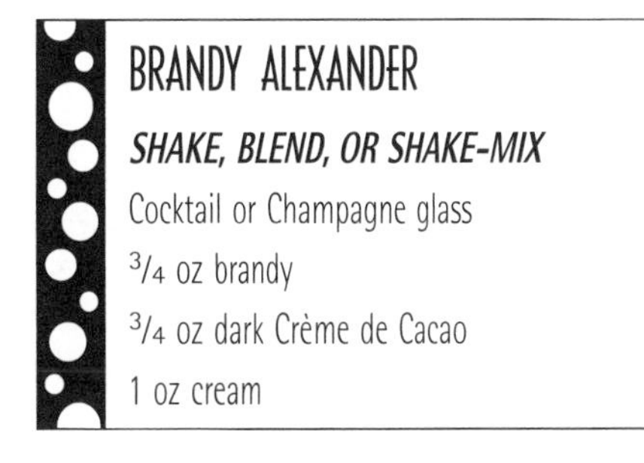

BRANDY ALEXANDER

SHAKE, BLEND, OR SHAKE-MIX

Cocktail or Champagne glass

3/4 oz brandy

3/4 oz dark Crème de Cacao

1 oz cream

The proportions of the ingredients vary from one house to another. Some use equal parts (from 1/2 ounce to 1 ounce of each), others use up to 2 ounces of cream and smaller amounts of the other ingredients, and still others use more of the predominant flavor or the major liquor if there is one. The total ingredients should add up to about 3 ounces; any more and you might have to use a larger glass. Light cream or half-and-half is typically used, but heavy cream makes a better drink. The cream must be very fresh. Whether you blend, shake, or shake-mix a cream drink, you follow the steps given for a sweet-and-sour cocktail. You may want to serve a cream drink with a pair of short straws. After mixing you must wash and rinse both your jigger and your glass or cup because the cream and liqueurs cling to the sides.

GRASSHOPPER

SHAKE, BLEND, OR SHAKE-MIX

Cocktail or Champagne glass

3/4 oz green Crème de Menthe

3/4 oz light Crème de Cacao

1 oz cream

Two familiar cream drinks are the Brandy Alexander and the Grasshopper. You can make an Alexander using any base liquor instead of the brandy. Apparently the earliest was the Gin Alexander, invented to disguise the awful bathtub gin of Prohibition days. Light Crème de Cacao is used when the base liquor is a light color, such as vodka, rum, and tequila. Dark Crème de Cacao is used with brandy and whiskies. An Alexander made with vodka sometimes is called a Russian Bear or a White Elephant. An Alexander made with rum becomes a Panama. The original cream concoctions spawned a whole menagerie of "animal" drinks:

- ***Pink Squirrel:*** Light Crème de Cacao, Crème de Noyaux, and cream
- ***Brown Squirrel:*** Dark Crème de Cacao, amaretto, and cream
- ***Blue-Tailed Fly:*** Light Crème de Cacao, blue Curacao, and cream
- ***White Monkey*** or ***Banshee:*** Light Crème de Cacao, Crème de Banana, and cream
- ***Purple Bunny:*** Light Crème de Cacao, cherry-flavored brandy, and cream

In addition to the critters, we have:

- ***Golden Cadillac:*** Light Crème de Cacao, Galliano, and cream
- ***White Cadillac:*** Light Crème de Cacao, Cointreau, and cream

- ***Velvet Hammer:*** Vodka or Cointreau, light Crème de Cacao, and cream
- ***Cucumber:*** Green Crème de Menthe and cream. Other versions add brandy or gin as the base ingredient.
- ***White Russian:*** A Black Russian with cream
- ***Golden Dream:*** Galliano, Triple Sec, orange juice, and cream
- ***Pink Lady:*** Gin, grenadine, and cream

Any of the cream drinks may be served on the rocks if the customer requests it. A cream drink on the rocks must be blended or shaken as for a straight-up drink, then strained over cube ice in a rocks glass. Sometimes a cream drink is built in the glass without stirring over cube ice in a rocks glass. Sometimes it is built in the glass without stirring, with the cream as a float. This makes a very different drink.

Other spinoffs of the after-dinner cream drinks are made when you add a mixer. They become highball-sized drinks. For example, the Colorado Bulldog starts off as a vodka-Kahlua-cream drink, shaken and poured over ice in a highball glass. Next, the glass is filled with cola. The drink is made using the shake-build method.

OTHER DAIRY DRINKS

RUM MILK PUNCH

SHAKE, BLEND, OR MIX

12-oz glass
3/4 glass cube ice
1 jigger rum
1 tsp sugar
4 oz milk
Sprinkle of nutmeg

In addition to cream other dairy products are sometimes used in mixed drinks. These are usually long drinks rather than cocktails, i.e., pick-me-ups or nightcaps rather than aperitifs or digestifs. They are simply too filling to precede or follow a meal, which may explain why they're not particularly popular. It is hard to say whether the current crop of milk drinks is a logical extension of the popular cream drinks or a modern version of old colonial libations. There seem to be some of each type.

Today's **milk punches** are clearly descendants of the older punch drinks, using milk instead of water and served either iced or hot, as the season—or the customer—dictates.

Family Characteristics

- **Ingredients.** Liquor, sugar, milk, cube ice, and nutmeg
- **Glass.** Collins
- **Mixing method.** Shake (or blend or shake-mix)

The liquors most commonly called for in milk punch are brandy, whiskey, rum, and gin. If you make your basic milk punch with brandy and add an egg you will make an Eggnog. You don't use ice in the Eggnog glass. The egg will add volume, and the drink does not demand the same ice-cold temperatures of most

most dairy drinks. Be sure to shake it with ice, however. You can add half a jigger of brandy to Rum Punch if you wish to pep it up. Some drinks of the highball family use milk or cream as a mixer, such as the Aggravation and the Smith & Kerns. Another milk drink is Scotch and Milk. It is served over ice in a highball glass like any Scotch highball. You can also substitute milk for cream in cream drinks if a calorie-conscious customer requests it.

An additional egg drink is the **Flip**, a cold, straight-up drink of sweetened liquor or fortified wine that is shaken with an egg and topped with nutmeg. This is the descendant of the Colonial Flip, which was drunk piping hot, either simmered over the fire or heated with a hot poker from the fireplace.

EGGNOG

SHAKE, BLEND, OR MIX

12-oz glass
1 egg
1 jigger brandy
1 tsp sugar
4 oz milk
Sprinkle of nutmeg

Ice-Cream Drinks

An ice-cream drink is, obviously, any drink made with ice cream. Many ice-cream drinks are variants of cream drinks, with ice cream simply replacing the cream. Others are made by adding ice cream to another drink, such as a Fizz. Figure 11.6 explains ice-cream drinks, including the family characteristics and the step-by-step mixing method. In addition to the equipment listed you will need a special freezer chest at the serving station for storing the ice cream, and your local health department will probably require you to have a special well with running water and an overflow drain into which to put your ice-cream scoops between uses. An alternative to all of this is to dispense your ice cream from a soft-serve machine. Two ice-cream drinks that may make the extra effort worthwhile are the Grasshopper Blend and the Ramos Fizz, a short one and a long one, respectively. In both drinks ice cream replaces the cream of the original recipe.

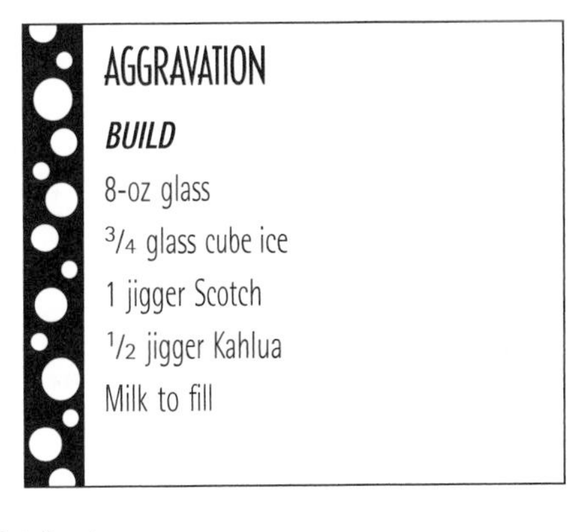
AGGRAVATION

BUILD

8-oz glass
3/4 glass cube ice
1 jigger Scotch
1/2 jigger Kahlua
Milk to fill

Few drinks can compare to the taste or appearance of a Brandy Alexander made with ice cream, and there are plenty of other drinks in which vanilla ice cream can replace cream, including the Velvet Hammer, White Russian, Pink Lady, and Golden Dream. Some Fizzes, such as the Royal Fizz and Silver Fizz, are sometimes made with ice cream.

The specialty-coffee craze opens up other hot sales possibilities for cold coffee drinks. Especially in warm weather people drink iced mochas, lattes, and cappuccinos. If you blend them with Tia Maria and Chambord and substitute two scoops of vanilla ice cream for the steamed milk, you will have a raspberry-flavored coffee cocktail.

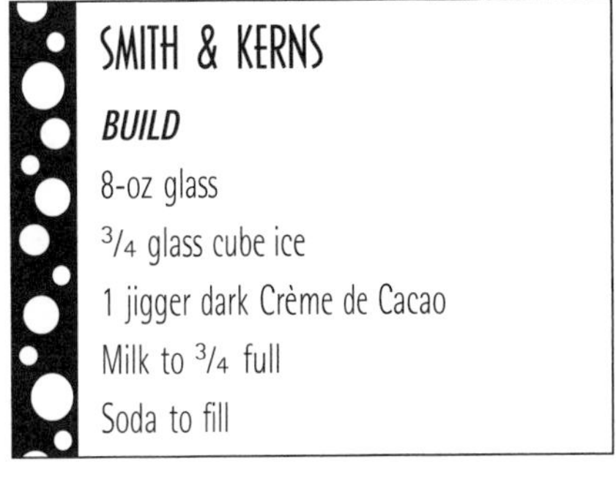
SMITH & KERNS

BUILD

8-oz glass
3/4 glass cube ice
1 jigger dark Crème de Cacao
Milk to 3/4 full
Soda to fill

HOW TO MAKE AN ICE CREAM DRINK

Ingredients
Liquor
Ice cream
Optional ingredients
Optional garnish

Glass
8- or 12-oz chilled

Mixing Method
Blend or Shake-Mix

Equipment and Accessories
Blender or shake mixer
Ice cream scoop, #20 or #24
Jigger
Barspoon
Straws
Cocktail napkin

step 1: Place prechilled glass on the rail.

step 2: Scoop ice cream into blender or mixer cup.

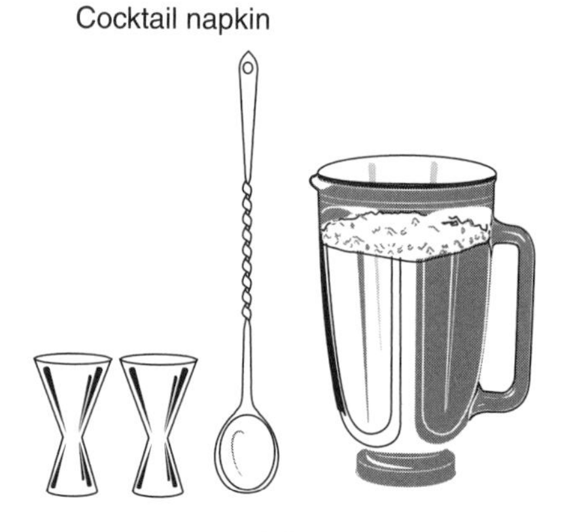

step 3: Add the liquor and other ingredients.

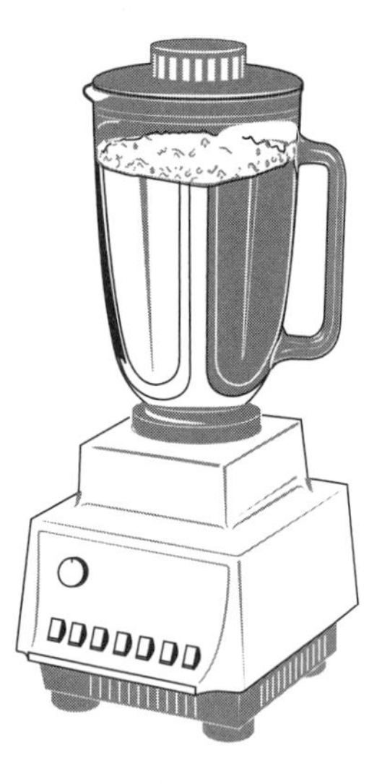

step 4: Blend or mix until ice cream has liquefied.

step 5: Pour the entire contents into the glass. Use barspoon to scrape cup.

step 6: Add garnish and straw and serve on a cocktail napkin.

FIGURE 11.6

Ice-cream drinks masquerading as "adult milk shakes" make good house specialties. For example the Chocolate Covered Banana is a blend of ice cream, Bailey's Irish Cream, Crème de Banana liqueur, chocolate syrup, and a ripe banana. The aptly named Death by Chocolate blends chocolate ice cream with Bailey's Irish Cream, Godiva Chocolate Liqueur, and vodka. You can invent your own: Not only do you have many drinks to start with, you have many flavors of ice cream to experiment with. Remember the rum raisin ice cream that topped the Mocha Rum Cooler? Consider exotic flavors, pretty garnishes, and special glasses for your frosty creations.

GRASSHOPPER BLEND

BLEND OR SHAKE-MIX

8-oz stem glass, chilled

1 scoop vanilla ice cream

1/2 jigger green Crème de Menthe

1/2 jigger white Crème de Cacao

Straws

BLENDED AND FROZEN DRINKS

For most bars there is a long list of benefits associated with blended drinks. For starters, they're tall and delicious, and they look great. As a group frozen drinks are extremely versatile and ounce for ounce they are also the most profitable. In terms of alcohol content they are less potent than their unfrozen counterparts. You can easily mix them as individual drinks or make them by the batch in special cocktail freezers. You can rent or buy portable "Margarita machines" that freeze premeasured amounts of perfectly smooth, slushy ice and dispense it on demand. The method is simple and straightforward: Simply blend crushed ice along with the ingredients of the drink until everything is homogeneous and the ice has refrozen to the consistency of slush (see Figure 11.7 for details). The flavors will vary according to which fresh fruits, juices, and packaged drink mixes you use. These can be combined with crushed ice, ice cream, frozen yogurt, and sorbet.

With such versatility and profitability beverage consultants are surprised by the fact that many bar blenders sit idle when they could be real profit centers. Bartenders often view the blender as a necessary evil. It's too loud, it takes too long to make a frozen drink, and using it can be a messy process, an attitude reinforced by outdated and/or poorly maintained bar blenders. If the appliance does not have the power to sufficiently crush ice it makes a grainy, inferior drink. As mentioned in Chapter 4 heavy-duty bar blenders are absolutely necessary. If noise is a problem commercial blenders can be fitted with noise-abatement chambers to muffle the sound. In many cases, however, bar owners feel that the whirr of hard-working blenders adds energy to the overall bar ambience and even prompts people to think about ordering a frozen drink.

RAMOS FIZZ

BLEND/BUILD OR SHAKE-MIX

12-oz glass, chilled

3 scoops vanilla ice cream

1 jigger gin

1 oz lemon juice

1/2 oz lime juice (or sweet-and-sour frothee mix)

1 egg white

1 tsp sugar

3–4 dashes orange flower water

Soda to fill

Straws

HOW TO MAKE A FROZEN DRINK

Ingredients
Liquor
Optional ingredients
Optional garnish
Crushed ice

Glass
8- or 12-oz stem glass

Mixing Method
Blend

Equipment and Accessories
Heavy-duty commercial blender
Jigger
Barspoon
Ice scoop
Short straws
Cocktail napkin

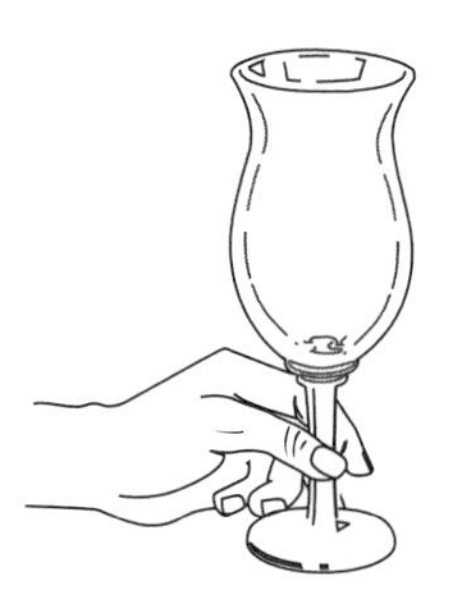

step 1: Place prechilled glass on the rail, holding it by the stem.

step 2: Pour cocktail ingredients into blender cup.

step 3: Using the scoop, add crushed ice to come just above liquor level.

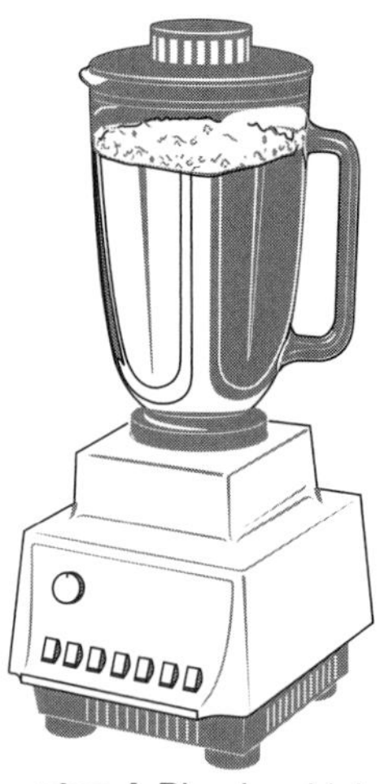

step 4: Blend on high speed until mixture blends and refreezes to a slush.

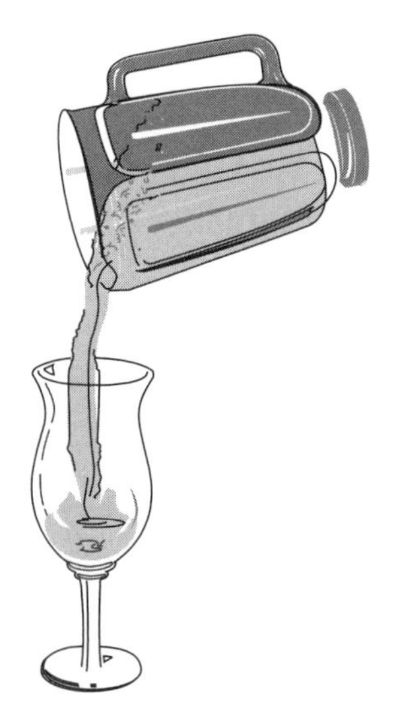

step 5: Heap contents of the cup into the glass. Scrape cup with barspoon.

step 6: Garnish, add straw, and serve on a cocktail napkin.

FIGURE 11.7

We believe that making blended drinks is a training issue and that every bartender should be familiar with the techniques. Several points are critical in making a successful frozen drink:

- All ingredients must be accurately measured, including the ice. In step 3 if you use too little ice you will make a drink without body; if you use too much ice you will make a drink without much taste.
- Blending time must also be consistent. In step 4 it takes quite a long time to reach the right consistency—several times as long as blending any other drink. Listen closely. When you no longer hear the bits of ice hitting the blender cup, the drink is ready to serve.
- In step 5 use the barspoon to scrape everything out of the cup. You should also have a routine for clean-up and sanitizing the blender and its parts, to get it back into service quickly and efficiently.

FROZEN STRAWBERRY DAIQUIRI

BLEND

8- to 10-oz stem glass, chilled

1 jigger rum

1 tsp lemon juice

2 tsp simple syrup

1 jigger pureed strawberries (or six fresh berries, cut up)

Crushed ice to submerge liquids

Whole berry garnish

The various Sours make the best frozen drinks because of their tangy flavors. Remember, when mixing ingredients, a bland drink will be even *more* bland when frozen. Many frozen drinks are sweet-and-sour drinks with fruit added, such as the classic frozen Strawberry Daiquiri and frozen Peach Margarita. These recipes require fresh fruit, although you can substitute frozen fruit if necessary. For the Peach Margarita you can use fresh peaches in season, blending the puree in advance with simple syrup and a dash of lemon juice. In winter simply puree frozen peaches. An important note: When using fresh fruit, add some simple syrup and/or a syrup or liqueur that is flavored with the same fruit. Otherwise the fruit flavor will be watered down too much with the addition of crushed ice.

Frozen tropical drinks seem to complement Mexican, Asian, and Caribbean cuisine. If you make them fun and casual people will order them year-round. Also look beyond the traditionally frozen classics (Daiquiri, Margarita, and Pina Colada) for crowd-pleasing ideas. Metropolitans, Bellinis, and Hurricanes can be made in frozen form. The following suggestions are from *Sante* magazine's May 2004 issue:

- Add liqueurs to the classics. There are Kahlua Coladas, Italian Coladas (with Amaretto), and "Gang Green" Coladas (with Midori melon liqueur). Make a standard Margarita into a "Meltdown" by drizzling a few teaspoons of Chambord on top to melt into the drink and add color. Other Meltdown liqueur favorites are Midori and Grand Marnier.
- Frozen Long Island Iced Tea is a possibility, and the use of ice lessens the considerable kick of this classic multiliquor drink. Variations include Iced Green Tea (add cranberry juice and Midori) and Raspberry Iced Tea (float Chambord).
- Frozen-lemonade concoctions capitalize on America's favorite hot-weather beverage. Blend lemonade and ice with Bacardi Limon Rum and a splash of grenadine for color. Add bourbon to frozen lemonade for a twist on the Whiskey Sour.

- Swirls require preparing two different blended drinks, then pouring them together in a specialty glass. Lightly swirl, but don't mix, the two colors before serving. An example is the Sapphire Swirl, developed by Blue Mesa restaurants in Dallas, Texas: Sauza Silver Tequila, Blue Curacao, Margarita mix, and a float of Sauza Hornitos Tequila, and garnished with a lime wedge and cherry in a 14-ounce stemmed glass. When swirling, remember to marry two drinks with different colors and complementary flavors.

FROZEN PEACH MARGARITA

BLEND

8- to 10-oz stem glass, chilled
1 jigger tequila
1/2 jigger peach liqueur
1 1/2 jiggers pureed peaches
Crushed ice to submerge liquids
Fresh peach wedge (in season)

The ability to make and market frozen drinks increases a bar or restaurant's appeal to a wide demographic span of potential customers, and some establishments choose to make it a signature. At Kahunaville in Wilmington, Delaware, ten frozen-drink dispensers crank out a variety of icy favorites to complement the casual, Caribbean-accented menu. The Dome, the cocktail lounge that revolves atop the Dallas, Texas, skyline at the downtown Hyatt Regency, sells more than 50,000 frozen cocktails a year (at $8.75 apiece) in logo-emblazoned souvenir glasses. Mino-Matic, a supplier of beer-dispensing equipment in Northridge, California, teamed up with Island Oasis, a maker of cocktail mixes in Walpole, Massachusetts, to invent an on-tap system for dispensing frozen drinks in high volume. Today these "draft" cocktails are available at such events as the Super Bowl and Mardi Gras.

ALCOHOL-FREE ALTERNATIVES

There are plenty of reasons why people who visit a bar choose not to drink alcohol but still want to enjoy the atmosphere with friends who do. For the non-drinking guest the typical alternative to a cocktail used to be a bar-gun-dispensed soft drink. Not anymore! Thanks to the ever-expanding ranks of bottled water, tea, juice, energy drinks, alcohol-free beers, and other nonalcoholic beverages, there are incredible options for making sophisticated and flavorful *mocktails,* as they are often called.

Alcohol-free drinks offer a serious opportunity for incremental sales. For instance, a good nonalcoholic-drink selection can pick up the slack in traditionally low alcohol sales periods, such as lunch. In addition these drinks appeal to a broad customer base: consumers who happen not to want a drink, as well as those who abstain. In a restaurant setting nonalcoholic beverages appeal to both children and adults. Moreover these drinks can generally be made with existing bar supplies, so inventory issues are minimal.

The key to a good nonalcoholic-drink program is to create the recipes and make the drinks with the same high mixology standards that you apply to regular cocktails and dessert drinks. You can charge "cocktail prices" for these libations—but only if you use quality ingredients and take great care in their preparation. Some operations keep the nonalcoholic-beverage price around $4, which guests find acceptable. Of course for you the profit margin is certainly better than selling a soft drink or iced tea at one third the price. As with other types of specialty drinks, the next step is to make customers aware of them. Have a separate nonalcoholic-drink menu or a creative table tent, or include them on your regular drink menu.

In the past nonalcoholic drinks were simply pale imitations of traditional mixed drinks. This is no longer true today and beverage managers' creativity is the only limitation. One way to jumpstart the mocktail creation process is to take your existing lineup of specialty drinks or dessert drinks, and make and taste each one without the alcohol. How can each recipe be modified slightly to make sure it delivers the panache of a "specialty" drink, alcohol-free? What can bartenders do with seasonal beverages, such as lemonade and cider, to spice them up for customers? How can you make them look as great as they taste?

An excellent source of nonalcoholic-beverage recipes is *The Original Guide to Alcohol-Free Beverages and Drinks* by Robert Plotkin (BarMedia, Tucson, Arizona, 2002). Since Plotkin usually writes about bartending, his expertise carries over into such topics as techniques and garnishing. On the Internet use the term **mocktail** and you'll be surprised by the number of easily accessible recipes. The following recipes are from the Liquor Control Board of Ontario, Canada, which lists 160 mocktails on its web site (www.lcbo.com):

- ***Tropical Spritzer.*** In a cocktail glass filled with ice, mix 3 ounces of mango juice and 3 ounces of peach juice. Fill with soda water and stir to mix. Garnish with a starfruit slice.
- ***Coco Colada.*** In a blender, add one cup ice, 4 ounces of pineapple juice, and 2 ounces Cream of Coconut (or 6 ounces Pina Colada mix). Blend until slushy and strain into an Old-Fashioned or Margarita glass. Garnish with an orange wheel.
- ***Cognac Craze.*** In a cocktail shaker filled with ice, combine 2 ounces of raspberry juice, the juice of one-eighth of a lime, 2 ounces of pineapple juice, and 2 ounces of cranberry juice. Shake until frothy and strain into a Hurricane glass filled with ice. Garnish with a skewer of fresh raspberries.
- ***Vienna Soother.*** In a cocktail shaker filled with ice, add 4 ounces of cold strong coffee, 2 ounces of cream, ¼ ounce chocolate syrup, and ½ teaspoon cinnamon. Shake well and strain into a tumbler. Top with whipped cream and shaved chocolate.

FILLING DRINK ORDERS

Most drinks are made to order drink by drink, but the orders seldom come in one drink at a time. The following tips on handling orders will help you to successfully meet this challenge:

- ***Speed.*** Keeping up with the orders.
- ***Quality.*** Getting the drink to the customer at its peak of perfection.
- ***Accuracy.*** Delivering the right drink to the right customer.

First deal with one set of orders, that is, one server's guest check or one party of bar customers. Set up all the glasses at once; this will help you remember what was ordered. Group the glasses according to the base liquor, setting them up in the same sequence as the liquor bottles in the well. (Have your servers "call" drinks—state their names to you—in this order, too.) In this way a good bartender can handle a fairly long list without taking time to refer back to the written ticket.

If the order contains several identical drinks that are not built in the glass make them together. Put extra ice in the mixing glass or the blender or mixer cup, multiply each ingredient by the number of drinks, and proceed as for a single drink. Divide the finished product among the glasses that you have set out for these drinks, but not all at once. Fill each glass half full the first time around, then add a little more product to each glass in another round or two until you complete all of these drinks evenly.

Make drinks in the following sequence:

1. Start frozen drinks and ice-cream drinks (they will be made in their machines while the rest are being poured).
2. Pour straight liquor drinks (straight shots, liquor on rocks).
3. Fix juice drinks and Sours.
4. Prepare cream drinks and hot drinks.
5. Mix highballs with carbonated mixers.
6. Pour draft beer.

This sequence enables you to make first those drinks that keep best and to make last those that don't hold well. Some places have the server call drinks in this sequence instead of in the well order.

When writing an order on a guest check use a standard set of abbreviations for drinks, liquors, brand names, mixes, and special garnishes. Figure 11.8 gives you some suggestions. Abbreviations vary from one bar to another. You can adapt these to your needs or create your own **bar shorthand**—just make sure that everyone on both sides of the bar knows and uses it correctly.

When you write a drink order a slash is used to separate the items in the instructions. For example a very dry Vodka Martini on the rocks with a twist is written: V MT/XX/R/TW. Bar shorthand might seem like Greek when you're first getting used to it, but soon you will find it indispensable—and if you use a computerized POS system, getting it right in order to enter the data is even more critical.

When a server takes a table order the best way to get the right drink to the right person is to pick out one seat as number 1—say, the seat closest to the bar. Then number each seat in order around the table. Next, write each drink on the check following the number of the customer's seat. Figure 11.9 is an example of a guest check for a party of six.

GUEST-CHECK ABBREVIATIONS

Liquors, etc.		*Drinks*		*Call Brands*	
Liquors		Bourbon and Water	B/W	Absolut	ABS
Bourbon	B	Black Russian	BRUS	Beefeater	BEEF
Brandy	Br	Brandy Alexander	BR ALEX	Canadian Club	CC
Gin	G	Barcardi	BAC	Chivas Regal	CHIVAS
Rum	R	Banana Daiquiri	BAN DAQ	Courvoisier	COUR
Scotch	S or SC	Bloody Mary	MARY	Cuervo Gold	C GOLD
Tequila	TEQ	Daiquiri	DAQ	Cutty Sark	CUTTY
Vodka	V	Fuzzy Navel	FUZ	Dewars White Label	WHITE or WL
Mixes		Godfather	GOD	Drambuie	DRAM
Coke	C	Gibson	GIB	Early Times	ET
Ginger ale	G	Gimlet	GIM	Glenlivet	LIVET
7UP	7	Grasshopper	GRASS	Grand Marnier	MARNIER
Soda	S	Irish Coffee	IRISH C	Hennessy	HENN
Sprite	SP	Harvey Wallbanger	BANGER	J & B	JB
Tonic	T	John Collins	JOHN	Jack Daniels	JD
Water	W	Kamikaze	KAM	Jim Beam	BEAM
		Manhattan	MAN	Johnnie Walker Black	BLACKS
Garnishes		Margarita	MARG	Johnnie Walker Red	REDS
Lime	LI	Martini	MT	Old Fitzgerald	FITZ
Olive	OL	Old-Fashioned	OF	Old Grand-Dad	DAD
Onion	ON	Ramos Fizz	RAMOS	Remy-Martin	REMY
Twist	TW or ~	Rob Roy	R ROY	Seagrams 7 Crown	7
		Rusty Nail	R NAIL	Seagrams V.O.	VO
Special instructions		Screwdriver	DRIVER	Sloe gin	SLG
Double	DBL	Scotch and Water	SC/W	Smirnoff	SMIRN
Dry	X	Tequila Sunrise	SUNRISE	Southern Comfort	SO C
Extra dry	XX	Tom Collins	TOM	Stolichnaya	STOLI
On the rocks	R	Virgin Mary	V MARY	Tanqueray	TANQ
Straight up	Up or a	Vodka Martini	V MT	Wild Turkey	WILD
Frozen	Z	Whisky Sour	WS		

FIGURE 11.8

RESTAURANT & BAR

GUEST CHECK

Server	Table No.	Guests	Date
CC	12	6	12-31-07

Line	Seat	Item	Price
1	1	V / MT / R / TW	4.75
2		XX / TANQ / MT / R / O11	5.50
3		7 / 7	4.75
4		Chivas / W	5.00
5		Br / Man / R	4.75
6	6	MARG/ Z / C GOLD	5.95
7			
8			
9			
10			
11			
12			
13			
14			

THANK YOU		
	FOOD	———
	BEVERAGE	30.70
	SUB TOTAL	
	TAX	———
	TOTAL	30.70

FIGURE 11.9 Guest check using typical abbreviations. Seat numbers are in the left column.

DEVELOPING DRINK MENUS AND SPECIALTY DRINKS

Once you have a thorough knowledge of drinks and the ways they are made, you will understand why planning the drink menu—the range and types of drinks you will serve—is one of your most important tasks. The drinks you serve will determine the sizes of glassware, the number and type of ice machines, the refrigerator and freezer space, the small equipment and utensils, and the space on the backbar. These drinks will also determine the skill level that you require of your bartenders and servers. And, of course, they will determine the kinds of liquor and supplies you buy and the number of items you must keep in inventory.

The Unlimited Bar Concept

If your menu concept is an **unlimited bar,** that is, one that serves the full spectrum of drinks, you must be able to produce those drinks. This means having the equipment that produces both cubed ice and crushed ice, glassware that will accommodate everything from the after-dinner liqueur to the Zombie, a freezer or soft-serve machine for ice cream, a means of chilling cocktail glasses, all the necessary small equipment, an ample draft-beer setup, and 100 or more different beverages in your inventory. In addition you must have skilled and knowledgeable bartenders, as well as servers who know how to take and transmit orders.

For many types of enterprises, the versatility of the unlimited bar is part of the bar's image. Even though the customer may order the same drink time after time (often without knowing what is in it or how much it costs), the assurance that that drink is available at that bar is important. It is also possible for a whole party of people to order widely different types of drinks to suit their individual tastes. The unlimited bar is essential to the expensive restaurant, where excellence in everything *is* its image.

The Limited Drink Menu

Many restaurant-bars today use printed drink menus. You may find them in restaurants where drinks are secondary to food or in trendy neighborhood bar-and-grills. Drink menus usually feature specialty drinks along with old favorites, with descriptions that raise the thirst level as they list the ingredients. An establishment may have a list of special drinks written in chalk on a blackboard at the bar. These drink menus are proving to be good sales stimulators. At the same time by focusing attention on a limited selection, they can eliminate some of the costs of a full-spectrum bar.

For example a well-designed specialty menu can reduce the extensive liquor inventory required in an unlimited bar. If you offer an attractive selection of 15 or 20 drinks—all carefully planned to be based on a few liquors, liqueurs, and mixes—you can cut the number of items in your inventory by half, at least. You should still be prepared to serve the standard highballs, Martinis, and Bloody Marys, and you will still need to carry a small selection of the popular call brands, but your customers will order up to 90 percent of their drinks from your printed menu.

The limited drink menu applies the philosophy of the limited food menu: Instead of offering everything anyone might want, you specialize in the same way that you develop a successful food menu. You combine a few basic ingredients using a skillful mix-and-match technique, in the same way that an Italian restaurant offers a long list of entrées by mixing and matching pastas and sauces.

The limited drink menu also shares some other advantages of the limited food menu. Properly developed, it can mean that less equipment is needed at the bar and that less space is needed for the smaller inventory—and, thus, less investment overall. This can mean that fewer skills and less experience are required of the bartenders, so you do not need to pay higher-skill wages. Your own training of personnel to prepare your selection of drinks can produce that sought-after consistency of product. In addition you can choose the base ingredients with an eye to keeping down costs: vodka and rum are cheaper than whiskies, and they mix well with a variety of flavor additions. Also, buying large quantities of fewer items might result in better quantity discounts.

For a limited menu to be successful the first requirement is that it must reflect the tastes of your customers. If you are already in business you have data on your most popular drink types. Include the favorites, then go from there to make new drinks by changing or adding flavors and flavor accents. If your enterprise is new find out what your target population is drinking in other places. Be sure to include house wines and a selection of popular beers—something for everybody.

Creating Signature Drinks

Signature cocktails are born from innovative mixology and clever merchandising—arguably the former is an art form; the latter, an acquired skill. A number of the drinks mentioned in this chapter and Chapter 10 are the specialties of particular bartenders, bars, or restaurants, and every bar should have them. But what makes any drink a "signature?" What gives it distinctive marketability?

A signature cocktail is often the result of brainstorming new drinks that match current trends. It must have a flavor that appeals to a variety of palates, and it should convey the spirit or theme of the bar or restaurant in which it was created. A bit of mystique, whether it's a funny story, an upscale image, or a top-secret recipe, never hurts. It is absolutely critical to keep the taste and quality of this drink consistent. The key is to take the "right" ingredients and make them your own. Since bartenders are experimenting all the time, it's up to you to cleverly substitute interesting new ingredients in tasty new ways and to vary the presentation just enough to be unique.

In case you haven't noticed, even the most famous bars have only one or two "signature" drinks. In New Orleans, it's the Hurricane at Pat O'Brien's, and the Brandy Milk Punch at Dickie Brennan's Steakhouse. Don't overwhelm your guests with a barrage of new drinks. This will scare customers away. Introduce the drinks seasonally or one every month, to see which ones sell and which ones have potential. Here are a few additional pointers about developing specialty drinks:

- ***Cater to your clientele and their preferences.*** Observe the basic drink structure discussed in Chapter 10. A successful drink has a base liquor, plus one or more flavor modifiers or flavor accents. The base liquor should be at least 50 percent of the liquor in the drink.
- ***Do not treat this as a contest to challenge your customers' taste buds.*** Choose flavor combinations that are compatible. Mixing orange juice and chocolate

probably will not work. Use popular flavors. Try adding a trendy flavor as a float atop a familiar drink, or be the first to make an old drink with a new product. Replace a plain liquor with an infusion that adds a new accent.

- ***Consider the use of fresh ingredients.*** Think about which flavors and items are already "signatures" in your local area. Use them to create drink recipes. Fresh, quality ingredients that can be obtained locally can help a cocktail become a "local favorite," which ironically helps sell it to visitors, too.
- ***Consider your equipment, glassware, and space.*** If you want to feature frozen drinks you must have an ample supply of crushed or flake ice and plenty of blenders, or enough demand for a single specialty to invest in a frozen-drink machine. If you want to serve ice-cream drinks, you must have ice-cream equipment at the bar. A custom cocktail deserves a custom glass, and you must be able to stock and store them in sufficient numbers.
- ***Consider your bartenders' skill level.*** If you want to serve flaming drinks, be sure that your personnel can make them without using a fire extinguisher. Do not introduce too many new items at once—it will confuse the staff and the customers.
- ***Keep the drinks fairly simple so they can be made quickly.*** Consider including a few *mocktails.* Dress them up handsomely and offer them free of charge to designated drivers.
- ***Consider your profit margin.*** Signature drinks are supposed to be high-volume items—at least, once they catch on—so keep your costs low when seeking out ingredients.
- ***Plan attractive visual effects, dream up catchy names, and blend it all into your image.*** This means using custom glassware, adding eye-catching garnishes, and coming up with drink monikers that are a play on words and/or fit the bar's theme, neighborhood, and clientele.

Promoting Your Wares

Making a commitment to creating specialty drinks means you will also need to promote them. A successful promotion should be consistent with your bar's "personality" or concept, as well as its clientele. A classy, after-work business crowd might not appreciate your rum drinks served in pineapple "bowls" with paper umbrellas in them, but they probably would appreciate an upscale Scotch selection and knowledgeable servers who can make recommendations about it. You have a goal when you run a promotion: either generating repeat business or generating more sales from existing customers. This is actually a long-term process, not a weeklong endeavor, so it might require spending a little of your hard-earned money to print collateral material: table tents, individual drink menus, or a list of drinks on your regular dining menu. A chalkboard list is another way to give guests the impression that they are trying something up-to-the-minute. Listing after-dinner drinks in a separate dessert menu is a good idea, as seen on the sample menu in Figure 11.10. A dessert menu is also the perfect place for touting coffee drinks.

BARTENDER PICKS: 2001–2004

One excellent way to keep up on bartending trends is to read the feature entitled "Bartender Picks," which appears regularly in the trade magazine *Market Watch.* The following are some samples from the last few years that we hope will spark your own signature creations.

2001

- Bartender *Steve Zell* at the Cypress Club in San Francisco is somewhat of a traditionalist. He says he began his bartending career at age 12 at home, pouring drinks for his dad! One of Zell's signature drinks is the Pink Thing, which is made with Absolut Vodka, orange juice, cranberry juice, and DeKuyper Blueberry Schnapps; shaken with ice; and served in a Martini glass.
- *Mike Smith* was a bartender at the Columbus Hotel in New Orleans for almost 20 years. In the Victoria Lounge his operating philosophy was to use the right ingredients and the right amounts when mixing cocktails. His signature drink, the Pretty Baby, made with Absolut Vodka, light Crème de Cacao, heavy cream, and a dash of grenadine, brought countless tourists to his bar pre-Hurricane Katrina. Smith shakes and strains this drink into a rocks glass over ice. The drink's name comes from the 1970s movie starring Brooke Shields, which was partially filmed at the hotel.

2002

- *Marcela Llodra* at the Champagne Bar/Lounge in Miami, Florida, offers 46 Champagnes by the bottle and by the glass and a mélange of Champagne-based cocktails. A native of Chile, she says that her signature drink is Pearl l'Orange, which is made with Absolut Mandarin, DeKuyper Pucker Watermelon Schnapps, and a splash of cranberry juice. The drink is served in a Martini glass rimmed with sugar and garnished with several fresh melon balls.
- *Joy Perrine* of Jack's Lounge in Louisville, Kentucky, has almost 40 years of experience behind the bar. She prefers bourbon, Kentucky's favorite, to create delicious drinks. One of her signatures is the Bourbon Ball, which is made with Woodford Reserve Bourbon, DeKuyper Dark Crème de Cacao, and Tuaca liqueur. Shake the ingredients with ice, then strain into a Martini glass, and garnish with a fresh, stem-on strawberry.

2004

- *Steve Burney* manages Oliver's Lounge in the Mayflower Park Hotel in Washington, DC. He takes great pride in the well-constructed cocktail. His signature drink is the Paradigm Shift, which is made with Ketel One Vodka, Bombay Dry Gin, Campari, and fresh raspberry sour, garnished with a Texas Ruby Red grapefruit wedge. Pour the ingredients with ice into a shaker, including the juice squeezed from the grapefruit wedge. Shake and strain them into a chilled Martini glass and garnish the drink with fresh raspberries.
- *Jodi Lee Smith,* bar manager at The Wave, the restaurant in Chicago's W Hotel, creates her own simple syrup with spices, an idea she credits to her chef, who supports the use of kitchen spices to make drinks. One of Smith's drinks, called Fresh, is made with Lichiko Vodka, pineapple juice, and her signature "Ice Bar Spice," shaken with ice, and served in a Martini glass. The drink is garnished with a cardamom-soaked pineapple slice and a sprig of mint.

DESSERT DRINK MENU

SUPER CREAMY DRINKS

FLYING GORILLA™
Fresh Banana, Chocolate, Ice Cream, Créme de Cacao and DeKuyper Banana Liqueur

KAHLUA KISSER
Kahlua, Créme de Cacao, Vodka and Ice Cream

STRAWBERRY CREAMSICLE®
Crushed Strawberries, Ice Cream, Vodka and DiSaronno Amaretto

CARAMEL TWISTER™
Vodka, Butterscotch Schnapps, Praline and Ice Cream with Swirls of Chocolate and Caramel

COFFEE DRINKS

IRISH COFFEE
Bushmills Irish Whiskey, Coffee and Whipped Cream

JAMAICAN COFFEE
Tia Maria, Myers's Rum, Dark Créme de Cacao, Coffee and Whipped Cream

DR. JIM'S COFFEE
Kahlua, Grand Marnier, Dark Créme de Cacao, Coffee and Whipped Cream

CAFÉ WYNNIE
DiSaronno Amaretto, Baileys, Tia Maria, Coffee and Whipped Cream

MEXICAN COFFEE
Sauza Hornitos Tequila, Kahlua, Coffee and Whipped Cream

CALYPSO COFFEE
Malibu Rum, Frangelico Liqueur, a Hint of Chocolate, Coffee and Whipped Cream

BAILEYS COFFEE
Baileys Irish Cream, Coffee and Whipped Cream

KEOKE COFFEE
Courvoisier, Kahlua, Dark Créme de Cacao, Coffee and Whipped Cream

COGNAC, PORT AND SHERRY

Courvoiser VS	Remy Martin VSOP	Hennessy VS	Sandeman Tawny
Fonseca Bin #27	Dry Sack	Hennessy XO	Harvey's Bristol Creme

FIGURE 11.10 Your dessert drink menu can be as fun as you want to make it. This selection is excerpted with permission of The Cheesecake Factory, Inc., Calabasas Hills, California.

The printed menu must catch the customer's eye, whet the appetite, and create a thirst. The menu should spell out the ingredients in each drink since your specialties will be new to the customer and the names that you give them won't mean anything. (Patrons might also be interested to read what their old favorites are made of.) Depending on your clientele and your budget, you might want to illustrate your menu with inviting photos or sketches of your drinks. Make the menu interesting to browse through; like your food menu, it is a promotional piece.

One national chain of Mexican restaurants cut its inventory to 35 liquors, 9 mixes, plus 4 wines, and 4 beers after conducting careful market research and planning. This is about one-third of the average unlimited bar. The chain's full-color printed menu offers 20 mixed drinks: frozen drinks, cocktails, and Slings, some new, some old. The lineup might seem unsophisticated, but it satisfies the tastes of the chain's youngish, blue-collar clientele. All the drinks are made from the same few base liquors, liqueurs, and made-to-order bottled mixes. This makes it possible to hire employees who have little or no previous bartending experience, train them thoroughly to mix each drink on the menu, and serve customers the same drink in Denver as in Tallahassee at an attractive price.

SUMMING UP

Many interesting and historical tidbits are associated with the development of the world's most popular drinks—including Manhattans, Martinis, and Cuba Libres—and these have made impressive comebacks in bars today. The younger generation enjoys the lore and drama, if you will, of bygone times and nightclubs that movies have painted as chic and glamorous.

If the drinks are not good, though, customers won't return. Behind the scenes the systematic development of drinks and a drink menu provides you with performance standards and products of consistent quality, and makes training easier for bartenders and cocktail servers. Standardization also facilitates accurately pricing drinks, controlling costs, and cutting losses, all of which enhance the profit picture. (These factors are discussed in upcoming chapters.)

In this chapter you learned about making from scratch the members of a number of drink families: Martinis, Manhattans, Sours, and Collinses, as well as shooters, tropical drinks, dairy and ice-cream drinks, and frozen drinks. The latter can be incredibly profitable, but only with the right equipment and staff training. We spent additional time on some of the most popular individual drinks, including the Martini, the Cosmopolitan, and the Margarita.

Most bars have a common form of shorthand (abbreviations used to write orders) and a system to "call" the drinks (place the order) at the bar. Planning a drink menu makes it much easier to order liquor, with fewer overhead costs and less storage space required. In short not every bar has to be able to make every drink. However, a thorough knowledge of drinks opens the door to fun and invention for you, your bartenders, and your servers. A few unique specialty drinks to complement your food menu are excellent merchandising devices.

POINTS TO PONDER

1. Why is it important to make a Martini or Manhattan in a chilled glass?
2. Why are some drinks known as "Sours"?
3. Why is the hand shaker used when blenders and mixers can do the job?
4. Explain the reasons for preparing a multidrink order in the sequence that this chapter recommends.
5. What is the difference between a Collins and a Fizz?
6. Why is it important for a server to use standard drink notations (bar shorthand) on guest checks?
7. From memory write down the standard Martini recipe given in this chapter. Then create your own version and explain why yours might have signature-drink potential.
8. What are the family characteristics of tropical drinks?
9. What is a shooter in your area? Provide two examples, and include how they are made and the amount of liquor they contain.
10. Develop a sample menu of about a dozen drinks. Use vodka, tequila, rum, up to four liqueurs, fruit juices, and your choice of condiments and garnishes. Write a description of each drink designed to interest your customers.

TERMS OF THE TRADE

bar shorthand
chaser
Collins
cream drink
Daiquiri
Fizz
Flip
Manhattan
Margarita
Martini
Milk Punch
mocktail
shooter
shot
signature drink
Sour
straight up
tropical drink
unlimited bar

A CONVERSATION WITH...JOSEPH TAKATA

Beverage Director, Hilton Hawaiian Village Beach Resort & Spa

You could say that Joseph "Joe" Takata just fell into his career in the bartending-and-hospitality industry. Although he was an education major at the University of Hawaii Joe found his calling through various hospitality industry jobs. Over the past 30 years Joe has worked in a wide variety of bar businesses, including stand-alone restaurants, dance clubs, showrooms, and large resorts, such as the Hilton Hawaiian Village Beach Resort & Spa.

Joe is currently the Director of Beverage for one of Hilton Hotels Corporation's largest hotels in the world, the Hilton Hawaiian Village Beach Resort & Spa. The Hilton Hawaiian Village spans 22 acres and offer 2,998 rooms. Joe oversees 8 bars and manages a staff of 37 servers and 49 bartenders and barbacks.

Q: What does a beverage manager do?

A: The role and responsibilities of a beverage manager depend on the type of operation. For example, in a freestanding restaurant the manager is in charge of the bar and often serves as the most senior bartender. The manager is also in charge of staffing and ordering supplies. The same position in a nightclub atmosphere would include these responsibilities; in addition the manager would coordinate advertising and promotions. In a hotel or resort setting the manager also coordinates all of the supply orders and works with the Human Resources Department for staffing needs.

Q: What is the most difficult part of the job?

A: The most difficult challenge of being a beverage manager or working in any large organization is communication. Communication is probably the hardest lesson to learn and the most challenging skill to perfect. In any career you work with a wide variety of personalities. It helps greatly if you have a positive attitude. You cannot get hung up on doing things a certain way, by micromanaging or by having the attitude that "I'm the boss!" You must learn to be flexible. You expect this of your employees, and so you too must be flexible and work as a team.

Q: Are your operations manuals and drink recipes standardized?

A: All our recipe and operations manuals are written down. Our measured pour is an ounce, and we also use a jigger. In the past we also have used mechanical pouring systems. The greatest concern with mechanical systems is the required ongoing maintenance, ensuring no leaks and that the system lines are clean. Sometimes you can have a pinhole leak that will spray a fine mist of alcohol, which evaporates, and you may never even notice the leak until your bottom-line costs and inventory don't match up.

Q: What kinds of precautions do you take to prevent theft?

A: To prevent theft we keep all liquor and wine bottles under lock and key when the bars and restaurants are closed. All ordering goes through a central purchasing office and all supplies are stored in one central, secured area. Each bar has a par stock that is issued, and we put our own sticker on each bottle that goes out of the storage area. The sticker serves as a quality check to ensure that someone is not bringing in their own bottle of wine, selling it, and pocketing the money. The sticker system helps to validate your costs at the end of the month. These simple steps help to control inventory and monitor costs, something that is essential to being a good beverage manager.

Q: When there is a problem, how is it handled?

A: If a theft occurs there are policies in place to investigate, and the investigation would be coordinated by the manager and a representative from the Human Resources Department. Theft can be grounds for immediate termination.

Q: What is your typical day like?

A: There is usually something new each day. It's always an adventure! I usually start my day at 9:00 A.M. with a site inspection, surveying all of the outlets to make sure everything is secure, equipment is in proper working condition, and needed supplies are on hand. Prior to a bar opening we have a 10- to 15-minute meeting before each shift. We also have a monthly food-and-beverage meeting to share restaurants and bars revenue status, promotions, and so on. After my site inspection I answer voice mails and e-mails. Since I am a beverage manager in a resort setting, our department also provides staff for banquet events. I thoroughly review the event orders and identify what assistance is needed from our department. Then

I review the prior day's labor costs and revenue generated to see if we are meeting our goals. Afterward, I return to the frontline to check on the status of the bars and check how my staff is doing. Quality customer service is paramount.

Q: Do your menus and drink recipes reflect anything unusual because your clientele is so international?
A: Customers visiting our Hawaii resort expect the standard tropical drinks, such as Mai Tais, Blue Hawaiis, Pina Coladas, and the like, but we also take special requests.

Q: What kind of training or prevoius experience do you require for new hires?
A: Required staff experience depends on the role they will be expected to fill. For example, if it's a fast-paced restaurant or bar we need seasoned staff who can keep the pace. If the pace is slower and the requests are straightforward (like soft drinks or beer), then I will hire someone with less or no experience if they have a positive attitude and a desire to learn. In the Hawaii resort market good bartender jobs are few and far between. I've worked in Hawaii for 25 years and I've seen people start off as a barback just to get a chance at the coveted bartender job.

Q: What are some of the most unusual situations that you've had to cater to?
A: The most unusual work situation I've experienced occurred in a prior position where we were asked to close all of the fast-food outlets and bars to make everything kosher for Passover. All of the products, even the glassware, were cleaned or we purchased brand new items that were then blessed by the Rabbi.

Q: What would you suggest for hospitality students to get real work experience?
A: Students should get a wide variety of experience by working as a barback, bartender, and host or hostess. You really need to be [a] Jack [or Jill] of all trades. Then when you're ready to move up to a manager position, you will have a much better understanding of your staff and how you can better support them to ensure a cohesive team that will better serve your customer. You can never say, "That's not my job, I'm the manager!" You have to be trained in all areas and open to rolling up your sleeves and pitching in! In any career flexibility in skill and attitude will lead you down the path of success.

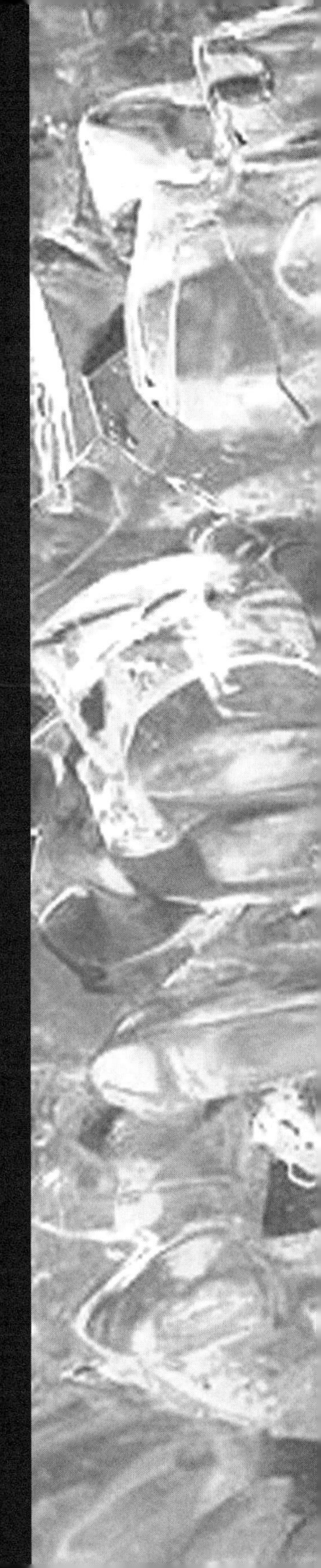

CHAPTER 12
EMPLOYEE MANAGEMENT

The people who deal with your customers represent your enterprise to the public. Your staff sells your wares and helps to create the ambience that keeps customers coming back. That's the upside. The downside is that employees are also among your highest costs and cause most of your headaches. High turnover, poor performance, and unreliability are frequent complaints among employers. Unfortunately the beverage industry is fraught with "people problems." Most of the employees are hourly, their shifts are irregular, their pay is variable, and they have few opportunities for advancement and many temptations along the way. Fortunately there are effective ways to approach these concerns. This chapter suggests ways to hire and train the right people, and to give them the impetus to become loyal employees.

THIS CHAPTER WILL HELP YOU . . .

- Become familiar with the types of jobs in the beverage industry.
- Write job descriptions and interview applicants.
- Develop effective training programs.
- Schedule personnel to meet daily needs.
- Supervise employees to avoid legal pitfalls.
- Meet federal and state compensation and record-keeping requirements.
- Figure wage and overtime amounts for various methods of payment.
- Understand the laws about tips and tip reporting.
- Decide which employee benefits to offer.

Never underestimate the importance of your employees. You can't be everywhere, and it is often up to them to make your customers feel welcome and important. They can help guests relax and celebrate, or prompt them to vow never to set foot in your place again! Your staff can please customers with their friendly style and efficiency, or turn them off with inattention, carelessness, bad manners, and/or dishonesty.

Employees affect your profits in many other ways. They are important links in any cost-control system. They are your best merchandising agents. To your customers, they represent you and your philosophy. So how do you go about finding the right people and putting them all together to function in a smooth operation? The kinds of employees you will need depend a great deal on your type of beverage business. First we'll look at the entire spectrum of staff positions, then we will consider how to determine your own staffing needs.

STAFF POSITIONS

The staff needs of bars are unique to each establishment, and there is probably no bar that has all of the positions that we describe. At one extreme is the small, owner-operated bar in which the owner is the manager, the bartender, and everything else. At the other end of the spectrum is the beverage service of a large hotel or restaurant chain. The organizational charts in Figure 12.1 show typical positions and their relationships in two types of beverage operations. The duties and responsibilities of the job described may vary greatly. In a small operation a single individual may handle the functions of three or four jobs, while only very large operations need a full-time beverage manager. Even the job of bartender or cocktail waitress varies from one bar to another.

The Bartender

The central figure in any beverage operation is the **bartender,** who is an amalgam of salesperson, entertainer, mixologist, and psychologist (seen in an amusing light in Figure 12.2). Of course the bartender's primary function is to mix and serve drinks for patrons at the bar and/or to pour drinks for table customers served by waiters or waitresses. Some say that is the easy part of the job. Less obvious, but no less important, are the roles of custodian and caretaker. These responsibilities include recording each drink sale, washing glassware and utensils, maintaining a clean and orderly bar, stocking the bar before opening, and closing the bar. In many operations the bartender also acts as the cashier. The bartender is typically a host and a promoter whose combination of skill and style translates into public-relations benefits that build goodwill and good business.

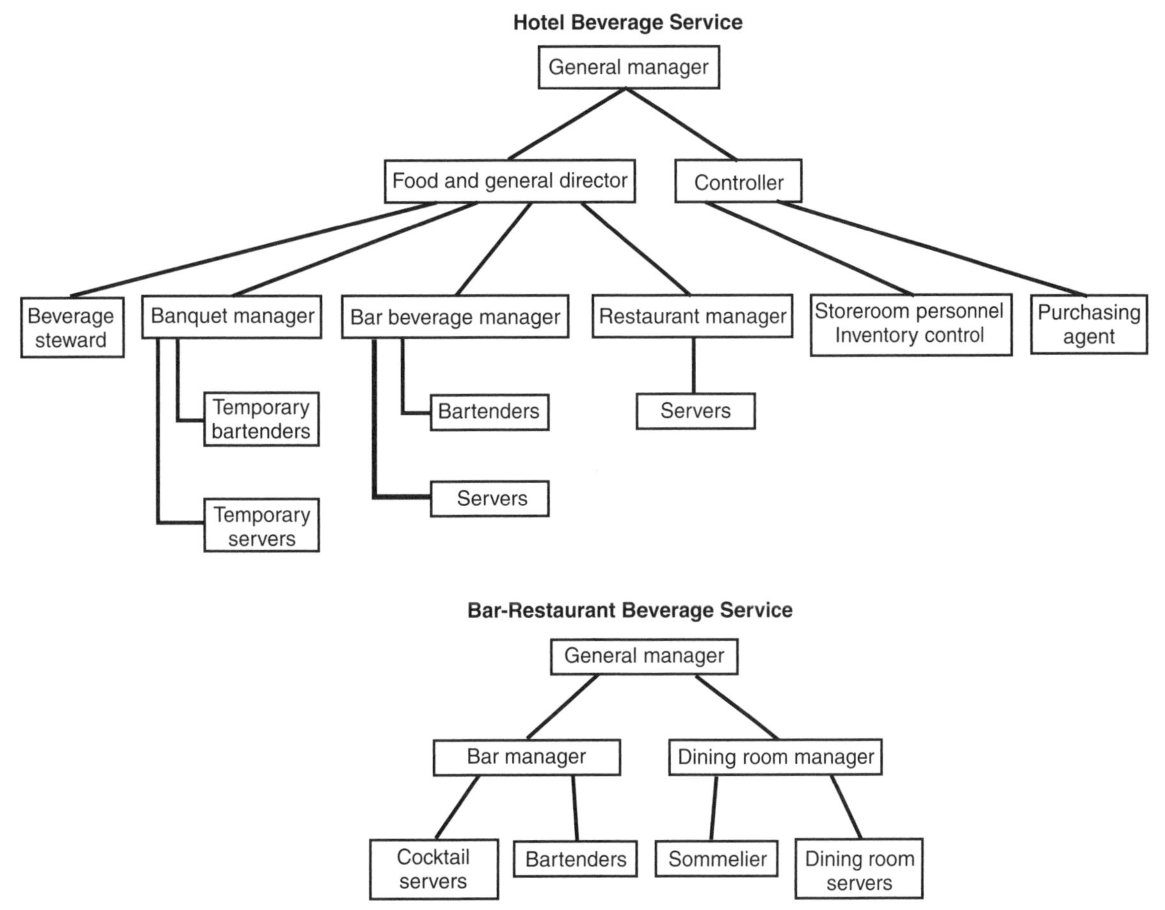

FIGURE 12.1 Organizational charts for two different types of bars.

Bartending is as wide-ranging a job as you can get in the foodservice business, and it is never as simple—or as glamorous—as it seems. The bartender is: the person who notices when the bar is getting crowded and crazy, and uses eye contact and a smile to buy time when newcomers or singles approach the bar; the person whose wit, wisdom, and approachability make him or her the center of conversation and the purveyor of both advice and drink concoctions; the person who can hold court behind a sleek bar at the ritziest private party or unclog the men's-room sink in a pinch. Bartending requires certain skills and aptitudes, not the least of which are patience, adaptability, and a good attitude. The bartender must know the recipes for whatever drinks the house serves (from dozens to hundreds, depending on the bar) and the techniques for mixing them, and must be able to work quickly and accurately. To this end the job requires dexterity and a good short-term memory. In a high-volume bar, often referred to as a *speed bar,* the ability to work quickly and under pressure is essential. A pleasing appearance and a pleasant personality

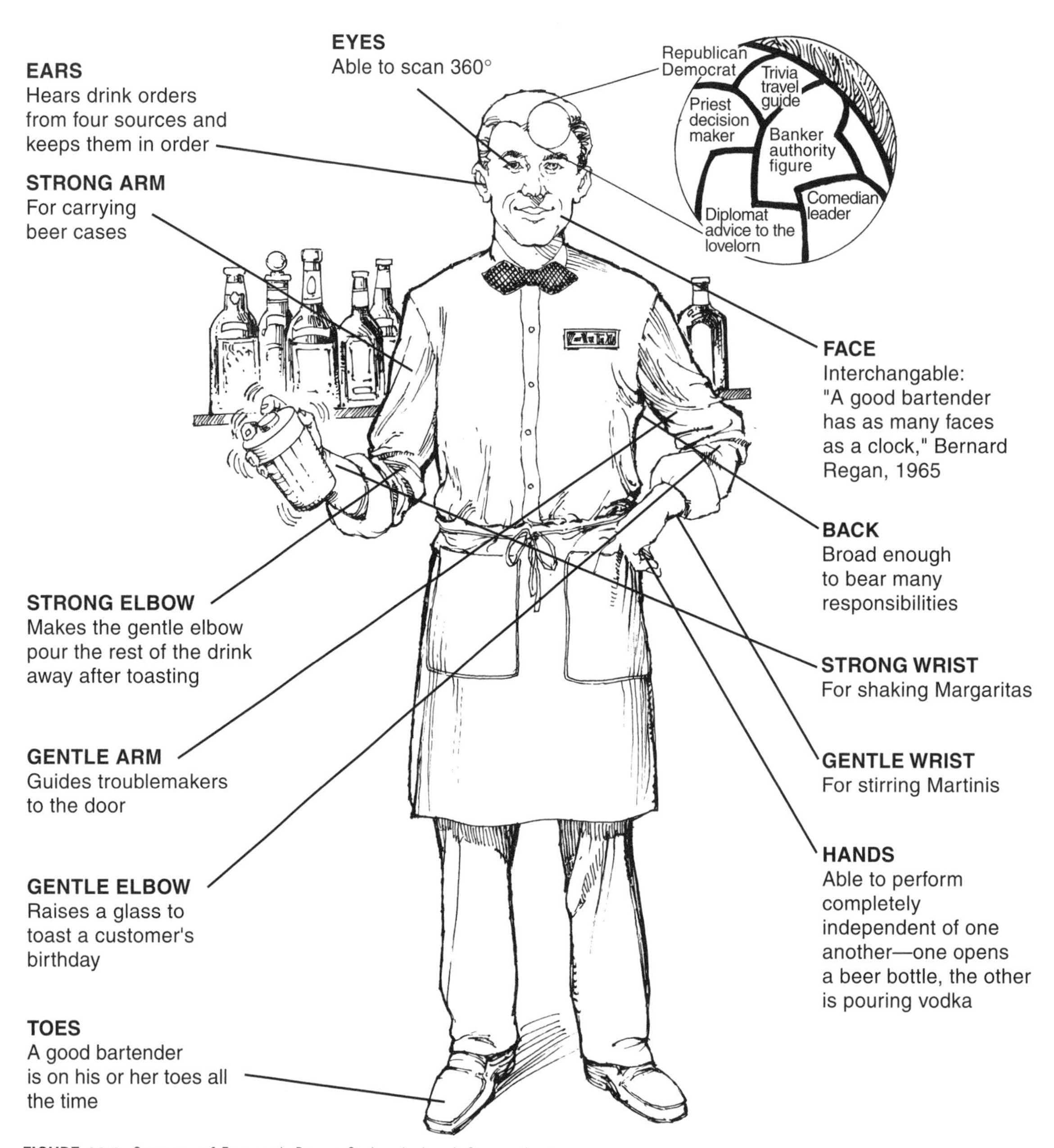

FIGURE 12.2 Courtesy of Foxwoods Resort Casino, Ledyard, Connecticut.

are essential in any bar, though less so in a service bar out of customer sight. Honesty is the most important quality of all and many bar owners insist, the hardest to find. When you're looking for candidates for a bartender job consider these points:

- ***Sex makes no difference.*** A good bartender is a good bartender, male or female. A good bartender can handle any situation in any bar at any time. For a long time the bar was a man's world, but this is no longer true. In fact some club owners feel that women bring a different temperament to bartending—that they have the ability to diffuse tense situations without becoming aggressive—and find them more willing to learn, practice, take notes, and ask questions.
- ***The bartender is a good host.*** The ideal person can get along with all of the other groups of employees: front of the house (servers, hostesses, etc.), the kitchen staff, management, and every guest who walks through the door. He or she can make people feel welcome, act as an icebreaker to introduce a new staff member or customers to others, apologize for slow service or a mishap, and generally keep "the party" running smoothly. Even when bartenders are busy, good ones can manage a smile and make eye contact with a newly seated customer—not just because they are friendly, but because they are alert.
- ***The bartender is a diplomat.*** Since a good bartender is observant he or she knows when to talk or joke around and when to be silent, knows when to gently but firmly refuse to serve more alcohol to someone who has had too much to drink, and knows the difference between someone who is being a nuisance and someone who is just trying to be friendly. The bartender's common-sense attitude in these situations is a major component of the bar's tone and atmosphere.
- ***The bartender is an authority figure.*** The man or woman behind the bar should be able to take control of the entire business, prioritize when things get busy, and step in to solve problems, all at the drop of a hat. When the manager is gone typically the bartender is next in command. A smart manager respects the bartender's judgment, allowing him or her to make those decisions that directly affect the bar operation. Leadership and the ability to make on-the-spot decisions are critical attributes of a good bartender.
- ***The bartender is a role model.*** As a representative of the bar or restaurant, the bartender's style and personality should reflect the type of business it is. But the rest of the staff should also be able to look up to the person who runs the bar. Ethics and honesty start at the top so this is one of your most important positions to fill. Since bartenders handle so much cash, there is a built-in temptation to steal. You want an employee who would not even consider stealing, and will model this exemplary behavior to others.
- ***The bartender knows how to mix a drink.*** Ironically this is not at the top of the priority list when most owners are asked what their prerequisites are for hiring a bartender. Some owners prefer to "hire character, not experience," then train the person to do things "their way." Others hire only those individuals who have had formal training at a bartending school. Still others promote from within their ranks; this is the norm in most national chains. But as master bartender

Dale DeGroff points out, "A bartender must know at least as much as the customers about the products he [or she] serves. And there are some very sophisticated customers out there." In addition the bartender follows the recipes, playing by the rules of portion control and presentation. There are no unnecessarily "stiff" drinks (containing more alcohol than normal) for friends or bigger tips.

- ***The bartender pays attention to detail.*** This includes everything from correctly cutting and storing garnishes, to cleaning up along the way, to keeping up with glass-cleaning, to maintaining a well-organized backbar and anticipating such needs as more ice and replacements for the well. (The use of a **barback** helps greatly here, but the lack of one does not excuse a messy workspace.) Another critical detail, especially on busy nights, is keeping up with the billing, which means preparing the check for each round of drinks as it is ordered.
- ***The bartender is imaginative and fun.*** Complacency kills the natural liveliness of a bar. Good bartenders make things happen by doing a little marketing at the point of sale, chatting knowledgeably about wines sold by the glass, and recommending something to a customer who is unsure about what to order. A good bartender has a sense of ownership about his or her station and what happens there. The bartender is confident enough to prepare a drink in front of the guest, and is able to add some good-natured flair for the customer's benefit. The bartender also should be interested enough in the profession to keep up on trends and make suggestions for recipes and improvements.

The Barback

A barback typically relieves the bartender of all chores except pouring the drinks and handling the customers and the cash register. A barback may be responsible for any or all of the following tasks: setting up the bar; preparing garnishes, special mixes, and syrups; filling ice bins; washing glassware and utensils; maintaining supplies of towels, napkins, picks, straws, stir sticks, and matches; keeping bar surfaces and ashtrays clean; washing fixtures; and mopping floors. The barback is also a *runner* or *gofer,* who goes for liquors, beers, wines, and other supplies as needed by the bartender. Often a barback is an apprentice bartender and may serve beer or mix simple drinks under the bartender's supervision. In short a barback program is an excellent way to always have people in training for bartending positions.

The Server

Beverage service at tables, whether in a cocktail lounge or in a dining room, is handled by waiters or waitresses, a group collectively referred to as *servers.* Servers record the customers' drink orders, transmit them to the bartender, pick up the drinks, serve the customers, present the tab, and collect payment. Servers also keep

THE UNITED STATES BARTENDERS GUILD

In Europe the food-and-beverage-service industries have long been treated like professions rather than jobs. The United Kingdom (UK) has had a Bartenders Guild since 1933, and a U.S. "chapter" of the organization was formed in California in 1948. In 1961 the U.S. group was granted a charter as the United States Bartenders Guild (USBG) by the International Bartenders' Association (IBA). The Guild's mission is to bring together journeymen bartenders who have a genuine interest in raising the professionalism of the industry. An individual must apply for membership, be sponsored by an existing member, and undergo a rigorous peer-review process that includes current USBG members observing the applicant at work. Check the group's web site (www.usbg.org) for more information. The UK Bartenders Guild web site (www.ukbg.co.uk) is also worth a look.

In a small pub or club the bartender might seem like a one-person show, performing each and every task behind the bar. In larger operations, there may be several bartenders and one or more helpers, known as **barbacks.** These are often apprentice bartenders whose job is to assist the bartender (see below). In the biggest bars the staff may be organized with a *head bartender* who has the overall responsibility for the bar function and acts as the supervisor for the other bar personnel. The head bartender may also participate in hiring and training new bar employees and in teaching cocktail servers how to describe drinks to customers, how to transmit orders, how to garnish drinks, and how to use the special vocabulary of the bar.

the serving areas clean and return empty glasses to the bar. In heavy-volume bar lounges servers may also help to prepare drinks by putting ice in glasses and adding garnishes. Sometimes servers use the cash-register systems to ring up their own tabs; in other places the bartender does this. Like the bartender, the server is also a host and a promoter. A few basic requirements for table servers include a pleasant personality, a neat and attractive appearance, poise, and a mind for detail. Serving personnel must be able to deal with both customers and bartenders pleasantly and efficiently. Being alert and observant is also key, whether it involves deciding if a customer has had too much to drink or spying a chipped or soiled glass before it gets to the table. But make no mistake: This is a sales job and is not appropriate for a shy, insecure, and/or uncommunicative person. Bar and restaurant owners worldwide debate ideas for how to maximize a server's ability to sell the customer any type of drink, from a single dry Martini, to a fine bottle of Bordeaux. Remember these two critical points:

- The server must actually *offer* cocktails, wine, or beer to every table. As elementary as it sounds, *failure to ask for the sale* is the principal reason that a sale

ALL I REALLY NEED TO KNOW I LEARNED BARTENDING

Everything I really need to know about how to exist in this world, personal or business, I learned bartending. This knowledge was shared with me by owners, managers, salesmen, waitresses, waiters, bartenders, and customers. Most of these teachers were successful in life's everyday challenges. These tips you cannot spend, they are the tips you keep for life:

Give everyone a fair shot.
If you haven't anything nice to say, don't say it.
Use the BEST premium products and you'll be the BEST.
Serve.
Be the solution to the problem, not part of the problem.
Don't drink and drive, don't let others.
Respect salesmen, you're one.
Don't take sides. You'll make two enemies.
Be NEAT.
Wear a clean shirt every day.
Don't cheat or steal.
Smile!
Keep your hands and fingernails clean.
Use Mr., Sir, or Ms. when talking to strangers.
Don't be a part of a rumor.
Keep your space clean.
Don't waste.
Be on time.
Help others when they're busy.
Don't use the easy way. Use the right way.
Don't give up. Follow your dream.

Courtesy of *Bartender* magazine.

is not made. And remember, there are numerous opportunities during every guest's visit when a selling suggestion is appropriate. A good training program should help servers learn these important cues.

- The server must make it known to customers that he or she is happy to *assist* them in selecting a beverage. Again, training gives your server these skills, which builds their confidence and improves your business. At the very least good bar service requires a basic knowledge of a broad array of drinks and some variations, so the server can pin down the customer's exact preferences: Does he want his Martini with an olive or a lemon twist? Does she want her Sour straight up or on the rocks? The best cocktail server's drink knowledge is almost as extensive as a bartender's. A server may even mix drinks to allow the bartender to take a break.

In many restaurants waiters and waitresses serve both food and drinks, including wine by the bottle, with the meal. Servers must be able to open a wine bottle properly, carry out the rituals of wine service, and answer questions about wines, specialty drinks, and recipes.

Like bartenders, most servers are actively involved in whatever control system management uses to keep track of beverages. Whether you call them orders, checks, or drink tabs servers literally "keep tabs" on what has been ordered and allow the payments to be recorded on the cash register. Carrying out check routines quickly, accurately, and honestly is an essential part of the server's job.

The Wine Steward or Sommelier

Fine restaurants that feature elegant service may have a management-level employee who handles the ordering and serving of wine. The **wine steward** (also called the **cellarmaster**, *winemaster, wine captain,* or *wine waiter,* all terms applying to both sexes) presents the wine list at the table, makes recommendations, discusses wines with customers, and takes care of serving the wines (see Figure 12.3). On busy evenings, this is a huge help to the rest of the wait staff.

The image of the stuffy, tuxedo-clad wine steward has changed, as has the job itself. Today's wine professional focuses on guest service: refilling water and wineglasses, setting up and replacing glassware, asking how the appetizers tasted, and generally keeping up a dialogue with customers. The "expert" status of wine waiters has given them an undeserved reputation for arrogance when this certainly does not have to be the case. One of the main functions of this job is in fact to translate an esoteric subject that continues to intimidate some guests, thereby making it fun and approachable. To that end it's important to simplify terminology as needed, and to make eye contact with *all* the people at a table, not just the one who's ordering the wine. The job also involves long hours and quite a bit of movement, on the floor, in the storeroom or cellar, behind the bar, at banquets and private parties.

FIGURE 12.3 Opening the wine bottles is just one of the responsibilities of the wine steward. Courtesy of PhotoDisc/Getty Images.

In addition to being part of the serving staff, a well-qualified wine waiter can become an integral part of the management team, who can do any or all of the following:

- Create a wine list that fits your atmosphere and menu.
- Deal with suppliers and importers and order wine.
- Negotiate exclusive deals to carry certain wines in your market.
- Control and keep inventory of the cellar or wine-storage area.
- Make purchasing decisions to maximize profits, in some situations this includes buying wines to store for future years' lists.

- Train your servers and other staff members in wine appreciation.
- Orchestrate and help publicize tastings, wine dinners, seminars, and other wine-related events for your business.

In some hospitality businesses this person is the expert on beverages in general: wines and aperitifs, cocktails and after-dinner drinks, even coffees and teas. A new generation of young, college-educated wine lovers has breathed new life into the profession. Some have spent time working in vineyards or for wine importers or distributors. Others have learned as apprentices or as serious hobbyists who decided to impart their love of the history and complexity of wine to others. They enjoy discovering wines from unexpected places, searching for new favorites from "undiscovered" vineyards, and seeking out good values to pass on to guests.

Those who are true connoisseurs of wines and wine service merit the title **sommelier** (SUM-el-yay or SOHM-ee-yay). This is the French word for *wine steward,* but it has come to be associated with excellence in this field. Sommeliers are usually found in upscale restaurants featuring expensive wines, extensive wine lists, and cellars containing thousands of bottles. This position is not an endeavor to be taken lightly; it is a full-time profession that requires ongoing education and a passion for the wine industry. It is attracting a growing number of people. Including both salary and tips sought-after wine experts can make from $50,000 to $100,000 a year.

Career sommeliers can study for the prestigious Master Sommelier (MS) Diploma, awarded by the Guild of Sommeliers of London, England. There are just over 100 Master Sommeliers, about half of them in the United States.

When you see articles in trade publications from authors with the designation MS after their names, it means Master Sommelier. Taking only the introductory course is sufficient for many wine-sales positions, which allows the designation *certified sommelier.* Only about a dozen U.S. women have joined the prestigious MS ranks, but it is important to note that more women are taking the advanced and masters-level courses of the three-level program.

The traditional symbols associated with sommeliers are a tasting cup called a **tastevin** (TAT-van or TASS-tah-van) that hangs from their neck on a cord or ribbon, a cellar key, and sometimes a leather apron. Occasionally a more modest enterprise may use these trappings and bestow the title of sommelier, cellarmaster, or even *wine director* on its most wine-knowledgeable employee to help create an upscale image. Although not everyone with these titles has an expert's level of wine knowledge, they must at least be thoroughly familiar with their own wine lists and competent in helping guests to select wines appropriate to the food they order.

An interesting new position that has emerged in the *beverage-expert* category is that of *beer sommelier,* for pubs or restaurants that specialize in exotic brews. The Four Points Sheraton Hotel in Los Angeles, for instance, pours 50 beers from at least 10 countries in its fine-dining restaurant called the Palm Grill. Beer sommelier Carlos Solis supervises tableside beer service and arranges beer seminars, tastings, and dinners. The menu includes beer recommendations for foods. If you cannot decide on a single brew, you can order six brews, a 3-ounce taste of each, for $9. Little wonder that half of the dining room's beverage profit now comes from beer sales. Customers enjoy the knowledgeable service and the attention to detail.

MICKEY MOUSE, MASTER SOMMELIER. . . ?

The greatest concentration of certified sommeliers in the world can be found in Orlando, Florida, at the Walt Disney World complex. More dining options are available on WDW's 47-square-mile property than in all the rest of the Orlando area. With more than $2 billion in annual food-and-beverage sales, the Disney complex is Florida's premier on-premise facility. Nationally it is second only to the Marriott Corporation. This success gives WDW bar managers incredible leverage in terms of pricing and obtaining some of the rarest and most strictly allocated wines in the world.

Even with high chairs dotting the dining rooms of the Walt Disney World hotels and restaurants, beverage sales account for about 25 percent of profits. Of this figure one-half is beer sales, but wine service is a top priority at the table-service restaurants. More than 200 certified sommeliers work here and many are studying for advanced-level spots.

Security Positions

Certain types of bars and nightspots that have no need for sommeliers may instead have a need for crowd control. This may come in the form of a doorman or door person. This person is expected to keep order if there are long lines to get in, to ask for customers' identification (and firmly but politely enforce a dress code or refuse to admit underage people), and to collect a **cover charge** at the front door. The cover charge is a fee for admittance to the bar, and is sometimes given to or split with the band if there's live music. A door person may perform small but significant acts of courtesy: opening doors for customers, walking unescorted female patrons to their vehicles, calling for taxis, and keeping the lobby area looking tidy. A door person may also be required to keep an overall headcount of incoming patrons or to fill out incident reports if customers get angry when they're turned away at the front door.

Security needs may also call for hiring one or more **bouncers**, who are generally fit (or somewhat tough-looking) men whose job it is to protect both bar patrons and employees from unruly behavior. Although the very word *bouncer* comes from ancient words that mean "to thump or strike," you want your bouncers to provide a sense of safety and order, not throw their weight around like all-star wrestlers. Legally a bouncer has no more authority than a private citizen so you must make the rules for this employee very clear. Exactly what is the bouncer supposed to do with disruptive customers? Does he ask them to quiet down or to leave the bar? At what point can the bouncer physically eject customers from the bar? How does the bouncer handle patrons who start a fight? At what point should police be called?

The bouncer should be impartial and professional, with the same people skills and ethics as any of your other staff members. Your hiring process should include a background check of these job candidates. Some bar owners have noticed that dressing the bouncer well—not in jeans and T-shirts—adds credibility to his image. Drinking on duty is strictly forbidden in this, and most other, bar jobs. The bouncer is on the lookout for disruptive conduct, but he should never use unnecessary or excessive force to eject a patron. You might ask the local police department to come in and talk with your security staff, to share advice about how to diffuse tense situations and when to call police.

Beverage-Management Positions

High-volume establishments, large hotels, private clubs, and restaurants with extensive wine cellars may have a person in charge of all wine and liquor purchasing, storage, receiving, requisitioning, and inventory control. This person must know a great deal about wines and spirits, the wine and spirits market, and the entire beverage operation. It is a position of considerable responsibility, and the official job title is typically **beverage steward.**

In very large operations the beverage steward may work for the *beverage manager* or *beverage director.* This is often a senior-management position, part of the team that runs a corporate operation: a hotel, a large nightclub, a high-volume restaurant, or an entire hotel or restaurant chain. The beverage director is in charge of hiring, training, and supervising all beverage-related personnel; purchasing all beverages and beverage equipment; establishing and maintaining inventory and control systems; setting standards; and making policy on matters relating to beverage operation.

The more sophisticated the corporation, the greater the mark that a good beverage director can leave on it. One of the best in the industry is Tony Abou-Ganim. At the Bellagio Resort and Casino in Las Vegas, Nevada, he oversaw 22 bars, 160 bartenders, and about 60 apprentices with an annual beverage-sales volume of $60 million. Abou-Ganim has all but banished the bar gun (or cobra gun), insisting instead that freshly squeezed juices be used in all drinks. He is passionate about using only fresh, hand-cut garnishes and chilled glassware. When you order an in-room cocktail when you stay at the Bellagio, it will be shaken right in your room, not at a hotel bar and delivered 10 or 20 minutes later. These might seem minor, but this kind of attention to detail might be the reason why, even in its first year of business, the Bellagio did a record $50 million in bar sales! (Abou-Ganim now operates his own consulting firm specializing in bar staff training and cocktail development.)

A beverage director is either part of, or reports to, top management. In some large organizations responsibility for food-and-beverage service is combined into one position called the *food-and-beverage director.* Such management positions require several years of industry experience, preferably firsthand experience in each area of responsibility. A beverage director must also have management training and/

or experience. This is a very public position so he or she must have the appearance, personality, poise, and wardrobe that are generally associated with management positions. This will ensure credibility when dealing with other management personnel, within or outside the company.

Even in a big hotel with multiple food-and-beverage outlets, each individual bar or restaurant usually has a *manager* who is in charge of all aspects of its operation. In a small business the owner is often the manager. If not, the manager is a surrogate, or stand-in, for the owner, running the show on the owner's behalf, whether the owner is an individual or a corporation. The owner sets the goals, establishes policies, and gives the manager the authority and responsibility for carrying them out. Within this framework the manager must make any and all decisions necessary to running a profitable operation.

It takes a great deal of savvy to run a bar, and not everyone can do it well. The January 2000 issue of *Restaurant Hospitality* magazine included the following list of qualities that you will find in the best bar managers:

- ***Business training.*** Well grounded in working knowledge of how business operates, their role in the business, and how each aspect of the business works together cohesively.
- ***Market knowledge.*** No business operates in a vacuum. A good manager knows his or her market well, what the competition is doing, and how to respond to competitive activity.
- ***Desire to lead.*** An effective manager is a leader. He or she easily grasps what has to be done, sees how it can be done, believes it can be done, and can energize the staff to get it done.
- ***Maturity and stability.*** It can be stressful working in a service industry with a young, socially active staff, a variety of guests, and a fiercely competitive business environment. The best manager can gracefully withstand the countless distractions and temptations.
- ***Financial wisdom.*** The best managers spend the business' money as it if were their own, with prudence and an eye for value.
- ***Street smarts.*** If a manager exerts too much control, the customers or staff members won't stick around. If a manager exerts too little, the place runs out of control. A good manager knows how to walk the fine line between the two.
- ***Legal knowledge.*** Running a bar involves some familiarity with liquor laws, health and safety codes, fire regulations, fair employment practices, and more. And that's just to stay in compliance! A good manager makes these topics into a continuing self-education program.

A manager's overall responsibilities may include hiring and firing; training, scheduling, and supervising personnel; forecasting and budgeting; purchasing beverages and related supplies or requisitioning them from a corporate commissary; maintaining records; carrying out control systems (the manager typically has the only key to the storeroom); handling cash and payroll; maintaining quality; and promoting the enterprise and the merchandise. All of this must be done in a way that meets or exceeds the owner's profit goals. (We'll discuss many of these activities in greater detail in later chapters.)

A good manager keeps everything running smoothly day to day. This means resolving staff problems, dealing with difficult customers, coping with emergencies, and often pitching in to do someone else's job. Interestingly, as of this writing there is a lawsuit pending by managers of a large, casual-dining chain. The suit claims that the restaurants are chronically understaffed, which requires the managers to do many hourly labor duties, such as washing dishes and cleaning; thus, managers work far longer hours than their salaries compensate them for. This should give you a sense of the wide range of duties that managers find themselves tackling. Their typical day is crowded with major and minor decisions, as well as new and different situations and challenges.

A manager should be well trained in every aspect of the enterprise and experienced enough at all jobs in order to be able to substitute in any one of them. He or she also should be able to relate to the people who do these jobs daily. A manager must be the kind of person who can make decisions easily and deal effectively with all kinds of people, both patrons and staff. Essential personal qualities are a good memory, a cool head, a positive attitude, sensitivity to people, leadership ability, self-confidence, and honesty.

HIRING AND SCHEDULING

Now that you've have learned what is expected of each major bar-related job, you can adapt the information by adding more detail about the specifics of your bar. For example, will your bartenders be working a service bar or public bar? Free pour, measured pour, or metered gun? How many minimum drinks per hour must they serve? What kind of person will maintain your image? This kind of information belongs in the *job description,* a written blueprint of what is required in each job.

Developing Job Descriptions

To create job descriptions you might take a hint from large organizations and perform a **job analysis.** This involves a couple of steps. First the **task analysis** lists each small task performed as part of a particular job: its purpose, how it is done, and what equipment and skills are required to do it. Then the **job specifications** are written. This list, identifies the knowledge, skills, and/or abilities a person must have to perform the tasks. Then these lists are combined in writing—it is important that they be written—to make up the job description.

The same technique can profitably be used in any size operation. A side benefit: Examining each job in such detail often reveals aspects of it that you had not thought of before. For example, is it too much work for one person, or is there not enough work to fill a shift? Are there ways to combine or divide jobs? Are there gaps in coverage? Do responsibilities overlap? Should you hire skilled people or train them on the job?

The next step is to list the qualifications for each job. Think about:

- Skills and aptitudes
- Physical characteristics
- Health requirements
- Mental ability and attitude
- Age requirements

The latter qualification is included because state laws prohibit underage persons from handling liquor, even if they do not drink or sell it.

The final step is to combine the data from your job analysis with your list of personal requirements to write a concise job description, as shown in Figures 12.4 and 12.5. In addition to duties, tasks, and qualifications, the job description should include the scope of the job, the workstation or area, the supervisor's title, and any positions supervised. The job description gives you a solid outline of points to cover during your employment interviews. It also informs an applicant of all aspects of the job so that he or she understands it fully before agreeing to take it. Used consistently, the job description will ensure that all of your employees have the same idea of what you expect from them.

Planning a Staff Schedule

How do you know how many employees you will need, both overall, and for specific time periods? It is impossible to staff a beverage operation without planning a detailed schedule. This means matching the days and hours of business and the peaks and valleys of customer demand with work shifts that make sense to employees and to your budget. A chart for each day of the week you are open, showing each hour that you must staff, is an indispensable planning tool (Figure 12.6). On the chart you can plot the highs and lows of customer demand, along with personnel needed to handle the volume at each hour of the day. Many would-be employees are looking for a full-time job with full shifts. Regular part-time jobs (fewer full shifts or several shorter shifts) are attractive to students, moonlighters, and others who do not depend entirely on your wages for their living, and they can help you deal with peak demand periods. Eight-hour shifts should include scheduled breaks for meals and short rest periods. Breaks should be scheduled during periods of low volume if possible; if not, your schedule must include someone who can take over the job during the break. An experienced server, for example, can tend bar for 15 minutes; or breaks can be staggered where there are several bartenders. Personnel on full shifts may have periods of time when there is little to do. You may be able to schedule tasks from other jobs during these periods, such as purchasing or restocking, training new employees, developing promotional

BARTENDER JOB DESCRIPTION

Description:

Bartenders work behind the bars and in back-of-the-house areas. They prepare and sell drinks to Cocktail Hostesses and customers. They prep their work area with several functions, measure and prepare drinks according to receipe, and make cash register transactions.

Bartenders must handle credit card tabs, note spills and overrings, and address the cash register immediately after preparing an order. They accept tips, but do not allow tips to remain on the bar or do not exchange tips or change with cash register monies prior to the end of their shift. Bartenders perform cleanup and register checkout functions at the end of their shift. They also stock products and supplies.

They perform "silent selling" and "upselling" techniques and inform customers of club activities and promotions. They serve customers by using "experience time" goals and create an upbeat, friendly environment in their work area. They must function as a team member with Barbacks, other Bartenders, and Cocktail Hostesses. They must learn and use alcohol management techniques and advise the management staff of intoxicated or unruly customers.

Due to the high level of customer interaction, the Bartender must perform all duties with great emphasis on cleanliness, personability, professionalism, and service. Bartenders are strongly encouraged to work up individual "Showtimes"—complete with costumes—to be performed throughout the evening with the Programmer.

Functions:

Prepare cocktails per recipe and serve per specifications.
Prep, clean, and stock work area—before, during, and after shift.
Accept credit cards, cash, and coupons for products.
Perform cash register functions, and checkout accurately.
Perform "silent selling" and "upselling" functions.
Monitor customers for intoxication, rowdiness, or need for drinks.
Have "Showtime" mentality.

Supervisors:

Bar Manager.
Management Staff.

FIGURE 12.4 A bartender job description developed after analyzing individual tasks.

BARBACK JOB DESCRIPTION

Description:

Barbacks work behind the bar areas and in back-of-the-house areas. Barbacks support the work of Bartenders by performing tasks of fruit cutting, juice making, filling of ice bins, removal of trash, and preparation of "speciality" cocktails. They have several opening and closing duties involving product stocking and cleanliness, and assist in keeping their work area clean through operating hours.

Barbacks do not accept tips or money from customers and do not handle transactions or register functions. They assist in the preparation of the Liquor Requisition form and advise the Bar Manager of needed supplies and products..

Barbacks only prepare frozen cocktails. They wash glassware and utensils, and supply the Bartenders with needed liquor, beer, and supplies. Because of the extensive customer contact, Barbacks must work with courtesy, energy, and speed. Barbacks are strongly encouraged to work up individual "Showtime" routines–complete with costumes–to be performed throughout the evening with the Programmer.

Functions:

Set-up the bars for operation.
Clean and mop the bars during operation and at the end of operation.
Stock glassware and product.
Change out condiments and juices for the Bartenders.
Prepare club "specialty" cocktails.
Monitor customers for intoxication, rowdiness, or need for drinks.
Have "Showtime" mentality.

Supervisors:

Bar Manager.
Management Staff.
(Directed by Bartenders during operating hours.)

Uniform:

Black work shoes or coaching shoes, black pants, white button-down oxford shirt (long sleeve), blue apron, blue bowtie, name tag, three club buttons, one button of choice, pen, lighter, and a smile.

Grooming:

"All-American scrubbed-up" look for hair. Clean and neat hair, nails, and skin. For men, no beards or earrings.

FIGURE 12.5 A barback job description developed after analyzing individual tasks.

BAR SCHEDULE

	10 a.m.	11 a.m.	12 p.m.	1 p.m.	2 p.m.	3 p.m.	4 p.m.	5 p.m.	6 p.m.	7 p.m.	8 p.m.	9 p.m.	10 p.m.	11 p.m.	12 a.m.	1 a.m.
Bar manager						XXXX	XXXX	XXXX	XXXX	XXXX	XXXX	XXXX	XXXX	XXXX	XXXX	
Asst. bar manager	XXXX	XXXX	XXXX	XXXX	XXXX	XXXX	XXXX	XXXX	XXXX							
Bartender	XXXX	XXXX	XXXX	XXXX	XXXX	XXXX	XXXX	XXXX								
Bartender							XX	XXXX	XXXX	XXXX	XXXX	XXXX	XXXX			
Bartender									XXXX	XXXX	XXXX	XXXX	XXXX	XXXX	XXXX	
Bar back	XXXX	XXXX	XXXX	XXXX	XXXX	XXXX	XXXX	XXXX								
Bar back									XXXX	XXXX	XXXX	XXXX	XXXX	XXXX	XXXX	
Cocktail server		XXXX	XXXX	XXXX	XXXX	XXXX	XXXX	XXXX								
Cocktail server			XXXX	XXXX	XXXX											
Cocktail server							XX	XXXX	XXXX	XXXX	XXXX	XXXX	XXXX			
Cocktail server									XXXX	XXXX	XXXX	XXXX	XXXX	XXXX	XXXX	
Sales per hour	0	0	$100	$250	$250	$200	$150	$250	$400	$350	$400	$400	$400	$400	$200	$100

FIGURE 12.6 A staff schedule for a busy bar with foodservice on a typical weekday.

materials, and answering the phone. (If yours is a state in which employees are unionized check with the union shop steward or the local union office to see if this is allowed.) Another way to handle peak volume without idle time at both ends is to stagger shifts.

A manager's work hours must be scheduled, just like everyone else's. The day is past when managers will work 80 hours a week—unless they are owners, too. Someone must be in charge in the manager's absence—an assistant manager or head bartender, for example—and the detail of such duties and extent of responsibilities must be carefully worked out on a job description. When determining the number of bar employees needed, you may find the following approximate figures useful:

- A good cocktail server can handle 40 customers, or 10 tables of 4.
- A good restaurant server can handle beverage orders for four or five lunch or dinner tables, along with foodservice.
- A bartender can pour 60 to 150 drinks an hour depending on dexterity, experience, types of drinks, method of pour, and efficiency of bar design.

Job descriptions and a tentative schedule form a sound, well-organized basis for recruiting and selecting the right people for the right jobs. For a small operation, it seems like a lot of paperwork, expensive in terms of time and effort. Whether or not they are formalized in writing, the same careful planning and analysis should take place. When hiring for a large enterprise, the written process is essential.

The Job Interview

The in-person interview of prospective employees should have two phases. First you as an interviewer should clearly explain the job being offered, using the job description as a basis for discussion. As a result both you and the applicant should be able to judge whether he or she has either the required skills or the capacity to develop them quickly enough to fill your needs.

The other phase of the interview should amplify the data on the application. Your initial probe of the information should have included a basic identity confirmation and criminal-background check. Then ask the following questions:

- Are there gaps in past employment? If so, why, and are the reasons good ones?
- What did this person like or dislike about previous jobs? Are there parallels in your job?
- If there are no former employers listed as references, ask why not.
- Would there be any transportation problems, any conflicts of schedule (such as school classes or the spouse's schedule)?
- Are there any difficulties with basic skills required for the job (such as handwriting or math)?
- Is there any history of frequent or chronic illness?

Unfortunately there is a fairly long list of topics that, in some cases, would be sources of conversation and points of natural curiosity in getting to know another human being that in employment interviews are strictly forbidden for a variety of legal reasons. These topics are listed in Figure 12.7.

What *can* you discuss in the personal interview? Ask the applicant about his or her skills, previous work experience, and reasons for applying for this particular position. Managers of small operations often find themselves too busy to sit and talk with applicants so they rely instead on intuition or even hiring based strictly on the written application. However the oral interview is where the applicant's personality and potential can best be assessed. The way a person responds to questions will tell you whether he or she is friendly, open, intelligent, and alert—and interested enough to ask *you* a few questions as well. Nonverbal clues are also important. The way a person sits, stands, moves, gestures, and speaks can indicate his or her capacity for speed and dexterity, as well as confidence and poise. Also of course, a personal interview is essential in judging appearance and the ability to relate to others.

Don't Ask	Why/Exception
Age/Date of Birth	There's no reason to ask about age unless you can prove that the job requires the person to be a certain age (for example, to qualify for licensing or for driving a car to pick up products or make sales calls). You may ask, "Are you eligible to obtain a driver's license?"
Gender	The only job this counts for is restroom attendant. Don't think of men as the sales staff and women as the service agents. There are lots of men who are great service people and plenty of women who are very successful salespeople.
Language spoken	In a biligual community it may be important for you to have bilingual staff. But where English is the community's single language, you may not eliminate an applicant because of a slight non-interfering accent. You may, however, require that applicants demonstrate ability to communicate effectively.
Parents' name/Maiden name	May reveal nationality or marital status.
Homeowner or renter	By asking this, you might be perceived to be discriminating against low-income people, who cannot afford to buy houses.
Number of children, child care	This is confidential information; you have no right to this information prior to hiring a person.
Club memberships	May reveal religious affiliation or ethnic background.
Emergency contact information	You have no right to this information prior to hiring a person.
Recent photo–height/weight	May reveal national origin, race, or physical disability.
Health status/Physical exam	May reveal physical disability. Physical disability must not be discussed until after hiring. You may ask if the candidate is able to lift a certain amount of weight, or sit or stand for long periods of time, if this is a requirement of the job.
Eye/Hair color	May reveal national origin or race of the applicant.
Arrest records	Don't ask. You may ask whether the person is eligible to be bonded, since this might be a requirement for some of your positions.
Citizenship/Place of birth	May reveal national origin of the applicant.
Military service	Don't ask how an individual was discharged from the service. You may ask about the types of training and education received while serving in the military.

FIGURE 12.7 Taboo topics during a job interview. Source: *Outfront* magazine, Fall 2000. Courtesy of Manufacturers Agents Association for the Foodservice Industry (MAFSI), Atlanta, Georgia.

The I-9 Form

For those people who are hired you have three business days from their date of hire to complete an *I-9 form*. This is the federal Employment Eligibility Verification form that lists the correct documents used to establish identity and eligibility to work in the United States (see Figure 12.8). It is your responsibility to obtain these forms from the Immigration and Naturalization Service (INS). The employee fills out and signs the first (top) section of the form; the employer fills out and signs the remainder.

You must keep a completed and/or updated I-9 form for each employee in your files for at least three years (or for one year after termination of employment) and be prepared to show these to an INS inspector. If you have hired someone whose documents do not prove eligibility or if you have failed to keep I-9 forms on file as required, you will be subject to a fine for each employee concerned. INS inspectors may check your files at any time after giving three days' notice. A detailed "Handbook for Employers" further explaining these requirements and employers' obligations is available from any INS office. Studying this hand book is well worth your time and effort as you plan your hiring program.

Food-and-beverage establishments are the category of operations most frequently fined for failure to comply with I-9 requirements, which raises a good point. A smart bar owner is organized about the way he or she collects the incoming paperwork associated with any job. For example you are legally required (by Title VII, Civil Rights Act of 1964) to keep all the written applications on file for six months after a job is filled or an applicant is rejected. Another federal law, the Age Discrimination in Employment Act of 1967, requires that applications be kept for a full year. Protect yourself! Don't just throw out these types of paperwork, and adopt a system to keep them secure and meet the federal requirements.

TRAINING THE STAFF

The first part of the manager's personnel responsibility, explaining jobs and assigning responsibilities, begins right after employees are hired. Every person must learn exactly what is expected of them: to whom they must report, whom they are supposed to work with or supervise, how to use the equipment and follow the house routines, what the menu includes, how to report work hours, whether tips are shared and with whom, and much more. It is quite a lot for a new person to absorb. Yet many a manager puts a new employee right to work, counting only on a bit of coaching as mistakes are made and questions asked. Often the coaching is left to another employee, who might resent the extra burden and who may not be the world's best teacher.

Department of Homeland Security
U.S. Citizenship and Immigration Services

OMB No. 1615-0047; Expires 03/31/07

Employment Eligibility Verification

Please read instructions carefully before completing this form. The instructions must be available during completion of this form. ANTI-DISCRIMINATION NOTICE: It is illegal to discriminate against work eligible individuals. Employers CANNOT specify which document(s) they will accept from an employee. The refusal to hire an individual because of a future expiration date may also constitute illegal discrimination.

Section 1. Employee Information and Verification. To be completed and signed by employee at the time employment begins.

Print Name: Last	First	Middle Initial	Maiden Name
Address *(Street Name and Number)*		Apt. #	Date of Birth *(month/day/year)*
City	State	Zip Code	Social Security #

I am aware that federal law provides for imprisonment and/or fines for false statements or use of false documents in connection with the completion of this form.

I attest, under penalty of perjury, that I am (check one of the following):
- ☐ A citizen or national of the United States
- ☐ A Lawful Permanent Resident (Alien #) A ____________
- ☐ An alien authorized to work until ________
(Alien # or Admission #) ____________

Employee's Signature	Date *(month/day/year)*

Preparer and/or Translator Certification. *(To be completed and signed if Section 1 is prepared by a person other than the employee.) I attest, under penalty of perjury, that I have assisted in the completion of this form and that to the best of my knowledge the information is true and correct.*

Preparer's/Translator's Signature	Print Name
Address *(Street Name and Number, City, State, Zip Code)*	Date *(month/day/year)*

Section 2. Employer Review and Verification. To be completed and signed by employer. Examine one document from List A OR examine one document from List B and one from List C, as listed on the reverse of this form, and record the title, number and expiration date, if any, of the document(s).

List A	OR	List B	AND	List C
Document title: ________		________		________
Issuing authority: ________		________		________
Document #: ________		________		________
Expiration Date *(if any)*: ________		________		________
Document #: ________				
Expiration Date *(if any)*: ________				

CERTIFICATION - I attest, under penalty of perjury, that I have examined the document(s) presented by the above-named employee, that the above-listed document(s) appear to be genuine and to relate to the employee named, that the employee began employment on *(month/day/year)* ________ **and that to the best of my knowledge the employee is eligible to work in the United States. (State employment agencies may omit the date the employee began employment.)**

Signature of Employer or Authorized Representative	Print Name	Title
Business or Organization Name	Address *(Street Name and Number, City, State, Zip Code)*	Date *(month/day/year)*

Section 3. Updating and Reverification. To be completed and signed by employer.

A. New Name *(if applicable)*	B. Date of rehire *(month/day/year) (if applicable)*

C. If employee's previous grant of work authorization has expired, provide the information below for the document that establishes current employment eligibility.

Document Title: ________ Document #: ________ Expiration Date (if any): ________

I attest, under penalty of perjury, that to the best of my knowledge, this employee is eligible to work in the United States, and if the employee presented document(s), the document(s) I have examined appear to be genuine and to relate to the individual.

Signature of Employer or Authorized Representative	Date *(month/day/year)*

NOTE: This is the 1991 edition of the Form I-9 that has been rebranded with a current printing date to reflect the recent transition from the INS to DHS and its components.

Form I-9 (Rev. 05/31/05)Y Page 2

FIGURE 12.8 Form I-9: Employment Eligibility Verification. The back of the form contains instructions for its use. Source: U.S. Department of Justice, Immigration, and Naturalization Services.

There are at least four good reasons for taking the time and effort to give employees a basic, all-inclusive orientation session before they start work:

- They will be able to work faster and with less confusion.
- They will feel more confident in their jobs, and this will be reflected in their attitude toward work and in the way they relate to your customers.
- They will more easily establish good relationships with coworkers.
- They will be more likely to stay if you ensure that they have a good experience from the very first day.

Some enterprises also develop an orientation manual to give to new employees. Certainly it is a sound idea to have all of the rules and information on paper so there is no possibility of misunderstanding or leaving something out. Make it modular, in notebook form, so that pages can be inserted or replaced as rules are added or changed. A completed form similar to the one shown in Figure 12.9 is the absolute minimum amount of written information for a new employee. In addition to job duties you can put information in the manual about vacation days, sick days, payroll, benefits, and other similar topics.

The Use of Uniforms

Orientation is the time to explain your dress code to employees, so we will discuss it here before moving on to specific types of on-the-job training. One of our pet peeves is not being able to tell the servers from the customers when you visit a bar or restaurant. Putting employees in uniform has many business benefits, and bar owners have devised cost-effective ideas that are almost as flexible as elastic waistbands! However, the quest for a uniform that fits the bar atmosphere, as well as employees of all shapes and sizes, can be challenging.

Owner-operators agree that attire has a psychological factor in job satisfaction and performance. It sends a positive message about professionalism even when the uniform itself is casual in style: A cool t-shirt or collared golf shirt with an interesting logo over a clean pair of blue jeans is often sufficient. But the use of uniforms is also a factor in the overall design and mood of the bar interior. An attractive uniform is a marketing tool. It fosters brand identity and colors the customers' first impressions of the server and the establishment.

Today there are uniform designers who take their jobs as seriously as any high-fashion designer. Uniform designers work with interior designers and owners to create the right combination of color and style that provides visual continuity and mirrors the bar's image and concept. Often the result is a classic style with custom accents, such as interesting ties, scarves, aprons, and belts. Employees are allowed to select from a palette of colors or several different separates, which makes them feel less like they've been "sentenced" to wear a prison uniform.

Uniforms not only have to look sharp but also be comfortable, durable, and easy to clean. Stretch fabrics, microfibers, and hydrophilic fabrics (often used in

TO OUR NEW EMPLOYEE:

Welcome!
We are glad you are joining us and hope you will enjoy working here.

Your hours are: ______________ Punch in and out on clock beside kitchen door.

Your days of work are: ____________________________

Your pay rate is: ____________ ($1\frac{1}{2}$ regular rate after 40 hours)

Payday is: ______________

Your supervisor is: __________________________________

You supervise: ______________________________________

You work with: ______________________________________

Dress: Conservative blue blouse, navy blue skirt or slacks, closed-toe shoes

Meals: You may buy your meals here at our discounted price.
You must eat on your own time.

Breaks: __________________________

Rules: Wash your hands as soon as you come to work. Make this a habit!
No smoking or drinking on the job.
Hair, nails, and clothing must be neat and clean.
Do not serve a minor any alcoholic beverage.
Do not serve an intoxicated person any alcoholic beverage.

Your duties are:

A menu, drink list, and wine list are attached. please study these. You will receive further personal orientation. Meantime, do not hesitate to ask questions.

FIGURE 12.9 A sample information handout for a new employee.

athletic wear) are popular. Cotton/poly blends (65-percent cotton, 35-percent polyester) have the feel and appearance of cotton, but they can last two or three times as long as all-cotton garments. Their colorfastness and wrinkle resistance also make them winners in foodservice.

Remember that shoes are part of the uniform. You might consider providing slip-resistant shoes for bartenders and servers since most employee accidents involve slipping. Many companies specialize in good-looking, hard-working work shoes for bar and restaurant wear. These shoes are fitted with traction for wet floors, reinforced (sometimes steel) toes for dropped knives or glassware, and antifatigue shock absorbers in the heels. The shoes are also "breathable," which keeps feet cool during long hours on the job.

All of this can be expensive but many of these items are now made overseas, thereby reducing costs, especially if they are bought in bulk. Depending on the type of bar, uniform budget, and amount of turnover, options range from paying for and issuing uniforms from head to toe, to providing only some of the uniform (for example a patterned hat and apron or a couple of t-shirts) and specifying the rest of the attire (such as a white dress shirt, black slacks, and black shoes). Some places give employees a clothing allowance or offer payment terms to enable them to deduct work-clothing purchases from paychecks. See the "Other Charges" discussion in in the "Compensation and Benefits" section on page 520 for elaboration on the federal rules about charging or reimbursing employees for uniform-related costs.

Bartender Training

There was a time when bartending was known as a way to earn some extra pocket money and, since most bartenders were men to meet women. While this might still be true it is also true that in many circles bartending has been elevated from a part-time job to a passionate profession—at least, among people who understand how to make a profit. As the Bellagio's former master mixologist Tony Abou-Ganim put it in the May 2002 issue of *Food Arts* magazine, "We don't have part-time bartenders working on other careers here."

However, with this added professionalism comes added responsibility. For managers this means more training and greater expectations of employees. For example a sharp bartender looking to improve his or her skills can take some cooking classes or, at least, spend time watching chefs. Courses in making sauces and pastry can be especially helpful because they involve the same kinds of precision that creating a drink recipe does. But any course that hones a person's knowledge about such topics as flavors, techniques, spices, use of kitchen equipment, menu or recipe development, and wine pairing can add to his or her skill set as a bar employee.

Some bars designate one person as the primary trainer for any new hire. The trainer should be an experienced employee with a positive attitude and a belief in your overall philosophy. You might set up a training system so that during the first two weeks on the job a newcomer works as a barback before graduating to bartender, or that he or she passes a test that combines written questions with a behind-the-bar demonstration of skills. You should test on an ongoing basis, not just during the first month on the job.

The success of Las Vegas's elegant Bellagio Resort and Casino, which has 22 bars and 160 bartenders, depends heavily on its well-trained bar staff. Training here is ongoing and is done onsite with the help of the beverage suppliers. Monthly classes are attended by 40 to 50 people, not just bartenders, but barbacks, servers, and porters. Although anyone on the hotel staff is welcome, the bar employees must dedicate 10 hours per year of their own time to attend these sessions.

During orientation each member of the Bellagio bar staff is issued a confidential recipe book. Its contents include more than 150 drink recipes (both classic and contemporary), drink terminology, historical facts about some of the drinks, and bartending tips, quotes, and advice culled from numerous sources. The resort also sponsors an in-house competition to create new cocktails, with dinners, trips, and coveted Las Vegas show tickets as prizes. As you might imagine, introducing a new cocktail in such an establishment is quite a feat and includes the following steps:

- Standardizing the drink recipe
- Pricing the drink
- Equipping the bars with ingredients and appliances (if applicable) to produce the drink
- Training the bartenders to use the equipment and ingredients to make the drink
- Reprinting the cocktail menus and otherwise advertising the "new" drink concoction
- Programming the computerized cash registers to track sales of the new drink
- Familiarizing the servers with the drink, including a taste of it, so that they can describe and sell it

Of course not every bar business has the need or the resources to train a small army of bar employees. For an establishment with fewer staff members we recommend an idea we first read about in the August 2002 issue of the trade publication *Sante*. "Bar Boot Camp" is a three-day training module designed around three full work shifts (about 7 hours each) for a bartender. Note that Days Two and Three take place during actual serving hours with real customers. The restaurant happens to be a chain, but the idea could be adapted to any type of bar business. The three days of training are outlined as follows:

- ***Day One.*** Review the service manual for the business, including the corporate identity and philosophy, style of service, and procedures for handling difficult customers. Take a first look at the wine list. Review a glossary of products, specialty items, and food descriptions. End the day with the trainees in the restaurant kitchen, identifying and "tasting their way through" as much of the menu as possible.
- ***Day Two.*** The trainees must arrive on time to learn about bar setup by being paired with experienced bartenders. The focus today is on maintaining a clean, well-organized workstation; learning what the par stocks are; where items are

stored and how to requisition them; opening and closing procedures; and so on. When actual service begins the trainees enter drink orders onto the computer system to become familiar with it. As business picks up the trainees will make drinks while the trainers take over at the computer. As time allows, it's back to the kitchen to review the Day One material; the shift ends at the bar, closing down for the shift.

- ***Day Three.*** The trainees are ready to work their first full shift from setup to closing, all under the direct observation of trainers or the bar manager. The manager is looking for customer interaction, product knowledge, "mechanics," neatness, a sense of organization, and of course speed—in short, will the trainee be able to represent the restaurant's bar business to its clientele? If the answer is yes they're put on the work schedule. If not, additional training is scheduled or perhaps the trainee is advised frankly that he or she did not make the cut.

Don't overlook what beverage suppliers may have to offer on the topic of training. They already train their own salespeople to sell their products, and in most cases they more than willing to participate in your staff training. For specialty products this can be incredibly helpful. There are even training programs for such ubiquitous beverages as beer. Anheuser-Busch has its "B-Lounge," a 45-foot motorcoach that serves as a mobile training facility for retailers and wholesalers. Among the topics covered are proper pouring and serving of beer, the importance of "fresh" beer, and some of the rich history of brewing.

Miller Brewing Company's instructional brochure, "The Perfect Glass of Beer," offers advice about pouring with a nod to consumer appeal and profitability, along with directions for cleaning lines and tapping kegs. Coors Brewing Company partners with the culinary programs at Metropolitan State College in Denver, Colorado, to offer classes at the Coors-owned Sandlot Brewery. Students get a look at the entire brewing process in a six-class course. With a lineup of all imported beers, LaBatt USA opened its "LaBatt USA Beer Academy" in 2002 in Arlington Heights, Illinois. LaBatt encourages retailers to send their key employees for a free one-day session in the simulated bar to learn about the various brands under the LaBatt umbrella.

Sales Training

The other great reason for training is to impart better sales and customer-relations skills, which are also critical to your bottom line. This type of training is ongoing: It can be done during short, weekly staff meetings or as monthly seminars, but it should definitely be scheduled on a regular basis. Your servers and bartenders sell not only your beverages, but your entire enterprise. They can turn your guests on or off at the very first contact. It is your job as owner or manager to teach and reinforce social skills—a smile, eye contact, enthusiasm, courteous attention, and prompt, accurate service—as well as grace under pressure. Teach employees what to do or say when a customer wants to send something back, when a cork crumbles in a wine bottle, when an order has been botched and must be rectified, and when someone walks out without paying.

This kind of training is a combination of the following:

- ***Product knowledge.*** Let employees taste new menu additions. Ask them to help you pick wines or beers that complement the foods that you serve. Ask distributors and suppliers to share wine information and sales tips. Record these meetings on audio or video so those who could not attend can still listen.
- ***Sales skills.*** Denver sales trainer and restaurateur Jim Sullivan says there are "right words" that can help trigger just about any type of sale. He also believes that there are five opportunities in any bar/restaurant setting to suggest a beverage sale. If you don't know them, you can bet your staff doesn't know them either. Invest in professional training that is designed specifically to increase your sales—and their tips.
- ***Guest psychology.*** This is certainly a sales skill, but it also includes how to deal diplomatically with problem customers: people who are loud or belligerent, who have had too much to drink, and/or who are making improper advances to staffers or other customers. It also includes safety training, what to do if you are robbed, harassed, or being faced with any type of emergency situation. The local police department might be willing to help with this type of training.
- ***Rules, etiquette, and technique.*** There are procedures that every bar adheres to because they help it to run smoothly and professionally. These procedures vary from place to place, but they typically include: the way drinks are ordered by the server (in a sequence, to help the bartender keep the orders straight), the use of a tray to carry drinks and other items, wiping the sides of glasses before they are delivered, and the types of garnishes used for each drink. If you have preferences about these issues you must regularly share these with your staff.

Training in Beverage Laws

This type of training is essential and should be taught immediately to serving personnel. Beverage laws are complex and sometimes antiquated, but they begin with the basic assumption that consuming alcohol—and therefore selling alcohol—is a privilege, not a right. If the privilege is abused, it can be taken away.

The following are three more general ideas on which beverage laws are based:

- Alcohol may be served only during the days and hours established by law in your area.
- It is against state law everywhere to serve alcohol to anyone under 21.
- It is against the law to serve alcohol to anyone who is clearly intoxicated.

Legal serving hours vary from one locale to another. Make sure that new employees know the legal hours in your area and that you expect them to observe these hours without exception.

The drinking age in every state is 21. At the time the order is taken, if there is any doubt at all about a customer's age, the server should ask for proof of age, such as a driver's license, passport, birth certificate, or special identification (ID) card issued by state- or local-government authorities. Some proof-of-age documents are easy to fake and even easier to borrow from a friend, so they must be examined closely. Your local law-enforcement agencies can probably provide examples of fake IDs and explain ways to spot the forgeries. Many state laws specify "a document with a signature, description, or picture." If the picture, description, and signature fit the individual, you as the seller are usually (although not always) presumed innocent in case there is trouble. The law sometimes contains a key word for your protection: You may not "knowingly" sell to anyone under legal age. You are also entitled to refuse to serve anyone you suspect is underage. Be aware: If your establishment serves an underage person, it does not matter that this young customer has broken the law by misrepresenting his or her age. Instead it is usually you, the seller, who is held responsible.

The other people you may not sell to, as you learned in Chapter 2, are those who have had too much to drink. It is all too easy for a busy or inexperienced employee intent on increasing check averages and tips to forget this. Not only is doing so against the law, it puts you at risk for third-party liability. The best you can do is to reduce the chances that someone will become intoxicated at your place of business. A number of good training programs have been developed to teach bar managers and servers how to tell when people are drinking too much and what to do about it. In these courses you can expect to learn how to:

- Keep track of the number of drinks served to each customer.
- Recognize behaviors that might indicate increasing intoxication.
- Understand drink equivalencies (how strong different drinks are).
- Observe guests' body types and sizes to determine how many drinks are "too many."
- Encourage alternatives to alcohol (snacks, a cup of coffee, dinner).
- Tactfully but firmly refuse to serve the person who can not handle any more ("I'm sorry, but I'm not allowed to bring you another drink.").

Suggestions are given to safely arrange for transportation home: calling a taxi service or a sober companion, getting a room at a nearby hotel rather than driving, or calling police as a last resort. A growing number of state and local liquor control boards now require bars to have their serving personnel trained and certified in a course or seminar approved by that agency. Some boards develop their own course or adapt an existing one to their state's requirements. Among the existing programs are:

Training for Intervention Procedures by Servers of Alcohol (TIPS). TIPS was developed by Health Communications Inc. under Morris E. Chafetz, the founder of the National Institute on Alcohol Abuse and Alcoholism. In a six-hour course using videotapes, written materials, and role-playing, servers are trained to recognize the onset of intoxication and to handle the inebriated customer. They are certified for three years upon passing a written exam. TIPS instructors have been trained in a two-day course and have passed a trainer-certification exam.

Responsible Beverage Service, Server Awareness Course. This course was developed by the Responsible Hospitality Institute. The Institute sends its own trainers to individual bars or restaurants for two three-hour sessions, then servers are certified by a written exam. This organization also offers a separate program for owners and managers.

Techniques of Alcohol Management (TAM). TAM is a creation of the National Licensed Beverage Association. This one-day seminar is tailored to the laws and requirements of each state.

ServSafe Alcohol™. Best known for its food-safety training (also under the ServSafe name), the National Restaurant Association Education Foundation revamped and renamed its former BarCode program in 2005. The new program includes a textbook, videos and DVDs, an instructor's toolkit, and written examinations. ServSafe-Alcohol certification is good for three years, unless local laws require more frequent recertification.

Serving Alcohol with Care (usually known as CARE). CARE was developed by the Educational Institute of the American Hotel/Motel Association. This program provides a 28-minute videotape, a leader's guide, and a server manual for developing your own seminar.

An excellent source of further information is the Responsible Beverage Service Council, a professional organization devoted to in-depth planning and promotion of beverage-service training programs and related activities. Individual communities are also developing programs suited to their own special needs and standards.

A staff of trained and certified serving personnel can reduce the cost of your liability insurance, as well as the risk that one of your guests will be involved in a drunk-driving accident. A trained, certified staff can also earn you the goodwill of customers, who will appreciate a caring approach to the problem and a skillful avoidance of unpleasant incidents.

No matter what kind of training you do it is usually more useful to present it as education or career development than as "penance." Make the training interesting, meaningful, and not too lengthy. If you require employees to attend be sure that they are paid for these hours. Servers dislike a hard sell as much as customers do, but some repetition and review will pay off. You must communicate to your employees what you expect them to get from the training, as well as how you expect them to use it.

The cost of training is high, but the cost of *not* training may be higher in the long run. You may find that the chief benefit of training is giving your staff a sense of professionalism that keeps morale high and retains good employees.

Learning from Employee Turnover

Although you have hired well and trained thoroughly, you must remember that not everyone in the hospitality industry stays forever. Turnover rates are commonly as high as 60 to 80 percent, which is incredibly discouraging for owner and managers who believe that they are working as hard as they can to keep employees as content as they do customers. Our advice on this persistent issue is to look at employee turnover as a symptom instead of a problem. In *The Consultant* magazine (second quarter issue, 2000) Bill Main suggests that managers find out why employees leave by conducting exit interviews with them, including the few simple questions listed in Figure 12.10.

Main also suggests that managers should not be the only employees who do periodic staff evaluations; he recommends that employees who are supervised should also have the opportunity to observe and critique the supervisor's work. Figure 12.11 is a simple but effective form to use for this purpose.

LABOR AND EMPLOYMENT LAWS

We have already begun to touch on labor issues in this chapter's discussion on hiring and retaining certain employee-related paperwork. As employers in any field are well aware today's work relationships are fraught with potential legal risks, from minor misunderstandings between workers that are settled informally, to million-dollar court judgments for alleged errors, injuries, pay disputes, and discrimination. Generally front-line managers and supervisors receive little or no training about how to handle disputed issues or what the consequences of a careless remark or simple decision might be. On the other hand some employers are so concerned about the risk of a lawsuit that they refuse to make difficult decisions, which results in reduced productivity, sagging morale, and inadequate communication with their workforce.

Increasingly when allegations are serious, an individual manager or supervisor is named in a complaint or lawsuit along with the company. As such managers and supervisors cannot be too careful when faced with a touchy situation. They should be trained to spot potential problems and to act in ways that reduce their employers' exposure to legal action. BNA Communications, Inc., of Rockville, Maryland, a company that conducts corporate training for managers, has created "10 Rules for Workplace Liability." These are:

Rule 1: Watch What You Say.

- ***Don't make threats.*** Occasionally in the course of a day's business managers will make a casual comment that seems threatening to an employee, who is trying to take advantage of those rights that are protected by law. The supervisor's ignorance of this employee's sensitivity may lead to litigation.

EMPLOYEE EXIT INTERVIEW

Name ______________________________ Date ______________

1. The type of work I was assigned was enjoyable.
   ❒ strongly agree ❒ agree ❒ disagree ❒ strongly disagree

2. My job was important to the company's success.
   ❒ strongly agree ❒ agree ❒ disagree ❒ strongly disagree

3. Wages are about average compared to other local restaurants.
   ❒ strongly agree ❒ agree ❒ disagree ❒ strongly disagree

4. My fellow employees were cooperative.
   ❒ strongly agree ❒ agree ❒ disagree ❒ strongly disagree

5. I was given adequate training for the job.
   ❒ strongly agree ❒ agree ❒ disagree ❒ strongly disagree

6. Working conditions are about average for the restaurant business.
   ❒ strongly agree ❒ agree ❒ disagree ❒ strongly disagree

7. My supervisor handles his/her job well.
   ❒ strongly agree ❒ agree ❒ disagree ❒ strongly disagree

8. The company was well-organized, scheduled, and controlled.
   ❒ strongly agree ❒ agree ❒ disagree ❒ strongly disagree

9. My specific work responsibilities were clear.
   ❒ strongly agree ❒ agree ❒ disagree ❒ strongly disagree

10. My abilities were well utilized.
    ❒ strongly agree ❒ agree ❒ disagree ❒ strongly disagree

FIGURE 12.10 Employee exit interview. © Bill Main & Associates, Chico, California. All rights reserved.

MANAGER EVALUATION BY EMPLOYEE

Date ______________

Manager's Name ________________________________ Return By ______________

Please answer the following questions to the best of your ability. A ⑤ is the highest score, and a ① is the lowest score.

1. How would you rate this person's grooming? ⑤ ④ ③ ② ①
2. How would you rate this person's ability to communicate? ⑤ ④ ③ ② ①
3. Does this person instill a sense of teamwork among those s/he supervises? ⑤ ④ ③ ② ①
4. Does this person have good training skills? ⑤ ④ ③ ② ①
5. How would you rate this person's ability to train management staff? ⑤ ④ ③ ② ①
6. Do you feel you can approach this person about subjects that trouble you? ⑤ ④ ③ ② ①
7. Does this person respond in an adult manner to criticism and suggestions? ⑤ ④ ③ ② ①
8. How willing is this person to help out in areas where s/he sees the need? ⑤ ④ ③ ② ①
9. Does this person deal fairly with everyone? ⑤ ④ ③ ② ①
10. Does this person show good judgment & common sense in emergencies? ⑤ ④ ③ ② ①
11. How well does this person follow through? ⑤ ④ ③ ② ①
12. Does this person leave his/her problems at the back door and concentrate on job performance? ⑤ ④ ③ ② ①
13. How well does this person adhere to company policy? ⑤ ④ ③ ② ①
14. Does this person help you to be the best employee you can be? ⑤ ④ ③ ② ①
15. How well do you like working with this person? ⑤ ④ ③ ② ①
16. In what one, single area should this person improve to increase his/her overall performance?
17. What one word would you use to describe this person?
18. What single thing does this manager do that makes you job easier?
19. What single thing does this manager do that makes you job harder?
20. Comments:

FIGURE 12.11 A manager evaluation by an employee. © Bill Main & Associates, Chico, California. All rights reserved.

- ***Don't make promises.*** At times, especially during tense situations, supervisors make promises to appease employees or to reward someone for outstanding performance. These promises, although not made in writing, can create legally enforceable expectations that can later hurt the organization.
- ***Don't denigrate.*** Never make any comment, on or off the job, that can be considered demeaning to a person's age, sex, race, religion, national origin, or type of disability. Such statements are not only illegal, they can be used as evidence of unlawful motivation in case of discharge, causing the employer to be liable for back pay, punitive damages, and other costs. Look at all employees as having valuable contributions to make.
- ***Don't ask improper questions.*** For example, by inquiring about an applicant's medical condition in a preemployment interview, you might be violating the Americans with Disabilities Act. By asking questions of one class of applicants that would not be asked of another class you could be creating evidence of discrimination, which violates Title VII, Civil Rights Act of 1964. By asking women and not men about child-care arrangements, for example, you could be perceived as discriminating against the women. If you insist that a green card is the only sufficient proof of a person's U.S. citizenship or right to work when other forms of identification are also accepted, you are violating the Immigration Reform and Control Act.

Rule 2: Keep Accurate Records of Hours Worked. In some work-related situations supervisors carelessly break the law when they ask employees to perform chores after hours without recording this overtime work. Another problem arises when employees who are eligible for overtime pay (which is 1½ times their regular pay rate) are not paid this higher rate for all hours worked over the standard 40-hour workweek. Swapping overtime in one week for time off the next week is also illegal. (Record-keeping is discussed in greater detail later in this chapter.)

Rule 3: Be Sensitive to Implications of Sexual Harassment. Supervisors must understand that their words can be taken out of context and more important, can be used against them in jury trials. Avoid using sexually oriented phrases, even in jest, as an attempt to create social relationships. Furthermore condoning pornographic material in the workplace can result in a charge of "Environmental Sexual Harassment."

Rule 4: Document Everything. It's not paranoia, it's smart business practice. A supervisor's memory of a discussion or incident might be hazy, especially in the absence of related documentation. Statistics show that in court juries typically will believe an employee over his or her supervisor.

Rule 5: Be Consistent. In an attempt to be nice supervisors may in fact expose their companies to potential lawsuits when they use different behavior or standards with different employees. An employee with a disability, for instance, can claim that he or she was treated differently on the basis of that characteristic, even if your intention was to make his or her duties less strenuous! And the Equal Pay Act prohibits employers from paying individuals differently based on their sex for doing the same jobs.

Rule 6: Be Safety Conscious. The Occupational Safety and Health Administration (OSHA) requires employers to document all work-related injuries that require medical attention other than minimal first aid or that result in a restriction of work assignments. Supervisors must also be sure that pushing for increases in productivity does not result in sacrificing safety rules or ignoring safety precautions. Employees will notice.

Rule 7: Seek Outside Help When Unusual Circumstances Arise. When a supervisor encounters any difficult or questionable situation that may involve an employment law, he or she should seek professional advice immediately. This may be the company's Human Resources department, an attorney, or a trade group, such as the National Restaurant Association or the American Hotel/Motel Association. Managers are not expected to know the intricacies of employment law, and even though a logical solution might be evident it might not necessarily be the correct legal solution to a problem with potential repercussions.

Rule 8: Consider All Implications of Any Special Request. A simple request for leave, which is a long period of time off work, can trigger obligations under a number of laws, including Title VII, which requires accommodation of certain religious requests; the Americans with Disabilities Act (ADA), which spells out the rights of persons with disabilities; and the Family and Medical Leave Act, which allows employees to take leave (even on an intermittent basis) to care for the medical needs of a spouse, child, or parent.

Rule 9: Take Seriously All Situations in Which Termination Is Implicated or Threatened. When employees threaten to quit take them seriously and immediately report this to your own superior or your company's Human Resources department. If employees are not given the opportunity to consult higher-ups about this decision before they actually quit, they could later argue that they were "forced" to quit, thereby entitling them to full back wages.

Rule 10: Be Aware of the Laws. New and veteran supervisors share one dangerous trait: They often believe that a commonsense approach to managing employees shields them from legal liability when employment disputes arise. Unfortunately few are aware of the complexity and changing nature of labor and employment laws. Take advantage of every opportunity to familiarize yourself with these laws, as well as to gain a fuller understanding of how they might impact your daily decisions as a manager. Seminars are offered at trade shows and conventions; by local and national trade groups, such as restaurant associations; and by business groups. Applying this knowledge on the job will save you and your organization time, money, and aggravation.

An Overview of Labor and Employment Laws

The following is a brief summary of the major federal labor and employment laws, those most frequently implicated in court actions. Remember, these are only the U.S. federal laws; many states have passed their own similar legislation about these topics that in some cases is more restrictive. An important note: These summary capsules are not a substitute for legal advice, which should always be sought from an attorney familiar with employment issues.

Americans with Disabilities Act (ADA). This act prohibits discrimination against disabled job applicants in privately owned companies with 15 or more employees. Employers are required to make "reasonable accommodations" to allow an otherwise qualified disabled person to be able to work, unless making the accommodations would cause "undue hardship" to the employer. The Equal Employment Opportunity Commission (EEOC) is responsible for enforcing this act. The ADA also covers accessibility in the overall design of your building.

Age Discrimination in Employment Act of 1967. This law states that companies with more than 20 employees may not discriminate against workers, or job applicants, who are over 40 years of age. The EEOC is responsible for enforcing this act also.

Equal Pay Act of 1963. This act requires equal pay for jobs that are substantially equal in skill, effort, and responsibility, and thus are performed under similar working conditions in the same workplace. This act is primarily designed to prevent sex discrimination in payment of wages, salaries, and other forms of compensation. The Equal Pay Act applies to private employers and all government employers, too. The EEOC enforces this act.

Immigration Reform and Control Act. This act prohibits discrimination against people for their national origin, citizenship, or intended citizenship, and it applies to any company with four or more employees (unless the company is already covered under Title VII, Civil Rights Act of 1964; see next paragraph). Termination of employment is also covered by this act, which is enforced by the Office of Special Counsel, U.S. Department of Labor.

Title VII, Civil Rights Act of 1964. This act says that employers may not discriminate against applicants or workers on the basis of their race, skin color, national origin, or sex. Title VII is a far-reaching act, which applies to all companies and all forms of government. Unlawful discrimination includes overt or "disparate" treatment, "disparate impact" treatment, sexual or racial harassment, and retaliation. The EEOC enforces this act.

Title VII, Sexual Harassment. This act applies not only to supervisors and managers, but also to employees—if their supervisor knows of their actions and does nothing to stop them. This type of harassment includes unwelcome sexual advances, requests for sexual favors, and other verbal or physical conduct of a sexual nature. In the case of a bar or restaurant the act also includes sexual harassment of your employees by guests if management is made aware of such activities and does not attempt to stop them. Sexual-harassment is difficult to prove since many people have different standards. To help, the EEOC, which enforces this act, has clarified a few points about what sexual harassment is:

- When submission to such contact is made a term or condition of an individual's employment, either explicitly or implicitly
- When submission to, or repetition of, such contact is used as a basis for employment decisions that affect an individual
- When such contact has the purpose or effect of reasonably interfering with an individual's work performance, or whether it creates a work environment for this person that is intimidating, hostile, or offensive

National Labor Relations Act. This act gives employees the right to form, join, or assist labor unions, and to bargain collectively through representatives of their own choosing. (It is also known as the Wagner Act, passed in the 1930s, which was amended by the Taft-Hartley Act in the 1940s.)

The act prohibits employers from interfering with, restraining, or coercing employees as they exercise their collective-bargaining rights. Companies cannot donate to unions or interfere with their operation; companies cannot discriminate against people for being union members; they can't encourage or discourage union membership, they can't refuse to negotiate in collective bargaining; and they can't fire or penalize a worker for using the act to file complaints against them. This act also covers unfair behavior on the part of unions. A union cannot coerce or restrain a worker in exercising his or her rights, cannot discriminate against employees who do not join the union, and cannot refuse to negotiate in collective bargaining. This is a far-reaching act with many implications for large employers and chain operators. The National Labor Relations Board (NLRB), a division of the U.S. Department of Labor, enforces the act.

Fair Labor Standards Act. This act is covered in detail in the next section, "Compensation and Benefits."

Family and Medical Leave Act of 1993. Any company with more than 50 workers must permit them to take leave (up to 12 weeks, unpaid) for family medical reasons. These might include the care of a newborn or newly adopted child or to care for themselves or a family member during a serious illness. The act requires that although the employer does not have to pay the workers' salary during their leave, it must maintain insurance coverage and hold a worker's job until he or she returns. The act also specifies the number of hours and years an employee must work to become eligible for this coverage. The U.S. Labor Department enforces this act.

Employee Polygraph Protection Act. Private employers cannot administer or require polygraph, or lie-detector tests, either to job seekers or current employees, except under certain circumstances. For instance, employees or applicants who have direct access to controlled substances as part of their jobs can be tested, prospective security guards can be tested, and employees can be tested if they are part of an investigation into workplace theft or other incidents that have caused an economic loss for the employer. This act is also enforced by the U.S. Department of Labor.

Occupational Safety and Health Act. This act prohibits employers who are "engaged in interstate commerce" from requiring their workers to perform tasks in unsafe places or unsafe manners. As of this writing new ergonomic standards are being discussed to include common ailments of the computer generation, such as carpal tunnel syndrome, tendonitis, and back strain. The act also requires employers to keep various types of records about on-the-job safety and accidents and prohibits employers from retaliating against workers who bring health- or safety-related claims against them. This act is enforced by the Occupational Safety and Health Administration (OSHA), an arm of the U.S. Department of Labor.

COMPENSATION AND BENEFITS

An employer may pay the members of a staff using several different methods, especially if some of them will receive additional income in the form of tips. The compensation picture is often made more complex by overtime pay, bonuses, commissions, incentive pay, and perquisites, while wage and hour laws, both federal and state, have many provisions that come into play when payroll is figured. Every employer must know the requirements well. We will look first at the usual ways in which various positions are compensated.

Methods of Compensation and Rates of Pay

Bar personnel are usually paid by one of two methods: hourly wages or a fixed salary. Tips add substantially to the earnings of bartenders and cocktail servers, while a supervisor or beverage director may receive a monthly bonus. Pay is also related to the type of ownership, with sole proprietors generally paying lower wages than partnerships and corporations. Other differences in pay may come from local and regional differences in prevailing wages and cost of living, local labor supply and demand, and union activity. Federal laws require every employer to give equal pay for equal work without regard to age, sex, race, national origin, religion, or skin color.

Federal Minimum-Wage Requirements

When you begin determining compensation you can use federal and state minimum-wage laws as a base. When the federal minimum wage was first created in 1938 it was 25 cents an hour. The federal Fair Labor Standards Act (FLSA) that sets the minimum wage was last amended in 1996, and the hourly rate is now $5.15. Congress occasionally debates the possibility of raising the rate to $6.15 an hour in two annual 50-cent increments, but this has not happened. In the meantime 18 states have enacted their own, higher minimum-wage rates: $5.70 an hour in Wisconsin, $6.15 an hour in Delaware and Florida, and $7.35 in Washington State. The most recent increases, which went into effect in 2006, were in the District of Columbia (now $7 an hour) and New York (now $6.75 an hour).

Paying the minimum wage to employees applies to any food-and-beverage enterprise grossing $500,000 a year. A special provision of the FSLA concerns wages of *tipped employees,* who are defined as persons receiving at least $30 per month in tips. The employer may consider the tips part of that person's salary, and pay him or her a smaller hourly rate of $2.13, allowing for a **tip credit** of $3.02. However if an individual's tips plus wages amount to less than the minimum wage ($5.15 an hour) in any workweek, the employer must make up the difference. It is the employer's responsibility to advise employees of the tip-credit provisions of the FSLA.

Suppose, for example, a waitress working a 40-hour week makes $85.20 in wages at $2.13 an hour and $150 for the week in tips, an average of $3.75 an hour in tips. Her tip average is well above the employer's tip credit of $3.02 an hour. (Remember, these amounts are calculated using year 2005 figures, which may change slightly over the years.) But the next week a spell of bad weather means less business. This waitress makes only $100 (or $2.50 an hour) in tips. Her employer must make up the additional 52 cents an hour to bring her total pay for the week up to the minimum wage of $5.15.

In 1990 the FLSA was amended to add a lower, **subminimum wage** for employees under age 20 during their first 90 days on the job. As of this writing this wage is $4.25 an hour. But employers are prohibited from getting rid of full-time employees or cutting their hours to hire lower-paid newcomers. The subminimum wage may also apply to full-time students in the workplace, some apprentice and trainee jobs, and individuals whose productivity is limited by a physical or mental disability. The idea was to encourage the employment of youth and disabled persons, but the use of the subminimum wage in these situations is decided by the U.S. Department of Labor on a case-by-case basis. The Labor Department has free publications that explain the subminimum wage and how it can be used.

Defining the Workweek

The FLSA also requires that minimum wage be computed on the basis of a **workweek,** whether the employee is paid weekly, biweekly, monthly, or at some other interval. A workweek is defined as a fixed and regularly recurring period of 168 hours: 7 consecutive 24-hour periods, beginning any day of the week at any hour of the day. In terms of computing minimum wages and overtime payments each workweek stands alone; this means that you can not average two or more weeks of different working hours to make your calculations. Employees must be paid for all hours that they work in any workweek, including breaks or rest periods of 5 to 20 minutes that occur within their work times. You do not have to pay employees for a meal period or lunch break, but you do have to pay them for short coffee breaks or rest periods. Also if "lunch" involves performing any work-related duties while employees eat, you must pay them for that time, too.

Tip Pooling

The FLSA specifies that all tips belong to employees. The employer cannot claim any part of the tip money for the business. However the employer may require **tip pooling.** This is when servers or bartenders **"tip out,"** or share a percentage of their tips with barbacks, busboys, and other service staff who have direct guest contact, that is, they are part of the "team" but generally do not receive tips. The tip-pooling requirement cannot apply to an employee until his or her tips have satisfied the employer's $3.02 tip credit. In other words the tipped employee does not pay into a tip pool until he or she has made enough in tips to bring his or her total hourly pay up to the minimum wage for the week.

In some cases, such as for large parties, there is a policy at many bars or restaurants of adding a compulsory service charge (of 15 or 20 percent) to the bill. Interestingly this charge is not considered a tip. Instead it is defined by the FLSA as part of the employer's gross receipts. In this case the employer must pay at least the full minimum wage to service personnel, and must pay applicable sales taxes on the full amount of the service charge.

Other Charges

Most bars, as part of their ambience, specify uniforms for both bartenders and servers, and some employers charge uniform costs to employees. The FLSA says that such charges must not reduce an employee's wages below the minimum wage. The employer must also reimburse employees the costs of laundering uniforms (as necessary business expenses for the employer) if such cost reduces employee wages below the minimum-wage level. Employers also cannot deduct from paychecks such occurrences as breakage of glassware or a shortage in the day's cash-register receipts if the deductions drop the total wages below the minimum-wage rate or if they reduce overtime pay that is legitimately due to the employee. It is important for both workers and their supervisors to keep accurate, written records of all of these factors: to ensure that everybody gets paid fairly and that no one feels cheated.

For all of the FLSA's technical complexity, there are some standard workplace issues that it does not address and does not require. These include: vacation, holiday, severance or sick pay; meal or rest periods; bonus pay for working holidays, nights, or weekends; pay raises or fringe benefits; or immediate payment of final wages to anyone who is fired. The FLSA does not even require that fired employees receive a reason for being terminated. It also does not limit the hours in a day, or days in a week, an employee can work if he or she is over age 16.

Supervisors as Exempt Employees. The FLSA exempts supervisors, managers, administrators, and executives from minimum-wage requirements. They are called **exempt employees,** while those covered by the act are called **nonexempt employees.** These regulations were revised in 2004 to spell out the conditions under which an employee may be considered "exempt." All three of the following tests must be met for the employee to be exempted from overtime pay:

1. **The salary-basis test.** The employee must receive a predetermined, fixed salary that is not subject to reduction because of variations in quantity or quality of the work performed—that is, it must be a fixed amount for every pay period that the employee works.
2. **The salary-level test.** The employee must make at least $455 a week (for an annual salary of $23,000) to be considered exempt.
3. **The duties test.** The employee must perform a job that for the most part involves executive, administrative, or professional duties. The "government-speak" that makes up these categories is as follows:
   - *Executive* means that the person's primary duty is to manage a recognized department, or that he or she "regularly directs" the work of two or more other employees, or that he or she has the authority to hire and fire other employees and/or recommend changes in the work status of other employees.
   - *Administrative* means that the person's primary duty is to perform office or nonmanual labor that directly relates to the management or general business operation of the employer or the employer's customers, and that in carrying out his or her duties the person must "exercise discretion and independent judgment."
   - *Professional* exemptions are further broken down into two categories:
     a. *Creative professionals* include some forms of culinary arts. For example, if the primary duties of a chef require invention, imagination, originality, or talent—such as that involved in regularly creating or designing unique menu items—this chef may be considered exempt from overtime rules.
     b. *Learned professionals* include those who have attained four-year, specialized academic degrees. Their work duties must require "advanced knowledge." Some executive chefs and sous chefs would meet this designation.

Again all three of the requirements must be met for the employee to be considered supervisory or managerial. If they are not met the employee is eligible to receive overtime pay. And that brings us to the next topic.

Calculating Regular and Overtime Pay

The FLSA requires that employees receive overtime pay for any time over 40 hours worked in one workweek. The act further specifies that the rate of overtime pay must be at least $1\frac{1}{2}$ times the employee's regular rate.

The **regular rate** for figuring overtime is always an hourly rate. No matter whether the employee's rate of pay is tied to the hour, the shift, the week, the month, or a percentage of sales, pay for a given week is translated into an hourly rate by dividing the week's pay by the number of hours worked that week. A week's pay includes all remuneration: wages or salary, commissions, attendance bonuses, production bonuses, shift differentials, and tips credited as part of a worker's wages (the *tip credit*). We will explain see how employers use the regular hourly rate to calculate the correct amount of overtime compensation for different methods of payment.

The Hourly Employee. To figure overtime for an hourly employee, begin with his or her regular hourly rate and simply multiply it by 1.5. For example, if an employee's hourly wage is $8.00 and she works 48 hours in one workweek, the calculation is as follows:

Regular rate: $8.00
Overtime rate: $8.00 × 1.5 = $12.00

40 hours @ $8.00 = $320.00
8 hours @ $12.00 = $96.00
Week's gross pay: = $416.00

The following another way to figure this:

Regular rate: $8.00
Overtime Premium: $8 × 0.5 = $4.00

48 hours @ $8.00 = $384.00
8 hours @ $4.00 = $32.00
Week's gross pay: = $416.00

The Salaried Employee Paid Monthly. The regular rate is computed by multiplying the monthly rate by 12 (months), then dividing by 52 (weeks per year) to find the weekly salary. This is divided by the number of hours worked to find the hourly rate. For this example let's assume that an employee's monthly salary is $2,500 and that he works a standard 40 hours a week. But in one busy week he works 48 hours. The calculation is as follows:

$2,500 × 12 (months) = $30,000.00 yearly salary
$30,000 ÷ 52 (weeks) = $576.92 weekly salary
$576.92 ÷ 40 (hours) = $14.42 is the standard hourly wage

The calculation for this person's overtime rate is as follows:

$14.42 × 1.5 ("time and a half") = $21.63
$21.63 × 8 (overtime hours) = $173.04 is the overtime pay for this week

Monthly gross pay would combine the regular monthly pay with the overtime pay:

$2,500 (regular) + $173.04 (overtime) = $2,673.04

The Salaried Weekly Employee Working Fewer Than 40 Hours a Week. The regular rate is computed by dividing salary by hours regularly worked. The employee is paid this hourly rate up to 40 hours and 1.5 times this rate thereafter. In this example the employee also earns $2,500 per month but works regularly only 35 hours per week. In a recent busy week she worked 45 hours. The calculation is as follows:

$2,500 × 12 (months) = $30,000 yearly salary
$30,000 ÷ 52 (weeks) = $576.92 weekly salary
$576.92 ÷ 35 (hours) = $16.48 is the standard hourly wage

When calculating this person's overtime rate, remember that the regular hours worked are only 35. As such, the first 5 hours of "extra" time are used to satisfy the basic workweek requirement of 40 hours. This worker will receive only 5 hours of overtime pay.

$16.48 × 1.5 ("time and a half") = $24.72 is the hourly overtime rate
$24.72 × 5 (overtime hours) = $123.60 is the overtime pay for this week

The employee's monthly gross pay would combine her regular monthly pay with the overtime pay. The calculation is as follows:

$2,500 (regular) + $123.60 (overtime) = $2,623.60

The Employee Paid a Fixed Salary for Varying Hours per Week. For this employee the regular rate for computing overtime will vary with total hours worked, so it must be computed for each workweek. Since the straight salary applies by definition to all hours worked, only the overtime premium (of 0.5 times the regular rate) is added. In this example an employee is paid a straight salary of $400 a week. In a month he worked 42 hours the first week, 50 the next, 45 the third, and 38 the fourth. The four calculations are as follows:

Week 1
$400 ÷ 42 (hours) = $9.52 regular rate
$9.52 × 0.5 = $4.76 overtime rate
$4.76 × 2 hours overtime = $9.52
Gross weekly pay: $400 + $9.52 = $409.52

Week 2
$400.00 ÷ 50 (hours) = $8.00 regular rate
$8.00 × 0.5 = $4.00 overtime rate
$4.00 × 10 hours overtime = $40
Gross weekly pay: $400 + $40 = $440.00

Week 3
$400.00 ÷ 45 = $8.89 regular rate
$8.89 × 0.5 = $4.45 overtime rate
$4.45 × 5 hours overtime = $22.25

Gross weekly pay $400 + $22.25 = $422.25

For week 4 his pay is $400 because the hours he worked did not exceed 40, the amount covered by his fixed weekly salary.

The Minimum Wage Employee with Tip Credit and Extra Pay. When you compute the regular rate the hourly wage is figured at minimum wage since the employee will receive it either in tips or from the employer. This wage is multiplied by the hours regularly worked. To this figure extra pay during the week is added. (This *will* include such items as bonuses or commissions, but *not* the balance of tips earned.) This total is then divided by the number of regular hours to arrive at the regular rate after computing overtime for that week.

For example, a tipped employee whose base pay is the minimum wage ($5.15 per hour) less the $3.02 tip credit, actually makes $2.13 per hour, which is paid by the employer. The employee is on the job 45 hours in one workweek and makes $150 in tips. In that same week she earns a commission of $40 on wine sales along with a $70 bonus for having the highest overall sales for the week. First we will calculate her standard weekly earnings under the minimum-wage law:

$5.15 × 40 (hours) = $206.00 + $40 + $70 (bonuses) = $316.00
$316.00 ÷ 40 (hours) = $7.90 regular hourly rate

The calculation for this person's overtime pay rate is as follows:

$7.90 × 1.5 ("time and a half") = $11.85 overtime rate
$11.85 × 5 hours (overtime) = $59.25 overtime pay

So altogether this waitress earned:

$316 (wages and bonuses) + $59.25 (overtime) = $375.25

However her tip credit must be deducted:

$3.02 (hourly tip credit) × 40 (hours) = $120.80

The employee's total weekly pay is her earnings, minus the tip credit:

$375.25 − $120.80 = $254.45 (gross weekly pay)

The following is an even simpler computation for minimum-wage employees with tip credits. For the first 40 hours that an employee works, you pay them the minimum-wage rate. To determine the overtime rate simply multiply the minimum-wage rate by 1.5, then subtract the hourly tip credit. For instance:

$5.15 (minimum wage) × 1.5 ("time and a half") = $7.73 overtime rate
$7.73 (overtime rate) − $3.02 (tip credit) = $4.71 net overtime rate

Suppose that an employee who receives customer tips works 49 hours in a workweek and makes $170 that week in tips. For the first 40 hours you pay him the tipped-employee rate, which is calculated as follows:

$5.15 (minimum wage) − $3.02 (tip credit) = $2.13 per hour
$2.13 × 40 (hours) = $85.20

Then add the overtime, which is calculated as follows:

$4.71 (overtime rate, less tip credit) × 9 (overtime hours) = $42.39
Gross weekly pay: $85.20 + $42.39 = $127.59

(To check whether the amount of reported tips is sufficient to cover the tip-credit requirements, divide the tip amount by the total number of hours that the employee worked. In this case the result is $3.46 per hour, which is more than the statutory $3.02 tip credit.) Hourly employees must be paid from the time that they report to work until the time they go off duty, whether they are working or not. Even if they go on working voluntarily beyond their normal hours, they must be paid for the extra time.

Contract Labor

Sometimes people are hired seasonally, on a part-time basis, or as consultants to help with a particular project. They may be paid hourly, monthly, or by flat fee, but with the special agreement that they will not be covered by the standard employee benefits and that no taxes or Social Security will be deducted from their paychecks. These people may refer to themselves as *contract labor, freelancers, consultants,* or **independent contractors.** No matter what you call them contract laborers are exempt from the minimum-wage regulations. However, it is important to carefully scrutinize the relationship between the worker and the business because the Internal Revenue Service (IRS) certainly will! Some companies have been reprimanded in recent years for firing standard, full-time employees, then rehiring them as "contractors" to avoid having to pay employment-related taxes. The IRS looks at the employee/business relationship with the following three criteria in mind:

- ***Behavioral control.*** If the employer has control over where, when, and how the work is to be done, the worker is an employee, not a contractor.
- ***Financial control.*** If the worker is reimbursed for all business expenses and has fixed costs—either profits or losses—then he or she can be considered a contract laborer.
- ***Type of relationship.*** This includes a number of factors, such as whether a written contract describes the relationship, whether the services are a key aspect of the business, and whether the relationship is permanent. It is smart to document these types of "freelance" working relationships in writing to protect both parties.

The following guidelines further distinguish between an independent contractor and an employee.

Be aware that the IRS is likely to scrutinize records of businesses that hire temporary workers as independent contractors who perform tasks similar to those of regular employees—something companies do all too often to avoid paying benefits to people. Misclassifying employees as contractors can lead to financial and administrative nightmares for you and your company. Attorneys who specialize in labor laws can assist with problems and questions on these topics as can accountants and the local IRS office.

EMPLOYEES OR CONTRACTORS?

They are employees if . . .

- You have the right to tell them when, where, and how to perform work, and have a continuing work relationship with them.
- You provide them with training.
- You generally integrate their services into your operation.
- You require them to provide their service in person.
- You hire, supervise, and pay any of the workers under their purview.
- You establish set work hours and expect them to perform their job on your premises and in the order you outline for the tasks.
- You require them to devote full-time to your business and (implicitly or explicitly) restrict them from doing other, gainful work during the same period.
- You require that they submit oral or written reports.
- You guarantee them a minimum salary, hourly wage, or draws against a bank account at stated intervals, and do not require them to repay any excess over the amount earned or drawn.
- You pay their job-related expenses, from travel, to tools, to equipment, to the necessary facilities to perform their work.
- You have the right to discharge them at any time, and they also have the right to end the work relationship at any time without incurring legal liability.

They are contractors if . . .

- They hire, supervise, and pay other workers to perform services for you.
- They agree to furnish labor and materials to attain a result, and are responsible only for attaining this result.
- They may choose when and for whom to work.
- They are customarily paid a commission on a per-job basis.
- They invest significantly in equipment that they use to perform their services.
- They can realize a profit (or a loss) from the provision of their services.
- They may work for more than one employer or company simultaneously.
- They make their services available to the general public.
- They usually agree to complete a specific job and in addition to being responsible for completing it satisfactorily, they are also obligated to make good for failing to complete it.

PAYROLL TAXES, BENEFITS, AND PERQUISITES

In addition to wages and salaries two other forms of compensation add to labor costs: payroll taxes and fringe benefits. Payroll taxes fund Social Security and unemployment programs. To employees these are both forms of deferred compensation, but to the employer they are real and present labor costs. As of this writing the employer's share of federal employment taxes includes the following:

Social Security Taxes, also Known as the Federal Insurance Contribution Act (FICA). This requires employers to pay 6.2 percent of each employee's wages and tips for workers who make $76,200 or less per year. You are also required to withhold another 6.2 percent from the employee's gross pay, which is his or her contribution to Social Security.

Federal Unemployment Taxes (FUTA). The employer pays this tax, which is 6.2 percent of the first $7,000 of all employees' wages and tips per year. However, most states give businesses a credit for this tax, which can effectively drop the rate to less than 1 percent. States also have unemployment taxes, which vary depending on the rate of unemployment claims against the employer.

Medicare. This is a tax of 1.45 percent of each employee's wages and tips that is paid by the employer; another 1.45 percent is withheld from the employee's paycheck. All wages and tips are subject to Medicare taxes; there is no upper income limit. Tax deductions from paychecks cause a great deal of employee grumbling because of the wide disparity between their gross pay and the much-reduced "take-home" pay. Every time that an income-tax rate or a Social Security rate increases, the take-home pay drops accordingly. At the same time though the payroll expense to the employer reaches considerably beyond the base pay.

The majority of hospitality-industry employers grant their workers, including bar personnel, paid vacations. As with other industries the number of weeks of vacation time increases as years of service increase. Some enterprises reimburse their management employees for job-related educational expenses and pay professional dues. Benefits that are related to specific jobs or job levels are known as **perquisites,** or *perks* for short. A car or car expenses for use on the job or a company credit card for business-related meals, travel, or other expenses are common perquisites. Sometimes interest-free loans are provided to top-level personnel. Benefits and perquisites are part of an employer's labor cost, while for the employee, with the exception of paid vacations and other cash benefits, they are tax-free additions to income.

The term **fringe benefit** refers to any tangible or significant compensation other than wages. The most common benefits are free meals and paid vacations. If you let employees eat meals at your business because it is convenient for you, the value of these meals cannot be charged to them as taxable income. Their value is not subject to income-tax withholding or any of the federal taxes listed above—that is, as long as the meals are provided free of charge and are consumed on your premises.

Insurance. Many employers also offer group medical insurance and group life insurance. These costs are also not considered part of employees' wages and are not subject to any federal taxes. Unlike other industries bars and restaurants offering health insurance to employees is still somewhat rare. But with rising medical costs, this is an increasingly valuable perk that today many of the large, casual-dining chains offer. One National Restaurant Association survey (skewed in this case to these national chains) concluded that 45 percent of the participants offer some type of health insurance, and, in most cases the restaurant and the employee split the cost of the insurance premium, with each paying half.

Starbucks has set the pace in this field, with a generous corporate insurance program that closely mirrors what you might expect in the corporate world. Conventional wisdom holds that young employees don't care as much about health insurance as older workers, but recent research has shown otherwise. For twenty-somethings, just out of college and off their parents' insurance policies, and for single parents caring for children, a group health insurance policy is far more affordable than individual coverage.

Dependent Care Accounts. Federal tax breaks allow businesses to offer some perks that benefit workers without increasing the bar or restaurant's labor cost, including pretax payroll deductions for such necessary services as childcare. Consider for example, a single mother who earns more than $20,000 a year as a server and puts two children in daycare, which costs $5,000 annually. If she puts this money in a pretax dependent-care account it is not taxed by the federal government; this saves the employee $935 in taxes. Employers also do not pay taxes on the amounts that their employees put into these pretax accounts. If the worker earns less than $87,000 per year, the employer saves $383 ($5,000 × .075) annually in payroll taxes for that employee.

Records and Reports

As soon as you become an employer you must fill out the form to obtain an Employer Identification Number (EIN) from the IRS. This is the nine-digit number that you use when you report and pay federal taxes. When you hire a new employee each one must also fill out an IRS W-4 form (and/or an **I-9 form**, seen in Figure 12.8). Use the W-4 information to determine the amount of income tax to withhold from each employee's wages and tips.

You must keep these forms on file and maintain records for each employee from his or her first day on the job. For workers who are subject to the minimum-wage laws, the FLSA says the following information must be kept:

Personal information: the worker's name, sex, home address, occupation, and birthdate (if under age 19). (You should keep the employee's Social Security number on file, too.)

- The hour and day when the person's workweek begins.
- The total hours that each person worked, by day and by workweek.
- The total daily or weekly "straight time" (regular pay) earnings.
- The worker's regular hourly pay rate for any week when overtime was worked.
- The overtime pay that the employee received, by workweek.
- Any deductions from, or additions to, wages.
- The total wages paid to the worker for each pay period.
- The dates of paydays and the dates included in each pay period.

You must file monthly, quarterly, and annual reports with the IRS and pay your share of federal taxes, as well as passing on the amounts that you withheld from employees' paychecks. To keep abreast of federal rate and regulation changes, be sure you have a copy of the current year's IRS Circular E, the "Employer's Tax Guide." It will also contain the latest details on reporting taxable tips.

Wage Complaints by Employees. The other good reason to implement thorough, accurate record-keeping procedures is in case of a challenge by employees who complain that they have not been paid or paid fairly. The U.S. Department of Labor's Wage and Hour Division can conduct investigations into these claims, or employees can hire a private attorney and file a civil lawsuit.

If the Department of Labor's audit of your records determines that the claims are valid, you can be liable for payment of back wages and penalties. This might be two years of back pay or if the violation has been determined to be "willful," it might be three years of back pay. Willful violations also carry a fine of up to $10,000 or even a prison term. You cannot intimidate or fire an employee who has brought such a claim during the investigation. That's a violation of the FLSA.

Reporting Tip Income. You should encourage service employees to keep careful daily track of their tips. Employees who are tipped directly, either by cash or credit card, must report their tips to the IRS as income, less the amount that they give up for tip pooling. As their employer you must also know how much they make in tips because you have to count tips as part of the employee's income when you deduct such items as income tax and Social Security amounts, and when you pay the company's part of Social Security or unemployment taxes.

It is also your responsibility to report tips, which are figured as a percentage of gross sales, to the IRS. As of this writing the percentage figure required from the employer and expected from the employee is not less than 8 percent of gross sales. The employer must report tips of more than $20 per person per month whether or not the employees report them.

You must also consider what will happen if your employees underreport the tip amounts they receive. The IRS is supersensitive to this very common problem and requires you to "allocate" tips. Here's how it works: Let's say that the combined food-and-beverage sales amount for your bar is $30,000, and you have 10 employees who receive tips. Each employee is allocated $3,000 of your total sales, and the IRS assumes that each one made 8 percent of the total sales figure (or $2,400) as tips, on which he or she must pay taxes. It might not seem like much for a waitress or bartender to pocket a few dollars tax-free. But tip-income totals more than $7 billion annually, and the IRS wants its share, just like any other type of income. Hiding or underreporting tip money has been such a problem that the IRS now has a voluntary program called the Tip Reporting Alternative Commitment (TRAC). It gives employers protection from IRS audits if they keep proper records and instruct employees about their tip-reporting obligations. Be forewarned, though: Both businesses and employees *will* be audited if the IRS suspects them of underreporting.

Other Types of Records. You must also keep information and withholding records for state insurance and tax programs, and you must file state returns and make the required payments. Each employee must be given a year-end statement, which is called a *W-2 form,* of the total wages or salary paid, deductions for the year, and tips reported. Copies of this form must also be sent to the IRS and the Social Security Administration. Record-keeping can be enormously simplified by computerized accounting programs. Almost all payroll functions can now be handled electronically.

SUMMING UP

After reading this chapter you might have a whole new appreciation for your own employers, past and present. Did you have any idea there were so many laws, rules, and potential pitfalls when it comes to hiring, scheduling, and paying employees?

There are also many reasons to proceed carefully in the bar business and to document as much as possible. This includes writing detailed job descriptions, offering comprehensive training programs, and detailing alcohol awareness and emergency procedures. It may also mean taking notes during staff meetings and after confrontations with employees or guests, keeping written schedules and time logs, and ensuring that state and federal paperwork is up-to-date. Be aware of the state and federal laws that govern hiring, alcohol service, and minimum wages since these occasionally change.

For prospective employees, a written application, background checks to verify identity and criminal history, and an in-person interview are essential.

The four good reasons to hold thorough employee-orientation sessions are detailed in this chapter. The basics should include information about uniforms and/or the on-the-job dress code. A training procedure should begin on the first day on the job for a new hire, and then should be an ongoing priority. Short, regularly-scheduled training meetings not only will get your rules and messages across, but will also serve the important function of motivating employees. This chapter details how several types of bars handle their training needs, including sales training and responsible alcohol-service training.

The plethora of wage-and-benefit-related laws require employers to tread carefully in everything from the hiring process to calculation of pay and overtime. This chapter offers an overview of labor laws, a close look at federal wage and hour laws and payroll taxes, and a summary of the most common benefits offered by bars and restaurants.

POINTS TO PONDER

1. List and briefly explain three reasons why it is important to hire good bartenders.
2. List three tasks that a sommelier should be able to perform for his or her employer, other than recommend and open bottles of wine for customers.
3. Identify the two things that you must do to create a good job description? (Hint: They are both types of lists.) Briefly describe each one.
4. List places where would you look for good potential employees for your bar.
5. What can a bar manager discuss in a job interview with a prospective employee?
6. Identify the three kinds of training that you should provide for employees. List them and write a sentence about the importance of each.
7. What are the basic ideas on which beverage laws are based?
8. Of all the workplace-liability topics that you read about in this chapter, did any surprised you? Explain why or why not.
9. What is a tip credit, and how do bar or restaurant owners use it?
10. A bartender earns a weekly salary of $600. Someone called in sick one shift, so he volunteered to work seven extra hours. During the week he received $180 in tips. Calculate his total pay for the week.

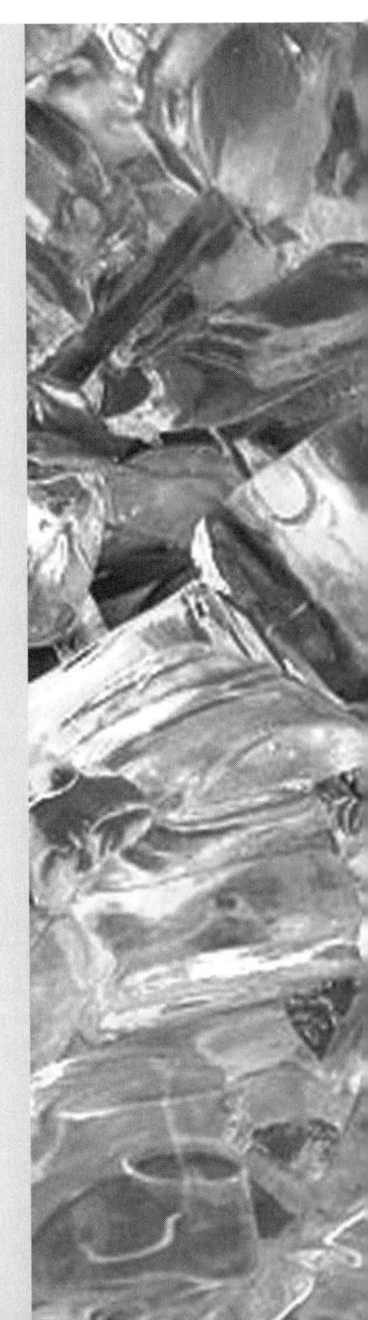

TERMS OF THE TRADE

barback
bartender
beverage steward
bouncer
cover charge
exempt employees
fringe benefits
I-9 form
independent contractor
job analysis
job specifications
nonexempt employees
perquisites
regular rate (for overtime)
sommelier (cellarmaster)
subminimum wage
task analysis
tastevin
tip credit
tip out
tip pooling
wine steward
workweek

A CONVERSATION WITH...CHRISTOPHER MANOLIS

Executive Assistant Manager
The Hotel Grande Bretagne
Athens, Greece

Christopher Manolis says that he was "practically born into the hospitality industry." His parents, both of Greek descent, owned two small hotels in Johannesburg, South Africa. Of their five children Christopher is the only one who pursued a career in the hospitality field.

After attending hotel-management school in Johannesburg, his first "non-family" job was as a waiter in a 600-room Westin hotel there. It did not take long for Manolis to become the manager of the hotel's prestigious Three Ships restaurant. He also worked in upscale private eateries before deciding that he wanted to gain international experience—and, indeed, the next 15 years took him on the career jaunt of a lifetime. He worked at luxury hotels in Greece, Bahrain, Manila, Australia, Japan, and the United States, and for some of the world's largest hotel companies: Intercontinental, Sheraton, and (what is now) Starwood Hotels & Resorts. In each instance he held positions in hotel management and/or food-and-beverage management.

Manolis's desire to return to Greece is what brought him back, first to a small, boutique hotel in Kifissia, then to his current position in 2002. The Hotel Grande Bretagne has been located in the same bustling, central Athens spot since 1874. Rich in history, in the 1940s this social landmark was closed to the public and commandeered—first by the Greek government, then by invading Germans, and finally by the British—as the lavish "headquarters" for their military leaders. In succeeding years it has remained the favorite hotel and watering hole of politicians and poets, and actors and directors from around the world.

In 2005 Condé Nast Traveler *magazine listed Alexander's Bar, which is right off the hotel lobby, as one of the world's top-ten hotel bars. It is a quiet, elegant space replete with potted palm trees and an enormous tapestry from the 1920s of a scene depicting Alexander the Great in the backbar area. The best-selling cocktails are Martinis, Mojitos, and Caipirinhas.*

Q: What is it like managing one of the world's great hotels, with such an illustrious history and reputation to uphold?

A: I realized from the day I put my foot in this hotel that the expectations would be high, not only from the international guests but also from the local community. Everyone here has grown up with the Grande Bretagne; it's "the" hotel, the grand dame of Athens. Being right across from the Greek Parliament, hosting politicians and celebrities and executives, I knew this would be a different ballgame. When I came here the hotel was being completely refurbished. I saw the plans for it and thought it would be a great opportunity to help bring the hotel back to its glory.

Tim Ananiadis [the General Manager] and I also realized that sitting in our offices is not the way to run this hotel. We need to meet people, and that means whoever walks through the door. Our guests love to be recognized and have someone talk with them. We also have to have a very high profile, operationally, to motivate the staff to really look after people. And we both have open-door policies–employees can talk with us any time, about anything.

One of Starwood's policies is that training is a huge aspect of the company. Each department has a monthly training program, as well as refresher courses. We've also instituted cross-training–our front-office people work in F&B, and vice versa. It exposes our employees to new things, and we've found it is motivational for them.

Q: What kinds of employees do well at the Grande Bretagne?

A: We've said from the beginning that skill wasn't the top of the priority list. We want young people who are friendly and pleasant and with the right attitude–we can teach them how to perform the jobs–but we look for the person who will take the basic knowledge a step further, to do more than just the basics. The ones who are best at it love working with people, and love what they're doing.

We don't hire anyone who doesn't speak English; most speak Greek, English, and at least one other language. I think everyone in this industry should be multilingual. Hospitality is truly a global job, and learning languages opens up so many opportunities.

Q: Tell us about working in Alexander's Bar.

A: Bartenders here start as assistants to learn the profession, just like cooks who work with chefs. It does help to have some work experience in good places, established places. That's where you can pick up what you can not read in a book. We have a beverage manager and a sommelier. When the bar is busy, we have at least four people working, including the beverage manager: two bartenders, and two servers. Their pay structure is not hourly; they are on a salary for 40 hours a week and 5-day workweeks. We have a union in the hotel and they are very strict on that. Waiters, busmen, and bartenders pool their tips.

Q: How has technology impacted the hotel?

A: Technology has allowed us to practically eliminate the storeroom, as such, both for the beverage and kitchen operations. We maintain small par stocks, do direct issues, and purchase more frequently, usually on a two-day cycle; with one e-mail, we can order almost anything fresh. Ordering within the European Union is fast and problem-free; there are no borders or customs to worry about—it is basically a distribution network. In terms of meats, fish, and produce, there's nothing frozen in the hotel. We sometimes buy wines at auction, but for the most part we order wine and liquor in the same way as food, on a two-day cycle and delivered directly to us, with small par stocks.

Technology also allows us to obtain "flash" food-and-beverage costs on a daily basis if required and monitor our expenses very carefully. We utilize a menu-engineering program that establishes your selling price of food-and-beverage items based on sales history and tracks your so-called "winners" and "losers" for any future menu-item changes. In a hotel like this the food cost percentage to sales is about 30 percent; beverage cost is about 16 to 17 percent. These numbers are the responsibility of the executive chef and the beverage manager, and their decisions can tremendously affect the bottom line. During the month we check the costs regularly to see if they are out of line. If we find something amiss we look at all the purchases and try to rectify it. Of course we look closely at the competition—the Inter-Continental, Hilton, Marriott, and so on—what are they charging, the same or a little more? In the food-and-beverage department keeping to budget is of major importance.

Q: Of all the places that you have worked, what was the most amazing hotel?

A: There were many of them, but the Yokohama Grand InterContinental in Yokohama, Japan, comes to mind. It is a beautiful property, built in the shape of a sail, 600 rooms with 11 different restaurant concepts in the same hotel. I didn't believe it in the beginning, but it was the highlight of my career because of the many different influences I was exposed to—Chinese, French, Italian, and Japanese cuisine; sushi and teppanyaki—and it was linked to a huge convention center, giving me valuable banquet experience.

The Japanese style of management is also something to learn from; they have long been known as hard-working, diligent employees and work in the corporate community appears large in the lives of the Japanese. Corporate synergy is practiced extensively and hierarchy in companies is demanded and respected. They are perfectionists and the culture respects age, especially in the corporate world. Jobs are almost lifetime jobs. This benefits all sectors including the hospitality industry. They are responsible workers; they take ownership in the job assigned to them and this helps when you managing a hotel.

Q: You've worked in some of the largest hotels in the world, and also in the upscale, boutique hotels. What would you say the differences are in terms of employment?

A: The large corporations don't pay especially well, but there are other benefits: the world travel, the interesting people you meet, and so on. There's also more job security, some stability in the larger business. You may move a lot, but you always have a job. The smaller companies actually headhunt in the large companies. They see a good person in a large hotel, for example, and offer them a bit more money. We lose some very good people that way. So I would say the loyalties are different, financial or personal, depending on the company.

Q: What advice would you give to students who may want to use their bar background to go into hotel management?

A: First of all I was not married when I did my world traveling, and I recommend that they get this experience when they are young and single. I married late in life, at age 48, and now that I have three children I'm not so easily transferable these days. I really enjoyed it, and I think young people in this industry should grab the opportunity to travel if it comes up—it broadens your mind to see the world and you think more laterally. I've already mentioned the importance of being multilingual, and I particularly think learning Chinese will be important in the hospitality industry. China is going to be a super economic power within the next 20 to 30 years.

You can play a very big role in this industry if you can learn the financial side behind hotel operations and, of course, marketing and sales skills are equally as important. Remember, with your academic studies as well as in the workplace "what you put in is what you take out—if you put zero in, you will get zero out of it." The industry is big and strict and harsh, and you may have to start at the bottom of the ladder. Be patient and persevere and if you love working with people and have a good attitude about life, you will succeed.

CHAPTER 13
PURCHASING, RECEIVING, STORAGE, AND INVENTORY

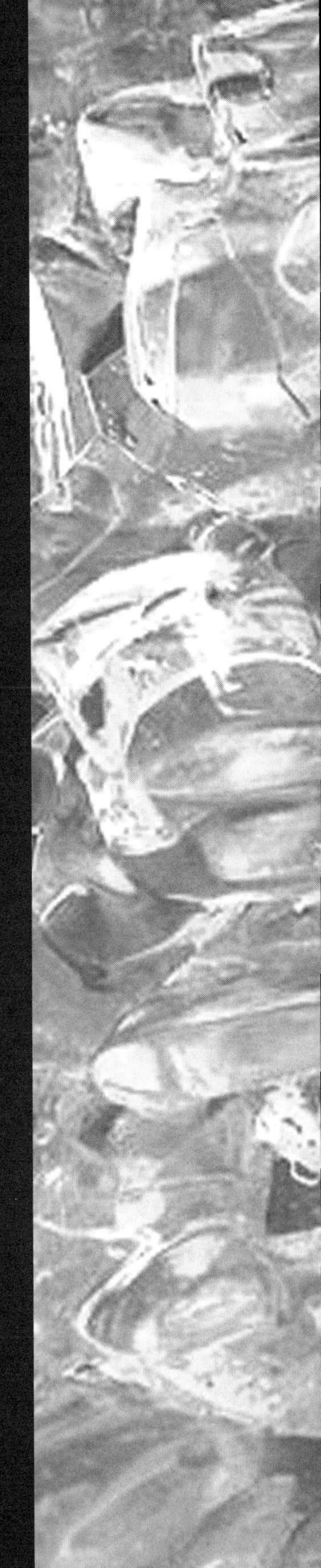

The remaining chapters discuss managing the business side of the bar, which begins with providing the beverages to be sold to customers. No matter how much experience a bar owner has, it is sometimes difficult to keep up with trends and how they affect beverage orders. Rarely is a liquor or wine order "standard" from week to week and month to month, yet a steady supply of product must be maintained and tracked to ensure that what is being purchased actually produces sales. Managing the storeroom is a third priority. This includes both physical care to maintain the quality of the products and theft prevention to maintain quantity.

This chapter examines purchasing policies and decisions; the routines of purchasing, receiving, and issuing; the inventory records and procedures commonly used; and the use of inventory figures to measure bar cost and purchasing efficiency.

THIS CHAPTER WILL HELP YOU . . .

- Decide what, when, where, and how much liquor, beer, and wine to buy.
- Decide what to look for when selecting suppliers and examining their prices and discounts.
- Establish par stock for each bar and minimum and maximum storeroom stock levels.

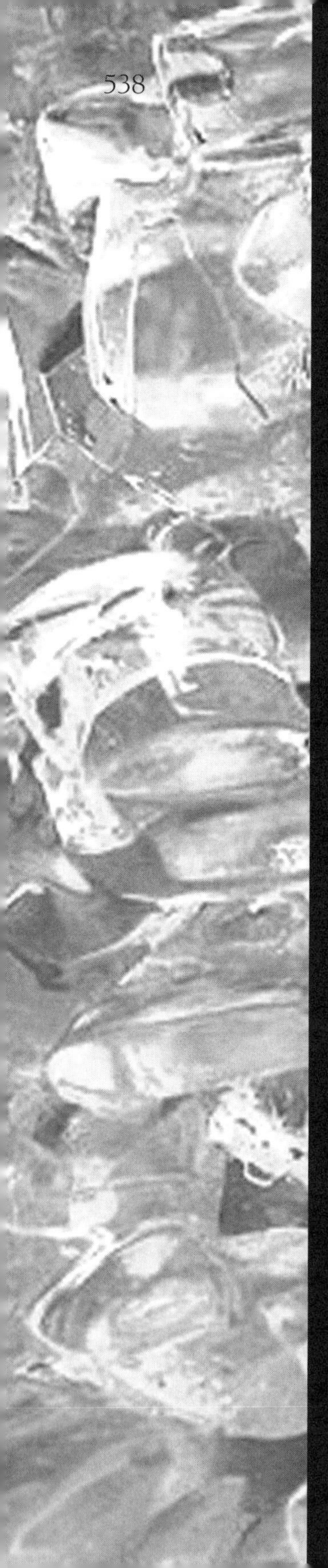

- Know the functions and relationships of purchase orders, invoices, and credit memos.
- Set up routines for ordering and receiving.
- Store each type of beverage properly, efficiently, and safely.
- Establish inventory procedures and conduct physical inventories.
- Determine inventory value, bar cost, and inventory-turnover rate.

You may wonder how such a straightforward subject as buying liquor and supplying it to the bar could take up so many pages. Part of the answer is that alcoholic beverages are an investment in income-producing stock and there are many facets to making the best investment for the least money. Another part of the answer is that the purchasing and record-keeping processes are critical to other aspects of the business. Still another part is that alcohol has an irresistible attraction for many people so if you don't keep track of it, it will "evaporate," so to speak.

The goal of beverage purchasing is to provide a steady supply of ingredients for the drinks you sell at costs that will maximize profits. The purchasing function moves in a continuous cycle with several distinct phases:

- ***Planning and ordering.*** Selecting what you need at the most advantageous prices.
- ***Receiving.*** Taking delivery of exactly what you have ordered—brands, sizes, and quantities—at the specified prices and in good condition.
- ***Storing.*** Keeping your beverage supplies in a place that is secure against theft and deterioration until needed.
- ***Issuing.*** Transferring your beverages from storeroom to bar, where they will be used to make drinks for your customers.

The sale of these drinks keeps the cycle revolving since you must continually replenish the supplies consumed. But the cycle does not revolve by itself; it must be managed. The process must be responsive to needs (sales volume and customer tastes), to the market (supply and price), to cash flow (money available for investment), and to indicators of change in any of these factors. The beverage manager must know what is going on at all times. In a small operation purchasing may be the responsibility of the bar owner or the head bartender. Large operations usually have a full-time beverage manager, while hotel and restaurant chains often have an entire department devoted to purchasing and other aspects of beverage management. However the principles and problems are much the same, no matter how big or small the enterprise is.

PLANNING THE PURCHASING

The term **purchasing,** as it applies to food-and-beverage operations, is usually a two-step process. The first step is the **selection process,** which involves making the decisions about what is to be served; which brands, sizes, and quantities to buy; what to make from scratch or to purchase premade. Selection also impacts the amounts, styles, and sizes of glassware to be used. These must also be ordered in sufficient quantity and kept in inventory.

The second step is the **procurement process,** or the method used for purchasing items. This involves choosing and working with vendors, using a standard system of ordering, deciding on a budget and sticking to it, and determining how often to replenish stock.

Many factors go into making purchasing decisions. Some are management policies that once established should be followed to the letter. Others are day-to-day decisions based on current situations. They all boil down to what to buy, where to buy it, how much to buy, when to buy, and what to pay.

What to Buy

Deciding what to buy involves two basic policy decisions: the quality of the beverages you will pour and the variety of items you will have available. To meet customers' needs and avoid overstocked bars and storerooms, today's bar managers use a policy commonly known as **category management.** This involves tracking what sells and what doesn't and using that information to create a beverage program that delivers the best product mix to customers and the maximum profit for the bar. Today's sophisticated point-of-sale (POS) system can be an invaluable tool in accomplishing this. The POS is very much like a personal computer. Its touch-screen technology and easy programmability give the user the ability to track multiple types of data, including the brands of alcohol used in a drink and the server who sold it. (Making note of servers who are not selling much is also valuable as an indicator of who needs additional training.)

In a large operation the POS terminals are workstations linked to a central computer, which is, ironically, also called a *server.* Another feature of these systems is the capability to keep a running inventory, automatically "deleting" the standard amount of each liquor that is used to mix each cocktail. Theoretically this should give a bar manager almost instant usage numbers, which can later be compared with the actual physical inventory. Some systems can even be programmed to draft purchase orders and e-mail them to a wholesaler when inventory reaches certain levels.

In a large chain computerization and category management are tremendously helpful. A company that operates several units can compare brand movement among locations and refine the menus, inventories, and promotional strategies accordingly. For example Ruth's Chris Steak Houses, a popular Southern fine-dining chain based in Louisiana, noted that one bar sold hardly any cognac. This was because the cognac was located in a seldom-seen portion of the backbar.

Market Watch magazine is an additional source that can be used to track beverage trends and desirable brands. According to the research firm Impact Databank, a "hot" brand is:

- An established brand with a minimum 20-percent annual growth rate.
- A brand that has experienced double-digit growth rates for the past three years.
- A product that is new but "significant" in some way. "Hot brands" must also meet annual volume requirements:
  - For spirits, 200,000 9-liter cases

- For major domestic-beer brands, 3.4 million 2.25-gallon cases
- For other, specialty-beer brands, 1.1 million 2.25-gallon cases
- For imported beers, 1 million 2.25-gallon cases
- For domestic wines, 250,000 cases
- For imported wines, 200,000 cases

These findings are published regularly in *Market Watch*. Computers and technology give bars and restaurants access to more specific brand information than ever before. This negates the old *shotgun-marketing approach,* in which a bar would try one idea, then another, and another, in hopes of "hitting" on something successful. With research the decisions are better informed and more likely to reap rewards.

Quality and Variety. Quality should be a primary consideration in brand selection because it depends on your clientele: what they expect and what they are willing to pay for. It would be foolish to buy premium brands or boutique California wines for a low-budget clientele, and equally foolish not to offer such items in a luxury restaurant. As in everything else you must know your customers.

Beyond this you must consider the quality of your **well brands,** which are the liquors that you pour in mixed drinks when the customer does not ask for a specific brand. Also known as **house brands** or *house liquors,* these represent about half of the liquor used in an average bar. Choose a set of well brands and stick with them for the sake of consistency in your drink recipes. Many bars use inexpensive brands in the well on the theory that customers can't tell the difference in a mixed drink. Other bars use familiar, advertised brands in the middle price range. Still others use premium brands—this is sometimes called a **premium well** or **super well**—that they feature with pride in their merchandising. By carrying premium brands in the well, in addition to making an impression, you eliminate having to carry well brands. This means less inventory and less cost. Premium brands are a good choice for bars where clientele is value-conscious, that is, willing to spend a little extra to receive a higher-quality drink. Superpremium brands have the advantages of strong name recognition and customer loyalty, but they will not be worth the extra expenditure if you don't do a good job of letting your customers know that these brands are being used.

Using cheap liquors in the well but charging higher prices for them is downright unethical—and if you think you are fooling your customers, you are only fooling yourself. Taste your own drinks and you will notice the difference, just as your customers will. You might save a few pennies per drink, but you will never know how many or why customers never came back and how many others they told about your "cheap, high-priced drinks!" Besides you don't save all that much. Take, for example, a liter of Scotch that costs $15 and one that costs $9. If the portion is 1 ounce the $15 Scotch costs 44 cents per drink and the $9 Scotch costs 26 cents, a difference of 18 cents per drink. Are the savings worth it when you may lose customers?

Since all drinks made using well brands are typically sold at the same price, you can calculate the overall cost of your well by averaging it. Take the wholesale cost of the six standard well products (gin, bourbon, Scotch, rum, vodka, and tequila), then divide by 6 to arrive at an average cost per liter. Divide that figure by 33.8 (and subtract any spillage allowance) to determine the cost per ounce of your well brands.

For further waste control arrange the sequence of well brands in your speed rail (the bottle-width rack in the underbar) in this fashion:

GIN BOURBON VODKA SCOTCH RUM TEQUILA

Light and dark liquors are interspersed so they are less likely to be used accidentally by a bartender in a hurry.

The second major decision is the variety of items you will stock. The average bar in the United States may carry as many as 130 liquors and liqueurs on the backbar, and a showy backbar lined with bottles is the hallmark of many operations. Some bars take pride in never having to tell a customer, "I'm sorry but we don't have that." Such a policy, while it can be good merchandising for some types of clientele, has the potential of expanding inventory indefinitely with items that do not move. Liquor that does not sell does not earn a penny of profit, except to the degree that it contributes to atmosphere and image on that great-looking backbar.

Many bars prefer to limit their offerings to popular and well-advertised brands of each item, with the number of brands varying with the type and size of the operation. If a customer calls for a brand that you don't carry, you probably won't lose either the sale or the customer if you can offer a well-known brand of comparable quality. But be sure to offer the alternate to the customer; do not try to substitute another brand without the customer's knowledge. That is a very bad practice that will only create an image of mistrust for your place and your bartenders. Still another approach is to deliberately limit the number of brands and items that you stock by developing a printed drink menu based on a small number of beverages, as discussed in Chapter 11. Most customers will respond to such a menu by ordering from the drinks listed; questions of call brands and unusual drinks seldom come up.

Where you draw the line on the numbers of brands and items that you stock will depend on your clientele, your type of enterprise, your volume of business, and the money available for such an investment. But it is wise to draw the line somewhere—then hold it. A common mistake is to let your inventory grow, over time, to unmanageable levels. Products do fall out of fashion, as in any industry. One way to avoid a proliferation of brands and bottles is never to add a new item of unpredictable demand without eliminating a slow-moving item from your list. In this case "*slow-moving*" means a product that takes nine months or longer to use up a single bottle.

You also need to keep up with new products and anticipate changes in customer tastes. One way to do this is to consult frequently with the salespeople for the wholesale buyers you deal with. They know who is launching a huge advertising campaign or coming out with a new light beer, as well as which new liqueur or imported beer is big in California or New York and is coming your way. Many beverage managers have a regular time for sales personnel to call. In this way the managers are not interrupted while immersed in some other task, and the salesperson has a receptive audience. Do not, however, let anyone tell you what you should buy. Consider suggestions, but measure them against your own ground rules and current needs.

Sales representatives will push their own products; that is their job. Compare what they say with what their competitors say and make up your own mind. Another way to keep up with trends is to read sales and market surveys in trade magazines, such as *Market Watch,* for their survey results of those hot new brands. For local trends remember to read the liquor-store advertisements in your local newspapers.

Beverage buyers can often peruse catalogs on CD-ROMs to find what they need. In many cases these have eliminated the bulky product notebooks and print catalogs the suppliers once used. If a beverage is available somewhere in the world and is distributed by someone, it is very likely that you can locate it on the Internet or on a particular supplier's catalog on disk. The next logical step is to link your own computer to the vendor's so that you can access current price lists, availability, and delivery information, and can place orders by e-mail. On some systems you can specify a replacement product that you would consider acceptable if your first choice is not available. The most sophisticated systems enable you to access historical data, such as how frequently you have ordered a certain product, or are set up to "cost" drink recipes.

No matter how sophisticated the ordering process, buying individual products is still mostly a matter of brand selection and common sense. When the liquor or beer brand concerns the customer, buy the brands that your customers will buy. For your well select the brands that make the quality of drinks you want to pour. This applies to your vermouth and liqueur choices as well. It is a good idea to taste your own mixed drinks with different brands of spirits and liqueurs. Generic liqueurs in particular can taste quite different from one brand to another, and the expensive imported brands are not necessarily the best.

Purchasing Wines

Buying wines is somewhat more complicated than buying beers and spirits. One reason is that customer demand is less clear-cut. For house wines more and more enterprises are replacing generic wines with inexpensive varietal wines in 1-liter and 1.5-liter bottles. Some restaurants pour house wines by the glass from 750-millileter bottles and have the same wines available for sale by the bottle. An alert waiter can often convert orders for two or three individual glasses to a bottle of wine for the table.

Wines for a printed wine list require a different approach. Because wines vary from one winemaker to another, one vintage to another, and one year of age to another, you must either rely on an expert or know a good deal about wines yourself. You can safely buy most young whites, rosés, and some of the simpler reds and sell them right away. The older the vintage date, the more skeptical you should be.

Fine whites and reds require special purchasing decisions. These wines should not be sold to customers before they are ready to drink. This means you must tie up your money in the wine cellar while they mature or take a chance on purchasing them later at higher prices—*if* they are still available. Keep supplies of the wines on your list in line with demand without overbuying. If you run out you lose sales and disappoint customers, but if you overbuy you have money tied up unproductively and may run the risk of having a wine outlive its lifespan in storage. (These factors reinforce the need for a good by-the-glass program.)

The Internet is becoming an important factor in wine sales: it has made it easier for bar owners and cellarmasters to find out what other people are paying for wines. All they need to do is peruse the Web pages of wine wholesalers and retailers around the country, as well as the wineries themselves. Distributors who pad their wholesale prices unnecessarily can easily be found out by your doing some online comparison-shopping.

eVineyard is an interesting case study and is still for the most part considered a grand experiment worth watching closely in the world of wine sales. This online wine-sales company has avoided the tricky interstate alcohol-delivery issues by obtaining retail licenses in each of the states it serves. The company passes along an order to a local wholesaler, who fills the order and delivers it to the user. eVineyard's average gross margin is 32 percent, which is good when you consider that the company carries no inventory and does not have to split its margin with retailers.

However, the earliest e-commerce wine sales companies, Virtual Vineyards and Wine.com (the latter now owned and relaunched by eVineyard), were part of the "dot-com" boom and bust. They had encouraging early sales figures but not enough long-term business savvy. Peter Granoff, the founder of California-based Wine.com, has pointed out that one problem with online wine sales is that the freedom of e-commerce naturally resists the rather old-fashioned constraints of the wine industry: a three-tiered sales hierarchy (winery/wholesale distributor/end user) and an outmoded regulatory system. Today with 26 states and the District of Columbia allowing limited direct shipments of wine to consumers, the Internet may simply be outgrowing the traditional ways of buying wine.

No one knows where this will lead but none of it is especially good news for wine distributors, whose ranks are already dwindling. To prevent large chains from grossly undercutting them in price, some of the smaller, independent fine-wine distributors are pooling their purchases to secure volume discounts. Others are being swallowed up by larger distributorships.

Internet wine sales were given a huge boost in May 2005 when the U.S. Supreme Court ruled that states that permit in-state wineries to sell directly to consumers cannot deny that right to out-of-state wineries. Opponents (including state governments, evangelical Christians, and Mothers Against Drunk Driving) argued that allowing direct wine sales to individuals could not ensure full tax collection on the sales, and would mean less control over underage drinkers' ability to obtain alcohol. Wine producers' representatives countered that in this age of distributorship consolidation, the smaller wineries are at a sales disadvantage—they have difficulty finding distributorships that want to take them on at all and can sell more wine by selling it themselves, no matter where the customers are located.

Distributors are still a crucial part of a successful bar business, and we'll discuss your relationships with them later in this chapter. For now remember that the distributor's sales force is knowledgeable about industry trends and will often bring news of wine bargains. You will need to decide which should you buy, and which should you pass up.

- *Post-offs* and *closeouts* are deals that help distributorships move slow-selling wines or to clear out a product line that they are soon planning to drop altogether. Look carefully at the offer and consider the background details. Why are these wines not selling? Are they too old? Not quite "good enough?" Were they overpriced to begin with and are just now being offered at a fair price for their quality?
- *Vintage clearances* are offered to make space in a distributor's warehouse for incoming newer wines. These offers usually come with a minimum number of cases that must be ordered to receive the discounted price, which means a sizable investment on your part. We suggest making the distributor an offer that you can afford. Yes, it's an investment of both cash and storage space, but you may be surprised at how much room for negotiation there is in this type of deal.
- *Exclusives* are deals offered to a buyer because of a solid relationship with a supplier, whether it's the sales rep who calls on you regularly or someone higher up in the organization. The word *exclusive* should indicate exactly what it means: that your business is the only bar in the area pouring this particular wine. (Retailers can sell that wine, but none of your competitors can.) Whether you participate in an exclusive deal depends mostly on the wine savvy of your customer base. If your customers will not necessarily appreciate the exclusivity of the deal or if the products are not upscale enough to warrant exclusivity, it is acceptable for you to pass it up. An exclusive arrangement may also come with minimum orders and other special requests by the distributor.

We should also mention that suppliers often offer very favorable discounts to feature a wine in your by-the-glass program so be sure to ask about that. It is also important to be wary of a discounted price for a wine that may be approaching deterioration. Taste wines before you buy them, then choose according to what you know about your customers' tastes and get as much expert advice as you can. (You might find it helpful to reread Chapter 7 on developing a wine list.)

Where to Buy

The beverage buyer does not always have a great deal of choice about where to buy. State laws, which vary from one state to another, govern the purchase and sale of alcoholic beverages. Local laws also come into play. First a buyer should study the laws of the state, county, city, and even precinct as they apply to liquor purchases. In 19 states or jurisdictions the *retailer,* the seller of alcoholic beverages to the consumer, must buy from state stores. These states are known as **control states** or **monopoly states.** In the remaining states, known as **license states,** and the

District of Columbia the buyer is typically allowed to purchase from any wholesaler licensed by the state and, in some states, from licensed distributors and manufacturers as well. Figure 13.1 lists the current status of each state. However, there may be local restrictions. For example, a county may have a law against buying in another county. To further complicate matters the requirements and limitations are usually not the same for beers and wines as they are for spirits.

In license states alcoholic beverages are sold to retailers by a number of wholesale liquor distributors. Each of these distributors will offer a wide variety of brands and will probably pride themselves in offering a few "exclusives," that is, products or brand names not available from other distributors in that market. Depending on your state's laws the makers of the products (or the importers, if they come from another country) may sell to distributors, and the distributors sell to the retailers. Almost always you will have to deal with several suppliers, who carry different items and brands. In some areas the healthy competition among suppliers works to your advantage since each one tries hard to come up with ways to please or

CONTROL STATES AND LICENSE STATES

Control States	*License States*	
Alabama	Alaska	Mississippi (retail only)
Idaho	Arizona	Missouri
Iowa[a]	Arkansas	Nebraska
Maine	California	Nevada
Michigan	Colorado	New Jersey
Mississippi (wholesale only)	Connecticut	New Mexico
Montana	Delaware	New York
New Hampshire	Florida	North Dakota
North Carolina	Georgia	Oklahoma
Ohio	Hawaii	Rhode Island
Oregon	Illinois	South Carolina
Pennsylvania	Indiana	South Dakota
Utah	Kansas	Tennessee
Vermont	Kentucky	Texas
Virginia	Louisiana	Wisconsin
Washington	Maryland	Wyoming (retail only)
West Virginia	Masschusetts	District of Columbia
Wyoming (wholesale only)	Minnesota	

[a] Iowa has no state stores; its control board, as sole wholesaler, sells to privately owned outlets it licenses to sell to retail consumers.

FIGURE 13.1

impress you, the customer. In many states, however, there are now only a few major distributors.

This has some important implications for the individually owned bar. First product choice may be limited, especially for less-well-known or unusual items. Second the fewer the vendors, the less likely it is that a buyer can negotiate for more "personalized" service, such as specific delivery times. The monopolistic trend forces smaller bars to conform to the dictates of the vendor.

In most license states, a master list is published monthly (by the state's liquor control authority) containing the names of all of the wholesalers in the state, the lines they carry, and the prices they charge. Monthly beverage journals list discount and post-off (sales) schedules. Individual wholesalers also have product catalogs and price sheets, quantity discounts, special sales, and promotional materials. As you learned earlier in this chapter at least some of this information is available on CD-ROM. Control states publish lists of all the brands available and their prices, along with the addresses of state stores. Dealing with sales representatives is often easier than working with lists. Although you may not be able to buy from them directly, they can tell you where you can buy their products. They can also keep you informed of special sales and promotions.

The Impact of Consolidation

The wine industry is as good a place to start as any in the discussion of consolidation, which is the overarching trend in the beverage business today. As with many other industries a few major, multibillion dollar international companies now dominate the scene. Constellation Brands has become the world's major wine marketer, surpassing longtime leader E & J Gallo Winery. Since 1999 Constellation Brands has acquired Robert Mondavi, Simi, Franciscan Estates, Paul Masson, Arbor Mist, and Sebastiani Vineyards, among others. The Gallo wine empire includes several Californians (Mirassou, Louis Martini, Turning Leaf), as well as vineyards in Australia (Black Swan), New Zealand (Whitehaven Wine Company), and Italy (Ecco Domani). Smaller California wineries and their brands have been snapped up by London-based Diageo, which owns Beaulieu Vineyards, Barton & Guestier, and Moet & Chandon; British-owned Allied Domecq owns Atlas Peak, Buena Vista, and Clos du Bois, to name a few, as well as vineyards in five other countries. Branches of long-respected wine family trees have been twisted, turned, and grafted by these megasales.

In the brewing industry the headlines are no less startling. South African Breweries (SAB) paid $5.6 billion to acquire Miller Brewing Company of St. Louis, Missouri, and renamed the company SAB-Miller. SAB went on to acquire Italian brewer Peroni and is (as of this writing) in a bidding war with Anheuser-Busch for the Harbin Brewing Group of China. The Adolph Coors Company and Molson, Canada's largest brewer, merged in 2004. Interbrew, a Belgian beer-maker, has merged with AmBev of Brazil to create what may be the world's largest brewer in terms of sales. The new company, InBev, will control 11.4 percent of the world beer market, surpassing Anheuser-Busch's 10.7 percent. In Australia (as of this writing) the Foster's Group (the beer conglomerate of Foster's Lager fame) is attempting a hostile takeover of the wine conglomerate Southcorp. If successful the result will be yet another major world beverage corporation.

These events do not exactly bring to mind the picturesque winery and the hardworking family who proudly tends to their vines and manages their business (we fervently hope that there will always be a place for the niche product and small organization). In the meantime retailers and restaurateurs must believe that consolidation in the supplier and wholesale tiers will have a positive impact overall. It might. It generally means more brand advertising aimed at consumers (paid for by the large companies) and serious marketing and training support for people who sell the products. So it is worthwhile to follow the news of these corporate incarnations and be alert to the changes that market consolidation brings.

Supplier Relations

When you have a choice price is certainly one reason to buy from one supplier rather than another, and you should always get competitive bids for large orders from different suppliers. But there are many other considerations, including which services a supplier does or does not offer. For instance:

- How often does the supplier deliver? The more frequently, the better; and daily is best, even though you do not order daily. You do not have to stock as much and can get something quickly in an emergency.
- Does the supplier alter quality, quantity, and/or delivery-time standards? You don't want to deal with someone who has basic organizational problems.
- Where is the supplier located? Suppose you are in a rural area and your suppliers must travel more than an hour to reach you. Does distance affect the delivery schedule? What about the weather? Will your wine or beer travel for hours in the hot sun? Will snow and ice interrupt service?
- What resources does the supplier have? Is it a large and varied inventory kept well stocked, or a small stock that is continually being depleted? Does the supplier have temperature-controlled warehouse facilities? Refrigerated trucks?
- Does the supplier give proper and systematic care to goods in storage or in transit? Are wines kept at proper temperatures? Are bottles kept on their sides or upside down if traditional corks are used? Are draft beers and unpasteurized package beers kept refrigerated?
- Is the supplier's office and warehouse organized, clean, secure, and professional overall? (A visit to these facilities can tell you quite a bit.)
- Must you buy a certain minimum per order? Is there a maximum? Can you adjust your orders to meet these requirements? Is it worth it?
- Does the supplier extend credit, and what are the terms? (This is not often a negotiable point because of government restrictions.)
- Can you buy mixes and accessories from the supplier at advantageous prices and quantities?
- What is the supplier's **lead time**, or the time between ordering and delivery? (You must estimate consumption and order far enough ahead to compensate for the gap. The shorter lead time, the better.)

- How much consultation and training of your staff members is the supplier willing to give? (Some wine distributors are willing, for instance, to organize winery tours for buyers and key staff members, even to other states or countries.)
- Is the distributor's staff willing to participate in sales-boosting activities, such as arranging wine tastings and dinners? Is the company willing to donate products for charitable events?
- What other services does the supplier offer: e.g., blank order forms, promotional materials, 24-hour telephone service?

The number of suppliers that a bar deals with usually depends on the variety of products it wishes to carry. You should consider more than one supplier for each category (beer, wine, spirits) because brands play such a strong role in your needs and because one vendor may be out of stock on one of your critical items. Not all suppliers carry all brands, by any means. If more than one supplier carries the same brand, go with the one that offers the best service and seems by all accounts to be running a profitable business. Avoid doing business with suppliers—at least, for the moment—if there are any signs of financial trouble.

The explosion of e-commerce has opened some new doors for purchase and, as you learned in the discussion of the 2005 U.S. Supreme Court decision, has created some new controversy. Alcoholic beverages no longer have to move within the traditional **three-tier system,** from producer, to distributor, to retailer. The business-to-business movement is still in its infancy with alcohol because it is more strictly regulated than most other types of products and because every state seems to have a tangle of different laws about selling it. But in the future these restrictions may be further weakened in court challenges.

Distributors stand to lose an estimated $25 billion in product markups if retailers could purchase every type of alcohol directly from producers: distilleries, wineries, brewers, and importers. But some forward-thinking merchants say that the cyber-marketplace actually makes it easier to do business with distributors. When price lists and orders can be e-mailed, instant or short-term specials can be offered via computer, and catalogs of items can be viewed and updated online, the bar manager or purchasing agent is the ultimate beneficiary.

One more point should be made, and it is about your own professionalism in dealing with beverage suppliers. These are generally hard-working salespeople who care deeply about their product lines and can bring a great deal of knowledge and enthusiasm to your beverage program. When you make an appointment with a beverage supplier, be sure to keep it. In fact it is a good idea to set regular meeting times specifically for them to present anything new that they have to offer. You certainly don't have to buy it all, but don't close your mind to interesting new items; be willing to try them in small quantities as your budget allows. Distributors also have events to which customers are regularly invited, such as open houses, trade tastings, and wine dinners. Attend them if you can. They are good networking events, where you will have a chance to learn more about your competitors, as well as the products that are being showcased.

How Much to Buy

This is a central question for the beverage buyer. The answer is enough but not too much: enough to serve your customers what they want but not so much that numbers of bottles stand idle on shelves for long periods, thereby tying up money you could put to better use. If you overorder the bottles will sit around too long; if you underorder you might find yourself running out of popular brands and unable to get more on short notice. Your goal is to never run out of your well brands, your house wines, your draft beers, the popular bottled beers, and call brands of spirits. But you might not reorder a slow-moving item until your last bottle is half gone.

Establish a **par stock** for each bar in your facility, using a form similar to the one in Figure 13.2. You can determine par stock needs from your detailed sales records. (If you are still in the planning stage you can "guesstimate" your rate of sale.) A general rule is to have enough of each type and brand to meet 1½ times the needs of your busiest day of the week. For a small restaurant bar averaging $500 in daily sales, this might work out to be the open bottle plus two full ones for each fast-moving brand, and the open bottle plus one extra for each slower-moving brand.

From par-stock needs for each bar, you can determine what you should have in the storeroom to back them up. This then becomes your par stock for the storeroom, or your normal storeroom inventory (that is, merchandise on hand). You can also use par stock to measure your daily consumption. The bottles it takes to bring the bar stock to par represent roughly the consumption of the day before. Over a week's time these bottles will yield an accurate figure of average daily consumption. This can guide your rate of purchase. Par stock is also a way of keeping up with customer tastes. You know which brands are moving quickly because you have par stock as a measure of their popularity. As such par stock tells you what to buy, as well as how much you are using. Whatever your buying interval, it is a good idea to set minimum and maximum stock levels for each item, to maintain your storeroom inventory. The minimum level may be supplemented by a reorder point that gives you lead time so that the stock does not drop below the minimum level before you receive delivery. Your maximum level represents the dividing line between enough and too much. Like the par-stock level at the bar, it should represent 1½ times what you expect to need before you replenish your supply.

There are several arguments for keeping a small inventory geared closely to your sales volume. The major point is that beverages are expensive, even at discount rates, and they tie up money that is not earning anything and may be needed elsewhere. When you finally do use a bottle of liquor that you bought months ago at a discount, it may have cost you far more in lost use of the money you paid than the money you saved in buying it.

Large inventories cause other problems, too. One is security: The more liquor you have, the more tempting it is to steal, the easier it is to steal, and the harder it is to keep track of. The larger the inventory, the more space and staff are needed

BAR PAR STOCK FORM

Bar Name
Address

Effective as of (date): ____________ Bar Outlet: ____________

Page ______ of ______ (total pages)

Item Number	Item Name	Size	Bar	Par	Item Number	Item Name	Size	Bar	Par

FIGURE 13.2 This all-important form is also shown as Figure 9.3.

and the greater the burden of record-keeping and taking physical inventory. Perishable items, such as beers, should never be overstocked; some wines also deteriorate quickly. Customer tastes may change suddenly, leaving you with items you will never use.

On the other hand some wines should be bought in quantity because they are scarce and will quickly disappear from the market. You will want to buy enough of them to last as long as your printed wine list does. Beverage wholesalers sell mostly in case lots, sometimes offering discounts for a certain number of cases. You

BOTTLE AND CASE SIZES

Bottle Size[a]	*Fluid Ounces*	*Units per Case*
Distilled spirits		
50 milliliters	1.7	120
100 milliliters	3.4	60
200 milliliters	6.8	48
375 milliliters	12.7	24
750 milliliters	25.4	12
1 liter	33.8	12
1.75 liters	59.2	6
Wine		
50 milliliters	1.7	120
100 milliliters	3.4	60
187 milliliters	6.3	48
375 milliliters	12.7	24
750 milliliters	25.4	12
1 liter	33.8	12
1.5 liters	50.7	6
3 liters	101	4
Beer[b]		
6 ounces	6	24 or 32
7 ounces	7	24 or 32
8 ounces	8	24 or 32
10 ounces	10	24 or 32
12 ounces	12	24 or 32

[a] Not all sized legal in all states.
[b] For draft-beer container sizes see Figure 13.6

FIGURE 13.3

can buy cases of spirits and wines in the bottle sizes shown in Figure 13.3. The size bottles you buy will depend on the type and size of your establishment and even more on the way you serve your beverages.

Some suppliers will sell a **broken case** or *mixed case,* which is a case of 12 bottles made up of several brands or items of your specification, and some will sell certain items by the single bottle or, for wines, a minimum of three bottles. The cost per bottle is higher for items in a broken case or by the bottle; the cost per bottle is lowest when purchased by the case or in multiple-case lots.

You should certainly buy by the case anything that you use a lot of—your well brands, house wines, domestic beers, and popular brands—to take advantage of cost savings and to ensure an adequate supply. From this point on, it becomes a matter of calculating your rate of use for each item and matching it with your purchasing intervals. As you decide what and how much to stock, you need to consider two more factors: **carrying costs** and **capital risk.** Your carrying costs are the total combined dollar value of the liquor, wine, beer, mixes, and supplies at the bar. This figure should not vary widely month to month. Capital risk is the risk you take when a bottle of liquor leaves the storeroom and goes to the bar, where it can be wasted, spilled, given away, consumed by employees, or otherwise not sold for profit. The way to control capital risks is to maintain a tight inventory, store as little as possible, and consistently enforce your inventory policies.

When to Buy

When and how often you place an order will depend on the volume of your business, the size inventory that you are willing to stock, the requirements and schedules of the suppliers, the scheduling of your receiving people, the specials you want to take advantage of, and such variables as holidays, conventions, special events, or even a run of bad weather. Some enterprises order daily, others once per accounting period, and still others somewhere in between. Some might buy wine once a year, spirits weekly, and beer every day. The more frequently you buy, the less inventory you have to cope with. On the other hand every order initiates the purchasing-receiving-storing routine, which may not always be labor-efficient.

Other factors affecting the timing of purchases are your cash position and the payment or credit requirements imposed by state regulations or by the purveyor. Some states allow no credit at all; all sales must be cash. Other states require payment monthly or semimonthly or within some other interval, such as 10 days after the week of sale or the second Monday after delivery. Fines and publicity may accompany late payments or nonpayment. These requirements make it very important to integrate your purchasing times with your cash flow so that you are not caught short on the due date.

What to Pay

In control states price markups are typically fixed by law and prices will be the same in all state stores. The only price decision the buyer must make is whether to take advantage of an occasional special or quantity discount. In license states it is often worth shopping around to find the best deal on the brands you want to buy. There are seldom large price differences because state laws are typically designed to avoid price wars. Manufacturers and distributors must give the same deals to everyone they sell to so the price structure is fairly homogeneous. Nevertheless in some areas suppliers are free to set their own markups, grant their own discounts, and run their own specials—and they do. So it is worthwhile to study price lists, talk to sales contacts, and look at the advertisements in the trade journals.

Several types of discounts are found in the wholesale liquor industry. In general they are: basic discounts, post-off discounts, size variations, and assorted discount structures.

A basic discount is usually volume-related, to entice buyers to purchase larger quantities. Suppose, for instance, that the list price of Brand Z Vodka is $100 per case (there are 12 bottles in a case). With a minimum 5-case order the price drops to $92 per case; for 10 cases, it drops to $88 per case; and for 15 cases, it might drop to $84. When you analyze this by cost per bottle, you will see that in a small order (4 cases or less), you are paying $8.30 per bottle; while in the largest order (15 or more cases) the price per bottle drops to $7.

There are no "standards" for basic discounts; they vary tremendously among brands. But often the liquors with the highest prices will also have the deepest discounts.

A **post-off discount** occurs when the distributor reduces the price of a particular brand to stimulate demand for it, either by the bottle or by the case. For example, Brand A Scotch has a $175-per-case list price. When a $9 post-off is announced for purchases of five or more, this drops the price to $166 per case.

Size variations also affect liquor's all-important cost-per-ounce numbers. You want to be familiar with this, particularly for spirits, because you pour and price them by the ounce. The cost per ounce is highest when the bottle size is smallest and decreases as the bottle size increases. The cost per ounce is higher for items purchased by the bottle or in a broken case than when purchased by the case. Figure 13.4 provides a price comparison of different bottle sizes.

PRICE COMPARISON OF DIFFERENT BOTTLE SIZES

Bottles/Case	Bottle Size	Fluid Ounces	Cost/Bottle	Cost/Ounce
12	750 ml.	25.4	$16.90	$0.665
12	1 liter	33.8	20.40	0.603
6	1.75	59.2	27.90	0.471

FIGURE 13.4

Just by changing your purchasing from 750-millileter bottles to liter bottles, the savings per ounce ($0.665 minus $0.608) equals $0.057, or a little more than half a cent. The savings per liter ($0.057 multiplied by 33.8 ounces) is $1.92. This is almost $2 per bottle. This works out ($1.92 multiplied by 12 bottles) to a few pennies over $23 for the same "Brand A" Scotch.

When you consider the larger, 1.75-liter bottle prices, remember that the number of ounces in a case of liters is greater than the number of ounces in a case of 1.75 liters; this is the difference between 12 bottles and 6 bottles, respectively. The case of liters contains 405.6 ounces; the case of 1.75 liters contains 355.2 ounces.

In addition to cost another very important consideration is convenience of pouring. What are your pouring station and backbar set up to handle? With an automatic dispensing system, the use of the largest possible bottle is no problem; in other situations, these bottles may be unwieldy.

The fourth popular discount option is a simple variation of the basic discount structure, called the **multiple brands** or **assorted discount.** An importer or distiller offers this discount to encourage the bar owner to buy a wider range of its products. The total number of cases purchased is what the discount is based on. It is a "buy five cases of anything, and get 10 percent off" kind of deal, but it varies greatly. Since some of the cases are already discounted when you buy five or more of them, this additional discount can offer the conscientious buyer substantial savings, especially when buying in large quantities.

Consider how a typical, assorted discount purchase might work. Suppose that a bar receives this price list from ABC Importers, its wholesale distributor:

Item	*Size*	*List Price per Case*	*5-Case Discount*	*10-Case Discount*	*15-Case Discount*
Vodka	liter	$144	$9.00	$16.00	$20.00
Scotch	liter	$235	$14.00	$22.00	$30.00
Gin	liter	$165	$9.00	$17.00	$21.00

The bar places an order for two cases of vodka, one case of Scotch, and one case of gin. The total ($288 for vodka + $235 for Scotch + $165 for gin) comes to $688. However, if the bar would order *one* or more cases, bringing the total to at least five, the discount really kicks in. Let's order one more case of vodka, and see what happens:

For vodka: List price $144 per case, minus $9 per case discount = $135 per case
For Scotch: List price $235 per case, minus $14 discount = $221 per case
For gin: List price $165 per case, minus $9 discount = $156 per case

When you total these individual costs, the price for the five cases is:

Vodka (3 cases)	$405
Scotch (1 case)	221
Gin (1 case)	166
TOTAL	$792

Of course, this sale would have cost $688 with only four cases purchased. The "extra" case of vodka ended up costing only $104. When you do find good buys, you must weigh the money that you save against your inventory size, rate of use, and other items that you could spend the money on. Sometimes the best price is not the best buy. Be wary, too, of the motives behind supplier specials. Sometimes these are intended to get rid of wines or beers approaching their freshness limits. Fortunately you do not have to worry about this when buying spirits, which do not deteriorate.

PLACING THE LIQUOR ORDER

Earlier in this chapter we discussed the idea of developing par-stock levels. Once you know what you will need you can use the **periodic order method.** This involves selecting a fixed calendar of ordering dates, then calculate what your bar will use (and therefore, what will be needed) for each time period between order dates. A person in charge of the bar, such as the manager or bartender, then selects the best time of day for the beverages to be delivered, and the supplier should be able to comply.

An alternative system is the **perpetual-inventory method.** In this system the order dates are variable and the amounts are preset. Inventory cards list purchases and issues, along with other information, such as par stock, and the lowest amount to which the item must drop in inventory before it is reordered. Someone checks the cards regularly, notes what is "running low," and orders it accordingly.

You must also develop a standard procedure for placing your orders. These procedures will be influenced by size and sales volume. At one extreme is the multicopy purchase order typically used by the large organization. At the other extreme is the informal verbal (oral) order given over the telephone or in person to a visiting sales representative. But even the verbal order should have a complete paper record to back it up. Every record, formal or informal, should contain the following information:

- Date of the order
- Name of the purveyor (seller)
- Name of the salesperson
- Purveyor's phone number
- Anticipated date and time of delivery
- Items, brands, and vintages ordered
- Sizes of containers (bottle and case)
- Numbers of bottles or cases
- Unit prices (price per bottle for each item)
- Name of person placing order

There are four good reasons for keeping a written record of each order:

- It gives the person receiving the delivery the data needed to check it.
- It gives the person paying the bills the data needed for checking the bill.
- It gives everyone concerned with the order—whether buyer, receiving agent, storeroom staff, accountant, bar manager, banquet manager, or bartender—access to exact data.
- It minimizes uncertainty, misunderstanding, and argument.

In a small operation this record may simply be a memo of a telephone order written on a form devised by the house, or it may be an order handwritten by a visiting salesperson. The only one concerned may be the owner/manager who buys, receives, and stores the merchandise; stocks and tends the bar; and pays the bills. In a large organization, where responsibilities are divided among many departments, a formal, multicopy **purchase order** (*P.O.*) may be used (see Figure 13.5), with the original going to the purveyor and copies sent to all concerned. Every purchase order has an order number (**P.O. number**), which is a key element in a network of paper records. It will be referenced on the purveyor's invoice and thus becoming the link between the two.

The **invoice** is the purveyor's response to the buyer's order. It reflects the information on the buyer's order sheet from the seller's point of view. It accompanies the delivery and must be signed by the buyer or the buyer's agent when delivery is received—which brings us to the second phase of the purchasing cycle.

PURCHASE ORDER

Name of Bar
Address

Date ______________________ Purchase Order No. ______________________
Purveyor ______________________ Salesperson ______________________
Phone ______________________ Date Needed ______________________
Address ______________________ Hour of Delivery ______________________

Item #	Quantity	Unit	Brand	Unit Price	Total

P.O. Total ______________________
Ordered by ______________________

FIGURE 13.5

RECEIVING THE LIQUOR ORDER

Technology is transforming today's wine wholesaler by automating transactions to an amazing degree. Cases of product may be tagged with radio-frequency identification (RFID) tags, making them easy for workers using handheld computers to find. These workers, known as *pickers*, can round up enough product to fill several orders at a time. Delivery trucks are outfitted with global positioning systems (GPS). The goals are to speed up large warehouse operations, minimize the margins for error, and eliminate breakage.

Despite all of the impressive technological safeguards the primary goal of the receiving process for the bar has not changed: to be sure that the delivery conforms exactly to what was ordered. The signing of the invoice by the purchaser has legal significance: It is the point at which the buyer, at least technically, becomes the "owner" of the merchandise. Therefore the delivery must be carefully checked before the invoice is signed. The person you give this responsibility to must be someone you trust, who has a good head for detail, and has been trained well for this assignment. There is no substitute for knowledgeable receiving personnel.

The first step is to check the invoice against the purchase order or memo. This must be an item-for-item check to see that the quantities, unit and case sizes, brands, vintages, and so on are listed as ordered and that the unit and case prices are quoted correctly. Then the math must be checked: the total costs per item, which are called **extensions** (the number of units multiplied by the unit cost) and the invoice total.

The second step is to check the delivery itself to see that it matches what is listed on the invoice. Each item must be checked as to quantity, unit, brand, vintage, and any other specification. Open cases should be verified bottle by bottle and examined for breakage, missing or broken tax stamps, and loose corks. Sealed cases should be examined for evidence of leaking bottles or weighed. The weight should agree with the weight printed on the case; a broken bottle will give a short weight. Beer should be checked for freshness by reading the pull dates on the containers, and for temperature by feeling the bottle or the keg. Kegs should be examined for signs of leakage. Their contents can be checked by weighing the keg, writing the weight on the invoice, and subtracting the **tare weight,** which is the weight of the empty keg, later. Figure 13.6 gives the correct net weights for draft beer. This process might seem like a hassle but you need to know if a beer keg is full or empty and you cannot do this simply by looking at it.

The third step is to request a **credit memo** for any discrepancies between the order memo and the invoice or the delivery itself. The credit memo includes items invoiced but not delivered, items invoiced and delivered that were not ordered, wrong merchandise (sizes, brands), items refused (overage beer, broken bottles, missing stamps, swollen beer cans), wrong prices, and math errors. At this point the credit memo is usually a notation right on the invoice showing the item, problem, and amount, but it might be a separate credit slip on which the invoice date and number are written. In either case the credit memo must be initialed or signed

BARREL AND KEG SIZES					
Container	*Gallons*	*Liters*	*Net wt/lb*	*Net wt/kg*	*Fluid Ounces*
Barrel	31	111.33	248	112.48	3968
½ barrel (keg)	15.5	58.67	124	56.24	1968
¼ barrel (½ keg)	7.75	29.33	62	25.12	992
⅛ barrel (¼ keg)	3.88	14.67	31	14.06	496

FIGURE 13.6

by the deliveryperson, and it too must be checked for accuracy. Only when everything has been checked, settled, and initialed does the receiving agent accept delivery by signing two copies of the invoice, one for you and one for the purveyor.

The purveyor will follow up the credit notation or memo with a confirmation that includes the invoice date and number (see Figure 13.7). A large organization may require the storeroom manager to repeat the check of merchandise using another invoice copy. When the storeroom manager signs for the beverages he or she accepts responsibility for them from the receiving agent. The beverages remain in the store room until they are requisitioned for bar use. The careful checking of deliveries has a double purpose: It is one-part protection against the purveyor's errors and one-part security against pilferage. Receiving a verified delivery is the first checkpoint along the system of controls that should follow your beverages from the time they enter your doors until they are poured at your bar and paid for by your customers.

STORAGE

The storeroom is the setting for the third phase of the purchasing cycle. This area performs three functions: security from theft, the physical care to maintain quality, and inventory maintenance and record-keeping. Computerized ordering has made it easier for bars and restaurants to order smaller amounts of goods more frequently, which may minimize the sizes of storage areas—but *nothing* will ever completely eliminate the need for storage.

The first essential step to running an effective storeroom is to limit access: Make the room off limits except for specific, authorized personnel. Anyone withdrawing

CREDIT MEMO

Customer:
Credit Memo No. ______________ Invoice No. ______________ Date ________

No	Item Description	Quantity	Unit Price	Total
1				
2				
3				
4				
5				

Amount of credit ______________

Reason for credit ______________________________________

Purveyor Signature ______________________________________

Receiving Bar Signature ______________________________________

FIGURE 13.7 This credit memo form serves as an order confirmation.

beverages does not enter the room; they must request what is needed from the storeroom staff or whoever has responsibility in a small operation. When open, the room must never be left unattended. If the person in charge must leave, even briefly, the door must be locked. This should be a substantial door with a deadbolt lock and only two sets of keys, one for the storeroom manager and one for emergencies, which is kept in the safe. Or it might have a combination lock that can be reset frequently, with only two people knowing the combination. If keys are used the locks should be changed often in case someone makes duplicate keys. Locks should always be changed when someone who has had keys leaves your employment.

Windows should be barred or covered with barbed wire. Alarm systems are frequently used to protect against off-hour break-ins. Some of these systems depend on light or noise to scare away intruders or summon help; others alert police or a private security system directly.

An orderly storeroom is both a security measure and a necessity for efficient operation. It should be divided into areas, each designed to stock a particular type of liquor. Each of these areas should be subdivided and clearly labeled so that each brand has a specially marked place. This also holds true for ancillary items, from cocktail napkins, to Champagne. A sample layout is pictured in Figure 13.8. When everything is systematically in place, anything amiss is soon noticed. Opened cases should be emptied immediately, their contents shelved, and the stock should be rotated so that the older bottles are in front.

Never leave a case half empty; flatten empty cases and remove them promptly. It could be easy to steal hidden bottles along with the trash. Shelving should be made of wire, heavy, and well braced because liquor is heavy. Select shelf units that are easy to assemble and add to, and that can be fitted with casters so they can roll. Technology now allows so-called "smart shelves" that sense when a bottle or case has been removed and can be programmed to reorder from the distributor of the product. Sealed cases can be stacked on low platforms until you need their contents.

Wine storage takes special care since wines are perishable and must be protected from temperatures that are too high, too low, or fluctuating; vibration; sunlight;

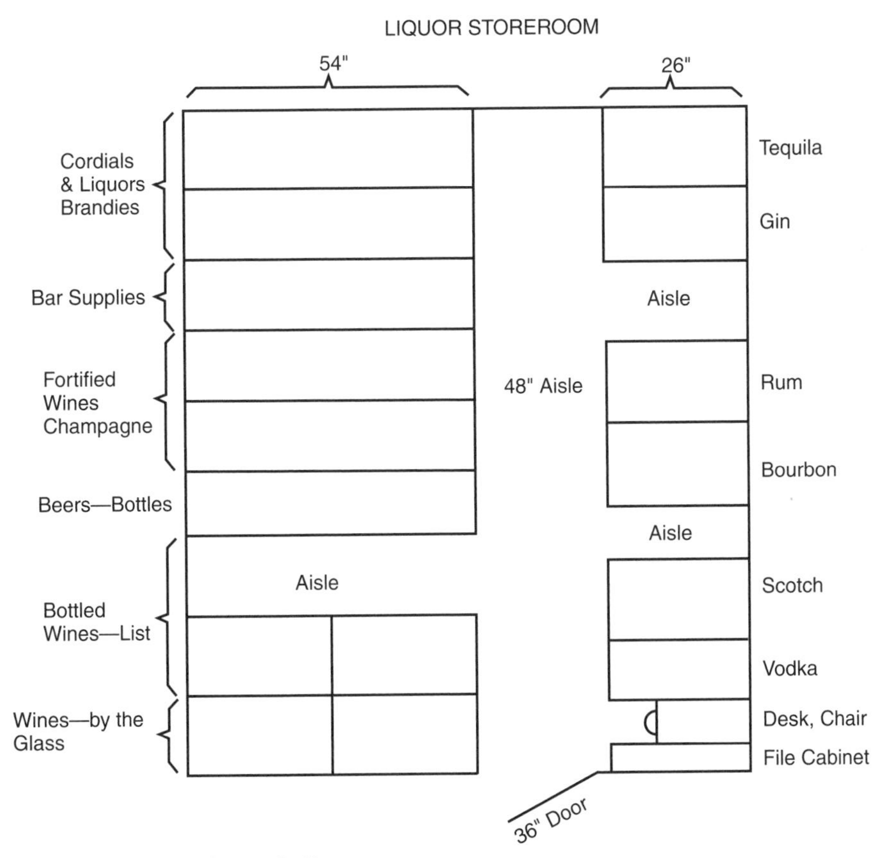

FIGURE 13.8 A sample layout of a liquor storeroom.

and excessive humidity, which causes mold to form around the foil cap. Wines survive best in a cool, dark environment between 50°F and 70°F (0°C to 21°C), with the ideal temperature being a constant 55°F to 60°F, which is known as **cellar temperature.** Wines that get too warm can leak through their corks and the seepage can stain or ruin the label. While high humidity is a problem low humidity (below 55 percent) can dry the cork and allow air in.

Move wines as little as possible and when you do handle them gently. Agitating a wine may upset both its chemistry and its sediment, making it unservable until the sediment settles again. For this reason newly imported wines should rest for 30 to 45 days before being served. However, since wines have limited life spans, rotating the stock becomes particularly important. Wine racks are the best places to store wine but not everyone has the room or money to purchase them. You can store wines on their sides or upside down in their sealed cases, but be careful not to stack them too high. More than five cases stacked on top of each other causes too much pressure on the necks of the upside-down bottles and can cause them to break. Also, the sediment collects inside the bottle's neck, sticking to the cork and making it difficult to extract when the wine is finally opened. Places *not* to store wine? Near loading docks, the dishroom, the kitchen, air-conditioning and heating-exhaust ducts, and never under stairways.

Beer has the most limited shelf life of all. Canned and bottled beers should be stored below 70°F (21°C) in a dark place and their pull dates should be checked periodically. Draft beers and some nonpasteurized canned or bottled beers should be kept refrigerated; ask your supplier about optimum storage conditions for these. Draft beer must be kept at an even 36°F to 38°F (2.2°C to 3.3°C) and should be used within 30 to 45 days. The best system of rotation has a handy acronym, **FIFO,** which means *first in, first out.* For beer storage consider keg racks or dunnage racks as shown in Figure 13.9. Most breweries have adopted pull-date systems, much like other perishable goods, with a cutesy new name: the **"born-on date" (BOD).** Anheuser-Busch uses the date that the beer was packaged and states that its shelf life is "110 days" after that. Other megabrewers list an expiration date.

FIGURE 13.9 A keg-and-dunnage rack for beer storage. Photo courtesy of KelMax Equipment © 1999, Decatur, Georgia.

As custodian of the storeroom contents the storeroom manager is responsibile for keeping track of the stock of each item at all times. This is an important part of any system because it helps to minimize pilferage. Some storerooms use a system of individual *bin cards* to log stock in and out. A card for each item is attached to the shelf where the item is stored. A typical bin card shows the brand name, bottle size, quantity on hand, and sometimes a bin number or code number. The amount of stock delivered is immediately added to the quantity on hand, and the amount of stock issued for use is immediately subtracted from the quantity on hand. The number of bottles shown on the bin card should always agree with the actual number of bottles of that item. Spot-checking stock against bin cards helps to keep track of inventory. The minimum and maximum stock levels may also be recorded on the bin cards, making it easy to be aware of purchasing needs. The cards are also a quick index to rate of use.

ISSUING LIQUOR

When you consider that the inventory levels at a bar change every time a bartender mixes a drink, you understand how difficult it is to keep track of what you have, where it is, and when you sold it. Like the other key points in the purchasing cycle the issue of stock as it passes from storeroom to bar must be correctly carried out and duly recorded, with a series of overlapping internal-tracking systems. The idea itself is not complicated and neither are the systems. What is hard is getting everyone to use them correctly, fill out the necessary paperwork, and turn it in promptly.

The document used to record the transfer of inventory from the storeroom to a specific bar or outlet is a **requisition form** or **issue slip** (see Figure 13.10). You might think of this as a sort of in-house purchase order, with the bar as the "buyer" and the storeroom as the "supplier." The bar lists the brand, size, and number of bottles for each item required, with the date and the signature of the person requesting the issue. The storeroom adds the cost and value information to complete the record, and the person issuing also signs. The person receiving the stock at the bar adds his or her signature to complete the transfer of responsibility. This means at least two or three signatures must appear on the requisition form, and is an important way of tracking who is handling the stock. Many bars require that the bottles emptied the previous day to be turned in with the requisition form. This is known as the **one-empty-for-one-full** system. The empties are collected and the requisition form is made out at closing time, as noted in Chapter 9. The manager double-checks the requisition form and the bartender's bottle count to be sure that they agree. Both are turned in to the storeroom the following day by the opening bartender and replacement stock is issued. In this way the supply is automatically maintained at par-stock level. As an additional benefit the empty-bottle system enables management to check the par stock at any time against the par-stock list to see if anything has disappeared. There should be a bottle for every bottle on the list, whether that bottle is empty or full.

Some enterprises mark each bottle with an identifying stamp when it is issued. Then if an empty bottle comes back without a stamp you know that somebody is up to something.

In multiple-bar operations each bar has its own par stock, which is requisitioned and issued separately. For public bars and service bars the one-empty-for-one-full system works well, but a different system must be used in supplying liquor for one-time events, such as banquets and conventions. This is a common situation in

REQUISITION FORM

Liquor, Beer, Wine, etc.
Bar Name
Address

Date: ______________________________

Issued from: ______________________________ (Storeroom)

Issued to: ______________________________ (Bar Outlet)

Item Number	Item Name	Size	Amount Ordered	Amount Issued	Perpetual Inventory Marked	Unit Cost	Extension
						Total	________

Requested by: ______________________________

Date: ______________________________

Received by: ______________________________

Date: ______________________________

Issued by: ______________________________

Date: ______________________________

FIGURE 13.10

hotels. In this case there are no empty bottles to replace and there is no specific par stock. The brands and amounts are estimated in advance for each event based on anticipated consumption, past experience, and a safety allowance, and are issued to the person in charge of the event using a special requisition form. The person in charge has the responsibility for returning all bottles, empty or full, to the storeroom when the event is over. The liquor used, which is represented by the empties, is charged to the cost of the event and the remaining stock is integrated into the storeroom inventory.

Sometimes the supply system breaks down during an unexpected rush or an emergency. If the storeroom is closed liquor is likely to be borrowed by one bar from another to prevent lost sales, and no one thinks to keep track. Eventually empties end up in the wrong place, the records are scrambled, and sooner or later something disappears. It is the manager's responsibility to avoid such emergencies and to keep the supply and record system on track.

INVENTORY

The beverage **inventory,** which is the amount on hand at any given time, is of central importance to the purchasing function. The buyer must be able to determine exactly what is immediately available and the rate at which it is being used in order to make intelligent purchasing decisions. In addition to storeroom records other means of keeping track of total inventory are needed. There are two reasons for keeping a constant check on inventory. One is to pinpoint losses quickly in order to put a stop to them. This has to do with controls, a subject discussed more fully in Chapter 14. The other reason has to do with purchasing. If you have lost stock due to theft, breakage, or error, you must buy stock to replace it so that you can serve your customers. Therefore you need to know what you really have on hand in order to plan each purchase.

Physical Inventory

The only accurate way to know what you have on hand is to take a complete **physical inventory,** which means counting each bottle and keg on a regular basis. Ideally you will perform a physical inventory weekly and again at the end of the accounting period. If possible the inventory should be taken by persons who do not buy liquor or handle it on the job. As a double-check it is best to have two people working together, one counting and the other writing down the count. With the growing popularity of RFID technology at least some of this process can be automated and computerized. No matter which system is used both people must initial or approve the results as they are completed. The inventory record should follow the arrangement of the storeroom, grouping items by category, within cat-

FIGURE 13.11 A storeroom or wine cellar should have everything well labeled and neatly organized. Photo courtesy of Culinary Institute of America, Hyde Park, New York.

egories by brand, and within brand by size. Figure 13.12 shows a sample inventory form.

The liquor at the bar is also part of inventory until it is sold, and it too is counted in an end-of-the-month physical inventory. It is inventoried in the same manner as the storeroom inventory except that there are opened bottles to be counted.

The simplest way to measure the contents of opened bottles is to estimate each bottle by sight and count the contents in tenths. Thus, a full bottle is 10/10, a half bottle is 5/10, and an empty bottle is 0/10. This gives you an approximate amount, of course, but it is close enough. If you have a metered pouring system you have a very accurate way of counting. The system counts the drinks that it pours. You multiply the count by the size of the drink and compare this with what is left in the partly used bottle. You have to count the liquor in each line from bottle to dispensing head as part of the inventory. The manufacturer's representative should give you this capacity at the time that the equipment is installed.

A bar owner or manager should conduct frequent audits of the actual inventory at the bar (excluding the storeroom) at different times during the week or on

PHYSICAL INVENTORY FORM

Bar Name
Address

Location: 1. Bar # ____________________. 3. Bar # ____________________.
2. Bar # ____________________. 4. Storeroom ____________________.

Date: ________________________
Inventory by: ________________________

Category (Circle One) Beer Wine Liquor

Item #	Item Name	Size	1	2	3	4	Unit Cost	Extension
							Total	________

FIGURE 13.12

different shifts. The frequency depends on sales volume: the higher the volume, the shorter time periods between audits. As you'll learn in Chapter 14, there are many ways for employees to be tempted, and security is a very real concern. The most powerful control tool you have is effective supervision.

One tool to speed the inventory process is the **bar-code scanner.** Since practically every item is labeled today with a **Universal Product Code (UPC),** a handheld model scanner can be used to scan each UPC label and instantly download its identity to a computer. A compatible scale can be used that is also able to read the UPC label, compute the bottle's total weight, subtract the tare weight (the weight of the identical bottle when empty), and the weight of the pourer if one is used on this particular bottle. Automatically the scale calculates the net weight and converts it to ounces. This method is precise enough to provide real cost controls for a manager. It is a computerized way to compare the volume of beverages the POS system says *should* have been used (based on sales) to *actual* usage (based on the bar-code scanner's readings). No matter which method is used the inventory must be taken all at once, from start to finish, and it must be done when the bar is closed so that nothing changes while the count is being taken. Weekly inventories of individual bars or the storeroom may supplement the overall end-of-the-month count.

A **depletion-allowance form** (see Figure 13.13) should also be kept handy at the bar each day to record any of the inventory that has been broken, spilled, transferred from one location to another (in large facilities), or given away as complementary beverages. Every bottle must be accounted for on a daily basis.

Perpetual Inventory. Another way of providing inventory information is to compile ongoing daily records from invoices and requisitions, adding each day's purchases and subtracting each day's issues for every item in stock. This task is typically performed by the accounting department and the results are known as a **perpetual inventory.** It is recorded by hand on a form (see Figure 13.14), a bin card (a separate card for each item), or by computer, which can report the stock record at any given moment with pushbutton ease. At any point in time the perpetual inventory is a paper record that should indicate exact quantities of every item that you have on hand. It does not tell you what you really have; only a physical inventory can do that. A perpetual inventory's primary function is to provide a standard against which a physical count can be measured item for item at any given time. If everything is in order the two inventories should agree. If separate records are kept on bin cards they should also agree: They, too, are a form of perpetual inventory.

The more inventory you have the more important it is that a perpetual inventory be kept. Since it should also clearly reveal a product's depletion rate it has the added benefit of making the ordering process more accurate. It also greatly assists in detecting employee theft. Finally it assists you in meeting your state's licensing requirements to maintain accurate records of the bar's alcohol purchases.

If the actual count and the perpetual inventory record do not agree, you are faced with determining whether there are errors in the records or the count, or the items themselves have disappeared. You can trace errors in the record by going

DEPLETION ALLOWANCE FORM

(Circle one) **Transfers, Spills, Comps, Broken**

Bar Name

Address

Date: ______________________________

Extended by: ______________________________

Date	Item	Size/Quantity	Purpose/Outlet	Liquor Cost	Wine Cost	Beer Cost	Manager's Signature
Totals							

FIGURE 13.13

PERPETUAL INVENTORY FORM

Bar Name
Address

Item Name: ____________________ Size: ____________________
Distributor: ____________________ Case Cost: ____________________
Item #: ____________________ Bottle Cost: ____________________

Date	Requisitioned/ Inventory/ Size	On-Hand Inventory/Size	Comments	Manager's Signature

FIGURE 13.14

back to the invoices and requisitions, and you can trace errors in the count by recounting. If you cannot find any mistakes you may as well assume theft and adjust your perpetual-inventory record accordingly. (Other ways of measuring discrepancies that are accurate enough for everyday use will be examined in Chapter 14.) Overall the most critical reason for a good inventory management system is this: If you do not have a way of knowing where you ought to be you cannot measure where you are now.

Determining Inventory Value, Bar Cost, and Inventory Turnover Rate. When you have completed a physical inventory for an accounting period you must determine the dollar value of the total stock. To do this begin by entering the unit cost of each item on the physical inventory form on which you have recorded the count (refer to Figure 13.12).

The next step is to multiply the unit cost by the number of units to find the dollar value of the stock for each item. Enter each total on the form in the last column. Totaling the values of all the items then gives you the value of your entire inventory. This number is known as the **ending (closing) inventory** for the accounting period. The same number becomes the **beginning (opening) inventory** for the next accounting period. Now you can use this figure to determine the value of all of the liquor used to produce your sales for the period, which is your **beverage cost.** Here is the way to do it:

To: Value of beginning inventory (*BI*)
Add: Value of all purchases made during period (*P*)
Equals: Value of total liquor available during period
Subtract: Value of ending inventory (*EI*)
Equals: Value of total liquor used during period, or cost (*C*)

This calculation in equation form is as follows:

$$BI + P - EI = C$$

For example:

$$\begin{array}{ll} BI & \$1{,}245.16 \\ +P & \$5{,}015.16 \\ \hline & \$6{,}260.32 \\ -EI & \$1{,}010.00 \\ \hline =C & \$5{,}250.32 \end{array}$$

The dollar cost for liquor used in a given period is usually expressed as a percentage of the sales for the same period. To determine this percentage, you divide cost by sales:

$$\frac{C}{S} = C\%$$

For example:

$$\frac{\text{Cost } (C)}{\text{Sales } (S)} \quad \frac{\$5{,}250.32}{\$28{,}720.50} = .1829 \text{ or } 18.3\%$$

This percentage is often referred to simply as **bar cost.** (We will discuss some uses of this figure in Chapter 14.)

You can also use the values for ending inventory and purchases for the period to determine your **inventory turnover rate.** This rate will help you to decide whether you are keeping too much or too little in inventory. To calculate this rate you must first determine the average inventory. To do this add the beginning and ending inventories for the period, then divide that sum by 2:

$$\frac{\text{Beginning Inventory} + \text{Ending Inventory}}{2} = \text{Average Inventory}$$

Then you divide costs for the accounting period by the average inventory number:

$$\frac{\text{Costs for the Period}}{\text{Average Inventory}} = \text{Turnover Rate}$$

For example if costs for the period were $1,500 and the closing inventory was $1,500, the turnover rate would be 1; i.e., you have turned over your inventory once during the period. If costs for the period were $1,500 and the closing inventory was $2,000, your turnover rate would be 0.75, while if the costs for the period were $1,500 and the closing inventory was $1,000, the turnover rate would be 1.5.

What is the significance of the turnover rate? Generally if your turnover rate is consistently below 1 you are probably stocking more than you need. If it runs above 2 you probably often run out of items that you need and you might increase your sales if you increased your rate of purchase. However, each type of business has its own optimum purchase rate, which may vary from industry norms. You really should calculate the turnover rates for beer, wine, and liquor separately because they are not necessarily the same. There are several other ways to calculate inventory turnover, but this is the simplest, though not the most precise.

You can apply the inventory turnover rate to help you buy beverages and remain profitable in several ways, which is the obvious goal of any good bar owner! We'll use wine in the following example but the methodology is identical for spirits and beer.

How much wine should I buy?

1. Project wine sales for the month. For this example let's say you expect to achieve $70,000 in wine sales.
2. Now consider your cost of sales on wine (that is, your wine cost percentage). Let's say it's 25 percent.
3. To determine how much wine to have on hand, multiply the projected sales times the cost percentage: $70,000 × .25 = $17,500.

4. Therefore, your wine purchases for the month should not exceed $17,500. If you want to include a margin of error—for example, to include 1.5 times your budget—the calculation would be: $17,500 × 1.5 = $26,500.

Remember to subtract the cost of the wine inventory that you already have on hand from either of these figures.

Next you need to know how much you should spend on wine purchases on a weekly basis. In this case take both the $17,500 and the $26,500 and divide them by 4. The results will be $4,375 (your weekly purchases) and $6,562.50 (your higher, margin-of-error figure), respectively. These two figures become your target point for weekly purchases. If you spend between $4,375 and $6,562.50 on wine for the week, you will stay within your budget.

PURCHASING BAR SUPPLIES

Purchasing supplies for the bar follows the same cycle as beverage buying: purchasing, receiving, storing, and issuing. However, buying supplies is much simpler because these are products not regulated by state or federal laws.

You can buy grocery items from grocery wholesalers and cocktail napkins from wholesalers of paper goods. But if you find beverage wholesalers who carry drink-related items, check their products and prices. (Some state codes do not allow liquor dealers to sell anything but liquor.) The prices might be better since the liquor dealer may get better quantity discounts on bar items, such as maraschino cherries and cocktail onions, than the grocery dealer does. Service might be better, too. The food wholesaler may pay little attention to your small order, whereas the liquor purveyor wants to keep your beverage business. The liquor dealer may also sell in smaller quantities than the grocery wholesaler, and if you have a small enterprise it may take forever to use a case of olives or a gross of napkins.

Keep in mind that liquor purveyors do not handle such items as lemons, limes, oranges, celery, eggs, milk, cream, and ice cream. You will buy your produce from a produce dealer and your dairy supplies and ice cream from a wholesale dairy. Such items must be refrigerated in the storeroom or go straight to the bar, ice cream must go straight into the freezer.

When working out your orders you will have a choice of can or bottle sizes for many items. The cost per olive or per ounce is nearly always cheaper in the larger container sizes. However, consider deterioration once the container is opened. If you use only half a can of something and have to throw out the rest, you have not saved any money.

Receiving, storing, and issuing bar supplies follow the same procedures used for alcoholic beverages. Like items must be stored together and the stock must be rotated at each delivery. All types of bar supplies are counted on the regular physical inventory. However, once a container is opened it is considered used and is not counted.

SUMMING UP

A good purchasing manager provides an adequate supply of beverages at all times without overinvesting in idle inventory. Purchasing involves both the selection and the procurement of everything needed to run the bar. The modern bar manager uses a category management system, tracking what sells well and what does not (most often by computer) and using the information to adapt the drink menu to deliver a beverage program that meets customers' needs and is profitable for the business.

It is important to maintain good relationships with suppliers and to understand their pricing systems so that you can evaluate the true values (to your operation) of the sales and discounts they may offer. The Internet has made it easy to check prices and obtain product information from a variety of sources; suppliers may offer product catalogs on CD-ROM, and your computer system may be linked to theirs to facilitate online ordering. But it is still important to maintain human contact with the distributor's salespeople and to build solid working relationships with them. Schedule regular appointments to taste new items, utilize the sales and training materials they can provide, and attend the events they host or sponsor. If you operate in a control state you must purchase your liquor from state-run stores or warehouses; good working relationships are just as important in these cases.

A careful system of records is maintained at all phases of the purchasing cycle. Start by determining the par stock necessary to outfit your bar to be ready for a business day, and be able to track the path of every bottle and its contents, from the time it is received to the time the empty is turned in. Through such records management can keep up with usage trends, as well as pinpoint possible problems (from thefts to slow sellers) and the responsibility for them at any stage along the way from purchase to sale.

Physical inventory at regular intervals provides the basis for figuring needs, costs, and losses. Written or computerized perpetual-inventory records provide standards against which the physical inventory can be measured. Storeroom areas should include strict security precautions and limited access. The system should include a series of forms for recording sales, discrepancies, par stock, and other standards. A well-organized, well-managed purchasing system can contribute to profits by keeping costs down, efficiency up, and supplies flowing.

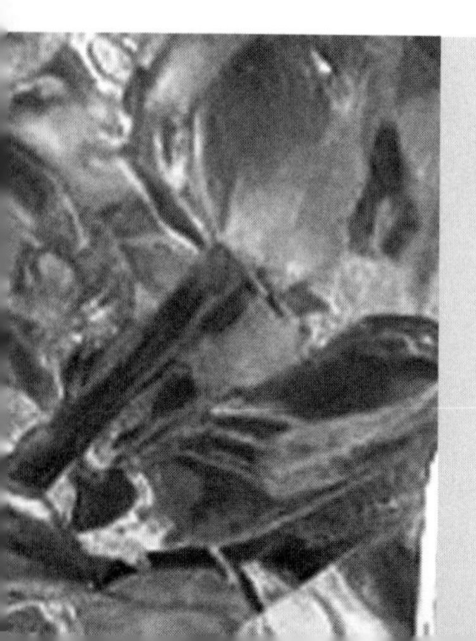

POINTS TO PONDER

1. What would your policy be on the quality of well brands and the variety of brands offered? Give reasons for your decisions.
2. Do you live in a control state or a license state? How does this affect purchasing?
3. Explain the relationship between the purchase order, the invoice, and the credit memo.

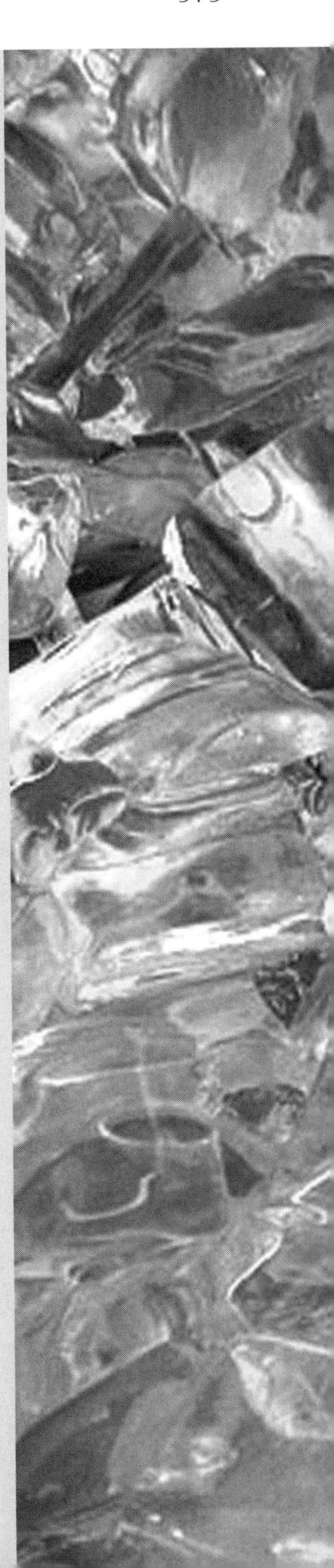

4. List and briefly discuss three qualities you would look for in a liquor supplier. Explain why they are important to you.
5. When buying wholesale liquor what is the difference between a post-off discount and an assorted discount?
6. Discuss the advantages and disadvantages of a perpetual inventory record. What would computerization contribute?
7. What kind of information should be listed on a bin card, and what is its function?
8. What does your inventory turnover rate tell you about your purchasing management?
9. Why should a physical inventory be taken by people who do not work at the bar or in the storeroom?
10. What numbers do you have to know in a bar business to arrive at its beverage cost or bar cost?

 TERMS OF THE TRADE

assorted discount
bar-code scanner
bar cost
beginning (opening) inventory
beverage cost
born-on date (BOD)
broken case
capital risk
carrying costs
category management
cellar temperature
control state
credit memo
depletion allowance form
ending (closing) inventory
extensions
FIFO
house brands
inventory
inventory turnover rate
invoice
issue slip
lead time
license state
monopoly state
multiple-brands discount
one-empty-for-one-full
P.O. number
par stock
periodic order method
perpetual inventory
perpetual-inventory method
physical inventory
post-off discount
premium well
procurement process
purchase order
purchasing
requisition form
selection process
super well
tare weight
three-tier system
Universal Product Code (UPC)
well brands

A CONVERSATION WITH...CRAYNE HORTON

Crayne Horton was a political-science professor at a branch campus of Heidelberg College . . . in Japan! An avid home brewer for many years he was finally pleased enough with his product to brew his own craft beer for sale when he moved back to the United States in 1992. He had, in his words, "absolutely zero business experience" when he wrote his business plan, put together a stock offering, and raised $200,000 to open a small brewpub, called The Fish Bowl, in Olympia, Washington.

More capital as raised to expand the business to include an 8,000-barrel brewery. In 2001 Fish Brewing Company purchased Leavenworth Brewery, another craft brewer in Washington State. In 2005 Fish Brewing Company added another 5,000 square feet to its brewing operations and acquired Spire Mountain Ciders, a local cider-making company in business since 1985. A second Fish brewpub opened in 2006 in Woodinville, Washington.

Fish produces about 7,500 barrels of beer annually, and is known for its organically brewed ales and a passionate commitment to environmental causes, particularly to protecting endangered fish species and their habitat.

Co-Founder, Fish Brewing Company Olympia, Washington

Q: What has the last decade been like in the craft- and regional-beer business?

A: It's been tough. Since 1996 all the major regional brewers added capacity—some by making large stock offerings—and this additional output created an oversupply. And there was also a bunch of ill will in the industry, with the craft brewers fighting against the major domestic brewers. It was a very public feud, and it made us look mean-spirited. A lot of quickly made, poorly made, beer hit the market and suddenly the craft-beer "fad" wore off. The growth that had been a predictable 40 percent per year went to 18 percent, to 3 percent, to flat. Lots of breweries went out of business, and mine almost didn't survive either. But today, the market appears to be growing again, at the rate of about 5 percent per year.

The next new fad, which is just starting now, is microdistilling of spirits. *American Brewer* magazine just changed its name to *American Brewer and Distiller.* It will be a smaller revolution, though, because the federal licensing for distillers is much more rigorous than for breweries. It'll keep a lot more people out.

Q: What is the hardest thing about this business?

A: The most challenging thing is that there are still too many competitors for the amount of business. It's too easy to get into the microbeer business—there are no real barriers to entry—and it's seen by a lot of people as a fun, charming, romantic way to make a living. Instead, it's a lot of hard, sweaty labor with very low profit margins. [The] Budweisers and Millers are successful because of volume so at low volumes and relatively low margins, there's no money to be made. And the amount of capital investment to get quality equipment is huge. For a small brewpub, with a 10- to 15-barrel capacity, there are bargains now because so many have gone out of business so you can purchase it used at $30,000 to $40,000. But new equipment is very expensive—a single, brand-new 2,000-gallon tank is going to cost you $15,000. Stainless steel is not cheap.

Q: What about the regulations? What is it like to deal with the different agencies, from local health departments to the Federal Bureau of Alcohol, Tobacco, and Firearms (BATF)?

A: The health department has almost no jurisdiction; we don't see them. The BATF is almost nonexistent except as a tax collector. They don't have the personnel. The closest office to us is in Cincinnati. If you pay your taxes and send in the appropriate paperwork on time, you might never see them unless you're newly in business and they come to do an initial inspection. Of course every label you produce has to pass BATF approval, and you can do that by mail. It's a procedure that must be followed very carefully, for every brand, every size of package, and it must be done well in advance because it can be a slow process.

The real problem is that each state you do business in has its own liquor laws, and none of them are the same. In some, we pay a lot of excise tax; others have different tax structures based on the strength of the alcohol product. Some have their own label-approval processes; others just accept the BATF approval. Some allow you to print alcohol amounts by volume on the label; others want it by weight; some won't let you print it at all! It is a huge management process that takes a lot of hours.

Q: What is it like working with distributors?

A: It's extremely frustrating. We have all Northwest distribution and good name-brand recognition, but you're not a large part of the dollars for any of these people. Their profit margins on your products are much better than on any of their domestic beers, but still there has been a dramatic consolidation among distributors over the last five years, so you have fewer choices of who you want to sell your product in a given market.

In my experience distributors don't "sell" product; they take orders and deliver product. You have to sell it yourself and make sure there is follow-through. You can hire a "rep" [representative] in a given market, and that's a lot more effective; they really keep an eye on the distributor and work with them.

There are some distributors who are really honorable, with quality salespeople who are well trained, out there representing your product. But some of them are just totally unscrupulous, with their hands out or trying to skirt the local laws by giving away product, for instance, or installing draft systems at their cost. In every market there are players of both ilk, and it takes a while to figure out which one you're dealing with.

Q: What role does your brewpub play in your overall business?

A: The pub is very profitable, and draft beer is where you make your money. The margins for bottled beer are even smaller than on draft.

We've changed the foodservice in the Fish Bowl every year we've been open. We used to do just smoked salmon and cream cheese, and little appetizer platters, from behind the bar. For a while, we owned a restaurant in the same building and managed that. We bought food from another restaurant for a while, and finally we installed a small kitchen of our own. Now we're doing great little panini sandwiches and a good, rich seafood soup. We have two rooms that each seat 40 or 50. It's a small output for a kitchen, but our pub is probably 30 percent of our overall sales for the company.

Q: Do you have advice for newcomers to the brewing business?

A: I would honestly discourage newcomers to the business at this point. There are so many good-quality beers being made in the world [that] you have to ask yourself, "Does the world need another pale ale?" No! I just don't think so. There are so many good choices now. The ones that are still in business have survived and are probably making good product. I just don't see the need from the consumer's standpoint. If you've got money to burn and just think it'd be fun, that's great. But just realize you're not going to make any money at it.

Q: What about the service area of the business?

A: Really knowledgeable beer servers are rare. I think it does help to have bartending experience. But anyone who wants to know more about beer as a server should know that any supplier or manufacturer is so happy to put information in their hands that they can share with customers. A good bartender or good server, really, is the one who sells the beer.

We have some specialty beers—Poseidon Imperial Stout and Leviathan Barleywine—that are aged six months or more in wine barrels. It's just like wine, 10- to 12-percent alcohol, lays down for a year, and is bottled in Champagne bottles or 3-liter jeroboams. These are on the wine lists of some wonderful restaurants, and Poseidon was just named one of the "Top Ten Cult Beers" in the United States. People chase these things down, and there's so much expert information to be had—it's much like wine in that way.

I do beer dinners, exactly like wine dinners, pairing foods and beers and working with chefs. So for servers food knowledge is a prerequisite. When you think about it the basic domestic beer from a major commercial brewery is a simply a beverage, whereas wine, or craft beer, is an extension of food. It is food itself! If you have food knowledge so much the better.

Q: Is there anything else you think hospitality students should concentrate on?

A: Yes, without a doubt, customer service. That is what makes or breaks a bar or restaurant. Be gracious, and don't act like you're doing someone a favor to wait on them.

CHAPTER 14
PLANNING FOR PROFIT

As you contemplate opening your own bar which parts of the dream appeal most to you? Is it the idea of owning your own business? Is it seeing a room full of people enjoying what you have created? Whatever the appeal your answer was probably not, "Because I love all the number-crunching." However if you fail to understand, monitor, and control the financial side of the bar, your dream business will likely fail, too.

A common mistake among bar owners is to look at the sales and profit figures on their financial statements, glossing over the rest as tedious details required to get to the totals. This chapter shows how and why, as the saying goes, "The devil is in the details."

Planning for profit means taking the necessary steps to structure the financial side of an operation to reach a profit goal. The budget becomes a profit plan that is used to measure the achievement of the profit goal. Every aspect of the business, from the number of employees, to the system for pricing drinks, is created and fine-tuned to maximize profits. Finally controls are established to ensure that the alcohol goes into drinks, the money goes into the cash register, and the profit becomes a natural offspring of a successful business plan.

THIS CHAPTER WILL HELP YOU . . .

- Establish a profit goal for a bar business.
- Prepare a budget that is aimed at a profit goal and measure progress toward that goal.
- Price each drink on the basis of beverage cost.
- Coordinate drink prices for maximum dollar sales.
- Use an income statement to measure achievement.
- Forecast cash flow.

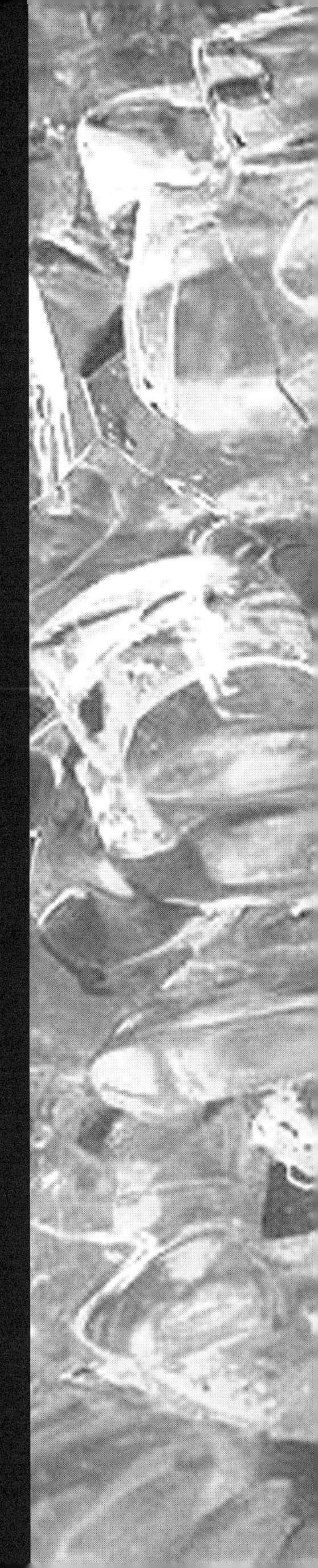

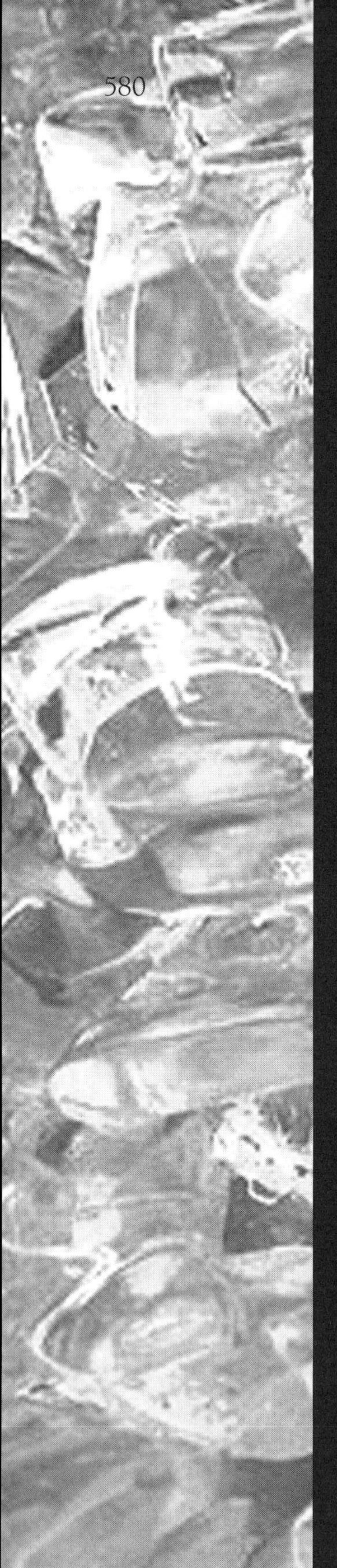

- Calculate a break-even point.
- Standardize drink size, recipes, and glassware.
- Establish a control system for detecting and measuring theft and other losses.
- Use par stock as a control tool.
- Establish a system of sales records and cash control.

How often have you been shocked to hear that a popular bar or restaurant was going out of business? If you ask what went wrong the offhand remark is usually something like, "Poor management" or "They didn't know what they were doing." These criticisms could mean almost anything but most likely money management was involved, and more than likely the failure also involved poor planning. A great many enterprises, especially small ones, operate with more enthusiasm than foresight and count on advertising, a particular trend, entertainment, or somebody else's successful formula to generate profits. The accountant is expected to take care of the financial end. But the shrewd entrepreneur knows that profit can and should be systematically planned for, budgeted for, and watched closely each day.

MANAGING THE NUMBERS

Your bar's ability to survive and prosper depends in large part on the "health" of three numbers: cash flow, pretax profit, and the level of debt you have assumed. Of these cash flow is the most critical. *Cash flow* is the month-by-month total of all of the receipts coming into the bar, minus all of the the sums being paid out. If the number on the bottom line of a cash-flow statement is not positive it usually means trouble. You may not be able to meet your payroll, insurance, and other financial obligations. You may have to close the doors. Clearly cash flow is a number to track at least weekly, and even daily if cash is tight.

Net profit or **pre-tax profit** is a figure on your monthly income statement. This number is the total monthly revenue, minus all of the expenses incurred in that same month. It includes all of the overhead expenses of the business, *except for income taxes.* Pretax profit is what some people refer to as "the bottom line." It shows what you are actually making before taxes are taken out. By comparing the pretax profit to your budget and to last year's performance you can spot expenses that are getting out of line. If this figure is decreasing it may also indicate that you are losing customers to your competitors.

The third major figure to review regularly is your *debt level.* This is a comparison of your *assets* (what you own) and your *liabilities* (what you owe). These two numbers appear on your business's *balance sheet.* (This is a document we will not cover in this text, nor do we attempt to wade into the subject of debt management in detail. However a few comments about it are appropriate for this discussion.) Assets include cash, inventory, real estate, equipment, and amounts that others owe to you. Liabilities are everything that you owe to others: bank loans that you are repaying, a mortgage on the building, payroll, and *accounts payable* (what you owe your vendors for the goods and services they have provided.) Your debt level shows, among other things, your ability to cover the payments on your debts within the year, as well as your capacity for growth: whether you have enough earnings to do *more than* just cover your debts. When you subtract the total value of the liabilities from the total value of the assets, the result is the *net worth* of your business. Your *net-worth capital* is the money you have available to operate the business. As your net-worth capital rises your risk is reduced because you have increased your ability to meet your current obligations.

If you go to a third party, such as a bank or a group of investors, for financing they will want to see these figures. There is nothing shameful about being in debt, especially in the first phases of business ownership. Investors understand that entrepreneurs often risk their own financial well being, including their home and personal savings. What is important is to have a plan for that business to steadily build net-worth capital.

You can pour yourself, all of your talents, and your heart and soul and energy into this business. You can even learn to crunch the numbers, like 'em or not. But you have to begin with a profit plan and this requires creating a realistic budget.

Budgeting for Profit

Profit is the primary goal of a beverage enterprise whether that goal is a hope, a dream, or a very specific target. But by itself profit does not indicate the degree of business efficiency. Indeed profit figures are not significant until they are expressed in relation to other factors, such as sales or return on investment.

A **budget** provides a closer look at what these figures mean, a strategy for reaching a target, and a tool for measuring progress along the way. A budget is a financial plan for a given period of time that coordinates anticipated income and expenditures to ensure solvency and yield a profit. The budget is a document with a dual personality. In the beginning it is a plan detailing in dollar terms the *anticipated performance* of the bar during the period to come: the expected sales, the expenses that will be incurred in order to achieve the sales, and the desired profit. As the budget period arrives the budget ceases to be a plan for the future and becomes a tool of control for the present. The budget now provides a basis for measuring *actual performance and results* against the performance goals of the plan. Perhaps it is more accurate to think of the budget as a continuing two-phase process or system rather than as a static or inflexible set of figures. The *planning phase* requires the manager to project the financial future in detail and make realistic forecasts of income and outgo in relation to the ultimate profit goal. This very process of thinking ahead, gathering data for forecasting, working your way through the facts and numbers, and applying them to a future that might change before it arrives may suggest operating adjustments that will help you to achieve your profit goal.

In the *control phase* the frequent measuring of actual results against a budget plan can signal threats to profits and identify the areas of trouble. Quick action may put the business back on course. On the other hand sometimes the original plan is unrealistic or circumstances change. The budget can then be modified to bring it into line with present reality. In this sense the planning process continues during the operating period. For the sake of simplicity while discussing the budgeting process we have ignored the fact that most enterprises combine some form of food service with beverage service. Wherever this is true most fixed expenses and some others are shared with the food-service side of the enterprise. It is customary in this case to lump fixed expenses and relate them only to total sales and to figure the bar's share of the remaining expenses as a proportion of total sales. For example if beverage sales are projected at 25 percent of a restaurant's total sales, you would budget the remaining shared expenses at 25 percent of the total projection for those expenses.

The Planning Process

The first step in developing a budget is setting your profit goal—a specific, realistic goal, not just "as much profit as possible." To do this think of it in terms of return on money invested. For example you have $100,000 invested in an established business or that you are going to invest that amount in a new project. What would this $100,000 bring you in a year if you put it in a savings certificate or mutual fund or invested it in real estate or some other "safe" (not-too-risky) venture? Suppose that it would bring you $10,000 a year. Now, double this figure (a rule-of-thumb safety margin because of the risks you are taking) for a total of $20,000. This is your projected *return on investment* (*ROI*) and your profit goal for the year.

Profit is the difference between income and expenses. Since your income comes from sales your next step is to forecast your sales for the budget period. The accuracy of this forecast will determine how realistic the rest of your budget is and whether or not you will reach your profit goal or indeed make a profit at all.

Understanding the relationships between profit, volume, and costs is essential to successfully budgeting by the month and forecasting for the future. To forecast your sales you must estimate the number of drinks that you expect to sell in each period of each day, week, and month of the year. Figure 14.1 is a useful form for such a forecast, and we stress that the best way to keep and track figures is to use a form, either on paper or on computer. (The International Guild of Hospitality and Restaurant Managers has templates for many forms online, which can be downloaded free of charge at its web site: www.hospitalityguild.com/templates.htm)

If you are already in business you can draw on your past sales data to forecast your sales. Break down the data in terms of the number of drinks sold on the noon shift, the afternoon shift, and the evening shift, and by the day of the week. Note the effect of price changes for special events or special drinks, as well as general price changes and the influence of holidays, conventions, and sports events. Make notes on high and low sales periods and seasonal variations. Then use this data to decide whether the upcoming year will be a rerun of the previous year, or whether you want to change your plans and whether external factors affect the forecast.

For example has your competitive position changed? Perhaps a new bar opened across the street. Is the general economy affecting your business? Are you going to make changes, such as renovating your facility or adding live entertainment and dancing? Do you have plans for special promotions? Adapt your historical figures to accommodate all of the changes that you foresee. If you are just starting out in

SALES FORECAST FORM

Period: *From* ____________ *To* ____________

	Date	Mon	Tue	Wed	Thu	Fri	Sat	Sun	Total Average
Shift 11–3									
Week ending									
Week ending									
Week ending									
Week ending									
4-week totals									
Shift 3–7									
Week ending									
Week ending									
Week ending									
Week ending									
4-week totals									
Shift 7–closing									
Week ending									
Week ending									
Week ending									
Week ending									
4-week totals									

FIGURE 14.1

the bar business make the same estimates on the basis of what you have found out about your chosen clientele, your market area, your competition, and your capacity (all of this is was discussed in greater detail in Chapter 3). Be sure to estimate conservatively!

Finally multiply the number of drinks that you forecast by the prices that you plan to charge in the upcoming year. This is your sales forecast and your anticipated income. Suppose that this figure is $100,000 for the year (see Figure 14.2). (The

TENTATIVE BUDGET

	Dollars	Percent of sales
Projected Sales	$ 100,000	100%
Variable Expenses		
Beverage costs	$ 24,000	24.0%
Payroll costs, variable portion	$ 13,500	13.5%
Administrative expenses	$ 4,000	4.0%
Laundry and supplies	$ 3,600	3.6%
Utilities	$ 3,000	3.0%
Advertising and promotion	$ 3,500	3.5%
Repairs	$ 1,500	1.5%
Maintenance	$ 2,000	2.0%
Miscellaneous operating expenses	$ 700	0.7%
Fixed Expenses		
Payroll costs, fixed portion	$ 9,000	9.0%
Rent	$ 6,000	6.0%
Taxes	$ 1,160	1.16%
Insurance	$ 2,400	2.4%
Interest	$ 800	0.8%
Licenses and fees	$ 2,200	2.2%
Depreciation	$ 1,800	1.8%
Amortization	$ 840	0.84%
Profit Goal	$ 20,000	20.0%
	$ 100,000	100.0%

FIGURE 14.2

figures in this example are low for today's realities, but they make the process easier to follow.)

Your next step is to estimate all of your expenses for the same period. You have two sources of information for these: the past year's history and any commitments that you have made for the period ahead, such as a lease or a loan from the bank. Again, gather your data and make your estimated expense figures as precise as possible.

Expenses are usually grouped into two categories: fixed and variable. **Fixed expenses** are those that are not related in any way to sales volume but are fixed by contract or simply by being in business. In other words you could not operate without them, yet they go on whether or not you sell a single drink. Your rent, for instance, remains the same whether your sales are zero or $1 million dollars; any increase in rent comes from your landlord, not from your volume of business. For the most part such items as payroll, insurance, licenses and fees, taxes (except sales taxes), interest on loans, and depreciation are fixed expenses. They continue independently of sales volume. The good news is that fixed expenses are easily predictable. Write them down in dollar figures as shown in the sample budget (see Figure 14.2). For example a fixed payroll at $750 a month or $9,000 a year, rent at $500 a month or $6,000 a year, and so on for taxes, fees, interest, insurance, depreciation, and amortization. Then add them all up for a total for the year.

Variable expenses are those that move up and down with sales volume. Chief among these are beverage and remaining payroll costs. Itemize these costs in dollars for the coming year, going back to your drinks-per-day figures to estimate the beverages and staff that you will need to produce these drinks. Notice that a certain portion of the payroll is considered a fixed cost. Salaried employees, such as a manager, must be paid whether you sell one drink or a thousand. A certain number of hourly employees also represent fixed costs because they must be there when the doors open for business. When budgeting some enterprises divide payroll costs between fixed and variable expenses (as in Figure 14.2), identifying the cost of a skeleton crew as a fixed expense and the cost of additional staff needed for the estimated sales volume as a variable expense. This produces a more finely tuned budget than lumping payroll all together.

A third category of expenses, **unallocable expenses,** is sometimes listed separately because it consists of general expenses that are neither fixed nor directly tied to sales. These expenses include promotion and advertising, but for simplicity's sake we include them under variable expenses. These dollar figures depend on your plans, which in turn depend on how much you think such expenditures will influence sales. A certain amount of advertising and promotion is often necessary just to keep your enterprise in the public consciousness and to maintain a certain sales level. Enter your planned dollar figures on your budget.

When you have estimated all your expenses for the year, add them up. Then go back and calculate each individual expense item as a percentage of your expected sales for the year (also as shown in Figure 14.2). The percent-of-sales figure is a precise way of expressing the relationship of a given expense to the sales it will help to produce. This critical relationship is watched closely in operation as a measure of performance against plan. The percent-of-sales figure is referred to in the industry as **percentage cost, cost percentage,** or **cost/sales ratio.**

When you have completed all of your percentage figures, enter your profit goal in dollar figures and again as a percentage of sales. Add the dollar profit goal to the total expenses and compare this sum with your sales forecast. Next, add up all the percent-of-sales figures for expenses and profit. If the dollar figure for expenses-plus-profit is the same as or less than the sales forecast and the percent-of-sales figure is 100 percent or less, you are in good shape. If expenses-plus-profit dollars are more than the dollar sales forecast and the percentage figure is more than 100 percent, you have some readjusting to do. To reach your profit goal you have two choices: to cut costs or to increase sales (raise volume or prices or both volume and prices). Whatever you do you must reach a balance. If all else fails you must reduce your profit goal. Your percentage figures can be very helpful in establishing a profit-yielding budget. You can see at a glance if any one category of expense is out of line. The percentages in Figure 14.2 are generally accepted industry norms, give or take a few points. Do not, however look at them as hard-and-fast goals for your budget. Your plan must reflect your own realities.

Longer-Term Planning

Figure 14.3 shows a sophisticated budget form. This type of form enables you to base your projections for the coming year on what has actually happened during the current year, that is, the year just ending.

You start with actual historical figures for the current year. These are year-to-date figures taken from your last income statement, showing the cumulative totals in each budget category (seen on Figure 14.3). Enter the figures in the two columns labeled *Actual,* both in dollars and in percent of sales. The next section, labeled *Change,* is the key to your budgeting for the coming year. In this section for each change you anticipate enter either a dollar figure (usually for a fixed expense) or a percent of last year's figure representing the anticipated change (usually for a variable expense). For categories that you expect to remain the same, do not enter anything.

The section labeled *Planned* combines the figures for the current year with the anticipated changes to give the figures for your new budget, which you enter in the *Planned* column. If a change is expressed as a percentage convert it into dollars, add it to the dollar amount from the *Actual* column and enter the total figure in the *Planned* column. If a change is expressed in dollars combine it with the dollar figures from the *Actual* column and enter the total figure in the *Planned* column. All of the dollar figures are then compared to calculate percent-of-sales figures for the total budget.

Financial statements that depict future period activity are called **pro forma statements** or *pro forma reports.* They represent what the bar is *supposed* to look like financially, based on a set of assumptions about the economy, market growth, location, and myriad other factors that affect that particular unit. You don't need a crystal ball to make these predictions. They won't be 100-percent accurate, but by using your own experience and common sense and by paying attention to industry trends as well as what is happening in your own town and neighborhood, you can do a good job. Keep in mind that even when you've made the predictions they are not sacred. Industry experts suggest that if they are off by more than 20 percent in a three-month period, you should redo them. If they are off by less than 20 percent, wait another three months and see what happens. Do not change them more than three months at a time unless you find that you have omitted a major expense item or discovered a new source of revenue.

You might be wondering why you need to make predictions at all. They are simply summaries of your business forecasts. The idea is not to impress anyone but to organize your data and let it guide you. First your lender(s) and investors

BUDGET

Comparative format

Actual (*Current year*)		Change		Planned (*Next year*)		
Dollars	*Percent*	*Dollars*	*Percent*	*Dollars*	*Percent*	
						Sales
						Variable Expenses
						Beverage costs
						Payroll, variable portion
						Administrative expenses
						Laundry and supplies
						Utilities
						Advertising/Promotion
						Repairs
						Maintenance
						Misc. operating expenses
						Total Variable Expenses
						Fixed Expenses
						Payroll, fixed portion
						Rent
						Taxes
						Insurance
						Interest
						Licenses and fees
						Depreciation
						Amortization
						Total Fixed Expenses
						Profit Before Taxes

FIGURE 14.3

will be interested so it is important to be methodical and thorough. You might err on the side of caution, slightly overstating expenses and understating sales figures. It is much better to exceed a conservative budget than to fall below an optimistic one. Second over time you will notice that most expenses and income are fairly predictable, which should make it easier to continue planning and budgeting. Suggested pro forma statements are also found in the *Uniform System of Accounts for Restaurants,* a useful guide published by the National Restaurant Association (NRA). (The most current version, the seventh edition, was published in 1996.) Two other kinds of forecasts are of great value, especially if you are opening a brand-new enterprise. One is your break-even point. The other is a cash-flow forecast. Many managers overlook these refinements of the budgeting process. They are also useful as the year goes on as you track your progress and analyze your performance.

Break-Even Point

A **break-even point** is the level of operation at which total costs equal total sales, which means that there is no profit or loss. Oddly enough this is the level that a new bar must reach fairly quickly if it is to survive. For food-and-beverage operations, break-even figures may be expressed in dollars or in "units," which means the number of guests served. But for bars these figures are generally expressed in dollars.

To calculate your daily break-even point, start with all of your fixed costs for one month. Add a month's wages and salaries for a *skeleton crew,* which is the fewest number of workers you can have to open your doors for business. Divide this total by the number of days in the month that you will be open. This is your basic daily labor cost. Next add the cost of a day's liquor supply and any extra staff needed to serve it. This will give you the number of dollars that you need in the register each day to break even.

A daily break-even point is useful at any time. When you use it over a period of days it can show you when you might cut back on staff and which days that it doesn't pay to open at all, or it may indicate that you need to do something to raise your general sales level.

Forecasting Cash Flow

A bar can do a high-volume business yet still run into trouble if there is not enough cash in the bank to meet payroll and pay bills. This can happen because, as anyone who has ever received a paycheck will attest, money does not come in and go out at the same daily rate. You may have lump-sum payments due at certain times. Customers may pay by credit card. You may spend a large sum to buy a special wine that is hard to get. Forecasting cash flow can help you avoid a crunch.

A **cash-flow forecast**, or *cash budget,* as it is sometimes called, is a short-term forecast of cash flowing into the bank and cash flowing out, week by week or

HOW TO CALCULATE A BREAK-EVEN POINT

We will determine a break-even point using the sample budget figures that appear in Figure 14.2

1. **Determine the projected monthly sales.** In this example we know that figure is $100,000.
2. Separate and list the monthly fixed and variable costs as follows:

Fixed Costs	
Fixed Payroll	$9,000
Administrative	4,000
Laundry and Supplies	3,600
Utilities	3,000
Advertising	3,500
Repairs	1,500
Maintenance	2,000
Miscellaneous	700
Rent	6,000
Taxes	1,160
Insurance	2,400
Interest	800
Licenses and Fees	2,200
Depreciation	1,800
Amortization	840
TOTALS	$42,500
Variable Costs	
Beverage Costs	$24,000
Variable Payroll	13,500
	$37,500

3. Divide the total variable costs by the total sales.

$$\$37,500 \div \$100,000 = .375, \text{ or } 37.5\%$$

4. Subtract the variable costs (as a percentage) from 1.000.

$$1.000 - .375 = .625, \text{ or } 62.5\%$$

5. To determine the break-even point divide the total fixed costs by the step 4 results.

$$\$42,500 \div .625 = \$68,000$$

This is the level of sales for this particular bar, at which there is no profit or loss. It means that in this case the bar has to make $68,000 per month just to break even.

Further we can factor in the $20,000 profit that has been budgeted by the hopeful owner and use the formula to come up with a new figure:

$$\frac{\text{Total Fixed Costs} + \text{Profit}}{1.000 - \text{Percent of Variable Costs}} = \text{Desired Sales}$$

Using our sample figures, the formula would look like this:

$$\frac{\$42,500 + \$20,000}{0.625} = \frac{\$62,500}{0.625} = \$100,000$$

As stressful as it may sound it is often useful to have a daily break-even point—a kind of quota so that you'll know how much business you should be generating. First decide how many days per year the bar will be open, say 350 days. Then divide your yearly break-even sales by the number of days that you plan to be open. For our fictitious bar we can figure it two ways: a true break-even point that includes no profit at all, and one that builds in a $20,000 profit goal. Here's how those look:

True Break-Even Point

$$\frac{\$68,000}{350} = \$194.28 \text{ needed per day}$$

$20,000 Profit Goal

$$\frac{\$100,000}{350} = \$285.71 \text{ needed per day}$$

month by month. It requires predicting each item that will put money in your bank account or take it out. If yours is already an established business you can use your monthly income statements from previous years and other records to help you to estimate variables accurately. Fixed expenses, such as rent, license fees, taxes, insurance, and loan payments, are typically due on fixed dates in fixed amounts. Figure 14.4 shows a detailed guide for setting up a cash-flow forecast. It is organized as a monthly forecast but can be made to work for any interval. The following list details each of the steps in the process:

1. **Cash sales.** Enter your estimated monthly sales based on last year's records, allowing for seasonal influences, inflation, and growth of decline in your business during the past year.
2. **Accounts receivable collections.** Enter receivables that you expect to be paid during the month.
3. **Other cash receipts.** Enter your anticipated cash income not directly related to sales.
4. **TOTAL CASH AVAILABLE.** Add items 1 and 3. This is the sum of all of the projected inflows of cash for the month.
5. **Purchase payments.** Enter the amount to be paid out for beverages. Estimate this from last year's records, using the cost/sales ratio for the corresponding month.
6. **Operating expenses.** Enter the anticipated operating expenses estimated from last year's income statement for the same month and last month's figures.
7. **Other cash expenses.** Enter all other anticipated cash expenses.
8. **TOTAL CASH PAYOUT.** Add items 4 and 7. This is the sum of all the projected outflows of cash for the month.
9. **NET CASH FROM OPERATIONS.** Subtract item 8 from item 4.
10. **Short-term financing.** Enter the cash that you expect to come in from short-term loans during this month.
11. **Long-term financing.** Enter the cash that you expect to come in from long-term loans during this month.
12. **Additional equity.** Enter any additional cash amount to be invested in the business by owners during this month.
13. **Repayment of short-term debt:** Enter the payments on principal and interest on short-term loans due during the month.
14. **Capital expenditure:** Enter the payments on a permanent business investment, such as real-estate mortgages, or equipment purchases due during the month.
15. **Repayment of long-term debt:** Enter the payments on long-term principal and interest due during the month.
16. **Cash withdrawals:** Enter owners' cash withdrawals anticipated during the month.
17. **NET MONTHLY CASH POSITION:** Add items 9 and 12, then subtract items 13 and 16.
18. **BEGINNING CASH:** Enter the previous month's cumulative cash (item 19 of the previous month's forecast or the actual cash position on the first of the month).

CASH-FLOW FORECAST

+ = Money coming in – = Money going out	Jan	Feb	Mar	Apr	May	Jun
+ 1 Cash sales						
+ 2 Accounts receivable collections						
+ 3 Other cash receipts						
4 TOTAL CASH AVAILABLE						
– 5 Purchase payments						
– 6 Operating expenses						
– 7 Other cash expenses						
8 TOTAL CASH PAYOUT						
9 NET CASH FROM OPERATIONS						
+ 10 Short-term financing						
+ 11 Long-term financing						
+ 12 Additional equality						
– 13 Repayment of short-term debt						
– 14 Capital expenditure						
– 15 Repayment of long-term debt						
– 16 Cash withdrawls						
17 NET MONTHLY CASH POSITION						
18 BEGINNING CASH						
19 CUMULATIVE CASH POSITION						

FIGURE 14.4

19. CUMULATIVE CASH POSITION: Add the beginning cash (item 18) to the net monthly cash position (item 17).

Industry Comparisons

On an annual basis the NRA and the accounting firm Deloitte and Touche team up to compile and publish a *Restaurant Industry Operations (RIO) Report*. This very helpful document includes numerous tables and exhibits that should enable you to compare your bar operation with the national averages.

The example offered here is from the *Operations Report* for 2004 (see Figure 14.5). It is a table of expense and sales ratios for full-service restaurants, with the cost of the average check (per person) under $15. The lower quartile, medium, and upper quartile are provided for each line item. It is best to use the median range when planning the budget for a new bar business.

You will also notice that these ratios are based on total sales, except for food-and-beverage cost ratios, which are based on their respective sales. This is only a small portion of the total information available in the annual *RIO Report*. There are also more detailed statistics with breakdowns based on the following:

- Metropolitan and nonmetropolitan restaurants
- Menu themes
- Average check
- Single-unit and multiunit restaurants
- Types of ownership: sole proprietors, corporations, partnerships
- Sales volume
- Leased space and owned space

The study also offers several reports broken down by state. NRA members can purchase the *Operations Report* from the association.

THE CONTROL PHASE

On paper your budget plan is a numerical blueprint for your operations during the coming year. To turn this "paper plan" into reality you must make whatever operating changes you have decided on to reduce costs and/or increase sales to match the numbers on the plan. From this point on you monitor the actual performance of the bar, using the budget as a standard of measurement and a tool of control.

The control process consists of the following three steps:

FULL SERVICE RESTAURANTS (AVERAGE CHECK PER PERSON UNDER $15)

Statement of Income and Expenses–Ratio to Total Sales*

	Type of Establishment					
	Food Only			Food and Beverage		
	Lower Quartile	Median	Upper Quartile	Lower Quartile	Median	Upper Quartile
Sales						
Food	100.0%	100.0%	100.0%	71.3%	82.3%	92.9%
Beverage	N/A	N/A	N/A	7.1	17.7	28.7
Total Sales	100.0%	100.0%	100.0%	71.3%	82.3%	92.9%
Cost of Sales						
Food	25.9	29.6	32.9	30.0	33.7	38.9
Beverage	N/A	N/A	N/A	25.8	30.1	37.4
Total Cost of Sales	25.9	29.5	92.9	29.7	32.9	37.0
Gross Profit	65.0	69.8	73.9	62.5	66.5	70.1
Operating Expenses						
Salaries and Wages (including Employee Benefits)	29.1	33.1	38.7	28.9	34.2	39.7
Direct Operating Expenses	3.1	6.6	9.9	4.2	6.7	9.5
Music and Entertainment	**	**	**	0.0	0.3	0.7
Marketing	0.8	1.6	3.7	0.9	1.9	3.3
Utility Services	2.9	3.6	5.0	2.4	3.2	4.1
Restaurant Occupancy Costs	2.9	6.6	10.5	2.8	4.9	7.5
Repairs and Maintenance	1.0	1.7	2.4	1.0	1.4	2.1
Depreciation	1.4	2.5	3.2	0.9	1.8	2.6
Other Expenses/(Income)	0.0	0.9	1.8	(0.5)	0.2	2.5
General & Administrative Expenses	1.1	4.0	6.5	1.1	2.7	4.9
Corporate Overhead	2.0	4.5	5.3	0.3	3.7	6.2
Total Operating Expenses	66.6	62.3	69.3	52.2	60.0	68.1
Interest Expense	0.2	0.7	1.9	0.1	0.7	1.7
Other Expenses	0.0	0.2	0.7	0.0	0.3	1.8
Income (Loss) Before Income Taxes	(0.4)%	4.8%	14.6%	(0.3)%	5.5%	11.3%

Note: Computations include respondents that provided zeros and numerical amounts.
* All ratios are based as a percentage of total sales except food and beverage costs, which are based on their respective sales.
** Insufficient data
N/A Not applicable

FIGURE 14.5 Source: *Restaurant Industry Operations Report 2004.* Excerpted with permission of the National Restaurant Association, Chicago, Illinois. www.restaurant.org

1. Compare performance with the plan to discover variations.
2. Analyze operations to track the causes of the variations.
3. Act promptly to solve problems.

These three steps are the links that connect the plan with the profit. Naturally the budget and the actual results are not going to correlate number for number every day or even every week or month. For example, you may spend a great deal of money to buy liquor to cover the American Legion convention, and the sales won't show up until the next monitoring period. So in one period both your dollar costs and your percentage costs rise, then in the next period your dollar costs are back to normal but your percentage cost drops because your sales went up during the convention. As such you need to learn how to judge when a variation is significant.

A **budget deviation analysis (BDA)** should be part of your monthly budgeting process. This is similar to taking a second look at the newly completed month's budget, to see where and how much the actual figures deviated from what you had expected. A sample BDA form is shown in Figure 14.6. To compare your business's performance with that of national figures, the NRA's *RIO Report* comes in handy.

To some extent the significance of any variation depends on what it is: a sales, labor, or beverage cost, or something else. It also makes a difference how large it is and how persistent. You can set an acceptable variation percentage based on past history for several periods. There are also a few basic rules. Generally a variation is significant if it shows up in both dollars and percent of sales. Less significant is a dollar variation by itself. Least significant is a percentage variation by itself. However you should look into any persistent variation or one that exceeds your permissible plan.

The Income Statement

The most useful tool you have for comparing your performance with your plan is the periodic **income statement** prepared by your accountant. This statement is part of the control phase because you measure results by it. It is also part of the planning phase because it is the basis for future decisions.

An income statement shows the kinds and amounts of revenue, the kinds and amounts of expenses, and the resulting profit or loss over a given period of time (see Figure 14.7). It is routinely prepared at the end of each month or each accounting period. When you compare it with your budget and with the statements of preceding periods, it tells you how you are doing. It also gives you the dollar data you need to figure the cost percentages you use for analysis and control. The income statement is management's most important accounting tool.

That said, it is trickier to produce an income statement than a cash-flow statement primarily because of the ways that expenses are categorized. As a result it is wise to leave this task to an accountant who is familiar with the hospitality industry. (You should also consider using the expense categories found in the NRA's *Uniform*

BUDGET DEVIATION ANALYSIS

From Income Statement for Month ________

	A ACTUAL	B BUDGET	C DEVIATION (B − A)	D % OF DEVIATION (C/B × 100)
TOTAL SALES				
Liquor				
Beer				
Wine				
TOTAL				
Less COST OF BEVERAGE SOLD				
Beginning inventory				
+ Purchases				
- Ending inventory				
GROSS PROFIT				
Less OPERATING (VARIABLE/CONTROLLABLE)				
EXPENSES				
Payroll Cost				
Administrative expenses				
Laundry and supplies				
Utilities				
Advertising and promotion				
Repairs				
Maintenance				
Miscellaneous operating expenses				
TOTAL VARIABLE EXPENSES				
GROSS OPERATING PROFIT				
Less FIXED OVERHEAD				
(NONCONTROLLABLE)				
EXPENSES				
Rent				
Taxes				
Insurance				
Interest				
Licenses and fees				
Depreciation				
Amortization				
TOTAL FIXED EXPENSES				
NET PROFIT BEFORE INCOME TAXES				

FIGURE 14.6

INCOME STATEMENT: SEPTEMBER 2006

	Liquor	Beer	Wine	September 2006			Year to Date		
TOTAL SALES									
Liquor $22,550.30								$67,230.20	
Beer 7,129.45								20,048.45	
Wine 13,743.85					$43,423.60	100.00%		37,965.00	
								$125,243.65	100.00%
Less COST OF BEVERAGE SOLD									
Beginning inventory	$2692.70	$1620.10	$2179.45						
+ Purchases	5101.35	2130.00	3603.10						
	$7794.05	$3750.10	$5782.55						
– Ending inventory	3622.24	902.10	1530.20						
TOTAL COST	$4171.81	$2848.00	$4252.35		$11,272.16	25.96%		$30,935.18	24.69%
GROSS PROFIT					$32,151.44			$94,308.47	
Less OPERATING (CONTROLLABLE) EXPENSES									
Payroll costs				$13,620.70			$40,075.90		
Administrative expenses				1,328.78			3,040.00		
Laundry and supplies				1,101.20			2,804.20		
Utilities				385.26			1,125.60		
Advertising and promotion				275.00			690.00		
Repairs				510.00			1,038.26		
Maintenance				874.00			2,196.00		
Miscellaneous operating expenses				162.00			250.44		
TOTAL VARIABLE EXPENSES					$18,256.94	42.04%		$51,220.31	40.89%
GROSS OPERATING PROFIT					$13,894.50			$43,088.16	
Less FIXED OVERHEAD (NONCONTROLLABLE) EXPENSES									
Rent				$850.00			$2,550.00		
Taxes				440.00			1,320.00		
Insurance				357.00			1,071.00		
Interest				818.00			2,454.00		
Licenses and fees				907.00			2,721.00		
Depreciation				774.00			2,322.00		
Amortization				320.00			960.00		
TOTAL FIXED EXPENSES					$4,466.00	10.29%		$13,397.00	10.69%
NET PROFIT BEFORE INCOME TAXES					$9,428.50	21.71%		$29,691.16	23.70%

FIGURE 14.7 A sample monthly income statement.

System of Accounts for Restaurants, most of which also apply to bars.) The income statement is compiled from the various revenue and expense accounts for the period. It shows a summary figure for each account, which is the account balance.

The way in which the income statement groups and presents these summary figures has a lot to do with its usefulness to the bar manager. Figure 14.7 shows an income statement structured for maximum usefulness. The two principles behind this arrangement are as follows:

- ***Responsibility.*** Revenues and expenses are grouped according to the responsibilities involved. Thus for each grouping the performance of the person responsible can be measured and evaluated.
- ***Controllability.*** Expenses are classified and grouped according to the extent to which they can be controlled. This income statement shows three levels of controllability: beverage expenses (directly related to sales and fully controllable), operating expenses (related to sales to some extent and controllable to some degree), and fixed expenses (uncontrollable overhead expense).

According to these two principles this income statement is separated into three successive profit levels. Its structure is shown in Figure 14.8.

- The first level is the **gross profit or contribution margin,** or the profit from beverage sales less beverage costs. The responsibility includes sales volume, beverage supply, and beverage cost control. This level of profit is the manager's responsibility.
- The second level is the **gross operating profit,** or the gross profit less the operating expenses. This responsibility, also the manager's, includes supplying items of sales-related expenses (labor, supplies, laundry, utilities, maintenance, promotion, and so on) in amounts that support and increase beverage sales, while controlling the costs of these items.
- The third level is the *net income* (also called the *pretax profit* or *net profit before taxes*), or the operating profit less the fixed overhead expenses, such as rent,

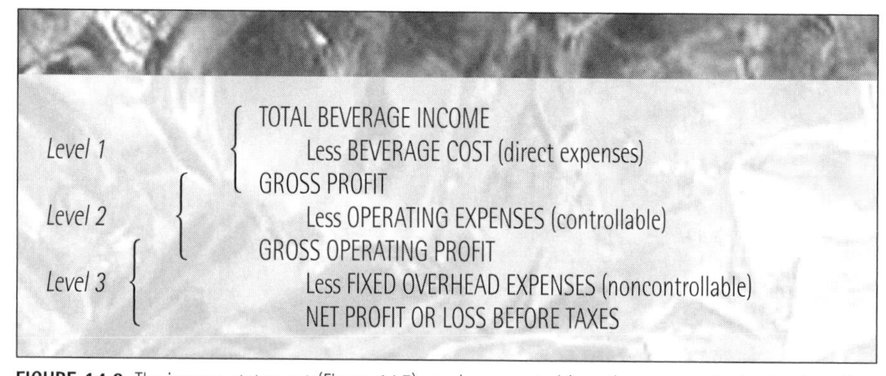

FIGURE 14.8 The income statement (Figure 14.7) can be separated into three successive levels of profit.

taxes, licenses and fees, insurance, interest, depreciation, and amortization. The responsibility here, to the extent that these expenses can be altered, involves finance and investment policy, contracts, and high-level decision-making. Those responsible for this segment of expenses and for the net-profit level are the owners of small businesses or top management in a large corporation. An important point: Although responsibility for net profit remains at the top as a practical matter, profitability depends on the extent to which the gross operating profit (Level 2) exceeds the fixed expenses. Since the manager is responsible for this level of profit profitability is in his or her hands.

Thus the goal should be to maximize gross operating profit, and the strategy should be to relate specific costs to the sales they produce, rather than simply thinking in general terms of maximizing sales and holding down costs. It is fine to spend money to make money. If increasing a cost increases sales by a more than proportionate amount, it is profitable to increase that cost. Each monthly income statement tells you how you are doing when you compare it with your budget and the statements of preceding periods. It also gives you the dollar data you need to calculate the cost percentages you need for analysis and control.

Data Analysis

The income statement is a form of data analysis. It arranges data in ways that show measurable relationships. If you carry the process further by translating cost and sales into percentage terms for specific budget items you can see and measure relationships in significant ways. Then you can make changes that will decrease costs or increase sales. In addition if daily data are gathered and organized by computer you can study what is happening almost as it happens. Two areas of analysis are especially important: sales, and operating expenses as they relate to sales. A third area, overhead expenses as they relate to sales, is also important, but since these expenses are fixed there is less that you can do about them.

All profits come from sales; therefore, increasing sales is one road to maximizing profits. To do this you need all kinds of information about sales, such as volume per drink, per price, per shift, per day, per week, per month, and per season. If you gather the data and calculate the *cost/sales ratio* you can see where the profit is being made and where to put your marketing emphasis. You can also measure the effects of any changes that you make. The other piece of the profit equation is cost: Profit equals sales less cost. A bar's operating expenses are the manager's responsibility. They are tied in varying degrees to the rise and fall of sales, and they are always examined in relation to the sales that they help to produce. Keeping close track of this relationship can tell you a great deal about what is happening to your profit day by day.

The two major categories of operating expenses, beverage cost and payroll expense, are called **prime costs** because they are the largest and most necessary items on which you spend your money. Beverage cost is the cost of the alcoholic beverages sold. Since the cost of these is dictated largely by customer taste the manager's primary focus is on controlling losses. So data analysis in the form of cost/sales ratios is a common way of detecting and measuring losses.

Payroll expense, the other prime cost, basically represents the cost of preparing and serving the products sold. Payroll costs should be correlated with sales for the same period in a cost-percentage figure and measured against the budget goal and percentages for previous periods. If your cost/sales ratio is high you should look for ways to avoid overtime or cut staff or hours worked. Other operating expenses, as well as overhead expenses, should also be closely watched in terms of cost/sales ratios and compared with budget goals and past history. The higher the percentage for costs, the lower the percentage for profits. A decline in the cost/sales ratio might indicate the need to step up promotion, to stay open longer, or to think about renovating your facility.

The control phase of any budget plan should conclude with several comparisons:

- ***With past performance.*** How did you do this year compared with last year?
- ***With industry performance.*** How did you do compared to your competitors and to the industry at large?
- ***With your own goals.*** How close did you come to reaching your profit goal?

The final and most important question you should ask yourself is: How can you use your experience with the past year's budget in structuring next year's budget to meet your profit goal?

Working with an Accountant

When competition is tough you will need every available advantage to succeed—a good accountant is one of those advantages. Accounting is a specialized profession and you should choose your accountant as carefully as you would choose an attorney, a doctor, or a chef for your kitchen. Make inquiries of other bar owners, ask bankers or attorneys for recommendations, and consult your local or state restaurant association for names. You are looking for someone whose strengths complement your own and who has had experience in accounting for bars or restaurants.

You should be able to record expenses and income on a daily basis, but it is the accountant who takes this information, compiles it into financial statements, and meets with you regularly to discuss these statements and whatever weaknesses or strengths they may reveal. It is wise to bring in the accountant at the very beginning of the business setup for ideas about which forms and software to use to best mesh with his or her system. An accountant can help you to make such decisions as whether to purchase additional equipment and whether it should be new or used, whether and how quickly you should expand the business, and what kinds of strategies you might use to maximize profitability.

Areas in which small businesses usually get into trouble are not separating personal and business expenses, not filing payroll information or paying payroll taxes correctly, not paying taxes in a timely manner, and submitting poorly prepared tax returns in general. These are all tasks that a good accountant can assist with; an accountant can also help you to keep track of myriad tax-law changes over the years. In short the accountant-client bond is a serious, long-term relationship in which trust and honesty is tantamount. Choose an accountant with whom you can build such a relationship.

PRICING FOR PROFIT

Profit is the difference been total sales and total costs. For a bar total sales are the number of drinks sold multiplied by their selling prices. The essence of profitable pricing is to set individual prices that produce the maximum difference between total sales and total costs. Several factors are involved: the cost of each drink, the effect of price on demand for the drink, the contribution of each drink to total sales, and the effect of the sales mix on profits.

The many different ways of pricing in the bar business are sometimes used consciously, sometimes unconsciously, sometimes simultaneously, and often inconsistently. Some managers set prices using a strict cost/price formula. Other managers set them by trial and error. Some charge whatever the traffic will bear. Many price according to neighborhood competition. Some copy the bar with the biggest business. Some set prices low, hoping to undercut their competitors; others set prices high to limit their clientele to people at a certain income level. A few lucky managers who are in charge of a unique facility, such as a revolving skyscraper lounge, set skyscraper prices because they assume that the customer expects them. Some managers use an impressive price/value combination as a basic merchandising strategy.

Two points need to be made here. One is that pricing works best when you choose and stick to a standard system—even if it differs for beer, wine, and liquor—that makes this part of the business much easier to keep up with and much less hassle when introducing new products. The second is that whatever the pricing policy the goal should be to set prices that will maximize the *gross profit* or *contribution margin* (the sales less the product cost). Each of the bar's many drinks should be priced to achieve this total outcome.

The Cost/Price Relationship

Any reliable method of pricing a drink should start with its cost. You can establish a percentage relationship between cost and price that will give you a simple pricing formula to work with. The cost percentage of the price pays for the ingredients in the drink, and the remaining percentage of the price (gross margin) goes to pay that drink's share of all of your other costs and your profit. The cost percentage will be about the same as the beverage-cost percentage of your budget (refer again to Figure 14.2), although it will not correspond exactly since the latter represents the combined percentages of liquor, wine, and beer. Generally your liquor cost percentage will be 20 to 25 percent, while wine and beer will run higher at 33 to 50 percent. Each enterprise must determine its own cost percentage to produce the profit needed. To find the price, divide the cost of the ingredients by the cost percentage:

$$\frac{\text{Cost}}{\text{Cost percentage}} = \text{Sales price}$$

For example:

$$\frac{\$0.80 \text{ (Cost of 1 1/4 ounce Scotch Mist)}}{0.25 \text{ (Cost percentage)}} = \$3.20 \text{ (Sales price for Scotch Mist)}$$

You can turn this formula around and convert the cost percentage into a multiplier by dividing it into 100 percent, which represents the sales price.

For example:

$$\frac{100\% \text{ (Sales price)}}{0.25 \text{ (Cost percentage)}} = 4 \text{ (Multiplier)}$$

$$4 \times \$0.80 \text{ (Cost)} = \$3.20 \text{ (Sales Price)}$$

When you price mixed drinks, the simplest version of this cost/price formula is to use the cost of the beverage alone. This is known as the **beverage-cost method.** In the Scotch Mist example above this cost figure is very accurate since Scotch is the only ingredient. However, most drinks have more than one ingredient, many of them nonalcoholic, such as mixers, garnishes, and cream. A truly accurate cost/price relationship must be based on the costs of all of the ingredients. The technique of determining total cost is based on the drink's recipe and is known as **costing** the recipe. The following is an example of a simple method of costing:

1. Start with the standard house recipe.

1. Recipe: 2 ounces gin
1/2 ounces dry vermouth
1 pitted olive

2. Determine the cost of the gin. To do this find:

a. Size of bottle and its ounce capacity
b. Bottle cost (from invoice)
c. Cost per ounce (divide bottle cost by ounces per bottle)
d. Recipe cost of gin (multiply ounce cost by number of ounces in recipe)

2. Cost of gin:

a. Liter = 33.8 ounces
b. $11.95
c. $\frac{\$11.95 \text{ (bottle cost)}}{33.8 \text{ (ounces per bottle)}} = \$0.35 \text{ per ounce}$
d. $0.35 cost per ounce
× 2 ounces in recipe
$0.70 recipe cost of gin

3. Determine the cost of the vermouth:
   a. Size of bottle and its ounce capacity
   b. Bottle cost (from invoice)
   c. Cost per ounce (divide bottle cost by ounces per bottle)
   d. Recipe cost of vermouth (multiply ounce cost by number of ounces in recipe)

3. Cost of vermouth:
   a. 750 millileters = 25.4 ounces
   b. $4.15
   c. $\frac{\$4.15 \text{ (bottle cost)}}{25.4 \text{ (ounces per bottle)}} = \$0.163 \text{ per ounce}$
   d. $0.163 cost per ounce
      × 0.5 ounce in recipe
      $0.081 recipe cost of vermouth

4. Determine the cost of the olive:
   a. Jar size and olive count (from invoice or lable on jar)
   b. Jar cost (from invoice)
   c. Cost per olive (divide jar cost by olives per jar)
   d. Recipe cost of olive (multiply olive cost by number of olives in recipe)

4. Cost of olive:
   a. Quart = 80 olives
   b. $2.20
   c. $\frac{\$2.20 \text{ container cost}}{80} = \$0.027 \text{ per olive}$
   d. 1 olive = $0.027 recipe cost

5. Total the costs. This gives you the standard recipe cost as of the date of costing.

5. Total costs:

Gin	$0.700
Vermouth	$0.081
Olive	$0.027
Standard recipe cost	$0.808

To arrive at the selling price of the drink, divide the cost by the cost percentage. This gives you the sales price:

$$\frac{\$0.808 \text{ Recipe cost}}{0.25 \text{ Cost percentage}} = \$3.232 \text{ Sales price (round off to \$3.25)}$$

A quicker although less accurate way to arrive at a selling price is to base the price on the cost of the **prime ingredient**—that is, the base liquor—instead of the actual recipe cost, adding a certain percentage for the extra ingredients. This is a refinement of the beverage-cost method. The following example uses a Martini:

$0.700	Prime-ingredient cost
+ $0.070	10% allowance for additional ingredients
$0.770	Cost base
× 4	Multiplier
$3.080	Sales price (round off to $3.10)

Pricing mixed drinks on the basis of the prime-ingredient cost is a quick, easy, and widely used method. It is typically used to establish a base price for all drinks having the same amount of the same prime ingredient, then the percentage is added for drinks having extra ingredients. Obviously the method is not as accurate as costing the recipe; you can see that the added percentage in the example does not reflect true cost. A single percentage figure will never be accurate for a whole spectrum of drinks.

A third method, the **gross profit method,** is used to express the amount of gross profit realized on the sale of one drink. It is determined by dividing the amount of gross profit by the sales price of the drink. Here's how it works: First subtract the cost of the drink from its selling price, then divide the result (the gross profit) by the selling price. This gives you the gross profit margin as a percent. For example:

Selling price: \$4.50
Cost of drink: \$0.75
Gross profit: \$4.50 − \$0.75 = \$3.75

$$\text{Profit margin: } \frac{\$3.75}{\$4.50} = 0.833, \text{ or } 83.3\%$$

You can of course "reverse" this method to set the prices of drinks. But first you must use the gross margin percent to get a reciprocal figure (a percentage of 1.000), then divide this reciprocal figure into the cost of the drink. Let's look more closely at how it works:

1.000 − 0.833 = 0.167, or 16.7%
(The "reciprocal" of the 83.3% gross margin is 16.7%.)
Divide the cost of the drink by the reciprocal amount:

$$\frac{\$0.75}{\$0.167} = \$4.491 \text{ (round up to \$4.50)}$$

As you can tell costing and pricing takes a great deal of time and can be tedious work. But to arrive at a sound price structure you have to establish the cost of each drink, one way or another. Only if you look at each drink by itself can you establish sound cost/price relationships and build a coherent overall price structure.

The Demand/Price Relationship

Costs and percentages are not the whole answer to pricing. Price is only one of two factors in total sales. The other, as you likely know, is the number of drinks sold. The price affects the number. The effect of prices on numbers is the elusive secret of successful pricing—elusive because no one ever knows precisely what effect a change of price will have on demand in any given situation.

If you increase the price of a given drink you increase the margin per drink sold since cost remains the same. But sales volume is typically sensitive to changes in prices. In a normal situation (whatever that is), there is a seesaw relationship: When the price goes up, the margin per drink goes up but the number of drinks sold goes down (demand falls). When the price goes down, the margin per drink goes down but the number sold goes up (demand rises).

DO DRINK PRICES CAUSE HANGOVERS?

In December 2005 the Los Angeles Business Journal reported on the skyrocketing prices of Martinis in the L.A. area. Among the top-of-the-line drink concoctions, Katana on Sunset Strip priced its Martini made with superpremium Ultimat Vodka at $18. The Hotel Bel-Air's Classic Vodka Martini cost $16. These made the Grey Goose Vodka Martini seem like a relative bargain at $14 at the Rooftop Bar of The Standard Hotel.

Bar owners and managers say the higher-end prices reflect the overall guest experience, not just the drinks themselves, and that high drink prices are a kind of "cover charge" for being part of the trendy crowd.

In a 2005–2006 Zagat survey average drink prices in a few major cities included the folliwng:

- San Francisco $7.27
- Los Angeles 8.26
- New York 8.83
- Las Vegas 9.42

That said, you seldom have a totally "normal" situation. In any given bar more than price is influencing demand. Other factors include drink quality, ambience, food, entertainment, individual capacity, other drinks, and competing bars. How much of a price increase for a given drink will cause a customer to order fewer drinks or switch to a lower-priced drink? At which lower overall price level will customers choose you over your competitors? At which higher price levels will customers start to patronize the bar next door instead? Where does the seesaw balance? Most bars operate in a competitive environment in which demand is fairly responsive to price changes. The trick is to know your competition and especially your customers, make shrewd guesses on demand/price sensitivity, and watch your sales to see how they respond. Your objective is to balance the seesaw for all the drinks taken together in a way that will bring the largest overall margin for your enterprise.

Coordinating Prices to Maximize Profits

When you have the whole detailed picture of cost-based prices you can round off and finalize drink prices with your eye on the seesaw of demand. The first modification of cost/price ratios is to simplify the picture by establishing several broad categories of drinks and setting uniform prices within each category. This makes it easier for everybody and enables bartenders and servers to complete sales transactions efficiently.

The following price categories may be useful; they should at least give you a point of departure for your own plan:

- ***Highballs.*** Two prices, one for highballs poured with well brands and one for those made with call-brand drinks. Generally highballs make up the lowest price category.
- ***Cocktails.*** Two prices, one for cocktails made with well brands and one for those made with call brands.
- ***Frozen drinks and ice-cream drinks.*** Two prices, one for well and one for call brands.
- ***After-dinner liqueurs and brandies.*** Two prices, one for ordinary liqueurs and one for premium liqueurs and French brandies.
- ***Specialty drinks.*** Two prices, one for well brands and one for call brands.

All pricing decisions involve interdependent relationships among drinks and drink prices. The price you charge for one kind of drink can affect the demand for others. For example if you raise your cocktail prices you may sell fewer cocktails and more highballs for fewer total dollars. On the other hand if you introduce a high-priced frozen drink with customer appeal, you may sell more of them and fewer of your lower-priced highballs and cocktails. A high-profit coffee specialty drink at a premium price may not affect demand for predinner drinks at all. You have to keep potential interrelationships in mind in order to arrive at a combination that maximizes the sum total of all drink profits. This is known as **total business pricing.**

As you create an overall pricing philosophy, ask yourself the following questions:

- Are the prices for liquor, wine, and beer integrated logically with each other?
- Is the pricing program organized into simple, easily monitored categories?
- How do the prices compare with competitors' prices? (You should check on this at least twice a year.)
- Are the drink prices in line with the food prices?
- Are we charging prices that are profitable, considering our budget?

Know your exact pouring costs and do not become too focused on low margins. By pouring premium brands, you can expect higher costs—but also more dollars to add to the bottom line because you can charge more for these drinks. It is also easy to get a high margin for specialty drinks and wines sold by the glass.

Of course some drinks always have lower margins because demand drops sharply as the price goes up. Among these are beer and wines by the bottle. You can use a lower-margin price as a way to increase volume by bringing in new customers. You can also reduce prices selectively to create a mood for buying other drinks. You might, for example, have a special low price on frozen Strawberry Daiquiris on a hot day and sell many other frozen drinks at their regular price just by planting the frozen-drink idea. Or you can reduce your standard prices on higher-priced drinks and raise them on lower-priced drinks, and you might come out ahead.

All of these price relationships must be calculated for your own enterprise. Some work well in some bars but not others. Whatever combination of prices gives you the best overall price-times-numbers-less-cost equation is the best set of prices for you . . . for the moment, at least. Things can change, so you must watch sales closely. It can be a fascinating and enlightening game.

Whatever your decisions it is a good idea to provide a list of standard prices, both for the customer and for service personnel. You can post prices at the bar (see Figure 14.9) or print them on a menu. Posted prices will eliminate arguments between employees and customers and will make it harder for unscrupulous employees to overcharge and pocket the difference.

The other side of the pricing philosophy is the bar's cost controls. Once the drink prices have been calculated, *costs must be controlled* to maintain the budgeted profit level. Ensuring that cost controls are in place means being able to answer the following questions affirmatively:

- Are discounts and promotional prices reflected on invoices from suppliers?
- Is the POS system properly programmed?
- Do distributors' sales representatives keep you informed about price increases?
- Are the bartenders tested for pouring accuracy? If so, how often? If not, why not?
- Are drink recipes readily available? Does everyone who makes drinks use them?
- Do new employees receive training on both drink pricing and drink mixing?
- Does the servers' training cover pricing and POS programming?

Running specials or promotions does not have to wreak havoc with your pricing policies and in fact, doesn't necessarily mean that you have to lower your drink prices. Marketing activities can be memorable and fun and they will do more to enhance your bar's image than merely offering cheap drinks. Partner with other businesses in your area to award such prizes as movie passes, music CDs, and sporting-events tickets. Your suppliers may also have fun, name-branded items to give away, such as t-shirts and hats.

Pricing Wines

In addition to the tips mentioned in Chapter 7 about wine list mapping and other ways to select wines in a variety of price ranges when creating a wine list, there are a couple of other ways to look at wine pricing as an overall strategy. Some restaurateurs (and bar owners) use a system that varies the markup with the type of wine. Instead of a standard "2.5 times wholesale price," their system looks like this:

Cost per Bottle	*Markup Percentage*	*Selling Price*	*Gross Profit*
$10	350% (3.5 times)	$45.00	$35.00
$20	250% (2.5 times)	$65.00	$45.00
$25	200% (2 times)	$75.00	$50.00

PRICE LIST

Restaurant Bar

Glass/Size	Drink Category	Drink Size	Drink Price
9 oz.	**HIGHBALLS**		
	Well	1.5 oz.	$3.50
	Call	1.5	4.00
	Premium	1.5	4.24
	Superpremium	1.5	4.50
7 oz.	**ROCKS**		
	Well	1.5	3.50
	Call	1.5	4.50
	Premium/Superpremium	1.5	4.75
1.5 oz. Jigger	**SHOTS**		
	Well	1.0 oz.	3.50
	Call	1.0	3.75
	Premium/Superpremium	1.0	4.00
7 oz. Rocks *or*	**MARTINI/MANHATTAN**		
4 oz. Cocktail	Well	2 oz./.25 oz.	4.25
	Call	2 oz./.25 oz.	4.50
	Premium/Superpremium	2 oz./.25 oz.	5.00
12 oz. Stemmed	**JUICE DRINKS:** Mary/Driver/Collins/Sling		
or	Well	1.5 oz.	4.00
12 oz. Tumbler	Call	1.5	4.50
	Premium/Superpremium	1.5	5.00
12 oz. Stemmed	**DAIQUIRI/MARGARITA/SOUR**		
or	Well	1.5 oz.	4.00
12 oz. Tumbler	Call	1.5	4.50
or	Premium/Superpremium	1.5	5.00
Speciality Glass			
12 oz. Snifter	**BRANDIES and LIQUEURS**		
	Well	1.5 oz.	4.00
	Call	1.5	5.00
	Premium/Superpremium	1.5	5.50

FIGURE 14.9 A basic drink price list. The more upscale the bar or restaurant, the higher the prices might be set.

7 oz. Rocks or Speciality Glass	**CREAM and TWO-LIQUOR DRINKS**		
	Well	1 oz. Plus 1 oz.	$4.00
	Call	1 oz. Plus 1 oz.	4.50
	Premium/Superpremium	1 oz. Plus 1 oz.	5.00
10 oz. Coffee Glass	**COFFEE DRINKS**		
	Well/one-liquor	1.5 oz.	4.50
	Well/two-liquor	1 oz. each	5.00
	Call/one-liquor	1.5 oz.	5.00
	Call/two-liquor	1 oz. each	5.50
10 oz. Glass	**WINES**		
	House Wine	6 oz.	4.00
		Bottle	14.00
	Premium Wine	6 oz.	5.00
		Bottle	See wine list
6 oz. Flute	**CHAMPAGNE**		
	Half-bottle	187 ml	8.50
	Bottle	750 ml	See wine list
12 oz. Mug/ 16 oz. Pint/ 32 oz. Pitcher	**BEERS**		
	Premium Draft	12 oz.	2.75
		16 oz.	3.75
		32 oz. Pitcher	5.50
	Superpremium Draft	12 oz.	3.25
		16 oz.	4.00
		32 oz. Pitcher	6.00
	Preium Bottled Beer	12 oz.	3.50
	Super/Premium Bottled Beer	12 oz.	4.00
12 oz. Wine	Bottled Water	Various	2.50
12 oz. Mug	Soft Drinks	No Liquor	2.00
12 oz. Wine	Nonalcoholic Drinks	No Liquor	2.50
12 oz. wine	Fruit Juices	No Liquor	2.50

FIGURE 14.9 *(continued)*

This system encourages the sale of more expensive wines (because of their lower markup) and maximizes the profits on the wines that cost you less to purchase at wholesale. This is an interesting alternative to the single-markup method because one markup percentage inevitably means that some wines are overpriced and others are underpriced.

Another way to view a wine-pricing strategy is to establish a limited number of selling prices or *price points,* and "force" wines of similar cost into a few distinct price categories. While both approaches have merit and are widely used, they also suggest that you follow some inflexible rules that may or may not meet your needs. We suggest that the pricing of wines is also influenced by the specific wine being offered, the existing market conditions, the type of clientele and their overall wine knowledge, and the ambience of the place where the wine is being served. With all this in mind, here are our suggestions for setting wine prices that are fair to both you and your guests:

- Remember that you are likely to sell more $30 bottles of wine than $100 bottles. Concentrate on pricing the lower-cost wines correctly, and on the price category that the majority of your customers would naturally associate with your operation.
- Indirect cost considerations, including location, ambience, and type of clientele, do allow some places to charge a little more. Your guests generally recognize these intangibles as value-added and accept the higher price, but you can get away with this only if you clearly understand your customer base.
- Reserve the highest markups for only those selections that are hard to get. Many of the rarest wines are not even appropriate for most bars' wine lists.
- Value-conscious guests usually choose a wine that is somewhere between the lowest- and highest-priced selections on the list. You can help shift sales to the price categories that are your most profitable by placing one wine that is significantly lower in price into the category. Suppose that you have two white wines on the list, one that sells for $25 and the other for $40. To round out the list add another white wine that sells for $20 and a fourth bottle that sells for $30. The $25 and $30 bottles appear to become "the best values."

The Pour-Cost Analysis

Another way to assess a bar's financial performance is to analyze its **pouring costs.** This is a way to compare the different cost percentages of wine, beer, and distilled spirits. Since each of these broad categories sell at substantially different cost percentages you should calculate each category separately. Pouring costs are figured by dividing the cost of the depleted inventory (*cost of goods sold*) by the gross sales earned over a given time period—say, one month. The owner or manager decides the time period, but the shorter the time frame, the more information you have about the bar's true financial state.

The following are sample calculations for a pour-cost analysis:

Opening inventory value	$12,720	
plus (+) Liquor purchases		$28,340
TOTAL Amount available for sale	$41,060	
Closing inventory value	$12,135	
plus (+) Cost of spillage		103
plus (+) Cost of complimentary drinks		427
plus (+) Transfers out from the bar		268
Adjusted closing inventory	$12,933	
Total available for sale		$41,060
minus (−) Adjusted closing inventory	$12,933	
Liquor cost		$28,127

$$\frac{\$28{,}127 \text{ Liquor cost (Cost of goods sold)}}{\$172{,}820 \text{ (Gross liquor sales)}} = 0.162, \text{ or } 16.2\%$$

This calculation may be further analyzed with the following operating factors in mind:

- If the bar is pouring the more expensive brands the well liquor will yield very favorable pouring cost percentages for this category.
- There is a wide disparity in beer quality and price among domestic, imported, and microbrewed brands. The pouring-cost percentages will be greatly affected by the beer-sales-mix percentages: what and how much you pour. If your customers drink more of the lower-cost bottled beers the pouring costs for beer will be lower overall.
- When you calculate the pouring costs of wines by the glass, two factors are critical: the cost per ounce for the wine and the portion size served. The industry standards for pouring costs, shown in Figure 14.10, come from the book *Successful Beverage Management* by Robert Plotkin and Steve Goumas (Bar Media, Tucson, Arizona, 2001).

The sales mix at the bar will also affect pouring cost. By "sales mix" we mean the percentages of total bar sales that are beer, wine, and spirits. Figure 14.11 shows a breakdown of bar sales and cost mix. For this table to be helpful you need to compare the *Monthly Sales Mix* column between reporting periods. As the sales mix increases in a category that has a high *Monthly Cost Percent* (the third column) pouring costs will also increase. So for the most favorable pouring costs, look for high sales-mix percentages in categories with low monthly cost percentages.

ESTABLISHING PRODUCT CONTROLS

In a bar business controls mean two things: tracking the incoming and outgoing beverages, supplies, and cash; and providing product consistency for customers. In Chapters 10 and 11 on mixology you learned what makes a successful mixed drink

PRICE LIST

Category	Cost Percentage Range
Liquor	
Well Liquor	9%–10%
Call Liquor	12%–14%
Premium Liquor	16%–18%
Superpremium	18%–20%
Top-Shelf Liquor	20%–24%
Overall Liquor Pour Cost	16%–20%
Beer	
American Bottled Beer	17%–33%
Imported Bottled Beer	20%–37%
Microbrews Bottled	25%–35%
Overall Bottled Beer Pour Cost	18%–28%
American Draft Beer	10%–20%
Imported Draft Beer	14%–35%
Microbrews Draft	22%–33%
Overall Draft Beer Pour Cost	16%–28%
Wine	
House Wine by the Glass	12%–18%
Varietals by the Glass	20%–25%
Varietal Bottled Wine (750ml)	33%–60%
Overall Wine Pour Cost	16%–33%

FIGURE 14.10 Industry standards for pouring costs. Source: *Successful Beverage Management,* Robert Plotkin and Steven Goumas, 2001, Bar Media, Tucson, Arizona.

and how to develop recipes for your drinks so that each drink served from your bar will taste the way you want it to. But how can you be sure that the recipes you have carefully developed will be faithfully followed by each bartender, keeping in mind that each has his or her own ways of pouring, and that bartenders sometimes come and go from the job at the normal rate for the species?

Not only do you want the drinks served at your bar to be your recipes, you want them to be prepared the same way every time that they are ordered. Product consistency is very important in building a clientele. New customers expect your Bloody Mary to taste the way a Bloody Mary should, and repeat customers expect your Bloody Mary to taste the way it did the last time. Meeting customer expectations is just as important to profit as setting your drink prices correctly is. This

BAR SALES/COST MIX

Category	*Monthly Sales*	*Monthly Costs*	*Percentage Cost/Month*	*Monthly Mix*
Liquor	$35,248	$ 7,627	21.6%	45.8%
Beer	22,730	6,913	30.4%	29.6%
Wine	18,970	7,016	36.9%	24.6%
TOTALS	$76,948	$24,679	32.0%	100.0%

(**NOTE:** In the Totals row, the 32 percent figure is obtained by dividing the monthly costs by the monthly sales.)

FIGURE 14.11

equation, sales price multiplied by sales volume, produces the profit that your budget stipulates. You cannot build volume on the basis of drinks that do not consistently meet customer needs and desires.

To achieve this consistency, you must establish standards for all drinks, that is, standard ingredients, quantities, portion sizes, and procedures for making them. When these standards are put into practice and everyone is required to follow them, the customer will get the same drink every time no matter who makes it. In addition to producing consistent drinks these standards give you ways of controlling the quantities of liquor used. If you can control the quantities, you also control the beverage costs. Further if you control the beverage costs, you can maintain your projected cost/sales ratio and protect your profit. To achieve all of this you must standardize three major elements for each drink: the drink size, the drink recipe, and the glassware in which it is served.

Standard Drink Size

In the vocabulary of the bar the term **drink size** refers to the *amount of the prime ingredient* used per drink poured, *not* the size of the finished drink. In each bar this amount is the same for most spirit-based drinks, with different standard amounts for a few drink types and special drinks. As such if your drink size is 1½ ounces, you will pour 1½ ounces of the base liquor in each drink, whatever it is. This is your **standard drink size.**

Each bar has its own standard drink size. Most bars pour a 1-ounce or 1¼-ounce standard drink but this varies across the industry from ¾ ounce to 2 ounces depending on the nature of the enterprise and the clientele. In each bar special drink types that vary from the standard will have their own standard drink size. You can see how this works in one bar by studying the *Drink Size* column in Figure 14.9.

To pour a standard drink the bartender must have an accurate means of measuring the liquor. As discussed at length in Chapter 10 there are several ways of measuring: hand measuring, metered or automated pouring, and free-pouring.

In a bar concerned with consistency and tight liquor controls, free-pouring is out of the question no matter how skilled the bartender. There is too much potential for variation. The most common way of measuring is to use a shot glass and stainless-steel jiggers of various sizes. All shot glasses should be the standard drink size. They will function as the jigger for the base liquor. Different sizes of stainless-steel jiggers will provide the means of measuring the smaller amounts called for in drinks containing more than one liquor, as well as the larger amounts for brandies and oversize drinks. If the bartender is well trained, skillful, and honest measuring with these hand measures will produce controlled, consistent drinks.

Even so overpouring and underpouring are hazards of the hand method, whether intentional or caused by the rush of business. In a bar with annual sales of $100,000 a steady overpouring of ¼ ounce per drink could add $3,000 or more per year to your costs. Many enterprises, large and small, use some method of controlled pour, either measuring pourers on bottle tops or an automated pouring system.

Several types of automated pouring systems were described in Chapter 4. Preset to pour the standard-size drink and to record each drink poured they eliminate overpouring, underpouring, and spillage and help to provide a consistent drink. Most systems pour only the major liquors however, so there is still more room for error, inconsistency, and loss.

Whatever the measuring method a list of drink sizes should be posted at the bar showing mixed drinks, wine, beer, and special drinks. Again refer to Figure 14.9 for a comprehensive list of drink sizes, glass sizes, and prices.

Standard Drink Recipe

The mixology discussions in Chapters 10 and 11 emphasize the importance of proportions in making a good drink and the wisdom of writing them down in recipe form. A recipe that specifies exactly how a given drink is made at a given bar is known as a *standardized recipe* (see Figure 14.12). It specifies the exact quantity of each ingredient, the size glass to be used, and the exact procedure for preparing the drink. The garnish is included, as is anything else that is necessary to the drink. If the recipe includes a picture of the finished drink in its assigned glass, so much the better. You should have a standardized recipe for every drink that you serve. Keep the recipes together in a looseleaf notebook with plastic page covers or better yet enter the the recipes in your computer. Use copies or printouts to train new bartenders, and make sure that every bartender, old and new, follows

INGREDIENTS

2 oz gin
½ oz dry vermouth
1 olive

DRINK: Martini

GLASS: 4-oz cocktail
7-oz rocks

PROCEDURE

Stir gin/vermouth with ⅓ mixing glass cube ice.
Strain into prechilled cocktail glass or over cube ice in rocks glass.
Garnish with olive.

INGREDIENTS		BOTTLE	BOTTLE COST					DRINK	DRINK COST			
	DATE:						DATE:					
Gin												
Vermouth												
Olive												
							DRINK TOTALS					

DATE
COST
PRICE
COST%

FIGURE 14.12 A standardized recipe card with room to record cost and price data.

the house recipes to the letter. If you can make this happen you will really have achieved control of quality and quantity.

The standardized recipe is the basis for the costing and pricing described earlier. Every recipe should be costed periodically, and the cost of each ingredient should be recorded on the recipe card, along with the date of costing. It is a good idea to review the whole recipe at this time to be sure you have not changed a garnish or a glass, or changed Cointreau to Triple Sec in your Sidecar without recording the change.

Standard Glassware

Each standard drink should be served in a *standard glass,* a glass of specified size and shape that is used every time that the drink is poured. The size is the more important feature since it controls both the quantity of the ingredients that must fill it and the taste, as explained in Chapter 10. But a standard, distinctive shape is important, too. It makes a drink look the same every time, as well as taste the same, and it reduces the possibility of using the wrong size glass. If you have two glasses of different sizes with the same shape it is easy to get them mixed up, and if you use the wrong one it will alter the drink considerably. (A word to the wise: Order replacements by both size and catalog number. It is difficult to judge capacity by appearance.) Some people equate glass size with portion size, and this has a superficial validity. But the real portion size is the drink size, and the base liquor is controlled by the shot glass or jigger. In most cases the drink glass has more to do with proportion than portion.

When standardizing your glassware choose whatever size and shape will give each drink the most appeal. This doesn't mean the glassware itself has to be special; it means that the drink in the glass should look appealing. For example a drink on the rocks looks skimpy if the glass is either too big or too small. A straight-up cocktail looks undersized in too large a glass. Shapes can make a big difference. A footed glass can make a drink look bigger than it does in a tumbler of the same capacity. Rounded shapes make a difference in the way the ice fits in, which changes the way the liquid fills in around the ice. You have to experiment. You must also allow for what the garnish will do to the drink. No glass should be so small that the measured drink fills it to the brim.

You can manage nicely with very few styles and sizes of glass if you wish: one glass for cocktails and Champagne, one for rocks drinks, one for highballs, one for tall drinks and beer, one for wine, and one for brandy and after-dinner liqueurs. The fewer the glass types, the fewer the mistakes in service. Your choices depend on your clientele, your drinks, and your image. The glass for each drink should be specified on its standardized recipe record, as well as on your drink list posted at the bar.

ESTABLISHING BEVERAGE CONTROLS

Ideally all beverages should be used to make drinks for which payment is collected and the paying customer consumes the product. But in real life liquor, beer, and wine may be overpoured, spilled, improperly mixed, or otherwise wasted. A beverage may cling to the sides of empty bottles. It may be rung up incorrectly. Customers may refuse the drink, avoid paying for it, or pay too little. It may be pilfered by your own employees. A bottle may slip and break. One way or another it is no longer available for sale. This kind of use, unchecked, can quickly deplete your bar's profit margin. The trouble is that as individual "events" these incidents do not seem all that problematic. It takes a keen eye and a knack for record-keeping to end patterns of loss and sloppiness before they become endemic.

One of the most interesting aspects of theft or **shrinkage,** as it is sometimes called, is that it often can be traced to a particular shift, a particular brand, or a particular bartender. Bevinco, an alcohol-auditing service, uses a combination of counting bottles, weighing kegs, checking records, and surveillance to get to the bottom of losses that often exceed 30 percent. Among the company's observations are that many bar owners leave it to their distributors to check and replenish inventory. This is a serious lack of oversight!

You can, for example, hire beverage auditors, conduct employee background checks, and offer rewards for information. But the most effective way to ensure the honesty of your workforce (and your suppliers and sales reps) is to remove the opportunity for theft. If you have standardized your cost percentages, drink sizes, recipes, prices, inventory procedures, and par stock, you have already minimized certain kinds of losses. You have also provided important tools for measuring loss. If measuring reveals that losses are indeed threatening profits you can track down the causes and "plug the leaks."

Three measuring techniques are commonly used. One is based on cost percentage, another compares ounces used with ounces sold, and the third measures potential sales value against actual sales. Each in its own way measures what you have to sell against what you actually sell.

The Cost-Percentage Method

The first technique of measurement compares the cost of liquor used during a given period to the sales of the same period. Then the resulting percentage figure is then compared to the standard-cost percentage. This method requires a physical inventory of the storeroom and the bar at both the beginning and the end of the period, plus purchase and sales figures for the period. With this information in hand make the following calculations:

1. To find the value of the liquor available for sale during the period, add the beginning inventory value to the value of the purchases:

   Value of beginning inventory
   plus (+) Value of liquor purchases
   = Value of liquor available for sales

TIPS FOR SETTING UP AN HONEST SHOP

- Pay attention to basics. Keep locks on all of the doors and take frequent inventories.
- Set the right example. If managers continually eat on the job and fail to ring up their food orders, for instance, employees begin to think that this is standard operating procedure.
- Let employees know just where the money coming in goes. Show how each dollar of income breaks down: i.e., so much for food and so much for salaries.
- Use the point-of-sale (POS) system to keep track of transactions. Once orders are entered into the system they are more difficult to alter. The system can also provide a track record of transactions if needed.
- Move quickly but discreetly when investigating suspicious activity.
- When criminal activity is involved, bring in the authorities. "You really want to send a signal to the other employees," says Isidore Kharasch, president of Hospitality Works in Lincolnwood, Illinois, a restaurant consulting firm.

(**Source:** *Restaurants USA,* a publication of the National Restaurant Association, Chicago, Illinois, January/February 2000.)

2. To find the cost of the liquor used during the period, subtract the value of the ending inventory from the value of the liquor available:

Value of liquor available
minus (−) Value of ending inventory
= Cost (value) of liquor used

3. To find the bar cost percentage, divide the cost of liquor used by the total dollar sales for the period:

$$\frac{\text{Cost of liquor used}}{\text{Total dollar sales}} = \text{Bar cost percentage}$$

The percentages for beer, wine, and spirits must be figured separately because they are all different.

The percentage figure can now be compared to the planned, or standard, bar cost percentage (your budget figure), as well as to the percentages of previous periods. If your bar cost for the current period is more than 1½ percentage points higher than your planned bar cost or the average bar cost of several periods, you should start looking for the reasons.

You probably recognize this procedure as part of the end-of-the-month inventory routine described in Chapter 13. But if you wait until the end of the month the damage will be done and you may not be able to trace the cause. It is better to take weekly or even daily inventories to keep track of your bar costs. Where only beverages are concerned, physical inventories are usually not major undertakings.

The Ounce Method

The second measurement technique compares the ounces of liquor used with the ounces of liquor sold. In this method taking beginning and ending inventories at the bar each day reveals the number of ounces sold. You take the beginning inventory before the bar opens but after the par stock has been replenished, and the ending inventory after the bar closes. Then use your data as follows:

1. Subtract the ounces of each type of liquor in the ending inventory from the ounces of liquor in the beginning inventory. This gives you the number of ounces used.
2. From your guest checks tally the drinks sold by numbers of each type. For each type multiply the ounces of liquor in one drink by the number of drinks sold. This gives you the number of ounces per drink type. Then add them up to find the number of ounces sold.
3. Subtract the number of ounces sold from the number of ounces used. This is a daily measure, and it assesses what is happening at the bar only, but it is accurate and it pinpoints this area of loss. Unfortunately it takes time—unless you have a computerized register that can replace the guest check and the hand tally. (We discuss the uses of computers at the bar on page 624.)

The Potential Sales-Value Method

The third method of measurement compares the actual dollar sales with potential sales value. Each bottle you buy represents potential dollars in the register. You can determine its potential sales value by using standard drink sizes, standard drink selling prices, and the number of drinks that can be served from each bottle. For example, if you pour 1-ounce drinks, sell each drink for $1.00, and use only liter bottles, you should have $33.80 in the register for each bottle you use.

In real life bar sales are more complex. Most bars have more than one drink size and more than one drink price. Therefore the potential sales value of each bottle must be adjusted for these variations. One method of doing this, the **weighted-average method,** is based on averages of drink sizes and prices for drinks actually sold over a period of time. The following example telescopes a time period into one typical day.

1. Find the average drink size for all of the drinks made with one kind of liquor—gin, for instance:

GIN-BASED DRINKS

Drink	*Drinks Sold*	*Ounces Sold*
Gimlet (1.5 ounces)	10	15
Martini (2 ounces)	40	80
Gin and Tonic (1.5 ounces)	12	18
	62	113

To complete this step divide the total ounces sold (113) by total drinks sold (62) to obtain an average drink size:

$$\frac{113 \text{ ounces}}{62 \text{ ounced}} = 1.82 \text{ ounces average gin drink size}$$

2. Find the number of drinks per bottle. If you divide the liter of gin (33.8 ounces) by the average drink size (1.82 ounces), you obtain the number of drinks per liter:

$$\frac{33.8 \text{ ounces}}{1.82 \text{ ounces}} = 18.57 \text{ average drinks per liter of gin}$$

3. Next, find the average selling price of these drinks:

GIN-BASED DRINKS

Drink	*Number Sold*	*Total Sales*
Gimlet @ $4.25	10	$42.50
Martini @ $4.25	40	$170.00
Gin and Tonic @ $3.75	12	$45.00
	62	$257.50

To complete this step divide total sales ($257.50) by the total drinks sold (62) to obtain the average drink-selling price:

$$\frac{\$257.50}{62} = \$4.15 \text{ average selling price}$$

4. Finally, find the potential sales value of each liter of gin by multiplying the average drinks per liter (18.57) by the average selling price ($4.15):

$$18.57 \times 4.15 = \$77.06 \text{ (Potential sales value of 1 liter of gin)}$$

In the same way you can figure the potential sales value of every bottle of liquor used in a given period. You can then compare the actual sales dollars with the potential sales value of the bottles to measure discrepancies. Ideally the actual sales should equal the potential sales value.

The weighted-average method assumes that the sales mix, liquor costs, and sales prices remain constant; when anything changes everything must be refigured. Moreover this method consumes many hours with a calculator in hand in order to approximate accuracy, and it requires further refinements to take into account drinks that contain more than one liquor.

There is another, simpler method of approximating potential sales value. It requires a test period of 45 to 60 days during which you enforce all standards to the letter and observe all bar operations continuously. At the end of the period you carefully determine bottle consumption from purchases, issues, and inventories, and translate it into potential sales value as though all of the liquor had been sold by the straight drink. Then you compare this value with actual sales during the period. The difference represents the varying amounts of liquor in your drinks, plus an inescapable minimum of waste and inefficiency. You convert this difference into a percentage figure and accept it as your *standard difference*. You can use this figure from then on to compare potential sales with actual sales. Any time that the percentage of difference is higher than the standard difference, an investigation is warranted. If costs and sales prices change the percentage figure is still applicable. If the sales mix changes a new test period is needed to determine a new standard difference.

The Role of Par Stock

We have already discussed par stock as a means of ensuring a full supply of liquor at the bar and as an inventory tool. Now you can see par stock in still another role: as a key tool of control at the bar, where it is a standard against which consumption can be measured at any time. With the one-empty-for-one-full system of requisitioning a manager has only to count the bottles at the bar and compare the number with the par-stock form to determine whether anything is missing. This can be done as part of a full-bar inventory or the manager can spot-check any given brand at any time. A wise manager will do so from time to time. Frequent checking is sometimes enough to prevent pilferage entirely. The more often you check the more closely you can pinpoint the possible culprits, and the less likely they will be tempted. Even if you are not actually preventing losses, you will have a measure of what is missing, how serious it is, and who is most likely responsible.

Par stock is the last step in the series of controls over the liquor itself. In Chapter 13 we followed the liquor controls in a large operation from receiving to sale. The receiving agent counted the bottles and assumed responsibility by signing the invoice. Then the liquor moved to the storeroom, where it was again counted and responsibility was transferred to the storeroom supervisor. The requisition, signed by both the storeroom supervisor and the receiver, transferred the responsibility to the receiver, usually the bartender, who again counted the bottles. There the responsibility lies until they are sold.

This chain of responsibility resting in the hands of a single person at all times is a system every manager would do well to follow. Even in large or highly computerized operations a single person must take responsibility. This does not guarantee security, but it discourages theft and facilitates finding the source of the problem and eliminating it.

In a small bar of course the owner/manager has all of the responsibilities that would be divided among several people in a larger establishment. Small bars (those that do less than $1 million in sales annually) tend to rely on manual control procedures that can be easily monitored. Measured pour spouts on all bottles and preprogrammed register keys for the various types of beverages served may be legal requirements in your area. The empty-for-full bottle-exchange system is common. Some bars mark all of the bottles when first checking them in to the inventory system, ensuring that they were purchased by the bar and not brought in illegally from another source. Small bars can also take daily inventories of beverages, allowing them to compare sales to consumption figures.

ESTABLISHING CASH CONTROLS

When a customer buys a drink you must have a way of making sure that the sale is recorded and that the money finds its way into the cash register. There are many systems of paying for drinks. The simplest procedure, and the riskiest, is for the bartender to pick up the cash laid out on the bar and ring it up on the register without the benefit of a guest check. The most complicated—and probably the safest, though most expensive—is a computerized system that prerecords the sale, pours the liquor, and rings up the sale on both the register and the guest check, with a receipt for the customer. In between are many different systems. Some bars may run on a pay-as-you-go system; others may use a running-tab system in which drinks are entered on the guest check but not paid for until the customer is ready to leave. In some places the customer pays the bartender. In others the customer pays the server, who pays the bartender or a cashier. In still others the customer pays the cashier directly. In busy bars the server may carry a "bank," a preset amount of cash and pay the bartender for the drinks when they are ordered, collecting and making change on the spot as each round of drinks is served.

Whatever system, you need standard procedures for handling cash and some form of guest check for the record. You need the record. You want the cash. Some of your personnel and your customers might want the cash, too.

When payment is routed through several persons it is usually intended as a system of checks and balances, but sometimes it works the other way. More people are exposed to temptation and opportunity, and tracking losses to the source is more complicated. On the other hand at the bar you have one person taking the order, filling the order, recording the sale, and collecting the cash, uninhibited by the controls that a division of responsibility might provide and surrounded by opportunity. For you this is a Catch-22 situation, magnified by the large number (you hope) of fast-paced individual transactions and an environment permeated with liquid gold and money changing hands. The following practices commonly make cash disappear. Most are at your expense, but sometimes the customer is cheated, and this can hurt your business, too.

The Bartender

- Fails to ring up sales and pockets the money
- Overcharges and pockets the difference
- Shortchanges customer and keeps change
- Brings in own liquor and sells it (using house mixes and garnishes)
- Brings in empty bottle, turns it in to storeroom, then sells from bottle that replaces it and pockets money
- Short-pours a series of drinks, then sells others from same bottle, keeping the money
- Sells liquor from one bottle without ringing up, then waters down the remainder to cover theft
- Substitutes well liquor for call brand, collects for call brand but rings up well price, keeps the change
- Smuggles out full bottles

The Server

- "Loses" guest check after collecting and pockets the money
- Reuses guest check and keeps the money
- Overcharges for drinks and pockets the difference
- Makes intentional mistakes in totaling guest check and keeps the overage
- Intentionally omits items from guest check to increase tip
- Changes items and prices on guest check after customer pays
- Gives too little change and pockets the balance

The Cashier

- Gives too little change and pockets the balance
- Fails to ring up guest check, pockets the money, and "loses" guest check (blame falls on server)

The Customer

- Walks out without paying
- Sends back drink or wine after half-emptying glass or bottle
- Uses expired credit card
- Pays with a bad check

The cash-control system that you devise to forestall all of these little tricks should both reduce opportunity and pinpoint responsibility. You need a system that you can enforce and that leaves a trail behind when it is evaded. Then you must continually assess its effectiveness. Wherever the system is not foolproof you must keep checking on it. If your employees know that you are policing the system they are likely to remain honest. Lax enforcement invites pilferage and, sadly, almost seems to condone it. We suggest the following system:

1. If there is no POS system to generate a computerized check, servers can use numbered guest checks with your bar's name or logo on which to take orders. Each bartender or server signs out a sequence of numbers for the shift and turns in the unused checks at the end of the shift. You keep the master list and check the used and unused checks. A missing check is a serious breach of work rules that justifies a severe penalty. Make this penalty very clear.
2. Direct staff to write all guest checks clearly and in ink. Prohibit alterations unless initialed by the manager on duty. Drinks should be machine-priced.
3. If possible use a precheck method of registering drinks. In this system the order is rung up before the drinks are poured. When payment is made another register (or another section of the same register) is used to ring up the same sale on the same check, but in a different record. The totals on the two records should be the same.
4. The bartender or cashier should ring up the sale, using the total on the POS terminal (or at least on an adding machine) to present the check to the customer for payment. Do not rely on the server's mathematics.
5. Instruct the server to print the amount received from the customer on the bottom of the check. A box on the bottom of the check for this purpose is useful.
6. Ring up each check individually when paid, and close the register drawer after each transaction. File the paid check in an assigned place, perhaps in a cash box or drawer that locks.
7. Give receipts to customers along with their change.
8. Allow only one person at a time to operate the cash register and to be responsible for the cash in the drawer. Train that person thoroughly in the register function and in your opening and closing routines, as mentioned in Chapter 9.

Other suggestions: Post prices for all drinks so that both customers and servers are informed. Position the register so that the customer can see the amount being rung up. Make access to the bar interior difficult, and lock up the liquor when the bar is closed. Check credit cards against lists of invalid cards provided by the credit-card companies.

TECHNOLOGY AT THE BAR

There is an entire service infrastructure in most bars and restaurants. Hidden from public view, it is complex and often incomprehensible to managers and employees. This infrastructure consists of *POS* workstations, computer servers, closed-circuit and/or satellite television, DSL or wireless modems, *electronic-data interface* (*EDI*) with suppliers, bar-code scanners, computer-controlled lighting and thermostats,

THE SKIMMING SCAM

Skimming is a $1 billion part of the growing problem of identity theft, and the majority of it takes place in restaurants and bars. An illegal device (smaller than a typical garage-door opener and available for only a few hundred dollars online) is used to *skim,* or surreptitiously read, the stored data on the magnetic strip on a credit card. Then counterfeit cards can be made using the same data and are used promptly—before the unsuspecting cardholder receives the next monthly billing statement.

Bars and restaurants are traditionally places where a guest and his or her credit card are parted, if only for a couple of minutes, when servers take the card to run it through the payment-authorization system and bring back a receipt. So criminals who specialize in skimming are known to prey on bar and restaurant staff, offering them a bonus of $20 or even $50 "per swipe" for using the illegal devices. The U.S. Secret Service and the California Restaurant Association teamed up for a 2002 study that estimated that 70 percent of all skimming takes places in restaurant/bar settings. (At least one credit card company, Visa, now offers a $1,000 reward for information leading to the arrest of these scam artists.)

To minimize the risk of skimming, consider purchasing other hand-held devices. Hand-held, wireless credit card processors are an innovation receiving a great deal of attention because they allow credit card transactions to be conducted in full view of the cardholder (see Figure 14.13). The card verification and receipt-printing unit is small enough to fit on a waist belt.

Skimming hurts the consumer, not the bar, because the bar gets paid; the credit card company holds the consumer responsible for the charges made on his or her account. However, the problem has become so pervasive that it is a good idea to ask for a driver's license when someone pays a bar tab by credit card as an extra measure of security against accepting counterfeit cards.

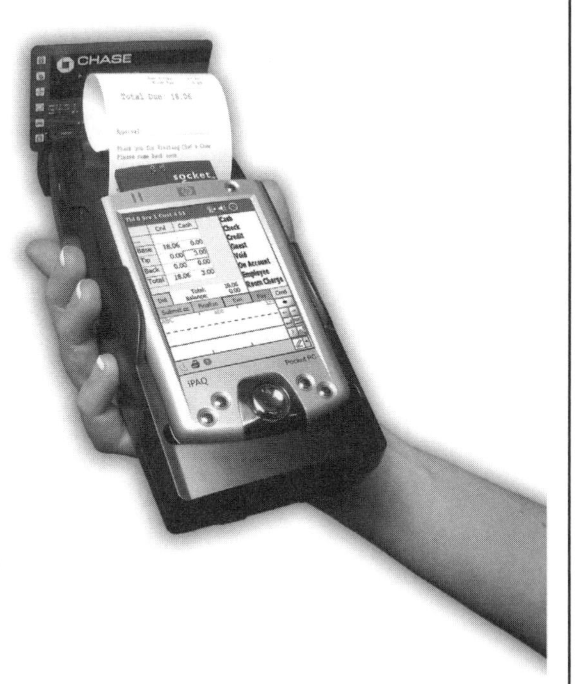

FIGURE 14.13 A hand-held POS unit allows transactions to be made and receipts to be printed without the server leaving the table. Courtesy of Action Systems, Inc., Silver Spring, Maryland.

LANS and WANS, and miles of cables and phone lines. You get the idea: We are all increasingly dependent on technology. You can't just hit an electronic cash register a certain way when it won't open. When a customer pays by credit card and the modem will not connect to the credit card clearinghouse, the customer remains at the table—when a new guest would otherwise have been seated by now. Technology works in your favor as a bar owner only when it accomplishes two things: Making the guest's experience a more pleasant one, and improving the profitability of the business. Profitability is increased by such factors as speeding up the service processes (ordering, payment), making theft less likely, keeping records accurately and consistently, and giving you the ability to track trends that affect your business.

Historically bars have used two types of sales-capture and cash-control devices: the computerized **point-of-sale (POS) system,** and the *electronic cash register (ECR)*. Until recently POS systems were used mostly in large chains and hotel-based operations; they were just too expensive for most small, independent bars, whose owners opted instead for a less sophisticated ECR. Even the smallest bar in the smallest town can own a cash register that provides sales breakdown by drink categories, sales periods, salespersons, and departments (see Figure 14.14).

This is just the beginning. Today you can purchase entire information systems that can track sales by product, by employee, by price point, and by time of day.

FIGURE 14.14 A bartender using a POS system. Courtesy of Action Systems, Inc., Silver Spring, Maryland.

The National Restaurant Association says that 8 out of 10 bars and restaurants in the United States now use computers to perform multiple business functions. Software can be purchased to assist with inventory management, payroll and accounting, sales tracking, employee attendance and other records, food and drink ordering, temperature monitoring and controls (for ambient temperature, utility conservation, and/or kitchen food safety), and credit and debit card processing.

Point-of-Sale Systems

The primary function of most POS systems is to track sales. A good system will be able to record the following information in hourly, daily, and month-to-date increments as needed: product sales mix, revenue (per shift, sales period, or server), an open-check report, a server-tips report (for tax purposes), and total revenue.

More sophisticated POS systems also interface with inventory and purchasing programs to follow beverages and other bar items from initial purchase, to use, to collection of revenue. All of this is valuable, especially for state tax audits (which are discussed in Chapter 16).

A computerized POS system can cost $10,000 or more, so before you buy you should have a clear understanding of what you expect it to accomplish and what you can afford to spend. Each bar and restaurant faces its own unique challenges in finding the system(s) that fit its needs. We suggest the following guidelines as you shop for a POS system:

- Compose a list of "must-have" features. The range of options can be overwhelming so don't rely on someone else's criteria; create your own list.
- Find out exactly what is included in the price of the system: only the software? Software and POS terminal? Cables? Installation? How much training? How much technical support, and for how long?
- Ask other bar owners and managers for their advice. What are the pluses and minuses of the systems that they use? What was the learning curve for their employees? Would they buy their systems again if given the opportunity to start over?
- Don't limit your search to the best-known industry leaders. Check out new software vendors, too. They've also been busy watching the leaders and just might have come up with something better.
- Match the size of the system to the size of your operation. How many users can the system handle at one time? How many different payment types can it process? Make the vendor demonstrate response times and speed during peak-volume processing.
- Choose software before choosing hardware. Your software will have minimum hardware requirements so be certain that the hardware you select exceeds them, allowing the capacity for upgrades.

- How often is the system upgraded? How often are there updates to fix bugs that have been discovered in the system? Are the updates free or do they cost extra—and if so, how much?
- Don't rush through the salesperson's demonstration of the system. Be sure that it includes a runthrough of every feature on your "must-have" list.
- Avoid customizing. The less you have to modify the basic system functions, the better. The fit should be good from the beginning.
- Never accept the standard contract. This is not just a sale; it should signal the beginning of an ongoing business relationship with this vendor. This gives you some negotiating power so use it to get the terms you want. Again pay special attention to the installation, training, and support after the sale that is offered. Include a test period and installation milestones.

Another list to consider is the special features that might prove helpful in running a bar. These apply not only to new systems, but as possible upgrades to an existing system. Perhaps you cannot afford all of them at the moment, but find out if they are available and compatible with what you are about to buy:

- *Automatic sales recording* should include the ability to work with an automatic dispensing system (such as the Bar Boy or Easy Bar brands) so that spirits or beers are tracked as they are dispensed from a bar gun or tap.
- *Menu description* is a function that enables a user to enter text to describe each menu item. This feature might include a reference guide that lets bartenders look up any uncommon drink recipes that are ordered.
- *Purchasing/recipe functions* enable the manager to input a list of ingredients for each drink or menu item. The data can be used to make shopping lists and to cost drinks when used in conjunction with product mix reports.
- *Settlement flexibility* makes it easier for a server to split checks among guests at a table, and to account for multiple payment options (some cash, some credit card, promotional coupons, and so on). It also allows an open check to be retained for the purpose of running a tab and applying taxes or discounts.
- *Time and attendance functions* track work hours, eliminating the need for separate time cards and time clocks. Employees can use their badge or an employee code number to check in and out at their designated workstations. The system can create summaries of these hours for specific days or pay periods.
- *Back-office or accounting functions* include a variety of individual reports that may also be shown as charts or graphs. The system can be programmed to produce them, and they are accessed as needed. Options include the revenue generated, taxes collected, server tip compliance, payroll data, and comparisons of figures from different time periods, and so on.
- *Customer or supplier databases* enable the operator to input sales and marketing information: names and addresses of customers and/or major suppliers. This is important because many bars and restaurants have their own web sites and send promotional news to a list of customers by e-mail, and because many suppliers allow ordering and billing by computer, using EDI.

The NRA also reports that more than half of its members use the Internet regularly, spending more than two hours a week online to do research, order products, and stay informed about local and industry news.

Two additional points: First no matter how your data is recorded—with a pen and legal pad or a top-of-the-line POS system—it is only useful if it is both accurate and timely. It takes a commitment of time and personnel to learn your system and maintain it. Second, remember that no records of any kind actually control costs; they only pinpoint losses. The flip side of controls—the effective side—is taking steps to stop the losses.

SUMMING UP

A budget is the financial plan for your business for a given period of time; it is a way to measure your actual performance and forecast your anticipated performance. Your first goals in a new business should be to set up a specific, realistic profit goal and to prepare a budget for reaching it. This also allows you to continuously measure the degree of success the bar is achieving in its operations. Your budget should work for you by allowing you to pinpoint variations, figure out why they are occurring, and correct any problems. One important figure to calculate is your break-even point, the amount that you must make in a business day to break even with costs and expenses.

Statistics are available from trade groups, such as the National Restaurant Association, that let you compare your own expenses and sales figures with those of other restaurants. Within this chapter are all the basic forms you will need to create a basic budget and profit plan for a bar business.

Since profit is the margin of sales over costs the profit plan sets up a two-pronged effort: to maximize sales and to minimize costs. On the sales side pricing is of strategic importance in maximizing profit per drink without inhibiting demand and reducing volume. In this chapter you learned three different ways to *cost* (determine what to charge for) a cocktail, as well as some tips to add to what you already learned in Chapter 7 about wine pricing.

On the cost side while every expense must be watched, the primary focus is on controlling beverage losses. There are two major ways to do this: to minimize the opportunities for pilferage and to set up control systems for measuring and pinpointing losses and take prompt action to stop them. Point-of-sale (POS) systems allow almost every facet of management—inventory, purchasing, sales, payroll, and accounting functions—to be tracked by computer, which offers additional safeguards. This chapter provides lists of popular features and considerations when purchasing a POS system.

No matter which kind of system is used, owners and managers must commit time, personnel, and resources to keeping accurate records and updating them on a regular basis.

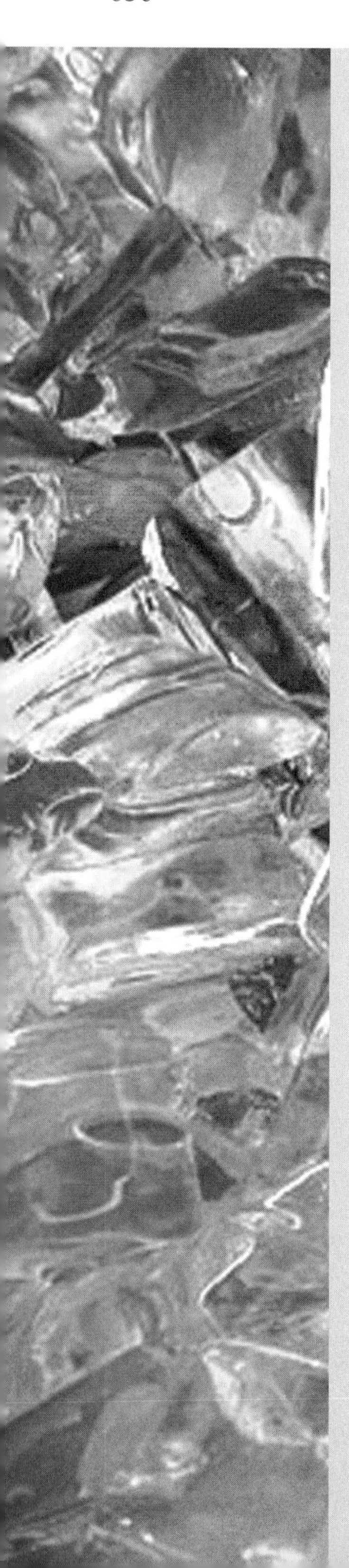

 POINTS TO PONDER

1. In what ways does making a budget depend on past history? On present conditions? On future hopes? On specific plans for change? Which elements do you see as most important and why?
2. How do you treat fixed costs when making a budget based on performance in the preceding year? Do you treat variable costs differently? If so, how?
3. What is a break-even point? Why do you need to know what it is for your bar?
4. How does competition affect price structure? Which pricing techniques can be used to gain a competitive edge, short of wholesale price-cutting?
5. What are the advantages of using standard drink sizes, standardized recipes, and standard glassware?
6. Where do you think liquor losses are most likely to occur? What can be done to stop them?
7. To what extent does an automatic (metered) pouring system control losses?
8. How would you evaluate the following methods of figuring losses: the **cost-percentage method?** The **ounce method?** The **potential sales-value method?** Give pros and cons for each method.
9. How does a system of sales records and cash controls operate to minimize losses? In your view, which two control measures would be the most effective?
10. How would you decide what to price a Tequila Sunrise? Use one of the three different costing formulas explained in this chapter and the recipe given in Chapter 10.

 TERMS OF THE TRADE

beverage-cost method
break-even point
budget
budget-deviation analysis
cash-flow forecast
cost percentage (or percentage cost)
cost-percentage method
cost/sales ratio
costing
drink size
fixed expenses
gross operating profit
gross profit (or contribution margin)
gross-profit method
income statement
net income (or net profit)
ounce method

point-of-sale (POS)
potential sales-value method
pouring costs
pretax profit
prime costs
prime-ingredient method
pro forma statement
shrinkage
skimming
standard (e.g., glass, drink)
total business pricing
unallocable expenses
variable expenses
weighted-average method

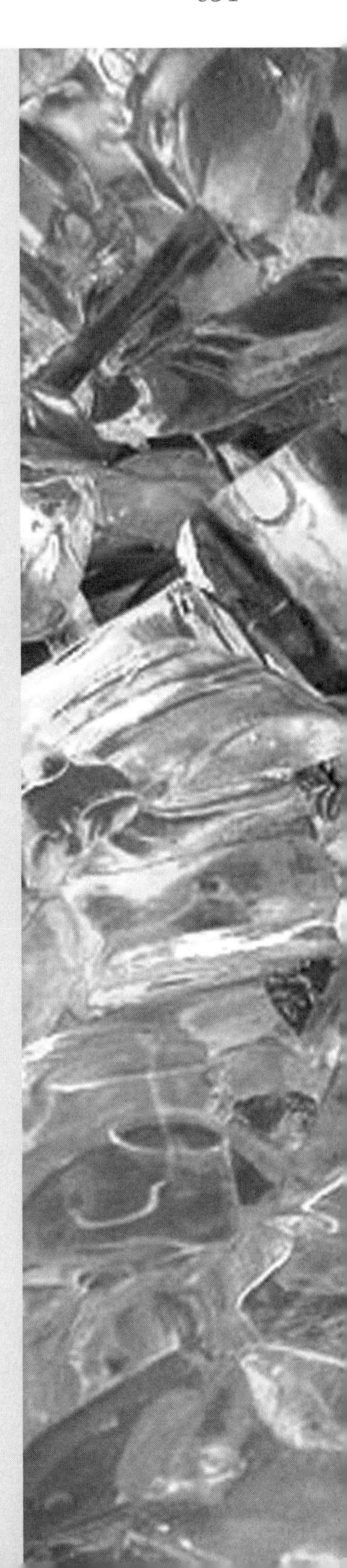

CHAPTER 15
MANAGING YOUR BAR BUSINESS

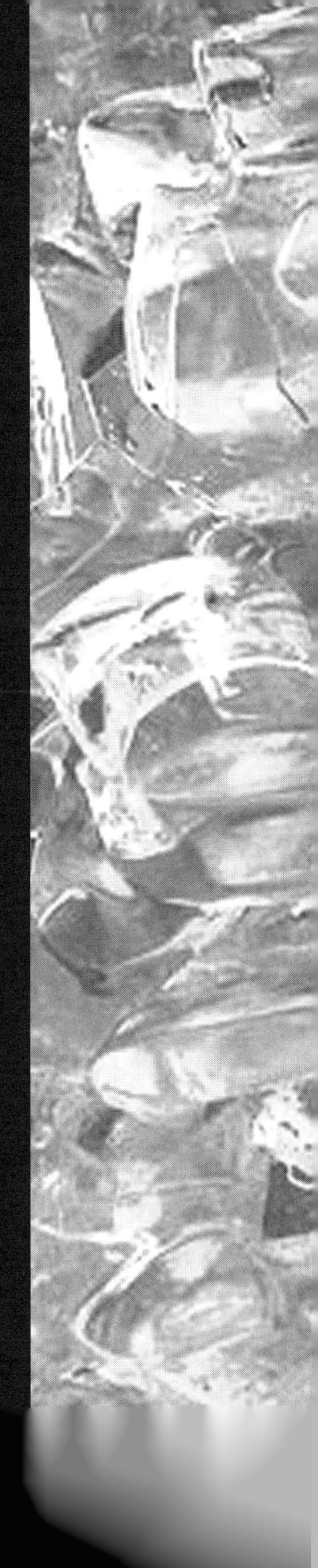

Despite the time and effort that you may put into pricing drinks and formulating a budget, it takes more than finances to determine the *true value* of your bar business. In today's highly competitive era, decent drinks at a bar are simply *expected.* Increasingly guests are paying *for the experience you provide.* If customers believe that the experience they had at your bar is worth the price they paid, then the time they spent there had value—regardless of the drink size, the theme, the décor, or the cool glassware that you've chosen for straight-up Martinis.

Marketing expert Adrienne Weiss posed the question this way at a restaurant-leadership roundtable mentioned in the April 2004 issue of *Restaurant Hospitality* magazine: "If your food and drinks were free, how much would your customers pay for the experience?" Weiss's theory is that if the amount a customer would voluntarily offer to pay is less than the amount of your average check, you have got problems. A good bar owner and/or manager should be able to pinpoint and solve such problems using the information in this chapter.

THIS CHAPTER WILL HELP YOU . . .

- Create and use a workable business plan for a bar.
- Determine the worth of your business.
- Position your business favorably in relation to your competitors' businesses.
- Create an atmosphere and menus appropriate to the chosen clien-

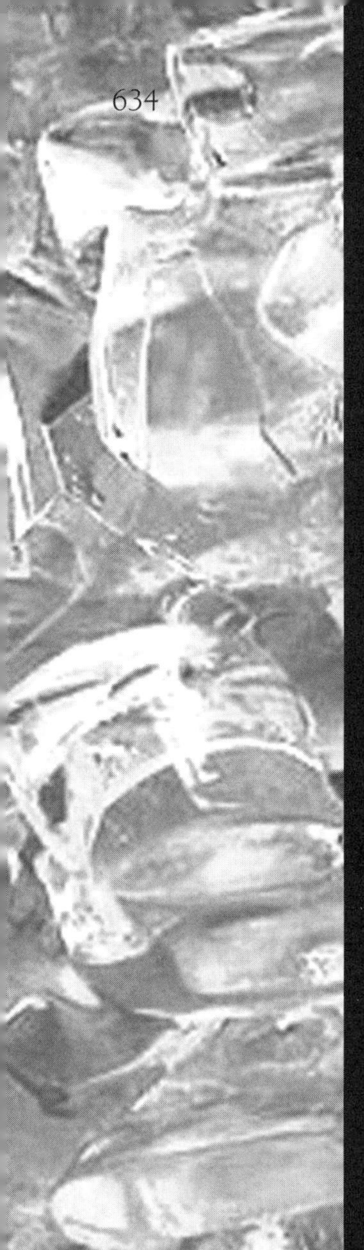

- Attract customers through low-cost or no-cost marketing activities.
- Use pricing as a merchandising tool.
- Make decisions about protecting and expanding a successful bar concept.

The scene may be loud and colorful or quiet and sedate but to a large extent people visit bars to relax and socialize, as a brief respite from the demands of daily life. To succeed in the face of tough competition you must analyze what your guests want and what your establishment means to them. How can you give guests the experience they seek so they think that patronizing your establishment is worth their time and money? It's about revamping a tired concept or even creating a new one. This chapter is about refining and rethinking how to relate to your guests in order to stay relevant to them. It is also about managing your bar wisely so that you can earn customer loyalty—which cannot be done of course unless you stay in business.

CREATING A BUSINESS PLAN

In Chapter 14 we discussed how to create a budget, but you also need to draft an overall business plan. This is the "résumé" of your business: an instrument that shows a seasoned consideration for all aspects of running it. A good business plan should accomplish three things:

- It should serve as your basic operating tool
- It should be useful to communicate exactly who and what you are
- It should be useful in obtaining financing

The process of writing the business plan is also useful. It requires objective thinking about the operation so that you can effectively set long-term goals for growth and income. In fact some management experts believe that a business owner should *never* write a business plan alone—that it should be the group effort of the owner and a trusted team of managers, investors, and/or advisers.

So what, exactly, should be in the business plan? The Business Plan Checklist of the National Restaurant Association (NRA) is a good starting point (see Figure 15.1). Once you answer the questions and assemble the related documents (e.g., tax returns and sample menus), if you are not much of a writer, you can hire a freelancer to spend a few hours organizing, editing, and making all of the plan components fit together.

Most experts suggest that you begin the research for this endeavor by deciding which beverages you are going to sell. The raw materials to make these drinks will take 20 to 25 percent of your gross sales. Estimating labor costs is the next task and typically the largest expense of any restaurant or bar. As much as one-third of your gross sales may be spent on employees' wages and benefits. Occupancy costs (rent or mortgage payment on the space, utilities, and maintenance) should be

BUSINESS PLAN CHECKLIST

____ **Cover Sheet**

____ **Executive Summary**

____ **Description of the Organization**
____ Management summary
____ Type of organization

____ **Description of the Concept** (Mission statement)
Note: It is not necessary to include the five questions (Who am I?, What makes me unique?, etc.) in the business plan.

Market Analysis and Marketing Strategy
Description of Target Market
____ Demographics/psychographics/lifestyle
____ Market potential (size, rate of growth)
____ Market share

____ *Pricing Strategy*

Location Analysis
____ Description of area
____ Commercial/residential profile
____ Traffic
____ Accessibility

Competitive Analysis
____ Number of competitors
____ Location
____ Sales and market share
____ Nature of competition
____ New competitors

Advertising and Promotional Campaign
____ Objectives
____ Techniques
____ Target audience/means of communication
____ Schedule

Other Information
____ Schedule of growth
____ Financing schedule
____ Schedule of return on investment

Financial Data

PROPOSED RESTAURANT
Balance Sheet
____ Pro-forma

Income Statement (pro-forma)
____ 1st year-detail by month
____ 2nd year-detail by quarter
____ 3rd year-detail by quarter

Cash Flow Statement (pro-forma)
____ 1st year-detail by month
____ 2nd year-detail by quarter
____ 3rd year-detail by quarter

EXISTING RESTAURANT
Balance Sheet
____ Previous three (3 years)

Income Statement
____ Previous three (3 years)

Cash Flow Statement
____ Previous three (3 years)

Tax Returns
____ Previous three (3 years)

Appendices
____ Sales projections
____ Organizational chart
____ Job descriptions
____ Résumés of management team
____ Legal documents
____ Leases
____ Licenses
____ Firm price quotations
____ Insurance contracts
____ Sample menu
____ Furniture, fixtures, and equipment (FFE)

FIGURE 15.1 A business-plan checklist. Excerpted from *A Guide to Preparing a Restaurant Business Plan*, with permission of the National Restaurant Association, Chicago, Illinois. www.restaurant.org

limited to 8 percent of annual gross sales. In addition to startup costs, it is wise to maintain a cash reserve of 6 months' operating expenses.

A next step might be to make a list of assumptions, including what kind of bar will it be, how many drinks will be sold in a given time period, and what the average drink price will be. These numbers will help you estimate annual gross sales. From this point you can figure out how much debt you can afford to take on, and how much return on investment you will be able to offer potential investors. Private investors may settle for as little as a 10-percent return but do not be surprised if they want 20 or even 30 percent. As you can see the numbers add up quickly, causing most would-be bar owners to lament, "Will there be anything left for *me* to live on?"

Using the Business Plan

As an operating tool a business plan should answer the following questions: Where are we now? Where do we want to be next year? Where do we want to be two or three years from now? How are we going to get there? Putting all of this in writing so that it can be referred to regularly is a constant reminder of the original concept of the bar and helps owners and managers stay on course. The business plan can be used as a benchmark to measure actual performance against expectations, and it can be used to guide management in making day-to-day decisions.

As a communications tool, many operations use their business plans to explain the bar's concept to the staff, the public, and prospective investors. It is important that your employees know what your goals are and how you plan to achieve them so why not let them read the business plan? And a written plan is a must if you are trying to obtain outside financing from bankers, venture capitalists, or even family members.

The NRA also recommends including three broad aspects of research in your business plan. These topics should be revisited periodically as long as you are in business. They are:

- ***Location analysis.*** This requires a detailed description of the physical structure (your building) and its neighborhood location. Factors worth including are traffic in the area (car and foot), zoning, accessibility, parking, and crime.
- ***Competitor analysis.*** This is a comparison of your operation's actual (or anticipated) performance against similar types of businesses. This forces you to figure out the activities, strategies, and strengths of your competition, and to decide how effective they are. (We discuss ways to thoroughly research your competition on page 642.)
- ***SWOT analysis.*** SWOT is an acronym for "strengths, weaknesses, opportunities, and threats." The first two items are *internal:* factors that you control. The other two items are *external:* factors that you can notice and react to. The real

objectives of this analysis are to identify weaknesses and turn them into strengths and to identify threats in order to turn them into opportunities. You might also notice that your weaknesses are your competitors' strengths, and vice versa.

If writing a business plan seems difficult, be aware that getting results from the plan can be just as hard. But the plan itself is nothing more than words on paper unless it includes realistic revenue projections. Any action that you undertake should have direct links to sales improvement, cost control, or both.

Many business owners (not just those in the hospitality industry) regularly track and monitor a variety of results, which is fairly easy to do by computer. But owners sometimes fall short by not taking the next step: trying to determine the specific actions that caused the results. This means asking direct, specific questions of front-line employees and managers: "What were the evening's sales? What was the average gross margin on the sales?" Open-ended questions probably will not provide the information you need to improve performance. Yes, it is difficult to hold people accountable, to set profit targets, and to establish consequences for missing them. Yes, you'll hear plenty of excuses: The weather, the competition, and the economy are three great reasons for a poor bottom line. But people are drinking, noshing, chatting, and dancing somewhere. *Why are they not doing this at your bar?* This is a crucial question that your business plan must answer if your original projections are not being met. Reward your staff members generously for helping you find the answers.

After you have been in business a while revisit the business plan with the following goals in mind:

- Instead of automatically increasing the budget determine what other actions might be taken or adjusted to improve your financial picture.
- Consistently evaluate whether the business is moving toward its bottom-line goal. Find a way to separate the results of any new strategic activity from what you have usually done so you can accurately measure success. For example, if an overall strategy is "to increase volume and profit through new customer visits," is it happening?
- Stand firm on the desired results but be flexible about the strategies used to get there. Don't be afraid to make changes and create a contingency plan if the original ideas are not working as well as planned.

Finally you must keep in mind that almost everyone fancies himself or herself an expert when it comes to offering advice about how you should run your bar. Listen politely if you like but base the final and/or major decisions on experience and research, not a smattering of friends' ideas. To reinforce this point we've listed a few of the ways that bar owners can trip themselves up, even with a well-thought-out business plan:

- ***Lack of follow-through.*** If you cannot translate ideas into action you are "running on empty."

- ***Much talk, minimal resources.*** The implementation of your goals requires you to continually scale back and perhaps even to eliminate portions of the plan.
- ***Procrastination.*** Quick, decisive action is often necessary to take advantage of a business opportunity. Think it over, but don't think too long. Delays often include throwing roadblocks in your own way, hoping a negative trend or persistent problem will disappear or right itself.
- ***Refining an idea endlessly.*** One way to ensure that nothing happens is to scrutinize portions of the plan forever.
- ***Focusing on the buy-in.*** This means getting everyone's opinion before acting. The idea of listening to others' viewpoints is valid—but not if it is used to avoid taking action.
- ***Lack of vision.*** Your bar must have a life, a feeling, a vision, and an attitude—that's how you connect with your guests. Without these attributes there is no reason why guests would prefer your bar to a competitor's.

What Is My Bar Worth?

Bar owners ask this question only occasionally, such as during a divorce, when making estate plans, or when mulling over the idea of selling the business. And yet, by asking this basic question on a semiannual or annual basis, he or she can take concrete steps to increase the value of the business.

There are many ways to view a bar's worth. It's a source of income, the culmination of hard work, a home away from home, a family legacy, or a retirement fund, to name a few. By most accounts the business is often its owner's largest single asset so it is logical to expect that its value should be maximized. In order to do this you must understand which factors impact the value of the business and how that value is determined. This requires understanding the difference between two key terms: *business valuation* and *business appraisal.*

By definition an *appraisal* is a procedure used to determine the value of something tangible or physical. You're probably familiar with real-estate appraisals before homes are sold or purchased; in the appraisal of a business, the building, real estate, and equipment values are taken into account. In contrast a *valuation* analyzes both tangible and intangible aspects of a company: the industry in general, the state of the economy, the competitive environment, the company's historical performance and projections, the company's customer base, proprietary rights, the management structure, the strengths and weaknesses of the business, and government licenses or regulations that affect the business. Clearly some factors are internal and others are external.

Business valuation also involves adjusting the assets of the business to reflect its *fair-market value,* not the depreciated value often used for tax purposes. Fair-market value is the price that a business could expect to bring if it were put up for sale under the current conditions for a reasonable time period, assuming that both the buyer and the seller were informed and neither was acting under undue pressure to buy or sell, respectively. To arrive at a bar's fair-market value, such items as

SOLVENCY RATIOS OF BARS, HOTELS, AND CASINOS

The bar-and-restaurant business has a more favorable solvency ratio than hotels or casinos, its cousins in the hospitality industry. This means that bar and restaurant owners as a group have less overall debt and a greater ability to make payments on the debt than the other two groups. A 1999 study by the University of Nevada Las Vegas found that the net profit of the bar-and-restaurant business was 9.25 percent, compared to hotels' 8.38 percent and casinos' 6.3 percent.

The study found several reasons for this profitable edge: Bars and restaurants require fewer assets in order to create the same amount of sales revenue. Their operating costs are lower and they don't depend as heavily on debt financing as the other facets of the hospitality industry. For every $100 invested in a bar or restaurant, the operation generated $16.04. Hotels generated $15.47, and casinos generated only $7.46.

The study pointed to a major downside, however. Most bars and restaurants have poor *liquidity,* which is the ability to pay off current liabilities without having to borrow. They generally owe a lot of money and keep low inventories on hand. In other words they don't have assets that they can easily sell if they need a quick cash infusion to pay bills or cover a major, unexpected expense. Poor liquidity subjects a restaurant or bar to high default risks and a higher closure rate.

Source: Study by Dr. Gu Zheng, associate professor, College of Hotel Administration, University of Nevada, Las Vegas, Nevada. Published in *The Consultant,* the quarterly magazine of Foodservice Consultants Society International, Louisville, Kentucky, Fourth Quarter 1999.

discretionary or nonrecurring expenses are added or subtracted as necessary. If the bar owner owns his or her building the valuation takes into account the fact that a new owner (of the business, not the building) would have to pay rent to remain there. The owner's *draw,* or salary, should be fair and reasonable for both the type of business and the industry norms.

Value is a highly subjective concept and you may hear several other terms in discussions of what businesses are worth:

- *Investment value* is used to determine what a business is worth to a potential investor, taking into consideration whatever assets (funds, staff members, expertise, and trademarks, and so on) the investors bring to the table.
- *Liquidation value* is most often associated with bankruptcies and foreclosures. It is how much the business's physical assets would sell for at an auction, which is probably a fraction of their original worth.

- *Intrinsic value* is what a bar is worth based on a perceived future outcome. Determining this value is a very hard task and the type of value that is most difficult to quantify and justify.

There are many reasons to ask, "What is my business worth?" Both appraisal and valuation processes offer opportunities to compare your bar's business performance with industry norms. You can use this information to improve profitability by identifying expenses that are higher than the norms, assets that are not being utilized efficiently, activities that may not maximize profit; and additional profit centers that you might consider.

MARKETING A BAR BUSINESS

All too often hospitality businesses implement marketing plans as a desperation move. The bottom line is dropping, or a keen competitor has just opened and is taking customers and/or grabbing media attention. Short-term results are sought even though a good marketing plan is meant for the long haul, to create and sustain loyal customer relationships over time.

Shaping your marketing plan involves the following three major steps:

1. Define your market. This is your chosen customer group or market segment. A **market segment** is a more or less homogeneous subgroup of the total consumer market; its members have similar needs and wants, attitudes, lifestyles, income levels, purchasing patterns, and so on.
2. Determine which products and services this market segment wants to buy.
3. After you have defined these two essentials you can take the third step: Shape everything about your enterprise to attract customers and sell the product at a profit. In the process you can *position* your enterprise in relation to the competition by creating an **image** that will set you apart from the rest.

Positioning Your Business

In a competitive marketplace it is not enough simply to choose your customers and the products and services that they want. You must position your enterprise in relation to all the others who are competing for the same market segment. Positioning involves two elements: customers and competitors. We will discuss both in greater detail.

The Patron. The success of your bar will depend to a large degree on your ability to know your customers, which does not always mean calling them by their first names or remembering what they drink, although those are certainly handy skills. Knowing your customers means keeping a watchful eye on the types of people who visit your establishment. How do they dress? What times of day are your rush hours? How do you think your business hours affect the types of people you attract? How often do people use credit cards to pay? Do people arrive in groups or as couples? Which cocktails seem to be the favorites? Does this change from month to month? Do cutomers order more domestic or imported beer and wine? More premium or superpremium brands? How do customers react to drink specials, price increases, and new products? Your service personnel and bartenders will be key players in helping you to keep up with these small but important details. But *you* are the most important key player. Walk around, introduce yourself, and talk to guests. Ask them to taste a new product that you are considering serving. Put comment cards on the tables and have a place for guests to turn in the cards as they leave. (Not many guests actually fill out these cards and those who do tend to be the ones who've had a problem. But it is one way to receive feedback.)

Guests are not statistics or concepts. They are people, and good bar owners make the study of people—their needs, their wants, their characteristics—a priority. If you want to call them "VIPs" use the term to stand for "very individual people." Then at your bar they will have very individual experiences. The overall **guest experience** is always affected by how the customer felt walking into the bar in the first place. A person who is happy about meeting up with friends for an after-work drink will have distinctly different needs from one who is walking into the same bar hoping he or she doesn't run into the same coworkers since he or she just got fired. The other components of the guest experience are:

- The **service encounter** is the moment of truth when a guest and server first converse and strike up a relationship, however temporary. In this moment the server represents the entire bar and can make or break a customer's experience. The **delivery system,** which involves getting the drink ordered, produced, and delivered to the customer, is part of the service encounter.
- The **service scape,** also called the *landscape,* refers to the environment in which the service encounter takes place. Some places make catchy service scapes their specialty: Hard Rock Café, Macaroni Grill, and Rain Forest Café, among others.
- The product itself affects the guest experience. Let's assume that the guest would not be in a bar if he or she did not want an alcoholic beverage. The experience includes whether the bar carries and the bartender can make what the guest wants; the presentation, portion size, and price of the product; and whether it is attractive and a fair value. The average bar stocks 125 to 140 liquors and liqueurs, and there are no clearcut guidelines about what, or how much, to stock.

The Competitors. We have already stressed the importance of studying your competition—not just other bars and restaurants in the area, but others anywhere in your town that might attract similar types of customers. This should give you a great deal of critical information. It will show you who else is competing for the entertainment dollars in your area, which will help you gauge the demand for your bar's services; allow a more objective and informed assessment of your planned location; and give you ideas (that you can adapt) about why other bars have been successful.

Primary competitors are those bars with concepts similar to yours. **Secondary competitors** are those bars that could be considered competition simply because they are located near your proposed site. Try to include a total of 10 competitors in your market survey within a 15-minute drive from your site. In fact if more than 10 bars are there already you should immediately question whether there is sufficient demand in the area to support your concept. Try to visit each place during busy periods to see how efficiently the staff handles a crowd. Take notes or use a form to record your observations (see Figure 15.2). You are looking for the following:

Physical Attributes

Location. How close or far is each bar from your proposed site? Is the bar in a mall, a hotel, or an office building? Is the bar part of a restaurant? What are the traffic patterns? Is the bar close to anything—e.g., a movie theater, other merchants—that helps generate business?

Accessibility. The ease with which a guest can drive or walk to the bar is extremely important to its overall success. Look for physical barriers, including a lack of parking, one-way streets, and entrances that are hard to locate. Can any of these be improved with valet parking, signage, and a request to the city or county for some type of variance, respectively?

Visibility. What kinds of signage are apparent from the street? Can you read them and make your decision to turn in within 400 feet?

Appearance. The business's exterior should be inviting and well maintained. Its interior should be attractive and clean, free from clutter and trash. Both should reflect the overall concept. A combination of factors gives a bar its unique feel or ambience. These include:

Ambiance Attributes

Menus and drink lists. How do you know what is served? Are there house specialties, signature drinks, and wines by the glass? How are these beverages presented to customers? How extensive are the food offerings?

Prices. Make careful note of what the drinks cost. Are there specials, happy hours, senior discounts, and so on? (The *happy hour* is discussed later in this chapter.)

Foodservice. Is food available in the bar? If so which kinds and which portion sizes? Are there complementary appetizers, mixed nuts, pretzels, or other munchies?

Service style. How are beverages delivered to guests? Are there separate servers for food and beverages? Who buses the tables? Do servers use trays? Does the bar use silverware, linen napkins, nice wineglasses, or plasticware, paper napkins, and less expensive glassware? How are the servers dressed?

EVALUATION FORM FOR MARKET RESEARCH

This can be organized on a numbered scale (1–5, with 1 being poor and 5 being excellent), or as "grades" (A–F). Add other categories if you feel they are pertinent.

Competitor ______________________ Date of Site Visit ______________________

Location ______________________ Evaluator ______________________

	Overall grade	Grade compared to competitors	Comments
Signage (Easy to find? Attractive?)			
Exterior (Attractive? Well-lit? Grounds well-kept?			
Parking (Adequate? Cramped? Well-lit? Convenient? Free or well-priced?)			
Foyer or entryway (Clean? Cluttered? Easy to figure out the 'system?')			
Food menu (Attrative? Easy to read? Prices clearly marked?)			
Menu appeal (Interesting selection? Fits the apparent target audience?)			
Drink menu			
Drink menu appeal			
Product consistency			
Pricing (Is it fair? A good value?)			
Speed of service			
Friendliness of service			
Apperance of servers (Sloppy? In uniform?)			
Overall quality of service			
Cleanliness, front-of-house			
Restroom cleanliness (toilet paper, soap, paper towels fully stocked?)			
Atmosphere (Colors, lighting, artwork)			
Climate control (Temperature, air quality)			
Furnishings (Comfortable? Cramped? Clean? Attractive?)			
Sounds (Hard to hear? Music, too loud or too soft? Noisy? Too Quiet?)			
Overall ambience			
Payment experience (Offers check promptly; picks up card or money and gives change promptly, pleasant "close" to the sale)			

FIGURE 15.2

Atmosphere. Estimate the numbers of barstools, cocktail tables, booths, and so on. Notice the layout of the space. Are the tables too close together or too far apart? Can you readily discern what the theme or concept is? Does the place look clean? Does the bar seem well organized or chaotic? Look at floor coverings, walls and ceilings, lighting and decorations, and fans and vents. What type of music is played? Is it live, on CDs, or from a jukebox? Overall how would you describe this bar in a couple of words: e.g., quiet, loud, romantic, businesslike, exotic, boring, lively, colorful?

Special characteristics. Make note of any special promotions or events that are being advertised, as well as any special design features: a sunken floor or dance floor, an elevated bar, an outdoor patio, or a private party room available for rent.

No, your guests will never look at your operation in this much depth. But this is exactly the kind of detail that you will need to make your own bar better in the long run. This is the reason why you are doing research. One other question must be answered by local bankers, the restaurant or merchant's association, or suppliers: Have bars gone out of business in this area, and why? Their answers may be revealing.

Put all of your market research in writing, and share it with your team as you create the marketing plan.

Components of Atmosphere

Your position in the market will be a positive image in the minds of customers that sets your enterprise apart. An *image* is, by definition, a subjective impression based on something unique or memorable about your place. It may come from a single feature or it may be the customer's total experience. Image is the element that you will emphasize in promotions, advertising, and on-site merchandising.

By this time you probably have a pretty good idea of the overall impression you want to create: the atmosphere, or *ambience,* of your place. These words are hard to define but you know what they mean. They have to do with what is seen, heard, touched, and tasted—the total of sensory impressions, to which the customer adds a psychological ingredient of response. Ambience may well be the most influential part of the customer's experience and it is likely to make its impact immediately.

One glimpse of the front of the building, one step inside the door, and the customer's reaction is immediately one of pleasure or disappointment. If you have done your job well this reaction will depend on the type of customer that comes to the door. What pleases the clientele you are after may well disappoint other potential customers.

Consider the groups of customers identified in Chapter 3. Diners are likely to be mature men and women, alone, together, or with children in tow. They want to enjoy their drinks and meals in comfort and relative quiet. They want to be able to read the menu without a flashlight, converse without shouting, watch other people like themselves, and feel well taken care of. They don't like loud music and noisy talk and don't come for fancy décor, although they don't object to it. For this group you might choose a fresh, friendly, low-key atmosphere, conservative but definitely not dull.

You should certainly offer a change of pace from eating and drinking at home. Leisure-time customers in search of entertainment or a partner for the evening are likely to want just the opposite type of atmosphere. They enjoy noise, action, crowds, and loud music. They respond to the newest in décor, as well as the latest in drinks, music, and activity—all of which contribute to the sense that something fun is going on.

A subgroup of these two groups is a more serious group of diners who are really leisure-time customers, for whom the entertainment *is* eating and drinking. The atmosphere takes its cue accordingly.

Drop-in customers are typically less involved with a special ambience. They want prompt service and good drinks, they like to have the experience move along briskly, and they usually enjoy a crowded, friendly bar. Neighborhood-bar customers want familiar, relaxed, and comfortable surroundings and an atmosphere of camaraderie. They are not interested in hype and they will provide their own entertainment.

There are many, many exceptions to and variations of these scenarios, but the message is clear: One person's meat can easily be another's poison. As you plan your bar's atmosphere look at it through the eyes of the group you want to serve. Your awareness of their view of the world is very important. Plan a décor that they will respond to. Offer services that they are looking for. Train a staff that knows how to deal with your desired clientele and is sensitive to their perceptions. If you can really get into this group's outlook on life and create an atmosphere that expresses it, you can make them think, "This is my kind of place." You are building an image. The consistency of the image is critical because loyalty is a function of a person's prior experiences at a bar. It can take only one negative experience to drive away even the best customer—and you might be surprised at how little it takes to create that bad experience.

You must address two major components when creating atmosphere: physical factors and human factors. Among the physical factors appearance and comfort are most important. Appearance has the most immediate impact, from the entrance and the interior as a whole, to the lesser details of uniforms, restrooms, tabletops, glassware, and matchbook covers. Restrooms deserve special attention; they can cancel out a previously favorable impression. The types and quality of food served may also be considered physical attributes of the bar.

Human factors include service components: speed, accuracy, friendliness, product knowledge, and even the server's appearance. Consider a real-life example: One of the coauthors of this book ordered a meal at a casual neighborhood pub from a young woman with a pierced-nose ring shaped like droplets hanging between her nostrils. The impression was downright unappetizing and the writer, who can choose many other places to eat and drink, has not been back to the pub. (Not offended, just grossed out!) Other human factors include the types of customers. Most people feel more comfortable in places where fellow guests appear to be of a similar age range or at least adhere to a similar (unwritten and unspoken) dress code.

Décor, Comfort, and Service

Using décor to create atmosphere was discussed at length in Chapter 3. You might want to reread that discussion in light of all that you have learned since. Think in terms of your total concept, your individuality, and your image. The look of your establishment is one of your most potent marketing tools: It's the packaging of your product.

Take all five senses into account when you are creating your bar. The B. R. Guest, Inc. restaurant group in New York City is masterful at this. Company founder Stephen Hanson has based the success of each of his 14 eateries on the "needs" of the particular neighborhoods in which they are located. Hanson judges what the area seems to lack and fills the void with a concept that provides it.

Décor creates the first impression; comfort has a slower but no less significant impact. Furnishings—part décor, part comfort—can be chosen to fill both needs. Lighting is also both décor and comfort, and sometimes a fine line of compromise must be drawn. Temperature is not important to the customer until it is too hot or too cold, then it becomes very important—too cold in front of the air-conditioning vent, too hot without it. A ventilation system that draws smoke away and keeps the air fresh is an essential element of a comfortable bar environment. Noise level is still another comfort factor that you can control according to customer tastes. Sight and sound provide the first impression, but human encounters provide the second and most lasting. Remember the "service encounter"? Customers of every group respond to the way you and your staff greet them, treat them, and deliver your products and services. Customers like to be cordially welcomed, to be served promptly and efficiently, and to feel that their needs are getting personal attention. This single element of your atmosphere is the one most likely to bring satisfied customers back and to inspire them to spread the word about your place to their friends.

The B.R. Guest, Inc., organization is also an example of a service-driven standard. Server training is tailored to match the restaurant concept but focuses on enhancing the food-and-beverage experience. First a "Wine High School" manual is issued for the basics, then servers attend "Wine College," an additional 16 hours of training focused on selling wines from around the world. The wine lists themselves vary according to the concept and location. Each day the servers have lunch and dinner preshift meetings with a manager, a chef, and a member of the chain's corporate beverage team. During these meetings, they are briefed on daily specials, new products, and "Beverage Points," tips on wine, beer, and spirits. Any service-related issues are resolved at this time, too. The goal is that by the time their work shifts begin, the servers and bartenders are fully briefed on what's happening, empowered with information and motivated to use it.

As you can see achieving customer satisfaction doesn't happen by itself. It depends on selecting friendly, people-oriented staff members and training them thoroughly in your products, serving routines, customer relations, and philosophy of service. Customer satisfaction also depends on your own performance with people, for your own personal impact and as the model you set for employees. It depends, too, on whether your employees are happy in their jobs and in your enterprise; their working atmosphere is certainly part of the overall atmosphere that you create. An employee at odds with management or one who feels like he or she is "flying blind" every day when taking orders or mixing drinks is likely to bring an obvious edge of frustration into customer relationships.

Another human ingredient of atmosphere is the customer. If you focus your **marketing** efforts on attracting a certain clientele you will have a compatible mix, and people will feel comfortable from the beginning, ready to enjoy their experience. Enjoyment itself is contagious. Yesterday's bar—a dark, mysterious place where people drank in isolated corners and dark booths, and could not see or be seen—no longer exists. In today's bar everybody is visible; people-watching and shared experiences are part of the fun. If you can foster a sense of belonging, i.e., if people feel that your bar or club is their own special place, you will encourage them to come for sociability, the way that the British enjoy their local pubs; the Germans, their beer gardens; and the French, their bistros. Developing a regular following is much cheaper than looking for new customers all the time.

Using atmosphere to attract customers is not just for the new enterprise; it can also revive one whose business is falling off. A certain amount of customer turnover is in the nature of the food-and-beverage industry: job transfers to other cities, marriages, babies, inflation, shifts in buying habits, sickness, and death can reduce your customer count at the rate of about 15 percent a year. Of course there are plenty of potential new customers: young people reach legal drinking age, new families move into the homes of those who have moved away, new offices and shops move into the area, and customers bring in friends. But not many of these people will become patrons unless you do something to attract them. Examine your premises with a critical eye and think about giving your place a new look and feel when it needs them.

Successful bar operators make frequent physical improvements, ranging from painting and lighting, to buying new furniture, opening up a patio, or renovating a facility completely. Customers are quick to spot neglect. Peeling paint, stained carpets, weeds in the shrubbery, and potholes in the parking lot raise doubts about whether you wash your glasses carefully and keep roaches away. Cleanliness invites the customer in and promises an operation with careful attention to product and service. Budget upkeep on a regular basis as part of the profit plan. In the process you can subtly modify and update your whole concept.

Bar Food and Snacks

What you serve says as much about your bar as how the room looks. More and more bars are replacing chips, popcorn, and pretzels with "real food," and charging for it. The simple addition of a bar menu can create a completely different atmosphere. Raising the quality of the food you offer, even if the menu is limited, has several important effects: It adds to the enjoyment of the drinks, it prompts people to spend a bit more time and money, and it slows the absorption of alcohol into the guest's system, thereby making the cocktail-drinking experience safer. In a competitive market, food quality can also tip the scales among competitors.

Menus that are well thought out and meet customer expectations should also make money for you with proper staff training and creativity on the part of the kitchen staff. An attractive menu is fully capable of prompting one more round of cocktails or by-the-glass wines at a table, both of which increase the check average. Remember, people "use" bars differently today than they did 10 or 15 years ago. Instead of stopping at a bar to have a cocktail on the way to dinner someplace else, today's customers is far more likely to go to a bar for drinks and appetizers instead of a big meal. So the bar menu can be positioned as a lighter, less filling, and less costly alternative to full-sized portions. Whether you call these dishes *tapas, hors d'oeuvres, appetizers, starters, small plates,* or *shareables* you have a whole new way of eating. The choices can be simple (hot wings and potato skins) or sophisticated (baked brie and oysters on the half-shell), and nobody really expects a bar menu to be extensive. Interestingly the smaller portion sizes often prompt guests to order more and to share them.

When deciding how extensive the bar menu should be, take the following factors into account:

- ***Understand your limitations.*** Consider how big and/or sophisticated the kitchen is. If you run a restaurant with a bar, can the kitchen be expected to produce different, additional food items for the bar, or should you seize the opportunity to cross-promote the restaurant's existing list of appetizers and desserts? A bar menu is not likely to take revenue from the restaurant menu. In fact properly managed the bar menu will increase overall revenue.
- ***Set hours, at least for hot-foodservice.*** If the menu is more extensive than simple snacks be sure that any printed menu lists the hours that the food will be available. Kitchens almost always close before bars close although in some states the hours of foodservice are dictated by state law: at least some food items must be available whenever alcohol is being served.
- ***Restaurant/bar combinations should function as a team.*** The kitchen staff must view the bar menu as an integral part of the operation, not just another element that slows down the "main-event" meals in the dining area. Guests will view the bar food as an extension of the restaurant so it must be comparable in quality, presentation, and price. The bar is actually a good place to "field test" new food-menu items.

- ***Be willing to update the menu regularly.*** If you have daily or weekly drink specials do the same for food items.
- ***Merchandise drinks and foods together.*** Pair signature cocktails with foods, from Margaritas and tacos, to Ports and chocolate desserts, to sake with sushi, to Champagne with caviar.

No matter what else you decide to serve in the way of food, in many bars a good snack mix is still a staple and a hungry customer's best friend: something crunchy, tasty, salty (to prompt thirst), and free of charge that is worth munching while decide on the rest of their order. Making your own bar mix is not difficult, and it is a low-cost endeavor. Just be sure that it is absolutely fresh and a bit distinctive: Add vegetable chips, raisins, or nuts to the mix. Season it with thyme, rosemary, or oregano, not just salt. Even better, try something really unique. Little Giant, a tiny restaurant on Manhattan's Lower East Side, makes its own vegetable chips by lightly frying and salting ribbons of fresh parsnip to serve in bowls at the bar.

MARKETING TOOLS TO ATTRACT CUSTOMERS

Let us assume that you have targeted a customer group, decided on your products and services, and created an atmosphere that will favorably impress your chosen clientele. But they won't be impressed unless they come through your doors. To make this happen you must send them messages that will make them want to come. The goal is to get the messages to the people you want to reach and in ways that you can afford. You should plan this in advance and in detail and prepare an ongoing budget. Many enterprises earmark 1 to 5 percent of sales as a ballpark figure for an advertising and promotions budget.

Paid advertising is an effective way to send your messages. Entire courses and books are devoted to the subject of how to advertise, so we will concentrate on options that are more or less free of charge and can work (with or without an advertising campaign) to keep your establishment top-of-mind with potential customers. These options include word of mouth, news releases, dining or entertainment reviews, feature stories, personal contact, and promotional events. First we will discuss the cheapest, the most effective, and perhaps the least controllable all of these methods.

Word of Mouth

By far the most effective marketing vehicle is one that an eager entrepreneur can approach only indirectly: **word of mouth,** that is, people telling other people about your place. If you have satisfied customers' needs and desires their comments will

VIRTUAL PUBS

Here's a list of just a few of the local brewpub Web sites around the United States. There are plenty more, but this gives you an idea of what some bar owners are doing to promote their businesses.

Pyramidbrew.com: This Seattle ale house features games and prizes on its Web site.

Toronado.com: This is a San Fracisco-based pub that gives customers a chance to suggest new brews on its Web site.

Maproom.com: The Map Room in Chicago includes an interesting "beer journal" on its site, plust a look at its menu.

Horsebrass.com: A Portland, Oregon, pub that has a curious history. Its Web site is personal, yet educational.

Mcmenaminspubs.com: This chain of Pacific Northwest pubs talks about its beers, bed and breakfasts, artwork, theaters, and more.

Drinkgoodstuff.com: You can find out when each of the kegs was tapped on this Web site for a brewpub company with locations in New Orleans and New York City.

be favorable and should encourage others to come. To initiate effective word-of-mouth promotion give customers something that they would really like to talk about. Be different. Be better. Be special. Offer something unusual. One way to stimulate talk is to have the most of something that is image-building, such as the world's largest collection of bourbons or the world's longest wine list. In Washington, DC, Brickskeller Bar has a nine-page beer list, with some 500 different brands from all over the world, and a display of antique bottles and cans. A few miles away Bullfeathers restaurant-bar has a collection of more than 50 single-malt Scotches. Such collections are not cheap and will move slowly but your customers will certainly talk about them; they will pay for themselves if they project an image, generate word of mouth, and bring in customers.

On a smaller scale unusual decorations or artwork on display, chosen especially with your clientele in mind, are items that your customers will want to tell their friends about. You can make deals with a local gallery to exhibit its wares and change them periodically. On an even smaller scale you can encourage such business-generating talk by providing take-home items with your name and logo. You can also personalize coasters, menus, and placemats or print out recipes for special drinks. Another option is to have glassware marked with your logo and invite the customer to take the glass home; you include the cost of the glass in the price of the drink. In the bar this promotes the sale of the drink; at home it becomes a word-of-mouth promotion piece. Anything that goes home with a customer becomes a conversation piece and an advertisement for your place. Make sure that it reflects your image.

Specialty drinks are also good for starting word-of-mouth promotions. If you invent a new one and dress it up in a special glass you might be lucky enough to capture the customers' attention and become the talk of the town. Two historic examples are Buena Vista's Irish Coffee and Cock 'N Bull's Moscow Mule; these drinks were invented more than 50 years ago and are still bringing people into the bars where they were created.

The classic example of using specialty drinks as a marketing technique is Victor Bergeron's drinks for Trader Vic's restaurants. In the 1970s he created an entire menu of drinks with a Polynesian theme, many of them oversized, designed a special glass for each one, and charged a price that made you know that you were getting something really special. But you don't really need the kind of word of mouth that makes a place famous. The best kind of "buzz" is simply spread by satisfied customers telling their friends that yours is the place to go. It helps if you can provide your own special twists that linger in the memory, such as your Café Diablo made with a flourish at tableside, your ocean view, your fabulous hors d'oeuvres, and your jukebox that plays everything from Bach to the Rolling Stones. Such features extend the conversation, and the detail sticks in the listener's mind far better than the vague general recommendation, "It was nice." You can do better than nice! If you meet the customer expectations outlined earlier and your guests go home eager to return, they will tell their friends.

One of the major components of customer satisfaction is the feeling of having been well served with person-to-person attention. Personal service is a facet of marketing in which the owner/manager has a golden opportunity. The proprietor who welcomes each guest personally is a refreshing holdover from the past. In today's impersonal world of machines, numbers, computers, self-service, and canned entertainment people are hungry for conversation. They want to feel special. As one of the last of the species of individual entrepreneurs the owner/manager has a unique chance to fill this need and to sell personality along with refreshment. The warmth of the boss, reflected in the equally warm attentiveness of the staff, will give customers something to tell their friends about. Don't underestimate its impact. People love it!

The downside of word of mouth is that you have no direct control over it. Unfortunately, unfavorable word of mouth is also easily triggered, e.g., a tale told by someone who was turned off on a bad night at your place when the bartender made an Old Fashioned with gin or filled up a short-poured drink with water from the rinse sink. In fact one of the most important ingredients of generating favorable word of mouth is to have well-trained, high-performing personnel as part of your image. Satisfied customers enthusiastically telling their friends about your establishment is the most solid kind of image-building word of mouth that you can have.

News, Reviews, and Feature Stories

You need not depend solely on your patrons' word of mouth to attract the numbers of new customers you want. A story in the newspaper, on radio, or on television can reach new people and increase the awareness of those who have already heard about you. In addition the only cost is time and effort or what you might pay someone else to write a news release.

In order to get a news story published or aired, it must be considered newsworthy by the person to whom you submit it: a newspaper editor or columnist, an assignment editor or feature reporter at a local television station, or the producer or host of a radio program. These people make their judgments on the basis of what will be of interest to their readers, viewers, or listeners. An entertainment editor might be glad to cover your grand opening or first-anniversary party, or the band that will play at your place on a certain Saturday night. Newspapers do not print only articles; they feature many small (one- or two-paragraph) "mentions" of local happenings. Details of your upcoming wine tasting, for instance, might run in the food or lifestyle section of the newspaper or in the dining critic's column. If you have regular entertainment—live music, comedians—be sure that the entertainment editor receives a regular list of "who's playing when."

Most local radio stations allow their deejays to read informative tidbits about a variety of events happening in the area, and they would be happy to include yours *if* they know about the events far enough in advance. If you sponsor or host an event for a local charity you are assured of at least some publicity. But again the amount and quality of the publicity depends on how effectively *you* get the word out. Think about *maximizing your mentions.* You might need to hire a local freelance writer to get you started and to familiarize you with what editors need and expect.

The standard vehicle for getting a news story published is a news release sent to the appropriate editor. The writer can help you with this too. A news release consists of a few short paragraphs providing the pertinent details about an upcoming event. It should be written simply, accurately, and well. Write it as though it will be published word for word (as it may well be by a smaller newspaper). Angle it to arouse the reader's interest immediately and in the first two sentences include the five Ws: who, what, where, when, and why. List all of the other essential facts in the first two paragraphs too. Less-important facts and additional interesting details can follow. If the editor decides to shorten the story, he or she can simply drop the last paragraph or two without eliminating anything essential.

Type the story double- or triple-spaced on one side of the page only. The story should be only one or two pages long. In a news release less is more. If it is more than one page, type "—More—" centered on the bottom of the page. At the end of the story type "—3O—" or "###" centered below the last line (this, in journalism jargon, indicates the end of the item).

Give the story a short, catchy headline to identify it for the editor. In the upper-right comer type the release date for example: "FOR RELEASE JUNE 22, 2006" or "FOR IMMEDIATE RELEASE." Check and double-check your spelling, grammar, and facts! Errors can be disastrous.

Put the story on your letterhead if you have it. If you do not, be sure that the release carries the name and address of your enterprise and the name and telephone number of a person to contact for more information. Most media outlets today have web sites on which these details are easy to find. Many also have specific instructions for e-mailing them information. Just be sure to send the story well in advance, that is, at least two weeks prior to its release date.

One important type of publicity is the review written by a columnist for a local newspaper or magazine. Many such publications systematically review the restaurants in town and publish lists with assessments of the product, atmosphere, and service, along with price-range information. This is a form of publicity over which you have no control. Usually you do not know when a reviewer is coming and most reviewers try hard to be anonymous anyway, so there is nothing you can do to influence the outcome of a particular visit. If you are newly open for business or if you have changed menus, concepts, locations, whatever—and you feel you are truly ready for a review, the best way to get on the list is to send a copy of your menu with a note to the reviewer.

If you have a shipshape operation and have trained your staff well both in skills and in customer service, chances are good that you will get a favorable review. If the column carries a recommendation you have one of the best kinds of word of mouth going for you: the word of a specialist. Then you can enlarge the review and display it on your front door or even quote it in paid advertisements. If you continue to serve your clientele well, your establishment might even get into the guidebooks of *Places to Go,* and then you will have it made—at least for a while.

On the other hand a critical review might hurt your place. The day that it was reviewed might have been the day a substitute bartender mistook the vodka bottle for gin and a new server spilled the wine. Perhaps the reviewer did not see your establishment through the eyes of your special clientele, did not share their values, and did not feel comfortable in your setting. In any case there is little you can do about a negative review except to learn from it. Think about it as free customer feedback. You can analyze the criticisms objectively, correct those that are legitimate, and invite the reviewer for another visit. But if you are pretty sure that the problem was a mismatch between the reviewer and your carefully created ambience and image, then you may as well forget the review. You really don't need customers who, like the reviewer, would not feel comfortable in your place.

Feature stories are yet another publicity vehicle. They are written by someone else at your suggestion and they must fill the writer's journalistic needs, for example to help fill the weekly food section or Sunday magazine with interesting reading. You do not control what is said, but if you and the writer develop the idea together the story is likely to be favorable. The starting point is an interesting or unusual angle to intrigue first the writer and then the reader. If you have renovated a historic house, this would be a good story idea for the Sunday magazine. You might have an employee with an unusual background and talent. Your head bartender and what she goes through on a busy Saturday night might make a good profile story or radio interview. Your interior design—that unique artwork you display—is worth a story somewhere. Such stories keep your image in the public eye and can increase your patronage.

Once you start thinking of story possibilities you will probably have many ideas. You might have a brainstorming session with your staff; it can be interesting for them and it will encourage their involvement and strengthen their spirit of teamwork.

Personal Contacts

Word of mouth and publicity stories are great when they work for you, but they are always in someone else's hands. There are ways to approach your market more directly. One is to use personal contacts. You can broaden your own contacts and you can ask people you know to bring in people they know.

One way to expand your contacts is to work for popular community causes, such as youth groups, church activities, and fundraising for charities—perhaps even assuming a leadership role. This can establish you as a respected working member of the community and broaden your acquaintanceship with other community leaders. Community goodwill is an important and continuing asset in any business, and this is especially true in the bar business. If in the process you offer your bar as a convenient place for meetings at quiet hours, this may also contribute directly to your business. But be careful that your involvement is not simply for personal gain. This motive quickly becomes apparent, people resent it, and it backfires.

Another way of using personal contact is to encourage your customers to bring in other customers. One way to do this is to give a party and ask your current customers to invite friends and coworkers. Print up invitations to a celebration of, for example, St. Patrick's Day, Greek Independence Day, or Halloween and ask your customers to pass them around to people they know. This is likely to produce a congenial group at the party. For your future use each invitation should have a place for the guest's name and address. This gives you the nucleus of a mailing list. One restaurant works through its customers by offering an "Angel's Check" to thank anyone who brings in a group of six customers. The "Angel's Check" reward is a gift certificate for $5 to be used on the next visit.

Still another idea for building a bigger clientele through your customers is to organize games or contests centered around their interests. You might even form a club and give members membership cards to pass out to their friends. Games and contests—darts, shuffleboard, pool, and videogames—are fun both to play and to watch. Interest builds if you form teams or set up tournaments, a good idea for slow evenings. Players may bring in friends to watch and cheer them on. A good crowd attracts additional business as passersby stop in to see what is going on. You will do a good business that night, and some of the new people will probably come back. This type of event is particularly appropriate for neighborhood bars and other enterprises catering to a clientele seeking entertainment and relaxation.

Another version of the game/contest idea is to sponsor an athletic team that plays in a league of teams sponsored by other establishments. Bowling leagues are a common type; you may also find interested baseball, softball, touch-football, and soccer leagues. A team of your own builds business—everybody adjourns to the bar after the game—and sports contests of any kind are usually good word-of-mouth generators.

Promotional Events

The two previous sections, about using the news media and personal contacts, may involve the creation of promotional events. Choose a charitable cause or civic group and donate a portion of profits—for a day, a weekend, or a whole week—to that organization. Offer to be a spokesperson for the event and/or to accompany the group's spokesperson to radio and television stations for on-air interviews, usually early mornings.

Holidays naturally lend themselves to promotions, but so do nonholidays. Pizza Hut, for example, has dubbed the Wednesday night before Thanksgiving as "Thanksgiving Eve," when (of course!) everybody's too busy preparing for Thanksgiving and would surely prefer a pizza. A bar in Philadelphia plays on the occurrences of Friday the 13th to promote fun drinks that ward off the bad luck associated with that particular date.

In addition to regular clientele think about the visitors and tourists in your area. For the most part they will want to go where the locals like to gather. Make it easy for "outsiders" by printing, perhaps a special flyer, drink menu, or coupon that the concierge in a nearby hotel can hand out.

In some markets where smoking is still allowed in restaurants and bars the "cigar event" is making a comeback. Call it a phenomenon, a fad, or a rebellion, but the persistent popularity of cigars is undeniable, fueled in part by the camaraderie created by events tailored to this high-end demographic. Some are expensive, black-tie, gourmet dinners for the well-heeled crowd; others are strictly casual events where people can sample and purchase various types of cigars and enjoy them with drinks and appetizers. The event can also be based on beers, wines, Ports, cognacs, single-malt scotches, Martinis, or an open bar. For some target audiences a beverage theme is unimportant—the cigars themselves are the draw. Other big decisions include whether to have the event indoors or outdoors, whether attendees will stand cocktail-party style or be seated, and whether or not there will be a guest speaker.

Every promotion must be planned, budgeted, fairly priced, and, to the extent that it is possible in advance, rehearsed. It must be marketed separately to the right target audience and the activity must be directed as it takes place. This requires an all-out commitment, a creative spark, and enthusiastic coworkers to help carry out the plans, usually while also maintaining (not neglecting) the everyday business. Ask your suppliers to get involved too. They'll have ideas for themes, speakers, decorations, point-of-sale (POS) materials, and special menus and drink recipes.

Suppliers also may be able to throw in prizes to give away to customers or offer a discount for items that you order for the event.

Checking Your Progress

You should recognize by now that a good bar is a work in progress. Even the best bars require subtle adjustments from time to time. These changes work best when they are guided by solid market research, which includes customer feedback. There are a number of ways to get this feedback, summarized as follows:

- ***Ask for it.*** Train servers and bartenders to ask things like: "Is there anything else I can help you with?" "How was your evening?" "Is there anything you can think of that we could do better for you next time?" These are not just pleasantries. Ask staff members to pay attention to how customers respond and to jot the comments down to share in staff meetings. In addition to soliciting comments staff members should also notice the questions that customers ask. As a rule if the same question comes up repeatedly over time it points to an issue that may need to be addressed: a brief explanation on a menu, descriptions of the beers or wines on a list, and so on.
- ***Provide a short questionnaire.*** The problem with this approach is that most people are ready to leave the bar when they receive the questionaire. But a brief, postcard format with a few questions like, "How did we meet your expectations?" and "Were you satisfied with the drinks and service you received?" may elicit a few comments. Bars can take a hint from restaurants and retailers that increasingly are asking their customers to go online to their web sites to fill out questionnaires. This can boost your mailing list (if you require name and email address information) and give the customer time to think about his or her answers. It is also a good idea to offer customers an online discount coupon, which is good on their next visit, for taking the time to answer the questions. Again, make it short!
- ***Hire mystery shoppers.*** Mystery-shopping firms send people out as eagle-eyed customers to report back about their actual shopping and dining experiences to client companies. Retailers use mystery shoppers extensively as do restaurant chains. The key to this type of research is the shopper's anonymity and ability to follow the directions of the bar owner in gathering specific types of information. The person (or couple) may have already seen a copy of the drink manual or menu, for example, and will ask questions about ingredients. A mystery shopper at a bar will notice cleanliness, the speed of service, the use of suggestive service, and the attentiveness of the servers and bartenders. The shopper might hint that he or she is having a birthday or anniversary, without making it obvious, just to see how the staff responds. They might ask for a special favor or complain about something once again to gauge the server's ability to handle the issue. In an example cited in *Market Watch* magazine (March 2004) a mystery shopper ran up a hefty bar tab and the bartender billed him only half the

amount, hoping to get a generous tip. When management confronted the bartender with the facts he was quite embarrassed.

Mystery-shopping companies usually work on contract, requiring visits one or two times per calendar quarter, and will provide written reports summarizing their findings and recommendations. As the eyes and ears of your guests mystery shoppers can be invaluable.

- ***Employee feedback.*** Ask for information from your front-line employees—servers, bartenders, host or hostess, and bus staff—who interact on a daily basis with customers. Schedule a monthly focus group (with different employees each month) to stay on top of any new issues or concerns. Ask employees what can be done to make their jobs better, how to handle certain situations and how to improve policies and procedures. Even if you are unable to change an unpopular policy, you'll learn what bothers the staff members and can explain why the policy is in place. Giving your workforce some input into their working environment is an important motivational tool, as well as a way to get new ideas.

PRICING AS A PROMOTIONAL TOOL

The role of pricing in promotion used to be viewed in terms of a simple formula: Reduce a price and you increase demand. Today most bar owners and managers look at this idea more soberly (pun intended). Not too long ago the universal means of applying the formula was the *happy hour,* a period of time in the late afternoon or early evening when all of the drink prices were reduced, or two drinks were offered for the price of one. Now, the happy hour is against the law in many states. Many managers sighed with relief since they generally only broke even during happy hours and went along with them only to remain competitive. Besides in today's climate few managers want to flirt with the risks of the intoxicated customer.

But lowering a price has subtler uses other than increasing the demand by each person for more drinks. One of these is to make a certain high-profit drink a "special of the day" by cutting its profit margin in half. Many people are bargain hunters by nature and the very idea of getting something for less excites them. In this way you reinforce their enjoyment of your place, yet you are not stuck with a lower price tomorrow. Another use of specials is to associate them in the minds of your customers with a special period of service that you are trying to promote, such as Sunday brunch. A specially priced Mimosa not only merchandises the drink, but also promotes the whole idea of Sunday brunch.

Still another way to use a special is to reduce the price of something expensive that your customer might not ordinarily buy at all—a good wine or a good brandy, for example. You may create a taste for it that will benefit you the next time the customer comes to your place. Since prices are directly related to image the overall level of prices should be kept stable. When increased costs force you to raise prices set them high enough so that you won't have to raise them again soon. Customers can take an occasional change in stride but several increases in a row can raise eyebrows and temperatures as well.

Even the most upscale bars can learn from quick-service restaurant chains about the practice of *bundling,* or packaging two or more items together and selling them at a fixed price. The Manhattan restaurant Cité offers a three-course dinner accompanied by four wines selected to complement the foods for $69. The **prix fixe** (fixed price) approach has netted not only loyal customers, but also some excellent media coverage. In New York City, known for its astronomical dining-out prices, the Zagat dining survey says Cité's offer "may be the best deal in town."

Above all else customers must feel that the value they receive from you is equal to or greater than the prices they pay: perceived value, a fair deal, their money's worth. It does not matter what the actual costs and money values are. If they think that they are paying too much for what they are getting, you have set your prices too high, and they won't be back. The marketing role of pricing must not interfere with its financial role. The two must continue together in a coordinated relationship; both are important to profitability.

PROTECTING AND EXPANDING YOUR CONCEPT

Many things go into making a bar a hit with locals: a strong concept, a distinctive design and décor, signature drinks, and a group of talented, dedicated employees. At some point owners of such a successful business might have to make a big decision: whether or not to open more locations. In the meantime today's business climate includes competitors who always seem to be trying to steal your thunder, hiring away your best people and copying your success formulas. How can you put a stop to this?

Protecting Business Identity

In general it is practically impossible to legally protect an idea or a concept. Even powerhouses like the Hard Rock Cafés could not, for example, prevent the creation of other rock-and-roll themed bars and restaurants. However in most cases the name of the bar can be **trademarked.** This is the legal process of registering the name to give you the exclusive rights to use it. The law firm of Spiegel and Utrera, P.A., with offices in seven states and the United Kingdom, describes a trademark as "a word, name, symbol, phrase, slogan, or combination of these items used to mark and distinguish goods or services to indicate their source or origin." (A *service mark* is a trademark for a service rather than a product.) Words that are generic in nature; such as "bar" and "lounge," do not qualify for trademarks.

Merely incorporating as a business in your state is not sufficient to claim that you have the sole rights to use the name you have chosen. You can trademark the name in one or more individual states, or nationally. This is why it is wise, when choosing a name in the first place, to search the Internet and see if you can find it being used elsewhere. You may also pay an attorney do a trademark search for you—has anyone already trademarked the name? If it's a different type of business in a faraway state, you might be able to ask them for written permission to use the name in your area, but an attorney is the best person to advise you of your rights in this situation.

Specific designs used to execute a concept or idea may also be protected. The U.S. Supreme Court has held that a business's **trade dress** may also be protected with a trademark or copyright. Trade dress is the image of a product or a business that makes it distinctive. This might include the size and shape of a container (or a building), graphics (logos, artwork, colors or color combinations used), and even the sales techniques used to market the product or business. In general if a bar's trade dress is distinctive enough that a competitor who copied it would be likely to confuse consumers into assuming that there is an association with the original, the competitor can be accused of infringing on the original business's trade dress or trademarks.

Copyrights are different than trademarks. As the federal law (17 USC Subsection 102a) reads, copyrights protect "original works of authorship, fixed in any tangible medium of expression . . ."—including books, music and lyrics, movies and plays, even architectural designs. As a rule copyright laws will not protect your individual drink recipes but they may protect your company's proprietary drink manual and the special names that you have given to particular, signature drinks. In order to keep bartenders from disclosing "secret" techniques, ingredients, or recipes, you'll have to ask them to sign an employment contract that contains a *noncompete clause* stating that they won't make your signature drinks for other bars, at least for a period of time after leaving your employ. An attorney can draft this clause, which is common in many industries.

After you've gone to the time and expense of taking legal-trademark and trade-dress precautions, you should monitor the marketplace for potential infringements. Surf the Internet looking for references to your business name and see what comes up. Encourage customers, vendors, and employees to let you know if they run across infringements. If you find a problem your attorney can draft a *cease-and-desist letter* asking that the other person or business stop using, for example, your trademarked name, logo, and color scheme. In some cases a court challenge might be necessary, but this step should be a last resort.

Branching Out

If your concept is good enough to copy, it may be good enough to clone—that is, to open more than one location. This is a huge decision and industry experts insist that smart businesses grow because they are truly better than their competitors, not simply because the owners find a "steal" on a piece of property in another area and decide to jump on it, opening a second location. If the first store does not have a strong business foundation and excellent profitability, it is not the time to begin building a multilocation empire. The key is to learn everything possible in the first unit, increasing operational efficiencies and fine-tuning the business plan to boost revenue over costs, before ever considering expansion. The following are the tasks at hand for the first bar:

- As you develop the market position of the first bar determine whether its appeal may be broader than in your existing market area: Elsewhere in your city or county? Could the appeal be statewide, national, or international?
- Establish a system to replicate the initial unit's success. Determine exactly what is required, and whether you and your business partners can afford to provide it.
- Ensure that you can deliver the same support—in terms of both staff members and funds—to the second unit as the first one enjoys.

Even in the same town the market factors for a second location may be different from those of the first bar. All the same market analyses are in order (just as if you were starting over): the relative strength of competitors with your target customers, local traffic generators, retail and residential growth, and real-estate costs, and so on. The good news is that sometimes real-estate brokers or developers will offer favorable incentives or loan terms to a successful bar to get it to open another location in a developing area. Multiple locations also increase leverage, with the ability to purchase at least some ingredients in greater quantity. Whether a second unit or a chain of bars will ultimately drain your energy and bank account depends entirely on your advance preparation and a realistic financial picture of expansion.

SUMMING UP

The creation of a business plan is the first step in deciding what types of marketing you need to do and how much you can afford to spend on them. This involves visiting at least 10 local competitors to see what they are doing and how well their concepts are working (or not working). Only after you complete this research can you position your business within that marketplace. The first part of this chapter focused on what should be in a business plan and identified some common issues that can prevent bar owners from successfully implementing and fine-tuning their plans.

Once you have identified a target clientele the entire enterprise should be shaped to meeting their needs, desires, and expectations. Create an ambience that these customers will respond to: serve drinks to their liking, from servers who care about them; add a menu of appropriate foods or snacks; and make their total experience memorable so that they'll come back and bring their friends. Check your progress by training servers to ask for feedback, using short customer questionnaires, and hiring mystery shoppers for an anonymous (but highly informed) guest's view of your bar.

You can depend on word of mouth for a certain amount of customer loyalty but advertising and promotion are the more serious and ongoing parts of marketing. This chapter focused on marketing tactics that can be used without much financial expenditure to boost business by creating fun events that can generate media publicity and community goodwill. Another part of marketing is the sales process itself. Displays, special drinks, and special prices are good promotional tools, but the real sellers are your serving staff. Individual attention and interpersonal communication are their highest priorities on the job.

Finally the chapter discussed bar owners' considerations in legally protecting the names, logos, and other distinctive elements of their concept from use by others as well as the factors inherent in making a decision to open more than one location.

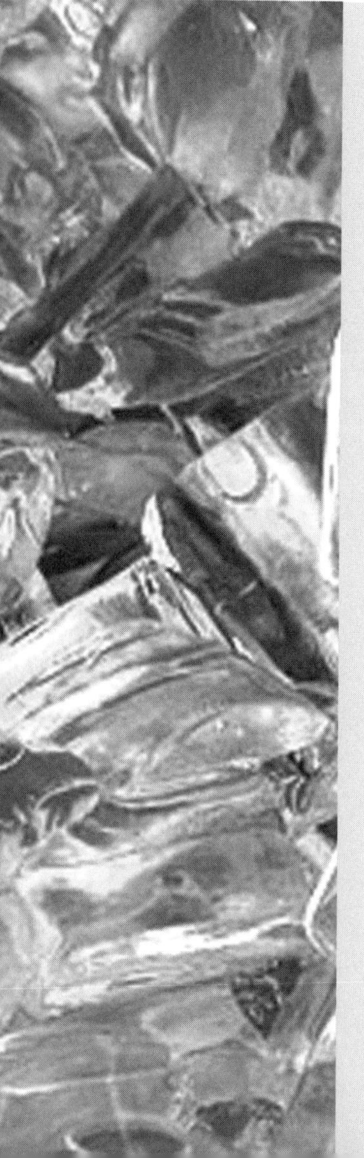

POINTS TO PONDER

1. Why is it important for a bar to have a business plan? Give two reasons. How is it different from a budget?
2. What are the three types of analysis that you should do when creating your business and marketing plans? Describe each type in one or two sentences.
3. What is a market segment?
4. Think of two groups of customers who are very different in their tastes and values. Make a list of three or four items that you might find in a bar that would attract one group but completely turn off the other one.
5. What makes up a guest experience at a bar?
6. List 10 details that you should know about the customers in any market segment. How can you use this information to create low-budget promotional events?
7. Identify three ways to keep your name circulating in public without spending a great deal of money on advertising. Write a few sentences about each, and explain how well you think they might work.
8. How do you feel about the idea of having a happy hour? Is it a valuable business-building tool for a bar or a way to create unnecessary problems?
9. Which snack foods would you serve free of charge in your bar to attract the following target customers: a.) the "Monday Night Football"-watching customer at a sports bar; b.) the female business executive; c.) the college-age customer at a casual bar near campus?
10. What steps should you take if you have trademarked your business name and find out that a bar in a neighboring state is using the same name? Do you think that it is acceptable to "share" your name with another business if that business is not located in your market area and/or is not doing anything that would cast a negative light on your business? Explain your answer.

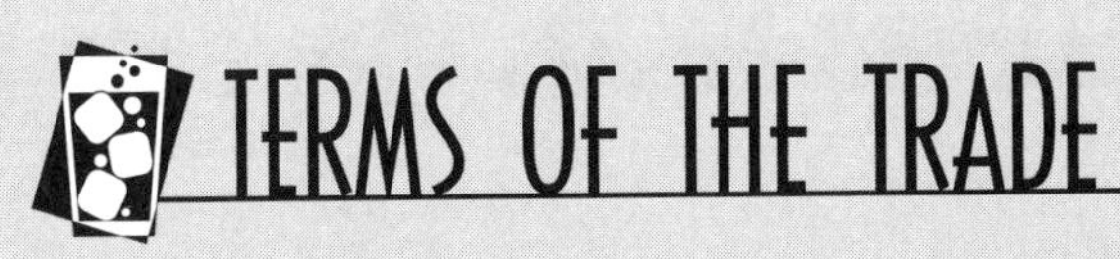

TERMS OF THE TRADE

delivery system
guest experience
image
market segment
marketing
presell
primary competitors
prix fixe
secondary competitors
service encounter
service scape
SWOT analysis
trade dress
trademark
word of mouth

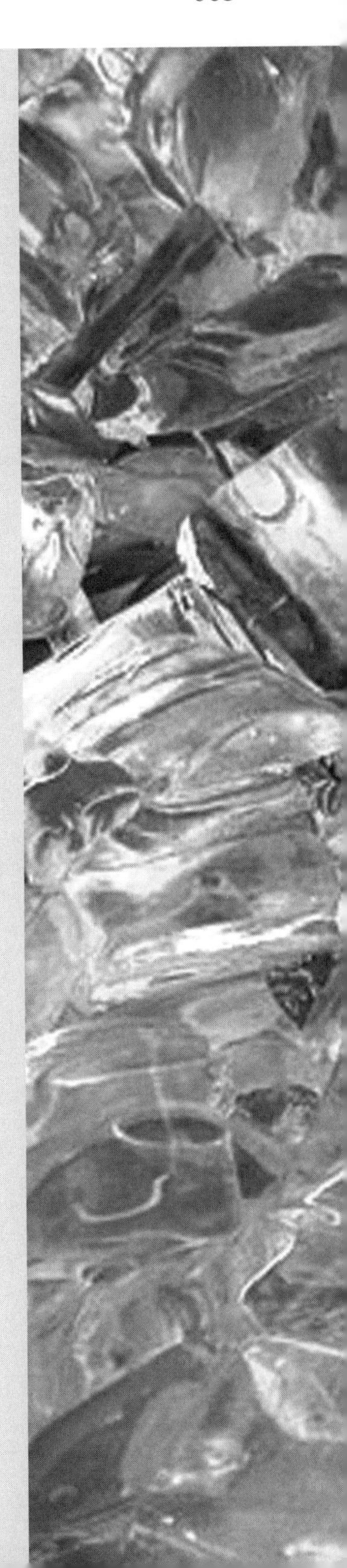

A CONVERSATION WITH...JULIE HANSEN

Regional Manager
Oregon Liquor Control Commission

Oregon is one of the control states, with a governor-appointed commission that regulates the sale and distribution of alcoholic beverages, issues licenses to vendors, and enforces the state liquor laws.

Julie Hansen got her first job with the Oregon Liquor Control Commission in 1981 as a secretary. She took advantages of an Upward Mobility Program within the organization and took additional college courses in business and law enforcement to become an inspector and license investigator before moving into management positions. Today Julie is a Regional Manager. She supervises five license investigators and five district inspectors whose territory is the Portland, Oregon, metropolitan area.

Q: Do you have any particular insight into the bar-and-restaurant business now that you've dealt with it as a regulator?

A: I have a certain amount of respect for the people who work in it; I know that it's a really tough business. I see lots of businesspeople who don't cause trouble, who obey the laws, but who still don't make it in business. They have not done their advance research or they don't have the financing to stay afloat for those first few months while they are building a clientele.

I'd like to encourage new bar or restaurant owners to become a part of the community where they're opening their business. Join the neighborhood association. Work with local law enforcement. It's understandable that neighbors may be worried about a bar that will be staying open till 2:30 in the morning. The customers who leave may be loud, get in fights, park in the wrong places. There is cause for concern, and it's important to be able to work through any problems with your neighbors. We ask prospective licensees to get local-government endorsement of their application to make sure neighbors get a chance to have input to the local government before the license is even issued.

Q: What do license investigators and inspectors do?

A: A license investigator goes through the application process with people who are trying to get a liquor license. They gather all the documentation they need to make a recommendation about their qualifications for the license—lease documents, proof of financial fitness, the individual's background or history. In Oregon a liquor license is a personal privilege, like a driver's license. So each person or corporation applies for their own new license, even if they're buying a business with an existing license.

An inspector is responsible for compliance with liquor laws for the licenses within their district. They have separate geographical areas, with up to 300 licensees in each area. Every inspector is required to make premises visits; they visit each of their licensees at least once every two years.

Q: What kind of things do the inspectors look for?

A: We have a checklist they take with them; whether the license certificate is displayed; whether the servers have a service permit; if the appropriate signs are posted about minors not being served; whether food is being served according to the state guidelines for food and alcohol service. In Oregon if you sell distilled spirits, there are food-service requirements. You have to have a cook on duty for a minimum of three hours during your meal periods, and you have to have at least five distinctively different menu items—sandwiches, burgers, entrées with side dishes. Even outside of meal periods you have to offer what we call "minimum foodservice," with at least five food items available at all times that distilled spirits are being served.

Q: What are some of the differences in requirements if you want to sell beer and wine, not distilled spirits?

A: If you have a license that allows you to sell beer and wine, there isn't any requirement that you also have food available. If you qualify you can sell beer between 7:00 A.M. and 2:30 A.M., and sell beer up to 14-percent alcohol, and sell wine up to 21-percent alcohol, for consumption on the premises. You don't have to have any food available but a lot of places do. There is more paperwork for a distilled-spirits license than for a beer and wine license, because you have to submit your menu and floorplan showing what seats are used for dining and what hours the dining will take place; and you have to document the hours that your cook is on duty, and so on.

Q: What are the most common problems you see with people, either accidentally or intentionally, breaking the law?

A: Both the OLCC and police departments around the state have minor decoy missions, where someone underage attempts to purchase alcohol, and that's where we see the most violations. Licensees need to be so careful about checking identification and not selling to minors, and the computer age has made teenagers very creative about making fake IDs. I got called to a bar downtown Portland recently where the security person had detained a boy from Australia. He had made his own "Australian" ID cards, in three different names, all with his picture on them! We see more and more very sophisticated IDs that look valid. And the trouble is, it sometimes *is* valid, but they have obtained it fradulently!

Another priority is overservice, and we do undercover observations in bars to make sure they're not overserving alcohol. Our law talks about visible intoxication, and we give lots of training to licensees to show them what they need to be looking for. The licensees attend Law Orientation, a half-day training session, before they even get their license. A bartender or cocktail waitress also attends a half-day training to get their service permit. They take a test and have to pass it, and they get a service permit card good for five years. To renew, they have to take the class again.

Q: How do you work in conjunction with the Federal Bureau of Alcohol, Tobacco and Firearms?

A: We do work closely together at times, but BATF has its own process and permits and fees that are completely separate from ours. It also has its own people who inspect all wineries, breweries, distillers—they focus on manufacturers of alcoholic beverages.

Q: Control states are, and probably always will be, controversial. Speak from your vantage point about the value of the system.

A: One of the concerns about privitizing alcohol and allowing it to be sold in supermarkets is that it would give minors so much easier access. And if, in Oregon, there were not a liquor commission, there wouldn't be as much focus on service to minors and overservice because law enforcement would have to do it all. They have to prioritize, and this might not end up on the top despite its very serious consequences.

The OLCC raised $540 million this biennium from license fees, fines, taxes, and liquor sales; $100 million of that goes into the state's General Fund.

Q: What about advice for students who are interested in this type of career?

A: I would highly recommend that they job-shadow an inspector or investigator to find out if they'd really like this kind of work. It's not police work, but it is regulatory work and we do work closely with licensees. We try to help them in lots of ways—education, training—we're not out there just to "nail" people. We try to work with them and teach them to do the right thing.

Q: Which personality traits would make a really good field person?

A: Somebody who is comfortable talking with people, a good communicator, in situations where you have to think on your feet. You've got to use good judgment and be fair in your dealings with people. And you've got to like working on your own. Every day is different; you not only deal with licensees, but with law enforcement, with parties or "keggers" involving minors, in schools doing outreach and education—those sorts of things. You work with quite a variety of people. I've liked every job that I've had here! I love this agency. I like regulation. It's really a challenge.

CHAPTER 16
REGULATIONS

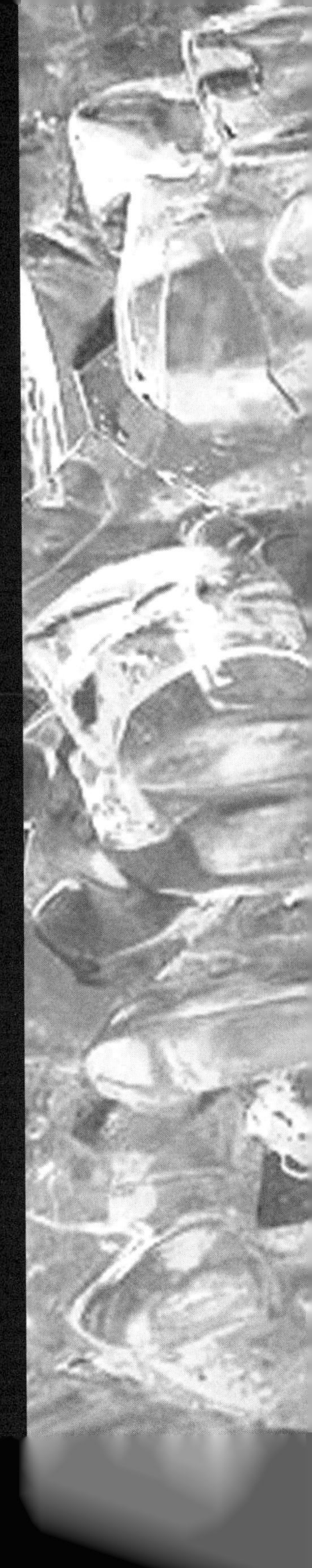

Many federal, state, and local laws apply to the sale of alcoholic beverages to be consumed on-premise, that is, at the same site where they are purchased. Some of these laws you are surely aware of, but others may never have crossed your mind. Breaking them, even unintentionally, can have serious consequences for bar owners, managers, and employees. So it is crucial for you to know the laws in your area as you open and run a bar or restaurant.

Overall the alcoholic-beverage industry is the most highly regulated business in the United States. Federal, county, city, and state regulations can affect where you locate, what you serve, whom you serve, the days and hours you stay open, how you train your employees, where you buy your supplies, which records you keep, when you pay your bills, what your advertising can and cannot say, what you do with your empty bottles—even your ability to conduct any business whatsoever.

The purpose of this chapter is to acquaint you with the major federal regulations and to make you aware of typical state and local beverage laws. Since local beverage laws vary greatly it is up to you to find out which laws are in force in your area.

THIS CHAPTER WILL HELP YOU . . .

- Research your state and local regulations before you buy or lease a property.
- Meet licensing, registration, and code requirements.
- Observe legal hours of sale and sell only beverages that you are licensed to sell.
- Avoid selling to underage or intoxicated persons.
- Buy your beverages from licensed suppliers.

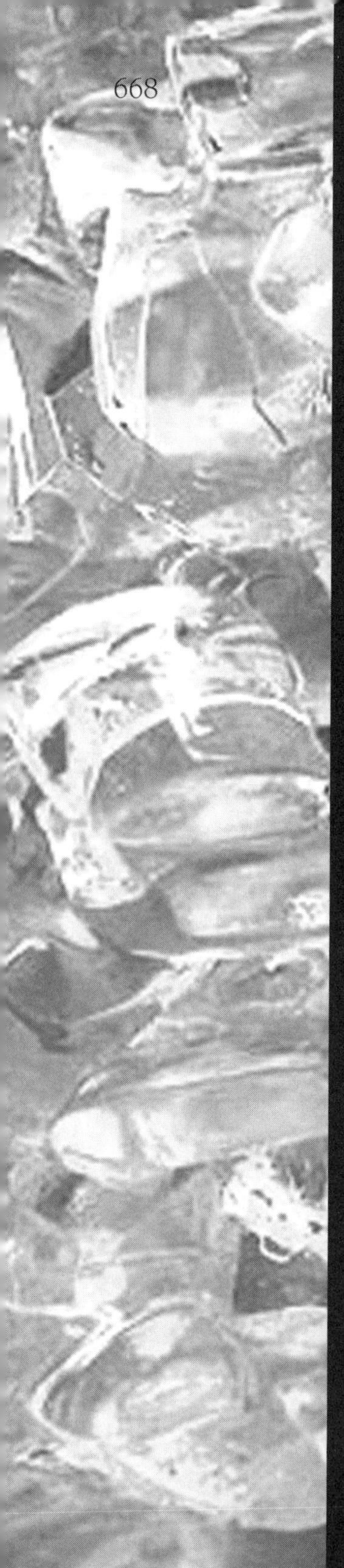

- Avoid illegal relationships with suppliers.
- Observe laws about record-keeping, bottle closures, empty bottles, and official inspections.
- Check product labels for legitimacy.
- Avoid illegal advertising.
- Train employees to be aware of and observant of beverage laws.

There is nothing new about the two overarching reasons for the plethora of alcohol-related laws: public revenue and public interest. Riotous drinking was the subject of legislation in Babylonia 4,000 years ago, and the tavern-keeper was punished for allowing it by losing a limb or even his life. In Colonial America laws restricted the hours of sale and prohibited selling to minors, drunks, Indians, servants, and slaves—often put just that bluntly. The tavern-keeper was selected and approved by the town fathers, and the tavern was hemmed in with rules for keeping it as respectable a part of the community as possible.

As for revenue, licensing fees brought income to early colonial towns and cities. British taxes on Dutch rum helped to spark the American Revolution. A tax on whiskey caused the Whiskey Rebellion in 1794. When President George Washington crushed the rebellion he firmly established the right and tradition of the federal government to tax liquor for general revenue. You'll learn more about current alcohol taxes in this chapter.

Today the mishmash of alcohol-related laws is fascinating. Some of them are unusual, impractical, and even downright comical. Nonetheless if they apply to your operation, noncompliance can create more problems than debating the merits of the laws themselves.

REGULATIONS: AN OVERVIEW

Today's regulations, many in the name of public interest, date from the repeal of Prohibition. They reflect the earnest desire of citizens and governments to prevent both the excesses of the pre-Prohibition era and the abuses by the illegal industry during the Prohibition years. Far outweighing the concerns of the past, however, are those of the present—the continuing toll of drunk-driving accidents, the effects of alcohol on fetuses and nursing babies, and the societal impact of alcoholism—addressing the 10 percent of drinkers who cannot seem to control their drinking. No matter how you feel about whose responsibility these real and present dangers are you are urgently advised to know and observe every regulation that applies to you.

Control States

How did the laws become so different in different areas? Following the repeal of Prohibition the federal government established the broad outlines of alcoholic-beverage control and with the Twenty-First Amendment to the U.S. Constitution turned over most aspects of administration to the states—where many were convinced that it had always belonged. The popular thinking was that the United States was too vast and its traditions and values too diverse to suit any specific standards of sobriety.

Today each of the 50 states still formulates its own laws and has its own administrative agency. The states in turn may authorize counties and municipalities to pass more stringent regulations. The resulting network of laws can be complex and bewildering. But from a practical standpoint the nation does at least accommodate the zeal of the "drys," the thirst of the "wets," and the obvious special interests of the liquor industry.

Today 18 states operate as *control states,* where alcoholic beverages are sold through stores run by the state, not by private industry. Two counties, both in Maryland, also use a control system. Bars that operate in control states also buy their wares from the state: sometimes only liquor, sometimes beer and wine as well. (Canada and some Scandinavian countries exercise similar controls.) The control states are as follows:

Alabama
Idaho
Iowa
Maine
Michigan
Mississippi
Montana
New Hampshire
North Carolina
Ohio
Oregon
Pennsylvania
Montgomery and Worchester Counties (Maryland)
Utah
Vermont
Virginia
Washington
West Virginia
Wyoming

The sales of distilled spirits in control states have consistently accounted for about 25 percent of the U.S. market, according to the National Alcohol Beverage Control Association, a trade group to which all of the jurisdictions belong. In a control state the government creates an agency, department, or commission that acts in a sense as a wholesale liquor distributor. Spirits (and sometimes beer and wine) are ordered and delivered to the agency's warehouses or central distribution points, then sold through a system of state-owned stores to consumers, bars, and restaurants. Alternately in some control states the liquor stores are privately owned but they have to buy their wares from the state. Again the setup and rules that govern each state vary widely, so check with your own state authority for specifics.

Some control states require a mark or stamp on bottles, indicating that taxes have been paid or that the bottle was purchased legally and in salable condition by the state.

Taxes and Revenue

Officials in control states walk a fine line between strictly regulating alcohol sales and trying to market the products in their warehouses and state-owned stores. This battle plays itself out in many state legislatures from year to year. Interestingly these states benefit most from the trend toward drinking high-end spirits. There are usually laws against—or at least rules that minimize—the advertisement of alcohol by the state. But even without promoting alcohol a few states have managed to make astonishing profits. The list of the most profitable control states has included the same five, in varying order, since the early 1990s: Michigan, Pennsylvania, Ohio, North Carolina, and Washington. As with private industry, flexibility and innovative operation have made them top performers.

Two types of federal taxes are levied: on the alcohol itself (known as an **excise tax**), and on the businesses that sell it. The latter is called a **Special Occupational Tax (SOT).** For both taxes the amounts paid depend on the type of beverage being sold.

Federal Excise Tax on Alcohol. In 1993 the federal excise tax on many luxury items (jewelry, yachts, upscale motor vehicles) was repealed—but it is still levied on alcoholic beverages. The federal tax rates have not changed since 1991. For beer each 31-gallon barrel produced includes $18 in federal taxes and another 5 cents for each 12-ounce can. Producing a wine of 14-percent alcohol or less, the winery pays $1.07 per gallon in federal tax and another 21 cents for each 750-milliliter bottle. Fortified wines, with their higher alcohol content, are taxed at higher rates: $1.57 per gallon and another 31 cents per bottle for more than 14-percent but less than 21-percent alcohol. Makers of sparkling wines are charged even more: $3.30 to $3.40 per gallon and another 62 to 67 cents per bottle, depending on whether the carbonation is natural (lower rate) or artificially added (higher rate).

Distilled spirits are taxed at $13.50 per "proof gallon," with credit given for any percentage of that gallon that is strictly wine or flavoring, not alcohol, and another $2.14 per 750-milliliter bottle. Bars pay these taxes when they purchase the alcohol for their mixed drinks, draft kegs, and wine lists, then pass them on to customers in their drink prices.

Special Occupational Taxes (SOT). Taxes on alcoholic beverage are owed by anyone who sells or provides alcohol, on or off their premises, including anyone who "provides alcoholic beverages as part of the cost of an item or service." These taxes apply even if the organization is exempt from income taxes and will not make a profit from the sale. SOTs are paid annually in the following amounts:

Retail liquor/beer dealer	$250
Wholesale liquor dealer	$500
Brewer	$500–$1,000
Distilled spirits plant, bonded wine cellar or warehouse, tax-paid wine-bottling house	$500–$1,000

A few *limited retail dealers* are exempt in certain circumstances from paying SOTs. These include fraternal, civic, church, labor, veterans', and other organizations, for events such as picnics, fairs, festivals, and so on. But these groups are still required to pay for permits to serve alcohol. Depending on the event it may be a single-use permit with a onetime fee paid to the city or county.

SOTs are paid to the **Alcohol and Tobacco Tax and Trade Bureau (TTB),** the newest agency under the U.S Treasury Department. The Homeland Security Act of 2002 split the Bureau of Alcohol, Tobacco, and Firearms (BATF) into two agencies with separate functions. The TTB collects taxes and is part of the Treasury Department; the BATF is now strictly an enforcement-related agency and is part of the Justice Department.

Perhaps the most important point to note about SOTs is that at least temporarily they have been suspended. Congress decided to give this perk to alcohol (and tobacco) sellers as part of the American Job Creations Act of 2004, possibly to free up a bit of cash to hire more workers. Between July 1, 2005, and June 30, 2008, no SOT amounts are due, although the sellers must still register every year as usual with the TTB. The agency stresses that the tax has not been eliminated, simply suspended for the three-year time period.

The federal taxes on alcohol bring billions of dollars into the U.S. Treasury. Today the retail price of a typical bottle of spirits is more than 50 percent taxes and fees paid into federal, state, and local treasuries. States have their own excise taxes on alcohol, generally ranging from $2 to $5 a gallon with a few over $6. Alaska's tax is perhaps the most unusual: $2.50 per gallon for alcohol content of under 21 percent, jumping to $12.80 for more potent spirits. As states struggle with fewer federal dollars, we predict that more states will turn to excise-tax increases for additional income. In 2005 lawmakers in Kansas, Missouri, and Washington proposed tax hikes on alcohol.

GETTING READY TO OPEN

If you own a bar or restaurant serving alcoholic beverages, you are defined in legal terms as an *on-premise retail dealer.* In this role you are subject to federal laws, state laws, and local laws. You must also meet the requirements of local zoning ordinances, building codes, health codes, and fire codes. State and local laws vary so widely this book cannot possibly cover all of them. But we can indicate the kinds of restrictions that are typical and what you should do before you take action.

Both you and your premises must meet several requirements in order to open at all. Some of them involve a good deal of time and legwork. You may have to attend a city council meeting, go before a judge, post a notice in a newspaper, and be fingerprinted—whatever the state and local laws require. First even before you sign a lease or buy a property, familiarize yourself with all the state and local regulations. Your local licensing agency will be able to provide them.

Local Option Laws

State laws generally allow the sale of mixed drinks in hotels, restaurants, and private clubs, although a few set limits and conditions, such as a related percentage of food sales. Several states limit the alcohol content of beer and other malt liquors, which might discourage you from opening a brewpub in one of these states.

Most states have **local option** laws; that is, the state allows the people of local communities to choose whether or not they will allow the sale of alcoholic beverages, and if so, how. Thus although state law may allow liquor to be sold by the drink, some communities or even voting precincts may not, even in different parts of the same city or county. The popular term for this mixture is *wet* and *dry* areas. "Wet" means alcohol is sold; "dry" means that it is not or, in some cases, not without the purchase of a special "membership." If your city or county is one of these areas, you should carefully check where the lines of demarcation are drawn. You must also find out which beverages are permitted in your locale because there are often different regulations for spirits, beers, and wines.

Even in areas that allow liquor by the drink, there may be zoning laws that prohibit operating a bar in your chosen location. For example, if you want to remodel an old house, you might discover that the area may turn out to be zoned for residential use only. In other instances an area zoned for commercial use may specifically prohibit the retail sale of liquor.

Many city ordinances have parking-lot requirements, for example one parking space for a certain number of square feet of customer floor space. Is there room on your chosen premises to abide by the parking rules? In many areas you cannot locate a bar within a certain distance of a church, school, or hospital—300 feet, 1,000 feet, or a city block. The way that the distance is measured—from lot line to lot line, or from door to door—may be enough to disqualify the premises you are planning to use. The most unusual situation we've heard of regarding this restriction is a New York City bar/restaurant combination in which distilled spirits are served in the bar but only beer and wine are available in the dining room because of the dining room's proximity to a public school.

Some local authorities limit the number of licenses they will grant. Some areas limit hours of sale more strictly than others. In some places sales of drinks must have a certain percentage relationship to sales of food. Many communities require you to sell food if you are going to sell alcohol. What you may find is that some areas' regulations are so restrictive that you will decide to do business elsewhere.

Licensing and Registration Requirements

Once you have determined that your chosen location meets both your requirements and the law's, you must secure the required state and local licenses and permits and register your place of business with the federal government before you open your doors.

A **license** and a **permit** for on-premise retail sales are essentially the same: a document granting permission to sell specific beverage types at a specific location by a specific business entity provided certain conditions are carried out. In some jurisdictions the two terms are used to distinguish between various types of permission: for instance a permit to sell wholesale and a license to sell retail, or a permit to sell mixed beverages and a license to sell beer (or vice versa).

The federal government does not issue licenses or permits for retail sales. Jurisdiction over retail sales is reserved for the state. The state may pass on the right to local bodies. In some places you must obtain a state license; in others, a local license; and in still others, both. In some states a state license must have local approval; in other states, it is the other way around. In some areas you must have separate licenses or permits for spirits, beers, wine, and mixed drinks. In short there is no practical way to cover exactly what you will need or what you will have to pay to become licensed in your area.

In some areas you can get a license to sell spirits only if you operate a private club. In a few places you must sell your drinks by the miniature bottle. Licenses and permits typically run for a year, requiring annual renewal and the payment of an annual fee. Such fees vary greatly. Some are flat fees, while others are tied to sales volume, the number of rooms in a hotel, or the number of seats in a restaurant. Amounts vary from as little as $50 for a beer license in Indiana, to $3,000 for a mixed-beverage permit in Texas, while Honolulu County in Hawaii, using a percent-of-sales system, sets its ceiling for hotel beverage licenses at $18,000.

In some areas a separate operator's license may be required in addition to the license for the business or premises. This may have such requirements as age (over 21), character ("good moral character"), U.S. citizenship, or residency of a certain length of time in the city or state. The penalties for selling alcoholic beverages without a license are severe. In fact you could put yourself out of the bar business forever.

When you have your state and local permits and licenses in hand or are sure that you are going to receive them, it is time to turn your attention to federal requirements. Federal law requires a retail dealer in alcoholic beverages to register each place of business owned and to pay an SOT for each place of business each year. In return the government issues a special **tax stamp** for each place of business.

As previously mentioned the SOT has been suspended until June 30, 2008. Nonetheless your business must still be registered with the TTB by filling out TTB Form 5630.5, which you can download from the TTB web site, www.ttb.gov. An SOT stamp serves as proof that you have registered and/or paid the necessary taxes for that year. *Do not lose the stamp!* It should be available for inspection by TTB or BATF officers. If you deliberately sell alcoholic beverages without registering (or after 2008 without paying the appropriate SOT amount) you may be fined up to $5,000 or imprisoned for up to two years or both.

If you move your place of business you must file an amended return (another Form 5630.5) within 30 days and send in your tax stamp to be amended accordingly. You cannot transfer your registration or tax stamp to anyone. If you sell your business the new owner must start over with a new TTB registration and new stamps. If you buy someone else's business you must start fresh. State and local license regulations have similar provisions for change of ownership. This is the government's way of ensuring accountability. The federal registration and tax payments do not permit you to sell liquor; they simply prohibit you from selling liquor without them. Registration is mainly a mechanism for keeping track of retail liquor dealers in order to enforce some of the public-interest laws concerning the liquor itself. We will discuss this topic later in this chapter.

Other Local Regulations

Your premises must meet the standards required by various other local codes. If you build or renovate a structure the finished work must pass the building-code inspection. Electrical work and plumbing must meet electrical and plumbing codes. The entire facility must meet the code of the fire district. This will include the requisite number and placement of exits, lighted exit signs, fire extinguishers, fire doors with panic bars that must open outward and be kept unlocked during business hours, smoke alarms, and sprinkler systems in kitchens and high-rise buildings. There is also usually an occupancy requirement limiting the number of persons allowed inside the premises at one time. There will also be specifications about employee training and fire drills.

When you are all set up and ready to open, your facility and personnel must pass inspection by the local health department. Usually you must have certain specified equipment, such as a triple or quadruple sink for dishwashing or a mechanical dishwasher and handsink. All of the equipment must be approved by the National Sanitation Foundation International (NSFI) and must be installed according to health department rules. For example your ice machine and other equipment with drains must have a minimum of 6 inches of space below that permits adequate cleaning. Other requirements pertain to floors (tile or concrete), counters, general cleanliness, proper food storage, proper temperatures for refrigerators and freezers, freedom from pests (rodents and roaches), such sanitary practices as keeping everything but ice out of the ice bin, air-drying glasses, and keeping bathrooms clean and stocked with soap, towels, and tissue. Finally you may not open for business until you have a Certificate of Occupancy (CO).

Health departments sometimes require that employees pass a health examination and that you keep their health certificates available for inspection. This practice is becoming less and less prevalent. Health departments also look for personal cleanliness and may require things like signs posted in bathrooms reminding employees to wash their hands. Generally smoking behind the bar is a violation of the health code. Some states allow bartenders to have a drink on the job but many do not. Health inspectors usually make periodic, unannounced visits to make sure that you comply with their requirements.

WHAT, WHEN, AND TO WHOM YOU MAY SELL

Usually the regulations governing drinks, hours, and customers are state or local laws, and you have already learned that there is considerable variation among them. The only federal requirements are that you may not sell any type of beverage for which you have not paid the SOT (in the years that it is due), nor can you sell any spirit that does not carry a portion of a strip stamp or other approved seal on the bottle.

What You May Sell

What you may sell is governed everywhere by the type of licenses that you hold (mixed drinks, wine, beer) and special restrictions such as mini-bottles in place of custom-mixed drinks or beers that do not exceed a certain alcohol content. Local laws may further limit what you may sell. The information that you are given when you receive your local license will specify the rules.

When You May Sell

Nearly all states have regulations governing the hours that an on-premise retail dealer may be open. These hours are usually fairly generous. Most states require closing for at least a few early-morning hours and many forbid the sale of liquor on Sunday for part or all of the day. Many states prohibit the sale of liquor on Election Day, at least while the polls are open. Many specify closing on certain national holidays; Christmas is most commonly mentioned. Many states allow local bodies to further curtail hours and days of service, with fines and/or jail time for violations. Pennsylvania recently (in 2003) began allowing 10 percent of its 638 state-owned liquor and wine stores to open on Sundays and to allow in-store wine sampling.

To Whom You May Sell

All 50 states and the District of Columbia prohibit the sale of alcoholic beverages of any kind to persons under the age of 21. This raising of the drinking age was brought about by the federal government, which denied federal highway funds to states unless they set the drinking age at 21. (In 2005 a few Vermont legislators unsuccessfully tried to lower the drinking age in that state to 18, but they were outvoted by others who pointed to the $9.7 million in highway maintenance funds that the state would lose if the measure passed.) The thrust of the law has been to curb the excess drinking associated with college students, and especially to reduce the number of drunk-driving accidents caused by the 18- to 21-year-old age group. As of this writing 15 states have laws that also prohibit the sale of nonalcoholic beer to minors.

You and your servers are part of the law-enforcement team but you will quickly be on the other side of the law if you are caught selling alcohol to an underage person. States set their own penalties, which are usually stiff. In Texas for example sales and/or "making alcoholic beverages available" to minors are both Class A misdemeanors with fines of up to $4,000 and/or one year in jail.

Chapter 2 discussed the importance of checking the age of anyone about whom you had doubts and the consequences of serving alcohol to someone underage. We suggest you review this material in light of all you have learned since.

The other category of persons you may not sell to is those who are **clearly intoxicated.** Many if not most towns and states have this law on their books. We suggest that you look into the various server-training programs available. Only nine states require that anyone who serves or sells alcohol must complete an approved training course; seven others have laws that recommend voluntary training. Illinois leaves the decision up to local communities but has created its own training standards. Reread the sections in Chapter 2 on the physiology of alcohol and third-party liability. In terms of the law these are the most important issues that you face. As of this writing 41 states and the District of Columbia have dramshop laws; nine states do not.

It is of course against the law to refuse to serve a customer on the basis of race, religion, skin color, sex, national origin, or disability. If you are dealing with an intoxicated person who could be the subject of such laws, you will be wise to make sure that you have witnesses to the intoxication in case the person involved charges discrimination.

Additional Liabilities and Insurance Coverage

There are other types of incidents related to drunken customers for which you may be liable under various laws. These include allowing injuries to take place on your premises, even when inflicted by other customers (stop the fight); allowing an intoxicated customer to drive away from your place (call a cab); and using more than "reasonable" force in dealing with an intoxicated person (call the police). In at least one state the law requires you to remove an intoxicated person from your premises entirely, including your parking lot. But one way or another you had better keep that person from driving even though the drinking wasn't done at your place; call a friend of the guest, a taxi, or the police if necessary.

As you can see bars and restaurants have a higher exposure to risk than many other types of merchants. Getting and keeping various types of insurance will take a greater amount of thought, time, and dollars than it did in the past. It is important to learn exactly what you are paying for when you purchase an insurance policy—what is and is not covered—and ask your agents plenty of questions. At least 60 days prior to the renewal date of any policy review the coverage and the cost, and shop around for alternatives.

The following list is a quick summary of the basic types of insurance that a bar owner might want to carry. In some cases your bank, investors, landlord, or municipality may require you to carry them.

- ***General liability.*** This type of insurance pays those sums that a bar or restaurant becomes legally obligated to pay as damages, due to personal injuries or property

CHECKING IDENTIFICATION

Identity thieves are not always looking for credit cards and bank-account access. Some of them are underage teens trying to get into bars. In an effort to stay ahead of the technologically sophisticated pastime of producing fake IDs, such as driver's licenses, Anheuser Busch, Inc., publishes an annual *Driver's License Booklet,* which every bar owner should have. It displays color reproductions of all current and valid driver's licenses issued by various states (and Canadian provinces). The booklet suggests the following steps for accepting or rejecting a license:

- Check the expiration date.
- Check for the word DUPLICATE. It means someone else has the original.
- Glue lines or uneven surfaces on the photo and/or birthdate line indicate tampering.
- Check for consistency on the sizes of numbers on both sides of the license.
- Look at the state logo. If it is partially missing, the license may have been altered.
- Pinholes on the license surface indicate bleach may have used to "erase" certain numbers.
- Look at the size, color, lettering, and thickness of the license. Compare it to your own.
- Compare the photo on the card with the actual features of the person in front of you.
- Ask for a second piece of identification.
- Quiz the person about information on the card, such as his or her zip code.

The Texas Department of Public Safety uses a handy acronym, FLAG:

- Feel for bumps or imperfections.
- Look at the picture—look at the person. Do they "match?" Does the description on the license match the person in the photo?
- Ask questions—date of birth, address, zip code.
- Go slowly, and return the ID to the individual.

You can politely refuse the sale if you suspect that an ID card is altered, borrowed, or fake. As a seller or server you do not have the authority to confiscate the card. But you can say, "I don't feel comfortable with this ID so I can't sell to you." Then contact local law enforcement as soon as possible.

damage that occurred on the insured's premises or in the normal course of business. It should include the costs of attorneys' fees. It may or may not cover liability claims from people who have been served alcoholic beverages.

- ***Liquor liability.*** Also known as *dramshop liability,* this is a specialized policy similar to general liability but for places that serve alcohol. This policy goes into effect as soon as a customer is served an alcoholic beverage and covers such off-premise occurrences as auto accidents of people who have left your property after drinking. An unnecessary expense? Think again. In 2004 a TGI Friday's franchisee in Louisville, Kentucky, paid $21 million to settle a lawsuit brought by the parents of two teenagers killed by a driver who had been drinking at the restaurant.

- ***Property insurance: for the building.*** This policy covers direct physical loss of or damage to the building. If you rent the space where your bar is located the building-owner's name will be on this policy, as well as (or in lieu of) yours. If there is a mortgage on the property the bank or investor who holds the mortgage will also be named on the policy. In a rental situation the landlord usually carries the property insurance but the tenant agrees in the lease to pay the premiums. Typical exclusions may be floods, earthquakes, mold, and terrorism. (Undoubtedly bars along the U.S. Gulf Coast are wrestling with these terms after the horrific, business-crushing, building-flattening hurricanes in 2005.)
- ***Property insurance: for the contents.*** This policy pays for the direct physical loss of or damage to furnishings, fixtures, and equipment owned or leased by a tenant. Be sure that it also includes coverage for theft, as some policies do not. The same exclusions apply for contents and building. It is a good idea to spell out in the lease agreement or an addendum what the renter owns and what the landlord provides, in terms of the specific contents of a leased space.
- ***Property insurance: leasehold improvements.*** This type of insurance covers direct losses or damage to any improvements that the tenant has made and paid for during the term of a lease. The same typical exclusions apply.
- ***Assault and battery.*** As its name suggests this type of insurance covers third-party liability claims arising from fights between patrons and/or employees.
- ***Loss of earnings.*** This insurance pays for the actual losses sustained when you have to shut down in order to rebuild or restore part of your operation because of another insurance-covered loss. (Again, think "2005 hurricane season.") If you are a renter make sure that the loss of rental income to the landlord is included. You probably won't want to have to pay rent if you are unable to open.
- ***Workers' compensation.*** This type of insurance is required in many states and is often administered by a state insurance agency or board. The policy provides coverage for employees or part-timers (independent contractors) who are injured on the job, including medical expenses for on-the-job injuries.
- ***Hired or nonhired auto.*** This policy covers liabilities related to the use of vehicles in performing business duties. Examples: One employee picking up another employee to go to work in his or her own car, delivering "to-go" orders using company cars or a worker's own vehicle, and sending employees in their own vehicles to pick up supplies from markets and stores. The limits are much the same as those of a general liability policy.

For almost any situation that may pose some risk most insurance companies offer specific types of coverage that can be added to a general liability policy in the form of an *endorsement*. Endorsements always increase the *premium*, which is the cost of the policy, so be sure that you need them before you enthusiastically agree to whatever your agent suggests. The following is a list of common endorsements that may be added to a business policy for a bar or restaurant limiting losses when damage or theft occurs in these areas of the business:

- Accounts receivable
- Automatic cooking protection systems
- Credit card receipts
- Exterior building signage
- Food spoilage
- Money and securities
- Off-premise utility failure
- Personal property loss from power failure
- Plate glass
- Valuable papers and records

After seeing the devastation that a hurricane, tornado, flood, or fire can cause you might be tempted to sign up for every possible type of insurance coverage "just in case." Remember, however, that the basic premise of insurance is to help you to limit your losses to an affordable amount should an unforeseen incident occur. It is not, and was never intended to be, a repayment instrument to protect your business against all losses. As such it is important to decide which types of coverage are absolutely necessary, as well as which risks you can afford to take on your own. To control the ever-increasing costs of insurance you should do the following:

1. Ask about increasing the deductible.
2. Ask about lowering the policy limits.
3. Ask about discounts for taking additional safety and security measures.
4. Ask about discounts for multiple policies with the same company.
5. Be aware of the amount of loss that your business could sustain and still survive, then insure against potential losses that would exceed that amount.

REGULATIONS THAT AFFECT PURCHASING

Federal, state, and local regulations may affect your purchasing, both directly and indirectly.

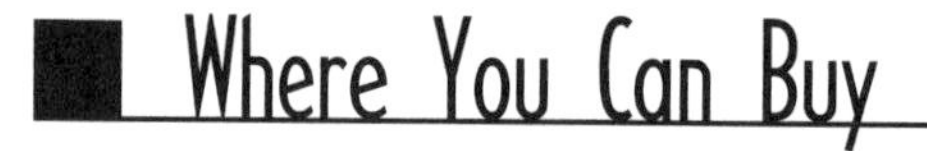

Where You Can Buy

As you have learned, in 18 states the sale of distilled spirits is a state monopoly, and bar operators must buy from state-owned stores or from stores authorized by the state to sell to your particular type of operation. Prices are the same in all state stores since each state mandates a markup formula. The amount of the markup plus state taxes varies from one state to another. Thus, although manufacturers' prices may be the same everywhere, the price that a bar operator pays varies from one state to another. Nevertheless you must buy within the state.

In the remaining states bar operators can buy only from suppliers that have the required state, local, and federal licenses and permits. The federal document is known as a **wholesaler's basic permit** and is free; the wholesaler must also typically pay the SOT. In some states you can also buy directly from state-licensed manufacturers or distributors. In Texas you can buy only from retail package stores that also hold a federal wholesaler's permit. This came about because the package stores opposed legalizing liquor-by-the-drink, which would cut heavily into their business; before that the customer took a bottle of liquor in a brown bag into the bar, and the bar host provided the setups and ice.

In most **license states,** the state does not control prices or markups. Prices may vary from one supplier to another although the manufacturer or distributor price must be the same for all wholesalers. Most license states require manufacturers and wholesalers to file brand and price information with the state beverage-control agency and to post prices and discounts. Publication of suppliers' prices is usually required. The overall objective is to prevent price wars and monopoly-building of the kind that damaged the beverage industry's reputation in the years before Prohibition. Many state laws specify that manufacturers' prices must be "no higher than the lowest price" offered outside the state. This gives the producers' price structure a certain national homogeneity, which varies somewhat by the amount of state and local taxes and fees.

Credit Restrictions

Nearly all states restrict credit that the supplier gives to the on-premise retailer, requiring either cash or payment within a specific time period, usually 30 days or less. Extensions of credit are prohibited in many states and federal laws prohibit extensions of credit beyond 30 days on goods involved in interstate commerce.

Relationships with Suppliers

State laws regulate or prohibit certain interrelationships between on-premise dealers on the one hand, and wholesalers, manufacturers, importers, and distributors on the other. The purpose of these laws is to maintain fair competition and prevent retailers from being controlled by other segments of the industry, as in the old days when the saloons were controlled by brewers. The following are some of the most important prohibitions typically found in state beverage codes:

- No **tied-house** relationships. No supplier may have a financial or legal interest in your business, premises, or equipment.
- Suppliers may not furnish equipment or fixtures.
- A supplier may not pay your debts or guarantee their payment.
- A supplier may not sell to you *on consignment,* that is, postpone payment until goods are sold with return privileges for goods unsold. (This is also a federal law.)
- Suppliers may not give you special discounts that are not available to all on-premise dealers.

- Suppliers may not give you gifts, premiums, prizes, or anything of value except specified items of limited dollar value for advertising or promotional purposes, such as table tents or a beer sign for your window, or consumer giveaways, such as matches, recipe booklets, napkins, and coasters.
- A supplier may not **induce you to purchase** all or a certain quota of your beverage supplies from his or her enterprise.
- Bribery for control of your purchasing carries severe penalties.

In sum suppliers may not own a piece of your business nor induce you to give them your trade. You too may be breaking the law if you accept such inducements. On the other hand there is no law against giving most or all of your business to one supplier if you make the choice without inducement. If you are tempted to accept deals and favors—which can easily happen because most people love to get something for less or for nothing—check out your state and local laws to be sure that the deal or the favor is legal and has no strings attached. Laws that maintain a competitive beverage market, although framed primarily in the public interest, protect you as an entrepreneur as well.

Internet Sales and Purchases

In Chapter 13 we first mentioned the topic of buying wines online as part of a discussion of the role of today's wholesale distributor and the future of the three-tiered distribution system through which most alcoholic beverages are sold. Typically the supplier of the product (a winery, a brewery, a distillery, an exporter) sells to the wholesale distributor, whose sales representatives call on bars, restaurants, and retailers. You will probably find it helpful to reread the "Purchasing Wines" section with a regulatory eye.

When Prohibition was repealed in 1933 Congress did not go so far as to declare that alcoholic beverages could flow freely across state lines. Instead as a nod to communities that still wanted to control consumption, Congress stipulated in the Twenty-First Amendment that the states would be free to write their own laws. As such some states require that all alcohol must move through their three-tier system or their state-run control system when it arrives from other states. Other states let alcohol enter only from states with similar, reciprocal laws. More than a dozen states already allowed direct sales to consumers. Some have allowed only in-state suppliers, such as wineries, to sell directly to in-state consumers, prohibiting out-of-state wineries from doing the same.

The latter issue prompted a case that went all the way to the U.S. Supreme Court, where a decision was issued in May 2005. New York and Michigan were challenged for not allowing out-of-state wineries to ship wine directly to their residents. The Supreme Court ruled that states have two ways to solve this inequity: They can either allow interstate shipments or ban all shipments, but they must treat all suppliers equally. The Court also ruled that the issue was a Twenty-First-Amendment case (which concerns states' enforcement of their own laws), not a Sixth-Amendment case (which concerns barriers to interstate commerce.)

What we don't know at this writing is exactly what the ruling means for Internet wine sales—greater volume for sure, but what other challenges will it reveal? Within months of the decision, New York and Connecticut had passed laws to allow both interstate and intra-state direct-to-consumer wine sales. Industry trade associations suggest that wineries could be licensed to provide direct home deliveries, with limits on the amounts that can be shipped to an individual consumer per month and a requirement to obtain a signature upon arrival from a person over age 21. But think about the potential problems. And what about beer? Spirits?

All of this points to major changes in the traditional three-tiered distribution system, which was originally created in the 1930s as an extra layer of enforcement to keep gangsters out of the liquor business. The system worked well for that purpose. But times have changed radically, and the Internet has created a new business dynamic that no one fully anticipated.

In the meantime direct sales via the Internet continue to grow. In 2002 at least 65 percent of California wineries were already selling wine on their own web sites. The numbers of their actual online sales are small, but growing.

REGULATIONS THAT AFFECT OPERATIONS

In addition to regulations that affect your buying and selling, other regulations, both federal and state, touch some of the smallest details of your beverage operation.

Policing the Product

During Prohibition the illegal production and sale of alcoholic beverages was widespread and much of the stuff was harmful and even deadly—two major reasons why Prohibition was finally repealed. It had proven impossible to control illicit production. The only solution was for the government to work hand in hand with a legal beverage industry and to set up controls to protect the public from unscrupulous producers and bad products.

Accordingly the federal government established Standards of Identity for each product, as well as systems of inspection and control at licensed distilleries, breweries, and wineries to see that the standards were met. Today federal regulations assure customers that the product inside the bottle is exactly what the label says. Labels must correctly state the product class and type as defined in the Standards of Identity, its alcoholic content (except for beer), the net contents of the bottle, and the name of the manufacturer, bottler, or importer. Periodic on-premise inspections by federal agents of the BATF ensure that a bottle's contents and its label agree. Bonded warehouses under lock and key are further controls against substandard merchandise. Imports are controlled in a similar manner through customs regulation, inspection, and labeling requirements. Federal control of the product extends right into your storeroom, speed rack, and backbar via the closure on the bottle and certain regulations concerning the bottle itself. The **strip stamp**, the red or green stamp that used to span the top of each bottle of distilled spirits, has generally been replaced by a **tamper-evident** type of closure, such as certain pull tabs or a screw top that leaves a thin, metal ring around the bottle neck when opened, although some countries still use strip stamps. No matter what type of bottle closure, it is a critical control in three federal government activities:

- Collecting revenue from distillers
- Maintaining product quality
- Preventing the sale of illegal spirits

The closure goes on the bottle at the time of bottling, when taxes are paid, then the bottle, its contents approved, leaves the warehouse. The closure is affixed in such a way that the bottle cannot be opened without breaking the closure. That closure must remain attached and unbroken until you open the bottle at your bar. It is your assurance that no one has tampered with its contents and that they are exactly as they were when they left the distillery.

If a delivery from a supplier includes one or more bottles with broken or clearly damaged closures you should not accept those bottles. It might be an accident, but it can also mean that the original contents have been altered and that you are not getting what you ordered. Besides the possession of bottles without proper closure is against federal law. Substitute closures are available but you should let your supplier deal with getting new closures. Send the bottle(s) back.

When you open a bottle you must leave a portion of the closure attached to the bottle. You must leave the liquor in that bottle and not transfer it to any other bottle. Make this very clear to all of your personnel. If you have liquors without portions of closures on your premises you are subject to a fine of up to $10,000 and/or imprisonment for up to five years. Again a bottle without a portion of its closure might be an accident, but if an inspecting federal agent should find it, it puts you under suspicion of having bought illicit goods. For you a broken or missing closure on a full bottle may be a clue that someone with access to your liquor supply has taken off with your good liquor and has substituted something else. Clearly the stamp or other closure can work for you as well as for the government.

It is also against federal law for you, or anyone, to reuse an empty spirits bottle for any purpose whatsoever. The primary thrust of this law is to prevent illegal distillers from refilling such bottles with their product and passing them off as the real thing. However it is also illegal for you to use an empty liquor bottle for your simple syrup or your sweet-and-sour mix, even if you label it as such.

Federal law does allow you to return empties to a bottler or importer that has federal permission to reuse them; to destroy the empties on your premises; or to send them elsewhere to be destroyed. Keep in mind that many state and local laws require spirits bottles to be broken as soon as they are empty. The clandestine production and sale of home-brewed moonshine are far from over and both federal and state beverage-control authorities are actively engaged in rooting it out. In 2001 "Operation Lightning Strike" pitted enforcement agents against moonshine-makers and bootleggers in Virginia and North Carolina who were allegedly turning out enough 100-proof illegal spirits to cost the U.S. Treasury more than $19 million in uncollected taxes.

There is also a federal law against adding *anything*—other spirits, water, any substance—to the original contents of a bottle. Oddly enough this forbidden practice is known as **marrying.** You may not even combine the contents of two nearly used bottles of an identical product, partly for sanitation reasons and partly as a precaution against illegal refilling. This is one reason why you should inquire first about making your own *infusions,* which are made by steeping fruits or herbs in alcohol (see Chapter 5). In some states your liquor bottles may carry an additional state stamp. This stamp may show that state taxes have been paid or it may have some other identification purpose. These state stamps should also always be left on the bottles.

Labels and Labeling Laws

In Chapter 6 we discussed how to read a wine label, but reading a label for government-required content is quite a different matter. Figure 16.1 is excerpted from a BATF pamphlet that explains the basics of wine label information.

The Alcohol Labeling and Formulation Division (ALFD) of the BATF is the agency responsible for issuing Certificates of Label Approval, both for domestic and imported alcoholic beverages. The ALFD a busy place, issuing more than 50,000 certificates a year. Applicants' formulas, ingredients, and manufacturing processes are verified, and the products are put into the correct tax classifications. While this might sound like a lot of busywork, the goal is noble: to prevent consumer deception and ensure that the product labeling gives consumers sufficient, accurate information about the identity and quality of what is in the bottle.

For example the BATF has seven requirements for wine labels:

- The brand name of the product.
- The type of wine (e.g., sparkling wine, table wine) or particular grape varietal (e.g., Cabernet, Chardonnay, Merlot).
- The alcohol content, usually a percentage by volume. For table wines, the percentage does not have to be shown as long as the alcohol content is less than 14 percent.
- The net volume of the contents (e.g., 750 milliliters, 1.5 liters).
- The bottler's name and location. Not every wine's brand name is the same as its bottler's name.
- The phrase *Contains Sulfites.* (We will elaborate on this in the next section on organic wines.)
- The health-warning statement. Whether the spirit is produced domestically or elsewhere, this wording must be present—and presented separately from any other information on the label. It is included in the label description in Figure 16.1.

WHAT THE WINE LABEL TELLS YOU

XYZ VINEYARDS

1994

ABC VALLEY

CABERNET SAUVIGNON

Produced and Bottled by
XYZ Winery, City, State
Alcohol 12% By Volume

Estate Bottled

Product of *(name of country)*

750 ml

Contains Sulfites

BRAND

The brand name is a name used by the bottler to identify the product. Any brand name is acceptable if it does not mislead the consumer.

VINTAGE DATE

A vintage date on the label indicates that 95 percent or more of the wine is produced from grapes grown in that year. If a vintage date is shown on the label, an appellation of origin, smaller than a country, must also be shown.

APPELLATION OF ORIGIN

Appellation of origin is simply another name for the place in which the dominant grapes used in the wine are grown. It can be the name of a country, state, county or geographic region called a viticultural area.

A country, state or county appellation on the label means that at least 75 percent of the wine is produced from grapes grown in the place named.

VITICULTURAL AREA

A U.S. viticultural area is a defined grape-growing region with soil, climate, history and geographic features that set it apart from the surrounding area.

A viticultural area appellation on the label indicates that 85 percent or more of the wine is produced from grapes grown in the particular area.

NET CONTENTS

The net contents of wine is stated in the metric system of measure and is the amount of product in the container.

VARIETAL DESIGNATIONS

Varietal designations are the names of the dominent grapes used in the wine. Cabernet Sauvignon, Chardonnay, Zinfandel, and Merlot are examples of grape varieties. A varietal designation on the label requires an appellation of origin and means that at least 75 percent of the grapes used to make the wine are that variety. (Except *"Vitis labrusca"* grapes such as Concord which require 51%).

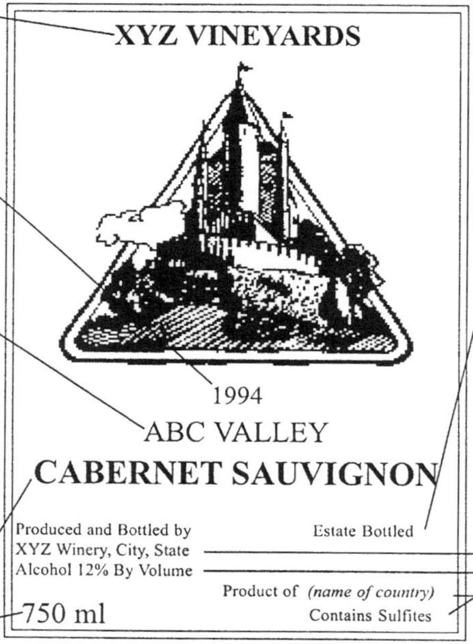

OTHER DESIGNATIONS

Wine labels are not required to bear a varietal designation. Other designations may be used to identify the wine. Examples are Red Wine, White Wine, Table Wine.

Designations such as Chablis, Chianti, or Burgundy include wines similar to those originally made in the geographic regions indicated by those names but now produced elsewhere. Such wines must include an appellation of origin to indicate the truw place of origin. For example *"California Burgundy."*

Some wines are designated with distinctive names which is permissible only on specific wines from a particular place or region within the country of origin, for example, Asti Spumanti from Italy and Bordeaux from France.

ESTATE BOTTLED

"Estate Bottled" means that 100 percent of the wine came from grapes grown on land owned or controlled by the winery, which must be located in a viticultural area. The winery must crush and ferment the grapes, finish, age, process and bottle the wine on their premises.

NAME AND ADDRESS

The name or trade name and address(es) of the bottler or importer must appear on the label. Domestic wines will state "**Bottled By:**" followed by the name and address of the bottler. Imported wines will state "**Imported By:**" followed by the name and address of the importer.

COUNTRY OF ORIGIN

A country of origin statement is required on all imported wines. For example, "**Product of *(insert name of country)***".

ALCOHOL CONTENT

A statement of alcohol content in percent by volume appears on most labels. As an alternative some bottlers prefer to label wine with an alcohol content between 7 and 14 percent as *"Table Wine"* or *"Light Wine."*

DECLARATION OF SULFITES

Required on any wine intended for interstate commerce that contains 10 or more parts per million (ppm) sulfur dioxide. Not required for wines only sold in intrastate commerce.

HEALTH WARNING STATEMENT

Required on all alcoholic beverages containing .5% or more alcohol by volume. "***GOVERNMENT WARNING***" must appear in capital letters and bold type. The remainder of the statement may not appear in bold type. The statement reads as follows:

GOVERNMENT WARNING:
(1) According to the Surgeon General, women should not drink alcoholic beverages during pregnancy because of the risk of birth defects. (2) Consumption of alcoholic beverages impairs your ability to drive a car or operate machinery, and may cause health problems.

FIGURE 16.1 Source: *What You Should Know About Grape Wine Labels,* Bureau of Alcohol, Tobacco and Firearms, Washington, DC.

The controversy about health labels is worth noting. In 1999 the U.S. government approved so-called *directional* labels for wines, which simply informed consumers to talk with their doctors about the health effects of wine consumption or to send for a government pamphlet on dietary guidelines. Figure 16.2 is an example of a California winery's label that the BATF disallowed even though the idea had originally been approved. The agency gave in to pressure from a number of groups, from the Federal Trade Commission, to the American Heart Association, to the Center for Science in the Public Interest. By 2003 the newly formed TTB was charged with coming up with new label language. The TTB decided that if a health claim was to be made, it must be accompanied by the following disclaimer:

> *"This statement should not encourage you to drink or to increase your alcohol consumption for health reasons."*

This statement created as much of an uproar in the industry as the original health statement. As of this writing wineries have opted to use neither the statement nor the disclaimer on their bottles. For the wine industry this refusal is about getting the government to admit that perhaps wine consumption has some benefits after all. This is an uphill battle, however, since our society in general has not adequately differentiated between simple enjoyment, such as wine appreciation, and alcohol abuse.

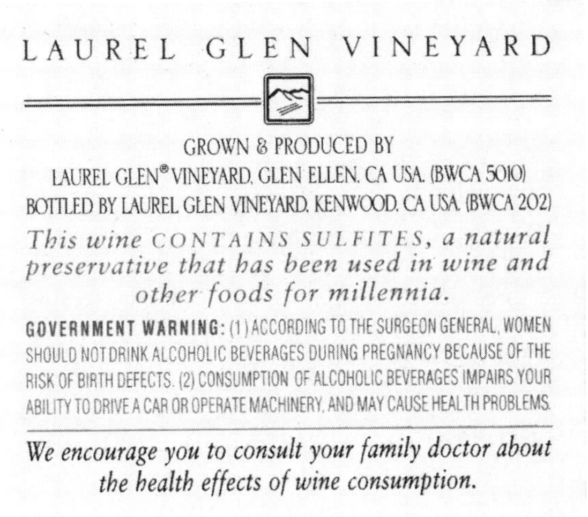

LAUREL GLEN VINEYARD

GROWN & PRODUCED BY
LAUREL GLEN® VINEYARD, GLEN ELLEN, CA USA (BWCA 5010)
BOTTLED BY LAUREL GLEN VINEYARD, KENWOOD, CA USA (BWCA 202)

This wine CONTAINS SULFITES, a natural preservative that has been used in wine and other foods for millennia.

GOVERNMENT WARNING: (1) ACCORDING TO THE SURGEON GENERAL, WOMEN SHOULD NOT DRINK ALCOHOLIC BEVERAGES DURING PREGNANCY BECAUSE OF THE RISK OF BIRTH DEFECTS. (2) CONSUMPTION OF ALCOHOLIC BEVERAGES IMPAIRS YOUR ABILITY TO DRIVE A CAR OR OPERATE MACHINERY, AND MAY CAUSE HEALTH PROBLEMS.

We encourage you to consult your family doctor about the health effects of wine consumption.

FIGURE 16.2 This back-bottle label is an example of an attempt to satisfy the federal government requirements with a friendly, common sense approach. Unfortunately the wording was disallowed. Label courtesy of Laurel Glen Vineyard, Glen Ellen, California.

Other label requirements, including alcohol content and proof, are spelled out depending on the specific type of beverage and the laws and rules in its country of origin.

The Organic Wine Debate

While some may argue that wine is a natural product, most wines are not made strictly from grapes grown in certified organic vineyards. Another controversy arose when winemakers began putting statements on labels in the 1980s to the effect that certain wines were "made from organically grown grapes." At issue here was not so much the source of the grapes as the small percentage of people have allergic reactions to *sulfites*. These antibacterial and antioxidant agents are routinely added to many wines to stabilize them during the winemaking process. Sulfur dioxide is often added even if the grapes are organically grown and in fact some sulfites are found naturally on the grapes themselves.

Beginning in 1987 another statement was required on the labels of all wines sold in the United States: "Contains Sulfites." If sulfur dioxide was not intentionally added, some wineries got away with the terms "Contains only naturally-occurring sulfites" or "No added sulfites." Either way the issue was confusing.

The U.S. Department of Agriculture (USDA) contended for years that the presence of sulfites makes wine a "manufactured" product, not "organic." After much industry debate the labeling rules adopted after 2000 for alcoholic beverages seem to suggest a bit of concession on that point. They are part of the USDA's National Organic Program, which the BATF has approved. The current labeling rules are as follows:

- If producers want to claim that a product is "100 percent organic," it must contain 100-percent organically produced ingredients (not counting added water and salt). The label must include an ingredient statement, and it can state that an ingredient is "organic," except for water and salt. It must also include the phrase "Certified organic by ______" and fill in the name of the Certifying Agent. Merely using the Certifying Agent seal is not sufficient. (The label may also include a "USDA Organic" seal, but this is optional.)
- To be called "organic" a product must contain at least 95-percent organic ingredients (again, not including water and salt). The remaining 5 percent can be "agricultural ingredients which are not commercially available in organic form," and other substances, including yeast, that are outlined in the federal Code of Regulations. The mandatory verbiage on the "organic" label is the same as the "100-percent organic" designation; optional details are to add the percentages of

THE NATIONAL LABORATORY CENTER

The National Laboratory Center in Ammendale, Maryland is a $108-million facility and the home of the Scientific Services Division of the TTB. The Center has been analyzing alcohol products (and other food and beverage items) since the 1880s.

Today technology can allow the lab to verify the geographic origins of wine, test for pesticide content, and authenticate types and amounts of varietal grapes found in the wines. Origin, for example, is confirmed by compaing trace elements found in the wine with soil samples from the vineyard and region. While so many factors in winemaking vary from year to year with different vintages and techniques, the trace-mineral content of soils and grapes remains relatively constant.

Wine samples are routinely tested for 150 different pesticides, harmful metal residues, and ethyl carbonate, a byproduct of fermentation that is a suspected carcinogen. Grape varieties are verified by analyzing the volatile organic compounds (VOGs) in the wine. This method has not been perfected for all varietals but scientists at the National Laboratory Center can now differentiate chemically between four white grapes (Chardonnay, Pinot Grigio, Riesling, and Sauvignon Blanc) and four red grapes (Cabernet Sauvignon, Merlot, Pinot Noir, and Zinfandel).

Then again, wine aficionados can probably do this a lot more cost effectively . . . by tasting them! The National Laboratory Center's annual budget for wine-testing tops $600,000.

(**Source:** Adapted from *The Wine Spectator,* San Francisco, California, January 15, 2005, issue.)

organic ingredients and the Certifying Agent seal. This classification of organic beverage cannot show the "USDA Organic" seal on its label.

In both cases the wine must not contain *added* sulfites, but it *can* contain a minimal amount of natural sulfites from the grapes themselves.

Records, Inspections, and Audits

The federal government requires you to keep records of all spirits, wines, and beers received: quantities, names of sellers, and dates received. You may keep this information in book form, on computer, or in the form of all of your invoices and bills. State and local governments may require you to keep daily records of gross sales, especially if you must pay sales taxes or collect them from the customer. You must keep all of your records for at least three years.

Your place of business, your stock of liquors, your records, and your special tax stamp and receipt are subject to inspection at any time by BATF officers, as shown

FIGURE 16.3 A BATF inspector checks the labels on alcohol bottles to ensure compliance with federal labeling and alcohol tax-payment requirements. Photo courtesy of the Bureau of Alcohol, Tobacco and Firearms, Washington, DC.

in Figure 16.3. An inspection is unlikely unless they think that you might have some evidence that would help them to trace someone who has broken the law. Your licenses and permits, your records, and your entire operation are also subject to inspection by state and local officials if your state and local codes so state—which they probably do. All such officials carry identification that they must show to you. Once you have verified their identity you must show them anything that they want to see.

If there are state or local sales taxes you will undoubtedly be required to collect them from your customers. To be able to prove that you have done so you must keep daily records of the sales of taxable items, with separate records for each category of taxables (beer, wine, spirits, mixed drinks) if the tax rates distinguish between them. The simplest way to keep these records is the point-of-sale (POS) cash register with a separate key for each category. Each category will be totaled separately, and you will have a printed record on the tape. You must keep your daily records for however long state and local laws specify.

You will be required to make sales-tax reports and payments at regular intervals, and your records will be subject to a revenue audit. In most states you can count on being audited at least once a year, often at random. The primary goal of the auditor is to verify that a bar's actual beverage sales match what the bar has reported to the state for taxes and fees. The auditor looks at the potential sales revenue for a single bottle of liquor by asking about the pour size or portion size—i.e., the number of drinks you can make from one bottle. The calculation is much like the basic beverage-costing method you learned in Chapter 14. If a 1-liter bottle holds 33.8 ounces of liquor and you pour 1.5 ounces per drink, you should be able to get 22 drinks per bottle. If you sell them for an average price of $4 each, the result is a potential sales revenue of $88 per bottle.

The auditor then asks to see your invoices. How many bottles has the bar purchased? The auditor will take an inventory of all beverages on the premises and subtract the existing stock from the purchases to determine how much was actually used. From this point it is a simple matter of multiplication: the total number of bottles purchased by the potential revenue per bottle to determine how much was sold. The taxes and fees that you owe will be determined by this method.

The process is contentious because there is a wide range of methods to account for *shrinkage*—that pesky combination of overpouring, spillage, and theft. Most state auditors allow up to 8-percent shrinkage. (Using the example above, 8-percent shrinkage translates into 1.76 drinks per 1-liter bottle.) Often however reality is not so formulaic. What about drink promotions, during which a bar sells one drink for $5 but a double for $8 (not $10)? If a bartender routinely overpours, giving customers 2 ounces instead of 1.5, the audit will show that the bar has underreported its sales by 25 percent! You'll be assessed additional taxes and perhaps penalties on drinks for which you received no revenue.

The following common-sense suggestions from experts will enable you to minimize audit-related problems:

- Eliminate overpouring, which can usually be accomplished through bartender training, the use of specific recipes, and continual reminders. A BEVINCO (independent inventory control firm) survey conducted for the California Restaurant Association found that the average bar loss due to shrinkage was 25 percent.
- Buy an up-to-date POS system that allows separation of spirits, wine, and beer sales by category and can track promotional activities. The more detailed your sales reports the better your evidence for auditors.
- During an audit be sure to give the auditor all of your pour sizes. Often they are as different as the drinks themselves, and the auditor take should this into account.
- Keep detailed notes on such items as sales promotions, changes in glassware sizes, mystery-shoppers' reports, and incidents of spillage and/or breakage for a period of at least three years. Most state auditors will consider all of the evidence that you can provide. A *complete lack of evidence* to support your assertions is what will get you into trouble.

Another frequent provision of state beverage codes concerns the credit that you may extend to customers. A few states forbid the practice entirely, requiring that all drinks be paid for in cash. Other states permit customers to charge drinks to their hotel bills or club-membership accounts or to pay by credit card. Still others have no **credit restrictions.**

Advertising Requirements

Nearly all codes set limits on advertising involving alcoholic beverages. The federal government has stringent regulations designed to prevent false, misleading, or offensive product advertising. Most states follow suit. Code provisions that might affect a beverage-service enterprise concern billboards advertising your bar or restaurant, the content of magazine and newspaper ads, signs identifying your place or your products, and window displays. Many beverage codes forbid ads associating your products with provocative women, biblical characters, and Santa Claus.

A final category of regulation involves keeping your enterprise an acceptable member of your community. The following are some of the kinds of actions for which, under some state or local laws, you may be liable for fines, imprisonment, or loss of license:

- Possessing or selling an illegal beverage
- Permitting lewd, immoral, or indecent conduct or entertainment on your premises (exposure of person, obscene language, disturbing display of a deadly weapon, prostitution, narcotics possession or use)
- Disturbing the peace

As you can see regulations pose plenty of potential pitfalls for bar owners and restaurateurs. Keep up with the current controversies, legal changes, and legal opinions by reading the industry trade journals. It can be frustrating that there seems to be no aspect of manufacturing, importing, selling, or advertising that escapes the scrutiny of at least one level of government. (That side of the story is beyond the scope of this book.) If you find the laws bewildering, contradictory, and time-consuming you are not alone. It helps to see them in the perspective of history and to realize that the seeming chaos simply developed in response to differing local needs and desires, with a good bit of emotion and politics thrown in to keep the regulatory process interesting. It also helps to realize that frustration and contradiction are not premanent but can be amended through education, the political lobby, and the voting machine.

Recognizing that many of the regulations benefit and protect you also helps. Thanks to regulations you have a product of guaranteed consistency and an environment of free and fair competition. Within the framework of regulation the beverage industry is an essential and respected element in the economic and social fabric of the United States. When it comes to profitability that is worth a lot in terms of goodwill.

So inform yourself of your local laws, pay your beverage taxes (budgeting them firmly into your profit plan), and comfort yourself with the thought that beverage laws are necessary precisely because the demand for your product is inexhaustible.

SUMMING UP

The sale of alcoholic beverages is highly regulated in many places and the beverages themselves are heavily taxed. There might be even more regulation if alcohol was not such a good source of revenue for all levels of government.

In some states alcohol is sold in stores like any other product. In other states the sale of alcohol is carefully regulated by liquor-control or alcoholic-beverage commissions, and sold only through state-run stores or authorized retailers who must purchase their inventory from the state system. Everyone who sells alcohol must have some sort of license or permit to do so; for a bar or restaurant you are licensed as an *on-premise retail dealer.* **On-premise** means that people consume the alcohol on your premises; **off-premise** means a store situation, where people buy the liquor then consume it elsewhere. There is also federal registration (and in most years, an annual fee) required by the recently created (in 2002) Alcohol and Tobacco Tax and Trade Bureau (TTB), which is part of the U.S Treasury Department. The Bureau of Alcohol, Tobacco and Firearms (BATF) continues to play an investigative and enforcement role in the picture, as part of the U.S. Justice Department. There are also plenty of city and county ordinances, including local health and safety standards and building codes, with which to comply.

The observance of existing laws, however absurd some of them might seem, is important for two reasons: One is for your own immediate good; the other is for the good of the industry as a whole. If the industry is to maintain a respected place in American life bar owners must all be law-abiding citizens. As a business owner, you can buy alcohol only from licensed wholesale distributors (or from the state, in a control state). A 2005 Supreme Court ruling allowed interstate wine deliveries to consumers who order online for home consumption, but it might not necessarily allow a bar owner to purchase for an on-premise business that way. As of this writing, the full impact of the ruling is still unclear.

There are long-accepted rules about what kinds of extras or "special" deals you can accept from wholesale distributors. A wholesaler cannot for instance have a financial or legal interest in your business, premises, or equipment, or make special payment arrangements for you that are not offered to others.

The bottles themselves must be sealed in such a way that you know that they have not been tampered with when you receive them. Furthermore empty bottles cannot be reused, and the contents of two partial bottles cannot be combined—all requirements of federal law. This chapter covered labeling requirements in some depth, and you will discover more on your own.

The laws—and all of the paperwork that you must keep current to prove that you are abiding by them—are reminders that the dual nature of alcohol is always with you and that you operate within the shadow of its dark side. It is important for anyone in the industry to keep up to date on legal issues and changes.

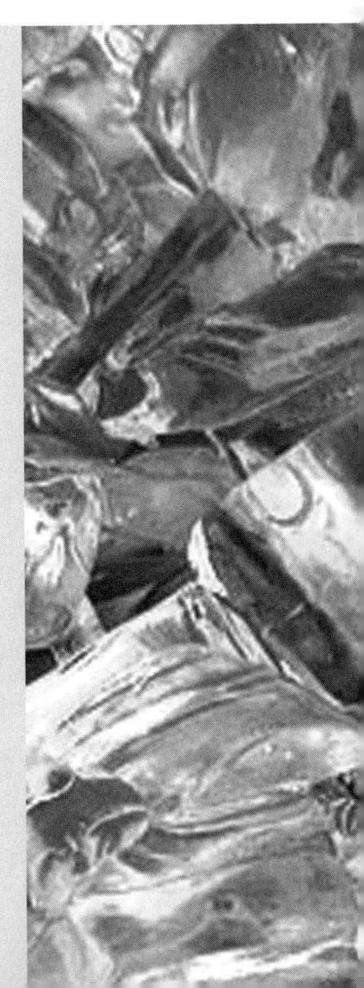

POINTS TO PONDER

1. In what ways does a bar operator benefit from government regulations that apply to alcoholic beverages?
2. Banning bars prevents what kinds of problems in a community? What kinds of problems does it create?
3. What is a local option law?
4. Why should a supplier not be allowed to own a bar or restaurant?
5. Why do you think federal taxes are higher for sparkling wines than for still wines?
6. In your community what are the procedures for obtaining the required licenses to operate a full bar?
7. Why should age be a barrier to buying a drink?
8. What is your opinion of online alcohol sales? If you were writing a realistic set of rules, what would be allowed and what would be illegal? Should the rules be different for beer, wine, and spirits? If so, how?
9. What is the purpose of the tamper-evident stamp on liquor bottles?
10. What kinds of records should you keep to be able to pay the proper amount of taxes for selling alcohol?

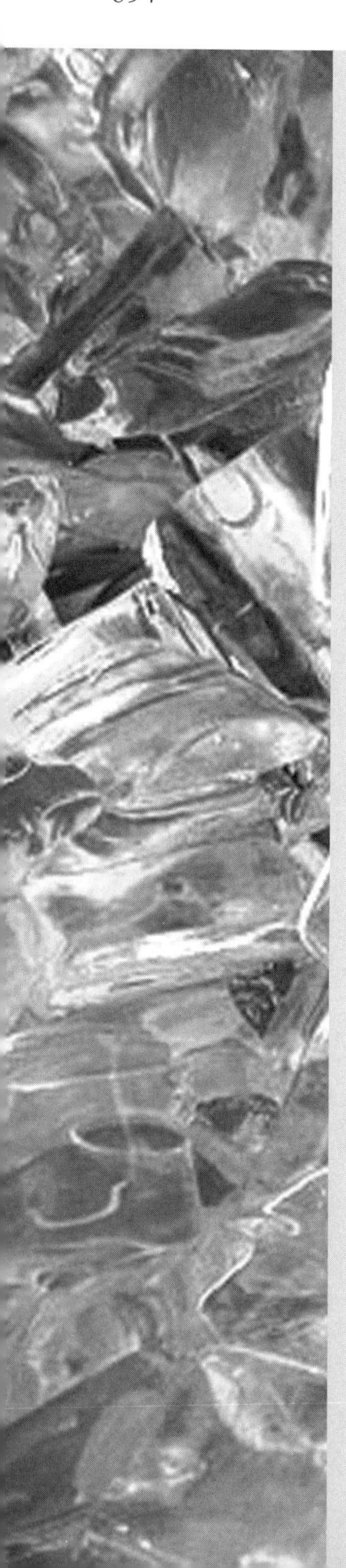

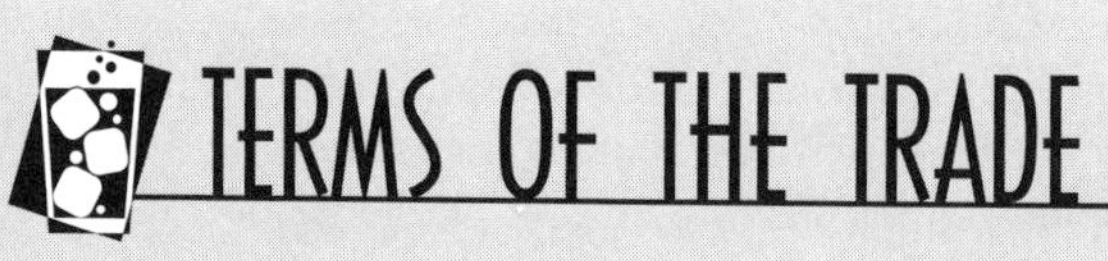

TERMS OF THE TRADE

Alcohol and Tobacco Tax and Trade Bureau (TTB)
Bureau of Alcohol, Tobacco and Firearms (BATF)
clearly (or visibly) intoxicated
control (monopoly) states
credit restrictions
dealer at large
excise tax
inducements to purchase
legal drinking age
license
license states
local option
marrying
off-premise
on-premise
permit
Special Occupational Tax (SOT)
strip stamp
tamper-evident closure
tax stamp
tied-house
wholesaler's basic permit

Glossary

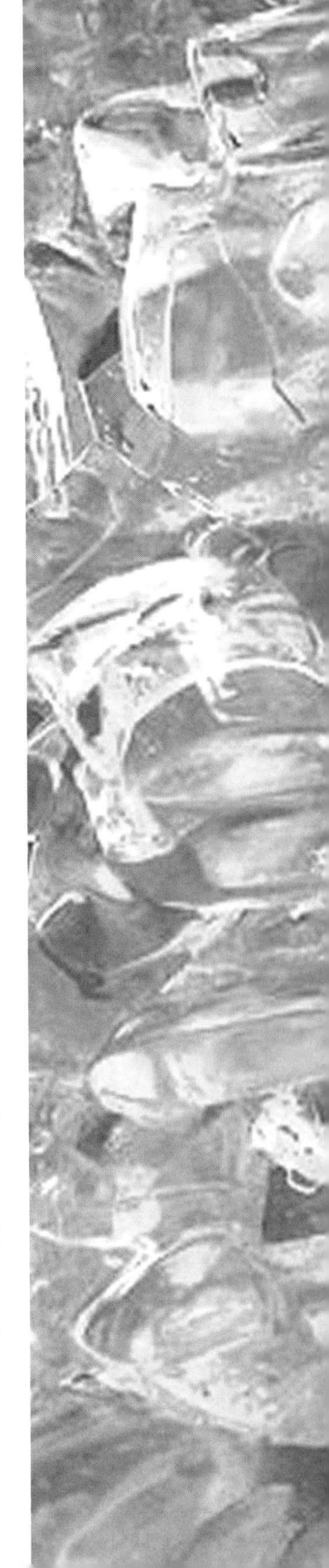

Absinthe. An herbal liqueur from France (also made in the Czech Republic and Bulgaria) that is strictly regulated for containing a small amount of a nerve-damaging ingredient called *alpha thujone*. It is illegal to purchase Absinthe in the United States due to its extremely high alcohol content.

Acetaldehyde. A by-product of the human liver when metabolizing alcohol that prompts inflammation and may stimulate the immune system.

Adjunct. Any cereal grain added to malted barley in making beer. Also called a *malt adjunct* or *grain adjunct*.

Aging. The storing of wine or spirits in wooden casks for a period of time to improve flavor.

Aguardiente (ah-GWAHR-dee-EN-tay). The Mexican name for rum whose sugar-cane-based spirits exceed 50 percent.

Ah-so. A wine-opening device that consists of two prongs, which are wedged into the neck of the bottle between the cork and the glass and twisted.

Alberino (al-behr-EEN-yoh). A grape that makes a popular Spanish white wine of the same name, full-bodied and lightly sweet.

Alcohol and Tobacco Tax and Trade Bureau. A federal agency in the U.S. Treasury Department responsible for licensing, taxing, and regulating the labeling of alcohol and tobacco products sold in the United States. Abbreviated TTB.

Alcoholic. A person who is addicted to alcoholic beverages.

Alcoholic beverage. A potable liquid containing .5 percent or more of ethyl alcohol (by definition under federal law).

Alcoholism. An addiction to alcoholic beverages.

Ale. A malt beverage (beer) made by top fermentation at lukewarm temperatures.

Alembic, alambic. A copper pot still used in distilling Cognac.

Altbier. German for *old beer*, made in a traditional Rhineland style using both ale and lager techniques. Known for a coppery red color and very hoppy flavor; top-fermented and cold-lagered.

Amaretto. An almond-flavored liqueur.

Ambience. Another term for *atmosphere*; the overall sensory and psychological impact of surroundings.

Amphora. Airtight clay containers that the ancient Greeks used for wine storage. See *pitching*.

Anejo tequila. A tequila that has been aged in wood for at least one year. The word *anejo* means "aged" in Spanish.

Angostura (ANN-goh-STIR-ra). Condiment bitters from Trinidad.

Anisette. A generic name for a sweet liqueur made with anise seed, fruit peels, and other herbs.

Annealing. The slow-cooling process used to harden melted glass; part of the process of making glassware.

Aperitif (a-PAIR-ih-TEEF). 1. A fortified wine flavored with herbs and spices. 2. A wine served as an appetizer before a meal.

Appellation controlee (ah-pel-la-SEE-awn kawn-tro-LAY). A phrase on a French-wine label indicating that the wine comes from the controlled area named and meets its strict legal standards.

Applejack. A U.S. brandy distilled from apple cider and aged in wood.

Apricot brandy. On a U.S. bottle, a brandy made from apricots. On an imported bottle, an apricot-flavored liqueur made from brandy.

Approved Viticultural Appellation. The U.S. counterpart of the European appellation system; the phrase is applied to a unique vineyard area officially defined and controlled. Abbreviated AVA.

Aquavit (ah-kwa-VEET). A Norwegian spirit (spelled *akvavit* in Denmark) much like vodka; made from potatoes, and most often flavored with caraway.

Aqua vitae (OCK-wah VY-tah). An early Latin term for a distilled spirit. The literal translation is *water of life*.

Arak, arrack. A brandy-like rum from Indonesia, aged in The Netherlands.

Armagnac (AR-mun-yak). A brandy made in the Armagnac district of France.

Aroma. A fruity or flowery scent of a wine, beer, or spirit.

Aromatized wine. A fortified wine to which aromatic herbs and spices have been added, such as vermouth.

Assorted discount. A price reduction based on quantity purchases: i.e., "Buy five cases and get a 20-percent discount." Also called a *multiple-brands discount*.

Astringent. A wine-tasting term referring to an aspect of the wine that makes the mouth pucker.

Auslese (AUSCH-lay-za). A German wine made from particularly ripe grapes picked very selectively in bunches.

Bacchus. The god of wine in Roman mythology; still used as a popular symbol of wines and drinking.

Backbar. The rear structure of the bar behind the bartender, including storage, equipment, glassware, and liquor displays.

Balance. A term in wine tasting that describes how the components in a wine relate to each other to form a "good" or harmonious overall taste.

Bank. The amount of starting cash 1. in the register, for making change; or 2. in some payment systems, the cash carried by each server.

Bank-count slip. A paper (similar to a deposit slip) on which a list of all of the bills and coins is made for the start and/or end of a business day or work shift.

Barback. A bartender's helper, usually an apprentice bartender.

Barbera (bar-BAHR-uh). An Italian red grape (also grown extensively in California) used primarily for blending with other reds.

Bar-code scanner. A handheld device that reads the Universal Product Code bar codes commonly affixed to most items sold today. See *Universal Product Code*.

Bar cost. See *beverage-cost percentage*.

Bar die. The vertical structure that supports the front portion of the bar and shields the underbar from public view.

Bar knife. A small to medium-size stainless-steel knife, such as a paring or utility knife.

Barley. The primary grain used to make beer and scotch. *Two-row* and *six-row* barley are used for this purpose, so named because of the numbers of rows of individual grains on the heads of each stalk.

Bar manager. The person in charge of all of the aspects of operation in a bar, or all of the aspects of beverage operation in a restaurant.

Bar mixer. A blender used strictly for making mixed and frozen drinks.

Barrel. 1. In beer-making, a 31-gallon glass- or stainless-steel-lined tank. Breweries' output is measured in barrels. 2. In making distilled spirits or wines, the wooden casks in which the liquid is stored to age and mature it.

Barrel house. The storage area for barrels at a bourbon-making distillery.

Barspoon. A shallow, long-handled spoon for mixing drinks, equal to 1 teaspoon.

Bar strainer. A round wire coil on a handle, used with a mixing glass or a shaker to strain a freshly mixed drink into a glass.

Bar sugar. A superfine sugar.

Bartender. A person who mixes and serves drinks to bar customers and fills drink orders for servers.

Base. The primary liquor in a mixed drink; usually at least a jigger.

Bureau of Alcohol, Tobacco, and Firearms. The U.S. Justice Department agency responsible for the enforcement of some laws related to these items. It works with the TTB to enforce alcoholic-beverage laws. Abbreviated BATF.

Beer. 1. A fermented beverage made from malted grain (usually barley), water, hops, and yeast. 2. A fermented grain mixture, or *wort,* from which whiskey or grain neutral spirits are distilled; distiller's beer.

Beer box. A refrigerator specially designed for a draft-beer system. Also called a *tap box.*

Beer-clean glass. A glass that is free of grease, soap, and lint.

Beerenauslese (BAHR-un-OUSCH-lay-zuh). A German wine made from individually picked, perfectly ripened grapes.

Beer gas. A mixture of carbon dioxide and nitrogen in a container used in a draft-beer system to keep the beer carbonated and to propel it through the lines from keg to tap.

Beer system. A draft-beer supply system, consisting of a keg of beer, a beer box, a tap, lines, and a carbon-dioxide cylinder.

Beginning inventory. The dollar value of the physical inventory at the beginning of an accounting period (which should be equal to the ending inventory of a previous accounting period).

Belgian ale. A beer made in Belgium, either by the Trappist-abbey-owned breweries licensed to make them or in the style of the traditional Trappist products. Also called *abbey ales* or *abbey beers.*

Benedictine. A prestigious French liqueur made by Benedictine monks from a secret recipe of herbs.

Beverage cost. The cost of spirits, wine, and beer for a given time period, determined by subtracting the beginning inventory from the ending inventory for that period.

Beverage-cost method. A formula for pricing mixed drinks based on the costs of their individual ingredients.

Beverage-cost percentage. A beverage cost expressed as a percentage of sales. Often called simply *bar cost.*

Beverage director, beverage manager. The person in charge of all phases of beverage operation in a large organization. Also may be called *beverage steward.*

Bin card. A storeroom card for each beverage item showing the bin number and the amount of stock on hand.

Bin number. A number assigned to each wine on a wine list, which makes it easier to organize and inventory, and easy for customers to refer to it by number if they cannot pronounce the name.

Binge drinking. Consuming four or more alcoholic beverages (for women; five or more alcoholic beverages for men) in rapid succession, usually in a party setting.

Bitter. A British-style ale, high in flavor and low in alcohol.

Bitters. Spirits flavored with such items as herbs, bark, and fruits, without the addition of sugar. *Flavoring bitters* are used in minute quantities as condiments; *beverage bitters* are potable beverages.

Blanc de blancs (blawn da BLAWN). A white wine made entirely from white grapes; usually a Champagne made from the Chardonnay grape.

Blanc de noirs (blawn deh n'WAHR). A white wine made from red grapes; usually Champagne made from the Pinot Noir grape.

Blend. 1. To mix, or *marry,* wines or spirits of different ages, character, or origin before bottling. 2. To mix a drink in a blender.

Blended American whiskey. A whiskey containing at least 20-percent straight whiskey plus neutral spirits, with no aging requirement.

Blended gas. A combination of carbon dioxide and nitrogen used in a draft-beer system. See *beer gas.*

Blonde beer. An ale or lager with a very light color and a medium-bodied flavor.

Blood alcohol content. The percentage of alcohol in an individual's blood; used as a measure of the degree of intoxication. Abbreviated BAC.

Blue agave. The type of desert plant used to make Tequila; grown in five specific government-authorized regions of Mexico. Also called *maguey* in some parts of Mexico.

Blush wine. A wine made from red grapes in which the grapes' skin is separated from the juice soon after crushing, giving the wine a pale (pink or peach) color instead of dark red.

BMSW. Abbreviation for Blended Malt Scotch Whisky. A blend of single-malt Scotch whiskies from more than one distillery. Also called *vatted malts* or *pure malts.*

Bock beer. A rich, heavy, dark, malty beer, high in alcohol, made seasonally in Germany; also made in various styles in the United States.

Body. 1. Of a wine, the feel of a wine in the mouth, the result of its alcohol, sugar, and glycerin content. 2. Of a spirit, the amount of flavor and aroma.

Bonded warehouse. A warehouse in which liquor is stored under government supervision.

Born-on date. A type of freshness dating, using the date on which a beer was canned or bottled. Abbreviated BOD.

Botanicals. Herbs and spices used as flavorings in spirits, especially liqueurs, and fortified wines.

Botrytis cinerea (bo-TRY-das sin-AIR-ee-a). A mould that dries ripened grapes, concentrating their sugar and flavor (French *pourriture noble;* German *Edelfaule*). The literal translation is *noble rot.* These grapes are used to make supersweet dessert wines of high quality.

Bottled in Bond. A phrase on a bottle's label indicating that the spirit inside is straight, distilled at 160 proof or less at one plant by one distiller, aged at least four years, and bottled at 100 proof in a bonded warehouse.

Bottom fermentation. A method of making lager beers in which yeasts act from the bottom of a fermenting tank at low temperatures.

Bouncer. A security person for a bar whose job is to be on the lookout for unruly behavior and underage patrons and to be able to deal with these issues firmly and politely.

Bouquet. A complex and interesting odor of a mature wine.

Bourbon. A whiskey made with 51 percent or more corn, plus other grains, and aged at least two years in charred new-oak containers.

Brandy. A distilled spirit made from wine or other fermented fruit juice.

Break-even point. The point in operating a business at which no profit is made and no loss is incurred. Handy to know because it enables you to track the minimum number of dollars that should be made each day to show a profit.

Breathe. A term for wine being exposed to air when it is first opened. Also called *aeration.*

Brewer's yeast. Special types of yeast used in beer-making. Also called *ale yeast* or *lager yeast.*

Brewpub. A bar/restaurant combination in which at least some of the beer served is brewed on-site.

Broken case. A case of 12 bottles made up of different items. Also called a *mixed case.*

Brown goods. A nickname for whiskies and brandies—spirits dark in color and with hearty flavors.

Bruised beer. A beer that has been warmed and cooled again, which may suffer in quality as a result.

Brut (BROOT or brutt). A French term on a Champagne label, indicating that the Champagne is *dry* (meaning the grapes used to make it contained little or no sugar); the driest style of Champagne.

Budget. A financial plan for a given period that coordinates anticipated income and expenditures to ensure solvency and to yield a profit.

Build. To mix a drink in its glass.

Bundling. Offering more than one item (for example, a bottle of wine with two dinner entrees) as a combination, often for a single or special price.

Cabernet Franc (CAB-ur-NAY fronk). A relative of the Cabernet Sauvignon grape; often used for blending.

Cabernet Sauvignon (CAB-ur-NAY so-vin-YON). One of the world's most important grape varietals; used to make red wines of Bordeaux in France; also in California, Australia, and other reds.

Cachaca (cah-CHOK-ah). A Brazilian-made rum made from unrefined sugarcane juice.

Call brand. A brand of liquor specified by a customer ordering a drink; a brand frequently requested ("called for") by name.

Cage. The wire hood that encases a Champagne bottle cork, holding it firmly in place.

Calvados (KAL-vah-dose). A French apple brandy.

Campari. A bitter Italian spirit, which is 48 proof; among the most popular of the beverage bitters.

Canadian whiskey. A blended whiskey imported from Canada; light in flavor and body; aged at least three years.

Capital risk. Financial risks that, through a number of ways, may be preventable, such as waste, breakage, and spillage.

Capsule. The foil or plastic cap covering the top of a wine bottle.

Carafe (kah-RAFF). A glass container used to serve house wines; holds two to four glasses.

Carrying costs. The total dollar value of your inventory; items for which you have already paid but have not yet been sold or used.

Cash flow. The cash that comes into and goes out of a business. Tracked as a *cash-flow forecast* or *cash budget.*

Cash register. A machine for recording and totaling sales. See *POS.*

Cask-conditioned beer. A secondary fermentation of beer, done by adding yeast and priming wort to a wooden cask called a *firkin.* The beer is served directly from the firkin.

Cask strength. A term used on a whiskey label that means that no water was added to the whiskey to dilute it before bottling.

Category management. Tracking specific sales to see what sells well and what does not, then using that information to make more profitable business decisions.

Cava. A Spanish-made sparkling wine.

Cellarmaster. See *sommelier* or *wine steward.*

Cellar temperature. For the wine storeroom, 55°F to 60°F (12.8°C to 15.6°C).

Chalice. A footed, wide-mouthed glass appropriate for European beer styles, such as ale.

Chambord. A French liqueur flavored with raspberries.

Champagne process. The French process of making Champagne, in which yeast and sugar are added to a bottle of still wine, which then undergoes a second fermentation in the bottle.

Chapitalization. In winemaking, the process of adding extra sugar before fermentation when grapes do not contain enough natural sugar of their own.

Chardonnay. One of the world's top white-wine grapes or the wine of the same name. It is also the grape used to make French Chablis and White Burgundies.

Charmat (shar-MAH) **process.** The method of making a sparkling wine in a large closed container under pressure rather than in individual bottles. Also called *bulk process* or *charmat bulk process.*

Chartreuse. A brightly colored, very expensive, herbal liqueur; made in a single monastery from a secret recipe since the seventeenth century.

Chaser. An additional liquid, such as beer or water, drunk immediately after gulping a *shot* of alcohol.

Chateau (shah-TOE). A vineyard in France. Some U.S. vineyards have picked up the term in naming their wineries.

Chateau-bottled. A wine bottled at the vineyard by its owner, made exclusively from grapes grown at that vineyard.

Chenin Blanc (SHEN-in BLONK). A popular white grape used to make wines of the same name, as well as the Vouvray wines (in France) and the Steen wines (in South Africa).

Claret. The British term for a red Bordeaux wine.

Classified growth. Wines from the chateaux of France that have been recognized for their high quality. The classification began in 1855 and lists the wineries (chateaux) by "first growth" (best and most prestigious) to "fifth growth" (also excellent). The classifications are subjective, and a great deal has changed since 1855.

Coarse salt. A salt that is larger than table salt and is used for *rimming* glasses. Also called *kosher salt* or *Margarita salt.*

Cobra gun. The dispensing head of an automatic beverage-dispensing system, for soft drink or liquor pouring. So named because of the lines that "snake" toward its head; the head itself has buttons on it that are pushed to dispense each beverage. Also called a *handgun* or *six-shooter.*

Cocktail. A mixed drink.

Cocktail glass. A stemmed glass with a flared bowl, usually holding 3 to 5 ounces.

Cognac (CONE-yak). A brandy made in the Cognac district of France.

Cointreau (KWON-trow). A brand-name liqueur that is a blend of several citrus fruits.

Collins glass. A tumbler that holds 10 to 12 ounces.

Collins mix. A sweet-and-sour combination of lemon juice, sugar, and club soda used to make Collins drinks.

Compound gin. A gin made or flavored by mixing high-proof spirits with the extracts of juniper berries or other botanicals.

Concept bar. A bar in which the décor transforms the space into an exotic place or another time period. Rainforest Cafés are examples of popular concept bar/restaurants.

Condiment. 1. A pungent or spicy product used to flavor drinks, such as bitters and Tabasco. 2. A garnish, used in this sense largely by manufacturers of condiment trays.

Condiment tray. A multicompartment tray in which garnishes (e.g., cherries, lemon wedges, and olives) are stored at a serving station.

Congeners (CON-jun-ers, or cun-JEEN-ers). Products present in minute amounts in fermented and distilled beverages; provide the beverages' distinctive flavors and aromas and certain features of a hangover.

Consultant. A specialist in design, market survey, feasibility, facilities design, and/or some other aspect of bar development or operation who works on a fee or retainer basis.

Continuous still. A continuously operating pair or series of interacting columns in which spirits are vaporized by steam. Also called a *column still,* a *patent still,* and a *Coffey still.*

Contract brewer. A brewery hired to make, label, and market private label brands for brewpubs, under contract. See *regional specialty brewery.*

Contribution margin. Sales less product cost. Also called *gross profit.*

Control. A means of preventing, detecting, measuring, or eliminating waste, error, and pilferage.

Control state. A state in which all alcoholic beverages are sold from state-run stores. Also called a *monopoly state.* Compare *license state.*

Cooler. 1. A bucket for wine service, in which wine is surrounded by crushed ice; a wine chiller. 2. Kitchen jargon for refrigerator. 3. A glass tumbler that holds 15 to 16 ounces. 4. A tall, iced drink.

Cordial. A brandy or other spirit sweetened and flavored with natural flavorers. Also called a *liqueur.*

Cordial glass. A stemmed glass that holds 1 to 3 ounces.

Corked. A term that describes a wine with an unpleasant taste, usually due to chemicals or substances on the cork coming into contact with the wine. See *2, 4, 6-Trichloroanisole.*

Cork retriever. The long wires on a handle that are used to grab a cork that has been pushed into a wine bottle and turned upright to remove it.

Corkscrew. A device with a spiral screw that is used to open a corked bottle. See *worm.*

Corn liquor. A whiskey made with 80 percent or more corn in the mash, aged in uncharred or used, charred oak barrels. Not common as a bar whiskey.

Costing. Establishing the exact cost of a drink by figuring the cost of each ingredient in its recipe.

Cost percentage. 1. A cost expressed as a percent of sales. 2. As a control method, a measurement of the actual bar cost percentage (based on a physical inventory) against standard bar cost percentages and past performance.

Count. The number of items in a container (necessary to cost a drink recipe).

Cover charge. A small entry fee charged at the door of a bar, usually when there is live entertainment; often used to pay the band or other entertainer.

CPU. Abbreviation for central processing unit, of a computerized register system (*POS*).

Craft brewery. Another term for *microbrewery.*

Credit memo. A seller's document crediting a buyer for short, broken, or otherwise unsatisfactory merchandise or mistakes on an invoice.

Crus classes (KROO clah-SAY). The formal quality ranking of chateaux wines in Bordeaux and certain other French wine districts. Also called *classified growths.*

Cruvinet (KROO-vin-AY). The brand name of a popular, temperature-controlled wine-storage cabinet.

Cryptosporidium. A common waterborne parasite that causes illness.

Cullet. Reused bits of broken glass, melted with soda, lime, and fine sand to make glass.

Curacao (KYOOR-a-sau). A liqueur made from the peel of a Caribbean fruit called the bitter orange.

Cup. 1. An 8-ounce liquid measure. 2. The metal can of a shaker or a blender. 3. A wine punch.

Cynar. A syrupy, dark brown Italian aperitif made of artichoke leaves.

Dash. A one-sixth teaspoonful, or about 10 drops of a liquid.

Dasher. A dispenser built into the neck of a bottle from which no more than a *dash* is usually dispensed, such as Tabasco or bitters.

Dealer at large. A liquor retailer who travels and makes sales in more than one state, such as a circus or carnival vendor.

Decant (dee-KANT). To carefully pour wine from a bottle to a carafe (or a *decanter*) so that the sediment remains in the bottle.

Delivery system. The process for ordering, producing, and delivering food and drinks to customers.

Demeraran rum. A rum made in Guyana; when specified in a drink recipe, it often means 151-proof rum.

Demi-sec. A French term on a Champagne label; the literal translation is *half dry,* but this is one of the sweetest styles of Champagne.

Demographics. Statistical data on population of a given area, such as age, income, dining habits, and lifestyle.

Denominazione di Origine Controllata (de-nom-ee-NATZ-ee-OH-na dee OR-ih-JEEN-ah KON-troh-LAT-ta). A phrase on an Italian wine label indicating that the wine comes from the controlled district named and meets its strict legal standards. Abbreviated D.O.C.

Denominazione di Origine Controllata Garantita. In Italy this label designation indicates that the wine meets even higher standards than the normal D.O.C. "Garantita" means *guaranteed.* Abbreviated D.O.C.G.

Depletion allowance form. A paper on which any problem with inventory is recorded: breakage, spills, transfers from one bar or site to another, or any beverage given away for any reason.

Dessert wine. 1. A class of fortified wines, often sweet, that includes port, sherry, Madeira, marsala, angelica, and muscatel. 2. Any sweet wine served at the end of a meal.

Detail tape. The paper tape made by a *POS* system or *cash register* as a way of documenting sales.

Diastase. The enzyme in *malt* (sprouted grain) that changes starches to sugars.

Die. A vertical structure that supports the top of the front bar and divides the customer's side from the bartender's side.

Dionysus. The god of wine in Greek mythology. Also called *Bacchus,* in Roman mythology.

Direct draw. The practice of serving draft beer most directly from the keg so that very short beer lines are required.

Distillation. The separation of alcohol from a fermented liquid by heating to vaporize the alcohol, then condensing the vapors.

Distilled spirit. An alcoholic beverage made by distilling a fermented liquid.

Doppelbock. German for *double bock,* this especially rich, strong bock beer is made as high in alcohol content as possible. See *bock beer.*

Doux. A seldom-seen designation on a Champagne label indicating extreme sweetness.

Draft beer. An unpasteurized beer drawn from keg to glass. The British spelling is *draught.*

Drambuie (dram-BOO-ee). A brand-named liqueur made from Scotch and honey.

Dramshop laws. State laws dictating (among other things) that the seller of alcohol to an intoxicated person may be held liable for damages caused by that person.

Drink size. The amount of base ingredient used per drink.

Dry. 1. Lacking in sweetness. 2. A person favoring the prohibition of alcoholic-beverage sales. 3. The term used for an area in which the sale of alcoholic beverages is forbidden.

Dry beer. A beer with less sweetness and little or no aftertaste; light and lively.

Dry gin. An English-style gin, as opposed to Dutch gin.

Dry stout. A beer made in the stout style, but without lactic sugar, creating a stout that is not sweet-tasting.

Dutch gin. A full-bodied, malt-flavored gin imported from Holland. Not a bar gin. Also called Hollands, *Genever,* and *Schiedam.*

Eau de vie (oh da vee). The French translation of the Latin term *aqua vitae,* or *water of life;* a general term for a spirit.

ECR. Abbreviation for electronic cash register; a computerized cash register.

Edelfaule (AY-dul-FOY-la). The German term for *botrytis cinerea,* or *noble rot.*

Edible cocktail. A term for the use of alcohol to create or enhance a dessert.

Eighty-six. 1. A signal to stop serving liquor to someone who has had too much to drink. 2. A sign that a supply of a product has run out.

Eisbock. A concentrated, highly alcoholic bock beer made by freezing the beer, then removing the ice crystals from it.

Eiswein. A rare wine, usually German, made from grapes that have frozen on the vine before harvesting, concentrating their richness and sweetness.

Ending inventory. The dollar value of physical inventory at the end of an accounting period.

Enology, oenology. The science of winemaking; a college degree in winemaking.

Estate-bottled. The term for wine bottled at the vineyard by the vineyard owner and made exclusively from grapes grown at that vineyard.

Ethanol. A type of alcohol found in spirits, beer, and wine.

Excise tax. A tax on items that the government considers nonessential, including alcoholic beverages.

Exempt employee. An employee who is exempt from federal overtime-pay requirements because of managerial or supervisory duties.

Extensions. On an invoice, multiples of the same item at the same price.

Extra. A term on a cognac label indicating that the cognac was aged at least 5½ years.

Extra sec. A term on a Champagne label; the literal translation is *Extra Dry,* but it means that the wine contains a small amount of added sugar.

Falernum. A sweet syrup with almond-ginger-lime flavors; 6-percent alcohol.

Farmhouse ale. A beer made in the home-brewed style of historic Belgium or France with added herbs, pepper, or grated orange rind, then bottled and stored like wine.

Feasibility study. A detailed analysis of whether a planned enterprise can make a profit on a given site.

Fermentation. The action of yeast upon sugar in a solution, which breaks down the sugar into carbon dioxide and alcohol.

Fetal alcohol syndrome. A pattern of birth defects in a child whose mother drank alcohol during pregnancy. Also known as *fetal alcohol effects* (abbreviated FAE). Abbreviated FAS.

FICA. Federal Insurance Contributions Act, commonly known as Social Security.

FIFO. Acronym for "first in, first out," a way to ensure freshness by rotating products in storage.

Filler cap. The rubber or vinyl top to a blender.

Financial statement. A statement showing the assets, debts, and net worth of an individual or enterprise.

Fine Champagne. A term on a cognac label indicating that the cognac was made from at least 50 percent of grapes from the Grande Champagne section of the Cognac district and the balance from the Petite Champagne section.

Finish. 1. The aging of wine in the bottle; bottle finish. 2. The aftertaste of a wine.

Firkin. The wooden cask used to store a certain type of beer. See *cask-conditioned beer.*

Fixed expenses. Expenses that remain the same regardless of sales volume.

Flag. A garnish of sliced orange or other citrus fruit on a pick, usually with a cherry.

Flaker. A machine that produces soft, snow-like ice used primarily to keep things cold, such as on a salad bar or in a wine bucket. Also called a *flake-ice machine*.

Flavonoids. Plant pigments found in fruits and vegetables that have antioxidant or anti-inflammatory benefits.

Flexhose. A flexible metal hose on which a *cobra gun* is mounted.

Flight. Several samples of different beers or wines purchased together, in lieu of a single glass or beer or wine, to encourage experimentation.

Float. To pour a liqueur or cream on the surface of a drink without mixing.

Flute. A Champagne glass, footed or stemmed, with a narrow, slightly flaring bowl.

Folio. A folder for enclosing the guest check for presentation to the customer.

Food and Beverage Director. The title of a management position in a restaurant, bar, or hotel that involves ordering products, developing menus, and hiring staff members. Also called *F-and-B*.

Footed glass or footed ware. A glass or glasses with a bowl that sits on a base or foot.

Foreseeability. The legal premise that a person can reasonably anticipate that a particular course of action, such as serving one more drink to an intoxicated person, could result in harm or injury to that person or a third party.

Fortified wine. A wine to which brandy or other spirits have been added.

Frangelico (fran-JEL-ih-koh). The brand name for an Italian liqueur flavored with herbs and hazelnuts.

Free-pour. To pour liquor for a drink without using a measure, estimating the amounts.

Fringe benefits. Compensation other than wages, such as free meals or paid vacations.

Frizzante (free-ZAHN-tay). An Italian term for slightly sparkling wine, such as Lambrusco.

Front bar. That part of a bar structure used by customers.

Frozen-drink dispenser. A machine that produces frozen, premixed drinks in large quantities.

Fruit-juice drink. A highball made with liquor and fruit juice instead of a carbonated mixer. A Screwdriver or a Salty Dog are examples of fruit-juice drinks.

Fruit squeezer. A hand-operated gadget used to squeeze half a lemon or lime for fresh juice for a single drink so that pits and pulp do not get into the drink.

Funnel. A cylinder with a sharply tapered end for pouring from large containers into smaller ones.

Galliano (GAL-ee-AH-noh). The brand name of an Italian liqueur that is yellow in color and made with herbs.

Gamay Beaujolais (GAM-ay BO-zha-lay). A light, fresh, and fruity red wine made from gamay grapes. The first wines of each vintage are released as *Nouveau Beaujolais* in an annual French celebration that has been adopted in other countries.

Gay-Lussac system. The percentage of alcohol in a spirit by volume; the label designation (instead of *proof*) commonly used in Europe.

Generic wine. A U.S. wine of a general style or type whose name is borrowed from a famous European wine, such as burgundy and chablis. U.S. law refers to these wines as *semi-generic*.

Geneva, genever (jeh-NEE-vur). A Dutch gin.

Gewurztraminer (guh-VURTS-tra-meener). A pinkish-colored grape from Germany and the Alsace region of France; used to make spicy, fruity white wines of the same name, as well as late-harvest whites. Also called *Gewurz* (guh-VURTS).

Giardia lamblia. A common waterborne parasite that causes flu-like symptoms when ingested.

Gin. A neutral spirit flavored with juniper berries.

Glass brush. A sturdy type of brush used specifically for cleaning glassware. There are glass brushes for use by hand, as well as motorized models.

Glass froster. A small, top-opening freezer in which to put glasses or beer mugs for chilling before use.

Glasswasher. A small, mechanical dishwasher made for cleaning and drying glassware that fits in an underbar or backbar area.

Glycerin. An odorless, colorless liquid found in wine as a by-product of fermentation; it is visible on the inside of a wineglass after swirling, clinging to the sides of the glass. These streams of glycerin are called *legs*.

Grain neutral spirits. Spirits distilled from a grain mash of 190 proof or higher.

Grand Cru (gron KRU). A French term on a wine lable indicating the highest classification of burgundy wines; the literal translation is *great growth* in French. Beneath Grand Cru is *Premier Cru* (PREM-ee-yay KRU).

Grand Marnier (GRAN marn-YAY). A French brand-name mixture of cognac and curacao.

Grande Champagne. A term on a cognac label indicating that the cognac was made from grapes grown in the Grande Champagne section of the Cognac district.

Grappa (GROPP-ah). A highly alcoholic liqueur made by distilling the leftover skins, stems, and seeds from winemaking. Although the name is used in many countries only Italy has the legal right to use it.

Grenache (gren-OSH). A red grape that makes a fairly sweet, light, red wine, such as France's Tavel rosé; also used in blending.

Grenadine. A sweet, red syrup flavored with pomegranates.

Gross operating profit. Sales less product costs and controllable operating expenses.

Gross profit. Sales less product cost. Also called the *contribution margin*.

Gross profit method. A formula for determining the percentage of profitability of a particular drink. The same method can be reversed to help correctly price that drink.

Guest experience. A guest's total impression of an establishment, from their mood when they walk in, to how they are treated and whether they enjoy what they have ordered.

Handgun. The dispensing head for an automatic soda or liquor system.

Hangover. The chemical imbalance experienced after overindulging in alcohol; common symptoms include headache, queasiness, stomach cramps, dizziness, and dehydration.

Happy hour. A limited period of the day, often early evening, during which drink prices are reduced.

Hard cider. A low-alcohol liquor fermented from apples or apple juice.

Hard lemonade. A low-alcohol product made by blending beer with lemonade.

Head. 1. The collar of foam at the top of a glass of beer. 2. In distilling, the top section of a pot still, where alcohol vapors are collected.

Highball. A drink made by mixing a spirit and carbonated water (or another mixer) and serving it with ice in a highball glass. Gin and Tonic or Scotch and Soda are examples of highballs.

Himbeergeist. A German-made raspberry brandy.

Hollands. A Dutch gin.

Hops. Blossoms of the female hop vine, which an essential flavor ingredient of beer.

Hourglass. The common term for a tall, slim, all-purpose beer serving glass of 10 to 16 ounces.

House brand. Liquors commonly poured when customers do not specify a specific brand. Also called *well* or *pouring brands.*

House wine. A specific wine that a restaurant sells by the glass or carafe.

Hydrochlorofluorocarbons. Chemical refrigerants used in icemakers and other refrigeration systems. These newer-style chemicals do not do as much damage to the atmosphere as *chlorofluorocarbons*, their predecessors. Abbreviated HCFCs.

Hydrofluorocarbons. Chemical refrigerants used in icemakers and other refrigeration systems. Abbreviated HFCs. See *hydrochlorofluorocarbons.*

I-9 Form. A government form for establishing a person's proof of identity and eligibility to work in the United States.

Ice bin. The container in which ice is stored.

Ice crusher. A machine that crushes cubed ice into smaller pieces.

Ice machine. A machine that freezes water to make cube ice. Also called an *icemaker.*

Ice scoop. A plastic implement for getting ice out of an ice bin; for bars, a 6- or 8-ounce capacity works best.

Ice tongs. Tongs used for handling one cube of ice at a time so that hands do not touch the ice.

Ignition Interlock law. A law that requires a person who has been convicted of drunk driving to use a device on his or her vehicle that tests for sobriety (by blowing into it) in order to start the vehicle or keep it running.

Image. A customer concept of the unique identity of an enterprise.

Imperial stout. A British-style stout beer, high in alcohol content; originally made for shipment to Russian royalty.

Income statement. A financial report showing kinds and amounts of revenue, kinds and amounts of expenses, and resulting profit or loss for a specific period.

India Pale Ale. A hearty beer style created for transport from Britain to colonial India; often copied by brewers today for its light color but full, sometimes fruity flavor.

Infusion. Flavoring a spirit by immersing fruit or spices in it and letting it marinate at room temperature.

Inlet chiller. A unit that can be added to an ice-making system that collects cold water as it drains away from the icemaker and recirculates it, chilling incoming water while saving energy.

Inventory. 1. The amount of stock on hand at any given time. 2. The process of taking inventory by counting each bottle on hand.

Inventory turnover rate. The speed at which you use up existing inventory; a figure used to decide if you are keeping too much or too little in inventory.

Invoice. A seller's document that specifies what goods were delivered as part of a customer's order.

Irish whiskey. A whiskey made in Ireland from several grains by a triple-distillation process.

Jamaican rum. A dark, full-flavored rum distilled from molasses; used in certain tropical drinks.

Jigger. A glass or metal measure for liquor; sized in ounces or fractions of ounces.

Job analysis. The process of creating a *job description* by listing individual tasks and the equipment and skills required to do them.

Job description. A written list of duties and responsibilities for a worker.

Job specifications. A list of the knowledge, skills, or abilities a worker must have to perform specific jobs or tasks.

Jockey box. See *pouring station.*

Jug wine. An inexpensive wine available in bottles, or boxes, larger than liters.

Kabinett (KAB-ih-net). A German quality wine made from grapes ripe enough to ferment without added sugar; one of five categories of a German quality designation for top-quality unsugared wines.

Kahlua (kuh-LOO-uh). A brand name of a Mexican-made liqueur that contains sugar-cane-based spirits flavored with coffee and vanilla.

Keg. A half-barrel of beer; contains 15½ gallons.

Kilning. The process of drying barley or other grain in a kiln.

Kirsch (keersh), **kirschwasser** (KEERSCH- voss-er). A wild-cherry brandy; usually from the Rhine River valley of Germany; colorless and unaged.

Krausening (KROY-zun-ing). In beer-making the addition of a small amount of newly fermenting wort to beer during the lagering stage, to induce additional fermentation and carbonation.

Krystal. A term on a German wheat beer label indicating that the beer has been filtered to eliminate the natural cloudiness that results from brewing with wheat.

Lager (LAW-gur) **beer.** A beer made by bottom fermentation at cool temperatures.

Lagering. Storing beer to mellow or condition it.

Lambic beer. A well-known style of wheat beer; often used as the base for adding fruits.

Lambrusco (lam-BROOS-koe). A red grape grown primarily in Northern Italy and used to make a sweet, fruity, red wine of the same name; has some natural "fizz" or carbonation.

Lawnmower beer. A slang term for a mainstream commercial beer that is nothing special, just something to drink when doing the chores.

Lay down. To store wine in the bottle; to age wine until it is ready to drink.

Layout. The arrangement of furniture, fixtures, traffic patterns in a room.

Lead time. The length of time between ordering items and having them delivered to you.

Ledger. One or more books of individual accounts for each category of assets, liabilities, and equity.

Lees. In winemaking the stems, skins, pulp, and seeds left over after grapes have been pressed and their juices removed. Also called *vinaccia* or *pomace* in other countries.

Legs. See *glycerin.*

Liabilities. The money owed by a person or business to others; debts.

License state. A state in which retail dealers may buy from any supplier licensed to sell to them rather than from state stores. Compare *control state.*

Light beer. A beer that is brewed to contain less alcohol and fewer calories than a regular or Pilsner-style beer.

Light whiskey. A U.S. whiskey distilled at 160 to 190 proof; light in flavor and body but not in alcohol.

Limited retail dealer. An organization, usually charitable or nonprofit, exempted from paying state liquor taxes for special events as long as they pay for a permit for the event. Church festivals and benefit concerts are examples of limited retail dealers.

Liqueur. A brandy or another distilled spirit sweetened and flavored with for example herbs, fruit, and spices. Also called *cordial.*

Local option. The state's ability to give a county, city, or voting precinct the right to choose whether to sell alcoholic beverages in that jurisdiction.

London dry gin. A gin in the English style, which is made with high-proof spirits redistilled with juniper berries or mixed with extracts.

Long. A slang term for a drink that totals more than five measures of fluid.

Long draw. A draft-beer system in which the kegs must be stored far enough from the taps to require long (more than 14 feet) beer lines.

Maceration. Steeping or soaking herbs or other flavor sources in a spirit to make a liqueur.

Macrobrewery. A large national or international beer-making business with multiple locations and an annual output of more than 500,000 barrels.

Maderized. The term used to describe a wine that smells overly sweet, such as a Madeira or port, when it is not supposed to; usually indicates that the wine has been improperly stored and may be bad.

Malt. A grain, usually barley, that is sprouted, then dried.

Malt beverage. The term used by a U.S. Standard of Identity in place of *beer* for a beverage made by fermenting malted barley with hops in water.

Malt liquor. A lager beer with a higher alcohol content, 5.5 to 6 percent or more, than Pilsner.

Malt scotch. An unblended whiskey made in Scotland entirely from malted barley.

Malternative. An industry slang term for alcoholic beverages made like beer but with additional ingredients, from caffeine, to flavorings, to other types of alcohol.

Marc. The French term for *grappa.*

Market segment. A subgroup of the total customer market having similar needs, attitudes, and lifestyles.

Marry. 1. To blend wines or spirits. 2. To add something to the liquor in a bottle.

Mash. In making beer or spirits to cook malt, with or without other grains, to convert starches to sugars; the resulting product is a mash.

Mash bill. An old-fashioned (American colonial) term for a beer-making recipe.

Mash tun. The container in which *mash* is cooked.

Mature (mah-TOUR). The term on a Champagne label indicating dry (little or no sugar). See *brut.*

Mega-tap bar. A beer bar that offers hundreds of beer brands on tap.

Merlot. A red grape or the mellow, uncomplicated red wine made from it; grown primarily in Bordeaux, Italy, and California.

Mescal. A white, tequila-like spirit made from agave plants that are not blue agave or located in one of Mexico's specific tequila-producing regions. Also spelled *mezcal.*

Metaxa (meh-TAX-ah). A Greek brandy; slightly sweetened.

Metered pour. A liquor-dispensing system that measures and controls drink size.

Myers's Rum. A brand name of a heavy, dark rum from Jamaica.

Microbrewery. A small, independent brewery that produces fewer than 15,000 barrels of beer annually. Also called a *craft brewery.*

Micron rating. The measure of how effective a water filter is at removing dangerous parasites and particles; the lower the micron rating number, the greater the filtration capabilities.

Minimum wage. The lowest amount that can be paid by federal law to most hourly employees. See *subminimum wage.*

Mise en bouteille au chateau (MEEZ on bou-TAY oh shah-TOW). A French phrase on wine labels indicating that the wine is chateau-bottled or estate-bottled. Also seen as *mise au chateau* or *mise du chateau.*

Mise en place (MEEZ ohn PLASS). A French phrase meaning "Everything in its place"; in bartending, this means that the bar is correctly set up, looks good, and is ready for business.

Mix can, mixing cup, mixing steel. The metal-cup portion of a shaker or shake mixer.

Mixed case. See *broken case.*

Mixed pint. The result of blending one beer with another, or with another type of alcohol, in a single glass.

Mixing glass. A heavy glass container in which drink ingredients are stirred with ice.

Mixology. The art or skill of mixing drinks containing alcohol.

Mixto. A commonly made tequila; half is derived from the blue agave plant and half from other sources (neutral spirits, corn, or sugarcane).

Mocktail. A cocktail made without the liquor.

Monopole (MONN-oh-POLE). In France a brand name or wine name that belongs exclusively to a particular wine producer or shipper.

Monopoly state. See *control state.*

Moonshine. The nickname for liquor brewed secretly in illegal stills.

Muddler. A wooden implement used for crushing fruit and sugar cubes and cracking ice.

Muller-Thurgau (MYOOL-ur TUR-gau). A popular white grape grown in Germany, used to make a variety of styles of table wine.

Multiple-brands discount. See *assorted discount.*

Multiple facings. Three or four bottles of the same liquor brand displayed together on the backbar.

Muscat. A popular grape used to make sweet, fruity wines, such as Italy's sparkling Asti Spumante, grown in both red and white varieties.

Must. The juice from crushed grapes before fermenting.

N2 canister. A container of nitrogen used in a blended-gas draft-beer system.

Napoleon Cognac. A cognac aged at least 5½ years. (No brandy actually dates from Napoleon's day.)

Nebbiolo (neb-ee-OH-loh). The red Italian grape used to make Barbaresco and Barolo wines.

Negociant (neh-GO-see-ahn). A French wine merchant and shipper, sometimes a blender and bottler as well.

Neoprohibitionism. A modern-day movement to outlaw the sale of alcoholic beverages.

Neotemperance. A modern-day movement to control alcohol abuse through legislation while allowing use of alcohol in moderation.

Net profit. Sales less all expenses.

Neutral spirits. Spirits distilled at 190 proof or above; almost pure alcohol, with no distinct flavor or odor characteristics; used in blending to make other types of spirits.

Ninkasi. The ancient Sumerian goddess of brewing.

Nitrogenated beer. A smooth, creamy beer style made by using a special flow restrictor in the *tap* to force nitrogen out of beer just before pouring.

Noisette (nwah-SET). A French brand-name, hazelnut-flavored liqueur.

Nonalcoholic beer. A malt beverage with the flavor of beer containing less than 0.5-percent alcohol.

Nonexempt employee. An employee who must be paid the federal minimum wage for hourly work.

151° rum. A rum that is 151 proof; used especially for flaming and as a float on mixed drinks.

Oatmeal stout. A beer made with a small percentage of oatmeal as the grain in the mash.

Off-premise sales. Sales of alcoholic beverages to be consumed at a different place from where the sale takes place. Supermarkets are examples of off-premise retailers. Compare *on-premise sales.*

Old Ale. A thick, sometimes fruity style of beer aged after fermentation. Usually made for winter consumption or for blending with other ales. Also called a *Winter Warmer.*

One-empty-for-one-full. A system for controlling losses by requiring an empty liquor bottle to be turned in to the storeroom for each full bottle issued.

On-premise sales. Sales of alcoholic beverages to be consumed on the same premises where the sale takes place. Bars and restaurants are examples of on-premise retailers. Compare *off-premise sales.*

On the rocks. Served over cube ice.

Orange flower water. A flavoring extract used in mixed drinks.

Orgeat (oar-ZHAY). A sweet almond-flavored syrup.

Ounce method. A liquor measurement and control technique that compares the total number of ounces of liquor used (based on a physical inventory) with the number of ounces sold (based on drink sales).

Ouzo (OO-zoe). A Greek anise-flavored liqueur.

Overhead expenses. Fixed expenses not related to sales volume or hours of operation.

Overproof. A spirit (usually rum) that has a higher-than-normal *proof,* or alcohol content.

Overrun. The percentage of air forced into a liquid drink mix by the pump in a frozen-drink machine. The overrun increases the overall volume of the mix, making the drinks light and slushy.

Overtime. The amount of time worked in excess of 40 hours in a workweek.

Oxidized. A wine that has gone bad because oxygen has gotten into the bottle, with a dull or rust color and vinegary or musty flavor.

Par stock. The amount of each liquor, beer, and wine to be kept at the bar at all times.

Participatory bar. A bar business that includes customers as part of the entertainment, such as playing pool or singing karaoke.

Pasteurization. In beer-making, heating briefly in the can or bottle to kill bacteria and remaining yeast cells.

Pear William. The English translation of *Poire William,* a colorless, unaged brandy made in France or Switzerland that usually has a whole pear encased in its bottle.

Peat. Decomposed vegetation that is harvested and burned for drying barley in making Scotch, giving the liquor a smoky favor.

Peaty. The smoky or ash-like character imparted to Scotch whisky from the use of peat fires to dry the grain or from its water source coming into contact with peat. Also called *peat-reek.*

Perceived value. The value of product/service in a customer's eyes, whatever its actual worth.

Percolation. In making liqueurs, adding herbs other flavors by pumping the spirit through them over and over.

Periodic order method. A system of reordering merchandise on certain dates every month.

Perpetual inventory. An ongoing daily record of purchase and issue for each inventory item, compiled from invoices and issue slips.

Perpetual order method. A system of reordering merchandise when existing inventory drops below a certain number.

Perquisites. Fringe benefits related to specific jobs or job levels. Also called *perks.*

Per se law. A law (in this case, a drunk-driving law) that says that police can use a single piece of evidence, such as a breath test or a driver's refusal to take the test, to determine guilt.

Peychaud's (PAY-shows). A brand of strong bitters from New Orleans.

pH. The abbreviation used to describe the amount of acidity in water, expressed on a scale of 1 to 14; an important component of the beer-brewing process.

Phenolic compounds. Natural antioxidants found in red grapes that give them their red coloring and the acidity known as *tannins.*

Physical inventory. Counting inventory in stock, bottle by bottle.

Pickup station. The section of the front bar where serving personnel turn in and receive drink orders and return empty glasses.

Pils. A cone-shaped glass with no stem or foot; used for serving Pilsner-style beers.

Pilsner. A mild, dry style of beer, usually 3.2- to 4.5-percent alcohol by weight (4 to 5 percent by volume). Sometimes spelled *Pilsener.*

Pinot Blanc (PEE-noh BLONK). A white grape used primarily for making sparkling wines in California, Italy, and France.

Pisco (PEES-ko). A Peruvian brandy.

Pitching. The ancient process of coating the insides of clay containers (*amphora*) with tar to keep them watertight.

Plymouth gin. An English-style gin with less alcohol (82.4 percent) than regular gin.

Point-of-sale system. A system in which a point-of-sale register functions as an input terminal for a central processing unit (CPU). Abbreviated POS system.

Pomace. The leftover seeds and skins from crushed grapes.

Pomace brandy. A brandy made from distilling the leftover skins, stems, and seeds from winemaking. Known as *grappa* in Italy and *marc* in France.

Pony. A slang term for 1 ounce.

Portable bar. A rolling bar unit, popular in hotel use, that can be positioned at a meeting, banquet, or reception for beverage service.

Porter. A dark, bittersweet specialty ale, about 5- to 7.5-percent alcohol by volume.

Positioning. Establishing an enterprise favorably in customers' eyes in relation to its competition.

Post-mix system. A system of dispensing carbonated beverages from a handgun by mixing carbon dioxide, water, and concentrated syrup from bulk supplies.

Post-off discount. Lowering the price of an item, usually if it is bought in quantity, to increase sales.

Potential sales value. Sales dollars that a given bottle of liquor would earn if all of its contents were sold; a control tool for measuring losses when compared with actual sales.

Pot still. A pot-shaped still in which spirits are distilled by using direct heat from below.

Pouilly Fuissé (POO-ee fweh-SAY). A well-known French white wine from the Macon region.

Pouilly Fumé (POO-ee foo-MAY). A well-known French white wine made from Sauvignon Blanc grapes from the Loire Valley; not to be confused with *Pouilly Fuissé*.

Pour. In a drink recipe to add an ingredient as is without straining it.

Pourer. A device that fits into the neck of a liquor bottle to reduce the flow of liquor to a controllable speed or a preset amount.

Pouring costs. A comparison of what it costs to offer beer, wine, and mixed drinks. Each category is determined by dividing the cost of goods sold by the gross sales for a given time period to arrive at a percentage.

Pouring station. The area of a bar where each bartender works, with his or her own supply of liquor, mixes, ice, glasses, and so on. Busy or large establishments have multiple pouring stations. Also called a *cocktail station, cocktail unit, beverage center,* or *jockey box.*

Pousse-café (POOS kaf-FAY). An old-fashioned after-dinner drink consisting of liqueurs floated in layers, one atop another, in multiple colors and densities.

Precheck. To ring up a drink order before the drinks are poured.

Premier Cru (PREM-ee-ay CROO). A French term on a wine label indicating the secondary quality designation for burgundy wines. See *Grand Cru.*

Premium well. A well that is stocked with upscale, more expensive name-brand liquors. Also called a *super-well.*

Premix system. A system of carbonating beverages from bulk supplies as they are dispensed from a handgun.

Preset. The key on a computerized cash register that is set to figure and record extensive information on a specific item sold.

Pressware. Inexpensive, commonly used glassware made by being pressed into a mold.

Pretax profit. The amount of money a business makes, including all income and expenses except for taxes. Also called *net profit.*

Primary competitor. A bar that vies for the same market segment because it has a concept similar to yours. See *secondary competitor.*

Prime costs. The largest and most necessary expenses to do business; in bars, these are beverage and payroll costs.

Prime-ingredient cost. The cost of the major ingredient in a drink (its *base* liquor); used as a basis for pricing the drink.

Prix fixe (PREE-FEEKS or PREE-FEE). The French term for *fixed price.*

Product/service mix. The combination of products and services offered to customers by a given enterprise.

Pro forma statement. A financial report that shows what a business should be making and spending, based on a set of assumptions about the industry, local economy, and other market factors.

Prohibition. The period of time in U.S. history (1920 to 1933) when the manufacture, sale, and transportation of most alcoholic beverages was illegal.

Proof. A measure of the alcoholic content of a spirit; each degree of proof is ½-percent alcohol by volume.

Proof gallon. In the United States 128 fluid ounces of 100-proof liquor.

Proprietary name. The brand name of a wine producer or shipper.

Pub. The popular British term for a casual, neighborhood bar. Short for *public house.*

Pull date. The date that a product should no longer be sold, after which it begins to deteriorate; typically pull dates are marked on cans, bottles, and other packaging.

Purchase order. A buyer's document specifying merchandise ordered. Abbreviated P.O.

Purchase-order number. The number that identifies a particular purchase purchase order. Abbreviated P.O. number.

Purchasing. The process of deciding what is to be served, which supplies are needed to produce these items, and procuring (ordering and buying) them.

Pure malt. See *BMSW.*

Qualitatswein (KVAHL-ee-tots-VINE). A German wine-quality category; medium-quality wine from a designated region. Abbreviated QbA.

Qualitatswein mit Pradikat (KVAHLih- tots-VINE met PRAD-dih-kut). A German superior-quality rating for wines having special attributes based on ripeness of the grape. Abbreviated QmP.

Rabbit. A much-imitated type of corkscrew, trademarked by the Metrokane company. Handles that look somewhat like a rabbit's ears are used to grasp the wine bottle's neck as a lever quickly extracts the cork.

Racking. In winemaking the process of draining the juice off the *lees* (skins and stems) and into a fresh cask.

Rail. 1. The recessed portion of a bar top closest to bartender, where drinks are poured. Also called the *glass rail, drip rail,* or *spill trough.* 2. On antique bars the brass footrest at the bottom front of the bar.

Ready-to-drink. A beverage category that includes premixed bottled or canned alcoholic-beverage products, such as *malternatives.* Abbreviated RTD.

Reasonable care. The legal term for what an ordinary, prudent person would do to prevent harm or injury.

Rectification. The alteration of a distilled spirit by blending, adding flavors or color, or redistilling to purify or concentrate.

Refrigeration circuit. The system of equipment that chills and circulates air and correctly humidifies refrigerated space.

Refrigeration cycle. The process of removing heat from a refrigerated space.

Regional brewery. A brewing facility that produces from 15,000 to 500,000 barrels of beer annually.

Regional specialty brewery. A brewery whose main or largest-selling product is a microbrew or specialty beer.

Regular rate. The hourly rate for determining overtime pay.

Relish fork. A long, thin two-tined fork for spearing such items as olives and cocktail onions.

Reorder point. The point at which supplies must be ordered to maintain minimum stock.

Reposado Tequila. A Mexican Tequila that has been aged 2 to 11 months by law. *Reposado* means *resting* in Spanish.

Requisition. 1. To request stock from the storeroom to be released for use at the bar. 2. The form for requesting the issue of stock and the record of such issue. Also called an *issue slip*.

Resveratol. An antioxidant that is found naturally in the skins of red grapes.

Riesling (REES-ling). A fruity white grape used to make many German white wines, including (when it is picked overripe) late-harvest and dessert wines.

Rim (or rimming). To coat (or coating) the rim of a glass with salt, sugar, or celery salt.

Rimmer. The device for rimming a glass evenly.

Rioja (ree-OH-hah). The Spanish wine district producing mostly red wines in the Bordeaux style; the red wine that comes from this district.

ROI. Abbreviation for return on investment; share of profit expressed as a percentage of amount invested.

Rosé (roe-ZAY). A wine made from dark-skinned grapes whose juice is allowed to ferment with the skins for only 12 to 24 hours, resulting in a light peach or pink color. Some rosés are in the *blush-wine* category.

Rotate stock. To put new supplies behind the existing stock so that the oldest will be used first.

Router. See *zester.*

Rum. A spirit distilled from molasses or sugarcane.

Rye. 1. A whiskey made with 51 percent or more of rye plus other grains, aged at least two years in charred new-oak containers. 2. In the East the popular term for blended whiskey.

Sake (sah-kee). A Japanese wine made from rice.

Sambuca (sam-BOO-kah). The generic name for a clear liqueur with a licorice flavor.

Sangiovese (SAN-gee-oh-VAY-zee). The red Italian grape used to make Chianti.

Sanitize. To destroy bacteria with a chemical solution.

Sauvignon Blanc (SO-vin-yon-BLONK). The adaptable white grape used to make many French wines, including white Bordeaux, Graves, Sancerre, Sauternes, and Pouilly Fumé. In the United States and elsewhere this grape is used to make the white wines Fumé Blanc and Sauvignon Blanc.

Schnapps. In the United States a sweet liqueur that is usually fruit- or mint-flavored.

Scotch. A whiskey made in Scotland; typically a blend of malt whiskies and grain neutral spirits.

Screw-pull. A type of corkscrew that twists into a wine-bottle cork and extracts it. Also called a *lever-pull.*

Seasonal ale. A specialty ale made for spring or fall release; has hints of spices.

Sec. A French term on a Champagne label; the literal translation is *dry* but this wine is slightly sweet.

Secondary competitor. A bar that competes with yours simply because it is located in the same area.

Sekt (zekt). A German term for sparkling wine.

Semillon (SEM-ee-YON). A white grape that had been used primarily for blending but is now bottled as its own varietal; a rich, fruity white wine.

Server. A waiter or waitress.

Service bar. A bar pouring drinks for table service only, often out of public view.

Service encounter. The server's first contact and subsequent "relationship" with a guest.

Service mark. A trademark for a service rather than a product. See *trademark.*

Service napkin. A clean, white towel or napkin carried by a wine server; used to wipe condensation off the bottle and to wipe the lip of the bottle before pouring. Also called a *serviette,* the French word for *napkin.*

Service scape. The environment in which a service encounter takes place. A service scape includes the décor, lighting, music, and anything else that affects the *guest experience.* Also called a *landscape.*

Shake. To mix a drink by shaking it in a shaker or using a shake mixer.

Shake mixer. A top-shaft mechanical drink mixer. Also called a *spindle blender.*

Shaker. The combination of a mixing glass and a stainless-steel container fitting over the glass, in which drink ingredients and ice, are hand-shaken.

Shelf life. The length of time that a beverage can be stored without loss of quality.

Sherry butt. A wooden cask in which sherry is aged.

Shooter. A small, straight-up drink served in a shot glass, typically consumed all at once, as in drinking a toast.

Short. A slang term for a drink that equals less than five measures of liquid.

Shot. The portion of liquor served straight in a shot glass with a glass of ice water or another liquid on the side.

Shot glass. The small glass in which a *shot* is served.

Shrinkage. Losses due to theft, spillage, and other occurrences.

Silica. The fine sand used in making glass.

Simple syrup. A sweetener for mixed drinks made of one part sugar and one part water.

Singani. A Bolivian-made brandy from grapes; a type of *pisco.*

Single-cask. The unblended Scotch from a single cask in a single distillery; usually the most exclusive (and expensive) type of Scotch.

Single-malt Scotch. An unblended malt Scotch from a single distillery.

Skimming. An identity-theft crime in which an illegal device is used to surreptitiously read (*skim*) the stored data on the magnetic strip of a credit card and to use the information to make a counterfeit card.

Slivovitz (SHLIV-uh-vits). A plum brandy made in central Europe.

Snifter. A footed glass with a large, rounded bowl in which brandy is typically served.

Solera system. A Spanish storage method for making some kinds of liquor, notably brandy. The system consists of rows of barrels filled with liquor of different ages; the oldest product is tapped and refilled with a younger product, and multiple vintages are blended for product consistency.

Sommelier (SUM-el-yay or SOHM-ee-yay). The person who handles the ordering and serving of wines in a restaurant, typically having considerable wine knowledge. Also called a *wine steward, cellarmaster, winemaster,* or *wine waiter.*

Sour. A family of mixed drinks made with lemon juice, served in a Sour glass, and garnished with cherry and orange. A Whiskey Sour and a Daiquiri are examples of Sours.

Sour mash. In whiskey-making a distilling method in which a portion of fermented mash from a previous fermentation is added to fresh mash.

Southern Comfort. A brand-named liqueur made from American brandy, peach juice, and other ingredients.

Sparkling wine. A wine containing carbon dioxide in solution that bubbles when poured.

Spatlese (SHPAYT-lay-zah). A German wine made from fully ripened grapes, late-picked after the official harvest date.

Special Occupational Tax. The annual federal tax that each liquor retailer is required to pay (to the *TTB*) for each place of business. Abbreviated SOT.

Speed bar. A very busy, high-volume bar that requires experienced bartenders who can work under pressure.

Speed rail, speed rack. A bottle-width rack for liquor bottles that is attached to the apron of underbar equipment.

Splash. A slang term for ¼ of an ounce.

Sports bar. A bar with a sports theme that attracts customers by showing a variety of sporting events, usually on big-screen television sets.

Spumante (spoo-MON-tee). An Italian sparkling wine.

Standard. Another term for the *tap* or faucet of a keg-beer dispensing system.

Standard cost percentage. A cost/sales ratio based on standardized drinks; provides a standard for measuring the actual cost/sales ratio.

Standard drink size. A standard amount of prime ingredient used per drink.

Standard glass. A glass of a specified size and shape for a given drink.

Standardized drink. A drink that is characterized by standard ingredients in standard quantities, a standard portion size, a standard glass size, and standard preparation procedures. See *standard.*

Standardized recipe. A recipe listing specific ingredients and amounts that all bartenders in the business must follow. See *standardized drink.*

Standards of Identity. The U.S. government's definitions of the various classes of spirits, wines, and malt beverages, including how it is made, what it is made of, its alcohol content, and the type of container in which it is aged.

Station. The area of a bar set up for a certain part of the drink-service process, such as a pouring station or a serving station.

Steam beer. A beer made by combining bottom fermentation with higher temperatures of ale fermentation. The name refers to the steam that is released when the barrels are tapped. Called *dampfbier* in Germany.

Stemmed glass or stemware. A glass with a foot, stem, and bowl.

Still wine. A wine without bubbles; nonsparkling.

Stir. To mix a drink by stirring its ingredients with ice in a mixing glass.

Stout. A full-flavored dark ale, usually imported, having an alcohol content ranging from 4 percent to as high as 10.5 percent by volume.

Straight. A liquor served "as is," without mixing in other ingredients.

Straight up. A drink served in a chilled glass without ice.

Straight whiskey. An unblended whiskey containing 51 percent or more of a single grain type, usually corn or rye.

Strainer, bar strainer. A wire spring with a handle and ears that fit over the rim of a measuring glass or cup.

Stripper. A hand tool used for cutting twists of fruit peel.

Strip stamp. A Federal stamp placed over the top of a sealed liquor bottle; now most often a tamper-evident closure of metal or plastic.

Structure. 1. The term for a combination of attributes of a wine: its sweetness, acidity, and the amounts of tannins and alcohol in the wine. 2. For a cocktail the components that are mixed together to make it: a base spirit, complementary ingredients to modify or enhance flavors, and a garnish.

Suberin oak. The type of tree from which natural cork is harvested.

Submicron filter. A water filter that removes most types of dangerous parasites from water systems.

Subminimum wage. A lower wage (lower than the federal *minimum wage*) allowed to be paid only to workers under age 20 and only during their first 90 days on the job. Also called a *training wage*.

Suggestive selling. The technique of offering or recommending additional items to customers.

Sulfites. Chemicals found naturally in many wines; a small percentage of people have allergic reactions to them.

Sweet-and-sour mix. A bar substitute for sugar and lemon or lime in mixed drinks.

Sweet stout. A beer made with milk (or *lactic*) sugar and fewer hops, resulting in a less bitter flavor that some compare to sweetened espresso.

Swizzle stick. A stir stick used to mix a drink in the glass.

SWOT analysis. An appraisal of four common business factors: **s**trengths, **w**eaknesses, **o**pportunities, and **t**hreats.

Syrah. An adaptable red grape that makes a tannic, full-bodied red wine; used often in blending. Called *Shiraz* in Australia.

2, 4, 6-Trichloroanisole. A harmless but smelly combination of mold, chlorine, and moisture that sometimes forms on natural cork, permeating the wine inside the bottle and tainting it with an off-putting, musty odor. See *corked*. Abbreviated TCA.

Table tent. A card folded into a triangle that stands on a table top; used to advertise specialty drinks or a short wine list.

Table wine. A grape wine (red, white, or rosé) with an alcohol content of up to 14 percent by volume.

Tafelwein (TOF-el-vine). The lowest-quality category of German wines; the literal translation is *table wine*.

Tall drink. A drink served in a large glass (Collins or larger) in which there is a high proportion of mix and ice to spirit.

Tamper-evident closure. A closure on a liquor bottle, part of which remains on the bottle when the bottle is opened.

Tap. 1. A beer faucet. 2. To set up a keg of beer for bar use by connecting one line to a carbon-dioxide tank and one line to the tap.

Tare weight. The weight of an empty container, which is used to calculate the weight or volume of its contents.

Tastevin (TAT-vin or TASS-tah-van). A wine-tasting cup that hangs from a cord or ribbon from the neck of a *sommelier;* a traditional part of his or her uniform.

Tax stamp. Proof given by the *TTB* to a retailer when he or she registers and pays the *Special Occupational Tax.*

Temperance. A word meaning moderation, self-restraint, and sobriety; used to label people or groups who believe in very stringent legal limits on drinking, or forbidding it altogether; the Temperance Movement historically had a powerful voice in the United States.

Tempering. In the glassmaking process the step in which cooled glass is reheated to high temperatures to "shock" it and make it more temperature-resistant. When the entire glass is tempered it is called *fully tempered*; when only the rim receives this treatment it is called *rim tempered.*

Tempranillo (TEMP-rah-NEE-yo). The primary red wine grape grown in Spain, used to make Rioja wines.

Tennessee whiskey. A whiskey made in Tennessee, filtered through maple charcoal; similar to bourbon and often considered part of the bourbon family.

Tequila (teh-KEE-lah). A distinctively flavored spirit from the Tequila district of Mexico; distilled at low proof from the fermented juices of the blue agave plant.

Tequila Puro. A Mexican Tequila distilled from 100-percent blue agave.

Tequillaria. (teh-KEE-lah-REE-ah) A bar or restaurant with a menu focused on tequilas and foods that complement them.

Tequiza. A brand-name beverage that is a blend of beer, tequila, and lime.

Third-party liability. The legal concept holding that the seller of alcohol to an intoxicated person may be held liable for damages caused by that person to a third party.

Three-tier system. An alcohol-sales-and-distribution method common in the United States, with a product going from a producer, to a wholesale distributor, who sells to retailers (including bars and restaurants).

Throw sediment. A wine that has been chilled or chilled too quickly, which causes solid crystals to precipitate on the cork or at the bottom of the bottle. The crystals (calcium carbonate) are harmless but off-putting to some consumers.

Tia Maria. The brand name of a Jamaican-made, coffee-flavored liqueur.

Tied-house. A financial or legal interest in a retail enterprise held by a brewer, distiller, or wholesaler; in most states this is a violation of the law.

Tip credit. The percentage of the minimum wage that an employer may subtract from the wages of tipped employees.

Tip out. The practice of servers sharing tips with busboys, barbacks, and other service people who are not commonly tipped as part of the service team.

Tipped employee. An employee who receives at least $30 per month in tips.

Tip pooling. The practice of servers combining all or a percentage of their tips and dividing the total amount among the staff.

Top fermentation. The method of making malt beverages in which the yeasts act from the top of the fermenting beverage.

Total business pricing. The concept that menu items must work together (some, expensive to make but popular; others, inexpensive and very profitable) to maximize total profit.

t-PA antigen. A beneficial enzyme in ethanol (alcohol) that helps prevent blood clots.

Trade dress. Elements of a product's or business's image that make it distinctive (e.g., logos, color combinations, and the size or shape of a building or container) from those of competitors.

Trademark. The exclusive right to use a business or product name after going through the correct legal process to register the name.

Training wage. For new employees under age 20, 85 percent of minimum wage, allowable for the first 90 days on job.

Trebbiano (treb-ee-AH-no). An Italian white grape used to make Soave wines and some sparkling wines.

Triple sec. The generic name for Curacao liqueur that is clear (colorless).

Trockenbeerenauslese (TROCK-un-BAHRun-OWSCH-lay-za). A rich, sweet German wine made from individually selected, overripe grapes shriveled with *Edelfaule* (*noble rot*).

TTB. The abbreviation for the federal Alcohol and Tobacco Tax and Trade Bureau.

Tulip. A stemmed glass with a tulip-shaped bowl. Some tulips are used specifically for Champagne; others, for beer.

Tumbler. A flat-bottom glass without a stem or foot.

Twist. A strip of citrus-fruit peel used as a garnish.

Tyramine. A chemical found in some types of wine and beer that interacts with some types of antidepressants to increase blood pressure, possibly to dangerous levels.

Ugni Blanc. A type of white grape used primarily in making cognac.

Unallocable expenses. Expenses that are neither fixed nor directly tied to sales.

Underbar. Equipment installed behind and under the front bar.

Universal Product Code. A series of vertical bars of varying widths printed on the packaging of most consumer products, which can be read by a computerized scanner for inventory purposes. Abbreviated UPC.

Upsell. To suggest that a customer have his or her drink made with a more prestigious or expensive liquor than the *well brand.*

Van der Hum. A South African brandy-based liqueur that is the equivalent of Curacao.

Variable expenses. Expenses that fluctuate, depending on the sales volume.

Varietal (va-RY-ah-tul). A wine named for its predominant grape.

Vatted Malt Scotch. A Scotch that is a blend of 100-percent malt whiskies from more than one distillery. Also called *Pure Malt Scotch.*

Vase. A Pils-style beer glass. Also called a *weizen glass.*

Vieille reserve. A French term on a cognac label indicating that the cognac has been aged at least 5½ years. The literal translation is *old reserve.*

Vienna lager. A light- to medium-bodied beer with a distinct red or amber color and a toasted malt aroma.

Viognier (VEE-ohn-YAY). A white-wine grape that makes a wine of the same name with distinctive, assertive fruit flavors and light sweetness; used in blending or bottled on its own.

Vini da tavola. A Italian table wine produced outside the government's D.O.C. quality standards, although not necessarily of lesser quality.

Vintage. A term on a wine label indicating the year that the grapes were crushed and the winemaking process began for that bottle.

Vintage-dated. A wine that has its year printed on the label, indicating all the grapes used to make it were harvested in that year.

Vitus vinifera. The ancient, original grape species from which almost all of today's wine grapes are descended.

Vodka. Neutral spirit treated to remove distinctive character, aroma, and taste.

VS. On a Cognac label, stands for Very Superior, aged at least one and a half years.

VSOP. On a Cognac label, stands for Very Superior Old Pale, aged at least four and a half years.

Waiter's corkscrew. A combination *worm* (the screw itself), small knife, and lever for extracting a cork from a wine bottle at tableside. The corkscrew folds up, much like a pocketknife. Also called a *waiter's friend.*

Weighted average. A method of determining the potential sales value of a bottle of liquor.

Weinbrand. A generic name for German-made brandy.

Well. 1. The supply of most-used liquors at a pouring station. 2. The area of the underbar in which these liquors are stored together; also called the *bottle well.*

Well brand. The brand of liquor poured when a customer does not specify a brand.

Wet area. An area (e.g., county or voting precinct) in which the sale of alcoholic beverages is legal.

Wheat beer. A top-fermented beer made with both *wheat malt* and barley malt; light in color, with a slightly fruity flavor and aroma.

Wheat malt. A beer made with malt that consists of half barley and half wheat.

Wheel. A round slice of lemon, lime, or orange used as a garnish.

Whiskey. A spirit distilled from grain. Also spelled: *whisky.*

White goods. An industry nickname for the colorless spirits such as vodka, gin, rum, and tequila.

White Zinfandel. A wine of pink or peach color made by crushing Zinfandel grapes but separating the juice from the grape skins early so that it does not take on the dark color of the red grape.

Wholesaler's basic permit. A federal permit that allows a liquor or wine wholesaler to sell to retailers.

Widget. A marble-sized pellet of carbon dioxide placed in some bottled or canned beers. The pellet bursts when the beer is opened, creating foam.

Wild fermented. A beer-making or winemaking process in which the liquid ferments by using natural yeasts found in the air rather than by the addition of yeast.

Wine. Fermented juices of grapes and occasionally of other fruits.

Wine bar. A bar with a theme of wine appreciation and featuring a wine list that encourages sampling and learning about different types of wines.

Wine basket. A wicker basket used for carrying a bottle of wine horizontally from cellar to table to avoid agitation.

Wine cabinet. A storage unit for wines in which partially full bottles are filled with inert gas to keep the remaining wine fresh. A popular brand name is Cruvinet.

Wine chiller. A bucket or container into which ice and water are placed to surround a wine bottle and chill it quickly.

Wine gallon. In the United States 128 fluid ounces of alcoholic beverage of unspecified alcoholic content.

Wine spritzer. A drink made by combining wine and sparkling water over ice.

Wine steward. A person who handles customers' wine orders and service. Also called a *sommelier.*

Wing corkscrew. A rather bulky style of corkscrew with handles, known as "wings," that rise as the screw or *worm* is twisted into the cork; the cork is extracted when the wings are pushed downward.

Wood management. A distiller or winemaker's system of using wooden casks or barrels to store, age, and blend liquids. Variables include the type and age of the wood, what was previously stored in the barrels, and whether they are charred or uncharred.

Word of mouth. Publicity generated by customer recommendations of for example a place of business.

Workweek. The fixed and regularly recurring period of 168 hours; seven consecutive 24-hour periods.

Worm. 1. In a still a coil in which the hot alcoholic vapors are cooled and condensed. 2. The spiral part of a corkscrew. Also called the *screw* or *augur.*

Wort. In beer- and whiskey-making the liquid in which starches have been converted to sugar.

Yeast. The ingredient responsible for fermentation in making alcoholic beverages by breaking down sugar into alcohol and carbon dioxide.

Zero Tolerance. The catchphrase for a strict no-drinking or no-drinking-and-driving policy.

Zest. The thin outer skin of a lemon or orange containing flavorful oils.

Zester. A tool that cuts a narrow strip of zest. Also called a *router.*

Zinfandel (ZIN-fun-DELL). An adaptable red grape that is used to make light, fruity White Zinfandel wines and the dark, full-flavored regular Zinfandels. Grown primarily in California.

Index